The Best of FRANCE

Revised Edition

Editor-in-Chief
Christian Millau

Editor
Colleen Dunn Bates

Translated by
Timothy Carlson, Kathy Compagnon, Yolande Depré, Robert Lever, Anne Weinberger, Patricia Wolf

Assistant Editor
Margery L. Schwartz

Operations
Alain Gayot

Directed by
André Gayot

Editorial Staff, French-language Guide
Jean-Louis Perret (Editor)
Guy Saint-Père (Editorial Director)

PRENTICE HALL ▪ NEW YORK

Other Gault Millau Guides Available
from Prentice Hall Trade Division

The Best of Chicago
The Best of Italy
The Best of Los Angeles
The Best of New England
The Best of New York
The Best of San Francisco
The Best of Washington, D.C.

Published by Prentice Hall Trade Division
A Division of Simon & Schuster Inc.
15 Columbus Circle
New York, New York 10023

Please address all comments regarding The Best of France to:
Gault Millau, Inc.
P.O. Box 361144
Los Angeles, CA 90036

Library of Congress Cataloging-in-Publication Data
The Best of France

Guide de la France. English.
The Best of France / editor-in-chief, Christian Millau; editor, Colleen Dunn Bates; translated by Timothy Carlson ... [et al.]; assistant editors, Margery L. Schwartz; coordination, Alain Gayot; directed by André Gayot. – Rev.ed.
p. cm.
Translation of: Guide de la France.
Rev. ed. of: The Best of France / Gault Millau. 1st ed. 1986.
Includes index.
ISBN 0-13-074022-5

1. France–Description and travel–1981–Guide-books.
I. Millau, Christian. II. Bates, Colleen Dunn. III. Gault,Henri, 1929- Best of France. IV. Title.
DC16.G3513 1989
914.4'04838–dc19 89-30942
CIP

Thanks to the staff of Prentice Hall Travel for their invaluable
aid in producing these Gault Millau guides.

CONTENTS

ABOUT THIS GUIDE
Read this short chapter before you go any further. How to find your way around *The Best of France* and how to decipher the rankings, prices, symbols and abbreviations. **1**

TOQUE TALLY
An index of the very best restaurants in France. **5**

PARIS RESTAURANTS
Find out why Paris is unquestionably the restaurant capital of the world. Grand temples of haute cuisine, convivial brasseries, welcoming neighborhood bistros—here you'll discover hundreds of incisive reviews of Paris's best restaurants. **7**

PARIS HOTELS
You'll find a home-away-from-home in this broad selection of Paris's hotels, whether your budget allows for opulent luxury or modest charm. **75**

PARIS SUBURBS
The best restaurants and hotels in Paris's outlying areas. Includes Versailles. **89**

FRANCE A TO Z
From Abbeville to Wimille, we've scoured France's cities, towns, villages and remote hideaways to uncover the country's best restaurants and hotels. Whether you're looking for a world-famous restaurant, a romantic resort or a charming village inn, you'll find it among these thousands of in-the-know reviews. Includes guides to the sights, cafés, bars, nightlife and food shops in the larger towns, along with maps of France's most-visited cities. **105**

FOOD TERMS

How to read a menu like a native. Includes Menu Savvy, a lexicon of frequently seen French food terms, and Regional Foods, a far-ranging guide to French regional cooking. **485**

INDEX

Cities classified by *départements*. **499**

MAPS

In and around France **506**

THE INNS AND OUTS

France: footloose and fancy-free. That could be the title of our guide aimed at tourists who, in ever-increasing numbers, travel on their own, usually by car, and who plan their own itineraries. Although most of these visitors limit their explorations to Paris and a few "classics," such as the Côte d'Azur, the Loire Valley châteaux and Périgord, we were unwilling to neglect France's other regions; at the very least, we hope to arouse the curiosity of the uninitiated to see them. Whether in one of the big cities or a small village, in Brittany or Alsace, Bordeaux or the Alps, Normandy or Haute-Provence, you are almost sure to find in our guide at least one listing of a good restaurant and a comfortable hotel. As you read these pages, you'll discover France's great dining institutions as well as small places whose gastronomic ambitions are more modest but that can still leave you with happy memories. It's not possible to lunch with Troisgros and dine with Senderens every day. And, anyway, even if you had the physical stamina and the financial means to do so, you'd be missing another France—delicious, usually warm in welcome and almost always inexpensive. Don't forget that, hidden by the glare of publicity lavished on the finest and most luxurious *maisons* (which remain the perfect place to celebrate special events, or simply to spoil yourself from time to time), there are innumerable charming and unpretentious little restaurants and hotels in the provinces that, considering the quality they offer, are among the least expensive in Europe. It's true that these are not as plentiful in the regions most visited by tourists, but there's never any difficulty finding one in the Southwest, Auvergne, the Pyrénées, the Alps or even Périgord. These bistros are often family-run businesses where Papa does the cooking and Maman serves the guests. They offer a simple cuisine, but one that is healthy and generous—and service is friendly, and prices incredibly reasonable.

Except for Easter, the month of July and the first three weeks in August, you can travel as free as a bird through middle France, as our countrymen have the deeply rooted habit of taking their vacations all at the same time. Still, it's a good idea to reserve your room or table a bit in advance, just to be on the safe side. Nor should you forget that in the country people tend to go to bed early, and if you drop by unexpectedly you run the risk of finding the hotel doors shut. Contrary to custom in Paris, where people generally order à la carte, almost all provincial restaurants offer menus, fixed-price meals that are less expensive but nonetheless usually trustworthy and recommendable.

It goes without saying that your dining habits should reflect the specialties of the regions through which your travels take you. The number and variety of cuisines are immense; every 60 to 80 kilometers (35 to 50 miles), you change not only landscape but also cooking styles, which take into account local foodstuffs. Don't hesitate to question waiters and restaurant owners about these differences. The same goes for wine: we believe that you should drink Burgundy in Burgundy, Bordeaux in Bordeaux, Côtes-de-Provence along the Mediterranean and Champagne in Champagne!

SYMBOL SYSTEMS

RESTAURANTS

Gault Millau ranks restaurants in the same manner that French students are graded: on a scale of zero to twenty, twenty being unattainable perfection. The rankings reflect *only* the quality of the cooking; decor, service, reception and atmosphere do not influence the rating. They are explicitly commented on within the reviews. Restaurants ranked thirteen and above are distinguished with toques (chef's hats), according to the following table:

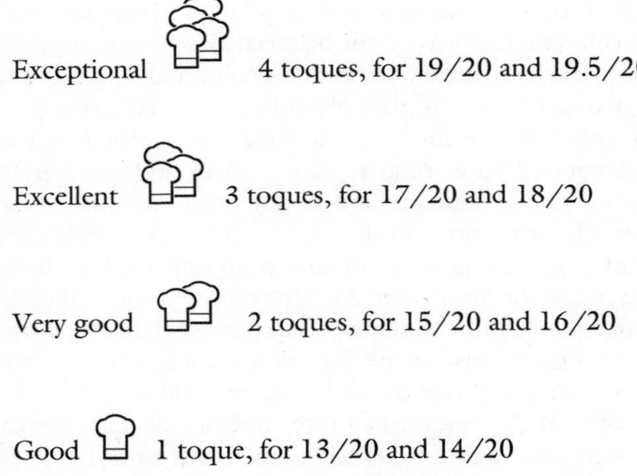

Exceptional — 4 toques, for 19/20 and 19.5/20

Excellent — 3 toques, for 17/20 and 18/20

Very good — 2 toques, for 15/20 and 16/20

Good — 1 toque, for 13/20 and 14/20

Toques in red denote restaurants serving modern cuisine; toques in black denote restaurants serving traditional food.

Keep in mind that these ranks are *relative.* One toque for 13/20 is not a very good ranking for a highly reputed (and very expensive) temple of fine dining, but it is quite complimentary for a small place without much pretension.

At the end of each restaurant review, prices are given— either à la carte or menus (fixed-price meals) or both. A la carte prices are those of an average meal (an appetizer, a main course, a dessert) for one person, including service and a half bottle of relatively inexpensive wine. Lovers of the great Bordeaux, Burgundies and Champagnes will, of course, face stiffer tabs. The menu prices quoted are for a complete multicourse meal for one person, including service but excluding wine (unless otherwise noted). These fixed-price menus often give diners on a budget a chance to sample the cuisine of an otherwise expensive restaurant.

Prices in red denote restaurants that offer a particularly good value.

In France, the service charge is always (by law) included in the price of the food. But it is customary to leave a few extra francs as an additional tip.

HOTELS

Our opinion of the comfort level and appeal of each hotel is expressed in a ranking system, as follows:

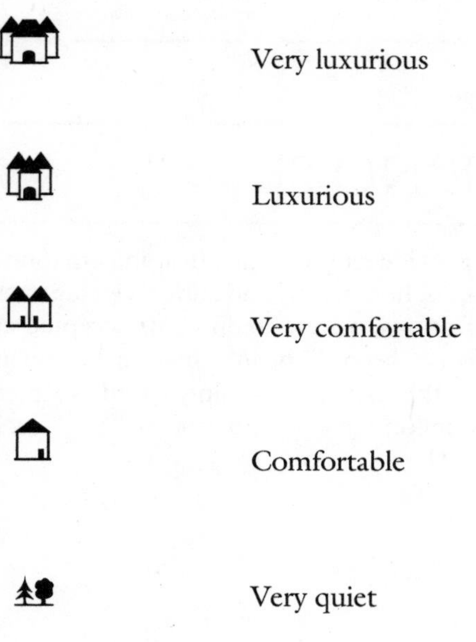

Symbols in red denote charm.

Hotel prices given are for the complete range of rooms, from the smallest singles to the largest doubles; suite prices are also given when possible. These prices are per room, not per person. Half-board and full-board prices, however, are per person.

Sadly, prices continue to creep up, so some places may have become more expensive than our estimates by the time you visit. You're best off expecting to pay a little more—then perhaps you'll be pleasantly surprised!

USEFUL INFORMATION & ABBREVIATIONS

Toques and grades: see Symbol Systems above

"Les Lauriers du Terroir": an award given to chefs who prepare noteworthy traditional or regional recipes.

M. (or MM. or Mme. or Mlle.): proprietor's, proprietors' or manager's name

Rms: rooms

Stes: suites

Seas.: season

Air cond.: Air conditioning

Half-board: rate per person for room, breakfast and one other meal (lunch or dinner)

Full board: rate per person for room and three meals

Oblig. in seas.: obligatory in season

Credit Cards

V VISA, or Carte Bleue

AE American Express

DC Diners Club

MC MasterCard, or Eurocard

How to read the locations:

Abbeville *(the town)*
280100 Abbeville - (Somme)
(the zip code) (the regional department)
Paris 160 - Amiens 45 - Dieppe 63 - Boulogne-sur-Mer 80
(kilometers to Paris and nearby major cities)

A FINAL NOTE

We have made a Herculean effort to provide as much practical information as possible: phone numbers, proprietors' names, hours, daily and annual closings, telex numbers, specific amenities and special features, prices, credit cards accepted and more. We've also made a tremendous effort to keep all the information current and correct. But establishments change such things with alarming speed, so please forgive us if you come across incorrect or incomplete information.

TOQUE TALLY

Red Toques: *Inventive/Modern Cuisine*; Black Toques: *Traditional Cuisine*

Four Toques (19.5/20)

Paris:
Lucas-Carton (8th)
Robuchon (16th)

France A to Z:
Georges Blanc (Vonnas)
Michel Bras (Laguiole)
Alain Chapel (Mionnay, see Lyon)
Michel Guérard (Eugénie-les-Bains)
Marc Meneau (Saint-Père-sous-Vézelay, see Vézelay)
Troisgros (Roanne)

Four Toques (19/20)

Paris:
Guy Savoy (17th)
Taillevent (8th)

France A to Z:
L'Aubergade (Puymirol, see Agen)
Auberge de l'Eridan (Annecy)
L'Auberge de l'Ill (Illhaeusern)
Jean Bardet (Tours)
Boyer (Reims)
La Côte d'Or (Saulieu)
La Côte Saint-Jacques (Joigny)
Pierre Gagnaire (Saint-Etienne)
Grand Hôtel du Lion d'Or (Romorantin)
Le Royal Gray (Cannes)

Three Toques (18/20)

Paris:
L'Ambroisie (4th)
Jacques Cagna (6th)
Carré des Feuillants (1st)
Le Divellec (7th)
Le Duc (14th)
Faugeron (16th)
Olympe (15th)
Michel Rostang (17th)
La Tour d'Argent (5th)
Les Trois Marches (Versailles)
La Vieille Fontaine (Maisons-Laffitte)
Vivarois (16th)

France A to Z:
Arzak (San Sebastian, see Hendaye)
Auberge des Templiers (Les Bézards)
Jean-Pierre Billoux (Dijon)
La Bonne Auberge (Antibes)
La Bourride (Caen)
Buerehiesel (Strasbourg)
Chabran (Pont-de-l'Isère, see Valence)
La Crémaillère (Orléans)
Le Crocodile (Strasbourg)
Le Flambard (Lille)
Lameloise (Chagny)
Léon de Lyon (Lyon/1st)
Le Louis XV (Monte-Carlo)
Le Moulin de Mougins (Mougins)
Georges Paineau (Questembert)
Pic (Valence)
Les Pyrénées (Saint-Jean-Pied-de-Port)
Restaurant de Bricourt (Cancale)
Saint-James (Bouliac, see Bordeaux)
La Tour Rose (Lyon/5th)
Vanel (Toulouse)

Three Toques (18/20)

France A to Z:
Paul Bocuse (Collonges-au-Mont-d'Or, see Lyon)

Three Toques (17/20)

Paris:
Apicius (17th)
Arpège (7th)
A. Beauvilliers (18th)
Le Bourdonnais (7th)
Au Comte de Gascogne (Boulogne-Billancourt)
Drouant (2nd)
Le Grand Véfour (1st)
Laurent (8th)
La Maison Blanche (15th)
Le Manoir de Paris (17th)
Le Pré Catelan (16th)
Jules Verne (7th)

France A to Z:
L'Abbaye Saint-Michel (Tonnerre)
La Bonne Etape (Château-Arnoux)
Le Centenaire (Les Eyzies)
Chabichou (Courchevel)
Chabichou (Saint-Tropez)
Château de Locguénolé (Hennebont)
La Cognette (Issoudun)
Daguin (Auch)
La Flamiche (Roye)
Le Goyen (Audierne)
Le Moulin de Martorey (Chalon-sur-Saône)
L'Oustau de Baumanière (Les Baux-de-Provence)
Pain Adour et Fantaisie (Grenade-sur-l'Adour)
La Palme d'Or (Cannes)
Passédat/Le Petit Nice (Marseille)
Le Président (Saint-Quentin)
Le Quéré (Angers)
Hôtel Radio (Chamalières, see Clermont-Ferrand)
Le Relais (Bracieux)
Restaurant Thibert (Dijon)
La Tamarissière (Agde)
La Terrasse (Juan-les-Pins)
La Toque Royale (Evian)
Le Vieux Moulin (Bouilland)

Three Toques (17/20)

Paris:
La Marée (8th)

France A to Z:
Barrier (Tours)
Le Chapon Fin (Bordeaux)
Hiély-Lucullus (Avignon)
Nandron (Lyon/2nd)
Jean Ramet (Bordeaux)
Rôtisserie du Chambertin (Gevrey-Chambertin)

PARIS

Restaurants

First Arrondissement

13 L'Absinthe

24, pl. du Marché-St-Honoré
42.60.02.45, 42.61.03.32

M. Malabard. Open until 11:30 p.m. Closed Sat. lunch & Sun. Terrace dining. Pets allowed. Parking. Cards: V, AE, DC.

A new chef and a new manager haven't changed the oh-so-Parisian style of this restaurant, which has been serving discerning diners for the past ten years. M. Malabard, the owner, keeps an attentive eye on his little 1900s-style dining room (a bit labored but highly decorative) and weathers the volatile tastes and times. His patrons—and they are never lacking—are primarily young, lively and appreciative of fine food. The cuisine is contemporary, with a touch of country flavors, and consistently well prepared: roast lotte with paprika, Basque-inspired grilled tuna steak and filet of lamb with eggplant au gratin. The terrace overlooking the Marché-St-Honoré is delightful for warm-weather dining.

A la carte: 300F.

14 Armand au Palais Royal

6, rue de Beaujolais - 42.60.05.11

M. Paillat. Open until 1 a.m. Closed Sat. lunch, Sun. & Dec. 23-27. Air cond. Pets allowed. Cards: V, AE, DC.

One of the few eating places in Paris whose continued success has not triggered a slight contempt for the less-than-affluent customer. And what a godsend, considering its spectacular location facing the arcades of the Palais-Royal. The lighting at night plays stunningly on the ancient stones, the welcome is cordial, and Jean-Pierre Ferron's selectively modern cuisine is just what discriminating theatergoers are clamoring for. The short à la carte menu changes frequently, but you'll always like the crayfish tails in tarragon butter, galantine of rabbit with foie gras, oxtail in red wine and those exquisite warm, thin apple tartelettes. There are some fine wines this side of 100 francs, though they won't help your check much.

A la carte: 350F. Menus: 170F (lunch only), 138F.

16 Gérard Besson

5, rue Coq-Héron - 42.33.14.74

M. Besson. Open until 10 p.m. Closed Sun., 3 weeks in July & last 2 weeks of Dec. Air cond. Pets allowed. Cards: V, AE.

Gérard Besson is happy in his little Les Halles restaurant, in which the mirrored walls reflect the light-colored furnishings, soft lights, sparkling crystal and white dinnerware. A distinguished chef (a national award winner) and disciple of Garin, Chapel and Jamin, Besson also knows how to make his customers happy—by serving tasty, classic dishes executed with a light, modern touch. Savory home cooking is given a fresh interpretation by a master chef: his "sausage" of foie gras with pistachios, terrine of duck with seasoned vegetables, salmon steak in red-wine aspic with a bell pepper mousse, and his unforgettable scrambled eggs à la Georges Garin with tomatoes, diced truffles, chives and mustard.

Excellent desserts (warm fruit tarts with ice cream, cream puffs with caramel ice cream, tea sorbet) and a sumptuous wine cellar housing some 45,000 bottles will send the check soaring unless you choose from the very reasonable lunch-only menu.

A la carte: 400-600F. Menu: 230F (weekday lunch only).

11/20 Bistro de la Gare

30, rue St-Denis - 42.60.84.92

See Sixth Arrondissement.

18 Carré des Feuillants

14, rue de Castiglion
42.86.82.82

M. Dutournier. Open until 10:30 p.m. Closed Sat. lunch (& Sat. dinner in July & Aug.) & Sun. Air cond. Pets allowed. Cards: V, AE.

Under the arcades of the rue de Castiglione, Alain Dutournier hung a sign a couple of summers ago that was tacky but highly informative: "Le Carré des Feuillants. Cuisine of the Southwest." After leaving Au Trou Gascon to woo the luxury dining trade and the place Vendôme, Dutournier opened this spectacular restaurant on the very site where the Feuillant ("constitutional monarchist") Club fanned the flames of the revolution, and promptly found himself the target of passionate debate. He has been accused of rejecting the culinary heritage of his Gascon birthplace merely to engage in a "sham race." There are complaints that the prices are out of sight. But Dutournier deserves a fair hearing, and, having followed his career since he opened his doors in Paris, we volunteer to provide it.

Let's begin with the decor. When you walk into the likes of a Roman palace (instead of an ordinary early-nineteenth-century home in southwestern France, as originally planned), Murano chandeliers cast a rather eerie blue glow, and there are just too many of those super-realistic still lifes hanging on the walls. The rest of the setting is delightfully theatrical, with one room opening into the next all the way back to the spectacular glassed-in kitchens. The pale trompe l'oeil woodwork is a visual treat. And the handsomely laid tables are set far enough apart to ensure quiet dining.

The cooking may not always be consistent—for instance, last time we were there the duck hearts with wild mushrooms had so much salt that the dish was virtually inedible. Another time, the cod, with its accompanying sea urchins in vinaigrette sauce, was a muddle of flavors. Dutournier's inventive spirit sometimes leads him astray, and he ought to stick closer to what he knows best: the produce of Gascony. His most successful Gascon dishes include escalopes of foie gras in duck juice served with an asparagus flan and sautéed asparagus tips; succulent Pauillac lamb with stuffed potatoes; and a superb cut of beef from Bazas, aged three weeks and garnished with marrow, shallots and a béarnaise sauce. The desserts are good but not breathtaking, especially the cinnamon crème brûlée, which could stand some improvement. But not so the wine cellar under Jean-Guy Loustau's able stewardship, which houses the treasures of Bordeaux, the southwest and Burgundy, as well as the unfamiliar tastes of wines from Chile, Spain and Australia.

So despite the critics, there is no reason to trundle the Carré des Feuillant's owner off to the guillotine, or to deny him his three toques.

A la carte: 400-600F. Menus: 230F (lunch only), 420F, 560F (menu dégustation, wine incl.).

12/20 Caveau des Chevillards

1-3, rue St-Hyacinthe
42.61.19.74, 42.61.60.21

M. Millemann. Open until 11 p.m. Closed Sat. lunch & Sun. Air cond. Pets allowed. Telex 210311. Cards: V, AE, DC.

The vaulted cellars of the Jacobin Club's headquarters during the revolution make a most pleasant 1980s setting, a comfortable, quiet place for business lunches and a charming spot for candlelight dinners (accompanied by live piano music). Caveau des Chevillards serves fine meats and a wide selection of light desserts. The menu is limited, but the bill isn't.

A la carte: 300F. Menu: 140F.

(13) Le Caveau du Palais

19, pl. Dauphine - 43.26.04.28

M. Dieuleveut. Open until 10:30 p.m. (11 p.m. in summer). Closed Sat. (off-season) & Sun. Air cond. Terrace dining. Pets allowed. Cards: V, AE.

Members of the legal profession—a pretty picky lot—patronize this two-level bistro, whose old stonework and beams are reminiscent of bygone days. The prices are beginning to reflect its charm, and its cuisine is well thought out by head chef Pascal Loué, who wisely limits himself to a simple repertoire of fresh, top-quality products served in generous portions: fisherman's catch (sole, salmon, lotte), a fricassée of kidneys and sweetbreads with honey and good grilled meats. Fine wines are sold by the glass at the bar that divides the rooms.

A la carte: 280-300F.

(14) Chez Pauline

5, rue Villedo - 42.61.79.01

M. Génin. Open until 10:30 p.m. Closed Sat. dinner, Sun., July 14-Aug. 17 & Dec. 23-Jan. 2. Air cond. Pets allowed. Cards: V.

Even without succumbing to the fresh truffles in puff pastry or the Breton lobster stew with noodles—neither of which is the type of dish you're likely to look for in this old-style bistro—you'll find that Andre Génin's prices have a painful sting. But who complains in the face of such generous portions, such fresh, high-quality ingredients and such good humor? Delicious terrines, wonderful red-mullet filets in a Chinese marinade, young asparagus from the Côte d'Azur under a velvety hollandaise, filet of turbot poached to perfection and served with a simple white-wine sauce, stuffed cabbage and an excellent molded rice dessert—in short, this is classic cooking adapted to modern life and the cost-of-living index. There's also a fine selection of Arabian coffees and an extensive wine cellar.

A la carte: 300F and up.

12/20 Chez Vong aux Halles

10, rue de la Grande-Truanderie
42.96.29.89, 42.86.09.36

M. Vong Vai Lam. Open until 1 a.m. Closed Sun. Air cond. Terrace dining. Pets allowed. Cards: V, AE, DC, MC.

Authentic Oriental antiques decorate both floors of these Gothic cellars turned mandarin palace. Other art objects, such as the cleverly sculptured vegetable displays created by the two chefs in charge of the kitchen, aren't as long-lived. These ornamental creations will appear on any banquet table you order—a day in advance, please. The cuisine seems to have reached a plateau: On our visit the dim sum were too expensive and uneven in quality, and while the glazed Peking duck and the chicken with ginger were in the tradition, a pork stew was dull. Sorry, the toque has gone.

A la carte: 300F.

(13) Au Cochon d'Or des Halles

31, rue du Jour
42.36.38.31, 42.36.33.14

M. Viart. Open until 10:30 p.m. Closed Sun. Air cond. Pets allowed. Cards: V, AE, DC.

The old meat markets of Les Halles are still alive in this once-famous bistro, which, with its choice cuts, french fries, oxtail terrine, grilled pork with garlic and delicious clafouti (warm fruit tart), deserves to remain so. Beaujolais goes well with all of the dishes, as do some of the excellent reds from Saumur or Anjou. At Au Cochon, a good, reliable and lively place to eat, the reception is cordial, the service is good, and the restful ambience allows for musing on Les Halles's colorful past—minus all the noise and commotion.

A la carte: 300F and up.

(13) L'Escargot Montorgueil

38, rue Montorgueil - 42.36.83.51

Mme. Saladin-Terrail. Open daily until 11 p.m. Closed Jan. 1, May 1 & week of Aug. 15. Pets allowed. Cards: V, AE, DC, MC.

Despite her best efforts, Kouikette Terrail, the charming sister of Claude (owner of La Tour d'Argent), still can't seem to whip her staff into shape and dispel what appears to be a chronically mild state of confusion in the kitchen—with the exception of certain traditionally fine dishes: escargots, obviously, in a variety of forms, foie gras and pigs' knuckles. In contrast, the sautéed veal kidney flamed in brandy was dried out, and, alas, those succulent strawberry fritters had vanished from the menu. The wine list isn't what it used to be, either. Thank heavens for the still-intact, elegant, attractive Restoration-period interior, with its splendid ceilings, wrought-iron staircase and antique mirrors that even now seem to reflect Sarah Bernhardt's presence.

A la carte: 350F. Menu: 184F.

(15) Espadon

(Hôtel Ritz)
15, pl. Vendôme - 42.60.38.30

M. Klein. Open daily until 11 p.m. Air cond. Garden dining. Parking. No pets. Telex 220262. Cards: V, AE, DC, MC.

You have to visit in the winter to taste the char (similar to trout), so rarely found in Paris, that Guy Legay brings in from a crater lake in the Puy-de-Dôme region. Cooked plain in its own juices, it is clearly the king of fish. Legay's talent rests on this very simplicity—a world apart from "the grand Ritz style," or worse, the pretentious elegance of Ledoyen's, where he trained for a short while. Though his gift for classic cuisine went astray temporarily, it has now found itself in the genuine everyday cooking we all appreciate: cod cheeks, salt-cured salmon, casserole of sweetbreads and tiny onions, roast chicken with thyme, tenderloin of herbed lamb. It is the type of cooking that thumbs its nose at the international set who pay the dinner bills in solid gold in this opulent Napoléon III–style winter garden. The service is among the finest in the world, and the sommelier, Georges Lepré, is a virtuoso.

A la carte: 600-800F. Menu: 295F.

11/20 André Faure

40, rue du Mont-Thabor - 42.60.74.28

Mme. Provost. Open until 10 p.m. Closed Sun. Air cond. Pets allowed. Cards: V.

A plain decor, whitewashed walls, narrow tables, rather hurried service and heaping plates (which the tourists love) in the evening: raw vegetables, steaks and chops, good confits and desserts. Beaujolais with the Duboeuf label.

A la carte: 150F. Menus: 60F (lunch only), 72F and 150F.

(14) La Fermette du Sud-Ouest

31, rue Coquillière - 42.36.73.55

M. Naulet. Open until 10 p.m. Closed Sun. Pets allowed. Cards: V.

You'd think you were entering an old-fashioned country inn, where the tables are crowded together and the regulars wouldn't give up their seats on any account. Butcher-turned-chef Christian Naulet, who sports a handlebar mustache and has the ruddy face of the Périgord region, lacks his native region's accent but has all the culinary know-how that makes his boudin (sausage) with onions and lard possibly the finest in Paris—not to mention his country sausage, duck and cured shoulder of pork. Naulet provides an hour and a half of honest dining pleasure just steps away from the limp fries and anemic burgers of the former Trou des Halles. You'd best avoid the stuffed quail and the apple tart, however; they're not as good as the gras-double (a Lyonnais tripe dish) with fennel and the Périgord pastry with crème anglaise. The wine list is on the short side.

A la carte: 200F and up.

(15) Goumard

17, rue Duphot - 42.60.36.07

M. Goumard. Open until 10:30 p.m. Closed Sun. Air cond. Pets allowed. Cards: V, AE, DC, MC.

Five days a week, Jean-Claude Goumard is one of the few Paris restaurant owners who bids for and obtains the very best food items at the Rungis market. That's the unseen side of his success. Ostensibly, his is one of the top seafood places in town because of the exceptionally high-quality produce that's delivered daily to the kitchens of head chef Georges Landriot. The rest is a matter of strict attention to detail (which results in consistency) wedded to a spark of talent—enough at least to combine crab rémoulade and smoked salmon into a marvelously fresh-tasting, appetizing dish or to turn poached lobster into a light, festive, delicious invention. A few desserts are worth three toques, like the feathery pear tart with caramel sauce. Expect a cordial reception by the owner's son and an attractive decor of blue and yellow Spanish tiles.

A la carte: 400-600F.

(17) Le Grand Véfour

17, rue de Beaujolais
42.96.56.27

M. Taittinger. Open until 10:15 p.m. Closed Sat. lunch, Sun. & Aug. Air cond. No pets. Cards: V, AE, DC.

The magic of the Véfour lies in the fact that you could dine among empty tables in perfect contentment, free to admire the exquisite surroundings that Jean Taittinger's good taste and family fortune have restored to their former glory: carved boiserie ceilings, graceful painted allegories under glass, lush carpeting, tables with white linens set among black-and-gold Directoire chairs. The place evokes memories of such immortals as Napoléon and Jean Cocteau, Victor Hugo and Colette, who once lounged on these very (or older) red-velvet banquettes in the soft glow of the Palais-Royal gardens. There would even be time to complain about the tasteless imitation-Empire chandelier hanging above your head.

But the Véfour is no place for solitary musings, having become a great crowd-drawer since its revival by the Taittinger group. Now, at the scene of important business luncheons and dinners, guests can rely on prompt and efficient service under the expert guidance of Marcellin Guillier. The pleasure of dining at the Véfour has taken a leap forward with the arrival of the 30-year-old chef, Jean-Claude Lhonneur, who had already made a name for himself in the Céladon's kitchens and at Les Célébrités, under the aegis of chef

Robuchon. But don't expect the kind of astounding creations turned out by his former boss, for Lhonneur, a native of the Berry region, favors a light, modernized classic cuisine. He strives for simple, uncontrived, delicate flavors expertly assembled and seasoned, as in his terrine of chicken livers; scrambled eggs with salmon roe and chives; firm, chunky filet of peppered sole; poached sea bass with perfectly prepared aromatic vegetables; and veal tenderloin in an herb sauce (served whole in defiance of the current foolish practice of cutting it up).

Lhonneur is doing many smart things. He also called in his brother Frédéric, an accomplished pastry maker, whose warm apple confections and bittersweet-chocolate-nut crusts with orange sauce are out of this world. And if the à la carte bill is also up there in the stratosphere, the lunch menu, including a wide variety of dishes, is a good buy because, with a fine Bordeaux selling for about 100 francs, you'll spend less than 400 francs in all and walk away with an unforgettable memory in the bargain.

A la carte: 600-800F. Menu: 290F (lunch only).

12/20 Gros Minet

1, rue des Prouvaires - 42.33.02.62

M. Nocchi. Open until midnight. Closed Mon. & Sat. lunch, Sun. Pets allowed. Cards: V, AE, DC, MC.

The decor is a '30s pub with up-to-date wiring and plumbing. Maurice Nocchi makes a splendid host. His bar is a period piece, and his customers, always animated and thirsty, keep the place lively until the wee hours. No-nonsense cooking with a southwestern French touch (cassoulet, roast duck) and a Madiran (red wine from the Hautes-Pyrénées) that you won't forget.

A la carte: 180F. Menus: 60F (lunch only), 98F.

10/20 Hippopotamus

25, rue Berger - 45.08.00.29

See Eighth Arrondissement.

(16) Hubert

25, rue de Richelieu
42.96.08.47, 42.96.08.80

M. Hubert. Open until 10:30 p.m. Closed Sat. lunch & Sun. Air cond. Pets allowed. Cards: V, AE, DC.

When we first met, M. Hubert was an able and ambitious 30-year-old master cheese maker. Today he's 56, and after a somewhat checkered career, he's become a chef of no small talent. He entered the kitchen relatively late in life and felt at a disadvantage. He has finally put down roots—midway between the Théâtre Français and the Fontaine Molière—in a setting that is, appropriately enough, faintly theatrical and, with its fake marble, fake blue sky dotted with fake clouds and distinctly pretentious service, lacking warmth. The chef's talent, however, has defined itself markedly, and he has mastered a growing repertoire of subtle, light creations to the point where we don't hesitate to raise his rating a notch. How could we not, after trying the warm oysters in a briny bouillon, rabbit pâté, delicious semismoked salmon garnished with a leek charlotte, a remarkably fresh-tasting duck foie gras flavored with tawny port, mixed aromatic seafood in a flaky crust, roast turbot basted with truffle juice, crab ravioli with veal flavoring, filet of veal in carrot juice, stir-fried meats cooked with pears in cider, and pot-au-feu of duck thighs? The pastries and desserts are always superb (orange-flavored chocolate rice charlotte; saffron-scented custard topped with brown sugar; caramel ice cream with candied orange). Pascal Martin, the young sommelier, has style and all the right labels. To fill his 40 seats twice a day, Hubert has developed a series of menus, the cheapest of which is not to be avoided.

A la carte: 350-550F. Menus: 220F (lunch only), 280F and 380F (dinner only), 300F.

12/20 Lescure

7, rue de Mondovi - 42.60.18.91

M. Lascaud. Open until 10 p.m. Closed Sat. dinner, Sun., July & Dec. 23-Jan. 1. Terrace dining. Pets allowed. Cards: V.

A cheerful family place with a menu that justly proclaims: "Our reputation goes back to 1919." The decor is abundantly rustic, the service instantaneous and expert, the clientele fanatic (the American Embassy practically lives here), and the cooking genuinely home style (pot-au-feu, aïoli, bourguignons and so on).

A la carte: 150F. Menu: 80F (wine incl.).

(14) Mercure Galant

15, rue des Petits-Champs
42.96.98.89, 42.97.53.85

M. Caille. Open until 10:30 p.m. Closed Sat. lunch, Sun. & holidays. Pets allowed. Cards: V.

After fifteen years at the helm of this attractive, authentic turn-of-the-century eating establishment, M. Caille can be justly proud of his uninterrupted success. On each of our visits to the elegantly faded restaurant, with its plush wall coverings, beveled mirrors and deep-cushioned banquettes, Caille also proved to be a first-rate host; the service was courteous, near perfect and prompt (business lunches are never allowed to drag on), and no detail was overlooked (appetizers, delicious dark bread and butter brought to the table immediately, excellent fresh petits fours). Chef Ferranti pays equally meticulous attention to his job, providing a choice of dishes that is modest (more so than the prices) and shows great care for the finished product. The vegetable terrine with a liver mousse is slightly overwhelmed by its carrot flavor, but the roast turbot with oysters and the sweetbreads in a light wine sauce with macaroni au gratin are faultless, as are the incredibly feathery millefeuilles. At dinner, excellent wines complement an inviting menu.

A la carte: 400-500F. Menus: 230F and 345F (dinner only).

(13) La Passion

41, rue des Petits-Champs - 42.97.53.41

M. Zellenwarger. Open until 10:30 p.m. Closed Sat. lunch & Sun. Air cond. No pets. Cards: V, AE, DC.

Gilles Zellenwarger, a bearded young chef who trained under Guérard and Pangaud, has taken over this rather staid but comfortable (in a pleasantly flowery sort of way) establishment. His à la carte menu may be conventional, but he has all the technical know-how to update a classic cuisine. Our meal included a savory rabbit terrine with a well-seasoned green salad, calf's head accompanied by sautéed sweetbreads and baby vegetables, and a light creamy molded rice dessert. The Beaujolais, on the other hand, was terribly mediocre.

A la carte: 250F. Menu: 180F.

12/20 Le Pavillon Baltard

9, rue Coquillière - 42.36.22.00

M. Tissot. Open daily until 1 a.m. Terrace dining. Pets allowed. Cards: V, AE, DC, MC.

After years of dust, excavation and street barriers, the gardens are actually being laid out in "the hole" (the excavation site of the old Paris markets now at Rungis); Le Pavillon Baltard stares straight out at them. So we'll have to visit there again (before the remodeling does away with Slavik's "farmhouse" decor) to sample the sausages, confits and choucroute (Sauerkraut).

A la carte: 230F. Menu: 138F.

(14) Pharamond

24, rue de la Grande-Truanderie
42.33.06.72

M. Hyvonnet. Open until 10 p.m. Closed Mon. lunch, Sun. & July. Terrace dining. Pets allowed. Cards: V, AE, DC.

The extravagant development that replaced the old Paris marketplace, Les Halles, is by no stretch of the imagination any more exotic or attractive than the beloved old open-air market. For instance, one of our favorite Les Halles restaurants is one of the old timers: the phenomenal Pharamond, the ancient temple dedicated to tripes à la mode de Caen, where you can also worship sausage from Jargeau and grilled pigs' feet. As the "modern" style wears thin, this bistro seems younger and livelier each year—with its wood paneling, flowered tiles, Belle Epoque fixtures and mirrors and intimate dining rooms. The cuisine is up to date and welcomes new ideas. Good wines in addition to pear and apple cider.

A la carte: 230-250F.

12/20 Au Pied de Cochon

6, rue Coquillière - 42.36.11.75

MM. Blanc. Open daily 24 hrs. Air cond. Terrace dining. Pets allowed. Cards: V, AE, DC.

Eighty-five thousand pigs' feet annually and one ton of shellfish daily and nightly. The most famous institution in Les Halles never closes its doors. Day and night, 365 days a year, it churns out nonstop pork dishes, seafood platters, onion soup and grilled meats. Run by the Blanc family and an able manager, the machine rattles on, while people in the street stare at the goings-on inside, fascinated by the sight of this venerable house suddenly left standing alone at the edge of "the hole," the site of the long-awaited gardens that are replacing Les Halles, Paris's former marketplace.

A la carte: 230F and up.

(15) Pierre Traiteur

10, rue de Richelieu
42.96.09.17, 42.96.27.17

M. Dez. Open until 10:15 p.m. Closed Sat., Sun., holidays & Aug. Pets allowed. Cards: V, AE, DC.

Quick, let's restore Pierre Traiteur's two toques, for its stuffed cabbage, its cod in the style of Auvergne, one of the best pot roasts in Paris, complete with vegetables from the pot, its amazing gratin dauphinois served with rack of lamb, its lean, tender, perfectly seasoned sausage, its extraordinary-tasting boar's head and its surprisingly delicate foie gras sliced as thick as your edition of *The Best of France*. In our last French-language edition, Daniel Dez, the new owner of this great regional bistro, did not receive the rating or the toques of his illustrious predecessor, Nouyrigat, as the restaurant changed hands at about the time we were going to press and the chef had flown the coop. His assistant, Roger Leplu, took on the job along with Didier Saux, and now the food in this cozy, prosperous Palais-Royal bistro, where they continue to uncork the most captivating little wines (the Chinon is out of this world), is as good as ever.

A la carte: 300-400F.

(14) Le Poquelin

17, rue Molière - 42.96.22.19

M. Guillaumin. Open until 10:30 p.m. Closed Sat. lunch, Sun. & Aug. 1-20. Air cond. Pets allowed. Cards: V, AE, DC.

On the brown-and-ivory-striped wallpaper are a host of engravings, some quite old, evoking the plays of Poquelin, alias Molière. And on Michel Guillaumin's menu are numerous reminders of his years at Taillevent and even of his years here when it was called Les Barrières, when Claude Verger ran the kitchens. Hence our impression of having tasted this cooking before: excellent and consistent, with the emphasis on updating traditional recipes and lightening classic dishes. Fine salads (like the chopped bottom round of beef with fresh tomatoes or the slices of veal kidney and crisp cabbage), well-prepared fish, choice wild game in season and delectable desserts (especially the famous flat tart à la Claude Verger). The wine list is still developing.

A la carte: 300F. Menu: 173F.

11/20 La Providence

6, rue de la Sourdière - 42.60.46.13

Mme. Schweitzer. Open until 11:30 p.m. Closed Sat., Sun. & holidays. Air cond. Pets allowed. Cards: V, AE, DC, MC.

An attractive reminder of what bistros used to look like, La Providence is a popular place, especially in the evening, to eat cured beef, Spätzle, Lorraine stew and several Alsatian specialties (the owner comes from there), washed down with Ottrott red wine at a modest price and, after dinner, mouth-watering white brandies.

A la carte: 150F. Menus: 73F (lunch only, wine incl.), 99F.

(13) Prunier Madeleine

9, rue Duphot - 42.60.36.04

M. Bernheim. Open daily until 10:30 p.m. Air cond. Pets allowed. Cards: V.

Seaworthy it may have been, but this venerable institution needed an infusion of bold Gascon blood to pry it out of dry dock and get it to hoist sail. Mustachioed Arnaud Daguin, son of the enormous André, did just that in 1987. But now along comes a brand-new chef, Mark Singer. Will he earn his captain's stripes? Just now, it's too early to tell, but he has been struggling valiantly to rid the menu of relics that must date back to the *Titanic*'s era. No more hollandaise and béchamel sauces smothering Prunier's sole and Vérilhac's turbot—now we have filet of sea bass in verjuice (the juice of unripened grapes), scallops with Sauternes and spices and grouper seasoned with juniper berries. But there's no reason to change those monumental platters of seafood or to redo the pleasant upstairs dining rooms, the glory of Prunier's. An attractive fixed-price menu at 150 francs is served on the ground floor, now known as Prunierskaia.

A la carte: 400F and up. Menus: 150F (wine incl.), 450F.

11/20 Le Samovar

14, rue Sauval - 42.61.77.74

M. Siew. Dinner only. Open until 1 a.m. Closed Sun. Air cond. Pets allowed. Cards: V, AE.

It's party time in the evening, with singers and balalaika players, pickled herring, blinis, shashlik and vatrouchka. With its attractive menus and delicious vodkas from all over served in carafes, Le Samovar is one of the best little Russian places in Paris.

A la carte: 230-300F. Menus: 130F (weekdays only), 170F, 320F (wine incl.).

(13) Saudade

34, rue des Bourdonnais - 42.36.30.71

M. Machado. Open until 11:30 p.m. Closed Sun., Aug. 1-Sept. 6 & Dec. 23-27. Air cond. No pets. Cards: V, AE, DC.

The great Portuguese food you kept looking for in Lisbon and Porto is found here, in a setting of rough-plastered walls decorated with tiles and folk art. The cooking is done by a skillful woman from traditional recipes and is served, minus fanfare and fads, with vintage port and surprisingly good Portuguese wines. There is cod and more cod (in a stew with cabbage—superb!), marinated roast suckling pig, an almond tart and a small wine-tasting bar.

A la carte: 200F.

11/20 Velloni

22, rue des Halles - 42.21.12.50

M. Cuccuini. Open daily until 11 p.m. Cards: V, AE, DC.

Lately we have been disappointed with this distinguished Italian restaurateur. Though the reception is always warm and the decor tasteful in this pink-and-black brasserie, the cheese ravioli was less than inspired and the sweetbreads with endive salad were quite ordinary on our last visit. Even if the saffron risotto and the mocha tart Procope are excellent, the cuisine lacks originality. The Italian wines are as good as they are costly.

A la carte: 250F.

12/20 Willi's Wine Bar

13, rue des Petits-Champs - 42.61.05.09

M. Williamson. Open until 11 p.m. Closed Sun. Pets allowed. Cards: V.

Mark Williamson is an extremely knowledgeable British wine expert who provides 200 wines to choose from, including an incomparable collection of Côtes-du-Rhône and rare labels from all over the world. Excellent selection by the glass. These beautiful wines will accompany a generous and fresh cuisine: roast duck, clams with herbs. Good fixed-price menu.

A la carte: 200F. Menu: 138F (wine incl.).

Second Arrondissement

12/20 L'Amanguier

110, rue de Richelieu - 42.96.37.79

M. Derderian. Open until midnight. Closed May 1. Air cond. Terrace dining. Pets allowed. Cards: V, AE, DC.

This delightful little chain is going strong, including its latest link in Chicago. The decor creates the illusion of a flower garden, the pastries look and taste marvelous (baked by Framboisier, same company), and the cooking is all quality and freshness: crab with cucumber, ravioli à la crème, lamb au gratin. Among the good choice of wines, none are too expensive.

A la carte: 180F. Menu: 100F.

(13) Auberge Perraudin

164, rue Montmartre - 42.36.71.09

M. Perraudin. Open until 11 p.m. Closed Sat. lunch (& dinner in July), Sun. & Aug. Air cond. Pets allowed. Cards: V, AE, DC.

The new decor, including a paneled ceiling and wall-to-wall carpeting, is a distinct improvement over the old, even if it does sacrifice individuality for comfort. Chef Perraudin, a disciple of Orsi and Bocuse and a true devotee of his art, appears to have lost a bit of steam, though his cuisine remains light and meticulously prepared. The à la carte selections are cautiously modern, but there is just one fixed-price menu (whose quality-to-price ratio is not as attractive as it has been in the past): a pungent terrine of mackerel, cod in puff pastry, an overripe Brie and a delicious warm apple tart. It can all be accompanied by a number of good little wines at ordinary prices.

A la carte: 250-350F. Menus: 150F, 250F, 320F.

11/20 Brasserie Gus

157, rue Montmartre - 42.36.68.40

M. Prigent. Open for lunch only; open for dinner Fri. until midnight. Closed Sat. & Sun. Pets allowed. Cards: V.

Good everyday cooking with an individual touch at moderate prices, served with sharp little wines by the pitcher. The nostalgic decor is typical of an old-time popular Alsatian brasserie and is the oldest in the city (it has been preserved intact since 1870). Try the filet of hogfish with eggplant, lobster in the shell (a Brittany specialty) or veal tenderloin with red currants.

A la carte: 200F.

(15) Le Céladon

(Hôtel Westminster)

15, rue Daunou - 47.03.40.42

M. Borri. Open until 10:30 p.m. Closed Sat., Sun. & Aug. 2-Sept. 2. Air cond. Pets allowed. Parking. Telex 680035. Cards: V, AE, DC, MC.

The spontaneous, inviting, intelligent cuisine of Joël Boilleaut, who recently took over from Jean-Claude Lhonneur (gone to Le Grand Véfour), is exactly what one would prefer to eat in these elegant yet informal surroundings, where the serpentine-green tile blends well with the willow-green silk and pale-rose chair covers. In short, neither the ambience nor the cooking evokes the ceremonial boredom common to luxury eating places. The new chef, former right-hand man to Michel Kérever at the Duc d'Enghien, creates precise, savory, decorative and thoroughly modern dishes. The crab ravioli with a light basil-flavored cream sauce and the cod steak with potatoes involve more technical expertise than imagination, and let's hope that in the future this young chef will develop more personality—perhaps in the style of his delectable pork filets en crépinette with a curry sauce. For a remarkable dessert, try the chocolate macaroons in a coffee crème anglaise. The good menu/carte combination at lunch keeps the check under 300 francs, including a Bordeaux wine.

Menu/carte: 270F.

15 La Corbeille

154, rue Montmartre - 40.26.30.87

M. Cario. Open until 10:30 p.m. Closed Sat. lunch & Sun. Air cond. Pets allowed. Cards: V, AE.

Spacious circular padded-leather banquettes, varnished wood, tall mirrors—all in all, a typical '50s interior, but one that Jean-Pierre Cario has redone and enlarged, surely for the greater enjoyment of the bankers and stockbrokers who flock here from across the street for the best cooking in the neighborhood. Following a stint on the heights of Salon-de-Provence, Cario brought with him the scents and flavors of that region, whose classics are liberally represented on the La Corbeille bill of fare. His market basket, as well as his remarkable fixed-price menus (the most expensive comes with several glasses of Bordeaux and one of a '77 port wine), is altogether sunny: fish stew steamed with basil; veal shank with crayfish prepared with fennel bulbs; coquilles St-Jacques with spaghetti-like strips of zucchini; skate wing with figs. Cario also serves a wide choice of wild game in season.

A la carte: 350F. Menus: 160F (lunch only), 265F and 340F (dinner only, wine incl.).

12/20 Coup de Coeur

19, rue St-Augustin - 47.03.45.70

MM. Namura & Oudin. Open until 10:30 p.m. Closed Sat. lunch & Sun. Pets allowed. Cards: V, AE, DC.

The interior is 100-percent gray (it's all the rage) with gorgeous but uncomfortable dining chairs designed by Philippe Starck. And the cuisine is in keeping with the rest: light, entertaining and up-to-date. Try the trout tartare, the brill (like sand dab) with lemon confit and the burnt-almond ice cream with pistachios. Good fixed-price menu, but the wines are too expensive.

A la carte: 230-250F. Menu: 118F.

17 Drouant

18, rue Gaillon
42.65.15.16

M. Bourdon. Open daily until 10:30 p.m. Air cond. Parking. Pets allowed. Cards: V, AE, DC.

This restaurant has the great distinction of hosting the monthly literary luncheons of the ten-member Prix Goncourt jury. Robert Sabatier, the gourmand of that prestigious group, warned his host: "Take it easy, now; my colleagues have classic tastes, so don't abuse their habits." James Baron listened reverently but went right ahead with his own plans. Being a "modern" chef, he had no intention of inaugurating the new Drouant's stoves by serving the literary lions lobster Thermidor and tournedos Rossini! The Tuesday before the Prix Goncourt (the most famous literary prize in France) was to be awarded, the jury gathered in its own special dining room, which has been moved down a floor and reconstructed pretty much as it was (except it is now oval and magnificently paneled). The members were surprised at the menu: oysters poached in their own juices with caviar and a lemon-flavored cream sauce; sole with a creamy watercress garnish; fried onions and tomato pulp; squab with fried celery; assorted cheeses from Authès; and a raspberry tart. Not exactly revolutionary, granted, but a fresh chapter nonetheless in the gastronomic epic of this illustrious body. The verdict was unanimous: Baron deserved the Prix Goncourt *de la cuisine*!

We can confirm this favorable report after tasting some half dozen dishes in the small room adjoining the celebrated Goncourt's (the demand for reservations is endless; it costs 1,500 francs to get in). This shouldn't be much of a surprise, since we awarded three toques to this culinary loner from the Vendée region, self-taught for the most part. He sprinted from Maxim's to Lenôtre and on to Troisgros before settling down in a small hotel opposite the railroad station in Cholet, the former capital of the handkerchief industry and not exactly a hive of gastronomic activity. His straightforward, inventive and flavorful cuisine arrived just in time to rescue the Drouant empire, founded in 1880 in the form of an oyster bar, from a steady decline. Not to mention providing a solid underpinning for the very spectacular metamorphosis of this venerable establishment on the place Gaillon.

After meticulously restoring this handsome building, the decorators Zanetti and Slavik completely redid the interior, with its splendid wrought-iron and marble staircase (considered one of Ruhlmann's masterpieces), to re-create the atmosphere of those wild years between the two world wars, exemplified by marquetry furniture, etched mirrors and Lalique-inspired sconces, such as you'd find aboard the great transatlantic liners of that era. The cool elegance is warmed by vases of vivid-colored flowers, by the subtle harmonies of carpeting, draperies and chair covers, by ideal lighting and by a series of striking Boldiniesque portraits of society swells gracing the walls of the main dining room, called "The Restaurant." There, for the 40 or so guests divided between the street floor and the mezzanine, Baron distributes his oversize menu—actually quite short but sufficiently eloquent to convey his talent: a light, crusty pastry filled with boned frogs' legs seasoned with garlic and anise, saffron-scented coquilles St-Jacques with poached oysters on a bed of fried spinach, red mullet with preserved zucchini, breast of duck with ginger and endive, herbed roast saddle of rabbit, tender and thick, garnished with a mushroom fricassée.

Le Café (the old Grill), to the left of the entrance, seats 60 under a pale-gold ceiling that, like the stairway, dates back to 1926. Cocteau remarked that the fish decoration resembled "the sky of the sea." The dark paneling, the mirrors, the marble, the soft-leather banquettes, the gray ostrich-skin wallpaper and the little yellow lamps on the tables have a most appealing effect. Two glamorous hostesses are there to receive you, and the service, exclusively by waitresses, could hardly displease the businessperson who may lunch until three in the afternoon on a plate of oysters, grilled salmon or a slice of roast beef served in the grand manner on a marble slab.

A la carte: 450-600F. Menu: 290F (dinner only at Le Café, wine incl.).

10/20 Hippopotamus

1, blvd. des Capucines - 47.42.75.70
See Eighth Arrondissement.

12/20 Isse

56, rue Ste-Anne - 42.96.67.76
M. Sudo. Open until 10:30 p.m. Closed Sat. lunch, Sun. & Aug. 1-15. Air cond. Pets allowed.

Fashion designer Kenzo's eating place needs a shot in the arm. The service and prices are as stiff as ever; fish dishes are spectacular in appearance and lunch menus are attractive, but you begin to find a sameness about everything. Try the raw live California-type lobster and the fluffy fritters.

A la carte: 300F. Menu: 110F (lunch only).

12/20 Perry Brothers Restaurant

20, passage des Panoramas - 42.33.31.80
MM. Perry & Zelaya. Open until 7 p.m. Closed Sat. & Sun. Pets allowed. Cards: V.

Chef Alan Perry is a sturdy Welshman whose approach to food is anything but insular. Inspiration for his cosmopolitan cooking comes from sources as diverse as northern Europe and Southeast Asia, via the Mediterranean and the U.S. Typical offerings from his menu—which, incidentally, he revises daily—might include delicate scallop ravioli in a creamy basil sauce, a hearty New York deli-style sandwich heaped high with pastrami and corned beef, a spicy chicken saté or a robust dish of poached finnan haddie (smoked haddock) in a smooth Cheddar sauce. Wine journalist Fiona Beeston has put together an equally international wine list, with representatives from Italy, Chile and Australia alongside the French contingent. Good news: Many bottles are priced around a hundred francs, and a selection of fine wines is always available by the glass. All this good eating and drinking goes on within the picturesque passage des Panoramas, in sleek silvery-gray and gray-green surroundings created by co-owner Jorge Zelaya, a professional graphic designer.

A la carte: 175F. Menu: 125F.

12/20 Le Petit Coin de la Bourse

16, rue Feydeau - 45.08.00.08
M. Andron. Open until 10:30 p.m. Closed Sat. & Sun. Pets allowed. Cards: V, AE, DC.

An amusing and typical turn-of-the-century Parisian bistro. The Belle Epoque decor is a bit faded though still appealing on the main floor and upstairs. The cooking also attempts to appeal: rabbit terrine with pistachios, beef filet in a wine sauce, thin tarts à la Verger.

A la carte: 280-300F. Menu: 150F (dinner only).

(14) Pile ou Face (Heads or Tails)

52 bis, rue Notre-Dame-des-Victoires
42.33.64.33
MM. Udron, Dumergue & Marquet. Open until 10 p.m. Closed Sat., Sun., Aug., Dec. 24-Jan. 1 & holidays. Air cond. Pets allowed. Cards: V.

The name of this restaurant belies the purposeful attitude of its ruling triumvirate. The cuisine of chef/partner Claude Udron, who, with no grand credentials, leaves nothing to chance, and the last few meals he prepared for us nearly warranted two toques: a sumptuous spinach soup, ravioli filled with herbed escargots, filet of beef with foie gras (pleasant echo of a tournedos Rossini) garnished with a delicious shredded potato pancake, filet of red mullet in olive oil with celery stalks, and a light, crusty apple pastry. Simplicity, freshness, exquisite presentations—all these, plus the homemade bread and petits fours, are points in favor. The wine list has blossomed, and the service is first-rate in an elegant if slightly confining decor.

A la carte: 300F.

12/20 Le Saint-Amour

8, rue de Port-Mahon - 47.42.63.82
Mme. Bouché-Pillon. Open until 10:30 p.m. Closed Sat. lunch (& dinner in July & Aug.), Sun., July 14-Aug. 15 & holidays. Air cond. Pets allowed. Cards: V, AE, DC.

A stone's throw from the main boulevards and their cheap eateries, this is a real restaurant: responsible, reliable and comfortable (the cozy interior is partitioned by banquettes on the second floor). A typical fixed-price menu: eggs poached in red-wine sauce, homemade duck confit, Brie from Meaux and tarte tatin.

A la carte: 250-280F. Menu: 170F.

11/20 La Taverne du Nil

9, rue du Nil - 42.33.51.82
Mlle. Khalil. Open until 8 p.m. Closed Sun. & Aug. 15-30. No pets. Cards: V, AE.

Tablecloths, napkins, a cordial reception (by a former member of the Marist Fathers of Byblos) and belly dancing on weekends can all be yours for a bargain price. You'll dine on mezze (an assortment of seven appetizers), falafel and chiche taouk (marinated chicken).

Menus: 71F, 90F, 120F.

12/20 Yaki

2 bis, rue Daunou - 42.61.71.31
Mme. Tamada. Open until 11 p.m. Closed Sun. Air cond. Pets allowed. Cards: V.

On the third floor of this Korean barbecue is an elegant, very Japanese sushi bar. Following the warm reception, three active sushi men, with artistry at their command, are there to serve you the freshest fish and shellfish with traditional rice, seaweed and finely chopped chive accompaniments.

A la carte: 230F. Menus: 75F (weekday lunch only), 110F to 195F.

Third Arrondissement

15 Ambassade d'Auvergne

22, rue du Grenier-St-Lazare
42.72.31.22

M. Petrucci. Open daily until 11:30 p.m. Air cond. Pets allowed. Cards: V.

Retired from his tripe and his cabbage soup, the delightful paterfamilias, Joseph Petrucci, scarcely ever appears in his "legation" barded with pork cuts and cured hams. But his diplomatic ministers—daughters, sons-in-law and a staff of loyal veterans—are adept at celebrating both the visual and the gastronomic delights of the Auvergne. The restaurant has just been refurbished from cellar to roof and looks even more characteristically Auvergnat: more rustic and even older. Gone are the calf's head with kiwis and lobster with currants. The latest culinary fashion in the Auvergne calls for lentil salad, pigs' feet with fourme cheese, daube of duck, boudin sausage with chestnuts, stuffed breast of veal and cured pork. Chateaugay or Saint-Pourçain are wines that go well with all of these dishes, and if you're really in the swing of things, you'll want to visit the table d'hôte, perhaps the last of its breed in Paris, and cut yourself a slice of Auvergnat pork. If you don't come from the Auvergne, a meal at the Ambassade will make you wish you did.

A la carte: 200-280F.

L'Ami Louis

32, rue de Vertbois - 48.87.77.48

M. De la Brosse. Open until 10:30 p.m. Closed Mon., Tues. & July 15-Aug. 31. No pets. Cards: V, AE, DC.

Sentiment motivated the two new owners from Ludéric, a company that specializes in home-catering services, in their purchase of this time-honored monument from famous chef Antoine Magnin, who passed away not long ago. They hasten to add that nothing will be changed, including the present layer of dust, and thus far they've kept their promise. Though Magnin no longer shuffles about behind clouds of smoke in his kitchen/museum, the dining room still offers the irresistible sight of the venerable stove pipe, the mold-ridden mirrors, the old paintings and the dining chairs that have grown rickety in his service. Best of all, you can still inhale those timeless, priceless cooking smells, the trademark of this last great Parisian bistro. We have sworn to celebrate the year 2000 at L'Ami Louis feasting on Burgundy escargots, foie gras, great slabs of beef rib roast, roast chicken (the best in Paris), duck confit, a divinely light apple béarnaise and burnt-almond ice cream. This will surely put us in proper spirits to face the next thousand years.

A la carte: 500-600F.

11/20 Chez Jenny

39, blvd. du Temple - 42.74.75.75

M. Siljegovic. Open daily until 1 a.m. Terrace dining. Pets allowed. Cards: V, DC.

The marquetry in the upstairs dining room is truly remarkable, which is more than one can say about the legendary varieties (five) of choucroute that are served here. The excellent Alsatian charcuterie is really what sells the choucroute.

A la carte: 200-230F.

12/20 Le Connétable

55, rue des Archives
42.77.41.40, 42.71.69.21

Mme. Wilcz. Open until midnight. Closed Sat. lunch & Sun. Air cond. Pets allowed. Cards: V, DC.

A pleasant bar on the main floor, an ancient cellar where you can listen to old French songs until late at night and an upstairs dining room in this handsome old Marais-district house with age-old beams and a fireplace. Unfortunately, the cuisine has slipped into banality (warm goat cheese, overgrilled lamb chops, tarte tatin).

A la carte: 250F. Menu: 100F.

12/20 La Guirlande de Julie

25, pl. des Vosges - 48.87.94.07

M. Grolier. Open until 11 p.m. Closed Mon., Tues. & Dec. 18-Jan. 18. Terrace dining. Pets allowed. Cards: V, AE, MC.

The pleasant new winter-garden decor highlights the superb beams of this historic house on the legendary place des Vosges. The new owner has designed an attractive 125-franc fixed-price menu based on a tasty pot-au-feu. The cuisine (mackerel rillettes, fish chowder, duck confit in cider and a bittersweet chocolate cake) is unpretentious and quite popular with the crowds that fill up the dining room and, on fine days, the terrace that overlooks the recently redesigned place des Vosges.

A la carte: 200F. Menus: 80F (weekday lunch only), 125F.

13 Taverne des Templiers

106, rue Vieille-du-Temple - 42.78.74.67

M. Bertrand. Open until 10 p.m. Closed Sat., Sun. & Aug. Pets allowed. Cards: V, DC.

With its intimate setting in a conventional but comfortable Louis XIII style, complete with a splendid beamed ceiling, the Taverne is a great place for a quiet lunch or a romantic dinner. The delightful neighborhood is right next door to the Musée Picasso. The owner's wife is all smiles, the service is unobtrusive, and Guy Bertrand's cooking conveys the bright, delicious country flavors of the Charente region, to which he adds his own personal and seasonal touches. From the short à la carte menu, we suggest the foie gras in wine aspic, warm oysters in a creamy herb sauce, herbed frog soup, fricassée of chevreau (kid) à la saintongeaise, parsleyed eel, lobster soufflé and one of the good regional wines at moderate prices.

A la carte: 250F.

Fourth Arrondissement

L'Ambroisie

18

9, pl. des Vosges
42.78.51.45

M. Pacaud. Open until 10:15 p.m. Closed Mon., Sun., 2 weeks in Feb. & 1st 3 weeks of Aug. Air cond. No pets. Cards: V.

The charming and discreet Pacauds left their cramped quarters on the quai de la Tournelle and moved to the majestic place des Vosges. Unfortunately, there is no view of it, as the dining room, which used to be a goldsmith's workshop, is windowless. But L'Ambroisie is spacious, handsomely proportioned and stylishly elegant, thanks to decorator François-Joseph Graf. Twenty-five guests can eat in the main dining room, fifteen more in a smaller one. To ornament the street level of this historic mansion, known as the Hôtel de Luynes during the tenancy of its seventeenth-century owner, a marvelous inlaid flooring of ancient tiles in various shades of ocher has been installed, as well as wood paneling, carved wood chairs, decorative objects displayed on a sideboard, a rich tapestry stretching the length of the central wall and soft lighting. In short, everything is in place to delight the eye and prepare for a celebration. Chef Pacaud offers a mousse of bell peppers with tomato purée, ravioli filled with crab cooked in shellfish broth, a combination of lobster and sweetbreads, spicy turbot filet, crayfish split and basted with tarragon butter, a feuilleté of fresh truffles, braised oxtail (Bernard Pacaud's trademark and a trademark of his menu) and a fabulous roast rib steak. The elegant but unpretentious meals have warranted one more point in this edition. The few desserts offered are remarkable: a traditional savarin, coffee mousse with melted chocolate, vanilla napoleons. The wine list, also short, is well balanced, including the best Côtes-du-Rhône and a nice selection from Languedoc.

A la carte: 600F. Menus: 255F (lunch only), 450F (tasting menu).

11/20 Auberge de Jarente

7, rue de Jarente - 42.77.49.35

M. Charriton. Open until 10:30 p.m. Closed Sun., Mon. & Aug. 5-Sept. 5. Pets allowed. Cards: V, AE, DC, MC.

A delightful place with Basque customers, a Basque atmosphere and chef and Basque cuisine: pipérade (Basque omelet), Béarn andouille (sausages) and two house specialties: paella on Friday and Saturday and cassoulet the rest of the week.

A la carte: 160F. Menus: 106F (wine incl.), 94F, 145F.

Benoit

14

20, rue St-Martin - 42.72.25.76

M. Petit. Open until 10 p.m. Closed Sat., Sun., March 20-27 & July 31-Aug. 21. Air cond. Terrace dining. Pets allowed.

Even though he's called the pope of Paris bistros, Michel Petit takes his customers quite seriously. The founder's grandson, Petit clearly intends to perpetuate the things that make his admirable restaurant, which opened in 1912, so attractive: the authentic stucco interior, the mirrors and light-oak cabinetry, the cordial service and, of course, the beef pot-au-feu à la parisienne (a mouth-watering cold stew that has been on the menu for 70 years), braised beef, cassoulet maison with plump beans that melt in your mouth, the best pot roast (sharing honors with Pierre Traiteur) and exquisite cod au gratin. In addition to exercising their talent for cuisine bourgeoise, Petit and his chef, Dany Bulot, borrow freely, almost cavalierly (though with authority) from the modern repertoire—for instance, skate with shallots and herbs in a pie crust, a small duck pâté in puff pastry with a memorable pear sauce, and poached salmon with a chiffonnade (minced sorrel, lettuce, parsley and chervil in butter). In short, Petit is a conservative who nevertheless marches steadily forward—along with the prices. Excellent wine cellar, strong on Beaujolais.

A la carte: 350F.

12/20 Le Bistrot de Clémence

4, quai d'Orléans - 46.33.08.36

M. Blanchet. Open until 10:30 p.m. Closed Sun., Mon. & Aug. Pets allowed. Cards: V.

This bright, genuine bistro along the Seine (opposite La Tour d'Argent) serves good wines by the glass and an inviting selection of cold and hot dishes (oxtail terrine, veal kidney with garlic and nice desserts).

A la carte: 150F. Menu: 135F.

12/20 Bofinger

3-7, rue de la Bastille - 42.72.87.82

M. Alexandre. Open daily until 1 a.m. Air cond. Terrace dining. Pets allowed. Cards: V, AE, DC, MC.

This brasserie, the oldest in Paris, is a typical one, with brass decorations, glass dome, marquetry, leather banquettes, aproned waiters and the lunch and dinner crowd hunched over choucroute, oysters and the chef's special of the day. The wine list is short but good.

A la carte: 250F. Menu: 149F.

10/20 Brasserie de L'Ile-Saint-Louis

55, quai de Bourbon - 43.54.02.59

M. Gueprattc. Open until 1:30 a.m. Closed Thurs. lunch, Wed. & Aug. Pets allowed.

The chef's name is Wagner, and he will sing, in key, all about Sauerkraut. It's Bayreuth in a cheerier mood, with froth-capped beer mugs and strings of sausages overhead.

A la carte: 180F.

Coconnas

13

2 bis, pl. des Vosges - 42.78.58.16

M. Terrail. Open until 10:15 p.m. Closed Mon., Tues. & Dec. 18-Jan. 20. Terrace dining. Pets allowed. Cards: V, AE, DC.

Every day, not just on Sunday, Claude Terrail (also owner of the famous Tour d'Argent) has something special for his guests—either on the short à la carte menu created by chef Denis Dumusois, or in the fixed-price meal "with no surprises," which includes, for instance, petit salé of duck, steamed hen with plenty of vegetables, a chocolate marquise and a half bottle of Côtes-du-Rhône. In warm weather, a few tables are set

under the arcades facing the majestic square. It's a marvelous sight (inside, the decor is less inspiring).
À la carte: 300F. Menu: 145F (wine incl.).

12/20 Le Coin du Caviar

2, rue de la Bastille - 48.04.82.93
M. Nebot. Open until midnight. Closed Sun. Air cond. Pets allowed. Cards: V, AE, DC.

Along the Champs-Elysées and at the Madeleine, caviar is a thriving business; near the Bastille, it's a tougher sell. The decor is attractive and the food of good quality, but prices are stiff and accidents can happen (like the salmon overcooked on one side). Good apple strudel.

A la carte: 250-300F. Menu: 132F (lunch only).

11/20 La Colombe

4, rue de la Colombe - 46.33.37.08
Mme. Rénata. Open until midnight. Closed Mon. lunch & Sun. Terrace dining. Pets allowed. Cards: V, AE, DC, MC.

Worth a visit for the superb location—a thirteenth-century house in the shadow of Notre-Dame and the charming little terrace that's choked with Virginia creeper in the summer. La Colombe has a few rather good dishes; others are less than exciting.

A la carte: 300-350F. Menus: 185F, 240F.

(15) Au Franc Pinot

1, quai de Bourbon - 43.29.46.98
M. Meyruey. Open until 11 p.m. Closed Sun. & Mon. Pets allowed. Cards: V, MC.

Get ready: This place has cellars reaching down to the level of the Seine in one of the oldest bistros in Paris, a beaming host, muted lighting (but not so dim that you don't notice the low-grade flatware settings), excellent wines by the glass or carafe (there's a wine bar on the main floor) and a kitchen that retains its two toques despite a few shortcomings. It's a pleasant restaurant for a quiet business lunch (superb warm oysters with zucchini, breast of chicken with baby vegetables, a cheese tray and a nut cake are about 200 francs, with a carafe of Anjou red) or a romantic dinner of exquisitely fresh-tasting squab vinaigrette; Scottish salmon just a shade overcooked with some wonderfully fragrant chanterelles that could stand being less sandy and better seasoned; excellent stuffed saddle of milk-fed lamb; and a delicate coconut flan (preferable to the apple tart or the pear with almond custard, both of which are below par). Patrice Guyader, who trained with Robuchon and has been cooking at Au Franc Pinot for many years, is a good technician and innovator, but he might do well to develop simpler, not-so-rich dishes.

A la carte: 350-400F. Menus: 150F (lunch only), 180F.

12/20 Au Gourmet de l'Isle

42, rue St-Louis-en-l'Ile - 43.26.79.27
M. Bourdeau. Open until 10:30 p.m. Closed Mon. & Thurs. Cards: V.

It gets elbow-to-elbow with loyal customers who flock here both to admire the 90-year-old owner's magnificent mustache and to eat the sensational andouillette (pork sausage) with kidney beans, the boudin (blood sausage) and the quince tart. Other trademarks include a beamed ceiling on the street floor, a handsome vaulted cellar and a good fixed-price menu.

A la carte: 180F. Menu: 100F.

10/20 Hippopotamus

1, blvd. Beaumarchais - 42.72.98.37
See Eighth Arrondissement.

(15) Au Quai des Ormes

72, quai de l'Hôtel-de-Ville - 42.74.72.22
M. Bourrier. Open until 10:30 p.m. Closed Sat. lunch, Sun. & July 29-Aug. 29. Air cond. Terrace dining. Pets allowed. Cards: V.

Mme. Masraff left to join her husband in New York, and this lovely house on the banks of the Seine, close to city hall, has found a new owner from Lyon: Yves Bourrier, a most likable mustachioed gentleman who recently gave up one of the best restaurants in Neuilly to come here. Bourrier's generous, inventive cuisine is based on the freshest produce. One can only regret that the prices are not as magnetic as they once were. Many of the Masraff's à la carte selections are still served, and the two fixed-price menus (the "bourgeois" at lunch and the low-calorie "to keep the ladies happy") are greatly expanded. Several delicious new dishes, such as the ravioli filled with sweetbreads and suprême of pheasant forestière, have appeared. The delightful view of the Seine and the Ile Saint-Louis from upstairs, above the relentless traffic along the riverside is delightful.

A la carte: 400F and up. Menus: 185F (lunch only), 210F, 350F (dinner only).

(13) Wally

16, rue Le Regrattier - 43.25.01.39
M. Chouaqui. Open until 10:30 p.m. Closed Sun., Jan. 15-30 & Sept. 15-30. Air cond. Cards: V, DC.

The masterly couscous of former camel driver Wally Chouaki is different from the ordinary liquid-doused, greasy couscous you find in Paris; here, it is perfectly dry, served without broth or vegetables. You can tell how light and finely ground the semolina is, and how tasty the accompanying merguez and grilled lamb are. This delicious dish is the centerpiece of the copious fixed-price menu (the only one offered), which includes a delectable b'stilla (a savory-sweet chicken and almond pastry) and stuffed sardines. The decor is also special: It resembles a luxurious tent ornamented with valuable rugs, Berber decorations and furniture tastefully inlaid with mother-of-pearl. Prompt service can be expected at the small tables separated by antique Arabian screens.

Menu: 260F.

Fifth Arrondissement

(13) Auberge des Deux Signes

46, rue Galande - 43.25.46.56
M. Dhulster. Open until 10:30 p.m. Closed Sun. (July & Aug.). Pets allowed. Cards: V, AE, DC, MC.

The musical feature of this impressive medieval setting, formerly the Chapel of St. Blaise, is unique: Customers select their meal from the "menu" of over 1,000 records of ancient music, some quite rare. It's a humorous touch from the good-humored owner, Georges Dhulster, whose name sounds Flemish but whose accent traces him to the Auvergne. The cooking reflects both influences, which is not surprising, as the new chef comes from Lamazère: savory pounti (a rustic casserole with bacon, onion and Swiss chard), served with a rather uninteresting salad of crisp cabbage; excellent medallions of veal from Cantal; goose confit with cèpes. The rest of the menu is not so exciting, the service snail-paced, and the atmosphere touristy. But in the evening, there is a marvelous view from the upstairs dining room of floodlit Notre-Dame and the church of Saint-Julien-le-Pauvre.

A la carte: 400-500F. Menus: 150F (dinner only), 180F (lunch only, wine incl.), 240F.

(15) La Bûcherie

41, rue de la Bûcherie - 43.54.78.06

M. Bosque. Open daily until 12:30 a.m. Air cond. Terrace dining. Pets allowed. Cards: V, AE, DC.

Lately, people have been going to La Bûcherie less for the food than for the pleasant atmosphere, the crackling fire, the friendly host and the fashionable clientele. But Bernard Bosque wants to avoid the reputation of running an "in" restaurant. He is, after all, an excellent cook, successful at adapting classic and bourgeois cuisine to modern tastes. He may have been off the mark in the past, but now he's back in form. We enjoyed two perfect meals worthy of two toques—one on the terrace facing Notre-Dame, the other in the back room, which is less cheerful—fresh foie gras with truffle juice, crayfish-stuffed cabbage, salmon soufflé with crayfish and dried cod, duck confit seasoned with sorrel, a light-as-a-bubble Black Forest cake and a pear tart with almond cream. The service is unusually courteous and attentive, and the table settings are becoming more and more elegant (new linens, attractive dishes). The wine cellar is heavy on Bordeaux and ought to include a few more affordable labels, some regional selections and more whites, which are practically nonexistent.

A la carte: 350F.

12/20 Chez René

14, blvd. St-Germain - 43.54.30.23

M. Cinquin. Open until 10:15 p.m. Closed Sat., Sun., July 27-Sept. 3 & Dec. 23-Jan. 3. Pets allowed.

The best things about this old, typically Parisian corner bistro are its Swiss chard au gratin, beef rib steak Bercy, country sausage and boeuf bourguignon—and, of course, the comfortable imitation-leather banquettes, genuine polished brass and unfailingly cheerful mood. The Chénas and Juliénas, bottled by the owner, have something to do with it.

A la carte: 180-200F.

12/20 Chez Toutoune

5, rue de Pontoise - 43.26.56.81

Mme. Dejean. Open until 10:45 p.m. Closed Sun., Aug. 15-Sept. 15 & Dec. 20-Jan. 3. Terrace dining. Pets allowed. Cards: V.

The famous fixed-price menu of blond Toutoune (a.k.a. Colette Dejean) is as reliable and substantial as ever, and the prices are steady; only the descriptions change. This year's offerings include a tureen of the soup du jour (as much as you can eat), herring or terrines, cod or the cook's daily special and chocolate soufflé. Wines by the pitcher are served in this whitewashed interior.

Menu: 147F.

12/20 Chieng-Mai

12, rue Frédéric-Sauton - 43.25.45.45

M. Takounseun. Open until 11:30 p.m. Closed Sun., Aug. 1-15 & Dec. 26-Jan. 9. Air cond. Pets allowed. Cards: V, AE.

Be prepared for syrupy music and a lot of bowing and scraping as you enter. The decor, though impersonal and without much character, is admittedly comfortable, and the Thai cuisine for the most part is authentic: grilled mussels with lemon grass, delicious breast of duck flavored with basil and pepper, and an attractive basket of fish wrapped in banana leaves, all of which can be accompanied by unusual rice wines. The inviting fixed-price menus feature an assortment of dishes.

A la carte: 160F. Menus: 129F, 153F, 166F.

(14) Clavel

65, quai de la Tournelle - 46.33.18.65

M. Piras & Mme. Clavel. Open until 10:30 p.m. Closed Sun. dinner, Mon., 1 week in Feb. & Aug. 8-29. No pets. Cards: V, AE, DC.

The new owners have elected to freshen up the place (this used to be Alain Passard's L'Ambroisie, which is now in the place des Vosges) with beige and black wallpaper, indirect lighting and flowers everywhere. The new chef is young Jean-Yves Guichard, who was trained by his pastry-making parents in the Vendée and by François Clerc at La Vieille Fontaine. If you like clever, elegant cooking, you won't be disappointed, though you will pay handsomely for it: lobster ravioli with chives, roast Bresse pigeon, skate wing with mustard seed and leeks, honey-glazed apple tart.

A la carte: 350-400F. Menus: 160F (weekday lunch only), 200F.

12/20 Au Coin des Gourmets

5, rue Dante - 43.26.12.92

Mme. Ta. Open until 10:30 p.m. Closed Tues. Terrace dining. No pets. Cards: V.

The cuisine used to be so good that you wouldn't even notice the dull decor. Now you notice it, since the squid with mint leaves and the fiery Indochinese duck have lost their charm. Reasonable prices.

A la carte: 160F. Menus: 79F (lunch only), 99F and 110F (weekday lunch only).

(13) Diapason

30, rue des Bernardins - 43.54.21.13

M. Olivier. Open until 10:30 p.m. Closed Sat. lunch & Sun. Pets allowed. Cards: V, AE, DC.

The appealing decor remains as it was when chef Duquesnoy presided here not long ago. It's not easy to compete with such a cooking talent, but we note that the young chef, Jean-Claude Olivier (who's making his debut at Diapason), has developed a well-planned, enjoyable menu at reasonable prices. We tasted the smoked frogs' legs in garlic butter (a tasty and unusual dish), veal kidney, Lyon sausage with plump beans and a sample of four chocolate cakes.

A la carte: 260-280F. Menus: 145F (lunch only), 180F (dinner only, wine incl.).

(15) Dodin-Bouffant

25, rue Frédéric-Sauton - 43.25.25.14

Mme. Cartier. Open until midnight. Closed Sun., Aug. 6-Sept. 7 & 10 days at Christmas. Air cond. Terrace dining. Pets allowed. Cards: V, DC.

Long after the departure of Jacques Manière, the slight misunderstanding that Dodin-Bouffant is the first-class bistro he created lives on. Hence some disappointed patrons, who discover a decor that's not terribly engaging, sometimes disorganized service, a clientele more noisy than elegant—in short, the lively, cordial ambience of a good brasserie instead of that of the stylish restaurant they expected to find. With this in mind, they'll agree with us that Dodin-Bouffant remains one of the most congenial spots on the Left Bank both at lunch and late in the evening. Apart from the short list of market-fresh offerings (primarily fish), the à la carte menu is devoted to a superb collection of shellfish, which may be selected directly from the huge saltwater holding tanks on the premises, and to traditional, lightened country-style cooking: ragoût of mussels and pasta shells, fricassée of cod provençal, daube of oysters and pigs' feet, calf's head fricassée with rosemary and generally good desserts. The wine list includes many regional selections for less than 100 francs.

A la carte: 330-360F. Menu: 155F (lunch only).

12/20 Han-Lim

6, rue Blainville - 43.54.62.74

M. Lee-Chul-Chong. Open until 10:30 p.m. Closed Mon. & Aug. Pets allowed.

Owner and son direct rare signs of welcome to the army of Korean lunch and dinner customers, who come here for the fine Korean-Chinese cooking: chicken wings sautéed in garlic, fresh homemade noodles and a sea-cucumber salad. The fixed-price lunch menu is a bargain.

A la carte: 150F. Menu: 50F (wine incl.).

10/20 Hippopotamus

9, rue Lagrange - 43.54.13.99

See Eighth Arrondissement.

(15) Miravile

(Gilles Epié)

25, quai de la Tournelle - 46.34.07.78

MM. Epié. Open until 11 p.m. Closed Sat. lunch & Sun. Air cond. Pets allowed. Cards: V, AE, DC, MC.

Gilles Epié gave up his Café Saint-Honoré for this little restaurant near La Tour d'Argent, whose longtime chef, Arthur Keller, has raised it to the top ranks of Paris bistros. The decor (sand-colored walls, café au lait–lacquered ceiling, excellent lighting) has been tastefully redone by Epié's charming wife, Muriel. A young chef who worked with François Clerc and for the Café de Paris in Brussels, Gilles's cooking is imaginative, generous and unpretentious: salad of pot-au-feu, daube of beef cheek, salmon with puréed cabbage, french toast with glazed apples. Prices have risen from their modest beginnings but are still reasonable, and the wine list includes a number of pleasant lesser-known and affordable labels.

A la carte: 250-350F. Menu: 150F (lunch only), 300F.

(13) Moissonnier

28, rue des Fossés-St-Bernard

43.29.87.65

M. Moissonnier. Open until 10 p.m. Closed Sun. dinner, Mon. & Aug. 1-Sept. 5. Pets allowed.

An unmistakable wine-country decor on the second floor and a bourgeois one downstairs. For 28 years, André Moissonnier has stuck to his country cooking, the cuisine of Bresse, Burgundy and the specialties of Lyon: gras-double (sautéed tripe) with onions, quenelles, a traveling salad bar from which you can make a meal, and whipped potatoes au gratin. For dessert, try the good wild-raspberry sherbet or oeufs à la neige, and throughout your meal sip a fine Brouilly or Bourgueil (served in the traditional mug), which the owner has tasted, selected from the grower and drawn for you from a barrel in his cellar.

A la carte: 200F.

(15) Au Pactole

44, blvd. St-Germain

46.33.31.31, 43.26.92.28

M. Magne. Open until 10:45 p.m. Closed Sat. lunch & Sun. Air cond. Terrace dining. Pets allowed. Cards: V, AE.

Slavik's new decor has revived the tired old Pactole, which was originally put together by Manière and later patched up by Noelle and Roland Magne. The cuisine had been suffering from a loss of identity; Magne's forte is not inventiveness. But things are looking a little brighter lately. His best efforts are in the classic vein: lobster salad with pasta, duck foie gras from the Landes, salmon with tarragon, roast beef with marrow in a salt crust, minced veal kidney seasoned with basil. All these consistent and savory dishes are well worth two toques.

A la carte: 250-500F. Menus: 180F (weekday lunch only), 280F.

(13) Le Paprika

43, rue Poliveau - 43.31.65.86

M. Csekö. Open daily until 11:30 p.m. Closed Sun. & July 13-Aug. 31. Air cond. Garage parking. Pets allowed. Cards: V, AE, DC.

Dominique Csekö, one of the owners, cooks this Hungarian cuisine, which is truly original and unfamiliar. Come some evening when music is playing (remarkable gypsy group) and taste the cinnamon-flavored cherry soup, Puszta crêpes stuffed with veal goulash, mushroom strudel and fresh pork with white beans, marjoram and smoked sausage. Many varieties of excellent sweet strudel, plus the famous layer cake (vanilla, chocolate, almond) and outstanding Tokays and the heavy red wine called "bull's blood."

A la carte: 300-350F. Menu: 85F (lunch only).

(13) Restaurant A

45, rue de Poissy - 46.33.85.54

M. Huynh-Kien. Open until 11 p.m. Closed Mon. Air cond. Cards: AE.

The plain though not inelegant interior is regularly decorated with extraordinary vegetable sculptures. Over the years, the owner has made a specialty of preparing those great Chinese banquet platters that have all but vanished from the Paris scene, including such dishes as imperial shrimp, the casserole of fish and shellfish simmered (for 48 hours) in a thick, fragrant broth, and the pork fritters Kowloon, a Cantonese specialty, with green peppers and pineapple.

A la carte: 200F. Menu: 90F.

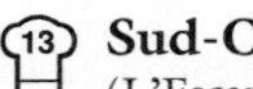

Sud-Ouest

(L'Escarmouche)

40, rue Montagne-Ste-Geneviève

46.33.30.46

M. Bourgain. Open until 10:30 p.m. Closed Sun. & Aug. Pets allowed. Cards: V, AE, DC.

This is the loveliest stone interior you'll find tucked away beneath the Montagne Sainte-Geneviève, an ancient arched crypt that sets off, with stunning elegance, the Louis XIII chairs and flower vases. Classic cuisine of southwest France is served exclusively, the best of which includes garlic-flavored tourin (onion soup), homemade foie gras, cassoulet with breast of duck, warm goat cheese with a nut salad and an array of desserts in addition to the excellent tart. Eating à la carte can be a bit costly, even with a little Gaillac wine for about 70 francs.

A la carte: 300F. Menus: 150F, 190F.

(18) La Tour d'Argent

15-17, quai de la Tournelle

43.54.23.31

M. Terrail. Open until 10 p.m. Closed Mon. Parking. Pets allowed. Cards: V, AE, DC.

Can a fairyland be privately owned? In Paris, one man can boast at least of being its tenant: Claude Terrail. At a recent summertime visit, under a threatening sky, the sunset over the stone facades of the Ile Saint-Louis and the towers of Notre-Dame created a special lunar glow that happens sometimes along the Seine. Auto headlights crossing the bridge beneath our feet coupled with lights dancing on the waves churned up by the excursion boats cast an enchanting spell outside the glassed-in room where we were dining.

We've said before that if there were to be a Nobel Prize for mashed potatoes, it would go to Joël Robuchon, but Robuchon now has to share the honors with Manuel Martinez, the new chef at La Tour d'Argent. Perhaps you think we're crazy to suggest that you reserve a table at one of the world's most famous restaurants just to taste a dish of lowly spuds puréed with olive oil, but trust us—there are more surprises in store. For one thing, the prices haven't gone up a dime in the last two years. The caviar is still just 635 francs, the fresh foie gras de canard only 225 francs, and the truffle ragoût a miserly 633 francs (and don't forget, service is included). Such a feast surely deserves no less than a Marquis de Laguiche Montrachet (2,898 francs) and a 1945 Latour (12,535 francs). Had we ordered that meal, two of us would have ended up paying the trifling sum of 16,889 francs. Yes, they've certainly kept the lid on prices here.

Terrail, who has a great sense of humor, surely would reply that the Tour d'Argent is fortunate to have well-bred clients who never look at prices and unflinchingly spend twice that amount. So let's spend a little more on our proposed dinner (which has, after all, been quite frugal until this point) and treat ourselves to a great old Cognac or a 100-year-old rum in the handsomely redecorated and enlarged cellar. Our bill has now doubled, but so what? Magic has no price tag. Anyway, who wants to come to Paris and not indulge in some wild extravagance? Martinez, who presided over the kitchens at Le Relais Louis XIII for seven years, has improved his own style here, becoming infinitely stylish and more flavorful. No audacious or dazzling creations, nor odd or confusing flavors, just clear and harmonious tastes that reflect the value of the products, all of which are first-rate.

A la carte: 700F and up. Menu: 330F (weekday lunch only).

(13) La Truffière

4, rue Blainville - 46.33.29.82

MM. Sainsard. Open until 10:30 p.m. Closed Mon. & July 24-Aug. 28. Air cond. Pets allowed. Cards: V, AE, DC, MC.

Like a lovely pike in a vulgar fishbowl, this delightful old bistro clings to its specialties—foie gras, a confit of gizzards and a Périgord cassoulet—in a neighborhood (the Contrescarpe) overrun by more or less greasy Middle Eastern and Oriental eateries. Under the high-beamed ceiling, the brothers Sainsard pursue both the bohemian life and truffles and foie gras. Alain is in the kitchen, trying to fashion all these rich ingredients into a distinctive cuisine. Though it isn't easy, he's often successful—truffle tarte, an assortment of three foies gras, breast of duck with périgourdine sauce, such top-notch desserts as warm feuilletés and bittersweet-chocolate mousse. Good selection of wines and Armagnacs.

A la carte: 300F. Menus: 85F (weekday lunch only, wine incl.), 130F, 210F.

12/20 Ugarit

41, rue Censier - 47.07.90.81

M. Doumid. Open until 11 p.m. Closed Sun. Terrace dining. Pets allowed. Cards: V, DC.

The Armenians in Paris consider Ugarit their star restaurant, a notion they share with language professors and all lovers of hummus, lissane (calf's tongue with pistachios), tarator (garlic-sauced chicken) and many more tasty items. The other dishes and kebabs are not terribly exciting.

A la carte: 150F. Menu: 60F (weekday lunch only).

12/20 Le Vieux Chêne

69, rue Mouffetard - 43.37.71.51

M. Tartare. Open until 11:30 p.m. Closed Sun. & Mon. Cards: V, AE, DC.

This former Apache dance hall and meeting place of the 1848 revolutionaries is strictly a dive, albeit a tidied-up one, that offers a colorful slice of Parisian life among all those dismal Greek bistros. You dine "from the blackboard" on breast of duck with kumquats or sweetbreads with crayfish. The food is good, inexpensive and served with a smile.

A la carte: 180F. Menus: 55F (weekday lunch only, wine incl.), 125F (dinner only).

12/20 Villars Palace

8, rue Descartes - 43.26.39.08

M. Pontoizeau. Open daily until 11 p.m. Air cond. Terrace dining. Parking. Pets allowed. Cards: V, AE, DC.

This modern bistro has a new owner, a new facade by the architect Kenzo and a new chef, Henri Morel. This young man has lots of enthusiasm but hasn't quite found a direction yet, resulting in some weak opening courses and desserts. On the other hand, the pan-fried red mullet filets are excellent, and the fish terrine and fried sole goujonnettes with cucumbers good. Service is nice but uneven; the wines are expensive.

A la carte: 350F and up. Menu: 160F (lunch only).

Sixth Arrondissement

11/20 L'Akvavit

15, rue Dauphine - 43.54.78.50

M. Rydeberg. Dinner only. Open until 10:30 p.m. Closed Mon., July 14-Aug. 15 & Dec. 24-Jan. 5. Pets allowed. Cards: V, AE.

This is one of the few, if not the only, authentic smorgasbords in Paris: a mountainous Swedish buffet with infinite salads, smoked products, marinades and stews. The check is as heavy as the cuisine.

A la carte: 225F (buffet).

12/20 Allard

41, rue St-André-des-Arts - 43.26.48.23

M. Bouchard. Open until 10 p.m. Closed Sat., Sun., Aug. & year-end holidays. Air cond. Pets allowed. Cards: V, AE, DC.

The new owner has caught the spirit of this legendary bistro, and Mme. Fernande Allard's departure and the head maître d's retirement have not disrupted the ambience—the reception is still relaxed and friendly, and the decor remains unchanged and pleasantly antiquated. Unfortunately, the cuisine has taken a turn for the worse: The beurre blanc couldn't mask the papier-mâché taste of the turbot filets we sampled recently. When you add a meager wine list, Allard certainly doesn't seem worth the 300 or more francs per person it costs to dine here.

A la carte: 300-350F.

11/20 L'Assiette au Boeuf

22, rue Guillaume-Apollinaire
42.60.88.44

M. Beaugrand. Open daily until 1 a.m. Terrace dining. Pets allowed. Cards: V.

The outstanding interior decoration by Slavik combines tastefully lit mirrored walls with elaborate woodwork. For years the standard menu of salads, grilled meats and french fries has provided the neighborhood with honest, no-frills fare for those in a hurry. Desserts are always good.

A la carte: 100-110F. Menu: 63F (wine incl.).

(14) Le Bélier

(L'Hôtel)
13, rue des Beaux-Arts - 43.25.27.22

M. Duboucheron. Open daily until 12:30 a.m. Air cond. Pets allowed. Telex 270870. Cards: V, AE, DC.

A longtime favorite for its atmosphere, pleasant piano bar, delightful fountain, flowers, tree trunk, the gorgeous evanescent creatures it attracts and the memories of Oscar Wilde and Mistinguett, Le Bélier has recently truly come into its own, serving a light, flavorful and authentic cuisine and wines from a small, attractive cellar. Try the saffron-flavored three-fish stew, duckling seasoned with lemon and honey, and rice made with milk and pine nuts.

A la carte: 250F. Menus: 150F (lunch only), 160F(dinner only).

11/20 Bistro de la Gare

59, blvd. du Montparnasse - 45.48.38.01

M. Bissonnet. Open daily until 1 a.m.

Bistro de la Gare boasts an authentic, well-restored turn-of-the century pub decor that makes up for the so-so cooking (which, at least, doesn't pretend to be more than it is): shellfish, salads, grilled meats, specials of the day. There's an endless (37) list of desserts, a few of which are quite good.

A la carte: 130-150F.

12/20 Brasserie Lutétia

(Hôtel Lutétia)
23, rue de Sèvres - 45.44.38.10

M. Scicard. Open daily until midnight. Air cond. Terrace dining. Pets allowed. Telex 270424. Cards: V, AE, DC, MC.

The sparkling, comfortable decor by Slavik and Sonya Rykiel has greatly improved this good brasserie, which serves both modern and rustic dishes (the latter are given a Parisian touch): fondant of rabbit in aspic, satiny and fragrant with tarragon; cervelas (spicy dried sausage) with lentils; fried andouille sausages; Sauerkraut; whole calf's head; filet of sander in a Bouzy wine sauce; and exciting desserts. You can also expect impeccable service, the best oysters around and a memorable Côtes-du-Rhône for 68 francs.

A la carte: 250-280F. Menu: 88F.

(18) Jacques Cagna

14, rue des Grands-Augustins
43.26.49.39

M. Cagna & Mme. Logereau. Open until 10:30 p.m. Closed Sat., Sun., Dec. 24-Jan. 2 & July 28-Aug. 28. Air cond. Pets allowed. Cards: V, AE, DC.

Intelligent (he speaks English and Spanish and is studying Japanese), with a scorching sense of humor and a passion for antiques and adventure, young Jacques Cagna, ex–merchant marine, is an appealing mixture of knockabout, Rive Gauche sophisticate and serious culinary professional. By dropping anchor in this old part of Paris and working hard, and with a little help from decorator Daniel Pasgrimaud, Cagna has transformed this fourteenth-century house into a most delightful little kingdom. It has original exposed beams, salmon-colored walls hung with Flemish still lifes, light-oak furnishings, trompe l'oeil paintings and a small salon at the foot of the stairs leading up to the dining room, which has a display of some fine old frescoes set into the wainscoting. All this works marvelously as a preface to a sound, well-balanced cuisine that is modern but not overrefined, light but not insipid, and bold enough to welcome a breath of country air—in the form of potato pancakes, salad of smoked goose and potted gizzards and a marvelous dish of pig's jowls with carrots and puréed potatoes, a recipe Cagna's mother gave him.

Cagna remains a country lad at heart, equally at home in a more sophisticated milieu, whose tastes are focused and whose blends of flavors are rarely off target, whether he's preparing cannelloni stuffed with cream of lobster, brill with oysters in a watercress sauce, veal fricassée with fresh ginger or squab sauced with honey and Sauternes. The menu varies, of course, but try not to miss the scrambled eggs with sea urchin, the scallops sautéed in truffle juice—if only for the delectable dwarf potatoes with chives that come with it. And if you've sworn off beef, have his filet of Scottish beef with truffles: It may restore your appetite for meat. Desserts rarely change on the menu, but we will never tire of the glazed almond mousse and the Queen of Sheba (chocolate nut cake with a custard sauce).

Cagna's 50,000-bottle cellar, an enormous number for a small restaurant, was assembled with great care and includes famous labels as well as lesser known Côtes-du-Rhône and Burgundies priced between 100 and 200 francs. All of the above explains the success of this restaurant, modest at lunch but overwhelming in the evening, when Cagna's sister, Anny, his partner for more than twenty years, plays hostess to the Parisian and international regulars who come here for a crash course in French culture.

A la carte: 500-700F. Menu: 235F (lunch only).

(13) Le Calvet

165, blvd. St-Germain - 45.48.93.51

M. Watelet. Open until 10:30 p.m. Closed Aug. 3-28. Air cond. Pets allowed. Cards: V, AE, DC.

The new management (1985) has replaced the worn red Hungarian decor with pale-rose table linens and velvet curtains that do wonders for the handsome stone walls. Chef Jean-Pierre Bouchereau, who rated a toque at Chez Nous in Montfort-l'Amaury, retains that ranking at Le Calvet, despite his timidity in properly reducing sauces and his lack of conviction with seasonings. It would take ever so little to improve the grilled sole, the rabbit stew, the blanquette of turbot with asparagus and lobster, and the mustard-flavored fricassée of lotte. The excellent pastries and delicate little tuiles need no improvement. Respectable wine cellar and two inviting fixed-price menus.

A la carte: 300F. Menus: 109F, 175F.

(13) Charly de Bab-el-Oued

9 bis, blvd. du Montparnasse
47.34.68.63

See Seventeenth Arrondissement.

12/20 Aux Charpentiers

10, rue Mabillon - 43.26.30.05

M. Bardèche. Open until 11:30 p.m. Closed Sun., Dec. 25-Jan. 1 & holidays. Terrace dining. Pets allowed. Cards: V, AE, DC.

The "daily special," an established Parisian tradition, is served in what was once a carpenters' guild hall that dates back to 1856 and retains its warmth and simplicity. The owner is a delightfully theatrical character, the aïoli, stuffed cabbage, petit salé (poached, lightly salted pork loin chop) and veal sauté are delectable, and the blood sausage is unforgettable.

A la carte: 180F.

(15) Le Chat Grippé

87, rue d'Assas - 43.54.70.00

M. Prunières. Open until 10:30 p.m. Closed Sat. lunch, Easter & Aug. Air cond. Cards: V, MC.

This little bistro, which opened a few years ago in an old butcher shop, has been run for the last four years by its owner, chef Marc Prunières, a native of Quercy, who has turned it into an attractive, relaxing, unpretentious place. The dark, mirrored interior, handsomely adorned with garnet velvet, is complemented by the friendly reception and efficient service. As for the food, since Prunières hired a young disciple of Senderens and Ferrero, it has improved markedly: a fricassée of fresh chanterelles seasoned with garlic and parsley, beef filet with fresh liver in a pie crust, and a savory saddle of lamb fragrant with rosemary. The expensive wine list is rich in Bordeaux and Cahors.

A la carte: 250F. Menus: 120F (weekday lunch only), 180F (dinner only).

12/20 Chez Maître Paul

12, rue Monsieur-le-Prince - 43.54.74.59

M. Gaugain. Open until 10:30 p.m. Closed Sun., Mon., Dec. 24-Jan. 2 & Aug. Pets allowed. Cards: V, AE, DC.

In this unassuming little corner restaurant, chef Gaugain has been turning out some of the best Savoyard cooking you'll find in Paris: fish stew in Arbois wine, coq au vin (in white wine), sweetbreads simmered in Château-Chalon and so on. Excellent Jura wines.

A la carte: 200F. Menu: 165F (wine incl.).

(14) Chez Tante Madée

11, rue Dupin - 42.22.64.56

M. Trama. Open until 10 p.m. Closed Sat. lunch & Sun. Terrace dining. Pets allowed. Cards: V, AE, DC.

Courteous, unassuming Alain Trama, with his athletic build and military beard, is in charge of this stylishly rustic dining room, which for years has been one of the top eating places in the neighborhood. His mother, Tante Madée, was one of the best cooks in Paris in this very same place. Trama learned a lot from her (she still helps him in the kitchen), but he's definitely his own man—imaginative, technically sound and guided by what looks best and freshest at market each day: perhaps a combination of scallops and asparagus, a seafood fricassée with fresh noodles, duckling in a bitter orange sauce with turnips au gratin, or a raspberry Bavarian. The single short fixed-price lunch menu is equally attractive and of gourmet quality: duck with four spices in pastry, casserole of calves' feet with fresh vegetables, assorted cheeses and a dessert special. A "wine of the month" (generally a medium-grade Bordeaux) is always offered—a good thing indeed, since the other wines are extremely expensive, like everything else. The homemade bread is delicious. Marie-Claude Trama is in charge of the dining room.

A la carte: 300-350F. Menus: 160F (weekday lunch only), 175F.

11/20 Dominique

19, rue Bréa - 43.27.08.80

M. Wiernik-Aronson. Open until 10:15 p.m. Closed Feb. school vacation & July 17-Aug. 16. Air cond. Pets allowed. Cards: V, AE, DC.

Dominique is the oldest, and still the best, Russian attraction in town, at least when you're talking about the combination bar/grocery store at the entrance, which draws discriminating customers from all over Montparnasse. Marvelous smoked salmon, borscht and herring.

A la carte: 200-300F. Menu: 152F (wine incl.).

11/20 Drugstore Saint-Germain

149, blvd. St-Germain - 42.22.92.50

M. Boutersky. Open daily until 1:30 a.m. Air cond. Pets allowed. Cards: V, AE, DC.

The omnipresent decorating hand of Slavik has done it again, this time transforming an old decor into a spectacle of metal palm trees and gigantic pineapple light fixtures. As for the cuisine, it has remained unchanged: salads, daily specials and ice creams.

A la carte: 160-180F. Menu: 60F.

(13) La Foux

2, rue Clément - 43.25.77.66

M. Guini. Open until 10:30 p.m. Closed Sun. Air cond. Pets allowed. Cards: V, AE.

Alex Guini, a dear, colorful fellow (growing stouter every year), has spruced up his pleasant modern decor that attracts publishing-industry types. He features the cooking of Nice and Lyon; his gras-double (tripe) is tops. Mme. Guini is there to welcome you. On winter Saturdays, there are choice tidbits (Lyon specialties) to whet your appetite.

A la carte: 300F and up. Menu: 145F (weekdays only).

10/20 Hippopotamus

119, blvd. Montparnasse - 43.20.37.04

See Eighth Arrondissement.

(14) Joséphine

(Chez Dumonet)

117, rue du Cherche-Midi - 45.48.52.40

M. Dumonet. Open until 10:30 p.m. Closed Sat., Sun. & July. Terrace dining. Pets allowed. Cards: V.

Always smiling and cordial as he caresses a bottle of Armagnac and strokes his beard, owner Jean Dumonet is an avid seafarer, though the menu in his venerable bistro gives no clue to this passion. Of course, you'll find skate (in a cream sauce with capers), sole (with a fondue of leeks) and John Dory (spiced with ginger); but what really draws the customers—who tend to be casual, perhaps socially prominent, sorts—are the leg of lamb (Wednesday lunch), truffled andouillette feuilleté, boeuf bourguignon with fresh noodles, navarin of lamb and duck confit. They also enjoy the elegant simplicity of the oak-paneled and etched-mirror decor. The wine cellar, too, is admirable, including fine estate Burgundies, Banyuls (a sweet apéritif or dessert wine) bottled by Dr. Parcé and a dozen or more prestigious 1961 Bordeaux from Le Clos Montmartre that cost a small fortune (920 francs)—plus other vintages that go as high as 9,000 francs a bottle. But never fear, an excellent Chinon can be yours for a mere 80 francs.

A la carte: 250-400F.

11/20 Lapérouse

51, quai des Grands-Augustins
43.26.68.04

M. Alexandre. Open until 11:30 p.m. Closed Sun. dinner & Mon. Air cond. Pets allowed. Cards: V, AE, DC.

The great Lapérouse disappeared ages ago, and it's most unlikely that the owner of the brasserie Bofinger, who performed the rescue operation, will ever resurrect the past. Decorator Pierre Pothier has salvaged the framework of this admirable turn-of-the-century monument, artfully combining genuine and fake elements, and has restored the six small dining rooms on whose mirrors the fortune-hunting ladies of that period inscribed, with their diamond rings, the names of their "protectors." Pothier also enlarged the ground floor and turned the third floor into one large, attractive room overlooking the quays along the Seine. Despite the striking effect of the new decor, the new chef indulges in heaviness and thick sauces, as seen in the fricassée of frogs' legs and escargots with chervil and the lotte-and-lobster navarin.

A la carte: 380-450F. Menu: 180F.

(13) Lipp

151, blvd. St-Germain - 45.48.53.91

Mme. Cazes. Open daily until 2 a.m. Annual closing varies. Air cond. Pets allowed. Cards: AE, DC.

After all sorts of rumors circulated recently when Roger Cazes departed for Aveyron, Lipp, which has been in the Cazes family since 1920, is back in the fold. There is no question that it's been acquired by "outsiders." Mme. Cazes, its sole owner, has turned over management responsibilities to her young computer-programming niece, who's made the switch from office machines to Sauerkraut. Sometimes you see her smiling presence behind the cash register, a bit out of her element in these surroundings.

Roger's second cousin, Michel Cazes, a man of exceeding courtesy who favors dark double-breasted suits, black ties and crew cuts, has taken the helm of the kitchen. He's 51, has worked at Lipp for 25 years and knows the ropes. Though too modest to say so, he's actually as unbeatable as Roger was about looking after the celebrities—real or phony—who turn up. Each morning he gets out a press release, reads his confidential mail, consults the rosters of officialdom and *Who's Who.*

Roger never wanted to write his memoirs, but Michel probably will; he's been taking notes for 25 years.

And neither Michel nor his able staff are about to challenge the tradition of blanquette of veal on Tuesday, boeuf à la mode on Wednesday, cassoulet on Thursday and either calf's head or brandade (paste) of cod on alternate Fridays. We nearly forgot to mention two events of cosmic significance: one is that the restaurant will be open every day of the year except Christmas,and the other is that after ten years of heroic resistance, Lipp finally accepts credit cards. All you have to do is show them your passport, driver's license, birth certificate, draft card and an affidavit from your landlady verifying your good morals.

A la carte: 200-300F.

11/20 La Lozère

4, rue Hautefeuille - 43.54.26.64

Mme. Almeras. Open until 10:30 p.m. Closed Sun., Mon., Dec. 24-31 & Aug. Pets allowed.

Dedicated to a celebration of the Lozère region—bracing mountain air and the robust cooking smells of tripoux vinaigrette (sheep's tripe and feet), goat cheese and herb sausage—La Lozère has a dignified interior of exposed beams and worn stones.

A la carte: 130F. Menu: 73F (lunch only, wine incl.), 90F, 109F.

(13) La Marlotte

55, rue du Cherche-Midi - 45.48.86.79

Mme. Agaud & M. Bouvier. Open until 11 p.m. Closed Sat., Sun. & Aug. Air cond. Terrace dining. Cards: AE, DC.

This is a happy marriage of good home cooking and pretty dinnerware. In the evening you dine by candlelight under a beamed ceiling on regional duck specialties, andouillette in white wine, sausage and veal confit—all first-rate and meticulously prepared. Your fellow diners will be people who want good cooking and know where to find it. The young owners keep an eye on everything, including the fine quality of their house wines and the price of your meal.

A la carte: 200-250F.

(13) Le Muniche

27, rue de Buci - 46.33.62.09

MM. Layrac. Open daily until 3 a.m. Air cond. Terrace dining. Pets allowed. Telex 201820. Cards: V, AE, DC, MC.

More power to the Layrac brothers, from the Aveyron country, for ferreting out such good little wines, for supplying the public with fresh oysters year-round, for keeping an honest country-style kitchen and for maintaining over the years one of the liveliest and most popular brasseries in town. If you're lucky enough (and the chances are dim indeed) to obtain a "box," you'll have what might be compared to a compartment on a sight-seeing train, along with an evening of noisy fun, and you'll be waited on by an attentive staff that manages to stay alert and smiling into the wee hours. You can dine on all kinds of Sauerkraut, rosy, thick-sliced calves' liver au gratin, duck confit, grilled pig's tail and ears, chicken in the pot and more.

A la carte: 220F. Menu: 127F.

11/20 Le Palanquin

12, rue Princesse - 43.29.77.66

Mmes. Tran-Van & Tran-Kim. Open until 10:30 p.m. Closed Sun.Pets allowed. Cards: V.

Apart from the beamed ceiling, the old stone walls and the cheerful reception, this is a perfectly unassuming, run-of-the-mill Vietnamese endeavor: pâté imperial, steamed lotte, stuffed duck. Political celebrities and others (like Catherine Deneuve) seem to like the place.

A la carte: 180F. Menus: 58F (lunch only), 92F.

(15) Paris

(Hôtel Lutétia)
23, rue de Sèvres - 45.48.74.34

M. Scicard. Open until 10 p.m. Closed Sun., Mon. & Aug. Air cond. Parking. Pets allowed. Cards: V, AE, DC, MC.

Jacky Fréon must have been so overcome in Lyon at being handed the coveted Bocuse award for gastronomic excellence by the master himself that he totally botched our lunch a week later. This delightful young chef has since recovered his balance, and in the sternly elegant art deco interior (inspired by Slavik and Sonya Rykiel) that replaced the Lutétia's dreary old tea room, he has succeeded in impressing us with a cuisine that explains why Joël Robuchon hired him as an assistant before letting him go to Nova Park. He is a sound technician who has a fine nose for subtle flavors: His fresh salmon in lobster sauce (which won him the Bocuse award), breast of duckling with foie gras, braised pork in cabbage leaves and his exquisite coffee-flavored baba manage to keep the tables filled. At lunch, these and other dishes appear on a fixed-price menu for 250 francs—a bargain in this neighborhood.

A la carte: 400-550F. Menu: 250F (lunch only).

10/20 Le Petit Saint-Benoît

4, rue St-Benoît - 42.60.27.92

M. Gervais. Open until 10 p.m. Closed Sat., Sun. & Aug. Terrace dining. Pets allowed.

At this most highbrow terrace in Paris, temporarily or permanently broke members of the fashionable set gather to eat shepherd's pie and roast veal.

A la carte: 80-100F.

(13) Le Petit Zinc

25, rue de Buci - 43.33.51.66

MM. Layrac. Open daily until 3 a.m. Air cond. Terrace dining. Pets allowed. Cards: V, AE, DC, MC.

Le Petit Zinc serves the same country cooking as next-door neighbor Muniche, emphasizing southwestern specialties: Corrèze sausage with chestnuts, duck thighs with apples and that famous heaping plate of grilled pork. Also, fresh seafood is served year-round, as is Sauerkraut and excellent calves' liver cut thick for two. Only the customers change: Nowadays they're quiet and better behaved. The decor hasn't budged in 30 years, since the time when its well-worn furniture, lace curtains and 1900s ambience introduced the "bistro" style to Paris.

A la carte: 250F. Menu: 127F.

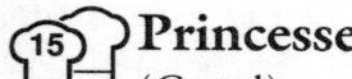

Princesse

(Castel)
15, rue Princesse - 43.26.90.22

M. Castel. Open until 1 a.m. Closed Sun. Air cond. Pets allowed. Telex 203835. Cards: V, AE, DC.

The Castel is like the Bank of France or Fort Knox: impregnable and everlasting. A hundred years from now there will still be a Castel in the corridor to welcome the chosen few and to turn away—from the Princesse club—those who don't belong but would like to. From cellar to attic, this establishment, one of the great dining spots in Paris, will continue to pack in the worldly set: to the discotheque to dance and drink; to Le Foyer on the main floor for a salad or a meat dish; or to the more formal dining room on the second floor for the menu, which includes scrambled eggs with sea urchins, mustard-flavored brill and squab stuffed with morels. Michel, who's been in charge of the dining room for the last 25 years, deserves an award for his reception. Right next to the Princesse club, Jean Castel opened an ultra-fashionable restaurant, Le Puzzle, which was superbly decorated by Philippe Starck. Count on spending 200 to 250 francs in Le Foyer and 400 to 600 francs if you eat upstairs.

A la carte: 200-600F.

Relais Louis XIII

8, rue des Grands-Augustins
43.26.75.96

M. Poindessault. Open until 10:15 p.m. Closed Mon. lunch, Sun. & Aug. Air cond. Pets allowed. Cards: V, AE, DC, MC.

This lovingly preserved site of the Grands-Augustins convent, where Louis XIII was proclaimed king on the evening following Henri IV's assassination, is probably one of the finest restaurants of its kind in the city. Sturdy beams, genuine patina and historical paintings (you dine beneath the gazes of Louis XIII, Anne of Austria and Francis I) lend the setting a distinct charm rather than comfort (some tables and banquettes are rather cramped). The kitchens, where Manuel Martinez reigned for the last eight years before leaving for La Tour d'Argent, are now in the hands of giant, debonair Georges Piron, 38, whose eyes reveal senses of daring and fantasy. The dishes reveal the same qualities: red mullet chaud-froid served as an amuse-gueule with vegetables tartare; a delicious cold nage of crustaceans with peppermint; devilish poultry wings stuffed with escargots; and sweetbreads with baby vegetables. For dessert, try the curious but refreshing grapefruit-orange terrine en gelée. You'll pay a king's ransom for this regal meal.

A la carte: 500-600F. Menu: 190F (lunch only).

12/20 Sur les Quais

53, quai des Grands-Augustins
43.25.45.94

Mlle. Nahan & M. Errandonéa. Open until 11 p.m. Closed Sat. lunch & Sun. Air cond. Cards: V.

Valérie-Anne, former president Giscard's daughter, has taken an adventurous leap into the whirlwind of Bordeaux wines and steak tartare. She and two associates have bought the old Cannelle and transformed it into a stylish (1950s-era) restaurant. The industrious trio plans to woo members of the 25-to-30-year-old crowd who, chic but not snobbish, have 200 francs maximum to invest in a rabbit stew with eggplant, spicy tuna tartare, fair steamed chicken breast and other simple dishes well presented by chef Didier Le Madec, a former pupil of Jacques Manière.

A la carte: 160-200F.

11/20 La Vigneraie

16, rue du Dragon - 45.48.57.04

M. Sabatier. Open daily until 1 a.m. Air cond. Terrace dining. Pets allowed. Cards: V, AE, DC.

A few solid (and expensive) daily specials (pot-au-feu, salmon filet) and good cold dishes are served with a respectable collection of wines by the glass (Bordeaux only). Good fixed-price menu and fast service at lunch.

A la carte: 250-280F. Menus: 75F (lunch only, wine incl.), 149F (weekdays only).

12/20 Yugaraj

14, rue Dauphine - 43.26.44.91

M. Meyappen. Open until 11 p.m. Closed Mon. Air cond. Pets allowed. Cards: V, AE, DC.

The cuisine of Hukum Singh, a native of Raajmahal in northern India, is strictly traditional. It was perhaps the best of its kind in Paris, but lately it seems to be slipping: dull chicken shat (salad) and timidly seasoned poulet tikka. Nonetheless, there are some good dishes worth trying, such as the grilled eggplant with onions, tomatoes and fresh herbs, the white lentils with aromatic vegetables, the pungent lamb in crème fraîche with raisins and cashews or, on Saturday nights, the whole lamb shank in a curry and ginger sauce. Courteous service in a setting that's a trifle silly and crowded.

A la carte: 220F. Menus: 82F (weekday lunch only), 150F (lunch only), 196F, 230F.

Seventh Arrondissement

(13) Antoine et Antoinette

16, ave. Rapp - 45.51.75.61

MM. Pernot. Open until 10:30 p.m. Closed Sat. (except dinner in summer), Sun. & Easter school vacation. Terrace dining. Pets allowed. Cards: V, AE, DC.

Film director Jacques Becker and scriptwriter Françoise Giroud used to lunch here with their film crew, and this tranquil restaurant is named after the heroes of their movie. The decor has been freshened up, the terrace overlooking the avenue is delightfully quiet in summer, and Jean-Claude Pernot's cooking relies on the best seasonal products. To compose his highly professional, nonhyperimaginative menu, he uses lotte with fresh spinach, good homemade duck foie gras, rack of lamb seasoned with thyme and some pleasant classic desserts (tarte tatin, pear charlotte). Expect a warm reception from co-owner Ghislaine Pernot.

A la carte: 300F.

17 **Arpège**
84, rue de Varenne
45.51.47.33, 45.51.20.02
M. Passard. Open until 10:30 p.m. Closed Sat. lunch, Sun. & Aug. Air cond. Pets allowed. Cards: V, AE, DC.

Alain Passard quit this address as an underling when it housed L'Archestrate. Having proved himself at the Duc d'Enghien, then the Carlton in Brussels, he has returned as owner. The "A" (for Archestrate) inscribed on the elegant Limoges dinnerware and the silverware now applies to Arpège. The threadbare furnishings in the small dining room are gone, and a coat of fresh paint and new fabrics have spruced things up. The decor is still unfinished, but instant success has encouraged Passard to make further improvements worthy of his cuisine. You'll agree that he's an extremely talented young chef after tasting his cabbage stuffed with crab in a mustard sauce, squab with lemon-flavored endive, saddle of hare with walnuts and cèpes (the meat is coated with ground nuts—a sensational dish!) and his superb desserts (licorice-flavored millefeuilles, tomato stuffed with a sweet filling, cocoa squares steeped in citrus fruits, macaroon with raspberry sauce). He's also to be congratulated for an exceptional fixed-price lunch menu at 150 francs (three courses plus cheese and dessert), which is undoubtedly one of the best values in the city. The new young wine steward deserves credit for developing the moderately priced wine list.

A la carte: 400-500F. Menus: 150F (lunch only), 375F.

11/20 **Babkine**
(Chez Germaine)
30, rue Pierre-Leroux - 42.73.28.34
M. Babkine. Open until 9 p.m. Closed Sat. dinner, Sun., Aug. & Dec. 24-Jan. 2. No pets.

Château dining on oilcloth. At this gold-medal address, the line forms on the sidewalk for the rabbit sauté, the coq au vin, the calf's head and so on.

A la carte: 60-68F.

12/20 **Le Balisier**
20, rue Rousselet - 47.34.66.29
MM. Lucas. Open until 10 p.m. Closed Sat. lunch, Sun. & Aug. Pets allowed. Cards: V, AE, DC.

This pleasant, simple, two-level little family restaurant recently spruced up its decor, but Mama is still in charge of the dining room and her son the kitchen. There are winners (remarkably cooked fresh salmon) and losers (sole smothered in almonds); it's just going to take a little time to sort things out. Excellent choice of wines.

Menus: 60F (lunch only, wine incl.), 100F (wine incl.), 145F (menu/carte).

12/20 **La Belle France & Le Parisien**
Eiffel Tower, Champ-de-Mars
45.55.20.04
M. Ody. Open daily until 10 p.m. Air cond. No pets. Telex 205789. Cards: V.

On the second floor of the Eiffel Tower, with a panoramic view of the city, Le Parisien is below (snacks and grilled meats) and La Belle France just above it (brasserie-style cooking).

A la carte: 200F. Menus: 85F, 170F.

16 **Bellecour**
22, rue Surcouf
45.51.46.93, 45.55.68.38
M. Goutagny. Open until 10:30 p.m. Closed Sat. lunch (& Sat. dinner in seas.), Sun. & Aug. 10-Sept. 1. Air cond. Terrace dining. Pets allowed. Cards: V, AE, DC, MC.

Gérard Goutagny has orchestrated a great comeback for this veteran bistro, which had seen better days. Only one or two of the Lyon specialties are still on the menu (primarily as a concession to the old regulars); André Plunian, the chef who took over a year or so ago, has his own way of doing things. We discovered Plunian a few years back at Château-du-Loir, then traced him to Le Mans, where, two years ago, we awarded him his second toque. This giant of a man is bursting with talent; he has ideas and direction, and his mastery of his art lacks only the aura of authority enjoyed by the greatest chefs. Anyway, he's on the right track with such dishes as raw salmon and caviar in a light cream sauce, crab wrapped in cabbage leaves, the distinctive, ultra-light wild rabbit pâté in puff pastry and the cod with white beans au gratin. For dessert, you can still count on the handsome creations of M. Goutagny, a trained pastry maker and former pupil of Bernachon: His glazed fig tart is delicious but could stand less sugar. There's a fine choice of Burgundies and Beaujolais. The service, provided by a competent, attentive young staff in a fine redecorated interior, is a welcome improvement. Call it a resurrection, or maybe a second birth.

A la carte: 300F. Menus: 200F (lunch only, wine incl.), 250F (dinner only).

15 **Bistrot de Paris**
33, rue de Lille - 42.61.16.83
M. Oliver. Open until 11 p.m. Closed Sat. lunch & Sun. Pets allowed. Cards: V.

As one of our colleagues once remarked, why would anyone ask when reserving a table, "Is the boss around?" Michel Oliver only bends over the stove for the TV cameras and to put the finishing touches on packaged foods that delight the customers of self-service food emporiums. Unlike others, he has the good sense and the integrity not to exploit his culinary fame, and he long ago turned over the Bistrot's kitchens to Jean-Pierre Frelet (the former chef at Le Camélia). Frelet is responsible for the clever dishes on the "modern" menu, which features eggplant and fresh cod caviar, marinated sardines, calves' liver with mashed onions, lemon fricassée of chicken, braised andouillette on Mondays and veal blanquette on Tuesdays. This light, bourgeois cooking generally turns out quite well. Once in a while it takes a tumble; most recently, neither the cassoulet, whose brown crust someone forgot to add, nor the cherry aspic on the pork that's all the rage made a good impression. But the bittersweet-chocolate cake, almond cream and glazed nougat are all marvelous. Ditto the Bordeaux—greater or lesser—listed at reasonable prices. The enduring Parisian atmosphere in this 23-year-old restaurant decorated like a century-old bistro—where business has perked up considerably since the nearby Musée d'Orsay

opened—makes lunch or dinner a truly relaxing, pleasurable experience.
A la carte: 300F.

Le Bourdonnais

113, ave. de La Bourdonnais
47.05.47.96

Mme. Coat. Open daily until 11:30 p.m. Air cond. Pets allowed. Cards: V, AE.

Micheline Coat has not yet decided whether to ditch the Bourdonnais's second name, La Cantine des Gourmets, which scarcely conveys the elegant refinement of this small, typically Parisian restaurant. Yet surely anyone would be overjoyed to have this kind of mess hall—a charming decor of mirrored walls hung with salmon-colored fabric, white woodwork, marvelous flowers everywhere. Coat has a knack for arranging a room—which is not so easy when the room is narrow—and for keeping her faithful customers (government and business personalities) happy by treating each as an individual. The chef is 26-year-old Philippe Bardau, who assisted previous chef Régis Mahé for four years and who, like Mahé, worked for a while at Maximin. Bardau has kept pretty much to the established style and seems to be quite at home with it. Clients surely will agree that Le Bourdonnais deserves to keep the three toques it was first awarded in 1986.

Coat, a superb hostess, and her staff present the menu and their recommendations to each table in a most charming manner. Perhaps they will suggest the tarragon-flavored loin of rabbit with kidney; sole and smoked salmon in aspic with a tarragon cream sauce; pan-fried sea bass with artichokes and rosemary; sea bream garnished with a fennel mousse and saffron-flavored fresh noodles; grilled duck with olive butter and Roquefort; or poached pigeon with a mousse of fresh peas. Desserts include glazed nougat and oranges poached in a raspberry purée with honey butter.

The 200-franc fixed menu at lunch includes wine, coffee and, for example, daube of duck and ham, broiled salmon with potatoes, and orange aspic.

A la carte: 300-400F. Menus: 200F (lunch only, wine incl.), 250F (dinner only, wine incl.), 380F (menu dégustation).

12/20 Le Champ de Mars

17, ave. de La Motte-Picquet
47.05.57.99

M. Gellé. Open until 10:15 p.m. Closed Tues. dinner, Mon. & July 15-Aug. 15. Terrace dining. Pets allowed. Cards: V, AE, DC.

The few excellent dishes here are prepared in the traditional fashion and served in a rustic, rather charming provincial decor by a squadron of motherly waitresses: delicious cold cuts, pike sauced with beurre blanc, calf's head, stuffed cabbage and so on. Good choice of regional wines.

A la carte: 230-250F. Menu: 106F.

13 Chez les Anges

54, blvd. de Latour-Maubourg
47.05.89.86, 45.55.69.26

Mme. Delmas. Open until 10:30 p.m. Closed Sun. dinner. Air cond. Pets allowed. Cards: V, AE, DC, MC.

For 30 years this peaceful house in the Invalides district has been serving poached eggs en meurette, excellent parsleyed ham, beef in wine sauce and calves' liver served in thick slices. It's getting a bit stale now and could use a touch of imagination in the cuisine and in the decor, which features wine-colored wood paneling and carpeting. But despite the unoriginality of the Burgundian cuisine of chef Bernard Labrosse, who has worked at Chez les Anges for fifteen years, it is nonetheless honest and classic: fish and shellfish steamed in a fennel-seasoned broth, lamb stew and a dessert of almonds, raisins, hazelnuts and figs covered with candied nougat. There's an impressive colony of government officials on hand at lunchtime; at night, you'll find candlelight, soft music and a more eclectic crowd, despite the steep prices.

A la carte: 400F. Menu: 200F.

13 Chez Françoise

Invalides Air Terminal - 47.05.49.03

M. Demessence. Open until 11 p.m. Closed Sun. dinner & Aug. Parking. Pets allowed.. Cards: V, AE, DC.

A miniature virgin forest besieges the glass wall, its greenery adding a cheerful note to the vast barn-like terminal. Many business people and government officials come here to park themselves in the comfortable wicker chairs set in the attractive, noisy but not hectic setting. The cooking is valiant, unpretentious bistro fare: roast lamb or rabbit, andouillette, salmon and warm apple tart or île flottante (floating island). Prices are high, except on the "parliamentary" fixed-price lunch menu, which contains just about the best this well-run restaurant has to offer. Good owners' Beaujolais is served in carafes.

A la carte: 250-300F. Menu: 130F.

Chez Muriel et Isabelle

94, blvd. de Latour-Maubourg
45.51.37.96

Mlle. Dechaut. Open until 10 p.m. Closed Sat., Sun., Aug. & Dec. 23-Jan. 1. Terrace dining. Pets allowed. Cards: V.

Muriel focuses on what's happening in the tiny dining room, with its daintily draped tables and ever-present flowers. Isabelle produces some inspired home cooking (hare terrine with cooked apples, young rabbit simmered with mustard and prunes) that has a distinct personality and favors the use—and overuse—of spices (she comes from Spain). We've had an interesting marinade of salmon and capitaine (a bony fish caught off the West African coast), except the flavors were dulled by too much herbs and ginger; tasty tuna terrine and broccoli with a mushroom-based sauce; excellent pan-fried calves' liver; and faultless vanilla crème brûlée. Wine is served by the glass, and in warm weather you can eat at one of two tables on the terrace facing the garden and dome of the

Invalides.

A la carte: 280F. Menu: 180F (lunch only, wine incl.).

13 Chez Ribe

15, ave. de Suffren - 45.66.53.79

M. Pérès. Open until 10:30 p.m. Closed Sun., 2 weeks in Aug., Dec. 25 & Jan. 1. Terrace dining. Pets allowed. Cards: V, AE, DC, MC.

Antoine Pérès knows how to run a bistro. He keeps a sharp eye on the quality of what he buys, as well as on the dining atmosphere and the generous portions he serves. The service is friendly, the tables roomy, and on the single fixed-price menu there are several simple, tasty dishes from the grill: fresh salmon, breast of duck or roast squab chicken "à l'américaine," and for dessert, a delicious chocolate cake with a light crème anglaise that's not too sweet. Even with a red Anjou at 42 francs, the bill is remarkably merciful.

Menu: 142F.

12/20 Le Crik

10, rue de Bellechasse - 47.05.98.66

M. Guillerand. Open until 8 p.m. Closed Mon. Pets allowed.

This is the bistro annex of next-door neighbor La Sologne. In the country-style snack-bar atmosphere, good low-priced wines are served by the carafe, and pleasant food, well cooked, is served promptly: herbed cottage cheese, grilled sausages, roast chicken and a variety of dessert crêpes. Ideal fixed-price menu.

A la carte: 100F. Menu: 60F.

16 Le Dauphin

(Sofitel Paris Invalides)

32, rue Ste-Dominique - 45.55.91.80

M. Potier. Open daily until 10 p.m. Air cond. Parking. Pets allowed. Telex 250019. Cards: V, AE, DC, MC.

The cuisine of the new chef, Marc Bayon, is about the only thing that unites the right and left wings these days at the nearby National Assembly. This Lyon-born chef comes by way of Marseille, bringing a burst of sunshine to the neighborhood. His "decorative" cuisine is so pretty we'd like to frame it, yet he doesn't rest on appearance alone. There's also plenty of flavor to be found in the stunning cold vegetable omelet (with slivers of smoked salmon); sweetbreads terrine with prawns and an onion-orange compote; Breton lobster cooked to perfection, married with olive oil; little "bundles" of red mullet, salmon and merlu surrounded by fennel roots and exquisite green vegetables; "pascalines" of lamb (noisettes, feet, sweetbreads, brains, tongue) with little Provençal stuffings; glazed nougat with fruit and creamed saffron; and crunchy chocolate with a pistachio mousse. Everything rings of powerful flavors, precise and sharp, that express the charm of Mediteranean cuisine.

A la carte: 350-500F. Menu: 210F (weekday lunch only).

13 Aux Délices de Szechuen

40, ave. Duquesne - 43.06.22.55

Mme. Lau. Open until 10:30 p.m. Closed Mon., Aug. 1-22 & Dec. 22-26. Air cond. Terrace dining. Cards: V, AE.

The cooking here is generally Chinese and occasionally Szechwan tailored to Western tastes, the decor is subdued Oriental with a lovely overhanging terrace, the service is excellent, and the clientele is stylish and from the neighborhood. As for the food, it's overwhelmingly civilized (no outrageous exotic items): crab-leg soup, sautéed chicken with walnuts, beef filet with spiced orange peel (it could stand more peel) and lovely coriander-flavored steamed turbot.

A la carte: 220F. Menu: 87F (weekdays only).

18 Le Divellec

107, rue de l'Université

45.51.91.96

M. Le Divellec. Open until 10 p.m. Closed Sun., Mon., July 29-Aug. 31, Dec. 25 & 1 week in Jan. Air cond. Pets allowed. Cards: V, AE, DC.

The blue-and-white dining room, with natural-colored fabrics and candles aglow in sparkling chandeliers, looks like an exclusive yacht club. And you should be aware that the maître d' in gray flannel who appears promptly at your table is not just anybody. His name is Antoine Ventura, an articulate, witty and, on occasion, sarcastic man who is the author of an amusing recently published book about his profession that you'd do well to glance at before you sit down.

Le Divellec himself is in complete charge of the kitchen, as he doesn't much care for socializing with the customers; he prefers fishing to fishing for compliments. At the moment, his great passion is Norway. There's nothing you can teach him about salmon or cod, and if the fish market suddenly shifts to the South Pole, you'll be sure to find him there. Whatever time he doesn't devote to finding the freshest fish, he spends cooking them. Unlike a Le Duc or an Allemandou (of La Cagouille), who worship simplicity, Le Divellec doesn't rule out sauces or complicated preparations; his talent lies in being able to produce elaborate dishes that preserve natural fish flavors—which is not an easy task. His most successful efforts include marinated small langoustes (spiny lobsters) combined with a slice of pan-fried foie gras; roast turbot sauced with cream of gray shrimp; red mullet with mushrooms in a chive sauce; a wonderful wine-based court bouillon swimming with shellfish and deep-sea fish; and pan-fried frogs' legs with foie gras. All these concoctions are both clever and delicious, but let's be frank and admit the truth. Among such fanciful creations, Le Divellec has slipped in a few simple, down-to-earth dishes, such as warm spider crab, langouste simmered with seaweed, and charcoal-grilled bass basted with olive oil and lemon. Something tells us that that's the type of cooking he likes best. So do we.

A la carte: 500-800F and up. Menus: 220F and 350F (lunch only).

(16) **Duquesnoy**

6, ave. Bosquet - 47.05.96.78

M. Duquesnoy. Open until 10:15 p.m. Closed Sat. lunch, Sun. & Aug. Air cond. Pets allowed. Cards: V, AE.

Jean-Paul Duquesnoy moved in during the summer of 1987 to a decor—willow-green walls framed by antique, well-lit paneling—that celebrated the glories of Burgundy. Although the atmosphere is less beguilingly feminine than in the other Duquesnoy on the rue des Bernardins, it's quite comfortable. Françoise Duquesnoy is there to greet you, and her staff actively looks after you. Chef Duquesnoy now operates in spacious kitchens instead of the cramped, smoky quarters he had before, and this alone has lifted his spirits. Not to mention the heady excitement of seeing his tables fill up (his next-door neighbors/customers are TV executives and government officials armed with their legendary expense accounts). His delicate cuisine doesn't vary much, but it would be hard to tire of the red mullet with flaked potatoes, the sweetbreads roasted in celery juice, the andouillette in puff pastry with a sauce Choron (béarnaise sauce with tomatoes) and the fondant of pigs' feet and foie gras en croûte that accompanies salad greens in walnut oil. But why is the salad disparaged by referring to it as "petite"? And why is the salmon in an herb vinaigrette? And while we're listing our complaints, we might as well let on that we can't rave about the terrine of eggplant and anchovies, and that the pasta in lobster ravioli was lumpish. Desserts, on the other hand, are feathery light, particularly the honey-and-nut glazed nougat with caramel sauce, which is superb. Excellent wine list at more or less reasonable prices.

A la carte: 400-500F. Menus: 220F (lunch only), 400F (menu dégustation).

(15) **La Ferme Saint-Simon**

6, rue St-Simon - 45.48.35.74

M. Vandenhende. Open until 10:15 p.m. Closed Sat. lunch, Sun. & Aug. 1-21. Air cond. Pets allowed. Cards: V.

Government officials pay closer attention to their lunch plates here at the farm (ferme) than to their morning sessions at the nearby Palais-Bourbon. The regulars are fairly prominent people who feel at home in this light interior—a trifle too ornate—extended by another smaller, cozier room opening into the winter garden, with its trellis and clumps of fake greenery hanging from the ceiling. Francis Vandenhende manages his Ferme Saint-Simon and his Manoir de Paris on the rue Pierre Demours (seventeenth arrondissement) down to the last detail. The same cordial reception awaits you, the same prompt service, and though the cuisine here isn't as ambitious as at the Manoir, it is inventive and flavorful: excellent ravioli with warm oysters and essence of seaweed, salmon filet in a butter sauce flavored with leeks, braised pigeon and a first-rate sautéed lamb with basil. The desserts are equally good: delicious apricot tarte soufflé and glazed millefeuilles. Good choice of wines, including twenty or so at about 100 francs. The bill for a meal of this caliber is quite reasonable.

A la carte: 300-350F. Menu: 185F (lunch only, wine incl.).

(14) **La Flamberge**

12, ave. Rapp - 47.05.91.37

M. Albistur. Hours & closings vary. Air cond. Pets allowed. Cards: V, AE, DC, MC.

Louis Albistur's new decor is light, cheerful and chic (tall mirrors, flowers at every table and patterned carpeting). For the longest time, he has been feeding TV stars from the rue Cognacq-Jay, and lately he has regained his form. The food is better than ever—well prepared, expensive and attentively served: prawn and artichoke salad, mixed roasted fish (salmon, sole, lotte, red snapper) served with a basil mousseline, and good desserts. And let's not forget the poached oysters in Champagne sauce, which are out of this world, as is the Délice de La Flamberge, a yellow plum soup with vanilla ice cream (though it could stand a fraction less sugar).

A la carte: 350F.

(13) **Le Galant Verre**

12, rue de Verneuil - 42.60.84.56

M. Cohen. Open until 10:30 p.m. Closed Sat. lunch, Sun. & Aug. Air cond. Parking. Pets allowed. Cards: V, AE, DC, MC.

The decor is worn and weary but maintains some shreds of charm. The lunchtime crowd of politicians of every stripe keeps the place lively. And friendly service accompanies a cuisine that's become progressively lighter: delicious pasta (too much of it) with a ragoût of mushrooms (too little); a well-composed mixture of foie gras and green beans, pleasantly spicy cod with herbs, and a rather weak chocolate-vanilla combination. There are a good many fine Bordeaux crux classés on the wine list.

A la carte: 350F. Menu: 220F.

(14) **Les Glénan**

54, rue de Bourgogne - 45.51.61.09

M. Brisbois. Open until 10:30 p.m. Closed Sat. lunch, Sun. & Aug. Pets allowed. Cards: V, AE, DC.

At lunchtime, government officials can order a light, refreshing, ideal meal—timbale of smoked salmon with mussels, filet of roast sea bream with zucchini, and a caramelized grapefruit—before heading back to their benches in the Chamber of Deputies. In the evening, however, you'll want to linger in the freshly redecorated dining room, over the fine seafood prepared by the new head chef, Jean-Luc Sanguillon. Though technically sound and curious to try out new combinations and contrasts of flavors, he still seems a trifle unsure of himself: too much raw fish, too many finely minced or shredded preparations and superfluous "exotic" afterthoughts (like those mangoes atop the superb tomato-garnished turbot). Surely he'll work things out—and judging from his delicious garlic-flavored cod soufflé and faultless apple tart, he's already starting to. Well-rounded wine cellar.

A la carte: 300F. Menu: 140F.

12/20 **L'Oeillade**

10, rue St-Simon - 42.22.01.60

Mmes. Kornicki & Papadopoulos. Open until 9:45 p.m. Closed Sat. lunch, Sun. & holidays. Air cond. Pets allowed. Cards: V, AE, DC.

Inspired by their success, Evelyne and Catherine are adding more fixed-price menus. The food is as good and fresh as ever, and the portions as generous. For example, for 120 francs you can order fig sorbet, melon and mango atop smoked breast of duck, leg of lamb in cumin butter and a delectable apple tart. With a small pitcher of Côtes-du-Rhône or Sauvignon for 10 francs, you won't be ruined.

A la carte: 150F. Menus: 82F (lunch only), 99F, 126F.

(15) Le Récamier

4, rue Récamier - 45.48.86.58

M. Cantegrit. Open until 10:30 p.m. Closed Sun. Air cond. Garden dining. Garage parking. Pets allowed. Cards: V, DC, MC.

Is it because he suspects that the publishers who patronize his restaurant really can't read that Martin Cantegrit has stopped revising his à la carte menu? In any event, this delightful Burgundian has no reason to worry; his Empire dining room and, on sunny days, the terrace—an oasis in this dead-end street that opens onto a minigarden—have been packed for years. So there's no point asking your waiter for the menu. Simply order eggs en meurette, wild mushroom terrine, and boeuf bourguignon or veal kidneys in Santenay wine. All the dishes are good and well presented; the wines, exquisite; the atmosphere, pleasantly subdued. So what's there to complain about? Only the tab, which tops the cooking!

A la carte: 350-450F.

12/20 Le Relais Saint-Germain

190, blvd. St-Germain
42.22.21.35, 45.48.11.73

Mme. Deutschmann. Open daily until 11 p.m. Air cond. Pets allowed. Cards: V, MC.

For years, this place has offered one of the best values in town. The menu is truly inclusive, with no surprises, and lists fresh duck foie gras, a medley of steamed fish, Brie or goat cheese and an apple tart, plus the house wine, red or white, bearing the Dourthe label. It's always crowded, naturally, even late in the evening.

A la carte: 160F (wine incl.).

12/20 La Sologne

8, rue de Bellechasse - 47.05.98.66

M. Guillerand. Open daily until 10 p.m. Closed Mon. Pets allowed. Cards: V, AE, DC.

The hunting decor is more rusty than rustic, and the service is completely lacking service. Unfortunately, the cooking seems to be following suit: The rolled duck livers with grapes is a catastrophe, and the wild fowl is well roasted and tasty but terribly presented and accompanied by tasteless vegetables. There is one good dessert, but that alone can't keep the toque.

A la carte: 250-300F. Menu: 120F.

(14) Tan Dinh

60, rue de Verneuil - 45.44.04.84

MM. Vifian. Open until 11 p.m. Closed Sun. & Aug. 1-15. Pets allowed.

Always packed (in the evening, at least), this inviting restaurant is done in light, modern tones and avoids any junky, "exotic" effects. M. Vifian Sr. and his two sons, Robert in the kitchen and Freddy, who manages the dining room and the sumptuous cellar, are men of great taste and refinement. They have absorbed French culture while retaining their Vietnamese heritage, and the outstanding success of their double cuisine is unparalleled in Paris. It's a modern version of traditional Vietnamese cooking—call it an Asian response to French nouvelle cuisine. After looking over the short menu (a relief from the customary telephone directory you have to wade through), you'll want to try the golden triangles stuffed with lobster and ginkgo nuts, scallop fritters with water chestnuts, salad of crab and mango, red mullet with coriander seeds, sea bream rolled in leeks and cumin, tender morsels of lamb simmered with lemon grass, ravioli stuffed with smoked goose, or lamb stew with a pungent oyster sauce. You won't believe your eyes when you see the wine list, which includes a fantastic collection of Pomerols that would impress even a Bordeaux vintner.

A la carte: 225-300F.

10/20 Le Télégraphe

41, rue de Lille - 40.15.06.65

M. Marck. Open daily until 12:45 a.m. Air cond. Garden dining. Pets allowed. Cards: V, AE, DC, MC.

Le Télégraphe represents an outstanding remodeling operation performed on a 1900-vintage building that once housed a branch of the postal, telephone and telegraph services. The spacious dining room is alive with a crew of efficient waitresses and a cuisine that slips down the gullet like a letter down a mailbox (scallops au gros sel, basil-flavored skate, roast meats).

Menu/carte: 175F (wine incl.).

12/20 Thoumieux

79, rue St-Dominique - 47.05.49.75

M. Bassalert. Open until 11:30 p.m. Closed Mon. Pets allowed. Telex 205635.

This old bistro has been redecorated in the Parisian style, but it didn't lose its Corrèze atmosphere in the process. Prices are kind to the wallet, and the plates are well heaped with serious, solid regional cooking: homemade cassoulet with duck confit, sausage from the Limousin and calf's head, among other entrées. The house red costs 30 francs and is fruity like a Cahors.

A la carte: 160F. Menu: 47F.

(17) Jules Verne

Eiffel Tower (2nd floor)
45.55.61.44

M. Ody. Open daily until 10:30 p.m. Air cond. Parking. Telex 205789. Cards: V, AE, DC.

Perched on the knees of a tower that recently celebrated its 100th birthday, Jules Verne is still just a kid: six years old in 1989, but what a bundle of health! Once the public's curiosity was satisfied, the success of this steel-and-glass landmark pinned to the Paris skyline could have tumbled faster than spent fireworks on the 14th of July. Yet the reservation book keeps filling up, and Parisians who haven't been back since they wore knee pants long to give it another go. Oddly enough, you see fewer foreigners than in the other great Paris restaurants. Instead of becoming a tourist attraction, Jules Verne has endeared itself to Parisians, who flock to its tables as eagerly as to Robuchon, Savoy and Taillevent. If Louis Grondard's cooking doesn't pretend to transport diners to seventh heaven, at least it doesn't let them down. Seamingly bolted to the narrow platform on which his stoves stand, this winner of the Meilleur Ouvrier de France (government award for excellence in a trade), formerly with Taillevent and Maxim's Roissy, cheerfully and doggedly puts up with the unique working conditions—not so different from life aboard a submarine. Despite the occupational hazards, he can be relied on for employing first-class ingredients; perfect timing; light, delicate sauces; and expert use of spices to come up with a cuisine that is solidly classic with contemporary overtones, and his kitchen operates as smoothly and efficiently as a Rolls-Royce motor. You won't encounter sudden sparks of genius or creative flights of fancy—that's not his style—but a well-constructed menu that reflects the four seasons: ravioli filled with mushrooms and snails or crab; exquisite salmon smoked over beech logs; squab dumpling with a minted salad; bass with vin jaune (yellow wine); veal tenderloin with lemon and vanilla; pigeon flavored with honey and spices; veal kidneys with shallots and cooked apples. There are a dozen good desserts (chocolate sablé with coffee sauce, honey-and-gentian ice cream, chocolate fondant with hazelnuts) that surely will keep reappearing on the menu. All these dishes have inspired us to put a third toque atop La Tour Eiffel.

On the other hand, those lugubrious black silk flowers planted by Slavik in the elegant gray and black decor would never be missed. The effect, though great at night when the halogen lamps are lit, in daylight adds only a funereal touch to the sophisticated ambience.

A la carte: 500F. Menu: 230F (weekday lunch only).

Eighth Arrondissement

12/20 L'Alsace

39, ave. des Champs-Elysées
43.59.44.24

M. Blanc. Open daily 24 hours. Air cond. Terrace dining. Pets allowed. Telex 280888. Cards: V, AE, DC.

The worst thing about this big corner brasserie that never sleeps used to be its pale pseudo-Alsatian decor. Then Slavik stepped in, bringing trompe l'oeil decorations, beveled mirrors and warm, rosy lighting, which can only attract more customers to the magnificent oysters and excellent Sauerkraut for which this restaurant is known. Very good Alsatian wines.

A la carte: 250F.

Les Ambassadeurs

(Hôtel de Crillon)
10, pl. de la Concorde - 42.65.24.24

M. Roche. Open daily until 10:30 p.m. Air cond. Terrace dining. No pets. Telex 290241. Cards: V, AE, DC, MC.

As we wrote these lines, the Crillon was changing chefs. Christian Constant, the replacement for André Signoret, had not yet had a chance to get in the door, so we cannot tell you what to expect. He certainly comes well heralded, and he will find the palatial, cold dining room of the Crillon an ideal setting in which to serve as royal a menu as he cares to.

A la carte: 600-800F.

12/20 L'Artois

13, rue d'Artois - 42.25.01.10

M. Rouzeyrol. Open until 9:30 p.m. Closed Sat., Sun., Easter, July 14-Sept. 1 & Dec. 25. Pets allowed.

A rustic, casual decor that hasn't changed for 30 years, and service by friendly waitresses under the direction of Isidore Rouzeyrol, the founder's son: Viva l'Auvergne! The cuisine runs to grilled boudin from Corrèze, homemade pork products, coq au vin de Cahors, apricot tart and good bottles of wine for about 70 francs.

A la carte: 210F.

11/20 L'Assiette au Boeuf

123, ave. des Champs-Elysées
47.20.01.13

See Sixth Arrondissement.

(13) Bacchus Gourmand

21, rue François-Ier - 47.20.15.83

M. Signoret. Open until 10:30 p.m. Closed Sat., Sun. & July 29-Aug. 4. Air cond. Terrace dining. Pets allowed. Cards: V, AE, DC.

A fortune went into the creation of this spacious restaurant in the cellars of the Maison de la Vigne et du Vin (House of Vineyards and Wine). The round interior is simple and luxurious, the waiters wear tuxedos and white gloves, and the bill is worth its weight in gold. The wine list has been greatly improved, but with food priced this high, one certainly can't expect to find many "little" wines. The cooking, after having gotten off to a great start, has become mired in needless complexities, costly ingredients and the confusion of form with substance. Why add both raspberry vinegar and juniper butter to smoked salmon? Why combine both capers and red onions with sweetbreads? And why serve magnificent veal ribs en croûte when the pastry arrives soggy? We're not saying that Bacchus Gourmand is unworthy of a toque, but it is unworthy of two. And is it worth the price?

A la carte: 500F. Menu: 250F.

(14) Baumann Marbeuf

15, rue Marbeuf - 47.20.11.11

M. Baumann. Open until 1 a.m. Closed Sat. lunch, Sun. & July 10-Aug. 28. Air cond. Terrace dining. Pets allowed. Cards: V, AE, DC, MC.

Guy-Pierre Baumann is the self-appointed ambassador of superlative Bazas beef in Paris. He ages the beef slowly in a cold-storage room before trimming it into loins, standing ribs and spareribs. Meat fanciers will also appreciate his Scottish beef and tartare dishes. The Baumann choucroute (with bacon, duck or fish) is famous, oysters and shellfish are on display in a large bed of ice, and there is a variety of desserts. The upstairs dining room has been remodeled by Slavik to resemble a Belle Epoque Viennese pastry shop. The chef is from Le Camélia; good wines are listed for less than 100 francs (excellent Riesling and Pinot Noir); and, best of all, the bill in your saucer won't give you a bellyache.

A la carte: 220F.

12/20 Le Boeuf sur le Toit

34, rue du Colisée - 43.59.83.80

M. Bucher. Open daily until 2 a.m. Air cond. Pets allowed. Telex 281396. Cards: V, AE, DC.

They say that everything Jean-Paul Bucher touches turns to gold, and he continues to cash in at this building, declared "historic," where business failures were once the norm. Each night a dinner crowd of well-heeled Parisians besieges the spacious dining room, redecorated in a 1925-era style; and now the siege extends to afternoon tea or cocktails. Also, if you're an overworked mother, the management will organize a special birthday celebration for your darling youngster. The kitchen, which for a while seemed to have run out of steam, has bounced back and is serving quite respectable brasserie fare: fresh foie gras, oysters (superb display at the entrance), cassoulet of goose, rib of beef, pigs' feet and the like.

A la carte: 200-300F. Menu: 350F (wine incl.)

11/20 La Boutique à Sandwichs

12, rue du Colisèe - 43.59.56.69

MM. Schick. Open until 1 a.m. Closed Sun. & Aug. Pets allowed. Cards: V.

Come here for delicious sandwiches: They're fresh and tasty, and there's a variety to choose from. A few regional (Valais) items and the famous pickelfleish (beef brisket à l'Alsacienne) are served at crowded tables on two levels in typical deli fashion.

A la carte: 130F.

11/20 Brasserie Löwenbräu

84, ave. des Champs-Elysées
45.62.78.63

M. Rath. Open daily until 2 a.m. Air cond. Parking. Cards: V, AE, DC, MC.

Brass fixtures, Tyrolean songs and dirndl skirts on the mezzanine, along with so-so choucroute served in an arena-like setting tucked away behind the shopping arcade. And, of course, draft beer is drawn from kegs shipped directly by the breweries.

A la carte: 250F.

(14) Le Bristol

112, rue du Faubourg-St-Honoré
42.66.91.45

M. Marcelin. Open daily until 10:30 p.m. Air cond. Parking. No pets. Telex 280961. Cards: V, AE, DC, MC.

When the city's luxury-hotel business is stumbling, Le Bristol marches resolutely forward, which is not surprising, as it is one of the two or three best hotels in town. Not that customers are knocking down the doors for a table in this elegant dining room, with its Louis XV chandeliers and pale woodwork, but the posh international set does maintain a steady presence. And when the warm weather returns, the restaurant shifts to its summer quarters around the delightful inner garden, hidden away in the heart of the Faubourg-St-Honoré, where you can enjoy a preseason country vacation in a rattan armchair. But if you had visions of a picnic on the grass in shirtsleeves, forget it! Summer and winter alike, one eats in style.

But all this insistence on the very best form has not kept the cooking from descending to some serious gaffes. It's up and down, depending on the day you eat here, but even on up days we have had an antiseptic red snapper consommé, limp prawns that could not be saved even by the excellent avocado and crab that came alongside, and mediocre oeufs à la neige. In memory of the shellfish salad, the John Dory with citronelle and the Provençal-style lamb we have left them a toque, but certainly not two. And before we finish, remind us to tell you about the wine list: it holds all the great Bordeaux châteaux, which is easy to assemble, but the Burgundy department is a hymn to mediocrity.

A la carte: 550-750F. Menus: 360F, 430F.

12/20 Café Terminus

(Hôtel Concorde-Saint-Lazare)
108, rue St-Lazare - 42.94.22.22

M. Blazy. Open daily until 11 p.m. Air cond. Parking. Pets allowed. Telex 650442. Cards: V, AE, DC, MC.

There's a piano in the entrance of this bistro, in which they serve excellent chef's specials and wine by the glass until late in the evening. In the attractive dining room decorated by Slavik and Sonya Rykiel you can order mérou (grouper) tartare with spinach sprouts and duck with raspberry vinegar. The regional menu changes each month.

A la carte: 250F. Menus: 138F, 182F.

(13) Le Carpaccio

(Hôtel Royal Monceau)
35-39, ave. Hoche - 45.62.76.87

M. Bouhellec. Open daily until 10:30 p.m. Closed Aug. Air cond. Parking. No pets. Telex 650351. Cards: V, AE, DC, MC.

Signor Paracucchi (of La Locanda dell'Angelo, near Pisa, one of the finest restaurants in Italy) drops in once in a while to check on the cuisine that bears his signature. The kitchen crew, after a long struggle to attain some degree of teamwork, has finally got its act together and is turning out a respectable product. Although nothing we tasted sent us into a state of ecstasy, the fettuccine with tomatoes and basil, the steamed giant shrimp from the Gulf of Genoa, the artichokes simmered in olive oil and their own juice, and the assorted fish from the grill warranted the toque that was about to be snatched away. A stylish international clientele partially fills the spacious, comfortable dining room, which looks pretentious and lacks warmth. The bill, on the other hand, will singe your fingers.

A la carte: 400-500F. Menus: 300F (dinner only, wine incl.), 250F (wine incl.).

(13) Le Chambellan

10, rue de La Trémoille - 47.23.53.53

M. Authié. Open until 11:45 p.m. Closed Sat. lunch & Sun. Air cond. Pets allowed. Cards: V, AE, DC.

In three years, the management and the chef have changed three times, the decor twice. But things seem to have settled down now with the arrival of André de Letty, formerly associated with Taillevent. De Letty prefers his own light, modern-classic cuisine to that of the Taillevent school. The fine fixed-price menu includes tempting terrines or ratatouille topped with cold poached eggs, fowl fricassée with cider, assorted cheeses and a bittersweet-chocolate mousse. Excellent service.

A la carte: 300F. Menu: 150F.

(13) Le Château de Chine

9, rue de La Trémoille - 47.23.80.90

Mme. Ting. Open until 11 p.m. Closed Sat. lunch. Air cond. Pets allowed. Cards: V, AE.

It's so comfortable lounging on the well-cushioned salmon-colored velveteen banquettes, being pampered by the charming Mme. Ting, who comes from Shanghai. The Chinese decor is tasteful, and the relatively short à la carte menu runs the gamut of basic, classic Chinese cuisine, attractively presented and impeccably served: five-fragrance chicken, grilled Oriental-style sole, fried ravioli and duck with pineapple.

A la carte: 200F.

(14) Chez Edgard

4, rue Marbeuf - 47.20.51.15

M. Benmussa. Open until 12:30 a.m. Closed Sun. Terrace dining. Pets allowed. Cards: V, AE, DC, MC.

If the system of "cohabitation" (between a Socialist president and a neo-Gaullist prime minister) has made anyone happy, it's "Monsieur Paul." Having been decorated by a cluster of ministers and honored with his name paraded on the front page of *The Wall Street Journal*, what's next for Paul Benmussa if not the Académie Française? Or perhaps the presidential palace (he has fervent support on both the left and the right). This Tunisian-born Frenchman, who might have made a respectable living running a neighborhood restaurant if he hadn't gotten the bright idea of wooing and winning the media powers-that-be, has enjoyed an amazing career. Articulate yet discreet, ambitious but realistic, he grew chummy with influential journalists (the Europe-1 radio crowd practically camps in his dining room) and incumbent and expectant ministers and secretaries of state—the people who rule and those preparing to do so. Like a magician, Benmussa orchestrates their comings and goings so that rivals never meet. Yet he still finds time to look after everyone personally, the somebodies as well as the nobodies. That's his secret: making his guests believe that each is a singularly important individual, and he does it without an ounce of flattery.

"Monsieur Paul" holds another winning card—his devoted, amiable and highly professional staff. So what about the cooking, you ask? It's good, reliable, not prone either to flights of genius or disasters (a new chef has just taken charge). Mérou with tomatoes and basil, John Dory with a caviar of eggplant, lamb stew with broad beans, sirloin steak with shallots, chocolate mousse and good wines (the great ones at unbeatable prices) flow in this spacious scarlet dining room, where there's always something going on to catch your eye and witty remarks to catch your ear.

A la carte: 250-300F.

(13) Chez Tante Louise

41, rue Boissy-d'Anglas
42.65.06.85, 42.65.28.19

Mme. Lhiabastres. Open until 10:30 p.m. Closed Sat., Sun., 1 week in May & 3 weeks in Aug. Air cond. Pets allowed. Cards: V, AE, DC.

The new owners of this cozy, 60-year-old bistro have found a deserving chef who does his best to justify the stiff tabs: well-prepared rabbit stew, for example (it's not simple), Challans duck in a light orange sauce and a perfect sauté of lamb à la printanière. The pastries (tartes, millefeuilles) are fresh and expertly made, and the everyday wines are good. The new decor is sunnier (yellow with a range of earth tones) than the last and even cozier, with nice carpeting.

A la carte: 300F. Menu: 170F.

12/20 Chez Vong

27, rue du Colisée
43.59.77.12, 45.63.61.65

M. Vong Vai Lam. Open until midnight. Closed Sun. Air cond. Parking. Pets allowed. Cards: V, AE, DC.

The carved wood dividers, the large, flower-decked, attractively set tables, the authentic decorations and the cozy corner dining spots for two make Vong one of the most elegant Chinese restaurants in town. It also used to be one of the best, but has fallen off a bit in spite of such enticing specialties as Cantonese dim sum, Vietnamese ravioli, chicken gros sel and the delicious Cantonese roast duck. Excellent service and parking attendant at the door.

A la carte: 230-250F.

(16) Chiberta

3, rue Arsène-Houssaye
45.63.77.90, 45.63.72.44

M. Richard. Open until 11 p.m. Closed Aug., holidays & end Dec. Air cond. Pets allowed. Cards: V, AE, DC.

Louis-Noël Richard is luckier with his toques than with his stars. It's hard to understand this restaurant's sudden fall from favor; as far as we can tell, chef Jean-Michel Bédier's cuisine hasn't changed one way or another. It's elegant—to match the lovely modern decor and floral arrangements—and clever. The only improvement we might suggest is that he amplify his flavors and seasonings to make them bolder. We'd also like to see the repertoire change more often. In any case, there is no finer restaurant in the Champs-Elysées area nor a more attractive setting for a business lunch or dinner party. Lobster tartare with fennel, young rabbit with mixed vegetables, turbot with pan-fried celery in anise vinegar, sole en crépinette with sea urchin roe, marbled red mullet, lamb kidneys in pesto, lemon- and ginger-flavored duck, truffled sweetbreads, crème brûlée with brown sugar, and sweet biscuit with a mousse of black-currant liqueur. Great Burgundies and Bordeaux.

A la carte: 400-700F.

14 Clovis

(Pullman Windsor)
4, ave. Bertie-Albrecht - 45.61.15.32

M. Rameau. Open until 10:30 p.m. Closed Sat., Sun., Aug. & Dec. 26-Jan. 1. Air cond. Parking. Pets allowed. Cards: V, AE, DC, MC.

The Uginox ceiling used to stick in our craw. But it disappeared, along with a tired-out decor, when this Frantel hotel restaurant was transformed into an elegant Pullman car. With its movable partitions, pastel tones, American blinds, well-spaced tables, comfortable chairs and abundant plants and flowers, the Clovis has become gracious, and can expect to attract the dinner crowd that previously snubbed it. Dominique Roué, who replaced chef Pierre Larapidie, is a talented young man who has worked with the best (La Tour d'Argent, Michel Rostang and Robuchon). His cuisine, however, did not strike us as being as good as his predecessor's. A dull oxtail stew, an overcooked scallop of sander with useless truffles, an excellent filet of veal with vegetables and good cheesecake left us thinking that we had just eaten at a one-toque restaurant. And so, for the moment, that's what it is.

Menus: 165F (dinner only), 235F (lunch only), 322F.

13 Copenhague & Flora Danica

142, ave. des Champs-Elysées
43.59.20.41

M. Engstrom. Copenhague: open until 10:30 p.m.; closed Sun., Jan. 1-7 & July 30-Aug. 27. Flora: open daily until 10:30 p.m. Air cond. No pets. Cards: V, AE, DC, MC.

Invented here in 1974 and eagerly adopted throughout the gastronomic world, the recipe for salmon "of purists"—grilled on one side only—remains the chief attraction on the menu. This remarkably pale, moist salmon is also prepared in a number of other ways: in cream sauce, smoked in the Danish fashion, poached in court bouillon or with spinach. Start with an array of extraordinarily tasty herring (fried, smoked, marinated, in sour cream), and don't hesitate to follow it up with reindeer tenderloin flavored with bilberries, Frikadellen (meatballs) with red cabbage, or cured duck. Excellent service both upstairs in the comfortable, sedate atmosphere of the Copenhague and downstairs in the luxurious snack bar and attractive summer patio of Flora Danica, where you can order just about the same dishes (for just about the same price).

A la carte: 250F (Flora Danica), 350F (Copenhague).

11/20 La Cour Saint-Germain

19, rue Marbeuf - 47.23.84.25

M. Ajalbert. Open daily until midnight. Air cond. Terrace dining. Pets allowed. Cards: V, AE, DC.

This small chain (four branches in Paris) has a single formula: salad sprinkled with nuts and a piece of beef (wine and dessert are extra). Pleasant winter-garden decor.

Menu: 68F.

15 La Couronne

(Hôtel Warwick)
5, rue de Berri - 45.63.14.11, 45.63.78.49

M. Muhle. Open until 10:30 p.m. Closed Sun. & holidays. Air cond. Parking. Pets allowed. Telex 642295. Cards: V, AE, DC, MC.

Let's forget earlier disappointments and crow about the recent faultless performance: pan-fried escargots with mushrooms and beef marrow, ravioli stuffed with sea urchins and creamed scallops, braised turbot with vin jaune (yellow wine) and mashed onions, lamb pot-au-feu, veal kidneys with mushrooms, orange-flavored custard, crème brûlée with brown sugar. All these display Van Gessel at his best, a solid, top-flight chef adept at combining bold flavors and fragrances. His talent permeates the Warwick's dining room, which would otherwise be mighty dull, with its commonplace, uninspired decor. There's a good choice of wines at affordable prices (the Saint-Emilion for 95 francs is a rare find on the Champs-Elysées). The fixed-price menu at 210 francs is also a good example of the Warwick's efforts to hold prices in check, a policy of savvy hotel managers who want to keep their rooms filled.

A la carte: 350-450F. Menu: 210F, 380F.

11/20 Drugstore des Champs-Elysées

133, ave. des Champs-Elysées
47.23.54.34

M. Masetti. Open daily until 1:30 a.m. Air cond. Pets allowed. Cards: V, AE, DC.

The decor is amusing, the grown-ups are funny to watch, and the children happily slurp butterscotch sundaes and banana splits. There are also grilled dishes, hamburgers and even some country fare that isn't half-bad (andouillette, confits). Fast, friendly service.

A la carte: 160-180F. Menu: 60F.

11/20 Le Drugstorien

(Drugstore Matignon)
21, ave. Matignon - 43.59.38.70

M. Anghelovici. Open daily until 12:30 a.m. Air cond. Pets allowed. Cards: V, AE, DC.

The pleasant terrace on the second floor boasts a panoramic view of what's doing over by the carré Marigny, the site of Marcel Proust's immortal foliage and the philatelic trade. The à la carte menu looks pretty tacky, but the cooking is quite respectable: good foie gras, sole with chopped chives, broiled tournedos.

A la carte: 280F. Menu: 144F.

16 Elysée-Lenôtre

10, ave. des Champs-Elysées
42.65.85.10

M. Lenôtre. Open daily 10:30 p.m. Air cond. Terrace dining. Parking. Pets allowed. Cards: V.

Cheerful, rotund Patrick Lenôtre, who used to cruise among the tables, wanted "to do his own thing." So Uncle Gaston gave him his approval and Patrick trotted off by himself, while his elder used the opportunity to reevaluate the tone of this ostentatious Pavillon des Champs-Elysées. After that, there was hardly any difference between upstairs and downstairs. The second floor dining room's conventional, colorless decor makes it look like a medical waiting room in a posh neighborhood, and down at garden level (the gilded gate opposite opens into the grounds of the Elysées Palace), you dine beneath an astonishing Belle Epoque ceiling featuring reclining goddesses and elaborate moldings. But a single menu now serves all the patrons. There used to be two, one for the VIPs, the other designed to attract ordinary folks (at 300 to 400 francs a head) to this pleasant winter garden that leads to a summer terrace. Lenôtre skimped a bit on the size of the menu but not on the quality of the cooking, which, for one thing, is no longer a carbon copy of Le Pré Catelan's. And it has never been as popular.

Gaston Lenôtre's kitchen, relying on a team of young professionals headed by Didier Lanfray, produces a polished cuisine with emphasis on bold flavors and minimal artifice, a style that brings out the garden freshness of zucchini flowers stuffed with an herb mousse; the firm flesh of red mullet en salmi (stew), "buttered" with their own livers and robed in an exquisite tomato and fennel sauce; the tenderness of roast veal basted with its own cooking juices and a hint of parsley and lemon verbena; and the elegant simplicity of a millefeuille with green cabbage and oxtail.

Didier Lanfray isn't giving anything away these days, and despite the nice, inexpensive little wines that Jean-Luc Pouteau unearths in the Loire and other regions, you'll run up a hefty bill. At lunch, however, an inviting fixed-price menu is served downstairs for 260 francs; if you happen to be on the second floor, ask for it. They won't refuse you.

A la carte: 500-700F. Menu: 320F (lunch only).

(13) Fakhr el Dine

3, rue Quentin-Bauchart
47.23.74.24, 47.23.44.42

M. Bou Antoun. Open daily until midnight. Air cond. Pets allowed. Cards: V, AE, DC.

This place serves one of the finest selections of mezze—those cold or hot hors d'oeuvres that you can make a meal out of as the Lebanese do—in town. Try the sanacel (salad of bone marrow), kebe naye (ground raw lamb and semolina), fatayers (meat patties with spinach), sojok (spicy sausage flamed and sprinkled with lemon) and the delectable grilled kafta (ground meat mixed with pine nuts and parsley and grilled over an open fire). This authentic ethnic fare, accompanied by potent Lebanese wines, is served in a friendly enough manner in a cozily exotic little room, all of which earns Fakhr el Dine one toque.

A la carte: 250F. Menus: 136F (lunch only), 130F.

(14) La Fermette Marbeuf 1900

5, rue Marbeuf
47.20.63.53, 47.23.31.31

M. Laurent. Open daily until 11:30 p.m. Terrace dining. Pets allowed. Cards: V, AE, DC, MC.

A reader writes from Villiers-le-Bel: "After waiting 45 minutes for a table at La Fermette Marbeuf, I sent you a letter of complaint. To my astonishment, Monsieur Laurent invited me and my family to be his guests. In all my experience, it's the first time a restaurant owner has acted so graciously." Now don't all of you bombard us with such letters. We don't want to bankrupt poor Jean Laurent, who sometimes has to deal with an impatient dinner crowd as dense as the subway crush. Mind you, he's not complaining and prefers it to an empty dining room.

La Fermette's year-round success is no stroke of luck. The Belle Epoque decor is enchanting (it's listed among the Monuments Historiques), the prices are reasonable (the 150-franc fixed-price menu is the best bargain in the neighborhood), there are no less than 32 wines listed for under 100 francs, and the dependable cooking avoids trendiness and concentrates on turning first-class ingredients into light, well-balanced, cleverly prepared dishes. Try the soufflé of snails with garlic butter in puff pastry, sherry-flavored omelet with potted goose, spiced escalope of bass, Bresse guinea-hen in a cream sauce with chopped chives, chocolate cake with bittersweet-chocolate icing and a glazed nougat with raspberry purée. In all, it's a cuisine created by a heroic team of culinary acrobats who withstand the daily assault of hundreds of hungry customers.

A la carte: 230-300F. Menu: 150F (dinner and Sunday and holiday lunch only).

12/20 La Fontana

26, ave. des Champs-Elysées
42.25.14.72

M. Giordani. Open daily until 12:15 a.m. Air cond. Garden dining. No pets. Cards: V, AE.

The site (remodeled) of the ephemeral Prunier-Elysées is now a new Italian restaurant owned by Signor Giordani (who used to run Il Beato on the rue Malar). The terrace facing the fountain is delightful, the staff is Italian to the hilt, and the calamari fritti, scampi and baked lasagne taste pretty good.

A la carte: 180-220F. Menu: 78F.

(13) Fouquet's

99, ave. des Champs-Elysées
47.23.70.60

M. Casanova. Grill: open daily. Restaurant: open until 12:30 a.m.; closed Sat., Sun. & July 20-Aug. 20. Terrace dining. Pets allowed. Telex 648227. Cards: V, AE, DC, MC.

He's been working at the same stove for more than 33 years, but chef Pierre Ducroux is no graybeard, although Fouquet's will soon observe its 100th year in business. There'll be a celebration dinner in honor of the occasion, and it's sure to be a success. When the kitchen crew decides to put on a show, they turn out exceptional dishes, especially if kept to simple, traditional fare. For example, Pauillac lamb with crunchy potatoes sarladaise, juicy and perfectly cooked; or mustard-coated brill with shepherd's pie; and, on Thursdays, an extremely popular pot-au-feu in three separate dishes. A good pastry chef prepares simple but flavorful creamy desserts and light, appetizing babas. It costs 300 francs and then some to lunch, dine or have late supper in this last bastion of Parisian civility on the forlorn Champs-Elysées, whose character, alas, is lost forever.

A la carte: 300-400F. Menu: 195F.

(14) Le Grenadin

44-46, rue de Naples - 45.63.28.92

M. Cirotte. Open until 10:30 p.m. Closed Sat., Sun., week of July 14, week of Aug. 15 & 1 week at Christmas. Air cond. Pets allowed.Cards: V, AE, DC.

Patrick Cirotte finally bought the porter's lodge next to his restaurant and transformed it into an exceptionally cheerful place, with lovely salmon-toned murals. His wife manages the dining room while he works in his pint-size basement kitchen. We liked the Sancerre ham smoked over grapevine trimmings, the thick-cut, undercooked Norwegian salmon with two sauces and the delectable bittersweet-chocolate marquise, not too sweet, with a pistachio crème anglaise. Good choice of wines, especially from Sancerre, the Cirottes' home turf, and delicious homemade breads.

A la carte: 300F and up. Menus: 180F (lunch only), 280F and 310F (dinner only).

12/20 Hédiard

21, pl. de la Madeleine - 42.66.09.00

Mme. Haug. Open until 10:30 p.m. Closed Sun. Air cond. Pets allowed. Cards: V, AE, DC.

Good, reliable cooking (on the whole) is served to a fashionable clientele at lunchtime (mostly businesswomen or their social-minded sisters) in a decor of wainscoting and pale fabrics above a catering shop. "Vintage" (skinned and boned) sardines in the can, roast Pauillac lamb and breast of duck are accompanied by expensive and wonderful house wines.

A la carte: 350F.

10/20 Hippopotamus

6, ave. Franklin-Roosevelt - 42.25.77.96

M. Guignard. Open daily until 1 a.m. Air cond. Pets allowed. Cards: V.

Sometimes you run into a tough piece of beef or a foul-mouthed waitress, but after twenty years in the fast-food business (this Hippo is the granddaddy of the chain), on the whole they deserve credit for serving good grilled meats with matchstick french fries and standard sauces, along with wines by the pitcher. Other branches in the eighth arrondissement: 42, ave. des Champs-Elysées (45.53.40.84); 46, ave. de Wagram (46.22.13.96); 20, rue Quentin-Bauchart (47.20.30.14).

A la carte: 150F. Menu: 73F.

(14) Indra

10, rue du Commandant-Riviére
43.59.46.40

M. Gupta. Open until 11 p.m. Closed Sat. lunch & Sun. Air cond. Pets allowed. Telex 670416. Cards: V, AE, DC, MC.

M. Gupta is your jovial host, and you'll probably feel slightly overwhelmed by the dark, hyperdecorative carved woodwork imported from his native India—as well as by the excellent Indian cooking that friendly, silent, incredibly polite waiters bring to your table. You'll enjoy tandoori specialties (from a special charcoal-fed oven); a variety of curries, including shrimp, chicken and lamb; marvelous mulligatawny (lentil) soup; coconut chicken and rice; salted or sugared fritters; and seven kinds of delicious breads. Or try the Indian-style eggplant and the lamb pilaf (shahjahani), with its outstandingly fragrant basmati rice. Several kinds of homemade lassi (fermented milk) are worth tasting.

A la carte: 230F. Menus: 160F (lunch only), 190F, 220F, 240F.

(13) Au Jardin du Printemps

32, rue de Penthiévre - 43.59.32.91

M. Tan Le-Bieng. Open until 11:30 p.m. Closed Sun. & Aug. Air cond. No pets. Cards: V, AE, DC.

The Tan brothers have a matchless flair for publicity: They love to see photos of themselves with the loyal Parisian celebrities who have been coming here for years. Perhaps the pretty decor has something to do with it, or the friendly atmosphere and consistently good Chinese-Vietnamese cuisine: shrimp flavored with mint or salted and grilled, roast chicken with lemon grass, brochette of beef marinated in saké.

A la carte: 250F.

(14) Le Jardin du Royal Monceau

(Hôtel Royal Monceau)
35, ave. Hoche - 45.62.96.02

M. Bouhellec. Open daily until 10:30 p.m. Air cond. Garden dining. Garage parking. No pets. Telex 650361. Cards: V, AE, DC, MC.

The Royal Monceau's vast inner courtyard becomes a picture-book flower garden in summer. A harpist plays in the evening, the notes echoed by songbirds; you'd think you were lost in the country, miles from the Champs-Elysées. Chef Gabriel Biscay's cuisine attempts to promote this gentle illusion—not by extravagant means but with light, richly flavored dishes that are elegantly presented: roast filets of red mullet with olive butter and cardamom, pan-fried lotte in red wine and chives, stir-fried lamb with lemon and saffron and delicious desserts. Light, appetizing dishes are served in a leafy setting around the hotel's splendid basement swimming pool.

A la carte: 450-500F. Menu: 260F.

(16) Lamazère

23, rue de Ponthieu - 43.59.66.66

M. Lamazère. Open until midnight. Closed Sun. & Aug. Air cond. Parking. No pets. Cards: V, AE, DC, MC.

The only thing Roger Lamazère can't manage to pull out of his magician's hat is a merciful tab. Even by ordering the least expensive (also the least interesting) items, you can't dine at Lamazère for less than 450 francs, including a half bottle of Cahors and coffee. And you'd better have handy an extra 300 to 400 francs in case you decide not to resist the foie gras (sumptuous goose liver cooked in its own fat in a cloth bag, or warm in the form of an escalope) with truffles, a specialty of this Toulouse-born chef for the past 30 years. Let's not even talk about the famous "Lamazère royal truffle," which arrives (practically under glass) with a healthy slab of foie gras, for this will add another 500 francs to your original bill of 800. And then, of course, you wouldn't dream of subjecting such ambrosia to the company of a pedestrian Cahors. To avoid a reputation for prices that are outrageous, Lamazère now serves a business lunch for 290 francs, including Cahors but minus the truffled foie gras, which is a relatively good deal.

Chef Daniel Tricaud isn't wedded to the regional cuisine of Toulouse. He also makes an excellent aiguillette of duck with leeks, a mixed seafood grill with fresh noodles, and a succulent roast Pauillac lamb with spicy vegetables. There's a lavish wine cellar stocked with fine Bordeaux and Armagnacs, along with a free-spending well-heeled clientele that enjoys drinking them in this spacious, luxurious, even ostentatious setting.

A la carte: 500F and up. Menu: 290F (lunch only, wine incl.).

Lasserre

17, ave. Franklin-Roosevelt - 43.59.53.43

M. Lasserre. Open until 10:30 p.m. Closed Mon. lunch, Sun. & July 30-Aug. 28. Air cond. Terrace dining. No pets. Parking.

Where in Paris can you eat lobster Newburg or a truffle in puff pastry made the way they were in 1950? Where else but Lasserre? Few restaurants can duplicate the Lasserre style of cooking even if they try. We say this in all sincerity, convinced as we are that the talent of chef Marc Daniel, a great admirer of Robuchon, is largely responsible for the success of these old-fashioned dishes. We also feel that the grandiloquent menu is properly accented by a staff trained to perform its stately ballet in the "grand manner" and by the intimidating starchiness of the lavish provincial decor, which lies open to the stars when the roof is retracted (the drapes have been cleaned; the carpeting is new). And, frankly, is it fair to insist on labeling Lasserre the repository of ostentation when René Lasserre has tried hard in recent years to evolve toward a less pompous style of cooking? In our last edition we were pleased to note a serious effort to simplify and fine-tune preparations.

Aside from a tenderloin of veal with sugar peas that was nothing to rave about, our latest meal within these venerable walls was nearly worthy of three toques: a light, fragrant feuilleté of golden, crunchy chanterelles; a perfectly poached turbot with the bone in and a faultless hollandaise sauce; followed by a marvelous cake of roasted hazelnuts and chocolate. A single question remains: Is it worth the astronomical price? You be the judge. The outstanding wine cellar is one of Paris's richest in Burgundies and Bordeaux, especially in great Bordeaux vintages. We'd like it better if the wine steward, who insists on serving reds at room temperature on the hottest days, didn't take offense at our request for a slightly chilled bottle.

A la carte: 700-800F.

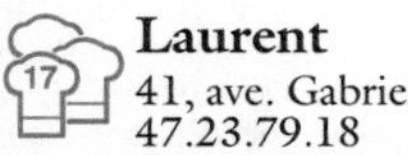

Laurent

41, ave. Gabriel
47.23.79.18

M. Ehrlich. Open until 11 p.m. Closed Sat. lunch, Sun. & holidays. Air cond. Garden dining. No pets. Parking. Cards: AE, DC.

Laurent did well to turn over the kitchens to Bernard Guilhaudin. This 36-year-old chef, who has worked for private households (including six years with art dealer Daniel Wildenstein) and trained under Chapel, has what it takes to do well here: a modified classic approach, free of the constraints of the grand style, with clear, bold flavors and a resourceful technique. His lobster with broad beans in an chilled consommé and his miniature lobster wrapped in a feathery light crust are magnificent dishes. His bass pan-fried in its skin; thick filet of sole garnished only with mushrooms; ravioli filled with foie gras and truffle essence; "American" charcoal-broiled steak; veal cutlet cooked on one side only and garnished with herb butter and a purée of celery stalks and tops; and such clever, elegant desserts as the "two soufflés" (warm chocolate and cold coffee) all mark the advent of a genuinely flavorful cuisine at one of the long-standing greats among Paris restaurants.

We almost forgot the wines! Philippe Bourguignon, one of the friendliest and most knowledgeable sommeliers in town, is certainly not neglecting his cellar, which he lovingly put together. Unfortunately, its prices don't make it any easier to face the final bill; there are two wines for less than 100 francs, but your dinner tab can still soar to 800 francs or more.

A la carte: 700F and up. Menus: 340F (lunch only), 680F (dinner only).

Ledoyen

Carré des Champs-Elysées - 47.42.23.23

M. Nessi. Closed Sun. Garden dining. No pets. Parking. Telex 642116. Cards: V, AE, DC.

While attending Régine's glittering housewarming for Ledoyen, her latest Parisian venture, we felt a distinct urge to make things more than just warm for decorator François Lamotte. Inspired, it appears, by the sublime sets of Visconti's classic film, *The Leopard*, Lamotte came up with a decor which the Leopard himself, that proud Sicilian aristocrat, would surely find (as we did) full of errors and lapses of taste—it's certainly not the sort of place where he would feel at home.

Were the building and gardens not so fine, were the volumes and proportions of the rooms not so remarkable, we wouldn't bother to make an issue of the decoration. But it's hard not to imagine—and regret—what might have been made of the place, given the enormous effort and sums of money that went into it.

The basic idea is appealing enough, and indeed there is a lot to like about this sumptuous collection of expensive bric-à-brac: the woodwork in the main dining room for example, and the handsome upholstery, the tubs that hold a lush profusion of plants, and the artful lighting. And how can one resist the droll, indescribably kitsch atrium, where stained glass, classical columns and campy torch-bearing bayadères parody the foyer of a high-class 19th-century bordello?

But it is precisely because Lamotte so nearly got it right that his slip-ups are all the more noticeable—and irritating. Why on earth did he choose that garnet-hued carpet, which manages to clash with every other color around it? Why are the "cloud-edged" ceilings so ineptly painted, and the bay windows dressed with silly, skimpy *bouillonné* curtains? And in the otherwise attractive blond-paneled bar, why—why?—did

Lamotte perpetrate that dreadful color scheme of orange on bordeaux? It certainly doesn't induce one to linger over a drink!

The four private dining rooms, with their movable partitions, are not wildly elegant. As for "Le Carré des Champs-Elysées," a room (with a terrace for fine days) designed with business lunches and dinners in mind, it is naturally done in a sober, subdued style. Yet it does seem to us that Lamotte might have tried a bit harder: the merest touch of charm or whimsy would have given the room a much-needed lift.

No fault can be found with the grand "Byzance" salon on the upper floor. Long left in a sorry state of neglect, its delightful "Pompei-style" murals, painted in the 1850s, have been restored to their original glory. But apart from that jewel, intended for receptions and other large gatherings, Ledoyen's new look falls regrettably short of the mark. Is it too late to set things right? Probably not. Régine, never one to walk away from a challenge, may just take it into her head to do it all over again.

As for the food, the jury is still—necessarily—out. Along with a few friends, I sampled a score of dishes in what were obviously exceptional conditions, since the restaurant wasn't due to open to the public for several days. Admittedly, the dice were loaded in our favor, but those were the rules we had to play by to meet our press deadline. That evening we had chef Jacques Maximin and his lieutenant, Philippe Dorange, as well as the entire kitchen brigade, the wine steward and the suavely expert dining-room staff all to ourselves. (I shall of course go back under more normal circumstances to judge the menu designed by Maximin, and carried out by Dorange.)

One wonders if this two-chef setup will prove to be workable: Maximin's attention is sure to be absorbed by the imminent opening of his own restaurant in Nice. We'll keep our fingers crossed, of course, and in any case we know that Dorange is a chef of solid talents.

Of the dishes set before us on our single visit, the hot offerings clearly surpassed the cold ones. The latter seemed bland overall, and reminded us of caterer's food (visibly prepared ahead, and made to withstand the passage of time). But Maximin's inimitable style came to the fore with the hot foie gras and prunes, the lobster ravioli with a touch of tomato, the ratatouille of shellfish with basil butter, prawns with "lace" potatoes, tian of lamb à la niçoise, and the gratin of lobster and macaroni, a veritable masterpiece.

We were less bowled over by the gratin of Belon oysters with leeks, the crayfish bouillon with girolles and a tomatoey Scottish salmon with fried rutabaga. What's more, we found the rice in the pigeon risotto to be unpleasantly pasty (but the pigeon was lovely and tender). Breast of guinea hen didn't elicit much interest either, though we liked its marvelous accompaniment of pumpkin with consommé-flavored butter. Sole with broccoli far outclassed lasagne with John Dory, but when dessert came around, our reaction was to send all of the superb pastries right to the head of their class. And in all my days of tasting and testing, I don't think I've ever sampled better fruit jellies than those cooked up by Ledoyen's young pastry chef, a Maximin protégé.

There. I've tried to be fair—neither too severe nor too indulgent. The reopening of Ledoyen is a major event on the Paris scene, and though it's anyone's bet whether the venture will succeed (they aim to serve 500 meals a day), we want to give Régine three cheers (and our encouragement) for having dared to take up the challenge.

Le Guépard: A la carte: 800F. Menus: 500F, 600F, 700F. Le Carré des Champs-Elysées: Menus: 250F and 350F (wine incl.).

13 La Ligne

30, rue Jean-Mermoz
42.25.52.65, 43.59.15.16

M. Speyer. Open until 10:30 p.m. Closed Sat., Sun. & Aug. Air cond. Pets allowed. Cards: V, AE, DC.

Jean Speyer has sold his restaurant to a new owner, who was in the process of rejuvenating the decor at the time of this writing. In contrast to some of our readers' experiences, we found a cheerful reception, efficient service and the good cooking of new chef Roger Pauly, who has a slightly complicated but elegant style: scallops and prawns in saffron, perfectly steamed bass filet in a lovely ginger sauce and a remarkable layered pastry of crêpes with kiwis, apples and oranges.

A la carte: 400F. Menu: 250F (wine incl.).

13 Le Lord Gourmand

9, rue Lord-Byron
43.59.07.27, 45.62.66.06

M. Borne. Open until 10:30 p.m. Closed Sat. & Sun. Pets allowed. Cards: V, AE.

Roland Borne, Le Lord Gourmand's new owner/chef, had barely gotten his feet wet when we ate at his restaurant, and still it was worth at least a toque. We expect this rating to be confirmed and even raised, just as soon as this well-trained young chef gains control of his new place, finishes his daytime military service and has a chance to improve the intimate but dog-eared decor. Try the grilled bass and skate in a cold bouillabaisse and the fatted Bresse fowl in a pot-au-feu with truffles. The dessert list needs rounding out and the prices rounding down.

A la carte: 300 and up. Menus: 165F (lunch only), 300F (dinner only).

19.5 Lucas-Carton

9, pl. de la Madeleine
42.65.22.90

M. Senderens. Open until 10:30 p.m. Closed Sat., Sun., July 29-Aug. 21 & Dec. 22-Jan. 2. Air cond. Parking. No pets. Telex 281088. Cards: V.

If Alain Senderens has a pet subject, it's the need for a culinary copyright. Imitators—and there are hordes of them—drive him up the wall, and he can't see why a special dish doesn't warrant the same artistic protection as a song or a couturier's design. The public doesn't care a bit about such futile debates. They don't want to hear who invented salade folle, truffle soup, stuffed zucchini flowers or bay scallop ravioli. They know that each "creation" is derived from a prior or parallel one, and what makes the difference is an element that defies protection: talent.

Everyone must have had the experience of turning out a second-rate copy by botching a recipe, not to mention an entire meal.

Lucas-Carton proved this not long ago with a dinner prepared by Senderens, but not Senderens at his best. This type of slip happens to every great chef—his clients also have their off days—and argues less in favor of artistic protection than simple modesty. But let's close the subject and recall the positive things... for instance, the new menu prepared by an inspired, meticulous artist. Instead of trying to taste everything, we concentrated on four dishes: baby zucchini with bay scallops and thyme; red mullet cooked in pastry, its liver served on a square of toast with fennel and black olives poached in basil; roasted sweetbreads garnished with assorted fried vegetables and herbs (sage, rosemary, parsley, fennel, coriander, celery, leeks and carrots); and, finally, wild duck with a salad of spinach with orange peel. No list can possibly convey the delectable succession of subtle flavors we enjoyed. We've tasted Senderens's cooking dozens of times, both at L'Archestrate and Lucas-Carton; some were memorable experiences, but this latest one was very special.

Let's see whether next time we'll feel as excited about the salmon steak poached in its own fennel-flavored juices in an earthenware pot, lobster with vanilla, minced lamb with puréed garlic and eggplant, coconut ice cream with raspberry sauce, mango soup with wild strawberries, and pineapple fritters à la piña colada. Some readers are immune to the "Senderens magic" and have bad reactions to the bills that accompany it. Not us. Luxury, as they say, has its price, and if you feel like spending 20,000 francs at Lucas-Carton for a bottle of Pétrus 1945, don't complain about it afterward to the Office of Consumer Affairs.

Anyway, despite a bad year or two for the restaurant trade, Lucas-Carton's handsomely paneled Belle Epoque dining room is doing well. Business has tripled since it reopened, and an elegant French and international crowd, greeted with an attentive and critical eye by Eventhia Senderens, who looks lovelier than ever, is on hand nightly.

Upstairs, indiscreet affairs once flourished over Champagne bottles, and on November 10, 1918, Clemenceau, Foch and the Allied command sat around a table and arranged the hour of the Armistice. Nowadays, the private rooms are reserved for business luncheons, while in the gray and blue "club room," Paris yuppies and entertainment people rub elbows and eat home-cooking for the price they would have to pay downstairs for a bottle of Meursault.

A la carte: 800-900F and up. Menus: 890F, 900F and 950F (wine incl.), 605F, 680F.

(13) Le Manoir Normand

77, blvd. de Courcelles - 42.27.38.97

M. Pommerai. Open until 10:30 p.m. Closed Sun. Terrace dining. Pets allowed. Cards: V, AE, DC.

Each day has its special dish: veal tenderloin with crayfish on Monday, chicken with mushrooms on Tuesday, veal kidney on Wednesday, and so it goes. What we like best of all is the succulent chicken that Rémi Pommerai roasts on a spit that you can watch turning in the huge fireplace, which, along with the two lobster tanks, false timbers in the ceiling and other "inventions," ornaments his fanciful manor house. The cooking is always reliable and not as heavy as you might expect, for Pommerai is an able craftsman. The excellent fixed-price menu includes a sausage-and-potato salad made with olive oil, a baron of rabbit with fresh pasta and a homemade tarte.

A la carte: 260-280F. Menu: 125F.

(14) Le Marcande

52, rue de Miromesnil - 42.65.19.14

M. Pouliquen. Open until 10:30 p.m. Closed Sat., Sun. & Aug. 5-28. Pets allowed. Cards: V, AE, DC.

We tend to expect something a little better from the teamwork of that great chef Michel Lorain (La Côte Saint-Jacques in Joigny), who plans the menu, and bearded Thierry Lemoine, a pupil of Lorain's who carries it out. Still, the poached eggs with wild asparagus, fresh cod and puréed garlic, and filets of red mullet in white sauce that we had at our last meal were not disappointing. And in summer, when you can escape the dreary dining room decor, the pleasure of eating in the delightful garden courtyard is dulled only by the shock of reading the bill. First-class service.

A la carte: 400F. Menus: 210F (lunch only), 380F (dinner only).

(17) La Marée

1, rue Daru
47.63.52.42

M. Trompier. Open until 10:30 p.m. Closed Sat., Sun. & July 29-Aug. 29. Air cond. Parking. Cards: V, DC.

We've reduced the rating of this long-established seafood restaurant one point for an overcooked turbot, a slipshod sauce in which the bitter tang of sorrel was covered up and lost, another sauce (mushroom) that was overreduced, a jellied bouillabaisse that probably sat too long in the fridge and hardened, and the famous tiny pastries that expanded but lost their delicate flavor in the process. Surely this will inspire owner Eric Trompier and chef Gérard Rouillard to set matters right. It shouldn't be too difficult for either Trompier, who loves the business his father left him and is a marvelous host, or Rouillard, a veteran of 22 years at the stoves whose classic repertoire has (until now) never failed to please. We've enjoyed his chiffonnade (sautéed minced fennel, lettuce, parsley and chervil) of shellfish, fricassée of rock fish, Belon oysters in Champagne, turbot with mustard sauce, and ramekin of lobster with tarragon. His daily specials include a savory "mosaic" of red mullet and John Dory, sea perch with creamed leeks and good meat and poultry dishes (there are a dozen among the 35 items listed), including a house specialty: fricassée of veal kidneys and sweetbreads with wild mushrooms.

Didier Bordas, who won a national award as the best young sommelier of 1983, may choose for you from a sumptuous cellar that includes such rarities as a 1928 Margaux and a 1961 Haut-Brion, an outstanding Chablis grand cru "Les Clos" from the domaine Raveneau, a fabulous wine with honeyed flavors. The menu, ranging from 75 to 4,400 francs, has never failed to attract a steady stream of politicians, senior civil servants and bankers, who fill the narrow, dark, ungraceful (except for two fine seventeenth-century paintings) dining room that still manages to radiate an unmistakable warmth, and in which a diligent staff provides faultless service.

A la carte: 450-700F.

Martin Alma

44, rue Jean-Goujon
43.59.28.25, 43.59.28.78

M. Casanova. Open until 11:30 p.m. Closed Sun. dinner & Mon. Air cond. Parking. Cards: V.

A favorite hangout of Paris socialites in the 1950s that subsequently fell from grace (for good reasons), Martin Alma was recently taken over by Charles Casanova and redecorated by Jean Dives (of *Maison et Jardin* magazine). Blue and black tiles, natural-wood dividers and comfortable zebra-striped armchairs make for an attractive, sophisticated backdrop for the humble couscous ritual. The cuisine remains North African (plus paella on Wednesdays), with magnificent appetizers (salad of roast peppers), lamb tajine (stew) with lemon, and couscous mechoui served with tasty spit-roasted lamb that you can watch turning. We give it one toque.

A la carte: 250F.

Maxim's

3, rue Royale - 42.65.27.94

M. Cardin. Open daily until 1 a.m. (except Sun. dinner in July & Aug.). Parking. No pets. Telex 210311. Cards: V, AE, DC.

Liane de Pougy is dead, Boni de Castellane is dead, Sem is dead, the Belle Epoque is gone, and Maxim's is not in good health. Is the little rosy light that has lit up Parisian nights for over a century about to go out? Pierre Cardin would assure you that Maxim's has never been so full of life. Reservations are booked for months ahead, and the once-deserted, shabby private salons are filled with cocktail parties and receptions. Now the place is open seven days a week, the staff is one of the best in the world, and the cooking, which underwent a temporary and superficial "modernization," has reverted to its bourgeois origins. All this would be fine if Maxim's hadn't ceased to be the focus of fashionable elegance and a fantasy fulfillment like no other. Its decline hasn't happened overnight, of course. There was hope that Pierre Cardin's arrival on the scene might halt the process. Instead, it accelerated it. Evenings go by when you wonder whether you're really on the rue Royale in the world's most beautiful, celebrated restaurant, or in a "Paris by Night" tourist bus gaping at Montmartre. Albert, a despotic high priest who, in the old days, used to screen new arrivals with a withering eye would be turning over in his grave. Even today, the aging maître d's, who are quite adept at sizing up people, cast contemptuous glances at tables of raucous guests and tipsy tourists.

Is it the end of an era? Or is it the fault of Maxim's for not having the sense to turn things around? We suspect the latter, for if the evening crowd occasionally appears loud and vulgar, the lunch customers are the cream of the business world. Lunch is the best time to capture what may be the last rays of a vanishing way of life, which we will miss—even if we don't fully admire it—when it is gone.

It's also a good time to sample meats from the traveling steam table: rare roast beef, pot-au-feu, beef in aspic and the best mashed potatoes in town, which chef Michel Menant ought to make more often. The bill, of course, is lighter at lunch than in the evening, when the orchestra has to be paid. For example, quail eggs with caviar (not an interesting choice) costs "only" 287 francs, whereas eight hours later you pay 322 francs. What a bargain!

A la carte: 450-700F (lunch), 800F (dinner).

12/20 L'Obélisque

(Hôtel de Crillon)
10, pl. de la Concorde - 42.65.24.24

M. Roche. Open until 10:30 p.m. Closed Sat. dinner, Sun. & Aug. No pets. Telex 290241. Cards: V, AE, DC, MC.

From his kitchens at Le Grand Véfour, André Signoret plans and directs food operations at the Crillon's luxurious quick-service restaurant, which has been redecorated by Sonya Rykiel, with paneling and velvet banquettes. You can expect a stylish clientele and fast-moving cuisine: sea trout with purée of leeks, mushroom lasagne, grilled chicken with carrot confit, excellent chocolate desserts.

A la carte: 230-250F. Menu: 170F.

Au Petit Montmorency

5, rue Rabelais
42.25.11.19, 45.61.01.26

MM. Bouché. Open until 10:15 p.m. Closed Sat., Sun. & July 29-Aug. 27. Air cond. Pets allowed. Cards: V.

It's like running an obstacle course when you turn off avenue Matignon into rue Rabelais, where the Israeli Embassy, through no fault of its own, makes life miserable for riverside businesses. Imagine: Barricades and police patrols are your introduction to a gastronomic experience. It's much easier if you come via the rue du Colisée. In any case, the talent of owner/chef Daniel Bouché, the hospitality of his wife, Nicole, and the serene ambience of their restaurant are well worth the detour. We were the first to applaud them, and we won't be the last to call Bouché not only engaging and disarmingly modest but also a most imaginative chef. Sometimes, however, his imagination plays tricks on him—a risk worth taking to develop one's abilities. Again he has presented us with several delectable creations: artichoke soup with fresh mushrooms accompanying foie gras on toast rounds, chervil-flavored custard with lobster tails, roast spiced lotte garnished with vanilla-flavored potatoes au gratin (don't grimace, this odd-sounding combination tastes wonderful), cod soufflé, pot-au-feu of beef and a potato pancake flavored with horseradish, and an incredible potato stew with pimientos. The desserts, particularly the chocolate soufflé with vanilla ice cream and the walnut "mal-brûlée," Bouché's version of crème brûlée, will make you his fan forever. You really ought to sample the cooking of this extraordinary chef, who would be doing a booming business on any other street.

A la carte: 350-700F.

(14) Le Pfister

8, rue de Miromesnil - 42.65.20.39

Mme. Pfister. Open until 10 p.m. Closed Sat. & Sun. Air cond. Pets allowed. Cards: V, AE, DC.

Philippe Pfister was a maître d' who longed to become a chef and did. A warm, friendly person, he tried unsuccessfully to make a go of it in the fifteenth arrondissement with a style of cooking that was a bit too far-out and which he has since toned down. Recently Pfister took over this small restaurant (formerly called Modeste) near the place Beauvau, leaving Jean-Pierre Coffe's decor intact. With fewer mannerisms and more precision, his cooking has definitely improved. We sampled a light shrimp salad with tomato-vinaigrette dressing, a ragoût of sweetbreads, cocks' combs with marrow, and a delectable fresh mango sablé with vanilla ice cream. Gracious but timorous reception from Mme. Pfister. Awesome prices, even on the ordinary wines.

A la carte: 350F.

(14) Prince de Galles

(Hôtel Prince de Galles)
33, ave. George-V - 47.23.55.11

M. Ferchaud. Open daily until 10:30 p.m. Air cond. Garden dining. No pets. Telex 280627 Cards: V, AE, DC.

Like the 140 rooms, with magnificent, wall-to-wall mosaic tile bathrooms and majestic art deco suites, the restaurant in this old hotel was refurbished from scratch by the Marriott people and is now unrecognizable. The 1930s patio has become a winter garden of soft lighting that extends to the dining room, with its paneling, autumn-colored fabrics and comfortable armchairs. Chef Dominique Cécillon, who used to assist Joël Robuchon, has added to this peaceful setting a cuisine that is sober but appetizing and unpretentious. In addition to the matchless fixed-price lunch menu and an extraordinary Sunday brunch served in the main dining room, there is a short list of selections that includes sea-perch ravioli with essence of truffle, whole steamed salmon with ginger, marinated beef filet and a host of exciting "nouvelle pâtisserie" desserts. The wine list still lacks affordable bottles.

A la carte: 400F. Menus: 190F (Sunday brunch only), 240F (Thursday only), 165F.

(14) Les Princes

(Hôtel George-V)
31, ave. George-V - 47.23.54.00

M. Bonnetot. Open until 11 p.m. Closed July 17-Aug. 20. Air cond. Garden dining. Parking. Pets allowed. Telex 650082. Cards: V, AE, DC, MC.

Competition from the Prince de Galles hotel next door, which Marriott recently spent a fortune redecorating, has pressured the new manager of the George-V to make some long-deferred improvements in the great dining hall (round tables and theater-like draperies), where the babble of millionaires mingles with the murmur of fountains in a most charming interior garden. The cooking has changed radically since Pierre Larapidie was brought in. This talented chef (formerly at Clovis) stripped away overnight a 50-year record of pompous culinary pageantry with such dishes as his taboulé of lobster, filet of sea bass with black pepper, roast calves' liver with puréed onions, and soufflé of red fruit pulp. There's a new fast-service grill in the gallery.

A la carte: 600F. Menus: 250F (weekday lunch only), 360F, 490F.

(16) Alain Rayé

49, rue du Colisée - 42.25.66.76

M. Rayé. Open until 10:30 p.m. Closed Sat. lunch & Sun. Air cond. Pets allowed. Cards: V, AE, DC.

Since the number-one chef in Albertville settled in Paris in 1986, he hasn't created much of a stir. Is it because he's shy or moody, or has it something to do with his off-the-beaten-track location, so close yet so far from the Champs-Elysées? Luckily, you don't have to rely on the gossip columns or on a packed house to make a living, and Alain Rayé does a good business in his dignified, elegant little dining room above the old Dariole address. An able, inventive chef, Rayé offers a short but enticing choice of subtle dishes that are quite personal. Try the oysters in lettuce and a lemon cream sauce, a ramekin of lobster with a crépinette of crab and leeks, semicooked salmon with artichokes in hazelnut oil, a superb saddle of rabbit stuffed with eggplant and baked in a pastry, deliciously crusty brains with creamed tomatoes, excellent calves' liver with Swiss chard and turnips, and a few first-rate desserts (a pistachio-chocolate soufflé and a mouth-watering concoction of dates, nuts and brown sugar).

The best wines are available—Didier, the young sommelier, is friendly and knowledgeable—and what you'll pay for them is reasonable. The fixed-price menu for 190 francs, served at both lunch and dinner, is a steal.

A la carte: 350-450F. Menus: 190F, 320F, 400F.

(13) Régence-Plaza

(Hôtel Plaza-Athénée)
25, ave. Montaigne - 47.23.78.33

M. Cozzo. Open daily until 10:30 p.m. Air cond. Garden dining. Parking. No pets. Cards: V, AE, DC, MC.

From ocean liner to grand hotel, chef Barnier, at the helm for 25 years, has dropped anchor but now wants to revive (though cautiously) his "aristocratic" repertoire, with a few concessions to the modern style—carpaccio with lemon grass, spicy tartare of sea perch, lobster ravioli with a basil-flavored cream sauce. An Italian influence has also crept in: Ravioli with asparagus and osso buco appear alongside calves' liver and grapes flamed in Armagnac and rolled slices of sole in a lobster sauce. The skillful, meticulous cooking and remarkable wines result in an explosive bill that rockets among the gilt-edged paneling in the château-size dining room and the flower-decked patio, where a fashionable international crowd parks its haunches in the summertime.

A la carte: 600-700F. Menu: 290F (Sunday lunch only).

Prices in red draw attention to restaurants that offer a particularly good value.

12/20 **Relais-Plaza**
(Hôtel Plaza-Athénée)
21, ave. Montaigne - 47.23.46.36
M. Cozzo. Open until 1 a.m. Closed Aug. 1-28. Air cond. Parking. Pets allowed. Cards: V, AE, DC, MC.

We're told that the smart set pays no attention to food, that what matters is having a regular table, knowing the maître d' and the waiters and surrounding yourself with the kind of people you wouldn't be ashamed to invite to your own home. The Relais-Plaza fits into this scheme perfectly. Who cares if the cooking is ordinary (except the beef in aspic) and the tab unreasonable? Some people will accept just about anything to be among kindred spirits who smell good and don't mistake a Karajan for a caravan of Jordan almonds. There's a special treat for those who like it: At the back of the 1930s ocean liner–style room sits a harpist who dispenses her syrup along with the iced cakes at teatime.

A la carte: 350-600F. Menu: 280F (dinner only, wine incl.).

12/20 **Le Saint-Germain**
74, ave. des Champs-Elysées
45.63.55.45
M. Hasegawa. Open until 10 p.m. Closed Sat. & Sun. Air cond. Parking. No pets. Telex 641566. Cards: V, AE, DC, MC.

Inside is a cheerful, spacious decor, even though it's tucked away below the street-level shopping arcade. The fixed-price lunch menu ought to bring in more customers: It includes an apéritif, appetizers, a plate of smoked fish, a lamb chop seasoned with thyme, dessert, coffee and a demi-carafe of red wine.

A la carte: 250-280F. Menus: 165F (lunch only, wine incl.), 250F (dinner only, wine incl.).

(13) **Saint-Moritz** ✿
33, ave. de Friedland - 45.61.02.74
M. Raichon. Open until 10:15 p.m. Closed Sat. & Sun. Air cond. Pets allowed. Cards: V, AE, DC, MC.

The prices are pretty steep, and the single menu/carte forces you to spend almost 300 francs with wine. But this is a luxury neighborhood, and the cuisine of Alain Raichon, who offers several specialties of his native Jura, is genuine and plentiful: excellent thick, perfectly pink foie gras marinated in vin jaune (yellow wine), roast pigeon (slightly overdone) with chanterelles, a good selection of ripe cheeses and pleasant desserts. The attractive decor is reminiscent of a mahogany-paneled English club room, with the addition of pretty pink tablecloths. Friendly waitresses look after you.

Menu/carte: 280F.

12/20 **Savy** ✿
23, rue Bayard - 47.23.46.98
M. Savy. Open until 11 p.m. Closed Sat., Sun. & Aug. Pets allowed. Cards: V.

Find yourself a seat at the end of the narrow corridor (called the "dining car," as at Maxim's) in the paneled dining room and order some of père Savy's hearty regional (Aveyron) fare: knuckle of ham with lentils, Auvergne-style calves' liver or Auvergne sausage with a purée of green peas. Friendly, cheerful atmosphere.

A la carte: 250F.

11/20 **Soma**
10, rue du Commandant-Rivière
43.59.46.40
M. Gupta. Lunch only. Closed Sat. & Sun. Air cond. Telex 670416. Pets allowed.

Open five days a week for lunch only, Soma is the fast-service annex to next-door neighbor Indra. The spotless interior in pale tones complements the light, popular Indian cuisine: fritters, curries and raw vegetables.

A la carte: 130F. Menus: 45F, 69F.

12/20 **Suntory**
13, rue Lincoln
42.25.40.27, 45.25.47.11
M. Hermitte. Open until 11:30 p.m. Closed Sat. lunch & Sun. Air cond. No pets. Cards: V, AE, DC.

At this luxury Japanese address with a sushi bar in the basement, the polite staff includes cooks who work expertly in plain view, making sashimi, teppanyaki, tempura and the like.

A la carte: 300-400F. Menus: 305F, 315F, 320F, 385F.

(13) **La Table de l'Astor**
(Hôtel Astor)
1, rue d'Astor - 42.65.80.47
M. Bidamant. Open until 9:30 p.m. Closed Sun. lunch & Sat. Pets allowed. Telex 642737. Cards: V, AE, DC, MC.

Formerly open only for private luncheon parties during the week, this elegant restaurant, whose 1930s decor lies hidden beyond the hotel's entrance hall, is now serving dinner as well. All the better, for the management is diligent and maintains high standards of service, and the new chef, Michel Legrand, is no novice. For proof, try his duck liver with raw spinach, stir-fried lobster with crisp vegetables, salmon cooked on one side only with chives, and good desserts. The fixed-price lunch menu is generally fine.

A la carte: 300F. Menus: 160F (dinner only), 210F (weekday lunch only).

(19) **Taillevent**
15, rue Lamennais
45.63.39.94
M. Vrinat. Open until 10:30 p.m. Closed Sat., Sun., Feb. school vacation & July 22-Aug. 21. Air cond. No pets. Cards: V.

Jean-Claude Vrinat is bound to open a restaurant one day in which he will be chef and his wife the wine steward. Though the idea would strike him as farfetched, even sacrilegious, we'll take odds on its success. This fastidious gentleman is like a sensuous cat; he knows good food and has been tasting, evaluating and analyzing Taillevent's dishes for so long that he's perfectly capable of running the kitchens. But he prefers to manage his busy place, which turns away as many customers as it accepts each day; to bolster the morale of chef Claude Deligne, who's celebrating his 32nd year of service; and to keep the Taillevent staff on its toes, as befits one of the great restaurants of France.

The cuisine is developing at its own unhurried pace, and though one of our critics was put off by "a meal without major blemishes but dull," he or she surely would have enjoyed the dishes we tasted most recently: a "cluster" of vegetables in a delicate lobster sauce, a near-perfect filet of sea bass au gros sel, and a superb tenderloin of veal with chervil, thick as a pillow and tender as down. Or, on another occasion, a warm terrine of wild mushrooms, grilled turbot with potatoes and sautéed lamb with black olives. Of course, you don't go to Taillevent expecting to see fireworks; the Taillevent cuisine is neither an exhibition nor an astounding gustatory experience. Of its kind—a great restaurant, an advocate of the "new classicism," where 90 seats are filled twice daily in two separate dining rooms that never quite empty—it is a model of good taste.

The style of cooking is in perfect harmony with its dignified setting, which once housed the Duc de Morny. In such elegant surroundings, others might feel called upon to serve the "grand cuisine" of pomp and ceremony. Jean-Claude Vrinat has opted for refined simplicity, and we applaud his choice. We also applaud the (relatively) moderate à la carte prices—as well as the wines that Jean-Claude and his wife, Sabine, are so good at picking and that still range from 110 to 250 francs.

A la carte: 550-800F.

12/20 **Toshka**

6, ave. George-V - 40.70.11.76

M. Richard. Open daily until 1 a.m. Garden dining. Pets allowed. Telex 250674. Cards: V, AE, MC.

After investing in Chez Francis on place de l'Alma, then Marius et Janette (Toshka's next-door neighbor), M. Richard, a coffee merchant who supplies most of the Paris bistros, moved a few steps up the avenue George-V and transformed a Givenchy boutique into a luxury caviar bar and restaurant called Toshka. (That's Caucasian for "the little place"—not to be confused with the French expression for "toilet"!) Claude Louboutin, the chef at Chez Francis, planned the menu, which includes four kinds of Russian caviar, smoked salmon (Norwegian, Scottish and Danish) served with marvelous blinis, a plate of smoked or marinated fish, excellent borscht with fresh herbs, hot salmon with noodles and succulent desserts. Last but not least, there's a great display of oysters and shellfish that also supplies Marius et Janette.

A la carte: 300F. Menu: 180F (weekday lunch only, wine incl.).

12/20 **Le Val d'Or**

28, ave. Franklin-Roosevelt - 43.59.95.81

M. Rongier. Lunch only. Closed Sun. & Dec. 23-Jan. 2. Cards: V.

Géraud Rongier has a gift for locating excellent little wines (from 6 to 10 francs a glass) to drink with his delicious open-face cold-cut sandwiches. A few well-prepared hot dishes are served in the basement, but the fun place to be is the crowded bar at street level.

A la carte: 200F.

12/20 **La Villa Pompéienne**

125, rue du Faubourg-St-Honoré

42.25.34.79

M. Benenati. Lunch only. Closed Sun. Air cond. Pets allowed. Cards: V, AE, DC.

This musical-comedy setting is held together by pink marble fabrics, a green ceiling, a large black-lacquer bar and clusters of artificial flowers (same look in the upstairs dining room). Also be prepared for a lively reception from the French and Italian staff and the friendly owner, and for good, if not exciting, Italian food (pasta, veal saltimbocca).

A la carte: 180F. Menu: 89F.

Ninth Arrondissement

11/20 **L'Assiette au Boeuf**

20, blvd. Montmartre - 47.70.91.35

See Sixth Arrondissement.

(14) **Auberge Landaise**

23, rue Clauzel - 48.78.74.40

M. Morin. Open until 10 p.m. Closed Sun. Pets allowed. Parking. Cards: V, AE, DC.

In these two pretty rooms, the tables are well spaced and dressed in impeccable linens. Around these tables are found hearty, happy business people enjoying southwestern French classics, notably a superb pipérade (a type of omelet), duck confit with delicious parsleyed potatoes and heaping portions of flawless cassoulet. Chef/owner M. Morin also prepares a thick cut of calves' liver for two and a hot foie gras with grapes. Mme. Morin bestows a warm greeting in the setting of whitestone walls and false beams that could almost pass for the real thing. Good, sturdy wines of the region, with the accent on Bordeaux, and an impressive array of Armagnacs.

A la carte: 250F.

11/20 **Bistro de la Gare**

38, blvd. des Italiens - 48.24.49.61

See Sixth Arrondissement.

12/20 **Le Boeuf Bourguignon**

21, rue de Douai - 42.82.08.79

Mme. Nattier. Open until 10 p.m. Closed Sun. & Aug. Terrace dining. Pets allowed.

Checkered tablecloths and white walls covered with movie posters dominate the house, including the newly added dining room. Nathalie Nattier, star of the famous film *Les Portes de la Nuit* (*The Gates of Night*), is still running the kitchen, which turns out good Parisian home cooking that favors ragoûts and bourguignons.

A la carte: 130-150F. Menu: 54F (wine incl.).

(14) **Cartouche Edouard VII**

18, rue Caumartin - 47.42.08.82

MM. Pocous & Laurent. Open until 10:30 p.m. Closed Sat., Sun. & July 24-Aug. 20. Air cond. Parking. Pets allowed. Cards: V, AE.

This elegant spinoff of Le Repaire de Cartouche (first arrondissement), which also specializes in Gascon dishes, is a resounding success, especially at lunch (despite competition from owner Raymond Pocous's newly opened wine bar across the street, Bacchantes). The hotel's English-style bar was transformed into a cozy, comfortable dining area (there's another dining room in the rear), and the serving staff is pleasantly talkative but diligent. Expect excellent wines from the southwest, moderate prices and generous cooking that relies on a number of regional products delivered to the door: the most beautiful plates of charcuterie in Paris, flavorful foie gras served cold or warm (steamed in a cabbage leaf), duck "steak" and superb cured fowl. The tourtière landaise (fruit pastry), however, is weak; you'll be happier with the lovely chestnut ice cream.

A la carte: 250F.

10/20 Chartier

7, rue du Faubourg-Montmartre
47.70.86.29

M. Lemaire. Open daily until 9:30 p.m. No pets.

Sadi Carnot was president of France in 1892 when Chartier opened its doors to ordinary hungry folks. In 1989, there's not a wrinkle in the admirable decor, and the cuisine is as philanthropic as ever.

A la carte: 60F.

12/20 Le Grand Café Capucines

4, blvd. des Capucines - 47.42.75.77

MM. Blanc. Open daily 24 hrs. Air cond. Terrace dining. Pets allowed. Cards: V, AE, DC.

The magic of the grand Parisian boulevards is resuscitated in the brilliance and gaiety of this room, whose new Belle Epoque decor is even more comfortable and sparkling than before. The food is good if you choose from the standard brasserie items: seafood, duck confit and pigs' feet. The fine cellar is strong in Loire wines.

A la carte: 250F.

12/20 Mövenpick

(Café des Artistes)
12, blvd. de la Madeleine - 47.42.47.93

M. Van Maenen. Open daily until 11:45 p.m. Air cond. Pets allowed. Cards: V, AE, DC, MC.

The decor conceals the lines and angles of this basement restaurant arranged around a pool. It's extravagant yet offers typically Swiss fast-forward service and five types of fixed-price menus, ranging from a gala breakfast to a full meal (excellent meats and oysters, spectacular frozen desserts) to a sandwich and salad. The wine bar is unusually good, and the list features frequent specials.

A la carte: 100-300F. Menus: 198F (Tuesday and Thursday only), 150F.

(13) Les Muses

(Hôtel Scribe)
1, rue Scribe - 47.42.03.40

M. Antoine. Open until 10:30 p.m. Closed Sat., Sun., holidays & Aug. Air cond. Parking. No pets. Telex 214653. Cards: V, AE, DC, MC.

Chef Christian Massault's new menu is a brief, intelligent selection of seasonal classics, exhibiting a deft touch. Witness the confit de foie gras pleasantly balanced with tart apples, the ample pot-au-feu of sole and shrimp, and the thick slice of rosy calves' liver with onions and potatoes. In other words, this is warm and generous cooking, served by a nicely inconspicuous staff in an elegant setting that was recently redone (wainscoting, smoky mirrors). Fine selection of wines.

A la carte: 300F. Menus: 290F (dinner only, on special order), 175F.

(14) Opéra Restaurant

(Café de la Paix)
3, pl. de l'Opéra - 47.42.97.02

M. Meyruils. Open daily until 11 p.m. Closed Aug. Air cond. Pets allowed. Telex 220875. Cards: V, AE, DC, MC.

The brochure states that the tableware is magnificent, the service and wine cellar superb, and the Napoléon III decor—designed by Charles Garnier, architect of the Paris Opéra—unmatched. This says nothing of the sumptuously elegant dining room, restored at great expense to its former gilded splendor, the comfortable chairs and pleasant lighting, the sparkling silverware and incredible collection of wines that makes up one of the finest cellars in the capital. The clientele, perhaps simply in contrast to all this, does not always measure up. The service, on the other hand, is exquisitely honed and discreet. So it's all the more a pity that we are forced to report that the cooking of the nationally recognized chef, Gil Jouanin, is becoming rather dull. The wonderful ingredients, the bountiful servings and his panache are not enough to disguise a certain lassitude in the kitchen. You would think this is the cooking of a chef who has lost interest, or one who isn't allowed to do what he wants (except in the dessert department, where all is still marvelous and superbly done). Taste the cold soup of shrimp, cucumbers, queen scallops and clams (though it's diminished by too much cold), the noteworthy seafood assortment and the salmis of duckling with wild mushrooms. A little more effort and they'll be back to two toques.

A la carte: 500F.

(13) Pagoda

50, rue de Provence - 48.74.81.48

MM. Tan Dinh. Open until 10:30 p.m. Closed Sun. & Aug. Air cond. Pets allowed. Cards: V.

For nearly twenty years, Pagoda's old chef Tang has been serving good, reliable Chinese cooking—not overly imaginative, but really delicious when he puts his heart in it. And his heart was in it when we had our last meal here: crabclaw fritters; crusty, fragrant spring rolls; and Peking duck, marvelously crisp and rendered of its fat. There's more room between the tables now, and co-owner/hostess Rosine is as cordial as ever.

A la carte: 200F. Menus: 95F (lunch only), 58F.

12/20 Le Quercy

36, rue Condorcet - 48.78.30.61

M. Simon. Open until 9:30 p.m. Closed Sun., holidays & Aug. Pets allowed. Cards: V, AE, DC.

Both the marvelous Rocamadour cabécou (little goat cheeses), and the highly recommended Quercy cassoulet with duck confit appear on the "suggested" menu of this beguiling restaurant with a country-inn decor. You'll also find excel-

charcuterie, which Mme. Simon "imports" from the Quercy region.

A la carte: 230F. Menu: 128F.

(15) La Table d'Anvers

2, pl. d'Anvers - 48.78.35.21

MM. Conticini. Open until 10:30 p.m. Closed Sun. & week of Aug. 15. Air cond. Pets allowed. Cards: V.

Gray walls and carpeting, a white central corridor, saffron-yellow support pillars, indirect lighting projected from black wrought-iron wall brackets: It's quite an "in" decor for a restaurant that sprang up suddenly in a working-class neighborhood. An original, you might say, like the Conticini family that owns it. Roger, the genial, voluble papa who had to leave the Bon Marché district when his restaurant failed, has reappeared with his two sons: Christian, who went to work in the kitchen (Roger manages the dining room), and the younger Philippe, a pastry chef. Christian had a great start, working first for Jacques Manière, then Christian Willer at Le Martinez in Cannes. He's highly inventive and capable of creating unusual and fanciful flavor combinations.

His idea of a fixed-price menu is in itself original: He offers a "vegetarian" meal with, for example, leeks cooked in walnut oil on a bed of mushrooms, and cabbage stuffed with eggplant, cereal grains and coriander-flavored vegetable juices. Another meal includes a choice of "spice" dishes (pungent salad of lamb's tongue, peppered salmon with artichokes cooked in cardomom); a third features "earth products" (delicious duck confit with hearts of celery); and a fourth lists "sweet-and-sour" offerings (smoked duck with mangoes and orange slices studded with cloves, lamb gratinée with cabbage and dates). There are some twenty other dishes to choose from, including chopped rabbit pâté in a delicious clear aspic, superb scallops happily coupled with salsify, crusty pigs' feet with mustard-coated turnips, and a savory casserole of pigs' jowls. As for Philippe, he's simply an extraordinary pastry cook. His chocolate, mocha and caramel cakes, his fruit gratins and his vanilla chaud-froid are all superb creations. Excellent value, but the service is still not yet there.

A la carte: 200-280F. Menus: 170F (weekday lunch only, wine incl.), 160F, 180F, 190F.

11/20 Taverne Kronenbourg

24, blvd. des Italiens - 47.70.16.64

M. Blan. Open daily until 3 a.m. Air cond. Terrace dining. Pets allowed. Cards: V, AE, MC.

Sauerkraut is king in this spacious, comfortable, lively place that has one of the last café orchestras, along with good Alsatian wines, first-rate grilled pigs' feet béarnaise, fresh seafood and excellent service.

A la carte: 180F. Menu: 64F.

12/20 Ty-Coz

35, rue St-Georges - 48.78.42.95

Mme. Lachaud. Open until 10:30 p.m. Closed Sun. & Mon. Pets allowed. Cards: V, AE, DC, MC.

A bracing breath of Brittany mingles with the pleasant scents of seaweed and salt butter, a fine complement to the spiffy Breton decor and smiling waitresses—not to mention the fine, if slightly tricked up, seafood (turbot with beurre blanc, lotte in cider) and traditional Breton cake. It's on the expensive side, even with a small pitcher of Muscadet.

A la carte: 300-400F.

Tenth Arrondissement

12/20 Brasserie Flo

7, cour des Petites-Ecuries - 47.70.13.59

M. Bucher. Open daily until 1:30 a.m. Air cond. Pets allowed. Telex 281396. Cards: V, AE, DC.

With its authentic, lovingly maintained 1900s decor, Flo is a lively spot famous for its formidable Sauerkraut, foie gras, fresh seafood and pastries served straight from the oven. A genuine, ever-fashionable brasserie.

A la carte: 200F. Menu: 113F (wine incl.).

(13) Casimir

6, rue de Belzunce - 48.78.32.53

M. Pujol. Open until 10 p.m. Closed Sat. lunch & Sun. Terrace dining. Garage parking. Pets allowed. Cards: V, AE, DC.

Plastered with famous wine labels, the decor is a bit bush-league and not overly cheerful, but it is inviting and well suited to this provincial corner of Paris, which you reach on foot via a steep, narrow street. The owners are delightful hosts, and Barthélemy Pujol flits in and out of the dining room in his chef's toque. His cooking seems to hover between two styles: bass with kiwis and excellent andouillette. The daily specials always turn up a few pleasant surprises, and the wine list has great treasures.

A la carte: 280-300F. Menu: 170F (wine incl.).

(15) Chez Michel

10, rue de Belzunce - 48.78.44.14

M. Tounissoux. Open until 10 p.m. Closed Fri., Sat., 2 weeks in Feb. & 1st 3 weeks of Aug. Air cond. Pets allowed. Cards: V, AE, DC.

It isn't the lobster salad with kiwi, or the rather stingy fixed-price menu for 170 francs, or even the ragoût of lobster and mushrooms for 305 francs that sends us running to Michel Tounissoux's place, where the frightening checks cast an aura of grand luxury over the small, ultra-provincial dining room. But let's give him credit for recently reducing the price of several wines, making it possible to have something to drink for 100 francs or less. As for the food, it remains pretty much the same: classic cuisine that is well prepared and solidly anchored in such standbys as lobster omelet, grilled turbot, John Dory with a purée of greens, sliced beef with béarnaise sauce, chicken with mushrooms, and honey-flavored ice cream with a dash of Chartreuse.

A la carte: 400F. Menu: 170F (weekday lunch only).

(13) La Grille

80, rue du Faubourg-Poissonnière
47.70.89.73

M. Cullerre. Open until 9 p.m. Closed Sat., Sun. & 8 days in Feb. & Aug. Cards: DC.

The menu rarely changes, ditto the prices and the quality of the cooking. In other words, the mouth-watering specialties served by chef/owner Yves Cullerre in his old-fashioned corner bistro behind iron railings have neither aged nor wilted. First and foremost is the magnificent whole turbot for two, grilled to perfection and served with a superb beurre blanc, as well as good herring filets, a so-so andouillette and heaping portions of broiled or pan-fried meat. Good Loire wines and a friendly reception from co-owner Geneviève.

A la carte: 200-250F.

12/20 Julien

16, rue du Faubourg-St-Denis
47.70.12.06

M. Bucher. Open daily until 1:30 a.m. Air cond. Pets allowed. Telex 281396. Cards: V, AE, DC.

Julien is the fifth feather in M. Bucher's cap (Terminus Nord and Boeuf sur le Toit are among his others), and it is breathtakingly lovely, with its 1890s brasserie decor and good food based on a menu common to its sister houses.

A la carte: 230F. Menu: 121F (wine incl.).

(14) Le Louis XIV

8, blvd. St-Denis - 42.08.56.56

M. Flottes-Descombes. Open until 1 a.m. Closed Mon., Tues. & May 31-Sept. 1. Parking. Pets allowed. Cards: V, AE, DC.

Watching squab, quail, legs of lamb and chickens turn on the spit in the center of the rather quaint 1950s-style restaurant; seeing your chateaubriand broiled to order; singeing your eyebrows in the heat of the charcoal grill; eating lobster Thermidor or lobster au gratin with your fingers—that's what dining is all about in this big, busy bistro where the tables practically rub against one another. It's lively, noisy, sometimes mad and always congenial. If you really want a good meal, order the excellent oysters, a large grilled sole, scallops or the seafood pasta. If it's hunting season, try one of the wild-game dishes for which this restaurant is known.

A la carte: 300F. Menu: 185F.

(13) Le New Port

79, rue du Faubourg-St-Denis
48.24.19.38

M. Fargeau. Open until 11 p.m. Closed Sat. lunch & Sun. Air cond. Pets allowed. Cards: V, AE.

After two years in this yacht-club setting, Francis Fargeau made a clean break from the old image of this veteran bistro well known to the denizens of Parisian nightlife. His new decor, enlivened with Dufyesque watercolors, is more comfortable and inviting than that at the mother branch, Les Algues in the Gobelins district. Le New Port welcomes seafood lovers who don't want their dinner ruined by astronomical bills. Prices are reasonable and everything is fresh and appetizing: salmon in puff pastry with cream of watercress, pike simmered with vegetables, fresh cod à la ratatouille. The desserts are making progress as well, and the wines are good. The toque is still warranted.

A la carte: 260-280F. Menus: 85F, 120F.

12/20 Paris-Dakar

95, rue du Faubourg-St-Martin
42.08.16.64

MM. Mamadou & Aziz. Open daily until 1 a.m. Pets allowed. Cards: V.

Two Senegalese men and their wives (gorgeous ladies who never step out of the kitchen) have transformed this former crêperie into an authentic little African restqurant presenting a short menu of true African classics: fish fritters, a poached fish stew (tiep-bou-dienn, the national dish) and chicken yassa (lemon-marinated and spicy).

A la carte: 160-180F.

(13) La P'tite Tonkinoise

56, rue du Faubourg-Poissonnière
42.46.85.98

M. Costa. Open until 10 p.m. Closed Sun., Mon. & Aug. 1-Sept. 15 & Dec. 20-Jan. 6. Pets allowed. Cards: V.

Michel Costa continues to serve native Tonkinese dishes, just as his father did, only he's Frenchified them a bit. His is an authentic yet personal cuisine, more seasonal than is customary in Vietnamese restaurants: crab with braised asparagus, a crisp fried cake made of seven vegetables, mérou (grouper) in a sweet-and-sour ginger sauce, stuffed duck "Lotus." Henri Costa, Michel's father, greets you warmly; the friendly, congenial atmosphere is reinforced by a loyal following of Indochinese expatriates.

A la carte: 200F.

12/20 Terminus Nord

23, rue de Dunkerque - 42.85.05.15

M. Bucher. Open daily until 12:30 a.m. Air cond. Terrace dining. Pets allowed. Telex 281396. Cards: V, AE, DC.

There's nothing exciting or stylish about a neighborhood around a rail terminal, but Jean-Paul Bucher (who also owns Flo, Julien, Vaudeville, etc.) is magician enough to pack his brasserie every night with a fashionable clientele. The clever Belle Epoque–Gay Nineties setting is just what the smart set adores, and the cooking, the best kind of brasserie fare, is wholesome and reliable: seafood, foie gras, choucroute and wines by the pitcher.

A la carte: 200-250F.

Eleventh Arrondissement

(13) Astier

44, rue Jean-Pierre-Timbaud
43.57.16.35, 43.38.25.56

M. Picquart. Open until 10 p.m. Closed Sat., Sun., holidays, Aug., 2 weeks in May & 2 weeks end Dec. Air cond. Pets allowed. Cards: V.

Owner/chef Michel Picquart, who wanders through his popular, crowded corner bistro (recently refurbished), is always in one of two moods: jovial or grouchy. And though it sets the mood at Astier, it has no effect on the surprising amplitude of his cuisine and menu. The terrines are superb, the salads seasonal, the home cooking strictly classic, and the breast of duck with cream of foie gras and the beef filet in Cahors wine well

prepared. Excellent choice of little-known growers' wines.
Menu: 100F.

(14) La Belle Epoque

(Holiday Inn)
10, pl. de la République - 43.55.44.34
M. Lutz. Open daily until 10:30 p.m. Air cond. Terrace dining. Garage parking. Pets allowed. Telex 210651. Cards: V, AE, DC, MC.

Surely it can't be much fun for a talented cook to work for a conference center like the Holiday Inn; Patrice Trincali is finding this out. Sadly, everyone seems to ignore him—except us, and we persist in admiring the freshness and individuality of his dishes: salad of snails and frogs' legs with sherry, whole roast salmon and a feuilleté of sweetbreads. We can understand his going through a slump now and then, for what cook wouldn't suffer from the critics' indifference? The desserts are superb, and the menu for dinner-dances is exceptional. Another point is warranted for the exquisite prawn ravioli with coriander, the salad of lobster and potatoes with sour cream and the red mullet in a tapenade cream sauce. The king-size 1930s decor is chilly but comfortable.

A la carte: 300F. Menus: 180F (lunch only, wine incl.), 230F (dinner only).

12/20 La Bonne Auberge du 11e

3, rue Crespin-du-Gast - 43.57.61.12
M. Basset. Open until 9:30 p.m. Closed Sun. & Aug. Air cond. Pets allowed. Cards: V.

A mecca for hungry tradesmen and diners on a tight budget, this place has an interminable handwritten menu featuring good daily specials, plenty of freshly prepared dishes and more then twenty desserts. And there's more: delightful little wines from Loire growers and a fixed-price menu at lunch that's unbelievable.

A la carte: 160F. Menus: 55F (lunch only), 95F.

(13) Le Chardenoux

1, rue Jules-Vallès - 43.71.49.52
M. Souvrain. Open until 11 p.m. Closed Sat. lunch, Sun. & Aug. Terrace dining. Garage parking. Pets allowed. Cards: V, AE.

The new owner is reviving this inviting turn-of-the-century neighborhood bistro. The authentic period decor, with its serpentine marble counter, wildly ornate carved moldings and acid-etched mirrors, is perfectly charming. The classic cuisine is simple, fresh and uncomplicated: appetizing specials (blanquette of veal or lamb, petit salé of pork, stuffed cabbage), excellent and hard-to-find shepherd's pie, stuffed tomatoes, genuine miroton (ragoût) and delicious lean boudin with sautéed potatoes and apples. Prices are quite reasonable, even on the good selection of growers' wines.

A la carte: 180-200F. Menu: 150F (wine incl.), 120F.

12/20 Chez Fernand

(Les Fernandises)
17, rue de la Fontaine-au-Roi
43.57.46.25
M. Asselinne. Open until 10:30 p.m. Closed Sat. lunch, Sun. & Aug. Air cond. Pets allowed. Cards: V.

M. Fernand, a good old Norman boy, knows the secret of friendly feasts that gladden the heart but don't sadden the purse. In this unpretentious neighborhood pub with a country-tavern decor, you can stop by for a friendly drink bolstered by a plate of pork, sausage, tripe, codfish au gratin, roast lamb, cider-basted duck or skate wing with excellent house-made Camembert. Fast-service annex next door.

A la carte: 180-200F. Menu: 95F.

(15) Chez Philippe

106, rue de la Folie-Méricourt
43.57.33.78
M. Serbource. Open until 10:30 p.m. Closed Sat., Sun. & Aug. Air cond. Pets allowed. Garage parking. Cards: V.

What looks like a village café is really a grand old Paris bistro that was familiar to merrymakers 100 years ago. The cooking is the best kind: generous, fresh, technically solid and free of modern clichés. After the food, the next best thing about this veteran neighborhood eating place is its owner: plump, gentle, quick-witted Philippe Serbource. Then there's the unpretentious interior, with low-hanging beams and a restful atmosphere, which attracts a steady stream of customers who like to slip off their jackets (but not their caps!) and relax. At the bar, Serbource uncorks magnificent Burgundies (at reasonable prices) for tasting, which stimulates conversation and an appetite for charcuterie, foie gras, rabbit stew, a near perfect goose cassoulet, an enormous rib steak marchand de vin and the best paella around. Desserts are less spectacular (good clafouti and pastries). Prices are climbing.

A la carte: 280-330F.

(13) Le Péché Mignon

5, rue Guillaume-Bertrand - 43.57.02.51
M. Rousseau. Open until 10 p.m. Closed Sun., Mon., Feb. school vacation & Aug. Air cond. Garage parking. Pets allowed. Cards: V.

Daniel and Evelyne Rousseau have gradually transformed this modest bistro in a working-class district into a sleek, elegant interior with raspberry-velvet accents and tulip-shaped sconces. There are comfortable banquettes, round and oval tables with pretty settings and a general ambience of good taste that complements the personal, flexible, seasonal menu: sauté of mixed fish in Sauternes, filet of roast brill with thyme leaves, filet of beef with garden vegetables (from which garden?). The six-course gourmet menu, well worth its fixed price, provides a good tour of the house specialties. Enticing desserts (apple feuilleté, chocolate fondant).

A la carte: 280F. Menu: 190F.

(13) Le Picotin

13, rue de la Pierre-Levée - 43.57.34.63

M. Malherbe. Open until 10 p.m. Closed Sat., Sun., Aug. 4-Sept. 3 & Dec. 23-Jan. 2. No pets. Cards: V, AE.

M. Malherbe's cooking is light, fresh and meticulous, and we hope this toque he has earned won't inflate his prices. On the menu are fragrant duck foie gras, filet of pike in a light basil sauce with delicious baby vegetables, and an excellent chocolate-and-orange charlotte. Adequate reception and service. The graceless, chilly interior is illuminated by a huge bay window with net curtains.

Menus: 85F (lunch only, wine incl.), 150F.

(14) Le Repaire de Cartouche

8, blvd. des Filles-du-Calvaire
47.00.25.86

M. Pocous. Open until 10:30 p.m. Closed Sat. lunch, Sun. & July 25-Aug. 20. Pets allowed. Cards: V, AE.

Jovial, mustachioed Raymond Pocous (who has just opened a wine bar, Les Bacchantes, that serves charcuterie and daily specials opposite his Cartouche Edouard VII) does a fine job with down-to-earth, honest country fare. The pleasure of eating is doubled by the reasonable prices, and the wine chosen from a wide selection of moderate-to-humble representatives won't ignite the bill. Southwestern specialties include ventrêche (smoked pork brisket), marvelous sausage and ham, hot or cold homemade duck foie gras, feuilleté of snails or mussels, sauté of duck confit, farm cheeses from the Pyrénées and tourtière landaise (not consistently good). Sturdy wood furnishings and excellent Armagnac.

A la carte: 230-250F. Menu: 90F (weekdays only).

(15) A Sousceyrac

35, rue Faidherbe - 43.71.65.30

M. Asfaux. Open until 10 p.m. Closed Sat., Sun. & Aug. Air cond. Garage parking. Pets allowed. Cards: V, AE.

The specialties of Quercy used to occupy center stage on the long handwritten menu at this old-fashioned, handsomely oak-paneled restaurant. But after 40 years, Gabriel Asfaux has stepped down and passed the crown to his son Patrick, who prefers high-quality Paris bistro fare to regional cuisine. Among the best dishes are Sousceyrac cassoulet (Wednesday and Friday), marvelous goose or duck foie gras, duck breast with wild mushrooms and, in hunting season, superb, rarely found hare à la royale. The rest of the menu includes such standard bistro items as andouillette, grilled pigs' feet, braised sweetbreads, pan-fried beef forestière and a daring and delicious combination of lamb's sweetbreads and lobster. Gabriel is in and out of the kitchen and dining room, where another son, Luc, acts as sommelier. The cordial, close-knit relationship between father and sons surely is an added attraction. Cahors is served in small pitchers or showcase bottles.

A la carte: 250-300F.

12/20 Le Wei-Ya

49, rue de Lappe - 43.57.62.58

Mme. Suen. Open until 11 p.m. Closed Sun. & Aug. No pets. Cards: V.

The owner/chef teaches a course in Chinese civilization every morning at the University of Paris (where he is on the faculty), and every night he practices, for his French friends, the fine art of Cantonese and Pekingese home cooking, which was handed down to him by his grandmother.

A la carte: 120F. Menu: 45F (weekdays only).

Twelfth Arrondissement

(13) Chez Marcel

7, rue St-Nicolas - 43.43.49.40

M. Trottet. Open until 9:30 p.m. Closed Sat., Sun., holidays & Aug. Pets allowed. Cards: V.

Bottles of Beaujolais, Muscadet and Cassis (added to dry white wine to make kir) are automatically brought in. You can eat all you want of the rabbit terrine with prunes; the smoked cured beef comes in portions big enough for three; and the vanilla-chocolate dessert is so thick and creamy that people often ask for a second helping. Tradespeople and office workers rub elbows at Chez Marcel, the oldtime bistro with leather banquettes and etched glass, where everything is tasty, well made and pleasantly served.

A la carte: 200F. Menu: 130F.

12/20 Le Drainak

18, ave. Ledru-Rollin - 43.43.46.07

M. Drai. Open until 10:45 p.m. Closed Sat. lunch & Sun. Terrace dining. Pets allowed. Cards: V, AE, DC.

The brothers Drai run this authentically restored 1900 bistro efficiently but have switched from home-style dishes to such things as gratin of prawns and zucchini, fricassée of sole and foie gras with fresh pasta. Not bad but pricey.

A la carte: 300F. Menus: 65F, 145F.

(15) La Gourmandise

271, ave. Daumesnil - 43.43.94.41

M. Denoual. Open until 10 p.m. Closed Sat. lunch, Sun., March 19-27 & Aug. 6-28. Pets allowed. Cards: V, AE.

Alain Denoual is a chef who prefers to stick to his stove and not to parade his toque among the customers. His angular dining room is tidy and comfortable, and he feels that the basic, old-fashioned decor—pink-velvet banquettes and well-lighted, attractively set tables—is fresh enough. The emphasis is on classic cuisine with a distinctively modern style. Denoual is a meticulous cook and technician (he worked at Tour d'Argent, Maxim's and Laurent, among others), a solid all-around professional who handles meats and variety cuts (superb sweetbreads and veal kidney with rice and essence of truffle) as imaginatively as he does fish (excellent salmon with crab mousse). Precise timing and expert seasoning transform an ordinary mackerel with aromatic herbs, or a terrine of leeks vinaigrette, or a filet of brill with chervil into extraordinary dishes. Desserts are not quite up to these high standards. The menu is limited but well balanced, and prices are holding steady.

A la carte: 250-300F. Menus: 165F (weekday lunch only), 260F (dinner only).

12/20 Le Jardin de la Gare

48 bis, blvd. de Bercy
(Gare de Paris-Bercy) - 43.40.82.48

M. Chazal. Open daily until 9:30 p.m. Garden dining. Parking. Pets allowed. Cards: V.

While you wait for your high-speed train or a Verdi opera at the sports palace, this garden restaurant stop atop the railroad station will serve you fast-cooked but well-prepared meals supervised by the Chazal kitchen team (which also operates Le Train Bleu in the Gare de Lyon): calf's-feet salad, andouillette with herbs and grilled steak.

Menu: 69F.

16 Au Pressoir

257, ave. Daumesnil - 43.44.38.21

M. Séguin. Open until 10 p.m. Closed Sat., Sun., Feb. school vacation & Aug. 1-27. Air cond. Parking. Pets allowed. Cards: V.

Henri Séguin's originality lies in his being *truly* original, which can't be said of too many others. Not only does his menu change frequently (and he offers a half dozen seasonal daily specials that don't even appear in print), but at least half the menu is devoted to dishes you've never eaten anywhere else—but which you'll surely see weeks later in other eating spots. Few restaurants can maintain the inventive spirit that rules this comfortable, unpretentious dining room, which could pass for a neighborhood bistro in spite of the carpeting and oak-paneled walls. It's best to come with an open mind; you might be offered a salad of fricasséed pigs' ears, puréed cod with asparagus, flaked bass with anise butter and carrot soufflé, orange-flavored veal kidney with a mushroom mousse, a gratin of prunes and pink grapefruit, or double-chocolate banana mousse. Everything is quite good, delicately flavored and beautifully presented. Son Jean-Jacques keeps the service humming and takes good care of the wine cellar. This meal is worth its price.

A la carte: 350-500F. Menu: 300F (menu dégustation).

13 La Sologne

164, ave. Daumesnil - 43.07.68.97

M. Médard. Open until 10:30 p.m. Closed Mon. dinner, Sun. & 1 week at Christmas. Air cond. Terrace dining. Garage parking. Pets allowed. Cards: V, AE.

M. Médard is fond of hunting, and during the season his menu of wild-game dishes rings out like a hunting cry for the entire neighborhood to hear. Excellent classic cuisine with an unrivaled array of prestigious traditional sauces: saddle of hare Saint-Hubert, wild pig sauce poivrade, roast leg of venison Grand-Veneur, tenderloin of yearling roe deer with a sauce Soubise and so forth. The "modernized" cuisine is not quite as distinguished when the hunting season is over.

A la carte: 250-350F.

12/20 La Tour d'Argent

6, pl. de la Bastille - 43.42.90.32

M. Solignac. Open daily until 1:15 a.m. Air cond. Terrace dining. Pets allowed. Cards: V, AE, DC.

This is no fraudulent annex of Claude Terrail's world-famous restaurant, but rather an old-time brasserie updated in keeping with the urban renewal efforts in the Opéra-Bastille neighborhood. The owner comes from the Aveyron region and knows his business: seafood, choucroute and daily specials. The food is generally good, not too expensive and served with a smile.

A la carte: 200-300F.

13 Le Train Bleu

20, blvd. Diderot
(Gare de Lyon, 2nd floor) - 43.43.09.06

M. Chazal. Open daily until 10 p.m. Pets allowed. Cards: V, AE, DC.

According to interior decorator Slavik, you need a neck brace to properly appreciate the ornate extravagance of this gilded 1900s monument, with its elaborately carved ceilings and woodwork, its frescoes and mammoth draperies, its leather and brass decorations. The cuisine is not quite so high-flying. The menu rarely digresses too far away from its programmed Paris-Lyon-Mediterranean circuit, including a medley of competent dishes (brill with sorrel, duckling with peaches) and a few remarkable ones (leg of lamb, milk-fed veal chop Foyot with noodles). The excellent service can be even faster if necessary for hurried travelers. The food is good enough to warrant one toque.

A la carte: 300F and up. Menus: 195F (weekday lunch only, wine incl.), 220F (dinner only).

16 Au Trou Gascon

40, rue Taine - 43.44.34.26

Mme. Dutournier. Open until 10 p.m. Closed Sat., Sun., last week in July, 1st 3 weeks in Aug. & last week of Dec. Air cond. Pets allowed. Cards: V.

Alain Dutournier has moved out, but his wife, Nicole, runs the place—with boundless competence, one might add—and loyal patrons are now enjoying the cuisine of Bernard Broux (formerly of Jamin), who cooks like a born-and-bred Gascon. Foie gras, sausage, farmer's ham, mushroom pâté with parsley juice, mutton stew with white beans, salmon with smoked bacon, roast fowl with mushroom juice and squab with broad beans—these and other dishes come rolling out of the kitchen of this former coachman's bistro. The original carved moldings and Belle Epoque charm remain in place. Excellent fixed-price business lunch. Claude, the maître d' and sommelier, will provide you with wines from all over at civilized prices.

A la carte: 300-400F. Menus: 390F (wine incl.), 190F, 290F.

Thirteenth Arrondissement

12/20 Boeuf Bistrot

4, pl. des Alpes - 45.82.08.09

MM. Amice & Garnier. Open until 10:30 p.m. Closed Sat. lunch & Sun. Terrace dining. Pets allowed. Cards: V, AE, DC.

A whiff of the Left Bank along the Butte-aux-Cailles, this amusing, meticulous, imaginative cuisine has beef as its theme: cured, with marrow bones and vegetables; tartare; filet; braised. You can order Beaujolais by the glass, and your bill won't suffer for it.
A la carte: 180-200F. Menu: 89F.

12/20 **Dao-Viên**

82, rue Baudricourt - 45.85.20.70
Mme. Vu Lan Phuong. Open daily until 10:30 p.m. Air cond. No pets. Cards: V, AE, DC, MC.
The various pho (noodle) dishes, chao-lon (Tonkin tripe) and barbecued beef (you wrap it in a thin rice crêpe) that come out of Mama Vu's kitchen are remarkably savory. Forget dessert: It doesn't exist. And the wines don't say much for themselves. Simple decor and attentive service.
A la carte: 100F. Menu: 55F.

12/20 **Fortune des Mers**

53, ave. d'Italie - 45.85.76.83
M. Remond. Open until 12:30 a.m. Closed Sun. & Mon. Terrace dining. Pets allowed. Telex 270352. Cards: V, AE, DC.
This combined fish market, restaurant, brasserie, bar and grill is devoted to seafood in a range of prices. Fish prepared simply is the best choice, and portions are generous.
A la carte: 120-300F. Menu: 86F (wine incl.).

(13) **Les Marronniers**

53 bis, blvd. Arago - 47.07.58.57
M. Lorenzatti. Open until 11 p.m. Closed Sun. & July 29-Sept. 7. Terrace dining. Pets allowed. Cards: V, AE, DC, MC.
This version of an "old-fashioned" establishment, with floral wallpaper and framed reproductions, is too provincial for words. It opens onto a delightful terrace shaded by tall chestnut trees that line the boulevard. Mme. Lorenzatti is a charming hostess, the waitresses are most obliging, and Gilbert Lorenzatti's cooking makes up in hearty, bold and flavorful dishes what it lacks in finesse. The excellent growers' wines include a dreamy Bourgueil.
A la carte: 280F.

(14) **Le Petit Marguery**

9, blvd. de Port-Royal - 43.31.58.59
MM. Cousin. Open until 10:15 p.m. Closed Sun., Mon., Aug. 1-Sept. 2 & Dec. 23-Jan. 3. Pets allowed. Cards: V, AE, DC, MC.
Michel and Jacques in the kitchen, Alain in the dining room—the three Cousins get along like brothers! It's a pleasure to watch them hard at work pleasing the contingent of lively, jovial regulars who appreciate the congenial atmosphere and fine cooking. The red and pink interior opens onto a pleasant sidewalk terrace, the staff is good-natured, and the wines are excellent and inexpensive (65 francs for a superb Bourgueil from Paul Maître). The cuisine is fresh and obviously seasonal, as the menu changes daily (handwritten in purple ink, of course). Choose from superb terrines, the best game dishes in the city, pan-fried mushrooms bordelaise, roast skate with ginger and mint leaves, delicious milk-fed roast lamb fragrant with marjoram and delicate dessert pastries.
A la carte: 250-300F. Menu: 250F (menu dégustation).

(13) **Les Vieux Métiers de France**

13, blvd. Auguste-Blanqui
45.88.90.03, 45.81.07.07
M. Moisan. Open until 10:30 p.m. Closed Sun. & Mon. Air cond. Pets allowed. Cards: V, AE, DC, MC.
The comically ultra-modern decor's accent is on fake stonework and beams on the ground floor of a modern building bordering the Butte-aux-Cailles. The cooking is genuine, however, and even though he's not much of an explorer, Michel Moisan makes an effort to update his classic cuisine. Try one of the terrines, grilled salmon with fresh noodles, sea scallops beurre blanc and beef tenderloin in wine... which brings us to the wines. The list is extraordinary in length and quality, including splendid aged port. And note that chef Moisan is a superb pastry cook.
A la carte: 350F. Menu: 195F.

Fourteenth Arrondissement

(13) **Les Armes de Bretagne**

108, ave. du Maine
43.20.29.50, 43.22.01.67
M. Boyer. Hours & closings vary. Air cond. Parking. Pets allowed. Cards: V, AE, DC, MC.
After a bad period, this once impressive little restaurant has regained its toque with its delicious seafood classics, such as fricassée of abalone and pan-fried sole with beurre blanc. The service is flamboyant and a bit affected, and the reception warm and friendly. The quite pleasant, comfortable Second Empire setting boasts large tables and roomy banquettes.
A la carte: 350F.

(13) **L'Assiette**

181, rue du Château - 43.22.64.86
Mme. Lucette. Open until 10:30 p.m. Closed Mon., Tues. & Aug. Pets allowed. Cards: V, AE, DC.
Lulu from the Basque country, her beret pulled down over her ears, keeps turning out heaping plates of first-class bistro fare: rillettes (cold paste) of mackerel, homemade pâté of poultry and foie gras or wildfowl, cured duck, veal kidneys in mustard sauce. These dishes suit her temperament as well as the old-fashioned butcher-shop decor—not to mention the tastes of her plate-cleaning customers. There are several delicious desserts, such as rhubarb-apple crumble and île flottante (floating island), and good wines from the Touraine. It's too bad that it has gotten so expensive, and that the service is so hopelessly slow.
A la carte: 280-300F.

12/20 **Auberge du Centre** ✿

10, rue Delambre - 43.35.43.09
M. Berthier. Open until 10:45 p.m. Closed Sat. lunch, Sun. & Aug. Pets allowed. Cards: V, AE.
The mustachioed owner, who hails from Saint-Pourçain in central France, seats his best customers at the "historic" bar where Hemingway,

Fitzgerald, Cocteau, Picasso and Gertrude Stein did their drinking in the 1920s, when this Montparnasse bistro was called Dingo. It still has a delightful atmosphere, along with good, hearty cooking from many regions. A recent plus: Seafood is now served year-round.

A la carte: 200F. Menu: 100F (lunch only), 148F.

12/20 Le Bistrot de la Gaîté

20, rue de la Gaîté - 43.22.86.46

M. Reissinger. Open daily until 11 p.m. Air cond. Garage parking. Pets allowed. Cards: V, AE, DC.

This place is among the last of those good old popular bistros, where patrons of the now-defunct Bobino music hall used to come to celebrate after the show. Plain, honest decor and a good standard cuisine: marinated herring, lamb stew, skate with hazelnut butter. Good little wines from the countryside.

A la carte: 180-200F. Menu: 76F.

(13) Didier Bondu

7, rue Léopold-Robert - 43.20.76.55

M. Bondu. Open until 10:30 p.m. Closed Sun. & Aug. Terrace dining. Pets allowed. Cards: V.

We don't mean to offend Didier Bondu, a most personable chef, when we say that his cooking is beginning to show signs of clumsiness and bad habits. The hot foie gras is delectable but cluttered with dull, uninteresting, half-cooked winter vegetables; the charlotte of young rabbit is savory but dense in texture; the braised calf's feet with foie gras and mushrooms, a splendid blend of flavors, arrives drowned in a torrent of sauce; and the mandarin orange soufflé has no delicacy. Although the cooking is generally satisfactory and the portions more than liberal, we can grant only one small (grudging) toque, despite the good wines (marvelous Sancerre and Champigny), Charlotte Bondu's cordial reception and the cozy comfort of the lilliputian, recently refurbished dining room.

A la carte: 300F.

(15) La Cagouille

12, pl. Brancusi - 43.22.09.01

M. Allemandou. Open until 10:30 p.m. Closed Sun., Mon., Aug. 13-Sept. 4 & Dec. 23-Jan. 3. Parking. Pets allowed.

Gérard Allemandou, with his Neptune beard and Bacchic belly, offers the freshest fish and shellfish in town (in company with Le Duc, Le Divellec and Le Bernardin). This jovial native of Charentes embarked on his culinary career with no more equipment than a gargantuan appetite, a few good tips on supply sources and extraordinary talent. He claims he has none, but what else would you call his ability to prepare fish as if he invented the species? It makes one lose patience with all those false purveyors of "grande cuisine" who smother seafood in layers of butter or pastry or stuffing and have yet to discover the real taste of black scallops from the Brest harbor, gilthead seasoned with herbs, flaked skate sauce gribiche (tangy mayonnaise sauce) or silver hake with mustard sauce. Where does Allemandou go to get the marvelously fresh creatures whose names are inscribed daily on the blackboard? No farther than Rungis, the Paris market complex, where he performs his miracle twice a week. There are a few desserts (the dark-chocolate fondant and a flat apple tart are excellent) and a limited selection of good wines, but the collection of Cognacs from local growers is remarkable. Allemandou can seat 60 guests in simple but pleasant surroundings, far less cramped and shabby than his old quarters on the rue Daguerre.

A la carte: 290-350F.

12/20 La Coupole

102, blvd. du Montparnasse
43.20.14.20

M. Boucher. Open daily until 2 a.m. Cards: V, AE, DC.

A corporation has recently purchased this Montparnassian institution from its owner/founder (he opened in 1927) but has assured the world—in press-release phrases worthy of a change of government—that its preservation is uppermost in their minds and hearts. The food was never the attraction in any case, and the picturesque interior will be lovingly restored. Montparnasse is in no danger, after all the legitimate concern, of having sold its "soul."

A la carte: 250F.

(18) Le Duc

243, blvd. Raspail
43.20.96.30

M. Minchelli. Open until 10:30 p.m. Closed Sat., Sun. & Mon. Pets allowed. Telex 204896.

Somehow (it just shows you how wicked we are) we always manage to visit Le Duc in midsummer to confirm our rating. Jean Minchelli was there that evening, as loquacious and affable as ever, though he kept glancing at his watch. He was about to dash off to his beloved Ile Praslin in the Seychelles, where a second Le Duc provides year-round dining pleasure to not terribly down-at-the-heels working folks. We had lost track of his brother Paul, the cook, yet our meal was superb. Tony, his assistant, of Italian-Scottish descent, must have learned to "reinvent" fish from his boss, as it was practically impossible to tell their cooking apart. This would be less surprising if the menu never changed, but for some time now, Paul, who occasionally mans the kitchens here (when he isn't working in Geneva or the Seychelles) has been bursting with energy. Perhaps in response to our comment that his menu appeared rockbound, he's come up with some marvelous new dishes: miniature lobsters sautéed for three seconds in palm oil; Scottish salmon like you've never tasted (the secret is simple—sprinkle the raw salmon with Guérande salt and let it sit for twelve hours, which partially "cooks" it, imparting a velvety texture and unforgettable taste). And that timeless masterpiece that makes a mockery of all the fancy sauces whipped up by the greatest chefs: Pyrex-fish (don't look for the name on the menu, because we made it up). Pyrex-fish is a bass, a silver hake, a salmon or any type of fish that Paul sets over a pot of boiling water between two Pyrex dishes. After a few seconds (timing is everything), he removes the fish, sprinkles it with sea salt (so tasty that you can eat it like candy), and that's all there is to it! Can you imagine going through such a silly performance in a cooking contest? Would any judge be crazy enough to admit that he'd just tasted the most delectable fish in the world?

But forget all of the above and take a seat in the combination dining room–ship's cabin, which looks a bit less dreary now that the Minchelli brothers have added wood planks on the walls, spotlights in the ceiling, mustard-colored velvet curtains at the windows and decorative touches—a tortoise shell, a sailing print and a carving of a spiny lobster—to the three portholes. It won't win any interior-decorating prizes, but for pure, elegantly simple seafood cuisine, "Captain" Minchelli's ship has no rival.

The rest of the menu includes sea bass tartare (which nobody else seems to know how to prepare), warm crab with mayonnaise, boned raw sardines "marinated" in sea salt, red mullet pan-fried in olive oil with skin, bones, entrails intact and—hang on to your hat!—the baba. Yes, a rum-soaked baba baked like a pound cake and cut in slices, better than any baba your expert pastry makers can turn out.

Le Duc needed to add one more point to its three-toque ranking, and here it is. We but wish we could decorate it less haphazardly, which would bring customers back more often to enjoy the soft-leather banquettes, the only note of refinement in this dismal dining room.

A la carte: 400-700F.

(13) Gérard et Nicole

6, ave. Jean-Moulin - 45.42.39.56

M. Faucher. Open until 10:30 p.m. Closed Sat. & Sun. Pets allowed. Cards: V.

Nicole's warm smile and Gérard's friendly face illuminate this charming country cottage with its false beams and woodwork, lost among the superettes and "studettes" (miniature studio apartments) off the busy Alesia intersection. Unfortunately, at our last visit the service had grown ostentatious, and the food, once so hearty and genuine, had taken on a pretentious, poorly done modern tone: The clumsy combinations and overdone sauces hardly warrant the new high prices. We'll have to knock off the second toque.

A la carte: 600F. Menu: 330F.

(14) Aux Iles Marquises

15, rue de la Gaîté - 43.20.93.58

M. Thery. Open until midnight. Closed Sat. lunch & Sun. Pets allowed. Cards: V, AE.

This narrow little restaurant shaped like a railroad car, with its funny shrimp-colored paintings, large mirrors and pretty nautical frescoes, represents the past glory of Montparnasse (in its heyday led by Edith Piaf). The food was never good until recently (1985), when Mathias Théry opened his fine seafood restaurant. Some of the main courses are no less than brilliant: crown of frogs' legs with watercress and hazelnut oil, and crab flan in the shape of a quenelle with a fine, thick, highly seasoned sauce. Excellent desserts (paper-thin tarts, millefeuilles with red fruit or citrus fruit) are provided by Mme. Théry, a rather timid but charming hostess, whose father is M. Demund, the great pastry chef in Bordeaux. The wine list and fixed-price menus are ideal, only one shouldn't have to ask for them when the à la carte menu is brought around.

A la carte: 300F and up. Menus: 110F, 140F.

12/20 Le Jéroboam

72, rue Didot - 45.39.39.13

M. Bon. Open until 10 p.m. Closed Mon. dinner & Sun. Pets allowed. Cards: V, AE.

This big, bright, attractive modern bistro on two levels, with red bricks and woodwork, is mobbed day and night for its buffet and daily specials (potted duck thighs, roast wild boar with noodles) and its shrewd wine list. The waitresses smile gamely but are clearly overwhelmed by the hectic pace.

A la carte: 150F.

(15) Lous Landés

157, ave. du Maine - 45.43.08.04

M. Rumen. Open until 11 p.m. Closed Sun. Air cond. Terrace dining. Pets allowed. Cards: V, AE, DC.

Ever since Georgette Descat, first lady of the Landes region in Paris, took off her apron, Lous Landés hasn't been the same. Jean-Pierre, her son, took over the kitchen for a while but recently made his own departure. Fortunately, the place couldn't have fallen into better hands: Hervé Rumen gave up his tiny dining room, Le Croquant (in the fifteenth arrondissement), for this large one, which is now practically unrecognizable in its new green outfit of plumage-decorated fabric that goes nicely with the coffee-bean curtains. The Descats' collection of bric-à-brac was amusing if coarse; the new decor is simple, friendly and quietly elegant.

The Landes isn't far from Périgord, and regular customers won't feel homesick having to choose from a shorter but still distinctly southwestern menu of duck foie gras served with brioche-like toast and truffles, farmer's ham, fricassée of wild mushrooms, cured breast of duck with foie gras sauce, pigeon in Madiran with coriander, cassoulet and knuckle of lamb with garlic juice. Rumen's simple, generous cuisine will be beyond reproach once he drops the habit of undercooking both his vegetables and his meats. There are a few good desserts (spiced apple tart, macao with dark chocolate and dark rum), a limited selection of wines, including the excellent Cahors from Gilis, and reasonable prices.

A la carte: 250-300F. Menu: 240F.

12/20 L'Olivier-Ouzerie

9, rue Vandamme - 43.21.57.58

M. Mavrroïdakos. Open until 11 p.m. Closed Sun. & July 30-Sept 3. Pets allowed. Cards: V.

This new and agreeable little Greek tavern is remarkable for its spotless tables, fresh interior decoration (facing a verdant patio) and satisfying cuisine: tarama, cucumbers in cream, grape leaves, moussaka, Greek-style cod. Pleasant, inexpensive white retsina.

A la carte: 150F. Menus: 49F (lunch only, wine incl.), 68F.

15 Pavillon Montsouris

20, rue Gazan - 45.88.38.52

M. Courault. Open daily until 10:30 p.m. Garden dining. Parking. Pets allowed. Cards: AE, DC.

It used to be a delightful place, but the food was no good. It's still delightful, and now the food is great. There's no doubt about it: Jean-Michel Bouvier, the young chef who's taken over the kitchens, is a good one. He might even turn out to be excellent. With Senderens and Guérard for teachers, he could have done worse, but Bouvier isn't here to repeat their lessons. Owner Yvan Courault, who was once with the Grand Véfour, is determined to revive this "historic" pavilion that has played host to Lenin, Trotsky, Mata Hari, Henri (Le Douanier) Rousseau, Braque and Prévert, but he doesn't intend to do it by engraving the customers' checks in gold leaf. From the start, he adopted and stuck with the policy of a single menu/carte for 210 francs, feeling that at that price, people weren't likely to complain as long as the cooking was decent.

This distinctive greenhouse bordering one of the city's most beautiful parks is so charming, with its pink walls and flower-shaped lamps, that you scarcely notice what's on your plate. But Bouvier's cuisine is not merely decent—it's brilliant. In a great restaurant, people would willingly pay twice as much for it. A miracle? Nothing of the sort—simply a rational approach to modern cooking. In concert with such restaurateurs as José Lampreia of La Maison Blanche, Bouvier has grasped the fact that one can serve good food for less than a fortune. It just takes a little thought: You have to rule out such costly items as truffles, foie gras and lobster and be creative with less-costly ingredients. On the menu this translates to a superb terrine of calf's feet with green peppers, warm skate filets on a bed of mixed salad with sherry vinegar, salmon trout with a highly seasoned oil-and-vinegar dressing, raw tuna steak, braised oxtail with cabbage, roast stuffed wild duck and a splendid platter of three raviolis filled with calf's feet, pork and lamb, the raviolis' distinct flavors are exceptionally delicate. We have one small suggestion for Bouvier: If he would use less concentrate and more juice in his sauces, his cooking would be even better.

Following a first course and a main dish, a delectable bittersweet-chocolate marquise with coffee syrup or an almond-cream layer cake with cherries arrives, and for 250 or 300 francs, including an excellent Chinon, you've got a steal in one of the liveliest, loveliest settings in Paris.

Menu/carte: 210F.

Fifteenth Arrondissement

12/20 L'Amanguier

51, rue du Théâtre - 45.77.04.01

See Second Arrondissement.

13 Ashoka

5, rue du Dr-J-Clémenceau - 45.32.96.46

M. Ashok. Open daily until 11 p.m. Terrace dining. No pets. Cards: V, AE.

From the dining room, with its towering ceiling that seems to crowd the sky, you can watch owner/chef Ashok moving around his glassed-in kitchens. One of the better Indian cooks in town, he specializes in chicken tandoori and lamb, fish and egg curries. His sauces are remarkably delicate—savory blends of onion, ginger, tomato, laurel leaf and chutney. Desserts aren't worth bothering with, and your meal arrives at a leisurely pace. The back room opens onto a pleasant little garden.

A la carte: 180F. Menu: 130F.

15 Bistro 121

121, rue de la Convention - 45.57.52.90

Mmes. Moussié. Open until 10:30 p.m. Closed Sun. dinner, Mon., July 14-Aug. 15 & Dec. 22-29. Air cond. Pets allowed. Cards: V, AE, DC, MC.

After 25 years on the scene, there's not a wrinkle on the calf's head sauce gribiche (tangy mayonnaise sauce), duck liver with verjuice (the juice of unripened grapes), casserole of stuffed chicken or wild hare à la royale (type of custard). Chefs from the Quercy region have come and gone, but the good Moussié ladies carry on, making the rounds of their restful dining room, with frilly lamps lighting each table.

André Jalbert, who energizes the chic clientele with dollops of truffle, warm leeks vinaigrette, duck confits and beef skirt steak in mustard sauce, and José, the bubbly Portuguese sommelier who delivers the finest Burgundies and Bordeaux, have been too busy to celebrate their years of service. Only that annoying little extra zero now clinging to the original 40-franc menu reminds you that it's time to turn your clock ahead.

A la carte: 400F. Menu: 250F (wine incl.).

11/20 Le Bistro Champêtre

107, rue St-Charles - 45.77.85.06

M. Dorr. Open daily until 11 p.m. (11:30 p.m. weekends). Air cond. Terrace dining. Pets allowed. Cards: V.

The menu that has made this bright, flower-decked restaurant such a success has expanded to include several hearty dishes, such as lotte with sea urchin coral and roast saddle of lamb with tarragon essence. Affordable, well-planned wine cellar.

A la carte: 130F. Menus: 135F (wine incl.), 63F.

12/20 Yvan Castex

2, rue Langeac - 48.42.55.26

M. Castex. Open until 10 p.m. Closed Sun. Pets allowed. Cards: V, AE.

The many-membered Castex family—mother, father, two sons and their wives—arrived recently from Tours to take over this cozy restaurant. Unfortunately, the once good cooking has proved disappointingly dull and careless of late. Perhaps Yvan Castex has been affected by the increasingly grand atmosphere—classical music and overdone appointments—but whatever the reason, his cuisine features overly thick shellfish ravioli, a wilted and unattractive salad of scallops, and an uninteresting sole bonne femme. Only the excellent desserts remain at one-toque level.

A la carte: 300F. Menus: 135F (wine incl.), 220F.

16 Les Célébrités

(Hôtel Nikko)
61, quai de Grenelle - 45.75.62.62

M. Iwasaki. Open daily until 10 p.m. Air cond. Parking. Pets allowed. Telex 260012. Cards: V, AE, DC, MC.

Those noble busts of Roman emperors leering down at your calf's tongue sauce gribiche (tangy mayonnaise sauce) may remind you of something. In fact, their twin brothers sit atop the columns in Robuchon's dining room. This is not surprising, since the same Japanese owners funded the decor that so delighted future culinary genius Joël Robuchon when he cooked here.

Since taking over these kitchens, Jacques Sénéchal isn't turning out the same style of cuisine that he did for twelve years at the Tour d'Argent, nor has he slipped into the "sub-Robuchon" category. He has a distinct talent all his own, which produces some superb, highly elaborate (and horrendously expensive) preparations—too elaborate on occasion—as well as exquisite sauces. (The most recent menu no longer included the Japanese-style cod, and we can't say we're sorry, because the saké-based sauce and mouth-puckering seaweed were more than we could handle.)

There are fewer Japanese (who regard the Nikko as their home away from home) than French in this panoramic dining room overlooking the Seine, and the latter tend to order the excellent foie gras, roast langouste (spiny lobster) with mushrooms, sea scallops with truffles, chevreau (kid) with mild garlic or superb lamb with tarragon cream sauce, all of which, along with Jean-Paul Mévin's magnificent desserts, make Les Célébrités one of the finest hotel restaurants in Paris.

A la carte: 450-650F. Menus: 260F and 290F (lunch only, wine incl.), 460F, 580F.

13 Charly de Bab-el-Oued

215, rue de la Croix-Nivert
48.28.76.78, 45.31.35.92

See Seventeenth Arrondissement.

12/20 Le Ciel de Paris

(Tour Montparnasse)
33, ave. du Maine - 45.38.52.35

M. Dufresne. Open daily until midnight. Air cond. Pets allowed. Telex 804418. Cards: V, AE, DC, MC.

Paris, vaporous and alluring, stretches out 300 yards below. The kitchen tries hard, and visitors from the countryside who flock to this immense glass cage perched high in the clouds are flabbergasted. Try the veal terrine laced with parsley and the desserts from Lenôtre.

A la carte: 250F. Menu: 135F.

14 Le Clos Morillons

50, rue des Morillons - 48.28.04.37

MM. Delacourcelle & Leguay. Open until 10:15 p.m. Closed Sat. lunch & Sun. Air cond. Pets allowed. Cards: V.

Philippe Delacourcelle has made great progress of late, and this restaurant, which he took over from Pierre Vedel a few years ago, is regaining its stature with a cuisine that is at once personal and improvised. The curried celery flan is a marvelous blend of contrasting flavors, the rabbit stew is tender and seasoned with a superb ginger sauce, the soy-flavored sauce accompanying the steamed salmon is a model of delicacy, and the rhubarb cake (actually a flan) topped with red-fruit sauce reminds us that this former pupil of Morot-Gaudry was also a pastry chef at Fauchon. Philippe's brother, Marc, puts out a short list of selected Loire wines (on the "discover the Loire Valley" menu; you may order them by the glass). The service staff is singularly aloof, but the new decor is more comfortable, with attractive round tables and a spacious, subdued interior lined with old photographs and mirrors.

A la carte: 260F.

13 Le Croquant

28, rue Jean-Maridor - 45.58.50.83

M. Bigot. Open until 10:30 p.m. Closed Sun., Mon. dinner & Aug. Pets allowed. Cards: V, AE, DC.

Hervé Rumen, the likable "croquant" (peasant) who made this restaurant so successful with his fine southwestern cuisine, has gone and opened Lous Landés (fourteenth arrondissement). The new chef's cooking, however, is uneven and lacks finish but is interesting nonetheless. The Norman oysters and mushrooms are disappointing, but the John Dory with shallots is nicely done. Several good Norman specialties are to be had, as well as excellent vanilla ice cream. Prices (including those of the modest cellar) are very fair, and Mme. Bigot, who greets you and takes care of the service all by herself (for now), is charming.

A la carte: 260-300F. Menus: 160F (lunch only), 230F.

13 Didier Délu

85, rue Leblanc - 45.54.20.49

M. Délu. Open until 10:30 p.m. Closed Sat., Sun. & Dec. 23-Jan. 2. Pets allowed. Cards: V, AE, DC.

Bocuse, Lameloise and Chapel have a few grateful pupils. One of them is Didier Délu, who honors their lessons on his menu and their faces on his walls. The new half-modern, half-nostalgic decor is pleasant and lively, but we were left with a few lingering question marks concerning the food after our last visit. Délu knows how to do fish, roll out flaky pastry and whip up a sauce, but his rabbit terrine with fines herbes, for example, was lackluster. You'll also find grilled red mullet with tomato pulp, a feuilleté of sweetbreads with glazed carrots, unusual whiskies, a good selection of wines and attractive fixed-price menus, if rather small portions.

A la carte: 300F and up. Menus: 150F (lunch only), 200F (dinner only, wine incl.).

14 Erawan

76, rue de la Fédération - 47.83.55.67

M. Napaseuth. Open until 10:30 p.m. Closed Sun. & Aug. Air cond. No pets. Cards: V, AE.

This is the best Thai cooking in Paris: colorful, fragrant, light and exciting, a happy blend of Chinese, Indian and Malayan influences. Specialties range from the shrimp soup with lemon grass and pimientos, the heavenly prawns (marinated in galanga, a fragrant root), the chicken wings stuffed with pork, crab and water chestnuts, the fish soup with celery, to the tender, subtle oven-browned flan with coconut milk. Hot or iced tea is the perfect beverage to set off such delicately spiced fare.

A la carte: 220-250F. Menus: 79F (lunch only), 158F, 164F, 175F.

13 La Gauloise

59, ave. de la Motte-Picquet
47.34.11.64

M. Aphécetche. Open until 11 p.m. Closed Sat. & Sun. Terrace dining. Pets allowed. Cards: V, AE.

La Gauloise's savvy clientele consists of well-known sports personalities, like Yannick Noah, and politicians (including Mitterrand) whose faces decorate the walls of this long dining room. The staff seems to take this as license for arrogant behavior. The new owners have changed neither the menu nor the decor—the latter a not exactly unpleasing affair in light brown, and the former basic bistro food, a little overdone and overpriced: tuna rillettes, excellent fish court bouillon with a velouté of mussels, good lemon tart. Fine selection of Bordeaux, enjoyable terrace dining on the boulevard and fearsome prices.

A la carte: 300-350F.

14 Kim-Anh

15, rue de l'Eglise - 45.79.40.96

M. Kim-Anh. Dinner only. Open until 11:30 p.m. Closed Aug. 7-25 & Dec. 25-30. Pets allowed. Cards: V.

Kim-Anhs fled to Paris from Saigon, where he imported American automobiles and a famous brand of French Cognac. This charming, articulate, pipe-smoking man has arranged his tiny dining room tastefully to accommodate twenty diners in an intimate, elegant setting of white woodwork, wicker panels, black walls and pleasant lighting. Flowers, white napkins and decorated chopsticks contribute to the refined atmosphere.

The lilliputian kitchen is his wife's territory. In split seconds, she prepares the tangy dishes sprinkled with fresh herbs and subtle spices that make Vietnamese cooking so appealing. Every dish is a revelation for the taste buds: light, crunchy nems, served in a nest of assorted greens and mint leaves (green on the outside, lavender inside, imported from Vietnam), with the compelling flavor of lemon grass; bo-bun, composed of sautéed shredded beef in a mixture of stir-fried green vegetables with vermicelli, peanuts and shallots marinated in vinegar; caramelized langoustines served with a remarkably fragrant Thai rice; stuffed crab; glazed duck; and a delicious creamed corn with coconut that, for a change, makes one eager to try a dessert in a Vietnamese restaurant. Even the coffee is good! Reservations are a must for this small room.

A la carte: 300-350F. Menu: 158F.

13 Les Lutins

29, ave. de Lowendal - 47.83.51.22

M. Lancry. Open until 10:30 p.m. Closed Sun. dinner, Mon. & Sept. 15-Oct. 3. Pets allowed. Cards: V, MC.

Two young men are partners: One acts as host and the other mans the kitchen, turning out respectable everyday cooking. Fresh, seasonal, high-quality ingredients mark the cuisine of this new restaurant, which deserves more recognition. Try the boned squab with turnips and the sponge biscuit with farm cheese. Desserts and prices require lighter treatment.

A la carte: 250-300F. Menu: 110F.

17 La Maison Blanche

82, blvd. Lefebvre
48.28.38.83

M. Lampreia. Open until 11 p.m. Closed Sat. lunch, Sun., Mon., 1 week at Christmas & Easter & 1st week of Sept. Air cond. Pets allowed. Cards: V.

Gilbert Le Coze and José Lampreia both bet their bottom dollars: Le Coze went off to make his fortune in New York, and Lampreia, setting up business in one of those all-gray boulevards named for French field marshals, soon became the talk of the town. When other restaurants are half empty, his place is mobbed. His recipe is simple: talent, taste, good looks (journalists like the latter, and so do customers), a ready smile, not taking oneself too seriously and a willingness to slave ten hours a day.

You must also understand three things. Number one is that a restaurant is a pleasure dome. And when you enter this all-white room—walls, tablecloths, even the 300 flowers that poke their heads out of one colossal vase—you suddenly become younger, more streamlined than in many eating places that make you feel ancient. La Maison Blanche quite simply reflects the trend of the times without being trendy. Number two is that diners don't want to spend a fortune even if they can afford to. The trick is to avoid luxury items, rely on seasonal produce and rack your brain to transform everyday ingredients into something special. If you want to use foie gras, use just enough to "grease" a superb potato cake moistened with a bit of truffle juice. How about sea urchins? Fill them with chopped pigs' feet for a divine combination. That's why, with few exceptions, nothing costs more than 100 francs. Other places charge as much for a first course as for a meat or fish dish, but here you pay only 70 francs for a delicious plate of haddock salad with dark radishes, and 85 francs for a beef marrow bone stuffed with cabbage and croutons. The third rule is to surprise your guests with innovative dishes that are in keeping with classic cuisine. You can see that Lampreia, working in his glass-bound kitchen dressed like a surgeon in immaculate white, never indulges in extravagant preparations.

This sophisticated Portuguese chef has a rustic streak in his veins—a smart peasant with good taste! He has won our admiration for his salad of calf's head; his turbot and whipped potatoes with olive oil; his sea bream, its skin all crusty with spices, garnished with raisin semolina; his velvety oven-browned rabbit; his parsleyed steak with potatoes au gratin; the marvelous desserts (gingered pear compote, praline-glazed macaroon, caramel leaves with red fruit, rhubarb tart with vanilla ice cream); and the excellent ordinary wines, ranging from 70 to 100 francs (and up, of course)—all of which bring your check to about 300 francs.

A la carte: 350-400F. Menu: 195F (lunch only).

16 Morot-Gaudry

8, rue de la Cavalerie - 45.67.06.85

M. Morot-Gaudry. Open until 10:30 p.m. Closed Sat. & Sun. Air cond. Terrace dining. Parking. Pets allowed. Cards: V.

If asked to name ten Paris restaurants we'd like to revisit, we wouldn't choose some of the more celebrated and highly rated ones, but Morot-Gaudry would definitely be on our list. Why do we love it? Because it's run by such an endearing couple. Jean-Pierre is smart and down-to-earth, unlike some of the celebrity chefs whose heads have grown too swollen to make it through their kitchen doors. His wife is gracious and smiling, the perfect hostess. Also, there's the picturesque setting of this 1930s converted garage, where you dine in an elegant mirrored room or on a verdant little terrace overlooking the rooftops. By craning your neck, you can glimpse the Eiffel Tower, which seems planets away. And we love it because of the discerning clientele (which comes here to dine rather than to be seen), the wine cellar (where great and not-so-great bottles are given equal place) and, of course, the constant care lavished on the cooking by Jean-Pierre.

His sweetbreads with mushrooms, veal kidney roasted whole in its own fat and Barbary duckling in Hermitage white wine are evidence of his mastery of classic principles. And when Jean-Pierre injects the sunny, herbal flavors of Provence into his creations, it conveys a style all his own. His latest summer fixed-price menu confirmed our high esteem for this food: a superb gazpacho flavored with lobster essence, tomato pulp, cucumber and sweet peppers; and a turbot filet with olive oil, basil, tomato sauce and coarse salt, which would have knocked the pins out from under the Côte d'Azur crowd. The chocolate desserts are delectable, as are the miniature fruit tarts and the caramelized apple in a light cream sauce. And the "businessman's lunch" is a spectacular bargain.

A la carte: 300-450F. Menus: 200F (lunch only, wine incl.), 400F (wine incl.), 280F.

18 Olympe

8, rue Nicolas-Charlet
47.34.86.08

M. Nahmias. Open until midnight. Closed Sat. lunch, Sun., Mon., Aug. 1-23 & Dec. 22-Jan. 4. Air cond. Pets allowed. Cards: V, AE, DC.

What a surprise—the extremely popular and superb Olympe has gone in an entirely new direction! After years of using all those expensive ingredients and rich dishes worthy of Maxim's or Tour d'Argent, Dominique Nahmias has turned an about-face to follow other impulses. We've always been happy here to pay a king's ransom to be royally fed, but now we're just as happy to be fed simpler, more accessible, home-cooked fare. We can imagine the shock of the show-biz clientele upon finding none of their old favorites—foie-gras-this and truffle-that (except the now famous and venerable dish of sautéed crayfish)—and paying a relatively inexpensive 300 to 350 francs for a meal of consistent, hearty, regionally inspired dishes. They'll find the rabbit terrine with liver; chicken with thyme; calf's-brains fritters with capers; big, beautiful skate wing with fresh coriander and olive oil; tuna with bacon and onions; thick, juicy veal chops; roast lamb shoulder with garlic and potatoes; roast duckling with stuffed cabbage; rabbit (Dominique's favorite food) in an artichoke pesto; and lots of good desserts like mother used to make (if you had a French mother, that is). All this is, of course, done in her own inimitable and unsurpassed style; no mere tasty bistro fare, it is prepared by a great chef with excellent technique and ingredients, light sauces, and subtle flavors. Paris used to lack a "mother." Voilà "Mère Olympe"!

A la carte: 300-350F. Menu: 250F (lunch only, wine incl.).

12/20 Le Petit Mâchon

123, rue de la Convention - 45.54.08.62

Mme. Moussié. Open until 10:30 p.m. Closed Sun., Mon. & July 25-Aug. 20. Terrace dining. Pets allowed. Cards: V.

This is one of Slavik's most handsome re-creations of an old-time bistro, and it's devoted to the cuisine of the Lyon area, just like its main branch next door (Bistro 121): rosette de Lyon (pork sausage), tripe, knuckle of ham with lentils and every Beaujolais in the book.

A la carte: 160-180F. Menu: 75F.

15 La Petite Bretonnière

2, rue de Cadix - 48.28.34.39

M. Lamaison. Open until 10 p.m. Closed Sat. lunch, Sun. & Aug. Garage parking. Pets allowed. Cards: V, AE.

Alain Lamaison is a smart man. Rather than underwrite the decorating trade, he preferred simply to make his tiny dining room more comfortable and cozy and to keep his prices down. By choosing raw salmon with parsley cream sauce, gâteau landais with truffle juice, caramelized grapefruit and a half liter of Madiran, you can enjoy a wonderful meal for 250 francs. For a trifle more, you can sample the innovative southwestern cuisine of this 28-year-old chef, who has a most engaging style: foie gras, terrine of duck, oyster soufflé gratiné, roast duck with mushrooms and apple tarte. There's a good choice of affordable wines from all over. Warm reception from Georgia Lamaison.

A la carte: 250-300F.

12/20 Pizzéria Les Artistes

98, blvd. de Grenelle - 45.77.79.70

MM. Dessez & Verrières. Open until 10:45 p.m. Closed Sun. & year-end holidays. Air cond. Terrace dining. Pets allowed. Cards: V, AE.

For the best pizza in Paris and pasta by the yard with every imaginable sauce and herb (if there are three of you, order the assortment), this is the required stop. Excellent fixed-price menu and an amusing collection of customers packed into an eye-catchingly decorated room under the elevated metro.

A la carte: 160F. Menus: 57F, 99F.

13 Raajmahal

192, rue de la Convention
45.33.29.39, 45.33.15.57

M. Kassam. Open daily until 11 p.m. Air cond. Pets allowed. Telex 692151. Cards: V, AE, DC.

Amin Kassam will never end his days on a bed of nails. Not satisfied with having recycled this former bathhouse on the rue de la Convention into a temple of North Indian cuisine, this flamboyant Bengali is now franchising a chain of takeout restaurants that are entirely predesigned, from the microwave ovens to the shape of the dining seats. Add to that an extensive business in spices, basmati rice, tea and coffee, and you can understand why Kassam is a busy man. A little too busy, it seems, when things don't run smoothly in his maharajah's palace with fishbowl lighting through a glass roof, when the service is confused and when the deliciously fragrant cooking is off its mark. But since he takes such pride and pleasure in his profession, he's sure to heed our advice and tighten the screws on his operation.

Specialties include meat-filled samosas, marinated lamb or chicken with mint and pimientos en brochette broiled over charcoal in the tandoor oven, Saturday's monumental lamb's-knuckle curry, biryanis of meat or fowl soaked in a diabolic sauce with at least twenty spices, and bread (both leavened and unleavened), all of which is so delicious that it more than makes up for the unabashed simplicity of the Indian desserts.

A la carte: 200-280F. Menu: 79F (weekday lunch only).

(16) Le Relais de Sèvres

(Hôtel Sofitel Paris)
8-12, rue Louis-Armand
40.60.30.30, 40.60.33.66

M. Ciret. Open until 10 p.m. Closed Sat., Sun., Aug. & 1 week at Christmas. Air cond. Garage parking. Pets allowed. Telex 200432. Cards: V, AE, DC, MC.

Just recently we got the news that chef Roland Durand is not leaving after all. So—by some perverse reasoning—the decision to revamp this wretched interior is therefore once again on hold. Once more we find ourselves facing the opportunity of sitting on kitchen stools at waxed tablecloths to eat the fare of this astoundingly inventive chef, who has made the Relais de Sèvres so successful in recent years. In fact, the dishes he prepared for us fell just short of the three-toque level: hot duck pâté baked in potato dough, crusty herbed snails, fresh cod stuffed with crab, oven-baked sea bream with pressed olives and macaroni gratin, calf's-head fricassée with mushrooms, rump of rabbit baked tandoori-style. This is distinguished, distinctive cooking, a far cry from traditional hotel dining, which is rooted firmly in classic and regional repertoires (Durand is from the Ardèche region). And his desserts prove once again that the best, most imaginative pastry makers are now in the restaurant business. His b'stilla of cinnamon-flavored pears, crown of hot caramelized apples, and compote of vanilla-flavored rhubarb and ginger-glazed nougat are truly magnificent. There's an excellent businessman's lunch, and the many wines priced at or around 100 francs (red Sancerre, Bourgeuil, Crozes-Hermitage, Pelouse) are far superior to anything you'll find elsewhere at twice the price.

A la carte: 350-450F. Menu: 290F (lunch only).

(14) Aux Senteurs de Provence

295, rue Lecourbe
45.57.11.98, 45.58.66.84

M. Dell'omo. Open until 10 p.m. Closed Sun., Mon. & Aug. 2-22. Cards: V, AE, DC.

Léonardo Dell'omo, the cordial owner of this neighborhood bistro, and his new chef, Christophe Agemeister, may not be the most likely candidates for promoting Provençal cuisine, but they do a good job of it. And now, alongside the bouillabaisse, aïoli (served on Wednesdays), bourride (on request) and lamb daube are a number of new and inventive dishes, such as a terrine of skate wing stuffed with capers and fresh herbs, and some beautiful prawns simply poached in a nicely scented fish coulis. The excellent desserts, however, remain on the rustic side. Good wines from Provence and excellent service under the baton of Dell'omo, who was maître d' at Lucas-Carton in its glory days.

A la carte: 300-350F. Menus: 160F to 180F.

(13) Uri

5, rue Humblot - 45.77.37.11

M. Cho-Ran-Ke. Open until 10:30 p.m. Closed Sun. & Aug. Air cond. No pets. Cards: V.

The chef for many years at the luxurious but disappointing Séoul, M. Cho finally opened his own place—or rather, "our place," which is what "uri" means. Two thousand Koreans in Paris have taken him to their hearts, and rightly so, because his fresh, appetizing cuisine reveals the unsuspected riches of an unfamiliar culinary tradition: chopped duck roll steamed in a cabbage leaf, deviled salad of raw skate, beef ragoût sauce piquante and exquisite soups, into which you dunk your white rice, as the French do their bread. Cordial reception by Mme. Cho and her son.

A la carte: 230F.

(15) Pierre Vedel

19, rue Duranton - 45.58.43.17

M. Vedel. Open until 10:15 p.m. Closed Sat., Sun., 2 weeks in July & 1 week at Christmas. No pets. Cards: V.

Still one of the best values in town: Including wine (and Pierre Vedel knows how to select it), the average price of a meal can still be kept around 220 francs. That's the key to the record success of this very Parisian bistro. Decorator Slavik's familiar hand can be detected in the white walls, fans, mirrors and old photos. Adored by his customers, Vedel—the nicest amateur weight-lifter you'll ever meet—ladles out hearty portions of mackerel filets, poached eggs in red wine, bourride "the way they make it down home" (he comes from Sète, like his old pal Georges Brassens, the poet), calf's head, duckling with turnips, and île flottante (floating island).

A la carte: 220-250F.

Red toques signify modern cuisine; black toques signify traditional cuisine.

Sixteenth Arrondissement

11/20 Auberge du Bonheur

Bois de Boulogne, Allée de Longchamp
42.24.10.17

M. Menut. Open until 11 p.m. Closed Sat. (off-seas.) & Feb. Garden dining. Parking. Pets allowed. Cards: V.

At this excellent little place in the Bois, you sit in the shade of 100-year-old chestnut trees, eat crisp salads and grilled meats and sip pleasant growers' wines at reasonable prices.

A la carte: 180-200F. Menu: 100F (wine incl.).

11/20 Brasserie Stella

133, ave. Victor-Hugo - 47.27.60.54

M. Guerlet. Open until 1:30 a.m. Closed Aug. Terrace dining. Cards: V.

The oyster bar poking out onto the sidewalk attracts the fashionable set from this fashionable neighborhood until late at night. The cheerful, boisterous crowd appreciates the good solid home cooking (pot-au-feu, smoked pork and the like).

A la carte: 200F.

(14) Paul Chène

123, rue Lauriston - 47.27.63.17

M. Chène. Open until 10:30 p.m. Closed Sat., Sun., July 30- Sept. 2 & Dec. 24-Jan. 3. Air cond. Parking. Pets allowed. Cards: V, AE, DC.

The outward appearance of a nice little neighborhood restaurant often hides its true character, just as the names of certain dishes leave diners puzzled (mackerel in Muscadet wine, fried "angry" silver hake). However, at Paul Chène it's the tastiest mackerel and the best "angry" hake, plus marvelous terrines, a real potted chicken Henri IV, goose confit with celestial parsleyed potatoes, and mouth-watering desserts like grandma used to make (apple fritters with currant jelly and caramel-flavored île flottante). The big problem is that this nice little neighborhood restaurant charges an arm and a leg. Everything is delicious and abundant, but before you can blink an eye your bill is up to 400 francs, and folks complain that that's too steep for a rustic, old-fashioned place where all you've eaten is rabbit afloat in a Riesling aspic and garnished with french fries (but delicious ones, to be sure), or daube of beef with wine and onions.

A la carte: 400F.

(15) Conti

72, rue Lauriston - 47.27.74.67

M. Ranvier. Open until 10:45 p.m. Closed Sat. & Sun. Air cond. Pets allowed. Cards: V, AE.

Fine cooking in a light, modern vein—call it French with Italian styling or vice versa. Michel Ranvier gives his own subtle, expert interpretations to ravioli (stuffed with cabbage and chopped sweetbreads), lasagne (with foie gras and herbs vinaigrette), scampi (superb miniature lobsters grilled with basil), polenta (with curried lamb) and a masterpiece sabayon (with port wine). Everything is light, beautifully presented and served with typical Italian courtesy and efficiency in a maroon-colored interior under a Murano chandelier. Try the generous pasta sampler, the fettuccine with black truffles and the magnificent, feathery-light Mascarpone cake. Excellent French and Italian wines.

A la carte: 350F.

(14) L'Estournel

(Hôtel Baltimore)
1, rue Léo-Delibes - 45.53.10.79

M. Lo Monaco. Open until 10 p.m. Closed Sat., Sun., Aug. & holidays. Air cond. Telex 611591. Cards: V, AE, DC, MC.

The decor of this circular hotel dining room is one of the few in Paris unlikely to develop early wrinkles. The crimson walls, Decaris paintings and simple, elegant furnishings recall the carefree atmosphere of posh prewar restaurants that never seem to go out of style. We wish the same could be said for the cooking, but with a rich international business clientele who are probably not the most demanding gourmets, chef Henri Boutier has not been kept on his toes. He has accustomed us in the past to more precise and subtle results than the overcooked hot oysters, jarring crab ravioli with orange sauce, overly honeyed duck breast and the needless, half-cooked apples in the exquisite rhubarb pastry. We must withdraw, therefore, our second toque. As always, however, you can expect an excellent wine list and impeccable service.

A la carte: 400F and up. Menu: 215F.

(13) Fakhr el Dine

30, rue de Longchamp - 47.27.90.00

M. Bou Antoun. Open daily until midnight. Air cond. Parking. No pets. Cards: V, AE, DC.

Upper-crust Lebanon in a jolting blend of white beams and paneling, beige fabrics and soft lighting. Local color need not apply! The doorman makes a mockery of traditional Lebanese hospitality and is likely to send you packing if you don't have a reservation and aren't from one of the rich families that come here to feed their nostalgia for the old country. Small, medium and large mezze (27 cold, 18 hot) are, in the opinion of those in the know, the best in Paris. After tasting the hummus (purée of chickpeas in sesame oil), moujaddara (purée of lentils), baba ghanouj (purée of eggplant with lemon), fatayers (pastry filled with chopped meat and spinach), kébbé (meatballs) and rkakat (cheese puff pastry), all of which make it pointless to read the rest of the menu (so-so brochettes, stuffed chicken and the like), we agree. The pastries are so light and flaky that you'll be lulled into thinking that you didn't really just consume a week's worth of calories.

Expect expensive wines—which doesn't mean they're all good—and a check of about 300 francs with a half bottle of ksara (a Lebanese wine) and a glass of arak.

A la carte: 300F. Menus: 136F (lunch only), 130F.

(18) Faugeron

52, rue de Longchamp
47.04.24.53

M. Faugeron. Open until 10 p.m. Closed Sat., Sun., Aug. & Dec. 23-Jan. 3. Air cond. Parking. No pets. Cards: V.

Henri and Gerlinde Faugeron have kept their word. And so has their decorator, which is rarer still. Recently the Faugerons reopened their restaurant and presented the redecorated dining room. Instead of fake flowers and drab brown fabric, they now have something a trifle fussy but pleasant and mild: blue and yellow silk wall coverings that blend nicely with the honey carpeting and pale-pink tablecloths. The golden sconces and clusters of halogen lights reaching down from the cream-colored ceiling add vibrancy and charm to the room. Two jarring notes are the flower paintings, which neither Sotheby's nor Christie's would look at twice (the lovely vases of cut flowers are a different story), and a shelf displaying liqueur bottles, bringing to mind a roadside tavern.

Anyway, Faugeron regulars seem thrilled, and no longer will we bemoan the gloomy, threadbare interior of one of the city's most hospitable restaurants. For Gerlinde is the cream of hostesses, and her staff, headed by Philippe Mathon, is absolutely tops. As for chef Henri, he has found his rhythm and his style but has no desire to make culinary waves. He simply does what is necessary to keep the menu lively and interesting. His "classics" reappear year after year, but who can complain when soft-boiled eggs with purée of truffles, house-smoked salmon (he was one of the first to make it), rabbit in aspic with foie gras, Challans duckling with broad beans, and roast duck with cider vinegar and stewed onions are prepared with such reverence for flavors? His creations are never disappointing; on our last visit he offered a salad of marinated mullet filets, salmon with yogurt, a hot salad of green vegetables with sweetbreads and mushrooms, flaked cod in a hazelnut cream sauce and lamb stew in aspic.

Many of these dishes appear on the excellent fixed-price menu that lists five starters, a fish special, five main courses and desserts, all of which will satisfy the appetite without overwhelming the expense accounts of business-lunch diners. Jean-Claude Jambon (who won the international award for Premier Sommelier) selects fine wines at affordable prices (like the sensational Mercurey 1982 put out by Raquillet) and great labels, familiar or unfamiliar, like the delicious Pomerol Vraye Croix de Gaÿ.

A la carte: 500-700F. Menus: 255F (lunch only), 440F (menu dégustation).

(16) Jean-Claude Ferrero

38, rue Vital - 45.04.42.42

M. Ferrero. Open until 10:30 p.m. Closed Sat. (except Sat. dinner in winter), Sun., May 1-15 & Aug. 5-31. Pets allowed. Cards: V, AE, DC.

Too many worries spoil the sauce, and no cook worthy of his toque expects to find inspiration in his lawyer's office. Jean-Claude Ferrero's problems at Le Marcande gave him plenty of headaches, but that's all behind him now. He has his own place: a small, detached Second Empire house with a lovely dining room full of contented customers attended to by the delightful Andrée; a vest-pocket garden with a fountain; and a new upstairs room that seats twenty and looks down on a flowery patio. He also has peace of mind—or close to it, for Ferraro is a restless spirit. This athletic-looking man devotes himself exclusively to one sport: cooking. City streets may not be the ideal location for a country lad born and raised in Briançon, where he used to collect mushrooms and shoot rabbits. Now he must wait for nature to come to him. Since his head is always brimming with recipes and new concoctions, dining is never a bore on the rue Vital. It seems that the minute Ferrero adds a dish to the menu, he replaces it with another. Spiny lobster in oil and lime juice (without salt or pepper), filet of bass with melon, stew of salted cod, two-liver pastry... the list of his inventions goes on and on. He adores working with mushrooms and truffles, which he adds to every sauce, and, in season, he celebrates with special "all-mushroom" (400 to 500 francs) and "all-truffle" (500 to 600 francs) menus.

This poet of the kitchen never allows his imagination to idle. He is better organized now and employs an adequate crew, which ought to reduce the tension and relieve his moody spells. In any case, we wouldn't mind if he worked a little harder at his desserts—some are good, others plainly mediocre. At one point, his wine list needed rounding out, as we suggested, and he and Robert Turlan have tried to improve it. He can certainly do the same for his pastries.

A la carte: 400F and up. Menu: 220F (lunch only).

(14) Le Grand Chinois

6, ave. de New-York
47.23.98.21, 47.23.99.58

Mme. Tan. Open until 11 p.m. Closed Mon. & Aug. Pets allowed. Cards: AE, DC.

Colette Tan is Cambodian, and she's polished to the tips of her long fingernails. A member of the family that operates Tan Dinh (seventh arrondissement), her shared interest in collecting great Bordeaux wines is understandable. These wines accompany some excellent dishes, such as shrimp with stir-fried vegetables, steamed Chinese cabbage with crab, glazed duck roasted on the spit and minced pigeon. The ultra-red, typically Chinese decor is cluttered but comfortable and permanently furnished with the poshest Chinese clientele in Paris.

A la carte: 250F and up. Menu: 110F (lunch only).

(16) La Grande Cascade

Bois de Boulogne,
near the Longchamp racetrack
45.27.33.51

M. Menut. Open until 10:30 p.m. Lunch only Nov. 1-April 14. Closed Dec. 20-Jan. 20. Garden dining. Parking. Pets allowed. Cards: V, AE, DC.

The iron and glass marquee of this graceful pavilion tucked away in the forest spreads its wings like a giant dragonfly speared on a pin. In summer, the broad terrace, which seats 120 people, is the setting of one of the most beguiling outdoor restaurants in Paris. It's too bad that Parisians ignore it, abandoning it to rich visitors from abroad. The same applies to the 1890s dining hall recently restored by a rather heavy hand. But whether settled outside beneath the umbrellas or inside beneath the decorated ceiling and glass roof, the service is impeccable under the able direction of André Menut and his son. This stylish Belle Epoque establishment, a favorite of Colette's, is best known for the consistently high-quality classic cuisine produced for the past several years by chef Jean Sabine. It may not be what you'd call creative cookery, but it is dependably fresh, tasty and surprisingly simple for such a posh address: fondant of rabbit with Chablis and herbs, fish poached in seaweed and basil, sweetbreads in truffle butter and a tart of green caramelized apples. Sumptuous Bordeaux wines, among many others.

A la carte: 500-700F. Menu: 240F (weekday lunch only).

16 Patrick Lenôtre

28, rue Duret
45.00.17.67, 45.00.20.45.

M. Lenôtre. Open until 11 p.m. Closed Sat. lunch, Sun. & July 13-Aug. 17. Air cond. Pets allowed. Cards: V, AE, DC.

His family name is practically a household word; now he wants to be a celebrity in his own right—"do his own thing," as he puts it. Lenôtre, a nephew of Gaston Lenôtre, served as chef at Le Pré Catelan for years and, more recently, at Les Jardins Lenôtre on the Champs-Elysées before buying Guy Savoy's old restaurant: a small, elegant dining place with light paneling, walls the color of marbled foie gras and a mirror in the back to create the illusion of space. Mauro Fratesi, who used to work at La Marée and Laurent, manages the dining room and presents guests with their menus, the caliber of which instantly places this restaurant among the finest in town: salmon marinated with parsley and white nettles, cold filets of sole en gelée (too bad the aspic was flavorless), sea trout with squid and fennel, excellent braised saddle of hare, beef flank with marrow, a magnificent hot soufflé of tropical fruits, sabayon flavored with tea and rhubarb, and delicious homemade breads, petits fours and chocolates. All told, it's a well-balanced, mouth watering repertoire that ought to make Lenôtre II a gastronomic idol. We would, however, like to see a few more affordable wines on the list, but Patrick Lenôtre obviously is no advocate of moderate prices.

A la carte: 450-600F. Menus: 220F (lunch only), 460F (dinner only).

12/20 A la Mandarine

120, rue de la Pompe - 45.53.47.18

M. Cho. Open until 11 p.m. Closed Sun. Terrace dining. Pets allowed. Cards: V, AE, DC.

The tables are too small, but the 1930s dining room, enhanced by a few decorative Chinese pieces, is elegant. To eat, try the fried ravioli, crisp Cantonese sweet pork and (surprise!) the good desserts.

A la carte: 160F. Menus: 79F (weekday lunch only), 110F.

16 Michel Pasquet

59, rue de La Fontaine
42.88.50.01, 45.20.13.38

M. Pasquet. Open until 10:45 p.m. Closed Sat. lunch, Sun., July 15-Aug. 15 & Dec. 23-27. Air cond. Pets allowed. Cards: V, AE, DC.

Something's out of order at Michel Pasquet's place. And that's too bad, for he's a talented chef. The gaps are between his elaborate cuisine, the would-be service on a grand scale (it doesn't work because there's not enough help) and the pleasant decor without any real style, in which the good elements (attractive pink banquettes, subdued lighting, handsome dinnerware) share center stage with the not-so-good (fake flowers and just the wrong shade of green wallpaper). This sense of disorder, compounded on the night of our visit by clusters of empty tables, doesn't do justice to the expert cooking, confirmed once again by a delicious plate of escargots in pastry; ravioli filled with lobster and leeks and sauced with a remarkable soy butter; a thick, tender turbot with chive butter; and excellent sweetbreads. Though the flavor of our desserts was slightly muddled, the petits fours were flawless. And the price was right. The 280-franc fixed-price menu has great variety, and the 160 franc lunch is a real bargain.

A la carte: 350F. Menus: 160F (lunch only), 300F.

16 Le Petit Bedon

38, rue Pergolèse - 45.00.23.66

M. Ignace. Open until 10:15 p.m. Closed Sat., Sun. & Aug. Air cond. Pets allowed. Cards: V.

"Petit Bedon" ("potbelly" or "spare tire") is a term from prewar days that evokes a flushed generation in plus fours that liked to stuff and guzzle. Christian Ignace has different tastes but was too timid to put up a new sign. So the name has become a joke, and in place of a country inn with massive wrought iron fixtures, we now have a bright, fresh, stylish little room out of *House and Garden*, a chef as slender as his customers and, instead of a high tide of rich sauces, a thoughtful, balanced cuisine prepared by a chef whose style is midway between classic and modern.

When Ignace worked for Raymond Oliver, his head bubbled with ideas. That's no longer the case, which is one reason why his dishes are successful, flavorful and reflective of the sunny spirit of the south that matches the vibrant Mediterranean colors of his dining room. Try his fresh crab with avocado mayonnaise, lobster ragoût with anise and mild garlic, soufflé of hogfish à la bouillabaisse, oven-baked rack of lamb with chicory and mint leaves, casserole of duck with vinegar honey, and Chinese-style mandarin orange preserves. The old Bedon has suffered a touch of sunstroke!

A la carte: 350-450F.

14 La Petite Tour

11, rue de la Tour
45.20.09.31, 45.20.09.97

M. Israël. Open until 10:30 p.m. Closed Sun. & Aug. Pets allowed. Cards: V, AE, DC.

Freddy Israël, who was tired of his cramped quarters on the rue de l'Exposition, recently bought this sleepy old neighborhood restaurant. He hasn't had the time to change the too-dainty decor, but his wife's warm reception, the comfortable banquettes and his good cooking calmed our impatience. The modest, polished cuisine rarely repeats itself (it will in time) and is light and meticulously prepared: lobster bisque, fresh duck-liver maison, sea urchin soufflé (a few spines wandered into our preparation), a remarkable mustard-flavored veal kidney, and desserts still in the development stage. No fireworks, but no

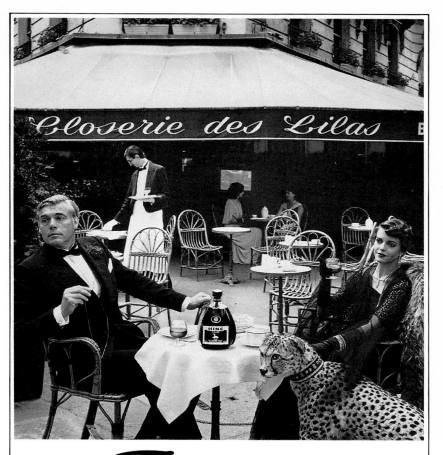

Time was when life's finer things such as Hine Cognac were the preserve of a privileged few.

Today, it is still the true connoisseur who appreciates the mature, mellow flavour of Hine.

The dictionary defines a connoisseur as "one who is an expert judge in matters of taste".

And who are we to argue.

BRASH, BOLD GUIDES
TO THE BEST OF THE VERY BES

Also available:

THE BEST OF CHICAGO
THE BEST OF NEW ENGLAND
THE BEST OF FRANCE
THE BEST OF PARIS
THE BEST OF LONDON
THE BEST OF ITALY

blunders either. Just good, solid, reliable dishes that the fashionable Passy crowd eats up.

A la carte: 300F and up.

17 Le Pré Catelan

Bois de Boulogne,
rte. de Suresnes - 45.24.55.58

M. Lenôtre. Open until 10 p.m. Closed Sun. dinner, Mon. & Feb. school vacation. Garden dining. Parking. Pets allowed. Telex 614983. Cards: V, AE, DC.

For years the food at Uncle Gaston's hadn't been anything to write home about—either at his place on the Champs-Elysées or here, where Denis Bernal presides as chef. But now, this 31-year-old cook, trained by Michel Guérard, along with his assistant and fish chef, is quietly but steadily weaning the house away from its "restaurant" cuisine. His dishes aren't just pretty to look at, they are flavorful, hearty and have real personality. For example, the firm-fleshed rock lobster in a delicate paprika sauce, the bouquet of lobster with baby vegetables, rock mullet "buttered" with its liver, lotte tail in a pistachio cream sauce, pan-fried filet of turbot steeped in vanilla and fresh mint and lightly sauced with beurre blanc, baron of rabbit with herb-stuffed ravioli and a dish that you rarely find in Paris, an exquisite goose filet mignon with "kitchen tobacco" (the name invented in the seventeenth century for powdered dried mushrooms).

Since top French chefs like Jean Bardet, Michel Trama, Pierre Gagnaire and Jacques Chibois have conditioned us to recognize truly outstanding desserts, we are all the more critical of Lenôtre's repertoire, knowing as we do that in his time he revolutionized French pastry making. Everyone has copied his gâteau opéra and worn out his mousse recipes. Of course, the napoleon with caramelized pastry cream, soufléed crêpes with bitter cherries and vanilla ice cream, and apricot rice suprême are fine desserts. But if the Lenôtre pastry squad really means to impress, they'll have to do it a lot more, and not merely repeat tried-and-true recipes. Lenôtre pastries are often oversugared, and we are beginning to tire of it. What we never tire of is the perennial charm of the Belle Epoque dining room, with its frieze designed by Caran d'Ache and, bordering the park, the marvelous terrace thick with greenery. Colette Lenôtre provides the reception, and the service is regal, if a trifle solemn.

Since the Bois de Boulogne is just outside the door, ask Denis Bernal or his assistant to tell you his secret places to find mushrooms (boletus and morels), not to mention the fat truffle he rooted out last winter, in true Périgord style.

A la carte: 600-800F. Menu: 500F (wine incl.).

12/20 Le Presbourg

3, ave. de la Grande-Armée
45.00.36.40, 45.00.24.77

M. Chaunion. Open daily until 1 a.m. Terrace dining. Pets allowed. Cards: V, AE, DC.

Le Presbourg's amusing, comfortable terrace, designed like a greenhouse, faces the Arc de Triomphe. The cooking attempts a variety of styles: delicious calf's head, hearty choucroute with pigs' knuckles, and a confused blend of fresh cod and oysters. Good wines by the pitcher and excellent service.

A la carte: 300F. Menu: 92F.

Prunier-Traktir

16, ave. Victor-Hugo - 45.00.89.12

Open until 10:30 p.m. Hours & closings vary. Terrace dining. Pets allowed. Cards: V, AE, DC.

First the Prunier-Madeleine and now the Traktir have left the hands of the Barnagaud family. The restaurant group that has just bought the place swears it won't touch a hair on the head of this stunning art deco monument and that Claude Barnagaud, great-grandson of the founder, will continue to run it. How long these promises are good for, no one knows; nor do we know what the new food will be like. In any case, the planned refurbishing of the second floor and the takeout area are long-overdue projects that even the most zealous devotees are not likely to argue with.

19.5 Robuchon

32, rue de Longchamp
47.27.12.27

M. Robuchon. Open until 10:15 p.m. Closed Sat., Sun. & July. Air cond. Pets allowed. Cards: V.

Joël Robuchon is without doubt an artist, but he's not a prima donna. Some of the greatest chefs are also egomaniacs—they're unbearable in the kitchen, can't stomach criticism, are vain as peacocks and mistake themselves for Michelangelo. Perhaps we journalists are somewhat responsible for the whirlwind that inflates chefs' toques like sea breezes swell sails. But then, how is it that the most gifted chef in France manages not to be tainted by the mountainous praise heaped upon him by the press? Simply because deep down, Robuchon, who is far less timid than reputation has it, has remained a craftsman whose tour of duty isn't over. To the endless, delirious acclaim he responds with simple words: discipline and work. He tells his raving admirers: "Cooking is, first and foremost, a technique—complicated in its simplicity, difficult to prepare and, once served, sobering," and "My competence is limited to 45 place settings!" He could serve five times as much—ten in New York!—judging by the number of clients he turns away each day. (Reservations run two months in advance.) But 45 meals, for this perfectionist, means 34 employees; any more than that and his little place would burst at the seams.

Like some others, he could give private lessons all over the globe, "supervise" a menu in Los Angeles and another in Tokyo, sell "consultations" right and left or waste time suing colleagues for stealing the recipe for his astounding simmered pig's head. Instead, he prefers to teach the technique of vacuum-packaging to young cooks, to help out his friends in the profession and to manage his restaurant with an iron hand. Don't dream of disturbing him at mealtimes. Any columnist who gets the bright idea of telephoning him during those sacred hours is told that the call will be returned later—quite the opposite of the celebrated chefs who come crawling whenever the media whistle. But if you could watch Robuchon at work in the kitchen, you'd understand his attitude. He seems to have eyes all over his head;

he doesn't miss even the smallest detail, and he won't let a single plate enter the dining room without his approval. How many "great" chefs take that trouble these days?

Let's forget the others and talk about Robuchon's dainty little dining room, with its green walls and pale gray-green coverings, redone recently by a team of Japanese decorators. The Asian touch is not evident, however, in the romantic flower prints wound with blue satin, white ceramic urns, busts of Roman emperors and glass screens that divide up space without shutting it out. This decor may not convey Robuchon's personality, but it is beguiling and a perfect setting for the miniature tableaux that arrive artistically arranged on each plate.

If you could treat yourself to only one sensational meal in Paris in this century, come here. But we're at a loss to tell you what to order. Since we've never left dissatisfied with any dish, it's hard to name the best ones. On our last visit we sampled hot foie gras with cream of lentils, truffled galette with onions and bacon, caviar aspic with cream of cauliflower, filet of bass with verjuice sauce (made with the juice of unripened grapes) and spiced rosy duckling with turnips au foie gras. Other wonderful creations appearing on the menu from time to time include lobster with coriander and baby vegetables, rack of lamb under a light coating of crumbled truffles, complemented by a salad of warm lamb's lettuce with vinegar, civet of rabbit with bacon, the astonishing simmered pig's head and a heavenly purée of potatoes with olive oil and crème fleurette that is Robuchon's passport to paradise.

Conclusion: Forget everything you've just read and give yourself over to Jean-Jacques, the dining room manager whose advice is always valuable, or else break open your piggy bank and buy a season ticket to Robuchon's so you can taste everything, including desserts: vanilla ice cream, gratin of mango with pineapple sauce, chaud-froid of apples and pistachios—we almost forgot to mention that Robuchon is hardly the worst pâtissier in town.

And lest we overlook the pretty, smiling lady in the corner behind the cash register, she's Joël's wife, Jeanine. Another name you should know is Antoine Hernandez, a sommelier with the key to one of the finest cellars in Paris (Robuchon got together with his friend Vrinat, proprietor of Taillevent, and amassed a wine treasury).

A la carte: 600-800F and up. Menus: 690F, 760F.

(14) Sous l'Olivier

15, rue Goethe - 47.20.84.81

M. Warnault. Open until 10:30 p.m. Closed Sat., Sun. & holidays. Terrace dining. Pets allowed. Cards: V.

The southern cuisine of this former Italian restaurant acquired a northern accent under the guidance of its new owner/chef, William Warnault, from Picardie. We miss the terrine of duck Amiens-style, the smoked eel with horseradish and the other home-style specialties that seem to have disappeared from his menu, probably deemed not worthy of this chichi neighborhood. We'll content ourselves instead with the exquisite galette of calf's feet with a tangy watercress sauce, calves' liver pan-fried in its own juices and seasoned with an astonishing clove sauce, buttered potatoes and a perfect Calvados sorbet. All this warrants an extra point, but the waitresses definitely need to shape up. There's a bright, comfortable blue and white decor on two levels.

A la carte: 250-300F. Menu: 150F (dinner only).

(14) Le Sully d'Auteuil

78, rue d'Auteuil - 46.51.71.18

M. Brunetière. Open daily until 10:30 p.m. Air cond. Terrace dining. Pets allowed. Cards: V, AE.

The most cheerful, luxurious and cozy railroad-station buffet in France (owned by the SNCF, the French rail system). This delightful Belle Epoque lodge at the Auteuil train depot, with its ivy-covered terrace and fresh, gilt-edged decor (salmon-tinted Japanese wallpaper, thick carpeting, Louis XVI armchairs, elegant dinnerware), owes its success not to enterprising railroad management but solely to the long-term efforts of a seasoned professional. That's Michel Brunetière, whose 45 years in the kitchen haven't dulled his boyish enthusiasm. He passes among the tables cracking jokes for the politicians and theater people who work in the district and enjoy the cordial reception (Brunetière's son-in-law doubles as host and sommelier), fine service and excellent food. Brunetière's teeming imagination sometimes carries him overboard, and nobody would object if he removed a number of puzzling, ill-defined entries from his overloaded à la carte menu or omitted the ham and melted cheese that asphyxiate his beautifully seasoned lamb filet with coriander. Desserts are clever but tend to be too sweet or too dense (like the apricot torte). Prices are pretty stiff.

A la carte: 380-400F.

(16) Le Toit de Passy

94, ave. Paul-Doumer - 45.24.55.37

M. Jacquot. Open until 10:30 p.m. Closed Sat. lunch, Sun. & Dec. 28-Jan. 9. Air cond. Terrace dining. Parking. Pets allowed. Cards: V.

In his rooftop restaurant, chef/owner Yannick Jacquot prepares a cuisine characterized by precise, distinct flavors: salad of pigeon and beans with purslane (an herb-weed for salads) in an exquisite hazelnut oil vinaigrette, John Dory filets with artichokes poivrade, rock lobster with citrus butter, parsleyed lamb with an eggplant compote and Brittany squab in salt pastry—not to mention a half dozen good desserts, including a millefeuille with red fruits, and a broad selection of wines. Don't expect affordability—you're also paying for a view of the Eiffel Tower.

A la carte: 400-500F. Menus: 225F and 270F (lunch only), 395F.

(13) Tsé Yang

25, ave. Pierre-Ier-de-Serbie
47.20.68.02

M. Tong. Open daily until 11 p.m. Cards: V, AE, DC.

This lavishly decorated opera set came, in sections, straight from Hong Kong. Along with the elegant porcelain dinnerware, very flashy cutlery and collection of ivories in display cases, this

Far-Eastern Versailles has cost M. Tong a small fortune, which he is rapidly recouping by charging the highest prices in town for Chinese food. But the luxury-hotel crowd in this neighborhood and the Mideast oil magnates don't seem to notice. The cuisine is meticulously prepared with the freshest ingredients—shark's-fin soup, roast duck with Chinese tea, sautéed shrimp with a spicy sauce—and choice wines are available.

A la carte: 350F. Menu: 195F.

(14) Vi Foc

33, rue de Longchamp - 47.04.96.81

M. Té Vépin. Open until 10:45 p.m. Closed Aug. 11-28. Air cond. Parking. Pets allowed. Cards: V, AE, DC.

M. Té travels all over the world and brings back recipes for his kitchen. It's a rare Oriental restaurant in which you can eat regularly without repeating a dish—but here you can sample from an ever-changing list of such items as a salad of fresh mangoes and sea scallops, eggplant stuffed with crab and shrimp, giant shrimp with mild pepper and duck with plum sauce. You'll find a distinguished Asian decor and good everyday wines, but the checks are getting daunting.

A la carte: 250-300F. Menu: 100F (lunch only).

(18) Vivarois

192, ave. Victor-Hugo
45.04.04.31

M. Peyrot. Open until 9:45 p.m. Closed Sat., Sun. & Aug. Air cond. Pets allowed. Cards: V, AE, DC.

What new surprises does that incredible man on his flying stove have in store for us? Claude Peyrot threatened to close up shop, supposedly to take off on some hazy adventure that would land him back in his native Ardèche via Morocco, where he planned to consult the culinary elders of Marrakech and learn their secrets. Hearing this, we had put his toques in the deep freeze—but the disappearing act never took place, and his cooking is greater than ever, so we had to restore them, remembering that for all his talk of going here or there, Peyrot has remained in the kitchen every minute of the last 23 years.

We enjoyed a marvelous meal composed of an exquisite brioche with onions (loaded with butter), asparagus with an extraordinary orange mousseline sauce, stuffed zucchini flowers (as good if not better than the dish first introduced at Maximin), a feathery-light feuilleté of saffron-seasoned mussels, bass en papillote stuffed with a savory fish-and-carrot mousse in a fennel-flavored shellfish sauce (the kind of dish you tend to avoid in restaurants but that in Peyrot's hands becomes a masterpiece), then a slice of lamb—more precisely, young mutton—that was strong but subtle in flavor, served in its own juices and seasoned with tarragon and garlic and, finally—accompanied by a magnificent Hermitage La Chapelle 1969 from Jaboulet—a celestial roast chicken with morel mushrooms, tender and fragrant in its satiny truffle sauce. To conclude this event, the honey-and-ginger ice cream atop a warm tart melted our hearts.

Everything tasted so perfect that it made the decor—even the cherry paneling and the gray marble slabs that used to look so forbidding—seem inviting and elegant. The Peyrots—she, always serene and cordial; he, excitable and fascinating—have added contemporary art and attractive lighting to give the room an appealing cosmopolitan look.

A la carte: 500F. Menu: 295F (lunch only, wine incl.).

Seventeenth Arrondissement

12/20 L'Amanguier

43, ave. des Ternes - 43.80.19.28

See Second Arrondissement.

(17) Apicius

122, ave. de Villiers
43.80.19.66

M. Vigato. Open until 10 p.m. Closed Sat., Sun. & Aug. Air cond. Garage parking. Pets allowed. Cards: V, AE.

In some restaurants the food is good but you feel uncomfortable; in others the food is second-rate but you feel relaxed. It's difficult to find comfort and good dining under one roof. At Apicius, however, you'll find the best of both worlds. The Paris carriage trade knows it, and at lunch and dinner, it packs the pastel dining room, where blond, fragile Madeleine Vigato waits to greet her guests.

Apicius is a fashionable restaurant, though it's not a social gathering spot where one comes to be seen. Rather, it's a place to sit back and enjoy its "rejuvenated" classic cuisine, designed not so much to dazzle the eyes as to tempt the palate with light sauces and natural flavors. We read somewhere that Jean-Pierre Vigato is on his way to stardom—sheer nonsense, considering that this tall, athletic-looking hulk of a man, who's actually rather timid, doesn't enjoy mixing with the public. His habitat is his kitchen, and he hasn't wasted his time there. Among other things, he has developed the budding talent that was manifested at Grandgousier at the foot of Montmartre. Today, he creates a short à la carte menu, plus several daily specials, all of which are based on sound principles of contemporary cooking, with excursions into hearty regional fare. His wife will enthusiastically describe them all for you. For instance, his "marbled" blend of sweetbreads and lobster; his medley of white fish, cooked separately, with olive oil (a good example of southern French cooking); his whole roasted scallops, firm and savory, with shallots and parsley; his John Dory with honey and vinegar (a contemporary blend of flavors); and his magnificent side of salmon, barely cooked through, with herbs and leeks.There are also such sturdy meat dishes as lamb tenderloin en crépinette with green cabbage, boned roasted pigs' feet in parsley-flavored juices, and calf's head lightly rubbed with lemon, which drives calf's head lovers wild with joy.

Of the ten or more desserts offered (they are among the best in town), we most like the coffee gratin with lemon cream glaze, a superb blancmange with almond milk, and an all-bittersweet-chocolate creation. If you want to sample some of the treasures of the small but choice cellar, consult Marc Brockaert, the knowledgeable, amusing sommelier we remembered from Guy Savoy and later at Le Divellec.

It's time for a third toque.

A la carte: 450-600F. Menus: 300F (lunch only), 420F (dinner only).

(16) La Barrière de Clichy

1, rue de Paris, 92110 Clichy
47.37.05.18

M. Le Gallès. Open until 10 p.m. Closed Sat. lunch & Sun. Air cond. Pets allowed. Cards: V, AE, DC, MC.

When Gilles Le Gallès took over this restaurant at the age of 30, it was a shambles. He repainted and refurbished it from cellar to attic with the help of decorator Michel Lussot (who did wonders with Duquesnoy on rue des Bernardins) and made it into a place of great charm and intimacy: pink and white tones, flowered fabrics and colorful lithographs. When he finally reopened, word traveled and the mink and chinchilla brigade flocked to investigate. They were delighted by the fine, light cuisine—hot oysters with coriander, squid stuffed with duck liver accompanied by a zucchini purée, mushrooms with cabbage and almonds, a superb John Dory with olives, filet of bass with walnuts, a bravura tenderloin of lamb with goat cheese—and by the comfortable, relaxed setting.

A la carte: 300-350F. Menus: 245F (lunch only, wine incl.), 330F.

(13) Le Bistrot d'à Côté

10, rue Gustave-Flaubert - 42.67.05.81

M. Rostang. Open until 10:15 p.m. Closed Sat. lunch, Sun. & Aug. 1-15. Terrace dining. Pets allowed. Cards: V.

Next door to his own restaurant, Michel Rostang opened this pleasant bar and grocery, in which he serves home cooking in the styles of Lyon and Paris: excellent duck rillettes and terrines, macaroni au gratin (so-so), andouillette (on the dull side) and delicious tripe. Modest wines and simple, friendly service.

A la carte: 180F.

(15) La Braisière

54, rue Cardinet - 47.63.40.37

M. Vaxelaire. Open until 10:15 p.m. Closed Sat., Sun., holidays, Feb. school vacation, May 1-8 & Aug. Pets allowed. Cards: V, AE.

Pinkish-beige walls, cretonne curtains, elegant tables (too close together) and attentive service: Bernard Vaxelaire's restaurant fits the perfect image of a large, prosperous Parisian bistro. This impression is confirmed by the confident, consistent cooking turned out for the past five years by a brilliant graduate of the hotel school in Strasbourg. The cuisine is resolutely modern in execution rather than inspiration. Vaxelaire values harmony over audacity; he loves fine products, precise timing and minimal sauces, but he's not interested in having a creative fling. All the same, his menu keeps in tune with the times, as evidenced by the tomatoes stuffed with snails and wild herbs, center cut of salmon cooked on one side, lotte bourguignon with tiny ravioli, and fondant of sweetbreads and squab. Desserts are wonderfully light, there's a large selection of wines, and prices are reasonable for such high quality.

A la carte: 350F. Menu: 185F (wine incl.).

(13) Charly de Bab-el-Oued

95, blvd. Gouvion-St-Cyr - 45.74.34.62

M. Drigues. Open daily until midnight. Air cond. Pets allowed. Cards: V, AE, DC.

This is the patriarch of the Charly chain that began some twenty years ago. In those days, along with the couscous decor you got a free performance by the boss, a delightful Algerian-born Frenchman who went from table to table regaling customers with Bab-el-Oued stories. Then Bernard Drigues became a businessman and became scarce here. Times have changed. Now a Japanese makes the couscous—which is excellent, light and distinctively garnished. In addition, there is lamb en brochette (méchoui), Algerian bestelles, good tajines (stew) and ultra-rich pastries. Warm reception and impeccable service.

A la carte: 200-250F.

(15) Chez Augusta

98, rue de Tocqueville - 47.63.39.97

M. Berton. Open until 9:30 p.m. Closed Sun., Aug. & holidays. Pets allowed. Cards: V, AE, DC.

One of the best fish restaurants in town, Chez Augusta already had that reputation when Marcel Bareste was in charge, and it has moved up a notch since Didier Berton came along a few years ago. He updated the menu, spruced up the decor and hired a young chef who, like himself, had worked at the Camélia in Bougival. Wisely, he has kept (and improved) certain house favorites that regular customers have been ordering for the past 25 years: the superb bouillabaisse with potatoes, simmered mutton tripe and trotters, and rack of lamb roasted in its own juices with potatoes Sarladaise (sliced and baked with goose fat). The menu changes every three months, not so much to reflect the market season as to refresh the repertoire. Thus, you can sample the delicious Augusta salad with seasonal shellfish, salmon with chives and first-rate langouste (spiny lobster) in court bouillon, and feast on exquisitely light, not-too-sweet desserts—the chocolate and cherry "delight" or the macaroon and pistachio creation. The splendid cellar holds great Bordeaux, rare Champagnes and good medium-priced wines.

A la carte: 400F.

(14) Chez Georges

273, blvd. Pereire - 45.74.31.00

M. Mazarguil. Open until 11:30 p.m. Closed Aug. Terrace dining. Pets allowed. Cards: V.

This is the best of Parisian family bistro atmosphere, noisy and fun, with all kinds of wonderful-smelling platters parading past your nose, borne by regiments of fast-moving if disorganized waiters. There is the roast lamb, a monument of smoked pork, a trainload of beef ribs, whole loins of roast pork and more. Cabbage, lentils, gratin dauphinois (one of the best in town), white beans and spinach accompany these robust entrées, which are carved tableside by adroit practitioners of the art. Chez Georges represents dependable, copious home cooking and country-style fare at its best. Great little local wines, and the bill is always reasonable.

A la carte: 250F.

16 Clos Longchamp

(Hôtel Méridien)
81, blvd. Gouvion-St-Cyr - 47.58.82.00

M. Bérardi. Open until 10:30 p.m. Closed Sun. Air cond. No pets. Telex 290592. Cards: V, DC, MC.

Our wishes have come true at last: The management has seen fit to put in a proper garden to give a little charm and intimacy to this restaurant in the biggest hotel in Western Europe. But bigger news than that has been the arrival of a new chef, Jean-Marie Meulien, a first-rate cook and a charming gentleman.

At the time of this writing, we had only the chance to taste his summer menu, which he called his transition menu, promising others to follow. But you needn't wait in order to enjoy some delightful cooking, an adroit synthesis of tradition, modern trends and even a touch of the exotic. The quality of the duck foie gras, the flavors of the steamed jumbo shrimp with Champagne vinegar and avocado, the succulence of the little prawns pan-cooked with fresh herbs and the perfection of the lightly steamed salmon in an astonishing marriage with yellow peaches and curried spices all promise great things. The meat dishes are just as admirable: filet of beef made into little sausages and put around slices of country ham; and, even better, the noisettes of rabbit sautéed in butter and served with liver and kidneys in a red-wine vinegar sauce, mixed with black currants, rosemary and sage. And we suspect that the dessert cart will very soon be up on the same level as the rest of the cuisine. The young sommelier is a fine example of the best of the new style in that profession: no flourishes and tendentious manner, just pleasant, intelligent wine service. Finally, the excellent table service is in the long-experienced and capable hands of maître d' Robert Bérardi.

A la carte: 380-500F. Menus: 220F (lunch only), 450F (dinner only).

15 Michel Comby

116, blvd. Pereire - 43.80.88.68

M. Comby. Open until 10:30 p.m. Closed Sat. (except dinner June-Oct.) & Sun. Terrace dining. Pets allowed. Cards: V, AE, DC.

The atmosphere is well behaved but not boring, the laughter muffled, the conversation in whispers, and you'll find the requisite sparkling silverware, fresh flowers and fine china—in short, this place has all the trademarks of an upscale private club. Michel Comby came here a few years ago with his maître d' and sommelier in tow, and the compliments began to pour in soon after, for which he was grateful after enduring years of neglect tending the ovens at Lucas-Carton in its dog days. The service under his wife's direction is alert, low-key and on the rapid side, much to the satisfaction of the business lunch trade (it's not quite so active at night). And the cuisine is classic from start to finish, with modern overtones of lightness. Some of the old dishes from Lucas-Carton appear on the menu, such as the ballotines and the famous sole with a mushroom duxelles. As for the snails with Chablis, the marvelous hot Lyon sausage, the boned frogs' legs in puff pastry and the crusty glazed apples, they are star productions well worth our toques. The cellar is small but select and fairly priced.

A la carte: 350-400F. Menus: 175F (lunch only), 235F.

12/20 Dessirier

9, pl. du Maréchal-Juin
42.27.82.14, 43.80.50.72

M. Robinet. Open daily until 12:30 a.m. Terrace dining. Parking. Pets allowed. Cards: V, AE, DC.

The best oysters in Paris have a standing contract with this 100-year-old brasserie, which has been transformed over the years into a luxuriously appointed restaurant. You can eat them year-round—from the best sources, opened and presented by a professional. Nevertheless this is not the wonderful seafood restaurant it once was. But if you ignore the prices and keep your attention instead on the silk-lined surroundings, the marvelous shellfish, and the simpler fish dishes, such as filet of sole or grilled salmon steak, you'll leave with memories of a nice evening. Excellent wines are served by the carafe (petit Chablis or Brouilly).

A la carte: 400F. Menu: 150F (wine incl.).

14 Epicure

22, rue Fourcroy - 47.63.34.00

M. Péquignot. Open until 10:15 p.m. Closed Sun. Pets allowed. Cards: V.

The Péquignots, a most civilized, engaging couple, have given up chasing two rabbits through the same field. They've sold their annex on rue Cardinet and are working full time in this restaurant. The modern, impersonal dining room, though awkwardly geometric and harshly lit, is comfortable, with small, well-dressed tables. Mme. Pequignot moves among these tables tirelessly, eager to please. The fixed-price lunch menu is remarkable: for example, a generous portion of foie gras, slightly cooked, in a fragrant aspic; followed by excellent homemade ravioli or minced veal kidney seasoned with coriander; and a thin, crisp apple tart. More or less the same menu applies at dinner and costs more; you can also order from the à la carte dishes developed by Alain Bergounioux, a former protégé of Dutournier's at Trou Gascon (oxtail in aspic with horseradish sauce, salad of smoked eel in a peppered vinaigrette). Lots of agreeable little wines sell for about 100 francs.

A la carte: 300-350F. Menus: 175F (lunch only), 195F (dinner only).

14 Epicure 108

108, rue Cardinet
47.63.50.91, 46.22.77.28

MM. Tourette & Goujon. Open until 10:30 p.m. Closed Sat. lunch, Sun. & holidays. Pets allowed. Cards: V, MC.

A new owner, a new chef and presto! We hear rounds of applause for this attractive "dining car" restaurant done in soothing shades of beige and pink. Chef Jean-Christophe Beaugon's credentials are minimal, but he is fast building a reputation for himself and his simple yet subtle cuisine, which is marked by clear, delicate flavors. Like the former owners, the Péquignots, the new management offers a single, changing à la carte menu and some of the same dishes: lamb's tongue with aromatic salad, a ruddy breast of duck flavored with honey, salmon steak with lentils and, for dessert, a flaky rhubarb turnover with caramel sauce. Good cellar with pleasant Loire wines and a memorable Brouilly.

A la carte: 185F.

14 L'Etoile d'Or

(Hôtel Concorde-La Fayette)
3, pl. du Général-Koenig - 47.58.12.84
M. Houin. Open until 10:30 p.m. Closed Aug. Air cond. Pets allowed. Telex 650892. Cards: V, AE, DC, MC.

The nightly piano music and formal dinner dancing on Fridays make this restaurant a great place to come for a romantic dinner and a chance to sample chef Joël Renty's contemporary cuisine. Try his salad of red mullet in hazelnut oil, northern cod in a soy sauce with chives, braised beefsteak with shallots, and honey-glazed nougat with apricot purée; the "symphony" of five chocolates is much too sweet. If it is all nicely done but lacks, well, inspiration, might that not be due to his having to supervise a staff of 80 across two restaurants and giant banquet rooms? The wine list holds several good values for about 100 francs, but that won't guarantee a merciful check, so it may be best to stick with the fixed-price menus, which are generous and attractive. Stylish modern decor and pretty brass lanterns.

A la carte: 400-600F. Menus: 198F (lunch only), 325F.

12/20 Goldenberg

69, ave. de Wagram - 42.27.34.79
M. Goldenberg. Open daily until 11:30 p.m. Air cond. Terrace dining. Pets allowed. Cards: V.

This is the place to come for pickled herring, pike caviar, stuffed carp, Yiddish-style cassoulet and kosher Beaujolais. You'll feel like part of the family in twinkly eyed Patrick Goldenberg's nostalgic, amusing Paris delicatessen.

A la carte: 180-200F. Menu: 98F (wine incl.).

12/20 La Gourmandine

26, rue d'Armaillé - 45.72.00.82
M. Dumonteil. Open until 10:15 p.m. Closed Sun., Mon. & Aug. 15-30. Pets allowed. Cards: V, AE, DC.

The cuisine of M. Dumonteil, a diploma-studded chef, makesonly the barest concessions to current fashion. The nearly perfect fixed-price menu includes, for example, a seasonal salad, curried fowl or stuffed pigs' trotters with foie gras and mushrooms, cheese, an excellent dessert and a regional wine. The nice wines are informatively listed.

A la carte: 250F. Menus: 145F (lunch only, wine incl.), 195F (weekdays only).

15 Guyvonne

14, rue de Thann - 42.27.25.43
M. Cros. Open until 10 p.m. Closed Sat., Sun., July 7-Aug. 1 & Dec. 22-Jan. 8. Terrace dining. Pets allowed. Cards: V.

For years this has been a quiet neighborhood eating spot, spared the turbulence of social success both by the moody reserve of the Monceau district and by owner Guy Cros's restrained ambition. The decor suggests a stylish little country inn, and your fellow diners will be informed food lovers, most likely regular customers who come to eat some of the finest cooking in town. And Cros never disappoints, especially with seafood, which he loves to prepare and to verbally describe for his guests: for example, grilled langouste (spiny lobster) with fresh artichokes, red-clawed crayfish that you won't find anywhere else in Paris (en cocotte with Chablis), oysters and clams with spinach and a few chanterelles, and pan-fried salmon with endives and watercress butter—evidence that he watches for seasonal products to come to market. Add to this impromptu menu a few excellent meat dishes, such as saddle of rabbit with chives, and old-fashioned desserts that melt in your mouth (superb fruit compotes). The prices are modest for such a high standard of quality.

A la carte: 350F. Menu: 195F.

13 Laudrin

154, blvd. Pereire - 43.80.87.40
M. Billaud. Open until 10:30 p.m. Closed Sat. & Sun. Air cond. Pets allowed. Cards: V, AE.

For the last 30 years, courtesy-conscious M. Billaud has been managing this lovely little yacht of a restaurant, with its mixture of nautical and Louis XVI decor and its comfortable booths. Chefs have come and gone; the present one maintains the high and (like the menu) unvarying standard of the bourride of lotte, Savoie-style beef rib steak Bercy and the remarkable "tripes de la Mère Billaud" (sliced thin). Plenty of fine wines are served in magnums (you pay only for what you drink).

A la carte: 300F and up.

15 Maître Corbeau

6, rue d'Armaillé - 42.27.19.20
M. Giral. Open until 10:30 p.m. Closed Sat., Sun., Feb. 18-27 & Aug. 5-22. Air cond. No pets. Cards: V, AE, DC.

Having vacated their elegant premises near the Château d'Anet, just west of Paris, Paul Giral, his chef, Guy Vallée, and the entire kitchen brigade have moved to the former site of the Auberge d'Armaillé near the Arc de Triomphe. The graceful decor reflects the owners' refined taste: pale paneling, muted lighting, colored lithographs lining the walls and lavish flower arrangements. The cuisine, an artful blend of classic and modern styles, is up to standards: avocado and shrimp mousseline, roast turbot with mushrooms, excellent calf's head, and bittersweet-chocolate ice cream coupled with mint sorbet. Good selection of top Bordeaux labels.

A la carte: 300-350F. Menu: 250F (wine incl.).

17 Le Manoir de Paris

6, rue Pierre-Demours
45.72.25.25
M. Vandenhende. Open until 10:30 p.m. Closed Sat., Sun. & July 9-31. Air cond. Parking. Pets allowed. Cards: V, AE, DC.

They talked about redecorating for three years, and it finally happened. This is classy stuff: Tiffany ceiling, mirrored pilasters, intricately carved white woodwork, flowers and greenery all over the place and, on the tables, little pink lamps that send out a seductive glow and put a sparkle in women's eyes. Pierre Pothier, who refurbished Maxim's, has done a great job here for Denise Fabre and Francis Vandenhende. Le Manoir, which never had anything going against it save its unappealing interior, has become one of the most attractive eating places in Paris. Chef Philippe Groult agrees. At one point he was ready to pack up and leave, complaining that the decor fell far short of the cuisine, but he soon unpacked his bags. Don't count on his being around forever, though; he'll open his own place one of these days unless they make him a partner.

Whatever the future brings, we have Pothier's remodeling to thank for perpetuating the cooking of one of Joël Robuchon's most gifted pupils. The cuisine even seems to have improved (not the first time that decor has affected a chef's morale), with more precise and substantial flavors. The calf's-foot aspic with a hint of truffle is incredibly subtle, the feuilleté of hot foie gras with spiced potatoes is lavish, and the ravioli stuffed with thyme-scented rabbit asserts the dignity of this pervasive pasta product, subjected nowadays to sauce baths of every description and color. Chocolate truffle cake, orange meringue and caramelized vanilla-and-chocolate ice cream are among the mouth-watering desserts. Excellent wines selected by Francis's brother are served by jovial Rémy Aspect, and the faultless service is under the baton of Charles Madeira, the solid, smiling pillar of Le Manoir.

A la carte: 400-600F. Menus: 310F (lunch only, wine incl.), 395F (menu dégustation).

(15) Alain Morel

123, ave. de Wagram - 42.27.61.50

M. Morel. Open until 10:30 p.m. Closed Sat. lunch & Sun. Terrace dining. Pets allowed. Cards: V.

Alain Morel has taken over these odd-shaped, dreary but comfortable premises, with off-white walls and the type of Louis XVI moldings you find in older apartments in the Ternes district. The atmosphere needs a dose of cheer, the waiters are young and polished, and the prices are appalling.

Some of Morel's less-charitable colleagues have called him a "swellhead"; we, on the other hand, find this thirtysomething chef anxious, eager to do well and rather modest. Take his menu, for instance, on which a sweetbreads salad, salmon with soy sauce and filet of lamb in pastry appear just that way, instead of dressed up in elaborate descriptions. This in itself would not be of great interest if the dishes didn't turn out to be so remarkable. Our latest sampling included potato salad with semicooked duck foie gras, lamb moussaka (a good way to utilize wonderful summer vegetables and tender morsels of lamb), and roast turbot in all its natural splendor, with nothing more than a touch of walnut-oil vinaigrette. For dessert we enjoyed that audacious pastry cone filled with seasonal fresh fruit in place of traditional raspberries or wild strawberries (the leafy frame really isn't necessary) and marvelous licorice ice cream with a muscular flavor. A terrace is open for meals in summer.

A la carte: 400-500F. Menu: 130F.

(15) Paul et France

27, ave. Niel - 47.63.04.24

M. Romano. Open until 10:30 p.m. Closed Sat., Sun. & July 14-Aug. 15. Air cond. No pets. Cards: V, AE, DC.

Do we dare admit that we miss the old haphazard but cozy decor, now that Paul et France looks like every other place around: pale woodwork, salmon-colored upholstery and smoky mirrors? Luckily, the southern vitality of Georges Romano and his smiling wife, Suzanne, and the mild euphoria of a fair-and-foul-weather following make up for it, and a Paul et France meal today is still a feast in miniature. Romano drifts among the tables describing his dishes in mouth-watering detail, dishes that reflect his temperament: sunny, colorful, simple, generous and delicious. His menu never stands still—he's a soccer fan and likes to keep things moving. His "market-basket cuisine" sets the kitchen humming, running from crab-filled ravioli to red mullet with oyster butter, from brill with red butter to turbot with cream of parsley, from braised lobster with noodles to breast of duck with truffle butter, from chocolate fondant to an extraordinary wild-blackberry sorbet. A little more attention needs to be paid to details, lest the food end up like the now-impeccable decor: boring. The ravioli at our most recent meal was oversauced, and the sweetbreads unattractively paired with regrettable pleurote mushrooms. Good wines are selected by an experienced sommelier.

A la carte: 350F. Menus: 250F (lunch only, wine incl.), 300F, 380F.

(16) Le Petit Colombier

42, rue des Acacias
43.80.28.54, 43.80.08.61

M. Fournier. Open until 10:30 p.m. Closed Sun. lunch, Sat. & Aug. 1-17. Air cond. Garage parking. Pets allowed. Cards: V.

While head of the Paris Association of Restaurateurs, Bernard Fournier also managed his own restaurant and kitchens. Now that he has stepped down as president, he'll be able to devote more time to his passion: cooking. No one knows better than Fournier how to roast a wild partridge or a well-aged cut of beef or how to make a classic coq au vin de Bourgogne. These delectable dishes are served in a pleasantly old-fashioned country inn with brass fixtures, pewterware and flower bouquets. You can also order molded pike, squab with no seasoning other than salt and pepper, a delicious chevreau (kid) with wild thyme, tasty desserts (blancmange with almond milk, chocolate fondant with a coffee crème brûlée topping) and the very best wines from a 35,000-bottle cellar. A meal at Le Petit Colombier is as soothing as a ride through the French countryside.

A la carte: 350-400F. Menu: 190F (lunch only, wine incl.).

Pétrus

(15) 12, pl. due Maréchal-Juin - 43.80.15.95

Mme. André & M. Berneau. Open until 11 p.m. Closed Aug. 6-Sept. 6. Air cond. Terrace dining. Parking. Pets allowed. Cards: V, AE, DC, MC.

If you order six Charente or New Zealand oysters, a feuilleté of hogfish with basil butter, a splendid cabbage stuffed with rock lobster and sponge cake with an almond-caramel frosting, you will have tasted the best of Gilbert Dugast's cooking. This excellent chef, with saltwater in his blood and the ocean at his fingertips, would select these dishes for himself if he were paying the bill. Every morning, 50 kilograms of fish are deposited on his doorstep and scarcely make it to the refrigerator before getting snapped up by eager diners. They know that the best poached turbot, grilled bass and sole meunière, in their natural state, can be found in this decidedly unstylish but warm and inviting dining room.

After a superb platter of cheeses come the several good desserts: île flottante (floating island), coffee parfait and the sponge cake with almond-caramel frosting. Jean Frambour, president of the national association of wine stewards, attends to your gullet; Jean Berneau and Monique André look after your comfort; and all you have to worry about is paying a check that rides the high seas, though at a relatively reasonable speed.

A la carte: 350-550F.

Michel Rostang

(18) 20, rue Rennequin
47.63.40.77

M. Rostang. Open until 10:15 p.m. Closed Sat. lunch (& dinner in seas.), Sun., holidays & Aug. 1-16. Air cond. Pets allowed. Telex 649629. Cards: V, MC.

Approaching 40 but still a boy at heart, chef Michel Rostang isn't one of those swellheads who philosophizes on the metaphysics of ravioli or chases after flattering comments from the press. Far from shy, he knows just how good he is and prefers not to shout about it. He loves to work hard. He's a craftsman—constructing his dishes as meticulously as a cabinetmaker assembles a fine piece of furniture—and an artist. It takes a solid technique, a refined sensibility and lots of drive to produce dishes of such purity, with clear, distinct flavors. And the remarkably consistent results are appreciated by his admirers. Unlike some of his celebrated colleagues, Rostang has no ups and downs, no "inspired" moments followed by nothing-goes-right days.

With a steady head, Rostang applies his creative talents to the bourgeois cuisine he produces with such flair. His inventive spirit is revealed in such dishes as elegant, crusty pastry shells filled with basil-flavored tomatoes and rabbit liver; calamari ravioli with saffron garnished with a julienne of raw beets; a superb roasted skate wing served with a chiffonnade of tender green cabbage; a viennoise of red mullet with black olives and fennel; a crisp, rosy-fleshed squab en crapaudine (backbone removed), its juices reduced with vinegar and honey; and a potato-and-turnip pancake. The traditional navarin (stew) of lamb, braised just long enough to turn the meat ruddy, tastes like nothing you've ever eaten—with its fresh noodles and garlic flan, it's irresistible. The goat cheese and the Saint-Marcellin are the same stunning products served by Rostang's brother at La Bonne Auberge in Antibes. Desserts are equally spectacular: cold caramelized soufflé of wild strawberries and passion fruit, warm rhubarb tart, chocolate millefeuille, raspberry clafouti. Wines are costly and of the best pedigree, but the engaging presence of young Mme. Rostang compensates somewhat for the stinging check. There are two attractive dining rooms filled with flowers: one a rosy shade of brick, the other mirrored.

A la carte: 500-700F. Menus: 230F (lunch only), 350F, 400F, 460F.

Guy Savoy

(19) 18, rue Troyon
43.80.40.61, 43.80.36.22

M. Savoy. Open until 10:30 p.m. Closed Sat. (except lunch Oct. & Easter), Sun. & July 14-Aug. 4. Air cond. Parking. No pets. Cards: V.

Four crowns—no, wait, four toques—for the house of Savoy. For some time now that fourth toque sat on the back burner while we waited for our bearded friend, who was fretting and fuming in his hideout on rue Duret, to simmer down. This was necessary, we felt, for his talent to really unfold. And it happened. At the site of the last Le Bernardin, which the Le Coze duo abandoned for New York (where they're making a fortune), Guy Savoy's dream came true: a spacious dining room and a modern, functional kitchen. In less than a month his decorator, Jean-Pierre Hanki, tore the place apart and did it over completely. Le Bernardin had been wrapped in eternal darkness, which was fine at night but at lunch made you feel as though you were entering a nightclub at an hour when the milkman should have been making his rounds. Savoy changed all that—now the decor is bright and cheerful (pinkish-beige walls and chairs that contrast nicely with the deep-green carpet), indirect lighting is hidden above the false ceiling, and the handsome prints reveal the chef's good taste in modern art.

Savoy has first-rate assistants: Jean Schuffenecker, formerly of La Barrière de Clichy, and Serge Polito, from Le Bernardin. The boss works just as hard as his helpers; for twenty years—he's just in his early 30s—that's all he's been doing. He was still in short pants when he started to help out his mother in the park refreshment bar she ran in his home town in the Isère. At seventeen, after flunking the entrance exam at the hotel school in Nice, he took over the bar and made it into a small restaurant. In 1970, he met the Troisgros brothers, who adopted him as an apprentice cook. Next came a stint in the Lasserre kitchens, military service, a job as pastry chef in Geneva, then to Outhier's in La Napoule and, in 1977, to La Barrière de Clichy, to which he was introduced by his friend Bernard Loiseau, now an all-star chef. "Almost deserves three toques," reported our *Guide de la France*, when we had just discovered this pearl. Three years later, having opened his own place on rue Duret, Savoy got his three toques and his first whiff of success.

The cuisine you eat here is very much Savoy's own "thing," but everyone seems to like it. The restaurant is packed twice a day. It's not surprising—he cooks with exuberance, and that makes for thrilling meals, extraordinary fusions of exquisite flavors. As, for example, when he couples sea scallops with roquette greens and dandelion leaves, spiny lobsters with cream of lentils, sea urchins with Chinese artichokes, filet of red mullet with sautéed chicken livers, or lotte with cabbage and caviar. Two ridiculously simple dishes that seem entirely out of place in a great restaurant assume, in Savoy's hands, princely dimensions: roasted cod with stewed onions and an ordinary pollock broiled to a crusty finish, set on a bed of puréed sweet garlic and accompanied by a few sliced potatoes and some black mushrooms. In another mode, the same can be said for his ramekin of wild mushrooms with asparagus purée and parsley, and a fabulous lobster in coral sauce with peas and string beans.

Enough of the litany. Savoy outruns his shadow, and it's impossible to keep up with his latest creations. Treat yourself to the pleasure of discovering the delights he has to offer on his ever-changing menu, making sure not to neglect the divine pastries and desserts (glazed rice and apples, spiced fruit pie, vanilla ice cream). Wines are presented by Eric Mancio, a young sommelier who "chants" his cellar with a storyteller's art, and you can rely on—but here the pleasure ends—a resounding bill.

A la carte: 350-800F. Menu: 540F (menu dégustation).

16 Sormani

4, rue du Général-Lanzerac
43.80.13.91

M. Fayet. Open until 10:30 p.m. Closed Sat., Sun., March 24-April 3, Aug. 1-22 & Dec. 24-Jan. 4. Air cond. No pets. Cards: V.

One of the finest and most brilliant Italian cuisines in Paris is produced by a Savoie-born Parisian, Pascal Fayet. For many years this remarkable chef was in charge of a good Italian restaurant, Conti, and having an Italian grandmother (whose name adorns the signboard) hasn't hurt. The delicacies you'll taste here seem to have been meticulously planned and executed, yet not a hint of this effort dilutes the bold and happy union of flavors. You'll find superb seafood pizza, tomatoes stuffed with spiny lobster, remarkably subtle red mullet in olive oil and basil, chaud-froid of salmon in tomato sauce and elaborate desserts to round off a perfect meal—provided you don't make the mistake of ordering the risotto with white truffles, which is curiously dry and lumpy. The bright-blue decor is a trifle chilly but chic (attractive tables, Louis XV armchairs, flowers galore); the service is low-key and vigilant.

A la carte: 350F. Menus: 300F (menu dégustation), 250F.

15 La Toque

16, rue de Tocqueville - 42.27.97.95

M. Joubert. Open until 9:30 p.m. Closed Sat., Sun., July 22-Aug. 20 & Dec. 23-Jan. 1. Air cond. Pets allowed. Cards: V.

Jacky Joubert certainly didn't learn interior decorating from Michel Guérard, with whom he trained. His tiny bistro is virtually crushed under the weight of velvet draperies and clutter, so it's best to rivet your eyes on the plates (which are breathtakingly elegant) and, more important, on what they contain. This excellent chef can't be faulted when it comes to stuffing his guests with a compote of duck in vegetable aspic, saffron-seasoned hogfish, snails fricassée, roast lamb with thyme, casserole of beef with shallots, caramel-glazed soufflé and dainty pastries (which certainly don't need their coatings of powdered sugar). While everyone complains of the stingy portions that come with modern cuisine, here it's the prices that are small. For about 500 francs for two, with a good wine, you can enjoy an excellent meal.

A la carte: 230-300F. Menu: 190F.

Eighteenth Arrondissement

17 A. Beauvilliers

52, rue Lamarck
42.54.54.42

M. Carlier. Open until 10:45 p.m. Closed Mon. lunch, Sun. & Sept. 3-17. Terrace dining. Cards: V, MC.

The best New Year's Eve parties in Paris, the most lavish flower arrangements, the prettiest terrace, the most adorable private salon (on display under glass are bridal bouquets from past wedding receptions), the most romantic restaurant, the most eclectic clientele. What else can we say, except that owner/chef Edouard Carlier is as crazy as ever. Crazy about parties, which he will organize at the drop of a hat, to honor his fellow cooks, to salute the new wine from Montmartre's vineyards or to celebrate birthdays. Even if you're not a "club member," you feel part of the fun in this converted bakery nestled against the Butte Montmartre, transformed into a pleasure dome by soft lighting, antique portraits and prints and a profusion of flowers.

Leaning on what looks like a Napoléon III counter, Carlier receives his guests with approving grunts, while his partner, Micky, checks the tables set with sparkling silverware to make sure that nothing is amiss. Michel Deygat, a tall, athletic-looking fellow who trained at the Nikko under Robuchon, then at Faugeron, doesn't venture onstage—he never leaves the kitchen. And that's where you'll find him, preparing standard dishes from his repertoire and developing new ones. There's no doubt that he is responsible for the reawakening of Beauvilliers, which was dozing on its laurels. You'll agree when you taste his boned rabbit braised in white Burgundy and seasoned with chopped parsley, fresh artichoke bottom with crab, poached egg with sautéed mushrooms, lamb's brains with bacon and sherry vinegar, and his remarkable roasted turbot with veal juice and roast filet of lamb with tarragon and Provençal vegetables (an Antoine Beauvilliers recipe that dates back to 1814). Begin with a glass of sherry (Carlier is crazy about it and stocks the finest sherries in town), then rely on sommelier Georges Bertet to help you choose from a vast collection of Bordeaux and Côtes-du-Rhône to suit everyone's taste.

A la carte: 450-700F. Menus: 175F (lunch only), 300F (lunch only, wine incl.).

(13) Chez Toi ou Chez Moi

8, rue du Marché-Ordener
42.29.58.24, 42.28.82.87

Mme. Sinclair. Open daily until 10:30 p.m. Parking. Pets allowed. Cards: V, AE, DC.

Caroll Sinclair, a self-taught cook, admits that taxis have trouble finding her place on its little street because they confuse it with the rue Ordener. She's thinking of leaving the neighborhood, but in the meantime, you won't regret dining in this captivating little candy box (whose decor needs redoing anyway), where you can expect a "surprise" menu and where vegetables have top priority. The service has its ups and downs (like the cooking), but it's a delightful spot. The expensive wine list does its best to build up the check.

Menu: 140F.

(14) Clodenis

57, rue Caulaincourt - 46.06.20.26

M. Gentes. Open until 10:30 p.m. Closed Sun. & Mon. Pets allowed. Cards: V.

Deny Gentes, who was one of the most enthusiastic chefs in Paris ten years ago, seems to have retreated from his highly creative beginnings. On the plus side, this has helped him maintain consistency in producing a set repertoire (which a Japanese chef is entrusted to repeat faultlessly day in and day out) using the finest ingredients. The decor has improved a good deal, and you'll never see a waiter drop as much as a spoon on the carpet. For all these reasons Clodenis remains one of the best eating places in this popular tourist area, especially when the warm weather comes and you can sit out on the delightful sidewalk terrace. Taste the smoked salmon maison perfumed with anise, cracked Brittany crab, brandade of cod the way they make it in Nîmes, hot foie gras with potatoes and feuilleté of red fruits.

A la carte: 350F. Menus: 180F (lunch only), 220F (dinner only).

11/20 La Crémaillère 1900

15, pl. du Tertre - 46.06.58.59

M. Bailly. Open daily until 12:30 a.m. Air cond. Garden dining. Pets allowed. Telex 232435. Cards: V, AE, DC.

This magic garden and charming 1900s-style place is located scarcely beyond reach of the noisy and touristy place du Tertre. Oyster bar and good, honest brasserie fare. Piano music at night.

A la carte: 180-200F. Menu: 77F.

(15) Les Fusains

44, rue Joseph-de-Maistre - 42.28.03.69

M. Mathys. Dinner only. Open until midnight. Closed Sun., Mon. & Sept. Terrace dining. Cards: V.

Bernard Mathys prefers to be known as a new chef rather than a former actor. As informed as he is engaging, this amateur cook has the right idea: He'll make more waves in the kitchen than in the theater, where he had a brief run. Cooking, it turns out, is his thing. Like most self-taught people, he throws himself into it heart and soul. More surprising is the degree of professional discipline Mathys brings to everything he does, beginning with his duties as host in his own dining room, with its cozy, candlelit tables and casual yet elegant atmosphere. There is only one menu—a fixed-price one—and it changes nightly, or quite often, according to the market. His dishes are simple and executed with great clarity. The other day we had a duck foie gras appetizer followed by a marvelously light salad of scallops and mushrooms; a fricassée of fresh chanterelles that tasted of the woods; and a precisely grilled salmon steak, moist and velvety, on a bed of tender sea fennel; followed by perfectly ripened cheeses and a pastry spree of apricot tarts, gratin of wild strawberries and hazelnut financière (small cake). Wines are expensive, but once you taste something as delectable as the Saint-Emilion Les Abeilles at 140 francs, you'll feel that they're practically giving them away.

Menu: 270F.

(13) Grandgousier

17, ave. Rachel - 43.87.66.12

M. Marzynski. Open until 10 p.m. Closed Sat. lunch, Sun. & 2 weeks in Aug. Parking. Pets allowed. Cards: V, AE, DC, MC.

A quiet bourgeois establishment on a back street that runs behind the cemetery, Grandgousier presents food that is good and consistent if not distinctive: refreshing fisherman's salad (raw fish perfumed with ginger and pink pepper), filet of red mullet, (unfortunately overcooked) in a delicate curry sauce and desserts that have made some progress (blancmange and a chocolate marquise). Nice wine list with stiff prices.

A la carte: 260F. Menu: 135F.

12/20 Le Maquis

69, rue Caulaincourt - 42.59.76.07

M. Lesage. Open until 10 p.m. Closed Sun. & Mon. Terrace dining. Pets allowed. Cards: V.

M. Lesage, who owns the nearby Clodenis, keeps an eye on quality and prices at Le Maquis, which has an amusing terrace decor. His extraordinary fixed-price menu and his market-basket à la carte dishes pack the house for lunch and dinner: brandade of cod, osso buco, scallop salad and feuilleté of lobster tails. Wine from the Gard region is served in carafes.

A la carte: 200F. Menu: 57F (lunch only, wine incl.).

Nineteenth Arrondissement

(15) Au Cochon d'Or

192, ave. Jean-Jaurès - 46.07.23.13

M. Ayral. Open daily until 10:30 p.m. Air cond. Pets allowed. Cards: V, AE, DC, MC.

Despite the blood sausage with puffed potatoes, the incomparable calf's head and the best meats in Paris served in truckload portions, the Cochon d'Or is no longer a "bistro," at least not in the sense it used to be when the meat butchers were here at Villette and the atmosphere was rough and zoo-like. Long ago the comfortable, homey decor and enlarged floor space (the immense wine cellar is spectacular) transformed it into a chic restaurant. Meat lovers and fans of hearty country fare like to come here for the filet mignon, the remarkable pigs' feet sauce Choron and the finest cuts. Still, if you look closely at the new urban clientele attracted by the gigantic cultural projects mushrooming just across the way, and if you carefully study the pretty menu (superb foie gras, delicately treated fish), you're bound to catch the whiff of smug trendiness pervading these sullen outskirts of the capital.

A la carte: 400F. Menu: 210F.

12/20 Dagorno

190, ave. Jean-Jaurès - 46.07.02.29

M. Abatécola. Open daily until midnight. Air cond. Cards: V.

The new brasserie look of the old Dagorno isn't exactly subtle, but it is cheerful and inviting. The cooking has yet to find its stride, and andouillette from Duval doesn't belong in such a posh setting. Nonetheless, you can expect some excellent dishes, whatever they are, along with good wines and faultless service.

A la carte: 300F. Menu: 150F (wine incl.).

15 Au Pavillon Puebla

(Christian Vergès)

Parc des Buttes-Chaumont - 42.08.92.62

M. Vergès. Open until 10 p.m. Closed Sun. & Mon. Garden dining. Parking. Pets allowed. Cards: V.

If you're an amateur decorator, you're bound to make mistakes, even if you have good taste. That's the story behind this Napoléon III hunting lodge near the entrance to the Buttes-Chaumont park. Revived after years of neglect, it became a little jewel—overpolished, as it turns out, since it's a jewel that would look better if it were left to glow in its own light. But on sunny days, the rooms and the winter garden remain charming reminders of the romantic past.

Not long ago we reported that Christian Vergès had come into bloom in this interior designed by him and his wife. The words were barely out of our PCs when he completely ruined our next meal with all kinds of elaborate, boring gimmickry. The next time around we were luckier; despite poky service, the wrong check delivered and errors in the "right" check, we rediscovered the fine flavors that characterize this self-made chef's elegant cuisine. The large, handsome menu includes stuffed baby calamari, hot curried oyster ravioli, poached lobster with leeks, oxtail miroton, tournedos of duck with foie gras (not very convincing), leg of lamb with chanterelles and nice desserts. The bill is no picnic, but there's a good fixed-price menu for 200 francs at lunch that attracts a steady stream of business people.

A la carte: 350-500F. Menu: 200F.

13 Le Plateau Gourmand

18, rue du Plateau - 42.45.79.39

Mme. Ols. Open until 9:30 p.m. Closed Sat., Sun. & Aug. 1-25. Pets allowed. Cards: V.

Idolized by his clients from the television industry (the Société Française de Production has its studios close by), young Benoît Revel is now doubling the floor space of his tiny bistro. This chip off the old block (Revel Sr. runs the charming Pot d'Argent in Dourdan) used to work at Le Servot on the Champs-Elysées. Despite a few miscalculations here and there (overly rich sauces and bright ideas that were never meant to be), his delicious duck breast with lemon peel and tasty lamb-and-mushroom mousse are inventive dishes. A la carte prices have rocketed, but nearly the same dishes may be ordered from the 165-franc fixed-price menu. Agreeable little everyday wines.

A la carte: 250-300F. Menus: 94F (lunch only), 165F.

Twentieth Arrondissement

12/20 Le Bistrot du 20e

44, rue du Surmelin - 48.97.20.30

M. Bihoues-Lechevallier. Open until 10 p.m. Closed Sat., Sun. & July. Pets allowed. Cards: V, AE.

This cute little restaurant in an old butcher shop features good, solid classic cuisine. Try the smoked salmon, charcuterie from the Landes and feuilleté of sweetbreads.

A la carte: 180-200F. Menus: 150F (dinner only, wine incl.), 80F.

12/20 Le Courtil

15, rue St-Blaise - 43.70.09.32

M. Azincourt. Open until 10 p.m. Closed Sun., Mon., March 28-April 1 & Aug. 1-26. Pets allowed. Cards: V.

A jazz duo on Tuesday evenings livens up this winsome restaurant. With a pocket-size garden in the rear, Le Courtil serves a modern cuisine that is in control, with an accent on vegetables (seafood salad, duck confit and Gamay wine in pitchers).

A la carte: 180F.

INDEX OF PARIS RESTAURANTS

Remember to call ahead to reserve your table—and allow a month or two advance notice for the very top restaurants.

PARIS

Hotels

First Arrondissement

Agora

7, rue de la Cossonnerie - 42.33.46.02
Open year-round. 29 rms 250-450F. TV in 8 rms. No pets. Cards: AE.

In the heart of the pedestrian district of Les Halles, these rooms are exquisitely decorated and well soundproofed. Lovely pieces of period furniture and engravings are found just about everywhere; the concern for cleanliness is impressive. No restaurant.

Castille

37, rue Cambon - 42.61.55.20
Open year-round. 14 stes 1,000-1,800F. 62 rms 700-1,280F. TV. Pets allowed. Telex 213505. Cards: V, AE, DC, MC.

The rooms and the superb duplexes of this small hotel are bright, hospitable and impeccably equipped. Bar and restaurant: Le Relais Castille (meals are served on the patio during summer).

Ducs d'Anjou

1, rue St-Opportune - 42.36.92.24
Open year-round. 38 rms 280-460F. TV. Pets allowed. Cards: V, AE.

Located on the delightful small place Sainte-Opportune, this ancient building has been restored from top to bottom. The rooms are small (as are the bathrooms) but quiet; those overlooking the courtyard are a bit gloomy. No restaurant.

Duminy-Vendôme

3, rue du Mont-Thabor - 42.60.32.80
Open year-round. 79 rms 390-800F. TV. No pets. Telex 213492. Cards: V, AE, DC, MC.

Duminy-Vendôme's rooms have impeccable bathrooms and lovely wallpaper; those on the sixth and seventh floors have slightly sloping ceilings. A small summer patio is located on the main floor.

Family Hôtel

35, rue Cambon - 42.61.54.84
Open year-round. 1 ste 1,000F. 25 rms 300-450F. Pets allowed. Cards: V, AE.

This is a small, quiet, well-maintained hotel. Ask for room 50 on the sixth floor, which offers a view of the Vendôme column; or for room 41, with its retro furniture. The rooms facing the street have double-glazed windows, so you'll sleep soundly. The rates are reasonable for the district. No restaurant.

Inter-Continental

3, rue de Castiglione - 42.60.37.80
Open year-round. 62 stes 2,940-9,085F. 393 rms 1,497-2,138F. TV. Air cond. Pets allowed. Telex 220114. Cards: V, AE, DC, MC.

Garnier, the architect of the Opéra, designed this vast hotel; three out of its seven immense and spectacular salons are ranked for their high standards. With its remarkably equipped conference rooms, it answers perfectly to the business world's needs; and as for charm and comfort, you'll find them both in the lovely patio filled with flowers, in the decor and the incomparable loveliness of many of the rooms (though some are tiny and gloomy), as well as in the small singles located in the attic, from which there is a fine view of the Tuileries. The suites (with Jacuzzi) are luxurious. Three restaurants: La Rôtisserie Rivoli, Le Café Tuileries and La Terrasse Fleurie (in summer).

Hôtel Lotti

7, rue de Castiglione - 42.60.37.34
Open year-round. 5 stes 3,740-4,620F. 123 rms 1,120-1,980F. TV. Air cond. Pets allowed. Telex 240066. Cards: V, AE, DC, MC.

This elegant hotel is very popular with the members of the Italian aristocracy. Each of the rather spacious rooms, whose comfort is worthy of their clientele, is uniquely decorated and offers outstanding facilities. The restaurant, the lobby and all the rooms were recently renovated.

Hôtel du Louvre

Pl. André-Malraux - 42.61.56.01
Open year-round. 10 stes 2,200-2,600F. 202 rms 880-1,900F. Half-board 125-200F (plus room). TV. Air cond. in 180 rms. Pets allowed. Parking. Telex 220412. Cards: V, AE, DC, MC.

From the door of the Hôtel du Louvre, one can see the Gardens of the Palais-Royal, the Louvre and the Tuileries. The guest rooms, under high ceilings, offer the decor and all the conveniences one expects from such a chain. The restaurant/brasserie, the bar, the lobby and the entire second floor were recently redecorated.

Meurice

228, rue de Rivoli - 42.60.38.60
Open year-round. 36 stes 3,440-9,500F. 151 rms 1,440-2,350F. TV. Air cond. in 120 rms. Pets allowed. Telex 230673. Cards: V, AE, DC, MC.

The Meurice has undergone substantial renovation these past few years. Most recently, the admirable salons on the main floor were redone; the rooms and suites (which offer a view of the Tuileries) were outfitted with air conditioning and tastefully redecorated; and the pink marble bathrooms are now ultra-modern and superb. The Meurice remains one of the best and most frequented grand hotels in Paris. There is a restaurant in the basement.

Novotel Paris Les Halles

Pl. Marguerite-de-Navarre - 42.21.31.31

Open year-round. 14 stes 850-1,250F. 271 rms 665-705F. TV. Air cond. Pets allowed. Telex 216389. Cards: V, AE, DC, MC.

This ultra-modern building constructed of stone, glass and zinc is located in the heart of the former Les Halles market. Its rooms offer perfect comfort, but their air conditioning (alas!) prevents one from opening the windows. The restaurant is open from 6 a.m. to midnight, and there is a bar on a terrace. The conference rooms can be tailored to size by means of movable partitions. Travel agency.

Ritz

15, pl. Vendôme - 42.60.38.30

Open year-round. 45 stes 5,300-39,410F. 143 rms 1,995-2,650F. TV. Air cond. Heated pool. Pets allowed. Parking. Telex 220262. Cards: V, AE, DC, MC.

The most famous hotel in the world has turned to state-of-the-art modernism, but without in the least betraying the distinctive character that won the Ritz its reputation. In other words, even if nowadays you can close the windows, change the video program or make a phone call without leaving your very bed or Jacuzzi tub (Charles Ritz was the first hotel owner to provide private bathrooms for his clients), nothing has altered the pleasure of stretching out on a wide brass bed surrounded by signed furniture. Add to that a full view of one of the most spectacular squares in the world, in an atmosphere of old-fashioned luxury so distinguished that a new word (ritzy) had to be invented for it. Recent improvements include an eighteen-meter swimming pool, a squash court, a gym and a heliport on the roof. Restaurant (see L'Espadon, first arrondissement); grill; several bars; summer terrace.

Royal Saint-Honoré

13, rue d'Alger - 42.60.32.79

Open year-round. 1 ste 1,200F. 77 rms 597-754F. TV. Pets allowed. Telex 680429. Cards: V, AE, DC, MC.

The Royal Saint-Honoré offers excellent, comfortable, quite peaceful rooms; those located on the upper floors have pleasant balconies. Bar and conference rooms on the second floor; restaurant.

Saint-James et Albany

202, rue de Rivoli - 42.60.31.60

Open year-round. 4 stes 1,500-2,000F. 203 rms 650-1,200F. TV. No pets. Garage parking. Telex 213031. Cards: V, AE, DC, MC.

Rated a "Residence-Hôtel," the Saint-James et Albany has studios, two-room apartments, suites and duplexes equipped with kitchenettes; they overlook a courtyard or an inner garden, and are perfectly quiet. Renovation should be complete on 40 of the rooms by the time you read this. There's a sauna, a bar with background music and a restaurant, Le Noailles.

Second Arrondissement

Gaillon Opéra

9, rue Gaillon - 47.42.47.74

Open year-round. 1 ste 630F. 25 rms 460-630F. TV. Pets allowed. Telex 215716. Cards: V, AE, DC.

This delightful little 26-room hotel (all have bathrooms and minibars) opened in 1983. There are plants everywhere and period furniture in an elegant setting, as well as a patio with flowers. No restaurant.

Westminster

13, rue de la Paix - 42.61.57.46

Open year-round. 20 stes 2,810-3,540F. 80 rms 1,250-1,820F. Half-board 250F (plus room). TV. Air cond. Pets allowed. Parking. Telex 680035. Cards: V, AE, DC, MC.

Recent and extensive renovation has completely transformed this charming little luxury hotel. Its lobby now is splendid and luxurious; its bar (with piano) is more than comfortable; its conference rooms are superbly equipped; and its air-conditioned rooms are impeccably modernized. Restaurant: see Le Céladon, second arrondissement.

Third Arrondissement

Pavillon de la Reine

28, pl. des Vosges - 42.77.96.40

Open year-round. 23 stes 1,100-1,800F. 30 rms 800-900F. TV. Air cond. Pets allowed. Telex 216160. Cards: V, AE, DC, MC.

The air-conditioned rooms, duplexes and suites, all equipped with marble bathrooms, are tastefully decorated; they artfully blend authentic antiques with lovely copies. They overlook either the place des Vosges and its garden or a serene inner patio filled with flowers. The utter charm of the setting almost makes up for the frosty reception. No restaurant.

Fourth Arrondissement

Les Deux Iles

59, rue St-Louis-en-l'Ile - 43.26.13.35

Open year-round. 17 rms 480-585F. TV. Pets allowed. Telex 375974.

This newly repainted hotel, like many buildings on the Ile-Saint-Louis, is a lovely seventeenth-century house. You'll sleep close to the Seine in small, pretty rooms decorated with bright Provençal fabrics. No restaurant.

Hôtel du Jeu de Paume

54, rue St-Louis-en-l'Ile - 43.26.14.18
Open year-round. 9 apts 1,200-1,500F. 23 rms 650-820F. TV. Pets allowed. Cards: V, AE, DC.

This is a seventeenth-century residence with a splendid wood and stone interior, and featuring a glass elevator to the rooms. There is a sunny little garden, and light food is available.

Lutèce

65, rue St-Louis-en-l'Ile - 43.26.23.52
Open year-round. 23 rms 480-620F. TV. No pets. Telex 375974.

A tasteful, small hotel for the lovers of Paris, this handsome old house has some twenty rooms with whitewashed walls, wooden ceiling beams and lovely bright fabrics. The bathrooms are small but modern and impeccable. No restaurant.

Saint-Louis

75, rue St-Louis-en-l'Ile - 46.34.04.80
Open year-round. 21 rms 410-510F.

The simple but stylish rooms of this delightful house (in which an elevator has recently been installed) have been freshly repainted and furnished with new beds and flowered drapes. The modern bathrooms have attractive blue-gray and brown tiles. No restaurant.

Fifth Arrondissement

Colbert

7, rue de l'Hôtel-Colbert - 43.25.85.65
Open year-round. 2 stes 1,200-1,450F. 38 rms 500-790F. TV. No pets. Telex 260690. Cards: V, AE.

Nearly half the rooms in this aristocratic eighteenth-century house look out upon Notre-Dame through their small-paned windows. The rooms are small and quite simply decorated; the bar, while large, is somewhat boring. The hotel was completely renovated in 1988. No restaurant.

Hôtel du Collège de France

7, rue Thénard - 43.26.78.36
Open year-round. 2 stes 870-970F. 25 rms 420-450F. TV. No pets. Cards: AE.

The simple rooms of Hôtel du Collège de France, located on a quiet little street, are wallpapered in light brown or green tones; the most pleasant of them, located on the sixth floor, have wooden beams, half-timberings and a view of the towers of Notre-Dame. No restaurant.

Le Jardin des Plantes

5, rue Linné - 47.07.06.20
Open year-round. 33 rms 300-490F. TV. Pets allowed. Telex 203684. Cards: V, AE, DC, MC.

This hotel, facing the Cuvier fountain, has appealing, delightfully decorated brand-new rooms. On the sixth floor, the flower-filled terrace overlooks the Jardin des Plantes. No restaurant.

Sixth Arrondissement

Abbaye Saint-Germain

10, rue Cassette - 45.44.38.11
Open year-round. 4 stes 1,200-1,400F. 44 rms 600-800F. No pets.

Set back from the street, this serene hotel located between a courtyard and a garden has charming, elegantly decorated rooms; the most delightful ones are on the same level as the garden. No restaurant.

Angleterre

44, rue Jacob - 42.60.34.72
Open year-round. 3 stes 660-730F. 26 rms 500-660F. TV. No pets. Cards: V, AE, DC.

Hemingway once lived in this former British Embassy building, which surrounds a patio decorated with flowers. Its impeccable rooms have been completely renovated; some are quite spacious, with high wood-beamed ceilings, and you'll sleep soundly in the immense beds. Luxurious bathrooms. There is a brand-new bar, as well as salon (with piano).

Aramis Saint-Germain

124, rue de Rennes - 45.48.03.75
Open year-round. 42 rms 375-600F. TV. No pets. Telex 205098. Cards: V, AE, DC.

These new, well-soundproofed and delightfully decorated rooms have soft lighting, modern equipment and perfect bathrooms. The service is especially attentive; room service (for breakfast) is available at all hours. No restaurant.

Danemark

21, rue Vavin - 43.26.93.78
Open year-round. 15 rms 500-630F. TV. Air cond. Telex 202568. Cards: V, AE, DC.

This small hotel, located in front of the rue Vavin's famous bathhouse, was completely renovated in 1987. Its refined, modern rooms have pleasant lighting, elegant wood furniture and gray marble bathrooms. Breakfast is served in the lovely cellar. No restaurant.

L'Hôtel

13, rue des Beaux-Arts - 43.25.27.22
Open year-round. 2 stes 2,300-2,700F. 25 rms 850-1,700F. TV. Air cond. Pets allowed. Telex 270870. Cards: V, AE, DC.

The little effort given to renovation explains the slightly faded character of the rooms in this delightful Directoire-style building—whether it's the room once occupied by Oscar Wilde, the Imperial room (decorated in a neo-Egyptian style), the Cardinale room (in purple and violet) or that once occupied by Mistinguett (on the fourth floor), which contains the art deco furniture from her Bougival home. The seventh floor houses two lovely suites. In the piano bar (open from 7:30 p.m. to 1 a.m.), you are sure to find a congenial clientele. Restaurant: see Le Bélier, sixth arrondissement.

Latitudes Saint-Germain

7-11, rue St-Benoît - 42.61.53.53

Open year-round. 117 rms 540-700F. TV. Pets allowed. Telex 213531. Cards: V, AE, DC, MC.

This spacious hotel, just opened in 1987, is located in the heart of Saint-Germain-des-Prés; it used to be a printing shop, and its gracious turn-of-the-century facade has been preserved. The large rooms are well equipped, elegant and part of a matchless setting designed, in the words of the management "for a charming stay amid the chic et choc of Paris." The shock is the list of extra charges, but the charming chic is real, except for the lax reception and pretentious piano bar. No restaurant.

Lutétia

45, blvd. Raspail - 45.44.38.10

Open year-round. 18 stes 2,200-2,800F. 275 rms 840-1,600F. TV. Air cond. in 150 rms. Pets allowed. Parking. Telex 270424. Cards: V, AE, DC, MC.

Sonya Rykiel has given the Lutétia a brand-new retro look. The twelve banquet rooms, bearing extremely pompous names ("Babylone," "Pompéi"), range from the very small to the very large and are decorated in gold, gray and purple tones with art deco frescoes and period chandeliers. As for the rooms, most of them have also been given a completely fresh look in the art deco style. Restaurants: see Brasserie Lutétia and Paris, sixth arrondissement.

Les Marronniers

21, rue Jacob - 43.25.30.60, 43.29.88.10

Open year-round. 37 rms 285-455F. No pets.

Set back a bit from the rue Jacob, this hotel has a small garden where breakfast is served. Chose a room just above this garden, or one of the rather bizarre but absolutely delightful (and bright) attic rooms on the seventh floor, which have views of the belfry of Saint-Germain-des-Prés. No restaurant.

Odéon Hôtel

3, rue de l'Odéon - 43.25.90.67

Open year-round. 34 rms 550-700F. TV. No pets. Telex 202943. Cards: V, AE, DC.

The highly rated Odéon Hôtel, located on a small, strategic street between the Odéon theater and the square of the same name, has some 30 rather small but appealing and well-equipped rooms (all have marble bathrooms). No restaurant.

Perreyve

63, rue Madame - 45.48.35.01

Open year-round. 30 rms 248-350F. TV. No pets. Telex 205080. Cards: V, AE.

Near the Luxembourg Garden and its foliage, the 30 comfortable rooms of the Perreyve have small but spotless bathrooms. There is a small provincial salon on the main floor. No restaurant.

Relais Christine

3, rue Christine - 43.26.71.80

Open year-round. 13 stes 1,150-1,700F. 38 rms 980F. TV. Air cond. Telex 202606. Cards: V, AE, DC, MC.

This sixteenth-century cloister was transformed into a luxury hotel in the early 1980s. Its spacious, comfortable, quiet rooms (all air conditioned) include marble bathrooms. Courteous reception. No restaurant.

Relais Saint-Germain

9, carrefour de l'Odéon - 43.29.12.05

Open year-round. 1 ste 1,595F. 9 rms 935-1,155F. TV. Air cond. Pets allowed. Telex 201889. Cards: V, AE, DC, MC.

About ten large rooms, all different from one another, are marvelously decorated in a refined and luxurious manner, with superb furniture, lovely fabrics, exquisite lighting and beautiful, perfectly equipped marble bathrooms. The tall, double-glazed windows open onto the lively Odéon intersection. You'll surely fall in love with Paris here. No restaurant.

Rennes-Montparnasse

151 bis, rue de Rennes
45.48.97.38, 45.48.85.02

Closed Aug. 41 rms 340-430F. TV. Pets allowed. Telex 250048. Cards: V, AE, DC, MC.

A small, modern, well-located and well-maintained hotel. Its rooms at the back (about ten) are perfectly quiet, but those on the rue de Rennes are rather noisy. Excellent equipment (such as the individual safes). No restaurant.

Sainte-Beuve

9, rue Ste-Beuve - 45.48.20.07

Open year-round. 1 ste 1,300F. 22 rms 600-1,000F. TV. No pets. Telex 270182. Cards: V, AE.

Sainte-Beuve's quite pleasant rooms (especially the attic rooms on the seventh floor) are fairly well decorated (lovely furniture and fabrics, but what ugly carpets!). Lots of comfort; fine equipment; delicious breakfasts. No restaurant.

Victoria Palace

6, rue Blaise-Desgoffe - 45.44.38.16

Open year-round. 110 rms 585-780F. TV. No pets. Telex 270557. Cards: V, AE, DC, MC.

This is a decorous, elegant and intimate little luxury hotel. Above its immense lobby, you'll find quiet rooms with double-glazed windows and flowered wallpaper; all have attractive bathrooms in beige, pink or black marble. Bar and restaurant.

Welcome Hôtel

66, rue de Seine - 46.34.24.80

Open year-round. 30 rms 225-380F. No pets.

You can almost forget the intersection of the nearby boulevard Saint-Germain behind the quiet-enhancing double windows in these small, bright, tidy rooms. If you want a taste of the bohemian life, you'll find it on the seventh floor (you can take the elevator!) under the wooden beams in the attic. No restaurant.

Seventh Arrondissement

Duc de Saint-Simon

14, rue St-Simon - 45.48.35.66

Open year-round. 5 stes 1,100-1,250F. 24 rms 700-1,000F. No pets. Telex 203277.

Back from the street and between two gardens, sits this quiet, elegant building from the nineteenth century. Redone and modernized a few years ago, it features exposed beams and period furniture, as well as a pleasant bar downstairs. No restaurant.

Elysées-Maubourg

35, blvd. de Latour-Maubourg
45.56.10.78

Open year-round. 2 stes 700F. 28 rms 450-650F. TV. Air cond. Pets allowed. Telex 206227. Cards: V, AE, DC, MC.

The 30 brand-new rooms are decorated without much originality, but they are superbly equipped and very comfortable. There is a Finnish sauna and a cafeteria in the basement, as well as a bar and a small flower-filled patio. No restaurant.

Les Jardins d'Eiffel

8, rue Amélie - 47.05.46.21

Open year-round. 5 stes 800-1,100F. 34 rms 400-590F. TV. No pets. Garage parking. Telex 206582. Cards: V, AE, DC.

The small, cozy, well-soundproofed rooms were redone in 1986; they include outstanding equipment (hair dryers, individual safes, color TVs, minibars...). Convenient individual parking spaces are provided; there is also a small but charming inner garden. Many services. No restaurant.

Lenox

9, rue de l'Université - 42.96.10.95

Open year-round. 2 stes 780F. 32 rms 395-550F. TV. No pets. Telex 260745. Cards: V, AE, DC, MC.

These petite but most attractive rooms were recently renovated with elegant wallpaper and stylish furniture; numbers 22, 32 and 42 are the most enchanting. The top floor includes two duplexes with exposed beams and flower-filled balconies. No restaurant.

Montalembert

3, rue de Montalembert
45.48.68.11, 45.48.61.59

Open year-round. 61 rms 560-780F. TV in 15 rms. Pets allowed. Telex 200132. Cards: AE, MC.

An intelligent management is discreetly modernizing this old eight-story townhouse; it regularly renews the upholstery and carpeting in the rooms, all the while preserving the lovely 1930s style. The bar (Le Décameron) is the rendezvous of the top Paris publishers. The guests include many Americans and Italians, along with writers from everywhere; some of them seem almost to have made the Montalembert their permanent residence. No restaurant.

Pont-Royal

7, rue de Montalembert - 45.44.38.27

Open year-round. 5 stes 1,900-3,000F. 75 rms 760-1,300F. TV. Air cond. Pets allowed. Telex 270113. Cards: V, AE, DC, MC.

Business types and movie actors have taken over the rather spacious and classic (but not terribly attractive) rooms where writers—from Faulkner to Sagan—once stayed. On the ninth floor, three rooms have terraces with views of all of Paris. Restaurant.

Saint-Dominique

62, rue St-Dominique - 47.05.51.44

Open year-round. 35 rms 350-490F. TV. Pets allowed. Telex 206968. Cards: V, AE, DC, MC.

The most modest of the three "Centre Ville" hotels is also the most charming, and the location is excellent. Its rooms are delightful, homey and comfortable. No restaurant.

Sofitel Paris Invalides

32, rue St-Dominique - 45.55.91.80

Open year-round. 4 stes 2,900F. 108 rms 1,170-1,430F. TV. Air cond. Pets allowed. Parking. Telex 250019. Cards: V, AE, DC, MC.

Located behind the Palais-Bourbon, this is an intelligently designed hotel of modest dimensions and sober decor. All the rooms, renovated in the summer of 1987, have soft lighting and agreeably functional furniture. Restaurant: see Le Dauphin, seventh arrondissement.

Solférino

91, rue de Lille - 47.05.85.54

Closed Dec. 23-Jan. 3. 1 ste 535F. 32 rms 227-535F. TV in 15 rms. No pets. Telex 203865. Cards: V.

Simple rooms with fresh colors, a lovely little salon, a balcony where breakfast is served and charming ornaments everywhere: The Solférino is both relaxing and pleasantly antiquated. Friendly reception. No restaurant.

Suède

31, rue Vaneau
47.05.18.65, 47.05.00.08

Open year-round. 1 ste 850F. 40 rms 441-693F. TV in 5 rms. No pets. Telex 200596. Cards: V, AE, MC.

The Suède offers attractive Empire-style rooms and one soberly and pleasantly decorated suite. From the fourth floor and up you'll have a view of the foliage and the parties given in the Matignon gardens. No restaurant, but there is a bar and a snack service from 6:30 a.m. to 10 p.m.

Varenne

44, rue de Bourgogne - 45.51.45.55

Open year-round. 24 rms 370-500F. TV. Pets allowed. Telex 205329. Cards: V, AE.

You have to make reservations well ahead of time for the pleasure of staying in one of the flower-filled rooms at this provincial little hotel, which includes an attractive salon and a delightful patio where breakfast is served on sunny days. No restaurant.

Eighth Arrondissement

Alison

21, rue de Surène - 42.65.54.00

Open year-round. 35 rms 330-560F. TV. No pets. Telex 640435. Cards: V, AE, DC, MC.

The 35 modern, functional rooms, as well as the lobby with its deep leather sofas and the breakfast room in the basement, are all decorated in orange, beige and brown tones. Impeccable bathrooms. No restaurant.

Astor

11, rue d'Astorg - 42.66.56.56

Open year-round. 128 rms 740-840F. TV. Telex 642737. Cards: V, AE, DC, MC.

Marble, dark oak woodwork, inviting leather sofas and huge vases of flowers year-round. The Astor's rooms are gorgeous, with their pale-green or beige wall hangings and stylish furniture. English bar. Restaurant: La Table de l'Astor.

Atala

10, rue Chateaubriand - 45.62.01.62

Open year-round. 2 stes 1,050F. 47 rms 650-870F. TV. Pets allowed. Telex 640576. Cards: V, AE, DC.

The cheerfully decorated rooms and suites open onto a garden and offer perfect comfort and new marble bathrooms. L'Atalante, the bar and restaurant, is also open to visitors. Excellent service.

Hôtel Balzac

6, rue Balzac - 45.61.97.22

Open year-round. 14 stes 2,500-5,000F. 56 rms 1,250-1,600F. TV. Air cond. Pets allowed. Parking. Telex 290298. Cards: V, AE, DC, MC.

One of the most recently opened little hotels in Paris, the Balzac has 70 rooms and suites that have been completely renovated and are spacious, quiet and discreet. Their soft pastel decor, their well-designed lighting, their comfortable furniture and their roomy beds ensure a truly lovely stay. The service is flawless.

Beverley Hills

75, rue de Berri - 43.59.55.55

Open year-round. 10 stes 9,400-30,000F (per week). TV. Parking. Telex 643868. Cards: V, AE, DC, MC.

This is a residence designed for Texas millionaires and sheiks: total electronic surveillance, huge apartments with dining rooms and all imaginable amenities. Piano bar and restaurant.

Bradford

10, rue St-Philippe-du-Roule
43.59.24.20

Open year-round. 2 stes 650F. 46 rms 480-570F. No pets. Parking. Telex 648530. Cards: V.

The large, bright rooms are meticulously clean and often pleasantly furnished; the staff is discreet and efficient; and there is a comfortable little Louis XVI salon. Four more rooms with showers were being built at the time of this writing. No restaurant.

Le Bristol

112, rue du Fg-St-Honoré - 42.66.91.45

Open year-round. 45 stes 4,400-7,685F. 155 rms 1,380-2,330F. TV. Air cond. Heated pool. No pets. Parking. Telex 280961. Cards: V, AE, DC, MC.

The elegance of its decor (genuine period furniture, as well as lovely imitations), the comfort of its rooms, the luxury of its suites and the quality of its clientele make Le Bristol one of the rare authentic luxury hotels in Paris (as well as one of the most expensive). There are ultra-modern conference rooms, a small heated swimming pool on the seventh-floor terrace and extremely spacious rooms with magnificent marble bathrooms and superb Louis XVth– and Louis XVIth–style furniture. An extraordinary restaurant (Le Bristol) opens onto the lawn and the flowers of a large garden. The staff is both cordial and impressively trained.

California

16, rue de Berri - 43.59.93.00

Open year-round. 3 stes 1,800-2,500F. 176 rms 860-1,230F. TV. Telex 660634.

The management has recently and successfuly turned this place around. The rooms are redone in extremely good taste, and open onto a quiet patio. Ornately frescoed restaurant.

Château Frontenac

54, rue Pierre-Charron - 47.23.55.85

Open year-round. 4 stes 1,000-1,200F. 99 rms 680-760F. TV. No pets. Parking. Telex 660994. Cards: V, DC, MC.

An excellent hotel whose rooms have been redecorated in either a classic or modern style, with a great deal of care taken to ensure their comfort and privacy. The soundproofing is good, but the rooms overlooking the rue Cérisole are still the quietest. Restaurant: Le Pavillon Russe.

Claridge-Bellman

37, rue François-Ier - 47.23.54.42

Open year-round. 42 rms 550-1,150F. TV. No pets. Telex 641150. Cards: V, AE, DC.

Though rather small (only some 40 rooms), the Bellman has made the best possible use of the lovely decor—paintings, precious ornaments, antique furniture—it inherited from the Claridge. Its pleasant rooms are soundproofed by double windows. The smaller attic rooms (on the seventh floor) are delightful.

Colisée

6, rue du Colisée - 43.59.95.25

Open year-round. 44 rms 430-630F. TV. Air cond. in 11 rms. Pets allowed. Telex 643101. Cards: V, AE, DC, MC.

Half the rooms were redecorated in 1988. Those whose numbers end with an "8" are more spacious than the others; the attic rooms on the top floor have wooden beams. There's a salon/bar but no restaurant.

Concorde Saint-Lazare

108, rue St-Lazare
42.94.22.22, 42.93.01.20

Open year-round. 324 rms 650-1,500F. TV. Pets allowed. Parking. Telex 650442. Cards: V, AE, DC, MC.

Slavik and Sonya Rykiel have combined their talents to restore the spacious lobby (it's on the list of Historical Monuments) and the billiard room (ten tables), which has been redone in a retro style. The result: a hotel that offers modern comforts without sacrificing tradition. Large bathrooms. American bar. Restaurant: see Café Terminus, eighth arrondissement.

Hôtel de Crillon

10, pl. de la Concorde - 42.65.24.24

Open year-round. 41 stes 3,500-15,000F. 148 rms 1,600-2,000F. Half-board 350F (plus room). TV. Air cond. Pets allowed. Parking. Telex 290204. Cards: V, AE, DC, MC.

The Crillon is the last of the Parisian luxury hotels to have remained authentically French: with its inner courtyards; terraces overlooking the most beautiful square in the world; superb salons; rooms that, though not always immense or well soundproofed, are exquisitely decorated; and the most beautiful suites one could hope for. Their windows overlook the place de la Concorde or the rue Boissy-d'Anglas, and bathrooms are completely redone in marble. Let's not forget the well-trained staff. Yes, the Hôtel de Crillon has reestablished its link with the elegant and intimate ambience of years past (Louis XVIth–style furniture, silk drapes, pastel walls and woodwork ornamented with gold leaf, well-hidden minibars). Relais et Châteaux. Restaurants: see Les Ambassadeurs and L'Obélisque, eighth arrondissement.

George V

31, ave. George-V - 47.23.54.00

Open year-round. 59 stes 2,950-11,380F. 292 rms 1,640-2,590F. TV. Air cond. Pets allowed. Parking. Telex 650082. Cards: V, AE, DC, MC.

The new management has succeeded perfectly in instilling new life and spirit into this "monument in decline." The bar and the restaurant (Les Princes; both open onto a delightful patio) have been redecorated, and the rooms have been renovated with as much concern for the elegance of the decor as for the modernism of the comfort (electronic panels located at the head of the beds allow guests to close the venetian shutters, control both the television and the air conditioning, call room service and so on). The lounges and the corridors, however, are faded, dull and depressing, and need attention. There are some precious objects (such as an admirable Regency clock), paintings (*Vase of Roses* by Renoir) and tapestries (from Flanders) estimated by Sotheby to be worth some 40 million francs. These and the elevator, with its plate glass, and the Galerie de la Paix, with its red and black marble, still radiate that George V charm. Perfect reception; attentive floor service. Restaurant: see Les Princes, eighth arrondissement.

Lancaster

7, rue de Berri - 43.59.90.43

Open year-round. 8 stes 2,990-6,325F. 51 rms 1,380-2,070F. TV. Air cond in 30 rms. Pets allowed. Parking. Telex 640991. Cards: V, AE, DC, MC.

Once you recover from the immense, breathtaking bouquet of flowers in the lobby, you'll notice that the general setting—furniture, draperies, paintings, ornaments—isn't really as refined and luxurious as you would wish. The small inner garden, with its flowers, fountains and statues (meals are served there on sunny days), lends an unexpected rural touch to this hotel located only a few steps from the Champs-Elysées. The rooms and suites all have period furniture and double windows; the decor, on the whole, is like something out of an interior design magazine. Excellent reception; attentive and punctual service. The small conference rooms have fine modern equipment.

Marriott Prince de Galles

33, ave. Georges-V - 47.23.55.11

Open year-round. 30 stes 2,800-5,500F. 141 rms 1,400-2,200F. TV. Air cond. No pets. Parking. Telex 280627. Cards: V, AE, DC, MC.

A coldly distinguished, Empire-style establishment rich in draperies and signed furniture. The rooms are decorated in a variety of styles (the finest ones are those furnished in a contemporary or 1930s style, with mosaic-tile retro bathrooms); their old fireplaces have been preserved, so you can treat yourself to the luxury of a fire in winter. Others have delightful balconies ideal for breakfast. Individual air conditioning; efficient soundproofing; video programs. Flowered terraces and pleasant patios. Restaurant: Le Panache.

Napoléon

40, ave. de Friedland - 47.66.02.02

Open year-round. 38 stes 1,290-3,350F. 102 rms 550-1,290F. TV. Pets allowed. Parking. Telex 640609. Cards: V, AE, DC, MC.

The decor is Empire style, and the comfort, equipment and service are all impeccable. The large rooms have a classic though not very cheerful decor. The pleasant banquet rooms (L'Etoile, for example) are much in demand for receptions and conferences.

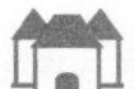

Plaza Athénée

25, ave. Montaigne - 47.23.78.33

Open year-round. 42 stes 4,950-8,240F. 220 rms 1,750-3,740F. TV. Air cond. Pets allowed. Parking. Telex 290082. Cards: V, AE, DC, MC.

At the Plaza, one finds nothing but discretion, efficiency and friendly courtesy. The rooms and suites are bright, generous in size and stocked with every available (or about-to-be-made- available) piece of hotel equipment. The rooms overlooking avenue Montaigne are perfectly soundproofed. At about 11 a.m., the guests staying here gather in the bar (where Mata Hari was arrested); and, from 4 p.m. to 7 p.m. in particular, you'll see them in the gallery (of which Marlene Dietrich was particularly fond). Two restaurants, Le Relais and Le Régence, are located just across from the wonderful patio, where tables are set in the summer among cascades of geraniums and ampelopsis vines. Dry cleaning services are provided, as well as a beauty salon, Dow Jones agency and so on.

Pullman Saint-Honoré

15, rue Boissy d'Anglas - 42.66.93.62

Open year-round. 1 ste 1,015F. 111 rms 560-730F. TV. Pets allowed. Telex 240366. Cards: V, AE, DC, MC.

Comfortable, luxurious and functional: This well-renovated hotel consists of seven stories of identically furnished, pleasant, modern rooms with impeccable bathrooms. Seven duplexes are located on the seventh floor; there is one suite on the eighth floor. The bar is open from 10 a.m. to 2 a.m. No restaurant.

Pullman Windsor

14, rue Beaujon - 45.63.04.04

Open year-round. 6 stes 1,950-2,200F. 129 rms 800-1,650F. TV. Air cond. Pets allowed. Parking. Telex 650902. Cards: V, AE, DC, MC.

This solid, austere building (built in 1925) hides a remarkably comfortable hotel, whose facilities (ultra-modern equipment for the business clientele) are constantly being improved. The rather large, bright rooms include sober, functional furniture (with minibars, color TVs and video programming). Room service. Restaurant: see Clovis, eighth arrondissement.

Résidence Maxim's de Paris

42, ave. Gabriel - 45.61.96.33

Open year-round. 39 stes 3,000-20,000F. 4 rms 1,800-2,000F. TV. Air cond. Pets allowed. Parking. Telex 642794. Cards: V, AE, DC.

Pierre Cardin himself designed the hotel of his dreams: He completely remodeled the interior of this bourgeois building opening onto the gardens of the Champs-Elysées. And the result is the most radically luxurious hotel created in Paris in a very, very long time. Needless to say, the rates of this little wonder deliberately exceed the means of most mortals. Restaurant.

Résidence Monceau

85, rue du Rocher - 45.22.75.11

Open year-round. 1 ste 760F. 50 rms 514-546F. TV. No pets. Telex 280671. Cards: V, AE, DC.

The Résidence Monceau opened in the summer of 1987 following a complete renovation. All its rooms have private bathrooms (with excellent equipment), color TVs, minibars and automatic alarm clocks. Good privacy; breakfast is served on a patio. No restaurant.

Royal Monceau

35-39, ave. Hoche - 45.61.98.00

Open year-round. 33 stes 3,600-12,000F. 186 stes 1,750-2,550F. TV. Air cond. Heated pool. Pets allowed. Parking. Telex 650361. Cards: V, AE, DC, MC.

The atmosphere is quite Parisian at this respectable, discreetly elegant palace, given refinement with a certain moderation. The rooms are brilliantly decorated and have magnificent marble bathrooms. Extras include a fashionable piano bar, a spacious health club (the Thermes du Royal Monceau, which has a sauna, Jacuzzi, swimming pool and massage), outstanding ultra-modern conference rooms and a well-equipped "business club." The rooms overlooking the charming flowered patio are the most sought after by the hotel's habitués. Two restaurants: see Le Carpaccio and Le Jardin, eighth arrondissement.

San Régis

12, rue Jean-Goujon - 43.59.41.90

Open year-round. 10 stes 2,000-3,600F. 34 rms 1,000-2,000F. TV. Air cond. No pets. Telex 643637. Cards: V, AE, DC.

This exquisite hotel, one of the most luxurious in Paris, was totally renovated and modernized in 1986. It boasts splendid period furniture, delicate fabrics, a discreet and refined decor, sumptuous bathrooms and lots of space, light and character. The staff is irreproachable. Restaurant.

La Trémoille

14, rue de La Trémoille - 47.23.34.20

Open year-round. 14 stes 2,070-5,290F. 97 rms 1,230-2,200F. TV. Pets allowed. Parking. Telex 640344. Cards: V, AE, DC, MC.

Cozy comfort, antique furniture, luxurious bathrooms, balconies filled with flowers and service worthy of a grand hotel. Several duplexes are brand new and remarkably comfortable. There is a delightful dining room/salon that's heated by a wood fire in winter. Restaurant.

Warwick

5, rue de Berri - 45.63.14.11

Open year-round. 4 stes 3,150-7,300F. 144 rms 1,500-1,980F. TV. Air cond. Pets allowed. Parking. Telex 642295. Cards: V, AE, DC, MC.

A new hotel whose bright, spacious rooms are designed more for relaxing and living in than for a quick stopover. Efficient soundproofing and air conditioning. There is an attractive bar with piano music in the evening and pleasant rooftop terraces. Room service 24 hours a day. Restaurant: see La Couronne, eighth arrondissement.

Ninth Arrondissement

Ambassador-Concorde

16, blvd. Haussman - 42.46.92.63

Open year-round. 7 stes. 298 rms 650-1,500F. Half-board 135F (plus room). TV. Air cond. in 50 rms. Pets allowed. /Parking. Telex 650912. Cards: V, AE, DC, MC.

Several rooms are ultra-modern, but most have been renovated in a fine retro style that better suits this establishment—they include painted wooden beds, lovely green and gold wallpaper and antique furniture. There is a hair salon for men and women in the hotel, as well as a gift shop and restaurant.

Bergère

34, rue Bergère - 47.70.34.34

Open year-round. 136 rms 380-660F. TV. Telex 290668. Cards: V, AE, DC, MC.

All the rooms (most of which overlook a courtyard garden) have been freshened up and modernized, including the bathrooms. The setting is modern and simple. Fine equipment.

Commodore

12, blvd. Haussman - 42.46.72.82

Open year-round. 11 stes 1,250-1,800F. 151 rms 650-1,150F. TV. Pets allowed. Telex 280601. Cards: V, AE, DC, MC.

This excellent traditional hotel is located a few steps away from the new Drouot auction house and its parking lot. All its rooms are decorated in a 1930s style (which is when the hotel was built). Remarkable and attentive service. Restaurant: Le Carvery.

Corona

8, cité Bergère - 47.50.52.96

Open year-round. 4 stes 780F. 56 rms 450-550F. TV. Pets allowed. Telex 281081. Cards: V, AE, DC.

In a handsome complex of 1930s-era buildings (all renovated) on the cité Bergère, these lovely, hospitable rooms include elegant gnarled-elm furniture and an unsurpassable view of the artists' entrance to the Théâtre des Nouveautés. No restaurant.

Grand Hôtel

2, rue Scribe - 42.68.12.13

Open year-round. 33 stes 3,500-7,150F. 482 rms 1,160-1,740F. TV. Air cond. Pets allowed. Parking. Telex 220875. Cards: V, AE, DC, MC.

The renovation of this grand hotel, built in 1862, is now complete (it follows the gorgeous work done on the Café de la Paix and the Opéra restaurant, which was decorated by Garnier). In the past ten years, this monumental Second Empire structure has recovered all the luster it had had when Empress Eugénie, on the arm of the banker Pereire, opened it—along with the additional comfort of the most contemporary equipment available, offices for business people, superb relaxation rooms, ultra-modern conference rooms, a sauna and much more. Excellent bar. Restaurant: see Opéra Restaurant, ninth arrondissement.

Hôtel Moulin Rouge

39, rue Fontaine - 42.81.93.25

Open year-round. 3 stes 650-800F. 47 rms 370-540F. TV. Pets allowed. Telex 660055. Cards: V, AE, DC.

A hotel full of charm and surprises, with its seductive Pompeiian-style lobby and large rooms (some of them are extended by a small terrace overlooking the inner courtyards). An excellent buffet-style breakfast is served until noon. No restaurant.

A red hotel ranking denotes a place with charm.

Royal Médoc

14, rue Geoffroy-Marie - 47.70.37.33

Open year-round. 41 rms 480-530F. TV. No pets. Telex 660053. Cards: V, AE, DC.

Ten minutes away from the Opéra and close to the main boulevards, this modern, functional building (with direct telephone lines and a multilingual staff) near the Bourse (the Stock Exchange) is perfect for international business types. No restaurant.

Scribe

1, rue Scribe - 47.42.03.40

Open year-round. 11 stes 3,200-5,000F. 206 rms 1,330-2,200F. TV. Air cond. Pets allowed. Parking. Telex 214653. Cards: V, AE, DC, MC.

The Scribe's Napoléon III facade is contemporary with the Palais Garnier, but its lobby, salons, bar, dining room (in the basement) and all six floors were completely redone several years ago. The rooms, suites and duplexes (with high ceilings; they include a room on the terrace, a living room that also serves as a dining room/office, a bathroom, dressing room and two entrances), are uniformly decorated in a lovely ocher and China red. The rooms on the street have double windows and either contemporary or Louis XVIth–style furniture; the ones on the courtyard are furnished with Louis-Philippe-style pieces and offer perfect tranquillity. All have color TVs and video programming. Room service is available 24 hours a day. Restaurants: see Les Muses, ninth arrondissement.

La Tour d'Auvergne

10, rue de La Tour d'Auvergne
48.78.61.50

Open year-round. 25 rms 300-480F. TV. No pets. Telex 281604.

This hotel was entirely renovated in 1986, each room with a decor from a different period; all are furnished with four-poster beds and double-glazed windows. A fine little establishment. Restaurant.

Tenth Arrondissement

Urbis Paris Jemmapes

12, rue Louis-Blanc - 42.01.21.21

Open year-round. 1 ste 700-1,100F. 48 rms 359-430F. TV. Pets allowed. Telex 211734. Cards: V, MC.

This brand-new business hotel is well designed and perfectly tailored for a busy clientele attending conventions and seminars. Its slightly chilly rooms are modernly and soberly decorated. Excellent equipment and generous breakfasts. No restaurant.

Eleventh Arrondissement

Holiday Inn République

10, pl. de la République - 43.55.44.34
Open year-round. 7 stes. 333 rms 950-1,200F. TV. Air cond. Pets allowed. Parking. Telex 210651. Cards: V, AE, DC, MC.

The architect Davioud, who designed the Châtelet, built this former Modern Palace in 1866. Today it belongs to the largest hotel chain in the world, which completely restored and modernized it in 1982. The rooms and suites are functional, pleasant and well soundproofed; the most attractive ones overlook the floral inner courtyard. Pleasant brasserie (with dinner-dancing); piano bar.

Twelfth Arrondissement

Le Cours de Vincennes

61, rue de la Voute - 43.45.41.38
Open year-round. 12 stes 700F. 35 rms 435F. TV. Pets allowed. Telex 215050. Cards: V, AE, DC, MC.

A brand-new, delightful little hotel with comfortable and well-furnished modern rooms.

Nouvel Hôtel

24, ave. du Bel-Air - 43.43.01.81
Open year-round. 28 rms 250-450F. TV in 22 rms. Pets allowed. Telex 240139. Cards: V, AE, DC.

The rooms of the Nouvel Hôtel are serene and attractive (the loveliest is number nine, on the same level as the garden). A pleasant little piano room is ornamented with a 1920s frieze. Inviting patio with flowers. No restaurant.

Novotel Bercy

85, rue de Bercy - 43.42.30.00
Open year-round. 1 ste 900F. 130 rms 530-560F. TV. Air cond. Pets allowed. Cards: V, AE, DC, MC.

This all-glass structure, right next door to the big Bercy arena, has handicapped access, bar and restaurant.

Le Zéphyr

31 bis, blvd. Diderot - 43.46.12.72
Open year-round. 52 rms 320-440F. TV. Air cond. No pets. Telex 216398. Cards: AE, DC, MC.

This charming new hotel, painted all in white, has been renovated in the art deco style. It offers quite pleasant, well-equipped rooms, as well as conference rooms. Restaurant.

Thirteenth Arrondissement

Mercure Paris-Bercy

6, blvd V.-Auriol - 45.82.48.00
Open year-round. 1 ste 960F. 87 rms 470-530F. TV. Pets allowed. Parking. Telex 205010. Cards: V, AE, DC, MC.

Just across the Seine from the new Finance ministry at Bercy, this is one of the chain's newest branches. Good-size rooms, pretty enough, are well-insulated; some have terraces. Bar open until midnight, and restaurant.

Fourteenth Arrondissement

Lenox

15, rue Delambre - 43.35.34.50
Open year-round. 6 stes 800F. 46 rms 380-490F. TV. No pets. Telex 260745. Cards: V, AE, DC, MC.

Everything is spanking new inside the Lenox, a three-year-old hotel in the heart of Montparnasse; its suites and rooms are bright and cheerful. There is no restaurant, but light meals are served at the bar until 2 a.m.

Méridien Montparnasse

19, rue du Cdt-Mouchotte - 43.20.15.51
Open year-round. 30 stes 2,750-4,500F. 920 rms 950-1,050F. TV. Air cond. Pets allowed. Parking. Telex 200135. Cards: V, AE, DC, MC.

This hotel, crammed with lush plants and shrubbery, is decorated in a handsome, modern style. The functional rooms are comfortable and pleasant (though their ceilings are low and the corridors seem endless). Three restaurants; bar; boutiques.

Pullman Saint-Jacques

17, blvd. St-Jacques - 45.89.89.80
Open year-round. 14 stes 1,345-1,515F. 786 rms 905-1,012F. TV. Air cond. Pets allowed. Telex 270740. Cards: V, AE, DC, MC.

The Pullman Saint-Jacques is the Parisian mega-hotel closest to Orly and Old Paris; it has 800 very small rooms with tiny but comfortable bathrooms. With its shopping galleries, nineteen conference rooms, beauty salon, entertainment (games; tours of Paris), bars and restaurants, its atmosphere is reminiscent of an airport.

Fifteenth Arrondissement

Capitol

9, rue Viala - 45.78.61.00
Open year-round. 4 stes 800F. 42 rms 420-480F. TV. Air cond. No pets. Telex 202881. Cards: V, AE.

This new hotel with its white stone facade offers cleverly arranged, eminently comfortable rooms, all decorated with muted fabrics and modern gray wood furniture. Cordial reception. No restaurant.

Fondary

30, rue Fondary - 45.75.14.75
Open year-round. 20 rms 285-330F. TV. Telex 206761. Cards: V, AE.

An excellent neighborhood address, with rooms still almost like new (they were completely redone in 1985), which feature a pleasant pastel decor, attractive fabrics and simple bamboo furniture. Good service and pleasant salon/bar. No restaurant.

Frantour Suffren

20, rue Jean-Rey - 45.78.61.08

Open year-round. 10 stes 760-1,500F. 397 rms 455-490F. TV. Air cond. Pets allowed. Parking. Telex 204459. Cards: V, AE, DC, MC.

The Frantour Suffren is a large, modern hotel located next to the Seine and the Champ-de-Mars. Its rooms are small, but comfortable and functional. Restaurant (Le Champ-de-Mars); bar; discotheque.

Hilton

18, ave. de Suffren - 42.73.92.00

Open year-round. 9 stes 5,000-8,600F. 453 rms 1,100-1,950F. TV. Air cond. Pets allowed. Parking. Telex 200955. Cards: V, AE, DC, MC.

The first modern hotel built in Paris after the war features spacious rooms, precise and organized service, free rates for children (whatever their age, so long as they share their parents' bedroom) and cable TV. Two restaurants: Le Western, La Terrasse; two bars; beauty salon; luxury boutiques.

Holiday Inn

69, blvd. Victor - 45.33.74.63

Open year-round. 90 rms 650-1,030F. TV. Air cond. Pets allowed. Parking. Telex 260844. Cards: V, AE, DC, MC.

The well-designed, air-conditioned (with individual controls) and soundproofed rooms all offer modern comfort; their remarkable bathrooms are equipped with radios, hair dryers and magnifying mirrors. Beautifully furnished restaurant.

Nikko de Paris

61, quai de Grenelle - 45.75.62.62

Open year-round. 22 stes 3,000-9,000F. 757 rms 945-1,550F. TV. Air cond. Heated pool. Pets allowed. Parking. Telex 260012. Cards: V, AE, DC, MC.

The ceilings on the Nikko's 31 floors are pitted with small concavities, giving the hotel much the appearance of an immense beehive. You can opt either for vaguely Japanese-style or modern, ultrafunctional rooms; their large porthole windows overlook the Mirabeau bridge. On the six upper floors are the luxury "Arc-en-Ciel 61" rooms, with personalized service. Boutiques, conference rooms, heated swimming pool with sauna, gym room and massage are also available. The bar has a pleasant view. Restaurant: see Les Célébrités, fifteenth arrondissement.

Sofitel Paris

8, rue Louis-Armand - 45.54.95.00

Open year-round. 2 stes 1,400-2,100F. 633 rms 700F. TV. Air cond. Heated pool. Pets allowed. Parking. Telex 200432. Cards: V, AE, DC, MC.

Thirty-seven meeting and conference rooms (with simultaneous translation available in five languages) are connected to a central administration office. The hotel also features all sorts of recreational facilities (exercise room, sauna and a heated swimming pool with sliding roof on the 23rd floor) and a panoramic bar. The rooms, with magnetic closing systems, are modern and comfortable, though a bit tiny. Restaurant: see Le Relais de Sèvres, fifteenth arrondissement.

Sixteenth Arrondissement

Alexander

102, ave. Victor-Hugo - 45.53.64.65

Open year-round. 2 stes 1,200F. 60 rms 550-830F. TV. No pets. Telex 610373. Cards: V, AE.

This is a comfortable and peaceful establishment, with a lobby paneled in light wood and superbly equipped and furnished rooms (the ones overlooking the courtyard are especially quiet). Two suites can accommodate two, three or four people. The reception is most courteous. No restaurant.

Ambassade

79, rue Lauriston - 45.53.41.15

Open year-round. 38 rms 330-430F. TV. No pets. Telex 613643. Cards: V, AE, DC, MC.

The rooms behind a lovely facade (recently repainted), are decorated with printed wallpaper and lacquered rattan furniture and are equipped with small gray-marble bathrooms. Their double windows overlook the street. No restaurant.

Baltimore

88 bis, ave. Kléber - 45.53.83.33

Open year-round. 1 ste 1,600-2,000F. 118 rms 700-1,280F. TV. Air cond in 19 rms. Pets allowed. Telex 611591. Cards: V, AE, DC, MC.

Six fine meeting rooms are located in the basement; the largest and most luxurious is the former vault room of the Banque Nationale de Paris. The 120 comfortable rooms were completely renovated in 1985 with a sober elegance that is well suited to the district and the tastes of the clientele. Restaurant: see L'Estournel, sixteenth arrondissement.

Garden Elysée

12, rue St-Didier - 47.55.01.11

Open year-round. 48 rms 700-1,300F. TV. Air cond. No pets. Parking. Telex 648157. Cards: V, AE, DC, MC.

Located in a brand-new building set back from the street and facing a flower garden, this hotel offers elegant, unusually spacious rooms, all overlooking the garden (where breakfast is served on warm days). The decor is fresh and modern, and the equipment is particularly fine (satellite television, individual safes, Jacuzzi). No restaurant.

Kléber

7, rue de Belloy - 47.23.80.22

Open year-round. 1 ste 796-840F. 21 rms 560-645F. TV. Pets allowed. Parking. Telex 612830. Cards: V, AE, DC, MC.

This impeccable little hotel has about twenty rooms spread over six floors, all equipped with double-glazed windows and lovely bathrooms. The decor is modern but warm. There is a bar on the main floor, but no restaurant.

Majestic

29, rue Dumont-d'Urville - 45.00.83.70
Open year-round. 3 stes 1,300F-1,500F. 27 rms 630-900F. TV. Pets allowed. Telex 640034. Cards: V, AE, DC, MC.

Richly furnished rooms (some with dressing rooms) and suites in the Louis XVth and Directoire styles. All have been (or are soon to be) renovated; soundproofing and air conditioning were recently installed throughout the hotel. On the top floor, a lovely penthouse features a small balcony filled with flowers. No restaurant.

Park Avenue

55, av. R.-Poincaré - 45.53.44.60
Open year-round. 16 stes 1,000-1,800F. 89 rms 700-1,280F. TV. Air cond. Pets allowed. Parking. Telex 643862. Cards: V, AE, DC, MC.

Behind the facade of the former mansion of designer Baguès hides this all new establishment in a little corner of English countryside. Its beautiful rooms are done in a '30s style, with kitchenettes. Restaurant: Le Relais du Parc.

Passy Eiffel

10, rue de Passy - 45.25.55.66
Open year-round. 50 rms 410-500F. TV. Pets allowed. Telex 612753. Cards: V, AE, DC, MC.

Five stories of spotless, comfortable rooms (though not all equally attractive); a pleasant breakfast room faces a tiny, glassed-in inner garden. No restaurant.

Queen's Hôtel

4, rue Bastien-Lepage - 42.88.89.85
Open year-round. 22 rms 230-470F. TV. No pets. Cards: V, AE.

About twenty rather petite but delightful, modern, quiet and comfortable rooms hidden behind a lovely white facade with flower-filled balconies. Excellent reception. No restaurant.

Raphaël

17, ave. Kléber - 45.02.16.00
Open year-round. 35 stes 1,950-5,000F. 53 rms 950-1,700F. Half-board 805-1,105F. TV. Pets allowed. Telex 610356. Cards: V, AE, DC, MC.

Built during those wild years between the two world wars, the Raphaël has maintained an atmosphere of relative privacy behind its freshly repainted facade. The Oriental rugs (authentic, according to the management) strewn upon the marble floors, along with the columns, woodwork, old paintings and period furniture, make it a luxurious palace; and while it may not be particularly charming, it is tranquil. The fairly spacious rooms (all with two beds) are luxuriously furnished in various styles and are equipped with modern bathrooms, small bars, flower terraces and a view of Paris.

Résidence du Bois

16, rue Chalgrin - 45.00.50.59
Open year-round. 3 stes 1,355-2,175F. 16 rms 940-1,320F. TV. Pets allowed.

The rooms of this small Napoléon III residence, all furnished in various period styles, are larger than the ones found in modern hotels; they overlook a delightful garden. The comfort is outstanding, and the service is efficient, discreet and impeccable. No restaurant. Relais et Châteaux.

Rond-Point de Longchamp

86, rue de Longchamp - 45.05.13.63.
Open year-round. 58 rms 520-600F. TV. Air cond. Pets allowed. Telex 620653. Cards: V, AE, DC.

A decent hotel with modern rooms, double-glazed windows and an attentive reception. There is an elegant restaurant with a fireplace, as well as a billiards room.

Trocadéro

21, rue St-Didier - 45.53.01.82
Open year-round. 23 rms 405-570F. TV. Pets allowed. Telex 643164. Cards: V, AE, DC, MC.

The management of the L'Etoile hotel (see seventeenth arrondissement) also supervises this small, serene hotel, which was completely renovated in 1986. The rooms are simple but quite comfortable, and the bathrooms are well equipped (including hair dryers). No restaurant.

Seventeenth Arrondissement

Banville

166, blvd. Berthier - 42.67.70.16
Open year-round. 39 rms 450-480F. TV. Pets allowed. Telex 643025. Cards: V, AE.

A fine small hotel, with flowers decorating the window sills and bright, cheerful rooms, all of which are made soundproof with thick carpeting—even in the marble bathrooms. No restaurant.

Centre Ville Etoile

6, rue des Acacias - 43.80.56.18
Open year-round. 16 rms 450-700F. TV. Pets allowed. Telex 206968. Cards: V, AE, DC, MC.

Attractive contemporary rooms with minitels (electronic telephone directories), satellite TV and excellent bathrooms. Breakfast is served in a quiet, inviting salon. Restaurant: Le Cougar.

Concorde–La Fayette

3, pl. du Général-Koenig
45.58.12.84
Open year-round. 27 stes 2,800-5,600F. 963 rms 850-1,450F. TV. Air cond. Pets allowed. Parking. Telex 650892. Cards: V, AE, DC, MC.

The Concorde–La Fayette is immense: It includes the Palais des Congrès and its 4,500 seats; banquet rooms that can accommodate 2,000; 60 boutiques; four movie theaters; two discotheques; and 1,500 parking places. Its 1,000 tiny rooms offer all the modern amenities available, including magnetic locks, color TV, adjustable air conditioning, soundproofing, minibars and clock radios. The top floor (the "executive floor") features the Top Club, which includes luxurious rooms and personalized service. Panoramic bar, Plein Ciel, decorated by Slavik. Three restaurants, including L'Etoile d'Or (see Restaurants, seventeenth arrondissemt).

Courcelles

184, rue de Courcelles - 47.63.65.30

Open year-round. 42 rms 490-580F. TV. Pets allowed. Telex 642252. Cards: V, AE, DC, MC.

All the rooms are equipped with remote-control color TVs, direct phone lines, clock radios and minibars. The most attractive ones are decorated in green tones with floral wallpaper. The furniture is modern; the bathrooms are flawless. There is a small salon/winter garden. Lovely bar.

Etoile

3, rue de l'Etoile - 43.80.36.94

Open year-round. 25 rms 405-570F. TV. Pets allowed. Telex 642028. Cards: V, AE, DC, MC.

L'Etoile is perfectly located between the place de l'Etoile and the place des Ternes. Its ultramodern decor is inviting; its large salon includes a small bar and a library. No restaurant. Courteous reception.

Etoile-Pereire

146, blvd. Pereire - 42.67.60.00

Open year-round. 5 stes 810-850F. 21 rooms 410-580F. TV. No pets. Parking. Telex 305551. Cards: V, AE, DC, MC.

Located at the back of a quiet courtyard, these spacious rooms have just been redecorated (the duplexes under the rooftop are the most attractive). More than twenty different varieties of delicious jams are served at breakfast. Both the atmosphere and service are charming and cheerful. No restaurant.

Frantour Berthier Brochant

163 bis, ave. de Clichy - 42.28.40.40

Open year-round. 648 rms 290-390F. Half-board 280F. TV. Pets allowed. Telex 660251. Cards: V, AE, MC.

These twin hotels with a common restaurant and lobby house pleasant rooms (with free cribs for infants); self-serve or à la carte breakfasts are served in the restaurant. Group dinners can be held for up to 220 persons.

Lenox Monceau-Courcelles

18, rue Léon-Jost - 46.22.60.70

Open year-round. 5 stes 950-1,200F. 13 rms 450-490F. TV. No pets. Telex 649949. Cards: V, AE, DC, MC.

This former bordello has been totally renovated. Its rooms are on the small side, but they're tastefully decorated and furnished. A large duplex on the top floor has a lovely terrace. Breakfast is served on the patio in summer. No restaurant.

Magellan

17, rue Jean-Baptiste-Dumas
45.72.44.51

Open year-round. 75 rms 410-435F. TV. Pets allowed. Parking. Telex 644728. Cards: V, AE, DC, MC.

Business people will appreciate the serenity and comfort of the rooms (they all have new bedding and furniture) in this peaceful hotel, particularly those overlooking the garden, where breakfast is served on warm days. No restaurant.

Méridien

81, blvd. Gouvion-St-Cyr - 47.58.12.30

Open year-round. 15 stes 3,700-8,000F. 995 rms 1,060-1,750F. TV. Air cond. Pets allowed. Parking. Telex 290952. Cards: V, AE, DC, MC.

The Méridien is the largest hotel in Western Europe, and one of the most exciting ones in Paris. The rooms are small but remarkably equipped—tailored for frenzied frequent fliers. There are boutiques, travel agencies, a bar, three restaurants (including the excellent Clos Longchamp—see Restaurants, seventeenth arrondissement), a coffee shop, vast conference rooms (accommodating up to 1,500 people), a sauna, massages and a discotheque (with a wild decor designed by Slavik and Pierre Pothier). Brunch is very popular on Sundays (with jazz music by Claude Bolling).

Hôtel de Neuville

3, pl. Verniquet
43.80.26.30, 43.80.38.55

Open year-round. 2 stes 800F. 26 rms 455-595F. TV. Pets allowed. Telex 648822. Cards: V, AE, DC, MC.

The former owner of Quai d'Orsay has just opened this lovely hotel on a quiet square. Its simple rooms are tastefully decorated with lovely floral fabrics and are equipped with fine bathrooms. Pleasant salon/winter garden and basement restaurant, Les Tartines.

Ouest Hôtel

165, rue de Rome
42.27.50.29, 42.27.21.44

Open year-round. 50 rms 180-290F. TV. Pets allowed. Cards: V.

This cozy establishment has thick carpeting, efficient double windows and modest, modern rooms. No restaurant.

Hôtel Pierre

25, rue Théodore-de-Banville
47.63.76.69

Open year-round. 50 rms 530-660F. TV. Pets allowed. Parking. Telex 643003. Cards: V, AE, DC, MC.

The Hôtel Pierre is a Mapotel–Best Western and features a spacious lobby, a small salon opening onto an inner garden and some 50 standard, admirably equipped rooms, plus a conference room and a dining room, where a generous buffet breakfast is served. No restaurant.

Regent's Garden Hotel

6, rue Pierre-Demours - 45.74.07.30

Open year-round. 1 ste 700-800F. 39 rms 475-825F. TV. Pets allowed. Garage parking. Telex 640127. Cards: V, AE, DC, MC.

This handsome Second Empire bourgeois-building, just a stone's throw from the place de l'Etoile, offers hugs rooms with high molded ceilings and lovely rustic furniture (but some of the rooms—especially the ones on the street—are rather noisy and a bit rundown). Lovely large flower garden. No restaurant.

Splendid Etoile

1 bis, ave. Carnot - 47.66.41.41

Open year-round. 3 stes 920F. 54 rms 580-820F. TV. Air cond in 10 rms. No pets. Telex 280773. Cards: V, DC, MC.

The Splendid Etoile features about 60 well-maintained, comfortably furnished, good-size rooms, all with double windows; some of the windows afford views of the Arc de Triomphe. The bathrooms are perfectly equipped. Attractive small salon. Restaurant: Le Pré Carré.

Eighteenth Arrondissement

Regyn's Montmartre

18, pl. des Abbesses - 42.54.45.21

Open year-round. 22 rms 280-350F. Pets allowed. Telex 650269. Cards: V, DC, MC.

Each of the rooms in this excellent renovated hotel has a direct telephone line, radio, color TV and bathroom; the decor is simple but pleasant. Lovely view of Paris. No restaurant.

Terrass Hôtel

12, rue Joseph-de-Maistre - 46.06.72.85

Open year-round. 13 stes 870-1,000F. 93 rms 570-860F. Half-board 570-740F. TV. Air cond. in 4 rms. Pets allowed. Telex 280830. Cards: V, AE, DC, MC.

Located on the slopes of the Montmartre hill, the Terrass offers a majestic, unsurpassable view of almost all of Paris. Its comfortable rooms are regularly redecorated in a luxurious style. The seventh floor features a terrace garden with a summer bar.

Utrillo

7, rue A.-Bruant - 42.58.13.44

Open year-round. 30 rms 200-300F. TV. No pets. Telex 281550. Cards: V.

Located behind rue Lepic in a still-typical Montmartre district, this building, which used to rent furnished rooms, has been totally renovated. The new rooms feature whitewashed walls and cheerful fabrics. Clean and hospitable. No restaurant.

Nineteenth Arrondissement

Le Laumière

4, rue Petit - 42.06.10.77

Open year-round. 54 rms 135-270F. Pets allowed. Cards: V.

This fine, modern small hotel is located a few steps away from the Buttes-Chaumont, in a district where modern hotels are not exactly plentiful. Well soundproofed and good moderate rates. No restaurant.

PARIS

Suburbs

Argenteuil

95100 Argenteuil - (Val d'Oise)
Paris 14 - St-Germain-en-Laye 15 - Chantilly 36

(13) La Closerie Périgourdine

85, blvd. Jean Allemane - 39.80.01.28

M. Senot de la Londe. Open until 10 p.m. Closed Sat. lunch, Sun. dinner & Mon. Pets allowed. Cards: V, AE, DC.

Maguy and Frédéric Senot de la Londe, the owners of this dark, rustic, suburban restaurant, are strong believers in truffles, cèpes, foie gras, preserves and the other delicacies of the Périgord. The homemade duck-wing jambon is delicious, the portions of duck liver, also homemade, are generous (you can take some home for an extravagant price), and the feuilleté desserts are beautiful. Contrary to what might be feared, this cuisine (especially the sauces) is as light as can be. There is also a good selection of Cahors and Bordeaux wines.

A la carte: 300F. Menus: 135F and 170F (wine incl.), 110F.

Bougival

78380 Bougival - (Yvelines)
Paris 18 - Versailles 7 - St-Germain-en-Laye 7 - Rueil 4

Château de la Jonchère

10, côte de la Jonchère - 39.18.57.03

Open year-round. 2 stes 1,000-1,500F. 45 rms 550-1,000F (Hôtel du Parc). TV. Pets allowed. Telex 699491. Cards: V, AE, DC, MC.

Twenty minutes away from the place de l'Etoile, in the middle of the verdant countryside and under new management, Château de la Jonchère boasts luxurious, lovely suites. At the other end of the park is a quite comfortable 40-room hotel (Hôtel du Parc de la Jonchère) under the same management. Restaurant.

(14) L'Huître et la Tarte

6, quai Georges-Clemenceau
39.18.45.55

M. Delaveyne. Open until 10 p.m. Closed Sun. dinner, Mon. & Aug. Pets allowed. Cards: V.

L'Huître et la Tarte's success has been astounding, and it is not likely to end soon. While Le Camélia, next door, is too often sadly empty, these tables, pushed close together in pleasant surroundings of pine and cashmere fabric, are much in demand at both lunch and dinner. It must be said that M. Delaveyne scored brilliantly when he opened this restaurant/shop, where the freshest and finest seafood is served at unbeatable prices: oysters year-round, smoked or marinated Norwegian salmon, a confit of exquisitely fresh anchovies, mussel soup, a gratin of macaroni with shellfish, seafood omelets, cod aïoli, a finely ripened Camembert worth its weight in gold, a delicious white cream cheese and a choice of tarts. You won't find lobster, crayfish or any exceptional fish that would weigh heavily upon the check, but you will find creative seafood dishes at freshwater prices: appetizers from 38 francs to 58 francs, six oysters with grilled sausages for 60 francs, entrées from 48 francs to 63 francs and tarts for 29 francs.

A la carte: 180-250F.

Boulogne-Billancourt

92100 Boulogne-Billancourt - (Hauts-de-Seine)
Paris (Pte de St-Cloud) 10 - St-Germain-en-Laye 15

(14) L'Auberge

86, ave. Jean-Baptiste-Clément
46.05.22.35

M. Veysset. Open until 10 p.m. Closed Sun. & Aug. 6-31. Pets allowed. Cards: V, AE, DC, MC.

Although he is experimenting more and more seriously with modern cuisine, the talented Jean-François Veysset has nevertheless remained loyal to the wholesome regional specialties from the Franche-Comté, for which he is famous (winter stew, Jésus de Morteau and so on). And he does not mind borrowing from neighboring provinces. His two young chefs are completely at ease with the recipes, which, despite their diversity, all share the lightness of a precise, graceful execution. The wonderful fixed-price menu is as popular as ever, and we can understand why—you choose from wild-rabbit rillettes with hazelnuts or assiette maraîchère; perch and eel pochouse (fish stew) or calf's knuckle with fresh pasta; a cheese plate from Cantin's; and cream of honey and almond milk. The well-stocked cellar houses some excellent Bordeaux wines, along with many good labels for less than 100 francs.

A la carte: 300F. Menu: 180F.

(13) L'Avant-Seine

1, rond-point Rhin-et-Danube
48.25.58.00

M. Pautrat. Open until 10 p.m. Closed Sun. & Mon. Air cond. Pets allowed. Cards: V.

Gérard Vié's Boulogne annex (he owns Les Trois Marches in Versailles) is as pleasant as ever. Pierre Pardaillon, the young award-winning sommelier, is gone, but he has left behind a cellar in good standing (and an ample selection by the glass). As for the cuisine, it is still magnificent for the price. The 103-franc fixed-price menu, for instance, offers a duck mousse with salad, a fricassée of young fowl and a pear millefeuille with pistachios.

A la carte: 300F. Menus: 103F, 155F.

17 Au Comte de Gascogne

89, ave. Jean-Baptiste Clément
46.03.47.27

M. Vérane. Open until 10:15 p.m. Closed Sat., Sun., Aug. & Dec. 24-Jan. 1. Air cond. Garden dining. Pets allowed. Parking. Cards: V, AE, DC.

Just before press time, a changing of the chefs was announced at this restaurant. So consider our ranking tentative—we'll have to leave it to you for the time being to see if the same level of mastery, imagination and nuance is still at work here. In any case, things are under the more-than-competent surveillance of owner Gérard Vérane, whom we can trust to maintain his tradition of modernized regional dishes, such as the hot duck livers and mangoes, roast duck breast in honey, young pigeon galettes with sage. We're sure we can count on his perfectionism and passionate love for his trade to keep us happy here, in his restaurant that looks like a private townhouse—with its mirrored entrance hall, its black bar and its luxurious tropical greenhouse under a movable, transparent ceiling.

A la carte: 500-700F. Menu: 400F (menu dégustation).

12/20 Le Poivre Vert

1, pl. Bernard-Palissy - 46.03.01.63

M. Vérane. Open until daily 11:30 p.m. Air cond. Cards: V.

This cheerful, attractive, small, unpretentious annex of Au Comte de Gascogne is located in a lovely green setting. The fixed-price menu includes an appetizer and an entrée (noisette of lamb in tarragon sauce). Try the delicious grilled andouillette and the duck confit. Dessert (nothing extraordinary) and wine are not included in the price.

Menu: 80F.

Châteaufort

78530 Buc - (Yvelines)
Paris 28 - Versailles 10 - Orsay 11 - Pontchartrain 23

16 La Belle Epoque

10, pl. de la Mairie - 39.56.21.66

M. Peignaud. Open until 9:30 p.m. Closed Sun. dinner, Mon., Aug. 12-Sept. 6 & Dec. 23-Jan. 5. Garden dining. Pets allowed. Cards: V, AE, DC.

The grumbling, opinionated yet immensely likable Peignaud, a native of Berry, is quite a character. It's always a pleasure to see him in the cheerful 1900s-style clutter of his old inn overlooking the Chevreuse valley. He acquired a taste for Brittany from his good friend Delaveyne and recently bought a house in the Finistère. So don't be surprised to see, next to the calf's head (the obligatory postwedding course in Berry), a Vendée squab, a tail of young rabbit "mère-grand," a soft goat curd, a pan of delicious small marinated sardines, a pollack with tasty potatoes from Goyen, a John Dory, a lobster steamed in seaweed or a salad of damselfish from Cherbourg (insufficiently seasoned), to which Peignaud adds a touch from his own region: exquisite melon grown in Berry's ancient peat bogs. Nor has this countryman forgotten his ties to Japan (he was chef at Maxim's in Tokyo), which find expression in his sweet peppers in an Oriental marinade, his effiloché of ray in a sour sauce with soybean sprouts, or his wakame, a Japanese seaweed that, once cooked, tastes much like green beans grown in the ocean. Peignaud's cuisine, however, remains essentially classical and cannot be noted for lightness. The desserts are good, especially the peaches with orange blossoms and the glazed nougat in a raspberry sauce. Among the Burgundies and Bordeaux, some delightful wines from the Loire valley accompany this somewhat baroque cuisine, which blends the flavors of Berry, Asia and Brittany in a delightful harmony.

A la carte: 350-400F.

Chennevières-sur-Marne

94430 Chennevières-sur-Marne - (Val-de-Marne)
Paris 17 - Lagny 20 - Coulommiers 51

14 L'Ecu de France

31, rue de Champigny - 45.76.00.03

M. Brousse. Open until 9:30 p.m. Closed Sun. dinner, Mon. & Sept. 4-11. Terrace dining. No pets. Parking. Cards: V.

Smart and spruce for long, this old place has begun to fall into neglect. The exterior is shabby and dilapidated, and the large provincial dining room, with its drab colors and faded carpet, is beginning to look antiquated. Still, one's eyes may feast on the Marne river and its cool greenery, as well as on the terrace close to the water that gives this restaurant its inimitable charm. The more modern dishes are decreasing in number, and the preparation is sometimes hasty. The well-prepared feuilleté is excessively garnished with long asparagus stems (instead of just the tips); slices of a rather bland lamb are cut too thin; but the pastries (if looks alone count) are appealing. The toque is proffered on probation.

A la carte: 330-350F.

Clichy

92110 Clichy - (Hauts-de-Seine)
Paris 7 - St-Germain-en-Laye 17 - Argenteuil 7

14 La Bonne Table

119, blvd. Jean-Jaurès - 47.37.38.79

M. Berger. Open until 8 p.m. Closed Sat. lunch, Sun. & Aug. 15-Sept. 15. Air cond. Pets allowed. Cards: V.

Gisèle Berger, a sincere, straightforward, generous woman, prepares a feminine cuisine in a simple and cheerful setting that suits her beautifully. The menu doesn't change much, but this self-made woman from Savoie is so charming that the lobster lasagne, the fish cassoulet (with fish sausages!), the fish choucroute, the eggplant stuffed with shellfish and the classic bouillabaisse assure lasting pleasure. René Berger keeps an excellent selection of shellfish. The wines (like everything else) are expensive.

A la carte: 400F.

Courbevoie

92400 Courbevoie - (Hauts-de-Seine)
Paris 11 - Asnières 3 - St-Germain-en-Laye 13 - Levallois 4

(14) La Safranée sur Mer

12, pl. des Reflets - 47.78.75.50

M. Ferreira. Open until 10:30 p.m. Closed Sat., Sun., Aug. & Dec. 24-Jan. 2. Air cond. Terrace dining. Parking. Pets allowed. Cards: V, AE, DC.

The top executives working in Courbevoie's business world for a long while have made La Safranée sur Mer their port of call. The clientele is almost exclusively male, and the setting somehow calls to mind the dining room of a luxurious private yacht anchored in some Mediterranean harbor. On sunny days, you can sit at a table under the tricolored umbrellas on the La Défense square, reveling in the bird's-eye view of the Arc de Triomphe. The new chef and new owner know how to make the most of a menu composed primarily of superb seafood: grilled red mullet, bouillabaisse, salmon braised in dill and so on. The dessert cake, a combination of raspberry mousse and Cointreau on a génoise shell, is disappointing, but the wine list is superb.

A la carte: 500F. Menus: 280F, 300F.

(14) Les Trois Marmites ❂

215, blvd. St-Denis - 43.33.25.35

M. Faucheux. Open until 10 p.m. Closed Sat., Sun., March 20-28 & Aug. 1-28. Pets allowed. Parking. Cards: V.

After cooking splendid bistro specialties at Pierre Traiteur's for many years, Marc Faucheux has created—in the midst of these modern, noisy, rather spiritless suburbs—a quaint and charming café where one feels immediately at ease. The handwritten menu revives the best themes from Pierre's: delicious jambon persillé, enchanting terrines, estofinado (poached cod with potatoes) from the Rouergues, green cabbage with bacon and the famous "boeuf à la ficelle ménagère" (beef suspended on a string and poached in broth) with tasty vegetables. The cellar holds the best vintages of Bourgueuil, Sancerre, Pouilly Fumé and Beaujolais. A young, pretty waitress ensured perfect service on our visits there.

A la carte: 330F.

Croissy-Beaubourg

77200 Torcy - (Seine-et-Marne)
Paris 29 - Melun 34 - Meaux 30 - Lagny-sur-Marne 10

(13) Hostellerie de l'Aigle d'Or

8, rue de Paris
60.05.31.33, 60.05.22.24

M. Giliams. Open until 9 p.m. Closed Sun. dinner & Mon. Garden dining. Pets allowed. Parking. Cards: V, AE, DC.

The Eurodisneyland developers need only drive a few kilometers to enjoy the shade of this old house, with its terrace overlooking a flower garden and the Croissy pond. The owner is an elegant, charming woman, the clientele is prosperous, and the wine lovers are plentiful (thanks to the wonderful cellar). Chef Hervé Giliams has taken tremendous pains with his cuisine, although it expresses itself in the not-so-appealing style of a slick hotel: salade des Princes (lobster, foie gras...), lobster blanquette in Champagne, filet of veal in a sauce of honey and morel juice. Service is excellent.

A la carte: 300-400F. Menus: 150F (weekdays only), 340F (weekend and holiday dinner only), 200F.

Enghien

95880 Enghien - (Val d'Oise)
Paris 18 - Argenteuil 16 - St-Denis 6 - Chantilly 32

12/20 Le Beau Danube Bleu

1, rue de la Libération - 39.64.66.29

M. Escherich. Open until 11 p.m. Closed Mon. lunch, Sun., end Aug.-early Sept., 1 week at Easter & year-end holidays. Pets allowed. Cards: V, AE, DC.

This cozy restaurant with plenty of ambience, next door to the train station, offers Camembert fried just as it's done in the Tyrol region, escalopes of veal Cordon Bleu (so-so) and a delicious Sachertorte prepared by the Austrian owner. And it's all served in a decor of wooden paneling, mirrors and lace curtains. It's a bit too expensive, particularly the wines.

A la carte: 280F. Menu: 110F.

(16) Duc d'Enghien

3, ave. de Ceinture - 34.12.90.00

M. Kéréver. Open until 10:30 p.m. Closed Sun. dinner, Mon. & Jan. 2-30. Air cond. Terrace dining. Parking. Pets allowed. Cards: V, AE, DC.

Ever since a powerful Anglo–South African group bought out Enghien's casino and then turned around and sold it to another group, everyone has been wondering what will happen on the lakeshore, particularly at the restaurant, the Duc d'Enghien, where chef Michel Kéréver has come from Rennes. One thing that is certainly called for is a thorough modernization of this rather rundown casino and shabby restaurant, whose sole charm up to now has consisted of a view of the tired lake.

It would be surprising if the new owners should bid farewell to a chef of Kéréver's caliber. No, they are intelligent enough to give him a setting worthy of his talent, which we confirmed once again by tasting his exquisite ravioli filled with tourteau (crab) covered with a strong crab sauce and a sprig of chervil, his extremely subtle ramekin of crayfish and mushrooms (though it could perhaps have been a bit more seasoned), his excellent fresh pasta with seafood and basil and his sensational turbot, which is roasted in buttered paper with lardons, small onions, young carrots and coriander. The à la carte menu features delicious sea bass, pan-fried in its skin, superb roast duck from Challans in a gravy of its own juice and liver, magnificent pan-fried rib of beef with marrow gravy, and divine desserts, including praline Paris-Brest with coffee sauce, unjustly forgotten by today's pâtissiers.

Most noteworthy among the offerings of the very good cellar (where the prices of even the greatest Bordeaux are not astronomical) is Hugel's rare Alsatian Pinot Noir, which could easily be confused with a beautiful Burgundy.

Under the management of a maître d' who possesses a rare graciousness and skill, the service is nothing short of excellent.

A la carte: 400-700F. Menus: 325F (lunch only, wine incl.), 360F.

Le Grand Hôtel

85, rue du Général-de-Gaulle
34.12.80.00

Open year-round. 3 stes 750-800F. 48 rms 390-565F. Half-board 460-660F. TV. Heated pool. Parking. Pets allowed. Telex 697842. Cards: V, AE, DC.

Though massive and unattractive, this building is located in a charming park, and the rooms are spacious and comfortable and furnished in a distinctive, classical fashion. Restaurant.

Juvisy-sur-Orge

91260 Juvisy-sur-Orge - (Essonne)
Paris 15 - Orly 6 - Longjumeau 26 - Viry-Châtillon 2

(13) Le Pays d'Oc

2, rue de Draveil - 69.21.50.62

M. Fort. Open daily until 10 p.m. Terrace dining. Pets allowed. Parking. Telex 690316. Cards: V, AE, DC, MC.

The Forts, who also manage the excellent Minotaure in the Hôtel California (see Paris Hotels, Eighth Arrondisement), prepare a simple, substantial, generous cuisine in this old and comfortable mariners' inn overlooking the Seine. The specialties include fish and dishes from southern France: beautiful seafood in season, foie gras, well-made winter cassoulet, fish soup from Saint-Raphaël and grilled meats. The fixed-price menus are most appealing, and the ambience and garden decor of this hospitable place are consistently elegant. Meals are served on a pleasant terrace in the summer.

A la carte: 250F. Menus: 85F, 120F, 170F.

Mapotel d'Occitanie

(See restaurant above)

Open year-round. 29 rms 230-439F. TV. Pets allowed.

All the rooms, tastefully decorated in a modern style, are well maintained; some have pleasant views of the Seine. The service is excellent.

Levallois-Perret

92300 Levallois-Perret - (Hauts-de-Seine)
Paris (Pte de Champerret) 7.5 - Neuilly 4 - Asnières 3

(14) Gauvain

11, rue Louis-Rouquier - 47.58.51.09

MM. Hude & Guillermou. Open until 10 p.m. Closed Sat., Sun. & Aug. 5-20. Air cond. Cards: V.

With only ten dishes on the fixed-price menu, which changes at least once a week, you can make your choice quickly and painlessly. The first formula entitles you to two dishes plus cheese and dessert, the second one to three dishes. No additions, no extras, no surprises—that is, except for one, and it's a big one. All the food, prepared by Jean-François Guillermou, a veteran from Maxim's, is deliciously simple, modern and light, whether you choose the warm oysters with leeks, the fricassée of lotte with bacon, the veal kidney with Meaux mustard or the rib of beef gros sel. Finish with the admirable marquise au chocolat. This is a great little place. We have found it both both lively and reliable on all of our visits. It was converted from a bakery shop, and its attractive decor is charming, bright and cheerful, and the service is always with a smile.

Menus: 175F, 210F.

Livry-Gargan

93190 Livry-Gargan - (Seine-St-Denis)
Paris 17 - Meaux 28 - Senlis 42 - Aubervilliers 13 - Aulnay 6

(14) Auberge Saint-Quentinoise

23, blvd. de la République
43.81.13.08, 43.81.74.01

M. Nicoleau. Open until 10 p.m. Closed Sun. dinner, Mon. & Jan. 15-Feb. 10. Terrace dining. Pets allowed. Cards: V.

Michel Nicoleau, who was an assistant chef at Oliver Sr.'s Grand Véfour, then chef at Oliver Jr.'s Bistrot de Paris, can prepare many great dishes, but he is particularly good with the generous, simple, yet devilishly savory provincial cuisine so famous at his last employer's: pot of "petit-gris" (small snails) in a golden crust, fresh cod with bacon and sautéed cabbage, lamb's tongue in piquante sauce, suckling lamb with sweet garlic and so on. The decor has been redone, and the courtyard garden is quite pleasant during Livry-Gargan's hot summers. The small wine list is nice, and the service, professional.

A la carte: 300F and up. Menus: 135F and 185F (weekday lunch only), 175F (weekday dinner only), 200F and 250F (weekends and holidays only).

Les Loges-en-Josas

78350 Les Loges-en-Josas - (Yvelines)
Paris 23 - Versailles 5 - Jouy-en-Josas 2 - Rambouillet 33

(13) La Ferme des Loges

Porte des Loges - 30.24.97.77

M. Woltz. Open until 9 p.m. Closed Sun. dinner, Mon. & Aug. 14-29. Air cond. Garden dining. Hotel: 6 stes 780-890F; 49 rms 470-670F; half-board 750-780F. Garage parking. Cards: V, AE, DC.

This large group of aristocratic buildings, once used as the "stables of the King's farm," is in the middle of a charming park where tables are set in summer. The park is, in fact, far more cheerful than the large, rather dreary country-style dining room. After an extremely promising beginning, young chef Eric Schneider's cuisine seems to have weakened a bit. His salade gourmande is adequate but stingy. The delicious noisettes of lamb are a touch overcooked, though they're served with a perfect zucchini gratin. And a good millefeuille with wild strawberries is given new life with a rhubarb sauce (though there is a bit too much cream topping it). The wine cellar is well stocked, particularly with Bordeaux.

A la carte: 350F. Menus: 190F, 240F, 320F.

Louveciennes

78430 Louveciennes - (Yvelines)
Paris 24 - Versailles 7 - St-Germain-en-Laye 6

Aux Chandelles

12, pl. de l'Eglise - 39.69.08.40
Hours, closings & credit card information not available.

Success first drove the prices up, then apparently led to the sale of this lovely house and enchanting garden. The new owner/chef had not quite opened for business at press time, but we will be most interested to see what he makes of this charming spot, and of his first venture.

Maisons-Laffitte

78600 Maisons-Laffitte - (Yvelines)
Paris 21 - Pontoise 18 - St-Germain-en-Laye 8

(14) Le Laffitte

5, ave. de St-Germain - 39.62.01.53
M. Laurier. Open until 9:30 p.m. Closed Tues. & Sun. dinner, Wed. & Aug. Pets allowed. Cards: V, AE.

His three "Rabelaisian" fixed-price menus win André Laurier a crown. The most expensive of the trio, with foie gras and lobster, plus fish, meat, cheese and dessert courses, may seem like a challenge to put away in one sitting, but Laurier is such a gifted cook that the meal goes down quite easily. The check, however, doesn't. The less daring ought to know that the so-called "small menu" is not exactly a consolation prize, and that the à la carte menu abounds in fine entrées, such as the salmon from Scotland with garden sorrel and the veal kidney sautéed in Pouilly wine. The cellar holds some excellent country wines for about 80 francs. The old-fashioned decor is quite pleasant.

A la carte: 280-300F. Menus: 200F, 270F, 300F.

(16) Le Tastevin

9, ave. Eglé - 39.62.11.67
M. Blanchet. Open until 10 p.m. Closed Mon. dinner, Tues., Feb. school vacation & Aug. 16-Sept. 10. Garden dining. Pets allowed. Parking. Cards: V, AE, DC.

The name of Michel Blanchet's restaurant alludes to his passion for fine wines. For the past fifteen years he has done such a good job collecting bottles that today his cellar is one of the best-stocked in the Paris area. And next to these great aged labels is a number of more modest vintages, priced well below 100 francs (a rosé Rully, for example, or a delicious red Menetou). This is all for the best, as the opportunities to spend money are not lacking in this well-to-do, bourgeois millstone house, built on the green edge of the Maisons-Laffitte park. Try the fondant of lobster, the marinière of palourdes (clams) with saffron, the turbot roasted with shallots in a meat juice, the sautéed langoustines or the escalopes of sweetbreads with creamed asparagus and truffles, all of which are prepared by this discreet and charming cook, whose command of sauces and preparations is nothing short of extraordinary. The solemn beige dining room is lightened with beveled mirrors that reflect a lovely flowering garden where meals are served in summer, just like in the country.

A la carte: 400F.

(18) La Vielle Fontaine

8, ave. Grétry
39.62.01.78
Mme. Letourneur & M. Clerc. Open until 10:30 p.m. Closed Sun., Mon. & Aug. Garden dining. Pets allowed. Cards: V, AE, DC.

In 1987, Catherine Deneuve and a number of other French celebrities called up favors owed to them by their most famous friends to christen the new decor of their Vielle Fontaine. Farewell to cuteness! Interior designer Elisabeth Malhettes opted for sobriety and discretion: mirrors, tons of flowers, black-lacquered armchairs upholstered in a splendid cashmere, walls of red and gray moiré and, above the park, an exquisite white winter garden. The effect is utterly charming. At the same time, longtime patrons of this grand white Napoléon III establishment will retain the comforting feeling that they aren't out of place.

Letourneur's gracious smile flourishes in these ideal surroundings, and Clerc's cooking has rediscovered a harmony and confidence of execution that for a time had seemed to waver. In any event, the new menu left us with favorable impressions, with its millefeuille of oysters and foie gras, oxtail and mutton sausage, marinière of lobster with watercress butter, oursinade of bass with fresh pasta, coquilles St-Jacques with vanilla and ginger, lambs' brains with coconut milk and curry, pot-au-feu with Pomerol and duck ragoût with apricots.

Clerc, assisted by Gilles Angoulvent, has gone beyond revising his cooking; he's created something totally original. His current efforts remind us that long before he became famous for his restaurant, he was a great chef. His new desserts—apple charlotte en brioche, a delicious pudding or cheese with cassis and raspberries—add just the right finish to a delightful meal, which is accompanied by perfect wines recommended by Hervé Besle, the young wine steward. Excellent menu/carte (a fixed-price menu with à la carte–style selections) at lunch.

A la carte: 450-800F. Menus: 480F (menu dégustation), 190F.

Meudon

92190 Meudon - (Hauts-de-Seine)
Paris 12 - Clamart 4 - Versailles 10 - Boulogne 3

(15) Relais des Gardes

42, ave. du Général-Galliéni - 45.34.11.79
M. Oudina. Open until 10 p.m. Closed Sun. dinner, Sat. & Aug. Terrace dining. Pets allowed. Cards: V, AE, DC.

Although Paris is quite close to Meudon, the Relais des Gardes seems hundreds of kilometers away. So soothing is the large dining room, with its tall fireplace, its etchings and its long-standing provincial clientele, that it takes us far away from the customary suburban bistros. Pierre and Simone Oudina manage this 200-year-old restaurant, which was patronized by the hunters and horse guards of the royal domain during the reign of Louis XV, with simplicity and graciousness. It's surely a fine place to be, as evidenced by the 40-year tenure of chef Daniel Bertholom. His cuisine is seasoned in a bourgeois or regional style, but it's much lighter, and noted for its generosity and simplicity. The charlotte of young rabbit en gelée and fresh herbs is delightful, as is the fish soup from Glénan, the filet of Charolais beef in wine and the pot-au-feu of duck à la saintongeaise. It is all accompanied by some voluptuous wines that aren't as expensive as one might think. The dinner menu/carte, with apéritifs and Champagne included, is enticing.

A la carte: 350-380F. Menus: 280F (wine incl.), 180F.

Neuilly-sur-Seine

92200 Neuilly-sur-Seine - (Hauts-de-Seine)
Paris (Pte de Neuilly) 8 - Argenteuil 9 - Versailles 16

(13) Carpe Diem

10, rue de l'Eglise - 46.24.95.01

M. Coquoin. Open until 9:45 p.m. Closed Sat. lunch, Sun., May 1-8 & Aug. 6-27. Pets allowed. Cards: V, DC.

In this small, pleasant, smartly decorated room, Serge Coquoin, a veteran from the Casino Royal in Evian, creates a lively, original, tasty cuisine—for example, the chevreau (kid) aspic with herbs, the salad of lamb's sweetbreads with a sea urchin vinaigrette, the millefeuille of salmon and oysters, the carp stew with Parma ham, the sautéed filet of lamb with pine nuts, the braised rabbit tail with asparagus tips, the crépinettes (flat sausages) of pigs' feet and lamb's sweetbreads with foie gras, as well as some excellent desserts, including a crème caramel with cherries. The fixed-price menu, for 145 francs, is lovely.

A la carte: 300-350F. Menu: 150F.

12/20 Le Chalet

14, rue du Commandant-Pilot
46.24.03.11

M. Brun. Open until 11 p.m. Closed Sun. Pets allowed. Cards: V.

In this old chalet-style restaurant, you can feel free to put both elbows on the wooden table and tuck a paper napkin under your chin. The grilled meats are good, the Raclette generous. The wine is served in pitchers, and the customers are congenial.

A la carte: 180-200F. Menus: 65F, 100F and 170F (wine incl.).

12/20 La Chevauchée

209 ter, ave. Charles-de-Gaulle
46.24.07.87

M. Valero. Open until 10:30 p.m. Closed Sat. lunch, Sun. & Dec. 26-Jan. 2. No pets. Cards: V, AE, DC.

Fantastic, this Chevauchée! It's one of the best little places in town. The dining room is cozy, the prices reasonable, and the cuisine has some nice "olé olé" touches (gazpacho, paella, crème catalane). The small fixed-price menu is astounding.

A la carte: 230-250F. Menus: 140F, 170F.

12/20 Chez Livio

6, rue de Longchamp - 46.24.81.32

M. Innocenti. Open until 10:45 p.m. Closed Sat. & Sun. in Aug. & Dec. 23-Jan. 2. Garden dining. Pets allowed. Cards: V.

This charming trattoria in beautiful Neuilly has been famous for a quarter of a century. The small but thick pizzas are unrivaled; the osso buco and pasta, perfect. Springtime dining on the large patio with an open ceiling proves especially delightful. An épicerie is located next door.

A la carte: 160-180F. Menu: 125F (wine incl.).

(16) Jacqueline Fénix

42, ave. Charles-de-Gaulle - 46.24.42.61

Mme. Fénix. Open until 10 p.m. Closed Sat., Sun., July 28- Aug. 29 & Dec. 22-Jan. 2. Air cond. Pets allowed. Cards: V, AE.

Iced tureen of salmon, salmon caviar, quail eggs and new potatoes, a slice of warm foie gras with a shallot spread, roasted langoustines with watercress, sole and vegetables en papillote with tarragon, grilled filet of duckling from Ganders, warmed cheese, marbré of bitter chocolate, lime and grapefruit paillettes... and all of this for less than 295 francs! It's a gift, in fact, from the beautiful Jacqueline to the ravenous public-relations people who come out here to discuss deals over lunch and return for personal pleasure at dinner. But don't be afraid: The advertising/PR agents aren't the only ones occupying the grounds. People come from just about everywhere to this flowery, very feminine atmosphere to savor the beautiful and tasty cuisine prepared by Albert Corre, formerly the sous-chef here under Michel Rubod. He also has perpetuated the style of the original creations of his former boss—a rémoulade of smoked salmon and duck with orange, a terrine of eel filets and chanterelles, a millefeuille of young rabbit with eggplant and rosemary, red mullet with duck or cod liver, and veal kidneys with crispy leeks. And one won't easily forget the classic Pauillac lamb with garlic and potatoes or the delicious country-style rib of veal casserole. As for the desserts—from the marbré of bitter chocolate to the hot waffles and madeleines with jam—they're just about unforgettable.

A la carte: 400-500F. Menu: 295F (menu dégustation).

(13) Les Feuilles Libres

34, rue Perronet - 46.24.41.41

Mme. Guillier-Marcellin. Open until 10:30 p.m. Closed Sat. lunch, Sun. & Aug. Air cond. Terrace dining. Pets allowed. Cards: V, AE, DC.

A brand-new little restaurant whose provincial charm will seduce you. This corner of Neuilly seems remote from Paris, and the small, square windowpanes, red floor tiles and banquettes give the place the air of an English teahouse. The proprietor, though not a cook, has exceptionally discriminating tastes, and his advice is always well taken. As for Patrice Hardy, the young chef, we have met him before at various toque-winning restaurants. The simple yet enticing fixed-price menu includes a half bottle of Muscadet or Bordeaux, a fondant of cauliflower with spices in a sauce we found a bit dull, delicious filet mignon of pork en croûte, and a perfect iced nougat in raspberry sauce. We award Les Feuilles Libres a small toque for its promising debut.

A la carte: 250F. Menus: 150F (lunch only), 230F (wine incl.).

(15) Jenny Jacquet

2, pl. Parmentier
46.24.94.14, 46.24.39.42

M. Jacquet. Closed Sat. lunch & Sun. No pets. Cards: V.

Having made the leap from the sixteenth arrondissement to Neuilly, Jenny Jacquet has landed on his feet once again. The decor of the former Truffe Noire is still not exactly inspiring, but it doesn't matter; we have eyes only for the fine cuisine of this Tours native, who makes full use of the time he spent at Papa Augereau's stoves in Rosiers-sur-Loire. That's where his taste for true country flavors, slowly simmering stews and refined sauces comes from (his "beurre nantais" is one of the best in the Paris area). Jacquet changes his menu every two months; if you happen to see his duck foie gras with Chaume wine, his pike mousseline with beurre blanc, his brill cooked with mushroom crumbs, his fricassée of sweetbreads with hazelnuts or his breast of duck with hot liver and celery, don't pass them up. There are no more than five or six desserts, always delicious (Jacquet spent several years at Lenôtre's), and the wines from the Loire, though few in number, are exquisite.

A la carte: 280F.

Neuilly Park Hotel

23, rue Madeleine-Michelis - 46.40.11.15

Open year-round. 24 rms 440-530F. TV. Pets allowed. Telex 612087. Cards: V, AE, MC.

This luxurious, elegant building, the newest of the small Neuilly hotels, has exquisite, well-furnished rooms, and its prices are excellent.

(13) La Tonnelle Saintongeaise

32, rue Vital-Bouhot - 46.24.43.15

M. Girodot. Open until 10 p.m. Closed Sat., Sun., Aug. 1-20 & Dec. 23-Jan. 5. Air cond. Garden dining. Pets allowed. Cards: V.

On sunny days, lunch here along the Seine feels almost like a garden party. When Joël Girodot opens his lovely terrace under the chestnut trees, the Ile de la Jatte becomes as beautiful as Cythera. Nicole Girodot makes dishes as beautiful as the setting: fricassée of snails, fish soup from Saintonges, young rabbit cooked in Pineau wine, small rounds of hot chèvre marinated in Cognac and her own versions of other delicious specialties from Charentes. The attractive dining room has been newly decorated with wood and stone.

A la carte: 250F. Menu: 200F (summer weekdays & on the terrace only).

Red toques signify modern cuisine; black toques signify traditional cuisine.

Orly

94396 Aéroport d'Orly - (Val-de-Marne)
Paris 16 - Corbeil 17 - Villeneuve-St-Georges 12

Altea Paris-Orly

Orly-Ouest, 94547 Orly Aérogare
46.87.23.37

Open year-round. 200 rms 355-435F. Half-board 90-300F. TV. Air cond. Pets allowed. Parking. Telex 204345. Cards: V, AE, DC, MC.

The comfortable rooms are done in bright, lively colors; the plumbing is of good quality. The staff is more numerous thanefficient. Tennis and golf facilities should be operational by the time you read this. Restaurant.

Hilton International Orly

Aérogare d'Orly-Sud - 46.87.33.88

Open year-round. 376 rms 680-910F. TV. Air cond. Pets allowed. Parking. Telex 250621. Cards: V, AE, DC, MC.

The rooms at this Hilton are as functional as they are comfortable, and very close to the airport (free shuttle). The conference facilities are exceptional. Restaurant.

(14) Maxim's

Aérogare d'Orly-Ouest - 46.87.16.16

M. Godeau. Open daily until 10 p.m. Air cond. Pets allowed. Parking. Telex 201389. Cards: V, AE, DC.

A comfortable grill serves as the anteroom to this twin of the Maxim's on rue Royale. With its exceptional fixed-price menu —country terrine of young rabbit with prunes and Armagnac, roasted meats (a beautiful, thick sirloin with marrow in a bordelaise sauce), lamb stewed with tomatoes and basil, cheese and salad, and a cart of desserts and pastries served with the best coffee to be found at the airport; all accompanied by an excellent wine, perhaps a Champigny or a fine Muscadet—it is one of the best places these suburbs have to offer. You'll feel as though you have wings, just like the huge Boeings on the runways before you. Next door, at the deep-red banquettes in the lively decor of Maxim's II, you'll have to pay a bit more to sample the paillasson of potatoes (like a potato pancake) topped with an escalope of duck liver, the lobster salad in walnut oil or the red mullet with saffron and olive oil. The cuisine is prepared by chef Jean Jorda, who is increasingly determined to abandon the chichi repertoire of the past. The cellar is most handsome, and the service consistently meets its high standards.

A la carte: 400F. Menu: 220F (in Grill only, wine incl.).

Le Perreux

94170 Le Perreux - (Val-de-Marne)
Paris 15 - Créteil 11 - Vincennes 6 - Lagny 17

(15) Les Magnolias

48, ave. de Bry - 48.72.47.43

M. Royant. Open until 10 p.m. Closed Sun., April 2-10 & Aug. 7-21. Pets allowed. Cards: V, AE, DC.

Les Magnolias is a small suburban house with vivid colors reminiscent of Utrillo's paintings.

The facade has just been repainted, and the interior will surprise you with its majestic decor: walls covered in burgundy linen, flourishing green plants, tables partitioned by light balustrades and elegant young waiters fluttering about in striped gray jackets. Gérard Royant, the chef/owner, takes the orders himself and keeps an eye on the service (according to our readers, he doesn't much care to be contradicted). The cuisine is original and on the whole quite well prepared, with an interesting fixed-price menu (but the à la carte dishes are costly): light zakuski (Russian hors d'oeuvres), a loaf of escargots in beurre blanc astutely seasoned with fresh herbs, breast of duck in a good wine sauce and delicious crêpes stuffed with raspberries. The wine cellar is small but perfect.

A la carte: 350F.

Pontoise

95300 Pontoise - (Val d'Oise)
Paris 34 - Beauvais 55 - Rouen 91 - Mantes 39

(15) Le Jardin des Lavandières

28, rue de Rouen - 30.38.25.55

M. Decout. Open until 9:30 p.m. Closed Sat. lunch, Sun., holidays, July 14-Aug. 15 & Dec. 23-Jan. 4. Air cond. Pets allowed. Cards: V, AE.

A murky stream running behind the parking lot testifies to the presence of a distant garden and the washerwomen who used to come here. It's enough to send those Parisians and Cergy natives, starved for a taste of the countryside, into pastoral dreaminess. When you step inside this old, still-charming house close to Notre-Dame, Chantal Decout's simple gracious smile greets you. Flowers fill the vases and decorate the walls, and with the beamed ceilings, the peaceful lighting and the atmosphere of natural freshness, you would indeed think you were in the country.

Jean-Louis, Chantal's husband, who once worked with Faugeron, cooks with as much attention and precision as a clock maker. Applying his genius to the finest of seasonal produce, without concocting extravagant combinations, he creates light, simple, yet elegant dishes whose flavors impress with their candor: salad of young leeks with truffles and foie gras, seafood and spinach en papillote, quail tourte with cabbage and grapes, lasagne of young rabbit and morels, and a waffle with wild strawberries. We have only one reproach for these delicious meals: One can't return too often, because the checks, although justified, climb quickly (the beautiful, expensive wine list is partially to blame), and Jean-Louis has not yet thought to offer his admirers the alternative of a smaller fixed-price menu.

A la carte: 300-350F.

A red hotel ranking denotes a place with charm.

Le Port-Marly

78560 Le Port-Marly - (Yvelines)
Paris 21 - Versailles 10 - Louveciennes 3 - St-Germain 3

(13) Auberge du Relais Breton

27, rue de Paris - 39.58.64.33

M. Chaumont. Open until 10 p.m. Closed Sun. dinner, Mon. & Aug. 10-Sept. 30. Garden dining. Pets allowed. Cards: V, AE.

Fifteen minutes from the porte Maillot and just a few steps from one of the most delightful landscapes along the Seine stands this old, thoroughly rustic inn, whose decor is reminiscent of Brittany. In its charming, intimate, leafy garden, one is served a lovely, lightly classical cuisine: hot oysters in Champagne, braised sole in lobster sauce, breast of duck with walnut butter. The beautiful desserts come from Flo-Prestige (whose owner is one of the inn's former managers).

A la carte: 250F. Menus: 195F (wine incl.), 149F.

(13) Le Lion d'Or

7, rue de Paris - 39.58.44.56

M. Cluzel. Open until 10 p.m. Closed Tues., Wed., March 1-15 & Sept. 1-15. Terrace dining. Pets allowed. Cards: V, AE.

Jean-Paul Cluzel, upon reaching 50, locked up his business, slipped the key under the door and left to study cooking with André Guillot, Jung, Darroze and Vié. Today he is an accomplished chef: serious, skillful, in full command of his techniques and original as well, as are all self-made people. That's why a visit to his old, quasi-historic inn (it appears in Sisley's painting *The Flooding of Port-Marly*), is always full of lovely surprises. Try the blancmange (jellied almond cream) of fowl, the duck cassoulet with beans, the small stuffed quails, the stuffed lamb and the exquisite farmers' cheeses from the Auvergne. Françoise Cluzel, a full-blooded native of Anjou, has collected some marvelous wines from her region. The terrace by the water is delightful.

A la carte: 250-300F. Menu: 120F, 220F.

Le Pré-Saint-Gervais

93310 Le Pré-St-Gervais - (Seine-St-Denis)
Paris (Pte de Pantin) 7 - Meaux 38 - Montreuil 5

(14) Le Pouilly-Reuilly

68, rue André-Joineau - 48.45.14.59

M. Thibault. Open until 10 p.m. Closed Sun., holidays & Aug. No pets. Parking. Cards: V, AE, DC.

We seem to be out in the country, in Père Thibault's native region of the Sologne, which abounds in wild game; but we're also in the land of chicken with crayfish, of andouillette in Pouilly wine, of paupiettes of Morvan-style ham (the way François Mitterrand likes it) and of fried fish. Actually, we're in a suburban restaurant with a high-tech, pale-colored decor and an extraordinarily cordial and friendly atmosphere. This place is one of the very few in which the noble bistro tradition survives. The black-aproned service, the exquisite little wines and Rolande's melting smile win out over the bad rustic imitations.

So why on earth doesn't the owner serve any tarte tatin? He is, after all, a native of Lamotte-Beuvron, where it was invented. He replaces it brilliantly, however, with a magnificent giant coffee éclair.
A la carte: 280-330F.

Puteaux

92800 Puteaux - (Hauts-de-Seine)
Paris 10 - Versailles 14 - Neuilly 3 - St-Germain-en-Laye 11

12/20 Le Bois d'Amour

4, blvd. Richard-Wallace - 45.06.47.79
Mme. Lebrun. Open until 10 p.m. Closed Sat. lunch, Sun., Mon. dinner & Aug. Air cond. Pets allowed. Cards: V.

The owners of L'Hippocampe next door offer a quite decent cuisine "à formule" here at Le Bois d'Amour: a good terrine of duck with pistachios and a very tender mignon of veal with fresh pasta and Roquefort sauce. For a few extra francs, one can order nicely prepared desserts and pitchers of Côtes-du-Rhône.
Menu: 65F.

Dauphin

45, rue Jean-Jaurès - 47.73.71.63
Open year-round. 30 rms 345-360F. TV. Pets allowed. Tennis. Parking. Telex 615989. Cards: V, DC, AE, MC.

The Dauphin is managed by the same family that runs the Princess Isabelle across the street (see below). In the lovely reception room, generous buffet breakfasts are served, and the rooms are serene and comfortable. The Dauphin is also a good spot for a quick meal at night. Free shuttle to the RER station.

Les Deux Arcs

34, Cours Michelet (La Défense 10)
47.76.44.43
M. Chevauche. Open daily until 10 p.m. Terrace dining. No pets. Parking. Telex 612189. Cards: V, AE, DC, MC.

Les Deux Arcs is an oasis of peace and comfort in a depressing environment of concrete and asphalt. The modern, cheerful decor is a perfect success, the staff courteous, the cuisine serious and good, and small touches of refinement can be found everywhere: roses on the tables, Echiré butter, delicious rolls. The terrine of fowl livers is flavorful, as is the duck confit with sautéed potatoes and the daube of beef, although its sauce, boiled down too far, is a little bitter. The iced nougat is perfect, and the Chinon wine from Gosset is delicious but too expensive.
A la carte: 300F and up. Menu: 270F (lunch only).

Sofitel Paris-La Défense

(See restaurant above)
Open year-round. 1 ste 3,200F. 149 rms 950-1,150F. Half-board 1,155F. TV. Air cond. Pets allowed.

This latest addition to the chain, decorated with golden mirrors and light marble, has a warm atmosphere. The quiet rooms have superb pink marble bathrooms. The service is outstanding, and breakfast is delicious. This hotel is well equipped for conferences.

(15) Gasnier

7, blvd. Richard-Wallace - 45.06.33.63
M. Gasnier. Open until 9:30 p.m. Closed Sat., Sun., holidays, Feb. school vacation & June 29-Aug. 2. Air cond. Pets allowed. Cards: V, AE, DC.

The area may not be exciting, nor the angular decor much fun, but Hubert Gasnier's Parisian heart contains a wealth of happiness. His cuisine from the southwest of France remains tremendously spirited, and his marvelous foie gras, charcuterie and fowl come from the best Basque and Béarn suppliers. His à la carte menu is graced with as much cordiality and warmth as one could wish for between Mont-de-Marsan and Castelnaudary. He takes great care to lighten his sauces, simplify his recipes and refine this earthy cuisine. For example, there is the perfectly balanced mesclun salad with foie gras and sweetbreads; the plump, tender aiguillettes of duck served with savory cèpes and chanterelles; the astounding cassoulet de Castelnaudary; and the andouillette braised in Jurançon wine. Maïté Gasnier's desserts, particularly her light, crusty apple feuilleté, are a perfect finish to these festive meals. And we mustn't forget the great wines and fabulous Armagnacs from the cellar.
A la carte: 300-350F. Menu: 240F (wine incl.).

Princesse Isabelle

72, rue Jean-Jaurès - 47.78.80.06
Open year-round. 1 ste 900F. 28 rms 510-530F. TV. Pets allowed. Tennis. Garage parking. Telex 613923. Cards: V, DC, AE, MC.

The rooms of this new hotel, very close to La Défense, are beautifully decorated and equipped with Jacuzzis or multijet showers. Some of the rooms are on the same level as the flowering patio. Free chauffeured-car shuttle to the RER station or to the Pont de Neuilly. No restaurant.

Syjac Hotel

20, quai de Dion-Bouton - 42.04.03.04
Open year-round. 4 stes 850-1,200F. 29 rms 380-710F. TV. No pets. Telex 614164. Cards: V, AE, DC.

This is a new building that escaped the triumphal style of architecture that characterizes its concrete neighbors at La Défense. The rooms are pleasant, huge and perfectly equipped. In addition, there is a pretty interior courtyard and a superb free sauna. No restaurant, but there is the possibility of room service.

Le Raincy

93340 Le Raincy - (Seine-St-Denis)
Paris 16 - Meaux 30 - Bobigny 6 - Livry-Gargan 3

(14) Le Chalet des Pins

13, ave. de Livry - 43.81.01.19
M. Aumasson. Open until 9 p.m. Closed Sun. dinner (July: Sun. & Mon. dinner & Tues.; Aug.: Sat. lunch, Sun., Mon. & Tues. dinner). Garden dining. Pets allowed. Cards: V, AE, DC.

The cooking of Fernande de Oliveira has all the virtues of a good feminine cuisine: generosity, forthright flavors, lightness and a careful technique. The raw salmon and sardines in raspberry vinegar, the émincé of lobster with fresh mint, the calf's head with fresh tomato, the roast salmon with truffle juice, the young rabbit with coriander and the excellent pastries (warm pear feuilleté) all have a degree of freshness and originality that goes beyond expectations. The rose-and-beige lacquered decor is elegant. Reasonable prices and a cellar rich with wines and spirits.
A la carte: 280-300F. Menu: 110F.

Roissy-en-France

95700 Roissy-en-France - (Val d'Oise)
Paris 26 - Meaux 36 - Senlis 28 -Chantilly 28 - Gonesse 7

Holiday Inn

1, allée du Verger
49.88.00.22, 39.88.00.22

Open year-round. 240 rms 640-880F. Half-board 835F. TV. Air cond. Pets allowed. Parking. Telex 695143. Cards: V, AE, DC, MC.

The rooms are large, bright and well equipped. There is a health club (gym, sauna, whirlpool), a free shuttle to the air terminals (from 6 a.m. to 1 a.m.) and a restaurant.

Maxim's

Aéroport Charles-de-Gaulle
48.62.16.16

M. Janisson. Lunch only. Air cond. Pets allowed. Telex 240270. Cards: V, AE, DC.

The concrete interior of Terminal 1 on the main floor, the mix of Boeings and business people, the chrome-pipe decor—none of this evokes the fancy, refined atmosphere promised by the restaurant's sign. Nevertheless, Maxim's is one of the better restaurants in the Paris region. Yet it is not necessarily one of the most expensive, provided you keep to the adjacent grill, which serves outstanding salads and appetizers and exceptional meats and fish grilled over a wood-burning fire. The food in the restaurant, although it is still technically superior to most, has lost its interest and individual accent. We therefore have removed a point, though one still dines very well here, particularly on Jacques Legrand's fixed-price menu, which he bases on his morning shopping. For example, he might offer a small salad of salmon and watercress followed by sea bass with basil, aiguillettes of duck in Santenay, excellent cheeses, a tray of splendid light pastries, and coffee. When you add a perfect Côtes-du-Rhône or a fruity red Sancerre (the cellar is exceptional), your check will scarcely exceed 300 francs per person. It's certainly worth doffing your hat for such seriousness and quality. The service here is faultless.
A la carte: 450-500F. Menus: 220F (in Grill only, wine incl.), 250F.

Some establishments change their hours and annual closings without warning. It is always wise to call ahead.

Sofitel

Aéroport Charles-de-Gaulle
48.62.23.23

Open year-round. 8 stes 1,200F. 344 rms 595-825F. TV. Air cond. Heated pool. Tennis. Pets allowed. Parking. Telex 230166. Cards: V, AE,DC, MC.

Located facing the runways, Sofitel is equipped with all the amenities one expects of this chain—from a disco and a sauna to a restaurant and a coffee shop.

Romainville

93230 Romainville - (Seine-St-Denis)
Paris 10 - Le Bourget 12 - Aulnay-sous-Bois 9

Chez Henri

72, rte. de Noisy - 48.45.26.65

M. Bourgin. Open until 9:30 p.m. Closed Sat. (except dinner off-seas.), Sun. & holidays. Air cond. Pets allowed. Parking. Cards: V.

The large, comfortable bistro of the faun-like and Rabelaisian Henri Bourgin may be as warm as its environment of suburban warehouses is icy and gloomy, but this has not been sufficient cause to draw large crowds to the grayish Romainville avenue, which features the city's refuse and a gas station as its major attractions. However, Bourgin is a remarkable cook, whose creativity and broad technical ability are rare indeed. Using his incredible knowledge of natural produce, he creates dishes whose appearance may not always be attractive, but which are truly original and admirably rich in flavor: quiche of fresh morels in truffle juice, a navarin of lotte with peas and baby onions, roasted John Dory with potatoes and baby carrots, leg of young rabbit with smoked bacon served on baby turnip tops. When leaving Chez Henri, you'll feel that you've never before tasted this type of cuisine. Nowadays, that's quite a compliment to pay a chef. The feuilleté desserts are enchanting, and the wine cellar is impressive.
A la carte: 400F. Menu: 200F.

Rungis

94150 Rungis - (Val-de-Marne)
Paris 13 - Corbeil 26 - Longjumeau 10 - Antony 6

La Rungisserie

20, ave. Charles-Lindbergh
46.87.36.36

M. Holzmann. Open daily until 11 p.m. Air cond. No pets. Garage parking. Telex 260738. Cards: V, AE, DC, MC.

Something new has happened to this huge building in the deserted zone between Rungis and Orly. For one thing, it is now rather elegant, despite the huge buffet of appetizers, erected like a catafalque under a blue-black linen cloth. For another, new chef Christian Petetin is cooking imaginative, clever dishes that would merit two toques were it not for the lack of seasonings (even in such country dishes as the calf's-foot salad). This may be due to the demands of an international clientele with an unsophisticated palate. So, for the time being, this restaurant's main attraction is its exceptional fixed-price menu: an infinite selection of appetizers and cold courses (as much as you can eat) and a special of the day or a grilled meat, followed by cheeses and desserts. Wine and coffee are included.

A la carte: 300F. Menu: 162F (weekdays only, wine incl.), 185F (weekdays only) and 75F to 200F.

Pullman Paris-Orly

(See restaurant above)

Open year-round. 2 stes 850F. 204 rms 565-820F. TV. Air cond. Pool. Pets allowed.

The perfectly soundproofed and air-conditioned rooms at the Pullman Paris-Orly, each complete with color television and direct-dial telephone, offer all the comfort you can expect of this hotel chain. There is also a continuous shuttle service to the airport, a panoramic bar, sauna, shops and new luxury rooms (called the "Privilège" rooms).

Saint-Cloud

92210 St-Cloud - (Hauts-de-Seine)
Paris 12 - Boulogne 3 - Versailles 10 - Garches 2

12/20 La Désirade

2, blvd. de la République
47.71.22.33

M. Cogé. Open daily until 10 p.m. Air cond. Terrace dining. Pets allowed. Garage parking. Telex 631618. Cards: V, AE, DC, MC.

The green and pink fabrics and cream-colored wood lattices on the first floor of the new Hôtel Quorum form a pleasant, exotic setting for the attractive waitresses in khaki dresses. Choose the remarkable fixed-price menu, which changes every day; perhaps it will include the egg casserole with ratatouille, the loin of pork with sage and the excellent Paris-Brest. The wine list needs expansion.

A la carte: 280F. Menu: 120F.

Hôtel Quorum

(See restaurant above)

Open year-round. 58 rms 360-390F. TV. Air cond. Pets allowed.

Everything, from the communal areas to the private rooms, is spanking new and brightly decorated in an elegant, modern, simple style; the rooms are large, with gray-marble bathrooms. Guests are cordially greeted.

Saint-Denis

93200 St-Denis - (Seine-St-Denis)
Paris 10 - Argenteuil 10 - Chantilly 30 - Pontoise 24

Mélody

15, rue Gabriel-Péri - 48.20.87.73

M. Balat. Open daily until 11:30 p.m. Air cond. Pets allowed. Cards: V.

Everything is new—first and foremost the prices, which have been cut in half; then the decor, now with big mirrors, paintings and small, crimson-velvet chairs; but especially the food, which is prepared in the best of the genuine, generous bistro style. Michel Balat has been extremely successful in carrying out his courageous, small "cultural revolution." No doubt many of his fellow restaurateurs would find the solution to their problems by following his example. Of course, they would have to do it the right way and prepare such dishes as the delicious herrings in oil, the perfect hot saucisson and the tender leg of lamb with beans that melts in your mouth. The wine list is good (Cabernet is served in carafes).

A la carte: 160-180F. Menu: 60F.

Saint-Germain-en-Laye

78100 St-Germain-en-Laye - (Yvelines)
Paris 21 - Chartres 81 - Dreux 70 - Beauvais 69

Cazaudehore

1, ave. du Président-Kennedy
34.51.93.80, 39.73.36.60

MM. Cazaudehore. Open until 10 p.m. Closed Mon. (except holidays). Garden dining. Pets allowed. Parking. Telex 696055. Cards: V, MC.

The Cazaudehores—father and son—have undertaken a huge renovation project at their beautiful large house in the middle of the woods. The new dining room wallpaper is fresh and tastefully floral. An immense veranda opens up directly onto the garden, which is a most delightful place to be: seated on the comfortable green chairs surrounding tables adorned with pink tablecloths, enjoying the cool shade of the old trees during the day and the light of the authentic Parisian street lamps at night. The chef's tasty cuisine, classical but light, is commendable and offers plenty of specialties from the southwest of France: tripe à la paloise (broiled tripe with green beans and potatoes), salmon roasted in olive oil and dill, lamprey à la bordelaise, lobster à la nage, loin of lamb with rosemary and on and on and on. The check mounts quickly, due to the selective wine list and the absence of a fixed-price menu.

A la carte: 350-500F.

La Forestière

(See restaurant above)

Open year-round. 6 stes 820F. 24 rms 560-650F. TV. Pets allowed.

Located in a large flower garden on the border of a forest, La Forestière has 24 recently renovated rooms and suites furnished with beautiful antique furniture; the walls are enlivened with fresh pastel colors. Relais et Châteaux.

Pavillon de la Croix de Noailles

Carrefour de Noailles - 39.62.53.46

M. Nakonieczny. Open until 9:30 p.m. (10 p.m. in summer). Closed Mon. dinner, Tues. & Feb. Garden dining. Pets allowed. Cards: V, AE.

This attractive eighteenth-century hunting lodge is built next to the most crowded intersection in the forest. But, surrounded as it is by splendid ancient oaks, the Pavillon isstill delightful, particularly in summer, when meals are served in the lovely garden under parasols. The hospitality is good, the waitresses are delightful, and the cuisine is still as light and well prepared as ever. We will, however, penalize it slightly for its lack of versatility and its indifference to the changing market and seasons. For instance, the mesclun salad with ray in raspberry vinegar is good but the greens aren't varied enough, and the aiguillettes of roast duckling are delicious but are served with large peas instead of the promised fresh beans. The tutti-frutti tart is a bit messy, but fresh and good.

A la carte: 350-400F. Menu: 145F (weekdays only).

Le Pavillon Henri-IV

21, rue Thiers - 34.51.62.62

Open year-round. 3 stes 2,200F. 42 rms 400-1,400F. Half-board 820F. TV. Pets allowed. Garage parking. Telex 695822. Cards: V, AE, DC, MC.

Nothing has been spared to make the 42 large rooms and suites of Le Pavillon Henri-IV extremely comfortable. The banquet rooms are magnificent (they were recently rated as ancient monuments), as is the incredible view of the immense park. Restaurant.

12/20 Restaurant des Coches

7, rue des Coches - 39.73.66.40

M. Corbel. Open until 10:15 p.m. Closed Sun. dinner, Mon. & Aug. 10-20. Air cond. Terrace dining. Pets allowed. Parking. Telex 699491. Cards: V, AE, MC.

Only the decor is still charming; everything else here has become so slipshod. The service is clumsy and condescending and the kitchen has fallen away: boring scallop salad, skeletal beef ribs with reheated potatoes, and desserts that are made too quickly (though the tea sorbet with prunes and cinnamon is good). No toque in this edition.

A la carte: 300F. Menus: 98F (lunch only), 190F, 250F.

Saint-Ouen

93400 St-Ouen - (Seine-St-Denis)
Paris 7 - St-Denis 4 - Pontoise 27 - Chantilly 34

Chez Serge

7, blvd. Jean-Jaurès - 40.11.06.42

M. Cancé. Closed Sun. & Aug. Pets allowed. Cards: V.

Mme. Cancé has left her stove, so Serge himself is in charge of the kitchen. The à la carte menu is short, but this is not a criticism, for it is versatile and uses fresh, seasonal produce purchased daily (with the exception of the marvelous foie gras in a Sauternes aspic, the calf's head and the homemade persillé, which are served year-round). Everything is delicious, honest and simply prepared, just like at home: calf's knuckle printanière, fresh cod with orange, real civet de lapin, and fricassée of Bresse chicken in truffle juice. The wine cellar is one of the most wonderful in these suburbs—not because of the number of bottles it holds, but because of its excellent selection and prices (twelve years ago, Serge made this restaurant famous when he won an award for the best wine selection). The provincial bistro decor may be unexciting, but the lively crowd lends a cordial atmosphere.

A la carte: 300-400F.

Le Coq de la Maison Blanche

37, blvd. Jean-Jaurès
40.11.01.23, 40.11.67.68

M. François. Open until 10 p.m. Closed Sun. Terrace dining. Pets allowed. Cards: V.

Le Coq is a big suburban bistro, as warm as the suburbs are gloomy, with a monumental white facade on the street corner that isn't exactly enticing. But the vast interior is cordial, with chocolate-brown drapes, a merry clientele of foremen and manufacturers and a young, vigorous and funny boss supervising a friendly staff. At the end of World War II, people came here to eat coq au vin à la Escoffier. Today the food, which has been prepared by André Gamon from Lyon for the past 30 years, is predominantly bourgeois and hearty. Generous, frank and seasonal: the jambon persillé, the terrine of skate with basil and a tomato coulis, the lobster salad with watercress, the perfectly grilled sole, the Loiret kid roasted with herbs, the numerous grilled meats (the pigs' trotters with sautéed potatoes are outstanding) and the chef's or granny's tasty desserts, including brioche with crème caramel. The Beaujolais is superb and the wine cellar well stocked.

A la carte: 250F.

Varennes-Jarcy

91480 Quincy-sous-Sénart - (Essonne)
Paris 29 - Corbeil-Essonne 14 - Evry 13 - Melun 20

Auberge du Moulin de Jarcy

69.00.89.20

Closed Tues., Wed., Thurs., 1st 3 weeks in Aug. & Dec. 25-Jan. 15. 5 rms 150-180F. No pets. Parking. Cards: V.

This old medieval mill located on the bank of the Yerre river has just five rooms, all of which are pleasant and quite comfortable. Restaurant.

Versailles

78000 Versailles - (Yvelines)
Paris 23 - Mantes 44 - Rambouillet 31 - Dreux 61

Sights. The Palace of Versailles (a must!), with more than 4 million visitors per year (from May to September its parks host the Grandes Eaux and the Fêtes de Nuit); the Trianon Palaces; the Salle du Jeu de Paume (recently opened to the public); Notre-Dame church (designed by Hardouin-Mansart); the king's vegetable garden (school of horticulture); the Carrés Saint-Louis (modest lodgings during the time of the Old Régime); the antiques and secondhand market (passage de la Geôle, next to the colorful market at Notre-Dame); the Hôtel des Ventes (former home of the Light Cavalry); the delightful Musée Lambinet (still underrestoration, with beautiful eighteenth-century paintings); the Couvent des Récollets.

Eating on the Run. Le Boeuf à la Mode, 4, rue au Pain (open until midnight, seafood specialties); Alain Chaminade, 44, rue de la Paroisse (varieties of teas, ice cream and quick lunches, open on Sunday); A La Côte Bretonne, 12, rue des Deux-Portes (more than 200 crêpes and pancakes); L'Entrecôte, 18 bis, rue Neuve-Notre-Dame (grilled meats, open daily until 11 p.m.); Le Feuille Thé, 2, rue Royale (fast lunches in a quiet courtyard); L'Orangerie, 4 bis, rue de la Paroisse (wine bar and fixed-price lunch menu); La Palette, 6, rue des Deux-Portes (near the Versailles marketplace and the antiques shops, regulars from the quarter); Le Roi Gourmet, 21, rue des Réservoirs (smoked fish and specialties from the southwest of France are sold in the shop next door); Tarte Julie, 104, rue de la Paroisse (savory and sweet tarts); L'Hôtel des Voyageurs, 12, rue Philippe-de-Daugeau (not too expensive, highly valued by the *tout* Versailles; pleasant terrace).

Bars & Cafés. La Civette, passage St-Pierre (a typical bar/tobacco shop with an old-fashioned decor); La Civette du Parc, 17, rue des Réservoirs (nice, conservative bar frequented by young locals).

Nightlife. There is no Saturday-night fever in Versailles; in fact, there isn't any fever the other days of the week either. L'Aiglon on the blvd. St-Antoine is nevertheless worth mentioning (very smart, also features a restaurant).

Shops. *Bakeries:* Galupeau, 20, rue des Chantiers (the cakes are beautiful and delicious); Joseph, 21, rue Carnot (for its pain au raisin); Didier Lhoste, 19,+ rue de Satory (for the paillasse, an excellent country bread). *Charcuteries:* Christophe, 62, rue de la Paroisse (*the* charcutier/caterer in Versailles); Gentelem, in the Versailles marketplace (game specialties); Le Roi Gourmet, 21, rue des Réservoirs (see "Eating on the Run"). *Chocolates:* Aux Colonnes, 14, rue Hoche (such specialties as the "favorites du Roy" and the golden palets). *Gourmet foods:* Hédiard, 1, rue Ducis (near the Versailles marketplace, with the same products as those sold at Hédiard on pl. de la Madeleine). *Cheese:* Michel Beignon, 6, rue Royale (Brie, cheeses from the Auvergne and goat cheeses). *Fruit and vegetables:* Castel, 49, rue Royale (there is permanent excitement around this "cours des halles," which sells beautiful fresh produce). *Pastries, confections:* Guinon, 60, rue de la Paroisse (a gourmet institution, try the délicieux and the picois); Pellisson, 44, rue de la Paroisse (sample the pavé de Versailles and l'Adélaïde, a chocolate specialty). *Wine and spirits:* Les Caves du Château, 9, pl. Hoche (a tremendous collection of great vintages, as well as the well-informed advice of M. Jean); Les Caves Royales, 6, rue Royale (good regional wines and some 50 kinds of Armagnacs).

12/20 Brasserie du Boeuf à la Mode

4, rue au Pain - 39.50.31.99

M. Vié. Open daily until 12:30 a.m. Pets allowed. Cards: V.

The Brasserie du Boeuf à la Mode is one of the latest additions to Gérard Vié's friendly little gourmet empire. A gifted former assistant chef at Les Trois Marches prepares anoverwhelmingly successful and delicious jambonneau of duck, an excellent boudin (blood sausage) with apples and a perfect chocolate terrine, all of which won't cost you more than 150 francs with a half bottle of Sancerre or Champigny wine.

A la carte: 160F.

Eden Hôtel

2, rue Ph.-de-Dangeau - 39.50.68.06

Open year-round. 24 rms 175-250F. TV. No pets. Telex 698958. Cards: V, AE.

Located on a fairly quiet street near the police station, equidistant from the train station and the palace, the Eden Hôtel features 24 newly decorated and modernized rooms. No restaurant.

(14) Le Potager du Roy

1, rue du Maréchal-Joffre - 39.50.35.34

M. Letourneur. Open until 10 p.m. Closed Sun. & Mon. Air cond. Pets allowed. Cards: V.

Here, in the redecorated dining room of Gérard Vié's old Trois Marches, which has been extended by a pleasant closed terrace, Philippe Letourneur serves two miraculous daily fixed-price menus that rate among the best in the region. The larger one includes a delectable pâté of blond liver or a mousse of coquilles St-Jacques, followed by veal kidneys in mustard sauce, cheeses and delicious eggnogs with cassonade (soft brown sugar). The handsome, short wine list composed by Les Trois Marches's sommelier should offer more half bottles.

A la carte: 300F and up. Menus: 105F, 150F.

(14) Le Rescatore

27, ave. de St-Cloud - 39.50.23.60

M. Bagot. Open until 10 p.m. Closed Sat. lunch & Sun. Air cond. Pets allowed. Cards: V, AE.

The enterprising patron of this restaurant, the sunniest and merriest in Versailles, draws his inspiration almost exclusively from the freshest possible seafood. The large windows, whose handrails are beautifully wrought, open onto avenue de St-Cloud, and the big, round tables are set in discreet elegance in the lovely, freshly wallpapered dining room. The cuisine provides many unexpected, original and (most of the time) happy combinations: the fricassée of scallops with Sauternes, the roasted oysters with slices of rare duck breast, the lotte with fresh ginger and the soufflé of sole with baby vegetables. All the dishes taste natural, and our only negative word is that Jacques Bagot stays too long with his creations instead of changing his à la carte menu more often.

A la carte: 300-400F. Menu: 225F (weekday lunch only).

(13) Rôtisserie de la Boule d'Or

25, rue du Maréchal-Foch
39.50.22.97

M. Saillard. Open until 10 p.m. Closed Sun. dinner & Mon. (except holidays). Pets allowed. Cards: V, AE, DC.

The friendly M. Saillard is passionately attached to his oldestablishment, one of the nine Versailles inns dating back to the era of Louis XIV (and famous even then). In his delightful, authentic and weathered dining room, where candlelight adds a soft gleam to the paintings by Mignard and Hobbema, Saillard's love of history has led him to compose a remarkable à la carte retrospective of the cuisine created by several great seventeenth- and eighteenth-century chefs. Next to this collection of dishes is a list of equally interesting specialties of Franche-Comté: terrine with morels, lotte in Château-Chalon and loin of lamb. The wine cellar is quite interesting.

A la carte: 400-500F. Menus: 115F and 155F (weekdays only), 224F (weekends and holidays only), 184F.

(13) Trianon Palace

1, blvd. de la Reine - 39.50.34.12

M. Marcus. Open daily until 9:30 p.m. Terrace dining. No pets. Parking. Telex 698863. Cards: V, AE, DC, MC.

This imposing old luxury hotel, built in 1912 in the Palace of Versailles's park, was recently refurbished. The magnificent main floor looks even more aristocratic than before, and the ambience of comfort and luxury is pleasant indeed, particularly in summer, when the high windows open onto the superb terrace. The cuisine of Jean-Jacques Mathou, an impressive collector of diplomas, is proof of a job well done. His delicious ravioli stuffed with supions (cuttlefish) and zucchini, his royal sea bream cooked to perfection with soft garlic, and his turbot pleasantly enhanced by fennel and purple olives win him one toque. The service is excellent.

A la carte: 450F. Menus: 190F (weekdays only), 260F (holidays only), 220F.

Trianon Palace

(See restaurant above)

Open year-round. 10 stes 1,785-2,990F. 110 rms 490-1,110F. Half-board 503-766F. TV in 95 rms. Pets allowed. Heated pool. Tennis.

Half of Trianon Palace's rooms were recently modernized; all the furniture was changed and an underground swimming pool and two tennis courts were being completed when we went to press. This old, neoclassical deluxe hotel has been transformed into a superb contemporary jewel.

(18) Les Trois Marches

3, rue Colbert (pl. du Château)
39.50.13.21

M. Vié. Open until 10 p.m. Closed Sun. & Mon. Garden dining. Pets allowed. Cards: V, AE, DC, MC.

With extreme discretion, Gerard Vié has built himself a small kingdom (in Versailles he has Le Potager du Roy, Le Quai No. 1 and La Brasserie du Boeuf à la Mode, and in Boulogne, L'Avant Seine and Le Bistro des Halles). This realm allows him to offer Les Trois Marches's clients the luxury of a historic building (it once belonged to the Gramont family), a garden for summertime dining, excellent service and cooking whose delicacy and finesse are reaffirmed year after year.

He even has an exciting project in the wings: a small luxury hotel to be built at the edge of the garden. It would fit inperfectly at Versailles, which suffers from a chronic shortage of rooms. Formerly an undignified pastiche of too many different colors and modern paintings that don't belong in this classic setting, the rooms are now handsomely restored in an honest, unfrilly period style.

These proper surroundings add so much to the pleasure of Vié's dishes—dishes that were once compromised by rather muddled flavors but are now quite precise. Some of the newer creations on Vié's menu include cold lobster with crushed tomatoes marinated in olive oil and ginger, rabbit in aspic with leeks, duck foie gras au rancio (a wine liqueur), and roast leg of baby lamb with garlic. Each is proof of a talent in full bloom. And everything surrounding these main dishes is also exquisite: The bread is marvelous, and the canapés, petits fours and coffee—particularly the Jamaican roast—are all sumptuous. Food fit for a prince, right under the rays of the Sun King.

A la carte: 450-700F. Menus: 230F (weekday lunch only), 325F, 435F.

Le Versailles

7, rue St-Anne - 39.50.64.65

Open year-round. 48 rms 310-380F. TV. Pets allowed. Garage parking. Telex 689110. Cards: V, AE, DC.

Next to the entrance of the Palace of Versailles and across from the Palais des Congrès, the location of Le Versailles is excellent. No restaurant.

Le Vésinet

78110 Le Vésinet - (Yvelines)
Paris 18 - Versailles 15 - St-Germain 3 - Pontoise 24

(16) A la Grâce de Dieu

75, blvd. Carnot - 34.80.05.44

M. Ballester. Open daily until 10 p.m. Air cond. Pets allowed. Cards: V.

Daniel Ballester, a native of Bougival and a student of Jean Delaveyne (that's why, being a perfectionist, he never stops experimenting), worked until recently in a delightful little restaurant in the village of Follainville, near Mantes. Not long ago, he bought an old brewery located between Chatou and Saint-Germain and redecorated it in a plain style. But here, at Le Vésinet, he wanted to strike it rich and fill his already crowded restaurant, so he devised a unique menu/carte for 110 francs. With a half bottle of good Beaujolais, your check won't exceed 145 francs and your meal will be out of the ordinary. The fresh ingredients Ballester uses are perfect (he goes to Rungis's central market four nights a week), the food is amusing and savory, and the presentations are simple yet always elegant. One may choose from a selection of ten appetizers, including a compote of rabbit en gelée, small marinated mackerel, beef shoulder with a tomato mousse, scrambled eggs with chanterelles, and fresh pasta with mussels; four fish dishes, including papillote of coalfish with herbs, salmon with sorrel, ray with fresh mint and turbot with an embeurrée of cabbage (this last dish will cost you an additional 35 francs); six meat dishes, including a civet of duck with fresh pasta, pigeon crépinette and leg of mutton with couscous; and six desserts, including a heavenly strawberry millefeuille. Let's add that the short wine list has been remarkably well composed by Guy Renvoisé. In conclusion, we suggest that you hurry and visit this restaurant to see what work, heart and talent can get you for 110 francs.

Menu/carte: 110F.

FRANCE A TO Z

Restaurants & Hotels

Abbeville
80100 Abbeville - (Somme)
Paris 160 - Amiens 45 - Dieppe 63 - Boulogne-sur-Mer 80

(13) Auberge de la Corne
32, Chaussée du Bois - 22.24.06.34
M. Lematelot. Open until 9:30 p.m. Closed Sun. dinner, Mon., Feb. 1-15 & July 1-15. Air cond. Pets allowed. Cards: V, AE, DC, MC.

True, the prices are a bit high, but then, a quality restaurant can afford to be expensive. The low, beamed ceiling makes the dining room a bit dark, but the fifteen tables, separated by a prow-shaped counter, are almost always occupied. You will enjoy the finest fish from the nearby Somme river: a generous dish of langoustines in celery butter (though the portion of baby vegetables is more generous than that of the langoustines), perfectly cooked lotte with sweet peppers, and pan-fried sole with cèpes (a bit heavy). Then finish with a double-chocolate charlotte, powerful yet a bit too sweet. The active and attentive patronne makes sure that the service is good, and the short wine list is well selected.

A la carte: 300F and up. Menus: 100F (weekday lunch only), 125F, 185F, 240F.

Les Adrets
83600 Fréjus - (Var)
Paris 886 - St-Raphaël 21 - Cannes 28 - Draguignan 45

12/20 Auberge des Adrets
N 7, toward Mandelieu - 94.40.36.24
MM. Sanchez & Lumediluna. Open until 10: p.m. Closed Mon. & Tues. (off-seas.) & Oct. 15-Dec. 15. Garden dining. Pets allowed. Hotel: 7 rms 160-200F; half-board 280-300F. Pool. Parking. Cards: V.

An imposing landscape surrounds the Auberge des Adrets. Inside, though, you'll find a baroque decor, a lovely hostess and simple food served in two tasty fixed-price menus. The first includes a salad of sweet peppers and smoked duck, rabbit with basil and fresh pasta, hot goat cheese and dessert. The historical retrospectives are dedicated to the legendary Baron des Adrets.

Menus: 170F, 205F.

Some establishments change their hours and annual closings without warning. It is always wise to call ahead.

Agay
83700 St-Raphaël - (Var)
Paris 902 - Cannes 30 - St-Raphaël 11 - Nice 63

Sol e Mar
2 km SW on N 98,
Le Dramont - 94.95.25.60
Closed Oct. 15-April 23. 47 rms 370-4510. TV in 40 rms. Pets allowed. Half-board 350-450F oblig. in seas. Pool. Parking.

At the extreme edge of the shore, these relatively isolated terraced rooms have superb views; there is also a saltwater swimming pool and a restaurant.

Agde
34300 Agde - (Hérault)
Paris 818 - Montpellier 57 - Béziers 22 - Sète 23

12/20 Nausicaa
4, pl. de la Marine - 67.94.71.08
M. Kreitmann. Open until 10 p.m. Closed Tues. (off-seas.). Garden dining. Pets allowed. Cards: V, AE, DC.

After wandering around the world for some time, the friendly Philippe Kreitmann has just put the finishing touches on his beautiful dining room, oriented toward an old, colossal fireplace. A touch of exoticism enhances his cuisine—émincé of mérou (thin slices of grouper) marinated in homemade chutney, roasted pigeon with ginger and mangoes—but he never forgets the traditions of Languedoc, such as mussels in fennel cream or a gilthead mousse with a purée of fresh sardines. We love the prices, both à la carte and on the fixed-price menus.

A la carte: 180-200F. Menus: 86F, 142F.

(17) La Tamarissière
21, quai Théophile-Cornu
67.94.20.87
M. Albano. Open until 9:30 p.m. Closed Mon. (except mid-June- mid-Sept.), Sun. dinner & Dec. 1-March 15. Terrace dining. Pets allowed. Telex 490225. Cards: V, AE, DC, MC.

Located amid the dunes between the canal and the sea, this big old café has, with the passing of the years, become one of the most comfortable country inns in the area and the best restaurant as well. Nicolas Albano, the owner's son, isn't just an inventive cook—when it comes to sauces, he's also an alchemist. He searches for combinations of subtle yet unmistakable flavors. These past few years have seen him make some praiseworthy efforts to add consistency and generosity to his repertoire and his fixed-price menus. The elegant table linens and china service, the terrace on the bank of the Hérault and the service (which is getting better but still needs improvement; on occasion it is too hasty and disorganized) will continue to enhance the clever and completely modernized cuisine of Languedoc. Highlights include a delicious grilled fisherman's plate with a zucchini flan, roasted pigeon with thyme flowers, sea perch with a morel cream sauce and an étuvée of red mullet and langoustines with anise. On the down side, the young rabbit pie and the sweetbreads that we tried were insipid. But let's not forget the fresh and beautifully prepared shellfish from the Thau basin, the real bourride (fish soup) or the exquisite Roquefort served with Banyuls wine. The regional wine list features a beautiful dry white Muscat. La Tamarissière deserves, and gets, a higher rating in this edition.

A la carte: 300-400F. Menus: 120F (weekdays only), 175F,235F.

La Tamarissière

(See restaurant above)

Closed Dec. 1-March 15. 33 rms 250-500F. Half-board 360-485F. TV in 25 rms. Pets allowed. Pool.

This pleasant stopover faces the Hérault estuary. Some of the rooms, newly decorated by Mme. Albano, have a view of the estuary, while others look onto the quiet vegetable garden. A small swimming pool was recently built in the garden.

IN NEARBY **Le Cap d'Agde**
(7 km SE on D 32E)
34300 Agde - (Hérault)

12/20 Le Braséro

Port-Richelieu II - 67.26.24.75

M. Millares. Open until 11 p.m. Closed Tues. (off-seas.) & Jan. 9-March 1. Terrace dining. Pets allowed. Cards: V, AE, DC.

The regulars are disappointed because the picture of the restaurant's founders in their birthday suits has disappeared from the menu. But it's still on the check, which is always reasonable, considering the freshness of the produce and the consistency of the cuisine: oysters, a cod turnover, poached fish and so forth. The terrace is quite pleasant.

A la carte: 180-220F. Menus: 100F (weekday lunch only, wine incl.), 120F (wine incl.).

Hôtel du Golfe

Ile des Loisirs - 67.26.87.03

Closed Nov. 15-March 1. 2 stes. 50 rms 310-550F. Half-board 469-660F. TV. Air cond. Pets allowed. Pool. Garage parking. Telex 480709. Cards: V, AE, DC.

This small, cozy, intimate hotel is tastefully decorated. An excellent breakfast is served, though there is no restaurant.

Le Matago

Rue du Trésor-Royal - 67.26.00.05

Annual closings vary. 90 rms 260-440F. Half-board 375-415F. Pool. TV. Pets allowed. Parking. Telex 480979. Cards: V, AE, DC, MC.

This newly built, modern hotel is about 900 yards from the beach and the port. Video. Restaurant.

Saint-Clair

Pl. St-Clair - 67.26.36.44

Closed Nov. 1-March 31. 82 rms 260-495F. Half-board 275-402F. TV. Air cond. Pets allowed. Pool. Garage parking. Telex 480464. Cards: V, AE, DC, MC.

Comfortable rooms and good facilities are found in this new hotel located a few steps from the port. Restaurant.

IN NEARBY **Marseillan**
(7 km NE on D 51)
34340 Marseillan - (Hérault)

12/20 La Roussette

Ave. de la Méditerranée - 67.21.97.63

M. Beltra. Dinner only. Open until 9:30 p.m. Closed Sept. 16- June 15. Terrace dining. No pets.

A fishmonger in the morning and a restaurateur at night, M. Beltra has created a restaurant that's a marvel of simplicity. His sunny beach decor is just right, his prices are a dream, and the fresh food he prepares is served without pretension, his sole concern being the precision of cooking. You must sample the clovisses (tiny clams) à la sétoise and the catch of the day. A fine restaurant.

A la carte: 180F.

Agen

47000 Agen - (Lot-et-Garonne)
Paris 647 - Tarbes 144 - Bordeaux 142 - Toulouse 108

Sights. The Musée Municipal (paintings by Goya); the Sénéchal house (and the entire medieval district); the bridge/canal (built in the fourteenth century, a magnificent cut-stone piece of work); the St-Caprais cathedral (romanesque choir, Gothic nave); the L'Ermitage hill (a beautiful view of Agen and of the Garonne river valley).

Eating on the Run. L'Apicius, 8, rue E.-Sentini; La Crêperie des Jacobins, pl. des Jacobins; Pizzéria Chez Philippe, 24, rue Voltaire; Le Toupin, 14, rue Grande-Horloge.

Bars & Cafés. Le Café des Arts, 2, rue Cessac (friendly); Le Café de la Bourse, 54, blvd. de la République (fashionable); Le Moderne, 43, cours Victor-Hugo (excellent beer); Le Pub Sentini, 3, rue E.-Sentini (young clientele).

Nightlife. Le Dandy, rue de Gergovie; Vallon de Vérone (young and not-so-young clientele); La Hulotte à Bon-Encontre (friendly and casual).

13 L'Absinthe

29 bis, rue Voltaire - 53.66.16.94

M. Geoffroy. Open until 10 p.m. Closed Sat. lunch, Sun. & July 15-31. Air cond. Pets allowed. Cards: V.

Pierrick Geoffroy is celebrating twenty years of restaurant cooking, but he has worked in this charming pink bistro in old Agen only since 1984. His talent and generosity are being rewarded with success. His cuisine is unpretentious and fresh, and his prices are fair. Geoffroy's specialties include mixed salads, fresh oysters with grilled sausages, lotte in a cream sauce with pink peppers, navarin of lamb with peas, confit of roasted duck with garlic, and refreshing sorbets. The proprietor is gracious, and the waiters are attentive.

À la carte: 220-250F.

Château-Hôtel des Jacobins

1 ter, pl. des Jacobins - 53.47.03.31

Open year-round. 2 stes 400-440F. 13 rms 220-440F. TV. Pets allowed. Parking. Telex 560800.

This ancient, aristocratic residence is tastefully furnished and looks out on the trees and the beautiful church of Les Jacobins. Some of the quiet, comfortable rooms are attractively decorated. No restaurant.

La Corne d'Or

Rte. de Bordeaux, 47450 Colayrac-St-Cirq (1.5 km N on N 113) - 53.47.02.76

Mme. Loisillon. Open until 9:30 p.m. Closed Sun. dinner, Sat., July 14-Aug. 7 & Dec. 17-27. Air cond. Pets allowed. Hotel: 14 rms 240-280F; half-board 220-240F. Parking. Telex 560800. Cards: V, AE, DC.

Jean-Louis Loisillon, trained by Sacha Guitry's ex-cook, is now the sole chef of this pleasant establishment just outside Agen (across the bridge/canal that spans the Garonne river). Loisillon's cuisine remains extremely cautious, consistent and generous but, alas, too expensive: fine avocado and duck-liver salad, perfectly prepared breast of duck in a subtle sweet-and-sour sauce of orange and pepper, decent millefeuille with red fruit. The wine list is well selected.

A la carte: 300F and up. Menus: 90F and 190F (weekdays only), 170F (weekends and holidays only), 140F, 280F.

Le Provence

22, cours du 14-Juillet - 53.47.39.11

Open year-round. 20 rms 150-270F. TV. Air cond. in 9 rms. Garage parking. Cards: V, AE, DC, MC.

Located in downtown Agen, this small, simple, well-kept and air-conditioned hotel offers a good value. No restaurant.

IN NEARBY **Puymirol**

(17 km E on N 113 & D 16)

47270 Puymirol - (Lot-et-Garonne)

L'Aubergade

(Michel Trama)

52, rue Royale - 53.95.31.46

M. Trama. Open until 9:30 p.m. Closed Mon. (except July, Aug. & holidays). Garden dining. Pets allowed. Telex 560800. Cards: V, AE, DC.

Michel and Maryse Trama are expecting—not a baby, but a new home for their restaurant. Actually, they already have one, and what a beauty! It's a thirteenth-century Gascon country house where the counts of Toulouse used to come to relax; today it sits in the heart of a hillside village. But how do you expect the Tramas to prosper or even survive if they can't offer their clients a bed or the means to discover this splendid countryside, which bears a strange resemblance to Tuscany?

Trama's growing fame profits the entire region. And when local authorities and the mayor of Puymirol (who did some splendid work rebuilding and equipping his town) learned that Trama would leave if he couldn't expand, they knocked themselves out to help him. Trama bought the two neighboring buildings, and the plans for his future country hotel are ready. The facade of old stones will be extended, the windows of the spacious rooms will open onto a delightful garden, and the current dining room, which was recently redone, will gain a view of the greenery. Thus, perfect harmony between the surroundings and the cooking will be attained, allowing the dazzling talent and inexhaustible imagination of this refined and sensitive man to flourish.

Trama took an interesting road to get where he is today. After studying sociology and psychology, he worked in the dining room and then in the kitchen as chef at a Greek restaurant. Then he owned a small bistro in La Contrescarpe before falling in love with Puymirol, a village of 794 inhabitants in the Séoune valley near Agen. Today, armed with his four toques, he is called to Japan every year to provide a week of gastronomic delight. Servair, a subsidiary of Air France, asked him to develop menus and dishes for its western SNCF (train) lines, and he may do the same for the TGV (superfast trains) and the Concorde. But despite all this, Trama has not become a phantom chef. His true passion is his restaurant and his cooking. You'll rarely see him in the dining room, since he's always busy working behind the scenes, following each meal with his team of young cooks from beginning to end.

It all begins with a treasure hunt, the daily quest for the fruits of the land that takes Trama into the surrounding countryside. Here, he gathers marvelous little vegetables grown by Saint-Exupéry's former cook; there, a none-too-ordinary Parisian pheasant; and in between, he fattens the best capons in the world and rabbits whose meat has nothing in common with mushy, bland, mass-produced rabbits. Fish from the Atlantic, beef from the southwest, farm chicken—when it comes to selecting hisraw materials, including the marvelous sea salt and the Italian balsamic vinegar that costs a fortune, Trama is as demanding as he is with the Havana cigars he puffs almost nonstop.

The last ingredient is a ton of talent, and voilà, your plate (a different color for each course) is filled with amazing blintzes with beans and pork sausage, a terrine of young leeks with truffles, langoustines fried with crackling pigs' ears, a preparation of lobster with cracked wheat that looks like a thick slice of sausage, the splendid "pressée de légumes" with basil vinegar (a terrine with the vegetables left whole), wild salmon with verjuice, the famous lemon capon with parsley sauce, sesame grilled pigs' feet, croustade de canard au cèpes presented as crunchy mushroom caps enveloping the mixture of duck and cèpes (the good Lord himself couldn't make this dish any better) and, lest we forget, salted cod with leeks à la ventrêche (thin slices of crusty pork)—a dish that couldn't possibly command a rating of less than 21/20.

Trama has discovered a fantastic pastry chef: himself. His delicate confit of apricots, combining apricots, fresh almond sorbet and almond and vanilla-bean cream, his crunchy biscuit with pain d'épice (wonderfully spicy cookie) ice cream, his griottines (small cherries) lightly dipped in chocolate and served in a Banyuls sauce, his millefeuille de nougatine glacée au pralin—any of these desserts would make nine-tenths of France's professional pastry chefs die of envy.

The wine list, presented by Maryse, her adorable daughter and her charming son-in-law, the first maître d'hotel, demonstrates the same concern for perfection, be it the best years of the great Bordeaux or the more modest wines from the southwest. With an old Armagnac and perhaps a fine Havana cigar to top it all off, you couldn't possibly make us believe that you aren't among the happiest of people.

A la carte: 350-500F. Menus: 120F (weekday lunch only), 250F, 400F.

L'Aigle

61300 L'Aigle - (Orne)
Paris 141 - Dreux 58 - Argentan 54 - Alençon 65

(13) Le Dauphin

Pl. de la Halle - 33.24.43.12

MM. Bernard & Leroi. Hours & credit card information not available.

The large dining room in this old coach house will soon lose its Anglo-Norman decor. The small room on the lower level will be redone, too, as will the entire inn, nestled in the Ouche district, so dear to La Varende and to the Countess de Ségur (*Les Mémoires d'un Ane* describes the open-air market that was held on the square just across from Le Dauphin). The traditional cuisine is cleverly innovative, though a bit weak in the finishing touches, as evidenced by the attractively presented salad of sweetbreads, which has too much vinegar, and the turbot, which is a bit overcooked (but not the beautiful vegetables that accompany it). An excellent dessert is the apples preserved in Calvados. In fact, there is an ample selection of Calvados fromthe regions of Normandy: Auge, Domfrontais, Perche, Avranches and so on. The reception and the service are improving.

A la carte: 350F. Menus: 104F to 300F.

Le Dauphin

(See restaurant above)

Closings & credit card information not available. 30 rms 296-430F.

The fair rooms have been redecorated with great care, while the common areas are in the best of provincial-bourgeois taste. A small shop located inside the hotel sells old Calvados.

> *This symbol stands for "Les Lauriers du Terroir," an award given to chefs who prepare noteworthy traditional or regional recipes.*

Aigues-Mortes

30220 Aigues-Mortes - (Gard)
Paris 750 - Arles 48 - Montpellier 32 - Nîmes 39 - Sète 65

(13) L'Archère

10, rue Amiral-Courbet - 66.53.72.68

M. Girard. Open daily until 11 p.m. (in seas.). Garden dining. Pets allowed. Garage parking. Telex 485465. Cards: V, AE, DC, MC.

At the foot of the tower of Constance, L'Archère successfully blends somber, contemporary luxury with old medieval stones. The geometrical dining room, decorated in peach and champagne tones, is superbly bare, and the tables are elegant. Jean-Claude Lanxade, a skilled chef who was Albano's assistant at La Tamarissière in Agde, prepares a fine, decorative cuisine. Earning L'Archère its toque: the melon soup with citrus fruit and Sauternes, which is nothing out of the ordinary but is fresh and attractively presented; the delicious raw salmon brushed with olive oil and seasoned with cod salt; and the light feuillantine with strawberries. The short fixed-price menus are outstanding, as is the service, and in summer, the patio is a pleasure.

A la carte: 260F. Menus: 90F (lunch only), 130F, 150F to 290F.

Saint-Louis

(See restaurant above)

Open year-round. 22 rms 256-316F. Half-board 360F. TV. Pets allowed.

The 22 spacious, well-equipped rooms have a fresh and pretty decor; the nicest ones have a view of the inside patio. Reception is cordial.

Hostellerie des Remparts

6, pl. d'Armes - 66.53.82.77

Closed Jan. 5-March 15. 3 stes 600-800F. 13 rms 250-430F. Half-board 230-320F oblig. in seas. Cards: V, AE, DC, MC.

This eighteenth-century townhouse, built into the outer walls of the city, now houses beautiful rooms with tasteful antique furniture. Restaurant.

Aïnhoa

64250 Cambo-les-Bains - (Pyrénées-Atlantiques)
Paris 768 - St-Jean-de-Luz 23 - Cambo 11 - Bayonne 26

(15) Ithurria

59.29.92.11

M. Isabal. Open until 9 p.m. Closed Tues. lunch, Wed. (off-seas.) & Nov. 15-March 15. Air cond. Pets allowed. Garage parking. Cards: V, AE, DC.

A more confident Maurice Isabal, captivated by the elegance of a light cuisine, has turned his magnificent old coach house (a historic monument from the seventeenth century) into one of the best restaurants in the Basque country. His fish is something of a miracle, his sauces have been lightened, and his interesting à la carte menu is filled with ideas. In a nutshell, Ithurria is a small revelation, one that deserves a second toque. We tasted and retasted the warm garden salad with two kinds of smoked, lightly steamed and exceptionally mellow salmon, the savory terrine of cèpes flavored with truffles, the ragoût of large langoustines with fresh, finely sauced pasta, the exquisite small red Espelette sweet peppers stuffed with cod; the grilled hake with tarragon cream and the outstanding homemade vanilla ice cream garnishing small poached pears in a strawberry sauce. The winecellar is excellent and the service superb.

A la carte: 300-350F. Menus: 120F, 210F.

Ithurria

(See restaurant above)

Closed Tues., Wed. & Nov. 15-March 15. 1 ste 580F. 27 rms 300-400F. Half-board 350-400F. TV in 16 rms. Pets allowed. Heated pool.

The large, beautiful rooms, more comfortable than charming, are spotlessly clean. Excellent reception by the ladies of the house, and a delicious breakfast.

Ohantzea

59.29.90.50

Closed Sun., Mon. & Nov. 15-Feb. 15. 10 rms 155-210F. Parking. Cards: V.

You'll love the authentic, ancient charm of this beautifully furnished village inn, as well as the cordial reception. Restaurant.

Aire-sur-l'Adour

40800 Aire-sur-l'Adour - (Landes)
Paris 708 - Tarbes 69 - Mont-de-Marsan 31 - Pau 31

13 Le Commerce

3, blvd. des Pyrénées - 58.71.60.06

M. Labadie. Open until 9 p.m. Closed Mon. Pets allowed. Hotel: 20 rms 90-180F. Garage parking. Cards: V, MC.

The gloomy decor is soon to disappear, and you may discover even before we do the cheerful new environment planned by the charming Dédé Labadie. Then there'll be a proper setting in which to sample his duck liver braised in herbs, salmon in Champagne, rabbit pot-au-feu and breast of duck with paprika. The wide selection of courses is a bit confusing, but everything is well prepared (particularly the grilled meats), and the portions are generous. The good-humored atmosphere will cheer even the most surly diner.

A la carte: 230-250F.

IN NEARBY **Ségos**
(9km SW on N 134 & D 260)
32400 Riscle - (Gers)

14 Domaine de Bassibé

62.09.46.71

M. Capelle. Open until 9:30 p.m. Closed Nov. 1-May 1. Garden dining. No pets. Parking. Telex 531918. Cards: V, AE, DC, MC.

The park-like grounds comprise nearly ten acres (and, beyond, thousands of acres spread majestically across the foothills of the Gers), an enticing swimming pool is framed by green lawns, and a happy, serene country atmosphere pervades: Such are the delights at this old hilltop estate, which has been thoroughly modernized by its owners, Jean-Pierre and Mayi Capelle. Recently, however, we were confronted by a slackness in the kitchen that was impossible to ignore. Though the brandade of cod with a tomato vinaigrette and the chocolate cake were up to snuff, the wan-tasting clams in an essence of tomato, the overcooked salmon and the little forcemeats of hake with a carrot and celery flan decidedly were not. Knowing chef Capelle, we have little doubt that this is merely a brief lapse that he will soon give us ample cause to forget. But for the time being, we'll have to leave his second toque in the cloakroom.

A la carte: 300-350F. Menus: 160F, 250F.

Domaine de Bassibé

(See restaurant above)

Closed Nov. 1-May 1. 3 stes 750F. 6 rms 440-590F. Half-board 510-590F oblig. in seas. TV in 6 rms. Pool.

An old estate renovated with exquisite taste now boasts bright, pleasant rooms artfully decorated by Mayi Capelle, perfect service and an outstanding breakfast. Relais et Châteaux.

See also: **Eugénie-les-Bains (Michel Guérard) Luppé-Violles, Plaisance-du-Gers Villeneuve-de-Marsan**

Aix-en-Provence

13100 Aix-en-Provence - (Bouches-du-Rhône)
Paris 760 - Nice 176 - Avignon 75 - Marseille 31

Note: The numbers following the telephone number in each review pinpoint the establishment's exact location on the accompanying map.

Sights. The superb Saint-Sauveur cathedral (with its sculptured portal and its triptych of the Blazing Bush); Cloister Saint-Sauveur (the very embodiment of grace); the city hall (and the adjacent clock tower); the archbishop's residence (a museum of tapestries and, in July, home to the Festival of Lyrical Arts); Musée Granet, located in the Knights of Malta's old priory (paintings from the French school of the sixteenth to the nineteenth centuries, as well as those from the Flemish, Dutch, German and Italian schools); Paul Cézanne's studio; the Vasarely Foundation; the cours Mirabeau itself with its fountains, and the many townhouses (more than 160) scattered throughout the city; the Museum of Old Aix (containing local artifacts); the Sainte-Marie-Madeleine church (with a fifteenth-century triptych of the Annunciation).

Eating on the Run. Al Dente, 14, rue Constantin (for its pasta); Brémond, 36, cours Mirabeau (menu for dieters); Le Diable Boîteux, 29, rue Fermée (a beautiful dessert buffet); L'-Empereur des Roses, 9, rue du Félibre-Gaut (salads and small Oriental dishes); Le Petit Verdot, 7, rue d'Entrecasteaux (you can order appetizers from the wine bar); Le Vésuve, 2 bis, rue Clémenceau (pizzeria); Le Vieux Tonneau, 6, rue des Bernardins (excellent quality for the price).

Brasseries. Le Cintra, 8, pl. Jeanne-d'Arc (a grand choice of beers); La Royale, 17, cours Mirabeau (classical).

Bars & Cafés. Le Blue Note, 10, rue de la Fonderie (jazz piano bar); Les Deux Garçons, 53, cours Mirabeau (an institution representative of an entire era); Le Festival, 67 bis, rue Espariat (youthful ambience); La Fontaine d'Argent, rue

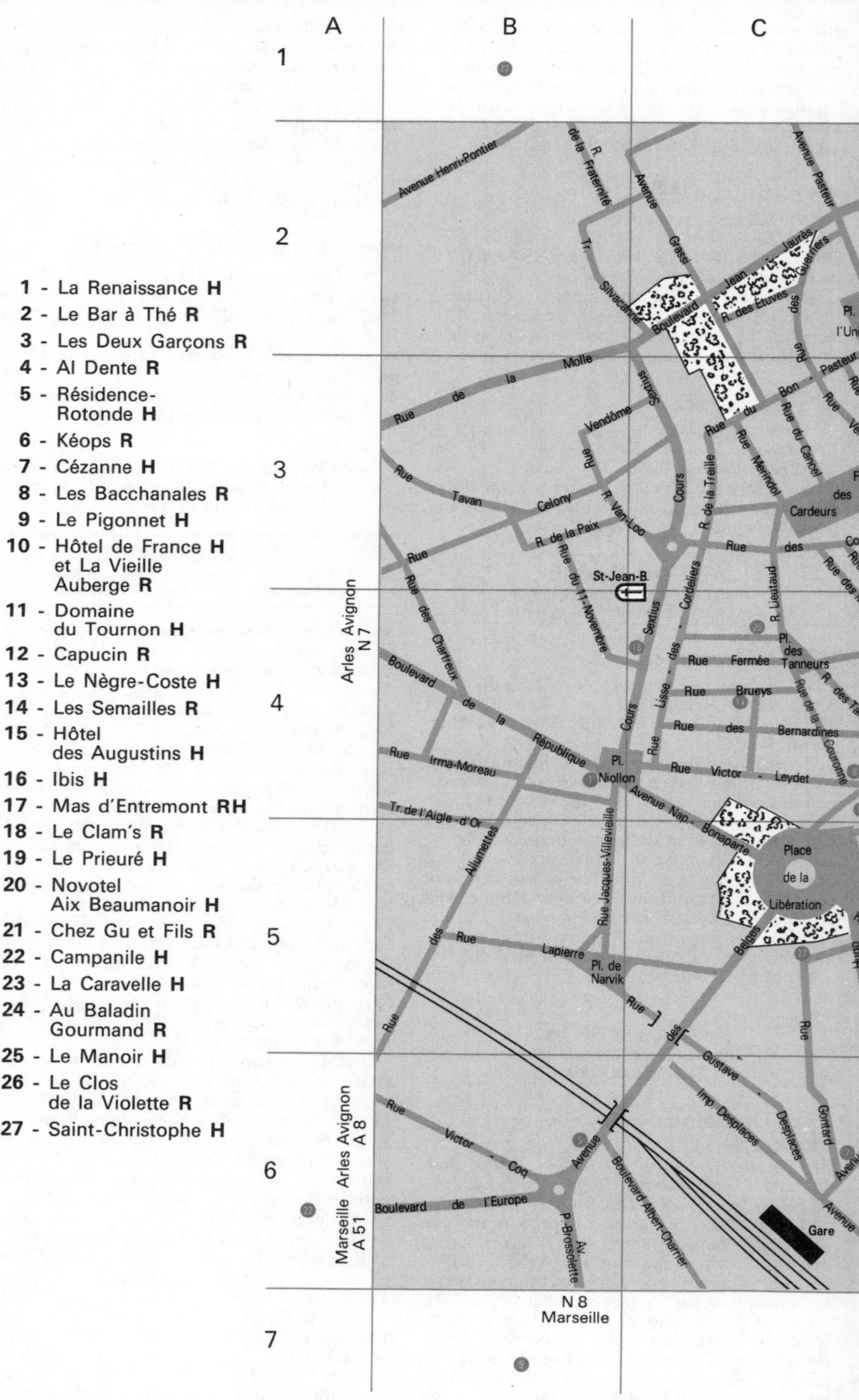
1 - La Renaissance H
2 - Le Bar à Thé R
3 - Les Deux Garçons R
4 - Al Dente R
5 - Résidence-Rotonde H
6 - Kéops R
7 - Cézanne H
8 - Les Bacchanales R
9 - Le Pigonnet H
10 - Hôtel de France H et La Vieille Auberge R
11 - Domaine du Tournon H
12 - Capucin R
13 - Le Nègre-Coste H
14 - Les Semailles R
15 - Hôtel des Augustins H
16 - Ibis H
17 - Mas d'Entremont RH
18 - Le Clam's R
19 - Le Prieuré H
20 - Novotel Aix Beaumanoir H
21 - Chez Gu et Fils R
22 - Campanile H
23 - La Caravelle H
24 - Au Baladin Gourmand R
25 - Le Manoir H
26 - Le Clos de la Violette R
27 - Saint-Christophe H
A
B
C
1
2
3
4
5
6
7
Avenue Henri-Pontier
R. de la Fraternité
Avenue Grassi
Avenue Pasteur
Tr. Silvacanne
Boulevard Jean Jaurès
R. des Étuves
Rue des Guerriers
Pl. de l'Univ
Rue de la Molle
Sextius
Rue Vendôme
Rue du Bon Pasteur
Rue du Cancel
Rue Mérindol
Rue Tavan
Rue Celony
R. Van-Loo
R. de la Paix
Cours
R. de la Treille
Rue du 11-Novembre
Rue des Cardeurs
St-Jean-B.
Rue des Chartreux
Rue des Cordeliers
Cours Sextius
R. Lieutaud
Pl. des Tanneurs
Rue Fermée
Rue Brueys
Rue des Bernardines
Rue de la Couronne
Rue Lisse des Cordeliers
Boulevard de la République
Rue Irma-Moreau
Pl. Niollon
Rue Victor Leydet
Avenue Nap. Bonaparte
Tr. de l'Aigle-d'Or
Rue des Allumettes
Rue Jacques-Villevieille
Place de la Libération
Belges
Rue Lapierre
Pl. de Narvik
Rue des Gustave Desplaces
Imp. Desplaces
Rue Gontard
Arles Avignon N 7
Arles Avignon A 8
Marseille A 51
Rue Victor Coq
Avenue
Boulevard de l'Europe
Av. P.-Brossolette
Boulevard Albert-Charrier
Gare
N 8 Marseille

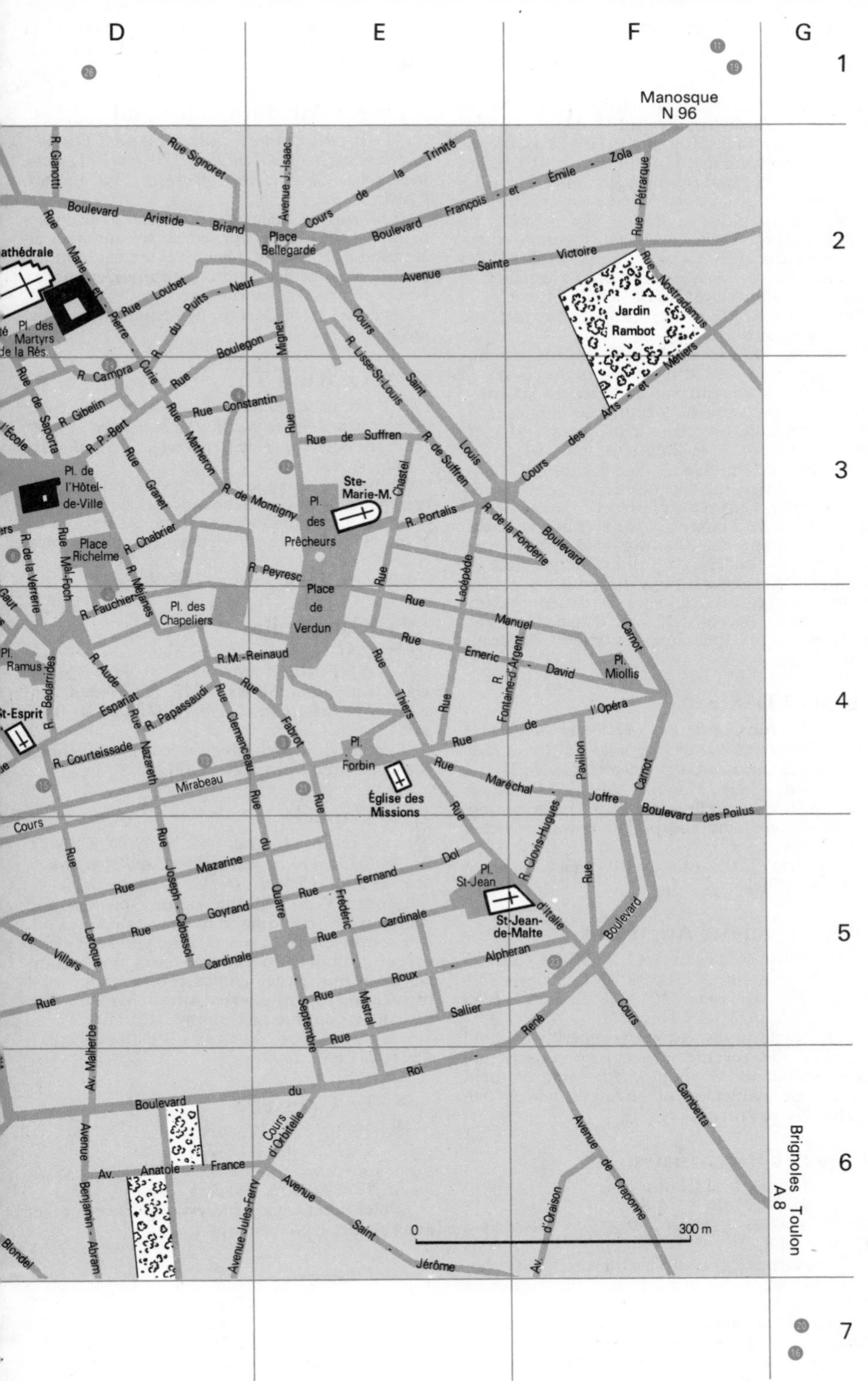

D
E
F
G
1
2
3
4
5
6
7
Manosque
N 96
Brignoles Toulon
A 8
Place Bellegarde
Jardin Rambot
Pl. des Martyrs de la Rés.
Pl. de l'Hôtel-de-Ville
Place Richelme
Pl. des Prêcheurs
Ste-Marie-M.
Place de Verdun
Pl. des Chapeliers
Pl. Ramus
St-Esprit
Pl. Forbin
Église des Missions
Pl. Miollis
Pl. St-Jean
St-Jean-de-Malte
Boulevard Aristide Briand
Cours de la Trinité
Boulevard François et Émile Zola
Avenue Sainte Victoire
Cours Saint Louis
Boulevard Carnot
Cours Mirabeau
Boulevard du Roi René
Cours Gambetta
Avenue de Craponne
Avenue Saint Jérôme
Av. Anatole France
Avenue Jules-Ferry
Cours d'Orbitelle
Boulevard des Poilus
Rue de l'Opéra
Rue Maréchal Joffre
Rue Manuel
Rue Emeric David
Rue Thiers
Rue Fabrot
Rue Clemenceau
Rue du Quatre Septembre
Rue Mazarine
Rue Goyrand
Rue Cardinale
Rue Fernand Dol
Rue Roux Alpheran
Rue Sallier
Rue Frédéric Mistral
Rue Joseph Cabassol
Rue Laroque
Rue de Villars
Av. Malherbe
Avenue Benjamin Abram
Blondel
Av. d'Oraison
Rue Pavillon
R. Clovis-Hugues
Rue d'Italie
R. Fontaine-d'Argent
Rue Lacépède
Rue Chastel
R. Portalis
R. de la Fonderie
R. de Suffren
Rue de Suffren
R. Lisse-St-Louis
Cours des Arts et Métiers
Rue Nostradamus
Rue Pétrarque
Avenue J.-Isaac
Rue Signoret
R. Gianotti
Rue Mignet
Rue Pierre et Marie Curie
Rue Loubet
R. du Puits Neuf
Rue Boulegon
Rue Constantin
Rue Matheron
R. Campra
R. Gibelin
Rue de Saporta
R. P.-Bert
Rue Granet
R. de Montigny
R. Chabrier
R. Peyresc
R. de la Verrerie
Rue Mal-Foch
R. Fauchier
R. Méjanes
R.M.-Reinaud
R. Aude
R. Bedarrides
Rue Espariat
R. Papassaudi
Rue Nazareth
R. Courteissade
0
300 m

de la Fontaine-d'Argent (depending on the hour, a piano bar, a crêperie or a café/theater); Le Grillon, 49, cours Mirabeau.

Nightlife. La Chimère, ave. de Lattre-de-Tassigny (lively and extremely selective); Club 88, La Calade N 7 (disco); Cousin-Germain, 15, rue d'Italie (jazz, same programs as Hot Brass, friendly and entertaining); Hot Brass, rte. d'Eguilles (the meeting place for local jazz musicians); Le Khoreia, 1 bis, cours Mirabeau (traditional, designed to please a middle-age crowd); Le Mistral, 3, rue Frédéric-Mistral (for the well-to-do and the over-30 set); Oxydium, rte. des Milles (disco); Rétro, 25, quartier Malouesse (fantastic sound, comfortable); Le Richelm', 24, rue de la Verrerie (one of the oldest clubs, but attracts the youngest patrons).

Shops. *Bakeries:* De Battista, 14, rue Montigny; Doze, 45, rue d'Italie (fabulous loaves of bread, fruit cakes and pain de Beaucaire). *Confections & chocolate:* Chocolaterie de Puyricard, 7, rue Rifle-Rafle (excellent chocolates and marzipan sweets); A la Reine Jeanne, 32, cours Mirabeau; Le Roi René, 7, rue Papassandi. *Charcuterie:* Olivier, rue Jacques-de-Laroque (everything is prepared on the premises). *Cheese:* Gérard Paul, 9, rue des Marseillais (the very best cheeses). *Pastries:* Brémond, 36, cours Mirabeau (many creations); Riederer, 6, rue Thiers (quite in vogue). *Santons* (sellers of small wooden Christmas figures): Paul Fouque, 65, cours Gambetta. *Wine:* Bacchus, 27, rue d'Italie; Les Vignobles, 5, pl. Richelme (excellent Bordeaux wines).

10/20 Al Dente

14, rue Constantin - 42.96.41.03 / D3-4
MM. Cerrito & Buti. Open until 11 p.m. Closed Sun. lunch. Air cond. Pets allowed. Cards: V.

Toulon, Nîmes, Marseille, Aix... Al Dente is a small pasta chain in Provence that's noisy, young, uncomfortable and cheap. The cuisine is heavy and hearty.

A la carte: 120F. Menu: 40F (weekday lunch only, wine incl.).

Hôtel des Augustins

3, rue de la Masse - 42.27.28.59 / D4-15
Open year-round. 3 stes 800-900F. 32 rms 360-680F. TV. Air cond. No pets. Parking. Telex 441052. Cards: V, AE, DC, MC.

The small rooms within the superbly restored walls of this seventeenth-century convent are comfortable and soundproofed; some of them have terraces with views of the Augustin friars' bell tower. No restaurant.

12/20 Les Bacchanales

10, rue de la Couronne
42.27.21.06 / C4-8
M. Poussardin. Open until 10:30 p.m. Closed Sun. Cards: V, DC.

Sample the egg casserole with sorrel, the excellent ramekinof sweetbreads and the ragoût of small calamari in a sauce piquante (a tangy vinegar-based sauce). This fresh, well-prepared cuisine has just one flaw: It's too expensive. But the wooden beams and stones provide an environment as warm and cordial as the reception from the friendly owners. The desserts are lovely.

A la carte: 280F. Menus: 69F (lunch only), 89F, 139F.

11/20 Au Baladin Gourmand

10, rue Campra - 42.96.60.43 / D3-24
M. Samtomocito. Open until 10 p.m. (11 p.m. weekends). Closed Sun. (off-seas.). Pets allowed. Cards: V, AE, DC.

In all fairness, success should crown the efforts of this small, newly opened restaurant with an amusing cellar decor. The prices are fair, and the cuisine is congenial and fresh: terrines, émincé of beef with paprika, lemon tart.

A la carte: 180F. Menus: 64F (lunch only, wine incl.), 85F, 125F.

10/20 Le Bar à Thé

66, pl. Richelme - 42.23.51.99 / D4-2
Mme. Girard. Open until 10 p.m. Closed Sun. & Aug. 15-Sept. 8. Terrace dining. Pets allowed. Cards: V, AE.

Le Bar à Thé is the noisy rendezvous spot for merchants from the Richelme market. The fresh, plentiful and spontaneous cuisine is prepared by Mme. Girard: vegetable terrines, scallop pies, chocolate cake.

A la carte: 160F. Menus: 70F, 90F.

Campanile

ZAC du Jas de Bouffon
42.59.40.73 / A6-22
Open year-round. 50 rms 230F. Half-board 215-340F. TV. Pets allowed. Telex 441273. Cards: V, MC.

Though close to the freeway, this modern hotel is well isolated from noise. Grill.

12/20 Capucin

7 ter, rue Mignet - 42.20.69.77 / E3-12
M. Jesset. Open until midnight. Closed Mon. lunch, Sun. & Aug. 15-Sept. 10. Pets allowed. Cards: V.

Capucin's early-Gothic decor, splendid and stately as it is, could stand to be warmed up a bit. The southwestern cuisine features good duck liver in coarse salt (it can be ordered warm, too, accompanied by fresh pasta), confits, properly rare breast of duck and expertly cooked lotte in Madeira. The restaurant continues to improve steadily.

A la carte: 230F. Menus: 100F (lunch only), 155F, 210F.

La Caravelle

29, blvd. du Roi-René
42.21.53.05 / F5-23
Open year-round. 30 rms 160-270F. TV. Pets allowed. Telex 401015. Cards: V, MC.

Fifteen rooms face a succession of lovely, quiet inner gardens. No restaurant.

Cézanne

40, ave. Victor-Hugo
42.26.34.73 / C6-7
Closed Jan. 2 stes 800-1,250F. 42 rms 390-900F. TV. Air cond. in 22 rms. No pets. Garage parking. Telex 403158. Cards: V, AE.

In this remarkable small hotel, with its fresh, bright, lovely rooms, the service is excellent and extensive. Particular care is given to breakfast. No restaurant.

12/20 Chez Gu et Fils

3, rue F.-Mistral - 42.26.75.12 / E4-21
M. Galasso. Open until midnight. Closed Sat. lunch, Sun. & Aug. Air cond. Pets allowed.

His cap perched atop his head, the jovial, mustachioed Gu, a distinguished local personage, has all of Aix rushing to his rustic bistro for his oysters "au coin du feu," his celery and anchovies, his pavé of beef Pierre Perret (a friend of the house) and his leg of lamb with cèpes. The wines are superb, the checks high-flying.

À la carte: 280-300F. Menu: 80F (lunch only).

13 Le Clam's

22, cours Sextius - 42.27.64.78 / C4-18
M. Fredenucci. Open until 10 p.m. Closed July & Aug. Pets allowed. Cards: V, AE, DC.

No one could say that Joseph Fredenucci goes out of his way to attract tourists to his lovely cork-walled restaurant. In fact, quite the opposite is true, since he closes the place for the summer. And his checks are indeed high, but that's because his exclusively seafood cuisine is understandably expensive to prepare—he chooses only the best fish, langoustines and lobster (patiently waiting in his fish pond), and only the freshest shellfish from his oyster seller. Try the marvelous plate of seafood steamed in algae, the tureen of fish in batter, the crab ragoût with cèpes, the turbot in olive oil and, to conclude, a perfect chocolate cake with bitter-orange sauce.

A la carte: 350F. Menu: 180F.

15 Le Clos de la Violette

10, ave. de la Violette
42.23.30.71 / D1-26
M. Banzo. Open until 9:30 p.m. Closed Mon. lunch, Sun., Feb. 20-March 7 & Nov. 1-21. Garden dining. No pets. Cards: V, AE.

It is clear that Jean-Marc Banzo's cuisine is that of a happy man. How, indeed, could one fail to be content in this harmonious bourgeois house at the end of a square garden shaded by chestnut trees in the most wonderful residential district of Aix-en-Provence? A small music room has been added to the dining room, which Brigitte Banzo has decorated in gray and blue. The subtle, precise cuisine, exquisitely served, is flavored with garden herbs and inspired by regional creations: Bouzigues mussels à la bohémienne (gypsy style), served in their shells and seasoned with a thyme sabayon, small sardines lightly marinated in spices, a fricassée of escargots with parsley,noisettes of young rabbit accompanied by a polenta with rosemary. The cheeses come from Gérard Paul—the best cheese producer in Aix—and the fresh soufflé with garden mint lends its lightness and freshness to the rest of the equally exquisite desserts. The cellar is well balanced. Le Clos de la Violette well deserves its second toque.

A la carte: 350-400F. Menus: 170F (weekday lunch only, except holidays), 260F, 330F.

Les Deux Garçons

53, cours Mirabeau - 42.26.00.51 / E4-3
M. Antonioli. Open daily until 2 a.m. Terrace. Garage parking. Pets allowed. Cards: V.

It's too early to say much about the food, which in any event is bound to be typical brasserie fare with a Provençal accent. But we can say how pleased we are to see the loveliest café in all of Provence rise up from its ashes. The "classical" gilded woodwork (dating from the first Empire), mercury mirrors and elaborate moldings look even better than before the fire, now relieved of centuries-old layers of grime. We cheer the resurrection of this historic café, where personalities from Raimu to Blaise Cendrars, from Mistinguett to Elisabeth Schwarzkopf – not to mention the thousands of festival-goers who descend on Aix in the summer – have lingered with pleasure. A la carte: 140-200F. Menus: 120F (weekday lunch only), from 180F to 300F (dinner only).

Domaine du Tournon

Les Pichinats - 42.21.22.05 / F1-11
Open year-round. 59 rms 240-360F. Half-board 370-450F. TV. Pets allowed. Pool. Tennis. Parking. Telex 441530. Cards: V, DC.

The rooms in this large, affluent townhouse in the heart of a twelve-acre park are quite comfortable. The hotel also houses special facilities for sports and recreation. Restaurant.

Hôtel de France

63, rue Espariat - 42.27.90.15 / C4-10
Open year-round. 27 rms 140-290F. TV in 15 rms. Telex 410777. Cards: AE.

The rooms and equipment have been completely renovated. Under new management.

Ibis

Chemin des Infirmeries
42.27.98.20 / G7-16
Open year-round. 83 rms 245-270F. TV. Pets allowed. Parking. Telex 420519. Cards: V, MC.

The rooms of this hotel next to the freeway are small but well maintained, and they offer a good value. Grill.

11/20 Kéops

28, rue de la Verrerie
42.96.59.05 / D3-6
M. Fathalah. Open until midnight. Closed Tues. Terrace dining. Pets allowed.

This place is never empty—Aix's young people flock to the small cellar, where, seated on stools, they sample the exquisite small crêpes, rolled and filled with fish, the meatballs and the sea bream with lemon preserves, all from Fathalah's Egyptian/Syrian repertoire. It is as fresh as it is inexpensive.

A la carte: 120F. Menu: 120F (wine incl.).

Prices in red draw attention to restaurants that offer a particularly good value.

Le Manoir

8, rue d'Entrecasteaux
42.26.27.20 / C4-25

Closed Jan. 15-Feb. 15. 43 rms 197-438F. TV in 30 rms. Pets allowed. Garage parking. Telex 441489. Cards: V, AE, DC, MC.

After spending a peaceful night in one of the large, nicely furnished rooms in this perfectly restored fourteenth-century cloister, you will enjoy a delightful Le Manoir breakfast. No restaurant.

11/20 Mas d'Entremont

Montée d'Avignon
42.23.45.32 / B1-17

M. Marignane. Open until 9 p.m. Closed Sun. dinner, Mon. lunch (except holidays) & Nov. 1-March 15. Terrace dining. Pets allowed. Parking. Cards: V.

Though the à la carte menu is a bit expensive, the fixed-price menus are perfect. And the charm of this large Provençal house is as splendid as its cool Provençal garden is priceless. Try the red mullet mousse with saffron, the fresh salmon marinière and the lotte with basil.

A la carte: 300F. Menus: 160F, 180F.

Mas d'Entremont

(See restaurant above)

Closed Nov. 1-March 15. 17 rms 380-650F. Half-board 400-500F oblig. in seas. TV. Air cond. Pets allowed. Pool. Tennis.

Located in a large, serene park in the Aix countryside, this beautiful, prettily furnished farmhouse, with its patio and terrace, offers outstanding reception and service.

Le Nègre-Coste

33, cours Mirabeau
42.27.74.22 / D4-13

Open year-round. 37 rms 310-470F. TV. Pets allowed. Garage parking. Telex 440184. Cards: V, AE, DC, MC.

Le Nègre-Coste is the oldest of the historic hotels in the center of Aix—its facade is from the eighteenth century—but all its rooms have been pleasantly modernized and are furnished with stunning antiques. The old-fashioned elevator and inside garage only add to its appeal. No restaurant.

Novotel Aix Beaumanoir

Résidence Beaumanoir
42.27.47.50 / G7-20

Open year-round. 102 rms 350F. TV. Air cond. Pool. Parking. Telex 400244. Cards: V, AE, DC, MC.

This hotel offers all the customary benefits of its chain: a swimming pool in the summer, special rates for children and modern, bright rooms that are regularly redecorated.Restaurant.

Le Pigonnet

5, ave. du Pigonnet - 42.59.02.90 / B7-9

Open year-round. 50 rms 350-750F. Pool. Cards: V, AE, DC, MC.

The rooms (and bathrooms) in this centuries-old country house set amid 100-year-old chestnut trees were recently modernized and redecorated. Its location in a two-acre flower-filled park will make you forget that you're in the heart of the city. The service is outstanding.

Le Prieuré

N 96, rte. de Sisteron
42.21.05.23 / F1-19

Open year-round. 30 rms 135-310F. No pets. Parking.

Facing the neatly pruned box trees of the Lenfant park (designed by Lenôtre), Le Prieuré is an exquisite, perfectly comfortable place for a rest. The decor is first-rate. No restaurant.

La Renaissance

4, blvd. de la République
42.26.04.22 / B4-1

Open year-round. 35 rms 188-285F. TV. Pets allowed. Telex 403521. Cards: V, AE, DC.

These well-equipped rooms in an old house have been prettily redone. No restaurant.

Résidence-Rotonde

15, ave. des Belges - 42.26.29.88 / B6-5

Closed Dec. 15-Jan. 15. 42 rms 175-300F. TV in 26 rms. Pets allowed. Parking. Cards: V, AE, DC.

A modern, functional and well-located hotel with lovely bathrooms and perfect sound insulation in the front rooms. No restaurant.

Saint-Christophe

2, ave. Victor-Hugo
42.26.01.24 / C5-27

Open year-round. 56 rms 170-270F. TV. Pets allowed. Garage parking. Cards: V.

Simple rooms, some with small terraces. No restaurant.

12/20 Les Semailles

15, rue Brueys - 42.27.23.44 / C4-14

M. Armitano. Open until 10:30 p.m. Closed Sun. lunch and Mon. Cards: AE, V.

The new owner seems to be doing a pretty good job in the kitchen: his sea bream with fresh herbs is attractively decorated and tasty to boot; the veal kidneys are cooked to a turn and napped with a savory mustard sauce; the raspberry charlotte is nicely made, with a fine, fresh flavor. Prices, however, are on the stiff side. We suggest that some of those profits be used to brighten and freshen the rather gloomy dining room.

A la carte: 250F.

(13) La Vieille Auberge

63, rue Espariat - 42.27.17.41 / C4-10

M. de March. Open until 10 p.m. Closed Wed. & Jan. 15-31. Cards: V, AE, DC.

A former chef at the Auberge de Bellet, where we had awarded him a toque, Albin Daïriam has now taken charge of the stoves at this bright, refreshing house bordering the old districts of Aix. His talent remains intact, if we can go by the flavorful terrine of sole, hogfish and a bouillabaisse aspic, the gâteau of red mullet with lobster mousse boldly seasoned with mint and the delicious filet of veal seasoned with sage and accompanied by a zucchini cake. But the desserts, we must report, are less than extraordinary. The tables are elegantly set, the wine list is handsome, and the reception by Bruno de March, the owner, is courteous.

A la carte: 260-280F. Menus: 100F (weekday lunch only), 150F to 250F (weekdays only).

IN NEARBY **Beaurecueil**
(10 km E on N 7)
13100 Aix-en-Provence - (Bouches-du-Rhône)

(14) Mas de la Bertrande

42.28.90.09

M. Bertrand. Open until 9:30 p.m. Closed Sun. dinner & Mon. (off-seas., except holidays) & Feb. 15-March 15. Terrace dining. Hotel: 10 rms 280-380F. Pets allowed. Parking. Telex 403521. Cards: V, AE, DC.

M. Bertrand, the cordial owner of this lovely farmhouse that bears his name, made a wise decision indeed when he employed Elisabeth Gagnaire, a skillful and serious cook. The dishes making up her creative cuisine depend upon the season; ingredients are purchased each day at the market, and they are always fresh, with bright, vibrant flavors. All is delicate and feminine, despite appearances, especially now that servings are no longer measured out under a watchful eye. Thanks to the variety of fixed-price menus, even with a good Côtes-du-Rhône (the choice is superb), your check won't be astronomical, especially if you order the short menu served on weekdays, which brings you a light millefeuille of blond livers served over an émincé of leeks, a delicious filet of beef with olives and a gratin of young turnips, some beautiful cheeses and a rich, black chocolate cake layered with crème anglaise. The choice of coffees and teas is excellent, and under the lovely white parasols on the terrace, amid flourishing greenery, you'll receive excellent service.

Menus: 169F (weekdays only), 279F, 205F.

(15) Relais Sainte-Victoire

42.28.94.98

MM. Jugy & Bergès. Open until 9 p.m. Closed Sun. dinner, Mon., Feb. & All Saints' Day school holidays. Air cond. Terrace dining. Pets allowed. Hotel: 5 stes 300-450F; 5 rms 200-260F; half-board 300-380F. TV. Air cond. in 5 rms. Pool. Tennis. Parking. Cards: V, AE, DC, MC.

The fire that destroyed their house two years ago only served to set ablaze the passion of M. Jugy, the owner of this large, pleasant country inn, and René Bergès, his son-in-law and cook. With its Provençal floor tiles, its pottery collection and its soft-oak paneling, the decor is even warmer and more hospitable than before. The wide windows allow the eyes to feast upon scenery whose colors inspired Cézanne. The family reception is gracious, and the well-spaced tables provide the degree of comfort needed for the long period you'll spend seated there: The gigantic, eleven-course "Cézanne" menu is prudently made available at 3 p.m. Bergès's ingenuity does not fail him: At our last visit, he once again offered such generous dishes as pan-fried filets of red mullet in lavender butter, Drôme pigeon with artichokes, and cod with a zucchini gratin. All these dishes are additions to the classical repertoire that simply mustn't be missed, particularly the pieds et paquets (Provençal mutton tripe and feet dish) with fresh mint and the lamb terrine with zucchini, not to mention the various desserts, whose deliberate rusticity is delightful.

Menus: 270F (menu/carte), 200F, 220F, 250F, 380F.

IN NEARBY **Puyfond**
(7 km N on N 96 & D 13)
13100 Aix-en-Provence - (Bouches-du-Rhône)

(13) Puyfond

Quartier Rigoulon - 42.92.13.77

Mme. Carbonel. Open until 10:30 p.m. Closed Sun. dinner, Mon., Feb. 15-March 9 & Aug. 24-Sept. 15. Garden dining. Pets allowed. Parking. Cards: V, AE, DC.

At first, one must take in the beautiful decor, the waxed furniture gleaming under the wooden beams, the old portraits, the lovely ornaments, the fresh bouquets and the flowered china. Everything is simple yet delightful, as is the ambience of this large house concealed among the trees. Mme. Carbonel's cuisine, spontaneous and generous, is the cuisine of a self-made woman (she used to be a nurse), pleasantly flavored with earthy tones: lasagne with lamb tripe, a cake of wild mushrooms, ramekin of escargots in garlic cream and iced nougat in orange sauce.

A la carte: 250F. Menu: 130F (weekday lunch only).

Aix-les-Bains

73100 Aix-les-Bains - (Savoie)
Paris 536 - Annecy 33 - Chambéry 14 - Lyon 112

(13) Ariana

Ave. de Marlioz - 79.88.08.00

M. Burnet. Open daily until 10 p.m. Garden dining. No pets. Parking. Telex 980266. Cards: V, AE, DC, MC.

The main floor of this large new house located in the heart of the Marlioz park, between the golf course and the forest, has an elegant but discreet prewar decor. The clientele is composed largely of people seeking the healthful waters and air, as well as the wholesome, sensible, light cuisine: salad of pan-fried langoustine tails, coquilles St-Jacques served with artichokes and a tomato fondue, and braised Bresse pigeon. The servings are a bit meager, but the service is excellent.

A la carte: 300-350F. Menus: 130F, 195F, 230F, 290F.

Ariana

(See restaurant above)

Open year-round. 5 stes 600-850F. 60 rms 380-750F. Heated pool.

Ariana's rooms, while small, are nevertheless quite comfortable, and their private terraces overlook the park. The outstanding recreation and leisure facilities include two swimming pools.

Le Manoir

37, rue George-1er
(behind the hot springs) - 79.61.44.00
Closed mid-Dec.-mid-Jan. 73 rs 200-395F. Half-board 248- 378F. TV. Air cond. in 11 rms. Pets allowed. Garage parking. Telex 980793. Cards: V, DC, MC.

Located in the middle of a park and flower garden, overlooking Aix-les-Bains and the lake, Le Manoir is a quiet and relaxing place. Though somewhat plain, it is nevertheless comfortable, and there's a free shuttle to the hot springs and the train station. Restaurant.

Ajaccio

see CORSICA

Albertville

73200 Albertville - (Savoie)
Paris 592 - Chamonix 66 - Chambéry 50 - Annecy 45

16 Million

8, pl. de la Liberté - 79.32.25.15
M. Million. Open until 9 p.m. Closed Sun. dinner, Mon. (except for lunch July 14-Sept. 1), April 24-May 10 & Sept. 18-Oct. 3. Terrace dining. Pets allowed. Hotel: 28 rms 250-500F. Garage parking. Cards: V, AE, DC.

To adequately describe the special features of Philippe Million's cuisine, we must first mention the remarkable conciseness of the small, handwritten à la carte menu. There are five appetizers and five fish and five meat dishes, then the simple clarity of the dishes, the constant creativity, Million's love of vivid flavors and fascinating, discreetly rewarding sauces and, finally, the precision of his cooking. We especially appreciate this professional who, ignoring the trend toward daintiness and one-upmanship, prefers to follow his own path; he doesn't hesitate to take great risks in his personal quest for simplicity and an authentic modern cuisine. That's how he created several wonderfully delicate dishes, whose precision of tone is close to great art: the foie gras chartreuse with poulet à la fermière, the wafers of salmon à la tombée d'oignon, the small filet of lotte in parsley sauce, the aiguillettes of duck potagère and the caramelized pistachio feuilleté with crushed sour cherries. The dining room is pleasant and comfortable, though the decor is somewhat plain. The terrace is delightful in summer, and the service has become even more gracious and efficient. Handsome cellar and good sommelier. Relais et Châteaux.

A la carte: 350-400F. Menus: 150F (weekdays only), 260F, 460F.

15 Chez Uginet

8, pl. Charles-Albert - 79.32.00.50
M. Guillot. Open until 9:30 p.m. Closed Tues., June 25-July 5 & Nov. 12-Dec. 5. Terrace dining. Pets allowed. Parking. Cards: V, AE, DC.

Eric Guillot, Alain Rayé's successor, did not have an easy job before him, especially on those days when the tourists going to the mountains arrived at Uginet weary and ill-tempered, almost overwhelming the dining room and the kitchen staff. But since Guillot accepts both criticism and compliments as long as they are justified, let's begin. Bravo for the beautiful 170-franc fixed-price menu served with a variety of delicious rolls (following Rayé's custom); for his exquisite feuilleté of veal and duck sweetbreads with asparagus; for his salmon seasoned with saffron cream; for his perfectly cooked guinea-fowl served with a stuffing of green cabbage and cream of fresh peas; and for his daring apple, lime and ginger feuilleté desserts. We did, however, find the filet of salmon with fennel slightly overcooked and the squab a bit dry. The new young sommelier, a consistent prize winner in the local wine-tasting competitions, is excellent. The service, overseen by the patronne, in a soft blue-gray decor, is charming.

A la carte: 300F. Menus: 110F (weekdays only), 250F (weekends and holidays only), 170F, 290F.

Albi

81000 Albi - (Tarn)
Paris 677 - Béziers 144 - Carcassonne 107 - Rodez 79

14 Le Cécilia

63.56.61.11
Mmes. Thuriès & Guibert. Open until 10 p.m. Closed Mon. & Jan. 3-20. Terrace dining. Pets allowed. Hotel: 4 rms 100-120F. Pool. Tennis. Parking. Cards: V.

A park, a swimming pool, two tennis courts, a private club—as many people come to Jacqueline Thuriès's large house for its recreational facilities as for her pleasant cuisine. The food is truly enticing, thanks to a young chef who trained with Robuchon and a pastry chef who trained with Yves Thuriès, the master of Cordes. The cuisine's flavors are controlled and fresh; dishes are prepared with ingredients purchased daily from the market. Clearly it's the result of excellent ideas, especially the John Dory with apples, garnished with a lemon and vanilla sauce, the feuilleté of guinea-fowl and foie gras and the pan-fried duck foie gras in mushroom sauce. The desserts are delicious as well: gratin of apricots and pistachios, millefeuille of iced mint chocolate. An additional point for the best restaurant in Albi.

A la carte: 300F. Menus: 58F and 80F (weekday lunch only), 190F (wine incl.), 95F to 220F.

Hôtel Chiffre

50, rue Séré-de-Rivières - 63.54.04.60
Open year-round. 40 rms 180-350F. TV. Pets allowed. Garage parking. Telex 520411. Cards: V, AE, DC, MC.

A handsome, well-maintained family hotel, whose rooms have all been recently redone. The restaurant opens onto a flower garden.

13 Hostellerie Saint-Antoine

17, rue St-Antoine - 63.54.04.04
MM. Rieux. Open until 9 p.m. Closed Sun. (off-seas.). Air cond. Pets allowed. Garage parking. Telex 520850. Cards: V, AE, DC, MC.

This inn, the oldest in the city, has belonged to the Rieux family for exactly 250 years. Wherever one looks, there is evidence of their dedication, consistency and professionalism, all enhanced by

the pleasures of a small, enclosed garden, which livens up the rather bourgeois dining room. The cuisine is discreetly yet sincerely modern, showing some regional color in the Languedoc-style confit and the tripe albigeoise. Sample the exquisite foie gras, the trout with herbs and the boned squab with red berries. Excellent Gaillac and Cahors wines are available at sensible prices.
A la carte: 250-300F. Menus: 90F, 130F, 180F.

Hostellerie Saint-Antoine

(See restaurant above)

Open year-round. 56 rms 280-550F. Half-board 300-480F. TV. Air cond. in 10 rms. Pets allowed.

Located right in downtown Albi, but in a quiet district, this comfortable hotel features elegant, attractively furnished rooms and a pleasant inner garden. Guests have free use of the swimming pool and tennis courts at La Réserve, the Fonvialane annex.

Le Jardin des Quatre Saisons

19, blvd. de Strasbourg - 63.60.77.76

M. Bermond. Open until 10:30 p.m. Closed Tues. lunch & Mon. Terrace dining. Pets allowed. Parking. Cards: V, AE.

The charming, rustic decor of this restaurant, which the young Bermond couple opened two years ago, has won over the people of Albi. The delicious coolness of the flowering arbors, the bougainvilleas, the geraniums and the smile of the lovely Martine are as much responsible for Le Jardin's success as is the light, precise, irresistibly inexpensive cuisine of Georges, her husband. The flan of haddock in lemon butter, the filet of mérou (grouper) à l'écossaise and the chocolate and orange cake—accompanied by a glass of Banyuls wine—definitely merit the toque. And the once meager wine list now boasts 18,000 bottles.
A la carte: 200F. Menus: 105F, 185F.

Alençon

61000 Alençon - (Orne)
Paris 195 - Rouen 145 - Le Mans 49 - Chartres 116

Le Chapeau Rouge

1, blvd. Duchamp - 33.26.20.23

Open year-round. 16 rms 120-270F. TV in 10 rms. Parking. Cards: V, MC.

Not long ago, the stylish rooms were tastefully redecorated according to the standards of a two-star hotel. No restaurant.

Au Petit Vatel

72, pl. du Cdt-Desmeulles - 33.26.23.78

M. Lerat. Open until 9:30 p.m. Closed Sun. dinner, Wed., 3 weeks in Feb. & Aug. 15-Sept. 1. Pets allowed. Cards: V, AE, DC, MC.

Located in the charming town made famous by its lace makers and the philosopher Alain, this exemplary provincial restaurant is the sweetest stopover you could possibly dream up. The career of owner M. Lerat reads almost like a Balzac novel. Here, during the past 30 years, Lerat has climbed the ladder to power, rung by rung, from bellboy to waiter to maître d' to kitchen assistant to chef and finally to patron. He is a most dedicated cook, faithful to tradition but at the same time taking care that his cuisine be visually pleasing as well. And he pays as much attention to the seasons as to his skill and lightness of execution. We recommend the duck jambon and home-smoked salmon, the filet of John Dory with plums, asparagus, peaches or grapes (depending on the season) and the young rabbit in a cucumber fondue. The split-level dining room is rich and subdued; the wines are handsome, particularly an excellent Bordeaux served by the pitcher.
A la carte: 300F. Menus: 108F, 168F, 208F.

Aloxe-Corton

see Beaune

L'Alpe-d'Huez

38750 L'Alpe-d'Huez - (Isère)
Paris 625 - Grenoble 63 - Briançon 79 - Bourg d'Oisans 13

Au Chamois d'Or

Rte. de Fontbelle - 76.80.31.32

M. Seigle. Open until 9 p.m. Closed April 30-Dec. 15. Terrace dining. No pets. Parking. Cards: V.

The elder Seigle has retired, so son Philippe, who had been assisting him for some time, has taken over his father's duties. The cuisine—consistent, solid, dedicated, classical without being boring—is still the best in the resort: gratin of langoustine tails with ètrille (crab) butter, warm oysters with fresh spinach, émincé of blanc de Bresse with truffle butter, iced raspberry parfait. The large dining room opens onto a wide, sunny terrace, where meals are also served, facing the ski slopes.
A la carte: 250-300F. Menus: 108F, 140F.

Au Chamois d'Or

(See restaurant above)

Closed April 30-Dec. 15. 3 stes 900F. 42 rms 450-550F. TV.

The rates at this hotel, with its south-facing terrace and its recently redecorated rooms, are quite reasonable; the customers are the real stars of the resort. Excellent service in a most agreeable atmosphere.

Le Christina

76.80.33.32

Closed April 30-early July & Aug. 20-early Dec. 27 rms 526F. Half-board 390-500F oblig. in seas. Tennis. Garage parking. Cards: V.

Le Christina is located on a sunny platform facing L'Oisans mountain. Its rooms are well furnished, but the decor is a bit impersonal. Restaurant.

Le Petit Prince

Rte. de la Poste - 76.80.33.51

Closed April 10-Dec. 20. 40 rms 350-550F. Half-board 360- 520F oblig. in seas. Parking. Cards: V, AE, DC.

Most of the comfortable, modern rooms face south, overlooking the valley and L'Oisans mountain. The public areas of the hotel,as well as its wide, sunny terrace, are quite lovely. Restaurant.

Royal's Hotel

Ave. des Jeux - 76.80.35.50

Closed April 15-June 26 & Sept. 4-Dec. 15. 3 stes 1,200F. 47 rms 480-1,100F. TV. Air cond. Pets allowed. Heated pool. Parking. Cards: V, AE, DC, MC.

These are luxurious rooms done in a warm, wood interior style. The hotel features fitness facilities that are more than complete. Restaurant and brasserie.

Althen-des-Paluds

see Avignon

Amboise

37400 Amboise - (Indre-et-Loire)
Paris 206 - Vendôme 50 - Blois 35 - Tours 25 - Loches 35

Château de Pray

2 km on D 751 - 47.57.23.67

Closed Dec. 31-Feb. 10. 16 rms 250-405F. Half-board 413-426F oblig. in seas. Garage parking. Cards: V, AE, DC, MC.

This ancient, peaceful, small Louis XIII castle, surrounded by a park, is located on the outskirts of Amboise, whose slopes overlook the Loire river. Restaurant.

14 Le Choiseul

36, quai Charles-Guinot - 47.30.45.45

M. Traversac. Open until 9:30 p.m. Closed Jan. 5-March 15. Garden dining. Pets allowed. Parking. Telex 752068. Cards: V, MC.

René Traversac has owned this beautiful complex of eighteenth-century houses built on an embankment of the Loire river since 1985. After he finished its renovation, he hired a new staff: Jean-Baptiste and Catherine Menneson, a charming young couple, are now the managers, and Gérard Hummel has just become chef. This experienced chef is in full control of a beautiful style of cooking that delights the tourist gourmets who pass through here. Try the slices of trout and sea bream with fennel, the remarkable oysters in seaweed aspic and cream of watercress, the savory ravioli filled with Sainte-Maure (a Loire goat cheese), a fine langoustine tart pan-fried with tourteaux (crabs), a tasty poultry served with artichokes and a flat corn cake and, for dessert, a lovely warm feuilleté with apples roasted in cinnamon. Most of the wines are from Tours. The service is good, but the dining room is too elegant to be comfortably hospitable.

A la carte: 300F. Menus: 190F, 240F.

Le Choiseul

(See restaurant above)

Closed Jan. 5-March 15. 4 stes 800-980F. 19 rms 380-680F. Half-board 480-630F. TV in 7 rms. Pool.

This old hotel, located on an embankment of the Loire, was recently completely redecorated and now comprises 23 comfortable rooms with antique furniture. Pleasant garden.

Amiens

80000 Amiens - (Somme)
Paris 135 - Rouen 116 - Lille 115 - Beauvais 60

Sights. The cathedral (UNESCO classified it as a "monument of the world's patrimony"); Musée de Berny (art and regional history); Musée du Costume (themes change twice a year); Musée de Picardie (archaeology and paintings); the "Water Market" (Thursday, and Saturday morning) and the excursion through the canals to the "hortillonages" (cultivated marshlands); the International Film Festival (mid-November); and the Jazz Festival (end of May).

Eating on the Run. Le Barbecue Khmer, 9, blvd. d'Alsace-Lorraine (generous servings at reasonable prices, as well as takeout food); Le Baron, 13, rue de Noyon (beautiful grilled meats); Le Buffet de la Gare, pl. A.-Fiquet (an honest restaurant with good seafood); Le Grenier, 14, rue Léon-Blum (home-style cooking); Le Pré Porus, 95, rue Voyelle (located inside the hortillonages, with outings by boat or water bicycle); Chez Richard (open until 3 a.m.); Le Sélect et Rhin, 69, pl. Goblet (open 24 hours); La Taupinière, 12, rue Cormont (very old house by the cathedral, large portions of grilled meats).

Brasseries. La Taverne de Maître Kanter, 2, rue Albert-Dauphin (Sauerkraut and seafood).

Bars & Cafés. Chez Froc, 69, rue de la République (jukebox, newspapers and cigarettes, open until 3 a.m.); Le Globe, 18, rue Ernest-Cauvin (for the well-to-do and the sports-oriented); Le Jockey, 3, rue Ernest-Cauvin (prewar facade and decor); Le Kent, 34, rue de Noyon (Caribbean music and punches, served by a former colonial); Le Mizrana, rue Morgan (the jukebox plays '70s rock 'n' roll until 1 a.m.); Le Winston Churchill, 16, pl. au Feurre (comfortable and not too expensive, inside the Hotel Le Postillon).

Nightlife. Le Clip, 18, rue du Faubourg-de-Hem (fashionable, videos on a giant screen); Lucullus (Chez Nasser), 58, rue de la République (good rock and contemporary music on a compact disc player, open until 3 a.m.); La Lune des Pirates, 17, rue Bélu (in the St-Leu district, a small theater room playing primarily jazz); Chez Marc, rte. d'Abbeville (catering to those in their 30s and 40s); L'Orange Bleue, rue du Marché-Lanselles (the only downtown club); Le Pavillon Bleu, ave. Louis-Blanc (retro, open weekends only); Le P'tit Paris, 5, blvd. de Beauvillé (restaurant/cabaret).

Shops. Chez Broutin and the Petit Poucet, both located in the rue des Trois Cailloux (regional specialties—Amiens macaroons, Picardie ficelle, leek tart, duck pâté).

Les Marissons

66, rue des Marissons - 22.92.96.66

M. Benoit. Open until 10 p.m. Closed Sat. lunch, Sun. dinner, Mon. & Jan. 2-8 & July 18-Aug. 17. Air cond. Parking. Cards: V.

With its yellow drapes and dark-blue velvet chairs, the new decor is remarkably suited to this perfectly restored fifteenth-century shipyard; the dining room windows afford a magnificent view of the cathedral. And the enticing patronne, Aude Benoit, is as fresh, appealing and young as the cuisine cooked by her husband, Antoine, who settled into this unique house four years ago. Brief and versatile, the à la carte menu offers a choice of four dishes per course. Sample the plate of smoked fish and red shrimp while savoring a glass of Tokay; the breast of duck seasoned with green pepper and orange zests, served in a remarkable sauce; and the delicious orange-flavored chocolate quenelles. It is clear that considerable effort is made with the vegetables; but more Picardie cheeses ought to be represented, instead of the flavored cheeses, such as the marinated Roquefort and the Saint-Florentin with pineapple, that are served. The quantity and quality of the wines are continually improving; several vintages are now served by the glass.

A la carte: 280-300F. Menus: 105F (weekdays only), 120F (weekends and holidays only), 142F, 175F.

Le Postillon

16, pl. au Feurre - 22.91.46.17

Open year-round. 37 rms 230-350F. Garage parking. Telex 140754. Cards: V, AE, MC.

Behind the magnificent facade and fountain of this small, nicely redone hotel are spacious, well-equipped rooms. Meals on trays. Pub on the main floor.

12/20 Le Prieuré

17, rue Porion - 22.92.27.67

M. Boulet. Open until 10 p.m. Closed Fri. dinner & Sun. Garden dining. Pets allowed. Hotel: 11 rms 185-285F; half-board 250-315F. Garage parking. Cards: V, AE, DC.

A freshly redecorated eighteenth-century hotel shaded by a cathedral is the home of this appealing restaurant. Its old-fashioned French decor is charming, despite the incongruous presence of a large aquarium in its center. The cuisine has been skillfully modernized and includes a marinière of lotte and salmon with basil and breast of duck in black-currant vinegar. The cheeses are beautiful. Located under superb Gothic arches is an extensive wine cellar.

A la carte: 220-250F. Menus: 100F, 142F, 200F.

L'Univers

2, rue de Noyon - 22.91.52.51

Open year-round. 41 rms 270-370F. TV. Pets allowed. Telex 145070. Cards: V, AE, DC, MC.

This superb hotel, well situated between the train station and the cathedral, faces a garden with very old, immense trees. The service, generous and efficient, runs 24 hours a day.

IN NEARBY **Dury-lès-Amiens**

(5 km S on N 1)

80480 Saleux - (Somme)

La Bonne Auberge

N 1 - 22.95.03.33

M. Beaussire. Open until 10 p.m. Closed Sun. dinner & Mon. Air cond. Terrace dining. Pets allowed. Parking. Telex 145861. Cards: V, AE, MC.

The interior of this lovely white roadside inn surrounded with flowers has become much more serene: The walls have been freshly painted and wallpapered, new carpeting has been installed, and the tables are more elegantly set. As for Raoul Beaussire's cuisine, it's as prolific and diversified as ever, and is consistently executed with great skill and attention to lightness. The à la carte menu is amazing—several dishes based on fresh market produce have been added, as well as several superb fixed-price menus at reasonable prices. Sample the homemade duck liver in a crust, the civet of eels from the Somme river and the cabbage chartreuse with sole and langoustines, while savoring some modest (or magnificent—you have your choice) wines selected from the extensive cellar.

A la carte: 350F. Menus: 78F (weekdays only), 149F (wine incl.), 110F, 145F, 199F.

Amilly

see Montargis

Ammerschwihr

68770 Ammerschwihr - (Haut-Rhin)

Paris 438 - Gérardmer 55 - St-Dié 49 - Colmar 8

12/20 A l'Arbre Vert

7, rue des Cigognes - 89.47.12.23

M. Gebel. Open until 9:15 p.m. Closed Tues., Feb. 8-March 20 & Nov. 25-Dec. 10. Pets allowed. Cards: V, AE.

The reception is nonexistent, but the service, performed by waiters wearing red Alsatian-style waistcoats, is charming and considerate. Traditional country or bourgeois cuisine—such as the warm goose liver in Pinot Noir, choucroute and chicken in Riesling—is served in an immense dining room paneled with light wood and decorated in the best of regional taste.

A la carte: 230-250F. Menus: 70F (weekdays only), 120F to 270F.

A l'Arbre Vert

(See restaurant above)

Closed Tues., Feb. 8-March 20 & Nov. 25-Dec. 10. 13 rms 100-200F. Half-board 180-240F oblig. in seas. TV in 10 rms.

The rooms of this handsome, large house located in front of the village fountain are pleasant and unpretentious.

Aux Armes de France

1, Grand-Rue - 89.47.10.12

M. Gaertner. Open until 9:30 p.m. Closed Thurs. lunch, Wed. & Jan. Pets allowed. Hotel: 2 stes 450F; 10 rms 300-400F. Parking. Telex 880666. Cards: V, AE, DC, MC.

Pierre Gaertner, a student of Fernand Point, has dazzled Alsace with his beautiful and rich cuisine for 40 years; unfortunately, he was recently stricken with illness and forced to give it up. But he placed his stoves in the capable hands of his son Philippe, who studied for a long time under Boyer, Bocuse and Senderens. Philippe has found his true talent at Aux Armes, with a balance between a traditional cuisine—such as the exquisite Pierre Gaertner goose foie gras, the filets of sole with noodles and the Fernand Point salad—and one that is discreetly contemporary:

the red mullet filets with fried vegetables and horseradish, the "beggar's purse" (a crêpe purse) filled with veal, sweetbreads and tarragon, and the éventail of pigeon in an apple sauce with saffron. All these exquisite creations are served in the cheerful, serene atmosphere of this beautiful family house surrounded by a vineyard. Presented by a charming sommelier who knows his job well, the wine list is among the richest and best-composed in all of Alsace.

A la carte: 500F and up. Menus: 190F (weekday lunch only), 280F, 380F.

Amou

40330 Amou - (Landes)
Paris 741 - Pau 49 - Orthez 14 - Mont-de-Marsan 46

(13) Le Commerce

Pl. de la Poste - 58.89.02.28

M. Darracq. Open until 9 p.m. Closed Mon. (off-seas.), 2 weeks in Feb. & 3 weeks in Nov. Terrace dining. Pets allowed. Hotel: 20 rms 140-220F; half-board 180-240F. Parking. Cards: V, AE, DC, MC.

Le Commerce is the mandatory rendezvous for all the gourmets of the region; they don't mind squeezing into the unexciting interior of this beautiful inn, surrounded by foliage and located at the foot of the village church. The cuisine is definitely local, whatever one may think of the incongruous presence, in the dessert section, of a banana split drenched with crème Chantilly. As for the rest, there is a beautiful foie gras delicately poached in a fine raisin sauce—though the croutons served as a canapé appear a bit meager—a smooth, savory Landes-style cassoulet and delicious goose or duck confits. The owner's reception is cordial and excellent, and the service is prompt, but the wine list is a bit weak.

A la carte: 180-200F. Menus: 55F (weekdays only), 90F, 135F, 170F.

Ancenis

44150 Ancenis - (Loire-Atlantique)
Paris 342 - Angers 53 - Cholet 47 - Nantes 42

(14) Auberge de Bel-Air

Rte. d'Angers - 40.83.02.87

MM. Gasnier. Open until 9:15 p.m. Closed Sun. dinner & Mon. Pets allowed. Parking. Cards: V, MC.

Jean-Paul Gasnier spent seven years at L'Assiette Champenoise in Reims before returning home (he was born in Champtoceaux) to open this beautiful house on a slope overlooking the Loire, across the railroad tracks (you have to get used to it). The decor is rather charming, particularly in winter, when a fire blazes in the hearth. The cuisine is devoted in large part to country dishes and seafood, which are lightly and freely interpreted (but sometimes slightly under or overcooked): perch escalopes with Nantes leeks, langoustine salad with crushed tomatoes and walnut oil, roast Barbary duckling with mustard and gherkins. Several desserts, rather more imaginative, are also excellent, especially the pear feuilleté in maple syrup and the gratin of exotic fruits in ginger. Geneviève, the patronne, will welcome you gracefully.

A la carte: 250F. Menus: 88F (weekdays only), 130F, 160F, 208F.

Val de Loire

Rte. d'Angers
(2 km E, Le Jarrier) - 40.96.00.03

Open year-round. 40 rms 185-232F. Half-board 172-243F. Parking. Telex 711592. Cards: V, MC.

Built in 1980, this small, hospitable, neatly efficient hotel is located amid vineyards and greenery. Restaurant.

Andorre

Principauté d'Andorre
Paris 895 - Toulouse 186 - Perpignan 166 - Foix 103

IN **Andorre-la-Vieille**

Andorra Palace

Prat de la Creu - 62.82.10.72

Open year-round. 40 stes 600-800F. 108 rms 290-390F. Half-board 430-720F. TV. Pets allowed. Heated pool. Tennis. Garage parking. Cards: V, AE, DC, MC.

Facing the mountain, this handsome little palace has outstanding facilities, including a sauna, exercise room and VCR-equipped rooms. Restaurant.

Sasplugas

Ave. Bisbe-Princep-Iglesias - 62.82.03.11

Open year-round. 26 rms 170-340F. TV. Garage parking. Cards: V, AE, MC.

The large rooms in this stunning residence are quite comfortable; a terrace overlooks the valley. Restaurant.

IN **Les Escaldes**

(14) Le 1900

11, carrer de la Unio - 62.82.67.16

M. Guitard. Open until 11 p.m. Closed Mon. & July. Pets allowed. Cards: V, AE, DC.

Away from the swarming crowds of Andorran shoppers, this attractive 1900s-style house is decorated in pale green and rose hues, which gives it a pleasingly intimate atmosphere. The best cuisine of the principality is served here. The boss, from Sète, and his chef, Alain Deprétz, have composed a clear, well-balanced menu; Deprétz pays particular attention to both the creativity and the presentation of the cuisine: red-mullet gazpacho with zucchini mousse, breast of duck with lentils, filetof beef served in a salt crust. The owner provides the cordial welcome, and the service is especially attentive.

A la carte: 300F. Menus: 190F (wine incl.), 270F.

Roc Blanc

5, pl. des Coprinceps - 62.82.14.86

Open year-round. 4 stes 800-1,850F. 236 rms 475-650F. Half-board 510-670F oblig. in seas. TV. Air cond. in 20 rms. Pets allowed. Heated pool. Tennis. Garage parking. Cards: V, AE, DC, MC.

One of the best hotels in the resort, with large rooms and complete facilities, including a hair salon, boutiques, exercise room, piano bar and restaurants. Outstanding trilingual service.

Anduze

30140 Anduze - (Gard)
Paris 720 - Montpellier 70 - Nîmes 49 - Alès 13

Les Trois Barbus

4 km NW on D 129 & D 50
Générargues - 66.61.72.12

M. Marvie. Open until 9 p.m. Closed Sun. dinner, Mon. & Tues. (Nov. 3-Jan. 1), Mon. lunch (April 1-Oct. 1) & Jan. 2-Feb. 28. Terrace dining. No pets. Parking. Cards: V, AE, DC, MC.

A former building contractor and the perfect example of a self-made man, the bearded Jean-François Marvie (his two brothers are just as bearded) has become an experienced cook whose talent is responsible for a cuisine worthy of this beautiful house nestled in the imposing natural scenery of the Cévennes and the Camisards valley. The beautiful, rustic dining room, the breathtakingly panoramic terrace, the grill next to the swimming pool and an air of blissful isolation—all this will make you feel that your hours spent at Les Trois Barbus are indeed those of a genuine vacation. You will be in the company of some very lovely dishes from the Lozère and Languedoc, such as the duck foie gras marinated in Beaumes-de-Venise, the fresh goat-cheese ravioli in a foie gras sauce and truffle juice, the duck with pears in a Gigondas wine sauce and the chocolate fondant in orange sauce. The reception is congenial, warm and casual; the wine cellar is well stocked.

A la carte: 300F. Menus: 100F (weekday lunch only), 150F to 250F.

Les Trois Barbus

(See restaurant above)

Closed Sun., Mon. & Tues. (Nov. 3-Jan. 2 & March) & Jan. 2- Feb. 28. 34 rms 190-410F. Half-board 270-390F. TV. Air cond. 17 rms. Pool.

This small but outstanding family hotel has a fantastic view of the Gardon valley and the Cévennes mountains. The rustic, comfortable rooms have attractive balconies overlooking grand scenery. The swimming pool is lovely, and there are many possibilities for splendid walks.

Angers

49000 Angers - (Maine-et-Loire)
Paris 305 - Rennes 126 - Tours 106 - Nantes 90

Sights. The castle (dating from the thirteenth century, don't miss the tapestry of the Apocalypse); the Saint-Maurice cathedral (twelfth and thirteenth centuries, stained-glass windows); Adam's house (fifteenth century, sculpted wood); the Préfecture (seventeenth century, Romanesque gallery); Musée des Beaux-Arts (Barrault's house); Musée Turpin de Crissé (Pincé hotel, antiquities, Japanese engravings); Musée Jean-Lurçat (including "The Song of the World" tapestry); Galerie David d'Angers (the former Toussaint monastery). In the surrounding areas: excursions to the vineyards (Brissac, Layon, Savennières, Bonnezeaux, the Aubance hills).

Eating on the Run. Les Antilles, rue Pocquet-de-Livonnière (good exotic cuisine); Boisnet, rue Boisnet (nicely prepared crêpes and pies); Clémentine, rue Delage (a friendly crêpes place); La Côte de Boeuf, rue Madeleine (the meat is generously served); La Cour Foch, 13 bis, blvd. Foch (good meats); Le Départ, 28, blvd. Ayrault (fish); Dolce Vita, rue Baudrière (pizza); L'Ecureuil, rue Pocquet-de-Livonnière (a pleasant bistro); La Marée, les Halles (seafood); La Taverne Alsacienne, pl. Mendès-France (interesting Sauerkraut).

Brasseries. Brasserie de la Gare, pl. de la Gare (friendly reception, good Anjou wines); Le Grand Cercle, blvd. Foch (diligent service, reasonable prices); Le Jules Verne, rue d'Anjou (consistent quality); Le Pub Saint-Aubin, 71, rue St-Aubin (lovely decor).

Bars & Cafés. Le Bar Belge, blvd. Henri-Arnault (caters to students, wide choice of beer); La Civette, pl. Romain (fashionable, caters to artists, terrace); Le Dupon t et d, rue Toussaint (students); Le Glacier, Jardin du Mail (pleasant decor); Le Kent, pl. Ste-Croix (pub, whiskies); Le Piano Bar, blvd. Foch (well-to-do, conservative clientele); Le Sunset, rue St-Laud (beautiful modern decor).

Nightlife. Le Boléro, rue St-Laud (disco); La Cabane Bambou and Les Rivières, at Juigné-sur-Loire (both a must for students); Le Manhattan, blvd. Bessonneau (original decor, the latest music); Le Paradise and Lady L, rue du Mail (cozy ambience).

Concorde

18, blvd. Foch - 41.87.37.20

Open year-round. 1 ste 590F. 72 rms 340-410F. TV. Pets allowed. Garage parking. Telex 720923. Cards: V, AE, DC, MC.

Located in downtown Angers, the Concorde has spacious, modern, well-soundproofed rooms. The reception is cordial, but the service is far from perfect. Breakfast, however, is good. Restaurant.

Hôtel d'Iéna

27, rue Marceau - 41.87.52.40

Closed Dec. 22-Jan. 4. 22 rms 170-265F. TV. Pets allowed. Telex 720930. Cards: V, AE, DC.

The rooms in this provincial hotel, located midway between the castle and the train station but not too close to downtown, are small, redecorated and fairly quiet. Restaurant.

Le Quéré

9, pl. du Ralliement
41.87.64.94

M. Le Quéré. Open until 9:30 p.m. Closed Tues. dinner, Wed., Feb. school vacation & July 1-20. Air cond. Pets allowed. Cards: V, AE, DC.

"A revelation!" we exclaimed in 1982, upon discovering Paul Le Quéré in this former hairdresser's salon. This seasoned veteran of culinary contests is now decorated with three toques, and he knows his Escoffier guide by heart. In front of his stove, however, he prefers to put into practice the brilliant lessons of Joël Robuchon. We were amazed to see such savoir-faire in the directing of a most contemporary and inspired repertoire. And we are still amazed by the control, the finesse and the cleverness of a cuisine unparalleled in the Anjou region.

Undoubtedly, such talent deserves a more flattering setting than the second floor of this plain building, which houses a motel. Still, Paul and Martine Le Quéré have worked very hard to turn their large, bright dining room into a comfortable and friendly place where round tables with lace tablecloths are set under brass chandeliers. Most importantly, though, Martine is in the room. This young woman, as communicative as her husband is quiet, is a wine enthusiast, and she is absolutely unbeatable on her knowledge of Loire bottlings. One could spend hours listening to her describe her impressive collection of wines from Anjou and the Touraine or analyze the subtle harmony of an aged Layon (it is, in fact, sublime) with the duck-liver terrine with asparagus; this marriage is indeed so harmonious that it is an absolutely mandatory beginning of any meal at Le Quéré.

Whether it is a Coteaux-de-l'Aubance, a Coulée-de Serrant, a Quarts-de-Chaume, a Bonnezeaux, a Saumur, a Quincy or a Chinon, it seems that the wines of the Loire have been especially created to enhance the subtle, clear flavors of the crayfish, red mullet and squab aspic, the eel feuilleté with leeks, the sea bass with chives in a cockle sauce, the Loire fish with Savennières, the carp with cabbage and smoked diced bacon, the wild duck with roasted prunes in Bourgueil wine or the veal kidney and sweetbreads with creamed morels. With the bitter-chocolate fondant, Martine will slip you a glass of white Anjou—an exquisite Château du Breuil 1971—of which this singular matchmaker keeps several bottles.

A la carte: 300-350F. Menus: 151F, 235F.

Saint-Julien

9, pl. du Ralliement - 41.88.41.62

Open year-round. 35 rms 140-260F. TV. Pets allowed. Telex 720930. Cards: V.

A small place well worth a recommendation. The Saint-Julien is located in the building that houses the best restaurant in town (see Le Quéré above), and the fairly spacious rooms are well soundproofed. Cordial reception.

13 La Salamandre

1, blvd. Foch - 41.88.99.55

M. Louboutin. Open until 9:45 p.m. Closed Sun. No pets. Garage parking. Cards: V, AE, DC.

Facing the stalls of a sumptuous flower market on Angers's wide main boulevard, this large neo-Renaissance room serves one of the most consistent and tasty cuisines in the region. Its themes are classic, but its spirit is modern. And the chef truly loves the good and flavorful produce of the region: pot-au-feu of foie gras with wonderfully prepared farm vegetables, perch paupiette garnished with vegetables and light beurre blanc, roasted squab with mushrooms. The desserts are somewhat weaker (the apricot tart is a bit heavy), but the wine cellar, featuring the wines of the Loire, is handsome indeed, and the homemade bread baked with beer is delicious. The blond patronne always has a ready smile.

A la carte: 280F. Menus: 92F (weekend and holidays only), 130F, 170F.

Hôtel d'Anjou

(See restaurant above)

Open year-round. 50 rms 180-390F. Half-board 272-482F. TV. Pets allowed.

This old hotel has been impeccably redecorated and modernized; the rooms are large and perfectly equipped.

15 Le Toussaint

7, rue Toussaint - 41.87.46.20

M. Bignon. Open until 9:30 p.m. Closings vary. No pets. Cards: V, AE, DC.

Michel Bignon was the first chef to dare to take Angers out of its swamp of sauces and compose a short seasonal menu of light dishes prepared with grace. His cuisine consists of a vigorous interpretation of country dishes for which he uses marvelous produce fresh from the market. Others may have caught up with him and even overtaken him—that is, after all, the rule of the game—but perhaps this former charcutier, an adroit professional who never ceases to take risks, has not yet had his final word. Of that we were certain, after sampling the rabbit compote served with an excellent herb aspic and delicate creamed parsley, the exquisitely flavored lobster sautéed in Bonnezeaux wine and the famous boned pigs' trotters stuffed with morels in a light Aubance wine sauce. The preparations are exquisite, and the sauces made with Anjou wines achieve a perfect clarity. This being said, since Bignon doesn't seem to be running out of imagination, he should bid farewell to some of his less interesting dishes, such as the quail eggs with "black pearls"; and we would have been happier if he hadn't used so much beurre blanc to garnish his perch, shad and pike (perhaps he does so because it's one of the best beurre blancs in the western part of France). The desserts, especially the pear charlotte and the lemon tart, are simply delicious. The wine cellar is impressive, and not just because of its Anjou wines.

A la carte: 380-420F. Menus: 155F, 220F.

13 Le Vert d'Eau

9, blvd. Gaston-Dumesnil
41.48.52.31, 41.48.52.86

M. Piers. Open until 9:30 p.m. Closed Sun. dinner, Mon. & Aug. 15-31. Pets allowed. Cards: V, AE, DC, MC.

A lovely, sensible Anjou cuisine disdaining clichés, strong and honest—this is what is served in the ruby-colored '50s decor (which no one will miss when the excellent Jean-François Piers decides to get rid of it). It is true that after World War II the Vert d'Eau was one of the most famous restaurants in western France. But we would guess that in those days we wouldn't have found such good Loire eels sautéed in chives and garlic, or a lamb so skillfully roasted to a perfect rare pink, garnished with a zucchini flan. The iced nougat with honey and pollen is a bit soft but marvelously flavored. The list of Loire wines is superb, and its prices are the best in Angers; there are some aged and mellow vintages as well.

A la carte: 280F. Menus: 85F (weekdays only), 165F, 200F.

IN NEARBY **Saint-Sylvain-d'Anjou**
(5 km NE on N 23)
49480 St-Sylvain-d'Anjou - (Maine-et-Loire)

(14) Auberge d'Eventard
Rte. de Paris (N 23) - 41.43.74.25

M. Maussion. Open until 10 p.m. Closed Sun. dinner, Mon. & Jan. 2-25. Garden dining. No pets. Hotel: 1 ste 350F; 9 rms 110-270F; half-board 250-350F. Parking. Cards: V, AE, DC.

The freeway under construction will soon ease traffic congestion on the highway built next to this old, rustic inn near the hippodrome, so you will be all the more comfortably seated in its elegant and recently redone dining room, whose decor now features a more modern, spacious motif in lieu of the somewhat stuffy Louis XIII that predominated before. The host likes things done the proper way, which is why he cooks with an almost religious devotion. His cuisine is light and classic, yet quite imaginative, and takes advantage of regional produce. Therefore the Auberge d'-Eventard wins back its lost rating point, thanks to the finely creamed fish navarin and young beans, the warm oysters seasoned with shallots and the rich pigeon served in its juice (the thigh is served separately, on a foie gras salad with Xérès). The goat cheeses are sumptuous; the desserts are, in general, a bit weaker, except for the beautiful chocolate creations; and the Loire wines are splendid, as is the maître d', the owner's nephew, who will skillfully help you make your selection.

A la carte: 300F. Menus: 110F (weekdays only), 230F (weekends and holidays only), 160F, 285F.

(13) Le Clafoutis
N 23, La Lieue - 41.43.84.71

M. Lebert. Open until 9:30 p.m. Closed Wed. & Sun. dinner, Tues., Feb. school vacation & Aug. No pets. Parking. Cards: V, AE, MC.

A big thank-you to Jean-Pierre Maussion, from the Auberge d'Eventard, who generously (such a spirit of fraternity isunusual in this profession!) directed us to his colleague and neighbor, Serge Lebert. A few years ago, Lebert and his wife, Violette, opened this simple but stylish rustic house. Both are solid professionals, and the cuisine they serve in this corner of Anjou is pleasantly surprising, with its seasonal liveliness and consistency of execution (not to mention its moderate prices). Your meal will be one of the most delicious you could imagine (light smoked salmon feuilleté with egg, lotte ragoût with mussels and saffron, garnished with delicious vegetables, a duck aiguillette that is skillfully prepared and beautifully pink, and exquisite desserts), especially if it is accompanied by one of the well-chosen, affordable regional wines.

A la carte: 200-230F. Menus: 70F and 110F (weekdays only), 130F.

La Fauvelaie
Rte. de l'Epervière - 41.43.80.10

Open year-round. 9 rms 100-200F. Half-board 173-233F. Parking. Cards: V.

Situated on a lovely, peaceful old farm, La Fauvelaie is a good place to stop if you want to discover Angers and the castles of Anjou. Restaurant.

Les Angles
see Avignon

Anglet
64600 Anglet - (Pyrénées-Atlantiques)
Paris 748 - Biarritz 4 - Bayonne 3 - St-Jean-de-Luz 18

Château de Brindos
Rte. de l'Aviation - 59.23.17.68

M. Vivensang. Open daily until 10 p.m. Parking. Telex 541428. Cards: V, AE, DC, MC.

Within this large Basque villa built on the shore of a 24-acre lake surrounded by greenery is a somewhat quaint, luxurious establishment offering a great deal of space, comfort and refinement. The classic cuisine is undoubtedly prepared with the best, richest ingredients: tartare of louvine (striped bass) with truffle juice, shellfish chartreuse, foie gras with raisins. The wine list is interesting, the service impeccable.

A la carte: 350-400F. Menu: 230F (weekdays only, wine incl.).

Château de Brindos
(See restaurant above)

Open year-round. 3 stes 1,750F. 12 rms 700-1,200F. Half-board oblig. in seas. TV. Pets allowed. Heated pool. Tennis.

Inside this large, Italian-style villa located between the lake and the forest is a rather pompous decor, but the rooms are extremely comfortable. Relais et Châteaux.

Hôtel de Chiberta et du Golf
104, blvd. des Plages - 59.63.88.30

Open year-round. 1 ste. 95 rms 240-506F. Half-board 373-623F. oblig. in seas. TV. Air cond. Pool. Golf. Telex 550637. Cards: V, AE, DC, MC.

In the heart of the famous golf course, on the lakeshore and close to the beaches, this double hotel has gorgeous rooms; its spacious salons open onto the greens. Hairdresser's salon and various shops. Excellent facilities for conferences. The restaurant, L'Orangerie, has a two vast terraces and a magnificent view.

Angoulême
16000 Angoulême - (Charente)
Paris 450 - Périgueux 85 - Bordeaux 116 - Limoges 103

Grand Hôtel de France
1, pl. des Halles - 45.95.47.95

Open year-round. 2 stes 550-600F. 58 rms 150-400F. Half-board 180-290F. TV in 12 rms. Pets allowed. Telex 791020. Cards: V, AE, DC, MC.

The quiet, beautiful rooms of the Grand Hôtel de France, newly redecorated, overlook the Charente valley. The garden is delightful, as is the reception. Restaurant.

Le Margaux

25, rue de Genève - 45.92.58.98

Mme. Pineau. Open until 11 p.m. Closed Sun., holidays, Aug. 1-15 & Dec. 23-Jan. 4. Terrace dining. Pets allowed. Cards: V.

The Angoulême chefs, seized with restlessness for some years now, are at it again. Francine Pineau, a self-made woman, and Alain, her oenologist husband (he trained with Alexis Lichine), have just moved into this centuries-old building. Reasonably priced late lunches and dinners are served on the main floor, which is decorated with furniture as amusing as it is uncomfortable. In contrast, however, the decor of the second floor is extremely refined, with elegant tables and lovely flower bouquets enlivening the otherwise plain white decor. This is the place to taste some marvelous Médocs (some are served by the glass) while enjoying an excellent feminine cuisine, especially the foie gras au torchon, the filet of turbot with leeks and the rack of lamb with mint.

A la carte: 250-300F. Menus: 51F, 120F, 200F.

La Ruelle

6, rue des Trois-Notre-Dame
45.92.94.64

M. Dauphin. Open until 10 p.m. Closed Mon. & Sat. lunch, Sun., Jan. 31-Feb. 13 & Aug. 15-31. Air cond. Pets allowed. Cards: V.

La Ruelle, a charming bistro, serves excellent grilled meats and fish (salmon, leg of lamb, breast of duck) and good wines by the glass. (There is another restaurant across the lane, whose atmosphere, with its pale stones, dark wooden beams and fireplace, is most congenial.) The service would be better if itweren't so formal, for the cuisine itself (created by Véronique Dauphin, the owner's daughter) is quite lively and refreshing: gâteau of warm rabbit in morel oil, roasted lamb filets with wild asparagus and a medallion of lotte with oysters. The chocolate cake is marvelous. Both the à la carte and fixed-price menu prices are reasonable.

A la carte: 250F. Menus: 115F, 180F.

IN NEARBY **La Vigerie**
(8 km W on N 141)
16290 Hiersac - (Charente)

Le Moulin Gourmand

45.90.83.00

Mme. Ménager. Open until 9:15 p.m. Closed Sun. dinner, Mon. (Jan. 1-March 31) & Nov.-Dec. Garden dining. Pets allowed. Parking. Telex 791053. Cards: V, AE, DC.

This beautiful large house, its architecture typical of the Charente region, was once a mill on the bank of the Nouère river. The owner, Mme. Ménager, had it redone in an ostentatious, characteristically Relais et Châteaux style. Now the enthusiastic industrialist is turning the large, pleasantly isolated estate into a more comfortable and hospitable place, and nothing is too fine or too luxurious. Deer wander freely in the manicured park; the dining room decor is refined (though it does lack a certain cheerfulness, despite the beautiful flowers from the garden); the service is elegant. The cuisine, which is also served on the garden terrace, has been constantly improving since Alain Samet, who trained at La Tour d'Argent and La Tour Rose, has taken over. The novelty of his personal and seasonal creations blends happily with his remarkably well-interpreted repertoire of regional dishes. Sample the duck ballotine and the terrine of young rabbit in a Sauternes aspic, the superb charcuterie prepared in a traditional style, the rolled salmon served with langoustines and green cabbage, the exquisite duck breast in a sweet-and-sour sauce and the light feuilleté of apple preserves and walnuts. The wine cellar is the home of magnificent Bordeaux and first-rate Cognacs, including a "fin bois" of the restaurant's own.

A la carte: 300F and up. Menus: 125F (weekday lunch only), 170F, 280F.

Le Moulin du Maine Brun

(See restaurant above)

Closed Nov.-Dec. 2 stes 950F. 18 rms 400-480F. Half-board 450-550F. TV. Pets allowed. Pool.

This old mill offers all the comfort and tranquility one could wish for. The large rooms are elaborately decorated and amply furnished with period pieces and faultless bathrooms. The facilities are impeccable and the service friendly. A good breakfast, including the patronne's own homemade preserves, is served. Tame deer wander in the beautiful park, and tennis courts and a golf course are located nearby. Relais et Châteaux.

Annecy

74000 Annecy - (Haute-Savoie)
Paris 547 - Lyon 142 - Chamonix 93 - Geneva 43

Sights. Musée de la Cloche; Old Town, with its canals and flower-decorated bridges; the churches of Saint-François and Saint-Maurice (featured in the Old Town festival in July); Saint-Pierre cathedral (built in 1535, Saint Francis of Sales officiated there); the castle (twelfth and thirteenth centuries, houses the historical museum of Annecy and the Haute-Savoie); the Semnoz and its forests (summer hiking, winter skiing); the lake and its shores.

Events. The Feast of the Lake (August); numerous film festivals—Italian Cinema (October), the International Festival of Animated Films (May–June, in odd-numbered years), the International Festival of Sports and Adventure Films (May, even-numbered years)—the Fantastic Haute-Savoie Festival (two weeks in January).

Eating on the Run. Café du Très Bon Lieu, centre Bonlieu (Lyonnaise bistro, managed by Marc Veyrat, serves until late at night); Le Wine Bar, cours du Pré-Carré (wines by the glass, good specials of the day).

Bars & Cafés. L'Abbaye, in Annecy-le-Vieux (piano bar, crowded); Le Saint-Mau, in Old Town (young, modern clientele).

Brasseries. Brasserie de l'Hôtel de Ville, pl. de l'Hôtel de Ville (a bit crazy, waiters wear different outfits every day).

Nightlife. Le Chardon d'Ecosse, 10, rue Vaugelas (large choice of whiskies, along with

VS
THE BEST
IN AIR TRAVEL
The best of the U.S.A. is connected with the best of France on Air France direct flights from New York, Washington D.C., Philadelphia, Boston, Chicago, Houston, Los Angeles, San Francisco.
Air France offers the best means to reach France in comfort and style. With Concorde the first supersonic commercial airliner, symbol of technical perfection and elegance, Air France is the only airline linking France to the U.S.A. in just 3 hours and 45 minutes. On board Air France has selected the finest meals and the most reputed wines and champagnes.
AIR FRANCE
For Reservations
in the U.S.A.:
CALL 1 (800) AF PARIS
1 (800) 237-2747
in New York City:
(212) 247-0100
or contact your travel agent
AIR FRANCE

EXTRA
12
SPECIAL
Johnnie Walker
BLACK LABEL

smoked salmon and foie gras; open until 4 a.m.); Le Garage, 36, rue Sommeiller (the most sought-after club).

L'Abbaye

15, chemin de l'Abbaye - 50.23.61.08

Open year-round. 3 stes 700-900F. 8 rms 350-550F. Half-board 335-585F. TV. Pets allowed. Parking. Cards: V, AE, DC.

The new, rather large and quite comfortable rooms have been beautifully decorated. Attentive service in a perfectly serene atmosphere. There is a lovely vaulted piano bar and an elegant but overpriced restaurant with a terrace.

16 L'Amandier

6, ave. Mandallaz - 50.51.74.50

MM. Guillot & Cortesi. Open until 9:30 p.m. Closed Sun. (except holidays) & 2 weeks in summer. Pets allowed. Cards: V, AE, MC.

Only five minutes from the train station, L'-Amandier islocated in a rather drab district of Annecy, but its new interior—modern, subtle, done in beige and pink tones—is charming. The formidable competition in the area, namely Marc Veyrat's successful Auberge de l'Eridan, has spurred Alain Cortesi, one of the owners, to new heights. The finesse and consistency of this self-made chef's cuisine has greatly improved; our last visits here convinced us that he is easily worth two toques: calamari salad with fresh mint, elegant hot-and-cold foie gras served with a glass of Sauternes, lotte in a honey-lime sauce, garnished with a small crown of refreshing and delicate zucchini, boned squab rosé in a beautiful Pomerol sauce and light, aromatic desserts, such as the flavorful cocoa sorbet and roasted peach in mulberry juice and caramel ice cream. Nicole and Jean Guillot, the other two partners, greet the customers cordially and offer remarkable wine service: They've brought back some excellent bottles from their native Bordeaux region. The prices are consistently fair.

A la carte: 300-350F. Menus: 145F (weekdays only), 175F, 240F, 300F.

19 Auberge de l'Eridan

7, ave. de Chavoires
50.66.22.04

M. Veyrat-Durebex. Open until 9:30 p.m. Closed Sun. dinner, Wed., Feb. & Aug. 16-Sept. 4. Air cond. Terrace dining. Pets allowed. Parking. Cards: V, AE, DC, MC.

In summer and winter alike, one could live quite happily in this large lakeshore chalet. A modest cottage until a few years ago, it will soon be the most beautiful restaurant in the region: The current dining room will become a lounge, and the new dining room will be located upstairs, behind a terrace overlooking a splendid panorama.

Three toques and, finally in this new guide, two more points and a fourth toque have rewarded Marc Veyrat's talent; everyone agrees that his is an exceptional talent. But he has had to struggle to fulfill this talent. Since 1983, this fiery man from Savoie (from the Manigod valley, a region of rough and, apparently, bad-tempered people) has needed all the tenacity and optimism he could muster to realize his dream, a dream far beyond the financial means of this former pastry cook turned chef (he worked for the Runel brothers in Montpellier, then at Bise and finally at L'Abbaye in Talloires). He would, at times, go so far as to throw out his customers, only to suddenly call them back for an absolutely unforgettable feast (and it is they who have become his most faithful clients). But he has mellowed. "Guidebooks, especially yours, have taught me to round off the angles," he says today. "I used to be a cook, now I have become a restaurateur."

In the area, word has traveled—when people want to celebrate, they go to Auberge de l'Eridan and nowhere else. François Mitterrand has often been found there, sitting several tables away from the young, brilliant Bernard Bosson, the mayor of Annecy and minister in charge of the European Economic Communities. We fully understand why they are here, for everything at Auberge de l'Eridan is delightful: Mme. Veyrat's greeting, the extremely attentive service and, of course, the pleasures of the table.

But is a fourth toque really warranted? You bet. For MarcVeyrat's talent has finally exploded. Gone is everything superfluous, any hint of over-balanced flavors and the last trace of presumptuous sauces. What's left is a perfect mastery of cooking, pure imagination and harmony, and subtlety itself. Words fail us—so let's move to the table, where we begin with an inspired combination of two foie gras, one mild, the other sharp. Next arrives the polenta ravioli containing delicately warmed gray truffles, an astoundingly flavorful dish served with baby carrots and an angelic mixture of herbs and spices that whispers of citronella, balm and cumin. A grand success! Then on to the filets of turbot rolled and poached in raw milk perfumed by pink palourde clams and accompanied by a perfect salad of wild spinach and pungent greens. Pike sausages are next, greenish from the presence of plant liqueurs; here for once is pike that tastes like pike. The sauce américaine is excellent, as are the accompanying shrimp. After the smoked lake trout with olive oil and exquisite little potatoes that follow, we now take wings toward perfection: a hot consommé of mushrooms with airy little puff pastries of fresh mountain cheese; fera (salmon-like lake fish) sauced with an astonishing coffee sauce; roast chicken whose breasts are "beaten" and served in flattened escalopes with lean and fat bacon and—the key—marjoram; and finally, in case you still have an ounce of resistance left, pigeon cooked in watercress with not a hint of butter or cream, whose marriage of flavors is ideal. So much for our "experimental" meal (how brave we are, you must be thinking). Next time it will be the farm-raised calf's head, the honey carrots, the wild duck and the rabbit with cocks' combs and basil. Meanwhile, the cheese tray provides the best and most complete tour of the delights of the Savoie region that we've ever seen, and the assorted desserts will bring tears to your disbelieving eyes.

A la carte: 400-700F. Menus: 250F, 350F, 600F.

(15) Le Belvédère

7, ch. du Belvédère
(2 km on rte. de Semnoz) - 50.45.04.90

M. Aubeneau. Open until 9:15 p.m. Closed Sun. dinner, Mon., 2 weeks in April & Oct. 25-Dec. 1. No pets. Parking. Cards: V.

Le Belvédère is a veritable festival of fish, especially those from the sea. The freshwater varieties don't seem to interest Jean-Louis Aubeneau (from La Rochelle) quite as much. If you want to save money, this beautiful contemporary dining room with its marvelous terrace is not for you. But if you want to feast on glittering fish, fresh from the sea and prepared according to your taste with an evangelical simplicity, such as the fish grilled over a wood fire or cooked in lovely, savory sauces (the sea bass à la bordelaise, for example, and the turbot pavé in spices), you should indeed pay Le Belvédère a visit. The crayfish and lobster go straight from the superb fish pond to the saucepans. The desserts are excellent.

A la carte: 300F. Menus: 170F (weekdays only), 240F (wine incl.), 330F.

Le Belvédère

(See restaurant above)

Closed Oct. 15-May 10. 10 rms 110-150F. Half-board 200-220F oblig. in seas. No pets.

Le Belvédère's rooms are large, quiet and clean; their charm lies in their magnificent view of Annecy's lake.

Carlton

5, rue des Glières - 50.45.47.75

Open year-round. 55 rms 276-373F. TV. Pets allowed. Garage parking. Telex 309472. Cards: V, AE, DC.

Located in downtown Annecy, facing a square, the Carlton has large, traditional and comfortable rooms. No restaurant.

(13) La Ciboulette

10, rue Vaugelas - 50.45.74.57

M. Paccard. Open until 9:30 p.m. Closed Sun. dinner, Mon. & July 1-20. Terrace dining. Pets allowed. Cards: V, AE, DC, MC.

Once the residents of Annecy have discovered Georges Paccard, it will be difficult to find even a small table available on his charming terrace in the cours du Pré Carré. At the time of this writing, the dining room was not very pleasant, but perhaps it will be redecorated and enlarged soon, thanks to the recent acquisition of the adjacent shop. This has been the chef's pet project for a while, along with his veal mignon with lemon (the quality of the meat is perfect, as is its execution); his fresh pasta with basil and warm goat cheese, which is marvelously well balanced; and his pleasantly thick, medium-cooked salmon. The wine list is short but rich in the best Savoie wines. The service is at the same time gracious and simple; both fixed-price menus are outstanding.

A la carte: 250-280F. Menus: 145F (wine incl.), 115F.

(14) Didier Roque

13, rue Jean-Mermoz - 50.23.07.90

M. Roque. Open until 9:45 p.m. Closed Sun. dinner & Mon. Terrace dining. No pets. Cards: V, AE, DC, MC.

Six years with Guy Savoy leave quite a mark on a man. Now, after working for two years at the Château de Faverges, Didier Roque is on his own, trying to impose his style and name upon a place that for so long had been the unquestioned establishment of "Monsieur" Salino. It's been a difficult task, but his wife helps greatly, greeting customers in a charming manner and decorating the terrace splendidly with flowers. For business lunches, Didier Roque suggests a 130-franc lunch menu; for all occasions, thereis the reasonable 175-franc fixed-price menu. This is a good idea, for the prices add up quickly when one orders à la carte. Sample the mussel-and-avocado gazpacho, which is fresh, savory and perfectly seasoned; the cold lobster soup, less convincing to the eye (its color is pinkish) but with the authentic taste of shellfish; the filet of perch with wonderful cèpes; the roasted sea bass with chanterelles, delicious in its simplicity; and the exquisite raspberry-and-orange crème brûlée. The wine list, inclusive and intelligently explained, is proof enough of the strength of this restaurant.

A la carte: 300F and up. Menus: 130F (weekday lunch only), 180F (weekday lunch only, wine incl.), 175F, 240F, 285F.

Super-Panorama

7, rte. du Semnoz - 50.45.34.86

Closed Mon., Tues. & Jan. 2-Feb. 11. 5 rms 175F. No pets. Parking. Card: V.

This simple, remarkably well-situated hotel faces the lake and the mountains. Terrace dining. Restaurant.

IN NEARBY **Chavoires**
(4.5 km SE on D 509)
74290 Veyrier-du-Lac - (Haute-Savoie)

---

(13) Pavillon de l'Ermitage

79, rte. d'Annecy - 50.60.11.09

M. Tuccinardi. Open until 8:30 p.m. Closed late Oct.-early March. Terrace dining. Pets allowed. Garage parking. Cards: V, AE, DC.

Book a table in the first dining room overlooking the lake—with its floral-patterned carpet, its older clientele and its incomparable view. Pavillon de l'Ermitage has preserved the now nearly obsolete charm once typical of spa-resort restaurants. Maurice Tuccinardi's cuisine can be summarized in two words: generosity and classicism. Those who yearn for the grandeur of an old-fashioned cuisine will have a splendid time with the warm pâté, a vol-au-vent (puff pastry case) of sweetbreads and chanterelles, such as we rarely see today, the Bresse chicken à la crème and a tasty, perfectly cooked rack of lamb. These ultra-bourgeois meals end with a pear praline or an iced nougat with nuts, followed by a series of petits fours and a tray of cream puff pastries. So we will forgive this good restaurant for using a pencil to cross out the price of the foie gras—110 francs—on the à la carte menu and write in 150 francs (though one really should be more discreet). The service is friendly, quick and efficient. The wine list includes some very old Bordeaux vintages at reasonable prices.

A la carte: 350F. Menus: 180F, 250F, 360F.

Pavillon de l'Ermitage

(See restaurant above)

Closed late Oct.-early March. 2 stes 450-480F. 11 rms 170-400F. Half-board 330-480F.

A delightful garden slopes toward the lake, which can be seenin its entirety from the beautiful rooms. The reception is charming.

IN NEARBY **Saint-Jorioz**
(9 km S on N 508)
74410 St-Jorioz - (Haute-Savoie)

La Cochette

La Magne (5 km S in St-Eustache)
50.68.50.08

Open year-round. 15 rms 90-160F. Half-board 145-230F. Pets allowed. Parking.

A chalet fit for a postcard, La Cochette overlooks the Annecy lake. Restaurant.

IN NEARBY **Talloires**
(13 km SE on N 509)
74290 Veyrier-du-Lac - (Haute-Savoie)

L'Abbaye de Talloires

Rte. du Port - 50.60.77.33

M. Tiffenat. Open until 9:30 p.m. Closed Sun. dinner & Mon. lunch (off-seas.) & Dec. 15-Jan. 15. Garden dining. Parking. No pets. Telex 385307. Cards: V, AE, DC.

The new chef in this noble building, a former Benedictine abbey that has been admirably restored and maintained by the Tiffenat family, fortunately hasn't changed the good traditions of the cuisine. It is still dedicated to handsome produce—regional whenever possible—and to the best specialties of Savoie. Whether seated on the terrace facing the enchanting lake or in the elegant dining room, you'll enjoy the lobster salad with citrus fruit, the trout with rhubarb, delicious lamb smoked at the abbey and garnished with a salad of string beans and mint, and the famous Reblochon fondue with green apples. Lovely wine cellar.

A la carte: 400-500F. Menus: 150F (weekday lunch only, wine incl.), 170F to 350F.

L'Abbaye de Talloires

(See restaurant above)

Closed Dec. 15-Jan. 15. 2 stes 925-1,420F. 30 rms 400-1,015F. Half-board 559-1,073F oblig. in seas. Pets allowed.

This old inn is extraordinary; the common areas (the cloister and the large gallery) have been redecorated with perfect taste. The garden is enchanting, the degree of comfort marvelous, and the service gracious. Many recreational activities. Relais et Châteaux.

Beau Site

50.60.71.04

Closed Oct. 1-May 15. 37 rms 190-400F. Half-board 260-350Foblig. in seas. Pets allowed. Tennis. Cards: V, AE, DC, MC.

Well isolated in a five-acre park, the appropriately named Beau Site has a private beach bordering the lake. The rooms are small but tastefully furnished; some overlook the lake. Restaurant.

Le Père Bise

Rte. du Port - 50.60.72.01

Mme. Bise. Open until 9 p.m. Closed Tues. (Sept. 14-July 9), Wed. lunch & Dec. 13-Feb. 18. Garden dining. Pets allowed. Telex 385812. Cards: V, AE, DC.

You won't be able to persuade the wealthy international clientele who have come here for years that this is not the authentic, grand French cuisine they think it is. Besides, you wouldn't want to, now that young Sophie Bise is working before the stoves. Bise didn't waste a moment when she started in summarily dismissing most of the dishes from the older, ostentatious repertoire, such as the rack of lamb Pompadour, the filet of sole in port and the chausson (turnover) filled with langoustines in a Nantua sauce. They seemed more appropriate for a culinary competition than for a restaurant, and fortunately they were replaced with such fine dishes as, for example, a delicious blanquette of lobster from Brittany in a light sauce, a perfectly cooked gilthead garnished with a twig of rosemary, an exquisite croustillant of sweetbreads with truffles served with carrots that melt in your mouth, and a bitter-chocolate cake, a little too rich but nevertheless delicious. The execution remains what it has always been—impeccable—but its spirit is more modern and its style livelier.

All this food is served with a flourish by waiters who, though a bit pretentious, are incredibly well trained; they are aware that they play a role in the preservation of the highest French culinary traditions. Michel, the maître d', is one of the best in France, and Sophie's mother makes her rounds twice during a meal. The gardens and flowers facing the mountains and the lake are enchanting. The wine cellar is impressive, but the coffee is insipid and the tuiles (cookies) are a bit soft.

A la carte: 600-700F. Menus: 280F (weekdays only), 380F, 550F.

Le Père Bise

(See restaurant above)

Closed Dec. 13-Feb. 18. 3 stes 2,000-3,800F. 31 rms 500-1,500F. Half-board 750-1,200F oblig. in seas. TV. Pets allowed.

A lovely complex of buildings nestled on the lakeshore in delightfully romantic surroundings. Ask for a room in the Villa des Roses, the beautiful new guest house on the other side of the small street. The rooms are extremely comfortable, the decor ultra-classic, and the view of the lake superb. Relais et Châteaux.

Les Prés du Lac

50.60.76.11

Closed Nov. 11-Feb. 2. 1 ste. 8 rms 1,165-1,375F. TV. Pets allowed. Tennis. Parking. Telex 309288. Cards: V, AE, DC, MC.

Separated from the lake by only a lovely garden, this hotelis ideally peaceful, and its delightful rooms are decorated in the Laura Ashley style. The facilities are both numerous and outstanding. No restaurant.

Annonay

07100 Annonay - (Ardèche)
Paris 546 - Valence 53 - Vienne 42 - St-Etienne 43

Marc et Christine

(14)

29, ave. Marc-Seguin - 75.33.46.97

M. Julliat. Open until 9:30 p.m. Closed Sun. dinner, Mon. (except holidays), Jan. 2-24 & 2 weeks in Aug. Garden dining. Pets allowed. Cards: V.

One can never be overly skeptical of a restaurant located next to a train station. Indeed, Marc et Christine isn't very cheerful, but neither was Troisgros years ago, and one certainly couldn't miss knocking at that door. So don't pass up the large dining room of this fairly new Annonay restaurant. Again, the exterior may not be so charming, and its interior proportions are rather clumsy, but there are some nice surprises in store. Ask for the rear dining room—it overlooks the garden, where meals are served in summer, and its pink and blue decor will put you in a fine mood. A large part of the cuisine is devoted to subtle regional dishes: quail with cabbage, émincés of sweetbreads, small white boudin sausages and a warm duck pâté with a confit of leeks and turnips. The filet of beef à la ficelle in a Saint-Joseph sauce is slightly overcooked (or perhaps slightly too marinated), which takes away some of its lightness, but the afternoon snacks from the Ardèche region possess all the charm of the robust, outrageously sweet desserts one finds in rustic cuisine. The chocolate cake in an eggnog sauce and the lavender ice cream with a honey sabayon testify to Marc Julliat's well-directed imagination. Christine greets the customers in an absolutely delightful manner. A good Vivarais cuisine is served in the annex (Le Patio).

Menus: 95F (weekdays only), 125F and 170F to 230F.

Hôtel du Midi

17, pl. des Cordeliers - 75.33.23.77

Closed Sun. (in winter) & Dec. 17-Jan. 15. 40 rms 95-195F. Pets allowed. Garage parking. Cards: V, AE, DC, MC.

Located just a few minutes away from Safari Park in the Haut-Vivarais area. No restaurant.

Antibes

06600 Antibes - (Alpes-Maritimes)
Paris 913 - Nice 22 - Cannes 11 - Grasse 28

Sights. The ramparts; old Antibes (the Provençal market, pl. Nationale); the marina. At Cap d'Antibes: La Garoupe hill; Thuret gardens (ten acres of Australian and South African trees); Notre-Dame-du-Bon-Port chapel (near the lighthouse, naves fromthe twelfth and fourteenth centuries). Museums: Musée Picasso (drawings, etchings, lithographs, ceramics and paintings Picasso did in the museum itself); Musée d'-Histoire et d'Archéologie (Antipolis since prehistoric times).

Eating on the Run. L'Arôme des Vins, 15, blvd. du Maréchal-Foch (wine bar and hors d'oeuvres); Le Cheap, 21, rue Dautheville (American dishes, chili); Le Clos des Moines, 8, rue Alazy (pizza, good grilled fish); La Côte à l'Os, 26, rue James-Close (jazz, hearty steaks); Il Giardino, 21, rue Thuret (pizza); Chez Olive, ave. Maréchal-Leclerc (pies and delicious tarts); Le Pistou, 18, rue James-Close (pasta, a small fixed-price menu); La Taverne Niçoise, pl. du Safranier (a modest fixed-price menu for 50 francs); Le Tea Pot, 44, blvd. Albert-Ier (salads, scrambled eggs, tarts, teas).

Bars & Cafés. Le Cristal (a large café/brasserie), Le Festival and Le Pam-Pam (ice cream, cocktails, live bands, often Brazilian)—all three are located on blvd. du Président-Wilson; Le Madison, ave. Alexandre-III (jazz).

Nightlife. Le Fort Carré, 11, ave. du 11-Novembre (huge, caters to a young clientele, especially popular on Saturdays); La Siesta, rte. du Bord-de-Mer (megacenter of modern nightlife—disco, lights, stretches of water).

Shops. *Bakeries:* Boulangerie Centrale Guelpa, 20, rue Clémenceau (bread with olives, small loaves baked in oil). *Charcuterie*: Jacques Girard, 4, rue Sade (excellent homemade products). *Gourmet foods:* La Corbeille, 10, blvd. du Président-Wilson (French and foreign products, a Fauchon subsidiary); L'Epicerie, 14, rue Lacan (tea, smoked fish, a Hédiard subsidiary). *Cheese:* L'Etable, 1, rue Sade (wide variety). *Wine:* L'Arôme des Vins, 15, blvd. du Maréchal-Foch (regional wines as well as famous vintages).

Bleu Marine

Les Quatre Chemins - 93.74.84.84

Open year-round. 18 rms 250-270F. TV. Parking. Cards: V, AE, DC, MC.

Each room in this new, modern hotel has a balcony/terrace facing the sea, where breakfast is served. No restaurant.

La Bonne Auberge

(18)

N 7, quartier La Brague
93.33.36.65

M. Rostang. Open until 10:30 p.m. Closed Mon. (off-seas.) & Nov. 15-Dec. 15. Air cond. Terrace dining. Parking. Pets allowed. Telex 470989. Cards: V, AE.

Every year Jo Rostang, whose mischievous little face seems to have been spared the nasty effects of the passing years, sings the same old song. He claims he's going to escape forever to the Caribbean, where he does in fact spend some time. There, he promises, he'll tan himself in the warm sun and supervise the kitchen of some sumptuous hotel. Yet every time we saunter into La Bonne Auberge—or rather the large, glassed-in terrace that precedes the ocher-and-rose dining room whose roughly plastered walls are adorned with a terrifying collection of clown paintings—Rostang is there, holding his post alongside his charming wife.

You see him dash for the kitchen, scurry back, only to return again, not exactly the sign of a calm retirement. And yet his 28-year-old son, Philippe, who has returned to the nest after a long voyage to some of the best restaurants in both the Old and the New World (Senderens, Delaveyne, Troisgros, Maître à Berlin, a stopover in Los Angeles), should hardly give him cause to worry. He recently served us a dinner that was perfect from start to finish: lobster ravioli in a coral sauce with black olives and fennel, marvelous sea urchins with apple mousse, a salad of red snapper subtly blended with artichokes, red beets and potatoes, a savory gratiné of young rabbit with cream and spinach (finally, rabbit that tastes like rabbit!) and very fine sweetbreads that would have been even better a little more golden and crusty; the beautiful finish to this elegant, harmonious, savory meal was a delicious lemon soufflé served on a chocolate cookie, along with an old classic that one could never tire of as long as it is prepared as it was here—cherries jubilee over vanilla ice cream. Absolute perfection.

The bill, which is hardly negligible, fails to faze the international clientele that dines here one night and at Vergé or Ducasse in Monte-Carlo the next. The service is perfect, as always, and among the finest Bordeaux, Burgundies and Côtes-du-Rhône, we found two or three wines from Provence that recently made a quiet appearance.

A la carte: 600F and up. Menus: 259F (lunch only), 340F, 460F, 500F.

(13) L'Ecurie Royale

33, rue Vauban - 93.34.76.20

M. Xhauflair. Open until 9:30 p.m. Dinner only in summer. Closed Mon. (in seas.), Sun. dinner-Tues. lunch (off-seas.) & Aug. 1-7. Air cond. Cards: V, AE, DC, MC.

The country decor of these former luxury stables combines large wooden beams, lace tablecloths, strings of garlic, rough stucco walls and wrought iron. Its ultra-traditional cuisine—dominated by the veal kidney à la liégeoise (Léa Xhauflair worked for quite a while in Belgium as a cook), the suprême of guinea-fowl with spinach, and a splendid parfait with Provençal honey and bitter chocolate—is served with an engaging attentiveness. The clientele is rather chic, and the checks are formidable.

A la carte: 350-400F. Menus: 170F, 240F.

(14) La Marguerite

11, rue Sadi-Carnot - 93.34.08.27

MM. Seguin & Tranchant. Open until 9:30 p.m. (10 p.m. in summer). Closed Sun. dinner & Mon. (June 15-Sept. 15: closed Tues. lunch & Mon.). Air cond. Pets allowed. Cards: V.

For the past ten years, La Marguerite has proven to be one of the most solidly successful restaurants on the Côte d'Azur. The two owners have created an outstanding small fixed-price menu, plus a brief à la carte list of subtle, beautifully presented dishes of a bold preparation. For example, for 155 francs you can sample the brandade of cod with olives and the fisherman's plate in a saffron cream, followed by beautiful cheeses and refreshing sorbets, or a light almond tart and pear au gratin. The contemporary decor is plain but comfortable, and the service is extremely good.

A la carte: 300F. Menus: 155F, 240F, 320F.

Mas Djoliba

29, ave. de Provence - 93.34.02.48

Closed Jan. 4-23. 14 rms 300-480F. Half-board 330-540F. oblig. in seas. TV. Pets allowed. Heated pool. Parking. Telex 461686. Cards: V, AE, DC.

The Mas Djoliba is well situated in the midst of a large serene park halfway between the beach and downtown Antibes. Private excursions can be arranged in Pullman minibuses. Restaurant.

Motel Mercator

Chemin des Groules - 93.33.50.75

Open year-round. 20 rms 265F. Pets allowed. Tennis. Parking. Cards: V, AE, DC, MC.

The Motel Mercator, tucked away in the peaceful Provençal countryside, has remarkably well-equipped studios. No restaurant.

(13) Restaurant du Bastion

1, ave. du Général-Maizières
93.34.13.88

M. Hammou. Open until 10:30 p.m. Closed Sun. dinner & Mon. (off-seas.) & Mon. lunch (in seas.). Terrace dining. Pets allowed. Cards: V, AE.

At the foot of the ramparts, the tables of the Restaurant du Bastion are elegantly set on a terrace shaded by an old gnarled fig tree. But this rather conspicuous place is not the tourist trap one might expect. On the contrary, it is a good fish restaurant run by a charming couple. The simple, subtle and fresh cuisine includes several noteworthy dishes served year-round: the panaché of three fish with pistou (pesto), the bouillabaisse and the grilled fish. And there are also several tasty appetizers, particularly the flan of sea urchins with saffron, as well as some well-prepared desserts. Alas, the à la carte prices are dangerously steep; but, thank goodness, there is a wonderful short fixed-price menu.

A la carte: 300F. Menus: 110F and 170F (weekdays only).

See also: **Cap d'Antibes**

Arbellara

see CORSICA

Arbois

39600 Arbois - (Jura)
Paris 393 - Lons-le-Saunier 39 - Dole 35 - Pontarlier 56

(16) Jean-Paul Jeunet

9, rue de l'Hôtel-de-Ville - 84.66.05.67

M. Jeunet. Open until 9:30 p.m. Closed Mon. dinner & Tues. (except Sept. & school vacations) & Dec.-Jan. Pets allowed. Garage parking. Cards: V, AE, MC.

Red toques signify modern cuisine; black toques signify traditional cuisine.

The deer antlers, the rustic ceiling lamps, the strings of garlic hanging from the wooden beams, the wine racks with cranks—the dated look that clashed so violently with the extraordinary élan of youth and modernism that Jean-Paul Jeunet has brought to his father André's restaurant—is now finally, and completely, gone. Sweeping aside all this Jurassic claptrap, Jeunet has done over not only the rooms of the hotel but more importantly the dining room in light, tasteful, modern style. Even the seemingly immortal bust of Pasteur, that glorious child of Arbois, is no longer perched powerlessly on his pedestal, watching the havoc being wrought by the encroaching contemporary cuisine in this former temple of poulard in yellow wine and pike soufflé in crayfish soup. Today's winners are modernized dishes composed of flavorful sauces, fresh seasonal vegetables, shorter cooking times, bold contrasts and an intelligent interpretation of regional dishes: shellfish consommé with oysters, court bouillon of red mullet served with a mousseline of sweet peppers, crépinettes of escargots with white beets, Jésus de Morteau with young cabbage in herb sauce, young rabbit ravioli in marjoram... The charming patriarch, André Jeunet, who recently has been feeling the effects of fatigue, witnesses this revolution with happiness, and now devotes himself solely to his wine cellar (handsome but rather incomplete), to his ample waistline and to his no less ample reputation, which he maintains by cordially coming and going among the tables. One more point in this edition.

A la carte: 300F. Menus: 100F, 149F, 300F.

Le Paris

(See restaurant above)

Closed Dec.-Jan. 18 rms 250-450F. Half-board oblig. in seas.

Completely modernized and redecorated, this is now a perfectly comfortable and well-equipped hotel, right down to the details. Lovely breakfasts.

Arcachon

33120 Arcachon - (Gironde)
Paris 627 - Biarritz 183 - Bordeaux 60 - Dax 141

Arc-Hôtel

89, blvd. de la Plage - 56.83.06.85

Open year-round. 3 stes 750-1,700F. 27 rms 298-790F. TV. No pets. Heated pool. Parking. Cards: V, AE, DC, MC.

Overlooking a large sandy beach and a swimming pool, the well-equipped rooms of the Arc-Hôtel are either modern or contain period furniture. Their terraces face the sea or the garden. No restaurant.

Le Boucanier

(Gérard Tissier)
222, blvd. de la Plage - 56.83.41.82

M. Tissier. Open until 10 p.m. Closed Mon. (in seas.), Sun. dinner & Jan. 1-Easter. Air cond. Cards: V, DC, MC.

Gérard Tissier's decor has taken a cheerful, exotic turn for the better. The cream-colored stucco walls, the soft lighting, the small, elegant tables and the clusters of flowers make for a lovely, fresh environment that adds a welcome touch to the cuisine, whose classicism and sobriety could sometimes bear a little livening up. The wild salmon marinated in dill is a bit bland, as is the brill, which is poached expertly but, alas, is served in a flavorless basil cream sauce. However, we found the maraîchère salad with small shellfish perfect and the filet of sole with mushrooms (cèpes or chanterelles) delicious. For dessert, the profiteroles with pistachios were satisfactory. The service could have been a bit more attentive.

A la carte: 300-350F. Menus: 95F (weekdays only), 125F.

Les Ormes

77, blvd. de la Plage - 56.83.09.27

Open year-round. 25 rms 250-550F. Half-board 280-431F oblig. in seas. TV. Pets allowed. Parking. Telex 570503. Cards: V.

This small, modern, pleasant and discreet hotel located in front of the beach has been thoroughly redecorated. The bright, spacious rooms have terraces. Restaurant.

Le Patio

10, blvd. de la Plage - 56.83.02.72

M. Falgueirettes. Open until 10 p.m. (11 p.m. in summer). Closed Tues. (off-seas.) & Feb. Garden dining. Pets allowed. Cards: V.

Chef/owner Bruno Falgueirettes is a prolific but conscientious saucier. The charming patio, along with the cordial reception proffered by his wife, lends an air of spontaneity to the entire place. Obvious efforts have been made, and the couple's enthusiasm is charming; this is a good restaurant whose prices have not yet gone crazy. Sample the beautiful oysters, the duck jambon with endives, the turbot blanquette with juniper berries and dill, and the handsome prime rib. The Bordeaux wines are good and their prices quite reasonable.

A la carte: 230F.

Point France

1, rue Grenier - 56.83.46.74

Closed Nov. 12-March 1. 34 rms 235-525F. TV. Air cond. Pets allowed. Garage parking. Cards: V, AE, DC, MC.

At this contemporary, intelligently designed hotel, some of the rooms (which are large and have lovely bathrooms) boast panoramic terraces overlooking the basin. No restaurant.

Pointe de l'Arcouest

see Paimpol

Les Arcs

73700 Bourg-St-Maurice
Paris 674 - Bourg-St-Maurice 12 - Val-d'Isère 43

Le Green

Arc 1800 - 79.07.25.17

M. Arnould. Open until 10:30 p.m. Closed April 15-June 15 & Oct. 1-Dec. 15. Terrace dining. Telex 980404. Cards: V, AE, MC.

A top-notch manager and maître d' have adeptly established an elegant, tasteful, relaxing tone here for the very appreciative après-ski in crowd.

A warm, blond-wood decor and a view of Mont Blanc are the setting for the fine food of Pierre Gagnaire, featuring salad of red snapper and prawns, medallion of veal with truffles and ravioli, good cheeses and a delicious bavarois made from spice cake with cinnamon ice cream. The prices for good food in an expensive resort are not too bad.

A la carte: 350F. Menus: 160F, 220F and 300F (dinner only).

Hotel du Golf

(See restaurant above)

Closed April 15-June 15 & Oct. 1-Dec. 15. 1 ste. 271 rooms. Half-board 381-672F oblig. TV in 12 rms. Pets allowed. Heated pool. Tennis. Golf.

Sporting facilities of all kinds, sauna, discotheque—this is a huge, well-equipped hotel with pleasant rooms.

Ardres

62610 Ardres - (Pas-de-Calais)
Paris 281 - Lille 87 - Boulogne 37 - Calais 17

Clément

91, esplanade du Maréchal-Leclerc
21.82.25.25

M. Coolen. Open until 9 p.m. Closed Tues. lunch (off-seas.), Mon., Jan. 15-Feb. 15 & May 1. Pets allowed. Garage parking. Cards: V, AE, DC, MC.

The "Grand Hôtel" Clément actually resembles a lovely little family house, with its white facade in front and green garden out back. Everything is clean, neat, full of flowers, rustic and well maintained, with stucco and ornaments on the dining room ceiling. The cuisine of François Coolen, the owner's son, is artfully modern, without excessive boldness, and beautifully personalized in its simplicity of execution. Try the plate of warm and cold duck foie gras, the fowl fricassée with cucumber and the turbot cressonnière; then, the tray of handsome desserts. The sommelier, a young girl fresh out of school, will explain the magnificent wine list. The Noilly-Champagne served as the house apéritif is a great success.

A la carte: 350F. Menus: 100F, 200F, 300F.

Clément

(See restaurant above)

Closed Mon. (except holidays), Jan. 15-Feb. 15 & May 1. 17 rms 175-275F.

The small, simple rooms feature rustic furniture. The reception is diligent, and the breakfast exquisite.

Argelès-Gazost

65400 Argelès-Gazost - (Hautes-Pyrénées)
Paris 812 - Cauterets 17 - Lourdes 13 - Tarbes 33

Thermal

Beaucens-les-Bains
(5 km SE on D 100) - 62.97.04.21

Closed Oct. 1-June 1. 30 rms 85-210F. Half-board 135-175F oblig. in seas. Heated pool. Parking.

Isolated in the countryside, in the midst of a nineteen-acre park, the Thermal hotel's pleasant rooms (some of which include kitchenettes) have views of the Pyrénées. Restaurant.

IN NEARBY **Saint-Savin**
(3 km S on D 101)
65400 Argelès-Gazost - (Hautes-Pyrénées)

Viscos

62.97.02.28

M. Saint-Martin. Open until 9:30 p.m. Closed Sun. dinner & Mon. (except school vacations & holidays) & Nov. 15-Jan. 14. Terrace dining. Pets allowed. Hotel: 16 rms 180-190F; half-board 174-209F. Parking. Cards: V, AE, MC.

This small, charming inn, located in an old village at the foot of the Pyrénées, somewhat isolated between Lourdes and the mountain peaks is a holiday home to a faithful clientele, both French and foreign. The terrace is cheerful, as is the rustic dining room with its fireplace. Jean-Pierre Saint-Martin prepares goose, duck and other tasty regional dishes with much earnestness and personality: foie gras in a caramelized Banyuls sauce, a small panaché of langoustines and foie gras, aiguillettes of duck with honey and seasonal fruit and, for dessert, a delicious warm apple tart in peach juice. The menus are interesting, the small local wines perfect.

A la carte: 250F. Menus: 90F, 115F, 195F.

Argenteuil

see PARIS SUBURBS

Argentière

74400 Chamonix - (Haute-Savoie)
Paris 627 - Annecy 103 - Chamonix 8 - Vallorcine 7.5

Becs Rouges

Montroc-le-Planet
(2 km NE on N 506 & VO 7)
50.54.01.00

Closed April 15-June 15 & Sept. 15-Dec. 20. 24 rms 263-360F. Half-board 255-296F. Parking. Cards: V, AE, DC.

Each room is soundproofed and has a balcony. Thoughtful provisions are made for taking out cold meals, if you wish, or for dining elsewhere with meal vouchers. Restaurant.

Grands Montets

340, chemin des Arberons - 50.54.06.66

Closed May 1-June 25 & Sept. 15-Dec. 20. 40 rms 350-500F. TV. Pets allowed. Garage parking. Cards: V, MC.

The rooms, some of which are duplexes and suitable for the entire family, are spacious. Ski lessons are available in winter, with tennis, golf and horseback riding in summer. No restaurant.

The prices given in this guide reflect what restaurants and hotels were charging at press time.

Arles

13200 Arles - (Bouches-du-Rhône)
Paris 727 - Marseille 92 - Avignon 40 - Nîmes 31

Sights. Blvd. des Lices and pl. de la République; the arenas and the antique amphitheater (circa 100 B.C.); hot springs of Constantine (fourth century B.C.); Alyscamps (one of the most beautiful Christian necropolises); Saint-Trophime cathedral and cloister; the forum's cryptoporticos; the Christian Lapidary Museum (said to be the richest in the world after the Vatican's, ancient Christian sarcophagi); the Pagan Lapidary Museum (Gallic and Roman antiquities); Musée Réattu (Provençal school of the eighteenth and nineteenth centuries); Musée Arlaten (founded by Mistral); annual celebration of the Guardians (May 1).

Eating on the Run. L'Affenage, 4, rue Molière (table d'hôte and regional specialties); La Grande Brasserie Arlésienne, 14, blvd. des Lices (shellfish and daily specials); Vitamine, 16, rue du Dr-Fanton (mixed salads and fresh pasta).

D'Artalan

26, rue du Sauvage - 90.93.56.66

Open year-round. 7 stes 310-540F. 42 rms 310-540F. Garage parking. Telex 441203. Cards: V, AE, DC.

The charming rooms of this ancient twelfth- and fifteenth-century building have lovely eighteenth-century Provençal furniture. Small garden. No restaurant.

(13) Lou Marquès

Blvd. des Lices - 90.93.43.20

M. Albagnac. Open until 9:30 p.m. Closed early Nov.-Dec. 21. Terrace dining. Pets allowed. Garage parking. Telex 400239. Cards: V, AE, DC, MC.

An authentic convent chapel displays its baroque facade in a garden enclosed by spindle trees, where in summer, Lou Marquès offers the greatest luxury to be found in Arles: pure and lovely peace and greenery. You'll book your table in this garden, of course, rather than in the austere, large dining room. The arrival of new chef Patrick Fer has hardly helped the cooking, however, whether in the old standards department, still acceptably done, in the local specialties or on the long and unimaginative dessert list. Only the prices have shown any initiative. We had to take away a point this year.

A la carte: 350F. Menus: 185F, 275F, 345F.

Jules César

(See restaurant above)

Closed early Nov.-Dec. 21. 3 stes 1,300-1,550F. 52 rms 350-850F. TV in 35 rms. Air cond. in 20 rms. Pets allowed. Heated pool.

This ancient convent, transformed into an elegant country inn, features a cloister, an inner garden, pleasant rooms and a new swimming pool. Relais et Châteaux.

Mas de la Chapelle

Rte. de Tarascon - 90.93.23.15

Open year-round. 1 ste 560F. 14 rms 310-540F. Half-board 375- 550F oblig. in seas. TV. Pets allowed. Pool. Tennis. Parking. Cards: V. MC.

The rooms in this beautiful hotel located on the border of the Camargue are clean and comfortable; some have views of the park. Horseback riding, golf practice. Restaurant.

(13) L'Olivier

1 bis, rue Réattu - 90.49.64.88

M. Cot. Open until 10:30 p.m. Closed Mon., Sun. (except July), Feb. 20-March 5 & Nov. 1-20. Terrace dining. No pets. Cards: V.

Charm, simplicity and freshness, but also a serious professionalism at all levels—that's what you'll find in this ancient house hidden away at the end of a small street in the old district of Arles. That's also why, in a short time, L'Olivier has won over the best clientele in town with a sensational fixed-price menu, a bright and sunny à la carte menu and a judicious wine list (which offers a wide choice of good vintages by the glass). You'll enjoy a handsome duck liver, served with a well-seasoned mesclun salad, and a gilthead roasted in laurel butter and citrus fruit, garnished with a zucchini tart. The pastries and sorbets are steadily improving. Charming summer courtyard.

A la carte: 260-300F. Menus: 138F, 190F, 250F.

Le Rodin

20, rue Auguste-Rodin - 90.49.69.10

Open year-round. 28 rms 240-305F. Half-board 338F. TV in 10 rms. Pool. Parking. Telex 420676. Cards: V, AE, DC, MC.

All of Le Rodin's rooms have balconies with views of the garden and pool; some have kitchenettes. No restaurant.

(14) Le Vaccarès

Pl. du Forum (entrance on rue Favorin)
90.96.06.17

M. Dumas. Open until 9:30 p.m. (10 p.m. in summer). Closed Sun. & Mon. (except holidays) & Dec. 20-Jan. 20. Terrace dining. Pets allowed. Cards: V.

Bernard Dumas's cuisine is perfectly suited to the soft, rustic decor of the beautiful dining room, whose long balcony overlooks the loveliest square in all of Arles. The least expensive of the fixed-price menus is inspired by such great classic regional dishes as the tureen of Camargue lotte and the sailor's broufado (marinated beef casserole). The à la carte menu lists a wide variety of dishes that are deliciously redolent of Provence: steamed sea perch garnished with an orange-and-lemon compote in olive oil, conger (eel), lamb with garlic cloves, a flan of red mullet with oysters, finely seasoned with a beurre fondu of anchovies. Because Dumas wants only the best wines of the Rhône valley for his wine cellar, his checks tend to be rather steep. But how can we blame him for his expensive wines, when they are so good?

A la carte: 300F. Menus: 150F, 190F.

Arnage

see Le Mans

Arnay-le-Duc

21230 Arnay-le-Duc - (Côte-d'Or)
Paris 287 - Autun 28 - Dijon 57 - Saulieu 28 - Beaune 34

15 Chez Camille

1, pl. E.-Herriot - 80.90.01.38

M. Poinsot. Open until 9:30 p.m. Closed Jan. 3-31. Air cond. Pets allowed. Garage parking. Cards: V, AE, DC, MC.

The courtyard of this sixteenth-century house (which used to be a horse relay station) is now a delightful and lush winter garden walled in by glass. That's where meals are served, under parasols at lunchtime and by candlelight under the stars at night. Monique and Armand Poinsot—she with her impeccable chignon, and he with his Englishman's mustache—are not just charming hosts; they are also well-experienced professionals who take great care of their restaurant, devoting to it limitless time and money. The cuisine is not exempt of small errors, but they seem attributive only to an excess of generosity. Sample the rabbit en gelée with tarragon, the escargots fondue garnished with a broccoli bouquet, carp au gratin cooked in Burgundy wine and especially the delicious capon. The wine cellar is interesting and varied; the wines are decanted and served out of carafes—a treat indeed.

A la carte: 250F. Menus: 156F, 198F, 260F, 268F.

Chez Camille

(See restaurant above)

Closed Jan. 3-31. 2 stes 500-750F. 12 rms 350F. Half-board 460-750F.

Chez Camille's excellent rooms have been charmingly arranged on the second floor of the building and in the attic. The facilities are both complete and modern. Sauna. Outstanding service.

Arras

62000 Arras - (Pas-de-Calais)
Paris 179 - St-Quentin 75 - Amiens 65 - Lille 51

13 L'Ambassadeur

Pl. Foch - 21.23.29.80

M. Chaveroche. Open until 9:45 p.m. Closed Sun. dinner. Pets allowed. Cards: V, AE, DC, MC.

Together with that of Valenciennes, the Arras train station offers the most beautiful buffet in all of northern France. Though somewhat solemn, this establishment is nevertheless perfectly comfortable; chef Yves Labrousse's traditionally inspired cuisine is never out of place. It's true that the long and rather conservative à la carte menu should list fewer dishes, such as the Danish salads, the escargots à la bourguignonne, the Périgourdine dishes, the piccatas Stroganoff and the Norwegian omelets, as well as more regional dishes, such as the wonderful Flemish herrings and the delicious andouillette with juniper berries. To sum up, the cuisine is a bit ostentatious and unabashedly conservative, but it is also authentic, well executed and quite generous.

A la carte: 300F. Menus: 120F, 175F.

14 La Faisanderie

Grand-Place - 21.48.20.76

M. Dargent. Open until 9 p.m. Closed Sun. dinner, Mon., Feb. school vacation & Aug. 1-22. Pets allowed. Cards: V, AE, DC.

When, in 1986, Jean-Pierre Dargent left his small family farm in the suburbs of Arras to come to the exquisite, unfortunately too-little-known Grand-Place, he caused more than a few Arras customs to be overturned. Today, despite the daunting checks, the success of this old stable, with its imposing arches and sandstone colonnades, proves that the local people are quite happy to finally have a luxury restaurant that serves an uncompromisingly contemporary cuisine. Dargent's ideas and technique are modern; he is also adamant about the quality and origin of his produce (fish from small fishing boats, Bresse poultry from Miéral's, Pauillac lamb, Landes liver), and he is quick to take advantage of any specials the market may offer. The pike grilled with grenouilles, the vegetable plate with smoked eels from the Somme bay, the rabbit kidneys with spinach-beets and goat-cheese ravioli, the turbot roasted in meat juice garnished with a potato purée, and the caramelized strawberries with ginger ice cream—these are creative, delicate, flavorful dishes that display to advantage the country's best products. The wine cellar is quite handsome.

A la carte: 350-400F. Menus: 150F, 205F, 310F.

Univers

3, pl. Croix-Rouge - 21.71.34.01

Open year-round. 36 rms 165-330F. Half-board 280-370F. TV in 12 rms. Pets allowed. Garage parking. Cards: V, AE, DC.

The well-restored ruins of a superb eighteenth-century monastery lend a peaceful charm to this elegant, tastefully furnished hotel. Inner garden and cloister. Stylish rooms, beautiful salons and a magnificent dining room.

Artzenheim

68320 Muntzenheim - (Haut-Rhin)
Paris 460 - Sélestat 20 - Colmar 17 - Mulhouse 49

13 Auberge d'Artzenheim

30, rue du Sponeck - 89.71.60.51

M. Husser-Schmitt. Open until 9 p.m. Closed Mon. dinner, Tues. & Feb. 15-March 15. Terrace dining. Pets allowed. Hotel: 10 rms 175-210F; half-board 175-205F. Parking. Cards: V, MC.

This charming inn with wooden beams and polished floors is bathed in the light and greenery of a small, manicured garden, which you have to share with the German clientele and with the families from Colmar out for a day in the country. The cuisine is doing well, the à la carte prices are still reasonable, and the small menu is perfect: house salad, flan of fresh cod with squid, grapefruit-port sorbet, ballotine of quail garnished with spinach, and caramel flan with pistachio ice cream. The wine cellar is quite nice.

A la carte: 280-300F. Menu: 135F.

Arz (Ile d')

56840 Ile d'Arz - (Morbihan)
Access from Vannes (ferry: 97.47.10.78) & from Conleau (ferry: 97.66.92.57)

L'Escale

Le Débarcadère - 97.44.32.15

Closed Oct. 15-March 25. 11 rms 125-270F. Half-board 151-223F oblig. in seas. No pets. Cards: V.

The rooms are perfectly maintained and the environment is superb. Very good prices. Restaurant.

Asnières

see PARIS SUBURBS

Aubazines

19190 Beynat - (Corrèze)
Paris 505 - Aurillac 86 - Tulle 19 - Brive 14

Lachaud

13

Pl. de l'Eglise - 55.25.71.17

M. Lachaud. Open until 9:30 p.m. Closed Sun. dinner & Mon. lunch (off-seas.) & Feb.1-20. Hotel: 19 rms 115-165F. Pets allowed. Cards: V.

A beautiful round dining room occupies the main floor of this centuries-old tower, whose narrow windows overlook the Corrèze valley and the Brives countryside. The lovely patronne, Arlette Lachaud, is a child of this region, as is Jean-Jacques, her timid, mustachioed husband, former cook at La Tour d'Argent and Lucas-Carton. Several years ago, Jean-Jacques took over this family village café, which made his grandmother famous. His cuisine is partly regional (confits, slightly cooked foie gras) and partly modernized-rustic (langoustine salad with duck, lotte with a bacon cream sauce, ramekin of escargots with a parsley cream sauce and frozen nut soufflé). The wine list features good Cahors wines.

A la carte: 200F. Menus: 55F and 75F (weekdays only), 100F, 150F.

Auch

32000 Auch - (Gers)
Paris 716 - Toulouse 77 - Tarbes 72 - Agen 71

Daguin

17

Pl. de la Libération
62.05.00.44

M. Daguin. Open until 9:30 p.m. Closed Sun. dinner, Mon. & Jan. Air cond. Pets allowed. Telex 520474. Cards: V, AE, DC, MC.

André Daguin has had this restaurant for 53 years. So who could boast of more success? For a while, he thought that his son Arnaud, who was assisting him, would take over, but the small family orchestra broke up. Now André is alone at the helm, which he holds steady and with panache—though we must say that his panache is unlike any other man's. This bulldozer from Gascony plows ahead at 100 miles an hour, nearly exhausting those around him. But the myth surrounding this character is not without truth. If you had heard his forceful speech a while back to the members of a prestigious culinary group that had bestowed on him the unprecedented honor to speak about his art, you would have been captivated by the power of his personality and the subtlety of his statements. Of course, speeches, even the best, don't fill up plates, or restaurants; and the clientele of the Hôtel de France certainly wouldn't think much of a feast composed only of beautiful words. Fortunately, Daguin is far too astute to bore his customers with words. He seldom appears in his dining room—a large, dark, red-and-white room decorated in the style of Napoléon III—preferring to let his cuisine speak for itself. And speak it does, for us at least.

Our most recent visit revealed a quite impressive talent, as evidenced by the daube of bull in a Madiran aspic: flavorful, admirably degreased and absolutely exquisite. Daguin manages to buy the bull that's the first to be killed (it's the least jumpy and the least nervous); after twenty days of aging, its meat becomes suitable for a real feast. We verified this later with the rib of bull cooked in Madiran, which equaled the best beef from the Chalosse, Bazas or Scotland. After this, Daguin insisted on waking up our palates with an extraordinary dish of kid liver gratinéed in vinegar with several meats—an explosion of highly concentrated tastes—followed by a suprême of capon stuffed with a confit of shallots, whose subtle juices tenderly steal over your mouth. At the end, your palate is tamed by the sweet bitterness of the four chocolates in a Banyuls sauce.

The great, very great Daguin will perhaps surprise us again next time, with warm foie gras, a simple breast of duck grilled to a pink in its skin, or perhaps lamb shank en gasconnade, farm chicken roasted in two kinds of mustard or roast Pauillac lamb garnished with young vegetables. Francis Miquel, the pleasant sommelier, will once more delight our palates when pouring his Colombards and Madirans: Elsewhere, we would sip them without paying them too much attention, but here (and we don't quite know why), they are simply delicious.

In the enclosed terrace located on the main floor of the small annex (Le Neuvième), Daguin serves a rustic cuisine at sensible prices (from 130 to 180 francs): terrines, cassoulets, daubes and blanquettes, accompanied by lovely little wines from thesouthwest of France.

A la carte: 300-600F. Menu: 410F (menu dégustation), 285F.

Hôtel de France

(See restaurant above)

Open year-round. 1 ste 900-1,200F. 28 rms 300-900F. Half-board 750-1,320F. TV in 15 rms. Air cond. in 15 rms. Pets allowed.

People always talk about André Daguin, but his wife, Jo—modest, charming and shy (sometimes a bit too shy)—deserves a sincere tip of the hat. With the patience of an ant, she has turned this old family hotel, where one never felt much like lingering, into a comfortable, hospitable establishment. After renovating the rooms and creating a Hollywood-style suite that even includes a Jacuzzi, she recently undertook the reception lobby. It's obvious she has succeeded: Now it draws us in, whereas before we never really felt at ease.

The Hôtel de France is well equipped for conferences. In addition, from October to April, two-day classes in duck and goose cuisine are offered. Relais et Châteaux.

Audierne

29113 Audierne - (Finistère)
Paris 588 - Quimper 35 - Pont-l'Abbé 32 - Douarnenez 22

Le Goyen

(17) Pl. Jean-Simon
98.70.08.88

M. Bosser. Open until 9 p.m. Closed Mon. (off-seas.), mid-Nov.-mid-Dec. & mid-Jan.-early Feb. No pets. Telex 941300. Cards: V, MC.

Adolphe Bosser, a knowledgeable cook, a great trainer of young talents (his former students are working in renowned restaurants throughout the French provinces) and a man of a powerful character, looks like a Bocuse from Brittany. He laughingly confesses to 35 years of experience in front of the stoves, and he possesses one of the most fertile and creative temperaments in Brittany. Bosser has managed to master the new trend of modern cuisine as few chefs his age have—to such an extent, in fact, that this cordial "professor" of the old school could teach the new generation a lot about enthusiasm, lightness and frankness. Today, two new elements have brought renewed energy to this colorful native of the south of France, now a resident of Cornouaille. First, he has found an extremely useful resource in Jean-Louis Leguyader, his outstanding assistant. Second, because he has quit smoking, he has rediscovered with rapture the subtle flavors that until now had been obliterated by tobacco. In short, Bosser is in great form.

His dishes fill us with enthusiasm: oysters accompanied by a tartare of coquilles St-Jacques, caviar and onion sprouts to spread on rye bread; creamy cockles with a julienne of lobster and truffles and a beaten egg white, served like a floating island; exotic crayfish salad garnished with a vinaigrette of passion fruit; sea bass and sliced potatoes served with a marvelous wine-sediment sauce; foie gras with two types of peppers (which he cooks at a cold, rather than warm, temperature,thus enhancing their flavor even more); and exquisite, elaborate iced desserts with fruit in season. The reception and service are those of an excellent restaurant but without any of the usual obsequiousness. A young and lovely brunette has recently taken charge of Bosser's sumptuous collection of Bordeaux wines.

A la carte: 350-400F. Menus: 120F, 195F, 245F, 345F.

Le Goyen

(See restaurant above)

Closed Mon. (off-seas.), mid-Nov.-mid-Dec. & mid-Jan.-mid- Feb. 5 stes 230-455F. 29 rms 202-255F. Half-board 265-340F oblig. in seas. TV.

The small rooms of this clean, well-maintained hotel are constantly undergoing modernization; most recently, they were being enlarged. The service is always provided with a smile. Breakfast is exquisite.

Audrieu

14250 Tilly-sur-Seulles - (Calvados)
Paris 240 - Caen 17 - Bayeux 13 - Deauville 60

Château d'Audrieu

(15) On D 158 - 31.80.21.52

M. Livry-Level. Open until 9:30 p.m. Closed Wed., Thurs. lunch & Nov. 27-Jan. 29. No pets. Parking. Telex 171777. Cards: V.

We have seen so many of these castles turned into hotels, either refurbished in patchwork fashion or made ostentatiously luxurious, that we are immediately tempted to run in the opposite direction, avoiding these places whose claim to nobility is so ill-founded. The Château d'Audrieu, however, is authentic; moreover, it's one of the most beautiful in the region: a superb mansion dating from the eighteenth century and facing French-style gardens in the midst of a 60-acre park. Miraculously, this historic monument still has its original decor, wainscoting and furniture. Of course, it needed to be restored and rearranged, but the Livry-Levels did such a lovely job when they turned the château into a hotel about ten years ago that it is impossible to find even the smallest error in taste.

Moreover, the couple had the excellent idea of placing the young Alain Cornet at the stoves. Because he trained at the Locguenolé château, then at Lucas-Carton, he now carefully avoids both the conventional and the chichi dishes one has come to expect of château-style cuisine. The beautiful dining room, which opens on both sides to the park and gardens, will certainly keep you from yawning with boredom. On the contrary, the Isigny oysters en gelée with herbs, the andouille (pork sausage) pie with quail eggs, the matelote (stew), the veal simmered in Pommeau, the lamb's feet with mushrooms, the cinnamon apple cooked in the traditional manner, the blancmange (jellied almond cream) in Calvados and the soft iced nougat in apple honey—these dishes promise a veritable festival of delights. Especially now that the competent chef, who at one time tended to overdo his dishes a little, adding small, superfluous touches,has begun to understand that supreme elegance and originality lie in simplicity. The service is excellent; the reception, in the customary château style, is cordial but not fawning. The checks are quite civilized, especially if you opt for the fixed-price menus, which are exemplary.

A la carte: 350-400F. Menus: 140F (weekday lunch only), 260F, 360F.

Château d'Audrieu

(See restaurant above)

Closed Nov. 27-Jan. 29. 3 stes 1,350-1,700F. 25 rms 400-950F. Half-board 575-800F. TV. Pets allowed. Heated pool.

The four beautiful suites are furnished with their original furniture (which has never left the castle); the bathrooms are remarkably well equipped; and the 24 charming and elegant rooms overlook the park and gardens of this splendid estate. A golf course is located fifteen kilometers away. Relais et Châteaux.

Aumont-Aubrac

48130 Aumont-Aubrac - (Lozère)
Paris 535 - Espalion 58 - Mende 42 - Marvejols 23

(16) Prouhèze

2, rte. du Languedoc - 66.42.80.07

M. Prouhèze. Open until 8:45 p.m. Closed Sun. dinner & Mon. (except July-Aug.) & Nov. 1-Feb. school vacation. Terrace dining. Pets allowed. Hotel: 29 rms 180-350F; half-board 240-290F. TV in 15 rms. Parking. Cards: V, MC.

Guy Prouhèze is establishing a solid position for himself as one of the best cooks in the Languedoc-Roussillon region. This former pupil of Michel Bras (his neighbor) has made great progress lately in giving his personal repertoire an authentic Lozère tone. Imagination, authority, magnificent country produce and a consistent generosity made our last meal here easily worthy of two toques, especially for such dishes as the lightly poached salmon garnished with crisp vegetables in a light shallot butter, marvelous, subtle guinea fowl ravioli flavored with bacon and mousserons (small mushrooms), aiguillettes of duck in honey sauce (or served with a black-currant sauce) and the spectacular feuillantine, garnished with every red fruit in season and served on a bed of melting vanilla ice cream. The marvelous wine cellar is one of the best in the region. The charming Catherine Prouhèze supervises the well-trained waiters (from the nearby Saint-Chély-d'Apcher hotel school) in a rustic dining room that's rather unexciting, despite its tapestries and large bouquets of flowers. Another point.

A la carte: 120-225F (menu/carte). Menus: 95F, 160F, 200F, 370F.

Auray

56400 Auray - (Morbihan)
Paris 474 - Lorient 36 - Quimper 97 - Vannes 18

(15) La Closerie de Kerdrain

14, rue Louis-Billet - 97.56.61.27

M. Corfmat. Open daily until 9:30 p.m. Garden dining. Pets allowed. Parking. Cards: V, AE, DC, MC.

The charming Fernand Corfmat and his wife, Martine, recently left their restaurant in Vannes for the place of their dreams in Auray: a charming, old little manor in the midst of a garden. Everything will be ready by the time you read these lines: Both the decor (antique wainscoting, Versailles flooring and beautiful silverware), which we have not yet seen, and the cuisine, which promises to be just as lovely. Practically a self-made man, Corfmat is lively, inventive and curious about everything. The meal we had recently at his former restaurant justly deserved two toques: warm oysters in a cider sabayon, cold bouillon of étrilles (small crabs) with langoustines and chervil, suprême of sea bass braised in old Pineau wine and garnished with sautéed artichokes, lamb's sweetbreads marinated with two types of peppers and fresh mint. The desserts, though well prepared, are less imaginative. Prices are still sensible.

A la carte: 250F. Menus: 80F (weekday lunch only), 120F, 150F, 220F.

(13) La Sterne

La Petite-Forêt - 97.56.48.33

M. Claussen. Open until 9:30 p.m. (10 p.m. in summer). Closed Mon. (except July & Aug. & for hotel residents). Air cond. No pets. Parking. Telex 951025. Cards: V, MC.

The owner is extremely attentive and charming, but since he is also the chef, we would prefer to see him spend more time at his stove than with his customers. Still, his cuisine is tasty, despite the slightly too-rich sauces and the frozen scallops we spied in one of the three small appetizer feuilletés (which were otherwise quite well prepared). The precisely cooked turbot has a beautiful garnish of puréed green apples, and the dark chocolate terrine with nuts is delicious. The wine cellar has a good selection of Loire wines. Finally, the pink decor is more attractive now, with its lovely fabrics and tables separated by screens.

A la carte: 250-300F. Menus: 70F (weekdays only), 98F, 129F, 160F, 200F.

Hôtel du Loch

(See restaurant above)

Open year-round. 30 rms 218-293F. Half-board 231-325F. TV No pets.

The rooms of this well-maintained hotel are more comfortable than attractive (despite the slightly narrow bathrooms and less-than-complete soundproofing). Breakfast is excellent.

Auribeau-sur-Siagne

06810 Auribeau-sur-Siagne - (Alpes-Maritimes)
Paris 926 - Cannes 16 - Grasse 8 - Nice 45

(13) Auberge Nossi-Bé

Pl. du Portail - 93.42.20.20

M. Rétoré. Open until 9:30 p.m. Closed Tues. dinner, Wed. & Jan. 10-Feb. 28. Terrace dining. Pets allowed.

The price of the fixed-price menu at this pleasant establishment leveled off recently after having increased 25 percent in one year. Of course, this doesn't make it cheap, but it is still a good deal. Jean-Michel Rétoré's delicate and generous cuisine is served by waitresses in harlequin costumes on a cool terrace overlooking the valley. It's even worth one toque now, thanks to the pink trout escalopes garnished with artichokes, the sweet-and-sour young duck civet and the outstanding feuilleté of green apples. Cheeses are also offered, but, though they are supposed to come from Ceneri's, they are best left unmentioned. The service is a bit slow, but Anne-Marie, the patronne, is charming, and the evening clientele is elegant. The wine cellar needs development.

Menu: 170F.

Auberge Nossi-Bé

(See restaurant above)

Closed Jan. 10-Feb. 28. 6 rms 175F. Half-board 185F.

A half dozen pleasant, perfectly tranquil rooms make up this small hotel, surrounded by greenery in the heart of a charming village.

Aurignac

31420 Aurignac - (Haute-Garonne)
Paris 780 - Toulouse 64 - St-Gaudens 35

(13) Le Cerf Blanc

Rue St-Michel - 61.98.95.76

M. Picard. Open until 9:30 p.m. Closed Mon. & Jan. 10-31. Terrace dining. Pets allowed. Hotel: 11 rms 120-250F; half-board 240-320F. Parking. Cards: V, AE, DC.

Located among prehistoric grottoes, castle ruins and an old church, this is one of the best restaurants in the lush Comminges area. Dominique Picard never takes the easy path of routine and expediency but instead takes his inspiration from the beautiful regional produce, fresh from the market each day, and prepares a cuisine that, in this somewhat isolated rural area, is becoming more and more personal and praiseworthy. You can sample duck escalopes with a rhubarb fondue, a roasted pigeon with vegetable crêpes, warm liver with melon and a mignon of white Comminges veal garnished with leeks and radishes. The wine cellar is handsome, the fixed-price menus are sumptuous, and the summer terrace overlooking the countryside is magnificent.

A la carte: 300F. Menus: 78F (weekdays only), 156F, 216F, 300F.

Autun

71400 Autun - (Saône-et-Loire)
Paris 300 - Nevers 103 - Dijon 86 - Chalon-sur-Saône 53

(13) Le Chalet Bleu

3, rue Jeannin - 85.86.27.30

M. Bouché. Open until 9:30 p.m. Closed Mon. dinner & Tues. Pets allowed. Cards: V, DC, MC.

The Bouché family has settled in what was formerly the Restaurant Meunier, located behind the town hall. Le Chalet Bleu looks younger and more cheerful now that it has a new decor, which includes a winter garden, wallpaper with botanic motifs and white rattan furniture. Son Philippe supervises the stoves now; he has some good ideas but not yet the precision of his father (the red mullet we tried was overcooked). Sample his tasty duck foie gras, his beef maraîchère with a shallot confit and his braised calf's head with simmered young vegetables. These solid dishes still deserve (but barely) one toque. In brief, this is still a good establishment but no longer the small miracle it once was.

A la carte: 200F. Menus: 75F (weekdays only), 95F, 165F.

Saint-Louis

6, rue de l'Arbalète - 85.52.21.03

Closed Sun. & Mon. (off-seas.) & Dec. 20-Feb. 4. 1 ste 385F. 51 rms 126-315F. Half-board 275-447F. TV in 13 rms. Garage parking. Telex 801262. Cards: V, AE, DC, MC.

This beautiful building dating from the seventeenth century is the epitome of the French hotel industry: aging but well maintained and regularly renovated. Patio with flowers. Restaurant.

Les Ursulines

14, rue Rivault - 85.52.68.00

Open daily until 9:30 p.m. 4 stes 380-460F. 25 rms 300-340F. Half-board 330-460F. TV. Pets allowed. Garage parking. Cards: V, AE, DC.

Though small, the pleasant rooms here are bright and cheerful, with modern equipment. These magnificent old buildings are quiet and their comfort outstanding. Restaurant.

Auvillers-les-Forges

08260 Maubert-Fontaine - (Ardennes)
Paris 210 - Laon 70 - Charleville-Mézières 30 - Rocroi 14

(16) Hostellerie Lenoir

Grande-Rue - 24.54.30.11

M. Lenoir. Open until 9 p.m. Closed Fri. (except holidays) & Jan. 2-March 1. Pets allowed. Hotel: 3 stes 365F; 18 rms 145-270F; half- board 265-400F. Parking. Cards: V, AE, DC, MC.

A quarter of a century ago, Jean Lenoir succeeded his ancestors, who were rustic village innkeepers, in this large,solid, almost luxurious house with flowered tapestries and a garden, located across from the school and the town hall in a large village in the Ardennes region. This excellent cook, who has been honored for years with medals from such impressive organizations as the Order of the Corsairs of Guadeloupe and President of the Lawyers, is also the purest, most famous French product of the Wallonian French cooking tradition. (The Namur restaurant school prides itself on having had him as a student during the postwar period). His cuisine is characterized by a great mastery of sauces and a precision in preparation, which strictly follows long-standing culinary tradition. His few attempts at a more modern style are less convincing, however; they quickly turn into something complicated and reminiscent of medieval times, such as the escalopes of goose liver with honey and jasmine. His general style has not been hindered by the recent arrival of Ginette Delaive at the stoves—she is a member of ARC (an association of women chefs) and professes the same taste as Lenoir for this sometimes imposing "chef's cuisine"; her penchant for pomp is typical of the '50s. Indeed, these tastes are still shared by the majority of the most faithful clientele from Champagne, Lorraine, Germany and Belgium, particularly during the hunting season, which draws to Maubert-Fontaine a crowd of people yearning nostalgically for game prepared in the traditional manner (particularly the superb saddle of roe with raisins). The rest of the year, the extensive menu includes mussel-and-shrimp ravioli in a saffron sauce (which is a bit too thin but remarkably well prepared); a perfect brill with cèpes and one truffle as a surprise; Brittany lobster or crayfish "retour d'Egypte" (with oranges or mandarins); salmon à l'Ardennaise (served en papillote); and a quantity of elaborate desserts, often too sweet (in the typical Belgian style) for our taste, especially the chocolate desserts. Lenoir, who was the best sommelier in France in

1968, now leaves the management of one of the most wonderful wine cellars in the whole of northern France to his son-in-law, Claude Delaive. The Champagnes are sublime. The owner's reception is most engaging, though slightly more reserved when it is from Mme. Lenoir.

A la carte: 400F. Menus: 215F and 235F (wine incl.), 300F, 390F.

Auxerre

89000 Auxerre - (Yonne)
Paris 174 - Dijon 148 - Bourges 145 - Nevers 112

Sights. Saint-Etienne cathedral (especially for its crypt and view of the Yonne river from its tower); the ruins of Saint-Germain abbey (the Romanesque cloister, the adjacent rooms, which have been turned into a cultural center and, above all, the Carolingian crypts); the facade of Saint-Pierre church; the small streets of downtown Auxerre, where the Tour de l'Horloge stands.

Eating on the Run. Le P'tit Bourguignon, 34, rue Joubert (a local regional bistro); La Primavera, 37, rue du Pont (Italian and Greek food, friendly atmosphere).

Bars & Cafés. Bistrot du Marché, 1, pl. de l'Arquebuse (well located); Le Pub, 3, rue Camille-Desmoulins (great variety of beer).

15 Le Jardin Gourmand

56, blvd. Vauban - 86.51.53.52

M. Boussereau. Open until 9:30 p.m. Closed Sun. dinner (off- seas.), Mon., Nov. 1-22 & Feb. school vacation. Garden dining. Pets allowed. Cards: V, AE, DC.

The terrace overlooking the lovely garden was recently expanded and redone, thus enhancing the fresh, cheerful decor of the dining room. This is one more reason to sample the versatile cuisine of Pierre Boussereau. He is truly a creative spirit and has all the accompanying anxieties, inspirations, illuminations and... inconsistencies; unfortunately, each of our visits here has verified this. On our last visit, we sampled exceptionally savory foie gras ravioli, lovely coquilles St-Jacques in mandarin butter, a plain John Dory and magnificent sweetbreads with ginger. Ultimately, the result was largely favorable—especially if we add to this the quality and finesse of the desserts, the beautiful Chablis (selected by Sylvie Boussereau, who is getting to be quite an expert), the discreet service and the elegantly set tables. Only those who never risk anything never err!

A la carte: 300-350F. Menus: 135F, 215F, 295F.

Le Maxime

2, quai de la Marine - 86.52.14.19

Open year-round. 25 rms 290-450F. TV. Garage parking. Cards: V, AE, DC, MC.

This decent provincial hotel, somewhat quaint, is nevertheless comfortable and well located on the banks of the Yonne river. Restaurant.

Normandie

41, blvd. Vauban - 86.52.57.80

Open year-round. 47 rms 180-220F. TV. No pets. Parking. Cards: V, AE, DC, MC.

The rooms of this downtown hotel, decorated with antique furniture and overlooking the garden, are pleasant and well equipped. No restaurant.

12/20 La Salamandre

84, rue de Paris - 86.52.87.87

M. Colas. Open until 10 p.m. Closed Sun. dinner, Mon. & Dec. 20-Jan. 5. Air cond. Pets allowed. Cards: V, AE, DC.

With a touch more personality and more refined sauces, all will bode well for this new fish restaurant located in the center of town. The attractive seafood is extremely fresh, and the reception is friendly and professional.

A la carte: 300F. Menus: 78F (weekdays only), 118F, 178F.

IN NEARBY **Chevannes**
(8 km SW on N 151 & D 1)
89240 Pourrain - (Yonne)

15 La Chamaille

4, rte. de Boilou - 86.41.24.80

M. Siri. Open until 9:15 p.m. Closed Tues., Wed., Feb., 1 week in early Sept. & Christmas week. Air cond. Pets allowed. Parking. Cards: V, AE, DC.

The valiant 50-year-old Pierre Siri has our complete trust—and it hasn't been betrayed since those long-ago days when we enjoyed his cuisine in his charming bistro on the Ile Saint-Louis. This adroit and consistent chef has succeeded with his moderate and precise style, without any accompanying fuss or moodiness. What strikes us as much as the rustic charm of his small manor that opens onto the countryside (although the painted ceiling is rather ugly) is the exactness of each preparation in a repertoire composed of the best of rich produce (game and fish in particular), as well as the simplicity of his dishes: a perfectly balanced warm liver with pears, a thick filet of brill garnished with fresh sautéed chanterelles, young lamb roasted with thyme, calves' liver with creamed lentils, and a lovely chocolate-mint sorbet. We award it a second toque, but wish that Siri would expand his wine cellar and show more interest in simpler dishes.

A la carte: 250-300F. Menus: 115F.

IN NEARBY **Vaux**
(6 km SE on D 163)
89290 Champs-sur-Yonne - (Yonne)

15 La Petite Auberge

2, pl. du Passeur - 86.53.80.08

M. Barnabet. Open until 9:15 p.m. Closed Sun. dinner, Mon., holidays, July 2-18 & Dec. 18-Jan. 10. No pets. Parking. Cards: V.

Young Jean-Louis Barnabet's small, pleasant, neorustic house never lacks for customers, perhaps because of the rooms overlooking the Yonne river (though at the moment, opportunities to enjoy the view within the somberly decorated rooms are rather scarce, but plans are underway to renovate). The real reason people come here is the quality of the cooking. The entire region appreciates quite as much as we do this sensibly modern, well-founded cuisine, whose basic principles, inspired by Escoffier, lie in the respect for both the produce and the clientele. Recently we had a truly exemplary and luminous meal here: delicious langoustines in Sauternes, savory beef à la ficelle and a heavenly apple tart. True class lies in simplicity, even if it is not immediately apparent. The good wines are scrupulously selected from the region by an open-minded and competent sommelier.

A la carte: 350F. Menus: 260F (wine incl.), 110F.

Avallon

89200 Avallon - (Yonne)
Paris 234 - Troyes 103 - Dijon 101 - Auxerre 52

(15) La Poste

Pl. Vauban - 86.34.06.12

Mme. Gachon-Millot. Open until 9:30 p.m. Closed Nov. 15-March 15. Terrace dining. Pets allowed. Garage parking. Telex 351806. Cards: V, DC.

This temple of Burgundian cuisine, marked forever by the memory of the Hure family, is slowly growing accustomed to the disappearance of Rolls-Royces and diamond necklaces. Its new owners would very much like to rejuvenate the rather old-fashioned image of their illustrious establishment; they intend to modernize the mezzanine decor, oldish and too ostentatious, by making better use of the delightful courtyard surrounded by houses and hidden among the greenery. We can only be glad of that. In the meantime, they have had to see to the essentials. After several trials and errors, they have finally found, in the person of the young and bearded Robert Wagonner, an excellent, modern chef. This adroit, meticulous technician has changed everything. If the truth be told, it has been well over ten or fifteen years since one has eaten so well at La Poste, thanks to the exquisite red-mullet filets with orange butter (alas, the fish is served with a distressing salad), the savory pigeon in an admirably subtle foie gras sauce and the fresh coconut and Bavarian lemon meringue. The prices remain formidable, but it no longer matters, because now they are fully justified. The wine cellar is rich in Burgundies, particularly Côtes-du-Rhône. The service still needs improving, but is less constrained than before.

A la carte: 300F. Menus: 100F (lunch only), 150F, 260F, 310F.

La Poste

(See restaurant above)

Closed Nov. 15-March 15. 5 stes 750-900F. 18 rms 250-900F. TV. Pool. Pets allowed.

This serene, luxurious, charming inn built in 1707 has comfortable, exquisite rooms that are still being extensively redecorated and modernized. A swimming pool is the latest addition.

IN NEARBY **Pontaubert**
(5 km W on D 957)
89200 Avallon - (Yonne)

Château de Vault-de-Lugny

86.34.07.86

Closed Nov. 21-March 17. 6 stes 1,350-1,950F. 5 rms 650-900F. TV. Pets allowed. Tennis. Garage parking. Cards: V, MC.

This noble and luxurious castle surrounded by a park has just eleven rooms and suites; the bathrooms are a dream. Restaurant.

See also: **Saulieu, Vézelay**

Les Avenières

38630 Les Avenières - (Isère)
Paris 504 - Grenoble 65 - Chambéry 40 - Lyon 76

(15) Relais des Vieilles Postes

Les Nappes - 74.33.62.99, 74.33.71.67

M. Thomas. Open until 9:30 p.m. Closed Sun. dinner, Mon. (except July-Aug.), March 26-April 11 & Dec. 22-Jan. 17. Terrace dining. No pets. Hotel: 17 rms 190-270F. Parking. Cards: V, DC, MC.

This former stagecoach relay station in the middle of the open country is one of the region's undisputed successes, and it's easy to see why. Chef/owner M. Thomas recently had the large park attractively rearranged by a landscape designer. On bright, sunny days, tables are set on the terrace shaded by a linden tree. The prices are reasonable, particularly during the week; the waiters are young, diligent and exceptionally gracious. The cuisine, which is in constant progress, is full of charm and freshness: medallions of lotte with zucchini cooked to precision, superb homemade foie gras served with a glass of Sauternes, excellent grenadine of veal rosé and exquisite iced nougat. The hotel features small, decent, quiet rooms. Beauty salon (Mme. Thomas is a hairdresser) in the lobby.

A la carte: 260-300F. Menus: 115F (weekdays only), 180F (weekday lunch only, wine incl.), 185F, 280F.

Avesnes-sur-Helpe

59440 Avesnes-sur-Helpe - (Nord)
Paris 213 - St-Quentin 66 - Maubeuge 18 - Vervins 33

(13) La Crémaillère

26, Grand-Place - 27.61.02.30

M. Lelaurain. Open until 9:30 p.m. Closed Mon. dinner & Tues. Pets allowed. Cards: V, AE, DC, MC.

Francis Lelaurain upholds the best tradition there is—one that never stagnates but follows the seasons, pursues beautiful produce and dispenses with useless heaviness. In this hospitable, rustic, old-fashioned inn, your meals will be both generous and light: broccoli charlotte with garden herbs, beautiful Licques poultry steamed with sage, fricassée of sole and langoustines and, for dessert, a smooth chocolate Balthazar. The wine cellar is varied and well composed. The service, supervised by Jeanne Lelaurain, is exemplary in its courtesy and attentiveness.

A la carte: 260F. Menus: 100F (weekdays only), 140F, 220F.

Avignon

84000 Avignon - (Vaucluse)
Paris 701 - Valence 128 - Nice 255 - Aix 75 - Marseille 100

Note: The numbers following the telephone number in each review pinpoint the establishment's exact location on the accompanying map.

Sights. Le Palais des Papes (a vast, magnificent Gothic palace/fortress) and the pl. du Palais (site of the cathedral, Hôtel des Monnaies, the Rocher des Doms park, the Palace of the Archbishops); La Balance district (remarkably well restored); the pl. de l'Horloge (an obligatory rendezvous); the fourteenth-century ramparts and the St-Bénézet bridge; Musée Calvet (paintings by Le Nain, Géricault, Manet); Musée Petit Palais (Italian primitives); Musée Vouland (French furniture, ceramics); Musée Lapidaire (Greco-Roman artifacts); the Roure Palace (Provençal ethnology and language); Musée Théodore Aubanel (literature and printing in Provence since the thirteenth century); the Chapel of the Black Penitents (baroque period); cruises on the Rhône river (boat/restaurant *La Mirio*, allées Oulle, 90.85.62.25); in Rochefort-du-Gard, the bust of Paul-Louis Meissonnier, the only cook to have had his statue erected during his lifetime (located in the square of the same name).

Eating on the Run. Assassino, 37, rte. de Lyon (good fresh pasta and meats); La Barbotine, 7, rue Racine (hearty brunches, homemade pastries); La Ferme, Mont-Blanc district; La Barthelasse (homemade cuisine cooked over a wood fire); Simple Simon, 27, rue de la Petite-Fusterie (owned by two English women, quite entertaining); Le Tastevin, 37, rue St-Michel (brief à la carte menu and good Côtes-du-Rhône).

Bars & Cafés. The wide terraces of the pl. de l'Horloge, of course, but also: Bar du Cintra, 44, cours Jean-Jaurès (comfortable and crowded); Bar du Sofitel, rte. de Carpentras (comfortable, modern and quiet); Bar du Vieux-Théâtre, 14, rue Crillon (young, intellectual clientele, opens onto an attractive pedestrian square); Le Régina, 6, rue de la République (large, centrally located, popular).

Nightlife. Le Galaxie, 23, rte. de Montfavet (a mixed crowd); Le Sévigné, at Entraigues (in the middle of the country, young clientele); Le Sholmès, Vaujus district in Rochefort-du-Gard (Parisian ambience tinged with exoticism).

Shops. *Bakeries:* La Fromenterie, 41, rue Carnot and ave. St-Ruf (small chain from Avignon still much in vogue). *Coffee:* Richard, 25, rue du Vieux-Sextier (the oldest and most esteemed). *Chocolate and pastries:* La Chocolaterie, 20, rue St-Agricol (delicious nougats and chocolate specialties); Roger Maurin, 62, blvd. Pasteur at Villeneuve-lès-Avignon (classical and outstanding); Au Petit Prince, in the central market (beautiful, delicate cakes). *Charcuteries:* Charcuterie Franco-Espagnole, 64, rue Bonneterie (authentic Mediterranean tone); Feste, in the central market (the best). *Fruit and vegetables:* Gaby Autard, in the central market (superb fresh vegetables and an excellent selection of fine herbs); Ferragut, 13, pl. des Corps-Saints (beautiful produce and exotic fruit in an artistic stall). *Wine and spirits:* Avidis, 101, rte. de Lyon (warehouse with an impressive selection).

(13) Auberge de France

28, pl. de l'Horloge - 90.82.58.86 / D3-6

M. Tassan. Open until 9:30 p.m. Closed Wed. dinner, Thurs., Jan. 4-27 & June 15-30. Terrace dining. Pets allowed. Cards: V, AE, MC.

The lofty decor of this restaurant, whose wide windows open onto a small terrace, is quite pleasant, with its spaciousness, comfort and sobriety. Its ambience is that of an elegant brasserie, located just a few steps away from the noise and stifling heat of the place de l'Horloge. Primo Tassan's cuisine isn't exactly known for its originality, but it is consistent and carefully prepared by an owner who knows his job well: duck with orange, Vaucluse lamb and walnut charlotte. Tassan's son, who trained at the Suze-la-Rousse wine school, is in charge of the interesting cellar.

A la carte: 300-350F. Menus: 200F, 300F.

Bristol Terminus

44, cours Jean-Jaurès
90.82.21.21 / C5-17

Closed Feb. 1-March 6. 91 rms 110-300F. TV in 50 rms. Pets allowed. Parking. Telex 432730. Cards: V, AE, DC, MC.

The rooms of the Bristol Terminus are conventional but also bright, spacious and comfortable. Restaurant.

(16) Brunel

46, rue de la Balance
90.85.24.83 / C3-24

M. Brunel. Open until 9:15 p.m. Closed Mon. (Oct.-May), Sun. & Feb. school vacation. Air cond. Terrace dining. Pets allowed. Telex 431938. Cards: V, AE, MC.

More and more people are insisting that Brunel is the best restaurant in Avignon. Indeed, there is more youth, imagination and lightness at Brunel's today than at Hiély-Lucullus. Let's not be too hasty, though. Roger Brunel does indeed present a formidable challenge, but he's not a champion just yet: At our last meal here, his fresh cod in spices was slightly overcooked, and his parfait was a bit too sweet for our taste. But these are minor flaws in a cuisine that is precise, honest and versatile, as evidenced by the superb ravioli filled with cockles and saffron and the noisettes of lamb with zucchini and eggplant that melted in our mouths. And we mustn't forget to mention the delicious sorbets flavored with fruit in season and the perfectmuscat grape soufflé. All these dishes admirably combine regional produce with Brunel's personal creativity. The newly decorated dining room, with its lovely Provençal fabrics and terrace garden, possesses wonderful charm and freshness and is enhanced by the cordial, smiling and relaxed reception proffered by Marc and Françoise Brunel. Roger Hennequin, their cousin, makes marvelous pastries. Côtes-du-Rhône is served in carafes—an intelligent way of

keeping the check reasonable.
A la carte: 350-400F. Menus: 130F (lunch only), 235F, 325F.

12/20 Café des Artistes

Pl. Crillon - 90.82.63.16 / C3-13
Mme. Demery. Open until 11:30 p.m. Closed Sun. (except June-Aug.) & Jan. 1-10. Terrace dining. Pets allowed. Cards: V, AE, DC.

The 1930s café setting, filled with flowers and frequented by a chic Avignon crowd, is truly a success, especially with its lovely patio-terrace facing the old theater. The cuisine is lively, seasonal and well prepared: fresh foie gras with pippin apples, sea perch with puréed tomatoes, feuilleté of chocolate nougat.
A la carte: 250F. Menu: 130F (dinner only).

11/20 Le Cintra

44, cours Jean-Jaurès
90.82.29.80 / C5-17
M. Mounier. Open daily until 11:30 p.m. Air cond. Terrace dining. Pets allowed. Telex 432264. Cards: V, AE, DC, MC.

The great brasserie of Avignon is full of charm, gaiety and gentle nostalgia, plus a smiling and friendly service staff. The wisely simple fare always makes a success out of such dishes as cabbage and ham hocks and lotte and aïoli, and it's all more than fairly priced. Good little regional wines.
A la carte: 160-180F. Menus: 50F, 66F, 76F, 80F.

Hôtel Cité des Papes

1, rue Jean-Vilar - 90.86.22.45 / D3-19
Closed Wed. & Dec. 18-Jan. 23. 65 rms 220-360F. TV in 38 rms. Air cond. Pets allowed. Telex 432734. Cards: V, AE, DC.

The spacious, comfortable rooms of this large and modern building located close to the Palais des Papes may be noisy, but they are equipped with air conditioning. No restaurant.

Danieli

17, rue de la République
90.86.46.82 / C4-10
Open year-round. 34 rms 270-290F. TV in 29 rms. Pets allowed. Cards: V, AE, DC, MC.

The rooms of this charming, small, centrally located hotel contain lacquered bamboo furniture and are decorated in vanilla and peach colors. No restaurant.

11/20 L'Entrée des Artistes

1, pl. des Carmes - 90.82.46.90 / E3-23
M. Parment. Open until 10:30 p.m. Closed Sat. lunch & Sun. Terrace dining. Pets allowed. Cards: V.

Though its price has rapidly increased, the fixed-price menu at L'Entrée des Artistes still remains a bargain in Avignon, particularly if you manage to book a table with a view of the place des Carmes. This menu includes scrambled eggs with cèpes, stuffed andouillette en croûte and dessert.
Menu: 90F.

Hôtel de Garlande

20, rue Galante - 90.85.08.85 / D4-7
Open year-round. 12 rms 170-255F. TV in 7 rms. Pets allowed. Cards: V, AE, DC, MC.

This small downtown hotel, a nicely renovated ancient house, is quite charming. The rooms have been carefully redone, and the bathrooms are well equipped. No restaurant.

11/20 Le Grandgousier

17, rue Galante - 90.82.96.60 / D4-3
MM. Reboul and Pastore. Open until 10 p.m. Closed Sun., Aug. 14-Sept. 7 and Dec. 24-27. Pets allowed. Cards: AE, V, MC, EC.

Hungry throngs always cram this glass-roofed restaurant wedged in between two townhouses in old Avignon. The decor is attractive indeed, the food is simple but generously apportioned, and a few cheerful country wines from the Ardèche region are poured by the glass. Try the pieds et paquets (sheep's tripe and trotters), or duck stewed in Séguret (a rustic local wine), or delicate chervil-scented oyster ravioli.
A la carte: 200F. Menus: 89F, 95F, 168F, 210F.

17 Hiély-Lucullus

5, rue de la République
90.86.17.07 / C4-14
M. Hiély. Open until 9:30 p.m. Closed Mon. (except July 5-Aug. 15), Tues., Dec. 31-Jan. 20 & June 20-July 5. Air cond. Pets allowed. Cards: V.

Pierre Hiély, who started his career right here at his father's side, recently celebrated his 60th birthday. If he is thinking about retiring, it's only halfheartedly; at any rate, it certainly isn't reflected in his cuisine or in the running of his restaurant. It was because of his single menu/carte, whose prices have always set an example, that he became famous—a fame that he has maintained, thanks to the excellence of his ingredients, the rigor of his technique, the subtlety of his dishes and the atmosphere of well-being in this traditional restaurant that he and his wife have never let lapse. So Hiély (who has granted our wishes and taken away most of the supplemental fare, which had become overwhelming) puts forth a 250-franc fixed-price menu/carte. Diners have the choice of a dozen appetizers (effeuillé of fresh cod with tomato vinaigrette, delicious eggplant gratin with a creamy herb sauce, feuilleté of crayfish tails, salad of lamb's brains and sweetbreads, among them); a dozen entrées (in particular, the outstanding young rabbit stuffed with its own liver in pepper sauce, the quail pie with foie gras in lemon sauce, the gilthead with sorrel and a mint butter and the exquisite pieds et paquets provençale); plus some delicate cheeses and desserts, all equally exquisite. For lunch, there is a beautiful 150-franc fixed-price menu. The wine list,which is truly splendid, includes the greatest names of the Rhône valley, as well as some excellent Côtes-du-Rhône served in carafes, starting at 100 francs.
Menu: 150F, 250F.

Inter Hôtel du Midi

Rue de la République
90.82.15.56 / C5-4
Open year-round. 57 rms 200-300F. TV. Pets allowed. Telex 431074. Cards: V, AE, DC, MC.

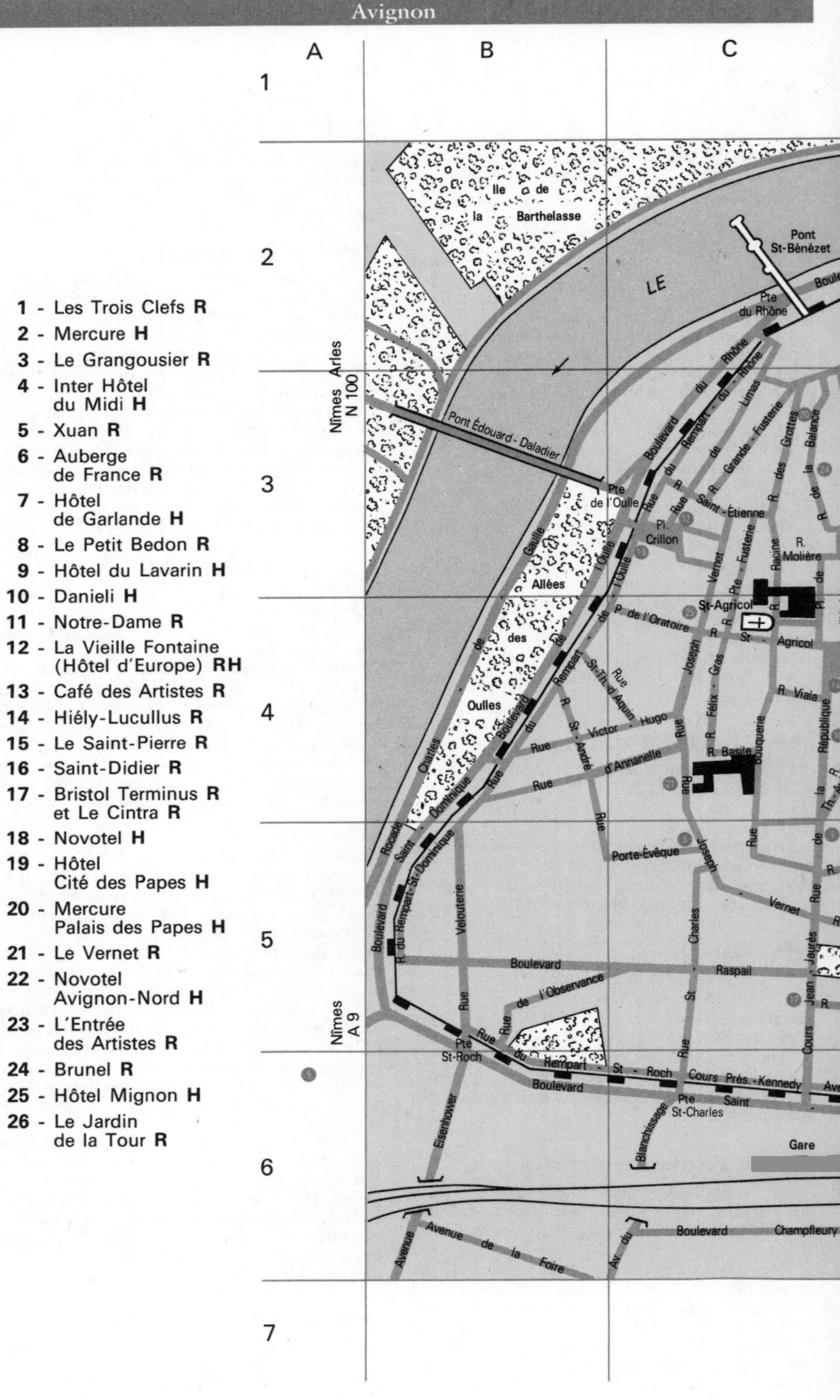
1 - Les Trois Clefs R
2 - Mercure H
3 - Le Grangousier R
4 - Inter Hôtel du Midi H
5 - Xuan R
6 - Auberge de France R
7 - Hôtel de Garlande H
8 - Le Petit Bedon R
9 - Hôtel du Lavarin H
10 - Danieli H
11 - Notre-Dame R
12 - La Vieille Fontaine (Hôtel d'Europe) RH
13 - Café des Artistes R
14 - Hiély-Lucullus R
15 - Le Saint-Pierre R
16 - Saint-Didier R
17 - Bristol Terminus R et Le Cintra R
18 - Novotel H
19 - Hôtel Cité des Papes H
20 - Mercure Palais des Papes H
21 - Le Vernet R
22 - Novotel Avignon-Nord H
23 - L'Entrée des Artistes R
24 - Brunel R
25 - Hôtel Mignon H
26 - Le Jardin de la Tour R
A
B
C
1
2
3
4
5
6
7
Ile de la Barthelasse
Pont St-Bénézet
LE
Pte du Rhône
Nîmes Arles N 100
Pont Édouard - Daladier
Pte de l'Oulle
Pl. Crillon
St-Agricol
Allées des Oulles
Boulevard du Rempart du Rhône
Rue de la Grande Fusterie
Rue Saint-Étienne
R. Molière
P. de l'Oratoire
R. St Agricol
R. Viala
Rue Victor Hugo
Rue d'Annanelle
R. Basile
Porte-Évêque
Rue Joseph Vernet
Rue de la République
Boulevard Raspail
Boulevard de l'Observance
Rue Velouterie
Rue St Charles
Cours Jean Jaurès
Boulevard Charles de Gaulle
Rocade Charles de Gaulle
Nîmes A 9
Pte St-Roch
Boulevard du Rempart St Roch
Cours Prés. Kennedy
Pte Saint St-Charles
Gare
Blanchissage
Eisenhower
Avenue de la Foire
Boulevard Champfleury

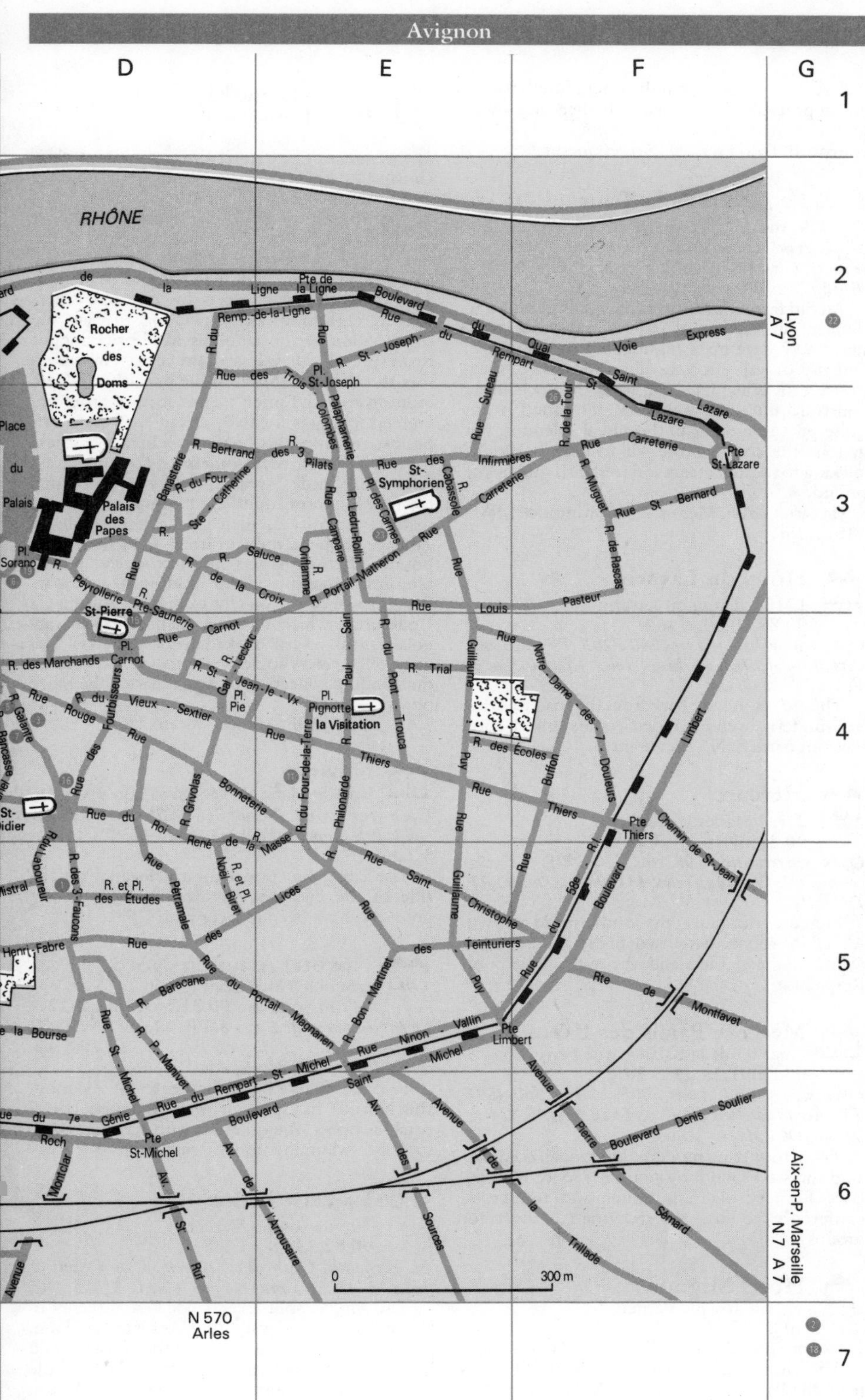
D
E
F
G
1
2
3
4
5
6
7
RHÔNE
Rocher des Doms
Place du Palais
Palais des Papes
Pl. Sorano
St-Pierre
Pl. Carnot
Pte de la Ligne
Remp.-de-la-Ligne
Boulevard du Quai St Lazare
Rue du Rempart
Voie Express
Lyon A 7
Pl. St-Joseph
St-Symphorien
Pl. des Carmes
Rue Carreterie
Pte St-Lazare
Rue St Bernard
R. de Rascas
Rue Louis Pasteur
R. Portail-Matheron
R. Ledru-Rollin
Rue Campane
R. Trial
R. du Pont Trouca
Rue Notre-Dame-des-7-Douleurs
R. des Écoles
Rue Buffon
Rue Guillaume Puy
Pl. Pignotte
la Visitation
Pl. Pie
R. des Marchands
Rue Vieux Sextier
Rue Thiers
Pte Thiers
Boulevard Limbert
Chemin de St-Jean
Rue Bonneterie
R. du Four-de-la-Terre
R. Philonarde
St-Didier
Rue du Roi René
R. et Pl. des Études
R. des 3-Faucons
Rue des Lices
Rue Saint Christophe
Rue des Teinturiers
R. Bon Martinet
Rte de Montfavet
Rue du Portail Magnanen
R. Baracane
Rue Ninon Vallin
Pte Limbert
Rue du Rempart St-Michel
Boulevard Saint Michel
Rue du 7e Génie
Pte St-Michel
Av. Moniclar
Av. St-Ruf
Av. de l'Arrousaire
Av. des Sources
Avenue de la Trillade
Avenue Pierre Sémard
Boulevard Denis Soulier
Aix-en-P. Marseille N 7 A 7
N 570 Arles
0
300 m

Its exterior is plain, but the Inter Hôtel's rooms are impeccably maintained, whether they overlook the street (these are soundproofed) or the courtyard. Good service. No restaurant.

12/20 Le Jardin de la Tour

9, rue de la Tour - 90.85.66.50 / F3-26

M. Larrue. Open until 10:30 p.m. (1 a.m. in season). Closed Sun. and last wk. of Aug. Garden dining. Pets allowed. Cards: AE, DC, V.

An old factory provides a fascinating setting to dine in; all manner of pulleys and other small machinery have been highlighted to advantage, and the overall effect is quite impressive. Outdoors, canvas awnings transform the enchanting courtyard into a dining room. The food is not quite on a level with all this visual splendor, but at least the chef has the wit to keep it simple, sticking to roasted meats and fresh fish sold by the pound.

A la carte: 280F. Menus: 290F (wine incl.), 98F, 145F, 195F.

Hôtel du Lavarin

1715, chemin du Lavarin
90.89.50.60 / A6-9

Open year-round. 44 rms 240-320F. TV in 21 rms. Pets allowed. Pool. Parking. Telex 432670. Cards: V, AE.

This new hotel, set back from the road to Arles, has modern, well-equipped rooms and a cool, pleasant garden. No restaurant.

Mercure

2, rue Marie-de-Médicis
90.88.91.10 / G7-2

Open year-round. 105 rms 320-390F. TV. Air cond. Pool. Parking. Telex 431994. Cards: V, AE, DC, MC.

Mercure is located at the southern end of town. All of its rooms have two beds; half of them overlook the garden and the swimming pool. Restaurant.

Mercure Palais des Papes

Quartier de la Balance, rue Ferruce
90.85.91.23 / C3-20

Open year-round. 3 stes 500F. 82 rms 360-450F. TV. Air cond. Pets allowed. Telex 431215. Cards: V, AE, DC, MC.

These rooms are modern, functional, comfortable and well soundproofed; the service is attentive. Remarkable equipment and numerous conference rooms. No restaurant (except for groups).

Hôtel Mignon

12, rue Joseph-Vernet
90.82.17.30 / C4-25

Open year-round. 15 rms 150-165F. TV. Cards: V.

This charming hotel, located about 200 yards from the Palais des Papes, is truly deserving of its name. The bright, small rooms are newly equipped and well soundproofed. No restaurant.

(14) Notre-Dame

34, rue Four-de-la-Terre
90.82.34.12 / E4-11

M. Bernadou. Open until midnight. Closed Sun. Cards: V, AE, DC.

A beautiful old statue of Notre-Dame standing on the dresser watches over the charming decor of this simple, rustic inn, which was built in the early 1900s and whose style is typical of the Languedoc region so dear to Jacques Bernadou. This delightful man greets his customers personally, enthusiastically explaining to each the composition of the fabulous fixed-price menus that express his deep love of the region, his ancestors and the joyful spirit of the pays d'Oc. These quite lively fixed-price menus feature an entire sautéed foie gras for two, served with capers or raisins, an enormous, marvelous breast of duck, the traditional three cassoulets (of Toulouse, Castelnaudary and Carcassonne), superb confits (made with goose, duck and poultry) and several rustic masterpieces, such as the large plate of cabbage soup—a meal in itself—and the rabbit boudin. Bernadou has just introduced a new bimonthly menu of dishes traditional to a particular town or region (for example, "Autour de Collioure," which includes such dishes as cargolade, a mixed grill cooked over vine stalks). The wine cellar offers some delicious Gaillacs and an outstanding collection of Armagnacs. One more point.

A la carte: 250F. Menus: 75F to 199F.

Novotel

Rte. de Marseille - 90.87.62.36 / G7-18

Open year-round. 79 rms 340-380F. Pool. TV. Air cond. Pets allowed. Parking. Telex 432878. Cards: V, DC, MC.

The large, functional rooms, located on the side of the highway, but well isolated in the greenery, have been redecorated. Grill.

Novotel Avignon-Nord

Avignon-Nord freeway exit,
84700 Sorgues - 90.31.16.43 / G2-22

Open year-round. 2 stes 800F. 98 rms 360-410F. TV. Air cond. Pets allowed. Pool. Tennis. Parking. Telex 432869. Cards: V, AE, DC, MC.

Five kilometers from the center of Avignon, this Novotel has spacious, well-equipped, comfortable rooms (the quietest, with terraces, overlook the swimming pool). Restaurant.

11/20 Le Petit Bedon

70, rue Joseph-Vernet
90.82.33.98 / C5-8

M. Ferigoule. Open until 10 p.m. Closed Sun. & June 15-30. Air cond. No pets. Cards: V, AE, DC.

The simple, split-level decor boasts plenty of flowers and attractive lighting. As for the cooking, it's not exactly consistent; and the service could stand a little more congeniality. Dishes include mussel soup with curry, pieds et paquets (a mutton feet-and-tripe dish) and trout vigneronne.

Menus: 80F (lunch only, wine incl.), 135F.

15 Saint-Didier

41, rue de la Saraillerie
90.86.16.50 / D4-16

M. Etienne. Open until 9:30 p.m. Closed Mon., Tues. & May 1- Sept. 8. Terrace dining. Pets allowed. Cards: V, AE, DC.

Christian Etienne, a friendly and enthusiastic native of Avignon, prepares a modern, fresh cuisine in which seafood and regional produce hold a prominent position. His small, redecorated dining room, enhanced by lovely engravings of horses, is an unpretentious place, where the reception is simple and friendly and the prices among the best in Avignon for the outstanding quality of the cuisine. This is particularly true of the first fixed-price menu, which features the best specialties of the brief à la carte list: duck saucisson with foie gras served atop a country salad, salmon cannelloni with cucumber in a green sauce, grilled red mullet garnished with a julienne of artichokes, roast lamb with eggplant in garlic sauce, beautiful small cheeses and a delicious nougat with grapefruit ice cream. The wine cellar is home to some handsome local wines, especially an outstanding Châteauneuf Vieux Télégraphe '84.

A la carte: 300F. Menus: 190F, 300F.

10/20 Le Saint-Pierre

10, pl. St-Pierre - 90.82.74.22 / D4-15

M. Labiche. Open until 11 p.m. Closed Tues. Terrace dining. Pets allowed. Cards: V, AE, DC.

On the quiet, tiny square facing the church and its gates of sculpted wood, you'll dine upon filets of John Dory with saffron, gratin of sweetbreads with langoustines and a fine apple tart for dessert. Congenial and inexpensive.

A la carte: 160-180F. Menus: 49F (weekday lunch only), 94F.

13 Les Trois Clefs

26, rue des Trois-Faucons
90.86.51.53 / D5-1

M. Mergnac. Open until 9:30 p.m. Closed Sun., Feb. 20-March 3 & Nov. 10-30. Air cond. No pets. Cards: V, AE, DC.

Located behind the ramparts, Les Trois Clefs is one of many lovely bistros in old Avignon. The decor, painted in trompe l'oeil, is elegant, intimate and bright; the patronne is charming; and Laurant Mergnac's cuisine follows the example set by its prices: It goes resolutely forward. Sample the terrine of eels from Saintes-Maries (based on a recipe by Frédéric Mistral), the minute of sea bass in veal juices served with sweet pepper and onion slices, the superb caramelized roast pigeon with sesame seeds and the pistachio mousseline in chocolate sauce.

A la carte: 300-350F. Menus: 150F, 220F.

14 Le Vernet

58, rue Joseph-Vernet
90.86.64.53 / C4-21

M. Clareton. Open until 9:30 p.m. (10 p.m. in summer). Closed Sun. dinner (off-seas.). Garden dining. No pets. Telex 431919. Cards: V.

Located in downtown Avignon, just across from the Musée Calvet, this beautiful eighteenth-century townhouse is perhaps the most pleasant summer restaurant in the inner city, especially with its vast garden, where 80 people can be seated in the shade of 100-year-old trees. From May to September, under immense and luxurious parasols, one may sample the intelligent cuisine of owner Claude Clareton. He uses lovely, fresh regional produce and local seafood, which is particularly appealing when one is on vacation: oysters and shellfish, l'océan salad with orange, a suprême of sea bass with new sorrel, a charlotte of Provençal kid with eggplant and a fricassée of flatfish with basil. The wines are rather expensive but well selected, the à la carte prices remain reasonable, and the fixed-price menus are always outstanding, particularly the brief lunch menu, with wine included.

A la carte: 300F. Menus: 110F (weekday lunch only, wine incl.), 150F, 250F.

13 La Vieille Fontaine

12, pl. Crillon - 90.82.66.92 / C3-12

M. Daire. Open until 9:30 p.m. Closed Sat. lunch, Sun., Aug. 15-21 & Nov. 1-20. Air cond. Terrace dining. Pets allowed. Garage parking. Telex 431965. Cards: V, AE, DC, MC.

With its superb classical dining room and the priceless tranquil and cool garden, this seventeenth-century house, located in the heart of Avignon, is absolutely delightful. The cuisine, serious and somewhat rich, is anything but boring: a soufflé of foie gras and Armagnac, lobster mousseline, young rabbit sautéed in honey. Handsome wines.

A la carte: 300F. Menus: 150F (lunch only, wine incl.), 190F (dinner only).

Hôtel d'Europe

(See restaurant above)

Open year-round. 5 stes 1,350F. 46 rms 390-1,350F. TV. Air cond. Pets allowed.

This venerable establishment, with its antique furniture and paintings, tapestries, display cabinets of precious objects, beautiful rooms and large marble bathrooms, is the most attractive and luxurious stopover in Avignon.

12/20 Xuan

6, rue Galante - 90.86.03.75 / D4-5

M. Vuvan. Open daily until 11 p.m. Air cond. Terrace dining. Pets allowed. Cards: V.

If this room done in light pine and matted walls is always crowded with diners, it's simply because the cuisine is better prepared and presented than in the standard Chinese restaurants that seem to clog Avignon. Here you can sample shrimp soup with curry, beef prepared on a hot plate and steamed sea bream. The service is excellent.

A la carte: 130-150F. Menu: 70F.

IN NEARBY **Althen-des-Paluds**
(13 km NE on D 942)
84210 Pernes-les-Fontaines - (Vaucluse)

---

13 Moulin de la Roque

Rte. de la Roque - 90.62.14.62

M. Lechenet. Open until 9:30 p.m. Closed Jan. 5-10. No pets. Parking. Telex 431095. Cards: V, AE, DC, MC.

This brand-new farmhouse adjoining an old mill is located at the end of a lovely lane lined with plane trees. The dining room is superb, the staff professional, and the cuisine of young Pascal Chambon (a former assistant chef at the Auberge de la Cassagne) full of noble promise: Vaucluse lamb in a salt crust, pan-fried red mullet and a subtle warm apple tart. The wine cellar is still young. This is a place to watch.

A la carte: 300F. Menu: 150F, 190F, 270F.

Moulin de la Roque

(See restaurant above)

Closed Nov. 15-March 20. 2 stes 1,000-1,200F. 28 rms 250-1,100F. Half-board 440-1,440F. TV. Pets allowed. Pool. Tennis.

Tranquility and freshness reign in this hotel located on the banks of the canal and the Sorgue river, ten minutes from Avignon. The spacious rooms are elegantly decorated and quite comfortable. Beautiful swimming pool, tennis courts and delightful garden.

IN NEARBY **Angles**
(4 km W on N 100)
30400 Villeneuve-lès-Avignon - (Gard)

L'Ermitage Meissonnier

(16)

Ave. de Verdun (rte. de Nîmes)
90.25.41.68, 90.25.41.02

M. Meissonnier. Open until 10 p.m. Closed Sun. dinner (Nov.-March) & Mon. (except dinner in July-Aug.). Garden dining. Pets allowed. Parking. Telex 490715. Cards: V, AE, DC.

This time, this is it! Michel Meissonnier has taken up the torch once carried by his glorious father, Paul-Louis Meissonnier, who isn't satisfied to be just the Maîtres Cuisiniers' traveling ambassador: He may move to Montpellier to embark on a new venture with his daughter (she recently spent several years in England and Japan, where she met with great success). It is true that last summer the master was still at L'Ermitage, at the side of his lovely wife; no grand farewell had yet been planned...

Be that as it may, Michel and his wife, whose good humor and cordiality make her greeting marvelous, have great plans in store. Quite possibly, a few months from now, we may not even recognize this small inn nestled in the greenery, whose rustic decor has about had it. At any rate, the terrace in the enclosed garden will still be just as pleasant, and its trees and high hedges will still make one easily forget the nearby road and urban environment, in which the famous Provençal charm is farfrom evident. The younger Meissonnier has spruced up the à la carte menu, which had begun to be incomprehensible, but its presentation and cover still lack elegance. Until several years ago, the father's talent was glorious; his son's still needs to assert itself. He has had a tendency to spread himself too thin, caught between the complicated munificence of a traditional rich cuisine and his not-always-convincing attempts toward something more creative. However, we have noticed an obvious improvement of late, particularly a more marked tendency toward simplicity. The more Meissonnier embraces a regional cuisine, with its southern aromas and sharp flavors, the greater his success will be. Of course, he has already triumphed with his red mullet, his seafood ravioli in a pistou soup, his delicious hogfish jowls and favouilles (tiny crabs) served in a bouillabaisse aspic, his zucchini and langoustines in a lemon sauce, his brochette of Vaccarès eels grilled à la béarnaise, and his profiteroles of young rabbit with thyme flowers (cooked to a golden crust in lavender honey). Not to mention his tender, savory noisettes of lamb with fresh mint, garnished with stuffing.

There are several fair desserts, such as the iced nougat, the fig tart and the Saint-Bénézet sabayon with orange. The wine cellar lists the best Côtes-du-Rhône. A clever system allows one to compose one's own meal by selecting two dishes (for 200 francs, with cheeses and wine) or four half orders (225 francs), which is an exceptional price for the quality. Also worth mentioning is the quality of the cheeses—picodon, Banon, pélardon, poivre d'âne (all goat cheeses) and Roquefort—and the four varieties of yeast rolls baked on the premises, all equally delicious.

A la carte: 380F. Menus: 150F (weekdays only), 210F, 240F, 380F.

Hostellerie l'Ermitage

(See restaurant above)

Closed Jan.-Feb. 16 rms 200-350F. Half-board 380-400F. TV in 5 rms. Air cond in 4 rms. Pets allowed.

The extremely comfortable rooms (each is equipped with bathroom, television set and minibar) are well insulated by double windows and separated from the restaurant by a beautiful garden, where breakfast is now served.

IN NEARBY **Montfavet**
(5 km W on D 53)
84140 Montfavet - (Vaucluse)

Les Frênes

(15)

Ave. des Vertes-Rives - 90.31.17.93

M. Biancone. Open until 9:30 p.m. Closed Nov. 30-April 1. Air cond. Garden dining. No pets. Parking. Telex 431164. Cards: V, AE, DC, MC.

This bourgeois house, without any particular charm itself, is transformed by the greenery and flower-studded lawns that surround it. Located close to Avignon, a stifling city in the summer, Les Frênes is a place to which everyone escapes when thethermometer rises. It's best to reserve a table behind the terrace's balustrade, facing the rosebushes, for the small dining room is somewhat confined, in spite of its elegance. There, in a tranquility disturbed only by the singing of the birds, you'll enjoy the classic, well-prepared cuisine of owner Jacques Biancone, enlivened by several Provençal specialties: crayfish salad in virgin olive oil, oysters en gelée with Champagne, roasted sea perch with basil and rack of lamb served in the style of the Provençal shepherds. The service, carried out by the patronne, is charming.

A la carte: 300-350F. Menus: 150F (weekdays only), 210F, 240F, 380F.

Les Frênes

(See restaurant above)

Closed Nov. 30-March 1. 5 stes 600-1,400F. 17 rms 400-1,400F. Half-board 705-1,005F oblig in seas. TV. Air cond. Pets allowed. Pool.

The rooms of Les Frênes, located amid the serenity of a delightful flourishing garden, are tastefully furnished. The swimming pool is superb, and the reception and service are impeccable. Relais et Châteaux.

IN NEARBY **Pontet**
(5 km NE on N 7)
84130 Le Pontet - (Vaucluse)

Auberge de Cassagne

Rte. de Vedène (D 62, exit Avignon-Nord Fwy.) - 90.31.04.18

M. Gallon. Open daily until 9:30 p.m. Garden dining. No pets. Parking. Telex 432997. Cards: V, AE.

Cypress trees, olive trees, a flower garden, a terrace shaded by a beautiful plane tree facing the swimming pool... you are miraculously taken away from the sterile bedroom communities outside Avignon. The young owners of this luxurious country inn (whose elegant decor and service are somewhat formal in the large, rustic, Louis XIII–style dining room) have hired the reliable and consistent services of Philippe Boucher, a young chef who trained with Blanc and Bocuse. His talent is certain, but more important, he has experience and an expert sense of precise, clear flavors. Sample the delicious émincé of squab (from the region) en gelée with foie gras, the red mullet pan-fried in lime and fresh tomato, the creative small rabbit chops cooked in bread crumbs and the decent though not exceptional desserts made by the new pastry chef fresh from Lenôtre. The handsome wine cellar, one of the best in the district, is tended by a perfect sommelier. A second toque in this edition.

A la carte: 450F. Menus: 280F, 380F.

Auberge de Cassagne

(See restaurant above)

Open year-round. 2 stes 790-990F. 14 rms 350-590F. Half-board545-665F oblig. in seas. TV. Air cond. Pets allowed. Pool. Tennis. Parking.

The rather tiny rooms, located in an annex facing the swimming pool, are all on the same floor. Good overall comfort, though on the whole, the quality doesn't meet the ambitions of the house. Good breakfast.

IN NEARBY **Villeneuve-lès-Avignon**
(2.5 km NW on N 580)
30400 Villeneuve-lès-Avignon - (Gard)

Le Prieuré

7, pl. du Chapitre - 90.25.18.20

M. Mille. Open until 9:30 p.m. Closed Mon. lunch (off-seas.), May 1 & Nov. 5-March 10. Air cond. Garden dining. Pets allowed. Parking. Telex 431042. Cards: V, AE, DC, MC.

The owner of this superb restaurant has clearly taken things into her own hands, whipping the dining room staff into shape and hiring a new chef, Serge Chenet. Less precious and more open thanwhen we knew him at his last restaurant, he offers here some very happy-making dishes: minced lamb's tongue and cabbage in a honey-caper vinaigrette, delicious cheese ravioli in an eggplant sauce, and roasted young pigeon. The pastry is very carefully prepared, and the lovely wine list boasts some irresistible Châteauneuf-du-Papes. It's time for another point.

A la carte: 350F. Menus: 210F (lunch only), 240F (dinner only).

Le Prieuré

(See restaurant above)

Closed May 1 & Nov. 5-March 10. 10 stes 1,100-1,700F. 26 rms 450-1,000F. Half-board 755-1,200F. TV in 33 rms. Air cond. Pets allowed. Pool. Tennis.

Whether it is the old priory adjacent to the church (its rooms are rather small) or its modern annex built on the edge of the large swimming pool (with larger rooms and a lovely view), one always finds the same luxury and refinement, far from the noise and crowds. The service is exceptional. Relais et Châteaux.

See also: **Les Baux-de-Provence, Noves**

Avoriaz

see Morzine

Ax-les-Thermes

09110 Ax-les-Thermes - (Ariège)
Paris 830 - Foix 42 - Carcassonne 104 - Andorre 61

IN NEARBY **Unac**
(13 km NW on N 20 & D 2)
09250 Luzenac - (Ariège)

L'Oustal

61.64.48.44

M. Descat. Open until 9:30 p.m. Closed Mon. & Jan. 5-Feb. 5. Pets allowed. Parking. Cards: V, AE.

Michel Descat and his solid team seem to beam with happiness in their restaurant in the heart of the Ariège mountains. For years Descat has been singing the praises of his little section of France: its beauty, its mysteries and its joie de vivre. His enthusiasm is understandable—it's hard not to fall in love with this beautiful setting and the old family building, which envelops you with the warmth of its lovely country furniture, blazing fireplace and sweet atmosphere. The cuisine is an ode to the region but not at the expense of personal interpretation: terrine of young rabbit with vegetables, eel stew (matelote), civet of duckling à la lauragaise, fish grilled over a wood fire(as is the whole duck breast) and good desserts. Fine wine cellar.

A la carte: 230F. Menu: 140F.

L'Oustal

(See restaurant above)

Closed Mon. & Jan. 5-Feb. 5. 6 rms 160-310F.

This is a warm, welcoming inn set in a beautiful countryside boasting some redone rooms as charming and comfortable as they are simple. Swimming pool and tennis are nearby.

Aytré

see La Rochelle

Azay-le-Rideau

37190 Azay-le-Rideau - (Indre-et-Loire)
Paris 254 - Chinon 21 - Tours 26 - Saumur 46

Le Grand Monarque

Pl. de la République - 47.45.40.08

Mme. Forest. Open until 9:30 p.m. Closed Nov. 15-March 14. Garden dining. Garage parking. Cards: V, MC.

An excellent traditional family restaurant situated amid lush greenery in the heart of a village, 200 meters from the château. The atmosphere is charming and the cuisine appealing: homemade foie gras, fish from the Loire, breast of duck with seasonal fruits, and fine desserts. Remarkable old Loire vintages.

A la carte: 250-300F. Menus: 90F (weekday lunch only), 140F, 190F, 205F.

Le Grand Monarque

(See restaurant above)

Open year-round. 2 stes 475-570F. 27 rms 145-330F. Half-board 235-410F oblig. in seas. Pets allowed.

This rustic, charming, simple yet comfortable hotel offers pleasant rooms on its second floor.

Baldenheim

67600 Sélestat - (Bas-Rhin)
Paris 440 - Marckholsheim 13 - Colmar 28 - Sélestat 9

La Couronne

45, rue Sélestat - 88.85.32.22

M. Trébis. Open until 9 p.m. Closed Sun. dinner, Mon. (except holidays) & Jan. 3-12. Pets allowed. Parking. Cards: V, AE.

Along the country road between Strasbourg and Colmar stands this delightful pink house just steps from the banks of the Rhine. The surroundings are immaculately flowered, and the dining room, subdued and elegant, is the domain of young Mme. Trébis, who gently supervises her attentive battalion of young waitresses. Her mother and husband reign in the kitchen, preparing a superb foie gras served in thick slices (though with too much aspic), wild salmon cooked to perfection in Alsatian sparkling wine and a fine selection of game in season. The wines are a bit expensive.

A la carte: 300-350F. Menus: 98F (weekdays only), 150F, 230F.

Bandol

83150 Bandol - (Var)
Paris 842 - Marseille 49 - Toulon 17 - Aix-en-Provence 74

Auberge du Port

9, allée Jean-Moulin
94.29.42.63, 94.29.78.00

M. Ghiribelli. Open daily until 9:30 p.m. (10:30 p.m. in summer). Pets allowed. Cards: V, AE, DC, MC.

You'll enjoy dining Roman-style under the stars in the new garden decor of the Auberge du Port (thanks to a sliding, removable roof). You'll also enjoy a view of the port while you sample Serge Fricaud's refined cuisine: rosettes of sea perch andcoquilles St-Jacques, fresh and delicious sardine filets with slivered peppers, terrine of lotte livers with dill and salicornes (natural plant salt), scorpionfish ravioli, remarkable red mullet in an anise-flavored sabayon sauce and a gratin of orange and grapefruit with almond cream. Expect a warm welcome from owner Jean-Pierre Ghiribelli, particularly when it's not too crowded. There's a good low-priced fixed menu, but the à la carte prices are steep.

A la carte: 350F. Menus: 85F (lunch only), 150F, 285F.

Délos

Ile de Bendor - 94.32.22.23

Closed Dec. 20-Jan. 30. 55 rms 380-700F. Half-board 560-720F oblig. in seas. TV in 5 rms. No pets. Pool. Tennis. Telex 400383. Cards: V, AE, DC, MC.

Comfortable, quiet rooms are decorated in various styles (generally colonial). There's a wonderful view of the sea and plenty of sports activities. Restaurant.

12/20 Les Oliviers

17, blvd. Louis-Lumière - 94.29.46.86

M. Barbier. Open daily until 9:30 p.m. Terrace dining. Pets allowed. Parking. Telex 400372. Cards: V, AE, DC, MC.

Simplicity is not the motto here, but the hotel cuisine is fresh and skillfully accomplished: a seafood pistou (pesto) with clam ravioli, roast loin of lamb en croûte, bitter-chocolate squares with a julienne of fresh mint. There's a superb view of the bay from the scenic terrace.

A la carte: 300-400F. Menus: 150F (weekends and holidays only), 175F, 330F.

Pullman Ile Rousse

(See restaurant above)

Open year-round. 2 stes 1,400F. 53 rms 650-1,090F. Half-board 235F oblig. in seas. TV. Air cond. Pets allowed. Heated pool.

Straddling a strip of land between the Bandol port and the beach (which you can access directly from the inside stairs), this very modern hotel boasts considerable comfort and excellent service. The room style is quite standard. Fitness club.

Bannegon

18210 Charenton-du-Cher - (Cher)
Paris 270 - Bourges 42 - Sancoins 18 - Moulins 63

13 Moulin de Chaméron

Rte. de Sancoins
48.61.84.48, 48.61.83.80

MM. Mérilleau & Cardoné. Open until 9 p.m. Closed Tues. (off-seas.), Jan. 5-March 5 & Nov. 15-Dec. 15. Terrace dining. Pets allowed. Parking. Cards: V.

Once a water-driven mill, this solid, rustic riverbank inn is meticulously well maintained. Jean Mérilleau, the owner's son-in-law, directs the restaurant and its cuisine. It's a good find in this region, which has a dearth of good dining spots. Try his eggs in a light wine sauce served with onion crêpes, his filet of lisette (mackerel) perfectly cooked in a delicate herbed butter sauce or his farm-raised chicken sautéed with red beans. Desserts need improvement, especially the strawberry marquise, which we found sickeningly sweet. Fine wine cellar. Service is a bit cool.

A la carte: 250F. Menu: 115F, 180F.

Moulin de Chaméron

(See restaurant above)

Closed Tues. (off-seas.), Jan. 5-March 5 & Nov. 15-Dec. 15. 1 ste 430-600F. 12 rms 185-340F. TV in 4 rms. Pets allowed. Heated pool.

Adorable rooms in a splendidly restored eighteenth-century mill on the edge of the Grand Meaulnes forest.

Banyuls-sur-Mer

66650 Banyuls-sur-Mer - (Pyrénées-Orientales)
Paris 960 - Perpignan 37 - Port-Vendres 7 - Cerbère 10

Le Catalan

Rte. de Cerbère - 68.88.02.80

Closed Oct. 15-May 1. 36 rms 230-400F. Half-board 370-470F oblig. in seas. Pool. Tennis. Garage parking. Telex 500557. Cards: V, AE, DC.

In this modern hotel facing the rugged coast of the Banyuls bay, all the rooms have ocean views. Piano bar. Restaurant.

15 Le Sardinal

Pl. Paul-Reig - 68.88.30.07

M. Buxéda. Open until 9:30 p.m. Closed Sun. dinner, Mon., Oct. 16-28 & Jan. 2-25. Terrace dining. Pets allowed. Cards: V, MC.

Chef Jean-Marie Patrouix has turned a former movie theater into a delightful bistro with flowers and rustic charm. His specialties are lightly cooked foie gras served in its own juices with a hint of the local wine vinegar; the catch of the day (grilled lotte, sea bream, bass and red mullet) served together in a tomato coulis; fish choucroute with creamed shallots; and Patrouix's famous crème brûlée Catalan. All in all, it's a magnificently savory example of Catalan cuisine. Genial owner Elie Buxéda, a former bandleader and saxophonist, speaks proudly of the local Banyuls wines, which are well stocked in his fine cellar. A second toque is in order.

A la carte: 300F. Menus: 70F, 150F, 190F, 260F.

Barbizon

77630 Barbizon - (Seine-et-Marne)
Paris 56 - Melun 11 - Fontainebleau 10 - Etampes 39

16 Le Bas-Bréau

22, rue Grande - 60.66.40.05

M. Fava. Open until 9:30 p.m. Closed Jan. 2-Feb. 18. Garden dining. Pets allowed. Parking. Telex 690953. Cards: V, AE, MC.

A weekend in the most beautiful inn in the Fontainebleau forest will obviously cost you an arm and a leg, particularly if you ask Jean-Pierre Fava for the sumptuous villa-bungalow at the back of the vegetable garden—but you'll be rewarded with a veritable feast for the eyes. Or stay in the charming historic inn where Stevenson wrote *Treasure Island* and have lunch in front of the fireplace, in the rustic dining room or in the lush interior courtyard. The food is pricey but savory: langoustines royales, lobster salad in hazelnut oil, fresh cod in truffle butter, aromatic braised turbot, spiced squab, remarkable veal cutlets with asparagus and, in season, sumptuous game (which doesn't taste like it's from the farmyard). The 280-franc fixed-price lunch menu includes wine and offers, for example, a delightful warm salad of red mullet and green beans, pan-fried brill, filet of Limousin beef with marrow in an exquisite bordelaise sauce, excellent cheeses (especially when Fava happens to find "coeur de Fontainebleau") and fine desserts. This place is practically an enchanted forest in itself.

A la carte: 600F and up. Menus: 260F and 300F (weekday lunch only, wine incl.).

Le Bas-Bréau

(See restaurant above)

Closed Jan. 2-Feb. 18. 8 stes 1,520-2,380F. 12 rms 880-1,300F. TV. Pets allowed. Tennis.

On the edge of the Fontainebleau forest, this inn, one of the nicest, most refined in the Paris region, is surrounded by roses and century-old trees and has a simple, pleasant atmosphere. There's one deluxe, astonishingly comfortable bungalow at the back of the vegetable garden. Relais et Châteaux.

12/20 Les Pléiades

21, rue Grande - 60.66.40.25

M. Karampournis. Open daily until 9:30 p.m. Closed Sun. dinner (off-seas.) & Feb. 6-26. Garden dining. Pets allowed. Garage parking. Telex 692131. Cards: V, AE, DC, MC.

On a flower-laden terrace on the street or in a quiet garden in back, you'll enjoy a fine 135-franc fixed-price menu of haddock and grapefruit salad, lotte in beurre blanc, cheese and dessert. We'll move the ranking up another point.

A la carte: 300F. Menus: 135F (weekdays only), 190F, 350F.

Les Pléiades

(See restaurant above)

Closed Sun. dinner (off-seas.) & Feb. 6-26. 3 stes 370-520F. 20 rms 250-330F. Half-board 350-370F. TV. Pets allowed.

The former house of the painter Daubigny was recently renovated from top to bottom. Pleasant rooms, most of which are quite attractive. The hotel boasts a beautiful, large flower garden on the edge of the Fontainebleau forest.

Barbotan-les-Thermes

32150 Cazaubon - (Gers)
Paris 686 - Mont-de-Marsan 43 - Condom 37 - Nérac 44

L'Ambassade Gourmande

62.69.53.75

M. Lamaison. Open until 9:15 p.m. Closed Tues., Jan. 31-March 15 & July 24-30. Garden dining. No pets. Hotel: 17 rms 240-300F; half-board 220-230F. Parking. Cards: V, AE, DC, MC.

We owe this delicious discovery to an ardent reader who urged us to make a visit, which is exactly what we did. We found a lovely, bright inn at the edge of the village, ringed by a shaded terrace. The tables were adorned with beautiful flowers, the staff was eager to please, and young owner Pierre-Yves Lamaison displayed remarkable care and attention to his cuisine, which blends his personal inventiveness with regional traditions. He likes vegetables and is an excellent sauce maker: salad of coquilles St-Jacques highlighted with an orange sabayon, savory rabbit pâté in a light, flaky crust, served with an onion compote, breast of duck and fresh liver with truffles, and fresh cod with artichokes and bell peppers. Several respectable local wines (such as Madiran) help top things off. Good fixed-price menus.

A la carte: 280F. Menus: 80F (weekday lunch only), 140F, 170F.

La Bastide Gasconne

62.69.52.09

M. Guérard-Barthélemy. Open until 9:30 p.m. Closed March 1- Oct. 31. No pets. Parking. Telex 521009. Cards: V, AE.

Michel Guérard reigns over this imposing, Armagnac-style eighteenth-century country inn overlooking the sulfur springs. The epicurean cuisine is French-country style, though sometimes lacking in some of the finer points: foie gras au torchon (wrapped in a cloth) that is velvety but rather bland, excellent grilled salmon in a thyme sauce (also rather flat), fine loin of lamb and exquisite desserts. The decor, created by Christine Guérard, is cheerfully elegant, in a lush and pleasant environment. Delicious wines, speedy service. Unfortunately, the lower-cost fixed-price menus have disappeared.

A la carte: 350-400F. Menus: 195F, 250F, 350F.

La Bastide Gasconne

(See restaurant above)

Closed March 1-Oct. 31. 2 stes 890-1,050F. 36 rms 370-555F. Half-board 470-580F oblig. in seas. TV. Pets allowed. Pool. Tennis.

This country inn is known for good living and for helping to invigorate rheumatism sufferers. The pool has an open-air grill beside it, and an immense pond is nearby. Plenty of water sports.

Château de Bégué

62.69.50.08

Closed Sept. 30-April 2. 14 rms 252-320F. Half-board 265-349F. Pool. Garage parking. Telex 531918. Cards: V.

Charming, quiet rooms (some with kitchenettes) in a huge, tranquil park. Restaurant.

Barcelonnette

04400 Barcelonnette - (Alpes-de-Haute-Provence)
Paris 740 - Gap 69 -Briançon 84 - Nice 209

12/20 Le Passe-Montagne

Rte. de la Cayolle, Uvernet (2 km S on D 902) - 92.81.08.58

M. Daneri. Open until 9:15 p.m. Closed Wed. & Nov. 15-Dec. 15. Terrace dining. Pets allowed. Parking. Cards: V, AE, DC, MC.

The 85-franc fixed-price menu is unbeatable: a ravioli-style potato tourte, followed by authentic, tender beef daube, local cheeses and fig soup. The cuisine is well done and charmingly regional. As a bonus, there's a clear view of the mountains, along with fine little wines.

A la carte: 180-200F. Menus: 89F, 122F, 180F.

IN NEARBY **Pra-Loup**
(8.5 km SW on D 902 & D 109)
04400 Pra-Loup - (Alpes-de-Hautes-Provence)

Auberge du Clos Sorel

Village de Clos Sorel - 92.84.10.74

Closed May 15-June 15 & Nov. 15-Dec. 15. 8 rms 320-640F. Half-board 450F oblig. in seas. TV. Pets allowed. Heated pool. Tennis. Parking. Cards: V, AE, DC.

This old farmhouse, restored with restraint and taste, faces a rugged mountain range. The rooms have character and are nicely decorated. Restaurant.

Motel Les Blancs

Molanès - 92.84.16.60

M. Deliance. Open until 10 p.m. Closed April 21-May 19 & Oct. 16-Dec. 14. Terrace dining. No pets. Hotel: 13 rms 140-200F; half-board 170-270F. Cards: V.

You'll find neither fast food nor health food here, just good traditional cuisine prepared by Pierre Deliance. His authentic regional dishes include ravioli of onions and potatoes, crouzets (akin to gnocchi) and longuettes (delicious four-sided tagliatelle). There's also a fine salad with warm chèvre and smoked mutton, and an original potée of winter vegetables, better than the disappointing filet of beef pan-fried in Sauternes. The young staff is nice, but the modern chalet decor lacks charm.

A la carte: 200-250F. Menus: 120F (dinner only), 65F.

IN NEARBY **Sauze**
(4 km SE on D 900 & D 209)
04400 Barcelonnette - (Alpes-de-Haute-Provence)

Alp'Hôtel

92.81.05.04

Closed April 23-June 4 & Oct. 22-Dec. 10. 10 stes 360- 1,050F. 24 rms 320-400F. Half-board 290-330F oblig. in seas. TV. Pets allowed. Heated pool. Garage parking. Telex 420437. Cards: V, AE, DC.

Located near the ski slopes, this alpine hotel has nice rooms with mountain views and many amenities: a garden, heated pool, terrace, fitness club and kitchenettes in the suites. Restaurants.

IN NEARBY **Super-Sauze**
(10 km S on D 9)
04400 Barcelonnette - (Alpes-de-Haute-Provence)

Op Traken

92.81.05.22

Closed Aug. 31-Dec. 15 & April 31-July 1. 12 rms 180-340F. Half-board 280-330F oblig. in seas. Cards: V, DC.

This recently built stone and wood inn with large rooms dominates the valley. Restaurant.

Barneville-Carteret

50270 Barneville-Carteret - (Manche)
Paris 336 - Coutances 48 - Cherbourg 37 - Carentan 43

(14) La Marine

11, rue de Paris
33.53.83.31, 33.04.91.71

M. Cesne. Open until 9:30 p.m. Closed Mon. lunch (except summer), Sun. dinner & Mon. (off-seas.), Jan. 5-Feb. 5 & Nov. 13- Dec. 25. Pets allowed. Parking. Cards: V, DC.

Laurent Cesne could show more audacity and imagination than his 24 years would suggest. But this self-taught chef nonetheless displays much skill and personality in his cuisine; his timing is perfect, his flavors precise. Even if certain dishes seemed banal (oysters in Champagne, émincé of kidney) or a bit confused (roast turbot, coquilles St-Jacques with caviar), we very much liked the salad of quail with pleurote mushrooms (despite a bit too much salt), the medallions of lotte in a perfect beurre rouge and the chocolate pavé with pistachio sauce. Wonderful seafood, notably the lobster, which is roasted with mushrooms or steamed in beurre blanc and is not too steep at 400 francs a kilo. The wine cellar is well stocked with modest wines. Service is a bit haphazard, but the large, bright dining room has a pleasant ocean view.

A la carte: 300F. Menus: 95F (weekdays only), 160F, 220F, 300F.

La Marine

(See restaurant above)

Closed Jan. 5-Feb. 5 & Nov. 13-Dec. 25. 2 stes 500-600F. 29 rms 220-390F. Half-board 265-335F. TV. Pets allowed.

Within this large, white pavilion facing the fishing port and the coast are quiet rooms with double-paned windows. Comfortable, well equipped and tastefully decorated.

Barsac

33720 Podensac - (Gironde)
Paris 608 - Bordeaux 38 - Libourne 45 - Langon 8

Château de Rolland

N 113 - 56.27.15.75, 56.27.19.20

Open year-round. 2 stes 450-550F. 10 rms 350-450F. Half-board oblig. in seas. TV in 3 rms. Pets allowed. Garage parking. Cards: V, AE, DC.

This attractive fifteenth-century monastery in the Sauternes wine region has been comfortably modernized. Pleasant garden. Restaurant.

Basse-Goulaine

see Nantes

Bastelica

see CORSICA

Bastia

see CORSICA

La Baule

44500 La Baule - (Loire-Atlantique)
Paris 463 - Rennes 133 - Vannes 72 - St-Nazaire 17

Sights. Nothing in La Baule itself other than the embankment and lovely beachfront with fin-de-siècle villas. In Guérande: fifteenth-century ramparts; the Roman-columned Collégiale Saint-Auban church (fine stained glass); the salt marshes. In La Brière: Fédrun Island at San Joachim; the clock tower of the church of Saint-Lyphard (beautiful view of La Brière); boat trips on the marsh.

Eating on the Run. La Barbade, on the beach between ave. du Général-de-Gaulle and ave. Lajarrige (reasonable prices, nice service); Le Bateau Ivre, 6, quai Jules Sandeau in Pouliguen (crêpes, oysters, mussels); Il Bertini, 14, ave. de Pavie (pleasant, good pizza); Le Nosy-Be, Plage de la Baule, blvd. Darlu (beach restaurant under the big removable top, salads, grilled meats and fishes, seafood).

Brasseries. Le Bistingo, on the casino terrace (dining to live music); Le Pavillon Rose, 44, ave. du Général-de-Gaulle (pizzeria, open until 3 a.m.); La Trattoria, casino terrace (slow service, pizza, orchestra).

Bars & Cafés. Bar de L'Hermitage, 5, esplanade François-André (good hotel bar); Bar du Pavillon Rose, 44, ave. du Général-de-Gaulle (comfortable, with video); Bar du Tennis Country Club, 113, ave. de Lattre-de-Tassigny (exotic cocktails, swimming pool); Le Safari, 157, ave. Général-de-Gaulle (good apéritifs); Les Terrasses du Chamey's, 24, ave. du Général-de-Gaulle (pleasant apéritif hour); Le Yachting, Bar du Royal, 2, ave. Pierre-Loti (chic, wood-paneled boat decor).

Nightlife. Le Churchill, rte. de Langon (private club in the swamp); Le Golf at Saint-Denac (where the high society of La Baule gathers, nice decor); Le Manhattan, rte. de Guérande (young, hip); Le Sako (disco, young crowd) and Le Tropicana (quiet, sweet), both at the casino.

Shops. La Baule's open-air market is held daily behind ave. de Lattre-de-Tassigny. *Chocolate:* L'Ami Pierrot, 69, ave. du Général-de-Gaulle (good chocolates and the best croissants in town); La Chocolaterie, 6 bis, quai de l'Herminier in Pouliguen. *Confections:* Chez Manuel, 2, ave. du Général-de-Gaulle and on the embankment (ice cream, waffles and its famous "niniches").

(14) Castel Marie-Louise

1, ave. Andrieux - 40.60.20.60

M. Fraenkel. Open daily until 9:30 p.m. Garden dining. No pets. Telex 700408. Cards: V, AE, DC, MC.

Despite the fact that the clientele remains rather advanced in age, the new proprietor has breathed new life into this enchanting villa in a lush, green setting. The bright, though not particularly cheerful, dining room boasts refined service, but on nice days the garden is the place to be. The cuisine's modern terminology belies its rich, traditional preparation: well-prepared smoked salmon bavarois with creamed shallots, warm oysters with spinach (too much sauce but well seasoned), a turbot confit with mushrooms, sweetbreads that are tasty but a bit heavy and a fine strawberry soup with pepper. The handsome wines are surprisingly well priced. Another point.

A la carte: 400F. Menus: 130F (weekday lunch only), 260F.

Castel Marie-Louise

(See restaurant above)

Open year-round. 2 stes 1,650F. 29 rms 900-1,200F. Half-board 1,150-1,420F. TV. Pets allowed. Heated pool. Tennis. Golf.

This large villa is undoubtedly one of the best and most pleasant hotels in all of France. The decor is classic (all rooms have been redecorated) without being banal, the comfort refined, the service remarkable, and the atmosphere warm and relaxing. A lovely garden faces the large beach. Inquire about the Lucien Barriére "getaway specials." Relais et Châteaux.

(15) L'Espadon

2, ave. de la Plage - 40.60.05.63

M. Cova. Open until 9:30 p.m. Closed Sun. dinner & Mon. (off-seas.) & Jan. Terrace dining. Pets allowed. Parking. Cards: V, AE, DC.

There are days when all is well in this top-floor, walnut-paneled dining room. The horizon, dotted with sailboats on a calm sea, is in full view. There are no storms brewing in the kitchen either, just good food: fresh red mullet seasoned with basil and served cold, bass with vegetables, a delicious loin of lamb in a creamy garlic-parsley sauce, pannequets (pancakes) with an orange-flower extract and a zesty orange confit, and exquisite hot rye rolls. Unfortunately, the service is a bit too haughty to be really enjoyable—and on not-so-good days, M. Cova's cuisine seems a touch repetitive (lobster à la parisienne, tortillons de sole in a puff-pastry twist, filet of beef with foie gras and truffles...).

A la carte: 400F. Menus: 104F (lunch only, in season), 173F, 322F.

(14) L'Hermitage

Esplanade François-André - 40.60.37.00

M. Le Naour. Open until 10:30 p.m. Closed Oct. 19-April 19. Air cond. Garden dining. No pets. Parking. Telex 710510. Cards: V, AE, DC, MC.

In the large, stately dining room, small, round tables are arranged very close together under sparkling chandeliers, which is great for those who like a festive ambience; the young, sharp (perhaps too much so) service, the flood of daylight coming through the tall windows and the plethora of fresh flowers also lighten much of the solemn atmosphere. But François Sierra's modern cuisine is more nouvelle on the menu than on the plate and, while undeniably well prepared, is not very adventurous. Our last meal fell a little shy of two toques, featuring as it did nice scallops mistreated by some disappointing melted butter, sea bream that was overcooked but served in a delicious sauce of lemon confit, and an excellent gratin of pears. The wine list offers some of the great bottles at unbeatable prices.

A la carte: 350F.

L'Hermitage

(See restaurant above)

Closed Oct. 19-April 19. 9 stes 1,360-1,730F. 228 rms 690-1,380F. TV. Air cond. Pets allowed. Heated pool. Tennis. Golf.

Remarkable luxury can be found in this grand, well-modernized hotel, which has spacious rooms and plenty of comfort. Extras include a private beach with restaurant, swimming pool with adjacent grill, sauna, massage, tennis and golf. Ask about the special tennis and golf packages. Service, unfortunately, is often lacking.

Hôtel Musset

15, allée des Cygnes - 40.60.24.08

Open year-round. 11 rms 210-260F. Half-board oblig. in seas. Cards: V.

Tucked inside a picturesque millstone villa are a salon and eleven rooms decorated in a romantic style; unfortunately, it's all aged a bit. Nice garden. Restaurant.

Royal

Esplanade François-André - 40.60.33.06

Open year-round. 4 stes 1,200-3,700F. 95 rms 490-1,470F. Half-board 250F (plus rm). TV. Pets allowed. Heated pool. Tennis. Golf. Parking. Telex 701135. Cards: V, AE, DC, MC.

Several superb rooms with spacious bathrooms are surrounded by a beautiful park and terraces. Modern meeting rooms. One of its restaurants is on the beach.

Remember to call or write in advance to reserve your room or your table.

Baume-les-Dames

25110 Baume-les-Dames - (Doubs)
Paris 433 - Besançon 30 - Montbéliard 49 - Pontalier 61

(14) Hostellerie du Château d'As

26, rue Château-Gaillard - 81.84.00.66

M. Aubrée. Open until 9 p.m. Closed Sun. dinner, Mon. & Dec. 15-end Feb. Pets allowed. Parking. Cards: V, AE.

This impressive residence on the village slopes has a quaint, charming decor and ambience; follow tradition and have an apéritif on the terrace. Mme. Aubrée, courteous and urbane, and her husband, Henri, greet diners after their meals. His cuisine is light, easygoing and classic: superb fresh goose liver, medallions of lotte cooked perfectly in a fresh tomato coulis, goujonnettes of sole and lobster with vegetables in a fine, light "américaine" sauce, and pan-roasted pigeon with a hint of garlic. For dessert, there's a marvelous almond charlotte and a coulis of red fruit. The wine cellar includes good Alsace, Burgundy and Jura wines, which Mme. Aubrée knows well.

A la carte: 400F. Menus: 130F (weekdays only), 220F, 275F.

IN NEARBY **Pont-les-Moulins**

(6 km S on D 492)
25100 Baume-les-Dames - (Doubs)

Le Levant

Rte. de Pontarlier - 81.84.09.99

Closed Nov. 1-Feb. 28. 15 rms 130-240F. Half-board 260F. TV in 6 rms. Pets allowed. Parking. Cards: AE, DC, MC.

On the lush banks of the enchanting Cusancin, you'll enjoy peaceful nights and fresh air. Restaurant.

Les Baux-de-Provence

13520 Maussane-les-Alpilles - (Bouches-du-Rhône)
Paris 714 - Salon-de-Provence 33 - Avignon 31 - Arles 19

Bautezar

Grand Rue - 90.54.32.09

Closed Mon. (off-seas.) & Jan. 5-March 15. 2 stes. 10 rms 260-350F. Half-board 480-550F (2 people). No pets. Cards: V.

An excellent small, charming hotel facing the La Fontaine valley and the Val d'Enfer (Valley of Hell). Comfortable rooms. Restaurant.

(14) Bérengère

Rue du Trencat - 90.97.35.63

MM. Auzet. Open until 9 p.m. Closed Tues. dinner, Wed. & Nov. 15-30. Air cond. Pets allowed. Cards: V.

Bérengère is practically at the top of the town. Three steps up a tiny staircase take you to the adorable dining room, which is a bit dolled up but warm and lively, thanks to the charming patronne, Denise Auzet. Four tables are enough for Bernard Auzet, son of the most famous baker in the Vaucluse, since he likes to work alone in his extraordinary kitchen carved into the rock. His à la carte menu features all the best flavors of Provence: pistou soup, delicate pastries filled with escargots and garlic-seasoned cream, bourride (a ragoût) of Mediterranean fish, stuffed young rabbit served atop a thyme-flavored cream sauce, mouth-watering noisettes of lamb seasoned with rosemary and so on. Each dish is cleverly and skillfully prepared with a personal touch. When the desserts reach the level of the rest of the food, everything will be truly heavenly. Good wines with easy-to-swallow prices.

A la carte: 300F. Menus: 145F, 215F, 310F.

(14) La Cabro d'Or

Val d'Enfer - 90.54.33.21

M. Thuilier. Open until 9:30 p.m. Closed Tues. lunch & Mon. (off-seas.) & Nov. 13-Dec. 20. Garden dining. Pets allowed. Garage parking. Telex 401810. Cards: V, AE, DC, MC.

Something is afoot in the domain of nonagenarian Raymond Thuilier—the arrival of Gérard Renébon, who has added several fresh dishes to the house repertoire: terrine de chevreau (kid) en gelée, mesclun salad with lamb's brains and tuna with mustard seed, all of which augment the Cabro d'Or classics (terrines, noisettes of lamb). As usual, the service is excellent, which adds to the happy moments one spends under the mulberry trees on the terrace. Thanks to the good local wines from the exceptionally rich cellar, the bill can remain reasonable. The fixed-price menus, alas, are nothing out of the ordinary.

A la carte: 350F. Menus: 150F (weekday lunch only), 245F, 320F.

La Cabro d'Or

(See restaurant above)

Closed Mon. (off-seas.) & Nov. 13-Dec. 22. 22 rms 420-660F. Half-board 450-600F. TV. Air cond. in 11 rms. Pets allowed. Pool. Tennis.

In a vast garden sheltered from the road stands this jewel of a Provençal farmhouse. Rooms are comfortable and generally tastefully decorated (some with a bit less taste). Cordial service. Horseback riding. Relais et Châteaux.

Mas d'Aigret

D 27 - 90.97.33.54

Closed Thurs. (off-seas.) & Jan. 4-Feb. 20. 2 stes 580F. 13 rms 290-755F. TV. Pets allowed. Pool. Parking. Cards: V, AE, DC.

A nice dwelling with rustic rooms, two of which are carved into the rock, like the restaurant. It sits at the foot of the château ruins. The pool is illuminated at night.

(17) L'Oustau de Baumanière

Val d'Enfer
90.54.33.07

M. Thuilier. Open until 9:30 p.m. Closed Thurs. lunch (Nov. 1-March 31), Wed. & Jan. 22-March 3. Air cond. Garden dining. Pets allowed. Garage parking. Telex 420203. Cards: V, AE, DC, MC.

A new cook has followed in the wake of Raymond Thuilier, the spry, delightful 91-year-old owner who welcomes you at the door. He is Thuilier's grandson, Jean-André Charial. This tall, slender young man trained with several great chefs before he joined the small family empire. At first, he was considered to be primarily an administrator and future heir of the empire, but it didn't take him long to develop a true passion for cooking.

Charial's specialties are not always written on the à la carte menu and are reserved for regular customers who trust the young chef to create meals for them. These include sweetbreads in a wheat crêpe, red mullet mousse in a sour sauce, young rabbit salad with foie gras and string beans (fine "angel's hair" beans picked each morning from the large vegetable garden), red mullet with anchoïade (anchovy paste), salmon with olives, a marvelous anise- and orange-seasoned gilthead, sweetbreads with parsley, and exceptional veal kidneys with fresh coriander. Charial is a truly gifted cook whose subtle use of herbs and spices releases authentic flavors and expresses, in the most refined simplicity, the spirit of Provençal cuisine. He has gotten rid of some overly rich sauces and dishes that had lingered on the menu, but we hope that Thuilier's favorite—leg of lamb en croûte—will stay forever. Baumanière could become a showcase for natural flavors, a place serving the freshest, most exquisite fish, fowl and vegetables prepared in an authentic regional style. And there could not be a more pleasant setting: lush greenery at the foot of an extraordinary stone building jutting into the clear Provençal sky. Shaded by an elm tree, the terrace is exquisite; and once the noisy parking lot located just below it has been moved farther down and hidden with landscaping, diners will experience perfect happiness around the lovely white swimming pool.

Try to coax one of the two excellent sommeliers, Gilles or Hervé, to pull from the cellar one of the remaining bottles of Domaine de Trévallon—the 1982 red Coteaux des Baux is definitely outstanding.

A la carte: 500-700F. Menus: 500F, 600F.

L'Oustau de Baumanière

(See restaurant above)

Closed Jan. 22-March 3. 13 stes 1,150F. 12 rms 700-850F. Half-board 1,000-1,150F. TV. Air cond. Pets allowed. Pool. Tennis.

Though not *truly* luxurious and equipped with every possible comfort, the suites and rooms open onto a delightful garden and, beyond, an extraordinary view of a white-rock formation and a perched village. One can also stay at La Résidence, a charming farmhouse nestled quietly in the greenery. Extras include a swimming pool, tennis and use of riding-club facilities at the Cabro d'Or. A nine-hole golf course is located two kilometers away. Relais et Châteaux.

(14) La Riboto de Taven

Val D'Enfer - 90.97.34.23

MM. Novi-Thème. Open until 9:30 p.m. Closed Sun. dinner (off-seas.), Mon. & Jan. 9-Feb. 25. Garden dining. Pets allowed. Parking. Cards: V, AE, DC.

This attractive old Provençal farmhouse opens onto a pleasant, cool garden nestled in the verdant belly of the Val d'Enfer (Valley of Hell); jagged rocks complete the extraordinary tableau. The luxurious setting, fine service, splendid wines and delicious cuisine are reminders that L'Oustau de Baumanière has no monopoly on excellence in these parts. Though a bit somber, the atmosphere is elegantly rustic and the terrace under the mulberry trees particularly attractive. Guests are showered with attention from the moment of their arrival, and the highly professional chef, Jean-Jacques Boissel, holds strictly to classic but light cuisine: terrine of guinea-hen with artichokes, a concoction of three raw fish in citrus fruit, bass in local olive oil and sage-seasoned loin of lamb, also locally bred. Portions could be less modest.

A la carte: 400F. Menus: 190F (lunch only), 240F, 350F.

Bavay

59570 Bavay - (Nord)

Paris 230 - Lille 76 - Valenciennes 23 - Mauberge 14

(13) Le Bagacum

2, rue d'Audignie - 27.66.87.00

M. Lesne. Open until 9 p.m. Closed Sun. dinner, Mon., Jan. 1-15 & July 1-22. Air cond. Pets allowed. Parking. Cards: V, AE, DC, MC.

Near one of the most beautiful archaeological sites in the region, this onetime barn has been refurbished and made into a comfortable, charming restaurant by the young owners. Brick walls, old beams, fine china, a large fish pond and a warm fireplace create a cozy atmosphere. The cuisine, though tasty, would benefit by being simpler, thus enhancing the preparation of the lovely local products: turbot in cider and apples, bass with morels, grilled lobster from Brittany and aiguillettes of beef with truffles. The à la carte menu could be shortened a bit. Good, comprehensive wine cellar.

A la carte: 250-280F. Menus: 80F, 150F.

Bavent

see Cabourg

Bayeux

14400 Bayeux - (Calvados)

Paris 251 - Cherbourg 92 - Caen 27 - St-Lô 36 - Vire 59

Churchill Hôtel

14-16, rue St-Jean - 31.21.31.80

Closed Nov. 15-March 15. 1 ste 420F. 31 rms 260-360F. TV in 15 rms. No pets. Parking. Telex 171755. Cards: V, AE, MC.

An attractive, small hotel recently opened in the heart of Bayeux. Its lovely rooms are well cared for. Pleasant veranda for breakfast.

(13) Le Lion d'Or

71, ave. St-Jean - 31.92.06.90

M. Jouvin-Bessière. Open until 9:30 p.m. Closed Dec. 20-Jan. 20. Garage parking. Pets allowed. Telex 171143. Cards: V, AE, DC.

The cheerful, neorustic decor gives a fresh feeling to this dining room, which has attractively set tables and lovely lighting. The affable owner displays professionalism in watching over the dining room and the kitchen, where a good, traditional, regional cuisine is prepared: lobster omelet, Norman-style skate with nettle tips, tripe and fricandeau (veal fricassée) with cider. The cheeses come from excellent local producers; the good wine cellar houses a delicious Auge cider.

A la carte: 180-250F. Menus: 100F (weekdays only), 135F, 165F, 240F.

Le Lion d'Or

(See restaurant above)

Closed Dec. 20-Jan. 20. 29 rms 125-350F. Half-board 225-480F oblig. in seas. TV in 23 rms. Pets allowed.

Located in the center of Bayeux, Le Lion d'Or has 29 rooms that face a flower-filled cobblestone courtyard.

Les Quatre Saisons

25, rue des Bouchers - 31.92.00.04

M. Morel. Open daily until 10 p.m. Garden dining. No pets. Parking. Telex 171663.

This large inn situated in the center of town was ravaged by fire a few years ago, but it has risen from the ashes and regained its former luxury. The large red dining room is decorated in opulent Louis XIII style, with coffered ceilings and high antique chairs; food is brought under elegant covers, with much attention to service. The young sommelier is proud of the 10,000-bottle wine cellar stocked with everything from an 85-franc Juliénas to a 1950 Pétrus at 10,000 francs. The cuisine is generous and rich, though a bit conventional, and it surely could improve in both its preparation and presentation. Entrées include crayfish gratinée, well prepared and seasoned, overcooked turbot with tomatoes and thyme flowers, and a veal kidney sautéed in a foie gras sauce. The fixed-price menus are magnificent.

Menus: 90F (weekdays only), 135F, 168F, 280F.

Grand Hôtel du Luxembourg

(See restaurant above)

Open year-round. 3 stes 1,200F. 19 rms 300-400F. Half-board 300F. TV. Pets allowed.

The huge rooms have been splendidly and luxuriously redone, with soft wall hangings, excellent bathrooms and elegant furniture. Interior garden. Private club in the cellar. Impeccable service.

IN NEARBY **Le Molay-Littry**
(13 km W on D 5)
14330 Le Molay-Littry - (Calvados)

Château du Molay

(Les Comtes de Normandie)
Rte. d'Isigny (4 km N on D 5)
31.22.90.82

M. Jouve. Open until 10 p.m. Closed Dec. 1-Feb. 28. Terrace dining. No pets. Parking. Telex 171912. Cards: V, AE, DC, MC.

We have nothing but good things to say about the atmosphere—a placid lake, a magnificent park where deer romp... all in all, a most alluring environment surrounding this late-seventeenth-century château. The château also features excellent service "sous cloche" (with the large, bell-shape dish covers). The cuisine, however, while fresh and well prepared, is lacking in dynamism. A more spirited seasoning is needed in the lovely salad of smoked duck filets and the curry sauce served with the lamb sauté (it has nice seasonal vegetables, though). And the mediocre cheeses don't do justice to Normandy's fine cheese-making reputation. Desserts are, on the other hand, remarkable, particularly the chocolate mousse with pistachios. Nice wine cellar.

A la carte: 280F. Menus: 145F, 190F, 250F.

Château du Molay

(See restaurant above)

Closed Dec. 1-Feb. 28. 40 rms 320-600F. Half-board 390-460F. TV in 10 rms. No pets. Heated pool. Tennis.

The Château du Molay has wonderful facilities, including an immense park, tennis, swimming pool, health club, billiards, bicycling, Ping-Pong, sauna, bar, library and more. All rooms have a view of the countryside.

Bayonne

64100 Bayonne - (Pyrénées-Atlantiques)
Paris 744 - Bordeaux 176 - Pau 107 - Biarritz 8

Sights. The impressive ramparts (two rings around Bayonne); the pedestrian zone in the old town (particularly rue du Port-Neuf); Le Château-Vieux (restored by Vauban); Sainte-Marie Cathedral and its thirteenth-century cloister; Musée Léon Bonnat (drawings, paintings) and Musée Basque (regional art, ethnography); the port and amphitheater; the distillery for Izarra liqueurs.

Eating on the Run. Bar du Théâtre, pl. de la Liberté; Le Biligou, 24, rue Maubec (crêperie); Le Rital, 30, rue Passemillon (Italian specialties); Le Salvatore, 6, rue de la Salle (pizza); Sur le Pouss, 2, rue Lormand (quick meals).

Brasseries. Aux Deux Rivières, 21, rue Thiers; Grand Brasserie, pl. de la Liberté; Le Perroquet, 2, rue 49e; Le Thiers, 3, rue Thiers; Le Victor-Hugo, 1, rue Victor-Hugo.

Bars & Cafés. Aux Deux Rivières, Le Bar du Théâtre, Grand Brasserie and Le Perroquet (see "Brasseries"); Le Pimm's, ave. Léon-Bonnat (large cocktail selection).

Nightlife. Centers around Anglet, 3 km away, particularly La Boucane and Sables d'Or; Le Columba, at the skating rink; Le Love, pl. du Dr-Gentille (piano bar for the ladies); in Saint-Pierre d'Irube (2 km south), La Perle (disco).

Shops. *Bakeries:* Hubert, 8, rue Pannecau (fine old-fashioned breads). *Chocolate:* Cazenav, 19, arceaux du Port-Neuf (century-old producer known throughout the region); Daranatz, 15, rue du Port-Neuf. *Eaux-de-vie:* Brana, at Saint-Jean-Pied-de-Port (exceptional plum and pear distillations from locally grown fruit). *Gourmet foods, cheese:* La Bergerie, 18, ave. Foch; Betbeder, 3, rue Bernadou (products from Fauchon's in Paris and an excellent Landais pie). *Bayonne ham:* Hargous, rte. de Cambo (old-fashioned curing methods); Montauzer, 17, rue de la Salle. *Pastries:* Andrieu, 33, blvd. d'Alsace-Lorraine; Barrères, 47, arceaux du Port-Neuf; Dodin, 7, rue Victor-Hugo; Mauriac, 23, arceaux du Port-Neuf.

(14) Béluga

15, rue des Tonneliers - 59.25.52.13

MM. Guédon. Open until 9:30 p.m. Closed Sun. & 1st 2 weeks of Jan. & June. Air cond. Pets allowed. Cards: V.

Some locals sulk about this charming spot in the old quarter of Bayonne. Is it because the prices are a bit steep or the quantities too measured? We must say that Jean-Claude Guédon, a skilled and professional chef, is paying somewhat less attention than in the past to the precision of his cooking—which is what is lacking in his otherwise magnificent coquilles St-Jacques served in a delicious parsley sauce, his haddock with cabbage and certainly his beautiful turbot, though it's saved by a fine lime-ginger sauce. He'll have to remedy these faults and serve more generous portions to remain the best restaurant in Bayonne. The wood-paneled decor is appealing, and patronne Dany Guédon made us feel welcome.

A la carte: 230-250F.

(15) Cheval Blanc

68, rue Bourgneuf - 59.59.01.33

M. Telléchéa. Open until 10 p.m. Closed Mon. (except July-Aug.) & Jan. 9-Feb. 6. Air cond. Pets allowed. Cards: V, AE, DC, MC.

Inside this very old Bayonne inn is a fresh new decor, pretty tables and elegant china—and a young chef who is steadily improving in his efforts to create a light cuisine. A native of the Basque region, Jean-Claude Telléchéa is already the most interesting chef in Bayonne, and some of his creations are worth two toques, such as the classic, warm foie gras perfectly cooked in a slightly creamy sauce and served with large morsels of aromatic truffles, or fresh and tasty paupiettes of striped bass with a compote of slightly cooked tomatoes. But the feuilleté of salmon and asparagus tips and the sweetbreads with green vegetables, though fine creations, are a bit less dynamic, and the marinière of langoustines with caviar is a bit too rich and seems out of place in this light, clever repertoire. The superb desserts include a fruit gratin with raspberry sorbet. The family gives a warm welcome, and the young maître d' is efficient. One point more in this edition.

A la carte: 300F. Menus: 115F, 176F, 235F.

Aux Deux Rivières

21, rue Thiers - 59.59.14.61

Open year-round. 1 ste 500F. 65 rms 225-340F. TV in 29 rms. Pets allowed. Garage parking. Telex 570794. Cards: V, AE, DC, MC.

A nice hotel in the center of town with a dated decor but spacious and well-maintained rooms. No restaurant.

Mendi-Alde

8, ave. du 8-Mai-1945 (3 km S on D 932)
59.42.38.44

Open year-round. 9 rms 100-175F. Garage parking.

A fine family hotel with several rooms facing the mountains. Garden. No restaurant.

IN NEARBY **Ustaritz**
(12 km SE on D 932)
64480 Ustaritz - (Pyrénées-Atlantiques)

---

(15) La Patoula

59.93.00.56

M. Guilhem. Open until 10 p.m. Closed Sun. dinner & Mon. (off-seas.) & Jan. 5-Feb. 15. Garden dining. Pets allowed. Parking. Cards: V.

This fine old house in its own park has become one of the most attractive spots in the region, with tiny dining rooms and a terrace overlooking the Nive river. But never mind that: Pierre Guilhem's masterful cuisine is, of course, the key attraction. His finesse and exactitude come through in the langoustines en papillote with leeks and a savory sauce of virgin olive oil, the salad of warm sole with a tasty garnish of fresh tomatoes and artichoke hearts, a fine array of fish (sole, turbot, salmon from the Adour) on a bed of carrots and leeks, and honey-strawberry gastembera (a velvety homemade curdled sheeps' milk). Elegant tables and fine service supervised by Mme. Guilhem.

A la carte: 250F. Menu: 120F.

La Patoula

(See restaurant above)

Closed Sun. & Mon. (off-seas.) & Jan. 5-Feb. 15. 9 rms 250-350F. Half-board 260-310F. Pets allowed.

Beautiful rooms and pleasant period furniture, along with well-equipped bathrooms and impeccable service, make La Patoula a worthy little hotel.

IN NEARBY **Villefranque**
(11 km SE on N 636 & D 137)
64100 Bayonne - (Pyrénées-Atlantiques)

Château de Larraldia

59.44.00.10, 59.40.90.00

Closed Oct. 15-May 30. 1 ste 1,200-1,300F. 19 rms 535-950F. Half-board 685-1,110F. Pool. Tennis. Parking. Telex 540831. Cards: V, AE, DC, MC.

This magnificent residence, now an annex of the Biarritz Miramar, has just undergone major renovation work that has transformed it into a truly charming hotel set in a 150-acre park. It features luxury rooms and facilities, along with a splendid view of the Pyrénées. A stay here can be complemented with visits to the spa at Miramar. Restaurant.

12/20 Iduzki-Alde

59.44.08.30

M. Vivier. Open until 9:30 p.m. Closed Wed., Feb. school vacation & Nov. 1. Garden dining. No pets. Parking. Cards: V.

True Basque charm is hidden away at Iduzki-Alde, off the beaten path and near the old church, the pelota court and the Nive riverbank. The unpretentious, generous cuisine served here also delights: escargots fricassée with herbs, squid in an inky sauce, a stew of hare in Rioja wine. Fine reception.

A la carte: 160-180F. Menus: 55F (weekday lunch only, wine incl.), 65F, 78F, 98F.

Beaugency

45190 Beaugency - (Loiret)
Paris 150 - Blois 31 - Orléans 25 - Châteaudun 41

12/20 L'Abbaye

2, quai de l'Abbaye - 38.44.67.35

M. Letellier. Open until 9:30 p.m. (10 p.m. in summer). Closed Dec. 5-27. Terrace dining. Pets allowed. Parking. Cards: V, AE, DC, MC.

The beautiful mezzanine rises majestically above the Loire, and the newly extended veranda overlooks the 22 arches of the marvelous Beaugency bridge. These stately buildings are part of a former abbey. The cuisine tries to be worthy of the decor, but it has its ups and downs, since chefs don't seem to stay long. Count our most recent visit in the down column: smoked goose filets in a runny onion marmalade, basic lotte with mushrooms, good desserts. The wine cellar may be fine, but we're still going to have to put the toque in mothballs for now.

A la carte: 300-350F. Menu: 175F.

L'Abbaye

(See restaurant above)

Open year-round. 5 stes 490F. 13 rms 380-500F. TV in 10 rms. Pets allowed.

This stately old abbey was recently renovated from top to bottom; it now has spacious rooms with a refined, sober decor. Marvelous view of the river and old bridge.

IN NEARBY **Tavers**
(2 km SW on N 152)
45190 Beaugency - (Loiret)

La Tonnellerie

12, rue des Eaux-Bleues - 38.44.68.15

M. Aulagnon. Open until 8:45 p.m. Closed Oct. 8-April 28. Garden dining. No pets. Parking. Telex 782479. Cards: V, AE, DC, MC.

The young chef at this delightful Touraine residence has struggled to invigorate the repertoire. He has been partly successful and hence deserves a toque, notably for his fine carp terrine, pork matelote with huckleberries and fresh pasta, chicken in Orléans vinegar and apricot bavarois. But he still needs to guard against sauces that are a bit too invasive and a sometimes excessive. Some totally uninteresting dishes (Lavallière trout with Cognac and raisins) could be taken off the à la carte menu, and the fixed-price menus could be more generous. Charming terrace in the garden courtyard.

A la carte: 250F. Menus: 160F to 260F.

La Tonnellerie

(See restaurant above)

Closed Oct. 8-April 28. 5 stes 460-550F. 21 rms 235-515F. Half-board 385-475F oblig. in seas. Pets allowed. Heated pool.

Several beautiful and comfortable rooms are decorated with elegance and simplicity, in a house where guests are greeted cordially. Next to the lush, tranquil Loiret river.

Beaulieu-sur-Mer

06310 Beaulieu-sur-Mer - (Alpes-Maritimes)
Paris 943 - Menton 20 - Nice 10 - Cannes 43

12/20 African Queen

Port de Plaisance - 93.01.10.85

M. Vissian. Open until midnight. Closed Nov. 15-Dec. 15. Air cond. Garden dining. Pets allowed. Telex 462428. Cards: V.

This waterfront terrace, simple but lively, is still a big success; it offers excellent salads, various pastas, fricassées, all sorts of brochettes and good local wine in carafes. Rapid service (aboard your boat if you like).

A la carte: 220F. Menu: 98F.

Carlton

7, ave. Edith-Cavell - 93.01.14.70

Closed Oct. 31-Jan. 1. 33 rms 450-950F. Half-board 175F. TV. Air cond. Pets allowed. Heated pool. Garage parking. Telex 970421. Cards: V, AE, DC, MC.

A nice, small hotel 300 meters from the beach. Pleasant pool. Restaurant with grill.

(14) Le Maxilien

43, blvd. Marinoni - 93.01.47.48

M. Demarche. Open daily until 10 p.m. (10:30 p.m. in summer). Air cond. Pets allowed. Cards: V, AE, DC.

We don't hold it against those who pass Le Maxilien by, since the bistros along the port are not appealing. Also, the decor is, quite frankly, ugly, and the service is a bit frazzled. But let's talk about a good chef, Jean-Jacques Ménanteau, who came here not long ago following a long stay in Holland and Luxembourg. His talent keeps the local habitués returning, and hotel concierges send guests who simply want to eat well. And eat well they do, thanks to the excellent duck foie gras, the light salmon mousseline with a carrot flan, and the tender young rabbit flavored with basil and served with a potato galette. Desserts are less inspired, and the wine cellar could be rounded out. The owner's wife and daughter are quite amiable. In summer, request a seat on the terrace facing the plaza.

A la carte: 300-400F. Menus: 98F, 160F, 195F.

Le Métropole

15, blvd. du Général-Leclerc
93.01.00.08

M. Badrutt. Open until 10 p.m. Closed end Oct.-Dec. 20. Air cond. Terrace dining. Pets allowed. Parking. Telex 470304. Cards: MC.

You'll discover the Côte d'Azur of bygone days at this luminous and lovely Italian-style villa done in white and ocher; its tiny park, with flower beds, palm trees and lush lawns,overlooks the sea. The luxury is subdued, and the diners are so discreet that only the personnel seem aware of their presence. And the cuisine, like everything else here, rings true. Refined and savory, it reminds us of the fare served to the bourgeois society of old, which lived too well to ever feel the need for surprises—one can have lunch and dinner here for two weeks straight without tiring. Chef Pierre Estival uses only first-rate products, particularly fish and shellfish, while respecting their purity of taste: red mullet with olive pulp, langoustines and eggplant in olive oil, young white turbot with fresh tomatoes (and a touch of Sauternes to enhance the flavor), baked bass, pink sea bream grilled with chervil butter, lobster with basil or, by special order, a marvelous bouillabaisse. All these dishes reflect the harmonious simplicity of this delightful villa in the sun.

A la carte: 500-700F. Menus: 370F, 410F, 440F.

Le Métropole

(See restaurant above)

Closed end Oct.-Dec. 20. 3 stes 2,680-4,840F (half-board for two). 50 rms; half-board 750-1,675F oblig. TV. Air cond. Pets allowed. Heated pool.

Old-world charm is combined with all the modern comforts in this superb villa, whose rooms and suites are soberly decorated in clear, cheerful tones. There's a wonderful view of the sea, and the coast seems to be miraculously unspoiled. A rare degree of efficiency and grace is found in the service, which is supervised by Jean Badrutt. Relais et Châteaux.

La Réserve

5, blvd. du Général-Leclerc
93.01.00.01

M. Maria. Open until 9:30 p.m. Closed Nov. 19-Dec. 22. Terrace dining. Pets allowed. Parking. Telex 470301. Cards: V, AE, DC.

The luster has not worn off this grand old residence on the Mediterranean, established in 1894. Its Italian decor retains the original charm and refinement that attracted the kings and queens of the Côte d'Azur to these enchanting shores before the great wars. But for several years it has been losing all the ground that its neighbor, Le Métropole, has been gaining in refinement and simplicity. The recent arrival of chef Joël Garrault, however, has rescued La Réserve from the torpor of elegant decline. The salad of spinach sprouts and shrimp, the cabbage-wrapped little shellfish and, above all, the excellent and perfectly cooked veal kidneys in sage all demonstrate a successful turnaround that does not sweep tradition under the rug. The dining room commands a dream-like view of the sea, the coast and, of course, the pool.

A la carte: 180-200F. Menus: 65F (weekdays only), 90F, 140F.

La Réserve

(See restaurant above)

Closed Nov. 19-Dec. 22. 3 stes 2,400-4,550F. 47 rms 530-2,100F. Half-board oblig. in seas. TV. Air cond. Pets allowed. Heated pool.

In a perfect location of absolute tranquility, this beautiful fin-de-siècle villa is meticulously maintained, with a luxurious 1950s atmosphere. There's a flower garden on the terrace, a heated pool overlooking the beach and a private dock for boaters to pull in for summer lunches.

Beaune

21200 Beaune - (Côte-d'Or)
Paris 312 - Dijon 40 - Autun 50 - Chalon-sur-Saône 31

Sights. The Hôtel-Dieu museum (courtyard, dormitory, Van der Weyden's 1443 polyptych, *Last Judgment*); Collegiate Church of Notre-Dame (portal, tapestries of the Virgin Mary behind the altar) and the narrow pedestrian roads nearby; the former hall of the Dukes of Burgundy (wine museum); Hôtel de Ville, which includes Musée des Beaux-Arts and Musée Marey (the inventor of chronophotography); Saint-Nicolas church; the wine cellars (not all!) and, several kilometers away, the Rochepot château and the Hautes-Côtes cliffs.

Eating on the Run. Le Bistro Bourguignon, 8, rue Monge (nice wine bar, light meals); Cafétéria Parunis, pl. Monge (new, lovely view); Le Caveau Saint-Gilles, 29, rue Carnot; La Papisienne, 1 pl. Madeleine (pizzeria); Le Saint-Flocel, 26, rue Paradis (small family restaurant).

Bars & Cafés. Pickwick's, 2, rue Notre-Dame (beer, intimate atmosphere); the cafés on pl. Monge (lively).

Nightlife. Le Galion, 5, pl. Ziem (small, pleasant American bar with video); Le Jazz Band, 11, rte. de Seurre (jazz, late-night grill).

Shops. *Bakeries:* A La Parisienne, 2, rue Monge (excellent breads). *Coffee:* Les Arômes de la Chancellerie, 18, rue Poterne (well-roasted coffees). *Cheese:* Tast Fromages, 23, rue Carnot (fine choice of regional products). *Fruit and vegetables:* Guiton, 24, pl. Madeleine. *Pastries:* Bazeron, 8, rue Carnot (croissants and various pâtisseries). *Tea salons:* Bouché, 1, pl. Monge (excellent ice cream).

Le Cep

27, rue Maufoux - 80.22.35.48

Open year-round. 49 rms 450-800F. TV. Pets allowed. Parking. Cards: V, AE, DC, MC.

The spacious, quiet rooms in this luxurioulsy equipped seventeenth-century residence are unoriginal but stylish nonetheless. There's a magnificent historic courtyard. Restaurant: see Bernard Morillon.

Dame Tartine

(Alain Billard)
3, rue Nicolas-Rolin - 80.22.64.20

M. Billard. Open daily until midnight. Terrace dining. Pets allowed. Cards: V, MC.

Alain Billard has given a new, chic look to his small restaurant well located near the Hôtel-Dieu. Oak paneling and purple fabrics dominate the decor, and the tables are always set with elegant flowers. The cuisine has recently taken a turn to traditional Burgundy specialties at good prices, in the process becoming simpler and tastier: salad of smoked breast of duck with duck foie gras in a delicate dressing of hazelnut oil and sherry vinegar; a poultry filet in an exceptional vinegar sauce; and perfect coq au vin made with Burgundy. One point higher in this edition, despite a disappointing poultry parfait. The price range is appreciated, and the wine cellar has good Burgundies of all vintages.

A la carte: 200-300F. Menus: 64F, 99F.

(14) L'Ecusson

Pl. Malmedy - 80.22.83.08

M. Senelet. Open until 9 p.m. Closed Tues. dinner (Dec.-March), Wed. & Feb. 21-March 16. Garden dining. Pets allowed. Cards: V, AE, DC.

All the charm is on the inside of this drab house in a lifeless quarter. Once in off the street, you'll feel like you're inside a comfortable club, with felt and soft carpet absorbing all noise. Chef Jean-Pierre Senelet is an excellent professional with all the right credentials. His à la carte menu is fine, but with such excellent fixed-price formulas, why bother? The 170-franc meal, for example, includes a delicious gelée of young rabbit with tarragon, sweetbreads ravioli in a young wine sauce, duck in an oxtail sauce, cheeses and sliced warm apples au jasmin. Remarkable wine cellar.

A la carte: 250F. Menus: 85F, 125F, 170F, 248F.

(14) Jacques Lainé

10-12, blvd. Foch - 80.24.76.10

M. Lainé. Open until 9:30 p.m. Closed Wed. lunch & Tues. (off-seas.); annual closing varies. Garden dining. No pets. Parking. Cards: V, AE, MC.

Jacques Lainé has been striving to cheer up this large merchant's house frequented by Beaune epicureans and wine connoisseurs, because the small, pearl-gray dining rooms in a Louis XVI–transition style are more comfortable than elegant. But the terrace over the tree-lined garden is one of the most agreeable spots around for a summer lunch. The cuisine is consistent, based on classics but with a personal style: baby vegetables in a warm vinaigrette, paprika-seasoned crayfish-tail salad, escargots bourguignon with leeks and baby onions, blanc de Bresse with baby vegetables, and excellent desserts (orange bavarois, charlottes). The service is less lethargic than it used to be, and the wine cellar is excellent (fine Burgundies) but pricey.

A la carte: 300F. Menus: 87F (weekday lunch only), 148F, 200F, 330F.

(13) Bernard Morillon

31, rue Maufoux - 80.24.12.06

M. Morillon. Open until 10 p.m. Closed Tues. lunch, Mon. & Feb. Garden dining. Pets allowed. Parking. Telex 351256. Cards: V, AE, DC, MC.

In a former shop next to the Le Cep hotel, Bernard Morillon has installed two large dining rooms under gorgeous ceilings. The rather conventional elegance lacks adroitness (particularly the curious Louis XV–style white porcelain objects) but offers excellent comfort, and the service and cooking do justice to the decor. The cuisine is prepared in regal Beaunois fashion: a marinated bass filet perfumed with anise and mint, a rich salade composée with foie gras, langoustines, sweetbreads (too much mustard), pleasant aiguillettes of John Dory with grapefruit, and superb chocolate desserts, which might be a trifle too rich for some.

A la carte: 420F. Menus: 160F, 250F, 320F.

La Poste

1, blvd. Clemenceau - 80.22.08.11

Closed Nov. 21-Easter. 4 stes 1,002-1,270F. 21 rms 695-845F. Half-board 703-1,282F.

Warm, attentive service can be found in this traditional hotel, which has been pleasantly renovated. View of the ramparts and the vineyards. Popular, solid restaurant.

(13) Relais de Saulx

6, rue Louis-Véry - 80.22.01.35

M. Monnoir. Open until 9:30 p.m. Closed Sun. dinner, Mon., Feb. 15-March 5 & Dec. 17-27. Air cond. No pets.

The rustic decor is typical of traditional Beaune: beautiful beams, stone walls and landscape paintings. The cuisine has its ups and surprising downs, but recently rather more downs—especially the lotte à la crème, with its wishy-washy sauce and morels that have seen better days, and the scraggly looking vegetables served with the spiced lamb rosette. But good marks go to the wonderful escargots cassolette in tarragon sauce and the roast pigeon (despite its fattiness). By all means stay away from the iced nougat. The dining room is noisy, and at times the service exasperates.

A la carte: 250F. Menus: 110F (weekdays only), 150F, 180F, 280F.

(15) La Rôtisserie de la Paix

47, Faubourg Madeleine - 80.22.33.33

MM. Dauphin. Open until 9:15 p.m. Closed Sun. dinner, Mon. & March. Garden dining. Pets allowed. Cards: V, AE, DC, MC.

Far from the historic center of town, this modestly redecorated former barn is not wildly cheerful. Its out-of-the-way location may seem problematic, but that keeps chef Jean-Luc Dauphin and his wine-connoisseur wife, Marie, safe from the ravaging crowds that plague the tourist centers. Despite a few slipups (like the rather dull black-currant crêpes), the cuisine is excellent—there's no cheating in either the products or the preparation. The fresh chèvre in a garlic-roasted galette is a fine dish, as is the salmon lasagne with parsley cream and the heavenly pigs'-feet cassoulet. Marie, daughter of a wine maker, makes sure the cellar is well stocked with the best Burgundies.

A la carte: 280-300F. Menus: 90F, 140F, 215F.

IN NEARBY **Aloxe-Corton**

(5 km N on N 74)

21420 Aloxe-Corton - (Côte-d'Or)

Clarion

80.26.46.70

Open year-round. 1 ste 685F. 9 rms 375-580F. TV. Pets allowed. Parking. Telex 351229. Cards: V, AE, DC, MC.

This beautiful seventeenth-century residence has been transformed into a charming hotel with comfortable, spacious rooms. Wine tasting. Babysitting. No restaurant.

IN NEARBY **Chorey-lès-Beaune**
(4 km NE on N 74)
21200 Beaune - (Côte-d'Or)

15 L'Ermitage de Corton

N 74 - 80.22.05.28

M. Parra. Open until 9 p.m. Closed Sun. dinner, Mon. & Jan. 20-Feb. 28. Garden dining. Pets allowed. Parking. Cards: V, AE, DC.

The ardent, passionate André Parra is Burgundy's Mr. Everything. Americans flip for the purple decor and curtains (we must say, though, that the atmosphere is in the most gaudy Hollywood style), those with big appetites swear by the generous servings, and wine lovers will be impressed by the fine collection of Côte-de-Beaune, Champagnes and grand Bordeaux tended by the eloquent young sommelier. There are faults in the cuisine—some heaviness and imprecisions—but fine qualities as well. On good days you'll find that the excellence of the products and the loving approach inspired by the tradition of a grand haute cuisine shine through. Try the innumerable amuse-gueules (tiny appetizers), fresh pasta in titanic portions (a meal in itself) with pan-fried foie gras and delicious truffles in equally generous servings, bass cooked to perfection with basil (but a bit lost in the plate of olive purée, tomatoes and assorted vegetables), superb pigeon rôti in a creamy garlic sauce, and the mouth-watering ice cream with mulberries or soft caramel.

A la carte: 450F. Menus: 125F (weekdays only), 325F (weekends and holidays only), 250F, 430F.

L'Ermitage de Corton

(See restaurant above)

Closed Sun., Mon. & Jan. 20-Feb. 28. 5 stes 800-1,500F. 5 rms 500-750F.

Grand luxury and grand style, with a Versailles decor and bathrooms worthy of the Pharaohs. The degree of luxury also comes through in innumerable details. Sensational breakfast.

IN NEARBY **Levernois**
(5 km SE on D 970 & D 111)
21200 Beaune - (Côte-d'Or)

16 Jean Crotet

Rte. de Combertault - 80.24.73.58

M. Crotet. Open until 9:30 p.m. Closed Wed. lunch & Tues. (except April 1-Nov. 30); annual closing varies. Garden dining. Pets allowed. Parking. Telex 351468. Cards: V, AE, DC, MC.

It is now a fait accompli: Jean Crotet has given up his place in Nuits-Saint-Georges for a setting more in line with his ambitions. Here in the countryside around Beaune, he found ten wooded acres with a river and numerous little bridges and footpaths, all surrounding a huge bourgeois residence, to which he has added a dining room whose decor is well lit if a little cold; it opens onto a formal garden. The kitchens, which are almost as spiffy as the famous ones at Troisgros, form a fine laboratory for the admirable chemistry of Crotet's technical skills, combined with his son Christophe's ideas. We expect nothing but the best from these two and are only waiting to see a little more precision once they settle down. The framework remains the same: a rock-solid technical base, the very best ingredients (especially fish and vegetables) and the meticulous professionalism of Crotet, who produces dishes with a traditional accent: snails in a pot with broth and a light pastry crust, warm house-smoked salmon with purée of watercress, and a fantastic terrine of pigeon that stands well above most terrines. The sauces are kept somewhat light, the vegetables are quite tasty, and the classic style needs only a little more individuality (like the wonderful tarragon sorbet served with the apple tart) to achieve perfection. The excellent wine list offers a white wine from the owner's own vineyard, and the service, like the cooking, is truly professional. A corner has obviously been turned here—we expect even higher ratings soon.

A la carte: 420F. Menus: 150F (weekday lunch only), 230F, 330F, 420F.

Hostellerie de Levernois

(See restaurant above)

Closed Tues. (except April 1-Nov. 30); annual closing varies. 12 rms 480-580F. Half-board oblig. in seas. TV. No pets. Golf.

Deep in the woods, under immense fir trees, sits this modern building done in a traditional style. The rooms are huge and comfortable, opening onto the forest and the lawns, and the facilities are more than complete. Marvelous homemade bread is served for breakfast.

Beaurecueil

see Aix-en-Provence

Belâbre

36370 Belâbre - (Indre)
Paris 312 - Châteauroux 57 - Argenton 36 - Le Blanc 13

15 L'Ecu

Pl. de la République - 54.37.60.82

M. Cotar. Open until 9 p.m. Closed Sun. dinner, Mon., Jan. 16-Feb. 13 & Sept. 7-15. Pets allowed. Hotel: 6 rms 150-220F; half-board 220-250F oblig. in seas. Garage parking. Cards: V, AE, DC, MC.

L'Ecu is a delightful surprise in this village deep in the Du Berry valley; it faces the church, whose bells ring at supper time. The rustic inn has a refined, generous cuisine and reasonable prices, while the decor, with its beams, copperware and artificial flowers on the tables, is unseemly but comfortable. Chef Daniel Cotar runs a strict kitchen that turns out classic dishes carried out with a modern execution. He features excellent sauces complementing a remarkably fresh and light repertoire: a well-balanced langoustine salad in orange butter, saffron sole with smoked bacon, classic breast of duck with three varieties of peppers, and delightful desserts. The congenial but reserved Joëlle Cotar greets diners. Another toque.

A la carte: 250-280F. Menus: 160F, 250F, 350F.

Belcastel

12390 Rignac - (Aveyron)
Paris 625 - Rodez 27 - Rignac 11 - Decazeville 27

(13) Le Vieux Pont

65.64.52.29

Mlle. Fagegaltier. Open until 9 p.m. Closed Sun. dinner (except July-Aug.), Mon. (off-seas.), Jan. 2-4 & Sept. 8-15. No pets. Cards: V, MC.

Along the banks of the Aveyron and facing an imposing château, Le Vieux Pont has a rustic atmosphere. The biggest surprise is the self-taught, 24-year-old chef, Nicole Fagegaltier, who is shy when it comes to customer relations (her sister handles that) but audacious in her culinary creations. For evidence of her skill, try her delicious walnut-Roquefort tart, her green-vegetable gâteau wrapped in cabbage with a leek sauce, her warm Scottish salmon in beurre d'oie and chou vert or her leg of lamb in a sauce of black olives and blette (strawberry spinach). Super prices.

A la carte: 220F. Menus: 75F, 120F, 180F.

Belfort

90000 Belfort - (Territoire-de-Belfort)
Paris 424 - Epinal 108 - Colmar 70 - Besançon 90

Sights. The fort (dating from Vauban); the Lion of Bartholdi (symbol of the 1870 resistance, 35 feet tall); the citadel (dominating the city, includes Musée d'Art et d'Histoire, with works from prehistoric times to the nineteenth century); the Saint-Christophe church (in red sandstone).

Eating on the Run. Marchal in Valdoie (excellent grill); L'Oasis, old town (fine couscous, congenial).

(15) Hostellerie du Château Servin

9, rue du Général-Négrier - 84.21.41.85

Mme. Servin. Open until 9:15 p.m. Closed Fri. & Aug. Air cond. Terrace dining. Pets allowed. Parking. Cards: V, AE, DC.

This opulent fin-de-siècle residence along the delightful Savoureuse river is a fine setting for the gastronomical creations of Dominique Mathy. The decor is luxurious though a bit heavy, with blue and gold velvet, lace tablecloths, real silver and fine china (the Louis XVI chairs could use a coat of paint). Mme. Servin is the perfect lady of the manor for her customers, many of whom cross the Rhine and park their Mercedeses in the elegant rose garden. Dining here could be merely a ruinous exercise in nostalgia, but professionalism reigns in both the refined service and the technically perfect cuisine based on classic opulence but with personality (and high prices): veal filet with bacon and truffles, warm salad with the catch of the day, foie gras, crayfish, grilled Breton lobster and duck à la rouennaise. Large wine cellar.

A la carte: 500F. Menus: 180F, 230F, 300F, 370F.

Hostellerie du Château Servin

(See restaurant above)

Closed Fri. & Aug. 1 ste 350F. 9 rms 280-350F.

A diverse style of decor is found in this "château," which is really more like a bourgeois manor. Pleasant garden.

(13) Le Pot au Feu

27 bis, Grande-Rue - 84.28.57.84

M. Guyotjeannin. Open until 10 p.m. Closed Sun., Mon., Jan. 1-8 & July 25-Aug. 20. Pets allowed. Cards: V, MC.

The rating slipped a point in our last French-language edition, but Le Pot au Feu has earned its toque back with a number of improvements. A sober but attractively decorated cellar, this cheerful bistro has become one of the best spots in town, offering excellent products (especially the meats) made into simple, light dishes. The menu is attractive, featuring fresh daily specials listed on a blackboard: salad of coquilles St-Jacques delicately pan-fried and accompanied by a fine ratatouille, home-style pot-au-feu that is worth a toque itself. Desserts are a bit plain, but the wine list is making progress.

A la carte: 250F. Menus: 80F and 140F (weekday lunch only), 240F.

IN NEARBY **Offemont**
(6 km NE on N 83 & D 46)
90000 Belfort - (Territoire-de-Belfort)

(14) Le Sabot d'Annie

5, rue A.-Briand, 90300 Valdoie
84.26.01.71

MM. Barbier. Open until 9 p.m. Closed Sat. lunch, Sun., Feb. school vacation & last week of July-mid-Aug. Pets allowed. Parking. Cards: V, AE.

This small house with little character sits in a colorless suburb of Belfort. The decor isn't the wildest, either, but it is comfortable and boasts fresh flowers and discreet good taste. Owner/chef Gérard Barbier is so shy he runs when he sees a customer. But in the kitchen he has an impressive command over the excellent smoked Norwegian salmon, the ramekin (soufflé) of scrambled eggs highlighted with duck liver, the noisettes of lamb (not original but perfectly cooked and garnished with assorted vegetables) and the tasty chocolate cake. Barbier has earned another point with this edition, due to fine execution rather than originality. Unfortunately, the prices are less easy to swallow than the good food—the Barbiers should perhaps change the name from the Sabot to the Silver Slipper. Service is good.

A la carte: 300-350F. Menus: 140F and 200F (weekdays only), 280F (dinner only).

Belle-Ile-en-Mer

56360 Le Palais - (Morbihan)
Quiberon ferry - 97.31.80.01

Le Cardinal

Sauzon - 97.31.61.60, 97.31.83.95

Closed Oct. 1-early April. 85 rms 140-430F. Half-board 260- 360F oblig. in seas. Parking. Telex 730750. Cards: V, AE, DC, MC.

A quite modern hotel amid the heather and evergreens with the sea all around. Small but attractive rooms. Restaurant.

Castel Clara

Port Goulphar - 97.31.84.21

M. Goumy. Open until 9:30 p.m. Closed mid-Oct.-mid-March. Garden dining. No pets. Parking. Telex 730750. Cards: V.

The pool, rooms with private balconies and lovely dining room in this luxurious, white, modern house all overlook a magnificent scenery of wind-swept coast, sky and ocean. What a pity, therefore, that the chef fails to give proper respect to the beauty and freshness of the ocean's ingredients in his cooking. The confusing dish of hot oysters in Champagne with stewed zucchini and leeks, the filet of turbot wrapped in cabbage leaves with overly rich foie gras, and the complicated sole soufflé with salmon mousse are barely worth the toque. We're going to knock this place down a point, despite the excellent apple tart and the good Loire wines.

A la carte: 300F. Menus: 130F (lunch only), 215F (Sunday lunch only), 255F (dinner only), 195F.

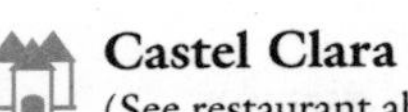

Castel Clara

(See restaurant above)

Closed mid-Oct.-mid-March. 11 stes 850-1,320F. 32 rms 590-790F. Half-board 460-625F. TV. Heated pool. Tennis.

These beautiful, spacious rooms have terraces facing the sea. A heated pool and tennis courts also help make Castel Clara one of the island's most pleasant spots. Relais et Châteaux.

La Forge

Rte. de Goulphar - 97.31.51.76

Mme. Mulon. Open until 9:30 p.m. Closed Nov. 11-April 1. Garden dining. Heated pool. Pets allowed. Parking. Cards: V, AE, MC.

The best of its type on the island, with a fresh, generous, unpretentious cuisine. There's no lack of imagination in the kitchen: crab in a tomato coulis, mussels with croutons, roast langoustine and turbot with cider butter. Inviting decor and good Anjou wines. Excellent fixed-price menu.

A la carte: 230-250F. Menu: 92F.

Grand Large

Port Goulphar - 97.31.80.92

Closed Nov. 12-March 15. 2 stes. 19 rms 190-280F. Half-board 240-310F oblig. in seas. TV. Pets allowed. Parking. Cards: V.

This well-maintained small hotel is perched on a cliff and therefore offers a superb view. Restaurant.

Manoir de Goulphar

Port Goulphar

97.31.83.95, 97.31.80.10

Closed Nov. 9-March 15. 52 rms 235-430F. Half-board 380-400F oblig. in seas. Parking. Telex 730750. Cards: V.

Overlooking a charming estuary, this large manor house has comfortable rooms, some with balconies facing the sea. Brasserie and restaurant.

Belle-Isle-en-Terre

22810 Belle-Isle-en-Terre - (Côtes-du-Nord)
Paris 503 - St-Brieuc 51 - Morlaix 36 - Lannion 28

Le Relais de l'Argoat

96.43.00.34

M. Marais. Open until 9 p.m. Closed Mon. & Feb. Pets allowed. Hotel: 10 rms 135-165F; half-board 190-210F. Parking. Cards: V, MC.

In this cute cottage in a lovely provincial village, you can expect an excellent reception from Pierre Marais, who likes fresh products and is generous with them. His stunningly lavish fixed-price menus include foie gras, lobster, squab, a delicious terrine of lisettes (small mackerel) in a tomato coulis, quail fricassée with morels and langoustines, cheeses and a fine dessert. All this earns Marais an honest toque. Pleasant wines and magnificent game in season.

A la carte: 150-180F. Menus: 65F, 110F, 140F, 190F.

Belleville

54940 Belleville - (Meurthe-et-Moselle)
Paris 313 - Metz 39 - Toul 28 - Nancy 19

Le Bistroquet

97, rte. Nationale - 83.24.90.12

M. Ponsard. Open until 10:30 p.m. Closed Sat. lunch, Sun. dinner, Mon., Jan. 2-Feb. 10 & July 15-Aug. 10. Pets allowed. Garage parking. Cards: V, AE, DC, MC.

The culinary traditions of the Lorraine don't appeal to chef Marie-France Ponsard—not even the region's marvelous hot mirabelle soufflé. So it's made by her husband, Jean, whose 1900s-style mustache matches the Belle Epoque decor (gramophone, lace tablecloths, posters). She, on the other hand, has mastered a style of light, well-prepared, modern cuisine: such classics as thick bass filet cooked to perfection in a delicate beurre blanc, delicious veal kidneys in wine and Bresse pigeon casserole. A good addition is the low-priced fixed menu that includes a house apéritif, Scottish salmon with a watercress cream sauce, aiguillettes of duck with grapes, splendid cheeses and a fruit gratin with vanilla ice cream. Top wines go for steep prices.

A la carte: 300-400F. Menus: 170F, 300F, 370F.

Belleville-sur-Saône

69220 Belleville-sur-Saône - (Rhône)
Paris 427 - Lyon 46 - Bourg-en-Bresse 39 - Mâcon 23

Le Donjon

St-Jean-d'Ardières - 74.66.51.41

M. Lobjoie. Open until 9:30 p.m. Closed Sun. dinner (Jan.-Feb.). Garden dining. Pets allowed. Parking. Telex 305772. Cards: V, AE, DC.

This delightfully restored castle is set in a lovely park designed by Le Nôtre with superb boxwoods. The dining room has been completely refurbished, retaining only the cuisine of Guy Santoro. He displays a level of skill, confidence and personality that is a pleasant surprise, mixing country with modern: sweetbreads terrine with

morels, sander poached in Morgon, roast spiced squab, delicate desserts. The wine list features an exceptional Côte-du-Py Beaujolais Morgon.
A la carte: 300F. Menus: 160F (weekday lunch only, wine incl.), 360F (wine incl.), 160F to 280F.

Château de Pizay
(See restaurant above)

Open year-round. 2 stes. 48 rms 400-460F. Half-board 370F. TV. Air cond. Pool. Tennis.

Beautiful large rooms, well equipped, overlooking the park and pool. Excellent facilities for conferences.

Bellevue
see Nantes

Bénodet
29118 Bénodet - (Finistère)
Paris 556 - Brest 88 - Concarneau 22 - Quimper 16

Kastel-Moor et Ker-Moor
Ave. de la Plage
98.57.04.48, 98.57.05.01

Closed Oct. 1-Easter (except for groups). 60 rms 300-400F. Half-board 370-410F oblig. in seas. TV. Heated pool. Tennis. Garage parking. Telex 941182. Cards: V, MC.

These twin hotels with plain decors lack a bit of imagination in the rooms. On the other hand, you can linger at the beach, the five tennis courts, the new squash club or the huge pool. Restaurant.

IN NEARBY **Saint-Marine**
(5 km W on D 44)
29120 Pont-l'Abbé - (Finistère)

Le Jeanne d'Arc
52, rue de la Plage - 98.56.32.70

M. Fargette. Open until 9 p.m. Closed Mon. dinner (except July-Aug.), Tues. & Sept. 30-March 25. Pets allowed. Hotel: 9 rms 120-155F; half-board 190-210F oblig. in seas. Parking. Cards: V.

René Fargette, a charming, ultra-classic cook, brought along some of the soul of Burgundy when he arrived at this attractive house close to the beach some 25 years ago. He also brought an imagination that is open to novelty, which has made for some unexpected and savory marriages of Bresse and Breton cuisine. Hence a Bresse-style lobster with vegetables (or in civet with Moulin-à-Vent), a Breton-style bouilleture (a matelote wine stew). The à la carte menu is full of originals, too, such as tiny cabbages stuffed with langoustines in a star-anis fumete, Burgundy escargots en croûte with Pinot Noir and noisettes of duck with cherry vinegar and green-pepper sauce. Remarkable pastries and a welcome low-priced fixed menu—but the à la carte prices are sheer folly.
A la carte: 350F. Menus: 140F, 210F, 340F.

Bénouville
see Caen

Bergerac
24100 Bergerac - (Dordogne)
Paris 522 - Angoulême 109 - Bordeaux 92 - Périgueux 47

Château-Hôtel Mounet-Sully
2 km N on D 709 - 53.57.04.21

Closed Nov. 1-April 30. 8 rms 170-350F. Parking. Cards: V, AE, DC.

This curious neofeudal castle in a park is located not far from central Bergerac. Its pleasant rooms are spacious and well equipped. No restaurant.

Le Cyrano
2, blvd. Montaigne - 53.57.02.76

M. Turon. Open until 9 p.m. Closed Sun. dinner (except July-Aug.), Mon., June 26-July 10 & March 9-20. No pets. Hotel: 11 rms 220-240F. Garage parking. Cards: V, AE, DC.

Jean-Paul Turon's fixed-price menus take you from the simplest (rillettes, pork chops grilled over an open fire and dessert) to the grandest (warm duck liver, fricassée of lotte in a pepper sauce, lamb cutlets grilled with tarragon, cheeses and desserts). He has earned his reputation as a quasi-regional chef with a liberal and skillfully prepared cuisine. He has also succeeded in brightening up this Bergerac house with a delightful decor. A la carte, you can order langoustines in wine and ginger, old-fashioned duck confit and a bavarois of creamed prunes in Armagnac. Delicious homemade bread. Gracious service.
A la carte: 250-300F. Menus: 100F, 160F, 220F.

IN NEARBY **Saint-Julien-de-Crempse**
(12 km N on D 107)
24140 Villamblard - (Dordogne)

12/20 Manoir Le Grand Vignoble
53.24.23.18

M. de Labrusse. Open until 9:30 p.m. Closed Dec. 24-Jan. 24. Garden dining. No pets. Parking. Telex 541629. Cards: V, AE, DC.

A magnificent 150-acre estate with buffalo and zebra roaming, this "manoir" is popular with sporting types who enjoy the pool, horseback riding and tennis. The dining room is in a charming old cottage, and the cuisine is making progress: a casserole of eggs and truffle cream, brill with braised vegetables.
A la carte: 250F. Menus: 125F, 175F.

Manoir Le Grand Vignoble
(See restaurant above)

Open year-round. 1 ste 425-475F. 30 rms 295-475F. Half-board 340-395F oblig. in seas. TV. Pets allowed. Heated pool. Tennis.

This aristocratic old building features some splendid rooms (soberly decorated), a long terrace on the park and a magnificent oak-paneled salon.

Berry-au-Bac

02190 Guignicourt - (Aisne)
Paris 149 - Laon 29 - Reims 19 - Soissons 47 - Rethel 44

(14) La Cote 108

N 44 - 23.79.95.04

M. Courville. Open until 9:30 p.m. Closed Sun. dinner, Mon. & Dec. 23-Jan. 28. Air cond. Pets allowed. Parking. Cards: V, AE.

Serge Courville is a chef with character, although his character is sometimes stormy. This gives some spunk and personality to his cooking, which is inventive and extremely light. It's hard to resist his blanc de Bresse (poultry breasts, sliced thin) in a lightly creamy gravy and pleurotes; his stuffed Reims-style pigs' trotters, in sausages with apples sautéed in their skins; or his John Dory grilled perfectly with fresh tomatoes. The Champagne-region wines are magnificent, but nearly as good are the Bordeaux and Burgundies. Geneviève is a most attentive mistress of the house. Pleasant view of the flower garden.

A la carte: 400F. Menus: 195F (wine only) and 140F (weekdays only), 250F, 365F.

Besançon

25000 Besançon - (Doubs)
Paris 390 - Nancy 199 - Belfort 90 - Dijon 91

Sights. The citadel and its ramparts (including the fascinating Musée Populaire Comtois); Musée des Beaux-Arts; Palais Granvelle (and the mansions along the main street); the astronomical clock; Sainte-Madeleine church (and its bell tower); botanical gardens (ave. de la Paix).

Eating on the Run. L'Annexe des Aviateurs, 11, rue du Palais-de-Justice (fashionable); Les Balladins, 9, rue Bertrand-Russell (simple, well-prepared food); La Caféteria du Casino, 52, rue de Belfort; Au Gourmand, 5, rue Mégevand (family cuisine); Le Grill du Saint-Pierre (good Franche-Comté cuisine).

Brasseries. Le Commerce, 31, rue des Granges (well-restored 1900 decor, reasonable prices); Granvelle, pl. Granvelle (one of the oldest in town, known for its shaded terrace and neorococo decor, prices moving up).

Bars & Cafés. La Bagatelle, 8, rue de Pontarlier (retro and quiet); Bar du Jura, 18, pl. Marulaz (lively, pleasant terrace); Bar 421, 109, rue de Belfort (saloon atmosphere); Le Coutsy, 21, rue de Dole (a favorite of the young crowd); Le Grand Vatel, 14, pl. du 8-Septembre (large café with terrace, fast service at lunch); Moto-Racing Bar, 18, rue Ch.-Krug (for car-racing fans); Le Select Bar, 90, rue des Granges (American bar); Le Starman, 3, rue Jean-Petit (gay bar, cocktails); Au Tonneau du Jura, 20, rue Ch.-Nodier (beer).

Nightlife. Excalibur and La Paloma, 2, ave. E.-Droz (disco bar and traditional bar, respectively); Le Privé, 1, rue A.-Janvier (very gay); Sypssi Club, pl. Granvelle (slightly old-fashioned, very bourgeois, piano bar); Les Tonnelles, rte. de Lyon in Mazagran (genuine tavern, good weekend ambience).

Altea

See Le Vesontio restaurant.

(15) Le Chaland

Pont Brégille, promenade Micaud 81.80.61.61

M. Bertin. Open until 10 p.m. Closed Aug. 1-15. Pets allowed. Parking. Cards: V, MC.

Inside a gorgeous houseboat moored on the lush banks of the Doubs in the heart of town is a comfortable setting and an ambitious cuisine (you can tell by the prices). At this family restaurant, young chef Bruno Bertin seems to think he has been appointed best rôtisseur in the world, while his brother was crowned top apprentice pastry chef in France. We don't know about that, but we will say that this attractive barge is one of the few restaurants in France to present a bread list (a dozen) for every taste and circumstance. And we'll add that the cuisine is getting better and better, particularly the escargots in anise-seasoned puff pastry, escalope of bass with oysters, turbot in young wine with morels, millefeuille of young rabbit and wild mushrooms and the excellent, generous desserts.

A la carte: 500F. Menus: 180F (lunch only), 265F (weekdays only), 320F.

Hôtel Epicure

159, rue de Dole - 81.52.04.00

Open year-round. 60 rms 285-340F. Half-board 320F. TV. Heated pool. Parking. Telex 360167. Cards: V, AE, DC, MC.

The former Hôtel Mercure has bright, well-equipped rooms and an inviting little pool. Restaurant.

Foch

7 bis, ave. Foch - 81.80.30.41

Open year-round. 28 rms 150-200F. TV in 2 rms. Cards: V, AE, DC, MC.

A pleasant view of the town can be had from this nice little modern hotel with rooms facing the train station. No restaurant.

(13) Le Poker d'As

14, square St-Amour - 81.81.42.49

M. Ferreux. Open until 9:30 p.m. Closed Sun. dinner, Mon., Dec. 25-Jan. 2 & July 9-31. Pets allowed. Cards: V, AE, DC.

The decor is a hodgepodge of a thousand things in a completely wacky Franche-Comté farm style. It's eccentric, entertaining and leads one to believe the cuisine will be at least original, with some exotic points and some baroque marriages. It is the creation of Raymond Ferreux, a self-taught, freewheeling and affable chef, who features a good salad of sweetbreads and langoustines, feuilleté (a bit overcooked) with bass (delicious and well cooked), veal mignon rosé with a classic foie gras sauce, and a lamb filet with crunchy cabbage in a minty sauce. Good Jura wines.

A la carte: 280F. Menus: 75F, 95F, 120F, 160F.

(14) Le Vesontio

3, ave. Edouard-Droz - 81.80.14.44

M. Navarre. Open daily until 10 p.m. Air cond. Pets allowed. Garage parking. Telex 360268. Cards: V, AE, DC, MC.

An immense bay window over the casino gardens filters a lovely light in the charming purple decor of the dining room. The angle of mirrors lends a glass-palace atmosphere that's comfortable and peaceful. There is also consistent efficiency and intelligence in the kitchen, as well as attention to detail (witness the delicious bread). Service remains a bit rough and slow, and the repertoire of classic (and some regional) dishes could use some updating. Taste the assorted fish with fresh olive oil (the salad of raw coquilles St-Jacques was too lemony), the feuilleté of sweetbreads with a sauce that's just creamy enough and the chateaubriand béarnaise with seasonal vegetables. There is also a well-devised light fixed-price menu for dieters (the "beauty" menu). Eclectic wine cellar.

A la carte: 280-300F. Menus: 90F, 126F, 153F.

Altea Parc Micaud

(See restaurant above)

Open year-round. 95 rms 300-400F. TV. Pets allowed.

Well-placed along the green banks of the Doubs river, the Altea is a well-managed, excellent hotel. Rooms have pleasant views, and the staff is perfectly trained. Fine breakfast and TV trays for dining in your room.

Besse-en-Chandesse

63610 Besse-en-Chandesse - (Puy-de-Dôme)
Paris 437 - Le Mont-Dore 31 - Issoire 35

15 Les Mouflons

Rte. de Super-Besse - 73.79.51.31

M. Sachapt. Open until 8:30 p.m. Closed Sept. 25-May 31. No pets. Parking. Cards: V, AE.

One day, we hope Antoine Sachapt will drag himself away from his mushrooms, herbs, pond trout and fine cheeses to add a bit of spice to the decor. The dining room is large, as it well must be, given the innumerable admirers of his excellent cuisine, which is rooted in the region but nonetheless light and personal: poultry terrine with sweetbreads, feuilleté of frogs and escargots, veal escalopes with fresh pasta and chanterelles, and délice of pears with strawberries. The delightful staff pays attention to detail.

A la carte: 250F. Menus: 100F (weekdays only), 150F (weekend and holiday lunch only), 205F, 250F.

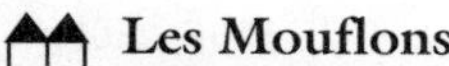

Les Mouflons

(See restaurant above)

Closed Sept. 25-May 31. 50 rms 270-340F. Half-board 300-420F. Pets allowed.

Facing the lovely village of Besse and the mountains, Les Mouflons has comfortable, pleasant rooms that were recently refurbished.

This symbol signifies hotels that offer an exceptional degree of peace and quiet.

Beuvron-en-Auge

14430 Dozulé - (Calvados)
Paris 224 - Caen 30 - Lisieux 28 - Cabourg 15

16 Le Pavé d'Auge

Pl. du Village - 31.79.26.71

MM. Engel. Open until 9 p.m. Closed Mon. dinner, Tues. & Jan. 23-Feb. 23. Terrace dining. Pets allowed. Cards: V, DC.

Despite her Alsatian roots, Odile Engel has become the best chef in Normandy. She has explored the region for its best—fish, poultry and rich dairy products—intelligently drawing the finest from country traditions without the heaviness. Her cuisine is solid, honest and earthy, balancing generosity and delicacy, tradition and creativity: mussel soup with cider, large sole cooked with the bone, mussels and andouillette, farm-raised chicken, duck with apples, incredible cheeses and tarte tatin. Her tasty, unpretentious cooking will win your heart and stomach. Prices are quite reasonable, unless you linger with some of the grand, age-old Calvados. Fine wines from everywhere.

A la carte: 200-350F. Menus: 125F, 200F, 250F.

Beuzeville

27210 Beuzeville - (Eure)
Paris 185 - Deauville 24 - Pont-l'Evêque 14

12/20 Le Cochon d'Or

Le Petit Castel,
pl. du Général-de-Gaulle - 32.57.70.46

M. Folleau. Open until 9 p.m. Closed Mon. & Dec. 15-Jan. 15. No pets. Hotel: 23 rms 110-280F; half-board 160-230F. Cards: V, MC.

A stone's throw from the highway, on the road to the Normandy beaches, lies this charming inn, which takes its customers seriously. The owner is a chef from the old school who can prepare everything: langoustines with a lettuce cream, Norman-style filet of sole, sweetbreads with tarragon and tournedos Rossini. Nice local wines.

A la carte: 230-250F. Menus: 65F (weekdays only), 90F, 140F, 190F.

Les Bézards

45290 Nogent-sur-Vernisson - (Loiret)
Paris 136 - Auxerre 76 - Orléans 69 - Gien 16

18 Auberge des Templiers

N 7
38.31.80.01

M. Depée. Open until 9:30 p.m. Closed Jan. 15-Feb. 15. Terrace dining. Pets allowed. Garage parking. Telex 780998. Cards: V, AE, DC, MC.

"The eternal mystery of des Templiers is that in these kitchens a new face appears every four or five years, which is enough to make you fear the worst. But on the contrary, the well-oiled machine continues to function as if nothing had happened." These words, which appeared in our last French-language guide, turned out to be a kind of premonition—except the machine turned faster than we expected. Yvan Levaslot has, in fact, just recently replaced Grégoire Sein, who had been preceded in turn by Christian Willier, Jean-Claude Rigollet and Jean-Charles Barrier. The new "master" of Auberge des Templiers is 33 years old and comes from Raymond Thuilier's L'Oustau de Baumanière, where he was second chef. Like the others, he has slipped quietly into his predecessor's shoes, and it would take an extremely clever customer to discern the difference.

In any case, this is hardly the kind of restaurant where the chef makes the rounds to collect compliments. The dining room is the territory of owner Philippe Depée, who has his strategy down pat. The restaurant has its own repertoire and a proven team, and when a new chef arrives, he merely blends into the scenery. After a while the new chef tests out his own dishes, and the best of them are added to the proven others—provided they receive the blessing of the cautious Depée. Resistant to revolutions of any kind, he is satisfied with his system. And how can we reproach him, since it's a system that works so beautifully? Obviously, neither creativity nor idiosyncrasy finds encouragement here, but then Depée is spared the possible moods of his chefs, and the cooking makes up in regularity what it loses in fantasy. And besides, we see all too often owners held hostage by their chefs and living in fear of losing them.

Thus, with complete confidence, you can return to this old relais, luxuriously disguised as a hunting pavilion, and take a table on the terrace bordered in flowers or in the ravishing dining hall. The terrine de canard à l'ancienne, salad of young rabbit in a mustard sauce with hazelnuts, cabbage soup with smoked pigeon, medallions of freshwater pike in Germiny wine, lobster in an herbed sauce with Sancerre, steamed Loire salmon à la berrichonne (braised cabbage, chestnuts, baby onions and bacon), young rabbit cooked slowly and lovingly with a marvelous foie confit with shallots, veal kidney wrapped in bacon, Challans duck for two, wild game in season—all are dishes that will make you want to linger at the table, longing for the pleasure to last just a little longer.

Above all, don't forget to order the crunchy vanilla-bean millefeuille at the beginning of your meal: It's one of the best desserts we've had in some time. And to make your feast complete, you will find sommelier Jean-Paul Martin a charming and knowledgeable guide who will lead you to discover the best wines from all of the vineyards of France, always with a prolonged stopover in Burgundy and the Loire valley, where you'll share his favorites.

A la carte: 400-700F. Menus: 250F (weekday lunch only), 320F, 480F.

Auberge des Templiers

(See restaurant above)

Closed Jan. 15-Feb. 15. 8 stes 1,100-2,800F. 22 rms 480-1,100F. Half-board 625-935F. TV. Heated pool. Tennis.

The beautiful and enchanting Françoise Depée welcomes you to her gorgeous home. She and her husband are always adding touches to make it even more delightful. Scattered among the gardens around the pool are the lovely buildings that house the elegant, comfortable suites in which you wake up to a sumptuous breakfast. The regular rooms were created with an equal concern for perfection. You can enjoy tennis in the gardens or golf and horseback riding in the surrounding area. You can even join the hunt in the forests of Orléans, on horseback or in a carriage. Relais et Châteaux.

Château des Bézards 

N 7 - 38.31.80.03

Open year-round. 4 stes 700F. 36 rms 250-450F. Half-board 430-820F. Heated pool. Tennis. Parking. Telex 780335. Cards: V, AE, DC, MC.

This large millstone house just off route Nationale 7 is well equipped for serious meetings. Several of the rooms are delightful; others need sprucing up. Restaurant.

Béziers

34500 Béziers - (Hérault)
Paris 839 - Montpellier 72 - Narbonne 27 - Perpignan 93

L'Ambassade

22, blvd. de Verdun - 67.76.06.24

Closed Sun. & Mon. 14 rms 90-220F. Half-board 257-325F oblig. in seas. Pets allowed. Cards: V, AE, DC.

A large private residence undergoing renovation. A gilded decor is found in some of the elegant, well-furnished rooms (the bathrooms are less cheerful). Restaurant.

(14) Le Framboiser

33, ave. du Président-Wilson
67.62.62.57

M. Yagues. Open until 9:30 p.m. Closed Sun., Mon., Feb. 12-28 & Aug. 16-31. Air cond. Pets allowed. Cards: V, AE, DC.

All of Béziers remembers the success of young Angel Yagues when he was supervising the kitchens at Olivier; that's why the town's gourmets crowd this small, delightful restaurant where he just moved. Reputed for his inspired sauces and perpetual creativity, Yagues has now applied himself to creating a simple, fresh and sensible cuisine at equally sensible prices: excellent foie gras, fish salad (smoked a bit too much), delicate warm oysters poached with sorrel, amusing lotte with squid, perfect veal kidneys with mustard and desserts that are plain but good. In all, it's a fine, generous cuisine that rings true and has found its stride. Agreeable regional wines, a sprightly young staff and a small, modern dining room. Another point.

A la carte: 250F. Menus: 95F, 170F, 250F.

(13) Le Jardin

37, ave. Jean-Moulin - 67.36.41.31

M. Santuré. Open until 10 p.m. Closed Sun. dinner, Mon., Feb. 12-27 & June 25-July 10. Cards: V, AE, DC.

The Santuré brothers manage their small restaurant with a great deal of efficiency. They replaced the artificial flowers in the garden-style decor with fresh ones, which did wonders for the ambience. Francis is an affable and eager host, while Jean-Luc produces a light, imaginative cuisine. Good ideas come out of the kitchen, and they should only get better with time: Bouzigues mussels lightly cooked with cod liver, lobster

navarin with a fine mild paprika sauce, salmon plate with a small gratin, and sorbets bursting with freshness. Good fixed-price menus.
A la carte: 230-250F. Menus: 95F, 135F, 230F.

Biarritz

64200 Biarritz - (Pyrénées-Atlantiques)
Paris 747 - Bordeaux 183 - Pau 115 - Dax 57 - Bayonne 8

Sights. The Basque coast (and its acrobatic surfers); Le Rocher de la Vierge (magnificent view); the old port and fisherman's port; pl. Clemenceau (lively center); L'Hôtel du Palais (villa of the empress Eugénie, today a famous attraction); Musée de la Mer (aquarium with fish from Biscay bay); the lighthouse (view as far as Spain); beach of the Chambre d'Amour ("Lovers' Room") and forest of Chiberta in Anglet; golf courses in Biarritz and Chiberta.

Eating on the Run. Côte Ouest, 1, ave. de l'Impératrice; Le Jam's, 2, pl. Bellevue; La Pizzéria, arceaux Lacombe.

Brasseries. Les Collonnes, 4, ave. Edouard-VII; La Coupole, 22, pl. Clemenceau; Le Radio-Bar, 4, ave. de la Marne (open late).

Bars & Cafés. L'Alambic, pl. Bellevue; Bar de l'Hôtel Miramar, 11, ave. de l'Impératrice (très chic); Les Colonnes, 4, ave. Edouard-VII; La Coupole, 22, pl. Clemenceau; La Désirade, 7, pl. Bellevue; Le Mannekenpis, 11, rue Gardère (marvelous beer and Belgian fries); Le Royalty, 11, pl. Clemenceau (meeting place for the elite in summer).

Nightlife. Le Baobab, Bellevue casino (discotheque for young set); La Canasta, 2, rue Gardère (very young crowd); Le Carlos, 1, blvd. Prince-de-Galles (live jazz); Le Caveau, 4, rue Gambetta (one room for gents, another for ladies); La Plantation, Bellevue casino (piano bar, live bands, singers); Le Port-Vieux, pl. du Port-Vieux (old tunes).

Shops. *Bakeries:* Guillou, 6, rue des Halles (old-fashioned bread); Lascaray, 16, ave. de Verdun (leavened breads cooked over wood fires). *Chocolate, pastries:* Daranatz, 12, ave. Maréchal-Foch; Dodin, 7, rue Gambetta; Henriet, pl. Clemenceau; Pariès, 27, pl. Clemenceau. *Gourmet food, cheese:* Arostéguy, 5, rue Victor-Hugo (from all over the world); Crémerie Saint-Charles, 17, rue Bergerie (magnificent cheeses, excellent smoked salmon); La Ferme Saint-Pierre, 14, ave. de Verdun (one of the best sugar refiners in the region); Les Mille et Un Fromages, 8, rue Victor-Hugo. *Old-style hams:* Baradat and Chassin in Anglet.

16 Café de Paris

5, pl. Bellevue - 59.24.19.53

M. Laporte. Open until 10 p.m. Closed Mon. (off-seas.) & Nov. 1-March 25. Terrace dining. Pets allowed. Cards: V, AE, DC.

Gone are the days when this was the only grand restaurant in Biarritz and even in the Basque country. In today's new gastronomical ball game, Pierre Laporte's famous dining spot—while still resplendent—is not what it once was. But, fortunately, the decor of the quasi-Belle Epoque dining room, where the elite from Biarritz and Spain strutted some twenty years ago, was recently refurbished. The colors are lighter and the furniture less massive, and there's once again a little zing in the atmosphere. As for the cuisine, one must compare it to that of its up-and-coming neighbors, and it would be unreasonable to give Café de Paris a better rating, unless we yielded to inflationary pressures. It's not that anything is bad here, it's just that we keep hoping the cuisine will find some new life. It is well prepared and has some fine moments, as the habitués know, including the mélange of langoustines, lobster and caviar; the sole stuffed with mushrooms; the loubine (bass) in watercress sauce; the squab with stuffed cabbage; the braised kidneys with cèpes and lentils; and the calf's head in a creamy gribiche sauce (to which the added lobster adds nothing special). It's all good, though not exceptional—just the same old thing. At the end of the meal come tasty, classic desserts, like the Saint-Honoré cake, warm cherries in a sherry sabayon sauce and fine bitter-chocolate cake. The wine cellar is still magnificent, filled with sumptuous Bordeaux, even the most famed of which are reasonably priced.
A la carte: 500-600F. Menu: 220F.

Carlina

Blvd. Prince-de-Galles - 59.23.03.86

M. Bégué. Open until 11 p.m. Closed Oct. 10-May 20. Terrace dining. Pets allowed. Hotel: 1 ste 900F. 30 rms 450-700F. Parking. Telex 550873. Cards: V, AE, DC, MC.

A young team with lots of spirit is working in this sunny beachfront spot on the Basque coast. Young chef Emmanuel Fonteyne prepares a light, modern cuisine based on masterful seafood cooking: Atlantic salmon grilled with its skin (served with a delicious fondue of zucchini and onions), baked sea bream with a fine lemon and white-wine sauce, turbot steamed with algae, and classic desserts perfectly prepared, such as chocolate fondant and wild strawberry tart. Wonderful terrace overlooking the ocean.
A la carte: 200F. Menu: 70F.

Château du Clair de Lune

Rte. d'Arbonne - 59.23.45.96

Open year-round. 1 ste 600-700F. 9 rms 290-500F. TV. Parking. Cards: V, AE, DC.

This quaint turn-of-the-century manor house is located in a large, splendid park. The spacious, quiet rooms are decorated with taste. Remarkable old-fashioned service. Good breakfast. No restaurant.

Le Galion

17, blvd. du Général-de-Gaulle
59.24.20.32

M. Barbé. Open daily until 11 p.m. Air cond. Pets allowed. Cards: V.

Michel Barbé recently left his tiny restaurant near the Bayonne train depot and set himself up in this large rustic-yet-modern building. The bay windows provide a view of surfers riding the waves (a small terrace is open in good weather). The cuisine, prepared by 24-year-old Monique Lissar, continues to improve. We haven't heard the last of her tasty crab terrine in a powerful "Eminence" sauce, medallions of lotte in a warm vinaigrette served with a perfectly seasoned salad, red mullet braised in a coulis of peppers (a wonderful dish well presented in a light red-pepper sauce), turbot filet soufflé with crayfish (a bit confused) and fine glazed nougat with a warm chocolate sauce. The wine cellar could be rounded out. Excellent prices.

A la carte: 200-250F.

16

Le Grand Siècle

1, ave. de l'Impératrice - 59.24.09.40

M. Mollin. Open until 10:30 p.m. Closed Nov. 15-April 15. Air cond. Terrace dining. No pets. Parking. Telex 570000. Cards: V, AE, DC, MC.

The big news in Biarritz these days is the revival of Le Palais, now called Le Grand Siècle, whose kitchens have been turned over to the highly respected Gérard Sein. The hotel (owned by the city) has renovated salons and a sumptuous mirror-paneled dining room with a rotunda facing the ocean. The superb menu still has an old "Palais" air but has been remarkably invigorated by the chef's imagination and light touch. Witness the fenouillette of opernes (a type of barnacle) with shellfish; salad of cold oysters with caviar; salad of langoustines dressed with thin slices of bacon and piperade (a Basque sauce of peppers, pimientos and tomatoes); duckling served in two courses (first the cold aiguillette en gelée with truffles and small onions, then the warm, crusty thigh with fries and a green salad). And the exquisite desserts, such as strawberries in a spicy red-wine aspic accompanied by an extraordinary soft Basque cake. The exceptional wine list offers an excellent dry Jurançon, and the service is good. Basque specialties are served until late in the evening (to music) at L'Hippocampe, at poolside.

A la carte: 450-600F. Menus: 230F (lunch only), 185F, 220F and 260F (dinner only), 350F.

Le Palais

(See restaurant above)

Closed Nov. 15-April 15. 20 stes 1,750-3,950F. 120 rms 800-950F. Half-board 330F. TV. Pets allowed. Heated pool.

The empress Eugénie's Basque playground is meticulously maintained in the tradition of fine hotels of old. Customers have high social standings and fat wallets, as befits the best hotel in Biarritz. Amenities include two bars, new meeting rooms, a lovely pool, sauna, solarium and ten television stations.

Plaza

Ave. Edouard-VII - 59.24.74.00

Open year-round. 60 rms 228-550F. TV. Pets allowed. Parking. Telex 570048. Cards: V, AE, DC, MC.

The Plaza has roomy accommodations with sunny terraces; all rooms have double windows. The beach and casino are within walking distance. Amiable, efficient staff. Restaurant.

Régina et Golf

(Les Jardins de l'Océan)

52, ave. de l'Impératrice - 59.41.33.00

M. Touati. Open daily until 10:30 p.m. No pets. Parking. Telex 541330. Cards: V, AE, DC.

This crumbling old luxury hotel on the cliffs has just found a new lease on life—an interior designer has turned it into a huge hotel that is at the same time posh, charming and livable. The restaurant received the same treatment and is now a relaxed, elegant and peaceful dining room that sprawls within the immense, roofed-over central court, with a view of the kitchens included. The young chef that the hotel's owners had the imagination to hire prepares a straightforward menu that is technically well done, light and tasty. It's already drawing some of the chic Biarritz crowd, thanks to such dishes as salmon steak on a hot tile, bass cooked perfectly in its coarse-salt-coated skin and a crab salad with tomato and zucchini confits. And the prices—at least for the moment—are very gentle.

A la carte: 200-220F. Menus: 175F, 220F.

Régina et Golf

(See restaurant above)

Closed Nov. 14-March 25. 10 stes 900-1,600F. 60 rms 503-856F. Half-board 668-918F. TV. Pets allowed. Parking. Telex 541330.

All the large rooms facing the ocean have been entirely and attractively renovated, and the bathrooms are truly magnificent. Well situated near the lighthouse, the Régina et Golf is now the second-best hotel in Biarritz (Le Palais gets top billing). Restaurant.

16

Relais Miramar

13, rue L.-Bodet - 59.41.30.00

M. Broch. Open daily until 10 p.m. Air cond. Garden dining. No pets. Parking. Telex 540831. Cards: V, AE, DC, MC.

A comfortable, rather conventional decor is found in this restaurant overlooking the sea and a pool. Still, it's one of the best in Biarritz. Chef André Gauzère has a new assistant, and their collaboration has resulted in good chemistry: marvelous fresh lobster with a fine orange cream sauce, warm smoked salmon, raw coquilles St-Jacques on a bed of apples and endive in an aromatic vinaigrette, and thick yet light-as-air bass in coarse salt cooked in its skin, exquisite chocolate desserts, and strawberry millefeuille with a raspberry-flavored cream. The cuisine is modern, based on excellent products prepared simply in either traditional (hare à la royale—hare in a bacon, vegetable and wine sauce) or regional (poultry, foie gras) styles. And let's not forget the extraordinarily gracious service, a perfect example of American efficiency with French charm. One more point.

A la carte: 400-600F. Menus: 250F, 320F.

Miramar

(See restaurant above)

Open year-round. 17 stes 1,000-1,900F. 109 rms 581-1,287F. Half-board 731-1,331F. TV. Air cond. Pets allowed. Heated pool.

Immense, pleasantly livable rooms, great for relaxing (some suites are right on the ocean), are accompanied by exceptional service worthy of a luxury hotel. It's an almost perfect hotel (though it could be livelier for long stays) that has every comfort; it fills up without trouble all year. Many come for Louison Bobet's marine spa.

Bidart

64210 Bidart - (Pyrénées-Atlantiques)
Paris 755 - St-Jean-de-Luz 9 - Biarritz 6 - Bayonne 12

Bidartéa Mapotel

N 10 - 59.54.94.68

Closed Sun., Mon. & Feb. 34 rms 288-336F. Half-board 320- 350F. TV in 12 rms. Pets allowed. Pool. Garage parking. Telex 570820. Cards: V, AE, DC, MC.

A large Basque-style chalet in the Rhune countryside. Terrace, pool and restaurant.

(15) Les Fréres Ibarboure

Ch. de Talienia - 59.54.81.64

MM. Ibarboure. Open until 9:30 p.m. Closed Wed. (except July, Aug. & Sept.). Air cond. Garden dining. Parking. Cards: V, AE, DC.

Cramped in their old place, the Ibarboure family dreamed for ages of a more spacious setting. Voilà—they're now set up in splendid quarters in an old Basque farm. Bay windows open onto the countryside in these three large, tastefully renovated dining rooms; the tables on the terrrace will put you even closer to the greenery. The Ibarboure brothers' wives see to the fine reception, the service is thoroughly professional, and the brothers' cooking has never been so attentive, precise and delicate: a salad of pan-fried prawns with an ultra-light shellfish vinaigrette, young pigeon cooked whole to order and served boned in its reduced juices with a zucchini-and-wild-mushroom stuffing, and desserts of unparalleled delight (like the grandiose lemon mousse with a citrus coulis). The lovely wine list is no bargain.

A la carte: 300-350F. Menus: 170F, 220F.

L'Hacienda

Rte. d'Ahetze - 59.54.92.82

Closed Mon. (off-seas.) & Jan. 6-Feb. 10. 13 rms 170-230F. Half-board 180-220F.

Two kilometers from the beach, nine rooms and five small bungalows are situated in a peaceful park. Restaurant.

Billiers

56190 Muzillac - (Morbihan)
Paris 458 - Nantes 86 - Redon 37 - Vannes 27 - Muzillac 3

(15) Château de Rochevilaine

Pointe de Pen-Lan - 97.41.69.27

M. Gasnier. Open until 9:30 p.m. Closed Jan. 5-Feb. 20. Garden dining. No pets. Parking. Telex 950570. Cards: V, AE, DC, MC.

More than a château, this large manor house is a landmark in the rocky coast right at sea level. It's surrounded by some dozen small buildings, which make a charming hamlet on the windswept Atlantic coast. Patrick Gasnier fought against the odds to make a name for this place and to attract the demanding summer crowd, avid for beauty, solitude and good fare. To that end, he has turned over the kitchen to well-schooled Patrice Caillault, known for fine seafood prepared with subtlety in such dishes as red mullet filet with a zucchini purée and blancmange of sole in a "coraillée" (lobster roe) sauce. In addition there are sweetbreads and morels in a delicious, light sauce and such excellent desserts as the "plaisir au chocolat," a superb praline-and-cocoa cake. The dining room features eleventh-century beams, precious antique furniture and ornaments.

A la carte: 350-450F. Menus: 240F (weekends and holidays only), 180F, 320F.

Château de Rochevilaine

(See restaurant above)

Closed Jan. 5-Feb. 20. 1 ste 1,350F. 27 rms 380-920F. Half-board 450-720F. TV in 14 rms. Heated pool.

This large Renaissance manor has spacious rooms and antique furniture, with just a touch of ostentation at times. Some rooms (the most charming) overlook the rugged coast, others the lovely flower gardens. Additional rooms are located in bungalows. Saltwater pool. Tennis and riding nearby.

Biot

06140 Biot - (Alpes-Maritimes)
Paris 922 - Antibes 8 - Grasse 18 - Nice 22 - Cagnes 10

(16) Auberge du Jarrier

30, passage de la Bourgade - 93.65.11.68

MM. Metral. Open until 9:15 p.m. Closed Mon. dinner, Tues., March 10-20 & Dec. 1-15. Garden dining. Cards: V.

Finally on the Côte d'Azur, where fine cuisine is created mostly by geniuses, prima donnas and star chefs, you can not only eat well but also spend some relaxing moments with unpretentious, gracious hosts who simply like to excel at their trade. You'll have that opportunity here if you make reservations well enough in advance (seating is limited to 25, and the place is always full) in this simple spot. Brigitte and Christian Metral treat their guests like old friends. Truly. And the cuisine seems to be getting even better. Christian makes the best of the season's produce and runs the kitchen with ease and a light touch: stuffed zucchini blossoms in a beurre blanc with chives and a fine tapenade (olive-anchovy paste), salmon steamed with a mouth-watering sabayon sauce with fresh herbs, and a civet of duckling thighs that represents extraordinary traditional cooking, with its tender meat and superb wine sauce thickened with foie gras. The caramel-strawberry millefeuille is worth nearly three toques. The food is so good you sometimes wish there was more (particularly when you order the small fixed-price menu). A top-notch sommelier has been brought in to complete the fine team here. Delicious summer terrace.

A la carte: 350F. Menus: 170F, 260F.

The à la carte restaurant prices given are for a complete three-course meal for one, including a half-bottle of modest wine and service. Menu prices are for a complete fixed-price meal for one, excluding wine (unless otherwise noted).

Biriatou

see Hendaye

Blaesheim

67113 Blaesheim - (Bas-Rhin)
Paris 493 - Strasbourg 17 - Molsheim 15 - Obernai 14

(13) Au Boeuf

183, rue du Maréchal-Foch - 88.68.81.31
M. Voegtling. Open until 9 p.m. (9:30 p.m. in summer). Closed Sun. dinner & Mon.; annual closing varies. Air cond. Parking. Cards: V, AE, DC, MC.

This is a large country inn like you might find anywhere in Alsace. Yet it has its virtues: respect for the clientele, nice Rhine wines and a good traditional cuisine, such as a barbue (brill) filet with leeks, tournedos strasbourgeoise (served between a potato galette and a thin slice of foie gras, garnished with choucroute) with a too-acid brown sauce, light génoise (sponge cake) with a lemon mousse filling. We'll award one toque, but we'll add that some originality wouldn't hurt.

A la carte: 280F.

Le Blanc

36300 Le Blanc - (Indre)
Paris 300 - Poitiers 60 - Châtellerault 53

Domaine de l'Etape

Rte. de Bélâbre - 54.37.18.02
Open year-round. 21 rms 170-320F. Half-board 220-430F. TV in 6 rms. Parking. Cards: AE, DC, MC.

Set in a 300-acre park with a 40-acre pond, the Domaine has well-equipped rooms. Riding. No restaurant.

Blois

41000 Blois - (Loir-et-Cher)
Paris 180 - Tours 60 - Orléans 56 - Le Mans 109

(16) Le Bocca d'Or

15, rue Haute - 54.78.04.74
M. Galland. Open until 9:30 p.m. Closed Mon. lunch, Sun. (except holidays) & Feb. 1-March 5. No pets. Cards: V, AE.

Patrice Galland is a man to watch. An exceptionally talented chef, he had loads of trouble establishing himself at Blois, a dyed-in-the-wool center of old-fashioned gastronomy. Yet his cuisine is so exacting, so top quality, with such directness, that he reminds us of Joël Robuchon at the Concorde Lafayette when no one (except us) seemed particularly interested. We wouldn't be surprised to see the lanky Galland wake up the slow-moving culinary atmosphere of this burg. He set up shop three years ago in the magnificent ribbed vaults of this fourteenth-century cellar. His debut was rather discreet, even cautious, but over time he has begun to unbridle his talents: salad of lentils, langoustine galettes, cold oysters and asparagus en gelée, paupiette of lotte with gherkins and a sweet-and-sour rosemary sauce, roast pigeon breast in its juice and served with giblets in a flaky pastry. Desserts are simple but delicate. In short, Le Bocca d'Or is not a discovery but a stunning confirmation well worth two toques, with a promising future. California-born Francine, mistress of the house, is a fine hostess. The wine cellar needs rounding out.

A la carte: 300F. Menus: 110F, 160F.

Campanile

Rue de la Vallée-Maillard - 54.74.44.66
Open year-round. 51 rms 205-225F. TV in 30 rms. Parking. Telex 751628. Cards: V.

These quiet rooms with direct access are well designed. Grill.

(13) Hostellerie de la Loire

8, Maréchal-de-Lattre-de-Tassigny
54.74.26.60
M. Renoult. Open until 9:30 p.m. Closed Sun. Pets allowed. Hotel: 18 rms 155-250F; half-board 275-410F. Cards: V, AE, DC.

The decor has a rusticism that was more in style during the '50s, but a pleasant terrace with a view of the old bridge has been added on. The new owner doesn't appear to be inclined to rejuvenate the cuisine of his predecessor. You'll have fine escargots accompanied by a Vouvray sorbet (which would be better if it was less sweet), lotte civet made with a fine Chinon sauce or breast of duck in an orange sauce. Good cakes and Loire wines.

A la carte: 250-300F. Menus: 120F, 160F.

Bonsecours

see Rouen

Bordeaux

33000 Bordeaux - (Gironde)
Paris 566 - Arachon 60 - Périgueux 120

Note: The numbers following the telephone number in each review pinpoint the establishment's exact location on the accompanying map.

Sights. Saint-Pierre district (chic, recently renovated, lots of shops), the heart of old Bordeaux, particularly lively with the health-food market on Thursday and Tuesday's exotic market, its four superb plazas—Parlement, Saint-Pierre, Camille-Jullian and Basque; the Saint-Michel district (undergoing transformation), with its large daily flea market around the Saint-Michel church and, steps away, the famous Capucins market, the "belly of Bordeaux" that starts at 2 a.m.; the Notre-Dame district, in the heart of the Chartrons, with its secondhand shops and video bars and, nearby, the large public gardens, with exotic trees and plants and its Muséum d'Histoire Naturelle; the heart of the city, the "magic triangle" defined by the allées de Tourny, pl. Gambetta and the Grand Théâtre; the wharfs and the pl. de la Bourse, a marvel of eighteenth-century architecture by Gabriel; the superb Saint-André cathedral (twelfth and fourteenth centuries); the Musée des Beaux-Arts (more than 2,000 paintings from the fifteenth to the twentieth century); Musée des Arts Décoratifs, Hôtel de Lalande, 33, rue Bouffard; La Galerie des Beaux Arts, pl. Colonel-Raynal; Musée des Arts Contemporains in the former Lainé warehouse, rue Foy (a superb, vast nineteenth-century hall with the most contemporary art in Europe); the Grand Théâtre, founded in 1773 (lively during "May musical").

Eating on the Run. L'Absinthe, 137, rue Tondu (cute and cozy, brasserie dishes); Le Bistro du Sommelier, 167, rue Georges Bonnac (fine wines at moderate prices, interesting evening wine tastings); Le Café du Musée, rue Ferrère (in the Musée des Arts Contemporains, good regional dishes); Déjeuner sur l'Herbe, 10, rue de la Devise (brunch, light local cuisine); Jegher, 36, cours de Verdun (fish tourtes and cinnamon biscuits); Joël D., rue des Pilliers-de-Tutelle (lively, friendly, oysters and white wine); Le Mably, 12, rue Mably (old brasserie, always packed); Lou Magret, 62, rue St-Rémi (grilled magrets—duck breasts—budget fixed-price menus); New Steak House, 14, rue de la Devise (fine grilled meats, charming wine-store decor); Palais des Thés, rue du Palais Gallien (daily specials, delicious cakes and teas); Le Piano en Croûte, 23, rue Neuve (summer terrace, great 50-franc lunch menu on the terrace in summer, 85 francs for dinner, live piano music Thursdays); Le Rital, 3, rue des Faussets (fresh pasta with cèpes or foie gras); Le Scopitone, 5, rue de la Vieille-Tour (fashionable, open late); Les Trois Arcades (generous salads) and L'Ombrière, both on Parlement plaza, with large terraces.

Bars & Cafés. *Cafés:* The terrace-cafés in vogue are still Le Régent, 46, pl. Gambetta; and across the way, Les Ducs du Cintra, 46, cours du 30 Juillet; Le Noailles (old landmark brasserie), 12, allées de Tourny; Le Grand Hôtel (more snobbish), facing the Grand Théâtre; Le Saint-Projet, 5, pl. St-Projet; Brasserie Montaigne and Café des Arts, both on cours Victor-Hugo; Chez Auguste, 3, pl. de la Victoire (chic student rendezvous, billiards, evening concerts). *Bars:* Bar des Grands Hommes, 10, pl. des Grands-Hommes (wine by the glass); Le Castan, 2, quai de la Douane (designer decor, oysters and white wine); Le Jardin Brésilien, 4, cours de Verdun; New York, 4, cours Pasteur (local press hangout, inexpensive, friendly brasserie); Le Pey-Berland, 3, rue Duffour-Dubergier (family atmosphere); bars of the big hotels—Mercure Pont d'Aquitaine, Pullman (piano bar) and Sofitel Aquitania.

Nightlife. Les Argentiers, 7, rue Teulère (jazz); Le Chat Bleu, 28, rue Maurice (video bar, open late); Le Fidji, 3, rue de Ruat (Caribbean ambience, open until dawn, in cellar); Performance, rue Ramonet (antiseptic decor, new-wave music); Le Salon Jaune, 32, rue Cornac (videos, loud music, hip); Sénéchal, 57 bis, quai de Paludate (disco, *the* place for the fashionable young set); numerous piano bars in center—L'Alligator, 3, pl. du Général-Sarrail; L'Aztecal, 61, rue du Pas-St-Georges (powerful cocktails, punch with punch, open from 9 p.m. to 2 a.m.); Le Cinq, 5, allées de Tourny (clean, sterile look); Le Comptoir des Iles, 2, pl. du Général-Sarrail; Le Cricketters, quai de Paludate (Scottish, pool, darts, music); Le Hangar, rue J.R. Dandicolle (immense two-level bar with videos, nightclub); Plantations, 41, rue des Augustins.

Shops. *Bakeries:* Boulangerie de la Martinique, 72, cours de la Martinique (fine old bakery); Dastarac, 9, rue Fondaudège (and nine other locations, known for its breads, brioches, layer cakes, quiche Lorraine). *Charcuteries, gourmet shops:* Le Comestible, 6, rue Porte-de-la-Monnaie (best regional products from La Tupina restaurant); Dardère, 18, rue St-James (excellent homemade preserves); Dubernet, rue Michel-Montaigne; Les Ducs de Gascogne, 52, cours du Chapeau-Rouge; Margoteau, 13, rue Michel-Montaigne (traditional and serious); Cerruti, 21, rue Voltaire (best gourmet shop in town); Comtesse de Barry, 2, pl. Tourney; Labeyrie, 10, rue Buffon (southwestern classics). *Cheese:* Jean d'-Alos, 4, rue Montesquieu (excellent selection and quality); Antonin, Grands-Hommes marketplace. *Pastries, chocolate:* Antoine, cours Portal; Buck, 11, rue Duffour-Dubergier (a Bordeaux institution, cinnamon pastries, Linzertorte); Cadiot-Badie, 26, allées de Tourny (sumptuous decor, exceptional choice of candies and chocolates); Darricau, 7, pl. Gambetta (prune turnovers); Saunion, 56, cours Clemenceau (best chocolates in Bordeaux). *Fish and shellfish:* Argonne-Maré, 77, cours de l'Argonne (grilled sardines); Brunet, 11, rue de Condé (for oysters); La Langouste, pl. des Capucins (branch of the famous Roscoff); Smith, 171, cours de la Somme (best fish). *Wine:* Badie, 62, allées de Tourny (excellent Médocs); Bordeaux Magnum, 3, rue Gobineau (superb selection); La Vinothèque, 8, cours du 30-Juillet (all varieties of Bordeaux).

(14) L'Alhambra

111 bis, rue Judaïque
56.96.06.91 / D2-3

M. Demazeau. Open until 9:30 p.m. Closed Sat. lunch, Sun. & July 14-Aug. 15. Air cond. No pets. Cards: V.

The prewar decor, with its country scenes and tones of pink, brown and soft green, is that of a somewhat modernized café. The owner's wife seems genuinely happy to greet you, and the service is attentive. As for the cooking, it's just what we like to find in such a place: simple and well prepared, with lovely products and light sauces. Sample the wild boar terrine with a powerful flavor of venison, the pot-au-feu of beef and calf's tongues served with tasty vegetables, the sea scallops with an endive cream sauce and the exquisite caramelized roast pear. On our last visit, we found a better wine list, even better food and a friendly reception—all of which adds up to another point.

A la carte: 250F. Menus: 90F (lunch only), 160F, 180F.

10/20 Bateau Alienor

Right bank, Garonne river, facing 27, quai des Queyries - 56.86.50.65 / E4-29

M. Baillard. Open daily until 8:30 p.m. Air cond. No pets. Parking. Telex 570553. Cards: V.

This large barge/restaurant will take you for a several-hours-long cruise along noble docks and famous vineyards; decent meals are served at reasonable prices.

Menus: 80F, 115F, 170F (plus 76-116F for cruise.).

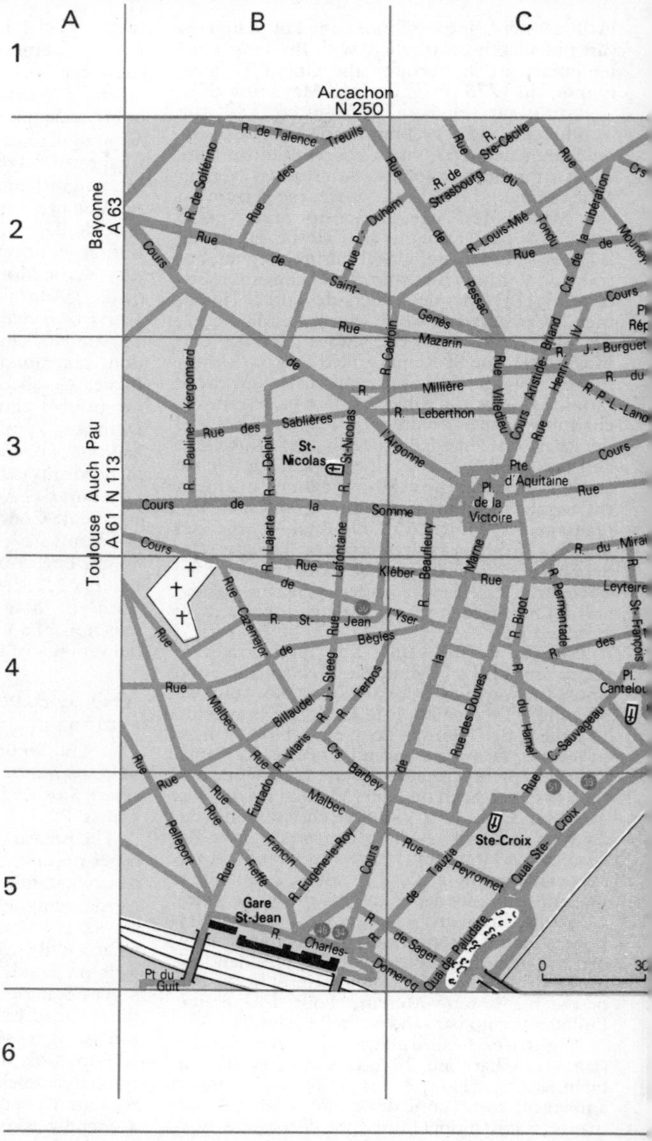

1 - Restaurant du Loup **R**
2 - Normandie **H**
3 - L'Alhambra **R**
4 - La Chamade **R**
5 - Sologa **R**
6 - Chez Philippe **R**
7 - Le Vieux Bordeaux **R**
8 - Bistrot du Clavel (Centre) **R** et Le Chapon Fin **R**
9 - Le Cailhau **R**
10 - Royal Médoc **H**
11 - Mercure Pont d'Aquitaine **H**
12 - Hôtel de Bayonne **H**
13 - La Téranèze **R**
14 - Pavillon des Boulevards **R**
15 - Hôtel Majestic **H**
16 - Le Buhan **R**
17 - Le Flore (Sofitel Aquitania) **RH**
18 - La Toque Blanche **R**
19 - Les Provinces **R**
21 - Campanile **H**
22 - Grand Hôtel de Bordeaux **H**
24 - Le Puits du Roy **R**
25 - Mercure Bordeaux-le-Lac **H**
27 - Le Bolchoï **R** et Le Rouzic **R**
28 - La Pelouse **H**
29 - Bateau Alienor **R**
30 - Au Chipiron **R**
31 - La Fortune du Pot **R**
32 - Hippopotamus **R**
34 - Hôtel Terminus **H**
35 - Le Piano en Croûte **R**
37 - La Ferme Saint-Michel **R**
38 - Le Meriadeck (Pullman) **RH**
39 - Le Cellier Bordelais **R**
40 - Novotel Bordeaux-le-Lac **H**
41 - Bistro du Sommelier **R**
42 - Dominique **R**
43 - Le Rital **R**
44 - Français **H**
46 - Bistrot du Clavel (Gare) **R**
47 - La Forge **R**
48 - Le Noailles **R**
49 - Jean Ramet **R**
50 - La Bonne Bouille **R**
51 - La Tupina **R**
52 - Chez Mau **R**

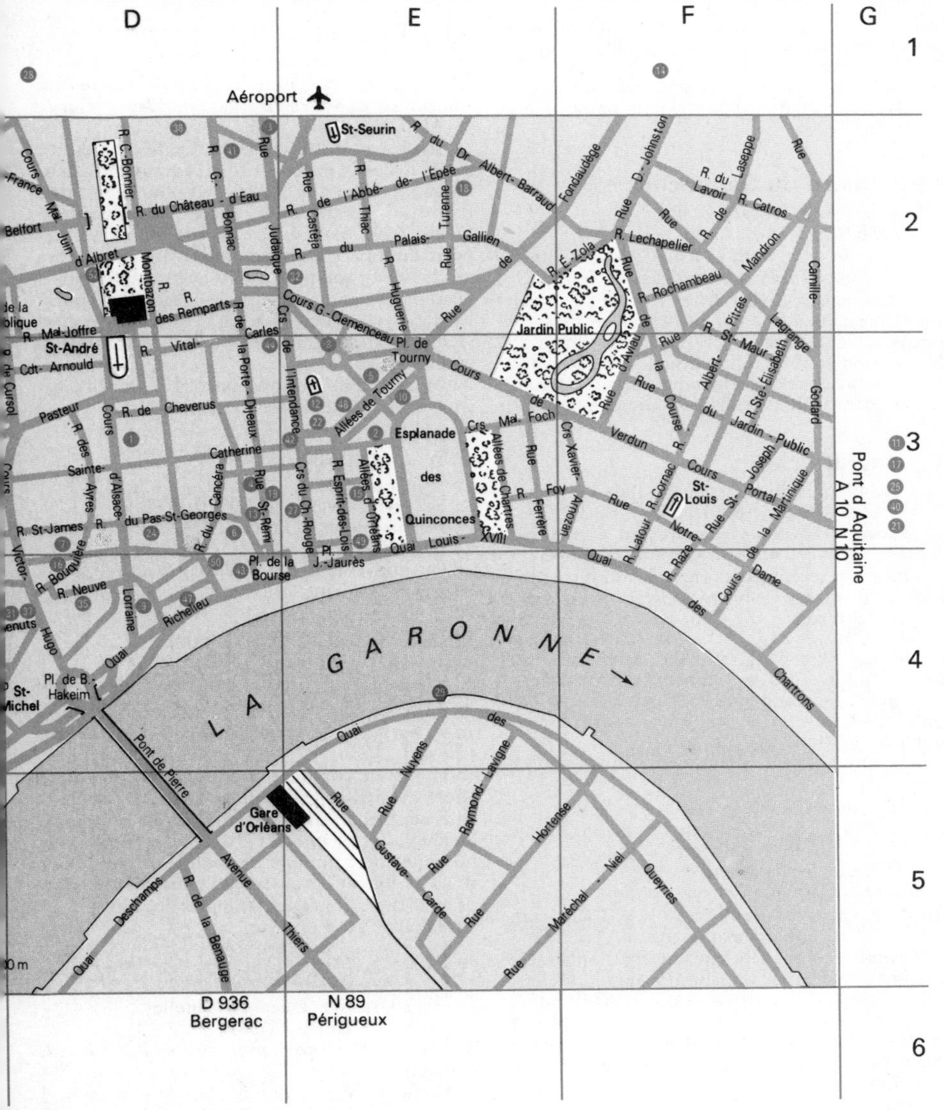

Hôtel de Bayonne

4, rue de Martignac
56.48.00.88 / E3-12

37 rms 155-230F. Pets allowed. Telex 570362. Cards: V.

Rather quiet despite its central location near the Grand Théâtre and the allées de Tourny. No restaurant.

(14) Bistro du Clavel

7, rue Montesquieu - 56.51.28.81 / E3-8

M. Garcia. Open until 11 p.m. Closed Sun. & Mon. No pets. Cards: V.

Francis Garcia can never be accused of resting on his laurels. It seems he opens up a new restaurant or gourmet shop every year, and apparently he can't keep the same decor for six months; he is already planning to change this one (though it's quite new and bright, with wonderful contemporary frescoes). One fears the worst, but Garcia comes up with the best: incredible prices, marvelous wines at reasonable tabs, an excellent staff and a cuisine that only grows more and more refreshing, generous and professional. We feel he'll soon outgrow his one toque (hence the move up to 14/20) with his delicious sautéed shrimp and caper salad, ramekin of escargots "vignerons"

(wine-maker style), baked lotte with three kinds of peppers, the zarzuela (a fish-shellfish ragoût) that he makes like no one else, the duck confit with cabbage and the good simple desserts.
A la carte: 200F. Menus: 140F (wine incl.), 115F, 160F.

11/20 Bistro du Sommelier

167, rue Georges-Bonnac
56.96.71.78 / D2-41

M. Valverde. Open until 11 p.m. Closed Sat. lunch, Sun. & Jan. 1-15. Pets allowed. Cards: V, AE.

A fine ex-sommelier from Dubern, M. Valverde presents a fine list of "small-great" Bordeaux, which is renewed every month following a blind wine tasting. His cuisine is honest and copious: breast of duck, blanquette, eel matelote.
A la carte: 150F. Menus: 54F (lunch only).

12/20 Le Bolchoï

34, cours du Chapeau-Rouge
56.44.39.11, 56.86.11.39 / E3-27

M. Gautier. Open until midnight. Closed Sat. lunch & Sun. Pets allowed. Cards: V.

Our most recent memories of this rather silly-looking Russian-style bistro above Le Rouzic restaurant (also run by the Gautiers) are not exactly overwhelming: Our zakuskis (Russian hors d'ouevres) were weak, and the vatrouchka tart heavy. But we can recommend the marvelous salmon, blinis, tarama and vodkas. Musicians play on Thursday evenings. Still, this place no longer warrants its toque.
A la carte: 250F. Menus: 96F (lunch only), 160F.

12/20 La Bonne Bouille

7, rue des Bahutiers
56.48.24.86 / D4-50

M. Gotrand. Open until 10:30 p.m. Closed Sat. lunch & Tues. Pets allowed. Cards: V, AE, DC.

Although completely new, this charming bistro was instantly filled with habitués and old friends. The owner/chef has two good, hearty budget fixed-price menus that include a seafood platter (crab, oysters, mussels) and lotte in a honey-vinegar sauce. He needs, however, a better wine selection.
Menus: 85F, 115F.

(13) Le Buhan

28, rue Buhan - 56.52.80.86 / D4-16

M. Brunel. Open daily until 10 p.m. No pets. Cards: V, AE, DC.

Jean-Claude Brunel's modern experiments (admittedly rare—there's a lobster salad with strawberry vinegar) don't interest him so much that he neglects his favorite repertoire. The terrine of semicooked foie gras, salmon with sorrel, tournedos Rossini and rack of lamb sarladaise are great classics, prepared with beautiful products and executed with a light touch. The decor is country-style but elegant, serene and warm (more so than the reception); it is pleasantly candlelit at night.
A la carte: 250-350F. Menus: 215F (wine incl.), 110F, 165F, 270F.

(14) Le Cailhau

3, pl. du Palais - 56.81.79.91 / D4-9

M. Juillard. Open until 10:30 p.m. Closed Sat. lunch, Sun. & 3 weeks in Aug. Pets allowed. Cards: V, AE, DC.

An elegant bistro cuisine, attractive tables in a lovely decor of exposed stone, young and attentive waiters wearing jackets and bow ties—that's the reason for the lasting success of Le Cailhau. Owner/chef Alain Juillard keeps a close rein on both the prices and the cuisine (the plates are nicely filled), and he keeps his menu up to date: a salad of sole and asparagus tips, catch of the day with an oyster sabayon sauce, sweetbreads in sherry and a spinach gratin. Good budget fixed-price menu.
A la carte: 250-350F. Menus: 145F (lunch only, wine incl.), 150F, 200F.

Campanile

Cours Charles-Bricaud
56.39.54.54 / G3-21

Open year-round. 132 rms 215-235F. TV in 90 rms. Parking. Telex 560425. Cards: V.

This convenient, modern hotel faces a spacious garden. Restaurant/grill.

12/20 Le Cellier Bordelais

30, quai de la Monnaie
56.31.30.30 / C5-39

M. Lafargue. Open until 11 p.m. Closed Sat., Sun., July 14-Aug. 15 & year-end holidays. Pets allowed. Cards: V, MC.

This place combines a brasserie decor—quite effective with its tall mirrors and old posters—with serious cuisine: sweetbreads in Sauternes, quail salad (too vinegary), tasty guinea-fowl vigneronne and a number of good Bordeaux, both small and great labels, served either by the glass or in bottles. Bordeaux's yuppies flock here.
A la carte: 200F.

(15) La Chamade

20, rue des Piliers-de-Tutelle
56.48.13.74 / D3-4

M. Carrère. Open daily until 10 p.m. Pets allowed. Cards: V.

Michel Carrère is one of the top two seafood chefs in Bordeaux, and of the two, he is the more imaginative, with an original and versatile repertoire. His baked bass filet is sumptuous—tender, fresh and cooked to perfection—though the zucchini and tomatoes accompanying it are disappointing. His wild fresh salmon from the Adour is one of the best we've had of late. Some of his desserts are worth more than two toques, most notably his "beehive honey" with a caramel-apricot sauce, while others are worth less than one toque, such as his pale strawberry mousse with mint leaves. The marvelous service is directed by a gracious maître d', and the elegant vaulted decor of white stone is soon to be renovated. A second toque is warranted.
A la carte: 350-400F. Menus: 140F (weekday lunch only), 200F (weekend and holiday lunch only).

(17) Le Chapon Fin

5, rue Montesquieu
56.79.10.10 / E3-8

M. Garcia. Open until 9:30 p.m. Closed Sun. & Mon. Air cond. No pets. Cards: V, AE, DC.

For six decades Le Chapon Fin was known as the Maxim's of Bordeaux, entertaining the most famous names of the Belle Epoque until World War II: Toulouse-Lautrec, Edward VIII, the Sultan of Morocco, Winston Churchill, Sacha Guitry and François Mauriac, among others. Then in 1960, Joseph Sicart, the brilliant chef who had run the place since its Belle Epoque heyday, departed, and the place went into a tailspin. When just recently Francis Garcia announced he would try to bring back the glory days to Le Chapon Fin, most of Bordeaux thought him crazy. After all, he had three successful restaurants (all named Clavel) and nothing to prove. Yet he fell in love with this enchanting place and personally took charge of the project. With the financial support of the Swiss restaurant chain Mövenpick (for which he's a technical adviser), Garcia realized his dream, and the elite of Bordeaux, skeptical at first, were quickly won over by the new Chapon Fin. The old ceiling—featuring a sky with swallows—was replaced with a movable glass roof that lets light flood in to brighten up the dining room. Repainted in white, the trelliswork and elaborate wood pillars have been preserved, as has the stunning rock decor. New features include a lavender carpet, round tables dressed with white linens, and black-lacquered bamboo-type armchairs with lovely floral coverings. The place has never looked so alluring and is once again the favorite of Bordeaux's high society, famed political figures and even foreign celebrities.

Francis Garcia has won his bet, and his cuisine, already delicious, is becoming even more refined. Take note of the subtle yet flavorful lobster gazpacho, Spanish-style peppers (Garcia hasn't forgotten his roots) stuffed with spider crab, squash flowers with mushrooms, a dish of hot and cold duck foie gras, excellent red mullet cooked in coarse salt and anise butter, salmon steak grilled in its skin with a pepper sabayon sauce. Or the pigs' feet stuffed with morels, delicious veal kidneys in their natural gravy with juniper berries, a pot-au-feu of poultry legs and a ballotine of young rabbit with an irresistible aroma of fresh thyme. Not to mention the delightful cheeses and heavenly desserts served on large plates (called "child's dream"). It's all served in a wonderful atmosphere with the precision of a Swiss watch. The wine list (it's really a book) includes an impressive choice of magnificent Bordeaux vintages (the more modest ones are a bit neglected). In addition to an à la carte menu that will allow one—on the condition that selections are made wisely—to enjoy a perfect meal for less than 400 francs, Garcia offers a regional fixed-price menu for 290 francs and a fixed-price business lunch for 200 francs.

A la carte: 400F. Menus: 200F (lunch only), 290F, 320F, 360F.

12/20 Chez Mau

50, cours d'Albret - 56.44.27.24 / D2-52

Mme. Vayssière. Open until 11 p.m. Closed Sat. lunch & Sun. Air cond. Pets allowed. Cards: V.

The narrow dining room with dark-red wallpaper seats about 30; its regulars are business people, mostly from the nearby courts of law. The cooking is generous and well prepared: fresh duck liver with raspberries, duck tartare, red mullet braised with foie gras and sea fennel. Good wine cellar.

A la carte: 250-280F. Menus: 85F, 150F, 220F.

(15) Chez Philippe

1, pl. du Parlement - 56.81.83.15 / D3-6

M. Techoire. Open until 11 p.m. Closed Sun., Mon. & Aug. Air cond. Terrace dining. Pets allowed. Cards: V, AE, DC.

Louis Pascual, who is celebrating ten years in the kitchens here, may not be the finest or most imaginative seafood chef in Bordeaux. Still, this large eighteenth-century bistro, flowery and friendly, remains the best seafood restaurant and the most deservedly famous in town. Owner Philippe Techoire has long understood that to keep up the reputation here, he has to stick to fresh products and natural methods. Thus the seafood is remarkably fresh and tasty, no doubt the best from the coast, and it's prepared with simplicity. The menu is short and rarely redone, which may lead the people of Bordeaux elsewhere someday to seek variety at better prices. But this is still the place to be, thanks to the seafood salad, bass with fresh grapes, turbot with sorrel, Mediterranean-style lotte and gargantuan (and ruinous!) seafood platters. Fine selection of white wines.

A la carte: 350-400F. Menu: 160F (lunch only).

12/20 Au Chipiron

56, cours de l'Yser - 56.92.98.59 / B4-30

M. Etchebest. Open until 9:30 p.m. Closed Sun. dinner, Mon., Easter school vacation & Aug. 28-Sept. 10. Pets allowed. Cards: V.

Wooden beams, a fireplace, hunting trophies—you'd think you were in an Ascain farmhouse. This impression is confirmed by a sensational soup luzienne offered as part of the budget fixed-price menu, followed by a homemade confit (a bit salty) and a tasty pastry. These dishes do not warrant a toque, though they are really quite decent. The reception is chilly, the service amateurish.

A la carte: 300F. Menus: 92F, 135F.

11/20 Dominique

1, cours de l'Intendance
56.52.59.79 / E3-42

M. Train. Open daily until midnight. Air cond. Pets allowed. Cards: V.

In this superb-looking site of the former Saint-James, facing the Grand Théâtre, fixed-price menus are offered (wine and dessert are additional). Especially noteworthy is the excellent beef rib bordelaise.

Menus: 78F, 150F.

(13) La Ferme Saint-Michel

21, rue des Menuts
56.91.54.77 / D4-37

M. Rivault. Open until 11 p.m. Closed Sun. & Mon. Pets allowed. Cards: V, DC.

The cosmopolitan Michel Rivault (25 years in the trade in all corners of the world) has dropped anchor in this modest but warm restaurant with his radiant wife, Catherine. His knowledge and love of fine food have been a big factor in his success. He has managed to maintain fabulous prices on his short à la carte list and daily fixed-price menus (110 francs for the latter, with fish or meat). Try the small calamari à l'encre, the oyster-cèpe ravioli, the beef ribs (a two-pound serving for two) and the marvelous hearth-cooked bread. Great selection of Bordeaux for less than 100 francs.

A la carte: 250F. Menus: 110F, 160F.

12/20 Le Flore

Blvd. du Lac - 56.50.83.80 / G3-17

M. Carrier. Open until 10 p.m. Closed Sat., Sun. & Aug. Air cond. Pets allowed. Parking. Telex 570557. Cards: V, AE, DC, MC.

This pleasant, fresh decor in pinks, whites and greens is refined, modern and comfortable. To boot, the service is amiable and efficient. But on our last visit, the cuisine seemed a bit tentative, especially the overcooked sea bass steak and the disappointing praline millefeuille. However, there are good mixed salads and excellent Pauillac lamb. A bit of effort is needed to regain the toque.

A la carte: 180-200F. Menu: 165F (wine incl.).

Sofitel Aquitania

(See restaurant above)

Open year-round. 8 stes 850-1,100F. 204 rms 545-615F. Half-board 260-320F. TV. Air cond. Pets allowed. Pool.

The rooms have been refurbished with great attention to comfort, and there is a luxurious new reception hall. Beautiful, well-equipped bathrooms. Lots of meeting rooms. Bar and disco.

11/20 La Forge

8, rue du Chai-des-Farines
56.81.40.96 / D4-47

M. Pouls. Open until 10:30 p.m. Closed Sun., Mon. & Aug. 15-Sept. 15. Pets allowed. Cards: V, AE, DC.

Consistency, simplicity and hearty generosity: top sirloin, leg of lamb, filet of shad (and sometimes shad roe), mussels marinière, lovely sheep cheeses and decent homemade tarts. The first two fixed-price menus are exemplary.

A la carte: 160F. Menus: 68F, 92F, 150F.

12/20 La Fortune du Pot

37, rue des Menuts
56.92.65.79 / D4-31

M. Rivierre. Open until 10:30 p.m. Closed Sun. & Mon. Pets allowed. Cards: V.

The name means "pot luck," and it will indeed be your good luck to eat at this tastefully redecorated wine shop, further charmed by the presence of a gracious young hostess. There are two hearty fixed-price menus served on lovely china, including one offering a velouté of liver and pleurotes (mushrooms), a light feuilleté of kidneys, loin of lamb with fresh pasta and a fine tart of the day.

A la carte: 160-180F. Menus: 60F (weekday lunch only, wine incl.), 100F, 160F.

Français

12, rue du Temple - 56.48.10.35 / D3-44

Open year-round. 4 stes 540F. 31 rms 320-420F. TV. No pets. Telex 550587. Cards: V, AE.

A traditional family hotel with attentive service and plain but well-maintained rooms.

Grand Hôtel de Bordeaux

Pl. de la Comédie - 56.90.93.44 / E3-22

Open year-round. 3 stes 760F. 95 rms 320-440F. TV. Air cond. Telex 541658. Cards: V, AE.

This three-star hotel is one of Bordeaux's most attractive, thanks to its superb white-stone facade. The rooms are a bit cramped but quiet behind double-pane windows. No restaurant.

10/20 Hippopotamus

39, pl. Gambetta - 56.44.00.39 / E2-32

M. Guignard. Open daily until 1 a.m. Air cond. Pets allowed. Cards: V.

Good meats are grilled over coals—the way it's done in all the Hippopotamus restaurants in France—and served in a bright, functional decor. Slow, slow service.

A la carte: 130F. Menu: 52F.

Hôtel Majestic

2, rue de Condé - 56.52.60.44 / E3-15

Open year-round. 50 rms 260-360F. TV. Garage parking. Cards: V.

A charming hotel with classic comfort, well situated behind place des Quinconces. No restaurant.

Mercure Bordeaux-le-Lac

Quartier du Lac - 56.50.90.30 / G3-25

Open year-round. 3 stes 450-750F. 105 rms 360-400F. TV. Air cond. Parking. Cards: V, AE, DC, MC.

This modern, functional hotel has rooms that are comfortable and well equipped (even with VCRs). Weekend packages include tours of the Bordeaux vineyards and golf lessons. Restaurant.

Mercure Pont d'Aquitaine

Bordeaux-le-Lac - 56.50.90.14 / G3-11

Open year-round. 2 stes 500F. 98 rms 360F. TV. Air cond. Heated pool. Tennis. Parking. Telex 540097. Cards: V, AE, DC.

Although austere, this modern building boasts a lovely pool, and all rooms have air conditioning, direct-dial telephones and color TVs. Poolside barbecue. Restaurant.

12/20 Le Meriadeck

5, rue Robert-Lateulade
56.90.92.37 / D2-38

M. Gajan. Open daily until 11 p.m. Air cond. Pets allowed. Telex 540565.

The reception and the service have clearly made progress, but that still won't help you to forget the morbidly dull decor of this chain hotel. Nor does it hide the defects of the overambitious cooking, which, apart from the very good lamb sausages in Pauillac wine, is no longer worthy of a toque (insipid cold lotte, overcooked gratin of oysters and scallops). The wine list, however, is

quite good.
A la carte: 300-350F. Menus: 98F, 160F and 230F (wine incl.).

Pullman

(See restaurant above)

Open year-round. 2 stes 1,800-1,950F. 194 rms 470-795F. Pets allowed.

Practical, functional, comfortable and rather dull, with a location in a stark, modern section of town. The Pullman is very well equipped, especially the "Privilège" floor, which has several luxury suites. Adequate service, good breakfast and free shuttle service to the airport.

11/20 Le Noailles

12, allées de Tourny
56.81.94.45 / E3-48

M. Hias. Open until 11:30 p.m. Closed Wed., 2 weeks in Feb. & July 6-28. Pets allowed.

Every day brings tasty, generous specials—leg of mutton, rabbit with mustard sauce, osso buco—in this old-fashioned brasserie, one of the few of its kind in Bordeaux.

A la carte: 180F.

Normandie

7-9, cours du 30-Juillet
56.52.16.80 / E3-2

Open year-round. 100 rms 190-380F. TV. Pets allowed. Telex 570481. Cards: V, AE, DC, MC.

This solid stone building facing the place des Quinconces and the port is a decent, traditional hotel. No restaurant.

Novotel Bordeaux-le-Lac

Quartier du Lac - 56.50.99.70 / G3-40

Open year-round. 173 rms 380F. TV. Air cond. Pets allowed. Pool. Telex 570274. Cards: V, AE, DC, MC.

This functional hotel facing the lake and the freeway features perfectly equipped rooms. Special equipment is available for groups. Restaurant.

Pavillon des Boulevards

120, rue de la Croix-de-Seguey
56.81.51.02 / F1-14

MM. Franc. Open until 10:15 p.m. Closed Sat. lunch, Sun., March 25-April 2 & Aug. 7-20. Garden dining. Pets allowed. Cards: V, AE, DC.

This is Bordeaux's rising star. We can't quite put a finger on what makes this place tick, but tick it does. The decor is fine, with a relaxing modern ambience and a veranda overlooking a small yard. Nelly Franc, lovely and quick-witted, runs the dining room with precision. The 21-year-old sommelier has the nerve to offer Burgundies "for a change," and to push a walnut wine or port with the fine sheep's milk cheeses. And the cuisine is progressing, with chef Denis Franc becoming more and more enterprising, original and precise. If you need proof of this, try his marvelous oyster salad with a lemon aspic or his squab "chinoiserie," the skin grilled with a honey sauce and the breasts and thighs served in a truffle gravy. The menu dégustation is a truly good deal (it includes fine red mullet filets with browned potatoes and rosemary). Though a bit sweet for our taste, the desserts are light and a feast for the imagination, especially the exquisite peaches roasted with almonds.

A la carte: 350-400F. Menus: 170F (lunch only), 250F, 350F.

La Pelouse

65, rue Pelouse-de-Douet
56.93.17.33 / D1-28

Closed Dec. 25-Jan. 1 & Aug. 6-21. 36 rms 180-260F. TV. Pets allowed. Parking. Cards: V, AE, DC, MC.

Although rather tiny, the rooms at La Pelouse are utilitarian and quiet. Easy parking. No restaurant.

10/20 Le Piano en Croûte

23, rue Neuve - 56.51.04.77 / D4-35

M. Esposito. Open daily until 11 p.m. Terrace dining. Pets allowed. Cards: V.

In this lively little bistro, a young and hungry clientele is served (somewhat haphazardly) simple, uncomplicated fare: mussels with sorrel, sirloin with shallots and so on.

A la carte: 150F. Menu: 95F.

12/20 Les Provinces

41-43, rue St-Rémi
56.81.74.30 / D3-19

M. Dumas. Open daily until 10:30 p.m. Pets allowed. Parking. Cards: V, AE, MC.

The decor is rather distressing, but the owner's reception, the courteous service and the consistently good quality of the cuisine all ensure the success of Les Provinces, where interesting regional "gastronomic encounters" take place: sea-bream tartare, veal grenadin with morels, orange soufflé.

A la carte: 260-280F. Menus: 72F (lunch only), 105F and 150F (wine incl.).

Le Puits du Roy

58, rue du Pas-St-Georges
56.51.23.57 / D3-24

M. Biamouret. Open until 10:30 p.m. Closed Sat. lunch, Sun. & 2 weeks late Aug.-early Sept. Pets allowed. Cards: V, AE, MC.

The most wonderful fixed-price menu in Bordeaux for the price will bring you a mouth-watering gâteau of carrots in carrot juices, a fine potato tart with foie gras, prunes in cinnamon wine, duck aiguillettes in ginger honey, a feuilleté of goat cheese and a salad or a cocoa sorbet and petits fours. As well, a fine regional selection is offered à la carte. Denis Biamouret, who took over Le Puits du Roy from Christian Clément, raised prices a bit but still provides excellent quality, from the salmon flan with a parsley cream sauce and the duck filet with mild pimientos to the delicious homemade prune ice cream.

A la carte: 280F. Menu: 120F.

Pullman

See Le Meriadeck restaurant.

Jean Ramet

17

7-8 pl. Jean-Jaurès
56.44.12.51 / E3-49

M. Ramet. Open until 10 p.m. Closed Sat., Sun., 3 weeks in Aug. & year-end holidays. Air cond. Pets allowed. Cards: V, AE, DC.

Jean Ramet prepares the most consistent, most natural cuisine in Bordeaux, so refined it gives the impression of being prepared effortlessly. There's more than just ambience here: It's a veritable habitat. Ramet and his wife, Raymonde, have created a wonderfully cheerful family atmosphere and take pleasure in receiving guests. You feel completely at ease in the intimate, though sparse, surroundings. The restaurant seats 30, and service is excellent and discreet in the sober, modern decor. Even the briefcase crowd doesn't detract from the family feeling. The cuisine is created from the best from the seasonal market: warm lobster salad with herbs and hazelnut oil on a bed of two kinds of lettuce (but why the lumpfish caviar?), butter-soft squab, completely deboned, with an extraordinarily delicate flavor, a panaché of the day's fish with marvelously fresh chanterelles and the desserts, still Ramet's strongest suit—from fruit feuilletés to the frozen praline délice and the honey ice cream with a raspberry purée. Sumptuous Bordeaux wines in all price ranges. Excellent fixed-price lunch menu.

A la carte: 350F. Menu: 190F (lunch only).

Restaurant Le Loup

14

66, rue du Loup - 56.48.20.21 / D3-1

MM. Boudin & Horeau. Open until 10:15 p.m. Closed Sat. lunch & Sun. Pets allowed. Cards: V, AE.

Jean-Claude Boudin, a former assistant at Clavel, is one of the rising young chefs in Bordeaux. His outstanding bargain fixed-price menu changes daily, as do his other fixed-price menus. For 172 francs, for example, you can feast on a mosaic of langoustines and spring vegetables, fresh cod in a soy sauce, lamb chops with cabbage, cheeses and an apple feuillantine with pistachios. Good wine cellar, attentive service and a charming decor that's perfect for romantic evenings.

A la carte: 300F. Menus: 100F, 172F, 235F.

10/20 Le Rital

3, rue des Faussets - 56.48.16.69 / D4-43

M. Ponzone. Open until 11 p.m. Closed Sat., Sun. & Sept. Terrace dining. Pets allowed. Cards: V.

A truly friendly Italian, M. Ponzone prepares tasty pasta al dente with foie gras or cèpes; his salads, however, are nothing out of the ordinary. Homey setting.

A la carte: 130-150F. Menus: 35F (lunch only, wine incl.), 42F.

Le Rouzic

16

34, cours du Chapeau-Rouge
56.44.39.11, 56.86.11.39 / E3- 27

MM. Gautier. Open until 10 p.m. Closed Sat. lunch & Sun. Pets allowed. Cards: V, AE, DC.

This place keeps getting better: Kinette Gautier directs the meticulously precise service, while her husband, Michel, becomes increasingly inventive in the kitchen. The pleasant, contemporary decor includes plenty of fresh flowers. The cuisine is also contemporary, with a rare creativity: fresh, light oyster ravioli in a Madras curry; lightly grilled langoustine tails with lamb's sweetbreads and morels; a large steak with shallots; a beautiful, quasi-Provençal "terrine of the sun" made from an assortment of fresh vegetables; and a delicious ultra-light coconut sorbet served with divine, small warm palmiers (cookies). Lately Kinette, who is a very knowledgeable oenologist, has been emphasizing her collection of "superior" vintages at modest prices—which is helpful, since the à la carte prices are rather steep.

A la carte: 300-400F. Menus: 250F (wine incl.), 195F, 350F.

Royal Médoc

3, rue de Sèze - 56.81.72.42 / E3-10

Open year-round. 45 rms 170-310F. TV in 30 rms. Parking. Telex 571042. Cards: V, AE, DC, MC.

A centrally located, clean, cordial, quiet hotel. No restaurant.

Sofitel Aquitania

See Le Flore restaurant.

12/20 La Téranèze

18, pl. du Parlement
56.44.43.29 / D3-13

Mme. Dubois. Closed Sun. (summer). Terrace dining. Cards: V, AE, DC.

Catherine Dubois, a former pupil of Daguin, prepares a valiant cuisine from Gascony, which is graciously served on a cool patio: foie gras, duck carpaccio, escargots with cèpes. Marvelous lesser Armagnacs.

A la carte: 200-250F. Menus: 59F (weekday lunch only, wine incl.), 89F to 190F.

Hôtel Terminus

Gare St-Jean - 56.92.71.58 / B5-34

Open year-round. 81 rms 258-434F. TV in 70 rms. Parking. Telex 540264. Cards: V, AE, DC, MC.

The amenities are minimal and the decor simple, but the Terminus is attentively maintained. Convenient basement parking. Restaurant.

12/20 La Toque Blanche

245, rue Turenne - 56.81.97.86 / E2-18

M. Gaudin. Open until 10 p.m. Closed Sat. & 1st week in Sept. Garden dining. Pets allowed. Cards: V, AE, DC.

This place has a lot going for it—an awning over the terrace that guards against sudden storms; a lively, delightful winter garden; lovely tables separated by dividers adorned with flowers; and a tasty regional cuisine whose prices have increased little in the past three years. Try the breast of duck stuffed with foie gras, lamprey bordelaise, homemade confit with walnut sauce and a handsome wine cellar filled exclusively with Bordeaux.

A la carte: 250F. Menus: 95F (weekday lunch only), 130F, 160F, 200F.

(14) La Tupina

6, rue Porte-de-la-Monnaie
56.91.56.37 / C5-51

M. Xiradakis. Open until 11 p.m. Closed Sun. & holidays. Air cond. Pets allowed. Parking. Cards: V, AE.

His roots are Greek, but Jean-Pierre Xiradakis is proud of his Basco-Bordelais territory; he is particularly enamored of its fine products, such as the Bazas beef. He has a flair for choosing the best Bordeaux vintages in all price ranges to accompany his veal flank on garlic bread, pot-au-feu with foie gras, blanquette of duck with fresh asparagus, stew of tripe and cèpes, Bazas beef and cassoulet. This gregarious man seems more gregarious with his tables of habitués than he is with passing tourists. He should also pay a bit more heed to the china and place settings.

A la carte: 300F.

(15) Le Vieux Bordeaux

27, rue Buhan - 56.52.94.36 / D3-7

M. Bordage. Open until 10:15 p.m. Closed Sat. lunch, Sun., holidays, 2 weeks in Feb. & 3 weeks in Aug. Pets allowed. Cards: V, AE.

Michel Bordage is a young, inventive chef who tries to create precise flavors with the season's products. His two fixed-price menus are among the best in town, and he has several excellent à la carte specialties: duck foie gras lightly cooked in its juices, langoustines with an oyster sauce, fresh cod with celery and wine vinegar and delicious Cenac pigeon with bacon and a garlic confit. The good Bordeaux wines start at 55 francs a bottle. Well situated near the old clock tower, Le Vieux Bordeaux has an attractive, modern decor. A second toque is well deserved.

A la carte: 300F. Menus: 110F, 170F, 220F (weekdays only).

IN NEARBY **Bouliac**
(9 km SE on D 10)
33270 Floirac - (Gironde)

---

(18) Saint-James

3, pl. Camille-Hostein
(Jardins de Hauterive) - 56.20.52.19

M. Amat. Open daily until 10 p.m. Terrace dining. No pets. Hotel: 20 rms 850-1,250F. Heated pool. Tennis. Parking. Cards: V, AE, DC.

When will it finally rise from the earth, the hotel that Jean-Marie Amat has so lovingly described in such detail so many times while strolling in his gardens that gently roll toward the Garonne river? Perhaps by the time you read these words... In any case, when that day finally arrives, the people of Bordeaux will stop saying that Amat was crazy to exile himself to the outskirts of Bouliac—a mere ten minutes from the center of Bordeaux, but in their eyes, Siberia. The charming rooms (so sadly lacking in the capital of Aquitaine) should have no trouble staying full in the midst of this pleasant countryside, and with such a view.

Already this talk of "exile" is heard less and less. Gradually, it became understood that you needn't empty the river to cross the bridge. So the good residents of Bordeaux started venturing over for a look, then coming back for more, and now they'll never let go of the man they consider to be their best chef. Thus, the anxiety of this eternally tormented chef was soothed. He smiles, he's calm, he's happy, and his kitchen is improving by leaps and bounds, forever onward. Applauded, even praised, the son of a little lady from Bacalan who once served snacks to dockworkers still has a clear head. "I'm a laborer," he says. "I never took myself for a good chef." If he means by that a "star," he's right. Amat is a worker, a taskmaster, who understands that to obtain simplicity, you have to go to a lot of trouble. It's a valuable lesson learned from his master, André Guillot. And through his struggle to fight off defeat, he has become a very good cook whose work is full of nuance and subtlety.

Sauces are made without flour and with the least possible amount of cream and butter; everything else that allows one to disguise and, in a way, to cheat the natural flavors has been cut out. His is a meticulous process that results in pure, clean flavors and savory cooking with no rough edges. There is a certain brilliance to this cooking, as seen in such dishes as morsels of eggplant with cumin, lobster in tartar sauce with watercress and the extraordinary Pauillac lamb with creamy garlic. Other times, his cooking seems mysterious and lightly veiled, like a September sky over a vineyard: the filet of sole with mussels, the duck consommé garnished with jambon d'oie and the ragoût of roast pigeon and vegetables, in which every ingredient retains its unique flavor.

We also must mention the wines—the incessant, unbelievable discoveries of Amat and his accomplice, Xiradakis. They never fail to turn a meal into a feast, and with every bottle, you find yourself jotting down yet another new and unknown name. Finally, we must mention the pleasure of sitting on the exquisite shaded terrace in front of the low, white-stone house, in which this lover of modern painting hangs his latest favorites.

A la carte: 450-500F. Menus: 200F (lunch only, wine incl.), 250F (dinner only, wine incl.), 400F.

IN NEARBY **Carbon-Blanc**
(1.5 km, Pont-d'Aquitaine)
33560 Carbon-Blanc - (Gironde)

---

(14) Marc Demund

5, ave. de la Gardette - 56.06.14.55

M. Demund. Open until 10 p.m. Closed Sun. dinner & Mon. Garden dining. Pets allowed. Parking. Cards: V, AE, DC.

Paradise can be found just a few minutes outside of Bordeaux on this terrace with century-old trees. The decor is sober, modern and refined, with flowers on the tables. The service is good when the staff isn't overloaded. And the cuisine is professional and improving, earning another point for the marvelous frogs' legs vinaigrette and the perfectly grilled bass steak with a spirited citrus sauce. One is very happy on this lovely terrace sampling the delicious, simple food: onions stuffed with rabbit liver, grilled tuna steak with tasty regional vegetables, light seafood ravioli and exquisite desserts (strawberries in a wine sorbet, frozen truffle horns).

A la carte: 350-400F. Menus: 110F (weekday lunch only), 150F, 190F, 290F

IN NEARBY **Pessac**
(6 km SW)
33600 Pessac - (Gironde)

(13) La Réserve

74, ave. de Bourgailh - 56.07.13.28
M. Flourens. Open until 9:45 p.m. Closed Nov. 15-March 1. Garden dining. Pets allowed. Parking. Telex 560585. Cards: V, AE, DC, MC.

La Réserve is located in a seven-acre park with a pond, a pleasant terrace, a renovated dining room and engaging hosts, Roland and Claudine Flourens. Chef Pierre Bugat's cuisine is classic but light and in tune with the seasons: sole matelote with a red Bordeaux sauce, pan-fried red mullet with a julienne of citrus fruit, breast of duck with its fresh liver. Superb desserts, especially the fresh-fruit sorbets, are offered, along with the best Bordeaux vintages and excellent Champagnes.

A la carte: 350-400F. Menus: 155F (weekday lunch only), 240F, 380F.

La Réserve

(See restaurant above)
Closed Nov. 15-March 1. 1 ste 950F. 19 rms 500-800F. TV. Air cond. in 7 rms. Tennis.

The rooms have been completely refurbished, and the park has been spruced up. La Réserve is quiet, and its service is impeccable. Relais et Châteaux.

Bormes-les-Mimosas

83230 Bormes-les-Mimosas - (Var)
Paris 890 - Toulon 40 - St-Tropez 35 - Le Lavandou 5

(13) La Cassole

Ruelle du Moulin - 94.71.14.86
Mme. Montanard. Open until 9:30 p.m. Closed Mon. (except holidays) & end Nov.-end Jan. Pets allowed. Cards: AE, DC.

The rear dining room is vaulted, with rough white plaster walls, and the front room has a paneled ceiling, but neither has and particular charm. Despite the picturesque view of the narrow, mossy, cobblestone street, a bit of effort in the decor would be welcome—especially since Gérard Pascal's cuisine deserves it. This new chef is responsible for a well-prepared 140-franc fixed-price menu: poultry salad with lemon and fresh mint, scorpionfish with bell peppers served with a little zucchini cake and fresh pasta, good cheeses and light, crunchy tuiles (cookies). You can expect attentive service and a good, unpretentious wine cellar.

A la carte: 300F. Menus: 300F (weekends and holidays only), 140F, 230F.

Safari

Rte. du Stade - 94.71.09.83
Closed Oct. 30-March 1. 32 rms 250-500F. Heated pool. Tennis. Parking. Telex 404603. Cards: V, AE, DC, MC.

In a wonderful location facing Lavandou bay, Safari offers rooms with large balconies. The grill is open in the evening.

(14) La Tonnelle des Délices

Pl. Gambetta - 94.71.34.84
MM. Gedda. Open until 10 p.m. Closed Nov. 1-March 15. Terrace dining. No pets. Cards: V.

The Gedda brothers have created a cheerful, flowery, impeccably kept terrace bistro that is a true delight. Guy, the chef, is a former grand pastry chef and a lover of Provençal cuisine. And that cuisine is even better now that the brothers have been joined by a veteran southern-French chef, Alain Gigant. The crab soup, hot rabbit-liver croquettes, young rabbit grilled in thyme-flavored wine and fish roasted in basil butter have never tasted so good, and the marvelous desserts are also better than ever (including a new one, the frangipane glacée). Mme. Gigant brings her experience and effervescence to the dining room, making everything seem right. And—mercifully—the prices are still honest. A good, reasonably priced Côtes-de-Provence comes from the Geddas' nearby wine maker.

A la carte: 230-250F.

Bosdarros

see Pau

Bouc-Bel-Air

13320 Bouc-Bel-Air - (Bouches-du-Rhône)
Paris 766 - Aix-en-Provence 11 - Marseille 21 - Gardanne 6

(13) L'Etape

Rte. Gardanne-Marseille - 42.22.61.90
M. Lani. Open until 9:30 p.m. Closed Sat. lunch, Fri. & Dec. 23-31. Air cond. Pets allowed. Hotel: 4 stes; 32 rms 165-230F; half-board 180-320F. Heated pool. Garage parking. Cards: V, AE, DC, MC.

The plain-looking white building on the road from Marseille to Gardanne has become an increasingly appealing way station (with tennis courts and a swimming pool in the works). And Lino Lani's two sons, Lucien and Joël, who take turns in the kitchen, have made considerable progress in livening up the cuisine with some fresh ideas: bass in anise, fricassée of lotte with spices and asparagus and delicious sorbets. Good-value fixed-price menus. Fine wine selection.

A la carte: 250F. Menus: 130F, 170F, 200F.

La Bouëxière

see Rennes

Bougival

see PARIS SUBURBS

Bouilland

21420 Savigny-lès-Beaune - (Côte-d'Or)
Paris 303 - Saulieu 55 - Beaune 15 - Dijon 45

(17) Le Vieux Moulin

On D 2
80.21.51.16
M. Silva. Open until 9 p.m. Closed Thurs. lunch, Wed. (except holidays) & Nov. 18-25. Garden dining. Pets allowed. Parking. Cards: V.

"Divine!" exclaimed one of our readers from Nice; "delectable," said another, from Belgium, though he added that he found the ambience deadly dull and the personnel ghost-like, and added that he is still waiting for the sommelier to come and take his order. It could be a long wait, for there is no sommelier... only a "sommelière": the charming, enthusiastic and knowledgeable 30-year-old Isabelle Silva who, evidently, "missed" our Belgian friend that day. But fair's fair, and he still sent his congratulations for the wine list—and rightly so, for none of its vintages, from the simple red Givry at 100 francs to the Mercury or the Hautes-Côtes-de-Nuit, can leave one indifferent.

The restaurant is in an old mill beside a trout-filled stream, and the dining room is done in an authentic country style (not from a slick magazine). Likewise, the young people waiting on you obviously haven't been trained at Maxim's, but the food they bring is so good that we easily forgive them. Thirty-year-old Jean-Pierre Silva, after a rather hesitant start, has finally uncorked his limitless talent and creativity. He still has a tendency to awkwardly juxtapose flavors, but most of his creations are happy marriages of traditional country and modern cuisine—witness the browned marrow with zucchini blossoms and mustard seed, or the lobster caramelized in real Burgundy with asparagus in a vervein (herb) broth. His carp "hamburger" with goat cheese and "house ketchup" sauce and his farm rabbit with a cold noodle salad may not be his best efforts—but try his lentils simmered with pigs' feet, his roast pike with herb vinegar, his frogs' legs in a wine-flavored leek stew, his ham-hock stew cooked in a flavorful broth of capers and red wine and then caramelized in the oven, his rabbit in a spicy sauce or his incredibly tender squab. These dishes have kept Burgundians (and since his third toque, the rest of the world) coming back to this lost little village in the hills.

Silva hides a superb pastry chef in his kitchen: himself. His millefeuille of crêpes with an apricot preserve, chocolate sauce and pistachio ice cream is perhaps Burgundy's best dessert, and his caramelized apple tart is no less than the best in the world. If you still need convincing about Silva's talents, try this: Instead of the mundane sorbet between courses, he serves a bowl of hot crayfish broth with celery. Your stomach will cry out with pleasure, and your appetite will be revived a second later. And Isabelle, who introduced us to the most exquisite 1980 Echezeaux, had a wonderful comment after a few moments' reflection: "Basically, a great wine goes with nothing. It goes only with itself." As you can see, you are among fine, unpretentious people. And the fantastic 150-franc fixed-price menu (three courses, cheese and dessert) undoubtably will not be able to convince you otherwise.

A la carte: 350-400F. Menus: 150F, 230F, 330F.

Le Vieux Moulin

(See restaurant above)

Closed Wed. (except holidays) & Nov. 18-25. 1 ste 800F. 11 rms 350-500F. TV. Pets allowed.

After recently completing construction on a quite comfortable hotel with four large rooms and one suite, 150 feet from Le Vieux Moulin in the middle of a field, the Silvas started refurbishing their mill, giving a new decor to the restaurant (see above), and adding a salon and several new rooms overlooking the river.

Boulogne-Billancourt

see PARIS SUBURBS

Boulogne-sur-Mer

62200 Boulogne-sur-Mer - (Pas-de-Calais)

Paris 242 - Lille 115 - Calais 34 - Arras 116

(13) La Matelote

80, blvd. Ste-Beuve - 21.30.17.97

M. Lestienne. Open until 9:30 p.m. Closed Sun. dinner, June 15-30 & Dec. 23-Jan. 15. Pets allowed. Cards: V, MC.

Right near the ocean, the ferries to England and the casino, this building has a plain facade that hides the elegant interior of a luxurious brasserie, with light colors, lots of flowers and well-polished silver. Unfortunately, it's rather cramped inside, and tables are squeezed too close. The owner's wife resembles actress Isabelle Huppert and is aloof. The staff tend to follow her example. Thankfully, the creative Tony Lestienne runs the kitchen with a great deal of attention to natural flavors and precision of cooking: escalope of salmon stuffed with herring (a perfect marriage, unfortunately complicated with a sorrel-spinach sauce), beef filet with (a few) fresh chanterelles, suprême of duck in a delicate vanilla sauce and a light apple feuilleté with cinnamon cream. The wonderful wine cellar is among the best in the region.

À la carte: 300-350F. Menu: 140F, 220F to 265F.

Métropole

51, rue Thiers - 21.31.54.30

Closed Dec. 20-Jan. 3. 27 rms 148-265F. TV. Cards: V.

A centrally located, comfortable, not-too-noisy hotel that is geared to the budget-conscious. No restaurant.

IN NEARBY **Pont-de-Briques**

(5 km S on D 940)

62360 Pont-de-Briques - (Pas-de-Calais)

(14) Hostellerie de la Rivière

17, rue de la Gare - 21.32.22.81

M. Martin. Open until 9 p.m. Closed Sun. dinner, Mon. (except holidays), Feb. school vacation & Aug. Pets allowed. Hotel: 9 rms 90-130F; half-board 230-290F oblig. in seas. Parking. Cards: V.

If you like classic cuisine made with a fresh, youthful approach, go see Jean Martin in his delightful, rustic bistro located between the river and the railroad tracks. His high-quality products, subtle sauces (so unlike the Normans) and precise cooking will combine in the most delicious meal you'll have in Boulogne. Try his shellfish fricassée with lobster sauce, braised turbot with apples, cider and Calvados, fish of the day steamed en papillote with fresh thyme, or roasted sweetbreads

with an herb cream sauce. Desserts are feather-light and delightful, notably the fine tart with apples melted in honey. Good wine selection.
A la carte: 280-300F. Menus: 130F (weekday lunch only), 195F, 260F.

IN NEARBY **Wimille**
(5 km N on N 1)
62126 Wimille - (Pas-de-Calais)

Le Relais de la Brocante

14

2, rue de Ledinghem - 21.83.19.31
MM. Janszen & Laurent. Open until 9:45 p.m. Closed Sun. dinner & Mon. Pets allowed. Parking. Cards: V, AE.

It looks rather like a plain roadside bistro, with an old baby carriage and battered copper wares outside. But it's actually a wonderful, tried-and-true restaurant in a pleasant eighteenth-century presbytery, with elegant tables and a young, courteous and attentive staff. Owners Claude Janszen (former maître d' at L'Atlantic in Wimereux) and Jean-François Laurent (from L'Atlantic, too, where he was executive chef) have great ambitions, so we won't quibble over details. Rather, we will talk about their generous cuisine based on fine, fresh products: lobster ragoût with foie gras, turbot à l'orange, veal kidneys with juniper berries and frozen nougat with red fruit (but we have mixed feelings about the asparagus ice cream). The parish garden, which, we are told, provides herbs and lettuce, is a curious little cemetery where physicist and aeronaut Pilâtre de Rozier has been pushing up daisies since 1785, when he crashed in his balloon on this very spot.
A la carte: 300F and up. Menus: 120F (weekdays only), 150F.

Bourbon-Lancy

71140 Bourbon-Lancy - (Saône-et-Loire)
Paris 308 - Autun 62 - Moulins 36 - Digoin 31 - Nevers 72

Grand Hôtel

Pl. d'Aligre - 85.89.08.87
Closed mid-Oct-mid-April. 22 rms 80-210F. Half-board 70F (plus room). Pets allowed. Cards: V.

A typical old hotel in this sleepy spa town, in a park teeming with birds. The rooms are hopelessly out of date but remarkably well maintained. A marvelous spot for romantic consumptives and nostalgic spa-goers. Restaurant.

Raymond

15

8, rue d'Autun - 85.89.17.39
M. Raymond. Open until 9 p.m. Closed Fri. dinner (except July-Aug.), Sun. (off-seas.), Sat. lunch, April 21-May 2 & Nov. 17-Dec. 9. Air cond. No pets. Hotel: 20 rms 95-210F; half-board 190-275F oblig. in seas. Garage parking. Cards: V, DC, MC.

The ferruginous waters of this old spa town don't attract the trendy spa-goers, and Gérard Raymond's excellent cuisine, served in this appealing family restaurant at the other end of Bourbon-Lancy, suffers a bit from this lack of popularity. Yet Raymond doesn't seem to mind. The cuisine he prepares is surprisingly creative and superbly executed, and its harmonies or oppositions of flavors are simply exquisite. The short menu includes several surprising finds, such as the light foie gras feuilleté with a chicken-gravy vinaigrette and the filet of sole with a parsley mousseline. Overall, the creations have an angelic simplicity—yet they are true masterpieces, notably the pan-fried beef ribs and the roast kidneys with mushrooms. A la carte prices are reasonable, and the fixed-price menus are even better. The wine cellar is a delight, especially the collections of Beaujolais and Burgundies.
A la carte: 300F. Menus: 75F and 105F (weekdays only), 170F, 230F, 280F.

Bourg d'Oisans

38520 Bourg d'Oisans - (Isère)
Paris 615 - Grenoble 50 - Gap 120 - Brianon 68

La Forêt de Marrone

Hameau de Chatelard
38520 La Garde-en-Oisans - 76.80.00.06
Closed April 20-June 10 & Sept. 20-Dec. 15. 12 rms 95-215F. Half-board 150-195F oblig. in seas. Pets allowed. Parking. Cards: V.

Well-situated in the Alpe d'Huez ski area, this hotel is pleasantly calm. Solarium, garden. Restaurant.

Bourg-en-Bresse

01000 Bourg-en-Bresse - (Ain)
Paris 425 - Lyon 61 - Mâcon 34 - Geneva 118

Auberge Bressane

15

166, blvd. de Brou - 74.22.22.68
M. Vullin. Open daily until 9:30 p.m. Terrace dining. Pets allowed. Parking. Cards: V, AE, DC.

Jean-Pierre Vullin is the indefatigable standard-bearer of the cuisine of the Bresse region; his repertoire is remarkably consistent from one year to the next. The pike quenelles aren't very light but are served with a perfect Nantua sauce, and the poultry liver cake is flawless, with its accompanying zucchini and pleurotes. He also produces a quite good dish of parsley-seasoned frogs' legs, although it is drowned in butter; roast pullet with cream or tarragon; and a sumptuous dessert cart featuring chocolate cake, meringues and hot brioches. None of this (nor the wines) comes at inviting prices. We would like, at these tabs, to see a bit of passion and an ounce of enthusiasm. The faultlessly maintained dining room offers a spectacular view of the Brou church and its ornate stone facade from the bay windows. On Sundays, tables are crowded together, forcing you to weave through the dining room to reach your place.
A la carte: 300-350F.

Le Commerce

1, ave. Pierre Sémard - 74.21.30.41
Open year-round. 23 rms 180-240F. Half-board 223-253F. TV. Pets allowed. Garage parking. Cards: V, DC.

It's been just two years since this old hotel was refurbished, and already new life has been brought to the place. It was a job well done. Large terrace, garden, snack bar.

La Galerie
(13)

4, rue Thomas-Riboud - 74.45.16.43

M. Reffay. Open until 10 p.m. Closed Sat. lunch, Sun., 1 week in early Jan. & late July-mid-Aug. Air cond. Pets allowed. Cards: V, AE, DC.

Cheerful, pleasant and fresh—but also professional, with an owner who trained in Lyon and a chef trained at Paris's Hôtel de Crillon. The young waitresses are delightful, and the prices make one jump for joy. So we're happy to bestow a well-earned toque on the émincé of young rabbit with rosemary served on a fine layered galette, the "choucroute" of fennel with smoked salmon (quite amusing and well done) and the émincé of calves' liver, lightly cooked and garnished with carrots and a sherry sauce. This place is also a mecca for great poultry. Sadly, the desserts are a bit plain, and the wine list needs developing.

A la carte: 160-180F.

Jacques Guy
(15)

Pl. Bernard - 74.45.29.11

M. Guy. Open until 9:30 p.m. Closed Sun. dinner & Mon; annual closings vary. Pets allowed. Garage parking. Cards: V, AE, DC.

Jacques Guy left his post at the Petit Relais in Coligny recently to take over this big, thoroughly provincial establishment in the center of town. He will keep his two toques for the delicious marinated salmon with marjoram and an irresistible salad of potatoes and truffles on a bed of lentils and green beans. On the down side, his young pigeon in casserole could stand a shade less cooking, and the young cheese server a shade less stinginess. With the help of his young son, Guy excels in making desserts: rich sorbets, a beautiful chocolate-and-hazelnut tart and a layered apple pastry with cinnamon. The long-enough wine list is not specific enough. Mme. Guy's reception is charming.

A la carte: 300F. Menus: 90F (weekdays only), 130F, 180F, 260F.

Le Mail
(13)

46, ave. du Mail - 74.21.00.26

M. Charolles. Open until 9:30 p.m. Closed Sun. dinner, Mon., July 10-25 & Dec. 24-Jan. 13. Air cond. Pets allowed. Hotel: 9 rms 170-270F; half-board 280-360F oblig. in seas. Garage parking. Cards: V, DC.

At Le Mail you'll find attractive prices, generous portions, a highly professional cuisine and service by gracious ladies. So do what the locals do: Forget about the rather stiff reception from Mme. Charolles, the keychain collection at the entry and the tacky brass sculptures. Then happily order the well-seasoned warm salad of bass filet, the poultry-liver terrine with hazelnuts, the frogs' legs with parsley, the fine creamed mushrooms, and the roasted Bresse chicken with a gratin dauphinois. Don't forget to leave room for dessert, some of which are worthy of two toques (particularly the crusty blueberry tart and the exquisite choux à la crème). Pleasant terrace in back.

A la carte: 250F. Menus: 120F, 150F, 185F, 250F.

Hôtel du Prieuré

49-51, blvd. de Brou - 74.22.44.60

Open year-round. 1 ste 560F. 13 rms 300-460F. TV. Pets allowed. Garage parking. Cards: V, AE, DC.

Some of the rooms in this all-new, modern small hotel have terraces overlooking the marvelous Brou church. No restaurant.

Terminus

19, rue Alphonse-Baudin - 74.21.01.21

Open year-round. 50 rms 218-292F. TV in 40 rms. Pets allowed. Garage parking. Telex 380844. Cards: V, AE, DC, MC.

The best hotel in town, the Terminus is delightfully situated in its own flower garden. All the rooms have been modernized. Friendly service. Restaurant next door: L'Albatros.

Bourges

18000 Bourges - (Cher)

Paris 226 - Nevers 68 - Dijon 245 - Châteauroux 65

Hôtel d'Angleterre

1, pl. des Quatre-Piliers - 48.24.68.51

Open year-round. 31 rms 270-330F. Half-board 244-416F. TV. Pets allowed. Garage parking. Cards: V, AE, DC.

This old Bourges hotel was meticulously restored in 1983. It has good plumbing and a polite staff. Restaurant.

Jacques Coeur
(13)

3, pl. Jacques-Coeur - 48.70.12.72

M. Bernard. Open until 9:15 p.m. Closed Sun. dinner, Sat., July 14-Aug. 13 & Dec. 24-Jan. 2. Pets allowed. Cards: V, AE, DC.

The chic spot in the '60s, this hotel has a decor that's smart (blue and gold fleur de lis) and service that's professional. The old-fashioned cuisine is rich and generous, and now more creative as well: duck with fresh dates, onion fritters with coquilles St-Jacques and, for a bit of exotic regionalism, a soft Caribbean tart made of apple and coconut.

A la carte: 260-280F. Menus: 140F, 175F.

Les Tilleuls

7, pl. de la Pyrotechnie - 48.20.49.04

Open year-round. 29 rms 152-220F. TV. Pets allowed. Garage parking. Telex 782026. Cards: V, DC.

Simple rooms, the best of which open onto a small flower garden. Modest prices. No restaurant.

IN NEARBY **Berry-Bouy**

(8 km NW on D 60)

18500 Mehun-sur-Yevre - (Cher)

La Guelardière
(14)

48.26.81.45

M. Poquet. Open until 10 p.m. Closed Mon. dinner, Tues. & Jan. 15-Feb. 15. Terrace dining. Pets allowed. Cards: V, AE, DC.

Recently we had the good fortune to discover Jean-Claude Poquet, a fine young chef in this charming burg in the heart of Berry. His modesty belies his talents: He is an inventive cook who combines care and remarkable execution. We suggest you go pay a visit to his lovely restaurant at the edge of the village, surrounded by chestnut trees. He has just spruced up the decor and redone one of the dining rooms, which overlooks a pleasant interior garden. Try the salad of Breton lobster, the langoustines with artichokes and ginger, the turbot grilled with spice bread and the marvelous caramel ice cream with a praline sauce. A bit more effort to give pizzazz to the hors d'oeuvres and to temper the use of rich products (even if they are quite reasonably priced) would be welcome. Betty Poquet is an excellent hostess.

A la carte: 250F. Menus: 98F (weekday lunch only, wine incl.), 170F, 210F, 310F.

Le Bourget-du-Lac

73370 Le Bourget-du-Lac - (Savoie)
Paris 527 - Chambéry 11 - Aix-les-Bains 9 - Belley 25

(16) Le Bateau Ivre

79.25.02.66

M. Jacob. Open until 10 p.m. Closed Tues. & Nov. 1-May 5. Garden dining. Pets allowed. Parking. Telex 309162. Cards: V, AE, DC, MC.

In the past, we have had some reservations about this lovely lakefront restaurant. Today we can offer our praises once again, particularly to Jean-Pierre Jacob, son of the owner, since he is now in charge of the kitchens in this superb seventeenth-century salt warehouse. The earlier inconsistencies (we're sorry to mention them) have been rectified, and the second toque is back thanks to the caviar aspic with a cauliflower purée and toasted brioche, the perfectly roasted young pigeon served with its own juice, the fine calf's-tongue salad from the first fixed-price menu, and the delicious chicken fricassée with cèpes that follows it. We almost feel like giving three toques to some of the desserts, such as the pistachio soufflé with bitter-almond ice cream—the young chef really outdoes himself with this one. An excellent wine list is now explained (out on the terrace during the dog days) by a willing young sommelier.

A la carte: 400F. Menus: 215F (weekday lunch only, wine incl.), 290F, 380F, 460F.

(15) Ombremont

2 km N on N 504 - 79.25.00.23

M. Carlo. Open until 10 p.m. Closed Sat. lunch (except July-Aug.) & Jan. 2-Feb. 4. Garden dining. Pets allowed. Garage parking. Telex 980832. Cards: V.

With a setting in a magnificent park with terraces, flower beds and a swimming pool, this fine, proud bourgeois house dating from 1925 is one of the best stopping places in the Savoie region. The dining room has a rich, comfortable Relais et Château decor and a marvelous panoramic view of the lake (and the terrace is even nicer), and the cuisine has improved since Jean-Jacques Barbot took over the kitchen. The owners' decision to stay open almost year-round has eliminated some of the seasonal irregularities in both the service and the cuisine. The latter is now consistently creative and fresh: a salad of foie gras confit with truffle vinegar, frogs'-legs ravioli with fresh herbs, lake trout with génépi (mugwort) and young pigeon breast with strawberry and spinach. Good selection of Savoie wines.

A la carte: 400F. Menus: 210F (weekdays only), 320F, 450F.

Ombremont

(See restaurant above)

Closed Jan. 2-Feb. 4. 2 stes 800-1,200F. 18 rms 425-750F. Half-board 650-800F oblig. in seas. TV in 14 rms. Pets allowed. Heated pool.

Spacious, modern and comfortable rooms and suites overlook the park. Billiards, a putting green, waterskiing and boat trips.

L'Orée du Lac

79.25.24.19

Closed Nov. 1-Jan. 31. 3 stes 1,050F. 9 rms 530-750F. Half-board 475-835F. TV. Pets allowed. Pool. Tennis. Parking. Telex 306773. Cards: V, AE, DC, MC.

An old residence has been transformed into a luxury hotel near the lake and the Bateau-Ivre. No restaurant.

Bouxières-aux-Chênes

54770 Bouxières-aux-Chênes - (Meurthe-et-Moselle)
Paris 321 - Nancy 14 - Eulmont 4 - Metz 44

(14) La Fine Aiguille

6, rue Nationale - 83.31.10.01

M. Schwinderhammer. Open until 9:30 p.m. Closed Sun. dinner, Mon., Feb. & 2 weeks in summer. Pets allowed. Parking.

This discreet restaurant alongside a national highway may surprise you, for inside there's an authentic rustic decor without gimmicks, as well as the fine cuisine of Guy Schwinderhammer. He is a professional, proud of making everything himself with products from all over France. All his dishes are personal and original: the cured ham from the Lorraine, the carp salad with gooseberries (or eel salad with raspberries), the duck foie gras served with honey bread, the carp with Burgundy, the remarkable andouille with a mustard cream, and the unforgettable Kirsch Munster. All are prepared with a simplicity and sincerity that you won't find elsewhere in the region. Excellent wines are selected by Guy's wife, Annie. All house products can be prepared to go.

A la carte: 260-280F.

Bracieux

41250 Bracieux - (Loir-et-Cher)
Paris 182 - Romorantin 32 - Blois 18 - Orléans 57

(17) Le Relais

(Bernard Robin)

1, ave. de Chambord - 54.46.41.22

M. Robin. Open until 9 p.m. Closed Tues. dinner, Wed. & Dec. 20-Jan. 31. Air cond. Pets allowed. Cards: V.

We were hoping to be able to promise you peaceful nights in the Bracieux forest here—but alas, Bernard Robin's waterside hotel isn't quite completed. In the meantime, at his restaurant, he followed our suggestion and replaced the dreadful paintings with more pleasant landscapes and still lifes. The natty dining room, decorated in pink fabrics and blond woods and facing well-manicured lawns, provides a delightful setting for the savory cuisine. We would prefer a repertoire that listed more dishes from Tourain and was less reliant on such dishes as fleurs de courgettes (zucchini flowers)—even though they are perfectly well prepared—chilled oysters with sea urchins à la crème (whose flavor is scant) and fresh cod with anchovies accompanied by a potato purée (nothing out of the ordinary). None of that will upset the gastronomical balance in France. Robin has won us over, though, with local specialties prepared in his own manner: the Chambord-style carp filet; salmon with chicken gravy and beef marrow; beef sautéed in Vouvray wine, accompanied by mouth-watering potatoes that are flavored slightly with vanilla; veal kidneys and feet with parsley, garnished with a salad of fresh beans and chèvre. And a marvelous oxtail shepherd's pie—hachis parmentier—with its gravy and diced fresh truffles. Dominique, the charming and knowledgeable sommelier and maître d', will help you choose from an astonishing collection of Loire wines: Valençays, Chevernys, Meslands, Montlouis, Beaugencys, Chinons and Jasnières, all of which will dazzle you. Try them with lemon-cream-filled crêpes topped with apricot sauce or a warm chocolate Pithivier (almond cream cake), both of which illustrate Robin's mastery of pastry making.

A la carte: 350-400F. Menus: 175F (weekdays only), 250F, 350F.

Brantôme

24310 Brantôme - (Dordogne)
Paris 480 - Périgueux 27 - Limoges 90 - Nontron 22

13 Les Frères Charbonnel

(Hôtel Chabrol)
59, rue Gambetta - 53.05.70.15

MM. Charbonnel. Open until 9 p.m. Closed Sun. dinner & Mon. (off-seas., except holidays), Feb. 10-28 & Nov. 15-Dec. 10. No pets. Hotel: 20 rms 220-400F; half-board oblig. in seas. Cards: V, AE, DC.

The plant-filled dining room is hung with Louis XIII wallpaper; the tapestries look a bit incongruous. Nonetheless, this large, opulent residence along the Dronne has a proud allure, and the dining room would be quite comfortable if the tables were not so close together. The mistress of the house is gracious and charming, the staff good humored, and Jean-Claude Charbonnel's menu monumental (his wine list even more so). The most difficult part is choosing in the face of such a magnificent array of products. Once more, we chose at random: the medley of seafood was plentiful and well seasoned with cider vinegar, the lotte in orange aspic was delicious, with a wonderful red cabbage–parsley mousse, and the Rossini squab had a powerful taste (though its sauce was too thick). And we can't forget the marvelous desserts, notably the large but light pear-caramel feuilleté served with fruits and sorbets.

A la carte: 300F and up. Menus: 105F and 160F (weekdays only), 170F to 230F, 310F.

15 Moulin de l'Abbaye

1, rte. de Bourdeilles - 53.05.80.22

M. Bulot. Open until 9:30 p.m. Closed Mon. & Nov. 5-May 5. Garden dining. Pets allowed. Garage parking. Telex 560570. Cards: V, AE, MC.

All the charm of Périgord can be found in this picturesque setting: the caverns carved into the cliffs, the abbey's bell tower where the abbot wrote his memoirs, the weeping willows above the waters of the Dronne and, at the foot of a bridge with uneven arches, the old mill covered with wild grapevines. Régis Bulot fell in love with the place and restored it from ruins, and now it's part of the exclusive Relais et Châteaux club (of which Bulot has been elected president). He has not abandoned his passion for gastronomy, but because of his two establishments (he also owns a hotel in Courchevel, where he goes in winter), he has turned over these kitchens to the young but well-qualified Christian Ravinel. On the flowery terrace overlooking the river, one discovers moments of true happiness, especially with the terrine of duck foie gras, shellfish stew with beans and chanterelles, leg of lamb with mild garlic, poultry with truffle butter, oven-roasted Rocamadour cheese, and apricots and gooseberries in Sauternes. Wines include Château La Gineste and Château de Chambert (also served by the glass), as well as a white Bergerac and, to accompany the copious "Richmont" fixed-price menu (330 francs), Brut Impérial Moët et Chandon.

A la carte: 350-450F. Menus: 165F (lunch only), 330F (wine incl.), 200F, 260F.

Moulin de l'Abbaye

(See restaurant above)

Closed Nov. 5-May 5. 2 stes 750-1,200F. 7 rms 460-650F. Half-board 580-780F oblig. in seas. TV. Air cond. in 4 rms. Pets allowed.

Air-conditioned rooms and suites are pleasantly decorated (although the paintings and some of the knickknacks are not in the best of taste) and complemented by marvelous views of the river and the old houses of one of the prettiest villages in France. Relais et Châteaux.

La Bresse

88250 La Bresse - (Vosges)
Paris 425 - Gérardmer 14 - Colmar 53

11/20 Les Vallées

31, rue Paul-Claudel - 29.25.41.39, 29.25.55.10

MM. Rémy. Open daily until 9:30 p.m. Pets allowed. Garage parking. Telex 960573. Cards: V, AE, DC, MC.

In this excellent inn geared to the winter-sports crowd, the decor is simple and functional, the service quick without razzmatazz, and the food generous and rather good: steamed turbot, breast of duck with cider, chocolate cake with cherries.

A la carte: 180F. Menus: 75F to 185F.

Les Vallées

(See restaurant above)

Open year-round. 60 stes 2,740-3,600F weekly. 54 rms 210-340F. Half-board 280-440F. TV. Pets allowed. Heated pool. Tennis.

These spacious rooms, including those in the annex, are perfectly equipped. Covered pool, sauna, weight room, disco.

Bresson

see Grenoble

Brest

29200 Brest - (Finistère)
Paris 590 - Rennes 244 - St-Brieuc 145

Sights. Cours Dajot (superb view of the bay at the mouth of the Elorn and the Albert-Louppe bridge); Musée (paintings from the seventeenth and eighteenth centuries); Musée du Vieux Brest (located in the fourteenth-century Tanguy tower); Musée Naval (marine history); botanical gardens of Stangalard, in Vallon; boat rides from the Port of Commerce to the bay, the Crozon peninsula and the isle of Ouessant.

Eating on the Run. La Chaumine, 16, rue Jean-Bart in Recouvrance (Breton, good crêpes); La Fleur de Blé, 11, rte. de Gouesou (good crêpes and galettes); Le Grand Pavois, in the Port de Plaisance marina (terrace with beautiful view); La Pensée Sauvage, 13, rue d'Aboville (comic-book library, good cakes); Vitamines, 4, rue Ernest-Renan (low-calorie menu).

Brasseries. L'Atlantide, ave. Clemenceau (spanking new); La Choucroutière, 14, rue Louis-Blanc in Saint-Martin (choucroute and fondue); Voyageurs, 15, ave. Clemenceau (central, paneled dining room, fast service).

Bars & Cafés. Le Conti, Square de la Tour d'Auvergne (Second-Empire decor); La Gentilhommière, 33, ave. Clemenceau (congenial); Loft, 30, rue St-Marc (exhibits, films); Le Macao, 11, rue de la Porte in Recouvrance (tea room, ice cream, videos); La Martingale, 26, rue Magenta (house punch, jazz, Caribbean music); Les Mouettes, 30, quai de la Douane at the Port of Commerce (house grog); Paris, pl. Sanquer (café/theater); Windsor, 8, rue Louis-Pasteur (pub, beer).

Nightlife. Le César, Port of Commerce (young, trendy); Melody, in Guipavas (students); Le Nautilus, rue de Siam (intimate, middle-age crowd); La Soute, 22 bis, rue de Lyon (English style, salty ambience); Le Stendhal, 18, rue Colbert (two floors, according to one's age). Late-night restaurants in the Recouvrance quarter: La Barcalla (decent pizza, piano jazz); L'Estocade (good paella); L'Osso Buco (best saffron rice in town); Sri Lanka (excellent curry).

Continental

Square de la Tour d'Auvergne
98.80.50.40

Open year-round. 1 ste 370F. 75 rms 170-350F. TV. Pets allowed. Telex 940575. Cards: V, AE, DC, MC.

Rather dated but not without charm, the Continental is a comfortable hotel that has a lovely lobby with a mezzanine, an impressive meeting room and impeccable service. Several rooms have been well renovated. Restaurant.

(15) Le Frère Jacques

15 bis, rue de Lyon - 98.44.38.55

MM. Peron. Open until 9:30 p.m. Closed Sat. lunch, Sun. & July 3-16. Pets allowed. Cards: V, MC.

It's true that the wine prices are a bit steep and the waiters surly, but otherwise, we can't find much to complain about at Le Frère Jacques. Claudine Peron is a delightful hostess, the 1930s wainscot decor has a pleasant exotic touch, and the china is superb. Jacques Peron's cuisine starts with some appetizers (delicious salmon and warm oysters) and ends with the fresh-fruit soup with a light cinnamon cream. In between, the portion of fried langoustines is a bit stingy, but it is accompanied by an excellent aspic, a light saffron cream and a blanquette of brill seasoned with seaweed (which Peron uses skillfully); and the lovely escalope of skate with a marvelous calamari ragoût tastes of Brittany.

A la carte: 300F. Menus: 145F, 190F, 270F.

(13) Le Poulbot

26, rue d'Aiguillon - 98.44.19.08

M. Martin. Open until 9:45 p.m. Closed Sat. lunch, Sun. & Aug. 13-Sept. 4. Air cond. Pets allowed. Cards: V, AE, DC, MC.

The bistro decor is sober and the cuisine full of pleasant surprises: an excellent plate of seafood steamed with soybeans and beurre blanc, lotte steak with sorrel and oysters, squab with mussels and young vegetables and the fresh-fruit "farandole" with a mint cream. Good wine cellar.

A la carte: 250F. Menus: 70F (lunch only), 118F, 152F, 240F.

11/20 Sofitel Océania

82, rue de Siam - 98.80.66.66

Open daily until 10 p.m. Pets allowed. Telex 940951. Cards: V, AE, DC.

The pleasant, multilevel modern decor in wood is reminiscent of luxury-liner cabins. The place is quite comfortable and well-conceived, but the cuisine lacks discipline: dull oceanic salad and veal kidneys with shallots in a flat sauce.

A la carte: 230-250F. Menus: 68F (weekday lunch only), 200F (weekends and holidays only), 85F, 135F.

Sofitel Océania

(See restaurant above)

Open year-round. 82 rms 320-530F. Half-board 405F. TV. Pets allowed.

A mere kilometer from the sea stands this imposing corner building. Pleasant bar, efficient and gracious service.

(14) Les Voyageurs

15, ave. Georges-Clemenceau
98.80.25.73

M. Lombard. Open until 9:45 p.m. Closed Mon. & July 21-Aug. 11. Air cond. Pets allowed. Hotel: 40 rms 115-290F; half-board 195-220F. Telex 940660. Cards: V, AE, DC, MC.

The planned renovation of the large upstairs dining room has been postponed, which is just as well, since the ocean-liner decor is perfectly comfortable, with a kitsch charm that is aging well (the ground-floor brasserie is designed like a ship's hold). The cuisine is professional, generous and fresh: magnificent seafood and fish (fried sole, poached brill, fresh salmon) and a great variety of mixed salads and grilled meats. The à la carte prices are a bit steep, but the fixed-price menus offer true seafood feasts for a song in the small first-floor brasserie.

A la carte: 300F. Menus: 48F, 67F, 180F, 210F.

Breuil-en-Auge

14130 Pont l'Evêque - (Calvados)
Paris 204 - Caen 55 - Deauville 20 - Lisieux 9

(14) Le Dauphin

31.65.08.11

M. Lecomte. Open until 9 p.m. Closed Sun. dinner, Mon. & Jan. 17-Feb. 10. No pets. Cards: V.

We can't hide our disappointment: Our most recent meals in this lovely Norman cottage pointed to a deteriorating cuisine. It's not that Régis Lecomte showed any laziness in his creative efforts; it was just rather sluggish execution. The dishes sound exciting and look appetizing but are lax in their preparation. Only the zucchini flowers stuffed with lobster mousse truly revealed the fine talents of this chef. Unfortunately, that wasn't the case with the skate fin, which was well cooked but had too strong a flavor from the hazelnut butter and was accompanied by insipid chanterelles; or for the pork filet mignon with a cider sauce served on a bed of potatoes and bland apple slices; or for the overrich rhubarb feuilleté (pastry cream plus caramel sauce plus brown sugar). On the up side, the decor features a hearth and fine old beams, the hosts are always gracious, and the cider has a delightful taste.

A la carte: 350F. Menus: 110F (weekday lunch only), 170F.

Breuillet

see Royan

Brignogan-Plage

29238 Brignogan-Plage - (Finistère)
Paris 538 - Brest 37 - Landerneau 26

(14) Castel-Régis

Pl. du Garo - 98.83.40.22

M. Plos. Open until 9 p.m. Closed Sept. 30-March 19. No pets. Garage parking. Cards: V.

Castel-Régis is situated at the tip of a small peninsula, placing the sea at your feet at high tide, and enticing you with its pleasant, rustic Breton decor. The young hostess is delightful, the owner's wife ever more so, the service as slow as it is remarkable, and the cuisine classic (even the "modern" section): buckwheat galette filled with crab, deliciously enlivened with a butter-curry sauce, an enormous bass steak with puréed langoustines (well made, but the beurre blanc is a bit thin), and an interesting and copious turbot with a rather strong pigs'-feet sauce. Don't miss the many wonderful desserts. Good fixed-price menus.

A la carte: 400F. Menus: 110F and 175F (weekdays only), 190F (weekends and holidays only).

Castel-Régis

(See restaurant above)

Closed Sept. 30-March 19. 17 rms 230-360F. Half-board 325-390F. Pets allowed. Heated pool. Tennis.

Spectacular scenery. The rooms, most of which are bungalows for two to four people, have marvelous views but plain interiors.

Brinon-sur-Sauldre

18450 Brinon-sur-Sauldre - (Cher)
Paris 188 - Bourges 64 - Cosne-sur-Loire 59

(13) La Solognote

Grande-Rue - 48.58.50.29

M. Girard. Open until 8:30 p.m. Closed Tues. dinner (except July-Aug.), Wed., Feb., April 16-26 & Sept. 13-28. Hotel: 13 rms 190-275F. Parking. Cards: V.

This little village house lives and breathes old bourgeois virtues. Tables are elegantly set in a deep-red decor, which features "art sketches" and dolls from the Sologne region. The staff is charming (though dawdling). As for Dominique Girard, the owner, he will have to fight harder to keep his toque. There's much banality on his menu these days (such as the émincé of haddock with poorly peeled lime, and the overly dry baked kidneys). On the other hand, he offers good curries of salmon and turbot and fine regional game in season. The prices are a bit steep.

A la carte: 250-280F. Menus: 135F, 210F, 260F.

Brive-la-Gaillarde

19100 Brive-la-Gaillarde - (Corrèze)
Paris 468 - Limoges 96 - Toulouse 212

(13) La Belle Epoque

27, ave. Jean-Jaurès - 55.74.08.75

M. Cherronnet. Open until 10:30 p.m. Closed Sun. dinner & 1 week for Feb. school vacation. Pets allowed. Cards: V.

Young owner/chef Thierry Cherronnet has been taken to task for virtually ignoring the local Brive cuisine. That's because he is an "immigrant" from Lyon. Besides, his plate of Brive specialties (foie gras, confit, duck saucisson and carpaccio) is so stingy that he might as well stop trying to work in a tradition whose generosity seems so foreign to him. On the other hand, he can be astoundingly good when me makes such dishes as lightly cooked breast of duck with a lovely sauce thickened with cocoa (an old Flemish recipe), seafood fricassée with zucchini and ginger, and his fine strawberry feuilleté. The staff is eager to please, though the decor (in blue and pink-ocher) is less than cheerful.

A la carte: 250-280F. Menus: 89F (weekday lunch only), 125F to 290F.

(15) La Crémaillère

53, ave. de Paris - 55.74.32.47

M. Reynal. Open until 9:30 p.m. Closed Sun. dinner & Mon. Garden dining. No pets. Cards: V.

Nearly everyone who has dined here will be happy to learn that Charlou Reynal has once again earned a second toque. (We say *nearly*, since one reader says he is still digesting an escargots feuilleté "from a tropical drought," as well as "sad and greasy" lamb chops à la provençal). We have always adored his sander with morels, his light ravioli of cèpes and foie gras, his salmon paupiettes with sweet peppers, his sublime cassoulet with confit, his duck petits salés with luscious white beans, and his vanilla ice cream—one of the best we've tasted recently—accompanied by warm caramel cherries. This passionate, bearded chef, who recently published an excellent book of regional recipes, has skillfully mastered the Brive cuisine, which he prepares with personality and modernism. Yet he maintains modest prices, even with his exceptional wine list—the best in Corrèze—that includes some outstanding Bordeaux. The rustic dining room is attractive, with plenty of elbow room, and Charlou and Régine are the perfect host and hostess.

A la carte: 200-250F. Menus: 120F, 160F, 200F.

La Crémaillère

(See restaurant above)

Closed Sun. & Mon. 9 rms 140-220F.

Located above the restaurant, this typical family hotel has several quite comfortable rooms with rather cold decors.

Mercure

5 km W, Le Griffolet - 55.87.15.03

Open year-round. 57 rms 345-375F. TV. Pets allowed. Pool. Tennis. Parking. Telex 590096. Cards: V, AE, DC, MC.

Near the Griffolet Château and its waters, in a tranquil five-acre park, the Mercure has rooms with terraces and new carpeting, along with a restaurant overlooking the pool.

IN NEARBY **Varetz**
(10 km NW on D 901 & D 152)
19240 Allassac - (Corrèze)

(15) Château de Castel Novel

55.85.00.01

MM. Parveaux. Open until 9:15 p.m. Closed mid-Oct.-early May. Pets allowed. Parking. Telex 590065. Cards: V, AE, DC.

Albert Parveaux, who owns two excellent hotels in the Alps and a château in the Dordogne region, remains nonetheless very much attached to this immense feudal castle, which has been restored throughout the centuries and in which Colette lived and wrote. With his elegant blond wife, Christine, Parveaux keeps an eye on every detail of the service and cuisine in this magnificent restaurant created by his father in 1956. Prepared by chef Jean-Pierre Faucher, the scrupulously light cuisine is based largely on regional specialties, with a few "modern" exceptions (on a special menu). It has won back its second toque with the world's best truffle omelet, the masterful pan-fried foie gras with cider, the roast turbot with coriander cooked "southern style" with a light olive-oil gravy, the duck pot-au-feu with scalded chestnuts and the chilled mousse with Corrèze chestnuts (the traditional desserts are a bit too complicated). You'll taste all of this in the small dining room in back, which was once Colette's library, or, even better, in the long room with beams and bay windows that offers a lovely view of the Limousin greenery. Good cellar with rare though ordinary-tasting Brive wines.

A la carte: 350-400F. Menus: 200F, 295F, 390F.

Château de Castel Novel

(See restaurant above)

Closed mid-Oct.-early May. 5 stes 900-1,360F. 32 rms. 330- 900F. Half-board 595-1,035F. TV. Pets allowed. Pool. Tennis.

The beautiful rooms are freshly decorated in cheerful and warm tones. The large park features tennis courts and a magnificent pool (complete with a lunch buffet). Less luxurious rooms are found in the annex, La Borderie. Excellent service.

Bubry

56310 Bubry - (Morbihan)
Paris 483 - Lorient 34 - Pontivy 22 - Vannes 53

Auberge de Coët-Diquel

1 km W on VO - 97.51.70.70

Closed Dec. 1-March 15. 20 rms 225-278F. Half-board 250-276F oblig. in seas. Pets allowed. Heated pool. Tennis. Parking. Cards: V, MC.

These rustic rooms are situated in a pleasant, large park on the edge of a trout stream. Special facilities for receptions and groups. Restaurant.

Le Bugue

24260 Le Bugue - (Dordogne)
Paris 525 - Périgueux 40 - Bergerac 48 - Sarlat 33

(14) L'Albuca

Pl. de l'Hôtel-de-Ville - 53.07.28.73

M. Rouffignac. Open until 10 p.m. Closed Mon. & Tues. lunch & Oct. 1-May 1. Terrace dining. Pets allowed. Garage parking. Telex 540710. Cards: V, AE, DC, MC.

The decor is a bit pompously classic but quite comfortable, with a large bay window that overlooks the Vézère river bubbling in the lush vegetation (it's illuminated at night). The cuisine is strictly Périgord, whether it's sumptuous (salmon pancakes with Catherine de Médicis cèpes, beef Talleyrand) or country-style (tourain—onion—soup with garlic, duck confit, nut cake). Several more creative dishes are skillfully prepared, such as langoustines with asparagus. Good fixed-price menu and magnificent regional wines, especially the Bergerac.

A la carte: 300F. Menus: 110F.

Auberge du Noyer

Le Reclaud de Bouny Bas - 53.07.11.73

Closed Nov. 20-March 24. 10 rms 180-340F. Half-board 240-300F. No pets. Pool. Garage parking. Cards: V, MC.

An English couple, who adore the Périgord region, have transformed this old farmhouse into a refined hotel with spacious, quiet rooms and lots of charm. Fine British reception and excellent breakfast. Restaurant.

Bussang

88540 Bussang - (Vosges)
Paris 435 - Mulhouse 50 - Epinal 60 - Belfort 43

Les Sources

12, rte. des Sources - 29.61.51.94
Closed Nov. 15-Dec. 15 (except by reserv.). 9 rms 185-250F. Half-board 195-220F oblig. in seas. TV. No pets. Parking. Cards: V.

This excellent little hotel near the source of the Moselle river has a congenial family atmosphere and a simple but well-maintained decor. Restaurant.

Buxerolles

see Poitiers

Cabourg

14390 Cabourg - (Calvados)
Paris 225 - Caen 24 - Deauville 19 - Lisieux 33

Le Balbec

Promenade Marcel-Proust - 31.91.01.79
M. Lauthelier. Open daily until 10 p.m. Terrace dining. Pets allowed. Telex 171364. Cards: V, AE, DC, MC.

Between the sea and municipal gardens, the Italian Renaissance–style facade of this grand hotel hasn't changed since it was popular during the days of Proust (the management had the good idea to gather mementos from those days in a special souvenir room). The dining room decor is not fabulous, but the cuisine is top-notch and consistent in every aspect: salad with two types of salmon and radishes, braised turbot with leeks and apples, and breast of duck with three fruits. Fine fixed-price menus and a comprehensive wine cellar.

A la carte: 300F and up. Menus: 150F, 190F.

Pullman Grand Hotel

(See restaurant above)
Open year-round. 2 stes 1,590-1,610F. 68 rms 600-740F. Half-board 210F (plus rm). TV. Pets allowed.

A magnificent marble lobby, some immense rooms and rather reasonable rates for a luxury hotel. Tea dances are held in summer, and a piano bar is open on weekends.

IN NEARBY **Bavent**
(7 km SW on D 513 & D 95A)
14860 Ranville - (Calvados)

Hostellerie du Moulin de Pré

Rte. de Gonneville-en-Aug
31.78.83.68
MM. Hamchin & Holtz. Open until 9 p.m. Closed Sun. dinner & Mon. (except holidays & July-Aug.), March 1-15 & Oct. Parking. Cards: V, AE, DC.

This small, unpretentious inn, recently built, is a true family restaurant, with a young self-taught owner, Jocelyn Holtz, at the stoves. Sit by the large fireplace at a macramé-covered table set with flowers, and try the vegetable terrine with duck foie gras, shellfish stew, sea trout back with leeks or smoked duckling thighs with cabbage. The recent effort to vary the vegetable garnishes has certainly been appreciated by the guests. Wild ducks gather in the small pond.

A la carte: 280-300F. Menus: 195F to 230F.

Hostellerie du Moulin du Pré

(See restaurant above)
Closed Sun. & Mon. (except holidays & July-Aug.), March 1-15 & Oct. 10 rms 125-235F. No pets.

Several lovely (though rather noisy) rooms decorated in pink face the countryside and a pond. Haphazard service.

IN NEARBY **Merville-Franceville-Plage**
(6 km on D 514)
14810 Merville-Franceville-Plage - (Calvados)

Chez Marion

10, pl. de la Plage - 31.24.23.39
MM. Marion. Open until 9:30 p.m. Closed Mon. dinner & Tues. (except school vacations), Jan. 2-Feb. 3. Terrace dining. Pets allowed. Hotel: 18 rms 130-265F; half-board 215-292F oblig. in seas. Telex 170234. Cards: V, AE, DC, MC.

For the last 40 years the Marion family has enjoyed a solid reputation for serving fine seafood in its large restaurant, which is, unfortunately, devoid of charm. The cuisine is prepared with intelligence, simplicity, generosity and talent: langoustines sautéed with fresh thyme, fried red mullet, braised turbot with coriander, bass steamed with lemon, young salmon grilled whole with chives. The prices are a bit steep but justified. Fine Loire wines (sparkling Vouvray, red Touraine) and a good selection of Calvados.

A la carte: 300F. Menus: 420F (weekends and holidays only), 93F, 170F, 230F.

Cabrerets

46330 Cabrerets - (Lot)
Paris 566 - St-Céré 64 - Figeac 41 - Cahors 34

Auberge de la Sagne

Rte. des Grottes de Pech-Merle
65.31.26.62
Closed Oct. 1-May 1. 10 rms 120-180F. Half-board 150-180F oblig. in seas. Parking. Cards: V, AE, DC.

Located next to the Pech-Merle caves, this beautiful stone residence has cozy rooms (with direct telephone lines) at very reasonable rates. Restaurant for guests.

La Pescalerie

65.31.22.55
Mme. Combette. Open until 9 p.m. Closed Nov. 1-April 1. Terrace dining. Parking. Cards: V, AE, DC.

Eight days at La Pescalerie will do you better than any hypnotherapy or rejuvenating spa. Every year, as soon as the manor opens on the edge of the romantic Célè river, the magic returns, as if time has no hold over this blessed place cradled between prehistoric cliffs; perhaps men were already savoring the sweetness of Quercy some 40,000 years ago at this spot. La Pescalerie is much like a house of old friends; you are awakened by the crowing of the cocks, and after a delicious breakfast enjoyed in a soft bed, you can linger on the terrace until lunchtime without a worry in the world. As for the kitchen, you'll find René Sarre there every morning with the fresh vegetables he's just picked from the garden, the trout just caught from the nearby stream, and all sorts of fine farm products from the Causse region. The master of the house, the indefatigable Roger Belcour, who hasn't yet retired from his medical practice, divides his time between the operating room and the dining room, where, rolling up his sleeves, he turns into a sommelier and sometimes even a waiter. People come here from the world over, yet they all have in common an appreciation for *l'art de vivre* and a refined simplicity that becomes veritable luxury. Strangely enough, rare are the guests who expect to find just another Relais et Châteaux, with everyone in monkey suits, silver bell covers on the plates and all the regalia. Here, the refinement is more subtle, including Sarre's cuisine, which is "home-style" cooking. You won't see flamboyance, just excellent garden salads, well-tossed and seasoned; farm-raised chicken roasted with sage and served with a remarkable clear gravy that contains a few morsels of smoked duck skin; rabbit confit with tarragon; grilled duck with honey; stuffed cabbage (the creation of Hélène, the mistress of the house). Not to mention lamb shoulder, artichoke ragoût with wild mushrooms, peaches stewed in Cahors wine, pear tourte and a red-fruit tart (the orchard's own strawberries, raspberries and gooseberries). It's natural, digestible and savory food, making this place one of those rare restaurants in which you can eat twice a day without tiring of it. Of course, as you've understood by now, La Pescalerie is more than just a restaurant.

A la carte: 250-300F. Menus: 195F, 240F.

La Pescalerie

(See restaurant above)

Closed Nov. 1-April 1. 10 rms 440-580F. TV in 5 rms. Pets allowed.

This lovely manor house sits along the Célè river in absolute tranquillity, amid lush greenery and magnificent rock formations. The decor in each of the ten rooms is distinct, with antique furniture, beautiful modern paintings and a variety of sumptuous bathrooms. Excellent service and a heavenly breakfast. Relais et Châteaux.

Cabrières-d'Avignon

84220 Gordes - (Vaucluse)
Paris 715 - Avignon 35 - Gordes 7 - Cavaillon 12

13 Le Bistro à Michel

Grande Rue - 90.71.82.08, 90.76.82.08

M. Bosc. Open until 9:15 p.m. Closed Mon., Tues. & Jan. 2-Feb. 6. Terrace dining. Pets allowed.

This place was a village café when we were last in the area, so it was quite a surprise to find such a lively cuisine full of freshness and imagination. But Michel Bosc didn't want to stop there. He redid the decor, added a terrace, upped the prices and created a new menu that isn't necessarily more attractive. Still, some wonderfully generous dishes and imaginative fish preparations have emerged, though there has been a decline in a few dishes, notably the veal kidneys in Madeira sauce and the aiguillettes of guinea-hen. Try the delicious pieds et paquets (mutton feet and tripe) and the exquisite house desserts.

A la carte: 180-230F. Menu: 95F.

Caen

14000 Caen - (Calvados)
Paris 222 - Rouen 124 - Cherbourg 119

Sights. The château and its museums (the Beaux-Arts, the Normandy); Musée d'Anthropologie and Musée de la Nature (natural history); Saint-Etienne church (men's abbey); Trinity church (women's abbey); the Saint-Sauveur district and the rue Froide; the old restored Vaugeux district.

Eating on the Run. Alcide, pl. Courtonne (good rustic dishes); Chantergrill, 17, pl. de la République (simple but fresh and fast); La Fringale, 20, rue du Vaugeux (casual, friendly and the best grill in town); Pizzeria Amalfie, 20, rue St-Jean (best pizzas); Le Ménestrel, 20, rue Porte-au-Berger (plain but convenient, open until 2 a.m.).

Bars & Cafés. American's Bar, 11, quai de Juillet (large selection of whiskies and extravagant cocktails); L'Inconnue, 12, rue d'Enfer; Pub Concorde, 7, rue Montoir-Poisonnerie (excellent beers); Le Rétro, 9, rue Fresnel.

Nightlife. Le Chic, 19, rue Prairies-St-Gilles; Le Jackspot, 20, rue Vauquelin (discotheque); La Lucarne, 15, rue Permagie (singles); La Poterne, 20, rue Porte-au-Berger.

Shops. *Bakeries:* Foucher, 1, rue Gailon. *Gourmet foods:* Poupinet, 8, rue St-Jean. *Chocolate:* Hotot, 13, rue St-Pierre; Témoins, 69, rue St-Pierre (for its Calvados-filled chocolates). *Cheese:* Au Chabichou, 10, rue Aimé-Lair; Galerie des Fromages "Les Pieds de Dieu," 2, rue des Chanoines (the best of the Norman producers and other varieties). *Pastries:* Stiffler, 72, rue St-Jean (eclairs). *Wines:* La Cave du Port, 56, quai Vendeuvre; Les Caves Thorel, 32, rue Neuve-St-Jean; Nicolas, 10, rue Bellivet. *Miscellaneous:* Librarie Générale du Calvados, 98, rue St-Pierre (bookstore with everything on Normandy).

18 La Bourride

15-17, rue de Vaugueux
31.93.50.76

M. Bruneau. Open until 9:30 p.m. Closed Sun., Mon., Jan. 3-24 & Aug. 16-Sept. 3. Pets allowed. Cards: V, AE, DC.

A new Bocuse? Why not? Like his compadre from Lyon, this hearty 38-year-old from Normandy understands that know-how is not enough. Still, Michel Bruneau writes, and not without a certain ingenuous wink, "Today, know-how is everything." As far as we know (except for Xiradakis in Bordeaux, who along with others puts out a publication for the promotion of regional products), Bruneau is the only chef who sends out a regular newsletter to his clients and the press. Actually, it should be called a letter of whim. Entitled "A Passion Called Cooking," it allows Bruneau, a real nut about cooking, to dip his pen alternately in vinegar and honey and let himself go wholeheartedly. He can write of his love for his region and take journalists to task for not writing about it enough; break with current wisdom to declare it a scandal that one or another of his colleagues was underrated in a guide; give a recipe and organize contests, with the prize money coming out of his own pocket.

Obviously, Caen is not Lyon, and the "Bruneau Gang," assuming he has one, will not replace the memory of the "Bocuse Gang" all that soon. Still, in the exuberance of this unique, captivating man you can see the same remarkable passion that twenty years ago inspired the young star of the Saône river and that shook the foundations of the culinary establishment. Unlike Bocuse—at least for now—Bruneau hasn't been dragged into the system or tempted by juicy contracts and international tours. He's perfectly happy in his little old house in Caen, he doesn't nurture any dreams of grandeur, and nothing so far could deprive him of the pleasure of taking his post in front of his ovens surrounded by his team. "I'm no dancer," he says, "and our clients pay enough to deserve a total feast."

It does, in fact, befit a feast to sit under the low ceiling of this four-century-old room. Its burnished furniture, old stones, antique knickknacks and bouquets of flowers create an inviting and timeless atmosphere. Lively and cheerful, Françoise Bruneau goes from table to table, giving out smiles and advice and describing the surprises of the "discovery menu" that her husband changes every day.

At the source of his cooking is a demand not only for irreproachable products, but for the best that can be found in Normandy's ports and markets. And he brings out the best in these products with an extreme sensitivity, a perfect mastery of proportions and a subtle sense of nuance that translates into personal dishes marked by an airy lightness. When you show up for your "initiation," don't hesitate to make it a long visit. In one sitting, we consumed a persillé of tourteau (crab) with leeks and aromatic herbs; a salad of calf's tongue with lentils and wine vinegar; a fricassée of regional andouille sausage in cider vinegar; turbot in a potato écaille (shell); a green-apple sorbet whose Calvados touched the tips of our toes, not invading the palate but waking it up. We moved on to a baby pigeon in a salt and vanilla-bean crust, a sliver of Livarot and another of Pont l'Evêque cheese (which we'll remember for years to come) and, finally, two or three desserts, such as the millefeuille in licorice cream and the chocolate marquise in vanilla cream. After all this, you, like us, will be so surprised that you still feel as fresh as a daisy that you won't know what to praise the most: your appetite or Bruneau's talent for whetting it.

And if you still have your doubts about the cooking of Normandy, try attacking his "Petit Normand" fixed-price menu. The crab terrine, oysters bathed in pommeau (apple juice and Calvados aged in oak), confit of tripes à la mode, veal filet in cider with a lightly smoked flavor, local cheeses and crêpe à la Bénédictine will sweep away your prejudices.

At our last visit, Françoise Bruneau and Eric Gilment, who are in charge of the wine cellar, were completely redoing their wine list. Since it was already quite fine, it can only become excellent.

A la carte: 300-500F. Menus: 175F (lunch only), 217F, 292F, 397F.

(14) Le Dauphin

29, rue Gémare - 31.86.22.26

MM. Chabredier. Open until 9:30 p.m. Closed Sat., Feb. school vacation & July 16-Aug. 12. Pets allowed. Parking. Telex 171707. Cards: V, AE, DC, MC.

This warm and intimate spot in a former priory near the château boasts elegant tables, a highly polished staff and a delightful patronne. Her husband, chef Robert Chabredier, prepares a largely regional repertoire but is continually trying to keep it light. It's a treat for those who like cream, cider, Calvados and pommeau (another apple brew) in their dishes. His ranking is climbing a notch, thanks to his fine mackerel marinated in cider, duck in a sweet-salty sauce with pommeau, ramekin of langoustines with fresh pasta and the delicious rhubarb charlotte. One of the best wine cellars in the region, though affordable wines are scarce.

Menus: 80F (weekdays only), 140F, 195F, 280F.

Le Dauphin

(See restaurant above)

Closed Feb. school vacation & July 16-Aug. 12. 21 rms 200-350F. TV in 18 rms. Pets allowed. Parking.

Pleasant little rooms, most with color televisions, and extremely attentive service.

(14) Les Echevins

Le Castel,
35, rte. de Trouville - 31.84.10.17

M. Régnier. Open until 9:30 p.m. Closed Sun. (except holidays), Feb. school vacation & July 9-31. Pets allowed. Parking. Cards: V, AE, DC, MC.

Not long ago, Patrick Régnier set himself up in this superb Anglo-Norman "castle" dating from 1882, situated in the middle of a park. A large entrance room and an opulent dining room in the "grand bourgeois" style, with elegant silverware on the tables, await you. The Paris-trained chef has expanded his horizons, developing his taste and talents for fine seafood: wonderful warm oyster mousseline with a broccoli purée, turbot with watercress and bacon croquettes, and warm smoked salmon with ginger and cucumbers.

A la carte: 300-400F. Menus: 135F, 205F, 275F.

12/20 Les Quatre Vents

116, blvd. du Maréchal-Leclerc
31.86.04.23

Mme. Mabille. Open until 10 p.m. Closed Sun. dinner (Oct. 15-March 15). Pets allowed. Garage parking. Telex 171106. Cards: V, AE, DC, MC.

Unfortunately, we have to rescind many of our nice comments from reviews past, because of the lackadaisical, noisy service and the surprisingly unimaginative and sloppy cooking that we encountered recently. We did not expect a dull rack of lamb, an uninteresting lobster and prawn salad and a gelatinous red-fruit mousse. So we must take back the toque.

A la carte: 260F. Menus: 85F, 135F, 195F.

Moderne

(See restaurant above)

Open year-round. 56 rms 170-480F. Half-board 291-471F. TV. Pets allowed.

This quiet hotel in the pedestrian zone near the center of town features stylish, cute, pleasant rooms. Direct access from garage.

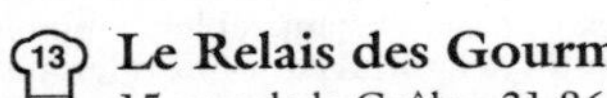

Le Relais des Gourmets

15, rue de la Geôle - 31.86.06.01

M. Legras-Daragon. Open until 9:30 p.m. Closed May 1. Garden dining. Pets allowed. Telex 171657. Cards: V, AE, DC, MC.

The owner of this solid provincial house (whose brand-new decor we haven't yet seen) is well connected with several Ouistreham fishermen, who save the best fish from the Seine bay for him. That's where the special charm of the cuisine, prepared by a young Alsatian chef, comes from: lobster millefeuille with cèpes, a braid of lotte and salmon with dill, and brill chausson with a leek cream sauce. There are also some excellent giblet dishes, a fine wine cellar stocked with 50,000 bottles and several wonderful old Calvados.

A la carte: 350F. Menu: 210F (wine incl.).

Le Relais des Gourmets

(See restaurant above)

Open year-round. 7 stes 550-760F. 20 rms 270-380F. Half-board 422-587F. TV. Pets allowed.

The modern rooms are conveniently situated near the château and the Saint-Pierre church. Good soundproofing, excellent service.

IN NEARBY **Bénouville**

(10 km NE)

14970 Bénouville - (Calvados)

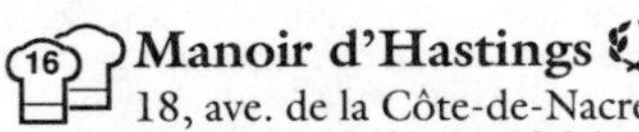

Manoir d'Hastings

18, ave. de la Côte-de-Nacre

31.44.62.43, 31.44.63.14

M. Scaviner. Open daily until 9:30 p.m. Pets allowed. Parking. Telex 171144. Cards: V, AE, DC.

Charming, 50-year-old Claude Scaviner, who made this former priory the top restaurant in Normandy, claims he is self-taught, which is probably true; but his son Yves, now in charge most of the time, can't quite make the same statement, simply because he is his father's pupil. This elegant young man would be well advised to liven up (and lighten up) the classic sauces tinged with regionalism that are the basis for the house repertoire. A good omen is the newly created turbot, perfectly cooked and served with carrots, apples and a delicious pommeau (apple juice and Calvados) sauce; there's also a perfect cold consommé of oysters and langoustines with coriander. The menu is still agreeably eclectic, including lobster with cider and tripe, a ragoût of truffles, fresh foie gras and ham with cider (with an exquisite blanquette of potatoes and leeks), oysters in sabayon sauce with asparagus tips, and lamb navarin. The desserts are more tasty than delicate, which is the case with the warm Norman tart (a whole apple cooked in a crust and dressed with a thin crêpe with Calvados). Unable to offer garden dining—the Norman weather is too changeable—the Saviners have transformed their salon/bar into a winter garden of sorts; it is a pleasant extension of their always inviting and cheerful dining room, with its beamed ceiling hung with scarlet fabric. Gracious service, fine wine cellar.

A la carte: 350F. Menus: 160F, 280F, 370F.

La Pommeraie

(See restaurant above)

Open year-round. 11 rms 500-850F. Half-board 660-720F. Pets allowed.

Set in a field, this white inn built by the Saviners isn't wildly alluring, but it does have eleven wonderfully comfortable rooms.

Cagnes-sur-Mer

06800 Cagnes-sur-Mer - (Alpes-Maritimes)

Paris 920 - Cannes 22 - Nice 13 - Antibes 11

Le Cagnard

Hauts-de-Cagnes, rue de Pontis-Long

93.20.73.21

M. Barel. Open until 10 p.m. Closed Thurs. lunch & Nov. 1-Dec. 18. Terrace dining. Pets allowed. Parking. Telex 462223. Cards: V, AE, DC, MC.

Delightful nooks and crannies, medieval vaults, low ceilings, antique furniture and a terrace surrounded by greenery and flowers—the small shingled houses (within the old ramparts of this perched city) that Felix and Mauricette Barel have patiently restored make for one of the most appealing and surprising Relais et Châteaux on the Côte d'Azur. The clientele is discreet and appreciates beauty, the staff is attentive, and the chef, Jean-Yves Johany, is excellent. In this enchanting atmosphere of romantic solitude, it's easy to imagine the quality of the pleasures await for you. The cuisine is consistent, though it's becoming increasingly expensive. Try the artichoke-eggplant cake, the sweetbreads in Noilly, the tian (casserole) of John Dory with Champagne butter and the pear flan with pistachio ice cream.

A la carte: 500F. Menus: 320F, 410F.

Le Cagnard

(See restaurant above)

Open year-round. 9 stes 550-1,000F. 11 rms 330-500F. TV. Air cond. in 3 rms. Pets allowed.

Exquisitely comfortable rooms, most with private terraces sheltered from prying eyes, are tucked into a charming residence behind the ramparts of the town. Relais et Châteaux.

Les Collettes

Chemin des Collettes

Closed Nov. 16-Dec. 25. 13 rms 253-346F. Pets allowed. Pool. Tennis. Parking. Cards: V, AE, DC.

This small hotel/motel (choose between the two options) has simple, rather pleasantly decorated rooms. No restaurant.

(13) Josy-Jo

Hauts-de-Cagnes, 8, pl. du Planastel
93.20.68.76

MM. Bandecchi. Open until 10 p.m. Closed Aug. 7-22. Terrace dining. Pets allowed. Cards: V.

This place has been full for the last twenty years, thanks to the delightful team of Jo and Josy Bandecchi. They take turns at the stoves in their adorable house in the greenery, with its wonderful terrace under the arbor. The cuisine is basic, unchanging and without pretense. But the quality of the products is impeccable—delicious Limousin meats, for example—and the execution is perfectly controlled: fish soup, stuffed artichokes, grilled fish, generous steaks (sirloin, T-bone), leg or rump of lamb, and calves' liver braised over a wood fire.

A la carte: 230-250F.

IN NEARBY **Cros-de-Cagnes**
(2 km SE)
06170 Cros-de-Cagnes - (Alpes-Maritimes)

---

(13) Picadero

3, blvd. de la Plage - 93.73.57.81

M. Miraglio. Open until 10:30 p.m. Closed Mon. & Dec. 1-15. Terrace dining. Pets allowed. Cards: V.

This rather homely bistro beside a noisy road has a loyal clientele of horse racing fans. The cuisine is professional and generous (the chef trained with Maximin), though not exactly light. One toque for the fine, fresh flavors: calamari fricassée, sweetbreads braised with thyme flowers and feuilleté of caramelized apples. The wine list is making progress.

A la carte: 250F. Menu: 98F (weekday lunch only), 135F.

(15) La Réserve

91, blvd. de la Plage - 93.31.00.17

M. Bertho. Open until 9:45 p.m. Closed Sat., Sun., holidays, June 30-Sept. 4 & Dec. 22-Jan. 2. Air cond. No pets. Cards: V, MC.

Loulou Bertho, a former law clerk and administrator, is a connoisseur of cuisine who hates slovenliness; he'd rather close his restaurant in summer than greet the bathing-suit-and-Bermuda-shorts crowd. His seafood is of only the very best quality—so when the three fishermen who cast their nets almost exclusively for him don't show up (perhaps due to a storm, or the pastis they've drunk), he serves only meat dishes: the best quality beef or lamb (raised in salt marshes) from one of Paris's top butchers and marvelously cooked over his wood-fire rotisserie. But seafood is definitely Bertho's strong point, so try his fish soup and his red mullet, bass, shrimp, mackerel or gilthead, all cooked to a meticulous precision en papillote, braised or steamed and served simply, retaining their delicate, natural flavors. This small restaurant, which looks like the many others on the highway along the sea, is in truth one of France's best seafood places.

A la carte: 400F.

(13) La Villa du Cros

On the port, blvd. de la Plage
93.07.57.83

M. Biccherai. Open until 9:30 p.m. Closed Sun. dinner, Mon. & Dec. 15-Jan. 15. Air cond. Terrace dining. Pets allowed. Parking. Cards: V, AE, DC.

Many of our readers tell us they are delighted by Jean Biccherai, the charming old-school chef who reigns here. The decor is a bit confined, but the terrace over the sea is lovely, the service cheerful and efficient, and the cuisine good and light: a langoustine cake flavored with basil, gnocchi in a tuna bourride and excellent fish (Biccherai has his own fisherman). The desserts are making progress. Select from the good wine cellar run by the knowledgeable Lucienne Biccherai.

A la carte: 300F. Menus: 170F and 250F (weekdays only), 210F (weekends and holidays only).

Cahors

46000 Cahors - (Lot)
Paris 569 - Rodez 121 - Brive 102 - Montauban 60

---

(14) Le Balandre

Ave. Charles-de-Freycinet
65.30.01.97, 65.35.24.50

M. Marre. Open until 10 p.m. Closed Sun. dinner & Mon. (off-seas.), Sat. lunch (in seas.), Feb. 1-20 & June 5-12. No pets. Garage parking. Cards: V, AE.

Gilles Marre has realized his dream of taking over the Hôtel Terminus and its restaurant, which was opened by his grandfather at the turn of the century. He had been a cook at the Elysée, then at the finest restaurants in Brussels (Villa Lorraine) before coming back to France (Taillevent and Haeberlin). He has maintained the authentic Belle Epoque decor (somewhat faded but still delightful) and created a cuisine that cleverly blends the local tradition (albeit lightened) with some of his own imaginative spirit. The thick lobster soup, the cod brandade (a preparation based on garlic, oil and cream) with warm oysters and curry, the poached pike with watercress butter, the warm escalope of foie gras with a sweet-and-sour sauce of honey and cinnamon, and the Quercy lamb panaché with juniper berries are some of his better creations. Also, don't miss his excellent desserts, particularly the walnut duchesse with chicory ice cream and the pan-fried millas (meal blend) with sugar and caramel ice cream. Lovely Cahors wines in every price range enhance this lively and generous cuisine, which is also light on the pocketbook.

A la carte: 280-300F. Menus: 100F, 175F, 230F.

Hôtel Terminus

(See restaurant above)

Open year-round. 31 rms 160-260F.

This solid, traditional family hotel faces the lovely Valentré bridge and has a pleasant terrace.

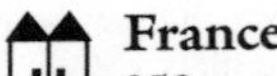

France
252, ave. Jean-Jaurès - 65.35.16.76
Closed Dec. 23-31. 80 rms 155-240F. TV in 37 rms. No pets. Garage parking. Telex 520394. Cards: V, AE, DC, MC.

Modern and comfortable, this hotel is located between the train station and the Valentré bridge over the Lot river. No restaurant.

IN NEARBY **Lamagdelaine**
(7 km N on D 653)
46000 Cahors - (Lot)

---

(14) **Marco**
65.35.30.64
M. Marco. Open until 9:30 p.m. Closed Sun. dinner, Mon., Jan. 3-March 3 & Oct. 22-Nov. 3. Terrace dining. Pets allowed. Parking. Cards: V, AE, DC.

Ten years of stubborn effort and enthusiasm have finally paid off for Claude Marco. In his attractive ivy-covered house, he has patiently created a most elegant and comfortable dining room under the stone vaults. In summer, though, diners sit on the terrace around the lovely fountain to sample some of his fine cuisine. The products are excellent, the execution more and more precise, and the herbs and vegetables from his garden (which he lovingly cultivates) contribute to such delightful dishes as tomato quenelles with cucumber served with lobster, truffled lamb kidneys with parsley and duck breast with caramelized endive. There are a number of new dishes, including the superb warm oxtail salad and lamb noisettes and kidneys with cèpes biscuits. Lise Marco is an outgoing, charming hostess. Regional wine cellar (primarily Cahors).

A la carte: 300F. Menus: 100F (weekdays only), 170F, 240F.

IN NEARBY **Mercuès**
(7 km N on N 20 & D 941)
46000 Cahors - (Lot)

(13) **Château de Mercuès**
65.20.00.01
M. Buchin. Open until 9:30 p.m. Closed Jan. 1-April 1 & Nov. Terrace dining. Pets allowed. Parking. Telex 521307. Cards: V, AE, DC, MC.

The large buildings and watch towers of the old fortress of Cahors' counts and bishops still rise above a beautiful country landscape. Recent renovations have considerably improved the stately dining room, and the cuisine has broken through to one-toque level, with fine foie gras–truffle ravioli, salmon tournedos with saffron and a feuilleté of caramelized pears. The wonderful wine cellar (dug into the rock) holds the best vintages of Georges Vigouroux.

A la carte: 300-350F. Menus: 180F, 250F.

Château de Mercuès
(See restaurant above)
Closed Jan. 1-April 1 & Nov. 7 stes 900-1,600F. 16 rms 500-1,000F. TV in 10 rms. Pets allowed. Pool. Tennis.

These rooms and suites overlook an immense, marvelous woodland landscape. Commendable renovation; fine bathrooms. Extras include a heliport and tours of local wine cellars. Relais et Châteaux.

Cala-Rossa

see CORSICA: Porto-Vecchio

Calais

62100 Calais - (Pas-de-Calais)
Paris 305 - Amiens 155 - Aras 113 - Dunkerque 39

12/20 **George V**
36, rue Royale - 21.97.68.00
M. Beauvalot. Open until 9:30 p.m. Closed Sat. lunch, Sun. dinner & Dec. 24-Jan. 6. Pets allowed. Parking. Telex 135159. Cards: V, AE, DC.

This very comfortable hotel restaurant has a curious neo–Haute Epoque decor. The cuisine is eclectic, and the young chef quite capable: fresh duck foie gras croquette, coquilles St-Jacques with Champagne and Cantonese-style gambas (prawns).

A la carte: 280-300F. Menus: 190F (weekends and holidays only), 140F.

George V
(See restaurant above)
Open year-round. 45 rms 110-260F. Half-board 210-280F. TV in 28 rms. Pets allowed.

Small but spanking new, George V has impeccable rooms, complete with fine bedding and good service.

Campigny

see Pont-Audemer

Cancale

35260 Cancale - (Ille-et-Vilaine)
Paris 360 - St-Malo 14 - Dinan 34 - Rennes 72

Pointe du Grouin
Pte.-du-Grouin - 99.89.60.55
Closed Tues. & Sept. 30-April 1. 18 rms 150-240F. Half-board 240-320F oblig. in seas. Pets allowed. Parking. Cards: V.

At the tip of the peninsula facing the Mont Saint-Michel bay, you'll find these comfortable but plain rooms and a panoramic view from the restaurant.

(18) **Restaurant de Bricourt**
1, rue Duguesclin
99.89.64.76
M. Roellinger. Open until 10:30 p.m. Closed Tues., Wed. & Dec. 15-March 15. Pets allowed. Cards: V, MC.

Now we know where to go to digest Olivier Roellinger's cooking—which is, of course, as light as air. Until recently, there was no really comfortable place to stay in Cancale. But our young three-toque chef just got hold of a fishing house in a wooded park 500 yards from the pretty setting where he opened his restaurant several years ago. So now you can sleep in one of six rooms that open onto the sea, the oyster beds and Mont Saint-Michel.

This is obviously a most agreeable plus, yet another reason to discover this unusual, warm chef, whose ratings have been skyrocketing in our guide. A former chemical engineer, Roellinger approaches his cooking with the eye of an alchemist. His greatest passion is the blending of flavors, and this destroyer of fat and executioner of needless sugar has proven his uncommon virtuosity. He may be crazy about Far Eastern spices (a great Malouine tradition), but he's learned to temper his usage, and only a fool would fail to grasp the fresh flavors, knowing simplicity and exquisite harmony of his idiosyncratic cooking. Artfully and intelligently, it celebrates the fruits of the sea and of Brittany.

One more time, we've fallen under Roellinger's spell from tasting or retasting his buckwheat galettes (typical of the region) with smoked salmon and langoustine tails, asparagus tips mixed with divine baby potatoes and fresh morels in Sauternes, Breton lobster sautéed simply with just a touch of parsley, raw bar (local fish) with aromatic herbs added with a lab technician's precision, white barbue (a variety of turbot) with girolle mushrooms and parsley in a strong but still subtle sauce, regional calves' liver with cardamom, an incomparable lamb from the saltwater fields of Mont Saint-Michel, and baby farm pigeons in Sureau vinegar with the breasts served separately in a bouillon of foie gras. And the feast continues with fruit gratins, bitter-chocolate cream puffs in coffee sauce, pannequets (a version of crêpes) in a slightly sharp sauce and the mangau with raspberries, a savory adaptation of a Breton dessert that Roellinger makes with fresh farmer cheese nestled in a meringue à l'italienne.

But don't expect this to be like any other restaurant. Here you're really in someone's home. They've just added a few tables in three little rooms authentically done in the eighteenth-century and First Empire style that was favored by the local celebrities. It's a place in which you speak softly, at least more softly than the rare ducks that cackle around the pond in the quasi-tropical garden (which, we might add, is beautiful). But if you go for country inns where they really make you feel at home, it would be wise to go elsewhere.

The Loire wines are excellent, and the prices are gentle (although the portions are not exactly gargantuan).

A la carte: 280F. Menu: 100F (weekdays only).

Hôtel de Bricourt

(See restaurant above)

Closed Jan. 1-March 15. 6 rms 500F. TV.

The sound of the waves from the other side of the little garden will lull you to sleep, so you may dream of the meal you have just eaten or are going to eat at the Restaurant de Bricourt. Chef Roellinger has just opened six rooms in this charming bourgeois house with a pretty English-style decor. The view of Saint-Michel bay is stunning, as is the breakfast.

Cancon

47290 Cancon - (Lot-et-Garonne)
Paris 595 - Agen 48 - Cahors 81 - Bergerac 41

(13) Château de Monviel

Monviel (11 km NW on D 124 & D 241)
53.01.71.64

M. Leroy. Open until 9:15 p.m. Closed Wed. & Nov. 15-April 15. Terrace dining. Pets allowed. Parking. Telex 571544 Cards: V, AE, DC.

This manor-house dining room is tastefully decorated and comfortable, with intimate nooks, white stone, modern paintings and a superbly pastoral environment. We were delighted by the return to fine form of the cooking: nicely done escargots pie, properly cooked salmon with a sweet-pepper cream sauce and kidneys in sweet wine. The reception is at once elegant and friendly.

A la carte: 250F. Menus: 120F, 180F, 250F.

Château de Monviel

(See restaurant above)

Closed Nov. 15-April 15. 1 ste 800F. 9 rms 390-590F. Half-board 425-525F oblig. in seas. TV. Pool.

You'll find a handful of spacious, luxurious lodgings for sleeping like a prince or princess in this beautiful seventeenth-century castle, recently renovated. It offers a sumptuous view of its seventeen-acre estate and lovely pool. The absolutely impeccable service is supervised by the refined lady of the house. Relais et Châteaux.

Candé-sur-Beuvron

41120 Les Montils - (Loir-et-Cher)
Paris 196 - Blois 15 - Tours 50 - Montrichard 23

(14) La Caillère

36, rte. des Moutils - 54.44.03.08

M. Guindon. Open until 9 p.m. Closed Wed. & Jan. 15-March 1. Garden dining. Pets allowed. Hotel: 6 rms 170-220F; half-board 298F. Parking. Cards: V, AE, DC, MC.

After feasting your eyes on the Renaissance castles, you can indulge your stomach in this bucolic cottage halfway between the royal châteaux at Blois and Chaumont (Cheverny is also nearby), while looking at a pretty flower garden along the Beuvron river. The amiable Jacky Guindon, alone for the past few years, has quickly created one of the best restaurants in the region. Despite his enthusiasm, imagination, simplicity and precision, he hasn't quite been discovered. We found just the slightest lack of discipline in execution during our last visit, which held us back from bestowing a second toque on the terrine of young rabbit en gelée (without much flavor) and the carp in cabbage leaves, a good idea that failed to make the grade (can one really do something special with carp?). On the other hand, the skate salad (sometimes replaced by sea bream) was exquisite, and the warm fruit millefeuille was delicious. Short and judicious wine list.

A la carte: 250-300F. Menus: 98F (weekdays only), 138F, 188F, 235F, 290F.

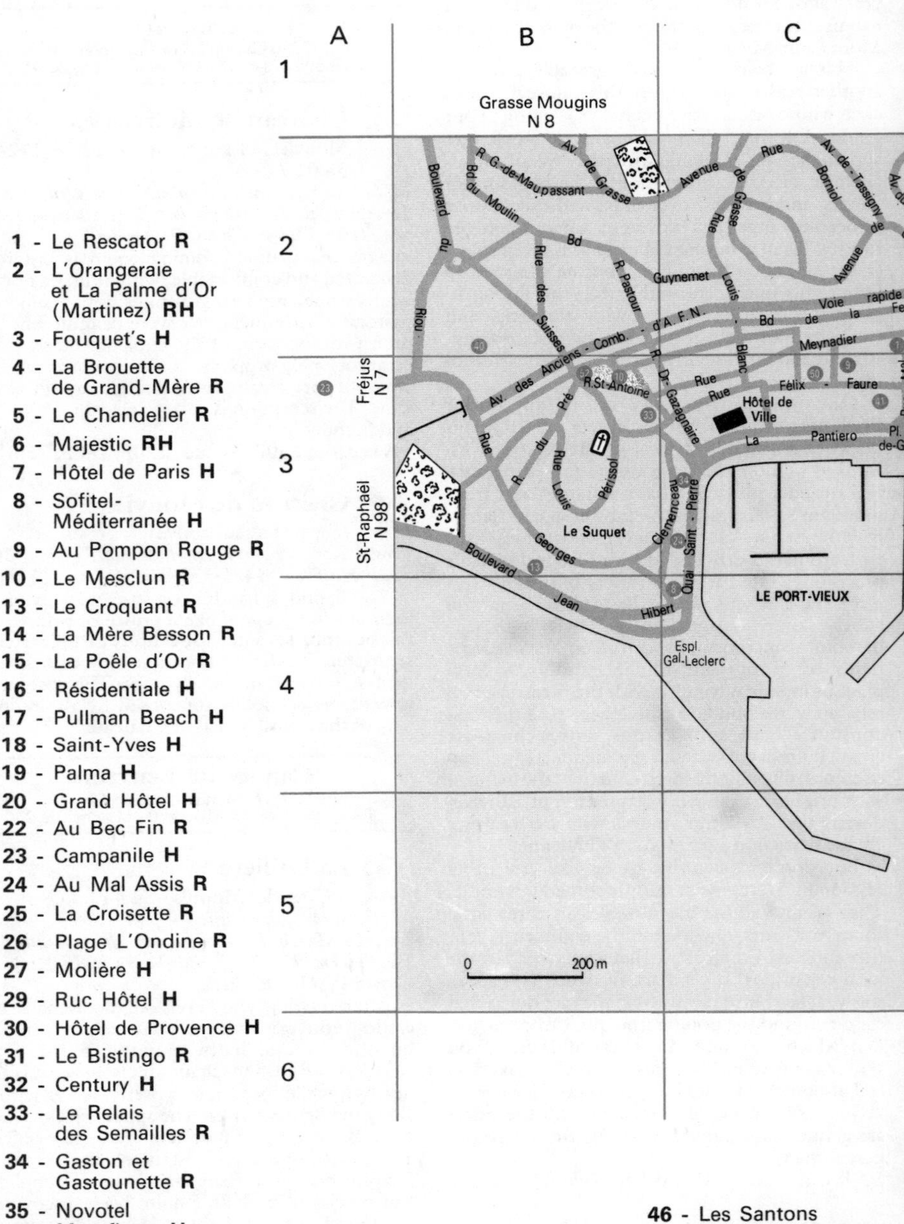

1 - Le Rescator **R**
2 - L'Orangeraie et La Palme d'Or (Martinez) **RH**
3 - Fouquet's **H**
4 - La Brouette de Grand-Mère **R**
5 - Le Chandelier **R**
6 - Majestic **RH**
7 - Hôtel de Paris **H**
8 - Sofitel-Méditerranée **H**
9 - Au Pompon Rouge **R**
10 - Le Mesclun **R**
13 - Le Croquant **R**
14 - La Mère Besson **R**
15 - La Poêle d'Or **R**
16 - Résidentiale **H**
17 - Pullman Beach **H**
18 - Saint-Yves **H**
19 - Palma **H**
20 - Grand Hôtel **H**
22 - Au Bec Fin **R**
23 - Campanile **H**
24 - Au Mal Assis **R**
25 - La Croisette **R**
26 - Plage L'Ondine **R**
27 - Molière **H**
29 - Ruc Hôtel **H**
30 - Hôtel de Provence **H**
31 - Le Bistingo **R**
32 - Century **H**
33 - Le Relais des Semailles **R**
34 - Gaston et Gastounette **R**
35 - Novotel Montfleury **H**
36 - Le Festival **R**
37 - Le Bouchon **R**
38 - Le Saint-Benoît **R**
39 - Les Quatre Saisons et Le Royal Gray (Gray d'Albion) **RH**
40 - Beau Séjour **H**
41 - Splendid **H**
43 - Escale de Chine **R**
44 - Le Monaco **R**
45 - La Côte (Carlton) **RH**
46 - Les Santons de Provence **R**
47 - Villa Dionysos **R**
48 - La Petite Maison **R**
49 - La Madone **H**
50 - Le Caveau "30" **R**
52 - La Mirabelle **R**

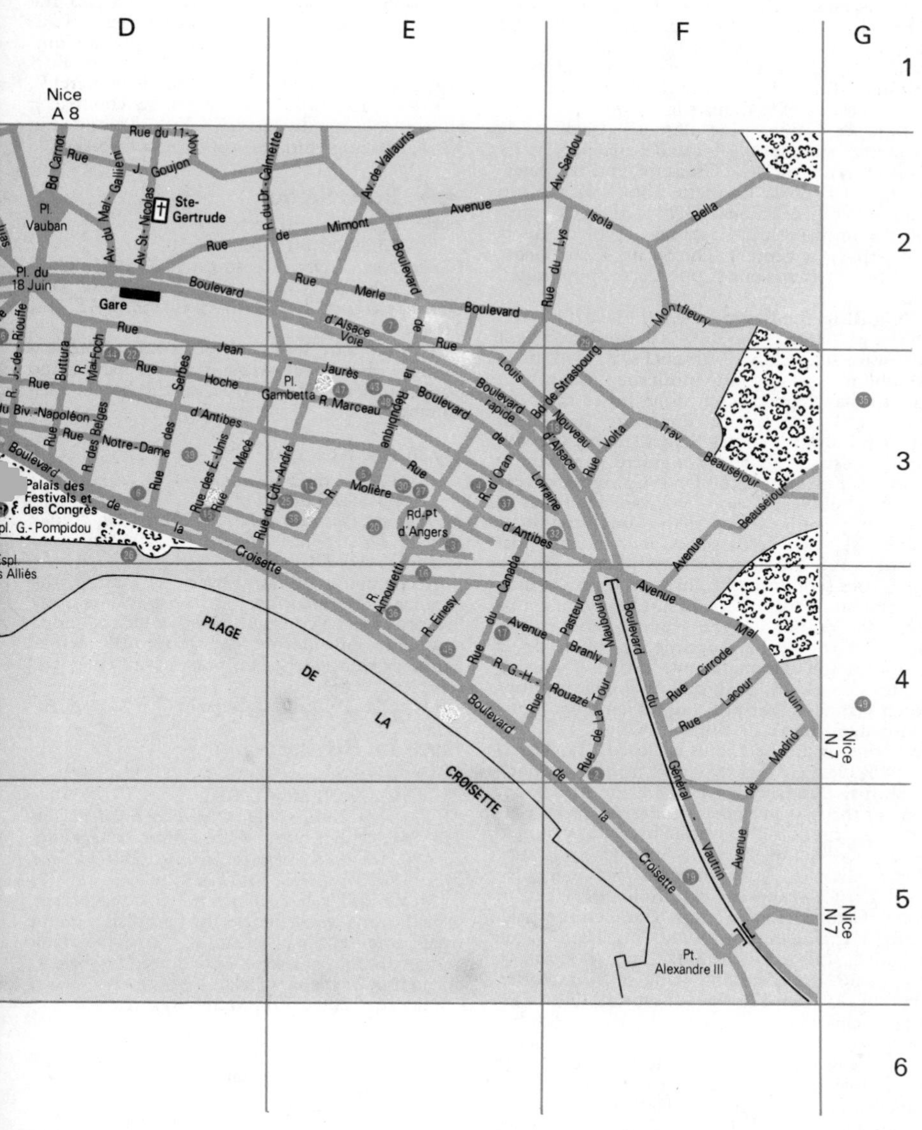

Cannes

06400 Cannes - (Alpes-Maritimes)
Paris 910 - Monte-Carlo 52 - Nice 33

Note: The numbers following the telephone number in each review pinpoint the establishment's exact location on the accompanying map.

Sights. Boulevard de la Croisette and its new Palais des Festivals; Le Suquet (old town); Musée de la Castre (archaeology, ethnography, regional history); the Old Port (boats to the Lérin islands); Observatory of Super-Cannes (fine panorama); Bellini Chapel (stunning Florentine baroque style, Bellini paintings); the Lérin islands—Sainte-Marguerite (Musée de la Mer, prison of the Man in the Iron Mask) and Saint-Honorat (old and contemporary monasteries).

Eating on the Run. Bart's, 67, blvd. de la République (cheerful and popular, shellfish); Maison du Caviar, 1 bis, rue Notre-Dame (foie gras, smoked salmon, caviar); Le Manhattan, 3, rue Félix-Faure (4 a.m.-8 a.m. and 7 p.m.-2:30 a.m.); Le Pirandello, 17, rue du Dr-Monod (Neapolitan style, lots of pasta); La Pizza, 3, quai St-Pierre (chic); Rohr, 62, blvd. de la Croisette (daily specials and wine by the glass).

Brasseries. The triumvirate at the pl. du Général-de-Gaulle—Le Claridge (lively), Le Cintra (young) and Le Noailles (trendy); Le Festival, 52, blvd. de la Croisette (hot festival spot); La Grand Brasserie, 81, rue d'Antibes (the rendezvous of the elite Cannes in crowd).

Bars & Cafés. Blue Bar, 48, blvd. de la Croisette (strategically located); the bars at Le Carlton, 58, blvd. de la Croisette, and Le Majestic, 6, blvd. de la Croisette (both with piano music); Bar du Martinez, 73, blvd. de la Croisette (very comfortable); Ragtime, 1, blvd. de la Croisette (jazz center); The Swan, 4, rue Georges-Clemenceau (young, pub decor, pop music, beer).

Nightlife. Bar Basque, 14, rue Macé (first stop on the gay circuit); Le Blitz, 10, rue Macé (best new-wave nightclub); Brummel's, 3, blvd. de la République (good young musicians); Cancan, 1, rue Emile-Négrin (charming hostesses); La Chunga, 1, rue Latour-Maubourg (late-night set); Club 06, 5, rue des Belges (nightclub with pizza); Disco 7, 7, rue Rouguière (transvestite show); L'Effronté, 5, rue Dr-P-Gazagnaire (very gay and bubbly); Galaxy, at Palais des Festivals (young people from good backgrounds, gamblers); Gent'l, 6, rue Commandant-Vidal (reopens at 5 a.m. for croissants); Jane's, 38, rue des Serbes (comfortable, chic, good restaurant); Le Kamasutra, 90, ave. de Lérins (less young); La Nouvelle Vague, 17, rue Jean-de-Riouffé (live jazz and rock); Le Ragtime, 1, blvd. de la Croisette (pivotal nightspot, excellent music); Studio-Circus, 48, blvd. de la République (top-notch Cannes nightspot, big-screen video, gift-and-gadget shop); Le Whisky à Gogo, 115, ave. de Lérins (when Le Circus is closed); Le Zanzi-Bar, 85, ave. Félix-Faure (classic men's hangout).

Shops. *Butchers:* Bruyère, 38, rue Meynadier (one of the best in France). *Bakeries:* Jacky Carletto, 2, rue Dr-P-Gazagnaire (old-fashioned bread); Collignon, 2, rue d'Alger (favorite supplier of the top chefs). *Gourmet foods:* Giry, 15, blvd. Carnot (excellent caterer for large receptions); Claude Traiteur, 6, pl. Gambetta (classic, perfect). *Chocolate, confections:* Angelica, 74, rue d'Antibes (glazed chestnuts, fine chocolates); Bruno, 50, rue d'Antibes (king of fruit confit); Maiffret, 31, rue d'Antibes (best selection of artisanal chocolate); Schies, 84, rue d'Antibes (Swiss and Alsatian specialties). *Gourmet shops:* Boutique des Landes, 13, pl. du Marché-Forville (fresh foie gras, excellent artisanal preserves); Canelle, 32, rue des Serbes (Fauchon products); Le Coin Gourmand, 14, ave. Buttura (foie gras, Italian sausage, good wines); La Côte d'Or, 107, rue d'Antibes (top-quality products, excellent "tea boutique"); François, 106, rue d'Antibes (exotic fruits, young vegetables); La Maison du Caviar, 1 bis, rue Notre-Dame (caviar, smoked fish, escargots); Ludovic Rovera, 50, rue Meynadier (the unfindable—chestnut, lupine flour). *Ice cream:* Alaska, 13, rue des Etats-Unis (great selection of ice cream and sorbets); Vilfeu, 19, rue des Etats-Unis (always has new flavors). *Cheese:* Agnèse, 114, rue d'Antibes (limited choice but excellent quality); Ceneri (La Ferme Savoyarde), 22, rue Meynadier (one of the best in France, exceptional selection). *Pasta:* Aux Bons Ravioli, 31, rue Meynadier (fresh-pasta champion). *Pastries:* Madame Ernest, 53, rue Meynadier (original cakes); Michel Rohr, 63, rue d'Antibes (specialist in textured pastries). *Wines and spirits:* Caves de la Peyrière, 7, pl. du Commandant-Maria (classic, good selection of Bordeaux and Burgundy); La Maison de la Bière, 7, rue des Alleis (200 beers from 25 countries); Sunshine, 5, rue du Maréchal-Joffre (founded in 1863, amazing vintages, 160 types of whisky).

Beau Séjour

5, rue des Fauvettes
93.39.63.00 / B2-40

Closed Nov. 5-Dec. 18. 46 rms 220-540F. Half-board 240-625F. TV. Air cond. Pets allowed. Pool. Garage parking. Telex 470975. Cards: V, AE, DC, MC.

This modern, well-equipped tourist hotel has rooms with terraces overlooking the garden and pool. Efficient service. Walk to the beach. Restaurant.

11/20 Au Bec Fin

12, rue du 24-Août
93.38.35.86 / D3-22

M. Hugues. Open until 10 p.m. Closed Sat. dinner, Sun. & Dec. 25-Jan. 26. Air cond. Pets allowed. Cards: V, AE, DC.

A champion of tasty, everyday cuisine, this excellent, unpretentious bistro has easy-to-swallow prices and a constant crowd, which is understandable considering the generously served daube provençal, the lamb sauté with curry and scorpionfish filet.

A la carte: 160F. Menus: 69F, 87F.

11/20 Le Bistingo

Jetée Albert-Edouard
93.38.78.38 / D3-31

M. Fighiera. Lunch only (& dinner until 11 p.m. Fri.-Sun. & July-Sept.). Closed Mon. (except July-Sept.). Air cond. Terrace dining. Pets allowed. Telex 970327. Cards: V, AE, DC.

Meats and fish (sea perch, pink sea bream) grilled over a wood fire are the best dishes on the small, unexceptional menu at this comfortable and prosperous brasserie, well located on the port at the foot of the new Palais Festival.

A la carte: 200-250F. Menu: 87F, 135F.

10/20 Le Bouchon

10, rue de Constantine
93.99.21.76 / E3-37

Mme. Tulasne. Open until 10 p.m. Closed Mon. & last 2 weeks of Nov. Terrace dining. Pets allowed. Cards: V, AE.

"Aïoli and duck à l'orange, daily" reads the sign at the door, but there's more: calf's head and a decent coq au vin. Le Bouchon is a real find in these difficult, hard-to-please days.

A la carte: 120F. Menus: 55F, 85F.

12/20 La Brouette de Grand-Mère

9, rue d'Oran - 93.39.12.10 / E3-4

M. Bruno. Dinner only. Open until 11 p.m. Closed Sun., June 27-July 12 & Nov. 1-Dec. 15. Air cond. Pets allowed. Cards: V, MC.

Situated in a provincial little Cannes neighborhood, La Brouette has been run for the last ten years by a former chef at Félix. Nothing ever

changes here, except the price of the fixed menu, which includes everything: apéritifs, appetizers, salads, steamed Bresse chicken, chèvre au gratin, a variety of desserts and coffee. House wine is served without limit.
Menu: 175F (wine incl.).

Campanile
Cannes-Mandelieu airport
(6 km W on N 7), 06150 Cannes-la-Bocca
93.48.69.41 / A3-23
Open year-round. 90 rms 225-270F. Half-board 318-385F. TV in 70 rms. Pets allowed. Pool. Parking. Telex 461570. Cards: V, MC.
Well situated, close to the airport and the ocean. Restaurant/grill.

Carlton
See La Côte restaurant.

12/20 Le Caveau "30"
45, rue Félix-Faure
93.39.06.33 / C3-50
M. Cassin. Open daily until 10:30 p.m. (11 p.m. in summer). Air cond. Terrace dining. Pets allowed. Cards: V, AE, DC.
Le Caveau "30" is the former Caveau Provençal, now decorated more comfortably in a '30s style. Good news: The classic, solid cooking hasn't changed, so you can still enjoy the red mullet terrine, bourride and seafood.
A la carte: 250F. Menu: 95F, 145F.

Century
133, rue d'Antibes - 93.99.37.64 / F3-32
Closed Nov. 30-Jan. 8. 35 rms 270-530F. TV. Air cond. Parking. Telex 470090. Cards: V, AE, DC.
A brand-new hotel in the center of town, the Century features spacious, soundproof rooms, individual air conditioning and television. No restaurant.

12/20 Le Chandelier
6, rue Tony-Allard - 93.38.51.31 / E3-5
Mme. Spampinato. Open until 12:30 a.m. Closed Sat. lunch & Sun. Air cond. Terrace dining. Pets allowed. Cards: V.
Candlelight dining in a pleasant tavern atmosphere with a lively player piano. The fresh fish, delicious grilled meats and Thursday couscous bring out the Cannes elite. Wines and desserts are rather simple. Owner Josée is a jovial hostess.
A la carte: 230F. Menus: 95F, 120F.

(15) La Côte
58, blvd. de la Croisette
93.68.91.68 / E4-45
Open daily until 10:30 p.m. Air cond. Terrace dining. No pets. Parking. Telex 470720. Cards: V, AE, DC, MC.
The Carlton dining room, decorated like a luxurious greenhouse, is one of the most attractive restaurants on the boulevard de la Croisette. And now the kitchen team is finally solidly in place, providing the unity and enthusiasm (previously lacking) that was needed to support the fine efforts of Sylvain Duparc. A second toque is warranted for the consistently marvelous dishes he is now capable of: red mullet mousseline with saffron cream, sweetbreads with celery in a fine langoustine ragoût, roast marinated lotte, lamb rumpsteak with a basil stuffing. The desserts are improving, and the wine list includes several good vintages by the carafe at reasonable prices.
A la carte: 450F. Menus: 180F (weekday lunch only), 315F.

Carlton
(See restaurant above)
Open year-round. 30 stes 4,620-7,705F. 337 rms 1,055-2,250F. TV. Air cond. Pets allowed.
"A precious reminder of the past." That's the least we can say about this monument with beautiful rooms, which are constantly undergoing renovation. Magnificent sea view, boutiques and a new covered restaurant on the beach.

11/20 La Croisette
15, rue du Cdt-André
93.39.86.06 / E3-25
M. Martin. Open until 10 p.m. Closed Tues. & Dec. 15-Jan. 15. Pets allowed. Cards: V, AE, DC.
For a place so close to the great hotels and its namesake boulevard, la Croisette, the two fixed-price menus are astoundingly reasonable and feature copious, simple daily specials: osso buco, sautéed rabbit, aïoli, paella, leg of lamb.
A la carte: 160F. Menus: 74F (lunch only), 82F (wine incl.).

(13) Le Croquant
18, blvd. Jean-Hibert
93.39.39.79 / B3-13
M. Peytour. Open until 9:45 p.m. Closed Mon.; annual closing varies. Air cond. Pets allowed. Cards: AE, DC.
Lucien Peytour's restaurant is famous for its graciousness, friendliness and constant effort to please. This brightens the limited and extraordinarily static Périgourdine cuisine he has offered for the last fifteen years: Landes fritons (a charcuterie), a quality pâté of foie gras, fine ham from the Landes and lentil cassoulet.
A la carte: 260F. Menus: 90F, 130F, 180F, 260F.

12/20 Escale de Chine
58, rue Jean-Jaurès
93.99.15.99 / E3-43
M. Chang. Open until 11 p.m. Closed Mon. & Tues. lunch. Air cond. Garage parking. Cards: V.
The Cantonese chef here makes delicious dim sum, light fritters and good steamed ravioli, along with several good meats grilled over a scented wood fire. It's worth putting up with the decor, which is becoming increasingly gloomy. Charming service.
A la carte: 160F. Menus: 49F (weekday lunch only), 89F (weekends and holidays only), 109F, 128F.

12/20 Le Festival
52, blvd. de la Croisette
93.38.04.81 / E4-36
M. Andréani. Open until 11 p.m. (in summer). Closed Nov. 26-Dec. 26. Air cond. Terrace dining. Pets allowed. Cards: V, AE, DC.

This enduring restaurant with its almost mythic terrace on boulevard de la Croisette has been made famous by the Cannes Film Festival since 1945. A cozy, luxurious decor is paired with impeccably correct (but cold) service. The cuisine is not ingenious, but it is fresh and generous: homemade foie gras, grilled tournedos béarnaise, young rabbit casserole and glazed nougat.
A la carte: 300-350F. Menus: 170F, 195F.

Fouquet's

2, rond-point Duboys-d'Angers
93.38.75.81 / E3-3

Closed Nov. 2-Dec. 26. 10 rms 360-990F. TV. Air cond. Pets allowed. Garage parking. Cards: V, AE, DC, MC.

A lovely little hotel, air conditioned and soundproofed, 300 feet from the beach. All rooms have a sitting room and terrace. No restaurant.

11/20 Gaston et Gastounette

6, quai St-Pierre
93.39.47.92, 93.39.49.44 / C3-34

M. Cassin. Open until 10:30 p.m. Closed Mon. (off-seas.) & Jan. 3-23. Air cond. Terrace dining. Pets allowed. Cards: V, AE, DC.

Gaston et Gastounette's terrace is particularly pleasant and well insulated from street noise. Its menu features fresh grilled fish, fish pot-au-feu and bouillabaisse; the prices, however, are steep.
A la carte: 300-350F. Menu: 145F (lunch only), 175F (dinner only).

Grand Hôtel

45, blvd. de la Croisette
93.38.15.45 / E3-20

Open year-round. 2 stes 2,600F. 74 rms 525-1,390F. Half-board 215F (plus rm). TV. Air cond. Pets allowed. Parking. Telex 470727. Cards: V, AE.

A remarkable little hotel in a pretty garden setting, with attentive service and a private park and beach. Restaurant.

Gray Albion

See Le Royal Gray restaurant.

La Madone

3-5, ave. Justinia - 93.43.57.87 / G4-49

Open year-round. 2 stes 720-870F. 21 rms 230-540F. TV. Pets allowed. Pool. Parking. Telex 470900. Cards: V, AE, DC, MC.

This quiet hotel, amid a verdant garden planted with palm trees and mimosa, features quaint, extremely comfortable rooms. No restaurant.

11/20 Majestic

14, blvd. de la Croisette
93.68.91.00 / D3-6

M. Bardet. Open until 10:45 p.m. Closed Nov. 15-Dec. 15. Air cond. Garden dining. No pets. Parking. Telex 470787. Cards: V, AE, DC, MC.

This stately hotel has a solemn cuisine (veal kidneys in sherry, prawns fricassée) and the most boring clientele in the world. It is far more interesting to eat on the beach, where you can join the movie stars and the beautiful people who prefer the "lunch-and-beach-towel" formula.
A la carte: 350-400F. Menu: 210F.

Majestic

(See restaurant above)

Closed Nov. 15-Dec. 15. 13 stes 3,220-5,720F. 249 rms 460-2,860F. Half-board 740-1,395F. TV. Air cond. Pets allowed. Heated pool.

An old-fashioned luxury hotel meticulously restored, overlooking the boulevard de la Croisette and a beautiful garden. Private beach. Excellent new conference rooms. Boutiques.

10/20 Au Mal Assis

15, quai St-Pierre
93.39.05.35, 93.39.13.38 / C3-24

MM. Olivero. Open until 10 p.m. Closed Mon. (off-seas.) & Oct. 10-Dec. 23. Terrace dining. Pets allowed. Cards: V, AE, MC.

On this spacious, cool terrace, one can watch the leisurely strollers, admire the yachts and dine on expensive bourride, bouillabaisse and grilled local fish.
A la carte: 300F. Menus: 110F, 170F.

Martinez

See La Palme d'Or restaurant.

13 La Mère Besson

13, rue des Frères-Pradignac
93.39.59.24, 93.38.94.01 / E3-14

M. Martin. Open until 10 p.m. (11 p.m. in summer). Dinner only in July-Aug. Closed Sun. (except holidays). Terrace dining. Pets allowed. Cards: V, AE.

With its plastic flowers and powerful garlic odors, this place is smart but without much charm or grace. Without old Mme. Besson, the clientele these days is primarily made up of tourists. Even though the place has lost much of its soul, the nephew who took over has worked hard to maintain the quality of the cuisine: delicious pistou (pesto) soup, rather ordinary Norwegian shrimp à la rouille (pimiento mayonnaise), respectable pieds et paquets (mutton feet and tripe), a generous aïoli served only on Friday and a pleasant homemade apple tart.
A la carte: 230F.

13 Le Mesclun

16, rue St-Antoine - 93.99.45.19 / B3-10

MM. Descoux & Guedon. Open until 11:30 p.m. Closed Wed. (off-seas.) & Feb. 8-March 16. Air cond. Pets allowed. Cards: V, AE, DC.

The two owners say straight out that they are professional cooks and prove it with laudably light dishes and some excellent creations: fresh cod rillettes with herbs, eggplant with a chervil stuffing, blanquette of lamb's tongue with hazelnuts. Though it's less expensive than the restaurants in Le Suquet, the prices are no bargains (ditto for the wines) for this neck of the woods.
A la carte: 300F. Menu: 150F (dinner only).

12/20 La Mirabelle

24, rue St-Antoine - 93.38.72.75 / B3-52

MM. Lucas & Slagmolen. Dinner only. Open until 11 p.m. Closed Tues., Dec. 1-23 & March 1-15. Air cond. Garden dining. Pets allowed. Cards: V, AE.

The charm is real here: the decor's lovely dry bouquets, the owners' amiability and Christian Maître's cuisine, which oozes personality and finesse. Try the salad of pan-fried skate with noodles and a fresh coriander sauce, red mullet grilled in an orange fondue or young rabbit pan-roasted with rosemary. (However, there is a certain pretentiousness in the names of the dishes.) The wines are well selected despite their steep prices, and the tiny veranda is always full, as is the intimate basement dining room. By the time you read these lines, there should be a new decor and a new regional-based menu.

A la carte: 300-350F.

Molière

5, rue Molière - 93.38.16.16 / E3-27

Closed Nov. 15-Dec. 20. 34 rms 240-450F. TV. No pets. Cards: V, DC.

Bright rooms with terraces, near the center of town. Pleasant garden. No restaurant.

11/20 Le Monaco

15, rue du 24-Août
93.38.37.76 / D3-44

M. Peisino. Open until 10 p.m. Closed Sun. & Nov. 10-Dec. 15. Pets allowed.

One of those little unpretentious and inexpensive bistros that are so rare in Cannes, this place serves professional, everyday cuisine: duck mousse en gelée, bouillabaisse, beef filet au poivre.

A la carte: 160-180F. Menus: 65F, 85F.

Novotel Montfleury

25, ave. Beauséjour
93.68.91.50 / G3-35

Open year-round. 1 ste 1,460-4,000F. 180 rms 450-1,000F. Half-board 640-690F. TV. Air cond. Pets allowed. Heated pool. Tennis. Parking. Telex 470039. Cards: V, AE, DC, MC.

In the heart of the ten-acre François-André park overlooking Cannes bay, this contemporary luxury hotel offers spacious rooms, modern furniture and a sea view from the fourth floor and up. Restaurant.

14 L'Orangerie

(Hôtel Martinez)
73, blvd. de la Croisette
93.68.91.91, 92.98.30.18 / F4-2

M. Duvauchelle. Open until 11 p.m. Closed Feb. & Nov. 10-Dec. 28. Air cond. Terrace dining. Pets allowed. Parking. Telex 470708. Cards: V, AE, DC, MC.

At the foot of La Palme d'Or, this elegant, inviting dining room with a terrace overlooking a pool enjoys great success, thanks primarily to the fixed-price menu, an excellent value in this neighborhood. For 190 francs, you get to taste Christian Willer's savory cuisine prepared in the "bourgeois provençal" style, including a warm tomato tart with marjoram, duck thighs with bacon and mild garlic, cheeses, cherries jubilee and chicory ice cream. The Sunday lunch buffet (190 francs) is magnificently generous.

A la carte: 250-350F. Menu: 190F.

Palma

77, blvd. de la Croisette
93.94.22.16 / F5-19

Open year-round. 5 stes 590-630F. 47 rms 196-470F. TV. Pets allowed. Parking. Telex 470826. Cards: V, AE, DC, MC.

Located on the famous boulevard de la Croisette, this lovely hotel done all in pink has rooms overlooking the sea. Its rates are surprising, given the good location. No restaurant.

17 La Palme d'Or

73, blvd. de la Croisette
93.68.91.91, 92.98.30.18 / F4-2

M. Duvauchelle. Open until 11 p.m. Closed Tues. lunch, Mon., Feb. & Nov. 10-Dec. 28. Air cond. Terrace dining. Pets allowed. Parking. Telex 470708. Cards: V, AE, DC, MC.

The grand chefs at fine hotels are a bit like generals: They stay holed up in command posts and rarely see fire. But Christian Willer, who is responsible for several hundred guests each day at Martinez, is on the front line in his kitchen, and it is *his* cuisine that makes it to your table. And it's a lively, inventive, cheerful and flavorful cuisine. An Alsatian by origin, Willer seems to give his dishes an almost Provençal sunshine. His magnificent menu offers delicious creations and clever marriages of tastes, such as the fine lobster broth with pistou, creamy lobster soup with wild mushrooms, the langoustines and sweetbreads with eggplant and parsley roots, oysters in a saltwater aspic, sea bream with supions (calamari) in a spicy sauce, gilthead royale with a fennel gravy and turbot with crusty potatoes.

Willer is an unparalleled maestro with fish, but his talents aren't limited to that arena. This is evidenced by his pigeon heart in a natural, fresh herb gravy, veal shanks with a large slice of grilled kidney, pigs' feet mixed with oxtail, lamb pie marinated in an aromatic sauce à la provençal and sumptuous desserts (crunchy leaves of coffee- and praline-flavored chocolate, caramelized pear soup with pistachio). You'll want to come back for more to this attractive, bright dining room with round, well-dressed tables, glorious black-and-white photos of old Hollywood stars on the walls and a stunning view of Cannes bay and the Lérin islands. If cautious, you can dine for less than 300 francs, though you'll be sorely tempted by some of Willer's specialties and by the rich wine cellar.

A la carte: 500-700F. Menus: 250F (weekday lunch only, wine incl.), 240F, 450F.

Martinez

(See restaurant above)

Closed Feb. & Nov. 10-Dec. 28. 15 stes 3,500-7,200F. 410 rms 565-2,200F. Half-board 190-200F (plus rm). TV. Pets allowed. Heated pool. Tennis.

The Concorde group has spent a bundle to revive the splendors of this 1930s palace. The rejuvenation has been carried out in the reception halls, bar and all the rooms. Several of the suites are pure chic (though cold). Eight TV stations, private beach and special weekend packages.

Hôtel de Paris

34, blvd. d'Alsace - 93.38.30.89 / E2-7

Closed Nov. 7-Jan. 20. 3 stes 760-2,200F. 45 rms 250-590F. TV. Air cond. No pets. Heated pool. Parking. Telex 470995. Cards: V, DC, MC.

The most pleasant rooms here overlook the small garden and pool. Good soundproofing. No restaurant.

10/20 La Petite Maison

4, rue Châteauneuf
93.39.31.98 / E3-48

M. Agnese. Open until 11:30 p.m. Closed Tues. lunch & Mon. Air cond. Terrace dining. Pets allowed. Cards: V, AE, DC.

At this rendezvous for journalists and photographers during the Cannes Film Festival, the decor is fresh and the prices affordable. Sample the salmon in lemon cream or rabbit with mustard sauce.

A la carte: 230F. Menus: 90F, 110F, 185F.

12/20 Plage L'Ondine

15, blvd. de la Croisette
93.94.00.49, 93.94.23.15 / D3-26

M. Ducroix. Lunch only. Closed Tues. (in winter) & Nov. 14-Dec. 23. Terrace dining. Pets allowed. Cards: V.

Léo, the owner, certainly does nothing for free, but his cooking is serious and meticulous (for the most part refraining from the shortcuts taken by most restaurants bordering the beach): quail or red mullet salad, seafood pot-au-feu, navarin of three fish. Young, fresh regional wines.

A la carte: 280-350F.

(14) La Poêle d'Or

23, rue des Etats-Unis
93.39.77.65 / D3-15

M. Leclerc. Open until 10 p.m. Closed Tues. lunch, Mon. & Nov. 15-Dec. 15. Air cond. Pets allowed. Cards: V, AE, DC.

The reception is cool, as is the atmosphere, especially in this severe contemporary setting. But the 135-franc fixed-price menu is one of the best deals in Cannes (sautéed frogs' legs, lovely sea bream à la marinière and glazed nougat with a crème anglaise), and the à la carte menu of owner/chef Bernard Leclerc has made leaps of progress. This is especially true in the seafood department, where you'll find shrimp stew with olives and fresh pasta and the warm smoked fresh salmon. The desserts are original and delicious, such as the waffles with cream and honey. There are too few simple wines on the list. A solid toque has been earned.

A la carte: 300-350F. Menus: 135F, 230F.

11/20 Au Pompon Rouge

4, rue Emile Négrin - 92.98.90.61 / C3-9

Mme. Caroz. Open until 10:30 p.m. Closed Mon. lunch, Sun., June 1-15 & Nov. 1-15. Air cond. Terrace dining. Pets allowed. Cards: V.

The king of Cannes bistros still offers the same lively, cramped decor, friendly service and generous cuisine—grilled boudin with potatoes "en l'air," calf's head and good, rich homemade cakes—which is washed down with fine Bandols. But the new, amiable owner seems to be pushing up the prices.

A la carte: 230F.

Hôtel de Provence

9, rue Molière - 93.38.44.35 / E3-30

Open year-round. 30 rms 190-400F. TV. Air cond. Garage parking. Cards: V, AE, DC, MC.

A Provençal decor is combined with modern comforts at this hotel, where a garden insulates the rooms from noise. Salon/bar and restaurant.

Pullman Beach

13, rue du Canada - 93.38.22.32 / E4-17

Closed Nov. 15-Jan. 25. 7 stes 735-1,470F. 87 rms 420-1,145F. Half-board 120F (plus rm). TV. Air cond. Pets allowed. Pool. Telex 470034. Cards: V, AE, DC, MC.

Steps from the boulevard de la Croisette, the Pullman is the last word in modern-hotel refinement. The beautiful, spacious rooms have all sorts of creature comforts, including programmable VCRs. Saunas, excursions, car rentals. No restaurant.

(13) Les Quatre Saisons

(Gray d'Albion)
38, rue des Serbes - 93.68.54.54 / D3-39

M. Turetti. Open daily until 10:30 p.m. Air cond. Pets allowed. Telex 470744. Cards: V, AE, MC.

This place wins the award for Best Short Subject in Cannes cuisine. It's produced and directed by Jacques Chibois and stars a stunning array of fresh ideas, daily market products, and a fixed-price lunch menu based on a different daily special (endive tourte with smoked salmon, lamb charlotte with eggplant and coffee, all for 95 francs). It also stars a generous weekend lunch buffet and theme meals on certain days—regional dishes on Wednesday, bouillabaisse on Friday and succulent specialties of the Lebanese guest chef on Saturday. The staff is young and charming, and several delicious wines are served by the glass in the lush garden setting on the first floor.

A la carte: 180-230F. Menu: 95F (weekday lunch only).

(13) Le Relais des Semailles

9, rue St-Antoine - 93.39.22.32 / B3-33

M. Saint-Vannes. Open until 11 p.m. Closed Mon. lunch, Sun., 3 weeks in March & Nov. 15-30. Air cond. Terrace dining. Pets allowed. Cards: V, MC.

The cuisine of this young chef/owner is delicate and appealing, befitting his "manor-style" decor: excellent bass seasoned simply with excellent olive oil, tasty fresh-fruit desserts (though the selection is limited). With a little extra effort, he has won himself a toque. Alas, the prices are climbing.

Menus: 170F, 230F, 260F.

Le Rescator

7, rue du Maréchal-Joffre
93.39.44.57 / C2-1

M. Bernard. Open until 10:30 p.m. Closed Sun. (off-seas.). Air cond. Pets allowed. Cards: V, AE, DC, MC.

Jacques Bernard recently came down from Angers to take over the kitchen at this luxurious mahogany-paneled restaurant. He has retained some of the fine seafood preparations of the former chef, André Clerc: lobster ravioli with a carrot julienne, warm lotte escalopes with flavored oils, bass filet with mussels and saffron. Everything is always skillfully done and well presented, but the prices are still steep for à la carte (for portions that often seem like an afterthought). The first fixed-price menu is, however, quite satisfying. The service is elegant but a bit aloof.

A la carte: 300F and up. Menus: 145F (weekends and holidays only), 265F.

Résidentiale

11, rue Lépine - 93.38.47.47 / E4-16

Open year-round. 35 stes 450-850F. 72 rms 350-730F. TV. Pets allowed. Pool. Pets allowed. Parking. Telex 970412. Cards: V, AE.

From studios for two to duplexes for six persons (with kitchenettes), the rooms in this residence are sumptuous and well equipped. Private bar. No restaurant.

Le Royal Gray

6, rue des Etats-Unis
93.99.04.59, 93.68.54.54 / D3-39

M. Dargham. Open until 10 p.m. Closed Mon. (except dinner July-Aug.), Sun. & Feb. Air cond. Garden dining. Pets allowed. Telex 470744. Cards: V, AE, DC, MC.

We all know that cemeteries are strewn with supposedly irreplaceable chefs. Still, to find a replacement for Jacques Chibois, you'd have to scratch your head for a long, long time. Truly worth his weight in gold, this 36-year-old man from Limoges just gets better with every birthday. He has the charming face of a choirboy who somehow managed to grow a mustache, and he has a way of smiling and carrying himself that immediately wins over clients; for his team, his slightest wish is their command. His sense of modesty is not at all false, and he invites criticism, as long as it's positive. He has an uncommon sense of organization, which allows him to manage the Royal Gray's kitchens as well as those of Les Quatre Saisons and Jane's (the restaurant and nightclub at the Gray d'Albion), the private beach and the reception rooms. And if asked to organize a dinner for 500 people at the Hoggar, there's no doubt he'd pull it off admirably. And that's not all! This technician, trained in the tough schools of Guérard, Delaveyne, Vergé and Outhier, is also an artist, a veritable poet when it comes to cooking. He's able to calculate the price of a leek to the nearest centime, and when he buys a local red snapper, a farm rabbit or fresh herbs, he does so not only with his heart but with his imagination, translating these raw materials into new flavors and sharp tastes.

In short, he is the complete chef, missing just one thing: his own restaurant. There's no doubt that Chibois dreams of it, now more than ever, having almost landed a superb villa above Cannes in which to set up shop. We were holding the presses hoping to announce Chez Chibois, but deals that size can be difficult, and he's yet to pull it off. In the meantime, we couldn't see holding off awarding his so richly deserved fourth toque. And we wish nothing but the very best for the humble, kind and dedicated Chibois and his long-cherished dream of finding a suitable setting of his own in which to practice his stupefying range of abilities and invention.

Our last meal started with lobster soup with baby vegetables. It was prepared with a Beaumes-de-Venise liqueur, which gave it a slightly sugary flavor that proved to be utterly irresistible. The faintly acidic bite of the next course, warm tuna cakes with chives, shallots and a touch of vinegar on a bed of finely chopped greens, was a perfect contrast. The loup de mer (literally, sea wolf) was one of the best we've ever tasted, and this "royal" fish can be rather blah. The lamb's sweetbreads were well browned to a light crustiness and garnished with stuffed morels, green onions and sorrel, a diabolic combination that proved to be a miracle of harmony. The butterflied langoustines with wilted basil, fricassée of morels with peas and sorrel, roasted lamb with fresh rosemary, crisp baby duck with white beets and mousserons (a variety of mushrooms) and even the simple roast leg of lamb were all greeted with the same enthusiasm. Finally come the desserts, all kinds of desserts, each better than the last. We ordered a mendiant provençal (a dessert made of almonds, figs, hazelnuts and raisins) covered with chestnuts and chocolate, a warm nut cake and a croustillant of wild strawberries in rhubarb sauce—and we were glad we did.

A la carte: 500-700F. Menus: 190F (weekday lunch only), 320F, 380F, 440F.

Gray d'Albion

(See restaurant above)

Open year-round. 13 stes 2,000-5,500F. 174 rms 650-1,350F. TV. Air cond. Pets allowed.

This is one of the most luxurious hotels in Cannes, if not necessarily the most charming. Both supremely comfortable and functional, the rooms are equipped with air conditioning, color TVs, direct-line phones (even in the bathroom) and, in the suites or in the rooms by request, VCRs with films. Discotheque, private beach, piano bar, shopping gallery.

Ruc Hôtel

15, blvd. de Strasbourg
93.38.64.32, 93.38.30.61 / F2-29

Closed Jan. 3-22 & Feb. 1-12. 30 rms 260-600F. TV. Air cond. No pets. Telex 970033. Cards: V, AE.

Lovely period furniture lends a special charm to this bourgeois house, which dates from the eighteenth century. Despite its age, the equipment is modern, with air conditioned rooms. No restaurant.

(13) Le Saint-Benoît

9, rue du Batéguier - 93.39.04.17 / E3-38
M. Bourgignon d'Herbigny. Open until 11 p.m. Closed Mon., Feb. 26-March 14 & Dec. 1-26. Terrace dining. Pets allowed. Cards: V.

The owner has created a pleasant, congenial ambience and allows Pascal Larrouy to do the rest with his cuisine: tagliarini with langoustines, braised veal cutlet with baby onions and roast duck breast in a Provençal wine sauce. Most of the dishes are expertly prepared and reasonably priced. All that needs to be done now is to liven up the desserts and the staff, who seem to be half asleep.

A la carte: 220-250F. Menus: 110F, 140F.

Saint-Yves

49, blvd. d'Alsace - 93.38.65.29 / F3-18
Closed Nov. 3 stes 500-800F. 8 rms 200-320F. TV in 3 rms. Pets allowed. Parking. Cards: DC.

A charming Côte d'Azur–style villa facing a splendid garden and palm trees. Several furnished suites are available for two-week stays or by the month. No restaurant.

12/20 Les Santons de Provence

6, rue du Maréchal-Joffre
93.39.40.91 / D2-46
M. Natali. Open until 10 p.m. Closed Mon. (except July-Aug.), Dec. 1-23 & Feb. 6-March 21. Air cond. Pets allowed. Cards: V.

The flamboyant regional decor has become more subdued, the table linens are new, and the lighting has been improved. As for the new chef, he's devoting his energies to instilling the unchangeable house repertoire with a bit of lightness: small farcis (stuffings) niçoise with basil, artichokes barigoule (stuffed with duxelles and wrapped in bacon), rabbit in herb aspic. The reception is excellent.

A la carte: 200F. Menus: 89F, 115F.

Sofitel-Méditerranée

2, blvd. Jean-Hibert - 93.99.22.75 / C4-8
Closed Nov. 20-Dec. 20. 5 stes 900-1,490F. 145 rms 350-1,090F. TV. Pets allowed. Heated pool. Parking. Telex 470728. Cards: V, DC, MC.

All the rooms here are bright, cheerful and pleasant, and many have terraces overlooking the old port. There's a heated pool on the roof. Excellent concierge. Restaurant.

Splendid

Allées de la Liberté
4-6, rue Félix-Faure
93.99.53.11 / C3-41
Open year-round. 2 stes 800-1,100F. 62 rms 400-780F. TV. Pets allowed. Telex 470990. Cards: V, AE, DC, MC.

Located on the old port, many of these comfortable, soundproofed rooms have kitchenettes. Personal service. No restaurant.

(16) Villa Dionysos

7, rue Marceau - 93.38.79.73 / E3-47
M. Verger. Open daily until 11 p.m. Air cond. Terrace dining. Pets allowed. Cards: V, AE.

Despite his 70 years, the formidable Claude Verger still displays remarkable enthusiasm. After leaving his well-known restaurant in Clichy, he began from scratch in this attractive downtown villa, creating a luxurious Italian-style decor with a deliciously sunny terrace and plenty of flowers. His chef is 24-year-old Véronique Boistelle, a lovely woman who has developed a simple, slightly rustic cuisine: savory young rabbit terrine, pigs' feet with cabbage, fresh cod with beurre blanc, oyster soup, duck with peaches and, of course, the famous warm, thin apple tart that Verger created twenty years ago (it was not quite perfect at our last visit). A magnificent wine cellar, reasonable prices and an excellent fixed-price menu also help make this place one of the best in Cannes.

A la carte: 350-450F. Menus: 180F, 270F.

IN NEARBY **Cannet**
(3 km NE)
06110 Le Cannet - (Alpes-Maritimes)

Château du Dauphin

Chemin de Garibondy
Open year-round. 39 rms 260-600F. Half-board 100F (plus rm). TV. Pets allowed. Heated pool. Tennis. Parking. Telex 970081. Cards: V, AE, DC, MC.

Recently opened in a large park with century-old trees, this original hotel has meticulously decorated rooms and excellent facilities. Large pool, eight tennis courts and a fine reception. Restaurant.

Le Cap-d'Agde

see Agde

Cap-d'Antibes

06600 Antibes - (Alpes-Maritimes)
Paris 923 - Antibes 10 - Cannes 21 - Nice 33

12/20 Eden Roc

Blvd. Kennedy - 93.61.39.01
M. Irondelle. Open until 10 p.m. Closed Oct. 12-April 20. Air cond. Terrace dining. No pets. Parking.

Overlooking the spectacular rock formations, the ocean and the playground of tanned millionaires trying to live the Gatsby life is this luxurious dining room. You'll pay solid-gold prices for a solemn but rather well-done grand hotel cuisine: langoustine salad, Bresse chicken fricassée, kidneys flambé. Excellent desserts and extremely stylish service.

A la carte: 500-600F.

Hôtel du Cap Eden Roc

(See restaurant above)
Closed Oct. 12-April 20. 10 stes 5,900-12,000F. 112 rms 1,450-5,300F. TV. Air cond. No pets. Heated pool. Tennis.

This superb luxury hotel in a large park has been admirably renovated and is popular with the very rich and those willing to face ruin for a few days of glorious opulence. The 34 new rooms each have a terrace-loggia fronting the ocean. Water sports.

La Gardiole

Chemin de la Garoupe - 93.61.35.03

Closed Nov. 5-Feb. 28. 21 rms 190-450F. Half-board 300-450F. TV in 5 rms. Pets allowed. Parking. Telex 460000. Cards: V, AE, DC, MC.

Bright, well-equipped rooms—some with ocean views—accent this family hotel tucked away in the pines. Wonderful terrace under clusters of grapes. Restaurant.

(16) Restaurant de Bacon

Blvd. de Bacon - 93.61.50.02

M. Sordello. Open until 9 p.m. (10 p.m. in summer). Closed Sun. dinner, Mon. & Nov. 15-Jan. 31. Air cond. Terrace dining. No pets. Parking. Cards: V, AE, DC.

This lovely house has a large, cool terrace with a view of the Antibes bay and, when it's clear, the Italian Alps. Once a tavern, it was transformed a dozen years ago into a comfortable restaurant that soon became one of the best seafood places on the coast. The two Sordello sons, who are as demanding as they are knowledgeable, buy their fish each day from local fishermen. Thus it's about as fresh as can be, and it's served in various ways: raw in a variety of salads, cooked in olive oil, grilled with fennel, à la nage with vegetables, simply steamed or blended in a marvelous bourride or bouillabaisse, which we think is the best in the world. The fish is prepared tableside, served in perfectly cooked filets (without a trace of bone), along with a bouillon for which you would sell your soul and a subtly sharp rouille (spicy garlic mayonnaise) that you greedily spread on croutons. The rather short repertoire is virtually unchangeable. Even the glazed nougat with a raspberry coulis is a (homemade) tradition. Only the prices seem to change, and rather painfully at that.

A la carte: 500-600F. Menus: 300F (weekday lunch only), 400F (weekend and holiday lunch).

See also: **Antibes**

Carcassonne

11000 Carcassonne - (Aude)
Paris 905 - Perpignan 107 - Toulouse 92 - Albi 107

(15) Domaine d'Auriac

4 km SE in Auriac, rte. de Ste-Hilaire
68.25.72.22

M. Rigaudis. Open until 9:15 p.m. Closed Sun. dinner & Mon. lunch (off-seas.) & Jan. 10-31. Garden dining. Pets allowed. Garage parking. Telex 500385. Cards: V, AE.

Whether it's served on the terrace overlooking a vast romantic park with 300-year-old trees, or in the château dining room, which was recently redecorated in salmon tones, Bernard Rigaudis's cuisine still lives up to its reputation for offering lots of quality, generosity and creativity. We've found fewer and fewer flaws, and he has even improved in lightness and technique. Two toques are in order for the Languedoc pigeon pot, salad of truffle and artichokes, delightful asparagus "citronette," salmon carpaccio with marinated anchovies, salad of skate with raspberry vinegar and an olive-oil dressing (a bit confusing), delicious veal kidneys in mustard sauce, perfect warm strawberry millefeuille and excellent chocolate soufflé with a rum-flavored crème anglaise. To complement this good cooking are a pleasant atmosphere, a well-trained staff and one of the best wine cellars in the region, rich with Champagnes, ports, Corbières, Minervois and Fitous.

A la carte: 300F. Menus: 120F (weekday lunch only), 160F, 210F, 250F, 300F.

Domaine d'Auriac

(See restaurant above)

Closed Sun. (off-seas.) & Jan. 10-31. 5 stes 700-780F. 18 rms 450-950F. Half-board 700-900F oblig. in seas. TV. Air cond. in 8 rms. Pool. Tennis. Golf.

We suggest you make reservations well in advance for one of the beautiful, spacious rooms in this lovely Relais et Châteaux overlooking the lush foliage of the immense park. The service is impeccable, and the atmosphere delightfully tranquil.

Les Remparts

3, pl. du Grand-Puits (in La Cité)
68.71.27.72

Closed Jan. 18 rms 190-250F. Pets allowed. Parking.

The rooms are well equipped and well maintained, but their most interesting characteristic is their location within the town's ramparts. No restaurant.

La Vicomté

18, rue St-Saëns (near porte Narbonnaise)
68.71.45.45

Open year-round. 3 stes 585-785F. 56 rms 285-585F. TV. Air cond. Pets allowed. Heated pool. Parking. Telex 500303. Cards: V, AE, DC, MC.

Time has not yet had a chance to grace this new replica of a traditional Languedoc building with the requisite patina. But there are plenty of amenities and a great view of Carcassonne to help pass the time until the charm sets in.

Carentan

505000 Carentan - (Manche)
Paris 293 - Cherbourg 50 - Bayeux 42 - Caen 69

(15) Auberge Normande

17, blvd. de Verdun - 33.42.02.99

M. Bonnefoy. Open until 9 p.m. Closed Sun. dinner, Mon., Feb. 1-15 & Oct. 10-25. Pets allowed. Parking. Cards: V, AE, DC.

We've been waiting a long time for the spark that would bring out the talent of Gérard Bonnefoy, and the time seems to have come. Served in the warm, gray-stone dining room (with dark carpet, bright-yellow tablecloths and a wooden ceiling), the cuisine of this hard-working chef has improved markedly, showing more imagination and sparkle. It's now well worth two toques: perfectly executed brill filet served with poached oysters atop spinach, a plate of lotte and smoked salmon garnished with a generous caviar cream with lemon juice, coquilles St-Jacques on cabbage leaves with basil butter (a classic with much character), lovely glazed nougat with red-fruit coulis and a crunchy caramelized orange fondant.

Though substantial, the wine list doesn't quite live up to the cuisine. The service staff, directed by friendly Anne-Marie Bonnefoy and a new maître d', is young and zealous—even a bit hasty, complained one of our readers, who also found the portions of the budget fixed-price menus to be a bit stingy.

A la carte: 300-350F. Menus: 95F, 158F, 230F, 300F.

Carnac

56340 Carnac - (Morbihan)
Paris 481 - Quiberon 18 - Auray 13 - Vannes 31

Novotel Tal-Ar-Mor

Ave. de l'Atlantique - 97.52.16.66

Closed Jan. 110 rms 350-485F. TV. Pets allowed. Heated pool. Parking. Telex 950324. Cards: V, AE, DC, MC.

This excellent, modern hotel specializing in "health and relaxation" programs is linked with a thalassotherapy center. Its lodgings are bright and roomy, and it boasts a covered and heated saltwater pool. Restaurant.

Le Relais du Sporting

Ave. des Druides
97.52.98.35, 97.52.16.66

Closed Tues. & Sept. 15-March. 8 rms 280-320F. Tennis. Cards: V.

These simple, almost new (1985) rooms are located near the beach. Two clay tennis courts. Restaurant.

Carpentras

84200 Carpentras - (Vaucluse)
Paris 683 - Cavaillon 26 - Apt 12 - Avignon 23 - Aix 82

Fiacre

153, rue Vigne - 90.63.03.15

Open year-round. 20 rms 140-300F. TV in 6 rms. Pets allowed. Parking. Cards: V, AE, DC, MC.

This pleasant eighteenth-century way station boasts spacious, well-maintained rooms, the quietest of which overlook a smart-looking patio. No restaurant.

IN NEARBY **Monteux**
(5 km SW on D 942)
84170 Monteux - (Vaucluse)

(14) Le Saule Pleurer

Quartier Beauregard - 90.62.01.35

M. Philibert. Open until 9:30 p.m. Closed Tues. dinner (except July-Aug.), Wed., March 1-20 & Oct. 15-30. Garden dining. Pets allowed. Cards: V, AE.

One needs lots of enthusiasm and stubbornness to survive in this countryside, where in winter the local clientele wants to be served traditional hearty meals at budget prices, rather than an inventive, refined modern cuisine. But Michel Philibert has bravely maintained his personal style, keeping things light and attractive: salad with an anise cream, Mediterranean fish with rosemary butter, veal kidneys with lavender honey, bodon (a cow's milk cheese served warm) with red wine and orange-grapefruit soup, all of which, as you can see, retain some of the local flavor. Nice wine cellar, pleasant shaded terrace.

A la carte: 300F and up. Menus: 110F (weekday lunch only), 165F, 215F, 280F.

IN NEARBY **Saint-Didier**
(6 km SE on D 4 & D 39)
84210 Pernes-les-Fontaines - (Vaucluse)

Les Trois Colombes

Ave. des Garrigues - 90.66.07.01

Closed Jan. 15-Feb. 28. 24 rms 260-280F. Half-board 240-250F oblig. in seas. TV. Pets allowed. Pool. Tennis. Parking. Telex 431067. Cards: V, AE, DC.

This new, comfortable and tranquil hotel in the countryside has a covered terrace overlooking a pool. Restaurant.

IN NEARBY **Venasque**
(11 km SE on D 4)
84210 Pernes-les-Fontaines - (Vaucluse)

(14) Auberge de la Fontaine

90.66.02.96

M. Soehlke. Open until 10 p.m. Dinner only (except lunch Sun.). Closed Wed. & Nov. 15-Dec. 15. Parking. Pets allowed. Hotel: 5 stes 590-690F. TV. Air cond. Cards: V, AE, DC, MC.

Climb the stairs of this old Provençal house facing a fountain to the inviting, cool dining room, with its waxed tiled floor and simple wooden tables. The unpretentious elegance is immediately apparent in the fireplace and little square windows. Its single fixed-price menu changes constantly and is one of the best values in Provence: small feuilletés à la tapenade (olive paste), bass mousseline, wild asparagus omelet, duck aiguillettes with mousserons (wild mushrooms), cheeses and a tarte tatin (unnecessarily flambéed with Calvados). You'll enjoy a warm reception, and newly added are some comfortable rooms to make the pleasure last.

Menu: 170F.

Carry-le-Rouet

13620 Carry-le-Rouet - (Bouches-du-Rhône)
Paris 768 - Salon 51 - Aix 40 - Marseille 27

(14) L'Escale

Promenade du Port - 42.45.00.47

M. Clor. Open until 9:30 p.m. Closed Sun. dinner, Mon. (except dinner in July-Aug.) & Oct. 30-March 1.

Gérard Clor's clients enthusiastically agree that Carry-le-Rouet is a unique little haven on the Côte d'Azur, especially when his wife, Dany, has seated them on this attractive terrace overlooking the crystal-green sea (you'd swear there wasn't a drop of pollution to be found), the port and the coves. These many faithful customers pay their weight in gold to sample the magnificent fresh Mediterranean fish that dominate the menu. Whatever faults existed in the past seem to have been corrected (aside from the plain clam ramekin). The roast lotte in truffle gravy is delicious, the bouillabaisse is positively sumptuous, and the langoustine mignonnettes with pepper and ginger is a delicate delight. The excellent wine list includes a remarkable white Châteauneuf and a Montredon.

A la carte: 400-500F.

Cassel

59670 Cassel - (Nord)
Paris 253 - Lille 53 - Dunkerque 29 - St-Omer 21

(16) Le Sauvage

38, Grand-Place
28.42.40.88, 28.40.52.06

M. Decaestecker. Open until 9:30 p.m. Closed Wed. dinner, Sun., Tues. & Feb. Terrace dining. Pets allowed. Cards: V, AE, MC.

The stately eighteenth-century facade of brick and stone shelters a clear, bright dining room with large bay windows. If this room lacks charm, no one seems to mind. That's because of the spectacular view of the Yser plains, the Boulonnais and the Lys valley from the summit of this glorious 600-foot-high hill (where the prince of Orange was routed in 1677)—and because Walter Decaestecker and his staff maintain such a friendly, warm atmosphere. This Flemish cook, dedicated and hard-working, also displays a remarkable generosity. Nothing is impossible for him: culinary-competition dishes, regional and seasonal cuisines, bold creations—all are listed on his exciting menu. In the opulent Flanders tradition, he offers potjevfleish (terrine of veal, bacon and rabbit) with juniper berries, young farm pigeon with sweetbreads and Sauternes, a feuillantine of vegetables with creamed peas, a plate of three kinds of fish with hops, and pear or nectarine roasted in cider and served with praline ice cream. Exceptional wine cellar with more than 600 vintages.

A la carte: 300-400F. Menus: 120F and 190F (weekdays only), 250F.

Cassis

13260 Cassis - (Bouches-du-Rhône)
Paris 803 - Toulon 44 - Marseille 23 - Aubagne 14

(13) La Presqu'île

Port-Miou Quarter - 42.01.03.77

Mme. Bertolotti. Open until 10 p.m. Closed Sun. dinner & Mon. (except July-Aug.) & Jan. 4-March 2. Terrace dining. Pets allowed. Parking. Cards: V, AE, DC, MC.

One of the finer points of this luxurious house is the canopied terrace that makes the Mediterranean seem like your own private sea (from the dining room's large bay windows you also get a fine view of the Canaille cape). Everything is sober, refined and impeccable, thanks largely to gracious Huguette Bertolotti and her staff. The cuisine is always good though not error-free. Thus, we are not giving more than one toque for the fine young rabbit salad with basil sauce, the red mullet filets lightly pan-fried with eggplant caviar (which is, in fact, a simple eggplant coulis) and the roast pigeon with a spiced gravy. The mango millefeuille was nothing out of the ordinary, and the petits fours served with the coffee were too soft.

A la carte: 350F. Menus: 170F, 260F.

Les Roches Blanches

Rte. des Calanques - 42.01.09.30

Closed mid-Dec.-Feb. 1. 35 rms 175-500F. Half-board 368-690F oblig. in seas. TV in 30 rms. Pets allowed. Parking. Telex 441287. Cards: V, AE, DC.

Beautifully situated on a promontory overlooking the sea, this hotel offers small rooms with modern comforts. Solarium, private beach. Restaurant.

Casteljaloux

47700 Casteljaloux - (Lot-et-Garonne)
Paris 657 - Agen 51 - Langon 40 - Marmande 23

Les Cadets de Gascogne

Pl. Gambetta - 53.93.00.59

Open year-round. 13 rms 150-280F. Half-board 200-310F oblig. in seas. Cards: V.

In this large residence, the owners greet you with a warm Gascon reception. Pleasant garden and a pretty restaurant.

(13) La Vieille Auberge

11, rue Posterne - 53.93.01.36

M. Bernard. Open until 9:30 p.m. Closed Sun. dinner, Mon., Feb. 27-March 6, May 29-June 13 & Oct. 16-31. Pets allowed. Hotel: 4 rms 80-140F. Parking. Cards: V.

The style is rustic, in a building typical of Old Casteljaloux, and the atmosphere is that of a residential hotel, with plenty of warmth; simple, attentive service; excellent prices; and a well-stocked wine cellar. Daniel Bernard remains attached to classic dishes and likes to make a show with flambées. You will have a delightful time, though, with the savory smoked breast of goose with an onion marmalade, duck aiguillettes in a tasty (though heavy) prune sauce, and civet of young wild boar in season. Excellent cheeses.

A la carte: 200F. Menus: 50F (weekdays only), 85F, 120F, 160F.

Le Castellet

83330 Le Beausset - (Var)
Paris 820 - Marseille 45 - Toulon 20 - La Ciotat 18

(13) Castel Lumière

Le Portail - 94.32.62.20

M. Matheron. Open until 9:30 p.m. Closed Tues. (off-seas.) & Nov. Garden dining. Pets allowed. Hotel: 6 rms 280-300F; half-board 320-350F oblig. in seas. Cards: V, AE, DC.

Even when he was serving a neomedieval cuisine, Jean Matheron knew how to keep it light, fine and well executed. Fortunately, he has created a more contemporary cuisine that features excellent lightly cooked foie gras, a delicate flan of bass and salmon and delicious glazed nougat with a red-fruit coulis. The decor is plain, but who cares? The luxuriant patio provides one of the best views in the world: Lecques bay over the Bandol

vineyards.
A la carte: 300F. Menus: 160F (weekdays only), 180F, 250F.

Castillon-du-Gard

Remoulins - (Gard)
Paris 690 - Nimes 25 - Avignon 27 - Pont-du-Gard 4

(15) Le Vieux Castillon

66.37.00.77

M. Traversac. Open until 9 p.m. Closed Jan. 2-mid-March. Air cond. Terrace dining. Pets allowed. Parking. Telex 490946. Cards: V.

This remarkable ensemble of antique stone houses overlooking the plain as far as Mont Ventoux was expertly restored by the Traversac family. The decor is bright, modern-rustic and luxuriously accented with the sober beauty of Gard stones. The staff has the efficient, gracious manners found in the grand restaurants. And Gilles Dauteuil's cuisine is spectacularly decorative, precise and forthright. A second toque is deserved for the squash flowers stuffed with a zucchini flan and accompanied by lightly poached langoustines, the red mullet with a potato mousse and caviar, a marvelous loin of lamb with a garlic cream and crisp vegetables and, to finish, the light ganache of white and dark chocolate with an unctuous crème anglaise. The wine list is good but rather confusing.

A la carte: 300-350F. Menus: 240F (except holidays), 310F, 360F.

Le Vieux Castillon

(See restaurant above)

Closed Jan. 2-mid-March. 2 stes 1,120F. 33 rms 540-1,120F. Half-board 600-890F (for double rooms only). TV in 7 rms. Air cond. in 13 rms. Pool. Tennis.

This wonderful cluster of houses is perched at the summit of the village, overlooking a magnificent landscape of plains and vineyards. Interior garden, luxurious large period rooms and a swimming pool. Relais et Châteaux.

Castirla

see CORSICA: Corte

Castres

81100 Castres - (Tarn)
Paris 727 - Montauban 96 - Albi 42 - Toulouse 72

(13) Au Chapon Fin

8, quai Tourcaudière - 63.59.06.17

M. Crespo. Open until 9:30 p.m. Closed Mon. & Feb. school vacation. Air cond. Pets allowed. Cards: V, AE.

Au Chapon Fin remains the best and prettiest restaurant in the region. This comfortable, rustic place in the old tanner's district along the Agout river provides a fine ambience for a cuisine that is solid yet light, classic yet personal: duck breast with cherries in a sweet-and-sour sauce, warm foie gras with two kinds of peppers, pigeon with peaches and cinnamon. Owner/chef Henri Crespo offers a warm greeting, and his prices are equally inviting, particularly those of the modest local wines and the fixed-price menus.

A la carte: 200-230F. Menus: 100F (wine incl.), 85F, 120F, 135F, 300F.

Cavaillon

84300 Cavaillon - (Vaucluse)
Paris 704 - Avignon 27 - Arles 43 - Aix-en-Provence 52

(14) Prévôt

353, ave. de Verdun - 90.71.32.43

M. Prévôt. Open until 9:30 p.m. Closed Sun. dinner & Mon. Air cond. Garden dining. Pets allowed. Cards: V.

Unfortunately, we arrived just days before Jean-Jacques Prévôt demolished his hideous boudoir decor, so we'll refrain from criticizing it. Fortunately, Mme. Prévôt was the perfect hostess: spontaneous, sincere and obliging. Her husband's cuisine has become increasingly convincing and personal, while retaining its traditional base: magnificent escalope of liver with apples, cherries and ears of corn; wonderful filet mignon garnished with a leek crêpe; tender, lightly cooked duck breast in an exquisite sauce of red pepper and cinnamon. Each dish is served with a different homemade bread (five in all), each delicious. The wine list is improving.

A la carte: 300F. Menus: 144F, 183F, 285F.

Hôtel Toppin

70, cours Gambetta - 90.71.30.42

Closed Jan. 2-20. 32 rms 130-250F. Half-board 170-210F. TV in 15 rms. Pets allowed. Garage parking. Telex 432631. Cards: V, AE, DC, MC.

Remarkably maintained and well situated in the center of town, the Toppin boasts a sunny interior terrace. The rooms are impersonal but clean, with a countrified flavor. Restaurant.

Cavalaire

83240 Cavalaire - (Var)
Paris 900 - Toulon 61 - St-Tropez 18

Hôtel de la Calanque

Rue de la Calanque - 94.64.04.27

Closed Oct. 4-March 15. 3 stes 570-625F. 30 rms 435-500F. Half-board 415-470F oblig. in seas. TV in 16 rms. Pets allowed. Pool. Tennis. Garage parking. Telex 400293. Cards: V, DC, AE.

This superb modern hotel is tucked into the rocks and surrounded by the sea. Large, bright rooms with a plain decor overlook the cove. Restaurant.

Cavalière

83980 Le Lavandou - (Var)
Paris 890 - Hyères 30 - St-Tropez 31

(15) Le Club

Plage de Cavalière - 94.05.80.14

M. Guillemin. Open until 10 p.m. Closed Mon. & Sept. 30-May 1. Air cond. Garden dining. No pets. Parking. Telex 420317. Cards: V, AE, DC.

Le Club continues to be a little miracle of comfort, luxury, ambience, relaxation, pleasantness—and, of course, cuisine. A miracle because it's unexepected from a place open just five months out of the year, and even more of a miracle because it doesn't gouge customers. The guests keep coming back, finding nothing on the coast to match the charm and refinement of Le Club. They are the sunbathers, sailors and tennis and "pétanque" (Provençal outdoor bowling) players who stay in the nearby bungalows on the adjacent beach, where there's a view of the Levant islands and some of the world's most beautiful women (on the beach, that is). Alain Gigant's cuisine is based on fish so fresh it looks you in the eye: cuttlefish soup with stuffed crab, bass en croûte with caviar butter, a fine salmon tarte au sel and bitter chocolates with a pistachio mousseline. Nice fixed-price menu.

A la carte: 400F. Menu: 220F (dinner only).

Le Club

(See restaurant above)

Closed Sept. 30-May 1. 27 rms 600-1,025F (half-board only). TV. Air cond. Pets allowed. Heated pool. Tennis.

One of the most pleasant hotels on the coast, even if its architecture isn't in the best taste (at the time of this writing it was being updated). The rooms have been redone, as have the pool and tennis court. Private beach, excellent service.

Cazaubon

see Barbotan-les-Thermes

La Celle-Saint-Cyr

see Joigny

Céret

66400 Céret - (Pyrénées-Orientales)
Paris 945 - Prades 55 - Perpignan 30 - Port-Vendres 36

La Châtaigneraie

2 km S, rte. de Fontfrède - 68.87.03.19

Closed Oct. 16-April 30. 8 rms 290-490F. Half-board 450-640F oblig. in seas. Pool. Parking.

A tiny but quite refined hotel. Several rooms have terraces with splendid views extending to the Pyrénées and the Mediterranean. Beautiful pool dug into the rocks, and lovely terraced gardens. Restaurant for dinner.

12/20 La Terrasse au Soleil

Rte. de Fontfrède - 68.87.01.94

Mme. Leveillé-Nizerolle. Open until 9:30 p.m. Closed Mon. (March & Nov.) & Dec.-Feb. Terrace dining. Pets allowed. Parking. Cards: V.

Nestled deep in rich greenery, this restaurant is relaxed and friendly, with parasol-covered tables on the terrace. But the cuisine has lost a little of its pizzazz (on our last visit, the grilled breast of duck with herbs was dry, the fruit feuilleté banal).

A la carte: 230F. Menus: 110F, 260F.

La Terrasse au Soleil

(See restaurant above)

Closed Dec.-Feb. 18 rms 380-480F. Half-board 375-425F oblig. in seas. TV. Pets allowed. Pool.

Seven kilometers from Spain, in a bucolic, luxuriant natural setting with Mt. Canigou in the background, La Terrasse has simple, pleasant rooms that are modern and quiet.

Cesson-Sévigné

see Rennes

Chablis

89800 Chablis - (Yonne)
Paris 182 - Auxerre 19 - Tonnerre 16 - Avallon 47

Hostellerie des Clos

(Michel Vignaud)
Rue Jules-Rathier - 86.42.10.63

M. Vignaud. Open until 9:30 p.m. Closed Thurs. lunch & Wed. (off-seas.) & Jan. 2-Feb. 3. Air cond. Pets allowed. Garage parking. Telex 800997. Cards: V, AE, DC.

The restaurant sits in the courtyard of the former Chablis hospice, whose buildings were recently restored to welcome tourists visiting this winery region. The relaxing, modern dining room is done in pink and apricot tones and offers a view of a beautiful interior courtyard. The local wine makers (co-sponsors of this enterprise with chef Michel Vignaud) have filled the marvelous vaulted cellar with a complete collection of the best Chablis vintages from 1962 to date. Moreover, the beautiful modern cuisine is prepared with care and with discreet regional touches: warm oysters in Chablis, lobster sauté with field mushrooms, roasted veal kidneys with fresh grapes, sander suprême with red wine. Fine service.

A la carte: 350F. Menus: 132F, 232F, 325F.

Hostellerie des Clos

(See restaurant above)

Closed Jan. 2-Feb. 3. 26 rms 180-320F. TV. Air cond. Pets allowed.

A nice, comfortable and simple hotel popular with Chablis buyers and tourists. Trips to wine cellars, wine tastings.

Chagny

71150 Chagny - (Saône-et-Loire)
Paris 330 - Chalon 17 - Beaune 16 - Mâcon 75

Château de Bellecroix

N 6 - 85.87.13.86

Mme. Gautier. Open until 9:30 p.m. Closed Wed. & Dec. 20-Feb. 1. Garden dining. Pets allowed. Garage parking. Cards: V, AE, DC.

A delightful Hitchcock-movie atmosphere reigns in the stately wainscoted dining room (with chevron-patterned parquet floors) located in an isolated former Knights of Malta command post perched at the top of an inviting park. The service has become pleasantly efficient and the cuisine respectable in a resolutely classic style: foie gras terrine, salmon in Noilly, young rabbit in an onion confit. Prices are skyrocketing.

A la carte: 300F and up. Menus: 95F, 180F, 280F.

Château de Bellecroix

(See restaurant above)

Closed Wed. & Dec. 20-Feb. 1. 19 rms 320-800F. Half-board 400-600F oblig. in seas. TV. Pets allowed. Heated pool.

Amid century-old trees on this estate is a new heated pool. Each of the lovely rooms is unique; the new ones are particularly spacious and meticulously kept.

Lameloise

(18)

36, pl. d'Armes
85.87.08.85

M. Lameloise. Open until 9:30 p.m. Closed Thurs. lunch, Wed. & Dec. 20-Jan. 18. No pets. Garage parking. Telex 801086. Cards: V.

He was a famous chef, King Jean, reigning over his escargots, the best rabbit pâté in the Western world and his Bresse baby pigeons en vessie (pig's bladder). Still, he must have felt just a twinge of regret or worry when he turned the place over to his son Jacques. But for the Lameloises, the story had a happy ending, and Jean soon discovered that there was no reason to fret. Jacques, who looks as gentle as a lamb, runs his kitchens with an iron hand. At first glance, you might wonder if he's capable of it, but he's tough. And though he's extremely modest about his cooking, he brings to his work an enthusiasm and a lightness that are a pleasure to witness.

And it's amazing how comfortable you feel in this ordinary building. Were it a mere 50 yards back, it would be in the middle of a garden; instead, it's at the corner of a busy street with constant traffic surrounding it. But as soon as you walk in, you feel as if you've found an old friend. The smile of Mama Lameloise, Simone, brightens the flower-filled entrance. That Lameloise smile must be contagious; Nicole, Jacques's pretty wife, certainly seems to have caught it. And when you find yourself in one of the three dining rooms, you'll see that smile again among the flowers, beautiful silver and paintings, and on the faces of the maîtres d'hôtel, wine stewards and young men in white jackets who carry trays not as if they're holding the Holy Grail but something that's really going to please you.

So here you are at the table, under the oak beams of the low ceilings. The lighting is soft, and you have so much elbow room that you hardly even notice the crowd—and this restaurant is always crowded. After a little glass of Montagny or Rully Clos Saint-Jacques, poured by Jean-Pierre Després, puts you at ease, you dive into the menu. And the feast begins!

Jacques is a cautious innovator. He watches over his basic dishes, which come and go with the seasons, like a father watching over his brood. Of course, something new shows up from time to time, but it never really shakes things up. There are enough dishes on the menu to eat a different meal for eight days straight, and since it's all good, we can't complain.

Sometimes not everything is exactly right, such as bits of sweetbreads poorly combined with cream, zucchini, thyme and crushed tomatoes (each ingredient is excellent, but together they fight one another). On our next-to-last visit, we were disappointed with the feuilleté of coquilles St-Jacques in a cream sauce with sea urchins and chervil, and before that, with sweetbreads that weren't quite golden. But that's hardly enough to condemn Lameloise, since the pigeon tart with foie gras, surrounded by a marvelous aspic and raspberries in vinegar, was a wonder, and the rouget-barbet (a variety of red snapper) revealed all of its delicacy on a bed of finely sliced fried leeks. The beauty of the vegetable pâté with Breton lobster and chervil would make any Japanese chef green with envy, and, even better, its exquisite flavor made our mouths water. If you have nothing against lobster, Lameloise stuffs ravioli with it, along with lime, green onions and garlic, and is it ever good. The thin slices of veal kidney with mustard and the lamb chops wrapped in rice pastry aren't bad either. In fact, they're superb. And if you know of a nougat glacé in vanilla sauce (the lime sauce was a mistake) or a black-cherry savarin that are better than these, let us know about it. Don't forget to try to steal the wine list. On blah days, we reread the section on Burgundies, and it cheers us up instantly.

A la carte: 500F. Menus: 270F, 420F.

Lameloise

(See restaurant above)

Closed Wed. & Dec. 20-Jan. 18. 1 ste 980F. 20 rms 280-800F. TV. Pets allowed.

Twenty rooms and one suite, all done in fresh colors and all quite comfortable, with well-equipped bathrooms and, come morning, a delightful breakfast.

Chailly-en-Bière

77960 Chailly-en-Bière - (Seine-et-Marne)
Paris 56 - Fontainebleau 11 - Melun 9 - Corbeil 20

Auberge de l'Empereur

(13)

27, rte. de Paris - 60.66.43.38

M. Héraud. Open until 9:30 p.m. Closed Thurs., Feb. & Aug. 10-25. Garden dining. Pets allowed. Cards: V, AE, DC.

Francis Héraud, owner of this inviting country inn, has remained loyal to his repertoire for the last fifteen years; the formula may be unchanging, but it's generous and diligently prepared. Try his ragoût of veal fraise (tripe) with cèpes, stuffed saddle of young rabbit or pigeon terrine with foie gras. All is done without pretense and served at reasonable prices in a lovely little garden; the setting reminds us of Angélus, the Millet painting.

A la carte: 250F. Menus: 95F (weekdays only), 150F.

Châlons-sur-Marne

51000 Châlons-sur-Marne - (Marne)
Paris 188 - Troyes 79 - Reims 43 - Bar-le-Duc 72

Jacky Michel

(14)

19, pl. Monseigneur-Tissier - 26.68.21.51

M. Michel. Open until 9:30 p.m. Closed Sat. lunch, Sun. (except holidays), July 2-23 & Christmas school vacation. Terrace dining. Pets allowed. Parking. Telex 842078. Cards: V, AE, DC, MC.

Facing the beautiful old church across the way, this restaurant has a new, ultra-modern decor: white ceilings, spotlights, blue-toned hangings, pastel curtains and light-oak armchairs. This successful renovation has enabled Jacky Michel to find his wings. Despite his classic training, his cuisine leans toward the modern and light. Still, he shows a taste for good technical execution and loves grand game dishes—noisettes of venison Saint-Hubert, saddle of young rabbit in Champagne brandy, partridge roasted with red cabbage—some of the most sumptuous dishes in the region. He is also an expert with mushrooms (in light feuilletés à la moelle) and is becoming increasingly interested in seafood (daurade filet au poivre with vinegar). The desserts he has come up with, such as the glazed figs with almond milk and a gooseberry pulp, are nothing short of marvelous. Fine choice of Champagnes.

A la carte: 350F. Menus: 150F, 200F, 260F, 310F.

Hôtel d'Angleterre

(See restaurant above)

Closed Sun. (except holidays), July 2-23 & Christmas school vacation. 18 rms 250-380F. TV. No pets.

Facing the beautiful Notre-Dame-en-Vaux church and its carillon, this rather quiet hotel is regularly modernized and redecorated by its new owner. Good breakfast.

Pasteur

46, rue Pasteur - 26.68.10.00

Open year-round. 29 rms 105-220F. TV in 26 rms. Pets allowed. Parking. Cards: V, AE, DC, MC.

Large, quiet rooms within the walls of a building that housed a former seventeenth-century religious order. No restaurant.

IN NEARBY L'Epine

(10 km E on N 3)
51000 Châlons-sur-Marne

(14) Aux Armes de Champagne

Pl. de la Basilique - 26.66.96.79

M. Pérardel. Open until 9:30 p.m. Closed Jan. 8-Feb. 15. Pets allowed. Garage parking. Telex 830998. Cards: V, AE, MC.

This rich country inn is from the old school, in the old French tradition, and it's solidly professional at that. Chef Hugues Houard, who once flipped the famous omelets at La Mère Poulard in Mont-Saint-Michel, is not one for extravagance. He uses his considerable talent and is progressively lightening his cuisine, producing interesting results: cassolette of escargots in Champagne, turbot in cèpe butter, roasted breast of duck in truffle gravy and Champagne vinegar. The dining room is impeccably comfortable, and the view spectacular: The lovely stone latticework of the Notre-Dame-de-l'Epine basilica is like a jewel against a dreary plain. Look at it, rather than the unsightly china.

A la carte: 300-350F. Menus: 90F (weekdays only), 165F, 235F, 320F.

Aux Armes de Champagne

(See restaurant above)

Closed Jan. 8-Feb. 13. 40 rms 145-410F. TV in 11 rms.

Much quieter since the owners closed the rooms on the street. Half the rooms have been modernized, and they overlook a lovely garden. Excellent service.

Chalon-sur-Saône

71100 Chalon-sur-Saône - (Saône-et-Loire)
Paris 346 - Mâcon 57 - Dijon 68 - Bourg 89

Sights. Saint-Vincent church and its cloister (on the plaza, colorful market on Fridays); Musée Nicéphore Niepce (photography, cameras); Musée Denon (nineteenth-century paintings, archaeology); the pedestrian zones (well-restored old quarter); Carnaval (two wild weeks in late February and early March).

Eating on the Run. La Maison des Vins, promenade Ste-Marie (Lyonnaise charcuterie and regional products); La Réale, 8, pl. du Général-de-Gaulle (traditional family place); Le Sphinx, blvd. de la République (authentic brasserie).

Bars & Cafés. Le Baryton, 5, rue des Cornillons (attractive bar, music); Club Philippe Martel, in Chamforgeuel (tennis, bowling and cocktails).

Nightlife. Le Bar O Loup, 8, rue de Strasbourg (a must); La Souris, 9, pl. St-Jean-de-Maisel.

(13) Le Bourgogne

28, rue de Strasbourg - 85.48.89.18

M. Chemorin-Reniaume. Open until 9:30 p.m. Closed Sun. dinner & Wed. (except July-Aug.). Pets allowed. Cards: V.

Young Stéphane Reniaume brought this restaurant, with its beautiful Louis XIII decor, out of the doldrums. The candlelight dinner—served more or less eagerly—features gratin d'escargots with spinach, salmon steak with a parsley emulsion and wonderful veal kidneys with a fine herb gravy. Prices have remained reasonable, both à la carte and in the fixed-price menus. A classic, rigorously executed, honest cuisine.

A la carte: 180-200F. Menus: 88F, 140F, 180F.

Mercure

Ave. de l'Europe - 85.46.51.89

Open year-round. 4 stes 430F. 84 rms 300-340F. Pets allowed. Pool. Parking. Telex 800132. Cards: V, AE, DC, MC.

A rather sterile environment but warm and efficient service and clean, functional rooms. Restaurant.

(17) Le Moulin de Martorey

2 km S, Saint-Rémy
85.48.12.98

M. Gillot. Open until 9:30 p.m. Closed Sun. dinner, Mon., Feb. school vacation & Aug. 23-Sept. 6. Garden dining. Pets allowed. Parking. Cards: V, MC.

Despite the risk of setting up shop at the autoroute interchange, Jean-Pierre Gillot (a pupil of Troisgros, Thuilier and Lenôtre) has made this place work, though it couldn't have been easy to attract the bourgeoisie with dishes as imaginative as oysters and frogs' legs en gelée, sander en nage, smoked goose and lobster with pigs' feet. Initially people come out of curiosity, then out of habit.

The area around this old mill has not yet been swallowed up by urbanization, and sheep and colts still roam the fields. Inside, you'll fall in love with the charming country-bistro dining room, which has been tastefully decorated.

Tourists are just beginning to poke their noses in here, so for now it's populated primarily with locals who come for a break from the mundane and to dine on such dishes as warm duck sausage with potatoes, homemade smoked salmon (served warm), carp steak with beurre rouge and fried leeks, sautéed veal rillons (crisply cooked veal belly) caramelized with lemon rind, veal ribs in verjuice (the juice of unripened grapes), young guinea-hen with turnip flowers and corn cakes, fruit gratin with verjuice and basil, and melon with saffron syrup—an inventive, ingenious, genuine cuisine. The wine list is rich, especially with local Challonais vintages, and the service is efficient and charming, directed by the lady of the house, a former English teacher. The fixed-price menus are light both on the pocketbook and the digestion.

A la carte: 340F. Menus: 95F (weekdays only), 140F, 190F, 270F.

Ripert

31, rue St-Georges - 85.48.89.20

M. Ripert. Open until 9 p.m. Closed Sun., Mon., April 2-10 & Dec. 25-Jan. 3. Pets allowed. Cards: V.

Located on a quaint old street behind the prefecture, Ripert boasts a beamed dining room that's refined and flowery. The cuisine is simple, fresh, sincere and generous. There are no à la carte dishes, just two fixed-price menus that change daily with the bargains Mme. Ripert finds at the market: perhaps a beef "nougat" en gelée with a small salad, a superb roasted duck breast in a fine poivre vert sauce, cheeses and an extraordinary choice of desserts, such as warm apple tarts or prunes stuffed with walnuts and pistachio ice cream.

Menus: 70F, 110F.

Royal Hôtel Best Western

8, rue du Port-Villiers - 85.48.15.86

Open year-round. 8 stes 460F. 42 rms 200-360F. TV. Pets allowed. Garage parking. Telex 801610. Cards: V, AE, DC, MC.

The rooms are a bit outdated but well maintained; some face a quiet little courtyard. Good service. Restaurant.

Saint-Georges

32, ave. Jean-Jaurès - 85.48.27.05

M. Choux. Open daily until 10 p.m. Air cond. Pets allowed. Garage parking. Telex 800330. Cards: V, AE, DC, MC.

The redone decor of the dining room is a nice improvement, but what one really notices here these days is the backsliding in the kitchen, particularly so as it comes at the same time as rising prices. The plate of three salads (rather heavy foie gras, dry shrimp) is not worth a toque any more than is the gratin of chanterelles and prawns surrounded by perfectly incongruous sweet red peppers. On the other hand, the Bresse pigeon with cabbage is superb and the desserts are worthwhile. The service is fine, but it's a point less this year all the same.

A la carte: 300-350F. Menus: 92F (weekdays only), 180F, 290F.

Saint-Georges

(See restaurant above)

Open year-round. 48 rms 220-320F. TV. Air cond. Pets allowed.

This good, classic hotel near the train depot has been modernized and boasts some spacious, comfortable rooms.

Hôtel Saint-Hubert

35, pl. de Beaune - 85.46.22.81

Closed Dec. 25-Jan. 1. 51 rms 166-290F. TV. Garage parking. Telex 801177. Cards: V, AE, DC, MC.

This old, central-city hotel has been well refurbished in Burgundy style; the rooms are rather small but quiet. Sauna, solarium. No restaurant.

Chambéry

73000 Chambéry - (Savoie)
Paris 560 - Grenoble 57 - Annecy 47 - Lyon 98

Grand Hôtel Ducs de Savoie

6, pl. de la Gare - 79.69.54.54

Closed July 15-30. 5 stes 600-660F. 45 rms 260-500F. TV. Air cond. in 10 rms. Pets allowed. Parking. Telex 320910. Cards: V, AE, DC.

Facing the train station, the fine rooms have been decorated with personality. Pleasant little garden. Disco. Restaurant.

Les Princes

4, rue de Boigne - 79.33.45.36

M. Zorelle. Open daily until 9:30 p.m. Air cond. Pets allowed. Cards: V, AE, DC, MC.

Jean-Claude Zorelle, known for twenty years for his inn at the other end of the region, recently reopened this old establishment located in the heart of town near the Fontaine des Eléphants. He renovated it from top to bottom and created a two-level dining room that's nice but lacks any particular style, though it does have the comforts and fine china of a top restaurant. This surly yet pleasant Savoyard is a culinary master, among the best in Burgundy; his repertoire includes a plate of two kinds of foie gras ("cru au gros sel" and in a terrine with port), marvelous shank of venison, veal mignon à la crème, precisely cooked John Dory with two kinds of peppers, unforgettable cheeses (Beaufort and Tomme), delicious homemade rolls, which customers secretly pilfer, and exquisite house chocolates (despite a mint coulis that's a bit too aggressive). Impeccable service and a good wine cellar, particularly in Bordeaux.

A la carte: 350-400F. Menus: 140F, 220F, 280F, 390F.

Les Princes

(See restaurant above)

Open year-round. 45 rms 220-340F. Half-board 300-380F. TV in 24 rms. Pets allowed.

Half the rooms at Les Princes, located in the heart of town, have been well renovated and soundproofed. The exposed beams work well with the lovely floral decor.

(13) Roubatcheff

6, rue de Théâtre - 79.33.24.91

M. Roubatcheff. Closings vary. Air cond. Pets allowed. Cards: V, AE, DC, MC.

An old family house noted for its strict conservatism and good Slavic food is beginning to break away from the conventional. Jean-Philippe Roubatcheff is proving his abilities as a first-class chef and delicate sauce maker. His fine surprises include salmon émietté (crumble) à la citronelle, salmon and pike perch in a langoustine aspic, and suprême de col vert (wild duck) with pink berries. The delicious desserts include a bitter-chocolate cake with sweet almonds. Beautiful Savoie wines.

A la carte: 300-350F. Menus: 150F (weekdays only), 230F, 400F.

(15) La Vanoise

6, pl. de la Gare - 79.69.02.78

M. Lenain. Open until 10:30 p.m. Closed Sun. dinner (off-seas.). Air cond. Garden dining. Pets allowed. Telex 320910. Cards: V, AE, DC, MC.

Parisian Philippe Lenain anxiously awaits fame and customers, no doubt including the rich, gourmand, casino-going crowd, in his bright Venetian-looking restaurant in a refurbished old hotel. He has gone to great lengths to beef up comforts, scrub the silver and polish the excellent fixed-price menus (one of which is a "Savoyard" formula). The cuisine is fine, appetizing and well updated: sea bream filet with artichokes, duck and langoustines in a vanilla infusion, breast of lamb with a tian of legumes and improving desserts by the pastry chef. The fine wine cellar is enriched regularly.

A la carte: 350F. Menus: 130F, 170F to 300F.

Chambray

27120 Pacy-sur-Eure - (Eure)
Paris 96 - Vernon 18 - Évreux 18 - Rouen 52 - Pacy 11

(15) Le Vol au Vent

19, pl. de la Mairie - 32.36.70.05

M. Lognon. Open until 9:30 p.m. (by reserv.). Closed Sun. dinner, Tues. lunch & Jan. 9-Feb. 1. Pets allowed. Cards: V, DC, MC.

This comfortable, neorustic inn on the village plaza lives up to its promises. Chef Christian Dupuis, an extraordinary culinary technician, produces the best pastry-based cuisine in France, reflecting an academic respect for the traditional marriage of flavor and ingredients and using a lot of butter and cream. Miraculous feuilletages (pastry leaves) play a big role here, as do precise sauces. His dishes represent a bastion of old-style cuisine and art de vivre: crab chausson (pastry), filet de boeuf Saint-Amand, sweetbreads feuilleté with morels, feuilleté of red fruits. Fine wine list and service directed by Gérard Lognon.

A la carte: 250-300F. Menus: 900F (for two, with reservations), 160F, 190F.

Chamonix

74400 Chamonix - (Haute-Savoie)
Paris 619 - Annecy 96 - Geneva 86 - Albertville 67

(15) Albert Ier et Milan

119, impasse du Montenvers
50.53.05.09

M. Carrier. Open until 9:15 p.m. Closed Wed. (off-seas.), May 8-25 & Oct. 23-Dec. 9. Garden dining. No pets. Garage parking. Telex 380779. Cards: V, AE, DC.

This restaurant is a place of mirth; it won't escape you upon entering the luminous dining room in the comfortable, charming chalet. Martine Carrier and her pleasant young staff are efficient, and the cuisine of husband Pierre, who is bursting with enthusiasm and ideas, is fresh and pleasant. Mont Blanc will keep you company if you are seated by one of the bay windows; otherwise you can admire the etchings that punctuate the wood-paneled walls. Try the exquisite house smoked salmon served with a caviar cream sauce, lobster ravioli with a nettle cream sauce, salad of pan-fried red mullet with a tomato aspic, roast pigeon in a salt crust and a fabulous lamb blanquette with fresh morels. Excellent desserts include the classic honey ice cream with raspberry coulis and the warm rhubarb tart with a caramel-honey sauce. The wine list has some good finds for about 70 francs. A pleasant garden for summer dining sits next to the pool.

A la carte: 350F. Menus: 150F, 230F, 350F.

Albert Ier et Milan

(See restaurant above)

Closed May 8-25 & Oct. 23-Dec. 9. 4 stes 660-760F. 30 rms 360-520F. Half-board 370-410F. TV. Pets allowed. Heated pool. Tennis.

This charming family hotel is without a doubt the nicest of its genre in Chamonix. The rooms are a bit worn but extremely comfortable and well equipped. Health club with sauna and Jacuzzi. A golf course was being added at the time of this writing.

12/20 Auberge de Bois-Prin

Les Moussoux - 50.53.33.51

M. Carrier. Open until 9:30 p.m. Closed Wed. lunch, May 8-June 1 & Oct. 9-Dec. 14. Air cond. Garden dining. Pets allowed. Garage parking. Telex 305551. Cards: V, AE, DC, MC.

This attractive chalet on the edge of Mount Brévent has one of the best views in Chamonix, with Mont Blanc directly opposite. The tiny dining room is inviting, and the service (in Savoyard costume) is simple and charming, but the cuisine is rather plain: generous salade gourmande, turbot à la tomate (nothing special), respectable breast of lamb with an uninspiring gratin savoyard. Good regional wines.

A la carte: 300F. Menus: 130F (weekday lunch only), 150F (weekdays only), 190F (weekends and holidays only), 320F.

Auberge du Bois-Prin

(See restaurant above)

Closed May 8-June 1 & Oct. 9-Dec. 14. 11 rms 480-890F. Half- board 450-680 oblig. in seas. TV. Air cond. Pets allowed.

A pleasant little family hotel with rooms warmly decorated, though without originality. Beautiful mountain view. Relais et Châteaux.

Beausoleil

60, allée des Peupliers
5 km NE on N 506, Le Lavanche
50.54.00.78

Closed Sept. 20-Dec. 20. 16 rms 160-280F. Half-board 170-260F oblig. in seas. Tennis. Garage parking. Cards: V.

At the foot of the needle-rock mountains, this charming hotel with lots of flowers is well isolated in the pastures. Adventurous visitors will be happy to know that the owner is a mountain guide. Restaurant.

Eden

Aux Praz, 2.5 km N - 50.53.06.40

M. Lesage. Open until 9:30 p.m. Closed Wed. & Nov. 15-Dec. 15. Pets allowed. Hotel: 10 rms 500F. Cards: V, AE, DC.

This large chalet on the edge of Chamonix may not be spectacular on the outside, but everything changes on the inside: The dining rooms are inviting and comfortable, with pretty white tablecloths, individual lighting, real silver and a tableside service that—a rare event—allows seconds. Gérard Lesage's cuisine is strictly classic and not always fascinating, but it's always well executed: trout with almonds, langouste au gratin, veal normande. The first fixed-price menu includes an excellent salad of warm duck livers, fish lasagne with a tasty salmon cream sauce, nice farm cheeses and fraisier (strawberry cake). Good Savoie wines.

A la carte: 260-280F. Menus: 90F (weekday lunch only), 130F, 190F, 300F.

Les Gentianes

5 km NE on N 506, Le Lavancher
50.54.10.85

Closed April 17-May 27 & Sept. 25-Dec. 20. 14 rms 130-295F. Half-board 145-260F oblig. in seas. Garage parking. Telex 385022.

These nice little rooms are located on the edge of a fir forest. Tennis and golf within three kilometers. Restaurant.

Le Matafan

Pl. de l'Eglise - 50.53.05.64

M. Morand. Open until 9:30 p.m. Closed Oct. 15-Dec. 15. Garden dining. Pets allowed. Garage parking. Telex 385614. Cards: V, AE, DC, MC.

The rustic/modern high-style decor revolves around a large central fireplace, which makes this place quite pleasant at night, particularly with the small lamps and the young, stylish staff. The son of the house, Yves Morand, creates a cuisine based on classics, with a personal touch and attention to good products: warm salad of new potatoes, lentils and marinated herring; pan-fried duck liver with wild mushrooms and a turnip confit; a fricassée of langoustines with Champagne butter. Desserts are well prepared, and the wine list is exceptional, notably the Mondeuses; some wines are served by the glass.

A la carte: 260-300F. Menus: 130F, 180F, 230F.

Le Mont-Blanc

(See restaurant above)

Closed Oct. 10-Dec. 15. 6 stes 840-1,416F. 44 rms 465-868F. TV. Pets allowed. Heated pool. Tennis.

This beautiful, traditional hotel, modernized and equipped with a sauna, pool and tennis courts, is located in the heart of Chamonix. Several splendid suites and a lovely garden.

La Sapinière-Montana

102, rue Mummery - 50.53.07.63

Closed April 8-June 17 & Sept. 23-Dec. 21. 30 rms 310-344F. Half-board oblig. in seas. Garage parking. Telex 305551. Cards: V, AE, DC, MC.

Comfortable rooms, pleasantly decorated, most with a large balcony facing Mont Blanc. Sauna. Restaurant.

Champagnac-de-Bélair

24530 Champagnac-de-Bélair - (Dordogne)
Paris 464 - Périgueux 33 - Brantôme 6 - Nontron 22

Moulin du Roc

At Moulin du Roc - 53.54.80.36

M. Gardillou. Open until 9:30 p.m. Closed Wed. lunch, Tues. & Nov. 15-Dec. 15. Garden dining. No pets. Garage parking. Telex 571555. Cards: V, AE, DC, MC.

Solange and Lucien Gardillou turned this former walnut-oil mill into a fine, friendly inn, working madly with all their heart, restoring and decorating every nook and cranny, so that the place now looks like a dollhouse. They probably tried too hard—too many mediocre knickknacks and table covers hide the fine antique furnishings. They might have better results if they toned things down a bit.

Solange, a lively young woman who took over the kitchen in a pinch and stayed on, brings freshness and vivacity to the cuisine. Yet a few things seem out of place, as with the decor, and we'd like to see her try to avoid mannerism and confusion of styles. Wild rice is always served with the fish of the day, as is fresh pasta (instead of vegetables). And on a short menu, we found fresh cod (a trendy dish) with pigs' feet, as well as pigs' feet stuffed with truffles. Too much! And is it really essential to stuff caviar in a salmon steak with lettuce? But we do have fond memories of a marvelous feuilleté au boudin, an exquisite warm terrine of cèpes, a tripe dish (her grandmother's recipe), a young-duck confit with sorrel and a beef filet with truffles, which were more definitive than the foie gras with honey and the unavoidable raspberry vinegar or the fresh pasta with truffles. And we have only praise for the wine cellar, which stocks some 50,000 bottles (some Mouton-Rothschilds and Pétruses practically at cost) and is the domain of son François, who seems to have grown as knowledgeable as his dad. We must also give praise to the fine desserts made by the other son: pear feuillantine, a tart (that is, good and tart) apple tart; and glazed vacherin (cake) with walnuts.

A la carte: 350F. Menus: 100F (lunch only, wine incl.), 190F, 270F, 350F.

Moulin du Roc

(See restaurant above)

Closed Nov. 15-Dec. 15. 4 stes 620-650F. 10 rms 380-550F. Half-board 520-650. TV. Pets allowed. Heated pool. Tennis.

The beautiful swimming pool is a welcome addition at this seventeenth-century mill, which has kept its machinery and its charm and added a romantic decor. The rooms and suites are perfectly comfortable and well equipped, but from the outside they're not in the excellent taste usually expected of the Relais et Châteaux group.

Champigny

see Reims

Champillon

see Epernay

Champtoceaux

49270 St-Laurent-des-Autels - (Maine-et-Loire)
Paris 367 - Cholet 48 - Angers 62 - Nantes 31

14 La Forge

1 bis, pl. des Piliers - 40.83.56.23

M. Pauvert. Open until 9:15 p.m. Closed Wed. dinner, Sun., Tues., Feb. school vacation & 2 weeks in Oct. Pets allowed. Cards: V, AE, MC.

Paul Pauvert has spent seven years at this charming, rustic restaurant, whose terrace overlooks the large towers of the château, which is wonderfully illuminated at night. His is a solid, professional cuisine with frank, clear tastes, relying on local products and two fishermen who supply him with shad, salmon and other Loire fish. Although his à la carte menu rarely changes—that's our only reproach—we still adore the shad mousseline with frogs' legs (well prepared with a Cabernet butter), a feuilleté of sweetbreads with spinach (slightly overcooked but with a subtle sauce), delicious warm chèvre served on a rye-nut bread and an exquisite poached pear stuffed with sorbet. Delicate wines, generous fixed-price menus and friendly service directed by Paul's wife, Joëlle.

A la carte: 230-260F. Menus: 120F and 145F (weekdays only), 175F, 270F.

Chamrousse

38410 Uriage - (Isère)
Paris 596 - Chambéry 80 - Grenoble 29 - Allevard 59

L'Hermitage

At the ski lift - 76.89.93.21

Closed April 15-Dec. 15. 2 stes 400-460F. 48 rms 320-440F. Half-board 360-420F. TV in 15 rms. Pets allowed. Garage parking. Cards: V.

Well situated on the ski slopes, L'Hermitage is a good, classic hotel with a rustic decor. It doesn't have much charm, but it is comfortable. Restaurant.

Chantilly

60500 Chantilly - (Oise)
Paris 42 - Compiègne 45 - Pontoise 36 - Senlis 10

Campanile

Rte. de Creil (3 km N on N 16), Gouvieux 44.57.39.24

Open year-round. 47 rms 210-230F. Half-board 182-202F. TV in 31 rms. Pets allowed. Parking. Telex 140065. Cards: V.

At the edge of the Chantilly forest, the Campanile is quiet, modern and well maintained. Restaurant.

14 Le Relais Condé

42, ave. du Maréchal-Joffre - 44.57.05.75

M. Rios. Open until 9:30 p.m. Closed Sun. dinner & Mon. Terrace dining. Pets allowed. Cards: V, AE, DC.

The nicest and classiest restaurant in Chantilly is located near the racetrack, under the frame of a nineteenth-century Anglican chapel. Young Patrice Lebeau creates a thoughtful, unpretentious, simple and consistently good cuisine: délice du Périgord (warm foie gras baked with a sauce made from eggs and fresh cream), lotte brochette with red bell pepper, perfect veal kidneys in mustard sauce and a beautiful three-chocolate cake with crème anglaise. Nothing spectacular, just fine work and generosity, especially on the two fixed-price menus. One of the nicest wine cellars in the region.

A la carte: 300F and up. Menus: 105F, 150F.

13 Relais du Coq Chantant

21, rte. de Creil - 44.57.01.28

M. Dautry. Open daily until 9:45 p.m. Pets allowed. Parking. Cards: V, AE, DC, MC.

This white cottage along the road lives up to its looks: a comfortable place for the "beau monde" of golfers and horse riders who frequent the region. The à la carte prices confirm the opulent tone, as does the decor—a mélange of pinks, flowered tapestries and the like. Try the scorpionfish with a delicious saffron aspic, the grilled turbot (though the béarnaise sauce isn't exactly light) and the raspberry gratin, which is quite nice despite a slightly oversweet crème anglaise. Fine fixed-price menus, good service.

A la carte: 350F. Menus: 89F and 159F (weekdays only), 148F and 287F (weekends and holidays only).

This symbol signifies hotels that offer an exceptional degree of peace and quiet.

IN NEARBY **Lamorlaye**
(7 km S on N 16)
60260 Lamorlaye - (Oise)

Hostellerie du Lys

63, 7e ave., Lys-Chantilly,
Rond-Point de la Reine - 44.21.26.19

Closed Dec. 21-Feb. 5. 35 rms 155-415F. Half-board 310-530F. TV. Pets allowed. Parking. Telex 150298. Cards: V, AE, DC, MC.

A beautiful, cozy weekend inn with comfortable rooms and a nice, quiet ambience. Tennis, golf and swimming are nearby. Restaurant.

La Charité-sur-Loire

58400 La Charité-sur-Loire - (Nièvre)
Paris 216 - Autun 127 - Auxerre 95 - Bourges 51

(14) A La Bonne Foi

91, rue Camille-Barrère - 86.70.15.77

M. Guyot. Open until 9 p.m. Closed Sun. dinner & Mon. Pets allowed. Parking. Cards: V, DC.

The decor of this provincial bistro is rather rudimentary, undoubtedly in need of a reworking. Yet appropriately, nothing is done in a hurry here. After spending ten years with Lenôtre, Didier Guyot has become a complete professional who cares about freshness and lightness: warm langoustine salad with green beans, foie gras pan-fried with asparagus, touraine beuchelle (sweetbreads, kidneys and morels in cream sauce) and delicate desserts (apple feuilleté with cinnamon ice cream, sorbets). Fine young staff.

A la carte: 300F. Menus: 120F, 160F, 210F.

Charleville-Mézières

08000 Charleville-Mézières - (Ardennes)
Paris 235 - Metz 160 - Nancy 205 - Reims 82

(13) Le Château Bleu

3, blvd. Pierquin-Warcq - 24.56.18.19

M. d'Orchymont. Open daily until 10 p.m. Terrace dining. No pets. Parking. Cards: V, AE, MC.

We admire the entrepreneur who creates an elegant and ambitious place in a depressed region. This large nineteenth-century house on a large wooded estate has a luxurious dining room decorated in pink and blue (laid on a bit too thick in places) in an Italian Renaissance style. The wonderful view and warm reception combine with Max Belloir's professional if sometimes affected cuisine: salmon seasoned with hazelnut oil and a dollop of caviar, tasty veal kidneys roasted in their own juices, langoustines in crustacean butter, good desserts. Good Champagnes at reasonable prices.

A la carte: 400F. Menus: 130F, 170F, 270F.

Le Château Bleu

(See restaurant above)

Open year-round. 13 rms 240-390F. Half-board 400-550F. TV. Pets allowed. Heated pool. Tennis.

Charming brand-new rooms, decorated in an Italian style, overlook the quiet woods or the noisy boulevard.

Charolles

71120 Charolles - (Saône-et-Loire)
Paris 370 - Autun 78 - Mâcon 55 - Roanne 59

(14) Moderne

Ave. de la Gare - 85.24.07.02

M. Bonin. Open until 9 p.m. Closed Sun. dinner (off-seas.), Mon. & end Dec.-early Feb. 1. Pets allowed. Hotel: 18 rms 125-260F; half-board 260-320F oblig. in seas. Pool. Garage parking. Cards: V, AE, DC.

From the outside, this huge, newly plastered house has about as much charm as the unemployment office, despite a cute terrace that overlooks the train station (where the once-weekly train is still a big event). In back, however, is a lovely, green garden with a pool, and inside are two large, bright dining rooms with nice antique furnishings and carefully chosen table settings. Jean Bonin's cuisine is quite professional: terrine of poultry livers with foie gras, sander filet in Burgundy, Charolais beef and wonderful meringue petits fours after dessert.

A la carte: 250-280F. Menus: 85F and 120F (weekdays only), 155F (weekends and holidays only).

Chartres

28000 Chartres - (Eure-et-Loire)
Paris 96 - Orléans 72 - Dreux 35 - Evreux 77

12/20 La Blanquette

45, rue des Changes - 37.21.99.36

M. Lavenir. Open daily until 10 p.m. Pets allowed. Cards: V.

This charming little find was recently opened by Bernard Roger as an annex of La Vieille Maison. Come here for good local wines by the glass and a generous bistro cuisine: joue de boeuf confiture, veal or fish blanquettes, clafoutis.

A la carte: 230F. Menus: 230F (wine incl.), 65F, 110F.

(16) Le Grand Monarque

22, pl. des Epars - 37.21.00.72

M. Jallerat. Open daily until 9:30 p.m. Terrace dining. Pets allowed. Garage parking. Telex 760777. Cards: V, AE, DC, MC.

Behind the eighteenth-century facade is a newly renovated dining room with a nice beige-tone decor, flowers, elegant tables and a peaceful winter garden. Georges and Geneviève Jallerat are still the perfect hosts, as they have been for some twenty years. The cuisine (prepared by well-qualified Bruno Letarte) is based on simplicity and the season. The à la carte list is short but always changing. Only the hors d'oeuvres seemed a bit overdone (a too-creamy sauce on the sweetbreads salad). Try the émincé of pigeon with fresh pasta, turbot grilled over a charcoal fire, young Challans duck with turnips and the famous pots de crême with café or chocolate. The wine cellar is thick with Loire and Bordeaux vintages. The steep à la carte prices are worth it, and the fixed-price menus are quite attractive.

A la carte: 350F. Menus: 180F, 269F.

Le Grand Monarque
(See restaurant above)
Open year-round. 3 stes 565-875F. 54 rms 247-410F. TV. Pets allowed.

The best hotel in Chartres has charming new rooms in two turn-of-the-century buildings surrounding a garden. Nice modern suites. Interior patio for breakfast.

14 Henri IV
31-33, rue du Soleil-d'Or - 37.36.01.55
Mme. Cazalis. Open until 8:45 p.m. Closed Mon. dinner, Tues. & Feb. Pets allowed. Cards: AE, DC.

The old and famous Maurice Cazalis is gone, but he has left the kitchen in good hands—with his trainee for some twenty years. Jacques Corbonnois perpetuates Cazalis's tradition of rich haute cuisine that is old-fashioned but rigorously executed, even when excessive. In reality, Corbonnois has been cooking alone for some time, and other than a reduction in cooking time, little has changed from the good old days. From the large dining room's windows, one views the famous Chartres cathedral's spire. The widow Cazalis is still a charming hostess, and her staff will bring you a delicious Chartres terrine of partridge and pistachios, a well-seasoned Henri IV salad (vegetables and shellfish), a remarkable lotte pot-au-feu (in fact, a sort of bouillabaisse) served with rouille (a garlicky, spicy mayonnaise), a blanquette of sweetbreads with creamed foie gras and such fine, old-fashioned desserts as Triomphe soufflé (à la liqueur) or bombe (pudding) with glazed chestnuts. The wonderful wine cellar is rich and varied.

A la carte: 300-350F. Menus: 165F (weekdays only, wine incl.), 220F, 275F.

15 La Vieille Maison
5, rue au Lait - 37.34.10.67
M. Roger. Open until 9:15 p.m. Closed Sun. dinner & Mon. Pets allowed. Cards: V, AE, DC, MC.

This is an antique restaurant with a young cuisine. Bernard Roger is a radiant, self-assured cuisinier who loves fine, strong flavors and creates dishes that are wonderfully rich (and costly). His à la carte menu is short but ever changing, inspired by the trends of the market. You'll find new asparagus accompanied by large, juicy langoustines, spring vegetables next to tender tournedos sauté, coquilles St-Jacques pan-fried in a foie gras coulis, an extraordinary Beauceron chicken stuffed with truffles under the skin and roasted with fresh lasagne au foie gras, pigs' feet stuffed with truffles, and desserts that are less imaginative but elaborate and well prepared. Prices are a bit steep (except for the first fixed-price menu), but we can't call them unjustified; everything is generous, successfully executed and served in a charming ambience, with little nooks dispersed throughout the dining room and the flowery patio.

A la carte: 350-400F. Menus: 160F (weekday lunch only, wine incl.), 160F (dinner only), 220F, 300F.

IN NEARBY **Saint-Prest**
(10 km NE on N 154 & D 6)
28300 Mainvilliers - (Eure-et-Loire)

11/20 Le Manoir de Palomino
37.22.27.27
M. Ribieras. Open until 9:30 p.m. Closed Sun. dinner, Mon. & Jan. 15-Feb. 15. Garden dining. Pets allowed. Garage parking. Cards: V.

This old manor house in the delightful Eure valley woods has been sumptuously restored. The scenery is magnificent, the dining room has exposed beams, and the owner displays charm and a desire to please. The cuisine has started out cautiously and rather plainly: salmon boudin with sorrel, generous duck confit. Intelligent wine list. We'll have to wait and see.

A la carte: 230-250F. Menus: 100F, 195F.

Le Manoir du Palomino
(See restaurant above)
Closed Jan. 15-Feb. 15. 1 ste 500F. 12 rms 150-400F. Half-board 300-600F. TV. Pets allowed. Tennis. Golf.

A fine weekend escape from Paris, for relaxing or for conferences. The 40-acre estate has golf and tennis, and the spacious, quiet, luxuriously decorated rooms have charm, flowers, beams and fine views of the landscape.

IN NEARBY **Thivars**
(7.5 km S on N 10)
28630 Chartres - (Eure-et-Loire)

13 La Sellerie
48, rue Nationale - 37.26.41.59
M. Heitz. Open until 9 p.m. Closed Sun. dinner (off-seas.), Mon. dinner, Tues., Jan. 9-24 & July 31-Aug. 22. Terrace dining. Pets allowed. Parking. Cards: V.

The dining room may look like an antiques dealer's shop, but the interior garden is pleasant, with plenty of flowers. Equally pleasant is the well-executed cuisine: tête de veau beauceronne, sole with a fennel cream sauce, sweetbreads and eggplant in a millefeuille. The fine wine list includes excellent Bordeaux. Service seems a bit stiff but is amicable.

A la carte: 300F and up. Menus: 115F, 260F.

Chasselay
69380 Lozanne - (Rhône)
Paris 448 - Lyon 22 - Villefranche-sur-Saône 15

14 Lassausaie
Rue de Belleuze - 78.47.62.59
M. Lassausaie. Open until 9:15 p.m. Closed Tues. dinner, Wed., Feb. 14-24 & Aug. Pets allowed. Parking. Cards: V, AE, DC.

This large Beaujolais country cottage now considers itself to be a *grand restaurant.* The flowered wallpaper has remained, but the gossip is that Guy Lassausaie won't. In the meantime, let's take note of the progress made here: a harmonious foie gras ballotine with apple and Sauternes, gilthead delicately cooked in fleurs de courgette (zucchini blossoms), excellent pigeon stuffed with coq kidneys, sander filet roasted with caramelized onions. Most of the desserts are also good (rather plain clafouti but fine banana sorbet and honey ice cream). The wine list and young staff are both good assets.

A la carte: 250-300F. Menus: 100F (weekdays only), 140F to 270F.

Château-Arnoux

04160 Château-Arnoux - (Alpes-de-Haute-Provence)
Paris 717 - Digne 25 - Sisteron 14 - Manosque 38

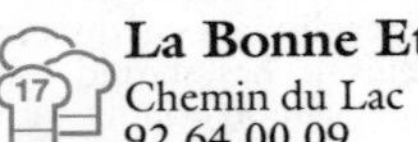

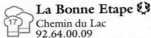

La Bonne Etape

Chemin du Lac
92.64.00.09

M. Gleize. Open until 9:30 p.m. Closed Sun. dinner & Mon. (off-seas.), Jan. 4-Feb. 15 & Nov. 20-27. Air cond. Pets allowed. Garage parking. Telex 430605. Cards: V, AE, DC, MC.

Even Pierre Gleize, with his radiant restaurant where people come for a once-in-a-lifetime experience, can't please everyone. We received a letter from one American reader who declared that his famous totènes (squid) with herbs and pine cones was lacking in taste; another found his cèpes ravioli indigestible (unless it was the Badoit at 25 francs a bottle). If we wanted to, we could also add that we found the pigeon confit salad a bit overcooked and the desserts lacking the imagination we expected. Still, we stand by our three toques, thanks to the marvelous house smoked salmon with cucumbers seasoned with wild marjoram, incomparable cèpes salad, Sisteron lamb of an unparalleled taste, perfectly cooked in a rustic gratin (but we regret the kiddie-portion cutlets), rolled young rabbit in hyssop (a mint-like herb) and fine goat cheeses that we've found nowhere else. Despite the minor flaws, La Bonne Etape produces an excellent fresh cuisine of the region, with the help of local farmers and markets. Despite the unfortunate urbanization hereabouts, this remains a bastion of quality, resisting the trend toward standardization.

A la carte: 400-500F. Menus: 190F, 300F, 350F, 380F.

La Bonne Etape

(See restaurant above)

Closed Sun. & Mon. (off-seas.), Jan. 4-Feb. 15 & Nov. 20-27. 7 stes 700-750F. 11 rms 280-600F. Half-board oblig in seas. TV in 14 rms. Air cond. Pets allowed. Heated pool.

Beyond the pleasant garden and pool are charming rooms that are well furnished and comfortable, some with terraces. And they're very quiet, except for those on the ground floor next to the parking lot. Marvelous breakfast. Relais et Châteaux.

This symbol stands for "Les Lauriers du Terroir," an award given to chefs who prepare noteworthy traditional or regional recipes.

Châteaubourg

35220 Châteaubourg - (Ille-et-Vilaine)
Paris 330 - Laval 50 - Rennes 20 - Vitré 15

Ar Milin'

30 rue de Paris - 99.00.30.91

M. Burel. Open until 9:15 p.m. Closed Sat. dinner, Sun. & Dec. 19-Jan. 7. Pets allowed. Parking. Telex 740083. Cards: V, AE, DC, MC.

Inside a nice, rustic dining room overlooking the river and the woods (too bad there are no tables outside) you'll find relaxed, fast service and intelligent realistically priced fare. The new chef prepares careful if not passionate dishes with good ingredients and an evident openheartedness. Try the salmon back grilled in its skin with fennel butter and the native wild duck in its juices.

A la carte: 230-250F. Menus: 85F (weekdays only), 200F (weekends and holidays only).

Ar Milin'

(See restaurant above)

Closed Sat. & Sun. (Nov.-Feb.) & Dec. 19-Jan. 7. 33 rms 158-340F. Half-board 305-340F. TV. Pets allowed. Tennis.

This large old mill in the woods has newly refurbished rooms; the nicest have terraces that overlook the river. Exercise room, Jacuzzi.

Châteaudun

28200 Châteaudun - (Eure-et-Loire)
Paris 132 - Chartres 44 - Orléans 48

Le Michel-Ange

33, rue des Fouleries - 37.45.23.72

Mme. Mertz. Open until 10 p.m. Closed Mon., Feb. 15-March 1 & Aug. 15-30. Air cond. Pets allowed. Garage parking. Cards: V, AE, DC.

The new owners of this grotto at the foot of the cliffs have toned down the rather impetuous rustic decor, though they kept the fantastic ironwork and the terribly uncomfortable wooden chairs. We put up with the discomfort because the food is made by a true cuisinier, Jean-François Ricard: lots of fresh mesclun lettuce with warm coquilles St-Jacques and foie gras, good red mullet filets steamed with seaweed (tasty but slightly heavy sauce) and a delicious caramel-pear feuilleté. Nice Bordeaux and Loire vintages.

A la carte: 230F. Menus: 130F, 180F, 280F.

Châteaufort

see PARIS SUBURBS

Châteauneuf-du-Pape

84230 Châteauneuf-du-Pape - (Vaucluse)
Paris 673 - Avignon 17 - Carpentras 24

Château des Fines Roches

2 km on D 17 toward Avignon
90.83.70.23

M. Estevenin. Open until 9 p.m. Closed Mon. & Dec. 23-Feb. 15. No pets. Hotel: 7 rms 390-650F; half-board 890-1,150F oblig. in seas. Parking. Cards: V.

This peculiar feudal castle amid the vineyards has spacious, more or less well-equipped hotel rooms and an elegant dining room. Jean-Pierre and Philippe Estevenin, the two sons of the house, prepare a good, light "vintner's" menu: salad of aiguillettes of duck with wine brandy, sole goujonettes in saffron with new vegetables, local chèvres and delicious desserts. Tastings of the magnificent Châteauneuf-du-Pape wine are offered by appointment.

A la carte: 400F. Menu: 320F (weekdays only), 195F.

Châteauroux

36000 Châteauroux - (Indre)
Paris 250 - Tours 109 - Bourges 65 - Vierzon 57

(15) Jean-Louis Dumonet

1, rue J.-J.-Rousseau - 54.34.82.69

M. Dumonet. Open until 10 p.m. Closed Sun. dinner (& lunch July-Aug.), Mon. & 2 weeks in Feb. Pets allowed. Cards: V, AE, DC.

The frilly decor hasn't changed since the days of the now-famous Jean Bardet, and the young chef—Jean-Louis Dumonet—he left behind to take over is truly coming into his own in this potentially intimidating position. His warm lobster salad with olive oil, his cream of cèpes du Barry with a slice of foie gras and the Scotch salmon with wild mushrooms go a long way toward soothing the disappointment of the owners (his parents) at losing one of the top chefs of France. Lovely wine list. The prices indicate Dumonet's ambition, yet he maintains two affordable fixed-price menus.

A la carte: 450F. Menus: 120F (weekdays only, wine incl.), 175F to 210F (weekends and holidays only), 150F, 310F.

Elysée Hôtel

2, rue de la République - 54.22.33.66

Open year-round. 18 rms 250-350F. TV. Cards: V, DC.

A pleasant, comfortable little hotel without pretense. Restaurant.

Château-Thierry

02400 Château-Thierry - (Aisne)
Paris 96 - Meaux 50 - Epernay 48 - Soissons 41

(13) Auberge Jean de la Fontaine

10, rue des Filoirs -23.83.63.89

M. Corbin. Open until 10 p.m. Closed Sun. dinner, Mon., Feb. 1-20 & Aug. 1-15. Pets allowed. Cards: V, AE, DC, MC.

The former shoemaker's shop that roguish Guy Girard has left for the glories of Paris won't overwhelm you with charm or elegance, particularly with its shamefully close tables. But the new owners seem intent on preserving the tradition here of excellent service and simple country cooking: excellent marinated fresh salmon, classic sliced duck breast in pepper, pike with sorrel (too many bones), sorry cheeses and decent desserts.

A la carte: 250F. Menus: 280F (Champagne incl.), 150F.

Remember to call or write in advance to reserve your room or your table.

Châtelguyon

63140 Châtelguyon - (Puy-de-Dôme)
Paris 375 - Clermont-Ferrand 21 - Vichy 47

Splendid Hôtel

5-7, rue d'Angleterre - 73.86.04.80

Closed Dec. 1-April 3. 1 ste 999F. 79 rms 315-800F. Half-board 439-919F. TV. Pets allowed. Heated pool. Telex 990585. Cards: V, AE, DC, MC.

An immense, solemn hotel amid flower gardens, with rooms that have been entirely redecorated. Nightclub. Restaurant.

Châtellerault

86100 Châtellerault - (Vienne)
Paris 305 - Cholet 128 - Tours 69 - Poitiers 34

(16) La Charmille

74, blvd. Blossac - 49.21.30.11

M. Proust. Open until 9:30 p.m. Closed Wed., Jan. 19-Feb. 18 & 10 days in Oct. Air cond. Pets allowed. Garage parking. Telex 791801. Cards: V, AE, DC, MC.

Christian Proust, a pork butcher turned innkeeper, hired himself as chef after a succession didn't satisfy him. His inn near the city hall is now one of the best in the region—it has such a modern, professional touch that some dishes appear almost as showpieces, perhaps even a bit too much so: a rich Charmille salad (with duck) topped with vinaigrette made from a duck glaze, langoustine soufflé en charlotte, salmon or turbot with a saffron cream sauce, ginger-seasoned sweetbreads in pastry and such ultra-light pastries as a wild strawberry feuilleté à la vanille. These dishes are becoming increasingly pricey, as are the fine Loire wines. But there is the impeccable service directed by Mme. Proust, who strives for elegance in the not-so-exciting fin-de-siècle decor.

A la carte: 300-350F. Menu: 160F.

Grand Hôtel Moderne

(See restaurant above)

Open year-round. 33 rms 200-440F. TV. Pets allowed.

Classic, comfortable and extremely well maintained.

Châtillon

39130 Clairvaux-les-Lacs - (Jura)
Paris 421 - Lons-le-Saunier 18 - Champagnole 23

Chez Yvonne

2.5 km E on D 39 - 84.25.70.82

Closed Mon. & Tues. (off-seas.) & Nov. 15-March 15. 8 rms 140-160F. Half-board 180F. Pets allowed. Garage parking. Cards: V.

An unpretentious cottage with unpretentious prices. The rooms are comfortable, with nice views of the Ain river below. Restaurant.

La Chaulme
63660 St-Anthème - (Puy-de-Dôme)
Paris 470 - St-Etienne 47 - Clermont-Ferrand 116

Creux de l'Oulette
73.95.41.16

Closed Wed. & Nov. 20-March 15 (except school vacations). 11 rms 65-160F. Half-board 118-148F. Parking. Cards: V, MC.

A pleasant, modest little house whose owner organizes ski trips for guests. Restaurant.

Chaumousey
see Epinal

Chavoires
see Annecy

Cheffes-sur-Sarthe
49330 Châteauneuf-sur-Sarthe - (Maine-et-Loire)
Paris 288 - Angers 19 - Château-Gontier 33

12/20 Château de Teildras
41.42.61.08

M. de Bernard du Breil. Open until 9 p.m. Closed Tues. lunch & Nov. 3-April 1. No pets. Parking. Telex 722268. Cards: V, AE, DC.

In the greenest part of the Sarthe valley stands this aristocratic old residence with the atmosphere of a real home, equipped with elegant hosts, fine furnishings and a naturally warm reception. But there are signs of carelessness everywhere: in the minimal service as well as in the slapdash cooking that's saved from the depths of mediocrity only by good ingredients. The salad of prawns is boring, the rack of lamb almost spoiled by excessive garlic, the apple tart acceptable.

A la carte: 300F. Menu: 190F, 290F.

Château de Teildras
(See restaurant above)

Closed Nov. 3-April 1. 11 rms 420-940F. Half-board 672-722F. TV. Pets allowed. Golf.

The delightful comfortable rooms, decorated in blues or pinks, are located in a magnificent sixteenth-century aristocratic residence. Disappointing breakfast. Service a bit abrupt. Relais et Châteaux.

Chenas
69840 Juliénas - (Rhône)
Paris 415 - Lyon 62 - Mâcon 17 - Juliénas 5

Robin
Deschamps - 85.36.72.67

M. Robin. Lunch only (except dinner Fri. & Sat.). Closed Wed. & early Feb.-mid-March. Garden dining. Pets allowed. Telex 351004. Cards: V, AE, DC, MC.

In his lovely country house with a terrace overlooking the Moulin-a-Vent vineyards and the Saône valley, Daniel Robin is both a fine host and an excellent chef, whose cuisine is rooted in the territory: Chenas andouillette (tripe sausage) with fines herbes, pike mousse, crayfish, coq au vin, Bresse poultry, Charolais beef à la bourguignonne. Nice wine cellar with local Beaujolais.

A la carte: 300-350F. Menus: 160F to 300F.

Chênehutte-les-Tuffeaux
see Saumur

Chennevières-sur-Marne
see PARIS SUBURBS

Cherbourg
50100 Cherbourg - (Manche)
Paris 360 - Caen 119 - Bayeux 92 - Avranches 134

Sights. Office of Tourism (2, quai Alexandre III); the cultural center, with its library, media center and museum of Thomas Henry paintings; Emmanuel-Liais park (botanical gardens, greenhouses) and its natural history and ethnographic museum; Fort du Roule (beautiful panorama); Musée de la Libération.

Eating on the Run. Aux Antilles, 13, rue de la Paix; Brasserie La Régence, 42, quai de Caligny (daily until 11 p.m.); Café du Commerce, 42, rue François-la-Vieille; Le Café du Théâtre, 1, pl. Général-de-Gaulle (choucroute specialist); Chabbi, rue de la Paix (Oriental cuisine); Crêperie de la Place Centrale, 3, rue Boël-Meslin; Au Drakkar, 17, rue de la Paix (grill); Le Mandarin, 38, rue Victor-Grignard (Chinese specialties); Marest, 15, rue Albert-Mathieu (good self-service place); La Pizza, 48, quai de Caligny.

Nightlife. Le Casino, 4, rue des Tribunaux (all ages); Le Paradiso, rue de l'Union; Le Piano Bar, 15, pl. du Général-de-Gaulle; Le Queen, Port Chantreyne (chic disco); Le Yalta, 46, quai Caligny (nighttime hot spot on the port).

Shops. *Wine:* La Cave du Roy, 47, rue Tour-Carrée. *Gourmet foods:* Basnier, 7, rue Thomas Henry; Aux Agapes, cour Marie; Boschet, 8, pl. de la Fontaine. *Fruit and vegetables:* Bébert l'Ami de la Ménagère, 9, pl. du Général-de-Gaulle (nice cheese, too). *Pastries and chocolate:* Lhuillery, 14, rue Grande-Rue; Yvard, 5, pl. de la Fontaine.

13 Chez Pain
(Le Plouc)
59, rue au Blé - 33.53.67.64.

M. Pain. Open until 10 p.m. Closed Sat. lunch & Sun.; annual closing varies. Pets allowed. Cards: V, MC.

No more wooden shoes and folk costumes for the waitresses here—now it's plaid blazers and a tasteful new decor, with individual lighting and wine-colored tablecloths. The cuisine has maintained its traditional base but is becoming more diversified and is using more seasonal products: crab stuffed into rather thick ravioli that nonetheless have an outstanding flavor, good bass Florentine (a warm mousse) with spinach, and lovely pear délice with a warm pistachio coulis. The wine cellar is a bit young but interesting.

A la carte: 250-280F. Menus: 120F (wine incl.), 150F, 230F.

12/20 **Le Clipper**

Gare Maritime - 33.44.01.11

M. Larbi. Open daily until 10:30 p.m. Terrace dining. Pets allowed. Parking. Telex 170613. Cards: V, AE, DC, MC.

You'll find a relaxing, subdued decor in this modern hotel dining room, which is lit well from the bay windows that open onto the port and the sea. You'll also find professional service and a respectable cuisine that could stand some improvement in its imagination and lightness: nice Landaise salad, (over) grilled salmon with basil, tasty cakes.

A la carte: 230F. Menus: 130F (weekday lunch only, wine incl.), 98F.

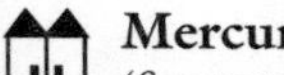

Mercure

(See restaurant above)

Open year-round. 81 rms 290-410F. TV. Pets allowed.

These rooms with ocean views are across from the port. Good for conferences.

Le Louvre

2, rue Henri-Dunant - 33.53.02.28

Closed Dec. 24-Jan. 1. 42 rms 130-270F. TV. Pets allowed. Garage parking. Telex 171132. Cards: V.

Next to the pleasure-boat port, Le Louvre has well-kept rooms with good plumbing. No restaurant.

Cherrueix

35120 Dol-de-Bretagne - (Ille-et-Vilaine)
Paris 343 - St-Malo 26 - Dol-de-Bretagne 9

(14) **Restaurant des Parcs**

99.48.82.26

M. Abraham. Open until 9:30 p.m. Closed Sun. dinner, Wed. & Jan. 5-Feb. 5. Terrace dining. Pets allowed. Cards: V, AE, DC.

The herbs in the vegetable garden provide the fragrance for the bay mussels served in their shells, the whiting goujonettes (with parsley and chervil), the savory shellfish consommé and the saddle of young rabbit. Restaurant des Parcs is a modest place near the church plaza, but it's bright and charming, one of the nicest restaurants in Brittany. Robert Abraham doesn't go in for the spectacular—he just tries to make everything simple, fresh and natural tasting, exactly what one craves while vacationing in Brittany. Fine desserts, including kiwi soup with warm fruit juices and sorbets made from seasonal fruit. The wine cellar is improving, and the decor was freshened up after the floods.

Menus: 95F (weekdays only), 125F, 180F, 240F.

The à la carte restaurant prices given are for a complete three-course meal for one, including a half-bottle of modest wine and service. Menu prices are for a complete fixed-price meal for one, excluding wine (unless otherwise noted).

Chevannes

see Auxerre

Chevreuse

78460 Chevreuse - (Yvelines)
Paris 32 - Rambouillet 19 - Versailles 16 - Etampes 45

IN NEARBY **Saint-Lambert-des-Bois**

(5 km NW on D 46)
78460 St-Rémy-les-Chevreuse - (Yvelines)

(15) **Les Hauts de Port-Royal**

2, rue de Vaumurier - 30.44.10.21

M. Poirier. Open until 9:30 p.m. Closed Tues. dinner, Wed. & Feb. school vacation. Terrace dining. Pets allowed. Parking. Cards: V.

The Poiriers opened their dream house a few years ago, doing everything in a meticulous and refined manner. The decor is rustic and romantic, with a charming English garden you can contemplate from the terrace on nice days, and an interior that is delicate without pretense: chintz and lace tablecloths, a beamed ceiling and an aquamarine carpet. François Poirier has become more inventive, more subtle and better all around in the kitchen since he left the Paris suburbs. Despite the steep prices, you can have some fine moments here, dining on langoustine salad with pink grapefruit, fish pot-au-feu with hazelnut oil, veal kidneys émincé with raspberries, veal noisettes with shallots and escargots and little almond horns with a pistachio cream. Charming service.

A la carte: 350F.

Chinon

37500 Chinon - (Indre-et-Loire)
Paris 282 - Tours 47 - Poitiers 95 - Angers 80

Chris'Hôtel

12, pl. Jeanne d'Arc - 47.93.36.92

Open year-round. 1 ste 600F. 39 rms 140-300F. TV in 10 rms. Pets allowed. Garage parking. Telex 751407. Cards: V, AE, DC, MC.

A large, well-dressed residence with pleasant, well-kept rooms. The service can be indifferent. No restaurant.

(16) **Au Plaisir Gourmand**

2, rue Parmentier - 47.93.20.48

M. Rigollet. Open until 9:15 p.m. Closed Sun. dinner, Mon. & Feb. 7-28. Air cond. Pets allowed. Cards: V.

Jean-Claude Rigollet, who hates playing a star in culinary show business despite his impressive credentials, has found a discreet niche for his talents. This is no reason to forget that he's one of the best chefs in the Touraine, in this charming old residence near a château's ruins. He keeps the prices modest and the haute cuisine simple, clear and "campagnarde." No fanfare, no pomp—this is the quiet provincial life, and the customers are the local (connoisseur) habitués. The decor in the 30-seat dining room facing the garden is opulent and cheerful. Daily specials are based on the offerings of the market, where Rigollet fills his basket twice weekly. A meal here might include turnip salad with poultry livers, a sweetbreads tourte and a pear gratin with almonds. Or perhaps lotte with mango and a saffron vinaigrette, salmon in Vouvray wine or veal mignon seasoned with red bell pepper. One's glasses are filled with excellent red or white Chinons and Bourgeuils (the best vintages), including a marvelous fruity young Chinon that comes from Rigollet's own acre of wine grapes.

A la carte: 280-300F. Menus: 150F, 195F, 260F.

IN NEARBY **Marçay**
(6 km S on D 749 & D 116)
37500 Chinon - (Indre-et-Loire)

---

(13) Château de Marçay

47.93.03.47

M. Mollard. Open until 9:30 p.m. Closed end Jan.-mid-March. Garden dining. No pets. Parking. Telex 751475. Cards: V.

The owner of this magnificent stone fortress went to a great deal of trouble to make it one of the best inns in the region, and he's just about achieved his goal. It's set in a lovely French garden estate, and the new dining room has been opulently decorated. The staff is a bit stiff but extremely efficient; the new chef, Gérard Côme, needs to put a little zip in his "classic" nouvelle cuisine. The presentation and execution are fine, but he must pay closer attention to seasonings, cooking times and sauces. He features a gâteau of young rabbit with onions, turbot blanc with seafood and truffles, young pigeon with vegetables, and a warm apple tart. Nice wines, including some exceptional local vintages.

A la carte: 400F and up. Menus: 135F (weekday lunch only), 480F (weekends and holidays only), 220F, 320F.

Château de Marçay

(See restaurant above)

Closed end Jan.-mid-March. 6 stes 1,025-1,290F. 32 rms 460-1,030F. TV. Pets allowed. Heated pool. Tennis.

The twelve new rooms in the castle wing, some with little gardens, provide a remarkable degree of comfort and charm. Top-notch service and a luxurious decor. Relais et Châteaux.

Cholet

49300 Cholet - (Maine-et-Loire)
Paris 350 - Angers 61 - Nantes 61 - Niort 106

---

(16) James Baron

15, pl. de la Gare - 41.62.00.97

M. Baron. Open until 10 p.m. Closed Sat. lunch & Dec. 24-30. Air cond. Pets allowed. Garage parking. Hotel: 21 rms 140-280F; half-board 240F. TV in 18 rms. Cards: V, AE, DC, MC.

It is rare that a cook is able to run more than one operation successfully—but it's evidently not impossible, as proven by James Baron. He is here only on weekends, spending the rest of his time as everyone knows behind the stoves of the celebrated Drouant restaurant in Paris (17/20). Naturally, he has left a solid, proven team behind in his absence; they are a small band of cooks remarkably dedicated to following the master's directives in everything concerning this fresh, inventive, open cuisine that is verging on three-toque status. Apart from a slight tendency toward too much cream, this is James Baron that you are eating, whether he is there or not: four "feuilletés gourmands" (lobster, foie gras, prawns, oysters), the pike perch and cucumber lasagne, the admirable roast turbot, the minced duck in a crust with preserved ginger, and the warm fruit salad in a sweet-sour sauce. As for Geneviève Baron, a budding wine expert, she is in charge of running the comfortable, modern dining room and does a superb, professional job, with grace and presence to spare.

A la carte: 300F and up. Menus: 95F, 150F, 220F.

(13) Le Belvédère

5 km SE on D 20, Lac de Ribou
41.62.14.02

MM. Thepaut & Inagaki. Open until 9 p.m. Closed Sun. dinner, Mon. lunch, Feb. school vacation & July 24-Aug. 23. Terrace dining. No pets. Parking. Cards: V, AE, DC.

The south terrace overlooks the man-made Ribou lake and the Mauges countryside. The customer's pleasure is the priority here, and the cuisine is beginning to get a nice modern flavor, from none other than its Japanese chef. Try the poultry breast gâteau with foie gras, bass in a madérisé Champagne and steamed langoustines aux choux. The sauces could lighten up, as could the prices. Good Loire (especially Anjou) wines.

A la carte: 280F. Menus: 98F and 180F (weekdays only), 150F and 200F (weekends and holidays only).

Le Belvédère

(See restaurant above)

Closed Sun., Mon., Feb. school vacation & July 24-Aug. 23. 8 rms 245-290F. TV. Pets allowed.

Pleasant and calm, with modern, well-equipped rooms. Fine reception.

Chorey-lès-Beaune

see Beaune

Ciboure

see Saint-Jean-de-Luz

La Ciotat

13600 La Ciotat - (Bouches-du-Rhône)
Paris 805 - Aix-en-Provence 49 - Marseille 32

12/20 Le Séréno

6 km E, Corniche du Liouquet
42.83.90.30

M. Biossi. Open until 9:30 p.m. Closed Sun. dinner (off-seas.) & Nov. 30-March 1. Air cond. Garden dining. No pets. Parking. Telex 441390. Cards: V, AE, DC, MC.

The bay windows overlook the pool and let in fresh ocean air, and the fixed-price menu aptly reflects the regional cuisine: authentic salade niçoise, light oyster-tomato soup. Desserts could

stand some improvement, but the service is charming.
Menus: 105F (lunch only), 165F, 225F.

Ciotel Le Cap

(See restaurant above)
Closed Nov. 30-March 1. 42 rms 465-695F. TV. No pets. Pool. Tennis.
With rooms set in little pavilions in the greenery, the Ciotel is amply equipped for sports and leisure.

Clermont-Ferrand

63000 Clermont-Ferrand - (Puy-de-Dôme)
Paris 389 - Limoges 191 - Lyon 183 - Moulins 96

Sights. Pl. de Jaude (lively center of town, with Bartholdi's statue of Vercingétorix); Notre-Dame-de-l'Assomption cathedral (thirteenth century, in Volvic lava); Notre-Dame-du-Port basilica (Roman style, eleventh to twelfth century); Musée Ranquet (local history, medieval sculpture); rue des Cordeliers, rue des Chaussetiers, rue du Séminaire, rue des Gras and rue Kléber (old, picturesque narrow streets).

Eating on the Run. L'Algarve, 14-16, rue St-Adjutor (seafood, Portuguese dishes, quick lunch); Le Buffadou, in train depot (rapid service, open late); La Cabane du Pêcheur, at the foot of the Altea (clean, unpretentious and prudent prices, open until 10 p.m.); Chez Michel (Aux Copains d'Abord), 96, ave. Marx-Dormoy (warm atmosphere, tripe stew and Auvergne potée—stew with bacon, sausage and vegetables); Pizzéria Chez Roger, 9, rue Nestor-Perret (simple, friendly, good value).

Brasseries. Brasserie de la Gare, 60, blvd. Gergovia; L'Européen, 50, ave. de Royat, Chamalières.

Bars & Cafés. Those at the big hotels (like the Altea, below); Sheldon (British club), 2 bis, pl. Allard (British club) and Les Diams (golf bar), both at Royat.

Nightlife. Le Grimoire, 12, rue Sous-les-Augustins (25- to 45-year-old set, rugby players and fans); Le Montmartre, 4, rue Montrognon (old-fashioned nightclub with orchestra); Le Phidias, in Orcines (the chic club in the region).

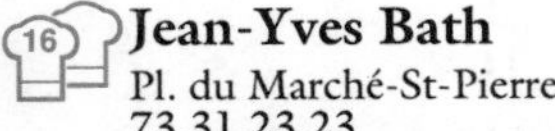

Jean-Yves Bath

Pl. du Marché-St-Pierre
73.31.23.23
M. Bath. Open until 10 p.m. Closed Sun., Mon. lunch, Feb. & Sept. 4-11. Air cond. No pets. Cards: V.
Jean-Yves Bath left the Auvergne countryside to come to the big city, setting up shop in a modern building over the new marketplace. His decor is also modern, with ebony panels, a large terrace overlooking the Puy-de-Dôme, nice lighting, a real fireplace, armchairs, round tables and flowers—the perfect environment in which to appreciate his fine cooking, which incorporates "a taste of the Auvergne," traditional cuisine and his own unique style. The pan-fried foie gras in eau-de-coing (quince), turbot kedgeree (a rice dish) with curry, and veal "epigram" (breaded cutlet and slice of breast) à l'orange are his own creations, evidence that Bath is among the best in the region. You can dine upstairs or in the ground-floor brasserie-bistro, Le Clos Saint-Pierre, where 150 francs will buy such fine simple dishes as a shellfish éclair, leg of lamb with gratin dauphinois and a chocolate-glazed soufflé. Good wines by the glass or the bottle.
A la carte: 300F. Menu: 160F (weekday lunch only, wine incl.).

12/20 Le Brezou

51, rue St-Dominique - 73.93.56.71
Mme. Duchet. Open until 9:30 p.m. Closed Sat., Sun. & Dec. 19-Jan. 2. Pets allowed. Garage parking. Cards: V.
This excellent family restaurant is perfectly maintained and lives up to its reputation, with easy prices and a consistently solid cuisine. Appetizing cooking featuring sweetbreads with mushrooms, fine fresh sole meunière and lovely desserts.
A la carte: 160-180F. Menus: 65F, 110F, 150F.

Mercure Arverne

16, pl. Delille - 73.91.92.06
Open year-round. 57 rms 305-375F. Half-board 230-245F. TV. Pets allowed. Garage parking. Telex 392741. Cards: V, AE, DC, MC.
Not far from the Notre-Dame-du-Port basilica, the Mercure was renovated in 1986. Spacious and comfortable rooms. Restaurant.

13 La Retirade

82, blvd. Gergovia - 73.93.05.75
M. Ganancia. Open until 10 p.m. Closed Sat. lunch, Sun. & Dec. 23-Jan. 2. Air cond. Pets allowed. Garage parking. Telex 392658. Cards: AE, MC.
Chef Gérard Trucheter needs to get back to basics: He's a skilled modern cuisinier with plenty of good ideas, but he has lacked imagination and execution (particularly in cooking precision and desserts). Still, he earns his (a solid) toque with the salad of coquilles St-Jacques with a tasty walnut-oil dressing, cod ragoût with croutons and the turbot filet with pleurotes. Magnificent Auvergne cheeses and exemplary service. The brown-tone dining rooms have little charm.
A la carte: 250-300F. Menus: 179F, 250F.

Altea

(See restaurant above)
Open year-round. 124 rms 300-550F.
In the center of town with a view of the Auvergne mountains, the Altea has quiet, air-conditioned guest rooms and nice meeting rooms.

IN NEARBY **Chamalières**
(3 km W)
63400 Chamalières - (Puy-de-Dôme)

---

17 Hôtel Radio

43, ave. Pierre-Curie
73.30.87.83
M. Mioche. Open until 9 p.m. Closed Sun. dinner, Mon. & Nov. 1-March 15. Pets allowed. Hotel: 1 ste 650-780F; 27 rms 250-520F; half-board 460-490F. Garage parking. Cards: V, AE, DC, MC.

The new 1930s-style decor works well, particularly in this art deco building; there is much light and comfort (despite the lace tablecloths that are more of an 1830s style), resulting in a luxurious ambience for the well-heeled clientele, which includes former president Valéry Giscard d'Estaing. Michel Mioche is a pro in the kitchen, blending his own inventions with traditional Auvergne cuisine (a new version of stuffed cabbage and cabbage soup, and a dish of salmon with lentils). We also like his salad of Breton lobster, spring panaché of three fish (salmon, lotte and turbot), lamb filet mignon with coriander grains, marvelous fresh-fruit feuilletés and Auverge "pompe aux pommes." The nice wine list includes Mioche's own Sauvignon from Issoire.

A la carte: 400-500F. Menu: 190F.

IN NEARBY **Durtol**
(5 km NW on D 941)
68330 Durtol - (Puy-de-Dôme)

Auberge des Touristes

D 941, rte. de la Baraque - 73.37.00.26

M. Andrieux. Open until 9:30 p.m. Closed Sat. lunch, Sun., May 1-7, July 15-Aug. 7 & Feb. school vacation. No pets. Parking. Cards: AE, MC.

An oddly placed roadside cottage with a refined, flowery decor, paintings and soft, comfortable armchairs. Owner Bernard Andrieux was unhappy (you read it right) to hear that we were upping his rating, thinking it undeserved. Despite his modesty, we persist in praising his delicious lightly pan-fried liver in a fine sauce of tart raspberries; excellent country ham made by his father-in-law; pan-fried langoustines with cabbage and a coriander gravy; fine game in season (wild boar, venison); and good chocolate desserts. In short, a real find that keeps improving. Magnificent wine cellar.

A la carte: 300-400F. Menus: 180F, 250F, 380F.

IN NEARBY **Orcines**
(8 km W on D 941A & D 941B)
63870 Orcines - (Puy-de-Dôme)

Le Dôme

73.91.49.00

Closed Oct. 1-May 1. 10 rms 118-230F. Half-board 195-270F. Parking.

This inn crowns one of the famous Auvergne hills, 1,500 meters high. A simple decor but absolute tranquility and great views, particularly in the rooms facing the volcanoes. Restaurant.

Pichon

Rte. de Limoges - 73.62.10.05

MM. Ray & Lille. Open until 9:30 p.m. Closed Sun. dinner, Mon., holidays & Jan. 1-Feb. 10. Pets allowed. Hotel: 2 stes 280F; 13 rms 178-240F; half-board 235-380F. Tennis. Garage parking. Cards: V, AE, DC.

"Good old-fashioned cuisine" is promised here. Good it is, but young Pascal Lille is hardly from the old school. In fact, his cuisine is quite the opposite, with lots of inventiveness and some affected names. It's light, with respect for fresh products: mussels gratinée with spinach shoots, perch nage in Corent wine, turbot "cardinal" with crab rolls, Auvergne farm chicken in a cassoulet with winter vegetables, joue de boeuf (beef jowl) in a pot-au-feu. The vaulted dining room is neorustic and not much fun. Good fixed-price menus, tasty wines.

A la carte: 200-250F. Menus: 85F (weekday lunch only), 130F, 210F, 270F.

IN NEARBY **Pérignat-lès-Sarliève**
(4 km SE on N 9 & D 978)
63170 Aubière - (Puy-de-Dôme)

Hostellerie Saint-Martin

73.79.12.41

M. Foulquié. Open until 9:30 p.m. Closed Sun. dinner, Mon. (except July-Aug.), Feb. & All Saint's Day school vacations & Dec. 24-30. Garden dining. Pets allowed. Parking. Telex 990536. Cards: V, MC.

One of the best dining spots in the region is found in this little castle at the foot of the Gergovie plateau. Once owned by the Michelin family, it was converted into a luxurious restaurant with six inviting little dining rooms, all subtle and refined. We've seen a big improvement in the food since the well-traveled Serge Lanoix took over the kitchens. His cuisine is a personal one, well-seasoned and executed with savoir-faire: noix de coquilles St-Jacques in a morel gravy, pan-fried foie gras with currant seeds, red-mullet filets in red wine, strawberry cake grilled with almonds and walnut cake. None of these are worth less than two toques. We are troubled, though, by a rather stingy spirit when it comes to the size of the servings. Good Burgundies in the cellar.

A la carte: 350F. Menus: 130F (weekday lunch only, wine incl.), 190F, 240F, 290F.

Hostellerie Saint-Martin

(See restaurant above)

Open year-round. 21 rms 200-450F. Half-board 350-550F. TV. Pets allowed. Heated pool. Tennis.

The lovely spacious rooms have been completely refurbished and are situated in a lush, green environment with lots of peace and quiet. Luxuriously equipped.

IN NEARBY **Royat**
(3.5 km W)
63130 Royat - (Puy-de-Dôme)

La Belle Meunière

25, ave. de la Vallée - 73.35.80.17

M. Bon. Open until 9:30 p.m. Closed Sun. dinner, Wed. 2 weeks in Feb & 3 weeks in Nov. Pets allowed. Hotel: 11 rms 180-250F; half-board 250-280F. Garage parking. Cards: V, AE, DC, MC.

Owner/chef Jean-Claude Bon maintains the elegant fin-de-siècle style from La Belle Meunière's glory days with the coffered ceilings, high mirrors, a lush garden and several dishes typical of French spa cuisine. Though lightened, the sauces are better (thanks to herbs from the garden), and the fixed-price menus are improving: nice calves'-liver salad with cèpes and sherry vinegar, roasted turbot with savory chopped chives, poached filet of beef à la ficelle. Desserts are too sweet, except for the excellent sorbets. Also, watch out for too much vinegar in the sauces.

A la carte: 280-300F. Menus: 145F (lunch only, wine incl.), 130F, 205F, 250F.

Métropole

2, blvd. Vaquez - 73.35.80.18

Closed Oct. 1-April 30. 5 stes 700-850F. 70 rms 170-520F. Full board 390-620F. Cards: V, MC.

Many of these lovely rooms overlook the park; common areas include fine salons and a showy dining room. Prewar thermal spa. Restaurant.

Clichy

see PARIS SUBURBS

Clisson

44190 Clisson - (Loire-Atlantique)
Paris 377 - Nantes 28 - Niort 124 - Poitiers 150

(14) La Bonne Auberge

1, rue Olivier-de-Clisson - 40.54.01.90

M. Poiron. Open until 9:30 p.m. Closed Sun. dinner, Mon., Feb. 13-28 & Aug. 13-Sept. 3. Pets allowed. Cards: V.

Chantal and Serge Poiron's tour de force was to transform this run-of-the-mill café into one of the loveliest inns in the region. While the exterior is still rather modest, the inside is a modern, harmonious blend of gray, white and pink with fresh flowers and pleasant lighting. The veranda on the garden adds a pastoral touch. Serge's cuisine is also making progress: It's inventive and fragrant and has a clarity of taste. Try the steamed lobster plate with baby vegetables and a light creamy tarragon sauce, Vendée duckling with truffle butter, bass roasted in its skin and the tasty caramel pear feuillantine. Excellent fixed-price menus.

A la carte: 300F and up. Menus: 75F (weekdays only), 122F, 185F, 280F.

Cloyes-sur-le-Loir

28220 Cloyes-sur-le-Loir - (Eure-et-Loir)
Paris 143 - Vendôme 27 - Chartres 56 - Châteaudun 12

Hostellerie Saint-Jacques

35, rue Nationale - 37.98.40.08

M. Le Bras. Open until 9 p.m. Closed Sun. dinner & Mon. (off-seas.) & Jan. 1-Feb. 15. Garden dining. Pets allowed. Garage parking. Cards: V.

Chef Simon Le Bras has departed this establishment, but fortunately he left the kitchen in the hands of his former number-two man of long standing, who knows the house repertoire thoroughly. It was still too soon to tell how the two-toque standbys of his former boss will fare, such as the poached farm egg with lobster, the rosettes of prawn with stewed vegetables or the roast young native pigeon. But we hope all will go well in this beautiful restaurant whose lovely garden descends to the Loire.

A la carte: 350F. Menus: 170F, 235F, 295F.

Hostellerie Saint-Jacques

(See restaurant above)

Closed Sun. & Mon. (off-seas.) & Jan. 1-Feb. 15. 1 ste 450F. 17 rms 280-390F. TV.

Several excellent rooms have been well equipped and renovated; others leave a bit to be desired. Good breakfast.

Cluny

71250 Cluny - (Saône-et-Loire)
Paris 396 - Autun 83 - Mâcon 24 - Tournus 38

(13) Bourgogne

Pl. de l'Abbaye - 85.59.00.58

M. Gosse. Open until 9 p.m. Closed Wed. lunch & Tues. (off-seas.) & Nov. 15-Feb. 10. No pets. Parking. Cards: V, AE, DC, MC.

This cuisine is lively, attractive, classic and served in a rustic cottage where one might not expect the modernity of the nage of fish with ginger, steamed turbot with morels or wild duckling with pink berries. Patrice Gosse, the well-trained son of the owners, creates a refined cuisine that could be more audacious. The pricey wines aren't all that special.

A la carte: 330F. Menus: 120F (lunch only), 190F, 260F, 350F.

Bourgogne

(See restaurant above)

Closed Tues. (off-seas.) & Nov. 15-Feb. 10. 2 stes & 14 rms 185-900F. Half-board 405-650F oblig. in seas. TV in 2 rms. Pets allowed.

Comfortable rooms face the abbey. Bourgogne is a nice way station with a pleasant interior garden.

Coaraze

06390 Contes - (Alpes-Maritimes)
Paris 970 - Nice 28 - Contes 10 - Lucéram 19

12/20 Auberge du Soleil

93.79.08.11, 93.79.34.82

M. Jacquet. Open until 9 p.m. Closed Nov. 16-March 15. Garden dining. Pets allowed. Cards: V, MC.

Fittingly named, this nice, sunny cottage has a terrace overlooking a breathtaking landscape. Yvonne's cuisine is equally bright: seasonal tourtes, aromatic rabbit stew and a good creamy potato gratin.

A la carte: 160-180F. Menu: 92F.

Auberge du Soleil

(See restaurant above)

Closed Nov. 16-March 15. 2 stes. 8 rms 195-360F. Half-board 220-290F. Pets allowed. Pool.

In the heart of the village but away from the noisy cars is a handful of refined, modernized rooms with fairy-tale views of the valley. One of the most peaceful and charming inns in the region.

Cognac

16100 Cognac - (Charente)
Paris 465 - Angoulême 42 - Niort 80 - Saintes 26

L'Echassier

72, rue de Bellevue (2 km S)
45.32.29.04

MM. Lambert & Goern. Open until 9:30 p.m. Closed Sun. Terrace dining. Pets allowed. Parking. Cards: V, AE, DC, MC.

Chef Bernard Lambert, a bit lost after leaving Angoulême, has returned with full glory to this fin-de-siècle-style restaurant at the edge of his hometown. The building looks like an old village schoolhouse; the inside has been transformed into a luxurious, modern, warm dining room. His savory cuisine (served under bell covers) has a strong authority and originality, freed from the influence of his teacher (Troisgros): lobster ragoût with grapes (generous and well balanced), rolled young rabbit au pistou with artichokes, and Charentais pot-au-feu with sorrel flanked by langoustines and warm oysters. Marvelous chèvre from the local farms and, less convincing, chocolate roulé with Cognac and ground orange rind. The thin tarts, however, are superb. Nice Bordeaux wines at good prices.

A la carte: 280-300F. Menus: 95F, 140F.

(14) Les Pigeons Blancs

110, rue Jules-Brisson - 45.82.16.36

MM. Tachet. Open daily until 9:30 p.m. Garden dining. Pets allowed. Hotel: 6 rms 190-280F; half-board 220-280F. Parking. Cards: V, AE, DC.

Jacques-Henri Tachet has excellent credentials, and he lets you know about them on the printed menus. We have a couple of criticisms, though: His cuisine is too static and sleepy and doesn't use enough of the quality ideas of the region. But it is good, light, fresh, distinct and consistent. You'll enjoy the capons with foie gras and a grape sabayon, the salmon pot-au-feu, the langoustine bouillon or the pan-fried lamb in truffle sauce. The wine cellar has some attractive, rather reasonably priced vintages. Pleasant family atmosphere. Nice terrace.

A la carte: 260F. Menus: 95F, 130F, 250F.

IN NEARBY **Saint-Laurent-de-Cognac**
(6 km W on N141)
16100 Cognac - (Charente)

Logis de Beaulieu

N 141 - 45.82.30.50

Open year-round. 1 ste 400F. 20 rms 100F. Half-board 250-370F. TV in 5 rms. Garage parking. Telex 791020. Cards: V, AE, DC, MC.

An imposing lodge amid the vineyards is surrounded by a pleasant garden. Activities include visits to the wine cellar and walks along the Charente river. Heavy but comfortable decor. Restaurant.

Cogolin (Plage)

83310 Cogolin - (Var)
Paris 880 - Ste-Maxime 8 - St-Tropez 7 - Cogolin 8

(13) Port-Diffa

Les Trois-Ponts sur la Giscle,
La Foux (N 98) - 94.56.29.07

M. Sibony. Open until 10 p.m. Closed Jan. 2-March 9. Air cond. Terrace dining. No pets. Parking. Cards: AE, DC.

A change of pace, Moroccan style, on the edge of the highway—poufs, carpets, waiters in fez, the whole treatment. To boot, there's an Oriental terrace overlooking the river, with a dock in case you come by runabout. Try the couscous with seven vegetables, pigeon b'stilla (a sweet-savory pie), briouats with zaalouks (vegetables) and honey-drenched Moroccan pastries, all prepared by the Marrakech-trained chef (who once worked for a sultan, no less).

A la carte: 250-300F. Menu: 135F.

Coignières

78320 Maurepas - (Yvelines)
Paris 40 - Versailles 18 - Montfort-l'Amaury 9

(13) Auberge d'Angèle

296, N 10 - 34.61.64.39, 34.61.64.62

M. Charrault. Open until 10 p.m. Closed Sun. dinner. Garden dining. Pets allowed. Parking. Cards: V.

This delicious cottage just outside Paris is perfectly suited for that romantic little dinner à deux, especially in summer, under the weeping willow in the courtyard. The dining room is decorated in blue tiles, with large round tables, lots of flowers and a warm fireplace (when needed). The new owners intend to preserve all of this—along with the steep prices. The food, on the other hand, is decidedly nonrustic, featuring classical dishes correctly if impersonally prepared with good ingredients: thick filet of lotte nicely cooked in a well-flavored sauce Noilly, tender filet of beef in two peppers and fine little pastries.

A la carte: 350-400F. Menus: 150F, 246F, 305F.

(14) Auberge du Capucin Gourmand

170, N 10 - 34.61.46.06

M. Lebrault. Open until 9:30 p.m. Closed Sun. (except holidays). Garden dining. Pets allowed. Parking. Cards: V, AE, DC.

The ravages of urbanization have left this former postal relay inn in a sorry state: in the middle of a shopping complex. Nonetheless, the thick walls do keep out some of the noise from the national highway out front, and it is pleasantly rustic inside, with a rear flower garden that's put to good use when the weather's mild. The fine cuisine is rigidly ultra-classic. The only movement is in the execution, which is even more rigorous and precise: pan-fried lotte salad with salmon and raw spinach, marvelous lightly cooked noisettes of lamb with pommes de terre Anna (potato casserole), plus eight green beans, (as a concession to nouvelle cuisine). To finish, there are exceptional cheeses and perfect desserts, notably the chocolate charlotte and the raspberry tart. Excellent wine selection.

A la carte: 400-500F. Menus: 200F (menu dégustation, dinner only).

La Colle-sur-Loup

see Saint-Paul-de-Vence

Collioure

66190 Collioure - (Pyrénées-Orientales)
Paris 955 - Perpignan 27 - Port-Vendres 4

Casa Païral

Impasse des Palmiers - 68.82.05.81

Closed Oct. 31-March 31. 2 stes 470-580F. 25 rms 260-440F. TV. Pets allowed. Pool. Parking. Telex 505220. Cards: V.

A lovely old Catalan residence with immense rooms, nice furnishings and a garden of paradise. No restaurant.

(13) La Frégate

24, quai de l'Amirauté - 68.82.06.05

M. Costa. Open until 10 p.m. Closed Thurs. dinner & Fri. (off-seas.). Terrace dining. Pets allowed. Telex 505072. Cards: V.

La Frégate's setting facing the château is remarkable, but some readers have complained about a few little things—the service, the prices and the cuisine. For our part, we found a delightful gourmet anchovy platter (fresh, marinated in oil), "tartare de la mer" (deliciously seasoned lotte), aromatic bouillabaisse and baked skatefish covered with tomatoes—nothing extraordinary, but a good job without cheating. Nice regional wines and pleasant service even in season.

A la carte: 250-280F. Menus: 98F (weekdays only), 155F, 195F.

Collonges-au-Mont-d'Or

see Lyon

Colmar

68000 Colmar - (Haut-Rhin)
Paris 445 - Strasbourg 69 - Nancy 141 - Basel 68

Le Champ de Mars

2, ave. de la Marne - 89.41.54.54

Open year-round. 1 ste 625-700F. 74 rms 305-380F. TV. Pets allowed. Garage parking. Telex 880928. Cards: V, AE, DC, MC.

Modern and well situated in a verdant municipal park, Le Champ de Mars has spacious, bright rooms. Meeting rooms. No restaurant.

(15) Au Fer Rouge

52, Grand-Rue - 89.41.37.24

M. Fulgraff. Open until 9:30 p.m. Closed Sun. dinner, Mon., 3 weeks in Jan. & 1 week in Aug. Pets allowed. Cards: V, AE, DC, MC.

Although from Alsace, Patrick Fulgraff has never been rooted in Alsatian cuisine; in fact, sometimes he even draws his inspiration from afar. We consider that a compliment, since he has been able to escape the heaviness and the bonds of the folk tradition of old Colmar. His cuisine is modern, inventive and personal. And it continues to improve in its execution: delicious artichoke hearts in a red dressing (beets) with noodles and sweetbreads, cold oysters with leeks and creamed shallots, marvelous turbot with a lobster coulis and fresh morels (though a stingy quantity of them), perfect suckling lamb with garden vegetables, breast of duck in its own gravy, remarkable orange millefeuille and an interesting warm peach tart with almond cream. Superb wines and a picturesque decor (beams, indirect lighting) are also found in this majestic 300-year-old house facing the old customs station.

A la carte: 400-450F. Menus: 195F, 295F, 395F.

(14) Les Hortensias

6, rue Henner - 89.41.44.89

M. Baroncini. Open until 9 p.m. Closed Sat., Sun. & Aug. 14-Sept. 8. Pets allowed. Cards: V, AE, DC, MC.

Régis Baroncini, trained in the Geneva hotel school, has thrived in this upscale neighborhood for a few years now. His mezzanine restaurant is cheerful, simple and elegant, and he has an alert staff. His short but original repertoire excludes meat, with the exception of foie gras (with a fig compote) and goose confit (in a warm salad with citrus). Good precision and personality in the kitchen clearly represent an effort to justify the steep prices (even though the German mark rules here): fine escalopes of bass in Bordeaux with an exquisite celery garnish, interesting langoustines pan-fried with choucroute and bacon in beer, nice glazed soufflé au kirsch with nougat. Original wines, including white Loire vintages.

A la carte: 300-400F. Menus: 130F, 180F, 210F, 230F.

Le Maréchal

5, pl. des Six-Montagnes-Noires
89.41.60.32

Open year-round. 2 stes 600-700F. 36 rms 200-500F. Half-board 270-350F. TV. Air cond. Pets allowed. Parking. Telex 880949. Cards: V, AE.

A large, beautiful old Colmar residence with a fine terrace over the Lauch. It's an opulent place, with some attractive beamed ceilings. Restaurant.

Le Rendez-Vous de Chasse

7, pl. de la Gare - 89.41.10.10

M. Riehm. Open daily until 10 p.m. Pets allowed. Telex 880248. Cards: V, AE, DC, MC.

A changing of the guard has been announced here, and the new chef will be the well-known Serge Burkel. Whether this richly done-up old establishment, with its position as an institution here in the heart of Alsatian wine country, will prove to be a congenial spot for the talents of the mercurial Burkel remains to be seen—as does whether he will stick around here longer than is his habit.

A la carte: 400-450F. Menus: 185F, 280F, 360F.

Terminus Bristol

(See restaurant above)

Open year-round. 10 stes 600-750F. 60 rms 300-450F. Half-board 410-520F. TV. Pets allowed.

Refurbished, modernized rooms in a beautiful traditional hotel are quiet despite the central location. Modern equipment and classic decor.

Saint-Martin

38, Grand-Rue - 89.24.11.51

Closed Jan. 24 rms 200-450F. TV. Pets allowed. Telex 375974. Cards: V, AE, DC, MC.

This little hotel, newly opened in a magnificent Louis XVI building, has lovely furnishings and a convenient location in the heart of town. No restaurant.

(16) Schillinger

16, rue Stanislas - 89.41.43.17

M. Schillinger. Open until 9:30 p.m. Closed Sun. dinner, Mon. & July 3-Aug. 1. Pets allowed. Cards: V, AE, DC.

Jean Schillinger says he is more concerned about his kitchen than his dining room. Yet his luxurious Louis XVI decor shows he can't be outdone in comfort, silver or service. We've always told him we'd rather see a wrong fold in the tablecloth or the waiter dropping a spoon (unthinkable here) in exchange for a bit more spontaneity and creativity. He does appear to have emerged from the doldrums, both physically and creatively, with some more audacious dishes, variations on old regional themes. He's still a master of execution and a terrific saucier: perfect red-mullet salad, nage of fresh sole and Breton lobster, braised sweetbreads with matignon (vegetable fondue) and a celeriac choucroute, Bresse pigeon en croûte de sel with a poivrade sauce, red-fruit millefeuille with dark chocolate and chibouste (vanilla cream). Ask to see the rich wine cellar, stocked with Alsace's best vintages of the last decade or so.

A la carte: 500F. Menus: 220F, 310F, 420F.

IN NEARBY **Niedermorschwihr**
(6.5 km W on N 415 & D 11)
68230 Turckheim - (Haut-Rhin)

12/20 Caveau Morakopf

7, rue des Trois-Epis - 89.27.05.10

M. Guidat. Dinner only. Open until 11 p.m. Closed 3 weeks in July, 1 week in March & 1 week in Nov. Pets allowed. Cards: V.

The lady of the house tends the kitchen, the man the vineyard. This is an authentic old country inn with true regional colors: good house wines in pitchers, presskopf (pork head cheese) vinaigrette, bibelskäs (fresh seasoned cheese), baeckeoffe (beef and pork stew), Kugelhopf (cake) and more. The locals get lively at night.

A la carte: 130-150F.

The prices given in this guide reflect what restaurants and hotels were charging at press time.

IN NEARBY **Wettolsheim**
(5 km SE on D 417)
68000 Colmar - (Haut-Rhin)

(13) Auberge du Père Floranc

89.80.79.14

M. Floranc. Open until 9 p.m. Closed Sun. dinner (off-seas.), Mon., July 2-17 & Nov. 14-Dec. 16. Pets allowed. Parking. Cards: V, AE, DC, MC.

This charming bourgeois village residence is typical of Alsatian wine growers: obliging service with the whole family around and a cuisine that is half traditional and half Alsatian. The terrine de foie gras, mascassin (young wild boar), ham, venison civet with spaetzle and very good Kugelhopf (cake) glazed with kirsch and served with remarkably light tuiles merit the toque. Interesting wines.

A la carte: 250-300F. Menus: 90F (weekdays only), 190F, 320F.

Auberge du Père Floranc

(See restaurant above)

Closed Sun. (off-seas.), Mon., July 2-17 & Nov. 14-Dec. 16. 1 ste 430F. 32 rms 190-430F. Half-board 290-430F. TV. No pets.

Comfortable rooms are tucked away in a peaceful inn with gardens. (Floranc is president of the Relais du Silence.)

See also: **Ammerschwihr, Illhaeusern (Auberge de l'Ill)**

Colroy-la-Roche

67420 Saales - (Bas-Rhin)
Paris 402 - Sélestat 30 - St-Dié 30 - Obernai 41

(14) La Cheneaudière

88.97.61.64

M. François. Open until 9 p.m. Closed Jan. 3-March 1. Air cond. Terrace dining. Parking. Telex 870438. Cards: V, AE, DC, MC.

Luxury and refinement are anything but sparse in this opulent, flowery inn, which is well cared for by the François family and features a spic-and-span decor, a delicious country setting, a sumptuous dining room opening onto the green Vosges landscape, elegantly dressed tables and romantic lighting. That's not to take anything away from the cuisine of Jean-Paul Bossée, except that this year we have to take back a toque, because as talented as he is, he does not seem to have the enthusiasm to produce his best on a consistent basis. This time the delicious salmon tartare—prepared tableside in a flourish of silver—was not so delicious, and the blini would have been better hot, and the perfectly grilled scallops on a bed of sorrel were strangely served in the company of two little, perfectly tasteless yellow and pink sauces. One of these reappeared later, lapping several hard little pieces of lukewarm lobster. Thank heavens for the lovely little red snapper filets served in an olive oil broth, and for the excellent dessert (almond-filled chocolate mousse in a sabayon of orange confit). The wine cellar is impresssive and stuffed with excellent Alsatian vintages but also some to be wary of. The service is omnipresent, if you like that sort of thing.

A la carte: 450F. Menus: 220F (weekday lunch only), 390F.

La Cheneaudière

(See restaurant above)

Closed Jan. 3-March 1. 4 stes 1,000-1,300F. 23 rms 470-700F. Half-board 515-930F. TV. Pets allowed. Tennis.

A large, quiet residence with lots of spacious and luxurious rooms; some have terraces overlooking the mountains and the woods. Private hunting grounds and trout fishing. Relais et Châteaux.

Combloux

74920 Combloux - (Haute-Savoie)
Paris 610 - Annecy 65 - Chamonix 33 - Megève 5

Au Coeur des Prés

50.93.36.55

Closed April 10-June 3 & Sept. 24-Dec. 20. 34 rms 350F. Half- board 250-310F (for two). TV in 10 rms. Pets allowed. Tennis. Garage parking. Cards: V.

Green in summer, white in winter and lovely all seasons, this hotel has delicately decorated rooms with terraces, 3,000-plus feet above sea level. Restaurant.

Rond-Point des Pistes

Le Rond-Point des Pistes,
Le Haut-Combloux - 50.58.68.55

Closed April 15-June 25 & Sept. 15-Dec. 20. 30 rms 200-400F. Half-board 255-380F oblig. in Feb. TV in 22 rms. Pets allowed. Parking. Telex 385550. Cards: V.

These rooms are intelligently equipped—some with balconies overlooking Mont Blanc—and located close to the ski lifts. Restaurant.

Compiégne

60200 Compiégne - (Oise)
Paris 82 - Amiens 77 - St-Quentin 64 - Beauvais 57

IN NEARBY **Elincourt-Ste-Marguerite**
(14 km N on D 142)
60157 Elincourt-Ste-Marguerite - (Oise)

Château de Bellinglise

44.76.04.76

Open year-round. 5 stes 820-870F. 42 rms 385-680F. Half-board 565F. TV. Tennis. Parking. Telex 155048. Cards: V, AE, DC, MC.

This immense Louis XIII–era castle in a 600-acre estate has been remarkably preserved and restored; guests can stay in one of the attractive rooms in the hunting lodge. Pond, tennis, conference facilities. Fine wood-paneled restaurant with a disciple of Robuchon and Fréon in the kitchen.

Concarneau

29110 Concarneau - (Finistère)
Paris 537 - Lorient 52 - Quimper 23 - St-Brieuc 130

La Belle Etoile

Le Cabellou-Plage - 98.97.05.73

Mmes. Raout-Guillou. Open until 9:30 p.m. Closed Tues. (off-seas.) & Oct. 30-March 15. Garden dining. No pets. Parking. Cards: V, AE, DC.

The talented and well-traveled Gérard Raimbault has taken over the kitchen at this charming spot on Concarneau bay. He has only a few steps to walk to the fishing boats that bring in fresh daily catches of turbot, John Dory and langoustes. Everything is Breton here, even the mineral water from Plancoët. Raimbault also makes the Viennese-style breakfast breads and his own sausages, but he prefers to work on fine seafood creations: good fritters (not greasy) of John Dory livers, cockles and clams with a ketchup-soy sauce, lightly cooked oysters in a lettuce butter with sea urchin tongues, poached lobster with young Léon artichokes, coral butter and fine herbs, and a marvelous John Dory filet cooked on one side only in a meunière sauce with vegetables and bacon bits. To top it off, try the airy chocolate millefeuille with Plougastel strawberries. The Baron de "L" Pouilly (whose only fault is its price) is the final touch for an exceptional meal. The two ladies who own the place supervise excellent service with attention to detail.

A la carte: 300F. Menus: 180F and 270F (dinner only), 145F.

La Belle Etoile

(See restaurant above)

Closed Feb. 30 rms 480-840F. Half-board 590-700F oblig. in seas. TV in 10 rms. Pets allowed.

This most pleasant large white residence faces the Cabellou beach. Spacious, well-kept rooms are in the two buildings in the middle of the gardens. Buffet served on the beach in summer.

Le Galion

15, rue St-Guénolé, Ville Close
98.97.30.16

M. Gaonac'h. Open until 9:30 p.m. Closed Sun. dinner (except mid-June-end Aug.), Mon. (except mid-July-end Aug.) & Jan. 15-26. Pets allowed. Telex 940336. Hotel: 5 rms 280-950F. TV. Pets allowed. Cards: V, AE, DC, MC.

There's an air of mystery and adventure in this quarter of Ville Close when the southwestern winds howl—which is when many take shelter behind the thick granite walls of Le Galion. Its inviting atmosphere comes from the heavy beams, huge stones and large round tables set with fine silver, china and flowers, not to mention the roaring fire in the hearth. Sample the delicious fricassée of girolles and trompettes-de-la-mort (mushrooms) with langoustines, perfectly cooked John Dory in a tart rhubarb sauce, pot-au-feu of young squab (a bit overcooked) with aromatic cabbages, and a remarkable fruit gratin. Nice Loire wines.

A la carte: 300F. Menu: 150F (lunch only, wine incl.), 135F, 210F, 280F.

(14) Restaurant de la Douane

71, ave. Alain-Le-Lay - 98.97.30.27

M. Péron. Open until 9:30 p.m. Closed Sun. (off-seas.) & Nov. 15-Dec. 15. Air cond. Pets allowed. Cards: V.

Jean-Marc Péron uses a short à la carte menu that changes with the seasons and his personality: Breton Belon oysters, home-smoked lotte filet, langoustine tails sautéed "à la diable"; a panaché of fish and shellfish with raspberries; young pigeon au chou and au foie gras; and exquisite desserts. These dishes make this place a laboratory of Concarneau cooking ideas. Good fixed-price menus and lots of originality are to be found at this narrow restaurant behind the port. Amusing bar where fishermen linger with the owners.

A la carte: 230-250F. Menus: 70F (dinner only), 100F.

Ty Chupen Gwenn

Plage des Sables-Blancs - 98.97.01.43

Closed Sun. (off-seas.), April 17-23 & Dec. 4-Jan. 4. 15 rms 215-340F. Cards: V, DC.

A superb view of Concarneau bay is afforded by this modern hotel built in an arc that curves along the beach. No restaurant.

Condeau

see Nougent-le-Rotrou

Condom

32100 Condom - (Gers)
Paris 680 - Auch 43 - Agen 38 - Toulouse 110

La Table des Cordeliers

62.68.28.36, 62.28.03.68

M. Dudouet & Mme. Sandrini. Open until 9:30 p.m. Closed Sun. dinner, Mon. (except July-Aug.) & Oct. 10-Feb. 10. Air cond. Terrace dining. Pets allowed. Garage parking. Cards: V, MC.

The setting is still superb in this fourteenth-century chapel with a cozy regional decor. But there's been a succession of chefs, and none has lived up to Jean-Louis Palladin, who's now working his wonders in Washington, D.C. The new man in the kitchen is a woman: Huguette Méliet, from the region. We like the service and the extremely reasonable prices, but the cuisine should be sharpened to keep the rating from slipping further: fresh foie gras salad, dull omelet with cèpes, aiguillettes of duck in Madiran (reheated and dry), but excellent iced nougat with raspberries.

A la carte: 260-280F. Menus: 70F (weekdays only), 100F, 160F, 230F.

La Table des Cordeliers

(See restaurant above)

Open year-round. 21 rms 180-300F. Half-board 192-302F. TV. Pets allowed.

Next to the chapel-restaurant (see above) is a new hotel in a quiet garden with well-equipped, functional rooms.

Condrieu

69420 Condrieu - (Rhône)
Paris 514 - Lyon 41 - Annonay 34 - Vienne 11

Beau Rivage

2, rue Beau Rivage - 74.59.52.24

M. Humann. Open until 9:15 p.m. Closed Jan. 5-Feb. 15. Garden dining. Pets allowed. Garage parking. Telex 308946. Cards: V, AE, DC, MC.

Paulette Castaing, the 76-year-old grande dame of cuisine, used to greet customers personally in a dining room flooded with light and flowers. Though her cooking as of our last visit still seemed as fresh as all outdoors, she has found the successor she was looking for to carry on. But for the moment she is staying on to advise and help direct what was certainly some of the best service in France and to help produce the delicious, high-toned cooking she is justly famous for. Try the asparagus in puff pastry, the hot foie gras, the scallops and glazed vegetables, the duckling in its own wine sauce and, above all, the familiar and delicious desserts. Of course, the excellent if expensive wine list remains, as will, no doubt, the formidable prices. We'll have to wait until our next edition to determine a rating.

A la carte: 350-500F. Menus: 250F, 370F.

Beau Rivage

(See restaurant above)

Closed Jan. 5-Feb. 15. 4 stes 770F. 22 rms 285-770F. TV in 22 rms. Air cond. in 2 rms. Pets allowed.

On the banks on the Rhône is this big, beautiful vine-covered residence with obliging service. Peace and quiet are assured in the large rooms, which are decorated in an old-fashioned style. Relais et Châteaux.

Conteville

27210 Beuzeville - (Eure)
Paris 184 - Deauville 28 - Le Havre 42

(15) Auberge du Vieux Logis

32.57.60.16

M. Louet. Open until 9:30 p.m. Closed Wed. dinner, Thurs., Feb. & Sept. 20-30. Pets allowed. Cards: V, AE, DC, MC.

This conservatory of grand Norman style, with its turned-wood chandeliers, pink tablecloths and pewter collection, has been made into the best restaurant in the region without betraying its Normandy heritage, thanks largely to the consensus among grand chef Yves Louet and his two young sons, who were trained in the best places in Paris. The generations are working together to create an intelligent, subtle and superbly executed cuisine. The exactitude is astounding—from the cooking precision to the sauces to the well-chosen produce. Try the fennel chicken aspic with duck foie gras; parsley-seasoned pigeon wings vinaigrette and thighs en croûte with baby vegetables and an exquisite aromatic sauce; saddle of young rabbit, rolled and cooked in cider; excellent Norman cheeses; and delicious, classic desserts. Mme. Louet is charming, but she really should change the china.

A la carte: 300F.

Contrexéville

88140 Contrexéville - (Vosges)
Paris 324 - Langres 66 - Epinal 48 - Nancy 76

Cosmos

Rue de Metz - 29.08.15.90

Closed Oct. 13-May 1. 6 stes 530-635F. 81 rms 287-340F. Half-board 477-488F oblig. in seas. TV. DG Parking. Cards: V, AE, DC.

This elegant hotel near the thermal springs offers easy sleeping in a quiet, pleasant park. Antique furnishings. Restaurant.

Etablissement et Souveraine

Cour d'honneur et parc thermal
29.08.17.30

Closed Sept. 22-April 1. 60 rms 130-327F. Half-board 326-485F oblig. in seas. Pets allowed. Parking. Cards: V, AE, DC.

Nicely situated inside the thermal park are two elegant old "palaces" that have been intelligently renovated. The decor and the atmosphere are very "spa," with plenty of attention to comfort. Lots of charm, too. Restaurant.

Cordes

81170 Cordes - (Tarn)
Paris 681 - Toulouse 78 - Montauban 71 - Albi 25

Grand Ecuyer

16

Rue Voltaire - 63.56.01.03.

M. Thuriès. Open until 9:30 p.m. Closed Mon. (except July-Aug.) & Oct. 25-March 25. Pets allowed. Cards: V, AE.

Dessert lovers flock to Cordes, a remarkable old village, and to this medieval inn—once a residence of the counts of Toulouse—where they find Yves Thuriès, one of the best pastry chefs of our time. Although the mustachioed chef wears an earring and apprentice's pants, he is a master of his trade who has an encyclopedic knowledge. Even better, he is also a complete chef, not just a pâtissier. His dishes include a perfectly balanced, technically perfect leek terrine with smoked salmon, sole torsade and salmon with turnip coulis, crusty turbot with mushrooms, and a large plate of Gascon duck. Remarkable wines are served by one of Belgium's best sommeliers. Fine desserts are the apex here, served hot, cold and frozen.

A la carte: 300-400F. Menus: 160F, 220F, 280F, 340F.

Grand Ecuyer

(See restaurant above)

Closed Oct. 25-March 25. 1 ste 1,200F. 12 rms 400-600F. Half-board 450-600F. TV. Pets allowed.

One of the noblest residences in the old village, with period furnishings and large fireplaces. Lots of charm, despite a few inconveniences.

Hostellerie du Vieux Cordes

63.56.00.12

Closed Mon. (off-seas.) & Jan. 15-Feb. 15. 21 rms 230-360F. Half-board 210F. Pets allowed. Garage parking. Telex 560323. Cards: V, AE, DC.

Yves Thuriès has entirely renovated this charming residence, putting twentieth-century comforts in a thirteenth-century environment. Restaurant.

Cordon

74700 Sallanches - (Haute-Savoie)
Paris 605 - Chamonix 30 - Sallanches 4

Le Chamois d'Or

50.58.05.16

Closed Sept. 15-Dec. 20 & April 15-end May. 32 rms 250-380F. Half-board 270-340F oblig. in seas. TV. Pets allowed. Heated pool. Tennis. Parking. Cards: V, AE, DC.

One of the most charming hotels in the Savoie region is located in a beautiful chalet with a superb view of Mont Blanc. The pleasant rooms are decorated with wood. Small summer pool and sauna. Restaurant.

Corrèze

19800 Corrèze - (Corrèze)
Paris 480 - Tulle 19 - Egletons 23 - Seilhac 17

La Sénorie

13

55.21.22.88

M. Renard. Open until 9 p.m. Closed Sun. dinner, Mon. & Jan. 2-Feb. 17. Terrace dining. Pets allowed. Cards: V, AE.

An impressive white granite building, a former girls' boarding school, has been lavishly refurbished as a restaurant/hotel in the heart of the countryside. A new chef, Francis Tessandier, replaced the first brief occupant of the kitchen, and now it's rumored that he too may leave. But for the time being, he is a good technician and an excellent saucier, though he sometimes lets his imagination go too far: The lobster with melon coulis combination and the mix of green peppers and cherries with duck are two cases in point. Instead, try the lovely crayfish salad with green beans, the John Dory blanquette or the langoustines with morels. Desserts, however, are too sweet. The decor includes old-fashioned square tiles, and the young owners are chic and cheerful. Prices are a bit steep.

A la carte: 300F. Menus: 120F (weekday lunch only, wine incl.), 140F, 195F, 260F.

La Sénorie

(See restaurant above)

Closed Jan. 2-Feb. 17. 26 rms 210-480F. Half-board 165F. TV. Pets allowed. Heated pool. Tennis.

A beautiful residence with spacious rooms, some with kitchenettes. Luxurious decor, excellent service.

CORSICA (CORSE)

Ajaccio

20000 Ajaccio - (Corse)
Bastia 153 - Bonifacio 140 - Calvi 163 - Porto 83

L'Amore Piattu

8, pl. du Général-de-Gaulle - 95.51.00.53
Mme. Maestracci. Open until 10 p.m. Closed Sun. & Oct. Air cond. Pets allowed. Cards: V.

This restaurant, in an opulent setting, will accept only about a dozen diners by reservation at its four inviting round tables. It's intimate, charming and friendly, and the cuisine changes with the season, based on the owner's mood and Corsican tradition: smoked trout with grilled peppers, cabri (kid) with quenelles of bruccio (mushrooms), farm-raised duck with turnips. Good Corsican wines.

Menu: 180F.

Dolce Vita

Rte. des Sanguinaires (8 km W)
95.52.00.93
Closed end Oct.-March 15. 32 rms 360-700F. Half-board 447-600F oblig in seas. TV. Air cond. Pool. Parking. Telex 460854. Cards: V, AE, DC, MC.

All the rooms, well renovated and air conditioned, have ocean views, as does the terrace. Beach, garden, nightclub and restaurant.

Eden-Roc

Rte. des Sanguinaires - 95.52.01.47
Open year-round. 5 stes 920-1,520F. 35 rms 530-920F. TV. Air cond. Pets allowed. Heated pool. Garage parking. Telex 460486. Cards: V, AE, DC.

This pleasant hotel overlooks the sea from a lush poolside garden. The rooms are spacious and modern, with terraces, and thalassotherapy and a heliport have been added. Virtually all water sports are offered, along with many amenities. Restaurant. Relais et Châteaux.

A Tinella

86, rue Fesch - 95.21.13.68
Mme. Multedo. Open until 10:30 p.m. Closed Mon. & Oct. 15- Nov. 9. Air cond. Cards: V, AE, MC.

The ground floor is bistro style, the cellar rather Andalusian—the decor in both could use a little freshening. But, happily, the cuisine is abundantly fresh. Dominique Molé is awarded a well-earned toque for his vegetable and poulty terrine en gelée, his marinated gulf-fish mélange (excellent lotte and scorpionfish, but which gulf do the salmon and coquilles St-Jacques hail from?—certainly not the Mediterranean), stuffed veal fricandeau and an excellent peach terrine (rather spoiled by the crème Chantilly). Good, relaxed service.

A la carte: 250-280F. Menu: 100F (weekdays only).

IN NEARBY Piscatello

(12 km E on N 196)
20129 Bastelicaccia - (Corse)

12/20 Auberge du Prunelli

Old rte. de Sartène - 95.20.02.75
Mme. Pittiloni. Open until 9:30 p.m. Closed Tues. & Oct. 1-Nov. 25. Terrace dining. Pets allowed. Garage parking.

The house produces the wines, the fruit and the vegetables; the rest comes from the mountain streams, the neighboring farms and the hunt. This is a true bastion of Corsican tradition. Try the Corsican soup, the merle (a cousin of whiting), the cabri (kid) or the mint-and-broccio (mushroom) omelet. Pleasant terrace.

Menu: 132F (wine incl.).

Arbellara

20110 Propriano - (Corse)
Propriano 11 - Sartène 16

Le Moulin d'Acoravo

Pont d'Acoravo - 95.77.06.56
Open year-round. Half-board 325F oblig. in seas. Pool. Parking. Cards: V.

Large, well-furnished rooms are nestled in a little love nest of a park, with a trout stream flowing through. Restaurant.

Bastelica

20119 Bastelica - (Corse)
Ajaccio 41 - Cauro 19 - Porticcio 34 - Corte 62

U'Castagnetu

95.28.70.71
Closed Tues. (except vacations) & Oct. 30-Dec. 15. 15 rms 158-195F. Half-board 188-213F oblig. in seas. Parking. Cards: V, AE, DC.

In an immense chestnut grove in a magnificent mountain village, with bright and well-conceived rooms, this hotel offers skiing, fishing and hiking. Restaurant.

Bastia

20200 Bastia - (Corse)
Ajaccio 153 - Porto 135 - Calvi 93 - Bonifacio 170

12/20 Chez Assunta

4, pl. Fontaine-Neuve - 95.31.67.06
Mme. Cianelli. Open until 10 p.m. Closed Sun. & Jan. 1-March 1. Air cond. Pets allowed. Cards: V, AE, DC.

The very lovely dining room has bricks, arches, flowers and a pleasant loggia terrace, despite the proximity to traffic. The affable owner has a knack for making good homemade pasta, pizza and huge, well-seasoned omelets.

A la carte: 200F.

Ile de Beauté

Rue de la Gare - 95.31.15.56

Closed Oct. 15-April 1. Parking.. Hotel: 2 stes 320-440F. 58 rms 300-400F. Pets allowed. Cards: V, AE, DC, MC.

Large rooms with spacious baths are found in this hotel filled with mirrors, carpets and marble—a kitschy Middle East style that is singularly antiquated. Strange but amusing. Restaurant.

L'Orient Express

26, rue du Général-Carbuccia
95.34.05.06

M. Delcourt. Dinner only in summer. Open until 11 p.m. Closed Sat. lunch & Mon. (off-seas.) & 1st week in June & Oct. Terrace dining. Pets allowed. Cards: AE, DC.

Francis Delcourt loves to search out new flavors and is particularly interested in those of the Far East. In his old two-level residence overlooking the port, he prepares a personal French cuisine with Sino/Vietnamese influences: lotte with lime and a mango coulis, ravioli fried in a sweet-and-sour sauce, fritters of lotte jowls in curry and a prune-blueberry charlotte. Excellent young service staff.

A la carte: 200F.

Piétracap

3 km N on D 80, Pietranera - 95.31.64.63

Closed Dec.-Feb. 22 rms 300-470F. TV. Pets allowed. Pool. Parking. Cards: V, AE, DC.

A resolutely modern hotel with a rather cold interior. The rooms are warmer and fairly spacious, and all have balconies. No restaurant.

Le Romantique

4 bis, rue de Pontetto - 95.32.30.85

M. Roncaglia. Open until 11 p.m. Closed Sun. (Sat. & Sun. lunch in seas.) & Feb. 1-March 15. Terrace dining. Pets allowed. Cards: V, AE, DC, MC.

In the evening, Le Romantique truly lives up to its name: The view of the lights along the port from the terrace is enchanting. Surprisingly, this is not a tourist trap. The service is charming and the home cooking classic and generous: mussels gratinée, salmon with strands of leeks, red mullet en papillote, duck civet forestière. Judiciously chosen Corsican wines.

A la carte: 250F. Menus: 95F, 120F, 138F.

Bonifacio

20169 Bonifacio - (Corse)
Ajaccio 140 - Bastia 170 - Corte 148 - Porto-Vecchio 27

Résidence du Centre Nautique

On the port - 95.73.02.12

Closed Nov. 5-March 10. 10 rms 285-310F.

In this hotel, which belongs to the yacht club, are rooms named after boats, and views from literally on top of the port. No restaurant.

12/20 Stella d'Oro

7, rue de Général-de-Gaulle
95.73.03.63, 95.73.03.12

M. Filippedu. Open until 12:30 a.m. Closed Oct. 1-June 30. Air cond. Pets allowed. Cards: V, AE, DC, MC.

Seventy-two-year-old Mama Filippedu still makes the best seafood cuisine in the neighborhood: grilled langoustines, bouillabaisse and, for a change, roast capon. Superb products combine with excellent cooking skills and a smooth operation. The decor includes an old oil press; crowds are big despite the heavy prices, plain desserts and bad coffee.

A la carte: 300F and up.

Calvi

20260 Calvi - (Corse)
Ajaccio 163 - Bastia 93 - Porto 80 - Corte 96

Les Aloès

1.5 km SW, Quartier Donatéo
95.65.01.46, 95.65.01.67.

Closed Oct. 1-May 1. 26 rms 230-380F. Parking. Cards: V, AE, DC, MC.

A nice little hotel hidden in the trees, not far from the beach, with a lovely view of the golf course and the Calvi citadel. No restaurant.

Grand Hôtel

3, blvd. du Président-Wilson
95.65.09.74

Closed Oct. 31-April 1. 58 rms 190-460F. Half-board 60-80F (plus rm). Air cond. Telex 460718. Cards: V, AE, DC.

These very comfortable lodgings are located a mere 100 meters from the beach. Stylish service and excellent view. Restaurant.

L'Ile de Beauté

Quai Landry - 95.65.00.46

M. Caumeil. Open until 10:30 p.m. Closed Wed. (except July 15-Sept. 15) & Sept. 20-May 1. Terrace dining. No pets. Cards: V, AE, DC.

A good restaurant on the port, with an inviting blue-and-white decor and an attentive staff. The new chef is serving up a very expensive menu that is heavy on the lobsters and foie gras; there are a few simpler items as well.

A la carte: 300-350F.

Le Magnolia

Rue Alsace-Lorraine - 95.65.19.16

Open year-round. 13 rms 330-600F. TV in 10 rms. Air cond. in 6 rms. Pets allowed. Cards: V, AE, DC, MC.

This adorable little hotel dressed in white and set in a green garden is decorated with taste, is well equipped and oozes charm and luxury. No restaurant.

12/20 U Spuntinu

Rte. de Bonifacio - 95.65.07.06

M. Apparu. Open until 11 p.m. Closed Oct. 1-May 15. Terrace dining. Pets allowed. Parking.

Ask the owner when you reserve your table to prepare one of his specialties: herbed soufflé,

estouffade (stew) of Corsican veal with bolets (mushrooms), or cabri (kid) with garlic and lemon. Grandiose mountain setting and a simple, clean decor. Regional products are also sold.
A la carte: 200F. Menu: 155F.

Canari

20217 St-Florent - (Corse)
Ajaccio 208 - Bastia 55 - Calvi 102

(13) U Scogliu

Marine la Cannelle - 95.37.80.06
M. Leonetti. Open until 10:30 p.m. Closed Oct. 10-April 1. Pets allowed. Cards: AE.

The sun, the wind and the sea set the scene here on the magnificent Cap Corse. It's a lovely fishermen's landscape, and this restaurant, housed in a former fishing hut, has been refurbished in a simple, fresh style. The whole family, including cousins, works here, and the ambience is relaxed and natural. Marie-Josée prepares a spontaneous, fresh cuisine that extols the tastes of the territory: delicious Corsican charcuterie, fisherman's salad with olive oil and garlic, herb tart, mussels with spaghetti, fish en papillote, excellent homemade canneloni and (more expensive) marvelous grilled langouste (spiny lobster) with crushed fennel seeds. Remarkable Corsican wines.
A la carte: 150-180F.

Cargèse

20130 Cargèse - (Corse)
Ajaccio 50 - Calvi 108 - Port 32 - Sagone 14 - Piana 20

Hélios

Ménasina - 95.26.41.24
Closed Jan. & Nov. 3 stes 250F. 10 rms 172-212F. Half-board 212-266F oblig. in seas. Pets allowed. Pool. Parking. Cards: V.

Functional and modern, Hélios is located on the edge of the village. The spacious rooms are clean and comfortable. Restaurant.

Cauro

20117 Cauro - (Corse)
Ajaccio 22 - Sartène 64

12/20 Auberge U Barracone

95.28.40.55
M. Massix. Open until 10 p.m. Closed Mon. (off-seas.) & Jan. 15-Feb. 25. Garden dining. Pets allowed. Parking. Cards: V, AE, DC.

The owner of this elegant inn, with its well-dressed tables, is a professional with traditional leanings: coquilles St-Jacques feuilleté, salmon with sorrel, tournedos with morels. He also offers some Corsican specialties, such as tripe, and well-chosen island wines.
A la carte: 250F. Menu: 98F.

Some establishments change their hours and annual closings without warning. It is always wise to call ahead.

Corte

20250 Corte - (Corse)
Ajaccio 83 - Bastia 70 - Calvi 96 - Porto 86

IN NEARBY **Castirla**
(12 km N on D 18)
20218 Ponte-Leccia - (Corse)

12/20 Chez Jacqueline

Pont de Castirla - 95.47.42.04
Mme. Costa. Closed Jan. 1-April 1. Terrace dining. No pets.

This tasty family cuisine has been passed down from mother to daughter for three generations, in a large residence near the bridge: brocciu (fresh sheep's-milk cheese) fritters, anchovies à l'aïoli, cabri (kid) à la stretta, fresh brocciu, homemade fiadone (flan). Lots of generosity.
Menu: 100F.

Ferayola

20260 Calvi - (Corse)
Ajaccio 144 - Calvi 24 - Porto 65 - Galéria 15

Auberge de Ferayola

95.62.01.52
Closed Oct. 1-May 15. 10 rms 150-250F. Half-board 220-240F oblig. in seas. Tennis. Parking. Cards: V.

A calm, relaxing atmosphere in the brush country. Restaurant.

L'Ile-Rousse

20220 L'Ile Rousse - (Corse)
Ajaccio 165 - Bastia 68 - Calvi 24 - Corte 72

Napoléon-Bonaparte

3, pl. Paoli - 95.60.06.09
Closed Oct. 15-March 31. 82 rms 430-580F. Pool. Tennis. Parking. Telex 460470. Cards: V, AE, DC, MC.

This large hotel with all the amenities sits right on the beach. Its rooms overlook the sea or the gardens and the mountains. There's an extra fee for tennis. Restaurant.

La Pietra

Rte. du Port - 95.60.01.45
Closed Nov. 1-March 31. 40 rms 250-450F. TV in 8 rms. Pets allowed. Parking. Cards: V, AE, DC.

This comfortable hotel is set in the rocks, near the Ile-Rousse lighthouse, on the water's edge. No restaurant.

Pioggiola

20259 Olmi-Cappella - (Corse)
Calvi 48 - Belgodère 20 - Olmi-Capella 4

12/20 Auberge Aghjola

95.61.90.48
M. Albertini. Open until 11 p.m. (in seas.). Closed Mon. & Oct. 15-Nov. 15. Terrace dining. No pets. Cards: V, AE.

In a rugged mountain hamlet, this warm, comfortable inn serves homemade charcuterie, stream

trout, game and tender suckling lamb. A "shepherd's menu" is available any time for a mere 50 francs (wine included), on the terrace.
A la carte: 150F. Menu: 50F.

Auberge Aghjola

(See restaurant above)
Closed Mon. (in seas.) & Oct. 15-Nov. 15. 12 rms 200-280F (half-board only). Pets allowed.
Very (!) far from the crowds, fascinatingly deep in Corsica. Simple but comfortable rooms with decent plumbing.

La Porta

20237 La Porta - (Corse)
Ajaccio 150 - Bastia 60 - Piedicroce 15 - Corte 47

12/20 Restaurant de l'Ampugnani

(Chez Elisabeth)
95.39.22.00
Mme. Mattei. Open until 9 p.m. Closed Mon. (off-seas.) & Jan.; open lunch only Nov.-Dec. Pets allowed. Cards: V.
The owner brews a mean eau-de-vie, which should be tasted after dining on the tripe, leg of lamb, gras-double (a tripe dish) and cannelloni. Pleasant service in a cheerful but dark dining room.
Menus: 100F (wine incl.).

Porticcio

20166 Porticcio - (Corse)
Ajaccio 19 - Sartène 80 - Bastia 153 - Calvi 163

(13) Le Caroubier

Pointe de Porticcio - 95.25.00.34
M. Obeuf. Open until 10:15 p.m. Closed Dec. Terrace dining. No pets. Parking. Telex 460708. Cards: V, AE, DC, MC.
Secluded on the edge of a rocky spur, this marine spa is modern and geometric, with a large, coldly decorated dining room. It is full of light and has a view from the terrace of the spectacular Sanguinaire islands. Louis Dulucq's cuisine has over the years become more like standard hotel fare, with (particularly in high season) a few shortcomings. Try the unusual pineapples stuffed Tahitian-style with raw fish, or the good denti (a cousin of gilthead) steak à la citronelle, but skip the sweetbreads overcooked in a bland sauce. Pleasant waitresses.
A la carte: 300-350F. Menus: 225F (off-season), 255F (in season).

Sofitel Porticcio

(See restaurant above)
Open year-round. 2 stes 1,230-3,100F (half-board only). 98 rms 655-2,350F (half-board only). TV. Air cond. Pets allowed. Heated pool. Tennis.
The rooms face the ocean and are remarkably comfortable, some with solariums and terraces. Private pier and access to thalassotherapy.

12/20 Le Maquis

95.25.05.55
Mme. Salini. Open daily until 10 p.m. Terrace dining. No pets. Parking. Telex 460597. Cards: V, AE, DC.
Nestled in the fragrant hills near the beach is one of the nicest little inns on Corsica, with a marvelous terrace and a charming antique decor. The classic, pricey cuisine is professionally prepared: nage of langoustines au pistou, veal médaillons with fresh morels.
A la carte: 300F and up.

Le Maquis

(See restaurant above)
Open year-round. 7 stes 2,000-3,000F. 19 rms 1,130-1,700F. Half-board 930-1,740F oblig. in seas. TV. Air cond. Pets allowed. Heated pool. Tennis.
This modern hotel on the sea has been intelligently constructed around an old house in the regional style. Simple, roomy lodgings. Pleasant garden.

Porticciolo

20228 Luri - (Corse)
Ajaccio 178 - Bastia 25 - Barcaggio 32

Caribou

At Luri - 95.35.00.33, 95.35.02.33
Closed Oct. 1-June. 18. 23 rms 520-550F half-board only. Pets allowed. Pool. Tennis. Parking. Cards: V, AE, DC, MC.
A pleasant hotel on the water with plenty of flowers on the terraces, a beautiful pool and comfortable rooms overlooking the sea and the island of Elba. Restaurant.

12/20 Torra Marina

95.35.00.80
M. Mattei. Open until 10 p.m. Closed Oct. 1-March 31. Garden dining. Hotel: 4 rms 200-250F; half-board 300-350F oblig. in seas. Parking. Cards: V, AE, DC.
The local fishermen save their best for this pleasant place facing the island of Elba. Try the mostelle (rockling) filets with fruits de mer, the little rock mullets and the grilled langoustines, and taste some of the best vintages of Haute-Corse. Warm reception.
A la carte: 250-280F. Menu: 120F (weekday lunch only, wine incl.).

Porto-Vecchio

20210 Porto-Vecchio - (Corse)
Ajaccio 133 - Sartène 63 - Bonifacio 27 - Bastia 143

Cala Verde

95.70.11.55
Closed Oct. 1-April 30. 40 rms 370-630F. Garage parking. Cards: V, AE, DC, MC.
These rooms face the ocean or the garden and mountains. All have large terraces and a functional, everyday decor. Tennis (for a fee) across the way. No restaurant.

Regina

Rte. de Bastia - 95.70.14.94

M. Gantner. Open until 10:30 p.m. Closed Nov. 1-April 30. Garden dining. No pets. Telex 460253. Cards: V, AE, DC, MC.

A while ago we tasted some of the best food in Corsica at Regina, located in an attractive group of new buildings in an oak grove. Most recently, not only were the flowers and the beautiful garden still there but the cooking had become the best on Corsica. We want to encourage with another toque such dishes as the crab cooked with oysters, the mixed seafood dish with gnocchi, the roast baron of lamb with anchovies and fresh mint, and for dessert the "frappé" of anise and warm apricot purée. The rest of the desserts could use a little more work and the cheeses are still not worthy of Corsica. We do think that Regina fills a need for an excellent restaurant on the island, and we think its status will be confirmed in the near future. The decor is not dazzling, but the terrace overlooking the pool is lovely. Good, unpretentious service.

A la carte: 400F. Menu: 190F (dinner only).

Hôtel Roi Théodore

(See restaurant above)

Closed Nov. 13-Jan. 31. 2 stes 540-1,160F. 37 rms 280-840F. Half-board 180-220F (plus rm). TV in 12 rms. Pets allowed. Heated pool. Tennis.

This extremely elegant new hotel, its pink in vivid contrast to the green surroundings, is unfortunately close to the road. The stylish, comfortable rooms have a rustic decor, and there are views of the pool from the flowery loggia terrace. The reception, however, was quite insufficient at the time of our visit.

IN NEARBY Cala-Rossa

(10 km E on N 98, D 568 & D 468)
20137 Porto-Vecchio - (Corse)

Grand Hôtel de Cala Rossa

95.71.61.51

M. Canarelli. Open until 10 p.m. Closed Nov. 1-April 29. Air cond. Garden dining. No pets. Parking. Telex 460394. Cards: V, AE, DC.

Have lunch on the lawn at noon, sheltered by the parasols and the pines and overlooking the beach, or dinner in the large, open dining room with a view of the gulf. Wherever you eat, you'll be received warmly by Marie-Madeleine Canarelli and one of the best staffs on the island. The cuisine is fresh and consistently good, and the prices are excellent, particularly at lunch. Try, for example, the red scorpionfish braised Corsican style, the lotte with squash and fresh pasta, and the chocolate-hazelnut feuilleté.

A la carte: 300-400F. Menus: 100F (lunch only), 400F (dinner only).

Grand Hôtel de Cala Rossa

(See restaurant above)

Closed Nov. 1-April 29. 55 rms; price not available. Half-board oblig. in seas. Tennis.

In a private 100-plus-acre park near the gulf, the Grand Hôtel has a view of the limpid sea. Its well-equipped rooms are situated a few yards from the fine, sandy beach. Excellent service.

Propriano

20110 Propriano - (Corse)
Ajaccio 74 - Corte 138 - Sartène 13 - Bonifacio 67

12/20 Le Lido

95.76.06.37

M. Pittilloni. Open until 10:15 p.m. Closed end Sept.-early May. Pets allowed. Cards: V, AE, DC, MC.

With your feet in the water, or almost, dine on baked langoustines, steamed catch of the day with fennel butter or respectable bouillabaisse. The repertoire doesn't budge, but the prices do. Pleasant shaded terrace.

A la carte: 300F.

Le Lido

(See restaurant above)

Closed end Sept.-early May. 17 rms 220-260F. Half-board 250-300F.

Modest but pleasant rooms overlook the beach. Good value for the money.

Saint-Florent

20217 St-Florent - (Corse)
Ajaccio 176 - Bastia 23 - Calvi 70 - L'Ile-Rousse 46

Hôtel Bellevue

95.37.00.06

Closed Jan. 10-March 10. 27 rms 270-600F. Heated pool. Tennis. Parking. Telex 460296. Cards: V, AE, DC.

The best hotel in Saint-Florent is located in a park with a pool and tennis courts, close to the golf course. The comfortable rooms were recently redecorated. Restaurant.

12/20 La Rascasse

Esplanade du Port - 95.37.06.99

M. Schneider. Open until 11 p.m. Closed Mon. (except June 15-Sept. 15) & Nov. 1-March 30. Air cond. Terrace dining. Cards: V, AE, DC.

This place puts forth plenty of variety in seafood, which is fresh and reasonably priced: scorpionfish matelote, bouillabaisse, langoustes, grilled fish of the day. Pleasant service on the terraces, which are nicely shaded.

A la carte: 200-220F.

Serriera

20147 Serriera - (Corse)
Ajaccio 83 - Porto 6 - Galéria 47 - Partinello 9

L'Aiglon

Plage de Bussaglia - 95.26.10.65

Closed Sept. 30-May 1. 18 rms 185-250F. Half-board 190-230F oblig. in seas. Parking. Cards: V.

In the brush country near the gulf of Porto sits this large stone house surrounded by oaks and pines. Bright rooms. Restaurant.

Venaco

20231 Venaco - (Corse)
Ajaccio 71 - Corte 13 - Sartène 128 - Aléria 41

Paësotel e Caselle

5 km E on D 43 - 95.47.02.01
Closed Sept. 30-April 1. 47 rms 315-410F. Half-board 327-450F oblig. in seas. Pets allowed. Heated pool. Tennis. Parking. Telex 460145. Cards: V, AE, DC.

The wild brush all around and a beautiful trout stream flowing under the windows make for a fine setting. Riding club, tennis courts, pool and some rooms with kitchenettes for weekly rentals.

Prices in red draw attention to restaurants that offer a particularly good value.

Cotignac

83570 Carces - (Var)
Paris 828 - Draguignan 36 - Toulon 70 - Brignoles 25

12/20 Lou Calen

Cours Gambetta - 94.04.60.40
Mme. Caren. Open until 10 p.m. Closed Wed. (off-seas.) & Jan. 1-March 18. Garden dining. Pets allowed. Hotel: 5 stes 420-460F; 11 rms 200-370F; half-board oblig. in seas. Pool. Parking. Telex 400287. Cards: V, AE, DC, MC.

This large, shady terrace facing a wild garden would be paradise if the cuisine hadn't started going downhill recently: assorted hors d'oeuvres, disappointing veal scallop zingara (a paprika-tomato sauce), two-chocolate mousse.

A la carte: 260F. Menus: 100F, 170F, 220F.

Courbevoie

see PARIS SUBURBS

Courchevel

73120 Courchevel - (Savoie)
Paris 653 - Chambéry 99 - Annecy 96 - Albertville 51

Les Airelles

Jardin Alpin - 79.08.02.11
Closed April 17-Dec. 15. 44 rms 525-1,330F (half-board only). TV in 40 rms. Pets allowed. Garage parking. Telex 980190. Cards: V, AE, DC.

Extensive renovations were made recently, but you'll still find the lovely terrace and many rooms overlooking the snowy fields. Les Airelles is well kept and quiet. Restaurant and bridge salon.

Annapurna

Rte. de l'Altiport, Courchevel 1850
79.08.04.60
Closed April 12-Dec. 18. 10 stes 4,600-5,300F. 59 rms 770-2,950F. TV. Air cond. Pets allowed. Heated pool. Parking. Telex 980324. Cards: V, AE, DC, MC.

In this hotel, one of the best in this ski town, indeed in all the French Alps, the spacious, superbly equipped rooms all have southern views of the mountains and the slopes. Indoor pool, game room, solarium, Jacuzzi, gym and more. Restaurant.

16 Le Bateau Ivre

79.08.02.46
M. Jacob. Open until 10 p.m. Closed April 15-Dec. 15. Air cond. Terrace dining. Pets allowed. Hotel: 48 rms 380-650F; half-board 800-850F. Garage parking. Telex 309162. Cards: V, AE, DC.

The Jacobs have the wind in their sails and a flair for business. (They recently made a hit on the Lac du Bourget with the opening of a second Bateau Ivre.) They have expanded and livened up the decor of the original restaurant, which, although elegant, was a bit dreary. So much the better for the cuisine of the increasingly accomplished son, Jean-Pierre Jacob, and for the exemplary reception by Jean Jacob, the father, and his lovely daughter-in-law, Josie; they deserve a more flattering environment. In the meantime, Jean-Pierre continues to develop the glowing talent that recently earned him an extra toque, with inventive and balanced dishes: lasagne with oysters and coquilles St-Jacques in a basil vinaigrette, escalope de foie gras de canard, filet of bass with artichoke hearts in a poultry sauce, and oeufs à la neige with pralines and pistachios. Alongside the priceless bottles in the proprietor's impressive wine cellar is his own selection of good wines at sensible prices.

A la carte: 400-450F. Menus: 220F, 340F, 420F, 480F.

Bellecôte

79.08.10.19
Closed April 20-Dec. 8. 2 stes 4,000-5,000F (full board only). 49 rms 980-2,600F (full board only). TV. Air cond. in 9 rms. Heated pool. Parking. Telex 980421. Cards: V, AE, DC.

A luxurious chalet boasting huge lovely rooms done in wood. Lots of services and a restaurant.

13 Byblos des Neiges

Jardin Alpin - 79.08.12.12
M. Virot. Open until 10 p.m. Closed Easter-Christmas. Air cond. Terrace dining. No pets. Parking. Telex 980580. Cards: V, AE, DC.

Perched on the peaks of Courchevel, in the most charming and forested section of the resort area, Byblos is at once spectacular, delicate, barbarian and refined. After three years, it has lost none of its power of surprise and seduction. The building's enormous trunks and Cyclopean pillars compose a sort of fairy-tale decor, halfway between the Carpathians and Walt Disney. Wide picture windows allow the forest and mountains to enter the luxuriously decorated dining room, and the dazzling service—among the best in any mountain resort—will keep you looking at the view instead of for your waiter. As for Serge Champion's cuisine, we would like to report that it is keeping up with all this, but we found recently that his expensive, classical cooking had lost its flair and gotten a little careless, especially with cooking times. You'll still find plenty of rich ingredients, high prices, remarkable desserts and a very professional sommelier.

A la carte: 400-500F. Menus: 250F (lunch only), 280F (dinner only).

Byblos des Neiges

(See restaurant above)

Closed Easter-Christmas. 8 stes 3,500-3,900F. 61 rms 1,300-3,100F. Half-board 1,200-1,870F. TV. Pets allowed. Heated pool.

In this veritable snow palace complete with ultra-luxurious rooms, sauna, whirlpool, piano bar and restaurants, there are sunny terraces, lounges with fireplaces and common areas decorated à la cyclops.

Caravelle

Jardin Alpin - 79.08.02.42

Closed April 17-Dec. 10. 3 stes. 57 rms 370-695F (half-board). TV in 44 rms. Pets allowed. Heated pool. Garage parking. Telex 980821. Cards: V.

This friendly, cozy chalet has warmly decorated rooms and offers numerous leisure activities (squash, gym, sauna, game room) and a restaurant.

(13) Carlina

Courchevel 1850 - 79.08.00.30

M. Bégué. Open until 10 p.m. Closed Christmas-Easter. Terrace dining. No pets. Parking. Telex 980248. Cards: V, AE, DC, MC.

An extra toque is warranted for the chicken sautéed in vinegar, the luscious bass with prawns and morel mushrooms, and even the tripe à la mode de Caen, which almost achieves—an impossible task for this dish—a light touch. None of this is earthshaking, but chef Maurice Fontanive, who favors a rich touch, is at least competent and sticks to reliable combinations of first-rate ingredients.

A la carte: 300-400F. Menus: 230F (lunch only), 260F (dinner only).

Carlina

(See restaurant above)

Closed Easter-Christmas. 2 stes 1,000-1,900F. 51 rms 400-1,600F. Half-board 400-1,150F. TV. Pets allowed.

Now there are ten fewer rooms, a half-board that is no longer obligatory and less frightening prices, but the Carlina still indulges its guests with impeccable comfort and an exceptional staff.

(17) Chabichou

Courchevel 1850, Quartier Les Chenus
79.08.00.55

M. Rochedy. Open until 10:30 p.m. Closed April 15-Dec. 15. Terrace dining. Pets allowed. Parking. Telex 980416. Cards: V.

Chabichou has undergone a dramatic face-lift. The new, unfinished-wood exterior on Maryse and Michel Rochedy's large house is a sign of their participation, together with the mayor and the people of Courchevel, in a fight against ugly architecture. And there is another battle, secret but formidable, firing up the ovens of Courchevel, for it is becoming necessary to fight not only on the decor front (Le Bateau Ivre is also being refurbished) but also on the culinary front. Unthinkable just a few years ago, the winter-sports clientele in this region now has the luxury of choosing between three remarkable restaurants, all rated at two toques. In fact, even if Michel Rochedy was the first to thaw the icy relations between ski resorts and gastronomy, he is no longer alone. Last year, with all the construction going on, there were understandably some lapses in the kitchen, but we are pleased to report that all is well again—in fact, it's even better: rolled smoked salmon with prawns, salad of lobster and skate, sea trout with mushroom butter, sweet-and-sour lamb tenderloin and the veal roast with stewed endives. We were delighted to rediscover Rochedy's frank, refined cuisine, prepared with admirable products from all over France that are hoisted up Courchevel's slopes and into this kitchen. He excels with his frogs' legs and lentil soup, tourte of John Dory with artichokes, oyster casserole with potatoes and chanterelles, filet of beef and lamb's brains in a meunière sauce, and souffléed hazelnut crêpes.

After the meal, guests can sit by the fireplace and enjoy wines from the most beautiful cellar in all of the winter-sports resorts, while mingling with the most sparkling of ski aficionados, attired in a mix of mink and après-ski outfits and unfailingly loyal to this first great restaurant in the snow.

A la carte: 500F. Menus: 135F (lunch only), 220F (dinner only), 320F, 450F.

Chabichou

(See restaurant above)

Closed April 15-Dec. 15. 22 stes. 20 rms 640-1,350F (half-board only). TV. Pets allowed.

Magnificently situated at the foot of the slopes, Chabichou's rooms are not very large, but they are charming and well equipped. Guests can take advantage of the sauna, solarium, billiards and the superb Savoyard brunches served each morning.

Les Ducs de Savoie

Jardin Alpin - 79.08.03.00

Closed April 15-Dec. 20. 70 rms 250-890F. Half-board 510-830F. TV. No pets. Heated pool. Parking. Telex 980360. Cards: V, AE, DC.

Located in the calm residential neighborhood of Jardin Alpin, this modern building has been redone in wood in the style of the Savoyard chalets. The layout is well conceived, providing a mountain view from the terrace of each room, and the service is remarkable. Restaurant.

Red toques signify modern cuisine; black toques signify traditional cuisine.

Grand Hôtel Rond-Point des Pistes

Courchevel 1850 - 79.08.02.69

Closed April 8-Dec. 19. 4 stes 1,990-2,300F. 51 rms 695F. Half-board 595-895F. TV. Pets allowed. Garage parking. Telex 980847. Cards: V, AE, DC.

Large, quiet rooms face the mountains, while the terrace gets the full southern sun. The Grand Hôtel also boasts expansive lounges, a discotheque and a restaurant.

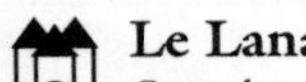

Le Lana

Courchevel 1850 - 79.08.01.10

Closed April 15-Dec. 15. 8 stes. 62 rms 1,025-1,300F (half-board only). TV. Pets allowed. Parking. Telex 980014. Cards: V, AE.

Facing the valley, at the center of Courchevel 1850, the large rooms of this superb, vast hotel overlook fields of snow. Guests take full advantage of the terrace, flawless equipment, sauna, massage services, gym and restaurant.

Hôtel des Neiges

79.08.03.77

Closed April 16-Dec. 17. 58 rms 810-1,020F (half-board only). TV. No pets. Parking. Telex 980463. Cards: V, AE, DC.

The in-season bonhomie at this hotel, located just 50 meters from the ski lifts, is maintained by a lively clientele. Most, but not all, of the rooms are pretty and spacious. Relais et Châteaux. Restaurant.

(14) Pralong 2000

Rte. de l'Altiport - 79.08.24.82

M. Parveaux. Open until 9 p.m. Closed April 9-Dec. 17. Terrace dining. Pets allowed. Garage parking. Telex 980231. Cards: V, AE, DC.

The Parveaux have closed (temporarily?) their excellent ground-floor restaurant, Le Paral. Pralong 2000, however, continues to serve its extensive buffets in the large dining room facing the slopes. The lovely cuisine is enriched in the evenings by a good portion of Le Paral's old southwestern-French menu. Try the marvelous truffles en croûte; the filet de boeuf in a foie gras sauce, accompanied by oven-browned potatoes and a mushroom ragoût; and the pear and almond gratin. The young, impeccable waiters, under the direction of the Parveaux, are ever attentive and pleasant.

A la carte: 350F. Menus: 250F (lunch only), 295F (dinner only).

Pralong 2000

(See restaurant above)

Closed April 9-Dec. 17. 4 stes 1,245F. 68 rms 460F. Half-board oblig. in seas. TV. Pets allowed. Heated pool.

This remarkably renovated hotel is perched by the ski lifts on the heights of Courchevel 1850. In addition to the afternoon video programs available in each room, amusements include a covered and heated pool, sauna, massages, a golf practice course, indoor tennis (a net returns the balls), a gym and a terrace/solarium. Nearby, and under the same management, is Crystal 2000, where the meals are not obligatory. Relais et Châteaux.

(13) La Sivolière

Courchevel 1850 - 79.08.08.33

Mme. Cattelin. Open until 10 p.m. Closed May 1-Dec. 1. No pets. Garage parking. Telex 309169.

Courchevel is a bit secretive about La Sivolière, an exquisite chalet that resembles a luxurious home more than a hotel. Every year the king of Spain and his retinue return to La Sivolière to savor the improvised cuisine (no menu) of owner Mado Cattelin, a former ski instructor. She serves her royal guests well-prepared, simple dishes, such as beef ribs, vegetables au gratin, numerous curries and, to finish, tartes and desserts that have made us feel like frolicking in the snow. Fine cellar with wines from the region.

A la carte: 200-250F.

La Sivolière

(See restaurant above)

Closed May 1-Dec. 1. 25 rms 555-615F. TV. Pets allowed.

This superb hotel is tucked in among the fir trees at the edge of the slopes. Its furnishings are refined, and its rooms are both intimate and functional, all with a splendid mountain view. Many leisure activities are available.

Courlans

see Lons-le-Saunier

Coutainville

50230 Agon-Coutainville - (Manche)
Paris 343 - St-Lô 40 - Coutances 13 - Cherbourg 77

(13) Hardy

Pl. du 28-Juillet - 33.47.04.11

M. Hardy. Open until 9 p.m. Closed Mon. (off-seas.) & Jan. 5-Feb. 5. No pets.otel: 17 rms 160-320F; half-board 220-310F. Cards: V, AE, DC, MC.

Emile Hardy won't let you regret getting your feet wet on the windy beach in this decidedly pretty, tucked-away corner of Normandy. His place is welcoming and cozy, his staff perfect and his cooking delicious, sometimes even inspired: langoustines with lime, bass with red Bordeaux and marrow, roast pigeon with cabbage. He offers two excellent fixed-price menus and seventeen well-equipped rooms—not to mention windsurfing in season.

A la carte: 300F. Menus: 80F (weekdays only), 165F, 260F.

Crest-Voland

73590 Flumet - (Savoie)
Paris 579 - Albertville 27 - Megève 14 - Annecy 56

Les Aravis

Le Cernix (1.5 km S on V.O.)
79.31.63.81

Closed April 18-July 1 & Aug. 31-Dec. 20. 17 rms 185-200F. Half-board 185-198F. Parking.

A tiny chalet nestled in the high mountain pastures, Les Aravis's rooms have large balconies overlooking the valley and mountaintops. Restaurant.

Croissy-Beaubourg

see PARIS SUBURBS

La Croix-Blanche

see Agen

La Croix-Valmer

83420 La Croix-Valmer - (Var)
Paris 879 - Toulon 62 - Le Lavandou 26 - St-Tropez 12

Les Moulins de Paillas

Blvd. de la Mer - 94.79.67.16

Closed Oct. 1-May 15. 30 rms 450-650F. Half-board 400-520F oblig. in seas. TV. Air cond. Pets allowed. Heated pool. Telex 970987. Tennis. Cards: V.

Against a pine-forest backdrop, the rooms are inviting and tastefully decorated. Excellent sports equipment and facilities—a pool, two tennis courts, a private beach, windsurfing, children's games—keep guests from having too lazy a vacation. Restaurant.

(14) Souleïas

Plage de Gigaro - 94.79.61.91

M. Yvon. Open until 9:30 p.m. Closed Nov. 1-March 15. Garden dining. Parking. Telex 970032. Cards: V, AE, DC, MC.

Since its opening more than six years ago, the luxurious Souleïas has become one of the most pleasant establishments on the Côte d'Azur and one of the most popular among chic society. They feel at home in the refined, modern decor and on the pine-shaded terrace with a sublime view of the coast just beyond the pool and the flowers. The service is of luxury-hotel quality, but without the customary stiffness. There is a pianist in the evenings and even a seventeen-meter yacht for cruising to the Iles d'Or.

In the few years that Georges Coquin, the former chef at L'Auberge de Noves, has reigned in the kitchen, progress has been ongoing; the dishes are becoming more inventive and the finishing touches more perfected. Our last meal was almost worth two toques: a harmonious fish in aspic with an orange and grapefruit confit, rock mullet with black olives, a simple farm squab casserole and a light apple feuilleté. Our good cheer was furthered by a sample from the exceptional wine cellar and made complete by the reasonable check.

A la carte: 300-400F. Menus: 160F (lunch only), 190F, 260F.

Souleïas

(See restaurant above)

Closed Nov. 1-March 16. 6 stes 890-1,200F. 41 rms 400-850F. TV. Air cond. in 16 rms. Pets allowed. Heated pool. Tennis.

With its modern construction and comfortable rooms, this hotel, tucked away in the flowers and greenery, is blessed with a stunning view of the sea—and a sailboat in which to enjoy it firsthand.

Croutelle

see Poitiers

Dax

40100 Dax - (Landes)
Paris 706 - Bordeaux 142 - Biarritz 57 - Pau 78

12/20 Le Parc

Pl. Thiers - 58.74.86.17

M. Pauthe. Open until 9:30 p.m. Closed Sun. & Dec. 15-Jan. 15. Terrace dining. No pets. Cards: V, AE, DC, MC.

The elegant dining room of the luxurious Le Parc hotel is located in the actual interior of the hot springs. After leaving the springs, guests can keep their strength up with the terrine of foie gras, grilled bass with crab, breast of duck with puréed onions, and various confits. Servings are generous, but the food is not always on the mark.

A la carte: 280F. Menus: 75F, 100F.

Le Parc

(See restaurant above)

Open year-round. 40 rms 200-350F. Half-board 300-450F oblig. in seas.

A posh new hotel at the thermal springs with light, fresh rooms facing the Adour and the Parc des Arènes.

Deauville

14800 Deauville - (Calvados)
Paris 206 - Rouen 89 - Le Havre - 72 - Caen 43

Sights. The famous promenade des Planches, which stretches along the beach and the boat harbor; the stunning gardens and elegant villas; the beautiful people who gravitate toward the luxury hotels and restaurants, especially for the international Bridge Festival (June-July), the polo matches and horse races (July-August), the sale of purebred foals (late August) and the American film festival (early September).

Eating on the Run. L'Ambassade d'-Auvergne, 119 bis, ave. de la République; Chez Boubou, 64, rue Mirabeau (good meats grilled over a wood fire); L'Entracte, 23, rue du Général-de-Gaulle (salads and hearty dishes); Chez Mioc-que, 81, rue Eugène-Colas (lively brasserie with choucroute); Le Mirama Mandarin, 82, quai F.-Moureaux à Trouville (formal); Pizzéria Santa Lucia, 15, ave. de la République.

Bars & Cafés. Bar du Normandy, 38, rue J.-Mermoz; Bar du Royal, blvd. Cornuché; Le Bagatelle, ave. du Général-de-Gaulle; Le Drakkar, 77, rue Eugène-Colas; Le Morny, 3, rue A.-Fracasse.

Nightlife. Régine's, at the Casino (elegant); Méduse-Club, 14 bis, rue Désiré-Le Hoc (for the young and very young); Mélody, 13, rue A.-Fracasse (for all ages).

Shops. *Chocolate:* Au Duc de Morny, 59 ter, rue Désiré-Le Hoc (the tradition); Léonidas, résidence Morny Palace, pl. Morny (the boutique of the famous Belgian chocolatier). *Gourmet foods, caterers:* Breton, 1, pl. Morny (caterer, poultry, charcuterie and prepared dishes); Cave Olliffe, 44, rue Olliffe (large selection of wines and liquors, foie gras, products from Fauchon); Chez le Gaulois, résidence Morny Palace, pl. Morny (marvelous country hams and sausages). *Pastries:* Lemonnier, 20, pl. Morny (tea room, chocolates—*the* pastry chef in Deauville).

Altea Deauville

Blvd. Cornuché, Port-Deauville
31.88.62.62

Open year-round. 70 rms 300-600F. TV. Pets allowed. Telex 170364. Cards: V, AE, DC, MC.

At the center of the lakeside village of Port-Deauville, the Altea Deauville has perfectly equipped rooms (especially for families) with balconies overlooking the port and the beaches, as well as a restaurant for groups.

13

Le Ciro's

Blvd de la Mer - 31.88.18.10

M. Barrière. Open daily until 9:30 p.m. (weekends until 10 p.m.). Terrace dining. No pets. Telex 171873. Cards: V, AE, DC, MC.

A glittering crowd that doesn't count pennies gathers here in this modern, seaside establishment for some of the better food in town. It's similar fare to that served at the Rotonde—the same chef is in charge—but here it is more carefully done: filet of sea bream with cuttlefish, prawns wrapped in cured ham and served with cream of lentils, filet of good beef with shallots.

A la carte: 350-450F. Menus: 175F, 290F (wine incl.).

Hélios Hôtel

10, rue Fossorier - 31.88.28.26

Open year-round. 44 rms 260-420F. TV. No pets. Heated pool. Telex 170053. Cards: V, AE, DC.

This new but traditional-looking hotel has a small pool in a garden courtyard and well-equipped rooms, but no restaurant.

14

Le Kraal

Pl. du Marché - 31.88.30.58

M. Chauvin. Open until 10 p.m. Closed Mon. (off-seas.) & Jan. 10-30. Air cond. Terrace dining. Pets allowed.

A few years ago, Jean Chauvin decided abruptly to abandon the old style of cooking, elaborate, flambéed and heavy. Happily, he has been rewarded for this bolt of inspiration: His lovely establishment has become *the* seafood restaurant in Deauville. He uses products of remarkable quality and freshness, cooked perfectly and served in light sauces. You can start with simple oysters, Norman mussels and stuffed shellfish, then move on to grilled turbot in a sharp Nantes butter, lobster cooked in court bouillon, sole meunière or sole filets with chive butter. The dining room on the second floor, which looks out onto the place du Marché, is the most cheerful.

A la carte: 400-500F. Menu: 165F (lunch only).

La Pommeraie

3 km S on D 278 - 31.88.19.01

M. Yvos. Closed Nov.-March. Terrace dining. Pets allowed. Parking. Telex 170448. Cards: V, AE, DC, MC.

The immense dining room of this luxury hotel, with its white satin walls and red chairs, opens onto the green expanse of a golf course beyond the monumental columns of its facade. The eagerly awaited arrival of chef André Plunian in this Marienbad of a dining room has, however, proved a serious disapointment, unheralded by the fine quality of his work elsewhere. Suspiciously peripatetic of late, and perhaps hemmed in or unsupported by the corporate management, this mustachioed giant is turning the faces of his customers as green as the links at having paid 300 francs and more for what tastes like reheated rubbery duck. We have removed the rating entirely until the chef returns to at least his former level of interest and promise.

A la carte: 350-400F. Menu: 175F.

Hôtel du Golf

(See restaurant above)

Closed Nov.-March. 9 stes 1,320-1,840F. 166 rms 440-920F. TV. Pets allowed. Heated pool. Tennis. Golf.

One of the great old French hotels. Happily, the many transformations and modernizations have not affected its luxurious art deco style. The service is impeccable, and the rooms, the most beautiful of which overlook the greens and the Seine, are spacious.

Normandy

38, rue Jean-Mermoz - 31.88.09.21

Open year-round. 22 stes 1,600-3,500F. 291 rms 630-1,440F. TV. Pets allowed. Heated pool. Tennis. Golf.

At this turn-of-the-century luxury hotel, many of the rooms cultivate a nostalgia for the sea. Nothing could alter the charm and seduction of the hotel, especially in the rooms on the lower floors, which are well protected from sea breezes. There is also a beautiful ocean view beyond the tennis courts, and a good restaurant.

13

La Rotonde

At the Casino, rte. Edmond-Blanc
31.88.29.55

M. Barrière. Dinner only. Open until 10 p.m. Closed Sept. 16-March 15. Air cond. Terrace dining. Parking. Telex 171873. Cards: V, AE, DC, MC.

Les Ambassadeurs has changed its name to La Rotonde, but its slightly solemn ambience lives on, as does its chef, Christian Girault, who was trained by Joël Robuchon at the Concorde Lafayette. The salade "folle" ("crazy") with foie gras, lobster and avocado, the filets of red mullet with eggplant and saffron, and the filets of roast lamb with garlic work well together to please the customers, none of whom bat an eye at the hefty tabs. This demanding clientele is spoiled with the utmost in service by Mario and his dining room staff.

A la carte: 400-500F. Menu: 175F (wine incl.).

Le Royal

Blvd. E.-Cornuché - 31.88.16.41

Closed end Oct.-early March. 17 stes 1,700-3,500F. 283 rms 570-1,500F. Half-board 360F (plus rm). TV in 250 rms. Pets allowed. Heated pool. Tennis. Golf. Telex 170549. Cards: V, AE, DC, MC.

Facing the sea and near the casino, this huge old-style luxury hotel offers classic-looking rooms, comfortable and plush, which are slowly being refurbished. Ask for the upper floors, where the view of the sea is beautiful. Lots of sports, and a restaurant.

Le Spinnaker

52, rue Mirabeau - 31.88.24.40

M. Angenard. Open until 9:30 p.m. Closed Wed. & Thurs. (off-seas.) & Nov. 15-Dec. 15. No pets. Cards: V.

Once a bar, Le Spinnaker has been transformed into a charming, rustic restaurant—one of the best in Deauville. The owner/chef, Pascal Angenard, is a young professional with experience from serious establishments in both Paris and the provinces. The foundation of his cuisine is classic, but it has both personality and honest simplicity. Taste the ragoût of lotte with tomatoes and lime, the long-simmered veal in rice with endive and the caramelized apples with vanilla ice cream and honey sauce. There's a decent choice of good wines for less than 100 francs.

A la carte: 300F and up. Menu: 140F (weekends and holidays only).

IN NEARBY **St-Martin-aux-Chartrains**
(8 km SE on N 177 & D 58)
14130 Pont-l'Evêque - (Calvados)

Auberge de la Truite

31.65.21.64

M. Lebon. Open until 9:30 p.m. (10:30 p.m. in summer). Closed Sun. dinner, Mon. & Feb. Garden dining. Pets allowed. Hotel: 7 rms 150-250F. Parking. Cards: V, AE, DC.

This beautiful Norman inn, with its lawn and flower garden in the back and its new, charmingly rustic dining rooms, is one of the best restaurants in the area surrounding Deauville. The owners—lovely Françoise Lebon and her husband, Jean-Michel, himself an excellent and generous cook—have recently recruited the former chef at Honfleur's La Ferme Saint-Siméon. The à la carte prices are "très Deauville" (pricey), but the first two fixed-price menus are quite reasonable. For 90 francs you can feast on skate with fennel and basil, guinea-fowl with a chicken-liver mousse, nicely enhanced by a peppered vinaigrette, salads, fruits and sorbets. A la carte, try the oysters and frogs' legs with thyme and the hot citrus-fruit soufflé. Nice wine cellar.

A la carte: 300F. Menus: 90F (weekdays only), 160F, 250F.

Les Deux-Alpes

38869 Les Deux-Alpes - (Isère)
Paris 641 - Grenoble 74 - Col du Lautaret 37

La Bérangère

76.79.24.11

M. Lherm. Open until 9 p.m. Closed May 1-June 30 & Sept. 1-Dec. 15. Terrace dining. No pets. Hotel: 63 rms 350-500F; half-board 350-520F oblig. in seas. Heated pool. Parking. Telex 320878. Cards: V, AE.

A winter annex of the family-run Saint-Céré inn, La Bérangère is a beautiful hotel in the snow, facing the mountains. The owners, from the southwest of France, have placed one of their sons in charge of the kitchen. He has studied under some of the country's top chefs (Daguin and Bocuse, among others), and everything he serves has a freshness and a generosity about it. Especially the duck foie gras, cooked till it's just pink (also served hot and accompanied by a potato pancake with truffles), the bass in white wine and herbs, and the filet of squab. To complete the gastronomic bliss, he also makes lovely desserts.

A la carte: 280-330F. Menus: 170F, 230F.

La Farandole 

76.80.50.45

Closed May 2-June 17 & Sept. 10-Dec. 2. 14 stes 1,000-1,800F. 46 rms 400-900F. Half-board 380-900F oblig in seas. TV. Pets allowed. Heated pool. Tennis. Parking. Telex 320029. Cards: V, AE, DC, MC.

Having recently undergone major reconstruction, this large chalet is remarkably comfortable and well equipped for socializing (piano bar), for relaxing (bathhouse, sauna) and for seminars. Restaurant.

Dieppe

76200 Dieppe - (Seine-Maritime)
Paris 185 - Rouen 58 - Abbeville 63 - Le Havre 103

La Mélie

2, Grande-Rue-du-Pollet - 35.84.21.19

M. Brachais. Open until 9:30 p.m. Closed Sun. dinner, Mon. & Feb. Pets allowed. Cards: V, AE, DC.

The former Quatre-Pain of Tocqueville-sur-Eau has moved into this old fishing quarter. You'll find the same chef and the same interesting cuisine: generous duck terrine, "creuille du pêcheur" (assorted fish in a basil sauce), filet of lamb in a garlic crème fondant, and apple pastries. The service is always friendly, though the decor isn't much to behold.

A la carte: 200F. Menu: 120F.

La Présidence

1, blvd. de Verdun - 35.84.31.31

Open year-round. 1 ste 500-750F. 88 rms 220-500F. TV in 80 rms. Pets allowed.

Spacious, perfectly equipped rooms (60 face the ocean), good accommodations for seminars, a popular English pub and a restaurant give La Présidence its appeal.

IN NEARBY **Saint-Aubin-sur-Scie**
(7 km S on N 27)
76550 Offranville - (Seine-Maritime)

(14) Auberge de la Bucherie

Rte. de Rouen - 35.84.83.10

M. Delaunay. Open until 9:30 p.m. Closed Sun. dinner, Mon., July 19-30 & Jan. 9-22. Pets allowed. Parking. Cards: V.

To eat well in Dieppe, all you have to do is leave it—and head for the suburbs, where you'll find this friendly hostelry in a flowering park. The decor is opulent and a sense of professionalism runs rampant, from the greeting of the distinguished owner to the young, competent staff and the attractively laid out tables. It all suits the classic yet light cooking style of Jacques Delaunay, whose dishes include a blanquette of fish with noodles of unparalleled freshness, veal kidneys cooked in their own fat and served pink with a delicate sauce, and feathery-light, hot feuilletés. The menu rarely changes (except for the prices, which climb steadily), but in its genre it is close to perfection. Good wine cellar.

A la carte: 350-400F. Menus: 110F (weekdays only), 160F, 240F.

Dieulefit

26220 Dieulefit - (Drôme)
Paris 633 - Montélimar 27 - Valence 72 - Nyons 31

IN NEARBY **Poët-Laval**
(4 km on D 540)
26160 La Bégude-de-Mazenc - (Drôme)

(15) Les Hospitaliers

Vieux-Village - 75.46.22.32

M. Morin. Open until 9 p.m. Closed Nov. 15-March 1. Terrace dining. Pets allowed. Parking. Cards: V, AE, DC, MC.

Atop a medieval village, where the knights of Malta kept watch over the borders of the Dauphiné and Provence, stands this extraordinary hotel complex. The rooms, common areas, pool, flower gardens and marvelous, shaded terrace (that faces a sublime panorama) are all perfectly integrated into the style of the village. The owner, a charming old man, is blessed with a son, Bernard, who cooks with consistency and lightness, resulting in meals that are always stunning in their variety and personality. Try, for example, the lamb's-brain fritters with cabbage and citrus butter, the médaillon of lotte in green lentil sauce or the splendid roast rack of lamb accompanied by a purée of flageolets and haricots verts. The desserts are a fine finish to a meal that now merits two toques.

A la carte: 300F and up. Menus: 170F, 210F, 245F, 350F.

Les Hospitaliers

(See restaurant above)

Closed Nov. 15-March 1. 20 rms 370-710F. Pets allowed. Heated pool.

Calm pervades these beautiful houses constructed in the style of the Middle Ages. The rooms are superb, all with modern furniture.

Digne

04000 Digne - (Alpes-de-Haute-Provence)
Paris 760 - Nice 155 - Aix-en-Provence 110 - Sisteron 40

(14) Le Grand Paris

19, blvd. Thiers - 92.31.11.15

M. Ricaud. Open until 9:30 p.m. Closed Sun. dinner & Mon. (off-seas.) & end Dec-early March. Terrace dining. Pets allowed. Garage parking. Cards: V, AE, DC.

Water gurgles under the plane trees that shade the summer terrace of this gracefully aging country house, where Jean-Jacques Ricaud prepares a traditional cuisine made with great respect and technique. The confit of vegetables with coriander is tasty but swimming in too much olive oil; although slightly overcooked, the salmon is of good quality, served with green tagliatelle; the lamb is impeccable, cooked pink and accompanied by fresh vegetables and a reduced sauce with Châteauneuf vinegar; the pastries are predictable, though well made; and the cellar is stocked with good wines from the Rhône and Provence. The atmosphere may be bustling, but the service by waitresses in regional dress is quite good.

A la carte: 350F. Menus: 145F, 180F, 200F, 290F.

Le Grand Paris

(See restaurant above)

Open year-round. 5 stes 500-600F. 27 rms 240-400F.

Although showing some signs of age, this provincial hotel offers modern comfort and is well maintained. The reception is a bit condescending.

Dijon

21000 Dijon - (Côte-d'Or)
Paris 310 - Reims 283 - Auxerre 146 - Lyon 192

Note: The numbers following the telephone number in each review pinpoint the establishment's exact location on the accompanying map.

Sights. Le Musée des Beaux-Arts, one of the richest in the provinces, and the new Musée de la Vie Bourguignonne (Museum of Burgundian Life); the crypt of the Cathédral St-Bénigne and the Musée Archéologique (in the old Abbaye St-Bénigne); the old Palace of the dukes of Burgundy; the Eglise Notre-Dame and the composite-style facade of the Eglise St-Michel; the Charterhouse of Champmol (in the gardens of the psychiatric hospital, with sculptures by Claus Sluter); the streets of Old Dijon (medieval and eighteenth-century structures); the marketplace (Tuesday, Friday and Saturday).

Eating on the Run. L'Assiette en Fête, 50, rue Chabot-Charny (formerly Petit Zinc); Café des Abattoirs, 34, rue Ernest-Petit (the excellent meat makes up for the decor); Les Congrès, 16, ave. Raymond-Poincaré (the best grill, though unfortunately out-of-the-way); Dijon-Ville, 77, rue Berbisey (quick meals downstairs, couscous upstairs); La Table Marocaine, 4, pl. Jacques-Prévert (splendid couscous, friendly); Le

Théland, 2, rue Monge (elegant, specializing in smoked fish); Le Vietnam, 57, rue de Tivoli (authentic food, restrained decor).

Bars & Cafés. Le Bistrot, 21, rue d'Ahuy (for beer worshipers); Le Brighton, 33, rue August-Comte (very popular, with a pleasant terrace); Bar de l'Hôtel de la Cloche, 14, pl. Darcy (peaceful, pretty, looks out on a garden); La Concorde, 2, pl. Darcy (nighttime brasserie); La Jamaïque, 14, pl. de la République (cocktails, young clientele, tropical decor); Messire Bar, 3, rue Jules-Mercier (the smallest, but the most crowded); Le Picadilly, pl. Jean-Macé (young and friendly, with video games); Bar de la Porte Guillaume, pl. Darcy (pleasant downstairs wine bar).

Nightlife. Bahia Brazil, 39, rue des Godrans (quiet, pleasant piano bar); Le Chic, 107, rue d'Ahuy (lives up to its name with much effort to create a lively place); Le Malibu, rte. de Troyes (for young people, relaxed atmosphere); Le New-Ambassy, 61, rue de la Liberté (skillfully refurbished to suit current tastes).

Shops. *Bakeries:* Faivret, 10, rue Charrue; La Gerbe d'Or, 12, rue François-Rude; Au Pain d'Autrefois, 47, rue du Bourg. *Butchers, charcuteries:* Durdyn, 5, rue de Champmaillot (always meticulous); La Fine Fourchette, 27, rue d'-Auxonne; Passemard, 47, ave. Maréchal-Lyautey; Pommey, 31, pl. du 1er-Mai. *Pastries, confections:* Carbillet, 84, rue de la Préfecture (chocolates, Bavarian cream); Pâtisserie Darcy, 25, pl. Darcy; Jeannenez, 51, rue du Bourg. *Gourmet foods:* Chenevoy, 1, pl. Grangier (it has everything); Les Saveurs Gasconnes, 75, rue Vannerie (specialties of the southwest). *Cheese:* Perrot, 28, rue Musette; Porcheret, 14, rue Bannelier. *Fruit and vegetables:* Collard, 10, rue Odebert (good selection); Tutti-Fruti, 14, rue François-Rude. *Wine:* La Cave aux Vins, 3, rue Jeannin (tasting, classes); L'Harmonie du Vin, 63, rue Monge (wise selection).

Altea

See Château Bourgogne restaurant.

Jean-Pierre Billoux

18

14, pl. Darcy
80.30.11.00, 80.30.12.3 / B3-4

M. Billoux. Open until 9:30 p.m. Closed Sun. dinner, Mon. & early Feb.-early March. Air cond. Garden dining. Pets allowed. Parking. Telex 350498. Cards: V, AE, DC.

Firmly established and well accepted by the people of Dijon, Billoux has no regrets about having left Digoin and his business-travelers' hotel. The magnificent Hôtel de la Cloche has been superbly restored, and Billoux occupies the best part of it. Here his talent is growing, and never has his cooking been so delicate and perfectly executed. He has, in fact, every reason to be happy in this enormous space that must be the envy of many chefs. How many square feet are in his realm? We didn't count them, but be prepared for a long walk if you want to tour the place in its entirety. It begins with an indoor country garden that borders on a large patio, where tables are set up, weather permitting. Just behind it is the bar, a comfortable place for a drink before dinner or a Cognac at the end of the evening. Then comes a large dining room, well lit and quite elegant, with festive chintz curtains and colorful engravings, where lunch is served. Finally, you enter the vaulted dining room, with walls of Burgundy's golden stone, where you'll enjoy a long dinner by candlelight. And if you open the doors to the kitchen, once again you'll be struck by the space, as well as the technical perfection. The tour complete, Marie-Françoise Billoux, whose warmth and humor make her one of the most charming hostesses in France, leads you to your table.

Our last meal started with a delicious slice of fresh duck foie gras au naturel, a bit of jambon persillé (tender ham dotted with bits of fat) made even more delectable by a touch of calves' feet, a simple but exquisite consommé of fresh peas, followed by a turnip broth with rabbit and tarragon. Then came a split baby pigeon, cooked to rosy perfection in the lightest wine sauce with just a touch of cream and surrounded by marvelous vegetable fritots (marinated and deep-fried carrots, baby peas, white turnips and greens). Finally, after perfectly ripened cheeses, came a spectacular dessert cart and, thank God, there wasn't a single mousse on it. But it did have a Saint-Honoré (a flaky, creamy confection named for the patron saint of bakers and pastry chefs) that was simply to die for. A weak point was the vanilla ice cream, which bordered on the banal.

So went the meal. Yours could just as easily be a stew of frogs' legs served with succulent little watercress crêpes, baked salmon on a bed of seaweed in a warm lobster sauce, a tureen of herbed farm chicken or Bresse duckling in an amazing Marsala sauce or an original pintade (guinea fowl, which is so much better than pheasant!) with duck liver and noodles. And be sure to take the time to stroll through the vineyards of Burgundy, guided by the excellent sommelier, Patrice Gillard, or Marie-Françoise, who also knows her way around. All the best Côte-de-Beaune and Côte-de-Nuits are on the list, but you can also linger a bit over a white Saint-Romain, a red Monthélie or even a modest but noble ordinary Burgundy.

A la carte: 450F. Menus: 220F (weekday lunch only, wine incl.), 380F.

Hôtel de la Cloche

(See restaurant above)

Open year-round. 4 stes 1,000F. 76 rms 460-520F. TV. Air cond. Pets allowed.

Entirely renovated, the Hôtel de la Cloche now has parquet floors, handsome false marble, Empire furniture and small but pleasantly modern rooms, as well as an indoor garden.

Breuil

1, rue de la Chouette
80.30.18.10 / C3-14

M. Breuil. Open until 10 p.m. Closed Mon. dinner & Tues. Pets allowed. Cards: V, AE, DC, MC.

The food here is serious but not boring, wise but not without personal touches. Christian Breuil is a most confident cook, able to achieve a discreet blend of the regional and the classic. His ingredients are consistently good, and his execution is professional and precise. Not long ago we tried fresh frogs' legs, firm and delicate and served with a light mustard sauce; a lobster tail and claws; a filet of bass perfectly cooked and served in a

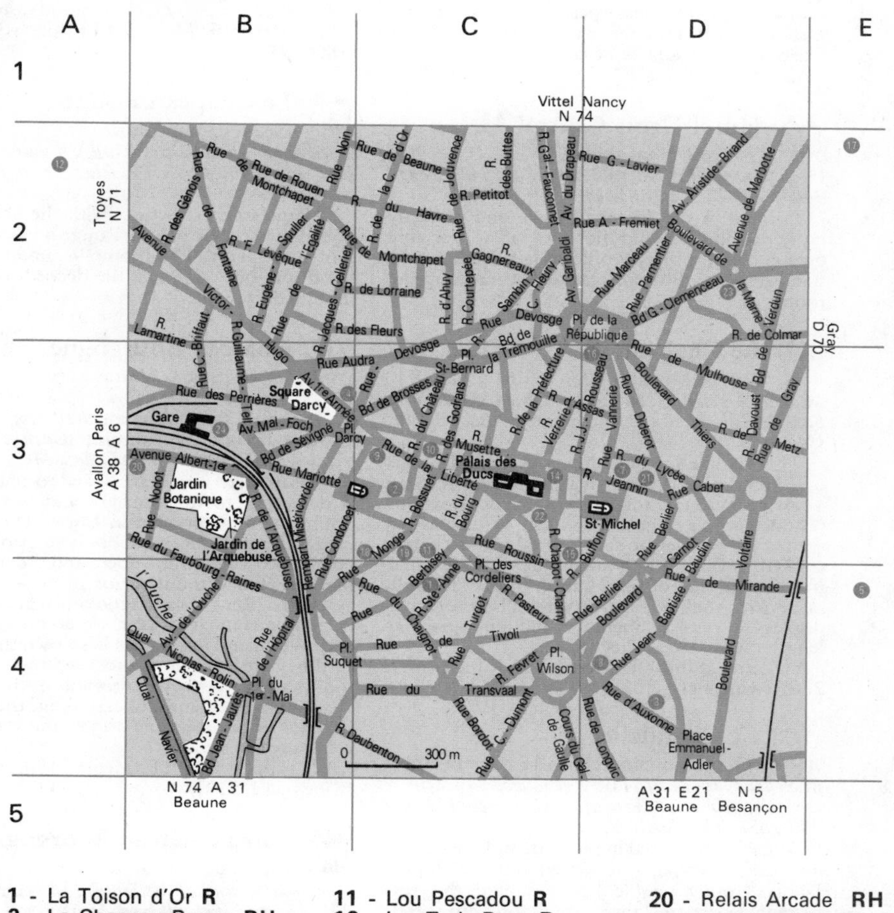

1 - La Toison d'Or **R**
2 - Le Chapeau Rouge **RH**
3 - Le Petit Vatel **R**
4 - Jean-Pierre Billoux (Hôtel de la Cloche) **RH**
5 - Les Relais Bleus **H**
7 - La Fringale **R**
8 - Restaurant Thibert **R**
9 - La Porte Guillaume **R**
10 - Central Grill Rôtisserie (Hôtel Urbis Central) **RH**
11 - Lou Pescadou **R**
12 - Les Trois Ducs **R** et Castel Burgond **H**
14 - Breuil **R**
15 - Le Rallye **R**
16 - Le Square République **R**
17 - Grésill-Hôtel **H**
18 - Le Chabrot **R**
19 - Restaurant Saint-Jean **R**
20 - Relais Arcade **RH**
21 - Le Chandelier **R**
22 - Pré aux Clercs et Trois Faisans **R**
23 - Château Bourgogne (Altea Château Bourgogne) **RH**
24 - Relais de la Gare **R**

reduction of red wine; a saddle of young rabbit stuffed with its liver and herbs; and ultra-classic desserts, like a hot apple tart. The wine cellar is respectable, and the Louis XV decor is a little cluttered but has style.

A la carte: 300F. Menus: 130F, 198F, 300F.

Castel Burgond

3, rte. de Troyes, Daix (2 km NW on N 71), 21121 Fontaine-les-Dijon
80.56.59.72 / A2-12

Open year-round. 38 rms 190-220F. TV. Pets allowed. Parking. Telex 350490. Cards: V, AE, DC.

This large geometric building located in the hills of Dijon is spacious, light and equipped with functional furniture. Restaurant.

(14) Central Grill Rôtisserie

3, pl. Grangier - 80.30.44.00 / C3-10

Mme. Belin & M. Jacquier. Open until midnight. Closed Sun. Air cond. Pets allowed. Telex 350606. Cards: V, AE, DC, MC.

Last year's redecorating, which included the installation of new, well-placed lighting (no windows), perfectly suited the style of this restaurant: efficient service provided by a mature personnel and copious dishes prepared without pretension. In addition to the uncomplicated grilled items are

a duck pie (slightly heavy pastry), a gratin of lotte with fresh pasta (the sauce could be lighter) and fine pastries. Modest wine cellar.
A la carte: 280-300F.

Hôtel Urbis Central

(See restaurant above)
Open year-round. 90 rms 230-280F. Half-board 340-420F. TV. Pets allowed.

Located in the center of town and perfectly modernized, this old hotel is of appreciably greater comfort than its official classification (two stars) suggests. But breakfast is not served in the rooms.

14 Le Chabrot

36, rue Monge - 80.30.69.61 / C3-18
M. Bouy. Open until 10:30 p.m. Closed Mon. lunch, Sun. & July 15-Aug. 16. Air cond. Pets allowed. Cards: V.

This humble-looking little fish establishment is being redecorated, which is all it needs to become a very good restaurant. The young chef treats his products with a commendable lack of fussiness, as seen in his Norwegian salad (diced salmon barely cooked, with pan-fried grapefruit segments) and his steamed filet of scorpionfish in a remarkable sauce. From behind his great mustache, the owner displays a rural exuberance and discourses at length on his wine collection.
A la carte: 280-300F. Menus: 59F (lunch only), 250F (wine incl.), 85F.

11/20 Le Chandelier

65, rue Jeannin - 80.66.15.82 / D3-21
M. Fedel. Open until 11:30 p.m. Closed Sun. dinner & Mon. Air cond. Pets allowed. Hotel: 128 rms 230-265F. TV. Cards: V.

The wine is offered in pitchers, and the hearty, inexpensive cooking is served until all hours. Dijon's young people have adopted this restaurant, where they dine on salmon with sorrel, veal kidney à la dijonnaise and duckling with a black-currant sauce. Le Chandelier's desserts, however, are not its strong suit.
A la carte: 180F. Menus: 60F (weekdays only), 70F, 86F.

16 Le Chapeau Rouge

5, rue Michelet - 80.30.28.10 / C3-2
M. Lagrange. Open daily until 9:45 p.m. No pets. Telex 350535. Cards: V, AE, DC.

After a couple of worrisome years, Dijon has rediscovered its classic, serious restaurant. Although even more classic and serious than ever, the cuisine now focuses on regional tradition, with clear, simple names. This all came to be with the arrival of Bernard Noël, the amazing saucier and cook who was number two at La Tour d'-Argent in Paris and then head chef at the same restaurant in Tokyo. Already the cuisine can be considered nearly great, as demonstrated by the exquisite-tasting frogs'-legs feuilleté, the poached fowl with tarragon, accompanied by pommes soufflés (the best anywhere) and perfect pastries, sorbets and hot soufflés. The new, young wine steward makes a great effort to be up to par with the substantial cellar. And the decor in this old stone house is relaxing and in good taste.
A la carte: 350F. Menus: 200F (lunch only, wine incl.), 170F.

Le Chapeau Rouge

(See restaurant above)
Open year-round. 2 stes 930F. 29 rms 380-520F. Half-board 400-465F. TV. Air cond. in 7 rms. Pets allowed.

A large stone structure, with the abbey's old stables intact, Le Chapeau Rouge is located in the center of Dijon. The rooms—soundproofed in the front—are calm, and the decor is charming, though disjointed.

14 Château Bourgogne

22, blvd. de la Marne
80.72.31.13 / D2-23
M. Bochaton. Open daily until 10 p.m. Air cond. Garden dining. Pets allowed. Garage parking. Telex 350203. Cards: V, AE, DC, MC.

This modern restaurant linked to a hotel chain is dedicated to functionality and is without a doubt the most popular in Dijon. The clientele ranges from families to business people, and, taking into account the prices and the number of meals served without major mishaps, everyone agrees that René Villard's cooking is generous and of good quality. This year, we do not. Evidently enthusiasm and inspiration has flown the kitchen of this giant operation and with them our two toques of last year. The dressing of the avocado salad was sugary and disheartening, the pathetic sole was of questionable origin, and the desserts were way too sweet.
A la carte: 280-300F. Menus: 150F and 165F (wine incl.), 210F.

Altea Château Bourgogne

(See restaurant above)
Open year-round. 7 stes 505F. 116 rms 340-440F. TV. Air cond. Pets allowed. Heated pool.

This excellent American-style hotel is in the new, rather dreary quarter of the Palais de la Foire, ten minutes from downtown. The rooms are modern, large and well air conditioned.

10/20 La Fringale

53, rue Jeannin - 80.67.69.37 / D3-7
Open until 11:30 p.m. Closed Sat. lunch, Sun. & Aug. 1-15. Air cond. Pets allowed. Cards: V.

This bright, simple, small bistro is frequented by the youth of Dijon, who come for its affordable prices and decent cuisine: beefsteak with shallots and breast of duck with cèpes.
A la carte: 200F. Menus: 55F (lunch only), 100F.

Grésill-Hôtel

16, ave. Raymond-Poincaré
80.71.10.56 / E2-17
Closed Aug. 16-25. & Dec. 26-Jan. 2. 47 rms 210-265F. TV. Parking. Telex 350549. Cards: V, AE, DC, MC.

This new, comfortable hotel is convenient, functional and well soundproofed. Bar/pub and restaurant.

11/20 **Lou Pescadou**

30, rue Berbisey - 80.30.34.71 / C3-11
Mme. Robadey. Open until 11 p.m. Closed Mon. lunch. Air cond. Pets allowed. Cards: V, AE, DC, MC.

In a congenial nautical decor, the energetic owner efficiently takes care of both the reception and the cooking. There is an ample selection (unique in Dijon) of fresh fish and shellfish: Nordic salad, poached turbot in beurre blanc and filet of sole with fresh noodles. The sauces, however, could clearly stand refining, and the tarte tatin could be prepared with a lighter touch.

A la carte: 300F.

12/20 **Le Petit Vatel**

73, rue d'Auxonne - 80.65.80.64 / D4-3
Closed Sat. lunch & Sun., 1 week in Feb. & 3 weeks in Aug. Air cond. Pets allowed. Cards: V.

A friendly, modestly furnished establishment, Le Petit Vatel features low prices and a young clientele. The cooking is simple and uses good ingredients: mussel salad with saffron, émincé of rabbit that is nicely livened up with onions. Generous desserts.

A la carte: 200F. Menus: 82F, 102F.

12/20 **La Porte Guillaume**

(Hôtel du Nord)
Pl. Darcy - 80.30.58.58 / C3-9
M. Frachot. Open until 10:45 p.m. Closed Dec. 23-Jan. 9. Pets allowed. Hotel: 2 stes 350-560F; 27 rms 150-300F. Telex 351554. Cards: V, AE, DC, MC.

There is a pleasant wine bar in the cellar and a spacious rustic-bourgeois decor under wooden beams on the main floor. The fixed-price menus are excellent: for 110 francs, you're entitled to tripe with rosé de Marsannnay, poached salmon vigneronne, cheeses and pear dijonnaise. The wine cellar is well selected and the service attentive.

A la carte: 250F. Menus: 90F, 110F, 180F.

12/20 **Pré aux Clercs et Trois Faisans**

13, pl. de la Libération
80.67.11.33 / C3-22
M. Fillion. Open until 11 p.m. Closed Sun dinner. Pets allowed. Telex 350394. Cards: V, AE, DC, MC.

This historic building, with its impressive beams and commanding exposed-stone walls, is reputedly the place where the canon Kir created his famous apéritif. A young local, M. Fillion, recently took over the restaurant, keeping its venerable staff in place but making the atmosphere more relaxed. He promised to introduce a more contemporary cuisine, but so far his trial-and-error attempts primarily have produced errors: dull terrine of smoked eel, lackluster filet of plaice (member of the flounder family) and an unsuccessful salmis of duckling. The subtle ragoût of rock lobster and the good desserts do not alone merit keeping the toque. The sommelier, a veritable fountain of knowledge, will be more than pleased to reveal the mysteries of his magnificent cellar.

A la carte: 280F. Menus: 95F to 260F.

Le Rallye

39, rue Chabot-Charny
80.67.11.55 / C3-15
M. Roncin. Open until 9:30 p.m. Closed Sun., holidays, mid- Feb.-early March & mid-July-early Aug. Pets allowed. Cards: V, AE, DC.

After becoming known as the pioneer of modern cuisine, this dependable Dijon restaurant has lost some of its preeminence. But it hasn't lost its direction, and the prices are better than ever. One after another, several young chefs-in-training have come to master their skills under the professional hand of François Minot. But this hasn't helped alleviate the uncertainties that the Rallye had hoped to be free of by now. The latest young chef to appear had not yet taken over the reins when we went to press, so we are unable to give a rating. The wine list is still in fine shape, and the restful, pretty decor is as always well maintained.

A la carte: 250F.

Relais Arcade

15, ave. Albert-1er - 80.43.01.12 / B3-20
Open year-round. 128 rms 195-225F. Half-board 185-261F. TV. Pets allowed. Parking. Telex 350315. Cards: V.

Currently undergoing renovation, the friendly Relais Arcade, near the train station, has well-conceived, quiet rooms. Restaurant.

Les Relais Bleus

Hameau de Mirande
80.66.32.40 / E4-5
Open year-round. 45 rms 235F. Half-board 289F. TV. Pets allowed. Parking. Telex 351653. Cards: V.

This brand-new hotel located along a strategic street features bright, modern rooms. Restaurant.

10/20 **Relais de la Gare**

Cours de la Gare - 80.41.40.35 / B3-24
M. Baudy. Open daily until 10 p.m. Parking. Cards: V, DC.

A cavernous room done up in leatherette and plastic (remember the 50s?) is the scene of a copious buffet spread, very popular at lunchtime. A quick and practical way for travelers to stoke up before they set off.

A la carte: 150F. Menu: 110F (weekends and hols.).

11/20 **Restaurant Saint-Jean**

13, rue Monge - 80.30.06.64 / C3-19
M. Zingerlé. Open until 2 a.m. Closed Sat. lunch & Aug. 15- Sept. 1. Pets allowed. Cards: V, AE, DC.

The new owner of this remarkable, small, late-night restaurant is a solid professional who prepares a cautious cuisine, less original and light than his predecessor's but still good for the price: escargots fricassée, lotte bourride and coq au vin. The wines, from local vineyards, are quite nice.

A la carte: 180-200F. Menus: 75F, 96F.

Restaurant Thibert

(17)
10, pl. Wilson
80.67.74.64 / D4-8

M. Thibert. Open until 9:45 p.m. Closed Mon. lunch, Sun. & 2 weeks in Aug. Air cond. Pets allowed. Cards: V, AE.

Although place Wilson won't knock you off your feet with its beauty, it did gain a touch of class in 1987 with the addition of Restaurant Thibert. Jean-Paul Thibert surprised Dijon by slipping a 1930s-style restaurant into the ground floor of a building of no particular character. While not of museum quality, the place still displays a certain elegance, albeit a rather cold one. Upon entering, guests are immediately enraptured by the warm smile of the slender Mme. Thibert, who appears timid until she delves into the wine list and comes up with a great Burgundy that would make a monastery of Benedictines tremble with pleasure.

Behind his ready smile, Jean-Paul Thibert hides a serious philosophy regarding the role of tradition in cuisine: It must be constantly evolving—but it must never be hurried along. That was the lesson he learned from Georges Blanc, who taught this young man (now in his early 30s) to become a remarkable technician. Like the great restaurateur from Vonnas, he has no desire to lose himself in audacious inventions. His credo: to create exquisite meals using the best ingredients. There are barely twenty first courses and main dishes on his menu, but it is constantly changing and always piques the curiosity. His dishes include baby cabbage stuffed with escargots; an exquisite smoked gâteau of larded pork with zucchini; scampi with peas and Burgundy truffles; and turbot with green olives in a light cream sauce, served with baby onions and a green salad, an unexpected combination but a delightful harmony of flavors. Finally—before the creamy goat cheeses and delicious (and original) desserts, like the dark and white chocolates filled with orange or passion-fruit sorbets—a dish is served that's a miracle of purity: a crisp saddle of lamb roasted with onions and sliced potatoes covered with sheep cheese. The prices are truly virtuous, with most of the dishes ranging from 48 to 98 francs.

Soon an extremely comfortable, 27-room hotel (Le Wilson, 80.66.82.50), which will share a common courtyard with the restaurant, will be opening.

A la carte: 320F. Menus: 155F (weekday lunch only, wine incl.), 95F (except Sat. dinner) and 150F to 270F.

Le Square République

(13)
10-12, pl. de la République
80.74.39.55 / D3-16

MM. Novack & Thibaut. Open until 11 p.m. Closed Sat. lunch, Sun., holidays, Feb. school vacation, Aug. 15-31 & Dec. 24-Jan. 2. Garden dining. Pets allowed. Cards: V, DC.

Previously a chef at the former Le Cygne in Dijon (15/20), Serge Thibaut and his partner, a maître d' at the same place, recently opened this fresh, modern bistro decorated in pink and white tones. Its success has been both prompt and well deserved (to which the exceptional small fixed-price menu has contributed greatly; the civil servants from the nearby prefecture are raving about it). Both the reception and the service are charming and relaxed, the wines are well selected and reasonable, and the cuisine bodes well for the future (though the appetizers and desserts could stand improvement)—delicious ragoût of escargots with garlic cream, fish pot-au-feu with basil and well-prepared calves' liver with reinette apples. But all of this still needs some fine tuning, which we hope the toque will encourage.

A la carte: 230F. Menus: 80F, 150F, 200F.

La Toison d'Or

(15)
18, rue Ste-Anne - 80.30.73.52 / C4-1

M. Barboso. Open until 9:30 p.m. Closed Sat. lunch, Sun., holidays, Feb. school vacation & July 30-Aug. 22. Pets allowed. Parking. Telex 351681. Cards: V, AE, DC, MC.

These sixteenth-century buildings clustered around a Gothic courtyard have been luxuriously restored and reflect the owner's passion for local history and wine. There are several formal banquet rooms and, downstairs, an interesting wine museum. A profusion of decorative effects shows off the beautiful old stone structure. The two Louis XIII dining rooms, filled with opulent-looking furnishings, paintings and tapestries, are infused with a folkloric yet solemn atmosphere. Nevertheless, La Toison d'Or has known great success due to its reasonable prices and the constant quality of its cuisine, which is classic but not tiresome. You can have a perfect dinner of coquilles St-Jacques, pan-fried and served on a bed of vinaigrette gently perfumed with ginger; filet de boeuf à la moelle (marrow) served with a gratin dauphinois; and nougat glazed with acacia honey. You'll find a nice selection of young wines at good prices, reception that lacks polish, and wine service that is more efficient than refined.

A la carte: 300F and up. Menus: 120F, 200F.

IN NEARBY **Daix**
(2 km NW on N 71)
21121 Fontaine-les-Dijon - (Côte-d'Or)

Les Trois Ducs

(15)
5, rte. de Troyes - 80.56.59.75 / A2-12

M. Piganiol. Open until 10:15 p.m. Closed Sun. dinner & Mon. Terrace dining. Pets allowed. Cards: V.

The second toque for the cuisine of young Emmanuel Joinville has been awarded with a gentle warning: His passion for researching combinations that are more and more subtle sometimes leads to an impasse of weak or confused flavors. But we will praise to the skies the spirit of research, the generous creativity and the great technique of Joinville, who was trained at the best schools (Lorrain, Troisgros, Le Duc). His mango-and-avocado terrine is a success, sharpened by an admirable vinaigrette; his salmon with asparagus tips is ravishing to the eyes, if a bit dull on the palate; and his desserts, such as the gratin d'oranges à la liqueur, are good but not otherworldly. Although the dining room in this modern establishment on the heights of Dijon is comfortable and spacious, it's too chilly—we would prefer they use the cozier room in back instead. The eclectic wine cellar boasts two reasonably priced, superb Condrieu whites, a rarity in Burgundy. The young waiters are relaxed and the fixed-price menus are inviting.

A la carte: 300-350F. Menus: 130F (weekday lunch only), 140F, 185F, 265F.

IN NEARBY **Marsannay-la-Côte**
(7 km SW on D 122)
21160 Marsannay-la-Côte - (Côte-d'Or)

---

16 Les Gourmets

8, rue du Puite-de-Têt - 80.52.16.32, 80.51.91.31

M. Perreaut. Open until 9:30 p.m. Closed Sun. dinner, Mon. & Jan. 1-Feb. 2. Garden dining. Pets allowed. Cards: V, AE, DC.

The modern dining room in this provincial restaurant may be on the garish side, but it's comfortable and has attractive contemporary paintings. And in the summertime, you can flee the confines of the rooms to dine in the shade of a plum tree on the terrace outside. Nicole Perreaut's service is skillful and friendly, and Joël Perreaut is masterful in the kitchen, with a great talent for sauces. He isn't far from attaining true perfection—if he would just shorten his cooking times and let his imagination soar, his cuisine could be worthy of God's own table. In the meantime, his saddle of rabbit is disappointing and his salade gourmande too quickly made. But everything else is elegant and well prepared, whether it be the asparagus with marrow, the coquilles St-Jacques with truffles and lobster roe, the lightly breaded sea bream filet with capers or the perfect sweetbreads in Sauternes, even the desserts (except for the too-sweet galette au chocolat). The splendid cellar is being expanded to include more affordable Burgundies and Marsannays.

A la carte: 350F. Menus: 135F (lunch only), 150F, 198F, 280F, 400F.

IN NEARBY **Val-Suzon**
(16 km NW on N 71)
21121 Fontaine-lès-Dijon - (Côte-d'Or)

---

15 Hostellerie du Val-Suzon

N 71 - 80.35.60.15

M. Perreau. Open until 9:30 p.m. Closed Wed. (off-seas.), Thurs. lunch (except holidays) & Jan. 1-Feb. 10. Garden dining. No pets. Parking. Cards: V, MC.

For years the Perreaus have been courting this second toque for their little inn. This time, it would have been unjust if we hadn't rewarded them for their hard work, professionalism and polished technique. We hope these laurels will encourage Yves Perreau, an excellent chef, to refine further his sauces and define his flavors, and perhaps to have more confidence in the excellent products he uses, allowing them to speak for themselves. The morel ravioli in foie-gras sauce is quite flavorful, but the cream sauce is a little too rich; the red mullet in red wine with turnips, zucchini and chervil is impeccable; the suprême de pigeon with mild garlic is admirable but slightly overcooked; and the millefeuilles and chocolate desserts are excellent. Everything is served in a newly designed room done in greens and pinks, and you dine looking out on the winter garden of the valley below. Good wine collection and gracious service.

A la carte: 400F. Menus: 130F (weekdays only), 190F, 290F.

Hostellerie du Val-Suzon

(See restaurant above)

Closed Wed. (except holidays in seas.) & Jan. 1-Feb. 10. 17 rms 200-320F. Half-board 350-480F oblig. in seas.

Both the house and the chalet offer rustic-style comfort, including modern plumbing, views of the trees and reasonable prices. By the time you read this, the proprietors hope to have a new swimming pool open for business.

Dinan

22100 Dinan - (Côtes-du-Nord)
Paris 370 - Lorient 150 - St-Brieuc 59 - St-Malo 29

---

13 Avaugour

1, pl. Du Guesclin - 96.39.07.49

M. Quinton. Open until 9:30 p.m. Closed Mon. (off-seas.) & Feb. Telex 950415.

For some time now, alarming rumors have warned us of Georges Quinton's decline. Sadly, they turned out to be only too well founded—our last visits to this lovely provincial house, endowed with a charming rear garden, left us with the impression of a stiff, unenthusiastic and at times erratic cuisine. Certainly, Quinton came through with a delicious langoustine-and-scallop salad with foie gras, an honest gratin de canard with baby vegetables and a well-executed hot apple tart. But with those dishes, we suffered through an assortment of fish that was covered in an unappetizing coating and then overcooked; coquilles St-Jacques with limp morels and a boring sauce; and a pear feuilleté drowning in alcohol. We're being kind by giving Avaugour a toque, and we hope this warning will be heard.

A la carte: 280F. Menus: 65F (weekday lunch only), 100F, 150F.

Avaugour

(See restaurant above)

Open year-round. 27 rms 250-350F. Half-board 300-350F oblig. in seas. Pets allowed.

Gisèle Quinton devotes all of her time and kindness to this big, pretty place. The rooms are extremely comfortable, and some have views of the garden and the ramparts.

16 La Caravelle

14, pl. Duclos - 96.39.00.11

M. Marmion. Open until 9:30 p.m. Closed Wed., Feb. school vacation & Oct. 15-Nov. 6. Pets allowed. Cards: AE, DC.

As you enter this rustic dining room, with its too-bright lighting and questionable orange-caramel tones, having passed through an austere facade and an entrance that resembles a snack bar, your first thought may be that the decor matches the budget price of the fixed menu. Once seated, however, you'll notice that the tableware is pretty, fresh flowers fill the room, the service is cheerfully attentive, and the presentation of the inexpensive menu is so enchanting that you'll think you've chanced upon the land of plenty. This fixed-price menu includes six oysters or a feuilleté of red mullet, a good slice of fresh Scottish salmon with cabbage, noisettes d'agneau (boned lamb chops) with tiny potatoes and a salad, several cheeses and a pastry. This incredible menu, one of the best in all of France, is the pride of Jean-Claude Marmion.

Advancing deeper into this inventive cuisine repertoire, not long ago we had an impromptu meal that was a joy from the first bite to the last: a thick escalope of foie gras on a bed of chanterelles, bursting with freshness; crayfish with peas and a subtle sauce of tarragon, orange zest and saffron; superb sweetbreads, dotted with tiny smoked lardons in a foie gras sauce; and a hot sauté of strawberries and figs in Sauternes with vanilla ice cream. Without hesitation, we're giving La Caravelle another point, but we hope, once again, that the Marmions will abandon their unfortunate decor. And for such excellent food, the wine cellar isn't quite up to par.

A la carte: 350-400F. Menu: 99F (weekday lunch only), 160F (weekdays only).

Dinard

35800 Dinard - (Ille-et-Vilaine)
Paris 370 - Rennes 72 - Diana 22 - St-Brieuc 67

Altaïr

18, blvd. Féart - 99.46.13.58

Mme. Leménager. Open daily until 9 p.m. Garden dining. Pets allowed. Hotel: 21 rms 230-290F; half-board 210-270F. Cards: V, AE, DC, MC.

One reader was unhappy with the reception, another with the service (having no ice bucket, the waiter suggested he put ice cubes in the wine!), a third with the kitchen (sandy coquilles St-Jacques), and a fourth with the rooms ("neglected"). Poor Patrick Leménager really took a bashing this year. So we set out for his restaurant, wearing dark glasses and phony beards, prepared for the worst. Yet, we discovered a charming and relaxed Mme. Leménager, friendly service and a cuisine that had not declined in the least—aside from a few seasoning errors and the unpalatable chocolates that were served with the coffee. The salade au foie gras was banal but well made; the bass steamed with seaweed, delicious; and the raspberry mousse, exquisite. So must we burn down this nice place?

A la carte: 230-250F. Menus: 65F to 250F.

Reine Hortense

19, rue de la Malouine - 99.46.54.31

Closed Nov. 15-March 20. 2 stes 1,200-1,400F. 10 rms 750-920F. TV. Pets allowed. Parking. Telex 740802. Cards: V, AE, DC.

Some souvenirs of Queen Hortense—or of her reign—and some truly picturesque furnishings are among this little hotel's distinctions. It also boasts a gorgeous salon with a Versailles-style parquet and the "Reine Hortense" room, which includes a silver bathtub. No restaurant.

Divonne-les-Bains

01220 Divonne-les-Bains - (Ain)
Paris 502 - Geneva 19 - Nyon 13 - Gex 9 - Bourg 120

Le Vendôme

Rte. de Gex - 50.20.00.32

M. Martin. Open until 9:30 p.m. Closed early Jan.-March 15. Terrace dining. Pets allowed. Parking. Telex 309033. Cards: V.

Patrons in the noble dining room of the gracious nineteenth-century Château de Divonne look out on the woods of the Gex countryside and its backdrop, Mont Blanc. Just outside is the rolling green of the Divonne golf course and the château grounds. Luxury and sensual delights, perfection and refinement... nothing less would suit the rich and difficult clientele from Switzerland and Germany who journey here year-round to view this latest acquisition of that lavish collector of châteaux, René Traversac (he owns Artigny, Esclimont and Isembourg, to name a few). But it is the food that makes this mansion one of the best in the region—or, at least, one with the most inventive, personal cuisine to be found in a solemn, luxury-hotel atmosphere. Guy Martin, the 30-year-old chef who was formerly with Troisgros and Robuchon, cooks meals that are expensive but well worth the price: foie gras and cabbage ravioli with truffle juice; salad with escargots, artichokes and beans; lake fish meunière that is simple and perfect; gratin of fresh figs with an aged-Port jelly; and feuilleté de chocolat with an almond mousse and pistachio cream. The only fault of this cuisine is that the sauces can be too rich and the pastries too sweet. The wines, particularly those from the Savoie, are excellent, and the service is delightful.

A la carte: 400-500F. Menus: 230F (weekday lunch only, wine incl.), 220F, 295F, 380F.

Château de Divonne

(See restaurant above)

Closed early Jan.-mid-March. 5 stes 995-1,585F. 23 rms 440-1,150F. Half-board 795-1,850F. TV. Pets allowed. Tennis.

Surrounded by natural beauty—Lake Léman (Lake Geneva), Mont Blanc, 50 acres of grounds—and an eighteen-hole golf course, this great château is one of the most luxurious spots in the region. Though renovated from top to bottom, its superb rooms still have the spaciousness of yesteryear—and, like yesteryear, it charms its guests with musical evenings. Relais et Châteaux.

Les Grands Hôtels

50.20.06.63

Open year-round. 6 stes 1,200-1,500F. 141 rms 540-910F. Half-board 507-710F. TV. Pets allowed. Heated pool. Tennis. Golf. Parking. Telex 385716. Cards: V, AE, DC, MC.

Here are three luxurious hotels whose rooms all face either the grounds and the Jura mountains or Lake Geneva and the Alps. Facilities include a cinema, a nightclub and a casino. Weekend and fitness packages are available, not to mention three restaurants.

Dol-de-Bretagne

35120 Dol-de-Bretagne - (Ille-et-Vilaine)
Paris 373 - St-Malo 24 - Rennes 54 - Dinan 26

(13) Les Roches Douves

80, rte. de Dinan - 99.48.10.40

M. Dufeil. Open until 10 p.m. Closed Sun. dinner & Mon. (except holidays). Pets allowed. Cards: V, AE, DC.

Diners will find all the seductions of a classic Breton house from the last century, carved in solid granite, decorated with pleasant furnishings and beams and heated in winter by a large, fourteenth-century fireplace that blazes almost as much as the hair of the gracious Catherine Dufeil. Her husband, Jean-François, who apprenticed in Paris, prepares a cuisine of fresh seasonal herbs and vegetables and overall fine ingredients. His dishes are imaginative and without complication: glazed asparagus with creamed peas, filet of bass steamed with basil, saddle of rabbit stuffed with thyme, and homemade sorbets. Small but well-thought-out wine cellar.

A la carte: 250F. Menus: 85F, 200F.

Douai

59500 Douai - (Nord)
Paris 203 - Lille 37 - Valenciennes 37 - Arras 27

(14) La Terrasse

8, terrasse St-Pierre - 27.88.70.04

M. Hanique. Open daily until 9:30 p.m. Air cond. Pets allowed. Cards: V.

Don't linger in the small, uncomfortable entryway; go right on in to the triumphant and comfortably rustic dining room. And more than the decor triumphs. Emile Hanique is a professional of tradition, yet he doesn't hesitate to challenge himself. His menu varies, and lately he's been offering a few new items, such as the fried goose liver served on a bed of lentils in ratatouille, the fresh salmon in curry and the émincé of duck with slivers of orange and lemon. The desserts from the cart are numerous and delicate, the wine cellar is rich with 750 different appellations, and the prices are distressingly harsh.

A la carte: 300F and up. Menus: 145F, 270F, 335F.

La Terrasse

(See restaurant above)

Open year-round. 28 rms 180-330F. TV. Pets allowed.

Facing the collegiate church of Saint-Pierre, the stylish rooms are cozy and well equipped, with good soundproofing. Excellent breakfast.

Douains

see Pacy-sur-Eure

Some establishments change their hours and annual closings without warning. It is always wise to call ahead.

Dourlers

59440 Avesnes-sur-Helpe - (Nord)
Paris 213 - Maubeuge 10 - Avesnes 8 - Lille 97

12/20 Auberge du Châtelet

N 2 - 27.61.06.70

Mme. Carlier. Open until 9 p.m. Closed Sun. dinner, Wed., holidays, Jan. 1-10 & Aug. 16-Sept. 15. Pets allowed. Garage parking. Cards: V, AE, DC, MC.

Where have all the enthusiasm and spirit of this great old country house gone? The à la carte menus have disappeared, along with the smiles and the goodwill. Instead of the former Talleyrand spectacle of provincial bounty, we have predictable dishes, such as fish in beurre blanc, lobster with small vegetables and so forth. All very nice, no doubt, but much more high-toned than toque-worthy.

A la carte: 210F and 300F (wine incl.), 95F.

Dreux

28100 Dreux - (Eure-et-Loir)
Paris 84 - Chartres 35 - Evreux 42 - Rouen 97

IN NEARBY **Montreuil**
(4.5 km N on D 928 & D 116)
28500 Vernouillet - (Eure-et-Loir)

(13) Auberge du Gué des Grues

Le Gué des Grues, Vernouillet
37.43.50.25

M. Caillault. Dinner with reserv. only. Closed Mon. dinner & Tues. (except July & Aug.). Terrace dining. Garage parking. Cards: V, AE, DC.

The charming name of this restaurant (Inn of the Cranes' Crossing) promises aquatic and rural pleasures. And the old Ile-de-France inn keeps its promise, situated in the delicate country between the Dreux forest and the Eure river, which flows beneath its windows. The old-fashioned, rustic decor is serene, and the atmosphere conforms perfectly to the good food, which is both classic and pleasantly light. The owner, Robert Caillault, is a professional chef whose experiences in the Far East give his dishes a certain exotic flavor: seasoned fricassée d'escargots; poached egg with Oriental spices; roast turbot with herbs; sweet-and-sour breast of duck.

A la carte: 280-300F. Menus: 150F, 230F.

Dunkerque

59140 Dunkerque - (Nord)
Paris 292 - Amiens 144 - Lille 73 - Calais 40 - Ostende 54

Sights. Le Beffroi (The Belfry, fifteenth century); L'Hôtel de Ville (majestic 1896 building); Le Musée Aquariophile (more than 150 species); Le Musée d'Art Contemporain (in the middle of a park filled with sculptures—600 works dating from 1950 to 1980); Le musée des Beaux Arts (remarkable naval gallery); pl. Jean-Bart and l'-Eglise Saint-Eloi (resting place of Jean Bart); La Tour du Menteur (the Tower of the Liar or "Leughenaer") the town's oldest monument, from the fourteenth century; the port (first French port in the ore trade; boat tours).

Bars & Cafés. Le Douglas (young and fashionable); Le Flore, pl. de la République (friendly and "in"); Le Moderne, 2, rue Nationale (young and preppy); on the seawall: La Fiesta.

Altea

Tour de Reuze, rue Jean-Jaurès
28.59.11.11

Open year-round. 122 rms 270-420F. TV. Telex 110587. Fax 28.63.09.69. Cards: V, AE, DC, MC.

These rooms, located on the twelfth through twentieth floors of the building—providing fantastic view of the harbor, out to sea and the Plaine de Flandres—are comfortable, clean and completely equipped. The service is excellent, and the hotel can accommodate seminars; it boasts fully equipped offices for business meetings. Convenient location in the heart of the city. This is by far the best hotel in the region. A restaurant serving local cuisine will be opening soon.

Borel

6, rue l'Hermitte - 28.66.51.80

Open year-round. 40 rms 240-280F. TV. Pets allowed. Telex 820050. Cards: V, AE, DC, MC.

Some of the rooms in this remarkable little family hotel look out on the port, and all are clean, light and well equipped. No restaurant.

12/20 Le Métropole

28, rue Thiers - 28.66.85.01

M. Bisiaux. Lunch only (& Sat. dinner until 10 p.m.). Closed July 15-Aug. 14. Pets allowed. Cards: V, AE, DC, MC.

In a beautiful old building at the center of town is a restaurant that is opulent yet lacks pretension. The fixed-price menus are generous, including the "grand"—three different wines accompanying a terrine of pâté de foie gras, baked crab turnover, beef ribs, cheeses and pastries.

Menus: 65F and 125F (weekdays only, wine incl.), 150F (wine incl.), 85F, 135F (lunch only).

IN NEARBY **Teteghem**
(3 km SE on D 4)
59229 Teteghem - (Nord)

16 La Meunerie

174, rue des Pierres - 28.26.14.30

M. Delbé. Open until 9:30 p.m. Closed Sun. dinner, Mon. & Dec. 25-Jan. 20. Air cond. Pets allowed. Garage parking. Telex 132253. Cards: V, AE, DC.

Jean-Pierre Delbé came to this old mill more than fifteen years ago, right out of hotel school and hasn't had another teacher since. During the more than ten years that we have been following his progress, we have seen him boost his confidence with the idea of being a self-made—and great—chef, capable of anything and no longer needing to prove himself. And he's not far from being absolutely right, though after our most recent experiences, we still have a few reservations that are keeping our enthusiasm in check. But his luxurious establishment is certainly one of the best restaurants in the north, as well as one of the most pleasant, with its succession of refined, flower-bedecked rooms; its Louis-Philippe chairs; its noble, solid-wood furniture; and its spectacular milling machinery. Mme. Delbé is an attentive hostess who maintains a cheerful, family-like atmosphere that adds to the enjoyment of this extremely precise, seasonal and original cuisine: delicate flan of curried celery and oysters, veal kidneys with an assortment of vegetables and foie gras sauce (which has a powerful flavor that throws the dish a bit off balance), filet of bass roasted in its skin with a Sauternes sauce, zucchini stuffed with langoustines in a sole-and-oyster sauce (a confusing dish, meagerly served), and Chinese tea and bergamot (a bitter pear-shaped orange) ice cream. The well-conceived fixed-price menus allow you to avoid the formidable à la carte prices, which are aggravated by the tempting but pricey wines.

A la carte: 480F. Menus: 170F, 280F, 330F.

La Meunerie

(See restaurant above)

Closed Dec. 25-Jan. 20. 1 ste 1,100F. 8 rms 350F. TV.

Upon entering this house through the restaurant and a gallery of glass, you will find nine luxurious rooms, each one unique and fitted with great attention to comfort and detail.

Durtol

see Clermont-Ferrand

Dury-lès-Amiens

see Amiens

Les Echets

01700 Miribel - (Ain)
Paris 445 - Bourg-en-Bresse 45 - Lyon 16 - Villefranche 26

14 Marguin

Rte. de Strasbourg - 78.91.80.04

M. Marguin. Open until 9:30 p.m. Closed Tues. dinner, Wed., Jan. 2-19 & Aug. 29-Sept. 9. Terrace dining. Pets allowed. Hotel: 9 rms 145-290F. Garage parking. Cards: V, AE, DC.

All is going well for Jacky Marguin; the most faithful of the Bocuse disciples has gotten his second wind. In his delightful country restaurant, we had a delicious meal of fresh foie gras in an aromatic aspic, unforgettable freshwater lotte with their livers, a rack of lamb cooked in its own juice, a good white cheese made with Marlieux cream, and a crème brûlée that was even better than the one made by Bocuse. The wine list is an exhilarating book; the staff a little young but competent. One more point in this edition.

A la carte: 300F and up. Menus: 130F, 185F, 275F.

Les Ecrennes

77820 Le Châtelet-en-Brie - (Seine-et-Marne)
Paris 70 - Melun 15 - Fontainebleau 20 - Nangis 14

13 Auberge Briarde

60.69.47.32

M. Guichard. Open until 9:30 p.m. Closed Sun. dinner, Mon., Feb. school vacation & Aug. 1-18. Pets allowed. Cards: V, AE, DC.

Settled now for a while in this old Brie building (we knew him before from L'Auberge du Velay in the Haute-Loire), Jean Guichard has not abandoned his great, classic style. His impressive menu includes several rich terrines, souffléed turbot, crayfish Thermidor in a bush, a tureen of sweetbreads and langoustines in puff pastry, breast of duck in a pale-looking bilberry sauce, good but frustrating calf's head (there really was nothing but the tongue), excellent Meaux and Melun Bries and fairly weak desserts (except for the good baba). Diners are received warmly beneath the old beams in front of the fireplace.

A la carte: 250-300F. Menus: 150F to 300F.

Elincourt-Sainte-Marguerite

see Compiègne

Enghien

see PARIS SUBURBS

Epernay

51200 Epernay - (Marne)
Paris 140 - Châlons-sur-Marne 32 - Reims 27 - Troyes 105

(13) Les Berceaux

13, rue des Berceaux - 26.55.28.84

M. Maillard. Open until 9:30 p.m. Closed Sun. dinner. Pets allowed. Hotel: 1 ste 290-436F. 28 rms 251-254F; half-board 303-484F. Cards: V, AE, DC, MC.

Luc Maillard and his wife, Gill, share their love for rich sauces, regional products and the wines of Champagne with the patrons in both their restaurant and adjacent wine bar, which offers a 90-franc menu, fifteen wines by the glass and a piano player on weekend nights. The decor is light and well soundproofed, and the carefully prepared cuisine features escargots au Champagne, turbot au Champagne and doe stew.

A la carte: 250-300F. Menus: 130F, 180F, 290F.

Champagne

30, rue Eugène-Mercier - 26.55.30.22

Open year-round. 32 rms 205-225F. Garage parking. Telex 842068. Cards: V, AE, DC.

This ultra-modern little hotel has rooms with color television, telephones and double-glazed windows. No restaurant.

IN NEARBY **Champillon**
(5 km N on N 51)
51160 Ay - (Marne)

(14) Royal Champagne

26.52.87.11

M. Dellinger. Open until 9:30 p.m. Closed 3 weeks in Jan. Pets allowed. Parking. Telex 830111. Cards: V, AE, DC, MC.

Situated on the heights of the vineyards, this old relais overlooks a large portion of Champagne and all of Epernay. Guests revel in the view from the high, glassed-in platform, from which the musicians of days past played for dinner dances. Down below, in the immense dining room, the service is a little stiff, reflecting the image of Jean-Claude Pacherie, a most academic chef. His cuisine is abundant in sauces, prepared with excellent products (duckling and white-liver salad, grilled bass with sorrel) and rich with excellent desserts (strawberry millefeuille, West Indian mousseline). As one would expect, there's a large Champagne selection.

A la carte: 400-500F. Menus: 200F (lunch only), 360F and 410F (Champagne incl.), 280F, 330F.

Royal Champagne

(See restaurant above)

Closed 3 weeks in Jan. 1 ste 1,300F. 25 rms 480-1,000F. TV. Pets allowed.

Looking out over the vineyards, the large white house provides a peaceful environment and newly renovated rooms. Relais et Châteaux.

IN NEARBY **Vinay**
(7 km S on N 51)
51200 Epernay - (Marne)

(14) La Briqueterie

4, rte. de Sézanne - 26.54.11.22

M. Guillon. Open until 9:30 p.m. Closed Dec. 24-26. Pets allowed. Parking. Telex 842007. Cards: V, AE, DC, MC.

We can find only good things to say about Guillon's beautiful hotel, which faces a hillside of white-wine grapes. Everything is bright, flowering and opulent, and the decor is both rustic and refined. You will find the personnel devoted and professional, the sommelier perfect (offering an impressive choice of Champagnes), and the traditional cuisine faithfully executed by Belgian chef Lieven Vercouteren. His rich (and expensive) menu includes fried langoustines in lemon juice, turbot in mustard with a Champagne sauce, veal kidneys with thyme in a Cointreau sauce and a superb fruit baba.

A la carte: 350F. Menus: 240F (lunch weekends and holidays only), 325F.

La Briqueterie

(See restaurant above)

Closed Dec. 24-26. 4 stes 490-570F. 38 rms 345-460F. TV. Pets allowed.

At La Briqueterie, surely the best place in the region for a quiet night's sleep in large, modestly decorated rooms, the vineyards stand in the background and the large garden at your feet. Pleasant service and good facilities for groups.

Epinal

88000 Epinal - (Vosges)
Paris 365 - Nancy 69 - Colmar 92 - Vesoul 82

(16) Les Abbesses

23, rue de la Louvière
29.82.53.69, 20.64.15.65

M. Aiguier. Open until 9:30 p.m. Closed Sun. dinner, Mon., 1st week in Jan. & 2nd week in Aug. Garden dining. Pets allowed. Cards: V, AE.

Epinal couldn't have improved its image in a better way than by welcoming Jean-Claude

Aiguier, who took over an imposing old mansion in the center of town, which (thanks to the decorating talents of his wife, Francine) is now both comfortable and cheery. Here we find the passionate cuisine of an alchemist who is rigorously searching for perfect flavors and contrasts. His dishes, even the most rustic regional specialties, are inventive and light, such as the escargots soup, the court bouillon of red mullet with ginger, the turbot in coconut milk and cinnamon served with wild rice, the tender rabbit with foie gras on a bed of cabbage, the special langoustine and lobster dishes, and the gratin of mirabelle plums in a blueberry sauce. The wine cellar is quite respectable (especially in Bordeaux).

A la carte: 350-400F. Menus: 200F, 280F, 320F.

(15) Les Ducs de Lorraine

16, quai du Colonel-Sérot - 29.34.39.87

M. Obriot. Open until 9:30 p.m. Closed Sun. dinner, Mon., Feb. 28-March 5 & Aug. 15-31. Air cond. Pets allowed. Cards: V.

Epinal has been shaken awake by a new cuisine, one that is light and inventive. After Jean-Claude Aiguier took over Les Abesses, Claude Obriot rescued this old restaurant, which was well on its way down the road to ruin. These two chefs have brought a deluge of toques to this little city, the capital of the Vosges. Let's just hope that Epinal will maintain its interest in excellent food and hold onto its new recruits for a long time to come. The Obriots have given their place a new look, with windows overlooking the Moselle river and a soothing blue-and-green color scheme. The service staff is young and devoted, and Agnès Obriot has the smile of a charmer. Claude's cuisine is a panoply of appetizing, personal dishes, although the menu is unnecessarily long. But that's a trivial complaint, especially considering Claude's substantial skill. Everything is perfectly mastered, whether it be the frogs'-legs salad, the filet of turbot grilled with aromatic herbs, the casserole of fricasséed quail and sweetbreads with morels, the blueberry pie or the hot mandarin feuilleté.

A la carte: 330F and up. Menus: 165F (weekdays only), 210F, 280F, 320F.

Relais des Ducs de Lorraine

(See restaurant above) - 29.34.35.20

Closed Sat. & Sun. 9 rms 170-380F. TV in 2 rms. Pets allowed. Garage parking. Cards: V, MC.

This traditional house on the banks of the Moselle serves breakfast in its elegantly furnished rooms.

IN NEARBY **Chaumousey**
(10 km W on D 460)
88390 Darnieulles - (Vosges)

(13) Le Calmosien

5 km between Epinal & Darney
29.66.80.77

M. Beati. Open until 9:30 p.m. Closed Sun. dinner & Mon. Pets allowed. Cards: V, AE, DC, MC.

To fill up their beautiful turn-of-the-century dining room as it deserves to be, the young owners of this delicious bistro on the Epinal road now offer fixed-price menus, which are varied and seasonal. Serge Vauzelle, one of the partners, continues to display his chef's talents: quail salad with mushroom mousse, filet of gilthead in white wine with vegetables and basil, filet of beef with vegetables, and crème brûlée with walnuts. The wine cellar is well stocked.

A la carte: 250F. Menus: 100F (lunch only, wine incl.), 135F, 190F.

L'Epine

see Châlons-sur-Marne

Erdeven

56410 Etel - (Morbihan)
Paris 490 - Vannes 32 - Lorient 28 - Carnac 9

Château de Kéravéon

15 km NE on D 104 - 97.55.68.55

Closed Sept. 15-May 15. 19 rms 595-700F. Half-board 500-562F oblig. in seas. Pets allowed. Pool. Parking. Cards: V, AE, DC, MC.

This large, classic château, with spacious, tastefully furnished rooms, has lovely grounds and is four kilometers from the Saint-Laurent golf course. Restaurant.

Erquy

22430 Erquy - (Côtes-du-Nord)
Paris 450 - Dinan 47 - Dinard 40 - St-Brieuc 35

(13) L'Escurial

Blvd. de la Mer - 96.72.31.56

M. Bernard. Open until 10 p.m. Closed Sun. dinner, Mon., Jan. 3-15 & Oct. 1-15. Cards: V, AE, DC, MC.

The red splendor of the Spanish-Regency decor has mellowed, but the view of the bay, the beach, the bathers and the boats is still marvelous. In season, the boats are busy harvesting the world's best oysters (Erquy is the mollusk capital of France), which Véronique Bernard prepares in a variety of successful dishes. The most popular is her fricassée, mixed with langoustines and fresh crab. Watch out for the cooking durations, though—the magnificent filet of bass with saffron we tried recently was a little overdone. The desserts, such as the nougatine with raspberry sauce, are pretty and not too sweet.

A la carte: 260F. Menus: 68F (weekday lunch only), 285F (wine incl.), 99F, 160F, 240F.

Espelette

64250 Cambo-les-Bains - (Pyrénées-Atlantiques)
Paris 761 - Pau 119 - Bayonne 22 - St-Jean-de-Luz 25

12/20 Euzkadi

Rue Principale - 59.29.91.88

M. Darraïdou. Open until 9 p.m. Closed Tues. (off-seas.), Mon., Feb. 9-20 & Nov. 15-Dec. 15. Pets allowed. Hotel: 32 rms 140-170F; half-board 200F. Cards: V.

André Darraïdou is a fervent promoter of traditional Basque cooking. People crowd into his immense banquet room to eat what they no longer fix at home: tripoxa (tripe), axoa d'-Espelette (veal with onions and peppers) and the rich ttoro (Basque-style fish soup). Good wines of the region.

A la carte: 160-180F. Menus: 65F, 100F, 120F, 140F.

Esterençuby

see Saint-Jean-Pied-de-Port

Eugénie-les-Bains

40320 Geaune - (Landes)
Paris 726 - Pau 53 - Mont-de-Marsan 25 - Dax 69

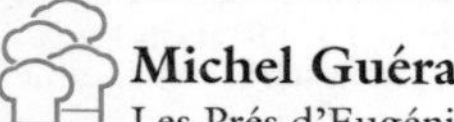

Michel Guérard

Les Prés d'Eugénie
19.5 58.51.19.50, 58.51.19.01

M. Guérard. Open until 10 p.m. Closed Dec. 30-Feb. 20. No pets. Parking. Telex 540470. Cards: V, AE, DC.

As you stroll past the sign that welcomes you to this small village in the Landes, you'll read "Eugénie-les-Bains, premier village-minceur de France" ("the top weight-loss town in France"), as a flock of geese, whose fattened livers will be transformed into the most succulent pâtés, wander along carefree... There you have it, a perfect image of this little village where several thousand people a year come from all over the world to get in shape and lose weight joyfully.

The town's success owes nothing to sheer luck and quite a bit to the Guérards. Ever since they opened their restaurant, Michel Guérard and his wife, Christine—a born decorator—have not stopped building, expanding and modernizing their establishment, making it the most charming spa in Europe. It's also one of the most perfect, with new spa facilities spread out over 2,500 square yards, reception rooms, recreation rooms, cabanas and pools. At the sight of it, guests are left stunned, gaping in admiration. But a battalion of 60 people scoops them up, coaxing, fussing, massaging and getting them back on their feet. Nonetheless, the Guérards haven't stopped; they are just about to open a delightful little hedgerow hermitage, "Le Couvent des Herbes," comprising eight suites whose windows open over the sage and rosemary fields, at the back of their grounds. They are thinking also of other spas, an eighteen-hole golf course and more.

Les Prés d'Eugénie, with its finely worked balconies reminiscent of New Orleans's Old Quarter, borders the hot springs. Here you'll find less of the health-conscious crowd and more of the followers of Robuchon and Senderens, who have come with different—indeed opposite—motives. The first group is here to watch their spare tires disappear with the help of the 1,000-calories-a-day diets—exquisite but superlight meals (no chef in the world has attained the degree of perfection, delicacy and flavor that Guérard has with his cuisine-minceur). The others, who don't have to worry about their waistlines, come to relax in the peaceful, beautiful setting, where every meal is a feast for the eye, the nose and the palate.

Unlike all the other weight-loss resorts, the Guérards' beautiful dining room, with its ravishing fabrics, old paintings, candles and silver pitchers, offers the same reception to dieters and to the already-thin. In fact, the dieters, who are served a cassoulet of escargots and langoustines with tomato butter, a tian of saddle of hare in a poivrade sauce (pepper and minced vegetables) and a cherry soufflé soup (a mere 500 calories for this royal menu!), haven't the slightest reason to gaze longingly at the other tables. Quite the opposite, in fact: At least once, nondieters will succumb to the desire to try this miraculous cuisine-minceur, which won't let you gain even an ounce.

All of Guérard's cooking deserves to be called minceur, since the fat content is calculated to the gram and the lightest sauces possible are used. We tried the robust "repas des champs" fixed-price menu and enjoyed the salad of duck carpaccio, a flaky galette with new vegetables in a sabayon sauce with fresh herbs (for many people, the herb garden at Eugénie is a shrine worthy of a pilgrimage), grilled salmon with potatoes sautéed in truffle oil, duck with baby onions and a huge dessert plate. And even after all of this, we didn't feel like taking a nap. Though contentedly full, we were already dreaming of dinner. Imagine the pleasure of eating a salad of lobster, freshwater cod and zucchini; sautéed langoustines with mousseron mushrooms; the fantastic lobster roasted over an open fire; duck-liver piccata grilled with asparagus; sumptuous baby rabbit cooked slowly in a bouillon of Pomerol wine; baby pigeon with cabbage and a potato millefeuille; white peaches in a lemon-verbena glaze; millefeuille Impératrice with an abundance of glazed fruits; and the dessert du Roi dressed "all in chocolate."

At our most recent visit, we discovered (or rediscovered) Guérard's subtle aromas and irresistible flavors. We keep thinking that one of these days he will botch at least one dish. But no, he continues to beat the odds. And despite his success, nothing has managed to tear him away from the ovens. In fact, since the departure of his highly talented, superb alter ego, Didier Oudill, if anything he has gotten a little more involved and creative in the kitchen. Another project, of course, is his vineyards. Someday soon we'll enjoy the fruits of that labor: wines lovingly nurtured in the soil of Bachenc. But his fervor for work and his demanding professionalism don't explain everything. Guérard has that something special, that intangible quality that is nothing less than a gift from God: talent. His is an enormous talent, and for once, money and success haven't managed to spoil it.

A la carte: 300-600F. Menus: 380F, 460F.

Les Prés d'Eugénie

(See restaurant above)

Closed Dec. 11-Feb. 20. 7 stes 1,357-1,403F. 28 rms 1,012- 1,150F. TV. No pets. Heated pool. Tennis.

Each of the rooms and suites is different and equally ravishing, with antique furniture, paintings and knickknacks. No more expensive than standard chain-hotel rooms, the accommodations are touched up or redecorated yearly. In 1987, just as they finished arranging the gardens and tennis courts and giving a Louisiana look to the Napoléon III facade by adding finely worked balconies and columns, the Guérards decided to build a beautiful gallery leading to the hot springs. Those too were enlarged and modernized, and today they're among the most attractive hot springs in France. And just so they don't lose their touch, Christine and Michel have decided to fix up rooms and suites in the adorable old building next to the herb garden, which was once a girls' school but has fallen into a sad state of disrepair. It promises to be so charming that people are already reserving rooms. A recent innovation is the offer of a weeklong package deal including a fitness cure, sports and full board (about 11,000 to 14,000 francs for one or 17,000 to 20,000 francs for two). Relais et Châteaux.

Evian

74500 Evian - (Haute-Savoie)
Paris 589 - Annecy 81 - Geneva 42 - Chamonix 113

Café Royal

South shore of Lake Geneva - 50.75.14.00

M. Lassalle. Open until 10 p.m. Closed Dec. 15-Feb. 5. Terrace dining. No pets. Parking. Telex 385759. Cards: V, AE, DC, MC.

The walls and ceiling of this marvelous dining room are covered with frescoes of flowers and fruits painted by a Swiss artist from the Belle Epoque. The ample windows open onto the grounds, and in the distance is Lake Léman and the hills of Lausanne. As we went to press, a new chef and a complete overhaul of the menu left us eager to taste the future of this beautiful spot, but we were unable to do so in time for a rating. Whoever is responsible, he is certain to enliven Café Royal's traditional cuisine with a dash of youthfulness and a less formal style. At the end of the dining room is another restaurant, La Rotonde, where clients ordering from the dietetic menu will find meals that are carefully prepared and anything but a punishment. In sunny weather, the "normal" meals are also served around the swimming pool.

A la carte: 300-500F. Menu: 290F.

Royal Hôtel

(See restaurant above)

Closed Dec. 15-Feb. 5. 29 stes 1,700-4,020F. 129 rms 300-1,880F. Half-board: 450-1,140F. TV. Pets allowed. Heated pool. Tennis. Golf.

Robert Lassalle has turned this grandiose turn-of-the-century luxury hotel, which was threatened with destruction, into a world-class resort for sports, health and even art buffs. Overlooking a spectacular panorama of Lake Geneva, the Royal provides reception and comfort that approach perfection. And one could never be bored here, with the eighteen-hole golf course, six tennis courts, pool, health club, sailing harbor, jogging track, grounds inhabited by deer and, in springtime, the internationally renowned chamber-music festival. This place is a dazzling success, confirmed by the exceptional rate at which it fills up.

(14) Les Prés Fleuris

Saint-Paul - 50.75.29.14

M. Frossard. Open until 8:30 p.m. Closed Oct.-end May. Garden dining. No pets. Parking. Telex 309545. Cards: V, AE, DC, MC.

The dining room is as filled with flowers as the fifteen acres of surrounding meadow, the view of Lake Geneva is sumptuous, and generosity is the principal quality of the new owners of this charming inn. Hot puff pastries are served the moment you arrive, and at the end of the meal, petits fours and chocolates are offered, as well as a selection of cigars. The staff encourages diners to take second helpings of each dish (even though the first servings are abundant). Unfortunately, this generosity also leads Roger Froissard, son-in-law and successor, to propose, during the same meal, fried salmon with a rich and perfect Nantes butter, then chicken with a no-less-rich tarragon sauce. But it is all perfectly created with remarkable ingredients. Discouraging prices.

À la carte: 400F. Menus: 220F, 280F, 320F.

Les Prés Fleuris

(See restaurant above)

Closed Oct.-end May. 5 stes 900-1,200F. 7 rms 750-950F. Half-board 600-1,000F oblig. in seas. TV. Pets allowed.

From a height offering fine views of Lake Geneva, Switzerland and the Alps, the rooms are large, comfortable and enveloped in peace. The atmosphere is charming and relaxed. Relais et Châteaux.

(17) La Toque Royale

(Casino Royal)

South shore of Lake Geneva - 50.75.03.78

M. Lassalle. Dinner only. Open daily until 11:30 p.m. Air cond. No pets. Parking. Telex 385759. Cards: V, AE, DC, MC.

At the Casino d'Evian, we recommend placing your bet on Michel Lentz. In calling him to the ovens of La Toque Royal, owner Robert Lassalle has picked a winner. This young chef—direct from positions in Paris at the Bristol and then the Crillon—is overflowing with talent, and we certainly haven't heard the last of him.

It is unusual to find a three-toque restaurant a few feet from the gaming tables, and the cuisine here deserves much more in the way of decor—La Toque Royale is separated from the gaming room only by a glass partition. The setting isn't unattractive, but its functional look is hardly inspiring, though the atmosphere, luckily, is improved by the lovely view of the lake and, in the evenings, by the lights of Lausanne. The tubs of artificial flowers are not exactly elegant, and it wouldn't hurt if they did away with the background music. Apart from that, guests are admirably welcomed and advised by François Félix, the maître d'hôtel, and immediately captivated by the intelligence and the finesse of Michel Lentz, who uses first-class products to blend flavors in perfect harmony.

Beautiful fixed-price menus—with almost angelic prices—enhance the à la carte menu, which is limited (the restaurant is open only in the evenings) but offers delicious dinners. Try the marvelous creamy soup of langoustines, cut lengthwise and gently seasoned "à la japonaise"; a cream of Breton oysters with the powerful yet subtle perfume of parsley; an excellent filet of red mullet in a Savoie Gamay sauce; slowly simmered sweetbreads with crayfish; a spit-roasted Bresse guinea fowl in its own juice; roast hare with smoked bacon; and hare coated with a blood sauce and accompanied by spätzle and celery "noodles." Don't miss trying a piece of aged tomme cheese, the fresh-peach sabayon, the purple fig stewed with wild honey or the sensational millefeuille cake with vanilla cream that is testimony to the pastry-making talents of Michel Lentz. Among the regional wines are excellent bottles from the Savoie, Monterminod and Bugey.

A la carte: 300-500F. Menus: 200F, 290F.

(13) La Verniaz

Neuvecelle - 50.75.04.90

MM. Verdier. Open until 9 p.m. Closed Nov. 30-Feb. 15. Garden dining. Pets allowed. Garage parking. Telex 385715. Cards: V, AE, DC, MC.

The beautiful La Verniaz overlooking the lake is popular for its flower gardens, terrace and pool. It is also admired for its classic regional food centered around Savoyard charcuterie, lake fish, spit-roasted Bresse fowl and delicious pastries. The small fixed-price menu, although a bit expensive, is often made on impulse from the best of the day's market (for example, asparagus, whole gilthead in a langoustine sauce and dessert).

A la carte: 280-300F. Menus: 180F, 220F.

La Verniaz

(See restaurant above)

Closed Nov. 30-mid-Feb. 15. 5 stes 700-1,500F (chalets). 35 rms 300-850F. Half-board 500-700F oblig. in seas. TV in 15 rms. Pets allowed. Heated pool. Tennis.

Located on spacious and peaceful grounds, this hotel offers a superb view of the Dent d'Oche in the Alps and Lake Léman. The rooms are in pleasant chalets scattered in the woods. Relais et Châteaux.

Evreux

27000 Evreux - (Eure)
Paris 100 - Rouen 51 - Mantes 44 - Dreux 44 - Caen 121

(14) Auberge de Parville

4 km W on N 13, 27180 St-Sébastien-de-Morsent - 32.39.36.63

M. Barrande. Open until 9:30 p.m. Closed Mon., Sun. & Wed. dinner. Terrace dining. Pets allowed. Parking. Cards: V, AE.

The reputation of this old, rustic inn had been tarnished to complete dullness when the Barrandes decided to get it back on its feet over four years ago. They put in a simple, fresh-looking decor around the old fireplace and asked chef Jacques Dehède, formerly with La Sologne in Paris, to create a menu with all the virtues: consistency, variety, lightness and personality. Their goals have been achieved with such dishes as a rabbit stew with tarragon, escalopes of salmon in a Sancerre sauce, and a saddle of young rabbit tucked into a delicate tart. The first two fixed-price menus have a country-style generosity. So in this edition, they have earned a toque.

A la carte: 250-300F. Menus: 100F (weekdays only), 165F (weekends and holidays), 140F, 195F.

(16) Hôtel de France

29, rue St-Thomas - 32.39.09.25

M. Rieser-Rogues. Open until 9:45 p.m. Closed Sun. dinner & Mon. Pets allowed. Garage parking. Cards: V, AE, DC.

The Iton, the many-branched river that crosses Evreux, bathes the charming garden seen from the terrace of the hotel's dining room. The tables, under old beams overhead, have garnet-colored cloths and luxurious settings, and the plates hold a cuisine that is both rich and wise. Chef Alain Rieser-Rogues, a product of the great brigades of the traditional luxury hotels (Crillon, Bristol, Normandy), often calls upon the shellfish classics, but he also has a personal style that reflects great precision in both cooking times and flavors. Most recently, he served us oysters in seawater aspic on a bed of Norman cream (and in a fritter with crushed coriander), parsleyed lobster in a rosé Sancerre aspic, roast turbot in beef juice, and fabulous chicken "de Loué" coated with cider vinegar. The cheeses are excellent, the desserts are works of genius, and the first two menus are staggeringly generous.

A la carte: 400-500F. Menus: 140F (lunch only), 160F, 205F, 320F.

Hôtel de France

(See restaurant above)

Open year-round. 1 ste 245-300F. 14 rms 105-205F. TV in 4 rms. No pets.

The top-floor rooms are quite charming, and the reception and service are faultless.

Les Eyzies

24620 Les Eyzies-de-Tayac - (Dordogne)
Paris 521 - Périgueux 45 - Sarlat 22 - Bergerac 57

Le Centenaire

D 170
53.06.97.18

MM. Scholly & Mazère. Open until 9:30 p.m. Closed Tues. lunch & Nov.-April. Terrace dining. Pets allowed. Garage parking. Telex 541921. Cards: V, MC.

Roland Mazère, the blond, still-young hermit of the famous prehistoric site where Cro-Magnons grilled their aurochs meat, prepares the most spectacular contemporary cuisine in the Périgord—and without any of the mad-dog feverishness for which he was known in the past. His technique has peaked, resulting in flavors that are blended with the thoughtful boldness of the best chefs. By using extraordinary regional ingredients, he has created a new country cuisine that is delicious, fanciful and light: the risotto with foie gras, truffles and langoustines; the escargots ravioli with smoked goose accompanied by a parsley gazpacho with farm cream; the pink salmon with Thai herbs; the entremets of goose confit or of sweetbreads served with a purée mousseline.

At our most recent meal here we experienced none of the little lapses that have marred our enthusiasm in the past. Always experimental and a little exotic, Mazère's cooking is now mature and experienced, with no loss of imagination in the process. What results are such exquisite dishes as the ravioli of snails with smoked goose and a parsley sauce; a stunning miracle of a ragoût of young vegetables and fresh morels, as concise as a Japanese poem and telling of glories to come for this chef; risotto with foie gras, truffles and prawns, bursting with flavor and doubtless the house best-seller; and young pigeon in a delicate, crunchy crust suffused with the flavor of minced cèpes. Not to mention the red mullet with oysters or the lobster with caviar, both grand successes, and the heavenly desserts, like cacao sorbet with a sauce made from an old bottle of Saint-Raphaël found in the wine cellar. This wine cellar is superbly chosen, if still not quite filled out.

A la carte: 450F. Menus: 200F, 300F, 400F.

Le Centenaire

(See restaurant above)

Closed Nov.-April. 3 stes 650-850F. 23 rms 270-500F. Half-board 400-550F. TV in 15 rms. Heated pool.

Guests staying in these modern, well-equipped rooms can take advantage of the five boutiques in the hotel's shopping arcade. When they tire of shopping, there's always the garden terrace, the swimming pool at the edge of the river, the gym and the sauna. Relais et Châteaux.

Cro-Magnon

53.06.97.06

M. Leyssales. Open until 9 p.m. Closed Wed. lunch & Oct. 10-April 28. Garden dining. No pets. Parking. Telex 570637. Cards: V, AE, DC, MC.

The chef at this large restaurant at the foot of the rocks is new, but the menu's still the same; unfortunately, the overall tone has sagged a bit of late. Certainly, Jacques Leyssales is an experienced restaurateur who knows how to do it all, particularly when it comes to choosing cooks, instructing them in his way of doing things (simple, fresh, straightforward food), and offering them the best products from this earth. Though our most recent meal was all in all very good, our vegetable gâteau in a poultry aspic was identical to the one we tasted two years ago, and our sole soufflé had an exquisite stuffing but a banal white-wine sauce. This cuisine needs some spunk to bring the less-than-stellar dishes up to par with the lotte in chive cream with leeks and zucchini, and the delicate desserts. Leyssales, a knowledgeable oenophile, has a sumptuous wine cellar. Outside, chestnut and plane trees shade a large terrace.

A la carte: 320F. Menus: 110F, 160F, 260F, 300F.

Cro-Magnon

(See restaurant above)

Closed Oct. 10-April 28. 4 stes 500-660F. 20 rms 280-400F. Half-board 300-380F oblig. in seas. Pets allowed. Heated pool.

With five acres of grounds and a swimming pool, the Cro-Magnon has many charming rooms, some of which overlook the greenery.

Le Moulin de la Beune

53.06.94.33

Closed Nov. 3-Easter. 20 rms 185-255F. Parking. Cards: V.

This remarkably restored mill sits on the beautiful cliffs of the Musée National de Préhistoire at the edge of the river. Its spacious rooms are nicely furnished. No restaurant.

Eze

06360 Eze - (Alpes-Maritimes)
Paris 959 - Nice 11 - Menton 18 - Monte-Carlo 7

Richard Borfiga

Pl. du Général-de-Gaulle - 93.41.05.23

M. Borfiga. Open until 10:30 p.m. Closed Mon. (except summer) & Jan. 1-Feb. 11. Terrace dining. Pets allowed. Cards: V, AE, DC.

Named for its owner, a young former student of Troisgros, Richard Borfiga has the double advantage of being open year-round and attracting the kind of clientele that just likes a good meal. Borfiga is an excellent cook, as proved by his aspic of leeks and foie gras (though there's too little of the latter), zucchini stuffed with aromatic herbs, filet of red mullet (nicely cooked, though too small) on a bed of tomato purée, and his delicious marquise of bitter chocolate with a true pistachio sauce. In sum, he displays dexterity and a good sense for flavors, which should be complemented in the future by a little more generosity. The round tables are well spaced and look out on the terrace and its pretty winter garden.

A la carte: 350F. Menus: 160F, 220F, 280F.

Cap Estel

Eze-Bord-de-Mer - 93.01.50.44

Closed Nov. 1-March 15. 47 rms 1,000-1,750F (half-board only). Air cond. Pets allowed. Heated pool. Telex 470305. Cards: V, DC, MC.

This great hotel lavishes its patrons with Hollywood-style luxury. Its five acres of lovely grounds, outdoor and indoor swimming pools, private beach, magnificently flowering terraces and ocean view from every room keep even the most demanding guest happy. Restaurant.

Château de la Chèvre d'Or

Rue du Barri - 93.41.12.12

M. Ingold. Open until 10:15 p.m. Closed Wed. (in March) & Nov. 30-March 1. Garden dining. Pets allowed. Telex 970839. Cards: V, AE, DC.

There are a thousand years of history behind this real-life château (hardly the likes of a Hollywood castle) clinging acrobatically to the rocks. Everything is precious, charming, wildly luxurious and irreproachably civilized. While lounging on the impressive poolside terrace, guests feast their eyes on the vast blue of the sea and their ears on high-society chitchat. The personnel bustles silently and smoothly in the distinguished but slightly fading dining room, while the owner of this eagle's nest, Bruno Ingold, carefully watches over the gentle way of life that is maintained here—an experience hard to find elsewhere on the Côte, even at the highest prices. The cuisine, though a bit formal, does have touches of splendor (lots of truffles, caviar and lobster), but it opens up with more spontaneous plates, such as the langoustine mousse with a coulis of haricots verts, the bass served with an émincé of zucchini, and the simple rack of lamb with its gratin dauphinois. The pastries are excellent and the wine cellar respectable.

A la carte: 400-800F. Menu: 310F (lunch only).

Château de la Chèvre d'Or

(See restaurant above)

Closed Nov. 30-March 1. 3 stes 1,950-2,050F. 11 rms 950- 1,950F. TV. Air cond. Pets allowed. Pool.

In this medieval château, reconstructed in 1920 and with an enchanting view of the sea, the newly refurbished rooms are all air conditioned. Relais et Châteaux.

Château Eza

93.41.12.24

Closed Nov. 2-March 20. 3 stes 2,000-3,500F. 6 rms 800-2,500F. TV. Air cond. Pets allowed. Cards: V, AE, DC, MC.

Six rooms, two suites and one apartment—all at insane prices—have been set up in authentically medieval stone houses. The colors may be a little too diverse (the furnishings are also of diverse quality), but the accommodations are perfectly comfortable and the service is impeccably attentive. On the restaurant side, the management is just closing a deal to bring the brilliant Bruno Cirino to the kitchen, which will provide more than ample reason to come up here in the future.

Faverges-de-la-Tour

38110 La Tour-du-Pin - (Isère)
Paris 530 - Lyon 65 - La Tour-du-Pin 10 - Chambéry 37

(14) Le Château

10 km E on N 516 & D 145 - 74.97.42.52

M. Tournier. Open until 9:45 p.m. Closed Mon. (except July & Aug.) & Oct. 12-May 6. Terrace dining. No pets. Parking. Telex 300372. Cards: V, AE, DC.

The succession rate here among chefs is dizzying and impossible to keep up with. The latest, Christian Alleaume from Brittany, is the fifth or so in four years. We don't know if you'll get a chance to taste it, but his cooking is very good, particularly such dishes as the millefeuille of foie gras with apples and potatoes, the remarkable noisettes of lamb served with a potato galette and a vegetable gâteau, and the gratinée of red fruits. But will he stay?

A la carte: 400F.

Le Château

(See restaurant above)

Closed Oct. 12-May 6. 3 stes 1,700F. 43 rms 400-1,200F. Half-board 700-1,225F. TV. Heated pool. Tennis. Golf.

The most beautiful rooms are on the second floor, decorated with much—sometimes too much—research. The furniture and tapestries are spectacular, but the overall look often lacks taste. There is an admirable view of the valley and the mountains, as well as a heliport and a nine-hole golf course. Relais et Châteaux.

Fegersheim

see Strasbourg

Ferayola

see CORSICA

Fère-en-Tardenois

02130 Fère-en-Tardenois - (Aisne)
Paris 110 - Château-Thierry 26 - Soissons 26 - Reims 46

(13) Le Connétable

Rte. du Château - 23.82.24.25

M. Pilati. Open daily until 9:30 p.m. Air cond. Garden dining. Pets allowed. Hotel: 4 rms 140-170F; half-board 230-350F oblig. in seas. Heated pool. Garage parking. Cards: AE, DC.

With its cozy atmosphere and beamed ceilings, this sweet forest inn welcomes its guests with good Champagne (135 francs a bottle) and fixed-price menus at friendly prices. The owner, an ex–pastry chef, also prepares excellent à la carte choices, including filet of perch with lemon and sweetbreads with prawns. He also offers four pleasant rooms and a pool.

A la carte: 280F. Menus: 72F and 115F (weekdays only), 120F and 150F (weekends and holidays only).

(15) Hostellerie du Château

3 km N on N 967 - 23.82.21.13

M. Blot. Open until 9 p.m. Closed Jan. 1-March 1. Pets allowed. Parking. Telex 145526. Cards: V, AE, DC, MC.

Do you know of many hoteliers who can pride themselves on having succeeded such luminaries as Robert de Dreux, the first of the Valois, the constable of Montmorency, the princes of Condé, the father of Philippe Egalité? No to mention less noble predecessors, such as the colony of rats and mice that at the end of the '50s had taken over the remains of this formidable château, with its ten towers, its sumptuous Renaissance gallery of finely carved wood (which inspired Catherine de Médicis to create the one at Chenonceaux) and its neighboring eighteenth-century manse fixed up under the reign of Viollet-Le-Duc. Although bestowed with this lofty legacy, the Blot family began with a modest boarding house in Bagnoles-de-l'Orne.

Above the fields and in the middle of the Tardenois woods, with its proliferation of wild game, the Blots have slaved away to restore the luster to this piece of royal turf inhabited over the centuries by many of the big names of historic France. The decor, which had become rather motley, has little by little been stripped down, and good taste and simplicity have gained ground. You will not be able to find a place this close to Paris (just an hour away) that's more country-like or pleasant to spend the night or, better, the weekend.

When the chef, Patrick Michelon, left for the Côte d'Azur in 1987, Gérard Blot brought in his 25-year-old son, Christophe, who had studied not only in the kitchens of the Elysée but also at Troisgros, Taillevent, Comme Chez Soi in Brussels and, finally, with Marc Meneau. He certainly has the talent, but before giving him the three toques of his predecessor, let's give him time to perfect his excellent, intelligent menu. Many of his dishes have enchanted us: the filets of sander with pickled turnips in a Chardonnay-chive sauce, the tender and flavorful squab and the pink and juicy loin of venison in perfect harmony with a mixture of cèpes and walnuts. Some others, however, have been a little less grand: lobster soup that was too sweet and had too much pumpkin flavor, and médaillons of sweetbreads that were pasty but were served with a very nice parsley purée. If you have forgotten the powerful flavor of true farm Brie, you'll rediscover it here, served before the exquisite desserts, such as the feuilleté of puréed apples, the Calvados sorbet and the red-berry macaroons. And if you have 200 to 300 francs to invest in a Burgundy, try the delightful Saint-Aubin La Pucelle or the Roux Chassagne-Montrachet whites or, for a red, the Dujac Clos-de-la-Roche or the Rousseau Charmes-Chambertin.

The prices are definitely those of a Relais et Châteaux, but the Blots are reasonable people, and the least-expensive fixed-price menu, which includes wine and coffee, is quite generous and well composed.

A la carte: 380-400F. Menus: 270F (weekday lunch only, wine incl.), 320F, 400F.

Hostellerie du Château

(See restaurant above)

Closed Jan. 1-March 1. 9 stes 950-1,300F. 14 rms 600-900F. Half-board 1,045-1,795F oblig. in seas. TV in 16 rms. Pets allowed. Tennis. Golf.

On more than 25 acres of grounds surrounded by a forest, the eleven rooms and twelve suites (two of which have whirlpools) are decorated in fresh tones and provide the best in comfort. This ideal weekend spot is especially appealing because the prices haven't changed in more than a year. Nine-hole golf course. Relais et Châteaux.

La Ferté-Bernard

72400 La Ferté-Bernard - (Sarthe)
Paris 164 - Chartres 76 - Le Mans 49 - Alençon 56

(14) Le Dauphin

3, rue d'Huisne - 43.93.00.39

M. Pasquier. Open until 10 p.m. Closed Sun. dinner, Wed. & Aug. 20-Sept. 20. Terrace dining. Pets allowed. Cards: V, DC.

A native of La Ferté-Bernard, like his parents and grandparents before him, Alain Pasquier returned home a few years ago to bring to this previously deprived region a fine restaurant. He was formerly a pastry chef nearby, and he spent nine years as chef in the classic kitchens of Ricordeau de Loué. His cuisine, served in this pretty place on a pedestrian street near the extraordinary Porte Saint-Julien, is personal and liberated. The seasonal dishes, written by hand on the menu and more numerous than the regular, printed items, include a feuilleté of asparagus and foie gras, fresh salmon with chive butter, roast kidneys with fresh vegetables, a large plate of duck (confit, filet and liver) and a charlotte with in-season fruits (among other exceptional desserts). The service is alert, and the dining rooms (the white one is preferable to the other, which is poorly lit) are adorned with splendid bouquets.

A la carte: 220F. Menu: 80F.

La Ferté-sous-Jouarre

77260 La Ferté-sous-Jouarre - (Seine-et-Marne)
Paris 64 - Château-Thierry 26 - Meaux 20 - Melun 63

(15) Auberge de Condé

1, ave. de Montmirail - 60.22.00.07

M. Tingaud. Open until 9 p.m. Closed Mon. dinner & Tues. Pets allowed. Parking. Cards: V, AE, DC, MC.

Twenty-seven-year-old Pascal Tingaud has taken the torch from his grandfather, Emile, the charming herald of the cuisine of sauces. The grandson has not yet relegated to oblivion the Vincent Bourrel filet of sole and the feuilleté of crayfish in whisky. Besides, revolution isn't his thing. He is extremely moderate, and if he allows some "fantasies" to slip onto the menu, like the turbot with caviar, the saffron bass or the brill with a leek fondue, his heart beats more for the lobster grilled with Nantes butter, the filet of sole with fresh pasta, the veal kidneys in port and the Bresse duckling. This young cook, trained by Pic and Troisgros, demonstrates a solid sense for cooking times and can turn out a good sauce.

In this opulent inn, with its fading but friendly decor, the reception is charming, the service worthy of a luxury hotel, and the Champagne list a book in itself. But the bill arrives like a bombshell, unless you take refuge in the (weekday) fixed-price menu, which isn't quite as shocking.

A la carte: 400-700F. Menus: 250F (weekdays only, wine incl.), 280F, 400F.

Figeac

46100 Figeac - (Lot)
Paris 559 - Cahors 71 - Aurillac 67 - Tulle 103 - Brive 92

(13) Hôtel des Carmes

Enclos des Carmes - 65.34.20.78

M. Tillet. Open until 9 p.m. Closed Sun. dinner (off-seas.), Sat. & Dec. 16-Jan. 15. Terrace dining. Pets allowed. Parking. Telex 520794. Cards: V, AE, DC, MC.

Sitting under an umbrella on the terrace overlooking the pool and the old village houses is surely the best way to take advantage of this friendly but not terribly charming modern building. The intelligent, personal regional cuisine comprises such dishes as the duck liver ravioli, the lotte with garlic and the parfait with bitter chocolate and fresh mint. The wine cellar is respectable, and the fixed-price menus are worthwhile (one includes an apéritif, wine and coffee).

A la carte: 280F. Menus: 95F, 170F, 260F.

Hôtel des Carmes

(See restaurant above)

Closed Sun. (off-seas.), Sat. & Dec. 16-Jan. 15. 40 rms 245-315F. Half-board 275-295F oblig. in seas. TV. Pets allowed. Pool. Tennis.

The modern, functional rooms are light, soundproof and well equipped. Guests enjoy conscientious reception and service, as well as a carefully prepared breakfast.

Flaine

74300 Cluses - (Haute-Savoie)
Paris 596 - Annecy 79 - Megève 49 - Chamonix 66

(14) Le Totem

50.90.80.64, 42.61.55.17

M. Miradoli. Open until 9 p.m. Closed April 15-June 30 & Sept. 4-Dec. 16. Terrace dining. Pets allowed. Telex 670512. Cards: V, AE, DC, MC.

From Le Totem's comfortable dining room overlooking the ski slopes is one of the most beautiful views imaginable. Considering that—and considering the elegant decor, well-trained personnel and high-class clientele—one would expect the bill to be formidable. But Pierrick Berthier's excellent cuisine is worth even more than the not-unreasonable prices. It is consistent, well balanced and classic but light: rosettes of scallops marinated in lime, breast of duck grilled with pickled turnips and chocolate cake with hazelnuts.

A la carte: 300F. Menu: 160F (lunch only), 190F (dinner only), 220F.

Le Totem

(See restaurant above)

Closed April 15-June 30 & Sept. 4-Dec. 16. 54 rms 290-520F. Half-board 300-560F oblig. in seas. TV in 30 rms. Pets allowed. Heated pool. Tennis. Golf.

This small, concrete luxury hotel in the snow is close to tennis courts and a heated pool. Summer packages.

Flavigny-sur-Moselle

see Nancy

Fleurie

69820 Fleurie - (Rhône)
Paris 420 - Lyon 58 -Mâcon 21 - Bourg-en-Bresse 48

(16) Auberge du Cep

Pl. de l'Eglise - 74.04.10.77

M. Cortembert. Open until 9 p.m. Closed Sun. dinner, Mon., Feb. 7-12, Aug. 1-6 & Dec. 12-Jan. 4. Air cond. Pets allowed. Cards: V, AE.

Situated in opulent-looking provincial surroundings directly across from the church, this village inn is one of the most discreet of the great restaurants of France. The owner, Gérard Cortembert, can be surly and unsociable, but he has the good soul of a cook with character. Here's a meal that will leave a happy taste in your mouth: hot cervelas (sausage) with pistachios, salad of poultry livers with artichoke hearts, braised scallops, filet de boeuf, squab casserole with pickled shallots, feuilleté of banana confit with a kiwi purée, and roasted pears with vanilla ice cream, accompanied by a bottle of Remoissennet or an '82 Moulin-à-Vent and finished off with petits fours and an aged rum that Cortembert likes to pass off as a great Cognac. Even the bill, severe but fair, won't spoil your good memories, particularly if you stick to the first fixed-price menu, which is certainly generous.

A la carte: 400F. Menus: 200F, 275F, 330F, 440F.

Fleurville

71260 Lugny - (Saône-et-Loire)
Paris 386 - Mâcon 17 - Tournus 13 - Pont-de-Vaux 5

Château de Fleurville

85.33.12.17

Closed Nov. 13-Dec. 25 & 1 week in Feb. 14 rms 360F. Pets allowed. Heated pool. Parking. Cards: V, AE, DC.

This pleasant château is located on lovely grounds and has seductive rooms that look out on the Mâcon vineyards. Restaurant.

(13) Le Fleurvil

85.33.10.65

M. Badoux. Open until 9:30 p.m. Closed Mon. dinner (off-seas.), Tues., June 5-14 & Nov. 15-Dec. 15. Terrace dining. Pets allowed. Hotel: 10 rms 90-220F. Garage parking. Cards: V.

The numerous and generous fixed-price menus allow you to sample much of this serious, well-prepared cuisine (although some dishes should be avoided, particularly the quenelles, which are more like semolina than poached pike dumplings, and the so-so desserts). Try the asparagus in a mousseline sauce, the marinated salmon, the grilled sander with béarnaise sauce and the pink rack of lamb. The wines are well selected and reasonably priced (carafes of Beaujolais and Mâcon). A toque for this rustic, flower-bedecked dining room.

A la carte: 180-200F. Menus: 85F, 105F, 128F, 180F.

Florensac

34510 Florensac - (Hérault)
Paris 810 - Montpellier 50 - Béziers 24 - Agde 9.5

(15) Léonce

8, pl. de la République - 67.77.03.05

M. Fabre. Open until 9:15 p.m. Closed Sun. dinner (except in summer) & Mon.; annual closing varies. Air cond. No pets. Hotel: 13 rms 120-200F. Cards: V, AE, DC.

The neochic, British-decorator-style decor is an unfortunate concession to modernity that the patron of this old village café/tobacco shop adopted a few years back. It is undoubtedly comfortable, but it is as sad as the cuisine of Jean-Claude Fabre, the owners' son, is spirited. This temperamental cook, still very young, studied at Septime's in Monte-Carlo and at Maximin's, where he was the saucier for two years. Everything he makes has panache, color and taste, and prices have remained quite fair despite the restaurant's considerable success. For about 250 francs you can eat marvelous oyster ravioli half poached in a quail-egg bouillon, Scottish salmon cooked on the spot with a basil cream sauce, rack of lamb roasted pink with its juice thickened with butter, and a hot apple tarte. The service is inconsistent and lacks warmth, and the table settings are quite ordinary.

A la carte: 250-280F. Menus: 115F (weekdays only), 185F, 260F.

La Flotte-en-Ré

see Ré (Ile de)

Fontainebleau

77300 Fontainebleau - (Seine-et-Marne)
Paris 65 - Melun 16 - Nemours 16 - Sens 53 - Orléans 88

L'Aigle Noir

27, pl. Napoléon-Bonaparte
64.22.32.65

M. Duvauchelle. Open daily until 10 p.m. Garden dining. Pets allowed. Parking. Telex 694080. Cards: V, AE, DC, MC.

Although finicky, the Cardinal of Retz would look with satisfaction upon the innumerable improvements that Pierre Duvauchelle has brought over the last few years to his old palace, whose windows open onto the gardens of Diana. Most recently, the Empire room got a face-lift that restored the tapestries and fabrics to their original splendor. But it is in the lovely garden, calm in the refreshing shade of green-and-beige parasols, that you can most enjoyably taste the lamb salad with thyme and the strawberry soup with mint. Chef Daniel Dumesnil's work is simple but executed perfectly and served graciously.

A la carte: 400F. Menus: 200F, 280F.

L'Aigle Noir

(See restaurant above)

Open year-round. 6 stes 1,025-2,500F. 51 rms 620-980F. Half-board 995-1,250F. TV. Pets allowed. Heated pool.

Facing the garden or the château, the luxurious rooms are decorated in Louis XVI, Empire or Restoration style. The renovation was only recently completed.

12/20 Chez Arrighi

53, rue de France - 64.22.29.43.

Mme. Amprou. Open until 10 p.m. Closed Mon. & Feb. school vacation. Pets allowed. Cards: V, AE, DC, MC.

Corsican food in the Emperor's old neighborhood? Why not? The "imperial" decor may be a bit faded, but not so the ravishing owner. Be sure to taste the migisca (a ragoût of lamb with red beans) and the sheep's cheese, accompanied by a powerful red wine from the region.

A la carte: 220F. Menus: 89F (weekdays only), 125F, 172F.

Hôtel Legris et Parc

36, rue du Parc - 64.22.24.24

Closed Dec. 20-Jan. 25. 3 stes 350F. 27 rms 210-350F. Half-board 325-465F oblig. in seas. TV. Pets allowed. Cards: V, MC.

Well situated in front of the entrance to the château's grounds, this old building has been pleasantly renovated. The better of the extremely comfortable rooms look out on the flowers of an interior garden. Restaurant.

Remember to call or write in advance to reserve your room or your table.

Fontaines-en-Sologne

41250 Bracieux - (Loir-et-Cher)
Paris 190 - Blois 23 - Chambord 13 - Romorantin 27

Auberge de la Fontaine aux Muses

La Gaucherie (7 km on D 765)
54.79.98.80

M. Soyer. Open until 9 p.m. Closed Tues. dinner & Wed. Garden dining. Pets allowed. Cards: V, MC.

Except for a few follies that the menu could do without (feuilleté of hot oysters with caviar, blanquette of sweetbreads in ginger), everything that Alain Soyer creates is proof of his intelligent imagination. His is a cuisine that brings joy to the table: terrine of bass with citrus fruit, sander in Gamay wine, spiced sirloin and a delicious fresh-fruit shortcake. In this obscure corner of France, Soyer is developing an original and inspired cuisine featuring lovely presentations of first-rate ingredients; this cuisine has earned him another toque as well as a following from all over. Go taste his vegetable terrine in aspic, his chicken in puff pastry with truffle sauce, and his heartwarming pot-au-feu of duck liver. Good local wines are offered for about 45 francs, and the pleasantly decorated dining room is heated in winter by a wood-burning stove.

A la carte: 220-250F. Menus: 150F, 160F, 190F, 280F, 290F.

Fontenay-Trésigny

77610 Fontenay-Trésigny - (Seine-et-Marne)
Paris 45 - Meaux 30 - Melun 26 - Provins 39

Le Manoir

Rte. de Coulommiers - 64.25.91.17

M. Sourisseau. Open until 9 p.m. Closed Tues. & Nov. 15-March 18. Garden dining. Pets allowed. Hotel: 2 stes 800-1,000F; 13 rms 400-700F. Heated pool. Tennis. Parking. Telex 690635. Cards: V, AE, DC, MC.

M. Sourisseau, the charming owner of this proud fin-de-siècle manor, thoughtfully installed an airstrip for those guests who arrive via private plane. He also has extravagant rooms, stunning salons with frescoes and a solemn dining room with a coffered ceiling and brocaded velvet tapestries. But this bucolic hostelry in the Brie region offers more than mere luxury: It has also become a very good restaurant since Denis Come, formerly of the Château de Locguénolé, took over the ovens. Come is attentive to both ingredients and finishing touches, and his rather classic repertoire does not lack personality: aiguillettes of beef sliced thinly à la tartare, warm mussel and vegetable salad and squab with broad beans. Tables are set on the terrace by the new pool.

A la carte: 350F. Menu: 200F (weekday lunch only).

Fontevraud-l'Abbaye

49590 Fontevraud-l'Abbaye - (Maine-et-Loire)
Paris 306 - Angers 70 - Chinon 23 - Saumur 16

(15) La Licorne

31, rue d'Arbrissel - 41.51.72.49
M. Criton. Open until 9 p.m. Annual closing varies. Garden dining. Pets allowed. Cards: V, AE.

In this glorious eighteenth-century building, with its carefully restored facade of half columns, is one of the best restaurants in the region. It's also one of the most obscure, since owner Jean Criton doesn't make an effort to attract the hordes of tourists who clog the royal abbey. His lovely dining room has just six tables, and the delightful garden shaded by a magnolia tree accommodates just a few more guests (when the season is right). It has all been arranged with comfort and pleasure in mind, and all in good taste. Chef Michel Lecomte is an excellent young cook who takes advantage of his training at Taillevent and Robuchon to prepare a short menu open to simplicity, creativity and honest flavors. His terrine of young rabbit with cauliflower cream, roast-langoustine salad, salmon pot-au-feu with olive oil, cod with a green pepper purée and delicate desserts have earned him a second toque. We just hope that the prices, already rather harsh for the region, won't go through the ceiling. The local wines are pleasant, and the reception and service attentive.

A la carte: 300F. Menu: 155F (weekdays only).

Fontvieille

13990 Fontvieille - (Bouches-du-Rhône)
Paris 711 - Tarascon 11- Avignon 30 - Arles 10

A la Grâce de Dieu

90, ave. de Tarascon - 90.97.71.90
Closed Wed. (off-seas.) & Jan. 5-March 15. 10 rms 270-320F. Half-board 270-300F. TV. Pets allowed. Parking. Cards: V, AE, DC, MC.

The stylish rooms are well equipped, and some have views of the Alpilles. Restaurant.

(13) Le Patio

117, rte. du Nord - 90.97.73.10
Mme. Rémy. Open until 9:30 p.m. Closed Tues. dinner, Wed. & Jan. 2-Feb. 6. Garden dining. Pets allowed. Cards: V, AE, DC.

It would be wrong to change the formula for success of this popular restaurant created out of an old sheepfold. On summer evenings the flowering terrace is crowded with boisterous young people, who are served meals that have the double merit of generosity and local color, sincerely expressed in the hot cod pie, the beef stew, the Alpilles lamb cooked over a wood fire and the cheeses in oil.

A la carte: 250F. Menus: 110F (weekdays only), 140F, 180F.

(13) La Régalido

Rue Frédéric-Mistral - 90.97.60.22
M. Michel. Open until 9 p.m. Closed Mon., Tues. lunch, Dec. & Jan. Garden dining. Pets allowed. Parking. Telex 441150. Cards: V, AE, DC, MC.

This old oil mill has been restored magnificently: Everything is simple yet refined, from the big, romantic rooms with flowering terraces to the vaulted dining room with large, round tables and beautiful cutlery. The cuisine of owner Jean-Pierre Michel is elegantly classic, making more use of simply prepared good ingredients than of imagination: bass mousseline with beurre blanc, bass cooked in a court bouillon with olive oil and leg of lamb in a casserole with garlic. The prices are steep, though there are a few good wines for less than 100 francs. During the summer, guests are served in the garden.

A la carte: 350-400F. Menus: 210F, 260F, 300F and 400F (weekdays only).

La Régalido

(See restaurant above)
Closed Dec. & Jan. 14 rms 550-1,200F. Half-board 580-900F. TV. Air cond. in 6 rms. Pets allowed.

Located in the heart of town, these comfortable rooms are furnished like little boudoirs and look out on a charming garden. Relais et Châteaux.

Forbach

57600 Forbach - (Moselle)
Paris 385 - Metz 60 - Sarreguemines 19 - St-Avold 23

(15) La Bonne Auberge

15, rue Nationale (2 km NE on N 3), 57350 Stiring-Wendel - 87.87.52.78
Mlles. Egloff. Open until 9:45 p.m. Closed Mon. dinner, Tues., 1st 2 weeks in July & 10 days at Christmas. Air cond. No pets. Parking. Cards: V, AE.

The Egloff sisters have made a great hit with this kitsch bistro decorated with flowers, 1930s chairs and modern dishes in lively colors. They have done their best to bring back the luster to this poor, collapsed mining area. And why not give Forbach a dose of charm as well? Isabelle Egloff is a young beauty who serves both as sommelier and maître d'hôtel; her sister, Lydia, prepares the delicious dishes: vegetables in aspic in a poultry marinade with a mild garlic cream, roast John Dory surrounded by potatoes, goose liver with langoustines, lamb's tongue and sweetbreads cooked in a court bouillon, a hot rhurbarb tart and a baba dipped in a fresh-fruit soup. The joy of inventiveness is present in all that emerges from the kitchen. The wine cellar is superb but expensive, like all the pleasures of this young, friendly restaurant.

A la carte: 350-400F. Menu: 198F, 340F.

Forcalquier

04300 Forcalquier - (Alpes-de-Haute-Provence)
Paris 775 - Aix 66 - Digne 49 - Manosque 23 - Sisteron 44

(13) Hostellerie des Deux Lions

11, pl. du Bourguet - 92.75.25.30
M. Audier. Open until 9:30 p.m. Closed Sun. dinner & Mon. (off-seas.) & Nov. 15-Feb. 28. Pets allowed. Garage parking. Cards: V, DC, MC.

Perched atop a peak in an old Roman village—but still steadily climbing the hill of success—this charming restaurant was once an old relay station for horses. After the open-arms reception of Mme. Audier, you will discover her husband's passion: the most stunning selection of cheeses imaginable, all perfectly ripe. But first you must taste the spontaneous and fresh cuisine of Michel Montdor-Florent, an intelligent interpreter of regional traditions: filet of bass in a broccoli cream sauce, filet of lamb with two types of grapes and a verjuice (the juice of unripened grapes) sauce, and delicious peach gratin. The wine list is perfectly composed by Jean-Luc Pouteau.

A la carte: 280F. Menus: 88F (weekdays only), 120F, 155F, 215F.

Hostellerie des Deux Lions

(See restaurant above)

Closed Sun. & Mon. (off-seas.) & Nov. 15-Feb. 28. 18 rms 160-225F. Half-board 235-295F. TV in 15 rms. Pets allowed.

This cheerful old relais features simple but impeccably maintained country-style rooms with some lovely furnishings and gentle rates.

Forges-les-Eaux

76440 Forges-les-Eaux - (Seine-Maritime)
Paris 113 - Dieppe 54 - Beauvais 50 - Rouen 42

15 Auberge du Beau Lieu

Le Fossé - 35.90.50.36

M. Ramelet. Open daily until 9:30 p.m. Garden dining. Pets allowed. Parking. Cards: V, AE, DC, MC.

Patrick Ramelet had the great idea of turning the house next to his Norman inn into a stunning dining room filled with antique furniture. And he had an even better idea when he decided to study under Marc Meneau. The dishes on his menu show his personality as a passionate, self-taught perfectionist: the sautéed langoustines with spices in a delicate Sauternes cream, the fried sweetbreads and veal kidneys with fresh pasta in a smooth mustard sauce and the caramelized pears with ice cream. Ramelet has earned an extra toque for having one of the best tables in Normandy, and a tip of the toque for the recently enlarged wine list.

A la carte: 300F. Menus: 110F (weekdays only), 200F (wine incl.), 180F, 210F.

Fougerolles

70220 Fougerolles - (Haute-Saône)
Paris 363 - Epinal 43 - Vesoul 38 - Luxeuil-les-Bains 9

16 Au Père Rota

8, Grande-Rue - 84.49.12.11

M. Kuentz. Open until 9 p.m. Closed Sun. dinner, Mon. (except holidays) & Nov. 19-Dec. 13. Pets allowed. Parking. Cards: V, AE, DC.

The big news at this place is that the decor, which we'd previously found so depressing, has finally been thoroughly renovated; now it's all bright, fresh and done in excellent taste. And what has always tasted good now tastes even better: the generous, enthusiastically prepared cuisine of Chantal and Jean-Pierre Kuentz. Their menu features lively creations that are cooked with precision and priced reasonably. The interpretation of the products and, in particular, the delicate use of local wines in Jean-Pierre's sauces have helped us discover some superb dishes: the goose liver in aspic, the duck salad with cabbage, the court bouillon of turbot and shellfish with wine and ginger, the fish in chive butter, and the baked cherry crêpes with Kirsch ice cream. The wine list is increasingly impressive, and the service is faultless.

A la carte: 300F and up. Menus: 125F and 185F (weekdays only), 165F (weekends and holidays only), 235F.

Fréjus

83600 Fréjus - (Var)
Paris 890 - Cannes 40 - St-Raphaël 4 - Ste-Maxime 21

13 Les Potiers

135, rue des Potiers - 94.51.33.74

M. Klein. Open until 10 p.m. Dinner only in seas. Closed Sat. lunch & Wed. (off-seas.), March 1-11 & Nov. 14-Dec. 15. Air cond. Pets allowed. Cards: V.

This is a friendly, peaceful place in the old part of town. Mireille Klein graciously serves her guests—in a modest decor—her husband's competent, classical cooking: blond livers with leeks, scorpionfish mousseline with a coulis of baby lima beans, sweetbreads with wild mushrooms, and tasty desserts. The smallest fixed-price menu is a good find.

A la carte: 230-250F. Menus: 135F and 160F to 190F (weekends and holidays only).

Résidences du Colombier

Rte. de Bagnols - 94.51.45.92

Open year-round. 3 stes 750F. 54 rms 385-420F. Pool. Tennis. Parking. Telex 470328. Cards: V, AE, DC.

The rooms of this modern complex are located in bungalows on the grounds. Restaurant.

La Fuste

see Manosque

Gan

see Pau

Garabit

see Saint-Flour

Garancières

78890 Garancières - (Yvelines)
Paris 52 - Houdan 14 - Pontchartrain 11

13 La Malvina

La Haute-Perruche - 34.86.45.76, 34.86.46.11

M. Borré. Open until 9 p.m. Closed Wed. dinner, Thurs. & Jan. 2-Feb. 3. Garden dining. Pets allowed. Cards: V.

Paris may be just a short drive away, but this little village is undoubtedly *country*. The forest is at its doorstep, and the dining room extends into a charming little garden. The owner, a solid, mustachioed man, is a serious product of the hotel school of the General Transatlantic Company. His cuisine is inspired by the repertoire of traditional cooking, but his execution is firm and his sauces light: duck confit with potatoes and cèpes, turbot in beurre blanc, beef ribs, fricassée of farm chicken. The wines of the southwest are intelligently selected.

A la carte: 230-250F. Menu: 190F (wine incl.).

Gassin

83990 St-Tropez - (Var)
Paris 877 - Le Lavandou 33 - St-Tropez 8 - Ste-Maxime 15

15 Domaine de Belieu

Rte. de St-Tropez - 94.56.40.56

M. Gourmelon. Open daily until 11 p.m. Air cond. Garden dining. No pets. Parking. Cards: V, AE.

By settling in at the edge of Saint-Tropez, in Gunther Sachs's former restaurant, M. Gourmelon, a young industrialist and multimillionaire, perhaps has not chosen the ideal place to preserve his anonymity. The Domaine de Belieu recently kept people gossiping—no one had ever seen such a sumptuous residence on the peninsula, a place full of mansions that make the Carrington's "château" on *Dynasty* seem shabby. Gourmelon has engaged a solid team of cooks, and now visitors flock there for the cuisine as well as for the curiosity of the place and its marvelous antiques. In pleasing contrast to the sumptuous decor, the cooking is wonderfully simple in the great bourgeois tradition: roasted prawns with marinated vegetables; seafood salad with green beans; fish with fennel; risotto of pigeon with truffles; stewed lamb with fresh thyme; and fine traditional desserts.

A la carte: 600-700F.

13 La Verdoyante

Montée de Gassin - 94.56.16.23

M. Mouret. Open until 9 p.m. Closed Wed. & Nov. 10-March 20. Garden dining. Pets allowed. Parking. Cards: V.

This little restaurant between the Saint-Tropez gulf and the vineyards has one of the most appealing terraces in the area. The cuisine is generously flavored, and the prices are decent (including those of the best wines of Provence): rabbit-liver pâté, mussel gratin with spinach, lotte in a saffron cream sauce, beef stew à la provençal, grilled fish. The reception and service are charming.

A la carte: 230F. Menu: 120F.

Gémenos

13420 Gémenos - (Bouches-du-Rhône)
Paris 794 - Marseille 23 - Toulon 50 - Brignoles 48

Relais de la Magdeleine

42.82.20.05

Closed Nov. 1-March 15. 20 rms 360-600F. Half-board 410-500F oblig. in seas. TV in 15 rms. Pets allowed. Pool. Parking. Cards: V.

Plane trees shade this eighteenth-century Provençal house with its beautiful, peaceful rooms and pleasant library. Magnificent grounds surround the pool, and the reception is perfect. Restaurant.

Gérardmer

88400 Gérardmer - (Vosges)
Paris 421 - Colmar 52 - Epinal 40 - St-Dié 30 - Belfort 77

Les Bas-Rupts et Chalet Fleuri

3 km on D 486 - 29.63.09.25

M. Philippe. Open until 9:30 p.m. Closed Dec. 5-20. Garden dining. Pets allowed. Garage parking. Telex 960992. Cards: V, AE, DC.

This large, family-run operation is a modern and opulent-looking chalet in the middle of the Vosges countryside, where it's pure green in the summer and pure white in the winter. Owner Michel Philippe has made it into one of the most welcoming hostelries in the region. Warm, comfortable and filled with light, it was freshened up recently (notice the lovely larch- and cherry-wood ceiling). Everyone seems happy to see you and to serve you. The owner himself is attentive to every detail, and his charming daughter-in-law, Marie-Hélène, manages an impressive wine list and doubles as a perfect hostess. The cooking is done by Philippe and his new chef, François Lachaud, based on a sensible repertoire that features regional flavors turned out with perfect lightness. The prices are reasonable, both à la carte and on the fixed-price menus, which are generous, reflect fresh ideas and use the finest produce. For 150 francs, for example, you will be served an exquisite ham cooked on the bone or unctuously creamy tripe in Riesling, a fish combination with fresh noodles, a salad topped with a grandiose Munster gratin, and glazed nougat with a fruit coulis. From the à la carte menu, try the fricassée of lobster with coriander, the salmon with a light Pommard wine sauce and the exquisite desserts made by daughter Sylvie.

A la carte: 280-330F. Menus: 110F, 160F, 190F, 260F, 340F.

Les Bas-Rupts et Chalet Fleuri

(See restaurant above)

Closed Dec. 5-20. 32 rms 250-480F. Half-board 300-450F. TV. Pets allowed. Tennis.

The rooms of this comfortable, modern chalet in the mountains are light, spacious and tastefully decorated. The service is discreet and the breakfast lovely. Outdoors, guests can take tennis lessons in the summer and can cross-country ski in the winter.

La Croisette

2, blvd. de Colmar - 29.63.24.10

Closed Oct. 15-Dec. 15. 32 rms 110-215F. Half-board 140-200F. Pets allowed. Garage parking. Cards: V, AE, DC.

The small rooms are well situated between the lake and the center of town. Restaurant.

(14) Au Grand Cerf

Pl. de Tilleul - 29.63.06.31

M. Rémy. Open daily until 9:30 p.m. Garden dining. Pets allowed. Garage parking. Telex 960964. Cards: V, AE, DC.

The large dining room/veranda has just been distinctively renovated in blue tones, with cascading curtains and Louis XVI chairs. It's a shame that it is open only on busy days. The rest of the time guests content themselves in the other dining room, which, with its new carpet and view of the garden, is actually quite pleasant. The cuisine remains well prepared (with remarkable cooking times) but too serious and not always executed as it should be: nice lobster pot-au-feu, sweetbreads with shellfish in a creamy but slightly overpowering sauce, Chartreuse of fatted chicken with cabbage and an insufficient choice of desserts, one of which is a tasty gratin of red fruit.

A la carte: 280-300F. Menus: 185 and 140F to 230F.

Grand Hôtel Bragard 

(See restaurant above)

Open year-round. 3 stes 600-850F. 57 rms 220-460F. Half-board 240-330F. TV. Pets allowed. Pool.

This excellent old-style hotel, with pretty, well-equipped rooms, a small pool, a sauna and a game room, was being renovated as we went to press.

Gevrey-Chambertin

21220 Gevrey-Chambertin - (Côte-d'Or)
Paris 310 - Dole 62 - Beaune 26 - Dijon 13 - Besançon 46

Les Grands Crus

Rte. des Grands-Crus - 80.34.34.15

Closed Dec. 1-Feb. 25. 24 rms 220-310F. Garage parking.

The comfortable rooms look out on either the famous vineyards or the old church. A pleasant breakfast is served in the garden.

(15) Les Millésimes

25, rue de l'Eglise - 80.51.84.24

M. Sangoy. Open until 9 p.m. Closed Wed. lunch, Tues. & Feb. Air cond. Pets allowed.arking. Cards: V, AE, DC, MC.

It would be difficult to celebrate the virtues of family spirit more than it is done at this magnificent underground restaurant situated beneath an old wine-press house. The cuisine is handled by Jean Sangoy and two of his sons. Mme. Sangoy and her daughter receive and serve the guests. And the wise Didier Sangoy has the heady responsibility of keeping a loving eye on the cellar, which could almost qualify as a national monument. He will guide you through one of the best wine lists in France (with 40 wines from Gevrey-Chambertin and some ineffable old vintages), without overwhelming you with too much of his knowledge on the subject, which is extensive. He won't overlook the more modestly priced bottles, but that still won't keep your tab reasonable, particularly if you order the delicate pan-fried liver salad, the salmon and foie gras brochette with a confit of carrots and honey, and the delicious and classic lemon millefeuille. Nevertheless, another toque is warranted for this energetic family.

A la carte: 400-500F. Menus: 175F, 240F, 340F, 440F.

(17) Rôtisserie du Chambertin

Rue du Chambertin
80.34.33.20

M. Menneveau. Open until 9 p.m. Closed Sun. dinner, Mon., Feb. & 1st week of Aug. Air cond. Pets allowed. Parking. Cards: V.

Pierre Menneveau can breathe easy now—he has finally found a chef and recovered his three toques. Since the disappearance four years ago of Céline, his wife, his experiments have not gone over well. But it seems that now, on the twentieth anniversary of the Rôtisserie, the worries have finally ceased. Chef Jean-Pierre Nicolas is as solid as the rock in which these deep caves were carved and the lovely stone-walled dining room was set up, animated by green tapestries and glittering candles. For twelve years he collaborated with chef Louis Outhier at La Napoule, so we know he went through tough and excellent training.

You won't find any of the dishes of the former "master," which is a good sign. Instead, Nicholas has kept a few of Céline's, paying her discreet homage by offering the "true old-style coq au vin" and the leg of pullet with morels in a wine sauce, which is a marvelous success. Everything else is from his own repertoire in the light classic style—with a perfect execution, Swiss-watch precision in cooking times and pronounced flavors highlighted by exquisite sauces that are never invasive. We almost wanted to ask Pierre to make up a bed for us in the restaurant, so we could prolong our stay and try the dishes we were so sorry to have missed: the frogs'-leg soup with watercress cream, the sweetbreads feuilleté, the veal kidneys with juniper berries and the cold pear soufflé. But it was enough to try the wonderful plate of fresh frogs' legs with a parsley coulis and a garlic mousseline, the hot duck liver with cherry sauce, the filet of sander in a wine sauce, the stuffed Bresse pigeon and the large dessert plate—all in all, evidence enough to condemn Jean-Pierre Nicolas to spend the rest of his life behind these stoves.

Pierre Menneveau has been thinking of making Nicolas a partner before eventually leaving the restaurant to the chef. But he would certainly shed a tear if he left behind the dizzying collection of Chambertins, Gevrey-Chambertins, Chapelle-Chambertins and Latricières-Chambertins, to speak only of the regional wines.

A la carte: 350F. Menus: 195F (lunch only), 230F, 370F.

Gex

01170 Gex - (Ain)
Paris 498 - Lons-le-Saunier 96 - St-Claude 44 - Geneva 17

11/20 L'Auberge Gessienne

Chevry - 50.41.01.67

M. Emery. Open until 9:30 p.m. Closed Sun., Mon., Feb. 1-22 & Aug. 1-16. Terrace dining. Pets allowed. Parking. Cards: MC.

It never was for the rough reception or the table-turning service that you made your way here in the past, but rather for the generous and well-prepared fixed-price menus. Unfortunately, that motivation no longer exists; the cooking is now dull and poorly done. Overcooked fish and tasteless chicken cause us to throw in the towel, and with it the toque.

A la carte: 280F. Menus: 62F (weekday lunch only), 110F, 145F, 220F.

IN NEARBY **Col de la Faucille**
(12 km N on N 5)
01170 Gex - (Ain)

La Mainaz

50.41.31.10

Closed June 15-July 1 & Nov. 1-Dec. 20. 10 stes 350F. 20 rms 295F. Half-board 420F. TV in 10 rms. Pets allowed. Garage parking. Telex 309501. Cards: V, AE, DC, MC.

The rooms in this vast chalet in the superb environment of Mont Blanc and Lake Geneva are warmly furnished.

Gien

45500 Gien - (Loiret)
Paris 154 - Orléans 64 - Bourges 76 - Cosne 41

(14) Le Rivage

1, quai de Nice - 38.67.20.53

M. Gaillard. Open until 9:15 p.m. Closed Feb. 6-28. Pets allowed. Hotel: 3 stes 390-570F; 19 rms 240-285F; half-board 311F oblig. in seas. Garage parking. Cards: V, AE, DC, MC.

Christian Gaillard, the owner of this beautiful place that faces the Loire and the old humpback bridge built by Anne of Beaujeu, sports a black handlebar mustache; his cheerful dining room sports gray and pink wall hangings and high-backed chairs in blue velvet. This active president of the Association of Young Restaurateurs of France prepares a cuisine that is more and more assertive, seasonal and regional. He makes expert use of fish from the Loire, game, local goat and garden produce to create such dishes as the delicious duck terrine with morels, the perfect sander from the Loire with a meadow-mushroom cream (light and balanced), the tasty émincé of veal kidneys with hazelnuts and the good gratin of oranges and wild strawberries.

A la carte: 300F. Menus: 135F, 165F, 255F.

Gimont

32200 Gimont - (Gers)
Paris 699 - Toulouse 51 - Auch 26 - Agen 85

(14) Château de Larroque

Rte. de Toulouse - 62.67.77.44

M. Fagedet. Open until 9:30 p.m. Closed Jan. 1-17. Garden dining. Pets allowed. Garage parking. Telex 531135. Cards: V, AE, DC.

André Fagedet and his charming sister, Rosemary, manage this delectable little neo-Renaissance château and its immense grounds. Guests dine in delicious peace on a lovely terrace or in the bright dining room while looking out at the greenery. The cuisine prepared by this excellent professional is growing in finesse, confidence and new ideas, and André is always attentive to the beauty of his products: magnificent goose stew with fresh pasta, cèpes and chanterelles, an original dish of duck hearts sautéed with cherry butter, and delicate glazed nougat with bitter oranges. There is a large selection of Bordeaux, but the regional wines are sparse.

A la carte: 300F. Menus: 125F, 180F, 240F.

Château de Larroque

(See restaurant above)

Closed Jan. 1-17. 1 ste 1,200F. 14 rms 330-720F. Half-board 480-550F oblig. in seas. TV. Pets allowed. Tennis.

This appealing Relais et Châteaux, located in the opulent Gascon countryside, has modern, well-cared-for rooms. Guests enjoy a breakfast of homemade bread and croissants on the pretty terrace. Activities include tennis and fishing.

Goumois

25470 Trévillers - (Doubs)
Paris 485 - Besançon 93 - Montbéliard 53 - Bienne 44

(13) Taillard

81.44.20.75

M. Taillard. Open until 9 p.m. Closed Wed. (off-seas.) & Nov. 15-March 1. Garden dining. Pets allowed. Hotel: 3 stes 290-310F; 14 rms 150-230F; half-board 245-290F oblig. in seas. Garage parking. Cards: V, AE, DC.

Life is sweet in this pretty country manor run by Jean-François Taillard. A large chalet, comfortable and full of light, sitting amid a sea of pastureland and fir trees, Taillard is a place where people can breathe deeply. They listen to the jingling of bells on the grazing flocks, and they settle down to dine on the terrace or in the beautiful dining room with its picture windows. There they partake of such dishes as the saddle of young rabbit with chive cream, the double-cream fondue with morels and the veal mignon with crayfish and fresh pasta. Now this is the good life, where you can sip the famous Arbois wines and savor the peace of the fields from your pleasant room.

A la carte: 250-280F. Menus: 95F (weekdays only), 125F, 200F, 280F.

Gouvieux

see Chantilly

La Grande-Motte

34280 La Grande-Motte - (Hérault)
Paris 747 - Nîmes 44 - Montpellier 20 - Sète 50

(15) Alexandre-Amirauté

Esplanade de la Capitainerie - 67.56.63.63

M. Alexandre. Open until 10 p.m. Closed Sun. dinner & Mon. (except July-Aug.), Jan. 11-Feb. 18 & school vacations. Air cond. Terrace dining. No pets. Parking. Cards: V, MC.

The beautiful Louis XV dining room looks out over the open sea through the picture windows along its veranda. This "admiralty" of the Alexandre family is without a doubt a little too chic to be seductive, although one could easily define seduction as being comfortably settled at a table directly above the Mediterranean, surrounded by an extraordinarily attentive staff and invited to taste, at reasonable prices, some of the best cooking on the Languedoc coast. Michel Alexandre is a saucier with a delicate touch and a great connoisseur of his region's resources, which he skillfully interprets without resorting to the ruinous myth of using luxury products. His two fixed-price menus are extremely generous and increase in price only slightly each year. The most modest one serves as a good introduction to his cuisine. It begins with an exquisite fish soup or Bousigues oysters, then (after some between-course spirits, the so-called trou languedocien) the lotte en bourride or the guinea-fowl with broad beans, followed by regional cheeses and the cart of desserts and ice creams that is paraded with solemnity by the patriarch, Paul Alexandre, a former grand-champion pastry maker.

A la carte: 300F. Menus: 175F, 290F.

Hôtel Azur

Esplanade de la Capitainerie - 67.56.56.00

Closed Dec. 5-Jan. 27. 3 stes 550-750F. 17 rms 390-490F. TV. Air cond. Pool. No pets. Parking. Cards: V, DC.

Each of these rooms has attractive furniture and looks out on the open sea. The hotel is far from the crowds but close to the quays, the boats and the casino. No restaurant.

Le Grand-Pressigny

37350 Le Grand-Pressigny - (Indre-et-Loire)
Paris 293 - Tours 58 - Le Blanc 43 - Loches 33

(13) L'Espérance

Le Carroir des Robins - 47.94.90.12

M. Torset. Open until 9 p.m. Closed Mon. & Jan. 6-Feb. 6. Pets allowed. Hotel: 10 rms 120-150F; half-board 165F. Parking. Cards: V, AE.

Bernard Torset is a good chef who is concerned with bringing classicism and regionalism together harmoniously on the plate. But sad to say his style recently has undergone some changes for the worse: less personality in his dishes and carelessness in accompanying vegetables—which used to be such a strong point with him. We found a straightforward warm salad of prawns and smoked salmon in olive oil, an uninspired and poorly cooked pigeon, and an excellent gratin of wild strawberries with orange butter. The pink, country-inn interior is charming, but noise from the backroom television seeps in. And the service by Mme. Torset includes some waits that would try the patience of Job.

A la carte: 280F. Menus: 70F, 95F, 140F, 165F.

IN NEARBY Le Petit-Pressigny

(9 km E on D 103)
37350 Le Grand-Pressigny - (Indre-et-Loire)

(16) La Promenade

47.94.93.52

M. Dallais. Open until 9:30 p.m. Closed Sun. dinner, Mon., 3 weeks in Jan. & 2 weeks in Oct. Cards: V.

Until recently this was the most unattractive old village bistro in the entire Indre-et-Loire area. Today, it may not be the most beautiful, but at least the contemporary furniture, apricot tones and painted beams lit by halogen lamps finally make it worthy of the enterprising and delicious cuisine of Jacky Dallais, whose propensity for research and taste for distinct flavors have blossomed in this new environment. His brief à la carte menu changes completely twice each week. As for his one fixed-price menu, it is an extraordinary poem, refreshed each day with glories from the marketplace. Dallais deserves two toques alone for the quality-to-price ratio: broccoli fondant in a red-pepper vinaigrette, filet of perch with a crayfish coulis, roasted chevreau (kid) with parsley, a cheese platter and fresh fruit gratin with almond milk. How much for this feast? A mere 93 francs! And for an additional 75 francs you can savor the best of the Chinon Blanc appellation, that of Olga Raffault. A confirmed revelation and worth an additional point for continued improvement.

A la carte: 260-280F. Menus: 93F, 150F.

Grane

26400 Crest - (Drôme)
Paris 598 - Valence 29 - Privas 28 - Montélimar 31

(14) Giffon

Pl. de l'Eglise - 75.62.60.64, 75.62.70.11

M. Giffon. Open until 9 p.m. Closed Sun. dinner & Mon. (except holidays), 1 week in Feb. & mid-Nov.-1st week of Dec. Air cond. Terrace dining. Pets allowed. Hotel: 9 rms 180-250F. Parking. Cards: V, AE, DC, MC.

Attentive to tradition, Jacques Giffon has nevertheless, in just a few years and with the help of his son, Patrick, made headway toward a more imaginative regional cuisine. The crayfish, the mousselines of American pike and the vermouth sauces have given way to better-composed dishes, like the quail salad with cabbage, the mussel soup with saffron, the fabulous spit-roasted rack of Drôme lamb and the gâteau ardéchois with chestnuts. The service is charming, and the terrace is pleasant, as are the Côtes-du-Rhône wines.

Menus: 120F (weekdays only), 150F, 190F, 250F.

Granges-les-Beaumont

see Romans-sur-Isère

Grasse

06130 Grasse - (Alpes-Maritimes)
Paris 938 - Nice 39 - Draguignan 56 - Cannes 17

11/20 Maître Boscq

13, rue de la Fontette - 93.36.45.76

M. Boscq. Open until 8:30 p.m. Closed Sun. & Mon. (off-seas.). Terrace dining. Pets allowed.

In the heart of the old village, with its winding, picturesque streets, Master Boscq fulfills the role of the neighborhood's great chef: cabbage stuffed with meat and vegetables, the local feast; snails in pesto and, of course, an aïoli platter. Congenial, not badly done and pretty cheap.

A la carte: 180F. Menus: 68F, 90F.

Hôtel du Patti

Pl. du Patti - 93.36.01.00

Open year-round. 50 rms 261-320F. Half-board 368-450F. TV in 30 rms. Pets allowed. Telex 460126. Cards: V, AE, DC, MC.

Marvelously situated in the heart of the old town, this is an exceptional hotel of its kind. The recently renovated rooms are inviting, luxuriously comfortable and equipped with beautiful bathrooms, and the service is in keeping with the decor. Breakfast is good. Restaurant.

Grenade-sur-l'Adour

40270 Grenade-sur-l'Adour - (Landes)
Paris 720 - Aire-sur-l'Adour 18 - Orthez 51

Pain Adour et Fantaisie

7, pl. des Tilleuls - 58.45.18.80

M. Oudill. Open until 10:30 p.m. Closed Sun. dinner (except July-Aug.), Mon. (except dinner July-Aug.) & Jan. 2-Feb. 13. Terrace dining. Pets allowed. Parking. Cards: V, AE, DC, MC.

At first we were a little surprised to learn that Didier Oudill had settled down less than ten kilometers from Michel Guérard, with whom he had been a close collaborator for ten years. But, thank goodness, everything is okay: They are still pals, even sending each other customers. Oudill played his cards in such a way that when you've eaten lunch at one place, you can only be curious about trying the other for dinner. Having contributed enormously to the success of Eugénie, he has enough of his own ideas to avoid rehashing his teacher's cuisine.

First of all, his prices are adapted to the means of the regional clientele, which favors the three-menu system—classic, fantasy (more creative and fanciful) and fish—new each day and at each sitting; these fixed-price menus are models of outstanding quality-to-price ratios. Then, Oudill knew that he had to establish a personal tone to avoid comparisons to or reminiscences of Guérard. His touch is evident from the hot eel pâté in sablé pastry to the asparagus feuilleté with chives, from the glazed purple artichokes in court bouillon to the mussels in a milk-fed lamb fondue that is simmered for hours (a great dish with an extraordinary aroma), from the pork and chicken stew to the wild strawberries and puff pastry feuilleté with cherries and crème anglaise, Oudill's precise and harmonious talent, his love for rustic flavors and his sensitivity show so well that, in the future, a treatment at the spa at neighboring Eugénie-les-Bains may include an obligatory meal in Grenade. Oudill and his young wife have become the bourgeois lords of this exquisite old manor, which they have embellished with antique furniture, paintings and floral arrangements. In good weather, tables are set on the terrace overlooking the Adour, and the regional wines don't last long in the glasses. Almost too good to be true—we gladly present a third toque.

A la carte: 250F. Menus: 135F, 195F, 260F.

Grenoble

38000 Grenoble - (Isère)
Paris 562 - Lyon 104 - Chambéry 57 - Geneva 148

Sights. Le Jardin de Ville (dear to Stendhal); Le Parc Paul-Mistral; Old Grenoble (the old Saint-Claire and Saint-André districts, with their markets and shops); L'Eglise Saint-Laurent (and its crypt); Le Musée de Grenoble (exceptional collections from the nineteenth and twentieth centuries); Le Musée de Saint-Marie-d'en-Haut (and its excellent regional expositions); Téléphérique (cable car) de la Bastille (a superb panorama); Musée de l'Automobile; walk through the garden of the Dauphins; Le Centre National d'Art Contemporain (CNAC); stroll the cours Berriat.

Eating on the Run. L'Ange Bleu, 4, rue Casimir-Périer (good crêperie, decor dedicated to Marlene Dietrich); Le Bistrot des Halles, 9, rue Chenoise; Le Brûleur de Loups, 4, rue André-Chevalier (more than 150 wines); La Calanque, 9, rue Col.-Denfert-Rochereau (pizzeria, open late); Le Mal Assis, 9, rue Bayard; Le Pain et le Vin, 3, rue Vauban (wine by the glass, regional open-face sandwiches); La Panse, 2, rue de la Paix; La Tête de Veau, 11, rue Dr-Mazet (pork specialties).

Brasseries. Pub Cambridge, 11, pl. Victor-Hugo, and La Taverne de Maître Kanter, 6, blvd. du Maréchal-Lyautey (two spots where people like to gather).

Bars & Cafés. Bar du Park Hôtel, 10, pl. Paul-Mistral (excellent hotel bar); Bar de la Renaissance, 1, rue du Palais (for an apéritif); Bar du Tribunal, 1, pl. St-André (a little later); Piano-Bar du Drac Ouest (see "Nightlife").

Nightlife. Le Club des Etudiants, in the St-Laurent district; Le Drac Ouest, 135, blvd. Paul-Langevin à Fontaines (bar, restaurant, club and hall for private parties); La Mare au Diable, at the Sonnant-d'Uriage; Le Palazzo, 7, ave. de Vizille (the most popular nightclub in town).

Shops. *Charcuteries, caterers:* Gilbert Goddard, 8, rue Pierre-Loti (open Sunday); Roger Gulliet, 135, cours Berriat; Maison Gambrelle, 4, rue Auguste-Gaché (sausage specialties). *Chocolates, confections:* Belval, 2, blvd. Gambetta (for Grenoble walnuts); La Forêt Noire, 5, rue Alphand; Godiva, 14, ave. d'Alsace-Lorraine; Zugmeyer, 4, blvd. Agutte-Sembat (the best chocolate in Grenoble). *Cheese:* Bayard, 16, pl. Bayard; Poisat, 30, ave. d'Eybens (Italian specialties). *Pastries:* Le Tyrol, 12, rue St-Jacques (Austrian specialties). *Tearoom/ice cream:* La Belle Hélène, 4, pl. de Gordes.

Angleterre

5, pl. Victor-Hugo - 76.87.37.21

Open year-round. 70 rms 250-435F. TV. Air cond. Pets allowed. Telex 320297. Cards: V, AE, DC, MC.

This well-conceived, modern hotel is situated on the largest square in Grenoble (converted into a park), before the Vercors mountains. No restaurant.

Lesdiguières

122, cours de la Libération - 76.96.55.36
Closed July 29-Sept. 2 & Dec. 18-Jan. 4. 36 rms 240-400F. TV in 9 rms. Pets allowed. Garage parking. Telex 320306. Cards: V, AE, DC, MC.

This excellent establishment serves as a training ground for hotel-school students. Pleasant rooms look out on expansive grounds. Restaurant.

(13) A Ma Table

92, cours Jean-Jaurès - 76.96.77.04
M. Martin. Open until 9:30 p.m. Closed Sat. lunch, Sun., Mon. & Aug. Pets allowed. Cards: V.

M. Martin, who studied extensively at numerous luxury hotels on the Côte d'Azur, devotes himself to a cuisine that is aromatic, light and varied—some of the most pleasant and consistent cooking in Grenoble. In an intimate, friendly setting, he offers a small à la carte menu that changes according to the season and the marketplace: terrine of young rabbit with basil and small lardons, fresh grilled salmon with tarragon and mustard, grilled filet of duck breast with baby vegetables. Michèle Martin is a gracious hostess. Nice reasonably priced wine from the Abymes (46 francs).

A la carte: 230-250F.

(14) Le Pommerois

1, pl. aux Herbes - 76.44.30.02
M. Bouissou. Open until 10:30 p.m. Closed Sat. lunch, Mon. & lunch in Aug. No pets. Cards: V, AE, MC.

This old restaurant located on the marketplace square has the same hours as the vendors. The dining room, on two levels, is decorated with antique furniture and exposed stone. The reception is a little cool and the service a bit amateur, but some of chef Philippe Bouissou's unique qualities deserve recognition. It's a shame that inconsistency is the rule, with a stunning moment deserving of three toques coming on one day and bitter deception the next. But based on our most recent experiences, we have given an additional point to this engaging cuisine, with its squab filets accompanied by ravioli with peas, and its sea bass with lean bacon and celery. Nice wine cellar; distressing prices.

A la carte: 400F. Menus: 150F(lunch only, wine incl.), 160F, 210F.

11/20 Taverne de Ripaille

10, pl. Paul-Mistral - 76.87.29.11
M. Ducret. Open until midnight. Closed Sun. dinner, July 29- Aug. 21 & Dec. 23-Jan. 2. Air cond. Pets allowed. Telex 320767. Cards: V, AE, DC, MC.

This simple, serious cuisine is served until late in the evening with infinite friendliness in the intimate and quiet atmosphere of the Park Hôtel: Russian-style tuna, marinated mackerel, lotte with mustard, braised veal kidneys.

Park Hôtel

(See restaurant above)
Closed July. 29-Aug. 21 & Dec. 23-Jan. 2. 3 stes. 56 rms 610-910F. TV. Air cond. Pets allowed.

This hotel is exemplary as much for its highly qualified staff as for its decor and the comfort of its rooms. There is a new conference room and small rooms for business lunches.

IN NEARBY **Bresson**
(7 km S on D 5 & D 264)
38320 Eybens - (Isère)

---

(14) Chavant

Rte. Napoléon - 76.25.15.14, 76.25.25.38
M. Chavant. Open until 9:30 p.m. Closed Sat. lunch, Wed. & Dec. 25-31. Air cond. Garden dining. No pets. Parking. Telex 980882. Cards: V, AE.

One never knows what to expect at this establishment, which so disapointed us last year that we could not rate it at all, following a two-toque performance the year before. Imagine our surprise this year to encounter delicious duck-liver ravioli, light and perfectly poached, and veal sweetbreads in a light and wholly successful lemon sauce. Even the now famous filet of beef in what could have been a boring treatment with foie gras and truffles was remarkable, and the chocolate cake faultless. In other words, a top-notch version of Chavant, equal to the opulent decor and the beautiful pool and garden. The service unfortunately suffers the house disease of unpredictability, running from charming to distressed, while, amid all of this, the wine cellar constitutes a haven in all of this of undisturbed excellence.

A la carte: 350F. Menu: 158F.

Chavant

(See restaurant above)
Closed Wed. & Dec. 25-31. 2 stes & 5 rms 380-680F. TV. Air cond. Pets allowed. Heated pool. Tennis.

Guests can breathe the pure air of the countryside from the seven lovely rooms.

IN NEARBY **Montbonnot-Saint-Martin**
(7.5 km NE on N 90)
38330 St-Ismier - (Isère)

---

(14) Les Mésanges

76.90.21.57
M. Achini. Open until 9:30 p.m. Closed Sun. dinner, Mon., 1 week in Feb. & 1 week in Aug. Garden dining. Pets allowed. Cards: V, AE.

At this dependable restaurant, guests can be assured of a pleasant reception and fine food. The dining room is a bit cramped, but the Achinis recently opened a lovely garden with a view of the mountains and pastures. This is a sure value in the Grenoble region, even if the cuisine shines less for its imagination than for its consistent generosity. Try the homemade foie gras, the blanquette of lobster and coquilles St-Jacques, the fricassée of sweetbreads and veal kidneys in green-pepper cream, and the hot apple feuilleté. Two of the fixed-price menus are quite reasonable, and the wine cellar is excellent.

A la carte: 300-350F. Menus: 95F (weekdays only), 140F, 185F, 290F.

IN NEARBY **Varces**
(13 km SW on N 75))
38760 Varces - (Isère)

L'Escale

Pl. de la République - 76.72.80.19, 76.72.84.07

MM. Brunet & Buntinx. Open until 9 p.m. Closed Sun. dinner & Mon. (off-seas.), Tues. (in seas.) & Jan. Garden dining. Pets allowed. Parking. Cards: V, AE, DC, MC.

The Brunets, who now take care of only their hotel, have left young Frédéric Buntinx the responsibility of maintaining the glorious reputation of their luxurious enterprise. He takes care of the dining room, brilliant with silver and Limoges dishes, its garden-facing veranda filled with flowers and birds. The cuisine can hold its own: foie gras in a truffle sauce, ragoût of frogs' legs and crayfish, and beef with walnuts and morels. The service is charming, but the prices are severe.

A la carte: 350-400F. Menus: 98F (weekday lunch only), 150F to 365F.

L'Escale

(See restaurant above)

Closed Sun. & Mon. (off-seas.), Tues. (in seas.) & Jan. 7 stes (chalets) 490F. Half-board oblig. in seas. TV. Air cond. Pets allowed.

The charming, air-conditioned chalets, located in a garden, provide comfort and calm, in spite of the proximity to the highway. Relais et Châteaux.

Gréoux-les-Bains

04800 Gréoux-les-Bains - (Alpes-de-Haute-Provence)
Paris 786 - Digne 62 - Aix-en-Provence 50 - Manosque 15

La Crémaillère

Rte. de Riez - 92.74.22.29

MM. Guérard. Open until 9:30 p.m. Closed Dec. 15-Feb. 14. No pets. Parking. Telex 420347. Cards: V, AE, DC.

Although there are more than 100 place settings, this contemporary dining room succeeds in being charming and almost intimate. The Guérards have created a marvelous garden atmosphere with modern paintings, wicker chairs and flowers on the tables. Professionalism is everywhere, with exacting service and a light, delicate cuisine by Jean-Paul Hartmann, trained at Eugénie-les-Bains: red-mullet salad with lemon herbs, exquisite but a bit small (a half mullet is not much); delicious squab turnover with Lubéron wine; perfect pear-and-chocolate millefeuille. Fine multiregional wine cellar.

A la carte: 330F. Menus: 165F, 285F.

La Crémaillère

(See restaurant above)

Closed Dec. 15-Feb. 14. 54 rms 305-342F. TV. Pets allowed. Pool. Tennis.

This lovely, recently rebuilt hotel welcomes those who have come to take the spa waters, and all those who love the restful calm.

Villa Borghèse

Ave. des Thermes - 92.78.00.91

Closed Dec.-Feb. 70 rms 290-500F. Half-board 340-630F. TV. Air cond. in 36 rms. Pets allowed. Heated pool. Tennis. Golf. Garage parking. Telex 401513. Cards: V, AE, DC, MC.

This attractive, modern hotel is located on grounds dominated by greenery and adorned with a lovely, small pool. The terraced rooms are furnished in good taste. Fitness packages are available, as well as free golf. Restaurant.

Grésy-sur-Isère

73740 Grésy-sur-Isère - (Savoie)
Paris 591 - Chambéry 37 - Albertville 19

La Tour de Pacoret

1.5 km NE of Grésy on D 201 toward Montailleur, 73460 Frontenex 79.37.91.59

Closed Oct. 1-March 1. 10 rms 200-320F. Half-board 230-280F oblig. in seas. No pets. Garage parking. Cards: V, AE, DC.

Beneath a fourteenth-century lookout tower, these ten well-equipped, comfortable rooms open onto a spectacular setting of mountains and forests. Restaurant.

Grimaud

83310 Cogolin - (Var)
Paris 857 - Hyères 45 - St-Tropez 10 - Ste-Maxime 13

La Boulangerie

Rte. de Collobrières - 94.43.23.16

Closed Oct. 15-March 28. 11 rms 445-660F. Half-board 450-650F oblig. in seas. Pool. Tennis. Parking. Cards: V.

This charming and intimate hotel has a superb view of the Maures mountain range. Videotheque and restaurant.

Les Santons

Rte. Nationale - 94.43.21.02, 94.43.35.11

M. Girard. Open until 10:30 p.m. Closed Wed. (except June-Sept.), Jan. 2-March 15 & Nov. 2-Dec. 23. Air cond. Pets allowed. Cards: V, AE, DC.

The crystal gleams, the silver shines, and the check is equally showy. But this simple and spacious restaurant inside a lovely village house is also a civilized, bright and animated place with an extremely courteous staff. Truffles, lobster, langoustines and foie gras still occupy the places of honor on the menu that, although considerably lighter, still reflects a bourgeois classicism: duckling terrine with truffled foie gras, scrambled eggs with truffles (250 francs), veal kidney casserole, roast rack of lamb with herbs. The cheeses are irreproachable (curiously, all of the goat cheeses are of the ash-coated style of the Loire Valley), and the desserts, fresh and diverse, are still one of chef Claude Girard's high points. So it is not surprising that, when night falls, the "summertime Saint-Tropez" crowd rushes to be seated at these tables.

A la carte: 400-500F. Menus: 200F (weekday lunch only), 265F, 385F.

Guérande

44350 Guérande - (Loire-Atlantique)
Paris 445 - Nantes 77 - La Baule 6 - Vannes 65

La Collégiale

63, Faubourg Bizienne - 40.24.97.29

M. Portner. Open until 11 p.m. (midnight in summer). Closed Wed. lunch, Tues. & Oct. 1-March 31. Garden dining. Pets allowed. Cards: AE, DC.

Good taste is everywhere, in the cuisine as well as the decor. Charming Christian Portner floats between the ravishing tables of his new dining room with red chintz (another room on an exotic veranda faces a garden paradise) and directs a battalion of decorative and efficient young waiters. The cuisine of his associate, Christian Mimault, is modern and exquisite, generally executed without fault; it would be perfect with less-buttery sauces: tasty shelled spider crab (excessive whipped butter), seafood pot-au-feu with excellent baby vegetables, delicious pear tarte with a pear coulis. Good but pricey wine cellar.

A la carte: 350F. Menus: 200F (weekdays only, wine incl.), 350F.

Le Havre

76600 Le Havre - (Seine-Maritime)
Paris 204 - Amiens 179 - Rouen 86 - Deauville 72

Sights. Le Musée des Beaux-Arts; Le Musée de l'Ancien Havre; Le Musée d'Archéologie (Graville Priory); Le Muséum d'Histoire Naturelle (pl. du Vieux-Marché); Le Parc de Loisirs de Rouelles; Le Cap de la Hève (view of Le Havre and the Calvados hillsides); La Cathédrale Notre-Dame. In Sainte-Adresse: La Chapelle Notre-Dame-des-Flots; the port (boat tours).

Eating on the Run. La Papillotte, 38, pl. Chillon; La Pizzéria Salvatore, 49, rue Richelieu.

Nightlife. La Bohème, pl. Amiral-Mouchez; L'Etable, 51, rue Bernardin-de-St-Pierre (discotheque and restaurant).

Bordeaux

147, rue Louis-Brindeau - 35.22.69.44

Open year-round. 31 rms 270-445F. TV. No pets. Telex 190428. Cards: V, AE, DC, MC.

This new hotel in the center of town faces the yacht harbor. Comfortable rooms. No restaurant.

La Manche

18, blvd. Albert-Ier - 35.41.20.13

M. Pimmel. Open until 9 p.m. Closed Sun. dinner, Mon. & July. Pets allowed. Cards: V, AE, DC.

The bourgeois-decorated room (being renovated) has large bay windows overlooking the magnificent spectacle of the harbor. Pierre Pimmel, the owner of this pleasant restaurant, receives his guests with great civility and offers a clear and well-balanced collection of dishes. Listed on the first fixed-price menu is mussel soup with saffron, a feuilleté of scrambled eggs with a leek fondue, white chicken meat with fresh lasagne, cheeses and a hot apple tart. We'll award another point for the controlled daring with which Pimmel interprets the classical tradition, as evidenced in his galantine of skate, his bavarois of haddock and watercress and his ragoût of lotte with oysters.

A la carte: 300F. Menus: 125F, 175F.

Mercure

Chaussée d'Angoulême - 35.21.23.45

Open year-round. 24 stes 450-500F. 72 rms 390-420F. TV. Pets allowed. Telex 190749. Cards: V, AE, DC, MC.

Right in the middle of town and next to the business center, this hotel offers comfortable lodging and several conference rooms. Restaurant.

IN NEARBY **Hode**
(18 km E on D 982)
76430 St-Romain-de-Colbosc - (Seine-Maritime)

Dubuc

On D 982 - 35.20.06.97

M. Dubuc. Open until 9:15 p.m. Closed Sun. dinner, Mon. & Aug. 6-21. Pets allowed. Parking. Cards: V, AE, DC.

The furniture is Henri II, but the cuisine is definitely Louis-Philippe. That's the name of the longtime chef at this large white structure sitting on a chalky hillside. Louis-Philippe Dubuc may be an old-school cook, but he likes nothing more than fresh, beautiful products and is not afraid to throw himself into a lighter, more personal style, which allows his great savoir-faire to blossom. Try the Puy salad daringly combining ham hocks, lentils and foie gras; red mullet with green peppers; a superb mixture of lobster and calf's head with pearl barley; classic and perfect roast pigeon; loin of lamb stuffed with its sweetbreads in a foie gras cream. The service is perfect, the wine list heavy on big bottles and the decor not unpleasant.

A la carte: 400F. Menus: 190F, 290F.

Hendaye

64800 Hendaye - (Pyrénées-Atlantiques)
Paris 777 - Biarritz 28 - St-Jean-de-Luz 13 - Pau 141

IN NEARBY **Biriatou**
(4 km SE on D 258)
64700 Hendaye - (Pryénées Atlantiques)

Bakéa

59.20.76.36

Mme. François. Open until 10 p.m. Closed Oct. 1-May 1. Terrace dining. Pets allowed. Hotel: 15 rms 140-280F; half-board 432-572F oblig. in seas. Parking. Cards: V, AE, DC, MC.

The cuisine of Claude François, served in his large Basque house overlooking the Bidassoa and Spain, remains as it was 25 years ago, and there is nothing that could make you hope that this Parisian (who spends his winters in California) will change a thing in the next quarter century. Doubtless his classic repertoire is carefully prepared overall, but there are certain simplistic items: the squab casserole with peas and the mediocre asparagus vinaigrette. The gulf turbot, admirably poached and served with simple melted butter was, however, a marvelous dish, and the chocolate cake was a perfect dessert. Mme. François is an excellent hostess.

A la carte: 300F and up. Menus: 120F, 180F.

IN NEARBY **San Sebastian**
(19 km W, in Spain)

Arzak

Alto de Miracruz
(943) 27.84.65

M. Arzak. Open until 11 p.m. Closed Sun. dinner & Mon. Cards: V, AE, DC, MC.

There may not be much reason for you to find yourself in this neighborhood other than the great Basque cooking available chez Arzak, but that is more than reason enough. Twenty-five autoroute-minutes from Bayonne will get you to this plush, warm, grand bistro with the Spanish-style woodwork. Jean-Marie Arzak is an extremely accomplished and sensitive cook who knows how to bring the classical, the traditional, the delicate and the hearty together into one great hymn to his love: the Basque country and its ways. He has spent time working under all the great French chefs to help equip him for his mission, and he will provide you with some truly extraordinary, absolutely unique dishes. Take, for example, his prawns sautéed with prunes and pimiento accompanied by an unusually scented white wine called Txakoli, or the crab in a sort of delicate dough served on a sauce of vermouth and saffron, or the cod steak grilled and served in a green sauce with clams. Or try some of the even more country-style dishes, such as the salad of gambas (prawns) with foie gras or the marvelous red beans and chorizo sausage. The wine list is stunningly rich and the service knowledgeable.

A la carte: 300-400F.

Hennebont

56700 Hennebont - (Morbihan)
Paris 482 - Vannes 56 - Concarneau 55 - Lorient 10

Château de Locguénolé

Rte. de Port-Louis
(4 km S on D 781) - 97.76.29.04

Mme. de la Sablière. Open until 9:30 p.m. Closed Mon. (off-seas., except holidays & for groups) & Jan. Garden dining. No pets. Telex 950636. Cards: V, AE, DC, MC.

One reader writes that a melon here tastes like a turnip. It wasn't particularly funny, but it was enough for the reader to conclude that the chef was a lemon. But we have found the new 29-year-old chef here to be one of our finest new discoveries. Denis Le Cadre has quickly demonstrated his ability to bring imagination and other flavors to Breton cooking. His lobster consommé with oyster brioche, tartare of mackerel with smoked salmon and lime mousse, extraordinary crab puff pastry, the scallops and asparagus tips in a hazelnut-oil vinaigrette, sea bream royale in a salt crust with a sublime butter à la badiane, whole roasted Challans duckling, melt-in-your-mouth lamb chops and original, beautiful desserts have earned an unheard of start-up rating of three toques from your astounded correspondents. Lovely reasonable wines, wonderful hosts... don't wait to hurry here.

A la carte: 350-500F. Menus: 130F (weekday lunch only), 190F, 280F, 460F.

Château de Locguénolé

(See restaurant above)

Closed Jan. 4 stes 690-1,637F. 31 rms 380-1,048F. Half-board 489-834F. Heated pool. Tennis.

The large, comfortable rooms, located in both the château and the annex, are furnished with antiques and feature exposed beams and old fireplaces. Breakfast is delicious. Activities include bicycling, hunting, sailing and fishing, as well as beaches a mere nine kilometers away, an eighteen-hole golf course twenty kilometers away, and an equestrian club nearby. Helicopter landing.

Le Hode

see Le Havre

Le Hohwald

67140 Barr - (Bas-Rhin)
Paris 424 - Strasbourg 47 - Sélestat 26 - St-Dié 46

Zundelkopf 

5 km SW on D 425, Col du Kreuzweg
88.08.30.41

Closed March 6-18 & Nov. 8-Dec. 12. 22 rms 110-200F. Half-board 155-180F oblig. in seas. Pets allowed. Parking.

The half-board prices are unbelievable in this modest but pleasant little Alsatian hotel on a hill, surrounded by a sea of fir trees. Restaurant.

Honfleur

14600 Honfleur - (Calvados)
Paris 192 - Le Havre 57 - Rouen 76 - Caen 60 - Lisieux 34

Le Cheval Blanc

14

2, quai des Passagers - 31.89.39.87

M. Samson. Open until 9:30 p.m. Closed Thurs. (except holidays), Jan. & Feb. No pets.

M. Samson would like this old house for post horses, with its rich, rustic decor opening onto the port, to be the best restaurant on this part of the coast. Having handed over the management of the hotel portion of the establishment to his son-in-law (returned from Vergé and Rostang), Samson now devotes himself entirely to perfecting his ambitious and attractive menu. Served with great respect, the rich, elegant meals put expensive products to good use and are well doused with Loire wines, notably the good Vouvrays produced by Samson: oysters in a creamy curry court bouillon, turbot with roasted oysters and chives, veal kidneys with pickled shallots.

A la carte: 300-350F. Menus: 130F, 200F, 280F.

L'Ecrin

19, rue Eugène-Boudin - 31.89.32.39

Open year-round. 20 rms 250-450F. Garage parking. Cards: V, AE, DC, MC.

This stunning manor has daring furniture, a neo–Haute Epoque decor and a savvy clientele. The huge rooms with canopy beds are extremely comfortable and the carpets and tapestries lovely. Billiards. No restaurant.

(14) La Ferme Saint-Siméon

Rue Adolphe-Marais - 31.89.23.61

M. Boelen. Open daily until 9:30 p.m. Garden dining. Pets allowed. Parking. Telex 171031. Cards: V.

This delightful seventeenth-century Norman house with slate walls is the original core of a vast hotel complex that has recently undergone expansion. Guests rave over the new covered pool and flower garden and the majestic "Pressoir Saint-Siméon," a Norman-style building with luxurious rooms recently added to the large manor, not to mention the grounds and tennis courts beside the ocean. However, it is at the Ferme (the former inn belonging to Mère Toutain, dear to the Impressionists) that you can put your feet under the table in the company of a clientele of rich foreigners attracted in hordes by the inimitable charm, the Seine bay and the prestige of the cultural aura that is carefully maintainted by the Boelen family. By bringing to the kitchen a former second chef from Laurent, the untiring Roland Boelen has certainly not disrupted this gourmand, lower-Normandy menu, but he has assuredly put an end to the languidness in the cooking. From now on everything you eat in this new and luxurious dining room will be seriously prepared and given a lovely finishing touch, whether it be the pigeon in wine vinegar, the brill with asparagus flowers or the rack of lamb. The wine cellar is excellent, and the prices formidable.

A la carte: 500-600F. Menus: 220F (weekday lunch only), 350F (weekday dinner only).

La Ferme Saint-Siméon

(See restaurant above)

Open year-round. 5 stes 1,810-2,590F. 33 rms 590-1,750F. TV. No pets. Tennis.

Next to the exquisite old farm, this Norman-style structure has seventeen new, luxurious rooms with ocean views and ravishing marble bathrooms. This hotel complex is one of the most beautiful and charming on the entire Norman coast. The service is high-class, and breakfast is of rare quality. Relais et Châteaux.

Houdan

78550 Houdan - (Yvelines)
Paris 62 - Chartres 50 - Rambouillet 29 - Dreux 21

(14) La Poularde de Houdan

24, ave. de la République - 30.59.60.50

M. Vandenameele. Open until 10 p.m. Closed Wed. dinner, Thurs. (except April-Aug.) & Feb. 6-23. No pets. Parking. Cards: V, AE.

We have no complaints with the recent improvements in the decor, which is now simple, comfortably modern and pleasant to be in, particularly in fine weather facing the garden and the river valley. We wish we had as little to say about the service and the fare, but we must report that the former was inexperienced, the latter careless. The establishment in general seems to have lost its way. A number of dishes were badly presented, and none of were deserving of two toques: delicious smoked salmon served with toast that was cold, foie gras stuck in some insipid jelly, an honest calf's head with potatoes and a delicate wine sauce, excellent rack of lamb and a dull chocolate cake with crème anglaise. Very nice wine list, but stay away from the house apéritif, "La Bicyclette."

A la carte: 400F. Menus: 150F (weekdays only), 200F (weekdays only, wine incl.), 250F.

Igé

71960 Pierreclos - (Saône-et-Loire)
Paris 394 - Tournus 30 - Mâcon 14 - Cluny 11

12/20 Château d'Igé

85.33.33.99

M. Jadot. Open until 9:30 p.m. Closed Tues. dinner & Wed. (off-seas.) & 2 weeks at year end. Garden dining. Pets allowed. Garage parking. Telex 351915. Cards: V, AE, DC.

The thick, noble stone walls beneath heavy beams, the elegant tables and the monumental fireplace set the atmosphere for this beautiful, small medieval château where the counts of Mâcon once lived. The cuisine is expensive but well prepared, though it certainly could stand some improvement. With great respect, the waiters will serve you beef and rabbit pâté with baby vegetables, the filet of grilled beef and the duckling with apples.

A la carte: 300F.

Château d'Igé

(See restaurant above)

Closed Nov. 15-March 1. 6 stes 650-850F. 6 rms 360-550F. TV in 10 rms. Pets allowed.

The atmosphere of this medieval minifortress, situated on its own grounds facing the Mâcon mountains, is excellent, and each of the pretty rooms is unique and perfectly comfortable. Relais et Châteaux.

L'Ile-Bouchard

37220 L'Ile-Bouchard - (Indre-et-Loire)
Paris 270 - Chinon 18 - Tours 40 - Ste-Maure 13

(13) Auberge de l'Ile

3, pl. Bouchard - 47.58.51.07

M. Guérin. Open until 9:15 p.m. Closed Sun. dinner, Mon. & Feb. Terrace dining. No pets. Cards: V, AE, DC.

No longer is this the back-room country bistro that we once knew. The decor (as well as the prices) has become elegant, and the cuisine has moved on from its former country accents. Philippe Guérin has talent and ideas, and it's understandable that he would be tempted to cook more like a fashionable chef. He is succeeding beautifully with such dishes as the marinated raw-fish combination with fresh mint, the médaillon of lotte with oysters, and the filet of roast duck with acacia honey. The old village and the Vienne river flowing below the terrace create an exquisite setting.

A la carte: 250F. Menu: 85F (weekday lunch only).

Illhaeusern

68150 Ribeauvillé - (Haut-Rhin)
Paris 448 - Colmar 17 - Sélestat 12 - Strasbourg 60

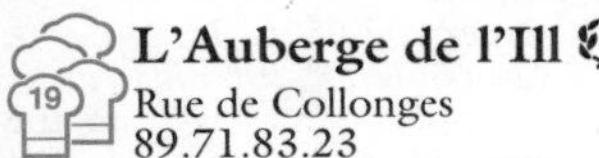

L'Auberge de l'Ill

Rue de Collonges
89.71.83.23

M. Haeberlin. Open until 9 p.m. Closed Mon. (except lunch in summer), Tues., Feb. & 1st week of July. Air cond. Pets allowed. Parking. Cards: V, AE, DC.

While many of his colleagues in Paris and on the Côte d'Azur were moaning about the tough tourist season a couple of summers ago, Paul Haeberlin was taking reservations three weeks in advance. His proximity to Germany clearly contributes to his popularity, but it doesn't explain everything. In the bright, warm dining room that opens onto an adorable garden, a small Alsatian farmhouse and willows that fall toward the romantic Ill, neighbors from across the Rhine are less numerous than the crowds from Paris, Burgundy, the Lorraine, Switzerland, Belgium, America and England. But above all, you will surely find a lot of local folks, whose merry faces brighten up the tables considerably as they gather for another culinary extravaganza.

A meal at the Haeberlins' is a feast for the eye and the palate, but also for the heart, for this marvelous family has a knack for infecting everyone with its happiness. And each member has his or her own special way of doing so. Paul's brother, Jean-Pierre, a subtle and sensitive artist, flits among the tables, offering a kind word and rectifying a jarring detail. Martine, Marc's petite and gracious wife, and her lively sister-in-law, Danielle, are stationed at the door, in front of the huge reservation book. In a black suit is Paul's young son-in-law, Marco, the maître d'hôtel. And hard at work in the kitchen is Paul himself, a stocky chef who clearly loves food. His son Marc follows in his footsteps, with less of a belly but just as much of his father's frank honesty and love for a job well done. And we certainly mustn't forget (although she rarely budges even to cross the street) the woman who makes everything shine in her beautiful old house: "Madame Paul," a real "maman-confiture" as only Alsace can produce.

In the shade of the willows, you've just drunk the last drop of a voluptuous Muscat from Hugel or Faller, and perhaps you saw the last invincible Illhaeusern fisherman pass by on his flat barge, casting his nets more by habit than conviction. Now you're seated in the large, white and green dining room, punctuated by paintings by Muhl. Open the white menu, on which Jean-Pierre's paintbrush has illustrated the landscape that lies before you, and you're on your way to the savory land of Haeberlin and son.

The clever menu answers the whim of every diner. It's a kind of classical music, conducted by the subtle hand of Paul, with all the specialties that established his fame: mousseline de grenouilles, brioche with truffled foie gras, salmon soufflé, lobster Prince Wladimir and the immortal truffe sous la cendre (truffles wrapped and baked buried in ashes). Or you can opt for more modern music: a salad of langoustes with mint, a terrine of smoked salmon and smoked coquilles St-Jacques, sea bass stuffed with crab, and medallions of lotte and filets of red snapper in red wine, dishes that seduce the locals who come to L'Auberge de l'Ill to enjoy what they can't find at home.

There is yet another song that charms us even more, one that is nurtured in the old soil of Alsace, with a few modern notes added by Paul and Marc. It accounts for the marvelous herbed eel roasted over hay that has almost magically shed its grease, allowing for a full expression of the delicacy of its meat; the warm green-lentil salad with bits of pork and foie gras; the ragoût of frogs' legs with choucroute and smoked bacon; and the venison noisettes wedded to roasted wild pears and fresh pasta—a marriage made in heaven.

The desserts are forever brilliant (though there's too much sugar in the rhubarb compote), the wine list towering and constantly restocked by a first-class steward—the best Muscat in creation; a Riesling Kastelberg to bring tears—and the service a marvel of elegance and good feeling. Once again we have had one of our best meals here. It is worth even the expanded prices.

A la carte: 500F and up. Menu: 490F.

La Clairière

46, rte. d'Illhaeusern, 68970 Guémar
89.71.80.80

Closed Jan. 1-March 3. 3 stes 700-1,000F. 25 rms 350-400F. TV. Pets allowed. Tennis. Parking. Cards: V, MC.

This is the place to get a good rest after your memorable meal at L'Auberge de l'Ill. Reserve far in advance. No restaurant.

Illzach

see Mulhouse

L'Isle-sur-la-Sorgue

84800 L'Isle-sur-la-Sorgue - (Vaucluse)
Paris 698 - Avignon 23 - Orange 41 - Apt 32

(13) Mas de Cure Bourse

Rte. de Cure-Bourse - 90.38.16.58

Mme. Donzé. Open until 9:30 p.m. Closed Sun. dinner & Mon. (except July-Aug.), Jan. 16-31 & Oct. 10-31. Garden dining. Pets allowed. Hotel: 1 ste 2,200F a week; 10 rms 220-330F; half-board 390-480F. Pool. Parking. Cards: V, AE, DC.

We have had a few unhappy readers, but if Françoise Donzé is a bit quirky, she also has a good sense of humor, and her large, rustic inn in the middle of the orchards is notable for its generous and personal cuisine. Formerly a chemist, Donzé is a purely self-taught chef; her dishes include a mousseline of scallops with curry, salmon en papillote (baked in buttered paper), lamb's tongue with an onion confit, and a warm pear-and- caramel cake. The tree-shaded summer terrace, next to the pool, is delightful. There are also a few pleasant, comfortable rooms.

A la carte: 250-280F. Menus: 98F (weekday lunch only), 144F, 178F, 228F.

Ispagnac

48320 Ispagnac - (Lozère)
Paris 610 - Mende 35 - Florac 10 - Sévérac-le-Château 50

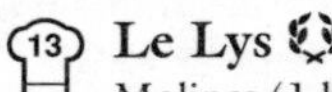

Le Lys

Molines (1 km W on D 707)
66.44.23.56

M. Plagès. Open until 10 p.m. Closed Oct. 1-April 30. Pets allowed.

Young students returned home after the excitement of May 1968, Noëlle and Michel Plagès traded their protesters' uniforms for those of restaurateur and cook. They have decorated their modern, loft-style dining room in good taste, and Noëlle has taken over the kitchen with passion and persistency. Today, this self-taught chef has become a real pro, attached to natural flavors and directing her inspiration toward the vegetables and fruits from her garden, regional mushrooms and other local products. Always anxious to do well, she never serves more than ten people at a time, which is all to the advantage of her morels in cream (discreet sauce), her grilled saddle of lamb with garlic cream and crisp baby vegetables, her tender beef rib roast accompanied by shallots in a ginger sauce, and her delicate rhubarb charlotte. Michel Plagés is a charming host.

A la carte: 260-280F. Menu: 130F.

Issoudun

36100 Issoudun - (Indre)
Paris 229 - Bourges 38 - Châteauroux 27 - Vierzon 34

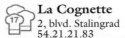

La Cognette

2, blvd. Stalingrad
54.21.21.83

M. Nonnet. Open until 10 p.m. Closed Sun. dinner, Mon. (except holidays) & Jan. 2-27. Air cond. Pets allowed. Parking. Cards: V, AE, DC, MC.

Since Jean Bardet left his beloved restaurant in nearby Châteauroux to settle in Tours, the locals swear they'll never suffer another such painful blow. They will cling to their other great chef—so now they are showing interest in this marvelous place, which you will find to be almost identical to the way Balzac described it in *La Rabouilleuse.* Here, 25 kilometers from Châteauroux, there is a great talent still waiting to be discovered, despite our three toques and enthusiasm. In a friendly hodgepodge from the Louis-Philippe empire, further complicated by an accumulation of family souvenirs, Alain Nonnet has always given in to the temptation of a rich, showy cuisine. But with his 50th birthday approaching, he has had the courage to reconsider. After training under Robuchon, he has finally put an end to his former ways. Nonnet no longer obscures his talent in frivolously fancy dishes. His cuisine has flavors that are forthright yet subtle, as in the duck fondant complemented by strawberry marmalade with vinegar and pepper, the lentil cream with truffles, and the beef and cèpes sandwich. These audacities perhaps upset the robust local appetites, which Nonnet appeases with large servings of chicken and Berrichon salad, among other simple, rural dishes, the kind of food honest people (like you and us) will always love. He offers a coffee and tea menu that is unique in France. The service of Mme. Nonnet and her daughter (whose husband is in the kitchen) is charming and the wine cellar remarkable.

A la carte: 350-400F. Menus: 180F (weekdays only, wine incl.), 150F to 400F.

La Cognette

(See restaurant above)

Closed Jan. 2-27. 3 stes 800-950F. 11 rms 270-600F. Half-board 420-650F. TV. Pets allowed.

Opened recently some 50 meters from the restaurant, this remarkable little hotel, with its large, stylish rooms and private garden, provides perfect comfort. The service and breakfast are marvelous.

Javron-les-Chapelles

53250 Javron-les-Chapelles - (Mayenne)
Paris 230 - Mayenne 25 - Alençon 36 - Le Mans 67

La Terrasse

30, Grand-Rue - 43.03.41.91

M. Bansard. Open until 9 p.m. Closed Sun. dinner, Mon., Tues., Jan. 2-16 & July 3-18. No pets. Cards: V.

Susan is English and charming. Her husband, Jérôme Bansard, met her at the Roux brothers' Waterside Inn, then again at Les Parveaux at the Castel-Novel de Varetz, where she was the pastry chef. Three years ago they settled down together in this rustic provincial (Louis XIII) house, to the great happiness of the region's gourmets. Everything here is seductive and carefully prepared, and the low prices will knock you over. Susan must still be making all of the desserts, because they are delicious and full of originality (warm banana feuilleté with cocoa butter, grilled chocolate truffle with coffee sauce). But first take a stroll through the lovely, and brief, menu prepared by Jérôme, where you will find inventive and personal dishes like cold asparagus soufflé with herbs, strips of rare lotte with an eggplant purée, filet of fatted duck with verjuice (the juice of unripened grapes), and sweetbreads lasagne with lemon rind. All this merits a toque, and we wager that it won't be just one for long. A number of Loire wines are available from the perfect cellar.

A la carte: 180F. Menus: 89F, 170F.

Joigny

89300 Joigny - (Yonne)
Paris 148 - Sens 30 - Auxerre 27 - Troyes 75

La Côte Saint-Jacques

14, Faubourg de Paris
86.62.09.70

M. Lorain. Open until 9:30 p.m. Closed Jan. 2-Feb. 2. Terrace dining. Pets allowed. Parking. Telex 801458. Cards: V, AE, DC.

People talk of the Lorains as they do of the Haeberlins or the Troisgros. It's a real family, bound together by affection and consumed by a singular passion: their restaurant, a humble auberge plunked on the edge of route Nationale 6, where 30 years ago their mother served coq au vin to business travelers. Today it has been transformed into a little Versailles of Burgundy and, above all, into one of the finest restaurants in France.

The Lorain family includes Jacqueline, a lively, charming blond who after a mere sniff of a glass of Burgundy can tell its origin, age and sometimes even the color of the winery owner's tie. Then there is Michel, a former pastry apprentice who, after winning numerous awards, including the Meilleur Ouvrier de France, slowly climbed the ladder of success toward a tranquil future as a master chef. And then suddenly understood when he hit 40 that the days of the old-boys' grande cuisine were numbered and that it was high time to throw some of his imagination and personality into his sauces. The day he realized that, the house of Lorain was destined for success.

And then there is Jean-Michel, Michel's son. While papa was breathing fresh air into his province, Jean-Michel found himself in the holy of holies of creative cooking: Freddy Girardet's in Crissier, Switzerland. When he returned home to Joigny in 1983, he found a Côte Saint-Jacques that clearly was on the rise, having already donned its third toque. Immediately, he and his father formed the most harmonious of duos, and just as rapidly, a shift occurred. An enormous talent was starting to emerge, and five years after the restaurant received its fourth toque, the father divides his time between his ovens and the management (no small task) of this imposing Relais et Châteaux. And now Jean-Michel is no longer the *other* Lorain but *the* Lorain. He is the author of a sensitive, intelligent cuisine, manipulating flavors, spices and aromas like a virtuoso. And he certainly has more surprises in store.

We have eaten in the elegant pale-gray and beige dining room—where lacquered woodwork, smoked-glass mirrors, soft lights, beautiful silver and bouquets of flowers create a warm, intimate atmosphere—on three occasions. And three times we found ultimate happiness as we dined on pigeon in aspic with artichokes, fennel and anise; another aspic with oysters, shallots and red wine (let's not forget that the "father" of oysters in aspic is someone else from Burgundy, Marc Meneau); and a delicately smoked sea bass (le bar) in caviar cream sauce (which posed a dilemma: Is it wise to smoke a light fish? That could, after all, diminish its flavor. But since sea bass has hardly any... regardless, it was quite good). There was also a wonderful combination of fresh morels and green asparagus in truffled butter, an exquisite sander cooked in its skin and accompanied by fine slices of celeriac marvelously blended with fried celery sticks, and the best saddle of rabbit we've had in a long time. It wasn't "sausaged" (a dismal preparation) but came in thick, tender, pink pieces with the kidneys and spaetzle in a voluptuous rosemary sauce. We should also mention, if only to delight in the memory, the effiloché of skate in balsamic vinegar, the farm pigeon and foie gras sautéed with baby turnips, the duckling breasts with wild rice and soy sauce, the lobster baklava with fresh fava beans, the three chocolate desserts, the crêpes with jellied grapefruit, the pears poached in wine and the caramel-praline ice cream.

And we should also say that the Lorains are the salt of the earth. Why? Because in this establishment, where "chic" is smack in front of your face, they dare to offer you an old-fashioned, family-style boudin noir with mashed potatoes. It's the same one Michel's clientele enjoyed before all the changes took place. Sure it's a detail, but it makes us love them all the more.

It's not yet known when the parking area will be converted into a garden. But while we're waiting, the Lorains have a small terrace, an extension of the dining room, on which one can dine while enjoying the fragrance of the greenery.

A la carte: 400-700F and up. Menus: 240F (weekday lunch only), 480F.

La Côte Saint-Jacques

(See restaurant above)

Closed Jan. 2-Feb. 2. 6 stes 1,500-2,300F. 12 rms 550-1,400F. Half-board oblig. in seas. TV in 15 rms. Air cond. in 15 rms. Pets allowed. Heated pool.

When Michel and Jacqueline Lorain dug an underground passage below the highway and decorated it with Roman flagstones and Mérovingian sculpted stones to provide their clientele with beautiful access to their new hotel, and when they took this cluster of old houses overlooking the Yonne and arranged suites of breathtaking size, comfort and luxury, their fellow restaurateurs thought they were crazy. And maybe they did overdo it a bit. But who cares? Once you've spent the night in this flamboyant Hollywood-à-la-Burgundy decor, you'll never forget it (ah, those enormous beds you sink down, down into, those dream bathrooms where not a single accessory has been forgotten). And isn't that what you should expect from a luxury hotel: a dream come true? The breakfast is sumptuous, and there's an indoor pool. Dogs are not only permitted but welcomed with open arms. The Lorains love them! Relais et Châteaux.

Joucas

84220 Gordes - (Vaucluse)
Paris 721 - Avignon 42 - Cavaillon 21 - Apt 15

(14) Le Mas des Herbes Blanches

90.05.79.79

M. Juillard. Open until 9:15 p.m. Closed Nov. 20-March 5. Terrace dining. Pets allowed. Parking. Telex 432045. Cards: V, AE, MC.

Facing the slightly strange landscape of an immense, barren plain between the plateau of the Vaucluse and the Lubéron, with the blue sky above, this old house of dried stone has been admirably restored with an air of monastic austerity. Pure lines, the beauty of stone, hearty vegetation—all of this was well thought out by Paul and Viviane Juillard, who, with all their will, want to avoid the traps of shortcuts and bad taste. Their new dining room is a perfect combination of soberness and elegance, and the cuisine of their chef, Patrick Deschamps, possesses a total rectitude of flavor, whether it be the foie gras millefeuille with truffle juice, the suprême of bass with caviar sauce or the sweetbreads au-Beaumes-de-Venise. Formerly at Lamelloise, Deschamps is an equally remarkable pastry chef, excelling in feuilletages (tarte fine, pear feuillantine). The prices are high, and the service is sometimes insufficient. Excellent wines from Provence.

A la carte: 350-400F. Menu: 200F (lunch only).

Le Mas des Herbes Blanches

(See restaurant above)

Closed Nov. 20-March 5. 2 stes 1,150-1,450F. 16 rms 670-1,150F. TV. Air cond. in 5 rms. Pets allowed. Heated pool. Tennis.

The sixteen stylish rooms are perfectly equipped (television, direct telephone, minibar), and most face the immense and grandiose panorama of the Lubéron. Relais et Châteaux.

Juan-les-Pins

06160 Juan-les-Pins - (Alpes-Maritimes)
Paris 920 - Nice 22 - Cannes 9 - Antibes 2 - Aix 160

Shops. See Antibes.

Auberge de l'Estérel

21, rue des Iles - 93.61.86.55

M. Plumail. Open until 9:30 p.m. Closed Sun. dinner, Mon., Feb. 1-8 & Nov. 15-Dec. 15. Garden dining. Pets allowed. Hotel: 15 rms 150-290F; half-board 200-215F. Parking. Cards: V.

The Plumails have freshened up the decor of their dining room, which is now better matched to the charm of their pleasant and peaceful establishment planted in the middle of a sumptuous garden. Success has in no way led to a compromise in the overall allure of this charming place, where even in high season the reception and service are cheerful and the cuisine of Christian Plumail filled with ideas and bursting with freshness. His ideas don't necessarily demand, like many others do, the use of the richest and most expensive products, which permits him to keep the prices under control. For example, he serves a creamy crab soup with basil accompanied by celery root, a sardine chartreuse in a white-wine sauce and a filet of haddock with endives and a potato purée with light soy butter. The portions are generous, and there is a good choice of Provençal wines, also reasonably priced.

A la carte: 280-300F. Menus: 150F, 225F.

Beauséjour

Ave. Saramartel - 93.61.07.82

Closed Oct. 1-Easter. 1 ste 1,480-1,750F. 30 rms 550-1,040F. TV. Air cond. Pool. Parking. Telex 470673. Cards: V, AE.

This small hotel is well situated in the green, residential quarter of Juan-les-Pins. The classic-style rooms have shaded terraces, and a lovely garden and barbecue are alongside the pool.

Belles Rives

Blvd. du Littoral - 93.61.02.79

Closed Sept. 10-March 25. 4 stes 2,240-3,610F. 41 rms 730-1,980F. Half-board oblig. in seas. TV. Air cond. Pets allowed. Telex 470984. Cards: V, AE.

The classic, ultra-comfortable rooms offer superb views of the entire bay as far as the Lérins islands. Improvements to the decor are constant. Private beach and boat launch. Restaurant.

Hélios

3, ave. Dautheville - 93.61.55.25

Closed Nov. 1-March 31. 2 stes 3,000-6,000F. 68 rms 500-1,200F. Half-board 600-1,100F oblig. in seas. TV. Air cond. Pets allowed. Garage parking. Telex 970906. Cards: V, AE, DC.

This luxurious hotel takes advantage of its private beach by serving lunches at the water's edge. The modern rooms are beautiful, and some have splendid terraces. Piano bar and restaurant.

Le Pré Catelan

22, ave. des Lauriers - 93.61.05.11

Open year-round. 20 rms 220-400F. Half-board 300-350F oblig. in seas. Parking. Cards: V, AE.

Set in a lovely garden planted with palm trees, this small hotel is 200 meters from the ocean. Restaurant.

La Terrasse

Ave. Georges-Gallice
93.61.20.37, 93.61.08.70

MM. Barache. Open until 10 p.m. (10:30 p.m. in summer). Closed Oct. 25-April 15 & lunch in July-Aug. Garden dining. Pets allowed. Parking. Telex 470778.

Good-bye Alain. Hello Christian! Alain Ducasse has left to make waves in Monte-Carlo, and Christian Morisset slipped into his position with such ease that the guests at the Hôtel Juana hardly noticed. It must be said that the two men have much in common. Morisset, like Ducasse, studied under Roger Vergé before conquering two toques at the Château d'Esclimont. Better yet, he worked there side by side with Ducasse, with whom he shares a taste for a cuisine that is spontaneous, lively, colorful and bathed in Provençal sunshine.

It is with brilliant subtlety and talent that Morisset prepares his crab ravioli with young spinach shoots, his zucchini flowers with langoustines embellished with a mustard-seed sabayon, his plate of aromatic Provençal vegetables with a light chive butter, his purple asparagus salad with a shellfish sauce, and his fresh local fish, such as the John Dory with clams or the red mullet roasted in olive oil. Then there are the escalopes of foie gras with chanterelles, the filet of veal with green peppers in a sherry sauce, the classic cherry clafouti, the bitter-chocolate fondant and the fried nectarines with peach-wine sorbet, each so precise that there is no reason to remove any of the toques from La Terrasse's head. On the terrace facing a flowered hill, palm trees and the lovely pool of this all-white 1930s hotel, you will discover happiness.

And, meanwhile, the runner-up Best Sommelier of France, Philippe Briswalter, will pamper you with the superb rosé of Provence from the house of Ott, Guigal's Condrieu, a Musigny from Comte de Vogué or the impressive Bandol from Château Pradeaux 1982. If you manage to leave after all that, you'll leave a deal poorer but infinitely happier and even eager to return and try it again.

A la carte: 500-800F. Menu: 495F (menu dégustation), 420F.

Hôtel Juana

(See restaurant above)

Closed Oct. 25-April 15. 5 stes 1,900-3,800F. 45 rms 670-2,500F. Half-board 325F (plus room). TV. Air cond. Pets allowed. Heated pool.

The Barache brothers have once again embellished this 1930s hotel, where the flower-filled terrace and the windows overlook the foliage of the municipal park. The superb pool makes this the best hotel in Juan-les-Pins, not to mention the more than 50 air-conditioned, comfortable rooms and suites. Unfortunately there are no grounds. Guests can enjoy lunch around the pool.

Juillan

see Tarbes

Jurançon

see Pau

Juvisy-sur-Orge

see PARIS SUBURBS

Kaysersberg

68240 Kaysersberg - (Haut-Rhin)
Paris 434 - St-Dié 46 - Colmar 10 - Munster 25

15 Chambard

9-13, rue du Général-de-Gaulle
89.47.10.17

M. Irrmann. Open until 9:30 p.m. Closed Sun. dinner, Mon. & Dec. 1-15 & March 1-21. Parking. Telex 88072. Cards: V, AE, DC, MC.

The name of this enterprise is that of its founder, one Marius Chambard. Pierre Irrmann is Chambard's successor at this luxurious place at the entrance of town, facing the Schlossberg vineyard and the old château. From the neo–Haute-Epoque dining room, the view through the bay windows looks out on the heart of town, the charming hometown of Albert Schweitzer, with its old bridge, its dense roofs and its grapevine-covered hills. The excellent chef's cuisine is classic and sauce-oriented on the one handtournedos 1900, fatted chicken with morels—and more modern on the other—foie gras pot-au-feu, seafood fricassée (which we prefer without tomatoes), grilled turbot with ginger, delicious hot figs with almond ice cream. Also noteworthy are two old standards beyond compare: the herring rémoulade and the mousse Chambard (chocolate). Irrmann spends less time now in the dining room, and the delighted kitchen staff no longer gives him grief for deserting his cuisine. But we miss him—his joviality was enchanting. The wine list offers the best of Alsace.

A la carte: 350-400F. Menus: 200F, 250F, 330F.

Chambard

(See restaurant above)

Closed Dec. 1-15 & March 1-21. 2 stes 400-500F. 18 rms 380-550F. TV. Pets allowed.

This pretty hotel with twenty remarkably decorated rooms and elaborate amenities fills the void of good places to stay in this highly touristy region.

Lacave

46200 Souillac - (Lot)
Paris 540 - Cahors 65 - Gourdon 26 - Rocamadour 10

13 Château de la Treyne

65.32.66.66

Mme. Gombert-Devals. Reserv. required. Open until 9 p.m. (10 p.m. in summer). Closed Nov. 15-Easter. Terrace dining. Pets allowed. Parking. Telex 531427. Cards: V, AE, DC, MC.

Truffles cooked in embers, duck confit with cèpes, hot foie gras with sherry vinegar... the cuisine isn't overflowing with ideas, but the new chef, Bernard Darcissac, demonstrates an excellent execution and handles the beautiful regional products with skill. The terrace, along the front of this marvelous château overlooking the Dordogne, is enchanting.

A la carte: 300F. Menu: 150F (lunch only), 200F (dinner only).

Château de la Treyne

(See restaurant above)

Closed Nov. 15-Easter. 1 ste 1,000F. 12 rms 700-1,000F. Half-board 950-1,250F oblig. in seas. TV in 4 rms. Pets allowed. Pool. Tennis.

This proud fifteenth-century château with luxuriously furnished rooms is perched just above the Dordogne. The terrace has a magnificent panorama.

14 Pont de l'Ouysse

65.37.87.04

MM. Chambon. Open until 9 p.m. Closed Mon. (off-seas.) & Nov. 11-March 1. Garden dining. Pets allowed. Parking. Cards: V, MC.

Not far from the great archaeological sites, on the path of our cave-dwelling ancestors, this family inn is a small paradise of greenery and tranquil beauty. Marinette and Daniel Chambon have, at great expense, restored and modernized this old house at the foot of the vertiginous peak crowned by the proud château of Belgastel. In summer, well protected from the processions of tourists, their shaded terrace above the Ouysse river has incomparable charm (the dining room is less seductive, but they plan to brighten it up). The owner's cuisine is one of the most inspired and adroit in the region, combining local ways with the lively personality of the autodidact: a lasagne made with crayfish ragoût and a watercress sauce, fried foie gras with capers, eels from the Ouysse in verjuice (the juice of unripened grapes) and a bitter-chocolate and fresh-mint millefeuille. Two impressive fixed-price menus and a well-stocked wine cellar.

A la carte: 300F. Menus: 120F, 170F, 220F.

Pont de l'Ouysse

(See restaurant above)

Closed Mon. (off-seas.) & Nov. 11-March 1. 13 rms 300-500F. Half-board 350F. TV. Pets allowed. Pool.

Most of the rooms have been ably renovated and now offer significantly greater comfort. The breakfast is delicious. Right outside is a fascinating landscape filled with caves.

Lagny-sur-Marne

77400 Lagny-sur-Marne - (Seine-et-Marne)
Paris 33 - Meaux 21 - Senlis 51 - Melun 42

15 Egleny

13, ave. du Général Leclerc - 64.30.52.69
M. Gaudet. Open until 9:30 p.m. Closed Wed. dinner, Thurs., Feb. 9-23 & July 26-Aug. 10. Pets allowed. Cards: V, AE, MC.

The arrival in Lagny of a young chef the caliber of Jean-Yves Gaudet is an event that could redirect a good number of gourmands headed for the new French Disneyland. Having opened not long ago in this lovely bourgeois building in an old village, Gaudet already seemed to have everything in place for great success when we dined there just a few weeks after the ovens were lit. The refined decor includes pale-pink tapestries and faces a sumptuous garden with flowering fruit trees. The waiters are young and spirited. The wine cellar houses many young wines, favoring the native Burgundy of the owner (he hails from Egleny, near Auxerre). And the cuisine brilliantly combines bourgeois tradition and modernity throughout a small repertoire of six appetizers, five fish dishes and six meats. Gaudet has worked at L'Archestrate, Le Vivarois and L'Espérance, where he picked up something valuable from each of the master chefs. His delightful cuisine is delicate yet honest: crayfish aspic in a court bouillon with anise, vol-au-vent (poultry quenelles, foie gras, sweetbreads and asparagus), remarkable pigeon salmi (stewed in wine and butter with Meaux mustard) served with cabbage stuffed with pork and duck, exquisite rolled lamb with fresh herbs, and strawberry feuillantine, among other wonderful desserts (frozen soufflé, chocolate fondant). Magnificent Brie cheeses. Gaudet earned his two toques immediately, and deservedly so.

A la carte: 350-400F. Menus: 180F (weekday lunch only), 280F.

Laguiole

12210 Laguiole - (Aveyron)
Paris 552 - Mende 85 - Aurillac 82 - Rodez 56

11/20 Auguy

Ave. de la Pépinière - 65.44.31.11
M. Auguy. Open until 9 p.m. Closed Sun. dinner & Mon. (off-seas., except school vacations), April 17-27 & Nov. 5-Dec. 25. Pets allowed. Hotel: 32 rms 110-200F; half-board 125-167F oblig. in seas. Parking. Cards: V.

Isabelle, the owner's daughter, presides with authority, if with inconsistency, over the ovens of this large provincial house, where the traditions of the region are strictly honored: salad of fried pork with walnut oil, pork feet with fresh pasta, duck confit with onions and prune parfait with Armagnac. Unfortunately, we encountered a few unpleasant surprises the last time we ate here: greasy lamb chops and a bitter cèpe cassolette.

A la carte: 180F. Menus: 63F (dinner only), 65F (weekday lunch only), 135F (summer only), 110F.

19.5 Michel Bras

(Lou Mazuc)
65.44.32.24
M. Bras. Open until 9 p.m. Closed Sun. dinner (except July-Aug.), Mon. & Oct. 15-March 23. No pets. Parking. Cards: V, AE.

Michel Bras—Super-Bras—came in 5,000th in the last New York marathon. It was the first big trip of his life. After the race, he returned to his village, without signing any solid-gold contracts in the States or lending his name to some hotel chain, the customary course for those who have become superstars of the pots and pans. Super-Bras, chef, poet and peasant, is never less shy, less modest and less frank than when at his mother's side, watching his pots or stirring his vats of jam.

If the 1,368 inhabitants of Laguiole (pronounced *La-iole*) still can't get over seeing Belgian Jaguars, German Porsches and English Rolls-Royces parked in their village, which not so long ago slept peacefully at the top of the wild and magnificent Aubrac, Bras doesn't seem to be affected by it. The fame, the pictures in magazines, the mammoth compliments of eleventh-hour discoverers... none of this seems important to him. What is important is being able to gallop up the mountain early in the morning and stop on the side of the road to pick gentian, amaranth and meadowsweet. And to then spread the fruits of his wild market on the kitchen table, and after numerous trials and failed guesses, his alchemist's knack transmutates the primary flavors of the basic ingredients into other flavors, which are infinitely more complex and subtle.

The purity of the sky and of the high plateaus of Aubrac, the extraordinary variety of plants and herbs that can be gathered there, and the poetic temperament and innate refinement of this self-taught chef came together to give birth to this new "nouvelle cuisine." There's little risk of it being imitated any time soon, and it's not likely that it will leave Bras's little realm. We can only imagine that someday, somewhere, such an exceptional being will once again encounter an equally exceptional natural surrounding.

Bras likes to say that his is an excessive ambition: the pursuit of simplicity. Is he really after simplicity? In the guise of the most natural of cooking, each of his dishes is in fact the result of rigorous construction and the product of a chemical analysis, which even if based on intuition approaches scientific value. In this system, vegetables play the role of seasonings, and flavors oppose and complement one another simultaneously. Each recipe is made up of one principal ingredient and two or three accompaniments—no more—with always-fresh herbs adding a strident or caressing touch as called for. Olive oil plays a greater role than cream or butter, which is used only to brown fish or meat.

From this process come dishes that you won't find anywhere else, with tastes that separate like rocket bursts. Having tried almost all of them, we'd like to describe them one by one, but we'd never finish. So we'll settle for remembering a few of the magical herbs. Genista flowers, for example, perfumed the juice of a lamb filet and sweetbreads grilled with young leeks. Gaillet (galium) gives a honey taste to the juice of a terrine of rabbit confit with garlic and baby turnips. Cistus (rockrose) throws a dash of anise flavor on the filet of loup (sea bass) au petit lait with sea salt and a marvelous bread quenelle seared with sage. Then there is the artemisia that strengthens the shallot broth used for cooking Mediterranean tuna ever so slightly. The curious but exquisite "potimarron" (a pre-Columbian vegetable that looks like a small pumpkin but has the sweet taste of a chestnut purée) and a dash of parsley made divine companions for sautéed whiting filets. Burnet (pimprenelle) slips a nutty flavor into the sautéed sole served in its juice with "burnt" bread and spinach leaves. The Aubrac tea, a menthol plant, has an incredibly savory effect on the infinitely pure juice of a filet of roast lamb, tender as an angel. A roast filet of rabbit was combined with truffles, turnips, skimmed cream and orache (a sort of wild spinach). And the exquisite Aubrac beef was sautéed and basted in a juice of roasted chicory root.

The desserts will simply make you fall over: bavarian cream à la recuite (whey from sheep's milk), a frozen gentian-and-lemon mousse on a coulis of black currants, a frothy ice milk flavored with licorice and soft butter caramel, a parfait with zests of citrus fruits, and crushed cooked oranges with cinnamon. Then come the unbelievably light hazelnut tuiles (wafers) that accompany the delicious coffee, which are the specialty of Sebastien, Michel's son, just 16 years old.

Everything is a family affair here. Papa Bras, a former iron worker blessed with common sense and uncommon ingenuity, plays the role of the receptionist in his own inimitable style (which doesn't necessarily please everyone). Michel's excessively kind sister takes reservations, and mama puts together the sausages and prepares the tripoux (tripe with mutton and veal) that you'll enjoy if you opt for the "petit menu" at 130 francs. And, finally, Ginette, Michel's wife, has become such a whiz at wines that in her cellar each region is represented by the best vineyards without the slightest error. She even managed to pull up a red Gaillac that was fruity, heavy and well above the usual level, a Manoir de L'Emmeille that stands well alongside the quite likable wines from the Auvergne, the sumptuous Côtes-du-Rhones and the most noble wines from Bordeaux and Burgundy.

And soon the old, vaulted cheese cellar that houses tables covered with bouquets of wildflowers will open onto a delightful herb garden.

A la carte: 300-500F. Menus: 130F (weekdays only), 280F, 400F.

Lou Mazuc

(See restaurant above)

Closed Sun. & Mon. (except July-Aug.) & Oct. 15-March 23. 13 rms 200-420F. TV. No pets.

Luxurious it isn't, but it is pleasant and full of character. Michel Bras himself designed the furniture and arrangements of these "studios à loggia" using sturdy local wood. Many of the rooms have windows that open onto the small herb garden, and the church bells awaken you just as the aroma of hearth cakes and toasted bread wafts into the morning air. Of course, you might prefer breakfast in the tradition of Aubrac: sausages, hams, old Laguiole cheese and a glass of Marcillac...

Lalinde

24150 Lalinde - (Dordogne)
Paris 574 - Cahors 90 - Périgueux 60 - Bergerac 22

(14) Hôtel du Château

1, rue de Verdun - 53.61.01.82

M. Gensou. Open until 9 p.m. Closed Fri. (except July-Aug.) & Dec. 1-March 1. Terrace dining. Pets allowed. Cards: V, AE.

Between the post office and the Dordogne sits this little neochâteau whose walls dip into the river. The dining room has plenty of charm, and the summer terrace, with its view of the verdant riverbanks, even more so. Guy Gensou is a professional who cultivates his classic dishes with a personal touch: duck foie gras with salt, sauté of langoustines in orange butter, frozen soufflé with walnuts. Homemade canned items are available for sale.

A la carte: 250F. Menus: 75F (weekday lunch only), 100F, 130F, 220F.

Hôtel du Château

(See restaurant above)

Closed Dec. 1-March 1. 8 rms 140-220F. Half-board 165-220F oblig. in seas.

These pretty rooms, several of which are just above the river, are gradually being modernized. The greeting is charming, and the prices reasonable.

Lamagdelaine

see Cahors

Lamastre

07270 Lamastre - (Ardèche)
Paris 582 - Le Puy 73 - Privas 56 - Valence 40 - Vienne 91

(15) Barattéro

Pl. Seignobos - 75.06.41.50

M. Perrier. Open until 9 p.m. Closed Sun. dinner, Mon. (except holidays & July-Aug.) & Dec. 15-March 1. Pets allowed. Hotel: 18 rms 150-300F; half-board 225-300F oblig. in seas. Garage parking. Cards: V, AE, DC, MC.

Aside from the prices (a bit high for the region), we have nothing but good things to say, once again, about this large and friendly family establishment. And all the more so since the small fixed-price menu, with its duck galantine (the likes of which you can rarely find these days) and veal liver with lime is still a real bargain for such quality. But let's linger over such beautiful dishes as the foie gras in a lime-blossom aspic; the half-cooked salmon with a shallot vinaigrette; and the always perfect house classic, the royal poularde de Bresse en vessie (fatted chicken in a pig's bladder), cooked with seasonings and a little foie gras, then carved before your eyes. The Ardèchois portions are generous, and Mme. Perrier knows how to revive declining appetites with her marvelous goat cheeses and stunning chestnut soufflé (better than the rather dull chocolate cake). The entire restaurant is scrupulously clean, with gladiolas on the tables and a staff that is attentive to the smallest detail. And the Perriers recently fixed up four rooms across the street, with a garden where breakfast is served. Their glory days have arrived! We salute them with an additional toque.

A la carte: 350F. Menus: 140F, 205F, 265F, 320F.

Château d'Urbilhac

2 km, rte. de Vernoux - 75.06.42.11

Closed Oct. 10-May 1. 13 rms 300-500F. Half-board 370-445F. Pets allowed. Heated pool. Tennis. Garage parking. Cards: V, AE, DC, MC.

Perched at an altitude of 500 meters on 150 acres of grounds, this sixteenth-century château has spacious, tastefully furnished rooms, a shaded tennis court and a pool with a panoramic view. Restaurant.

Lambesc

13410 Lambesc - (Bouches-du-Rhône)
Paris 740 - Marseille 51 - Apt 38 - Salon-de-Provence 21

14 Moulin de Tante Yvonne

Rue Benjamin-Raspail - 42.92.72.46

Mme. Soliva. Open until 9 p.m. Closed Tues., Wed., Thurs., Feb. & Aug. Pets allowed.

Superb armoires, tall buffets and a monumental table shine immaculately beneath the lovely arches of this old mill, where you'll find the smiling and mischievous André Soliva and the cuisine of the most famous of the "mothers" of Provence, from the Lubéron to as far away as Arles. And she can still prove (thank goodness!), as she approaches her 80th year, how her original cooking can be full of both energy and finesse: for example, her extraordinary creamed fish served with garlic croutons; leg of lamb stuffed with herbs and served cold under a light, aromatic cream; and her magnificent yet simple stew. Some welcomed imaginative dishes include the crayfish flan and the rolled veal with foie gras. Soliva serves an excellent dessert with an almond cream base and good wines from Visan.

A la carte: 250-300F.

Lamorlaye

see Chantilly

Landerneau

29220 Landerneau - (Finistère)
Paris 571 - Morlaix 39 - Brest 20 - Quimper 70

13 Le Clos du Pontic

Rue du Pontic - 98.21.50.91

M. Saoût. Open until 9 p.m. Closed Sat. lunch, Sun. dinner & Mon. Pets allowed. Hotel: 38 rms 200-240F. Parking. Cards: V, AE.

This vast, turn-of-the-century manse (with some unfortunate modern touches) rises from lovely grounds bursting with rhododendrons. The pleasant, intimate dining room extends out to a terrace. Mme. Saoût is charming and loquacious, and the cuisine of her chef, Claude Barbé, is generous and carefully prepared: a copious plate of raw fish (turbot, bass and salmon) with lime, sweetbreads braised in mead vinegar (with a rich accompaniment of seasonal vegetables) and good pastries. The toque has been solidly confirmed.

A la carte: 280-300F. Menus: 82F, 120F and 180F (weekdays only), 140F and 190F (weekends and holidays only).

Landersheim

67700 Saverne - (Bas-Rhin)
Paris 433 - Strasbourg 24 - Saverne 14 - Haguenau 31

15 Auberge du Kochersberg

Rue de Saessolsheim - 88.69.91.58

M. Klipfel. Open until 9:30 p.m. Closed Sun. dinner, Mon., holidays, Jan. 30-Feb. 15 & July 24-Aug. 16. Air cond. Pets allowed. Parking. Telex 870974. Cards: V, AE, DC, MC.

For a long time and with much panache, the people in charge of this vast restaurant next to the Adidas factory took on the challenge of assuming the role of both company canteen and luxury restaurant. It's difficult to discern who were the happiest and the best treated—the factory personnel who came to eat lunch here every day for less than 10 francs, or the rich public running up bills of more than 300 francs. The sparkling Alsatian decor seems to include as much wood as the neighboring Forêt Noire (Black Forest). The immense dining room (150 seats) has a slightly crude rustic look, but the cuisine of Patrick Klipfel and his chef, Armand Roth, has slipped a bit this year from its rank as one of the best in Alsace. Undistinguished fish platters and undistinguishable flavors left us to find solace in the still wonderful cheese and dessert possibilities, like the white peach with ginger sabayon and vanilla ice cream or the poached pear in mocha with frozen honey cream. As for the 80,000-bottle wine cellar, it covers every region of France, as well as nearly all of the countries of the world (Alsace is well represented, including its eaux-de-vie), and Jean-Marie, the competent chief wine steward, will give you a tour of his "museum."

A la carte: 400F. Menus: 200F, 270F, 330F.

Langon

33210 Langon - (Gironde)
Paris 604 - Bordeaux 47 - Marmande 37 - Libourne 54

15 Claude Darroze

95, cours du Général-Leclerc
56.63.00.48

M. Darroze. Open until 9:30 p.m. Closed Oct. 15-Nov. 6. Garden dining. Pets allowed. Hotel: 16 rms 180-340F. Garage parking. Cards: V, AE, DC, MC.

The reception and service at this rich-looking and euphoric restaurant, at one time legendary, were at half mast when we dropped by the other day. The waiters were tired, and the wine steward contented himself with just filling our glasses (with such a good cellar, you would think he would want to talk about his wines). As for the cuisine, there weren't only good things to report. The spring salad with foie gras and asparagus was too salty, and the accompanying filet of goose was too fatty; the fried lamb's sweetbreads in a salad with white truffles and cèpes was tasty and balanced; there was nothing exciting about the filet of beef with foie gras (in spite of the delicious meat); and the milk-fed lamb from the Médoc was a bit dry. A delicious dessert of fruit steeped in wine preceded some disappointing petits fours, ending a meal that, fortunately, was followed by a return visit, which resulted in a pleasing and satisfying meal. If this shows anything, it's that Claude Darroze is still quite inconsistent.

A la carte: 350-400F. Menu: 140F.

Laon

02000 Laon - (Aisne)
Paris 139 - Amiens 115 - St-Quentin 46 - Reims 47

13

La Petite Auberge

45, blvd. Pierre-Brossolette - 23.23.02.38

M. Zorn. Open until 9:30 p.m. Closed Sun. dinner, Sat. & July 15-Aug. 15. No pets. Parking. Cards: V, AE, DC.

Almost directly across from the train station, in the unappealing quarter that stretches out at the foot of the more admirable upper part of town, this "rustic Louis XV" restaurant with thick walls and a monumental fireplace, has become the best in Laon, after two years under the direction of the young (23-year-old) Marc Zorn. Because Zorn's cuisine is ultra-modern, it lends itself to some technical risks, which have not all been quite mastered. It is ambitious (in the good sense of the term), imaginative and personal, in spite of the chef's numerous reflections on such chefs as Meneau (sauces), Rostang and Thuriès (pastries). Try, for example, the foie gras of raw duck, the roast young rabbit (a little overdone) with potatoes in puff pastry, the perch filets with a mango purée, and the nougat with honey and pistachios. The prices are a bit high for a beginner, but the toque is amply confirmed.

A la carte: 350F. Menus: 130F, 180F, 245F, 350F.

Laval

53000 Laval - (Mayenne)
Paris 291 - Tours 140 - Le Mans 75 - Angers 73

16

Le Bistro de Paris

67, rue du Val-de-Mayenne - 43.56.98.29

M. Lemercier. Open until 9:30 p.m. Closed Sat. lunch, Sun. & last 3 weeks in Aug. Air cond. No pets. Cards: V.

Would you like to know about a perfect place? Then hurry to Laval, but make your reservations several days in advance, because when you can find excellent food at heavenly prices, served with graciousness in an attractive decor with all kinds of exquisite wines... well, you can just imagine the competition for tables. What is Guy Lemercier's secret? He earns a good living, maintains a staff of seven cooks and seven charming waiters, has a new decor and enlarged dining room and offers meals for less than 200 francs, everything included. His small, seasonal menu is a marvel, brilliant in its presentation, and every appetizer is priced at 55 francs (except the foie gras at 70 francs), every main dish at 70 francs and every dessert at 30 francs. Perhaps he'll offer you a fricassée of langoustines, chicken and squid served with shiitake mushrooms and exquisite cèpes; a large plate of assorted small appetizers, including chunks of crab and smoked eel, frogs'-leg fondant with a touch of garlic, and a salad of duck and escargots seasoned with rosemary; then a stew of young rabbit, pig's ear and lamb's foot (marvelously rustic); pigeon loaf presented in slices with rare liver and a subtle juice; and, finally, a chocolate feuille-à-feuille with a caramel sorbet that is worthy of three toques. You understand now why people come here from as far away as Nantes, Angers and even Paris: There are only three or four such restaurants in all of France.

A la carte: 200-250F. Menus: 90F (weekdays only), 105F, 200F.

14

La Gerbe de Blé

83, rue Victor-Boissel - 43.53.14.10

M. Portier. Open until 10 p.m. Closed Sun. dinner & Mon. No pets. Hotel: 2 stes 450-520F; 6 rms 320-430F. Cards: V, AE, DC.

This little hotel that wasn't much to look at is becoming a nice, comfortable inn. Pierre Portier has just modernized the rooms and brightened up the heavily rustic look of the dining room with new curtains, lights and tablecloths. The cuisine is still testimony to his savoir-faire in the creation of an eclectic repertoire, which now includes more and more light versions of respectably executed regional dishes: matelote of eel and pike cooked in Montlouis wine, paupiettes of veal in cider, peach sabayon, a millefeuille "minute" of bitter chocolate and orange. Some exotic reminiscences still hold their own (sweet-and-sour, salted-sweet, curries). Both fixed-price menus are impressive, and the wine cellar is exceptional.

A la carte: 280F. Menus: 120F, 215F.

Grand Hôtel de Paris

22-28, rue de la Paix - 43.53.76.20

Open year-round. 2 stes 230-250F. 38 rms 101-250F. Half-board 200-300F. TV in 12 rms. Pets allowed. Garage parking. Cards: V, AE, DC, MC.

The rooms of this good hotel located at the center of town and on the banks of the Mayenne river are relatively quiet and well maintained. Restaurant.

Le Lavandou

83980 Le Lavandou - (Var)
Paris 887 - Toulon 41 - St-Tropez 38 - Cannes 104

L'Algue Bleue

62, ave. de Général-de-Gaulle
94.71.01.95

Mmes. Doering & Dal Sasso. Open until 10:30 p.m. Closed Wed. (off-seas.) & Oct. 30-Easter. Garden dining. Pets allowed. Parking. Cards: V, AE, DC, MC.

As you sit facing the harbor on the expansive terrace, with its flowers, crystal and silver, a young, smiling staff serves you. Everything runs smoothly, and everyone seems happy to be working. René Théveniot's light, inventive cuisine is also on the right track, but guests these days need more and more money to enjoy it. The first fixed-price menu, however, is almost a bargain: escalopes of salmon with shallots and green peppers, sliced filet de boeuf with thyme, cheeses and pastry.

A la carte: 350F. Menus: 190F, 250F, 350F.

La Calanque

(See restaurant above)

Open year-round. 2 stes 864F. 36 rms 500-650F. Half-board 510-690F oblig. in seas. TV in 2 rms. Pets allowed.

Located on pleasant grounds on Iles d'Hyéres and the Lavandou harbor. Luxury suites are planned for the future.

L'Orangeraie

Plage de Saint-Clair (1.5 km on N 559) 4.71.04.25

Closed Oct. 1-April 30. 2 stes 336-394F. 18 rms 180-378F. Parking. Cards: V, AE, DC, MC.

At 100 meters from the beach at Saint-Clair, without even a road to cross, this hotel offers comfortable, modern rooms, some with kitchenettes and private gardens. No restaurant.

Hervé Vinrich

17, rue Patron-Ravello - 94.71.00.44

M. Vinrich. Open until 9 p.m. (11 p.m. in summer). Closed Mon. (off-seas.); annual closing varies. Terrace dining. Pets allowed. Hotel: 13 rms 220-320F; half-board 260-310F oblig. in seas. Cards: V, AE, DC, MC.

A small pedestrian walkway stands to one side and the ocean to the other. Between the two is this charming Provençal dining room with a large press (refreshments are envisioned for the near future), a bit of a terrace abounding with flowers and a view of palm trees, the harbor and the islands. Hervé Vinrich, the owner, is a spunky autodidact who is at home with imaginative food, as is demonstrated by his red mullet tart with vinaigrette, his langoustine fricassée with vanilla and saffron, and his braised lobster in Muscat from Provence. The desserts, such as the frozen anise mousse with orange sauce, are equally delicious. Rather expensive but well-selected regional wines.

A la carte: 300-350F. Menus: 140F, 205F.

IN NEARBY **Aiguebelle**
(4.5 km E on D 559)
83980 Le Lavandou - (Var)

Les Roches

1, ave. des Trois-Dauphins - 94.71.05.07, 94.71.05.05

M. Fauchie. Open until 10:30 p.m. Closed Oct. 15-Easter. Air cond. Terrace dining. No pets. Garage parking. Telex 430028. Cards: V, AE, MC.

A cascade of stairs leads to this exotic garden restaurant among the cacti, just above water level. It is the most extraordinary terrace on the Varois coast. Under a ceiling of stretched sails at the edge of a dream-like rocky inlet are simple, widely spaced tables and a decor that is discreet, so nothing distracts the eyes from this marvelous piece of nature. The new owners of this beautiful place that was on the road to ruin have invested wild amounts of money to get it back on its feet, and have no intention of stopping there. To start, they have found a perfect young chef, Laurent Tarridec, who came from Rochedy after five years under the tutelage of Jo Rostang at La Bonne Auberge, and who will surely be one of the next revelations on the Côte. Taking advantage of a kitchen that would make the Troisgros jealous, this Breton affirms an exceptional talent by the extreme honesty of his flavors, created with products he buys from the numerous excellent vegetable farmers and fishermen who live and work between the Hyères Islands and the peninsula.

You will be won over, as we were, by the ragoût of tiny, young purple artichokes; the fine, crispy tuna in puff pastry; the tian of duck (an extraordinary little checkerboard of foie gras and duck-wing meat constructed between thin lasagne noodles); and the simple cod filet, fresh and served with potatoes mashed with a fork and seasoned with chives and olive oil. Tarridec possesses true talent and an ease with getting the best out of simple, good-quality products. The desserts are so remarkable—crispy caramelized apples, chocolate delicacies (including a delicious sorbet)—that you ask yourself how the pastry chef to come could do any better. The wine list is excellent, with a few interesting discoveries and moderate prices, but the service needs refinement.

A la carte: 300-350F.

Les Roches

(See restaurant above)

Closed Oct. 15-Easter. 4 stes 1,500-1,900F. 34 rms 350-1,250F. Half-board 650-2,200F. TV. Air cond. in 20 rms. Pets allowed. Pool.

The Côte d'Azur's new luxury hotel is situated high above the ocean and the rocks. The spacious rooms were recently entirely renovated with splendor, as were the common areas. A superb pool is dug into the rocks, and water sports are available.

See also: **Bormes-les-Mimosas, Cavalière, Levant (Ile du)**

Les Lecques

83270 St-Cyr-sur-Mer - (Var)
Paris 812 - Marseille 39 - Toulon 29 - Bandol 10

Grand Hôtel

94.26.23.01

Closed Oct. 20-April 15. 58 rms 318-650F. Half-board 302-500F oblig. in seas. Tennis. Parking. Telex 400165. Cards: V, AE, DC, MC.

An exquisite flower garden surrounds this vast hotel overlooking the sea. Some of the rooms are quite small and others spacious. Restaurant.

Lembach

67510 Lembach - (Bas-Rhin)
Paris 460 - Strasbourg 56 - Haguenau 24 - Wissenbourg 15

Auberge du Cheval Blanc

4, rue de Wissembourg - 88.94.41.86

M. Mischler. Open until 9 p.m. Closed Mon., Tues., Feb. 6-24 & July 3-21. No pets. Parking. Cards: V, AE.

This massive old post house presides over the center of town, with its beautiful courtyard of big paving stones that still seem to resonate the clacking of horse-drawn diligences (French stagecoaches). A nondescript hall leads into a vast, formal dining room with an enormous fireplace, carved ceilings and handsome Louis XIII pieces. A batallion of friendly waiters in black jackets and bow ties attends to some 150 bon vivants (most having come from across the Rhine), even addressing them in their mother tongue. This opulent northern Alsatian inn has been run by the Mischler family—without skipping a generation—since 1908. The imperial Fernand offers an immense repertoire that covers many genres with good results. The products are magnificent, the execution more than conscientious, and the quality consistent. Everything here expresses the strictness and the expertise of great professionals. The sautéed frogs' legs provençales and the veal steak are not the best souvenirs to take away from Lembach. Rather, try the shellfish salad, the hot goose liver, the turbot with oysters and the Strasbourg-style pigeon. Extensive wine cellar.

A la carte: 350F. Menus: 130F, 170F, 230F, 300F.

Lestelle-Bétharram

64800 Nay - (Pyrénées-Atlantiques)
Paris 790 - Pau 23 - Lourdes 16 - Laruns 35 - Nay 9

13 Le Vieux Logis

59.71.94.87

M. Gaye. Open until 9 p.m. Closed Jan. 15-March 8. Terrace dining. Pets allowed. Hotel: 15 rms 150-190F; half-board 235-300F oblig. in seas. Parking. Cards: V, MC.

The winding road that leads to the Bétharram caves meanders in the lush exuberance of the Pyrénées forest and leaves you at the foot of an impressive restaurant. Here Pierre Gaye and his son, Françis, work euphorically and with a love for their region to create a magnificent and generous cuisine. The tender salmon with sorrel, the excellent duck confit accompanied by fresh cèpes, and the thick filet of fatted duck with green pepper and an émincé of pears and Vichy carrots are all abundant but not heavy. And they are complemented perfectly by wines of the region. We happily grant them a toque and hope that they will soon make some improvements in decor.

A la carte: 200-300F. Menus: 90F, 110F, 160F.

Levallois-Perret

see PARIS SUBURBS

Levant (Ile du)

83400 Hyéres - (Var)
Embarkation: Cavalaire, Le Lavandou, Hyéres

La Brise Marine

Pl. du Village
94.05.91.15, 94.71.69.44

Closed Oct. 15-May 1. 23 rms 220-340F. Half-board 347-410F oblig. in seas. Pets allowed. Heated pool. Cards: V, AE, DC, MC.

These lovely rooms facing the sea have bathroom facilities (a luxury for this island) and are grouped around a Spanish-style patio crawling with flowers. Beautiful pool. Restaurant.

Lezoux

63190 Lezoux - (Puy-de-Dôme)
Paris 390 - Clermont-Ferrand 27 - Thiers 16 - Vichy 42

Château de Codignat

Bort-l'Etang (8 km SE on D 223 & D 115E) - 73.68.43.03

Closed end March-Nov. 4. 4 stes 930-1,700F. 12 rms 575-1,020F. Half-board 680-915F oblig. in seas. TV. Pets allowed. Heated pool. Parking. Telex 990606. Cards: V, AE, DC, MC.

This château has preserved its machicolations, wrought iron and armor. The suites are luxurious and the spacious rooms are decorated in Haute-Epoque style, opulent and heavily furnished. Restaurant. Relais et Châteaux.

Liepvre

68160 Ste-Marie-aux-Mines - (Haut-Rhin)
Paris 488 - Colmar 36 - St-Dié 30 - Sélestat 14

13 A la Vieille Forge

Bois-l'Abbesse - 89.58.92.54

M. Woerth. Open until 9 p.m. Closed Mon. dinner, Tues., June 20-July 7 & Nov. 15-Dec. 1. Pets allowed. Parking. Cards: V, AE, DC, MC.

Every kind of decorative treasure hoarded by country antiques stores (bellows, grandfather clocks, copperware) has been put to use in this old roadside (and hence noisy) inn. Together they create a warm atmosphere, which is matched by the friendly reception and service. Marcel Woerth recently has proven to be one of those rare chefs of the old school who are willing to rethink their stiff classicism. In his case this has meant that the great tradition has taken on some individuality, and his technique has grown noticeably lighter, even in the rediscovered regional dishes, such as the calf's tongue in a pot-au-feu with horseradish or the beef filet Strasbourg-style. We must also suggest trying his crispy stuffing of sole and salmon and the seafood ravioli with saffron, while enjoying the warm and rich dose of rusticity. Excellent wine cellar.

A la carte: 250F. Menus: 98F, 160F, 220F.

Lille

59000 Lille - (Nord)
Paris 219 - Dunkerque 80 - Brussels 116 - Arras 51

Sights. Old Lille (century-old streets and houses); Musée des Beaux-Arts (one of the best in France); Hospice Comtesse (and the Musée des Arts et Traditions Populaires); Musée d'Art Religieux (Notre-Dame-de-la-Treille); Ancienne Bourse (The Old Stock Exchange—a splendid testimony to seventeenth-century Flemish architecture); Citadelle (the genius of Vauban); Le Métro (the jewel of French technology).

Eating on the Run. L'Atrébate, 45, rue du Priez (friendly and fashionable); L'Entrecôte, 28, rue de Paris (grilled meats); La Cloche, 13, pl. du Théâtre (wine bistro); Café de la Poste, 158 bis, rue Colbert (cheerful, fast service); La Rotonde Opéra, 10, rue Léon-Trulin (for its terrace and salads); La Petite Taverne, 9, rue Plat (as friendly as it is fast).

Brasseries. Brasserie Jean et Végastore, pl. du Théâtre (facing the Opera, numerous beers); La Chicorée, 15, pl. Rihour (the only place serving food and drink around the clock); Le Président, 21, pl. du Général-de-Gaulle (classic, close to the famous bookstore, Le Furet du Nord); La Taverne Flamande, 55, rue Nationale (quite pleasant).

Bars & Cafés. Bar de l'Echo, 20, pl. du Général-de-Gaulle (large beer selection); Bar du Royal Hôtel, 2, blvd. Carnot (popular, an excellent bartender); Café de la Plage, rue Solférino (the "in" crowd starts arriving at 6 p.m.); Circus Bar, 36, rue d'Angleterre (subdued decor, in old Lille); The Queen Victoria, 10, rue de Pas (faithful to its reputation, mahogany decor).

Nightlife. Cantina, 104, rue St-André (South American specialties and shows); Les Dessous de Louise, pl. Louise-de-Bettignies (vaulted cellar with shows); Joséphine's Club, 1, pl. des Reignaux (bar/club, exotic cocktails); Le Majestic, 11, rue des Arts (piano bar, *the* place to be seen in Lille).

Shops. *Beer:* Les 300 Bières, rue du Molinel (impressive choice of the great beers of the north). *Bakeries:* Aux Délices Lillois, 151, rue Nationale (favorite baker in the town center); Boulangerie du Parvis St-Maurice; Poilâne, rue Esquermoise. *Chocolate:* Léonidas, 49, rue Faidherbe and 6, rue St-Genois (Belgian chocolate); Verdonck, pl. Gambetta. *Cheese:* La Prairie, 33, rue de Sec-Arembault (the best of the classic northern cheeses: boulette d'Avesnes, vieux-lille, maroilles); Le Pré Vert, rue Nationale (excellent selection). *Pastries, ice cream:* Meert, 27, rue Esquermoise (creator of the "lillois," imitated everywhere); Yanka, 75, rue Nationale (master pastry and candy maker). *Fruit and vegetables:* La Boutique, 64, rue de Paris (excellent quality, large selection).

(13) La Belle Epoque du Victoria

10, rue de Pas - 20.54.51.28

M. Louguet. Open daily until 10:30 p.m. Air cond. Pets allowed. Cards: V, AE, DC, MC.

The new owner of this charming restaurant has followed in the footsteps of his predecessor, and you will find that neither the atmosphere nor the cuisine has changed. In the evenings, the dining room is still exquisite, its turn-of-the-century decor set aglow by the light filtering down from the stained-glass ceiling. And after twelve years, Christian Leroy is still executing a conscientious cuisine. Imagination isn't his strong suit, but consistency and nice finishing touches—whether it's his escalope of sweetbreads and lobster (the cream sauce lacks a bit of finesse), the ordinary but delicious saddle of lamb or the respectable strawberry and mint bavarois—are. The wine cellar is extraordinary and the service courteous, though a bit stiff.

A la carte: 300-400F. Menus: 250F (Sunday and holidays only, wine incl.).

Carlton

3, rue de Paris - 20.55.24.11

Open year-round. 4 stes 895-1,200F. 57 rms 315-470F. TV in 40 rms. Pets allowed. Telex 110400. Cards: V, AE, DC, MC.

Here across from the Opera you'll find pleasant, spacious rooms, with good acoustic insulation. On the ground floor is the famous Brasserie Jean.

(13) La Coquille

60, rue St-Etienne - 20.54.29.82

M. Deleval. Open until 10:30 p.m. Closed Sat. lunch, Sun., Jan. 2-9 & Aug. 1-21. Pets allowed. Cards: V.

The clientele is young, the brick decor a success, the atmosphere relaxed and the prices always attractive for a cuisine as generous as it is fresh: roast saddle of young rabbit with bay leaves and baby onions, curried lotte with a watercress sauce, white-chocolate marquise. Some good regional wines.

A la carte: 250F. Menus: 68F (lunch only), 102F (weekdays only), 165F (wine incl.), 172F (dinner only).

(15) La Devinière

61, blvd. Louis-XIV - 20.52.74.64

M. Waterlot. Open until 9:30 p.m. Closed Sun. Air cond. Pets allowed. Cards: V, AE, DC.

A small restaurant comprising eight tables, an exciting little à la carte menu and plenty of good cheer. In an effort to improve the decor and comfort of his modest dining room, Bernard Waterlot has freshened it up and filled it with flowers to create a spacious, handsome look. This is especially true since the charming Mme. Masclet, whose husband assists Waterlot in the kitchen, has been supervising the exemplary service. The spirited cuisine is a creation of the seasons, the marketplace and their whims, combining country tastes and the subtleties of invention without friction. At our last visit we tried the red mullet and squid soufflé, the langoustine cakes in a shellfish bisque, the fricasséed lamb tongue in a garlic confit and the simple and perfect roast duck with young vegetables. Delicious Loire wines—the specialty of the house—will keep your bill down, particularly with the judicious fixed-price menus.

A la carte: 350-400F. Menus: 258F (menu dégustation), 148F.

(18) Le Flambard

79, rue d'Angleterre
20.51.00.06

M. Bardot. Open until 9:30 p.m. Closed Sun. dinner, Mon. & Aug. Cards: V, AE, DC.

When Robert Bardot set up shop in Lille more than fifteen years ago, he was quite proud of the beautiful MOF (Meilleur Ouvrier de France) medal he had just received. At the time, we didn't skimp on encouragement, nor did we go easy on criticisms of his cooking, then still too academic and willfully grandiloquent. With the modesty of the truly great, Bardot claimed that we were right and that he understood. Since then, not only have we never been disappointed, but each time it improves—so much so that for the last few years, we have regarded his cooking as among the best, the most knowing, the most audacious "within the tradition" available in France today. Without a doubt, Bardot is one of our greatest chefs. His cooking shows an exceptional agreement—the work of a true master—between spontaneity and technique at its highest level. This is clearly what prompts us to add a point to his rating and to stand in awe at the infinitely delicate fruits of his labor.

The warm fisherman's salad with shallots is a monument to technical perfection, with every delicate fish from the day's market cooked to exact precision. We had a roast turbot in écailles (shells) of potatoes flavored by a first-rate sauce of leek greens and smoked eel. The rosy roast pigeon with peaches and spices was extremely delicate, prepared in the sweet-and-sour Flemish spirit with Belgian endive. An infinitely light warm millefeuille was served with ice cream flavored with roasted local chicory. And we will never forget the delicious cheeses, such as the mariolle with beer, the roasted rigotte with chives and the Roquefort with Armagnac.

To do Bardot justice we should add that, based on our experience, he is one of the most imitated chefs in France, as well as one of the least acknowledged. Le Flambard's wine cellar is one of the richest in the north, especially for Champagnes. Jannie Bardot receives guests most attentively, and the exemplary service is directed by M. Deneuville, a native of Pas-de-Calais who was trained at Le Barrier at its height. The comfortable brick decor has been agreeably relieved of useless accessories, and the dining area will soon become larger when Bardot's house is adjoined to the neighboring house, which also dates from the seventeenth century.

A la carte: 400-500F. Menus: 210F, 340F, 440F.

(16) L'Huîtrière

3, rue des Chats-Bossus - 20.55.43.41

M. Proye. Open until 9:30 p.m. Closed Sun. & holiday dinner & July 22-Sept. 1. Air cond. Pets allowed. Cards: V, AE, DC, MC.

After catching a whiff of the fresh fish wafting from the marvelous fish store, with its turn-of-the-century mosaics, you'll encounter the heady smell of the polish that is rubbed into the oak paneling in this formal dining room every day. Walking into this neo–Louis XVI decor, where for ages the strictly aligned tables draped with immaculate white cloths have been fixed beneath the twinkling chandeliers, is like a fantasy. It may be perfectly bourgeois, but it's not at all boring, making some interesting statements within its provincial distinctiveness. And because it is always jam-packed with diners and abuzz with a cheerful (and large) staff, what could have been the most somber eating establishment in Lille is perhaps the most lively. As for the cuisine, if food from the sea were intoxicating, you could get blind drunk from this menu, a vast and luxurious repertoire introducing every creature from the North Sea and all the traditional seafood recipes (plus a number of other daring dishes). The dazzling products on one hand, and the seriousness and consistency of the precise execution on the other, have for years assured the reputation of this great restaurant: escalope of lotte accompanied by baby vegetables and lobster butter, magnificent bouillabaisse (no shells or bones), exquisite seasoned shellfish soup, roast bass with parsley sauce, fried whiting Colbert (the best in the world, along with that of Prunier). The desserts aren't all memorable (slightly dry almond tart) but on occasion can be exceptional, like the clafouti with morello cherries topped with a perfect Kirsh sabayon. The wine cellar is immense and serious.

A la carte: 350-400F.

Novotel Lille Centre

116, rue de l'Hôpital-Militaire
20.30.65.26

Open year-round. 8 stes 600-1,100F. 94 rms 480-505F. TV. Air cond. Pets allowed. Telex 160859. Cards: V, AE, DC, MC.

This inviting, modern hotel is conveniently located behind the Grand-Place. The rooms are comfortable, well lit and functional. Grill.

(15) Le Paris

52 bis, rue Esquermoise - 20.55.29.41

M. Martin. Open until 9:30 p.m. Closed Sun. dinner & early Aug.-early Sept. Pets allowed. Cards: V, AE, DC.

This spacious, nondescript dining room was certainly not a model of charm and seduction, so it's a good thing that Loïc Martin has finally improved the decor: a cozy monochrome brown with velvet banquettes, gracious chairs and pleasant lighting. Nothing so very original, but it's easy to feel happy and relaxed here, basking cozily in provincial luxury. There are beautiful damask cloths, impressive flower arrangements, sparkling silver and a personnel that knows its job well. The cuisine is exemplary in its consistency, precision and simplicity. Gérard Chamoley, whose twelve years of fidelity to Martin show at least that this Breton is not as difficult a restaurateur as he is reputed to be. He was trained at Point and Chapel but clearly has ideas of his own. His menu is one of the most varied in Lille: roast veal liver with anchovies and nasturtium butter, warm pea salad with stuffed squid, eel pâté with mustard flowers, fresh Flanders escargots with walnuts, a large selection of seasonal game and superb hot and chilled desserts. The choice of wines is very good, and although he gives well-advised recommendations, Martin does not pressure his guests into imbibing.

A la carte: 350F. Menus: 176F, 280F.

(16) Le Restaurant

1, pl. Sébastopol - 20.57.05.05

M. Arabian. Open until 10 p.m. Closed Sat. lunch, Sun., 1 week at Easter, 2 weeks mid-Aug. & 2 weeks at Christmas. Pets allowed. Parking. Cards: V, AE, DC, MC.

Each year Ghislaine Arabian, who directs the two young brigades at Le Restaurant, further refines her image as a great chef. She is a woman of character who took her time to mold her experiences and familiarize herself with every station in the kitchen—from baking bread to preparing fish to creating pastries (where she excels). What a fortunate place! During the same time in which she scaled the ranks to stand among the best in the north, Jean-Paul Arabian, a great professional in the dining room (he trained at the Oasis de la Napoule and the neighboring Flambard), helped make their place the most elegant and fashionable in Lille. The 1930s decor—in which the purple watered fabric, the deep-red velvet and the pink marble shine gently under handsome light fixtures—is a vision of cheerfulness and comfort. Everything invites you to be relaxed under the eye of an attentive host and an exacting and smiling staff. As for the large winter or summer menu, it is a festival of inventions that are both light and generous, as shown by the fried wild mushrooms, the risotto with squid in their ink, the coquilles St-Jacques with romaine lettuce and the squab with chanterelles. Two excellent young wine stewards supervise the exceptional cellar, which holds numerous superb Champagnes for less than 200 francs and good proprietary wines for about 80 francs.

A la carte: 450-500F. Menus: 150F (lunch only), 180F, 250F, 350F.

Le Varbet

2, rue de Pas - 20.54.81.40

M. Vartanian. Open until 9:30 p.m. Closed Sun., Mon., holidays, July 10-Aug. 18 & Dec. 22-Jan. 3. Cards: V, AE, DC.

Small, mustachioed and of Armenian origin, Gilles Vartanian is a reserved man who rarely leaves his kitchen. As a chef, he fluctuates a little, but his form and inspiration have been at their peak for some time now, so we'll take this opportunity to give him back the point that he had lost. He has earned it with his oyster crêpes garnished with seasoned morels, his sweetbreads croustade (in a light pastry shell), his grilled filet of sole in a clam sauce and his great desserts (hot apple feuilleté, marquise au chocolat). The decor, redone recently, still has its 1950s-style wood paneling. The atmosphere is quite friendly, thanks to its collection of regulars and the presence of the lively (too much, some have complained) Arlette Vartanian.

A la carte: 350F. Menus: 260F (dinner only), 130F.

IN NEARBY **Marcq-en-Baroeul**
(5 km NE on N 350)
59700 Marcq-en-Baroeul - (Nord)

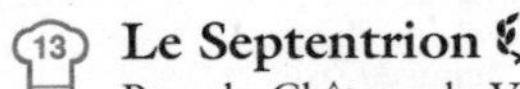

Le Septentrion

Parc du Château du Vert-Bois
20.46.26.98

M. Lelaurain. Open until 9 p.m. Closed Thurs. & Sun. dinner, Mon., 1 week in Feb. & Aug. 1-22. Pets allowed. Parking. Cards: V, AE, DC.

In the evenings on these magnificent grounds, floodlights in the trees illuminate the ornamental ponds afloat with great white swans. But this large, tastefully decorated restaurant is equally enticing at lunchtime. Gilbert Lelaurain dreams of bringing to this extraordinary, lush environment the luxurious and modern hotel that the area is lacking. In the meantime, he contents himself with being a chef—and an intelligent and enthusiastic one at that—combining personal ideas with lighter versions of classic regional cuisine: turbot with fresh fennel, young rabbit thigh braised in beer, veal kidney sautéed with juniper berries. Nice, inexpensive wines.

A la carte: 250-300F. Menu: 210F.

IN NEARBY **Prémesques**
(10 km NW on D 933 & D 952)
59840 Pérenchies - (Nord)

La Fringale

497, rue Roger-Lecerf - 20.08.71.51

M. Coopman. Open until 9 p.m. Closed Sun. dinner & Wed. Pets allowed. Cards: V, AE, DC.

Such a good restaurant with such minimal decor is a surprise in these quiet suburbs. And it's a surprise that's lasted for ten years, because Christian and Jeannine Coopman have wisely limited their ambitions to this tiny dining room with five tables (reservations are advised). The cuisine of the Périgord, which used to be a large part of the menu, is now losing importance to a repertoire that still focuses on fish but is more imaginative. The large menu dégustation with nine dishes is definitely the best choice. It is extremely generous, uses the freshest products from the marketplace and is created from the whims of this good and scrupulous chef: roast foie gras with watercress, sole with asparagus butter, sweetbreads with endives and thyme cream, fresh-fruit fondue with hot chocolate. There is a wide selection of excellent wines from the southwest, as well as premium liquors and cigars.

A la carte: 330F. Menus: 190F, 250F.

See also: **Roubaix, Tourcoing**

Limoges

87000 Limoges - (Haute-Vienne)
Paris 374 - Poitiers 118 - Angoulême 103 - Niort 161

Sights. La Cathédrale Sainte-Etienne and the old houses that surround it; Le Palais de l'Evêché (The Bishop's Palace, and its gardens), which houses the Musée Municipal (remarkable collection of Limoges enamels); the old bridges of Saint-Etienne and Saint-Martial (at the foot of the old Abessaille quarter); the beautiful houses of the pl. du Présidial; the 10,000-piece collection of ceramics in the Musée National Adrien-Dubouché; the churches of Saint-Pierre-du-Queyroix and Saint-Michel-des-Lions; the marketplace at the pl. des Bancs; the picturesque rue de la Boucherie.

Eating on the Run. A l'Entracte, rue du Temple (brunch); Aux Vikings, 19, ave. du Général-de-Gaulle (until 1 a.m., omelets, salads, daily specials); Café des Girondins, 12, pl. des Bancs (1900s decor, small and unpretentious); La Parenthése, 22, rue du Consulat (small lunch menu, nice teatime pastries); Le Saint-Amour, 14, rue Elie-Berthet (wine bar and hors d'oeuvres); Le 7e Art, 3, ave. du Général-de-Gaulle (grilled meats and good tartares); Le 13-15, 4, rue Charles-Michels (crêpes and puff-pastry cakes); Le Trianon, 7, blvd. Georges-Périn (popular and friendly, good daily specials).

Bars & Cafés. Cotton Club, 6, blvd. Victor-Hugo (lively); Les Deux Cités, pl. de la République (the excellent bar at the Royal

Limousin); Le Pacha Club, 16, rue Charles-Michels (chic and mellow, good cocktails); Le Royalty, pl. de la République (the place to be seen for those who like to be seen).

Nightlife. Apart from the Cotton Club and Le Pacha Club (see "Bars & Cafés"), Limoges's night owls frequent the Cat's Club, rue du Temple; The Cute, rue des Rafilhoux; Le Moulin des Cendrilles, rte. de Nexon; and, the youngest one, Le Tiffany, rue Victor-Duruy.

Shops. *Charcuteries:* Chez Roger Eustache, 37, rue de la Boucherie (marvelous decor and admirable salted ham). *Chocolate, confections:* Buissière, 27, rue Jean-Jaurès (truffles and almond-paste goodies); Dissoubray, 20, rue Adrien-Dubouché (for its "châtaignes du Limousin," or chestnuts with rum); Puymérail, 10, pl. Denis-Dussoubs (delicious liquor-filled truffles). *Cheese:* Garrot, 14, rue Ferrerie (cheeses from the Auvergne). *Pastries:* Bidaud, pl. St-Pierre (for its hazelnut pastry and vacherin with chestnuts). *Porcelain:* Prestige de Limoges, blvd. Louis-Blanc (the best and the largest selection). *Miscellaneous:* Marché Broussaud, 8, rue Broussaud (secondhand goods sold Saturday through Monday: porcelain, regional furniture, tapestries and so on).

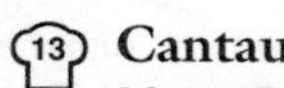

Cantaut

10, rue Rafilhoux - 55.33.34.68, 55.30.12.18

M. Cantaut. Open daily until 9:30 p.m. Pets allowed. Cards: V.

A spiral staircase takes you down to the dining room in the deep Roman cellar. In the kitchen on the main floor, you can hear the bearded Patrice Cantaut coach his assistants—ever since he was accused of "sleeping" on the job, this amiable chef is full of life. There are no more problems with the service; he has taken charge himself. And there is much less hesitation in the style and execution of his cuisine. Cantaut seems to have taken up the good old country traditions (especially with duck) that he practiced in the past at his restaurant in Pierre-Buffière. Our "fine bouche" salad (with vegetables, cèpes and foie gras), the magnificent duck consommé with garlic and fresh pasta, the catch of the day (fried bass with star anise or turbot with orange zest) helped him earn back his toque. These dishes will be even more valuable to him when his desserts (otherwise interesting) are less sweet. Good selection of Bordeaux and Cahors wines.

A la carte: 280F. Menus: 85F (weekdays only), 130F, 215F, 285F.

Caravelle

21, rue Armand-Barbès - 55.77.75.29

Open year-round. 39 rms 185-320F. TV in 30 rms. Garage parking. Telex 580733. Cards: V, MC.

The building is old, the accommodations are modern, and the service is friendly. Some of the rooms overlook onto the greenery of the Champ-de-Juillet. No restaurant.

Le Champlevé

1, pl. Wilson - 55.34.43.34

M. Amardeilh. Open until 10 p.m. Closed Sat. lunch, Wed., Jan. 2-9 & Aug. 16-Sept. 6. Air cond. Pets allowed. Cards: V, AE, DC.

The good news for the citizens of Limoges is that they no longer need to leave the city center to eat a good meal in a refined setting. Nothing is left to chance in this little place, which opened two years ago in the heart of the city on a pretty, tree-lined square. A plush decor in salmon pink; good china and silver; perfect service that isn't stiff; and a light, delicate, open-hearted cuisine—everything has been seen to. Taste the periwinkle salad in orange butter, the perfect young pigeon filets with cèpes and the marvelous honey flan with an apricot coulis. The wine list is intelligent and growing steadily, and the prices are very reasonable.

A la carte: 250F. Menus: 95F (lunch only, wine incl.), 120F (weekdays only, wine incl.), 150F, 210F, 300F.

Luk Hôtel

29, pl. Jourdan - 55.33.44.00

Open year-round. 54 rms 210-450F. Half-board 260-550F. TV. Pets allowed. Telex 580704. Cards: V, AE, DC, MC.

The decor is rather luxurious (if cluttered), and the comfort is indisputable. Restaurant.

Royal Limousin

1, pl. de la République - 55.34.65.30

Open year-round. 1 ste 1,200F. 74 rms 285-505F. Air cond. in 7 rms. Telex 580771. Cards: V, AE, DC, MC.

This modern, intelligently conceived and well-situated hotel has spacious, bright rooms. No restaurant.

IN NEARBY **Saint-Martin-du-Fault**
(11 km NE on N 147 & D 35)
87510 Nieul - (Haute-Vienne)

Chapelle Saint-Martin

55.75.80.17

M. Dudognon. Open until 10 p.m. Closed Mon., Jan. & Feb. Garden dining. No pets. Garage parking. Cards: V.

To one side is the road—which you don't notice beyond the high walls of the estate—and to the other is the admirable Limousin countryside, stretching out beyond ponds and through a gap in the trees. The Dudognon family mansion is becoming more and more lovely, the ambience more and more seductive (the new decor in the dining rooms is exquisitely sophisticated), and the cuisine better and better since Gilles Dudognon was given free rein of the kitchen by his father. Though young, he had a solid apprenticeship with Gaudin, at Taillevent and especially at the side of Jean-Marie Amat, with whom he stayed for four years. His cuisine is quite ambitious, already full of authority, intelligently reliant on the marketplace and combining the best of the past and the present: mackerel with olive oil and garden vegetables, steamed bass with herb vinaigrette, grilled pigeon with spices, clarified duck bouillon with ravioli, exceptional calf's head with vegetables. The desserts are making progress, the wine cellar is excellent, and the service, like the reception, is most courteous.

A la carte: 350F. Menus: 180F (weekday lunch only, wine incl.), 320F.

Chapelle Saint-Martin

(See restaurant above)

Closed Jan. & Feb. 1-8. 3 stes 890-980F. 10 rms 420-750F. Half-board 650-700F. TV in 6 rms. Tennis.

A wing has been added to this elegant mansion, with its spacious and exquisitely furnished and decorated suites. The other rooms have also been done in delicate good taste. The view of the grounds is splendid and the service exemplary. Relais et Châteaux.

See also: **La Roche-l'Abeille**

Lisieux

14100 Lisieux - (Calvados)
Paris 173 - Evreux 72 - Caen 49 - Deauville 28

12/20 La Ferme du Roy

122, blvd. Herbet-Fournet - 31.31.33.98

M. Gouret. Open until 9 p.m. Closed Sun. dinner, Mon. (except holidays), June 30-July 9 & Dec. 18-Jan. 18. No pets. Parking. Cards: V.

This old farm, with beautifully restored wood, is a place where generosity, freshness and friendliness come together to greet the notables of the neighborhood. There are many good homemade items (smoked duck and salmon, ice creams), and the fixed-price menus are inventive. Inexpensive Loire wines.

A la carte: 250F. Menus: 150F, 200F.

Hôtel de la Place

67, rue Henry-Chéron - 31.31.17.44

Open year-round. 6 stes 350F. 27 rms 250-350F. TV in 27 rms. Garage parking. Telex 171862. Cards: V, AE, DC, MC.

The entirely renovated rooms look out on Saint-Pierre Cathedral. They are spacious, perfectly equipped and effectively soundproofed. Efficient staff. No restaurant.

IN NEARBY **Ouilly-du-Houley**
(11 km NE on N 13 & D 137)
14590 Moyaux - (Calvados)

12/20 Auberge de la Paquine

31.63.63.80

Open until 9 p.m. Closed Tues. dinner, Wed. & Jan. 16-March 1. Garden dining. No pets. Parking. Cards: V.

This handsome Norman inn stands in a picture-postcard village on a riverbank. The cuisine is rich and well prepared, and the prices are stiff, except for the perfect fixed-price menu, which offers a fricassée of rabbit in wine with baby vegetables, sliced beef, cheeses and a hot apple tart.

A la carte: 300F. Menu: 115F.

Liverdun

54460 Liverdun - (Meurthe-et-Moselle)
Paris 306 - Toul 20 - Nancy 15 - Pont-à-Mousson 25

(15) Les Vannes et sa Résidence

6, rue Porte-Haute - 83.24.46.01

M. Simunic. Open until 9:45 p.m. Closed Mon. (except holidays) & Feb. Pets allowed. Hotel: 2 stes 420-450F; 9 rms 225-380F (dinner oblig. in seas.). Parking. Cards: V, AE, DC.

One Simunic greets the guests, another creates splendid cakes, and a third manages Lorraine's best wine cellar. But the difference in the last few years is that there is no chef Simunic. The young Jean-Loup Martin, who had raised the level of this glorious restaurant considerably, has left his position to Robert Saint-Pol, who has in turn now bowed to the young but authoritative and certainly talented Vincent Dalle. Apart from a few minor quibbles, we think everything is being carried out quite well and with great imagination: witness the spinach-and-scallop salad, the filet of turbot in a red-wine sauce and the pigeon with vegetable confit. Getting rid of the remaining standbys and toning down the use of truffles and caviar would only add to the promise of this venerable establishment's fresh start. Deliciously complicated desserts made by the son of the house will thrill the connoisseur of such delicacies as pear gratin with almonds and cassis sorbet. You'll be superbly welcomed to these rich rooms, which are more comfortable than charming—the best reason to lift your head is to admire the Moselle river winding its way through the immense, deep-green landscape.

A la carte: 350-400F. Menus: 250F (weekdays only), 155F, 242F, 316F.

Livry-Gargan

see PARIS SUBURBS

Les Loges-en-Josas

see PARIS SUBURBS

Lons-le-Saulnier

39000 Lons-le-Saulnier - (Jura)
Paris 407 - Besançon 88 - Bourg-en-Bresse 61 - Dijon 102

IN NEARBY **Courlans**
(6 km W on N 78)
39000 Lons-le-Saunier - (Jura)

(16) Auberge de Chavannes

84.47.05.52

M. Carpentier. Open until 9 p.m. Closed Sun. dinner, Mon. & Jan. 15-Feb. 15. Garden dining. Pets allowed. Parking. Cards: V, AE, DC.

This restaurant, in a simple building overlooking an orchard, just a few minutes from the center of Lons, is indisputably the greatest in this department of France, where you'll find cooking of remarkable purity. The blond, bearded chef, not affiliated with any culinary clique, has guided the love of his work to the threshold of perfection. He has endeavored to ennoble the qualities of simplicity and frankness with an enlightened technique applied to perfect products (vegetables picked twice a day from the garden, seafood from Dieppe, shellfish from Brittany, farm poultry). Carpentier is a professional in the style of André Guillot, a perfectionist who is immersed in contemporary ideas but attached primarily to redefining all aspects of traditional cuisine. Try the airy café mocha feuilletés served as an appetizer, the garlicky sausage of young rabbit stuffed into a chicken neck (simply miraculous), the fricassée of langoustines, the filet of red mullet with foie gras, and the smooth desserts, all served with impeccable confidence. So are the great wines of the Jura, about which Mme. Carpentier is very knowledgeable.

A la carte: 320F. Menus: 150F, 250F.

Lorient

56100 Lorient - (Morbihan)
Paris 491 - Quimper 68 - Vannes 56 - Rennes 145

Novotel Lorient

Zone commerciale Bellevue - 97.76.02.16

Open year-round. 88 rms 340-380F. TV. Pets allowed. Heated pool. Parking. Telex 950026. Cards: V, AE, DC, MC.

This pleasant enough place is located on wooded grounds at the edge of town near the beach. The rooms boast comfort and simplicity. Restaurant.

(14) Le Pic

2, blvd. Franchet-d'Esperey - 97.21.18.29

M. Le Bourhis. Open until midnight. Closed Sat. lunch, Mon. (except holidays), 1 week in March, 2 weeks in June & last 2 weeks of Dec. Pets allowed. Cards: V.

A display of oysters on ice, with the obligatory oyster sheller, have for a while now defended the entrance to this inviting bistro—a symbol of its partiality to seafood. But Pierre Le Bourhis, a true Breton, likes his products to come from the land as well, so he balances out his menu with some excellent meat dishes: stewed cheek of beef, roast andouillette, duck confit with sautéed potatoes. However, Le Bourhis's strong points remain the tender salmon, the enormous grilled langoustines, the émincé of squid and the sautéed lotte. Another strong point is the wine cellar, one of the best in Brittany.

A la carte: 250F. Menus: 75F, 130F.

(14) Le Poisson d'Or

1, rue Maître-Esvelin - 97.21.57.06

M. Rio. Open until 10 p.m. Closed Sun. (except July-Aug.), Sat. lunch, Feb. school vacation & Nov. 1-15. Pets allowed. Cards: V, AE, DC.

Located within splashing distance of the yachts and facing the Palais des Congrès, the Poisson d'Or is steadily progressing. We're not wild about the strange decor—blue lacquered ceiling and mauve velvet walls—but at least you feel at ease here, seated before lovely dishes and sparkling silver. Michel Rio is an active and sociable owner who likes to keep an eye on his guests and circulate among the tables, as well as watch over the cuisine. He has earned another point for his cabbage stuffed with crab; his giant langoustines presented live and then returned, an instant later, split in two, grilled and served with butter and almonds; and his oyster-and-foie-gras feuilletés. Well-stocked wine cellar.

A la carte: 250F. Menus: 90F, 130F, 180F, 250F.

Loué

72540 Loué - (Sarthe)
Paris 228 - Laval 49 - Le Mans 28 - Sablé 25 - Alençon 61

(16) Laurent

11, rue de la Libération - 43.88.40.03

M. Laurent. Open until 10 p.m. Closed Jan. & Feb. Garden dining. Pets allowed. Parking. Telex 722013. Cards: V, AE, DC.

Having barely left the Saint-Etienne region, Gilbert Laurent took it upon himself to revive this old Ricordeau inn, which seemed to have taken its last breath. The great structure, which dates from the first empire, stands at the heart of a rather ordinary village surrounded by lovely countryside where a famous breed of chickens pecks about (but is rarely seen). The facade has rediscovered its nobility, the 22 hotel rooms are now fresh looking and comfortable, the two dining rooms have been repainted and hung with pink fabric (which doesn't take away from the ceilings and their handsome moldings), and the reseeded garden has been extended to the edge of the river, which has a new footbridge. And by the time you read this, the dilapidated annex buildings that spoiled the environment will have been removed. In brief, this has become a perfect weekend spot, just two hours from Paris at the entrance to Le Mans.

While his wife and daughter handle the reception and supervise the waiters, and one of his sons serves as wine steward, Laurent is assisted in the kitchen by two other sons. There were whispers, for a brief while, that he wasn't spending enough time in the kitchen, but we didn't notice anything abnormal. And if his buckwheat galette with new vegetables shocked us (delicious vegetables, but the galette, or pancake, was heavy, and the concept of the dish totally uninteresting), we were quite pleased with the scrambled eggs with caviar. And even more so with the mussels in a frothy radish cream, the marvelous Loué pigeon loaf with lentils, the classic chicken (also from Loué) in a wild-mushroom cream (which could have been cooked a bit longer), the hot apple tart and the millefeuille with pralines. Nonetheless, Laurent's cooking has suffered a bit in attention to detail and in personality. We can only hope that he now will put down his trowel and get back to the pots and pans—and back on the path toward a third toque.

A la carte: 400F and up. Menus: 190F (weekday lunch only, wine incl.; except holidays), 260F, 350F, 450F.

Laurent

(See restaurant above)

Closed Jan. & Feb. 6 stes 700-1,200F. 16 rms 280-700F. Half-board 500-950F. TV. Pool.

The sixteen rooms and suites are cozy, even a little cutesy, but they are perfectly comfortable. A large garden extends to the river, where guests can go canoeing and fishing. Breakfast is remarkable, and the service, under the direction of Mme. Laurent, is perfect. Relais et Châteaux.

Louhans

71500 Louhans - (Saône-et-Loire)
Paris 378 - Dijon 83 - Tournus 29 - Bourg 56 - Dole 69

(13) Le Moulin de Bourgchâteau

Chemin de Bourgchâteau - 85.75.37.12

M. Clément. Open until 10 p.m. Closed Sun. dinner & Mon. (off-seas.) & Jan. 2-Feb. 15. Pets allowed. Garage parking. Cards: V, AE, DC.

This old mill on the Seille river, with its imposing turbines still intact, is one of our most recent discoveries. Open for less than two years, the large dining room, with an antique pink decor, is on the second floor facing the sluice and centered on the shaft of the millstone. The young chef studied under Lameloise and Blanc, and it shows in his good technique, his balanced sauces and his personal accents. Try, for example, the curious but delicious filet of gilthead cooked in its skin and served with a melon sauce, and the marvelous Bresse chicken served whole for the entire table with sautéed potatoes and salad. Good selection of wines.

A la carte: 250F. Menus: 75F (weekdays only), 90F, 140F, 180F.

Le Moulin de Bourgchâteau

(See restaurant above)

Open year-round. 17 rms 180-230F.

The modern, new rooms smell of wood and flour. The greeting is charming, but the breakfast coffee is not.

Lourdes

65100 Lourdes - (Hautes-Pyrénées)
Paris 797 - Pau 40 - Tarbes 20 - Argelès-Gazost 13

Gallia-Londres

26, ave. Bernadette-Soubirous
62.94.35.44

Closed Oct. 15-April 15. 90 rms 450-650F. Half-board 500-600F oblig. in seas. TV in 12 rms. Air cond. in 12 rms. Parking. Telex 521424. Cards: V, AE, DC.

The atmosphere and the stylish rooms reveal that this is a classic luxury hotel. Garden and restaurant.

Mapotel de la Grotte

66, rue de la Grotte - 62.94.58.87

Closed Oct. 20-March 29. 3 stes 1,000-1,500F. 85 rms 300- 520F. Half-board 250-510F. TV in 60 rms. Pets allowed. Garage parking. Telex 531937. Cards: V, AE, DC, MC.

From the balconies on the upper floors is one of the most delightful views in Lourdes, overlooking the Gave (the mountain stream), the sanctuaries and the Pyrénées. Lovely garden on the Adour river. Restaurant.

(13) Le Relais de Saux

Hameau de Saux - 62.94.29.61

Mme. Héres. Open until 9:30 p.m. Closed Jan. 3-15. Garden dining. No pets. Hotel: 8 rms 230-450F; half-board 255-365F oblig. in seas. Parking. Cards: V, AE.

Far from the crowds and the busy markets, this old house is hidden at the end of a path, its garden facing the Pyrénées and its deliciously irregular decor a mishmash of old furniture and knick-knacks. The owner is an energetic woman (the daughter of hoteliers from Lourdes) who has created the style and charm of the entire place, from the reception to the cuisine. The latter is prepared with great fervor by a chef who makes use of the owner's taste for regional products: fresh duck liver with caramelized pears, warm oysters with a smoked-duck mousse, squab baked with honey vinegar and lamb's sweetbreads with fresh pasta and spinach. Pleasant hotel rooms.

A la carte: 300F. Menu: 150F.

Le Tara

6, ave. Peyramale - 62.94.22.33

Closed Oct. 8-March 21. 73 rms 160-240F. Half-board 255-365F. TV in 4 rms. Telex 531937.

This new, nine-story hotel on the edge of the Gave (mountain stream) has functional rooms that are simple and bright, two minutes from the sanctuaries. Restaurant.

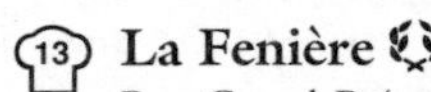

Lourmarin

84160 Cadenet - (Vaucluse)
Paris 736 - Salon 36 - Apt 18 - Avignon 56

(13) La Fenière

Rue Grand-Pré - 90.68.11.79

M. Sammut. Open until 9:30 p.m. Closed Sun. dinner, Mon., Jan. 2-16 & 1st weeks of March, July & Oct. Air cond. Pets allowed. Cards: V, AE, DC, MC.

Do you like the cuisine of Elisabeth Gagnaire at Le Mas de la Bertrande? Or that of Anne Carbonnel at Puyfonds? Then you can finish the triangle of women's Provençal cooking at this refurbished barn in Lourmarin. The Sammuts have purposefully created a stark decor, leaving lots of room for the warm reception of Guy and the delicious cuisine of Reine, who had wanted to be a dentist but is doing quite well preparing her stunning upside-down tart with potatoes, truffles and foie gras; her saddle of young rabbit cooked with herbs; and her fondant of chocolate and orange confit. Some fine cooking takes place in this rustic atmosphere, in which a perfect sense of the characteristic flavors of the region emerges.

A la carte: 300-350F. Menu: 120F.

Hôtel de Guilles

90.68.30.55

Closed March 1-15. 28 rms 230-480F. Half-board 640-800F (for 2 people). TV. Pets allowed. Pool. Tennis. Parking. Cards: V, AE, DC, MC.

At the foot of the Lubéron, among the grapevines, stands this cleverly restored old farm. The rooms are spacious; weekend packages are available. Restaurant.

Louveciennes

see PARIS SUBURBS

Loyettes

01800 Meximieux - (Ain)
Paris 468 - Bourg 51 - Lyon 33 - Vienne 48

15 La Terrasse

Pl. des Mariniers - 78.32.70.13

M. Antonin. Open until 9:30 p.m. Closed Sun. dinner, Mon. & Feb. school vacation. Cards: V, AE.

In mild weather you can take full advantage of this terrace at the edge of the Rhône, especially evenings when the regulars swarm out to the tables, finding the lighting in the dining room a bit dreary. Gérard Antonin is a chef with a personal touch and great consistency: admirable hot duck pâté, coquilles St-Jacques with salt, poached salmon with baby vegetables (thick and nicely cooked but a bit dull), delicate squab cooked rare and accompanied by cabbage, and exquisite desserts (crème brulée and little chocolate and coconut tarts, among them). The Beaujolais wines are well selected, and their reasonable prices will temper your bill. Mme. Antonin does everything she can to be charming, which she achieves with ease (particularly when she serves coffee with her delicious cherries soaked in eau-de-vie).

A la carte: 300F. Menus: 100F, 155F, 230F, 340F.

Lumbres

62380 Lumbres - (Pas-de-Calais)
Paris 266 - Arras 86 - Montreuil 48 - Boulogne 40

13 Moulin de Mombreux

Rte. de Bayenghem - 21.39.62.44, 21.39.13.13

M. Gaudry. Open until 9:15 p.m. Closed Dec. 20-Jan. 10. Pets allowed. Hotel: 7 stes 550F; 17 rms 430F. Parking. Cards: V, AE, DC, MC.

The Bléquin river passes beneath the paddle wheel of this proud, remarkably restored eighteenth-century mill. The sluice and its little cascade, the magical gearworks and the green riverbanks are irresistibly rustic. We were delighted that Jean-Marc Gaudry had the good idea to open twenty comfortable rooms in a nearby annex, allowing us to linger over his coquilles St-Jacques in a court bouillon with basil and asparagus, his crayfish and langoustines in a white sauce with morels, and his roasted veal kidneys with vegetable noodles. The prices are becoming rather formidable, even with the most modest wines.

A la carte: 300-350F. Menus: 173F (weekdays only), 220F, 276F, 345F.

This symbol stands for "Les Lauriers du Terroir," an award given to chefs who prepare noteworthy traditional or regional recipes.

Lunéville

54300 Lunéville - (Meurthe-et-Moselle)
Paris 340 - Strasbourg 124 - Metz 92 - Nancy 35

16 Château d'Adoménil

Réhainviller-Adomenil - 83.74.04.81

M. Million. Open until 9:30 p.m. Closed Sun. dinner, Mon. & Feb. Garden dining. Pets allowed. Parking. Cards: V, AE, DC, MC.

Today, when innkeepers make châteaux out of every shack, you can be assured that this elegant nineteenth-century residence, set amid expansive grounds, has not stolen its title. It offers pure seduction with its pinnacled chapel, its moats swimming with fish, its old wine press, its peacocks admiring their glorious reflections in the water, and its entryway where tables are set alongside the lawn and flowers. Still more château-like is the ravishing decor of the dining room: wood paneling, round tables set in sober refinement, old parquets. The relaxed and lively atmosphere is maintained by the cheerful Bernadette Million, who is also in charge of purchasing the magnificent wines; she will gladly help you find a suitable accompaniment to your selections from her husband's brief menu. He is a knowledgeable cook and an expert saucier, as evidenced by his warm crayfish with orange vinaigrette, filet of red mullet with basil, filet of squab and hot plum soufflé.

A la carte: 400F. Menus: 180F (weekdays only), 290F, 330F.

Château d'Adoménil

(See restaurant above)

Closed Sun., Mon. & Feb. 5 rms 600F. TV. Pets allowed.

Next to the old wine press, the comfortable rooms are luxurious but not ostentatious and are almost reasonably priced. Breakfast is exquisite.

Luppé-Violles

32110 Nogaro - (Gers)
Paris 700 - Pau 62 - Condom 55 - Auch 69 - Tarbes 66

14 Le Relais de l'Armagnac

62.08.95.22

M. Azam. Open until 9:30 p.m. Closed Mon. & Jan. Garden dining. No pets. Hotel: 10 rms 160-230F; half-board 255F. Cards: V, AE.

It was not evident at all that, in succeeding the impressive Roger Duffour and his marvelous goose tripe, stews and ragoûts, daughter Marie-Martine would be able to fill papa's shoes. Although full of energy and charm, Marie-Martine's twelve years as a flight attendant didn't exactly leave her ideally qualified to step in front of the hallowed ovens of the Relais. The doubts proved well founded, and the locals were happy to see the arrival of a true professional to carry on. The new chef has picked up where Duffour left off while adding his own distinction to the great regional classics of this generous house (the fixed-price menus are exhilarating). All of the favorites are in place: the foie gras, the famous tripe, the stews and the confits. But we can't forget to mention the exquisite duck and goose hearts with cherries en papillote; delicious filet of sole with beurre rouge and cèpes; and a few good desserts, like the strawberries in chocolate with a cardamom-flavored crème anglaise (for those few who resist the prune tart served with Armagnac). The rustic decor is pleasant and simple, extending out to a rear terrace that faces the garden.

A la carte: 250-300F. Menus: 65F, 135F, 180F, 335F.

Lurbe-Saint-Christau

64660 Asasp - (Pyrénées-Atlantiques)
Paris 795 - Lourdes 60 - Pau 42 - Oloron-Ste-Marie 9

Au Bon Coin

59.34.40.12

M. Lassala. Open until 9 p.m. Closed Mon. (off-seas.) & Nov. Terrace dining. Pets allowed. Hotel: 14 rms 100-180F. Parking.

Thierry Lassala is a young cook with talent, a unique personality and a nice touch, which he no doubt acquired from his training with Guérard and Arrambide. We would like to see him abandon certain archaisms that aren't appropriate to his age, like the langoustines flambéed with whisky, and even free himself from the sole meunière and the tournedos béarnaise, which add nothing to his repertoire. The small menu proposes other, delicious dishes, such as the salmon cured in lime (wonderfully delicate); the warm langoustine-and-mullet salad with tomatoes, chives and virgin olive oil; and the pigeon prepared in the regional style, sautéed with cèpes and grapes in a light juice. The pear tart, with an excellent crème anglaise served on the side, is worthy of Lassala's teacher, Guérard. The rustic decor is neat and charming. A good restaurant, progressing quickly.

A la carte: 220F. Menus: 70F, 100F, 165F.

Relais de la Poste et du Parc

Via N 618 - 59.34.40.04

Closed Dec. 1-Feb. 28. 5 stes 350-475F. 38 rms 188-230F. Half-board 250-389F. TV in 3 rms. Pool. Tennis. Parking. Telex 550656. Cards: V, DC, MC.

These peaceful, classic, restful rooms are in the middle of the vast hot springs and above a small lake, around which are planted ancient trees. Restaurant.

Luynes

37230 Luynes - (Indre-et-Loire)
Paris 248 - Tours 13 - Langeais 14 - Saumur 55

Domaine de Beauvois

4 km W on D 49 - 47.55.50.11

M. Taupin. Open until 9:15 p.m. Closed Jan. 9-March 5. Pets allowed. Telex 750204. Cards: V.

This lovely residence nestled in the enchanting greenery of the Touraine countryside is classic Relais et Châteaux material, the kind of place American tourists dream of: mansard roofs, endless acres of grounds, a pepper-box tower, oak trees from the era of Louis XIV, a looking-glass pond and a pool designed to look like a pond. Each of the rooms is comfortably proportioned, whether it's the salons by the fireside or the handsome dining room where the stylish staff keeps busy. Chef Daniel Tauvel's cuisine is somewhere between the old and the new. You'll find classic dishes (relieved of their heaviness) alongside a few compositions that are completely off the beaten path. Try the langoustines sautéed with ginger, the John Dory with Vouvray and the local squab with truffles, but don't forget the catch of the day, which may include sander, salmon and pike. There are excellent wines from the region, as well as others.

A la carte: 400-500F. Menus: 185F and 210F (lunch only), 220F and 320F (dinner only).

Domaine de Beauvois

(See restaurant above)

Closed Jan. 9-March 5. 3 stes 1,290-1,785F. 37 rms 495-1,195F. Half-board 702-900F. TV in 35 rms. Heated pool. Tennis.

One of the most beautiful Relais et Châteaux in the Touraine, the Domaine's immense rooms are attractively furnished and constantly modernized. Guests can fish, ride horses and visit the wine cellars following the grape harvest.

Lyon

69000 Lyon - (Rhône)
Paris 462 - Marseille 315 - Grenoble 106 - Geneva 190

Note: The establishments in Lyon are classed by arrondissement. At the end of the city, an alphabetical index lists the arrondissements (and the neighboring towns) in which all of the mentioned establishments are located.

The numbers following the telephone number in each review pinpoint the establishment's exact location on the accompanying map.

Sights. Vieux (Old) Lyon (the neighborhoods of Saint-Jean, Saint-Georges and Saint-Paul), in which the most beautiful ensemble of European Renaissance architecture is found (including La Cathédrale Saint-Jean, the private homes and the famous covered passageways that link the streets and pass through courtyards and buildings; in some of these buildings the Canuts wove silk threads); in Fourvière: panoramic view from the observatory of the basilica, Le Musée Gallo-Romain (the mosaics of Le Grand Théâtre, with more than 10,000 seats, dating from 15 B.C.) and Saint-Irénée church (fifth-century crypt and, in the vicinity, vestiges of the old Lugdunum); in La Croix-Rousse, fourth arrondissement: La Maison des Canuts, 10, rue d'Ivry, the baroque Saint-Bruno church and the numerous covered passageways; tours called Lyon Insolite (Unusual Lyon) are organized by the Office du Tourisme, 5, pl. St-Jean, 78.42.25.75; Les Musées de la Presqu'île, first and second arrondissements: Le Musée des Beaux-Arts, Le Musée des Arts Décoratifs, Le Musée de l'Imprimerie (printing) et de la Banque, Le Musée des Hospices Civils at the Hôtel-Dieu (general hospital), with its Louis XIII apothecary, and the rich and fascinating Musée des Tissus (fabrics), whose permanent exhibition rooms have just reopened after two years of renovation; Le Musée Saint-Pierre d'Art Contemporain, L'Elac (espace Perrache); more contemporary art at Le Nouveau Musée in Villeurbanne; the banks of the Saône and the river boats that cross both rivers; Le Parc de la Tête d'Or (rose garden and zoological garden), sixth arrondissement; Le Musée de l'Automobile in Rochetaillée (at the edge of the Saône, toward Trevoux); the medieval village of Pérouges (35 km toward Geneva on the rte. nationale).

Bouchons (charcuterie restaurants). Some of the most authentic that we didn't have room to cover in the following pages: Abel-Café-Comptoir, 25, rue Guynemer, 2nd; Le Café du Musée, 2, rue des Forces, 1st; Le Garet, 7, rue du Garet, 2nd; Chez Marcelle, 71, cours Vitton, 6th; La Mère Jean, 5, rue des Marronniers, 2nd; Tante Alice, 22, rue des Remparts-d'Ainay, 2nd; Tante Paulette, 2, rue Chavanne, 1st.

Bars & Cafés. Le Bar du Bistrot, 64, rue Mercière, 2nd (for apéritifs); Le Bar du Pullman, 129, rue Servient, 3rd (excellent); Le Chantaco, 21, quai Romain-Rolland, 5th (early evening and late night); Le Cintra, 4, rue de la Bourse, 2nd (for apéritifs); Eddie et Domino, 6, quai Dr-Gailleton, 2nd (all night, large whisky selection); Le Melhor, 20, quai Dr-Gailleton, 2nd (the bar at the Sofitel, best cocktails in town); Moana, 20, quai Pierre-Scize, 9th (to find a soul sister); Le Saint-Louis Bar, 61, rue Mercière, 2nd (jazz in a steamboat decor).

Nightlife. Actuel, 30, blvd. Eugène-Deruelle, 3rd (big discotheque, patrons screened at the door); L'Aquarius, 43, quai Pierre-Scize, 9th (rather small, attracts young jet-setters); Le First, 14, rue Thomassin, 2nd (to wrap up the night); Le Onze, 11, quai des Etroits, 5th (disco music and gay clientele, losing popularity); Le Quartier Latin, 7, quai St-Vincent, 1st (the newest).

Shops. *Meat:* Gauthier-Grande Boucherie des Monts-d'Or, 13, rue Montebello, 3rd (neighborhood of the butcher shops); Schumacher, rue du Dr-Gallarvadin in St-Priest (very popular); Maurice Trolliet, 6, rue Paul-Verlaine in Villeurbanne (the best). *Bakeries:* Boulangerie des Jacobins, 7, rue Jean-de-Tounes, 2nd (bread to eat with foie gras and cocktails); Boulangerie du Pont, Halles de Lyon, 3rd, and 4, cours Aristide-Briand in Caluire; Mano, 92, Grand-Rue de la Guillotière, 7th (an artist—breads with carrots, seaweed, currants); Marius Petit, 9, rue Lanterne, 1st (pain de campagne). *Charcuteries:* Besson (called Bobosse), 66, rue de Bonnel, 3rd (for its andouillette, among others); Chorliet, 12, rue du Plat, 2nd (fatted chicken from Bresse, truffled pork sausage called saveloy); Delangle–Au Chapon Fin, 26, ave. du Maréchal-de-Saxe, 6th (foie gras and quenelles); Gast, Halles de la Part-Dieu, 3rd (Alsatian charcuterie); Colette Sibilia, Halles de la Part-Dieu, 3rd. *Chocolate:* Bernachon, 42, cours Franklin-Roosevelt, 6th (world famous); Pierre Ginet, 9, rue de la Charité, 2nd (supplies Fauchon and La Maison de la Truffe, more than 80 varieties); Aux Palets d'Or, 96, ave. Jean-Jaurès in Saint-Fons; Palomas, 2, rue Col-Chambonnet, 2nd. *Gourmet foods:* Bocuse-Bernachon, 49, rue de Sèze, 6th (wines and preserves); Boutique des Landes, 29, quai St-Antoine, 2nd (products from Le Grand Larrocq, raw, partially cooked and preserved foie gras); Boutique de la Tour Rose, 2, pl. Neuve-St-Jean, 5th (fine wines, conserves, dishes to go); Clostan, 10, cours Vitton, 6th (Fauchon products); Comptoir de la Gastronomie, 125, rue de Séze, 6th (vacuum-packed products to go). *Cheese:* Maréchal (carefully selected farm cheeses) and Renée Richard (the best Saint-Marcellin in the world), both in the Halles de la Part-Dieu, 3rd. *Pastries, ice cream:* Bonniaud, 64, ave. des Frères-Lumière, 8th (as artistic as they are delicious); La Minaudière, 5, rue de Brest, 2nd (cakes, ice creams and sorbets); Jean-Paul Pignol, 17, rue Emile-Zola, 2nd (an institution). *Fish and shellfish:* Durand, Goguillot, Pupier and Rousseau (the best oyster shucker in Lyon), all in the Halles de la Part-Dieu, 3rd. *Wine:* Beaujolais and Côtes-du-Rhône (Hermitage, Saint-Joseph, Condrieu, Cornas) at Malleval, 11, rue Emile-Zola, 2nd, and the Relais des Caves, 32, ave. du Maréchal-de-Saxe, 6th; La Vieille Réserve, 1, cours Franklin-Roosevelt, 6th; the Vinothèque, 1, montée des Carmélites, 5th.

Shows & Festivals. February: Grand Prix de Tennis de Lyon at the Gerland Stadium, from the 8th to the 14th (excellent "chefs village" with the best of Lyon). May: Floralies (Flower Show), April 29-May 29; Mai de Lyon (traditional festivals that run through June) with, as the grand finale, Les Pennons de Lyon (horse race inspired by the Palio of Siena). June: Fête sans Frontière, the largest humanitarian festival in Europe, at the Parc de la Tête d'Or. September: Biennale de la Danse (alternating every other year with the festival Berlioz). October: Octobre des Arts (contemporary art festival throughout the city, lasting into November). November: Fêtes du Beaujolais Nouveau, the 3rd Thursday of the month, in the bistros and entertainment spots. December: Fête Traditionnelle du 8 (December 8), with a light show toward Fourvière, every window lit with candles, and the peninsula closed to cars.

First Arrondissement

The "Peninsula" of Lyon between the Rhône and Saône rivers, at one time considered the center of town, is at the foot of the Croix Rousse.

12/20 L'Assiette Lyonnaise

19, pl. Tolozan - 78.28.35.77 / Z1-24

M. Gros. Open until 11:30 p.m. Closed Sat. lunch, Sun. & Aug. 1-16. Terrace dining. Cards: V, AE, DC.

Located at the lower end of the silk merchants' quarter, this pleasant eating place, with its marble tables and greenery, has the sort of reception one expects of a grand restaurant. The service is brisk and attentive, and the cuisine, though impersonal, is nevertheless well prepared: sweetbreads with fresh noodles, enticing daily specials, such as a young pork stew, and a perfect crème brûlée.

A la carte: 180-200F. Menus: 75F, 110F.

12/20 Boname

5, Grande-Rue-des-Feuillants
78.30.83.93 / Z1-53

M. Boname. Open until midnight. Closed Sat. & Sun. (in seas.) or Sun. & Mon. (off-seas.). Air cond. Pets allowed. Cards: V.

Among the hills of the Croix Rousse, in a decor that more closely resembles a textile factory than a bistro, is one of the finest eating places in the

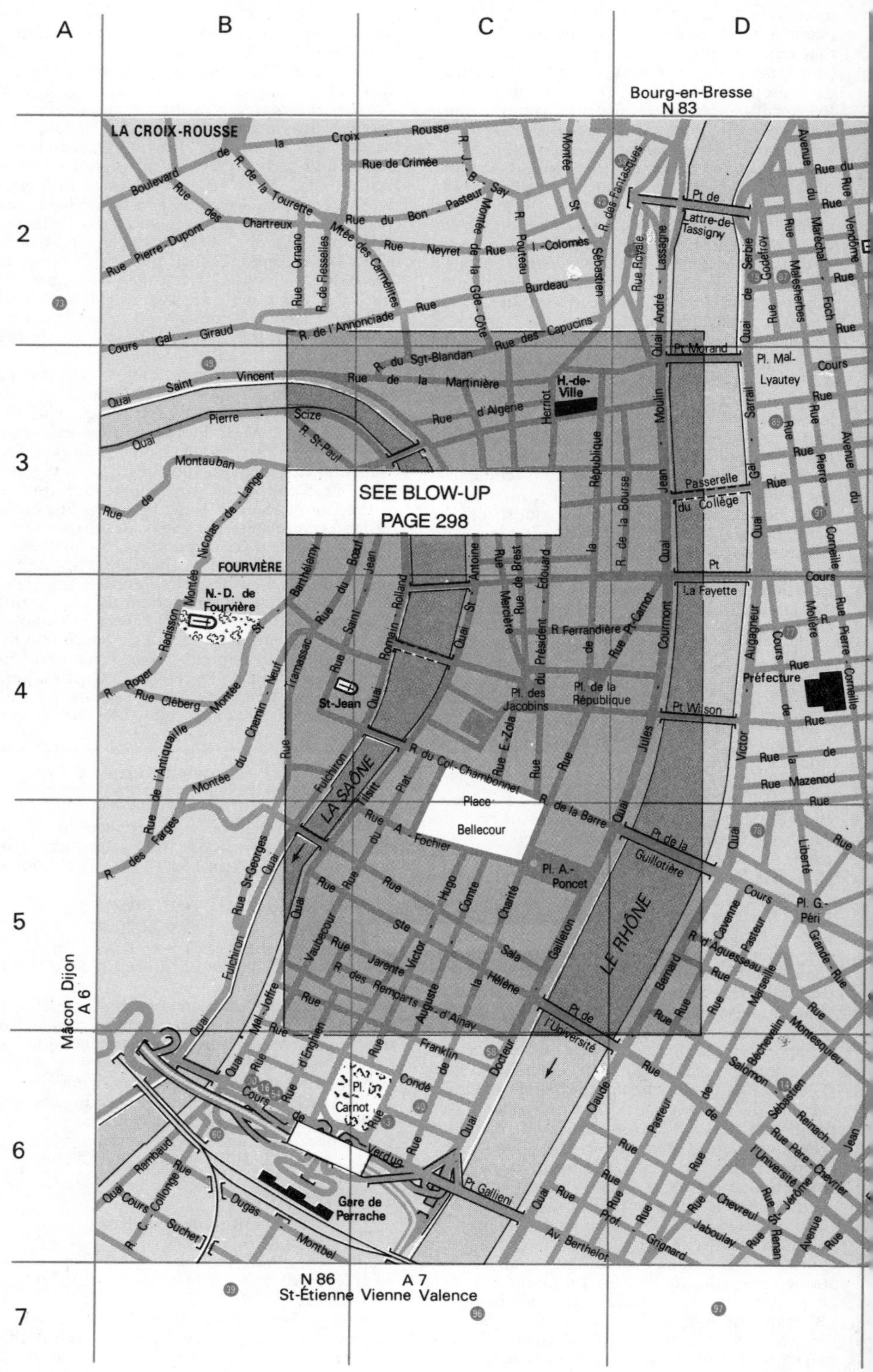

A
B
C
D
2
3
4
5
6
7
Bourg-en-Bresse
N 83
LA CROIX-ROUSSE
Boulevard de la Croix Rousse
Rue de Crimée
R. J. B. Say
Montée St Sébastien
R. des Fantasques
R. de la Tourette
Rue des Chartreux
Rue Pierre-Dupont
Rue du Bon - Pasteur
Mtée des Carmélites
Rue Neyret
Montée de la Gde-Côte
R. Pouteau
Rue I.-Colomès
Rue Ornano
R. de Flesselles
Rue Burdeau
R. de l'Annonciade
Rue des Capucins
Cours Gal. Giraud
R. du Sgt-Blandan
Quai Saint Vincent
Rue de la Martinière
H.-de-Ville
Rue d'Algérie
Quai Pierre Scize
R. St-Paul
Rue de Montauban
Montée Nicolas-de-Lange
SEE BLOW-UP
PAGE 298
FOURVIÈRE
N.-D. de Fourvière
Rue Royale
Quai André Lassagne
Pt de Lattre-de-Tassigny
Quai de Serbie
Rue Godefroy
Rue Malesherbes
Avenue du Maréchal Foch
Rue Vendôme
Rue du
Pt Morand
Pl. Mal. Lyautey
Cours
Quai Jean Moulin
Quai Gal. Sarrail
Passerelle du Collège
Pt La Fayette
Rue Pierre Corneille
Avenue du
Cours
Rue Molière
Rue de la Bourse
Rue de la République
Herriot
Rue de Brest
Rue Mercière
Rue Président Édouard
Quai St Antoine
Rue du Bœuf
Rue Saint Jean
Rue Romain Rolland
R. Ferrandière
Rue Pt-Carnot
Quai Jules Courmont
Quai Victor Augagneur
Cours
Préfecture
Rue Barthélemy
Montée St Barthélemy
R. Roger Radisson
Rue Cléberg
Montée du Chemin Neuf
Rue Tramassac
St-Jean
Quai
Pl. des Jacobins
Pl. de la République
Pt Wilson
Rue E.-Zola
Rue
Rue de l'Antiquaille
Montée du
Rue des Farges
R. des
Rue Fulchiron
LA SAÔNE
Tilsitt
R. du Col.-Chambonnet
Place Bellecour
R. de la Barre
Rue du Plat
Rue A.-Fochier
Rue Mazenod
Rue de la
Pt de la Guillotière
Pl. A.-Poncet
Quai
Cours
Pl. G.-Péri
Grande-Rue
Rue de la Liberté
Quai St-Georges
Quai Fulchiron
Quai
Rue Vaubecour
Rue Ste Hélène
Rue Jarente
Rue Victor Hugo
Rue Comte
Rue de la Charité
Rue Sala
Quai Gailleton
LE RHÔNE
R. des Remparts d'Ainay
Rue Auguste
Pt de l'Université
Rue Bernard
R. d'Aguesseau
Rue Pasteur
Rue Cavenne
Rue Marseille
Rue Montesquieu
Mâcon Dijon
A 6
Quai Mal-Joffre
Rue d'Enghien
Rue Franklin
Docteur
Rue Salomon
Rue Béchevelin
Rue Sébastien
Rue Reinach
Jean
Cours de Verdun
Pl. Carnot
Rue de Condé
Rue Claude
Rue Pasteur
Rue de l'Université
Rue Père-Chevrier
Rue St-Jérôme
Rue Chevreul
Rue Renan
Avenue
Quai Rambaud
Cours Gare de Perrache
Rue Dugas Montbel
R. C. Sucher
Pt Gallieni
Quai
Av. Berthelot
Rue Prof. Grignard
Rue Jaboulay
N 86
St-Étienne
A 7
Vienne Valence

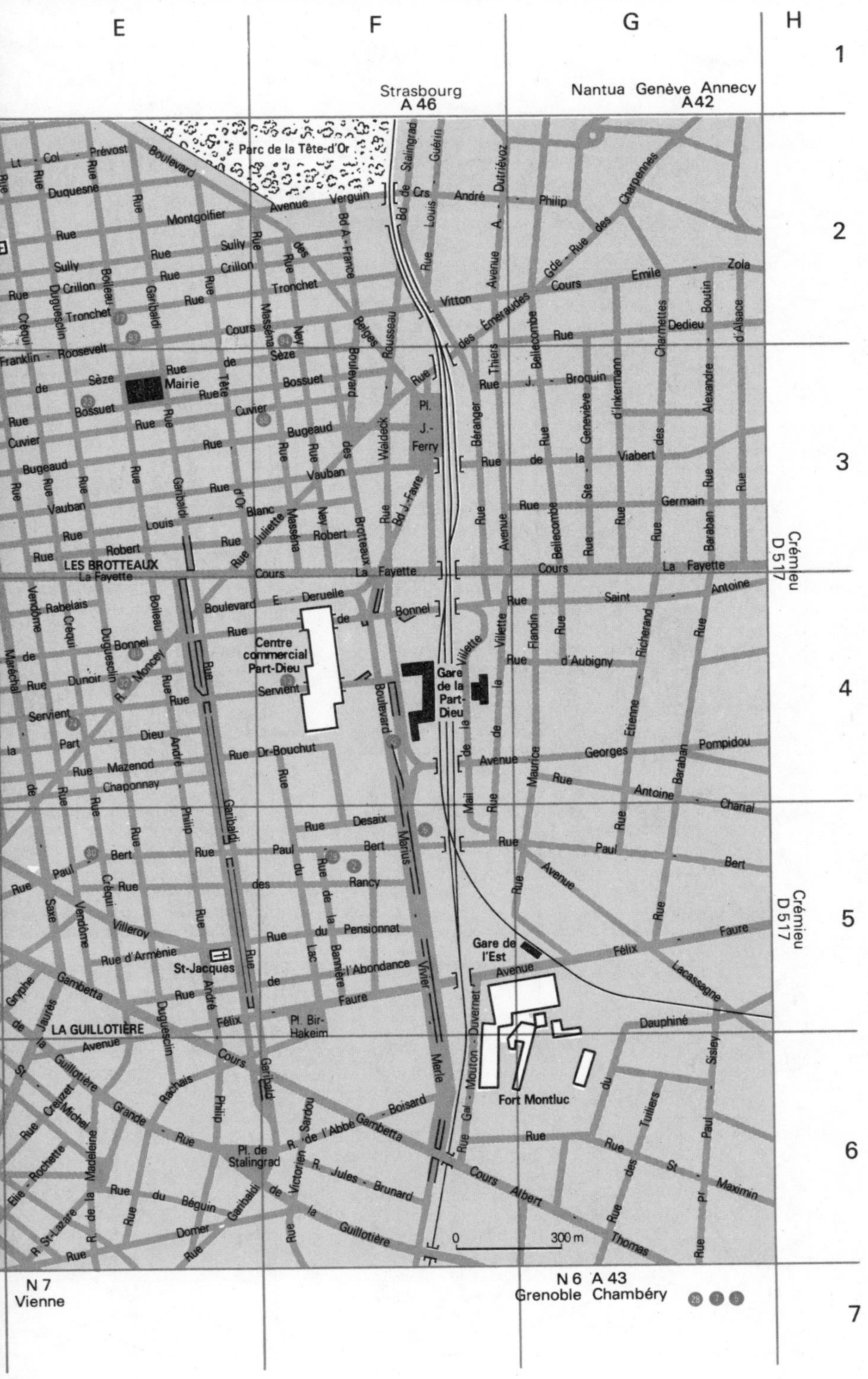
E
F
G
H
1
2
3
4
5
6
7
Strasbourg A 46
Nantua Genève Annecy A42
Parc de la Tête-d'Or
Crémieu D 517
N 7 Vienne
N 6 A 43 Grenoble Chambéry
LES BROTTEAUX
LA GUILLOTIÈRE
Centre commercial Part-Dieu
Gare de la Part-Dieu
Gare de l'Est
Fort Montluc
Pl. J.-Ferry
Pl. Bir-Hakeim
Pl. de Stalingrad
St-Jacques
Mairie
0 300 m

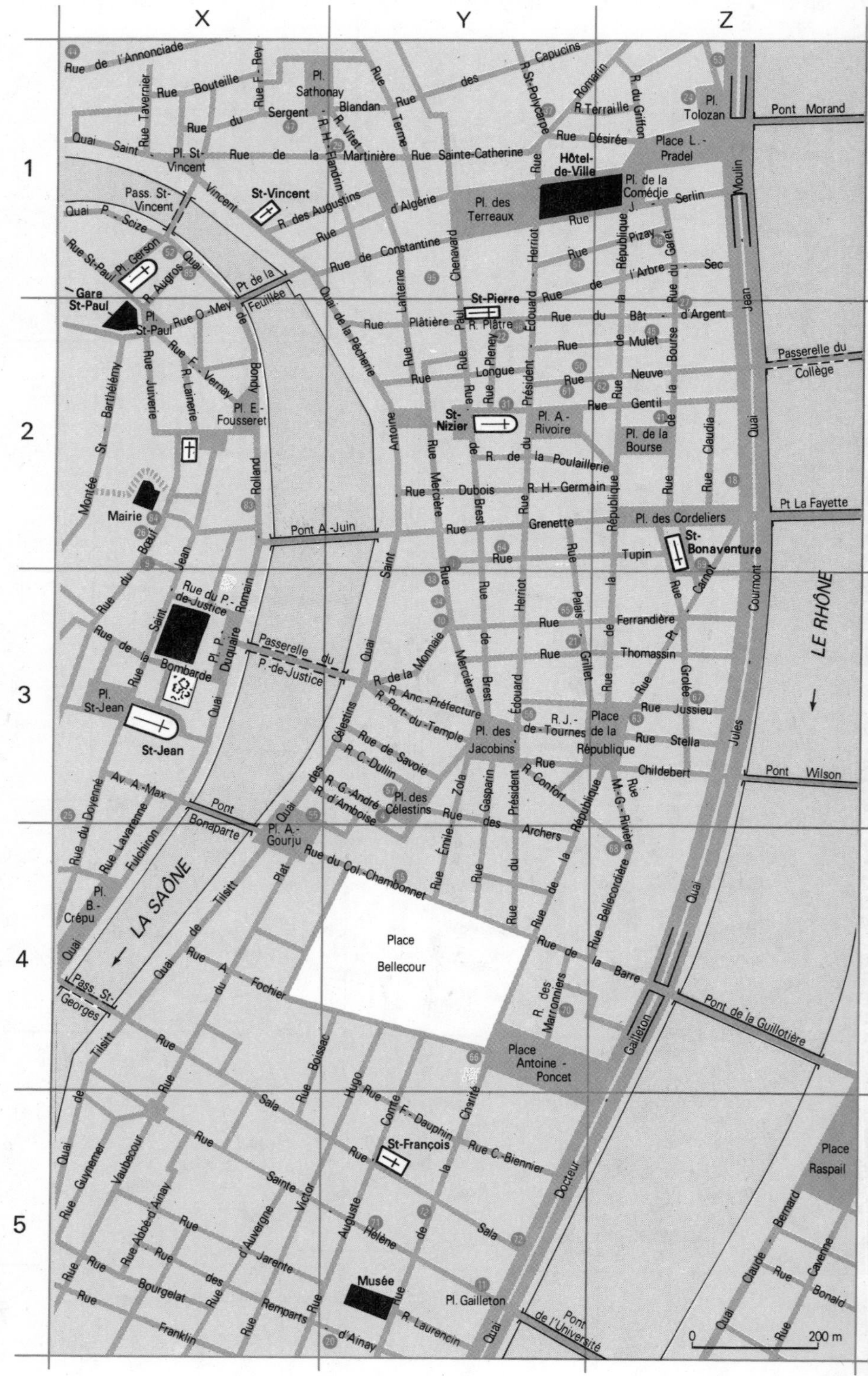

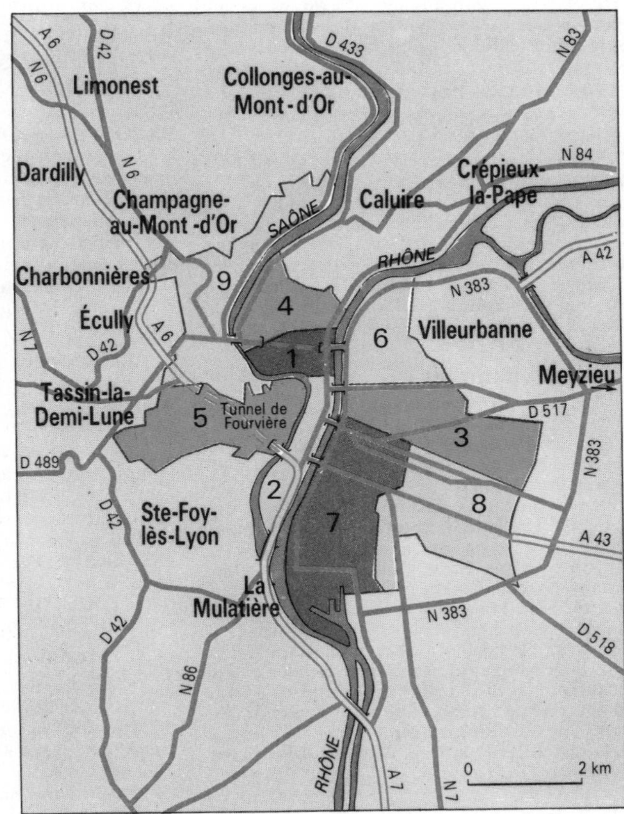

- Daniel et Denise (2e) **R**
- Chez Pino (3e) **R**
- Institut Vatel (2e) **R**
- Christian Bourillot (2e)
- Laennec (8e) **H**
- Carro (3e) **R**
- Altea Park Hôtel (8e) **H**
- La Mère Brazier (1er) **R**
- Comptoir du Bœuf (5e) **R**
- Le Bistrot de Lyon (2e) **R**
- Le Vivarais (2e) **R**
- La Tassée (2e) **R**
- L'Arc-en-Ciel (Pullman Part-Dieu) (3e) **RH**
- La Grille (7e) **R**
- Vettard (2e) **R**
- Bristol (2e) **H**
- Cazenove (6e) **R**
- Nandron (2e) **R**
- Le Restaurant des Gourmets (6e) **R**
- Les Visiteurs du Soir (2e) **R**
- Le Sarto (2e) **R**

2 - Léon de Lyon (1er) **R**
3 - Le Fulton (6e) **R** et Le Roosevelt **H**
4 - L'Assiette Lyonnaise (1er) **R**
5 - Le Prestige Thaïlandais (5e) **R**
6 - La Tour Rose (5e) **R**
7 - La Corbeille (1er) **R**
8 - Auberge Savoyarde (8e) **R**
9 - Henry (1er) **R**
0 - La Mère Vittet (2e) **R**
1 - La Rose des Vins (1er) **R**
2 - L'Alexandrin (3e) **R**
3 - Au Temps Perdu (1er) **R**
4 - Le Bouchon aux Vins (2e) **R**
6 - Georges (1er) **R**
7 - Alain Janiaud (1er) **R**
8 - Le Mercière (2e) **R**
9 - Tourinter (2e) **H**
0 - Au Petit Col (2e) **R**
1 - Les Fantasques (2e) **R**
3 - Le Champier (1er) **R**
4 - La Mandarine (1er) **R**
5 - Le Tonnelier (1er) **R**
6 - Le Passage (1er) **R**
7 - Chevallier (1er) **R**
9 - L'Estragon (1er) **R**
0 - La Meunière (1er) **R**
1 - Hugon (1er) **R**
2 - Phénix (5e) **H**
3 - Boname (1er) **R**
4 - Brasserie Georges (2e) **R**
5 - La Voûte (2e) **R**
56 - Grand Hôtel des Beaux-Arts (2e) **H**
57 - Chez Jean-François (2e) **R**
58 - Le Shalimar (2e) **R**
59 - Café Gambs (2e) **R**
60 - Terminus Lyon-Perrache (2e) **H**
61 - Kun Yang (2e) **R**
62 - Le Nord (2e) **R**
63 - Carlton (2e) **H**
64 - Café du Jura (2e) **R**
65 - Guy Garioud (2e) **R**
66 - Royal (2e) **H**
67 - Grand Hôtel Concorde (2e) **H**
68 - Eriksen (2e) **R**
70 - Chez Mounier (2e) **R**
71 - L'Assiette en Douce (2e) **R**
72 - Les Trois Dômes (Sofitel) (2e) **RH**
73 - Hôtel de Lyon Métropole (4e) **H**
74 - Wœhrlé (3e) **R**
77 - Chez Rose (3e) **R**
78 - A Ma Vigne (3e) **R**
79 - Le Gourmandin (3e) **R**
80 - Péquet (3e) **R**
81 - Le Val d'Isère (3e) **R**
82 - Mercure (3e) **H**
83 - Le 21 (5e) **R**
84 - Cour des Loges (5e) **H**
85 - Les Saisons (5e) **R**
87 - Le Quatre Saisons (6e) **R**
88 - Christian Grisard (6e) **R**
89 - La Soupière (6e) **R**
91 - Gervais (6e) **R**
93 - Pierre Orsi (6e) **R**
94 - La Romanière (6e) **R**
95 - Café des Fédérations (1er) **R**
96 - Mercure Pont-Pasteur (7e) **H**
97 - Le Fédora (7e) **R**

silk merchants' quarter: filet of beef with shrimp and marrow, seafood stew with crab bisque and glazed nougat with honey. Mâcon wines are served in jugs.

A la carte: 180-200F.

12/20 **Café des Fédérations**

8, rue du Major-Martin
78.28.26.00 / Y1-95

M. Fulchiron. Open until 9:45 p.m. Closed Sat., Sun. & Aug. Pets allowed. Cards: V, AE, DC.

In a weather-beaten decor garlanded with sausages, the Café des Fédérations serves an unchangeable menu worthy of Lyon's legendary gastronomy: salads, terrines, pot-au-feu, "tablier de sapeur" ("fireman's apron," a grilled tripe dish) and numerous jugs of Morgon wine.

Menu: 115F.

(13) **Le Champier**

10, rue des Fantasque
78.28.41.33 / C2-43

M. Cantat. Open until 9:30 p.m. Closed Sun. dinner, Mon. & Aug. 15-Sept. 1. Air cond. Pets allowed. Cards: AE, DC.

People come to Le Champier for the food, not the decor. The latter is comfortable but without much other interest, except for the superb view of Lyon over the Croix Rousse tunnel. Daniel Cantat was trained by the great traditionalists but has little taste for retrospective cuisine. He is a man of personality and inventiveness, which is what we like in his best dishes, such as the ocean trout, the cassoulet of hot oysters with leeks, the filet of lamb stuffed with kidneys and eggplant, and the terrine of chocolate with coconut. He offers Côtes-du-Rhône from Guigal.

A la carte: 250F and up. Menus: 90F (except Sat. dinner), 145F, 190F.

12/20 **Chevallier**

40, rue du Sergent-Blandan
78.28.19.83 / X1-47

MM. Coutant & Tuset. Open until 9:45 p.m. Closed Tues., Wed., Feb. 13-23 & July 3-Aug. 3. Air cond. Pets allowed. Cards: V, AE.

Within Chevallier's bright, comfortable and prosperous bistro decor (which M. Coutant's prices do their best to reflect) you'll find serious, well-prepared, Lyon-style brasserie fare: quail salad with fresh foie gras, homemade sea-pike quenelles, tablier de sapeur (grilled tripe), breast of duck with two kinds of peppers and lovely desserts.

A la carte: 200F. Menus: 78F (weekday lunch only), 98F (dinner only), 130F, 150F.

12/20 **La Corbeille**

21, rue du Bât d'Argent
78.27.74.50 / Z2-27

M. Randu-Hordé. Open until 10 p.m. Closed Sat. lunch, Sun. & Aug. 1-22. Terrace dining. Pets allowed. Cards: V, AE, DC.

The cuisine may not exhibit much creativity, but at least it's copious and meticulously prepared: all kinds of salads, tasty sweetbreads with a lovely cream sauce, several fresh fish (depending on the catch of the day) and a good homemade cake. The amusing bourgeois decor is done in candy pink.

A la carte: 180F. Menus: 54F and 65F (lunch only), 90F, 120F, 160F.

12/20 **L'Estragon**

27, rue St-Vincent - 78.28.14.51 / B3-49

M. Lauro. Open until midnight. Closed Sat. lunch & Sun. Terrace dining. Pets allowed. Cards: V.

The fashionable nightlife crowd and theatergoers have made this their new rendezvous spot. In an amusing setting, under pleasant lighting, the former chef of the Bistrot de Lyon prepares an intelligent cuisine: fresh seafood, good rabbit with tarragon and fresh pasta, and ganache au chocolat (chocolate, whipped cream and butter).

A la carte: 160F.

12/20 **Georges**

8, rue du Garet - 78.28.30.46 / Z1-36

M. Foulquier. Open until 10 p.m. Closed Sat., Sun. & Aug. 15-Sept. 1.

The decor isn't lively, but the owner is, which comes through clearly in his tasty, traditional Lyon-style cooking, which is enhanced with several creative seasonal specials: tablier de sapeur (grilled tripe), marrow meunière and sea perch with olive oil. The wines (served in jugs) are well selected.

A la carte: 130-150F. Menu: 72F (lunch only).

(15) **Henry**

27, rue de la Martinière
78.28.26.08 / Y1-29

M. Balladone. Open until midnight (with reserv.). Closed Sat. lunch & Mon. (except holidays). Pets allowed. Cards: V, AE, DC.

Vanished are the memories of this old corner bistro as it was in the days when diners with great appetites ready for a hearty meal wandered down from the covered passageways. Today it is a luxurious brasserie with a decor that combines glass, carpeting and steel with, beneath the high ceiling, superb canvases by the Lyon painter Truphémus. Swiss-born Pierre Balladone, M. Henry's son-in-law, is an energetic and professional cook trained by Vergé and Senderens. His cuisine has great appeal, including a mastery of the most difficult sauces: lobster and crayfish salad with truffle butter, médaillons of lotte with coriander, boeuf bordelaise. The 160-franc fixed-price menus is exceptional, and the service irreproachable.

A la carte: 300-350F. Menus: 160F, 230F.

11/20 **Hugon**

(Le Bouchon Lyonnais)
12, rue Pizay - 78.28.10.94 / Y1-51

Mme. Hugon. Lunch only. Open until 3 p.m. Closed Sat., Sun. & Aug. Pets allowed. Cards: V.

Don't expect too much of this cuisine (chicken with vinegar, sabodet—a hearty sausage—stew and pot-au-feu), but do expect plenty of atmosphere and graciousness. Excellent Côtes-du-Rhône and Beaujolais (in jugs).

A la carte: 150F. Menu: 120F (wine incl.).

(13) Alain Janiaud

9, rue St-Polycarpe - 78.28.15.31 / Y1-37
M. Janiaud. Open until 10 p.m. Closed Sat. lunch & Sun. Pets allowed. Cards: V, AE, DC.

New owner Alain Janiaud is an example of the result of a good, Lyon-based education (Bourillot, Mère Brazier, Douillé and Nandron). He has landed in this classic and inviting bistro with the goal of performing well and varying his repertoire (the menu changes about once a month). For the moment, his cuisine is of a thoughtfully modernized classicism, with such strong points as the delicious grilled pigs' feet with beurre blanc, the loin strip of veal with garlic cream and the light fricassée of poultry and sweetbreads. The apple tart isn't exciting, even with the added vanilla ice cream and raspberry sauce. The wine cellar is small but has good labels. Monique Janiaud is a charming hostess.

A la carte: 230-250F. Menus: 85F, 128F.

(18) Léon de Lyon

1, rue Pléney
78.28.11.33
M. Lacombe. Open until 10 p.m. Closed Mon. lunch, Sun. & Aug. 6-21. Air cond. Pets allowed. Cards: V.

Now there are two Mme. Lacombes. There is Gisèle, the good, sweet "maman" (they don't come any more Lyonnaise) who still pays a visit every now and then. She comes to breathe in the sacred emanations of the kitchen and to remember the good old days when Paul, her joker of a husband, would get together with a few friends to concoct a clever response to the latest mystification to emerge from Bocuse. And as of a year or so ago, there's the daughter of Georges Duboeuf, who recently married Jean-Paul Lacombe and who's in charge of the company's bookkeeping. And make no mistake, this is a real company, one that employs no less than 85 people in Léon de Lyon, Le Bistro de Lyon and Le Bouchon aux Vins. And, with consideration being given to opening a restaurant in Paris, it may be getting even bigger. Fortunately, Jean-Paul does not spread his talent too thin, concentrating instead on the cuisine at this Lyon monument, where novelty gathers strength from a solid tradition.

The antique building is a delightful, relaxing place. On its two floors, waiters wearing long blue aprons as in days of old wind their way through the small, delicate dining rooms furnished with dark woodwork, old paintings and cooking utensils. Faithful to the hot sausages, Lyonnaise salads, rich and juicy double-gras, fish quenelles, deboned pigs' feet and cervelle de canut (soft cheese, herb and cream misture) that have always marked Léon as a conservator of Old Lyon, Jean-Paul, a sensitive and imaginative chef, always astounds us with a dish of his own creation that slips into this classic repertoire with amazing ease. It might be, for example, a terrine of pois gourmands with lobster, a feuilleté of langoustines with fresh morels, roasted red snapper and John Dory in a warm aïoli sauce. Or perhaps a marvelous veal filet studded with calves' feet and celery; sautéed baby lamb with fava beans sprinkled with its juices and a touch of cream; a delicious baby lamb ragoût in a garlic sauce accompanied by a divine little feuilleté garnished with lamb's sweetbreads, heart, tongue and liver; or a Bresse baby pigeon in a salt crust with a cake of its liver in a hazelnut-oil vinaigrette. Though these dishes are light and subtle, the tastes are well defined. The desserts—a cocoa feuilleté, a chocolate mousse without eggs, a strawberry croustillant—are exquisite, as are the Beaujolais, Burgundy and Côtes-du-Rhône wines from the worthy wine cellar. The prices are extremely reasonable, including the "petit" fixed-price menu that changes daily and that the people of Lyon consider a real bargain.

A la carte: 400-450F. Menus: 210F, 395F.

(13) La Mandarine

10, rue Rivet - 78.28.01.74 / X1-44
M. Perrier. Open until 10:30 p.m. Closed Sat. lunch, Sun. & Aug. Pets allowed. Cards: V, AE, DC.

The bourgeois cooking served at La Mandarine is always admirably prepared, and the clientele is composed of lively, rather young diners who come to celebrate in groups in an uncomfortable but amusing '60s-style decor. The fixed-price menu is based on home-style cooking, and you'll find fresh, copious dishes à la carte: scorpionfish and salmon tartare, spinach cake with langoustines, and breast of duck with turnip confit. For dessert, try the tasty chocolate cake.

A la carte: 280F. Menus: 80F (lunch only), 110F, 195F.

(16) La Mère Brazier

12, rue Royale - 78.28.15.49 / D2-8
Mmes. Brazier. Open until 9:45 p.m. Closed Sat. lunch, Sun. & July 29-Aug. 29. Pets allowed. Cards: V, AE, DC.

It wouldn't take too many places like this to make you want to move to Lyon. The wine cellar is so wonderful (ah, those legendary Burgundies), the presence of Carmen Brazier and her daughter Jacotte so friendly, and the charming little dining room so lively that you'll ask yourself if there could possibly be another restaurant in this city where you could be so content. And the "miracle" of Mère Brazier doesn't stop here. To have attracted for more than 60 years the most important members of the political, legal and business societies, this restaurant has maintained perfection, consistency and professionalism in its delicious demi-deuil chicken (cooked with truffles under the skin), artichoke hearts with foie gras, rack of lamb au gratin, calves' liver with parsley and macaroni gratin, kidneys in mustard, apple tart and ice cream with hot chocolate sauce. And would you believe that the repertoire is virtually unchanged since 1921, yet gives the impression of having been conceived yesterday?! Everything is perfectly executed and without unnecessary heaviness (it's actually quite light). You can believe us when we say that the additional point in this edition is certainly not a stolen one.

A la carte: 300-350F. Menus: 250F, 285F.

12/20 La Meunière

11, rue Neuve - 78.28.62.91 / Y2-50
M. Debrosse. Open until 9:45 p.m. Closed Sun., Mon. & July 14-Aug. 16. Pets allowed. Cards: V, AE, DC.

The salads are creative—lamb's tongue, tripe with a provocative seasoning—and the whole kidney is cooked to precision. There's also a magnificent dessert buffet, handsome wines and a delightful atmosphere, typical of an authentic Lyon tavern.

A la carte: 160F. Menus: 60F, 80F, 110F.

(15) Le Passage

8, rue du Plâtre - 78.28.11.16 / Y2-46

M. Carteron. Open until 9:45 p.m. Closed Sat. lunch, Sun. & holidays. Terrace dining. Pets allowed. Cards: V, AE, DC.

The à la carte prices are those of a fancy restaurant, and the place itself, squeezed into one of the old covered passageways, painstakingly reconstitutes the atmosphere of the bistros of yesteryear. Vincent Carteron's restaurant features stone floors, bistro tables, a comfortable bar and walls resplendent with paintings by Braque, Derain and Dali—good copies, that is. But the deception ends there. The brilliant Daniel Ancel reaffirms the success he enjoyed at Quatre Saisons. His only fault is that he too brazenly avoids the traditional cuisine of Lyon, even its adaptations, cooking only what comes to mind: one day a plate of warm foie gras with asparagus tips or a ragoût of crab and fatted chicken, another day a marvelous blanquette (ultra-modernized), a roasted stuffed saddle of lamb or a fricasséed Breton lobster with cumin served with extraordinary lentils with bacon. Everything is generous and appetizing. For those watching their wallets, the lunchtime fixed-price menu will be a happy surprise, and there are wines from everywhere for less than 100 francs.

A la carte: 300F. Menus: 140F (lunch only), 200F, 250F.

12/20 La Rose des Vins

5, rue de la Fromagerie
78.28.48.22 / Y2-31

M. Bleton. Open until 1 a.m. Closed Sat. lunch, Sun. & Aug. 15-31. Terrace dining. Pets allowed. Hotel: 11 rms 150-250F. Cards: V, AE, DC, MC.

La Rose des Vins features about ten modern, small rooms upstairs; in the dining room downstairs, the large contemporary decor is as pleasant as it is original. Here you'll be served a hearty bistro fare: cassoulet, confit with beans and superb regional cheeses, all of which is accompanied by 80 well-selected vintages, about twenty of which are also served by the glass.

A la carte: 160-180F. Menu: 65F (lunch only, wine incl.).

11/20 Au Temps Perdu

2, rue des Fantasques
78.39.23.04 / D2-33

Mmes. Daru & Aardenburg. Open until midnight. Closed Sat., Sun. & Dec. 24-Jan. 1. Pets allowed. Cards: AE.

A lovely view of the old town and tasty home cooking prepared by one or both of the charming owners: various salads, breast of duck with onion confit, pan-fried calves' liver with macaroni au gratin and delicious fruit tarts.

A la carte: 160F.

11/20 Le Tonnelier

10, rue Mulet - 78.28.05.48 / Z2-45

M. Faure. Open until 9:30 p.m. Closed Sat. dinner, Sun. & July 14-Aug. 16. Air cond. Pets allowed.

With hot saucisson (cured sausage) and coq au vin, M. Faure's budget menu is satisfying indeed to all the neighborhood noshers. Lovely cakes.

A la carte: 130F. Menus: 42F, 70F, 85F, 115F, 160F.

Second Arrondissement

Home to the oldest of the Lyon families, this arrondissement includes the neighborhoods of Bellecour, Perrache and Ainay.

12/20 L'Assiette en Douce

31, rue Ste-Hélène - 78.92.93.54 / Y5-71

MM. Reverchon & Fougerat. Open until 11 p.m. Closed Sat., Sun., Jan. 28-Feb. 12, June 17-25 & Sept. 2-17. Air cond. Pets allowed. Cards: V.

Success came quickly to this cheery bistro, where a fashionable crowd and good food meet. You'll find a good gâteau of poultry liver, roast lotte with a vanilla-and-saffron sauce and a delicious dark-chocolate cake. Good gold-medal Coteaux-du-Lyonnais for 52 francs. Endearing prices.

A la carte: 180F. Menus: 45F, 55F and 65F (lunch only).

(13) Le Bistrot de Lyon

64, rue Mercière - 78.37.00.62 / Y3-10

MM. Carr & Lacombe. Open until 1:30 a.m. Closed May 1-Dec. 25. Air cond. Terrace dining. Pets allowed. Cards: V.

On the evenings of theater premieres, there's always a high- society crowd. The rest of the time, when late night rolls around, the patrons change over to their business-breakfast mode. Chef Dominique Fesseteaux prepares a soup with peas or ravioli, escalopes of tuna with fresh pasta and daily specials. Excellent wine cellar.

A la carte: 200F. Menu: 130F (weekday lunch only, wine incl.).

(14) Le Bouchon aux Vins

62, rue Mercière - 78.42.88.90 / Y3-34

M. Caro. Open until midnight. Closed Sun. & May 1-Dec. 25. Air cond. Terrace dining. Pets allowed. Cards: V.

Here, in a former electronics store, is the best of Lyon's premiere wine bistros. In this superb, cozy setting, you'll find perfect waiters with the traditional black aprons worn by wine growers, a marvelous choice of wines by the glass or in bottles and an intelligent cuisine that's served for quick meals at the counter or for more leisurely repasts at the tables. Everything has the signature of Jean-Paul Lacombe and Jean-Claude Caro, the associates of the Bistrot de Lyon next door. Dishes include beef carpaccio with olive oil and pepper, fried-beef tenderloin with a macaroni gratin, lotte with red-pepper cream and such exquisite desserts as the apricots stuffed with bitter oranges and cooked in Muscat from Beaumes-de-Venise or the chocolate tart with an orange and pistachio sauce. Forty wines are served by the

glass, from 16 francs (white Duboeuf Beaujolais) to 56 francs (1980 La Vaillières Côte-Rôtie).
A la carte: 180-250F.

(15) Christian Bourillot

8, pl. des Célestins - 78.37.38.64 / Y3-4
M. Bourillot. Open until 10 p.m. Closed Sun., holidays, July & Dec. 25-Jan. 2. Cards: V, AE, DC.

Bourillot is an institution, a restaurant that seems to forge ahead on its own against the winds and tides of fashion. The facade is discreet, like Christian Bourillot himself, a middle-of-the-road chef unshakeable in his consistency. But behind it all lies a man of great character, a hard worker who knows exactly what he wants. And what he wants is to create a great cuisine, classic but modern: highly perfumed foie gras, poultry in cream served with truffles and a ragoût of potatoes (his grandmother's recipe), excellent filet of beef with a light morel-and-butter sauce, smooth sorbets, superb tarte tatin and a not-too-exciting feuilleté of pears. That is what you will be served—a bit too casually, in fact—in this triumphantly bourgeois room with pistachio-colored ceiling moldings and mahogany paneling. The wine cellar covers a wide range of prices, and Anne-Marie Bourillot's reception is very relaxed.
A la carte: 350F. Menus: 190F, 290F, 360F.

12/20 Brasserie Georges

30, cours de Verdun
78.37.15.78 / B6-16
M. Rinck. Open until 11 p.m. Closed May 1. Terrace dining. Pets allowed. Telex 310778. Cards: V, AE, DC.

The new owner, Didier Rinck, wants to instill a youthful touch in one of the oldest (1836) and largest (650 square yards of ceiling suspended without pillars) brasseries in all of Europe. The good Rinck draught beer and honest choucroutes are served in a superb ambience. As for food, it's just the classics, but they're very well done. Another point is called for.
A la carte: 180F. Menus: 130F (weekends and holidays only), 55F and 85F (weekdays only), 80F.

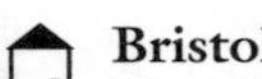

Bristol

28, cours de Verdun
78.37.56.55 / B6-16
Open year-round. 131 rms 165-360F. TV in 100 rms. Telex 330584. Cards: V, AE, DC, MC.

These regularly maintained rooms face the Perrache interchange. No restaurant.

12/20 Café du Jura

25, rue Turpin - 78.42.20.57 / Y2-64
M. Josserand. Open until 10:30 p.m. Closed Sat., Sun., 3 weeks in Aug. & 1 week at Christmas. Terrace dining. Pets allowed. Cards: V.

The owner's young wife recites most of the repertoire's "lyonnaiseries" the way an old local woman would: calves' liver, andouillette, tablier de sapeur (grilled tripe) and braised veal shank. But she does it gracefully, in her own style. The decor—that of an old Lyon pub—is dark, restful and altogether lovely.
A la carte: 160F.

(13) Café Gambs

4, rue du Pdt-Carnot
78.92.89.78 / Z2-59
MM. Birmant & Zelmati. Open until 10 p.m. Closed Mon. dinner, Sat. lunch & Sun. Terrace dining. Pets allowed. Cards: V, AE, DC, MC.

The white, black and gray decor designed by Jacques Aupetit, one of Lyon's renowned interior designers, has turned Gambs into a modern bistro that's now attracting the trendiest clientele in town. The service is as lively as you'll find anywhere, but Marc Chazelle's cuisine is quite the opposite—it's cautious, serious, meticulous and consistent: foie gras, raw-fish salad with lime, breast of duck with pink berry essence and glazed nougat with raspberry juice. There are some "dietetic" dishes for weight-watching gourmets, as well as a lovely Côteaux-du-Lyonnais for 45 francs.
A la carte: 200F. Menus: 65F (lunch only), 95F, 125F.

Carlton

Pl. de la République
78.42.56.51 / Z3-63
Open year-round. 87 rms 260-375F. TV. Air cond. in 35 rms. Garage parking. Telex 310787. Cards: V, AE, DC, MC.

All the rooms have been redone and soundproofed. Good equipment and gracious reception. No restaurant.

12/20 Chez Jean-François

2, pl. des Célestins - 78.42.08.26 / Y3-57
M. Courtois. Open until 10 p.m. Closed Sun., holidays, Easter & July 25-Aug. 25. Air cond. Pets allowed. Cards: V.

Despite the rather cold and unappealing decor, the elegant, famished clientele emerging from the Théâtre des Célestins wastes no time devouring the dishes included in the lovely budget fixed-price menu: small Lyonnaise salad, good navarin of lamb with a hearty serving of vegetables, and chocolate cake. The service, unfortunately, couldn't be slower.
A la carte: 180F. Menus: 72F, 120F.

11/20 Chez Mounier

3, rue des Marronniers
78.37.79.26 / Y4-70
M. Mounier. Open until 10:30 p.m. Closed Wed. dinner & Mon. Pets allowed. Cards: V.

This discreet tavern located behind the place Bellecour has a decidedly Lyon-style decor and atmosphere. The owner's wife is adorable; the cooking, without any surprises, is devoted to quenelles, tripe and hot saucisson. Côtes-du-Rhône and Beaujolais are served in jugs.
A la carte: 100F. Menus: 48F (weekdays only), 50F (weekends and holidays only), 71F, 85F.

(15) Daniel et Denise

2, rue Tupin - 78.37.49.98 / Y2-1
M. Léron. Open until 10 p.m. Closed Mon. lunch, Sun. & Aug. 1-15. Air cond. Pets allowed. Cards: V, AE, DC, MC.

Daniel Léron is reputed to be an inspired sauce chef and king of the kidney casserole and asparagus mousseline. Such a reputation is certainly warranted; he is a meticulous technician whose confidence and precision never disappoint. The strength of this virtue results in a rather serious attitude here—it's not the kind of atmosphere that attracts frivolity and people-watching. Rather it's one where you can have a nice meal with the family, including such dishes as superb sautéed langoustines with leeks and asparagus tips, a filet of lamb en croûte with a tarragon sauce and delicious desserts. The Beaujolais and Côtes-du-Rhône are of top quality.

A la carte: 350F. Menus: 155F, 250F.

12/20 Eriksen

28, rue Louis-Paufique
78.38.01.90 / Z4-68

M. Revol. Open until 11 p.m. Closed Sun., Mon., Jan. 1-10 & Aug. 1-17. Terrace dining. Pets allowed. Cards: V, AE, DC.

This is the local trendsetters' favorite Scandinavian place. In the beautiful modern dining room upstairs, done in yellow and blue tones, salmon is served in a variety of ways (all Scandinavian), along with smoked fish with tasty vegetable confit and a delicious homemade gingerbread.

A la carte: 200-250F. Menus: 72F and 92F (weekday lunch only), 186F (dinner only), 135F.

(15) Les Fantasques

53, rue de la Bourse
78.37.36.58 / Z2-41

M. Gervais. Hours, closings and credit card information not available.

The beauty of the seafood on display at the entrance to this comfortable, traditional restaurant that faces the Stock Exchange tips you off to the type of cuisine that awaits you. Claude Gervais is passionate about seafood—not capricious dishes (as suggested by the name of his establishment) but proven ones: bouillabaisse as good as that found at the best restaurants on the Côte d'Azur, lobster terrine, red mullet with fennel and grilled fish. It's all prepared simply and without pretension, as well as with great skill and unfailing consistency. Your meal will be accompanied by excellent white wine (particularly the Côtes-du-Rhône) and finished off with a delicious pear feuilleté (among other excellent desserts).

A la carte: 400F.

(13) Guy Garioud

14, rue Palais-Grillet
78.37.04.71 / Y3-65

M. Garioud. Open until 10 p.m. Closed Sat. lunch & Sun. Air cond. Terrace dining. Pets allowed. Cards: V, AE.

Guy Garioud will surprise you with its brand-new decor—the tables are set farther apart from one another, and the comfort is now more worthy of the lovely cuisine prepared by this former disciple of Paul Bocuse. At any rate, you'll be able to sample a tasty tureen of mussels en croûte, a ramekin of escargots with cèpes and almonds and the interesting house specialty: a precisely cooked filet bouillabaisse. The pastries are lovely. Congenial "fast cooking" is served in the bistro annex, Le P'tit Garioud.

A la carte: 250-300F. Menus: 182F (wine incl.), 98F, 154F, 218F.

Grand Hôtel Concorde

11, rue Grôlée - 78.42.56.21 / Z3-67

Open year-round. 3 stes 1,200-1,600F. 137 rms 450-650F. TV. Air cond. Pets allowed. Garage parking. Telex 330244. Cards: V, AE, DC, MC.

This huge, central hotel has spacious, remarkably soundproofed rooms, traditional reception and service and numerous conference rooms. Restaurant.

Grand Hôtel des Beaux-Arts

73, rue du Pdt-Herriot
78.38.09.50 / Y3-56

Open year-round. 79 rms 240-470F. TV. Air. cond. in 60 rms. Pets allowed. Telex 330442. Cards: V, AE, DC, MC.

Located in the center of town and recently renovated, the Grand Hôtel des Beaux-Arts features comfortable, modern rooms, almost all of which have air conditioning. No restaurant.

12/20 Institut Vatel

8, rue Duhamel (Ecole Hôtelière Privée)
78.38.21.92 / C6-3

M. Sebban. Open until 8:30 p.m. Closed Sat., Sun., Aug. & Dec. 20-Jan. 4. Air cond. Pets allowed. Cards: V, AE.

This restaurant belongs to a small, private cooking school. Its decor is pleasant, its atmosphere subdued, and its service performed by young, intelligent students under the direction of a somewhat hieratic teacher. The cooking is of superior quality, either classic (flambéed kidney) or bold (delicious risotto with coconut), depending on the chefs/teachers, and the wine cellar is lovely. Plans for a hotel are in progress.

Menus: 95F, 120F, 150F.

12/20 Kun Yang

12, rue Neuve - 78.39.98.12 / Y2-61

MM. Kan. Open daily until 10:30 p.m. Air cond. Pets allowed. Cards: V, AE, DC.

The Oriental-palace decor hasn't aged well, nor have some of the dishes listed on the long menu. But Kun Yang is to be recommended for its dim sum, its crisp nems and its specialties cooked on hot plates (an excellent filet of beef with soy sauce). The desserts, however, are distressing.

A la carte: 250-300F. Menus: 110F, 165F, 250F.

(13) Le Mercière

56, rue Mercière - 78.37.67.35 / Y3-38

M. Manoa. Open daily until 11:30 p.m. Terrace dining. Pets allowed. Cards: V, AE, DC.

Jean-Louis Manoa's cuisine makes us hungry even before it gets to our plates. Whether it's traditional Lyonnaise dishes, classic bistro specials or seasonal creations, its generosity and charm cannot be hidden. Neither the common nor the sophisticated Lyon residents ever tire of the hearty, lively meals served here: escargots with chervil and tomato purée, Scottish salmon pot-au-feu with hollandaise sauce, pickled pork with lentils, gratinée lyonnaise and calf's head. The service is entertaining and lively in a warm, simple bistro/bar setting.

A la carte: 230-260F. Menu: 90F.

12/20 La Mère Vittet

26, cours de Verdun
78.37.20.17 / B6-16

M. Vittet. Open daily 24 hours. Closed May 1. Air cond. Pets allowed. Telex 305559. Cards: V, AE, DC, MC.

Under the sharp eyes of Mme. Vittet, majestically seated behind her cash register, you'll discover a regional, Lyon-style cuisine. And whether traditional or modern, cheap or outrageously expensive, during the day or at night, you'll always dine with equal pleasure here. Our galette of sweetbreads with morels was tasty indeed, the seafood was extremely fresh, the choucroute decent (the sausages were delicious), and the filet of lamb cooked in its own juice with mild garlic simply perfect. We must tip our hats to the service, which is incredibly gracious and efficient, even when crowds overrun the immense establishment.

A la carte: 280-300F. Menus: 110F, 135F, 210F, 280F.

17 Nandron

26, quai Jean-Moulin
78.42.10.26 / Z2-18

M. Nandron. Open until 9:45 p.m. Closed Fri. dinner, Sat. & July 29-Aug. 28. Air cond. Pets allowed. Cards: V, AE, DC.

Just when cooking styles are going every which way, and sometimes haywire, Gérard Nandron has introduced his new menu ("Escoffier du Jour") as a return to classical traditions, long-simmered dishes and liberal servings. Is he pulling our leg? No. He says, of course, that he'll make the "necessary adjustments" to these old-style dishes, but he is serious about continuing the spirit of his tradition while offering some new items on his time-tested menu, along with keeping prices down. This is Nandron's big plan: Having decided that prices were getting too high, he is unveiling an entirely new menu. We did not have a chance to sample dishes from this new list before press time, but we expect that his policy will prove to be a good idea. And we salute Nandron's vision and courage, particularly after our last meal of his estimable classics: oxtail salad, mushroom terrine, baked eggs and truffles, duck terrine, and unimportant desserts, which left us thinking that some sort of change might be in order in this beloved establishment. The reception and the service in this venerable series of low-ceilinged, plush old rooms, in which all of Lyon meets to eat, should remain exactly as they always have been: perfect.

A la carte: 350F. Menus: 250F, 360F.

13 Le Nord

16-18, rue Neuve - 78.28.24.54 / Z2-62

M. Chassonnery. Open until 10:30 p.m. Closed Mon. dinner & Sat. Air cond. Terrace dining. Pets allowed. Cards: V.

As you are seated comfortably in this homey room, Geneviève Chassonnery watches over her staff with an eagle eye. The cuisine of her husband, Alain, son-in-law of Auguste Pralus, is of the classic genre with massive portions, but it is decidedly well prepared. The brasserie dishes in particular have brought him success: sole with noodles, baeckeoffe (meat stew), choucroute. The desserts are superb, and the wine cellar attractive.

A la carte: 250-280F. Menus: 80F and 100F (weekdays only), 148F, 185F.

12/20 Au Petit Col

68, rue de la Charité
78.37.25.18 / C6-40

M. Junet. Open until 10 p.m. Closed Sun. (except holidays) & Aug. 1-25. Air cond. Pets allowed. Cards: V, AE.

The new owners, who left their Terrasse in Thizy recently, have brightened up the pleasant bourgeois decor, given the tables more space and enhanced the lighting. The cooking is off to a good start as well, featuring many tasty terrines and several clever seasonal dishes: cod with crab sauce, sea perch with eggplant fondue. The desserts are simple, the wines excellent.

A la carte: 250-280F. Menus: 100F (weekdays only), 145F, 200F.

Royal

20, pl. Bellecour - 78.37.57.31 / Y4-66

Open year-round. 90 rms 300-700F. TV. Air cond. in 60 rms. Garage parking. Telex 310785. Cards: V, AE, DC, MC.

Facing the admirable place Bellecour, this traditional hotel features period rooms that have been well modernized and well equipped. The service is good, the bar quiet. Numerous meeting rooms. No restaurant.

14 Le Sarto

20, rue Palais-Grillet
78.37.49.64 / Y3-21

M. Battini. Open until 10:15 p.m. Closed Mon. lunch & Sun. Air cond. Pets allowed. Cards: V.

Le Sarto was recently taken over by a "youngster" who was in charge of the kitchens at the Ministry of Defense when the great Charles Harne ate there. The deputy mayor of Villeurbanne has spared no effort in helping the Battini family with its two-level restaurant. Find a seat on the main floor (the pizzeria decor upstairs isn't very interesting) to judge for yourself the worthiness of this result of civic pride. Ange Battini, assisted by his brother, offers exceptional fixed-price menus. The 85-franc menu, for example, brings you a delicious smoked salmon with light crêpes, young rabbit roasted with garlic, cheeses and a hot apple tart (served with dull ice cream). There are some imaginative à la carte dishes (ravioli with spinach and a pea gratin, delicious hot crêpes with hazelnuts). The pricey à la carte menu really calls for Battini to replace his worn silverware and provide a more pleasant reception.

A la carte: 300F. Menus: 95F, 145F, 200F.

11/20 Le Shalimar

39, quai Gailleton - 78.42.18.20 / C6-58

M. Tariq. Open daily until 11 p.m. Air cond. Pets allowed. Cards: V.

Turbaned waiters, a raja decor and a long procession of spicy Indian dishes—fritters, curries, tandooris—softened with almond, pistachio, cinnamon or mint milks.
A la carte: 160F. Menus: 100F.

Sofitel
See Les Trois Dômes restaurant.

(13) La Tassée
20, rue de la Charité
78.37.02.35 / Y5-12
Mme. Borgeot. Open until 10:30 p.m. Closed Sun. & Dec. 24-Jan. 2. Pets allowed. Cards: V, DC.
La Tassée is a wonder of a bistro, whichever way you look at it: the simple but warmly homey decor (large frescoes and imitation-leather banquettes), the sweet but spirited reception by the two Borgeot ladies, the modest and great wines of Papa Roger (who was the best sommelier in France a quarter of a century ago) and, finally, the clever Lyon-style cuisine of son Jean-Paul, who really knows his business: delicious calf's feet rémoulade, superb hot pork, salmon with fresh noodles, sirloin grilled with tarragon.
A la carte: 250F. Menu: 90F, 130F, 160F, 185F.

Terminus Lyon-Perrache
12, cours de Verdun
78.37.58.11 / B6-60
Open year-round. 2 stes 1,000-1,200F. 133 rms 340-530F. TV. Air cond. Pets allowed. Garage parking. Telex 330500. Cards: V, AE, MC.
This pleasantly modernized late-nineteenth-century hotel has retained its superb wood paneling and old-fashioned charm. The rooms are spacious and comfortable, but they can be rather noisy. An airport shuttle leaves every twenty minutes.

Tourinter
23, cours Charlemagne
78.92.81.61 / B7-39
Open year-round. 119 rms 260-360F. TV. Parking. Telex 380401. Cards: V, AE, DC, MC.
This double hotel (Charlemagne and Résidence) has beautiful rooms with either contemporary or period furnishings. The Perrache train station is 200 meters away. Restaurant.

(14) Les Trois Dômes
20, quai Gailleton - 78.42.72.50 / Y5-72
M. Seiss. Open daily until 10 p.m. Air cond. No pets. Parking. Telex 330225. Cards: V, AE, DC, MC.
The famous three domes rise above the rooftops before your eyes from the dining room of this eighth-floor restaurant (which was just recently refurbished). The view from here—a marvelous panorama of the entire eastern part of the city and of the Rhône—is better than from any other restaurant in Lyon. And, to make things even better, it is a restaurant whose cuisine has been a model of consistency for some ten years. The brilliant technique of chef Guy Girerd has developed a certain originality, which has resulted in some fine dishes: a magnificent grilled salmon, a fish combination with endives, a flan of coquilles St-Jacques in a saffron sauce with mussels and a marinated saddle of young rabbit served with corn. The desserts, prepared by Maxime Durand, are enchanting. In the Sofishop on the main floor, a simpler cuisine is graciously served until the middle of the night.
A la carte: 300-350F. Menus: 168F, 215F, 288F.

Sofitel
(See restaurant above)
Open year-round. 6 stes 1,800-2,500F. 194 rms 785-1,105F. TV. Air cond. Pets allowed.
These remarkable modern rooms are furnished with taste; most overlook the Rhône and the city. Extras include a piano bar, nineteen conference rooms and a gallery of shops.

(16) Vettard
7, pl. Bellecour - 78.42.07.59 / Y4-15
M. Vettard. Open until 7:45 p.m. Closed Sat. dinner (in July), Sun. & end July-Aug. Air cond. Pets allowed. Telex 330949. Cards: V, AE, DC.
Behind its wine-colored double facade and looking out at the majestic splendors of the place Bellecour, Vettard maintains its reputation as a monumental institution in Lyon, a temple to quenelles, to calves' liver and to poularde en vessie (fatted chicken in a pig's bladder), as if nothing had changed since Edouard Herriot, since the epic of the Beaujolais (its legend was born here), since the glorious reign of the original Vettard, Marius. But even though the quenelles remain a sure thing, what is impressive is that Jean, the son, has for fifteen years known how to marvelously adapt and brighten up the enterprise passed on to him by his father. At our last visit he was beginning a renovation of the decor (let's hope the sculpted ceilings and lacquered paneling will be preserved) that included accents of lively colors, elegant dishes and superbly set tables, around which Lucien, one of the best maîtres d'hôtel in Lyon, circulates busily. And not content to just give a new touch to traditional cuisine, Jean has totally revamped the cooking to create an intelligently modern repertoire, combining simplified local traditions with a continuum of new ideas: lotte fondue with a parsleyed lobster sauce, pasta shells with foie gras and spinach, small plates of hot seafood, poultry with mixed vegetables and exquisite and delicate desserts. Nothing is given away—even if you are content with a pitcher of the delicious Saint-Joseph (the Burgundies are fabulous and not all high priced)—but it's all so incredible!
A la carte: 500F. Menus: 230F, 300F.

12/20 Les Visiteurs du Soir
34, rue des Remparts-d'Ainay
78.37.22.23 / Y5-20
M. Bobenrieth. Open until 10 p.m. Closed Sat. lunch, Sun., Feb. school vacation & Aug. 7-22. No pets. Cards: V, AE, DC.
Bare stone walls, old wooden beams and muted lighting lend an air of a '60s nightclub/pizzeria to Les Visiteurs du Soir. There's an excellent 80-franc fixed-price menu that includes a terrine of young rabbit with tarragon (a bit bland), beautiful fowl in vinegar sauce with avocado con-

fit, and a fragrant vanilla ice cream. The service, unfortunately, is rather spiritless and slow.

A la carte: 250F. Menus: 85F (weekdays only), 110F, 150F, 190F.

12/20 Le Vivarais

1, pl. Gailleton - 78.37.85.15 / Y5-11

M. Duffaud. Open until 10:30 p.m. Closed Sun., holidays, July 10-30 & Dec. 24-31. Air cond. Pets allowed. Cards: V, AE, DC, MC.

The new owner/chef is a distinguished professional (he worked at Chapel and at Bourrillot) who prepares a tasty, simple Lyon-style family cuisine: calf's head with two sauces (vinaigrette and gribiche, a tangy mayonnaise), marvelous rabbit in aspic and an orange-and-rice cake. Fine Beaujolais is served in pitchers. Reasonable prices.

A la carte: 180-200F. Menus: 85F, 110F.

(13) La Voûte

Chez Léa

11, pl. Antonin-Gourju - 78.42.01.33 / X3-55

M. Rabatel. Open until 9:30 p.m. Closed Sun. & July 9-31. Air cond. Pets allowed. Cards: V, AE, DC.

Léa, the last great "mother" in Lyon to retire her apron, has not been betrayed. The spirit of her tasty, creamy cuisine has been scrupulously applied to each of the dishes prepared by her successor, Philippe Rabatel: the hot poached sausage, the quenelles, the chicken in vinegar and the tripe (among other age-old Lyon specialties), all of which have also maintained the charm of their gentle prices. The decor is innocuous, and Mme. Rabatel's greeting, which is assisted by Léa's niece, is charming.

A la carte: 160-180F. Menus: 90F, 110F, 140F.

Third Arrondissement

This is the new Lyon, the business quarter in the center of the city, with the Part-Dieu train station and the commercial center.

(14) L'Alexandrin

83, rue Moncey - 72.61.15.69 / E4-32

MM. Alexanian. Open until 9:15 p.m. Closed Sun. dinner, Mon. & Aug. Air cond. No pets. Cards: V.

Véronique Alexanian gracefully ushers her guests to tables set with pink tablecloths facing the glassed-in kitchen, from which the chef can keep an eye on the dining room while keeping the clattering of the dishes, pots and pans behind closed doors. The menu is reassuringly short, and after ordering the first fixed-priced menu we were duly enchanted: savory creamed zucchini with gingered potato croquettes, white poultry meat with a parsley flan. Alain Alexanian is also adept at preparing deliciously rare tournedos. Even from the small fixed-price menu, you can choose from the entire dessert list: a pistachio crêpe with orange slices, a pineapple-chocolate dish with a rum crème anglaise, and three or four others that are equally good. This young chef, both subtle and daring, has all the assets needed for success: a most unique personality and a solid base of training from Condrieu's Mme. Castaing. This isn't the first time this great lady has turned out something good.

A la carte: 250F. Menus: 95F, 135F.

(14) L'Arc-en-Ciel

129, rue Servient - 78.62.94.12 / F4-13

M. Fleury. Open until 10 p.m. Closed Mon. lunch, Sun. & July 14-Aug. 16. Parking. Telex 380088. Cards: V, AE, DC, MC.

Of the two meals we had not long ago in this restaurant on the 32nd floor of the Crédit Lyonnais tower, the first didn't deserve so much as a single tiny toque, but the second was worth at least two. The uncertainty in the air and the sense of a change of cooking style are regrettable reflections on this cuisine. But in the long run, it seems that François Galabert, the successor to Jean Fleury (now chef at Bocuse), is pulling himself together. In any case, it looks like he has totally "digested" this difficult succession. Let's forget, then, the confusing plate of artichokes and marinated salmon and the overcooked filet of bass with lime, and just remember the remarkable rabbit-and-wild-mushroom salad, the sweetbreads and veal kidneys served in aspic as a pot-au-feu (exquisitely fresh), the half-cooked salmon cutlet and the dark-chocolate charlotte with mango sauce. But the newfound reassurance of these dishes will have to spill over into the stiff reception and awkward service before the people of Lyon become attached once again to this restaurant, which now has a new, warmer decor (tones of pink and gray) and still has, as always, a splendid view of Lyon and its peninsula.

A la carte: 350F. Menus: 205F (lunch only), 175F, 225F.

Pullman Part-Dieu

(See restaurant above)

Open year-round. 2 stes. 243 rms 420-680F. TV. Air cond. Pets allowed.

Europe's tallest hotel, the Pullman Part-Dieu has some magnificent rooms with fantastic views of Lyon and its environs. The decor is lovely and the furniture functional.

12/20 Carron

65, blvd. Vivier-Merle
78.60.28.61 / F5-6

M. Léron. Open until 10:30 p.m. Closed Sat. lunch, Sun. & Aug. Air cond. Cards: V, AE, DC.

Daniel Léron can now seat 200 people in his newly expanded dining room located next to the Bistro de la Gare. This large brasserie close to the TGV train station is an outstanding restaurant, serving a consistent, unpretentious cuisine at inexpensive prices: various pork cold cuts, butcher's-cut beef with Roquefort cheese and a selection of grilled meats.

A la carte: 150-180F.

12/20 Chez Pino

21, rue de la Rize - 78.60.09.37 / F5-2

M. Criado. Open until 10 p.m. Closed Mon. dinner, Sun. & 1 week in Aug. Air cond. Pets allowed. Cards: V, AE, DC, MC.

Sylvana Criado, the owner's elegant wife, reigns over a crew of cooks that prepares excellent, classic, light dishes typical of the Lyon peninsula:

fritto misto, tagliatelle with scallops, rabbit stew with polenta. The luxurious brasserie decor is pleasant, and the prices reasonable.
A la carte: 180-230F.

13 Chez Rose
4, rue Rabelais - 78.60.57.25 / D4-77
M. Astic. Open until 9:15 p.m. Closed Sat. lunch, Sun., July 29-Aug. 22 & Dec. 23-Jan. 2. Air cond. No pets. Cards: V, MC.

Nothing that pertains to traditional Lyonnaise cuisine is foreign to Gérard Astic, the owner of this adorable family bistro in which Raymond Barre likes to feed his modest politician's paunch: tablier de sapeur (Lyonnaise grilled tripe), salads, gratins, hot sausage and the famous "soupe à la jambe de bois" ("wooden-legged soup").
A la carte: 250F. Menu: 90F.

16 Le Gourmandin
156, rue Paul-Bert - 78.62.78.77 / F5-79
M. Abattu. Open until 9:15 p.m. Closed Sat., Sun., holidays & Aug. 10-20. Air cond. Pets allowed. Cards: V, AE, DC.

The main road cuts right through the city, then heads for the melancholy of the suburbs. But along the way, if you take refuge behind the Gourmandin's wine-colored facade, you can easily escape these suburbia blues. The dining room is the ultimate in comfort, with its modern yet rustic decor and its lovely paintings. And Daniel Abattu, former maître d'hôtel for Paul Bocuse, is a perfect host. Every six weeks the chef, Jean-Paul Lechevalier (also formerly with Bocuse), proposes a new menu, in which fresh products are put to better use by this remarkable technician: terrine of wild boar with spice bread, creamed mushrooms with frogs' legs and a liver gâteau, wild duck with peaches, Bresse poultry with crayfish, and white-chocolate parfait. The selection of Côtes-du-Rhône is exceptional.
A la carte: 300F and up. Menus: 180F, 260F.

12/20 A Ma Vigne
23, rue Jean-Larrivé
78.60.46.31 / D5-78
Mme. Giraud. Open until 9 p.m. Closed Sun. & Aug. Cards: V.

The crowd is especially large at lunchtime in this old harbor eatery, popular for its marvelous frites (french fries), as well as for its mussels, tripe, roast ham and orange tart. Lucien, the owner, always has good luck with his choice of Côtes-du-Rhône.
A la carte: 130-150F.

Mercure
47, blvd. Vivier-Merle
72.34.18.12 / F4-82
Open year-round. 122 rms 395-450F. Half-board 210-250F (groups only). TV. Air cond. Garage parking. Telex 306469. Cards: V, AE, DC, MC.

Only a few steps from the TGV train station, this hotel encloses inviting, soundproofed rooms. Restaurant.

13 J.-C. Péquet
59, pl. Voltaire - 78.95.49.70 / E5-80
M. Péquet. Open until 9:30 p.m. Closed Sat., Sun., July 14-31 & Dec. 23-Jan. 2. Air cond. Pets allowed. Cards: V, AE, DC, MC.

Behind the contemporary facade of a financial institution hides a comfortable restaurant, replete with tapestry-covered chairs, carpeting and tablecloths in orange and bordeaux, as well as flowers on every table. The service is alert, and the cuisine is diligent and reliable: a salad of warm lamb's sweetbreads, fresh duck liver, veal kidneys and a hot-and-cold chocolate dessert. This is the kind of consistent restaurant you can recommend with your eyes closed, even more enthusiastically because of the reasonable prices.
A la carte: 250F. Menus: 100F, 140F, 180F.

Pullman Part-Dieu
See L'Arc-en-Ciel restaurant.

11/20 Le Val d'Isère
64, rue de Bonnel - 78.71.09.39 / E4-81
M. Dandel. Lunch only. Closed Sun. & July 1-Aug. 7. Pets allowed. Cards: V, AE, MC.

Spacious, modern and well lit, Val d'Isère is located (despite its name) just across from the Lyon markets. Bobosse, the king of andouillette, has made it his favorite cantina, as have many other chefs, who come for the pigs' feet, tripe and so on.
A la carte: 120F.

12/20 Woehrlé
156, rue de Créqui - 78.60.66.53 / E4-74
M. Woehrlé. Lunch only (dinner Tues. & Fri., with reserv., until 8 p.m.). Closed Sat. lunch (in June), Sun. & Aug. Pets allowed.

As his name indicates, M. Woehrlé is Alsatian, so he's particularly fond of his beautiful Sauerkrauts, accompanied since 1929 by pork cuts prepared in the shop adjacent to his friendly old establishment.
A la carte: 150F.

Fourth Arrondissement

The Croix-Rousse, with its old quarters and its covered passageways, is a working-class, but not overcrowded, neighborhood.

Hôtel de Lyon Métropole
85, quai Joseph-Gillet
78.29.20.20 / A2-73
Open year-round. 120 rms 380-470F. TV. Air cond. Pets allowed. Pool. Tennis. Garage parking. Telex 380198. Cards: V, AE, DC, MC.

These large rooms are furnished in modern good taste. The view to one side is of the Saône, and to the other, the Olympic-size swimming pool and surrounding greenery. Restaurant.

Fifth Arrondissement

Old Lyon, Saint-Paul, Saint-Jean and Saint-Georges are the most beautiful examples of Renaissance architecture in Europe.

12/20 Comptoir du Boeuf

2, pl. Neuve-St-Jean - 78.92.82.35 / X3-9
M. Chavent. Open until midnight. Closed Sun. Terrace dining. Pets allowed. Cards: V.

About 30 good vintages from various regions are offered by the glass. This is just one surprise in this congenial annex of La Tour Rose, where the tables overflow onto the sidewalk. M. Chavent's cuisine includes pickled pork with lentils, pot-au-feu, veal shank and other delicious daily specials.

A la carte: 170F.

Cour des Loges

6, rue du Boeuf - 78.42.75.75 / X2-84
Open year-round. 10 stes 1,700-2,700F. 53 rms 950-1,300F. TV. Air cond. Pets allowed. Heated pool. Parking. Telex 330831. Cards: V, AE, DC, MC.

This fabulous new hotel, unequaled in Europe, is located at the heart of the renovated Renaissance quarter. The architects have created a masterpiece in daring good taste, integrating steel, glass (in Italian-style galleries) and the most modern materials and forms into this historic setting. The luxurious rooms are surrounded by terraced gardens. Sumptuous breakfast, a tapas bar and a small restaurant.

Phénix

7, quai Bondy - 78.28.30.40 / X1-52
Open year-round. 36 rms 125-275F. TV in 18 rms. Cards: V, AE, DC.

At the center of old Lyon, on the banks of the Saône, stands this favorite stopover for artists and actors passing through town. No restaurant.

12/20 Le Prestige Thaïlandais

1, rue Bellièvre - 78.42.05.75 / X3-25
Mme. Véron & M. Xunebane. Open until midnight. Closed Tues. dinner, Aug. 2-24 & Dec. 20-Jan. 4. Terrace dining. Pets allowed. Cards: V, AE.

This is one of the best exotic eating places in Lyon—not because of its decor (modern, without lacquer or dragons) but because of its cuisine, which is fresh and exciting (that is to say, amateurs will find it very spicy): subtly seasoned Thai soup, breast of duck with coconut milk, basil-seasoned chicken. The fish dishes aren't as successful. Frédérique Véron, the blond French co-owner, is a charming hostess.

A la carte: 180-200F. Menu: 119F.

12/20 Les Saisons

8, quai de Bondy - 78.28.47.55 / X1-85
Mme. Hardy. Open until 10 p.m. Closed Sun., Mon., July 14- Aug. 15 & Dec. 24-Jan. 2. Air cond. Pets allowed.

Yvette Hardy may be from the West Indies, but it takes some coaxing to get her to prepare her native dishes. She devotes herself, instead, to the traditional cuisine of Lyon: calf's foot salad, quenelles, andouillette, calves' liver and so on. The wines include a Duboeuf Beaujolais.

A la carte: 180F. Menus: 48F(lunch only), 58F, 78F, 125F.

La Tour Rose

18

16, rue du Boeuf
78.37.25.90 / X2-26
M. Chavent. Open until 10:30 p.m. Closed Sun. & Aug. 6-20. Air cond. Pets allowed. Cards: V, AE, DC.

It hasn't always been rosy at La Tour Rose. Several times, Philippe Chavent almost threw up his arms and bailed out of glorious but shabby Old Lyon, where he was bold enough to open a luxury restaurant. But he held on, and today he's about to hit the jackpot. The sumptuous, Florentine-style Renaissance quarter has been cleansed of its grime; it's fast becoming a tourist mecca and is no longer snubbed by the locals, who used to be leery of venturing onto its streets. In the meantime, Chavent has gained faith, and never has his cuisine, which at times had lapsed into mannerism, been as inspired or successful as it is today. His fried red mullet with sea urchins, ragoût of frogs' legs and crayfish with star anise, potato salad with caviar cream, roast loin of lamb with artichokes, foie gras and basil, marvelous oeufs à la neige with toasted almonds, and strawberry gratin with almonds are making Lyon roar with pleasure.

For Chavent, an unexpected stroke of good luck was the opening, just a few steps away, of La Cour des Loges, a fabulous hotel equipped with amazing talent. La Tour Rose is now virtually the dining room annex of La Cour des Loges, and by the time you read these lines, the restaurant may have moved a little farther down the street into a large Renaissance structure. The new location will have more light and be larger and better adapted for cooking than the superb but dark current setting, which will in turn be converted into reception rooms at the disposal of La Cour des Loges.

In the meantime, enjoy lunch or dinner in this handsome place, without forgetting to take a glance at the courtyard of the elegant pink tower ("tour rose") that adjoins the main body of the building. While you are passing by, take pity on the poor cooks who slave away in the cavernous kitchen on the ground floor... And if you find that terribly depressing, leave yourself in the hands of the capable sommelier, who has in reserve some of the very best Côte-Rôtie and Châteauneuf-du-Pape you could ever dream of.

A la carte: 600F. Menus: 285F, 395F, 480F.

11/20 Le 21

21, quai Romain-Rolland - 78.37.34.19, 78.37.30.35 / X2-83
M. Caro. Open until 2 a.m. Closed Sun. Air cond. Terrace dining. Pets allowed. Cards: V, MC.

This young and friendly bistro, located on a noisy upper floor decorated in 1930s style, offers an innocuous but generous cuisine: terrines, salads, breast of duck.

A la carte: 180-200F.

Sixth Arrondissement

The chic quarter, with the Brotteaux and the park, is near the Part-Dieu and is home to both businesses and residences.

(14) Cazenove

75, rue Boileau - 78.89.82.92 / E2-17

M. Orsi. Open until 10 p.m. Closed Sat., Sun. & July 30-Aug. 29. Air cond. Pets allowed. Telex 305965. Cards: V, AE.

Business people lingering over lunch amid the lovely Belle Epoque decor of Pierre Orsi's annex give way to an elegant clientele at night, often just emerging from the theater. Whatever time of day, the young waitresses in their long Laura Ashley dresses and the magnificent variety of specials offered by young chef Emile Bouet—Lyon-style tripe, Cazenove salad with foie gras and shellfish, sander filet with marrow and mushrooms, saddle of young rabbit with mustard, and chocolate fondant with coffee sauce—do wonders for this happiest, most popular of the luxury Lyon bistros. Lovely wines from all regions are listed, including some fine young Bordeaux and an excellent Beaujolais-Village served in a pitcher.

A la carte: 280-300F. Menus: 180F (lunch only), 260F (dinner only).

11/20 Le Fulton

25, rue Bossuet - 78.52.60.93 / E3-23

M. Bargues. Open until 11 p.m. Closed Sat. lunch, Sun. & July 29-Aug. 29. Air cond. Pets allowed. Telex 300295. Cards: V, AE, DC, MC.

The modern gray-and-black decor is rather chilly. There's a dietetic fixed-price menu (500 calories), which politician Raymond Barre (who comes here from the nearby Roosevelt hotel) wisely refuses, ordering instead the andouillette and the brains favored by the Canuts (Lyon's silk weavers).

A la carte: 200F. Menus: 70F and 80F (lunch only), 180F, 250F.

(13) Gervais

42, rue Pierre-Corneille
78.52.19.13 / D3-91

Open until 9:45 p.m. Closed Sun., holidays & July. Air cond. Pets allowed. Cards: V, AE, DC.

This small restaurant is consistency itself, with its gracious owner; its young, smiling, efficient waitresses; its faithful and contented clientele; and its chef, who knows intuitively how to please them all. Don't expect many novelties, but you can be sure you'll never be disappointed with the sweetbreads salad, escalopes of hot duck liver, veal kidney with white port and poultry fricassée with sherry. The wine cellar is complete but expensive.

A la carte: 300F. Menu: 150F.

(13) Christian Grisard

158, rue Cuvier - 78.24.77.98 / F3-88

M. Grisard. Open until 10:30 p.m. Closed Sun., Mon. & Aug. Pets allowed. Cards: V, DC.

Christian Grisard's repertoire won't make much of a contribution to modern, personal cuisine, and his dining room decor is not wildly cheerful, even for Lyon. But this very serious cook, who trained at Bernachon and La Tour Rose, knows his business remarkably well, and his graciousness and generosity are exemplary. You'll be able to taste an excellent winegrowers' Beaujolais (Domaine La Madone) while dining on a salad of sweetbreads with truffle juice, cervelat of coquilles St-Jacques with beurre blanc and poultry fricassée with sweet red pepper.

A la carte: 250F. Menus: 98F, 130F, 160F, 220F.

(16) Pierre Orsi

3, pl. Kléber - 78.89.57.68 / E2-93

M. Orsi. Open until 9:30 p.m. Closed Sun. Air cond. Pets allowed. Telex 305965. Cards: V, AE.

A former student of Bocuse, Pierre Orsi had the most enticing and imaginative menu in Lyon at the beginning of the '80s (along with that of Léon de Lyon). Today, it is a model of seriousness, barely accented here and there with some emotion; it has been turned completely toward the rigors of an academic execution. And so it is with the salade gourmande, where the lobster, the foie gras and the artichokes celebrate (rather melancholically) their twenty years of marriage; and with the fried tournedos with green peppers, the squab with garlic cloves and the many other dishes engraved on the menu for nearly ten years. These include the delicious steamed John Dory with a fresh bitter tomato sauce, the salad with Lyon sausage or the Williams pear drizzled with hot chocolate. All of these are usually excellent (marvelous lobster soup with anise and other herbs), extremely light and admirably presented (superb crayfish with coconut, topped with caviar), along with being perfectly enchanting to that sizable percentage of eaters with traditional tastes. And it is these same guests who are equally enamored of the luxury and preciousness of this restaurant, with its crystal chandeliers, mirrors, antique paintings, pink decor and, finally, young waitresses in long dresses who serve with great kindness. The wine list is still a little weak in Côtes-du-Rhône from the north.

A la carte: 400F and up. Menus: 180F, 300F.

(13) Le Quatre Saisons

15, rue Sully - 78.93.76.07 / D2-87

M. Bertoli. Open until 9:30 p.m. Closed Sat. lunch, Sun. & Aug. 1-16. Air cond. Pets allowed. Cards: V, AE, DC.

This is the archetype of a good restaurant—comfortable, discreet, pleasant looking and consistent—made from a mold created to satisfy the demanding clientele of this residential neighborhood, one that doesn't care for unpleasant surprises and dreads anything drastically new. Lucien Bertoli is a concerned owner who rules his place with unyielding discipline. He watches over the quality of the service, which is a bit emphatic but quite well done. But he is even more preoccupied with the cuisine, which he does not prepare but for which he takes responsibility (going so far as to wear a chef's uniform): hot escalope de foie gras, whole kidneys cooked in their own fat, beef ribs, seasonal game. The cheeses from chez Richard are sublime, but the desserts are singularly lacking in imagination. Excellent wine cellar.

A la carte: 350F. Menus: 170F, 290F.

(13) Le Restaurant des Gourmets

14, rue de Godefroy
78.89.37.13 / D2-19

M. Ricci. Open until 10 p.m. Closed Sat. lunch, Sun. & Aug. 1-16. Pets allowed. Cards: V, AE, DC.

After having played maître d'hôtel for twenty years at L'Abbaye de Collonges, Luigi Ricci has taken over the ovens at his own charming bistro where, in his 51st year, he has the enthusiasm of a young man. Combining his Italian spirit (he was born in Siena) and a wonderful style, his cuisine is generous, uncomplicated and always fresh: red mullet salad with herbs, marinated salmon, breast of duck with green pepper. The Côtes-du-Rhône are perfect, and Mme. Ricci is a smiling hostess.

A la carte: 350F. Menus: 170F, 290F.

12/20 La Romanière

129, rue de Sèze - 78.24.23.42 / F2-94

M. Rossignol. Open until 10 p.m. Closed Wed. dinner, Sun., Feb. school vacation & 2 weeks in Aug. Pets allowed. Cards: V, AE, DC.

The owner is always smiling, the decor is a success, and the young clientele appreciates the copious food and reasonable prices. Try the warm langouste salad with sweet-and-sour sauce, the filet of sea perch with cream of fennel and the liver and sweetbreads with green cabbage and bacon. Small but handsome wine cellar.

A la carte: 200-220F. Menus: 68F (weekdays only) and 90F to 165F.

Le Roosevelt

25, rue Boussuet - 78.52.35.67 / E3-23

Open year-round. 3 stes 408-446F. 87 rms 283-356F. TV. Air cond. Garage parking. Telex 300295. Cards: V, AE, DC, MC.

Ultra-modern and well maintained, this hotel is excellent for business travelers (the rooms even have telex hookups). Room service is efficient, and there are good facilities for conferences.

(14) La Soupière

14, rue Molière - 78.52.75.34 / D3-89

M. Peyrard. Open until 10 p.m. Closed Sun., Mon., Aug. & Dec. 24-Jan. 3. Air cond. Pets allowed. Cards: V.

Some days everything seems blessed: the lamps, the chairs, the pralines in the île flottante (floating island on a sea of custard), even the patronne's dress—they're all rose colored. So is life here, for that matter: Christian Peyrard, an able chef who trained at Lamazère and La Marée, prepares a discreetly seductive cuisine, including mussel soup with saffron, grilled sea perch with a touch of anise and fennel purée, filets of red mullet with truffles and warm foie gras and noisettes of lamb with basil. The reception and service are spirited and charming. We'd like to see more good small wines in the cellar, however.

A la carte: 250-300F. Menus: 130F, 180F, 300F.

Seventh Arrondissement

This new quarter in the new section of Lyon is still undergoing development. In it are Gerland stadium and the Ecole Normal Supérieur (teachers' training school), as well as research and industry.

(16) Le Fédora

249, rue Marcel-Mérieux
78.69.46.26 / D7-97

M. Judéaux. Open until 10 p.m. Closed Sat. lunch, Sun. & Dec. 24-Jan. 3. Air cond. Garden dining. Pets allowed. Cards: V, AE, DC.

In nice weather, the vivacious Catherine Judéaux opens up the large, flowering patio that hides this ordinary-looking restaurant from the confluence of the Rhône and the Saône and from the Gerland stadium. Beneath the canopy that filters in a peaceful light, you are suddenly far removed from the grayness of Lyon—somewhere at the edge of the invigorating ocean, for which Daniel Judéaux has developed a great passion, as if to exorcize the powerful memory of the slaughterhouses that were once fixtures in this quarter. For a reasonable price (the price range is prudently broad), you may dine on excellent products and a skillful cuisine. Our good memories come from the prawn salad with a slightly acid tomato aspic, the flavorful squid ragoût, the ray with oranges and the exquisite desserts. The choice of Côtes-du-Rhône, particularly the whites, is perfect.

A la carte: 350F. Menus: 130F (weekdays only), 210F, 460F.

12/20 La Grille

106, rue Sébastien-Gryphe
78.72.46.58 / D6-14

M. Gillet. Open until 10 p.m. Closed Sat. lunch, Sun. & Aug. Air cond. Pets allowed. Cards: V.

The successor to Marinette, the legendary former owner of La Grille, is full of good intentions, but it's no longer quite the same in this glum Lyon-style decor: The terrines are rather poor, though the scorpionfish filet is quite decent (if a bit salty), and there's always the good sabodet (a beef and pork sausage) from Bobosse. Wines are served in pitchers.

A la carte: 200F. Menus: 110F, 198F.

Mercure Pont-Pasteur

70, ave. Leclerc - 78.58.68.53 / C7-96

Open year-round. 194 rms 380-500F. TV. Air cond. Pets allowed. Heated pool. Garage parking. Telex 305484. Cards: V, AE, DC, MC.

A modern hotel (built in 1984), with perfectly comfortable rooms and fine conference facilities. Restaurant.

Eighth Arrondissement

Facing the Alps, East Lyon is a working-class section of the city.

Altea Park Hôtel

4, rue du Pr-Calmette
78.74.11.20 / G7-7

Open year-round. 72 rms 285-350F. TV. Pets allowed. Garage parking. Telex 380230. Cards: V, AE, DC.

This vast, traditional hotel has some renovated rooms. The patio restaurant is open in summer, and the lounges are pleasant.

12/20 Auberge Savoyarde

72, ave. des Frères-Lumière
78.00.77.64 / G7-28

M. Blache. Open until 9:15 p.m. Closed Sun. Air cond. No pets. Cards: V, AE, DC.

This seriously traditional restaurant is as well equipped for large family or society meals as it is for light fondue or Raclette suppers. The cuisine is classic and well prepared (calves' liver, coq au vin), and the wine cellar has nice Burgundies and Côtes-du-Rhône. The owner is charming and devoted.

A la carte: 200F. Menus: 70F (dinner only), 100F.

Laennec

36, rue Seignemartin
78.74.55.22 / G7-7

Open year-round. 14 rms 205-310F. TV. Garage parking. Telex 310111. Cards: V.

The neighborhood around this small, reasonably priced modern hotel is quite peaceful, particularly at night. No restaurant.

IN NEARBY **Champagne-au-Mont-d'Or**
(9 km N on N 6)
69410 Champagne-au-Mond-d'Or - (Rhône)

Les Grillons

18, rue Dominique-Vincent
78.35.04.78

M. Duthion. Open until 9:30 p.m. Closed Sun. dinner, Mon., Feb. school vacation, Easter & 3 weeks in Aug.-Sept. Garden dining. Cards: V, AE, DC, MC.

In an attractive turn-of-the-century building with a garden for sunny days, this restaurant is delicately decorated in tones of blue and cream and has fancy table settings with prices to match. Fernand Duthion, it's true, doesn't play around with his ingredients, and he is certainly a generous chef. Nevertheless, 120 francs for a slice of foie gras and 135 francs for fried turbot with raspberry vinegar is rather steep for a cuisine that is quite thoughtful but not exactly in Bocuse's league. The small fixed-price menu and the wine cellar are both high points.

A la carte: 300-350F. Menu: 125F, 178F, 225F, 325F.

> *The prices given in this guide reflect what restaurants and hotels were charging at press time.*

IN NEARBY **Collonges-au-Mont-d'Or**
(9 km N on N 51)
69660 Collonges-au-Mont-d'Or - (Rhône)

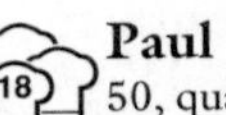

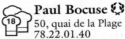

Paul Bocuse

50, quai de la Plage
78.22.01.40

M. Bocuse. Open daily until 9:45 p.m. Air cond. Pets allowed. Telex 375382. Cards: V, AE, DC.

Here, finally, is a job worthy of the mighty Paul: to win back his four-toque rating from a guide that he is less and less fond of. Understand us correctly—the loss of a toque does not signify any real slippage on his part but simply the tremendous advances made by the next generation of Bocuses: Michel Bras, Pierre Gagnaire, Didier Clément, Marc Veyrat and Michel Trama, who fight like schoolboys to be better and still better, and who succeed. How then to avoid diminishing, in relative terms, their acheivements while continuing steadfastly to grant the same top marks to someone slightly behind them? Of course, it is a difficult decision to make when the someone is of enormous international stature and past accomplishment, a single mighty tree for whom one cannot see the forest of talent beyond—and especially when it is Paul Bocuse, for whom we have undiminished feelings of admiration and camaraderie.

Bocuse chose, quite deliberately, his own destiny; he dreamed of being the most famous chef in the world, which he clearly remains. He aimed at being the ambassador of French cooking to the rest of the world, and no one now would dispute that title. Add to that his polished media skills and his golden business touch, and you have the measure of the man: incontestably the strongest in the field. Meanwhile, he has been vunerable to the dangers of too much time out of the kitchen that await the superstar chef, so he has therefore assembled a solid, superbly professional, well-oiled machinery in his restaurant. Roger Jaloux, Jean Fleury and Christian Bouvarel are the high priests of Bocusianity and all that it means.

With those men at the controls, there is danger of neither derailment nor gradual decline. But if the restaurant here at Collonges, in all its bright new tropical plumage, is thus assured of consistent success, it has also insured itself against any bolts of inspiration that might strike it. There is no place amid this solid, repetitive competence for the risks of creativity and renewal, not to mention a grain of folly, that distinguish the truly great cuisines from the rest. To be precise, the world-famous truffle soup; the filet of sole Fernand Point with fresh noodles; the artichoke and foie gras salad; the plate of salmon, lobster, lotte and sea bass; the bass en croûte; the pigeon in puff pastry; the veal kidneys Dijon style and the fatted Bresse fowl in a bladder (beautifully carved) all make for a very tasty meal, to be sure. And that's to say nothing of the cheeses from (holy) Mère Richard, the crème brûlée Sirio (recipe from Le Cirque in New York) and the chocolate caraque Maurice Bernachon.

In the end there remains the matter of a rating, and we can certainly proclaim all this to be a delicious, eighteen-point, three-toque feast. Our assurance is based on several anonymous visits, all of which resulted in exemplary meals, all confirming the same impresssions.

At the same time, it should not be overlooked that Bocuse's prices are more than fair; you can easily eat much worse and less famously for more money elswhere. With a good Burgundy or Beaujolais, three excellent dishes plus cheese and dessert won't exceed 600 francs.

A la carte: 600F. Menus: 400F (weekdays only), 470F, 510F, 560F.

IN NEARBY **La Mulatière**
(SW)
69350 La Mulatière - (Rhône)

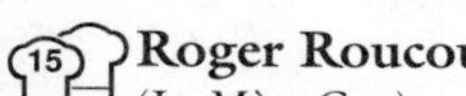

Roger Roucou

(La Mère Guy)
35, quai Jean-Jacques-Rousseau
78.51.65.37

M. Roucou. Open until 9:30 p.m. Closed Sun. dinner, Mon. & Aug. Air cond. Terrace dining. Pets allowed. Parking. Telex 310241. Cards: V, AE, DC.

For Roger Roucou's cuisine to generate enthusiasm, it needs only to be perfect. A native of the upper Languedoc, Roucou combines, in the strict framework of Escoffier-style rigor, the styles of the Landes and Périgord (truffle surprise, foie gras either braised or in a brioche) with the tastes of Lyon and Bresse (fatted chicken, crayfish tails au gratin). One more thing to Roucou's credit: His honorable perpetuation of the ceremony that gave classic French cuisine its reputation. The cuisine from the beginning of this past half century is captured here at its best. Bravo for the Bresse poultry in a gently spiced sherry-vinegar sauce, the braised sweetbreads with morels, the tournedos Cendrillon (with artichokes and foie gras) and the desserts, such as the spectacular bavarois and the marvelously sweet chocolate cake with pralines. Jacqueline Pignol, Roger's daughter, is the most charming hostess in Lyon. Also worthy of mention is Rémy Le Nahour, the attentive yet discreet maître d'hôtel, a classic vestige of his profession whose style should set an example for all of today's hotel schools. The admirable wine cellar is one of the most complete in the Lyon region.

A la carte: 400-600F. Menus: 210F, 320F, 400F.

IN NEARBY **Rilleux-la-Pape**
(7 km N on N 83 & N 84)
69140 Rilleux-la-Pape - (Rhône)

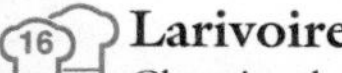

Larivoire

Chemin des Iles (on the banks of the Rhône) - 78.88.50.92

M. Constantin. Open until 9:30 p.m. Closed Mon. dinner, Tues., Feb. 15-March 8 & Sept. 1-8. Terrace dining. Pets allowed. Garage parking. Cards: V, AE, DC.

Larivoire is one of the best places to eat in the environs of Lyon. It's also one of the most pleasant, when good weather opens up the beautiful terrace that stretches out to the Rhône from the prawn-pink walls of the restaurant. Bernard Constantin is the third-generation owner of this inn, which has been run by his family since 1904. In just a few years he has succeeded in ridding the place of its reputation as a hall for wedding receptions and large banquets. First, he turned the decor completely inside out, creating a friendly atmosphere with elegant tables, Venetian mirrors and lovely salmon-colored wall hangings. Then, at the same time that he expanded his dining room staff and brought in an excellent sommelier, he let loose his talents as the all-around chef who was trained at such top-notch places as Bocuse, La Marée and Chez Pauline. The quality of his products and a search for simplicity are teamed with a daring personality, which is responsible for the charm of his frogs' legs in parsley cream with a subtle celeriac, John Dory with berries accompanied by crispy artichokes, and rabbit au jus with rosemary and wild rice. The desserts are delightful (including freshly made ice creams), and the wine cellar is superb, with plenty of inexpensive offerings.

A la carte: 300-350F. Menus: 170F, 280F, 330F.

IN NEARBY **Tassin-la-Demi-Lune**
(6 km W on N 89)
69160 Tassin-la-Demi-Lune - (Rhône)

---

(13) Le Jardin Tassinois

5, rue de la Liberté - 78.34.00.47

M. Frigo. Open until 9:30 p.m. Closed Sun. & Aug. Garden dining. Pets allowed. Cards: V, AE, DC.

The interior garden here has been transformed from a sort of cathedral on a small street in one of the "good" suburbs of Lyon. Le Jardin is quite popular in spite of the fairly high à la carte prices, but the setting is one that puts you immediately at ease, and the cuisine of Christian Frigo is faultlessly fresh and generous, although without much personality: foie gras terrine, grilled duck, bass with artichokes, roast pigeon with truffles, fruit tarts. There are very good Alsatian wines, rare for this region, and a delicious Courbis white Saint-Joseph.

A la carte: 300F. Menus: 99F to 350F.

INDEX OF LYON HOTELS AND RESTAURANTS

Lyons-la-Forêt

27480 Lyons-la-Forêt - (Eure)
Paris 107 - Rouen 36 - Gournay-en-Bray 25

(14) Le Grand Cerf

Pl. du Marché - 32.49.60.44

M. Colignon. Open until 9:30 p.m. Closed Tues., Wed. & Jan. 15-Feb. 15. Pets allowed. Hotel: 8 rms 200-250F; half-board 270-370F. Cards: V, AE, DC, MC.

There's always a storm brewing in Philippe Colignon's head—the impressive, mustachioed owner of this rustic wood-paneled inn racks his brains to interpret, in his own fashion, opulent and old-fashioned cuisine. Its charm is in its light touch and its inclusion of seasonal offerings: duck "au sang," veal from a 1740 recipe, deboned pigeon stuffed with foie gras. Top it off with such Norman desserts as douillon (stuffed pears) with apples. Good Duboeuf wines.

A la carte: 280-300F. Menu: 170F.

Mâcon

71000 Mâcon - (Saône-et-Loire)
Paris 395 - Lyon 68 - Bourg 34 - Chalon-sur-Saône 58

Sights. Musée Lamartine (in the beautiful Régence hotel); remains of the old Saint-Vincent church; Musée des Ursulines (wonderfully provincial); Maison de Bois and the "baby tower" of the old hospital; interesting side trips—the vineyards, the frescoes at Berzé-la-Ville, the new Musée Solutré.

Eating on the Run. Le Café de Lyon, pl. Gérard Genèves (warm, friendly); L'Elysée, 2, rue Victor-Hugo (brasserie-pizzeria); Le Jardin de Tiffany, 1, rue Gambetta (lots of foliage and pleasant lighting, good prices); Le Lamartine, 259, quai Lamartine (wonderful 1900s decor); Le P'tit Goulu, 2, rue Dufour (crêpes and hamburgers, amusing and inexpensive); Le Réstique, 56, rue St-Antoine (folk decor with lots of antiques, nice ambience, honest Lyonnaise cuisine); La Vigne et les Vins, 42, rue Dufour (simple, comfortable, beautiful meats).

Bars & Cafés. Le Café du Palais, 11, rue de la Préfecture (elegant and relaxing); Café du Phénix, 10, pl. de la Barre (teenage meeting spot, good fruit juices); La Maison du Bois, 13, pl. aux Herbes (piano bar with cocktails, pleasant decor); Pub La Traboule, 47, rue Carnot (good choice of imported beers and liquors, Irish pub decor); La Rondelle Pub, 343, rue de Paris (sampling of artisanal products—beer, goat cheese, sausages, estate-bottled wines); Le Vieux Saint-Vincent, rue de Strasbourg (vaulted arch is a registered landmark).

Bellevue

416-420, quai Lamartine - 85.38.05.07

Open year-round. 1 ste 480F. 24 rms 255-480F. TV. Pets allowed. Parking. Telex 800837. Cards: V, AE, DC, MC.

This traditional hotel with excellent comforts faces the marketplace and the Saône. Restaurant.

(13) Au Rocher de Cancale

3, quai Jean-Jaurès - 85.38.07.50

M. Mabon. Open until 9:30 p.m. Closed Sat. lunch, Sun. dinner, Mon., Jan. 2-9, June 5-26 & Nov. 13-20. Pets allowed. Cards: V, AE, DC, MC.

The short menu, with daily specials based on the market's offerings, is devoted to the best of family-style cuisine, consistent, generous and professionally prepared: andouillette, tournedos, fabulous roast chicken with a garlic-clove confit, steamed salmon with a classic sorrel accompaniment. The decor is nothing thrilling in this plain old house along the Saône. Very good prices for wines by the carafe (Duboeuf Beaujolais is 35 francs).

A la carte: 250F. Menus: 75F, 120F, 160F.

IN NEARBY **La Croix-Blanche**
(14 km W on N 79)
71960 Pierreclos - (Saône-et-Loire)

(14) Le Relais du Mâconnais

Berzé-la-Ville - 85.36.60.72

M. Lannuel. Open until 9 p.m. Closed Sun. dinner & Mon. (off-seas.) & Jan. 3-Feb. 3. Terrace dining. Pets allowed. Hotel: 12 rms 140-230F: half-board 260-350F oblig. in seas. Parking. Cards: V, AE, DC, MC.

We discovered this simple, serious restaurant a few years ago, and we didn't predict good things for its cuisine. Fortunately for Christian Lannuel, we were wrong. He has established himself as the best chef in the neighborhood, despite a rather spare decor, cool service and a lot of shouting in the kitchen. His creations are inventive, personal, exacting, generous and extremely diversified, as evidenced by the warm vinaigrette with the coquilles St-Jacques and the frogs' legs, as well as by his technically complicated and exquisitely delicious pigeon feuilleté. Ambitious wine list, particularly in the Bordeaux.

A la carte: 250-300F. Menus: 100F (weekdays only), 200F (weekends and holidays only), 160F, 260F.

Magescq

40140 Soustons - (Landes)
Paris 698 - Dax 17 - Soustons 10 - Bayonne 42 - Castets 12

(13) Le Cabanon

N 10 - 58.47.71.51

Mme. Hanff. Open until 9:30 p.m. Closed Sun. dinner, Mon. & Oct. 1-Nov. 1. Garden dining. Pets allowed. Parking. Telex 540660. Cards: V.

The new chef is a native of the region who trained with Joël Robuchon and is now back home in this old farmhouse amid the oaks. Try his delicious terrines, farm-raised chicken with cèpes, glazed nougat and homemade sorbets. There's also a good selection of wines, whiskies and coffees, which can be bought for home use. The staff, bearded members of a nearby religious community, is charming.

A la carte: 200-250F. Menus: 96F, 152F.

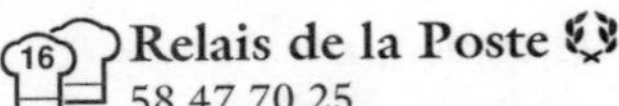

Relais de la Poste

58.47.70.25

MM. Coussau. Open until 9:30 p.m. Closed Mon. dinner, Tues. (except July-Aug.) & Nov. 12-Dec. 24. Air cond. Pets allowed. Garage parking. Cards: V, AE, DC.

This picture-book country inn from bygone days is actually posh and comfortable (though the modern paintings don't go with the stone walls). It is also a house of traditional Landaise cuisine. Bernard Coussau is fiercely rigorous and classic, directing the dinner service like a ballet master. In the kitchen, with the help of son Jean, he prepares admirable foie gras, both raw and cooked; confits; duck breasts; cèpes; game; and some incredibly beautiful sauces (including the béarnaise that accompanies the grilled salmon steak). And we found the thick prune tart to be the best imaginable. We must applaud Coussau for taking advantage of seasonal products, such as local asparagus, fresh girolles and seasonal fruits (which go into the sorbets). The "all duck" fixed-price menu is excellent; the list of wines and Armagnacs and the cigar cellar are equally impressive.

A la carte: 350F. Menus: 310F (weekends and holidays only), 260F.

Relais de la Poste

(See restaurant above)

Closed Mon., Tues. (except July-Aug.) & Nov. 12-Dec. 24. 2 stes 650-750F. 10 rms 400-500F. TV in 6 rms. Heated pool. Tennis.

A large, peaceful Landaise house overlooking a vast park, with recently refurbished, well-equipped rooms.

Magny-Cours

58470 Magny-Cours - (Nièvre)
Paris 251 - Moulins 42 - Nevers 12 - Bourges 80

La Renaissance

Old N 7 - 86.58.10.40

M. Dray. Open until 9:30 p.m. Closed Sun. dinner, Mon., end Jan.-early March & 1st week of July. Pets allowed. Parking. Cards: V, AE, DC, MC.

This opulent inn has been a local fixture for some 30 years, since before the route Nationale 7 made its detour. We haven't known it that long, but long enough to know Jean-Claude Dray's bold and vibrant cuisine. He has recently settled into a routine that is seasonal but less inventive, a celebration of powerful aromas; clear, natural flavors; and a rustic, light style. He uses fine Charolais meat for his showcase dish, beef filet with a morel cream sauce, which brings all the gourmets from the region running to his plush provincial-looking restaurant. Some of his regional favorites include the tapenade Morvandelle and Arleuf ham with three purées. There are also plenty of other generous, well-prepared dishes: pan-fried lotte with pistachios and tarragon and a mélange of veal kidneys, sweetbreads and liver with a chive cream sauce. Beautiful wines.

A la carte: 500F. Menus: 180F, 280F, 320F, 400F.

La Renaissance

(See restaurant above)

Closed Sun., Mon., end Jan.-early March & 1st week of July. 1 ste 440-640F. 9 rms 210-390F. Half-board 500F. TV in 2 rms.

These quiet, tastefully redecorated rooms are located several minutes from the famous automobile race course. Breakfast is exceptionally good, served on the terrace in summer.

Maisons-Laffitte

see PARIS SUBURBS

Malataverne

see Montélimar

Malbuisson

25160 Malbuisson - (Doubs)
Paris 467 - Besançon 75 - Pontarlier 15 - St-Claude 73

Le Lac

81.69.34.80

M. Chauvin. Open until 9 p.m. Closed Nov. 20-Dec. 18 (except weekends). Pets allowed. Parking. Telex 360713. Cards: V, DC, MC.

This large lakefront restaurant with an elegant Louis XVI decor is impeccably and professionally managed by the Chauvin family. The father shops in Rungis and chats with customers at the tables. His daughter supervises the service and the wine cellar. And Jean-Marie Chauvin, who spent 26 years at Lasserre, bases his masterful cuisine on intelligently revisited classicism: excellent sauces, precise cooking and remarkable desserts. The sensational fixed-price menus are terrific values: For 140 francs, for example, you get house foie gras, sweetbreads in walnut sauce and glazed nougat with a raspberry coulis and mignardises (pastries).

A la carte: 260F. Menus: 70F and 100F (weekdays only), 140F, 160F, 200F.

Le Lac

(See restaurant above)

Closed Nov. 20-Dec. 18 (except weekends). 54 rms 115-254F. Half-board 150-210F oblig. in seas.

A pleasant stopover to recharge one's batteries; it's perched at an altitude of 3,000 feet, and has large, comfortable, newly redecorated rooms. Charming staff and an invigorating breakfast.

Mallemort-Pont-Royal

13370 Mallemort - (Bouches-du-Rhône)
Paris 721 - Avignon 43 - Sénas 9 - Salon-de-Provence 8

Moulin de Vernègues

N 7, exit Sénas - 90.59.12.00

Open year-round. 35 rms 580-900F. Half-board 650-900F. TV. Pets allowed. Heated pool. Tennis. Telex 401645. Cards: V, AE, DC.

These beautiful, old-fashioned rooms near the highway are much in demand for top-flight conferences and seminars. Hunting trips and skeet shooting can be organized, and the grounds are extraordinarily lovely. Restaurant.

Manosque

04100 Manospue - (Alpes-de-Haute-Provence)
Paris 767 - Aix-en-Provence 53 - Digne 57 - Sisteron 52

IN NEARBY **La Fuste**
(6.5 km SE on D 907 & D 4)
04210 Valensole - (Alpes-de-Haute-Provence)

16 Hostellerie de La Fuste

92.72.05.95

M. Jourdan. Open until 9:30 p.m. Closed Sun. dinner & Mon. (off-seas., except holidays) & Jan. 9-Feb. 15. Garden dining. Pets allowed. Cards: V, AE, DC, MC.

Lobster, foie gras, truffles and rich sauces play a big part in the cuisine of this glistening country inn with a rather affected air. On top of that, the opulent decor is becoming adorned with more and more extravagant accessories and stately furniture. And don't think it's unintentional. M. Jourdan is among the most charming of men, and he's always striving intelligently to do better. The decor is solemn, despite flowers, pretty Moustiers china and the smiling Lydia, daughter of the house; the summer terrace, in the shade of the sycamore trees, is the nicest in the region; and the cuisine is based on top-quality produce. We suggest you make a meal from the "three-night" smoked salmon (salted, desalted, smoked and marinated in oil), the stuffed fresh vegetable plate with an aïoli of pesto, a fine gratin of summer cèpes from the region, lightly cooked young pigeon, fresh pasta (Jourdan brought back a pasta machine from his Italian vacation), stuffed lamb's sweetbreads poached in duck broth. And for dessert, try the vanilla ice cream with mint from the garden and red fruits.

A la carte: 400-500F. Menus: 190F, 280F, 330F.

Hostellerie de La Fuste

(See restaurant above)

Closed Sun. & Mon. (off-seas., except holidays) & Jan. 9-Feb. 15. 2 stes 1,000F. 7 rms 400-960F. Half-board 500-900F oblig. in seas. TV. Pets allowed.

Spacious, comfortable rooms (though a couple of them are in need of renovation) are found in this beautiful country cottage. Excellent service and breakfast. Boutique for regional products.

Le Mans

72000 Le Mans - (Sarthe)
Paris 216 - Rennes 145 - Chartres 120 - Tours 81

Sights. The old city (Gallo-Roman belt along the Sarthe); Maison de la Reine Bérengère (history museum); Saint-Julien cathedral (apse, south portal); Sainte-Jeanne d'Arc church; Notre-Dame de la Couture church; Musée de Tessé; Notre-Dame de l'Epau abbey (along the Huisine, 4 kilometers); auto racing (Bugatti, 24-hour racing, automobile museum).

Eating on the Run. L'Adresse, 1, rue des Remparts (budget fixed-price menus, pleasant ambience); Le Berry, 29, pl. de la République (popular, good ice cream); L'Etna, 37, rue des Ponts-Neufs (Italian style, pleasant veranda in summer); Maïo, 45, rue des Ponts-Neufs (good low-priced pizza); Le Panier à Oeufs, rue des Ponts-Neufs; Le Roy d'Ys, 30, rue des Ponts-Neufs (best crêperie in town).

Brasseries. La Bourse, 11, pl. de la République (crêperie upstairs); Félix, blvd. René-Levasseur (wine bar, reasonable prices).

Bars & Cafés. Along rue des Ponts-Neufs—Le Café Crème (trendy, jazz piano on Monday), Les Dix Vins (new wine bar, Greek decor) and Le Sherlock Holmes; Le Moderne, 23, pl. de la République (lots of people); Le Satan, pl. de l'Eperon (quiet, good cocktails).

Nightlife. L'Aristophane, 30, rue Wagram (private club, steep prices); Le Darling, rue Ledru-Rollin (men's-club atmosphere); La Louisiane, ave. du Général-Leclerc (restaurant open until 2 a.m., reopens at 4 a.m.); Le Privé, 23 ter, rue Halleaux Toiles (billiards, mixed crowd); Le Tropicana, 43, rue des Ponts-Neuf (lively crowd, gloomy decor).

Central

5, blvd. René-Levasseur - 43.24.08.93

Open year-round. 38 rms 170-320F. Half-board 320F. TV in 27 rms. Telex 722878. Cards: V, AE, MC.

These stylish, renovated rooms overlook a quiet courtyard. Restaurant.

14 Concorde

16, ave. de Général-Leclerc - 43.24.12.30

Mlle. Naudès. Open daily until 10 p.m. Pets allowed. Garage parking. Telex 720487. Cards: V, AE, DC, MC.

The elegant dining room in this fine, friendly little provincial hotel is done in salmon pink, with great chandeliers and Louis XVI chairs—just the setting to sample the cooking of the new chef, Michel Frey, who worked most recently on the Côte d'Azur. Still more influenced by the Mediterranean than by the Le Mans region, this technically adept chef offers a wide and well-balanced choice of dishes, such as a terrine of leg of lamb with a garlic confit, accompanied by a julienne of mushrooms in walnut oil, an excellent preparation of goosefish in an orange cream with little seasonal vegetables, and a beautiful passion-fruit soufflé with a mango coulis. The list of Loire wines is very well selected, but service is a little sloppy.

A la carte: 300F. Menu: 110F.

Concorde

(See restaurant above)

Open year-round. 2 stes 500F. 66 rms 320-490F. Half-board 110F. TV.

These beautifully renovated rooms are located halfway between the train station and the old town. Free locked parking. Special sports and getaway packages.

IN NEARBY **Arnage**
(9 km SE on D 147 & N 23)
72230 Arnage - (Sarthe)

15 Auberge des Matfeux

289, rte. Nationale - 43.21.10.71

M. Souffront. Open until 9 p.m. Closed Sun. & holiday dinner, Mon., Jan. & July 17-31. Parking. Cards: V, AE, DC, MC.

To look at this large, plain-looking inn near the Le Mans raceway, you wouldn't think it would hold any treasures. But in fact, it's a little Louis XV palace with proud, shining-silver bell covers, candlesticks, plates and serving carts—not to mention the remarkable table linens, upholstered velour armchairs and the plush carpet that absorbs any noise the waiters make as they move about. Alain Souffront, the bon vivant chef, has trouble containing his enthusiasm, and his only fault is that he tries to do too much. He's a skillful cook, highly knowledgeable about the products of the region and full of grandiloquence. Bravo for all the little details he attends to (like the cocktail snacks), his excellent bargain fixed-price menus and his dishes: fine langoustines ravioli, seafood pasta, saddle of young rabbit stuffed with sweetbreads and superb local farm produce (suckling veal and lamb, young hens).

A la carte: 300-350F. Menus: 295F (menu dégustation), 245F (wine incl.), 98F, 195F, 290F (wine incl.), 250F.

Mantes-la-Jolie

78200 Mantes-la-Jolie - (Yvelines)
Paris 60 - Evreux 44 - Rouen 81 - Versailles 44

La Galiote

1, rue du Fort - 34.77.03.02

Mme. Coutureau. Open until 10 p.m. Closed Feb. 8-21 & July 5- 25. Pets allowed. Cards: V, AE.

Mélanie Coutureau's cuisine is simple, authoritative, masterfully executed and based on fine products. We only wish she'd show less indifference to seasonal produce (well, she does have a magnificent variety of fresh mushrooms). Overlooking the Seine, the dining room is elegant and subdued; La Galiote remains a best bet for a classic, generous meal in a delightful atmosphere: exquisite pan-fried girolles, Bresse hen with cream and morels, roast gilthead with a fresh tomato-and-Sauternes sauce and excellent desserts. Interesting Jura wines.

A la carte: 300-350F. Menu: 140F.

Marçay

see Chinon

Marcq-en-Baroeul

see Lille

Prices in red draw attention to restaurants that offer a particularly good value.

Margaux

33460 Margaux - (Gironde)
Paris 598 - Bordeaux 22 - Lesparre-Médoc 20

13 Le Relais de Margaux

56.88.38.30

M. Iversen. Open until 10:15 p.m. Closed Jan. 1-March 1 & Dec. Terrace dining. Pets allowed. Parking. Telex 572530. Cards: V, AE, DC.

After some ups and downs, the kitchens at this luxurious blond-stone inn (a former wine shop, facing the vineyards) have been turned over to the impressively credentialed Daniel David, who trained in Biarritz and Bordeaux's top restaurants. His cooking is uneven, ranging from the dull (tomatoes stuffed with langoustines, with a syrupy taste) to the nearly excellent (fresh duck foie gras with spices and a remarkable accompaniment of apples, corn and hazelnuts). David also presents some farfetched names and substitutions (a cress flan instead of fresh pasta), good, classic desserts; and excellent wines. We hope the service becomes less clumsy and the reception more cordial.

A la carte: 350F. Menus: 140F (weekday lunch only), 180F, 280F.

Le Relais de Margaux

(See restaurant above)

Closed Jan. 1-March 1 & Dec. 3 stes 1,440-1,800F. 28 rms 725-1,400F. TV. Air cond. in 11 rms. Pool. Tennis.

There's an attractive decor in the handful of rooms and suites that overlook the quiet Garonne river and its lush surroundings. Breakfast needs some improvement, as does the service, which is markedly off. Tennis (on synthetic turf). Relais et Châteaux.

Marlenheim

67520 Marlenheim - (Bas-Rhin)
Paris 437 - Strasbourg 20 - Haguenau 35 - Molsheim 12

Hostellerie du Cerf

30, rue du Général-de-Gaulle
88.87.73.73

M. Husser. Open until 9 p.m. Closed Tues., Wed. & Feb. school vacation. Terrace dining. Pets allowed. Parking. Cards: V.

Robert Husser is a wise man who cultivates a garden of greens and aromatic herbs—just one of the things he does to assure the quality of the cuisine served at his fine roadside inn. Although he has turned the kitchen over to son Michel, a smart young man with excellent training, he still keeps an eye on things. Father and son get along perfectly, creating a regional cuisine that blends the old and the new: excellent oxtail terrine with a sorrel mousseline, frog cassoulet with Riesling and barley, hake that was slightly overcooked but had a marvelous Provençal accent and saddle of veal with kidneys and tarragon. We'd like to add that this old postal relay station along the famous route du Vin has an amazing wine cellar, and that its new decor—bright, comfortable and warm—has all the charm of the territory (wainscoting, earthenware furnace, antique buffets).

A la carte: 400F. Menus: 195F (weekday lunch only, wine incl.), 290F, 410F.

Hostellerie du Cerf

(See restaurant above)

Closed Tues., Wed. & Feb. school vacation. 2 stes 500F. 15 rms 250-380F.

A charming hotel, typical of the villages in Alsace, built around a flowery courtyard, with several excellent, well-modernized rooms.

Marsannay-la-Côte

see Dijon

Marseillan

see Agde

Marseille

13000 Marseille - (Bouches-du-Rhône)
Paris 771 - Lyon 315 - Nice 188 - Arles 92 - Toulouse 400

Note: The numbers following the telephone numbers in each review pinpoint the establishment's exact location on the accompanying map.

Sights. The Vieux Port (ferry service recently instituted); the fish market (quai des Belges); La Bonne Mère cathedral; the coves (east of the city); minifishing ports (Auffes valley, Goudes cove); Château d'If and Le Frioul (boat trips from the Vieux Port); Musée Cantini (decorative arts, modern art, surrealism); Musée des Beaux-Arts (eighteenth-century Provençal paintings); Musée d'Histoire de Marseille (around the Roman ruins); Musée du Vieux-Marseille (curious sixteenth-century captain's residence); Musée Gobret-Labadié (5,000 objets d'art in a nineteenth-century mansion); Musée de la Marine; the Roman docks; Musée de la Vieille Charité (in a restored hospice); Muséum d'-Histoire Naturelle (Mediterranean and tropical fish) and the zoological park behind it; Borély Park, whose château includes an archaeological museum (second-finest collection of Egyptian artifacts in France, after the Louvre); Saint-Victor's Basilica (eleventh-century abbey with tombs dating from the third century A.D.); La Cité Radieuse (famous residence designed by Le Corbusier).

Eating on the Run. Chez Angèle, 50, rue Caisserie (ravioli, immense pizzas); Antoine, 35, rue du Musée (pasta, osso buco, pizza); L'Artisan du Chocolat, 43, cours d'Estienne-d'Orves (salads, daily specials, excellent pastries); L'Avant-Scène, 59, cours Julien (chic spot, Anglo-American cuisine); Castelmuro, 37, rue F.-Davso (large provincial bistro, excellent prices); L'-Entracte, 10, rue Fortia (tartares); Le Poussin Bleu, 17, rue Armény (lunch only, charming little annex of a caterer); Taverne de Maître Kanter, 38, cours d'Estienne-d'Ovres (oysters, beer, choucroute).

Bars & Cafés. Sofitel bars—Vérandah and Astrolabe (facing the Vieux Port); the Pullman Beauvau, 4, rue Beauvau (famous in the 1950s as Le Cintra); Le New-York, 7, quai des Belges (nice terrace for an apéritif); Le Petit Pernod, 10, quai du Port (locals); Le Pelle-Mêle, cours d'Estienne-d'Ovres (very hip); Seaport Café, 16, rue Lulli (wine bar).

Nightlife. L'Abbaye de la Commanderie (old operatic musical refrains) and Ajaccio (Corsican music), both on rue Corneille; L'Ascenseur, pl. Thiars (offbeat); Le Blue Note, rue Fort-Notre-Dame (small jazz spot/restaurant); Le Duke, rue Beauvau (late-night grill); O'Stop, pl. E.-Reyer (simple dishes served all night, colorful owner); Le Roll's, corniche Kennedy; Le Satellite, corniche Kennedy (also on the beach in summer).

Shops. *Butchers:* Lombardini, 8, ave. du Maréchal-Foch (Charolais meats, lamb from the Hautes-Alpes); Melquinon, 2, ave. de la Grande Armée (customers from all over Marseille); Sambuc, 50, ave. F.-Davso (whole lambs, cut for free). *Bakeries:* Boulangerie Aixoise, 45, rue F.-Davso; Le Founil du Mont, 7, pl. Notre-Dame-du-Mont (delicious sourdough baguettes); Michel, 33, rue Vacon (traditional Provençal bakery); De Stéphanis, 41, chaussée de Gibbes (Marseille's master baker). *Chocolate:* L'Artisan du Chocolat, 43, cours d'Estienne-d'Orves (nearly perfect); Puyricard, 155, rue J.-Mermoz, and 30, blvd. Clemenceau (traditional). *Gourmet foods:* Bataille, 18, rue Frontage (nice wines, best cheese in town); Epicure, 2, blvd. Chave (products from the southwest); Fromagerie Blanc, 19, ave. Prado (cheese, roe, Bresse poultry); Marrou, 15, pl. Castellane, and La Tour d'Argent, pl. Castellane (products from Fauchon). *Seafood:* Barone, 43, rue Vacon (good advice and prices); Chez Blaise, rue Consolat (good packaging for transporting shellfish); Henri, 2, rue Montaigne (fresh, large selection). *Ice cream:* Maison de la Glace, 96, rue Sainte (classic, professional). *Pastry makers, caterers:* Amandine, 69, blvd. E.-Pierre (light pastries); Castelmuro, 31, rue Paradis (Marseille's "grand" caterer); Le Moule à Gâteau, 7, pl. Castellane (reasonably priced for the quality); Planchut, 168, La Canebière (oldest pastry maker in Marseille); Le Poussin Bleu, 85, rue Paradis (the caterer in vogue); Villedieu, 16, La Canebière.

Altea

See L'Oursinade restaurant.

12/20 Les Arcenaulx

25, cours d'Estienne-d'Orves
91.54.39.37 / D5-6

Mmes. Laffitte. Open until 1:30 a.m. Closed Mon. dinner, Sun. & Aug. 1-15. Air cond. Garden dining. Pets allowed. Cards: V, AE, DC.

A charming hostess, an attractive rough-stone decor with large beams and an amusing menu capable of granting your every wish, whether it's for Grisons meats, tasty marinated sardines, scrambled eggs with tapenade (an anchovy, olive and caper paste) or mutton stew with artichokes. Good wines are served by the glass. Adjoining bookshop.

A la carte: 180-200F.

1 - Le Tire-Bouchon **R**
2 - Byblos Prado **R**
3 - New Hotel Astoria **H**
4 - Chez Fonfon **R**
5 - Le Régent **R**
6 - Les Arcenaulx **R**
7 - Concorde Prado **H**
8 - Au Pescadou **R**
9 - Cousin Cousine **R**
10 - Chez Madie **R**
11 - Le Zinc **R**
12 - L'Oursinade (Altea) **RH**
13 - Le Caribou **R**
14 - Ibis **H**
15 - Lutétia **H**
16 - Maurice Brun **R**
17 - Concorde Palm Beach **H**
18 - Bagatelle **R**
19 - La Table d'Albret **R**
21 - Calypso **R** et Michel **R**
22 - Esterel **H**
23 - Grand Hôtel de Genève **H**
24 - Le Charolais **R**
25 - Pullman Beauvau **H**
26 - Résidence Sainte-Anne **H**
27 - New York **R**
28 - A la Folle Epoque **R**
29 - Caï-Bat **R**
30 - Bompard **H**
31 - Peron **R**
32 - Les Trois Forts (Sofitel) **RH**
33 - Au Jambon de Parme **R**
34 - Caruso **R**
35 - Le Petit Nice **RH**
36 - L'Oursin **R**
38 - La Garbure **R**
39 - Patalain **R**
40 - Chez Loury **R**
41 - L'Epuisette **R**
42 - Le Chaudron Provençal **R**
43 - Grand Hôtel de Noailles **H**
44 - Miramar **R**

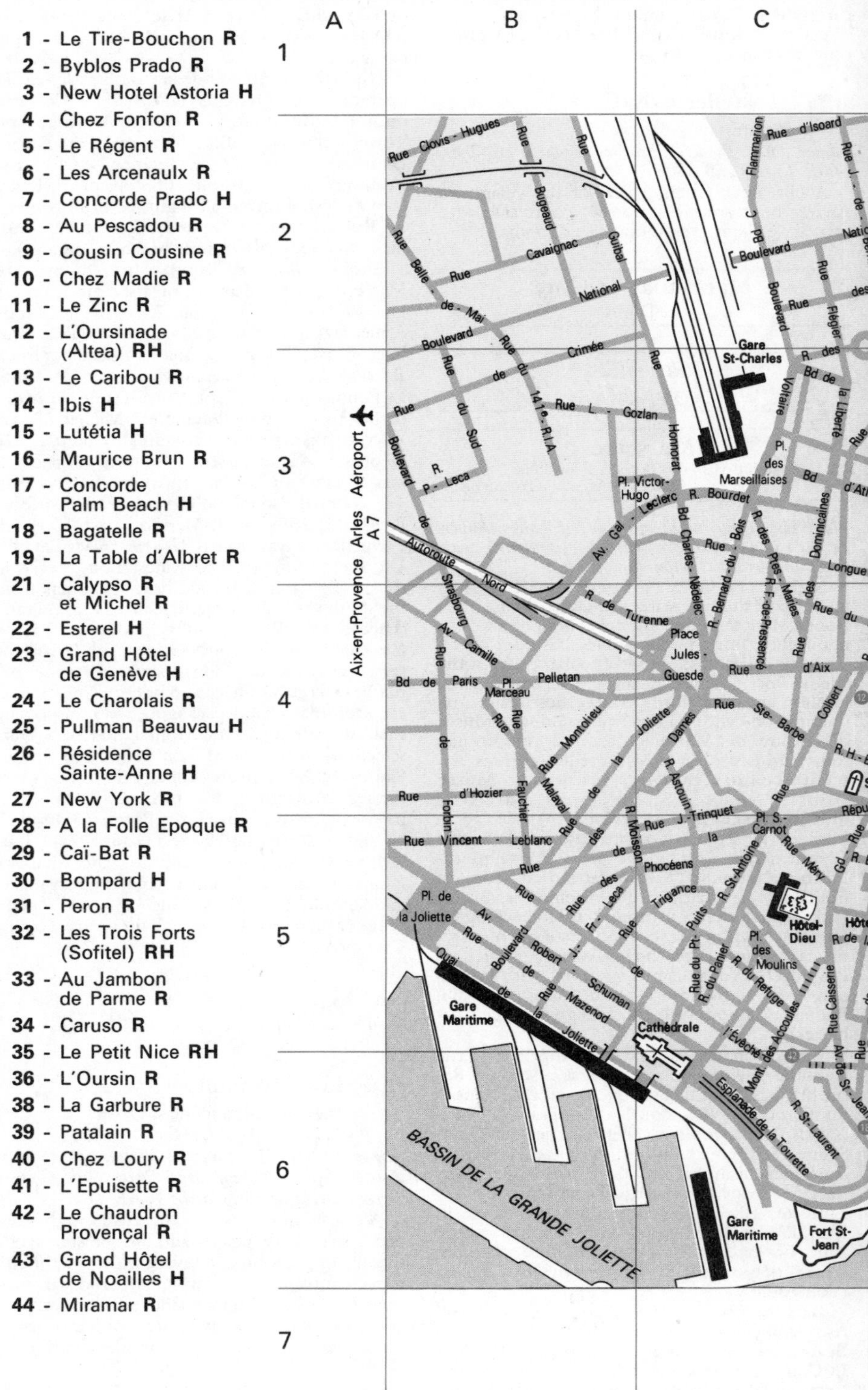

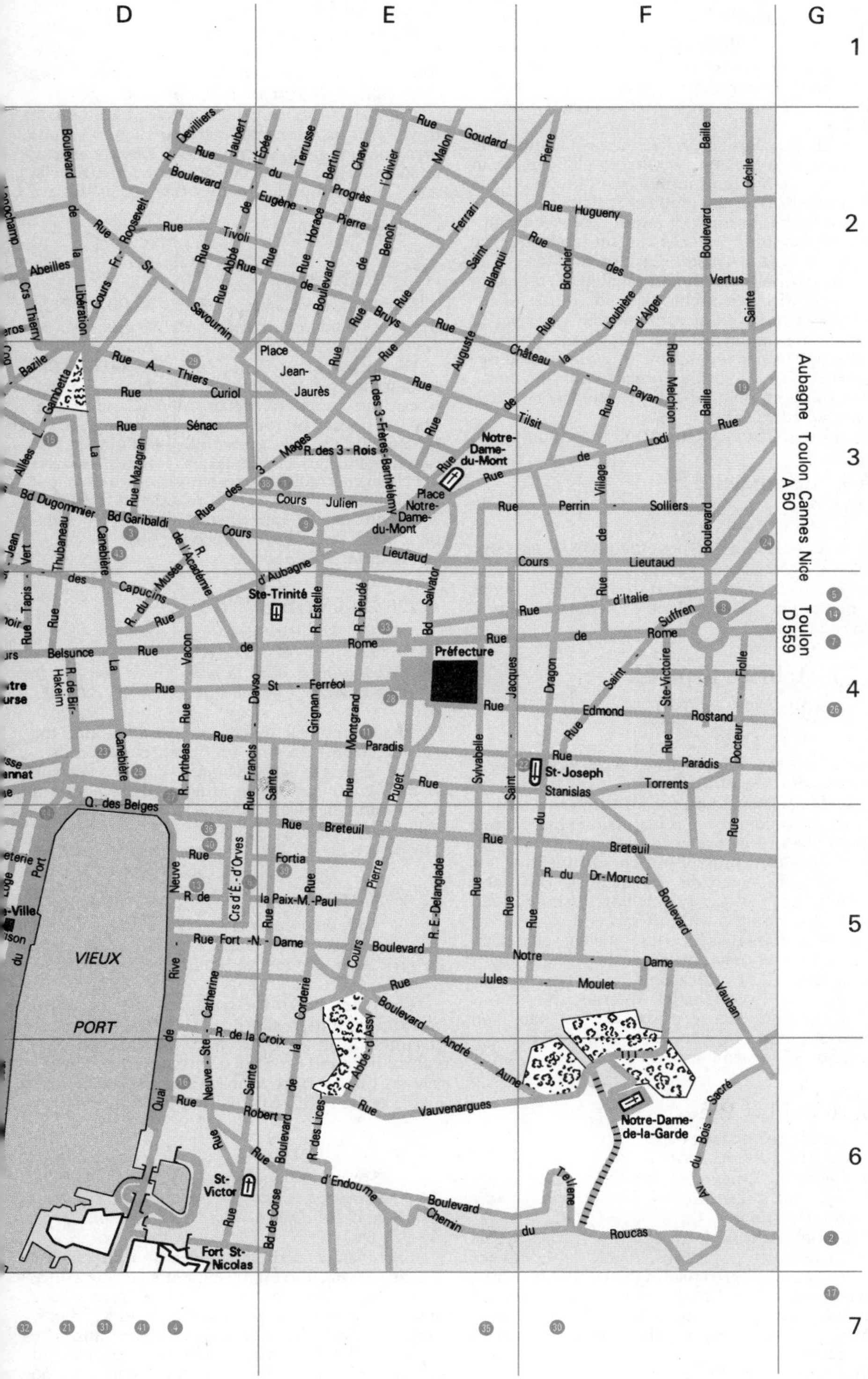

D E F G

1 2 3 4 5 6 7

Boulevard de la Libération
Cours Fr. Roosevelt
Rue Devilliers
Rue Jaubert
Rue de l'Épée
Rue du Terrusse
Boulevard Eugène Pierre
Rue Tivoli
Rue Abbé de l'Épée
Rue Horace Bertin
Rue du Progrès
Rue Chave
Rue de l'Olivier
Rue Malon
Rue Goudard
Rue Pierre
Rue Ferrari
Rue Saint Pierre
Boulevard de la Blancarde
Rue Benoît
Rue de Bruys
Rue Auguste Blanqui
Rue Brochier
Rue Hugueny
Rue des Loubière
Boulevard Baille
Rue Cécile
Boulevard d'Alger
Rue Vertus
Rue Sainte Cécile
Rue Abeilles
Crs Thierry
Rue St Savournin
Rue Château Payan
Rue de la Loubière
Rue Melchion
Rue de Tilsit
Rue de Lodi
Place Jean-Jaurès
Rue A. Thiers
Rue Curiol
Rue Sénac
Allées L. Gambetta
Rue Bazile
La Canebière
Rue Mazagran
Rue des 3 Mages
R. des 3 Rois
R. des 3-Frères-Barthélemy
Notre-Dame-du-Mont
Place Notre-Dame-du-Mont
Cours Julien
Rue du Village
Rue Perrin Solliers
Bd Dugommier
Bd Garibaldi
Rue Thubaneau
Rue des Capucins
R. du Musée
R. de l'Académie
Cours Lieutaud
Rue d'Aubagne
Ste-Trinité
R. Estelle
R. Dieudé
Bd Salvator
Rue d'Italie
Rue Suffren
Rue de Rome
Rue Tapis Vert
Rue Belsunce
Rue Vacon
Rue Davso
Rue St Ferréol
Préfecture
Rue Grignan
Rue Montgrand
Rue Paradis
Rue Sylvabelle
Rue Saint Jacques
Rue Dragon
Rue Edmond Rostand
Rue Ste-Victoire
Rue Saint Sébastien
Rue Docteur Fiolle
R. de Bir-Hakeim
Rue Pythéas
Rue Francis
Rue Sainte
Rue Puget
Rue Stanislas Torrents
St-Joseph
Q. des Belges
Rue Breteuil
Rue Fortia
Rue Neuve
R. de la Paix-M.-Paul
Crs d'É.-d'Orves
Cours Pierre Puget
R. E.-Delanglade
R. du Dr-Morucci
Boulevard Vauban
Rue Fort -N.- Dame
Boulevard Notre Dame
Rue Jules Moulet
VIEUX PORT
Quai de Rive Neuve
Rue Neuve - Ste - Catherine
R. de la Croix
Boulevard de la Corderie
Boulevard André - Aune
R. Abbé-d'Assy
R. des Lices
Rue Vauvenargues
Rue Sainte
Rue Robert
Rue d'Endoume
Bd de Corse
Rue Tellène
Notre-Dame-de-la-Garde
Av. du Bois - Sacré
St-Victor
Fort St-Nicolas
Boulevard Chemin du Roucas

Aubagne Toulon Cannes Nice A 50

Toulon D 559

14 Bagatelle

1, ave. St-Jean - 91.91.52.00 / C6-18

M. Bagatta. Open until 10 p.m. Closed Sat. lunch, Sun., Mon. dinner, 2 weeks in winter & 2 weeks in summer. Terrace dining. Pets allowed. Cards: V, DC, MC.

From old Marseille stock, Pierre Bagatta, after working with Maximin at the Hôtel Negresco in Nice, traded his uninspiring restaurant on the rue des Trois-Rois for this grand old café ear the Vieux Port. There is a touch of maroon on the cream-colored freestone, and the elegant tables and the large veranda overlook La Bonne Mère. The cuisine is vibrant, fresh and intelligent: fish soup enriched with sea urchin, a cold soufflé of artichokes and zucchini with smoked cod liver (a marvelous summer dish), sardine gâteau, potatoes and eggplant perked up by an audacious anise-tomato coulis, and broiled pigeon with cinnamon, an example of pointed and precise flavors. Well-constructed wine list.

A la carte: 280F. Menu: 100F (lunch only).

Bompard

2, ave. des Flots-Bleus
91.52.10.93 / F7-30

Open year-round. 47 rms 240-315F. Parking. Telex 400430. Cards: V, AE, DC.

This quiet hotel, located in a park 500 meters from the sea, has excellent conference facilities. No restaurant.

Maurice Brun

(Aux Mets de Provence)
18, quai Rive-Neuve
91.33.35.38 / D6-16

M. Brun. Open until 9 p.m. Closed Sun. & Mon. Pets allowed. Cards: AE, DC.

A Marseille standard for 50 years, this austere Provençal dining room is maintained by Maurice Brun. The liturgy has been the same for so long that we can't muster much enthusiasm for describing it: tapenade (an anchovy, olive and caper paste), anchovy quichettes, spit-roasted meats, fish cooked without salt and so on. The routine, it seems, has grown somewhat stale. Also, we are a bit troubled by the steep prices, in light of the fact that Provençal cuisine was never meant for the rich. Even Charles Maurras, the famous former political figure whose likeness hangs on the walls, might be growing weary of all this.

Menu: 350F (wine incl.).

11/20 Byblos Prado

61, promenade de la Plage
91.22.80.66 / G6-2

M. Chagouri. Open until 10:30 p.m. Closed Sun. dinner, Mon. & Dec. 15-Jan. 10. Air cond. Terrace dining. Pets allowed. Cards: V, AE, DC.

A stone's throw from the beach, the Byblos Prado features a spacious, comfortable terrace where, while children play in the sand, diners feast on majestic hot and cold Lebanese mezze: falafel, tabouli, hummus, moussaka and other good things. Courteous service by the owner's daughters.

A la carte: 130-150F.

11/20 Caï-Bat

43, rue Adolphe-Thiers
91.42.33.7 / D3-29

Mme. Duong Thi Thanh. Open daily until 11 p.m. Garden dining. Pets allowed. Parking.

Caï-Bat is the only Vietnamese restaurant in town with its own small garden; there, in summertime, you may dine on such dishes as can-tiou (a spicy soup), sea bream grilled with citronella and Chinese fondue. Many other specialties are also available.

A la carte: 150F.

13 Calypso

3, rue des Catalans - 91.52.64.00 / D7-21

Mme. Visciano. Open daily until 10 p.m. Pets allowed. Cards: V, MC.

We are sorry that Mme. Visciano, who runs this restaurant and the neighboring place, Michel, doesn't attempt to rejuvenate Marseillaise cuisine. She goes heavy on the fennel (massacring the sea bream) and the alcohol, sinfully indulging in certain nostalgic gourmand tastes. Nonetheless, this is a cheerful, traditional restaurant, with excellent bouillabaisse and baskets of wonderful fresh fish. The wine list is inadequate, the service inexperienced. Prices have dipped slightly.

A la carte: 300-350F.

11/20 Le Caribou

38, pl. Thiars - 91.33.22.63,
91.33.23.94 / D5-13

M. Catoni. Open until 11 p.m. Closed Sun., Mon. & June 1-Oct. 1. Pets allowed. Cards: V, AE, DC, MC.

The prices will make you shudder, but the cuisine, based on fine products, is generous—grilled fish, tarragon-flavored kidney, venison grand veneur (a brown sauce with red-currant jelly)—and the lovely convivial atmosphere is typically Marseillaise.

A la carte: 300F and up.

12/20 Caruso

158, quai du Port - 91.90.94.04 / C5-34

M. Zanaboni. Open until 10 p.m. Closed Sun. dinner, Mon. & Oct. 15-Nov. 15. Terrace dining. Pets allowed. Cards: V, AE.

The chef at this classic Italian restaurant remains faithful to all the specials that have made it famous: carpaccio, fresh pasta, Venetian-style calves' liver and osso buco with noodles. There's a large, quiet terrace at one end of the Vieux Port.

A la carte: 230F. Menu: 130F.

12/20 Le Charolais

56, ave. de Toulon - 91.25.94.51 / F3-24

M. Lemaire. Open until 10 p.m. Closed Mon. dinner, Sun. & holidays. Air cond. Pets allowed. Cards: V, AE, DC.

The change in the kitchen hasn't altered the quality of this fine establishment's cuisine. Since a butcher now manages the place, meats have become savory and tender. We suggest, in particular, the pan-fried calves' liver and the Charolais beef en croûte. The relaxing, elegant decor is extremely pleasant in the evening. Good service.

A la carte: 250F. Menus: 90F (lunch only), 145F.

12/20 Le Chaudron Provençal

48, rue Caisserie - 91.91.02.37, 91.56.26.88 / C6-42

Mme. Paul. Open until 10:15 p.m. Closed Sat. lunch, Sun. & July 3-24. Air cond. Pets allowed. Parking. Cards: V, AE.

The restaurant has been extended (there's a dining room upstairs), and the decor embellished (with trompe l'oeil paintings). The cuisine, prepared and served with good humor by the Paul family, is among the most honest in Marseille in its own special way: bouillabaisse, sea perch cooked in salt, small sautéed calamari. Fine little wines and excellent prices.

A la carte: 200F.

12/20 Chez Fonfon

140, vallon des Auffes 91.52.14.38 / D7-4

M. Mounier. Open until 10:30 p.m. Closed Sat., Sun., Oct. & Dec. 24-Jan. 2. Air cond. Cards: V, AE, DC.

Alphonse (nicknamed "Fonfon"), an old local character, cleverly negotiates his way with the fishermen in the vallon des Auffes. Fish and shellfish leap directly from the boat onto your plate: tasty bourride and bouillabaisse, grilled fish just like everywhere else (be sure to demand specific cooking times) and stuffed capon provençal.

A la carte: 300F and up.

12/20 Chez Loury

3, rue Fortia - 91.33.09.73 / D5-40

M. Loury. Open until 11 p.m. Closed Sun. Terrace dining. Pets allowed. Cards: V, AE, DC, MC.

In September, try the delicious sea urchins roasted with herbs; year-round, you can dine on a seafood fricassée with excellent olive oil and poultry sautéed with mild garlic. The mustachioed chef/owner is convivial, and there's a pleasant terrace facing the pedestrian zone.

A la carte: 200F.

12/20 Chez Madie

138, quai du Port - 91.90.40.87 / C5-10

Mme. Minassian. Open until 10:30 p.m. Closed Sun. dinner, Mon. & Feb. 1-20. Terrace dining. Pets allowed. Cards: V, DC.

Marie-Odile Minassian, a true Marseille mama, has moved to the sunny side of the Vieux Port and serves—on the terrace or in the two-level dining room—scorpionfish, clams with thyme, baked fish and Provençal alouette (lark). Her food is a good value.

A la carte: 200F. Menus: 95F and 120F (wine incl.).

Concorde Palm Beach

2, promenade de la Plage 91.76.20.00 / G7-17

Open year-round. 3 stes 1,360F. 139 rms 465-520F. TV. Air cond. Pets allowed. Pool. Garage parking. Telex 401894. Cards: V, AE, DC, MC.

All the rooms in this large hotel complex, which is built against the high rocks, have balconies overlooking the sea. The functional decor has no particular charm. Indoor swimming pool. Restaurant.

Concorde Prado

11, ave. de Mazargues 91.76.51.11 / G4-7

Open year-round. 1 ste. 99 rms 465-520F. TV. Air cond. Pets allowed. Garage parking. Telex 420209. Cards: V, AE, DC.

A modern luxury hotel near the Palais des Congrès with pleasant, rather office-style rooms and a nearby pool and beach. Shopping gallery, meeting rooms and restaurant.

13 Cousin Cousine

102, cours Julien - 91.48.14.50 / E3-9

M. Sellam. Open until 10:30 p.m. Closed Sun., Mon., Oct. 1-15 & Feb. 15-28. Terrace dining. Pets allowed. Cards: V, AE, DC.

The decor here—smart, polished, with clinging plants and a country buffet chest—is perhaps more comfortable than warm. Tables are nicely set, which puts diners at ease for sampling the unique cuisine of Jean-Luc Sellam, who has found a perfect balance between tradition and creativity. The short but intelligent list of offerings includes a millefeuille of salmon and duck liver, bass filet with a green dressing, roe purée and olive oil, a galette of potatoes and sweetbreads with morels, and divine desserts. We're sorry to report that the budget fixed-price lunch menu has disappeared.

A la carte: 280-300F. Menus: 130F, 180F.

12/20 L'Epuisette

Vallon des Auffes - 91.52.17.82 / D7-41

M. Bonnet. Open until 10 p.m. Closed Sat., Sun. & Dec. 24-Jan. 30. Terrace dining. Pets allowed. Parking. Cards: V, AE, DC.

Since his place has all the charm of the vallon des Auffes, plus that of a small wooden terrace above the water, the owner hardly needs to fish for clients. The key to this cuisine is its regionality: bouillabaisse, bourride, grilled fish and a delicious piece of fresh salmon grilled with coarse salt.

A la carte: 300F and up.

Esterel

124, rue Paradis - 91.37.13.90 / F4-22

Open year-round. 28 rms 164-284F. TV. Air cond. Parking. Telex 420425. Cards: V, DC, MC.

Air-conditioned rooms (most of them soundproofed) in a residential district. Numerous services. No restaurant.

12/20 A la Folle Epoque

10, pl. Félix-Baret - 91.33.17.26 / E4-28

M. Costantini. Open until 11 p.m. Closed Sun. Terrace dining. Pets allowed. Cards: V.

Clever Marseille-style brasserie cooking is served good-naturedly under the energetic direction of a Corsican-Lyonnaise owner: haddock brandade with small beans, swordfish steak with shallots, navarin of lamb with artichokes, fresh chèvre with crushed strawberries. The decor has

been redone in a blandly picturesque style.
A la carte: 200-250F. Menus: 95F (lunch only), 125F.

12/20 **La Garbure**

9, cours Julien - 91.47.18.01 / E3-38
M. Lafargue. Open until 10:30 p.m. Closed Sat. lunch, Sun., Mon. & Aug. 1-17. Air cond. Pets allowed. Cards: V.

The vaults of this lovely candlelit cellar are quite well suited to the wonderful Gascon and Béarn culinary traditions: foie gras, breast of duck with chanterelles, fresh noodles with foie gras and duck, and tourtière (meat pie) with Armagnac. Choose from Madiran and Cahors wines, as well as fine Armagnacs.
A la carte: 250F.

Grand Hôtel de Genève

3 bis, rue Reine-Elisabeth
91.90.51.42 / D4-23
Open year-round. 4 stes 396F. 45 rms 148-330F. TV in 33 rms. Telex 440672. Cards: V, DC.

This old but modernized hotel is located near La Canebière, in a relatively quiet pedestrian zone. It holds classic, comfortable, beautiful rooms. No restaurant.

Grand Hôtel de Noailles

68, La Canebière - 91.54.91.48 / D3-43
Open year-round. 4 stes 450-700F. 66 rms 250-540F. Half-board oblig. in seas. TV. Air cond. in 45 rms. Telex 430609. Cards: V, AE, DC, MC.

In the center of Marseille, at the top of La Canebière, the Grand Hôtel de Noailles features large, quiet rooms with double-paned windows and bathrooms. Restaurant.

Ibis Prado

6, rue de Cassis - 91.25.73.73 / G4-14
Open year-round. 118 rms 240-290F. TV. Air cond. Pets allowed. Parking. Telex 400362. Cards: V, MC.

Located near the Palais des Congrès, the Ibis offers functional rooms that were recently redone. The hotel is well equipped. Restaurant.

12/20 **Au Jambon de Parme**

67, rue de la Palud - 91.54.37.98 / E4-33
M. Giravalli. Open until 10:15 p.m. Closed Sun. dinner, Mon. & July 14-Aug. 17. Air cond. Pets allowed. Cards: V, AE, DC, MC.

Au Jambon de Parme, still in all its splendor, carries on Marseille's elegant bourgeois tradition. The flower-filled decor is both comfortable and refined, and the service is professional and impeccable. But the cooking is slowly declining: The salad with two salmons tasted as if it had sat in the refrigerator (was it prepared in advance?), though the beef with green pepper was decent. The pastries were nothing extraordinary. No longer worth one toque.
A la carte: 250-300F.

Lutétia

38, allées Léon Gambetta
91.50.81.78 / D3-15
Open year-round. 29 rms 189-209F. TV. Pets allowed. Cards: V, DC.

Located on a quiet street near the porte d'Aix, the recently redone rooms are now modern and bright. No restaurant.

13 **Michel**

6, rue des Catalans - 91.52.64.22
See Calypso (across the street).

15 **Miramar**

12, quai du Port - 91.91.10.40 / D5-44
MM. Minguella. Open until 10 p.m. Closed Sun., Aug. 1-22 & Dec. 23-Jan. 9. Air cond. Terrace dining. Pets allowed. Cards: V, AE, DC, MC.

The ultra-kitsch dining room is marked by wrought iron, parchment lamp shades and a terrace that overlooks the port. Marseille's high society fills this place and swoons over young Dominique Passeron's cuisine: sardines marinated in a lemon confit, warm artichoke mousse with a mussel cream sauce, whole bass braised in raspberry vinegar, bass steak lightly sautéed with oranges, sumptuous bouillabaisse (also one of the lowest priced along the port). The Miramar's is among the best cuisine in Marseille, and clearly it is headed for glory. The lively, friendly service is directed by the chef's brother, Pierre. Light homemade pastries and cleverly chosen wines.
A la carte: 300F and up.

New Hotel Astoria

10, blvd. Garibaldi - 91.33.33.50 / D3-3
Open year-round. 58 rms 220-280F. TV. Air cond. Cards: V, AE, DC.

This small hotel, newly renovated, is located near La Canebière. Bright, large well-equipped rooms. No restaurant.

13 **New York**

7, quai des Belges - 91.33.60.98, 91.33.91.79 / D4-27
Mme. Venturini. Open daily until 11:30 p.m. Air cond. Pets allowed. Cards: V, AE, DC, MC.

This is one of those rare places where a superb view (in this case, of the most beautiful port under the Mediterranean sun) isn't a smokescreen for a ruinous, sloppily prepared, poorly served cuisine. One of the most brilliant crowds in Marseille frequents this small southern "Lipp," with its comfortable '50s decor. The Venturinis are delightful hosts, and the short menu lists some irreproachable dishes: rock fish soup, lotte bourride and calf's head.
A la carte: 250F.

11/20 **L'Oursin**

14, cours Jean-Ballard
91.33.34.85 / D5-36
M. Cazanave. Open until 11 p.m. Closed July-Aug. Pets allowed. Cards: V.

Urchin omelets, sorrel-flavored lotte, shellfish platters and other varieties of fresh, unpretentious seafood are promptly served in a convivial, all-white setting. Find little wines.

A la carte: 180-200F.

16 L'Oursinade

Rue Neuve-St-Martin (Centre Bourse)
91.91.91.29 / C4-12

M. Pelaud. Open until 10 p.m. Closed Sun., holidays & Aug. Air cond. Terrace dining. Pets allowed. Parking. Telex 401886. Cards: V, AE, DC, MC.

Lyon native René Alloin, trained by Alain Senderens, has been in the kitchens here for ten years, in a restaurant with an ultra-functional but harmonious ambience in a modern hotel in the center of town. The cuisine can best be described as modern and earthy, combining creativity and the use of the region's favorite, stunning products: shellfish tartare with salmon marinated in anise; crayfish and oyster cassolette with white Bandol wine; sole and salmon enlivened with roe; breast of duck with apricot and lime. Also served are excellent cheeses from Georges Bataille and wonderful, feather-light desserts (grapefruit and bitter-chocolate sorbets). Next door is L'Oliveraie, a fine quick-bites place serving salads and grilled dishes. Beautiful fixed-price menus.

A la carte: 300F and up. Menus: 165F, 200F, 239F.

Altea

(See restaurant above)

Open year-round. 1 ste 1,050F. 198 rms 400-650F. TV. Air cond.

The perfectly equipped, modern rooms are elegantly decorated. Situated near the Vieux Port and La Canebière, with direct access to the shopping gallery of the Centre Bourse.

12/20 Panzani

17, rue Mont-Grand
91.54.72.72 / E4-11

M. Panzani. Open until 9:30 p.m. Closed Sat. lunch (& Sat. dinner in summer), Mon. dinner, Sun., 3 weeks in Aug. & Dec. 25-Jan. 2. Air cond. No pets. Cards: V, AE.

The decor, with its booths, soft lighting and carpets, is now pleasantly warm; and M. Panzani's cuisine, consisting of good, seasonal, uncomplicated dishes, is still tasty: galinette (Mediterranean fish) tartare, lobster brouillade (stew), veal kidney with pickled lemon. We'd like to make a suggestion: Le Zinc's business clientele would surely appreciate the addition of a reasonably priced fixed lunch menu.

A la carte: 230-250F.

17 Passédat

Corniche Kennedy, Anse de Maldormé
91.52.14.39, 91.59.25.92 / E7-35

M. Passédat. Open until 10 p.m. (11:30 p.m. in summer). Closed Mon. (except dinner in summer) & Jan. 2-31. Air cond. No pets. Garage parking. Telex 401565. Cards: V, AE.

The father-and-son team of Jean-Paul and Gérard Passédat is flying high with a fine haute cuisine and prices to match. Although steep tabs and fine food do not always come together, Gérard's many stunning dishes merit their prices. It is now clear that he is indeed a serious practitioner, not just a playboy, as will attest the Marseille-style truffled cod, the little vegetables in an anchovy dressing, the thick soup of frogs' legs, pigs' trotters and basil, the marvelous tart of zucchini flowers and potatoes. Or the oyster and sage soup under a rye crust, the delicious red snapper and the firm, surprisingly tasty bass filet in olive oil—not to mention the lobster with tomato and mixed grains and the sweetbreads with purple artichokes and a clove cream.

So what is all this worth? Three toques for sure and one day maybe even more. We only hope that Gérard Passédat doesn't get thrown by his success, that he keeps a level (and unswollen) head and continues to marshal his imagination in the service of an honest and serious cuisine. And that the who's who in Marseille begin to discover his superb fixed-price lunch menu. In any case, Passédat, where they do all the little things right, remains unrivaled for an enchanting evening. In summer or spring, with the sea and the islands as a backdrop, the floodlit garden is a tropical paradise.

A la carte: 550-700F. Menus: 270F (weekday lunch only, wine incl.), 460F, 500F.

Le Petit Nice

(See restaurant above)

Closed Jan. 2-31. 4 stes 2,100-2,200F. 14 rms 800-1,000F. Half-board 1,350-1,750F oblig. in seas. TV. Air cond. Pool.

A remarkable hotel, several minutes from the Vieux Port, with a small number of luxurious lodgings. Most of the suites overlook the sea and a pleasant garden. Large baths, saltwater swimming pool. Relais et Châteaux.

12/20 Patalain

49, rue Sainte - 91.55.02.78 / E5-39

Mme. Quaglia. Open until 10:30 p.m. Closed Sat. lunch, Sun. & Aug. 1-Sept. 2. Air cond. Pets allowed. Cards: V, AE, DC.

Mme. Quaglia's cooking is improving by leaps and bounds: coquilles St-Jacques in a light herb broth, scorpionfish filet in a perfect marrow sauce, precisely cooked farm pigeon and lovely accompanying vegetables. We can report progress on all fronts, including the regional fixed-price menu and the marvelous new decor. So we'll up the rating two points.

A la carte: 250-280F. Menus: 140F (lunch only), 260F.

12/20 Peron

56, corniche Kennedy
91.52.43.70 / D7-31

M. Frittoli. Open until 9:45 p.m. Closed Sun. dinner, Mon. & Jan. Pets allowed. Cards: V, AE, DC, MC.

The superb terrace facing the road gives the feeling, because of its air shaft, that one is lunching on the promenade deck of an ocean liner. The cooking is thoroughly conventional (bouillabaisse, grilled fish, bourride and so on), but its execution is meticulous—quite enough to make it original.

A la carte: 280-300F.

12/20 Au Pescadou

19, pl. Castellane - 91.78.36.01 / F4-8

M. Mennella. Open until 11 p.m. Closed Sun. dinner (off-seas.) & July-Aug. Air cond. Pets allowed. Telex 402417. Cards: V.

The new, bright, inviting dining area overlooks a large Napoléon III fountain. The cuisine remains classic, though it has been supplemented with some lightness: superb shellfish, shellfish quenelles and a complete array of grilled fish. The prices are almost reasonable for this type of seafood, especially in Marseille.

A la carte: 250-300F.

Pullman Beauvau

4, rue Beauvau - 91.54.91.00 / D4-25

Open year-round. 1 ste 1,200F. 71 rms 500-650F. TV. Air cond. Telex 401778. Cards: V, AE, DC, MC.

Entirely renovated, this splendid hotel, well situated on the Vieux Port, has not lost its charm. The comfortable, bright rooms are well soundproofed. Room service is offered until one in the morning.

12/20 Le Régent

324, ave. du Prado - 91.22.05.05 / G4-5

M. Rossi. Open until 10:30 p.m. Closed Sun. Air cond. Pets allowed. Cards: V, AE, DC.

Le Régent is a prosperous-looking place on the second floor of the most prestigious tower in town. The new owner, a former chef at La Cabro d'Or, is a serious and experienced cook who prepares assorted seafood in a warm marinade, saffron-flavored turbot and veal kidney cooked in its juice. The service is youthful and efficient.

A la carte: 280-300F. Menu: 180F.

Résidence Sainte-Anne

50, blvd. Verne - 91.71.54.54 / G4-26

Open year-round. 43 rms 250-280F. TV. Air cond. Parking. Telex 441082. Cards: V, AE, DC.

Located close to the Prado square, Résidence Sainte-Anne is a comfortable, quiet, modern hotel. Restaurant.

Sofitel

See Les Trois Forts restaurant.

(13) La Table d'Albret

5, rue Ste-Cécile - 91.80.07.93 / F3-19

Mme. Moreni-Garron. Open until 10 p.m. Closed Sat. lunch, Sun., Jan. 1-7 & July 20-Aug. 31. Air cond. Pets allowed. Cards: V, AE.

A loyal following returns every day to this lively, smart little restaurant with a low ceiling and lots of flowers. A southwest accent can be detected in the cuisine, which is presented generously and with much finesse. Jeanne Moreni-Garron has a light touch, even when she prepares her fine cassoulet or fresh pasta with foie gras and morels. Breast of duck is prepared in a variety of ways. And the confits and the daube with wine aren't to be missed. Fine Madiran wines and Armagnac.

A la carte: 250F. Menus: 100F (lunch only), 150F.

> *Red toques signify modern cuisine; black toques signify traditional cuisine.*

(13) Le Tire-Bouchon

11, cours Julien - 91.42.49.03 / E3-38

M. Richard. Open until 1:30 a.m. Closed Sun. & Mon. Terrace dining. Pets allowed. Cards: V, DC, MC.

Only impromptu, seasonal cuisine finds favor with Jean-Claude Richard, a latecomer (but with such enthusiasm!) to imaginative cuisine. The menu is handwritten, of course, and is completed by a slate that lists last-minute dishes: a basket of asparagus with coquilles St-Jacques, a raw-fish salad with mango and ginger, duck leg roasted with honey and spices and an émincé of calves' liver in butter with sweet red pepper. Catherine, the owner's wife, is an exuberant hostess, and a pitcher of red or rosé Côtes-du-Rhône won't make your check too steep.

A la carte: 250F.

(13) Les Trois Forts

36, blvd. Charles-Livon
91.52.90.19 / D7-32

M. Chadel. Open daily until 10 p.m. Air cond. Pets allowed. Garage parking. Telex 401270. Cards: V, AE, DC, MC.

Since two-toque chef Marc Bayon left, the kitchen here is in the hands of young Philippe Noël, whose talent justifies a little more attention to the quality of his ingredients and to the dowdy decor of the dining room. There is clearly, however, much to look forward to from this young talent, not to mention the pleasure he's already providing with his cauliflower in a raw tomato coulis, perfectly cooked fresh cod in aromatic herbs and the dainty, prepared-to-order desserts. The curious wine list includes several half bottles that cost less than half the price of a full bottle.

A la carte: 300-350F. Menus: 150F (lunch only, wine incl.), 150F (dinner only).

Sofitel

(See restaurant above)

Open year-round. 3 stes 1,650-1,950F. 127 rms 550-650F. TV. Air cond. Pets allowed. Pool.

Near the Vieux Port and facing the Pharo palace and its gardens, the Sofitel is comfortable, well climatized and soundproofed.

Mauzac

24150 Lalinde - (Dordogne)
Paris 545 - Périgueux 62 - Sarlat 54 - Bergerac 29

La Métairie 

Rte. du Cingle-de-Trémolat
53.22.50.47

Closed Nov.-April 28. 1 ste 785F. 9 rms 525-670F. Half-board 475-685F oblig. in seas. TV in 6 rms. Pool. Parking. Telex 572717. Cards: V, MC.

This lovely Périgourd residence, relaxing and beautifully rustic, sits in a park with a delightful pool. Relais et Châteaux.

Meaux

77100 Meaux - (Seine-et-Marne)
Paris 54 - Reims 98 - Melun 57 - Compiègne 69

IN NEARBY **Poincy**
(6 km NE)
77470 Trilport - (Seine-et-Marne)

(14) Le Moulin de Poincy

Rue du Moulin - 60.23.06.80
M. Abit. Open until 9:15 p.m. Closed Tues. dinner, Wed. & Christmas school vacation. Garden dining. Pets allowed. Cards: V, AE, DC.

Armel Abit recently set up shop in this old mill on the banks of the Marne, seeking to restore not only the building but the restaurant's reputation, which declined following the war. The beamed-ceiling dining room opens onto a pleasant garden, where one can dine in good weather under the linden trees. The staff is young, cheerful and inexperienced, and the cuisine is full of curiosity and a concern for lightness: a wonderful salad of lobster and foie gras, served generously with green beans (slightly overcooked), turbot grilled in its skin with an exquisite beurre rouge sauce, Challans duckling with fresh figs, and a gigantic, old-fashioned strawberry feuilleté (a bit heavy). Unfortunately, the bearded Abit sometimes tries to do too much—too many sorbets, for example. Good regional cheeses.

A la carte: 300F. Menus: 175F (weekdays only), 280F.

IN NEARBY **Sancy-lès-Meaux**
(12 km S on N 36 & D 228)
77580 Crécy-la-Chapelle - (Seine-et-Marne)

Demeure de la Catounière

1, rue de l'Eglise - 60.25.71.74
Closed Aug. 16-31 & Dec. 15-31. 22 rms 320F. Half-board 370- 530F oblig. in seas. TV. Heated pool. Tennis. Parking. Telex 690375. Cards: V, AE, DC, MC.

An old estate has been transformed into a weekend inn, with a covered pool, tennis, riding club and spacious rooms with excellent facilities and views of the woods.

Megève

74120 Megève - (Haute-Savoie)
Paris 613 - Chamonix 35 - Geneva 72 - Lyon 197

12/20 Auberge Les Griottes

Rte. de Megève - 50.21.24.43
M. Allesiardi. Open until 9:30 p.m. Closed Mon., Easter school vacation-May 15 & end Oct.-end Nov. Garden dining. Pets allowed. Parking. Cards: V, DC, MC.

A former Cannes Film Festival director opened this agreeable Savoie chalet. The Paris-trained chef's fish-based cuisine is pleasant: cod aïoli, brill suprême. The reception is cordial, the prices low.

A la carte: 180-200F. Menus: 70F (lunch only), 105F, 150F.

Chalet du Mont d'Arbois

(See restaurant above)
Closed April 18-June 18. 1 ste 3,100-4,700F (half-board). 20 rms 550-1,900F. Half-board 880-2,400F for 2, oblig. in seas. TV. Pets allowed. Heated pool. Tennis. Golf. Cards: V, AE, DC, MC.

This beautiful and comfortable mountain chalet was decorated with excellent taste in Savoyard style. Eight new rooms and a new suite are planned as part of the ongoing renovation. Restaurant. Relais et Châteaux.

Au Coin du Feu

Rte. de Rochebrune - 50.21.04.94
Closed April 15-July 1 & Sept. 1-Dec. 15. 4 stes 1,240-1,350F (half-board only). 19 rms 700-1,040F (half-board only). TV. Pets allowed. Cards: V.

Much warmth is evident in the decor of these charming rooms. Sauna and steam bath. Two restaurants, one serving Savoyard specialties.

Le Fer à Cheval

Rte. du Crêt-d'Arbois - 50.21.30.39
Closed April 15-July 1 & Oct. 15-Dec. 15. 19 stes 850-1,150F. 27 rms 600F. Half-board 400-450F oblig. in seas. TV. Pets allowed. Garage parking. Cards: V.

This elegant little chalet was renovated recently, and its rooms now have lots of character and warmth. Attractive salon with fireplace; dining in the evening only.

Mont-Blanc

Pl. de l'Eglise - 50.21.20.02
Closed April 9-June 1 & Sept. 17-Oct. 30. 6 stes 1,650-2,850F. 44 rms 650-1,650F. Half-board 950-1,450F. TV. Heated pool. Parking. Telex 385854. Cards: V, AE, DC, MC.

The Mont-Blanc remains a luxury hotel of charm, the most sought-after residence in the region. It offers attractive rooms with elegant furnishings, a beautiful interior terrace with a pool, in front of which you can have lunch in the sun. A sauna, a nightclub and a restaurant.

(13) Le Mont-Joly

Rue du Crêt-du-Midi - 50.21.26.14
M. Philippe. Open until 9 p.m. Closed Easter-June 15 & Sept. 15-Dec. 20. Terrace dining. No pets. Hotel: 22 rms 500-540F; half-board 480-550F oblig. in seas. Parking. Cards: V, AE, DC, MC.

This clean, comfortable little hotel (fairly quiet despite its central location), has just hired a new young chef who seems eager to make his mark. The attention he pays to the accompanying vegetables, the fine sauces and the refined presentation is already making this one of the better spots to eat in the resort area. Try the very light gâteau of young rabbit, the ravioli of prawns in a vinaigrette and the lamb with eggplant. The unfortunate decor is hardly worthy of such good food, which is served elegantly and efficiently.

A la carte: 280-300F.

La Résidence
Rte. du Bouchet - 50.21.43.69

Closed April 15-June 15 & Sept. 15-Dec. 15. 56 rms 400-890F. Half-board 405-605F oblig. in seas. TV. Pets allowed. Heated pool. Tennis. Garage parking. Telex 385164. Cards: V, AE, DC, MC.

This luxurious hotel is located at the foot of the Rochebrune ski lift. The atmosphere is young and lively, and there's lots to do (shopping arcade, piano bar, discotheque). Restaurant.

Ménerbes
84560 Ménerbes - (Vaucluse)
Paris 713 - Cavaillon 16 - Apt 21 - Bonnieux 12

Le Roy Soleil
Rte. des Baumettes, Le Fort - 90.72.51.54

M. Derine. Open until 9:30 p.m. Closed Wed. lunch & Nov. 15-March 25. Garden dining. No pets. Parking. Cards: V, MC.

The vaulted stone arches make for an alluring decor that's elegant though lacking originality. The ambience is a bit ceremonious, in the image of the cuisine, which tries too hard to be chic. We'd like to see more ideas, variety and lightness, but we must admit that the execution is skillful and the products of excellent quality: crab feuilleté in a shellfish sauce, breast of lamb with sauce royale, sweetbreads in Champagne.

A la carte: 250-300F. Menu: 160F (lunch only).

Le Roy Soleil
(See restaurant above)

Closed Nov. 15-March 25. 2 stes 850-950F. 12 rms 320-700F. Half-board 380-640F oblig. in seas. TV. Pool. Tennis.

An old, skillfully renovated stone farmhouse is set in gardens and surrounded by vines and cherry trees, with the Luberon landscape as a backdrop. The rooms are comfortable and cheerful. This makes for a delightful vacation way station.

Menton
06500 Menton - (Alpes-Maritimes)
Paris 961 - Nice 31 - Cannes 63 - Monte-Carlo 9

Europ Hôtel
35, ave. de Verdun - 93.35.59.92

Open year-round. 33 rms 300-500F. TV. Air cond. Parking. Telex 470673. Cards: V, AE, DC, MC.

A modern hotel on a courtyard 200 meters from the old town and the sea. Spacious, comfortable rooms. No restaurant.

12/20 L'Oursin
3, rue Trenca - 93.28.33.62

M. Casademont. Open until 10 p.m. Closed Wed. Terrace dining. Pets allowed. Cards: V, AE, MC.

The owner makes it a point of honor to serve only local fish, which he grills simply with lemon and oil. The result is good and inexpensive, which is why it's always crowded here. Excellent aïoli is served on Fridays. If only all the bistros on the coast were like this one!

A la carte: 220-250F.

IN NEARBY **Ponte San Ludovico**
(1 km E, in Italy)

Balzi Rossi
(Les Rochers Rouges)
Piazzale de Gasperi - (184) 38.132

M. Beglia. Open until 9:30 p.m. Closed Sun. dinner (in winter), Mon., Tues. lunch (in summer) & Nov. 13-30. Air cond. Pets allowed. Parking. Cards: AE, DC.

The modern, flowery decor is highlighted with beige marble and turquoise curtains, and the view extends as far as Cap Martin and Menton bay, but from the Italian perspective. How can one resist such a fine cuisine, even if it means crossing customs and driving a kilometer into Italy? Try the rabbit terrine au spumante (sparkling) with an onion confit, tagliolini with pesto, baked scampi with braised leeks and breast of duck with lentils. This charming family house serves 100 other fine dishes, all of which are well seasoned and have a lightness that's not exactly common in Italian-mamma cuisine. The prices, unfortunately, are growing increasingly hard to swallow.

A la carte: 450-500F. Menus: 200F (lunch only), 300F (wine incl.), 375F (weekdays only).

Mercuès
see Cahors

Mercurey
71640 Givry - (Saône-et-Loire)
Paris 348 - Autun 40 - Chalon 13 - Mâcon 70 - Chagny 12

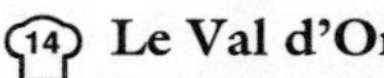

Le Val d'Or
Grand-Rue - 85.45.13.70

M. Cogny. Open until 9 p.m. Closed Sun. dinner (off-seas.), Tues. lunch (in seas.), Mon., Aug. 27-Sept. 4 & Dec. 17-Jan. 17. Air cond. No pets. Hotel: 11 rms 195-320F; half-board oblig. in seas. Garage parking. Cards: V.

Delightful one year, disappointing the next—that's the situation that confronts returning customers here. The place doesn't lack wagon wheels and other rustic paraphernalia; instead, it lacks consistency in the cooking: an excellent salmon-and-pike custard but a sad, woefully overcooked lamb chop. Desserts also run this unfortunate gamut (a delicious sorbet, for example, is waylaid by some nasty profiteroles). Despite the warm reception and excellent wine list, we have to move the ranking down one point.

A la carte: 300-400F. Menus: 130F, 190F, 290F.

Méribel-les-Allues
73550 Méribel-les-Allues - (Savoie)
Paris 637 - Chambéry 93 - Albertville 45 - Annecy 90

Altiport Hôtel
79.00.52.32

Closed April 20-June 25 & Sept. 25-Dec. 20. 8 stes 900F. 34 rms 500-600F. Half-board 690F oblig. in seas. TV. Heated pool. Tennis. Golf. Garage parking. Telex 980456. Cards: V, AE, DC.

A comfortable chalet pleasantly decorated in the most modern taste, with extremely attractive rooms in a rustic style. In summer, tennis, golf and bridge workshops are offered. Restaurant.

Belvédère

79.08.65.53

Closed April 15-Dec. 15. 17 rms 255-450F (half-board only). No pets. Parking. Cards: V, AE, DC, MC.

Recently renovated rooms are located in a nice large wooden chalet beautifully situated near the ski lifts. Large south-facing terrace for meals.

(13) L'Estanquet

Résidence La Tougnette - 79.08.65.43, 79.08.64.25

Mme. Arbulo. Open until 10 p.m. Closed April 15-Dec. 1. Pets allowed. Cards: V, AE, DC.

When the north wind blows, Pépette Arbulo leaves Estanquet in the Landes for this modern ground-floor restaurant. Postcards, vegetable confit and a pleasant atmosphere help re-create the atmosphere of a family bistro. On the first floor, Arbulo serves modest wines from back home with large tartines (open-face sandwiches), and on the mezzanine he serves Landaise salads with country ham and cou farci (stuffed goose neck), duck aiguillettes, escargots ragoût and a warm and delicious tourtière (fruit pastry). Needless to say, you should avoid the fantasy (untraditional) dishes in such a place (the sole pot-au-feu had a watery taste). Prices are climbing rather quickly.

A la carte: 250-300F. Menus: 130F, 160, 240F.

(14) Le Grand Coeur

79.08.60.03

M. Buchert. Open until 10 p.m. Closed April 17-June 30 & Sept. 4-Dec. 15. Garden dining. Pets allowed. Parking. Telex 309623. Cards: V, AE, DC.

This cozy cottage-inn has become the darling of this resort town since the new owner hired an excellent chef, Patrick Beekes. His is a lovely cuisine, simple yet knowing and demonstrating technical mastery. Our latest meal in this pleasing beamed dining room almost earned the two toques he wore at his former post: half-cooked salmon in a wonderful lemon marinade, very fine bass with a delicate ratatouille and saffron, locally raised milk chevreau (kid) roasted with rosemary and perfectly flavored desserts (pear charlotte, blueberry tart, citrus salad). The wine list is a bit of a mess, though it does offer some good Savoie selections.

A la carte: 350-400F. Menus: 135F (lunch only), 240F (dinner only).

Le Grand Coeur

(See restaurant above)

Closed April 17-June 30 & Sept. 4-Dec. 15. 9 stes 1,980F-2,600F. 42 rms 850-1,700F. Half-board 530-1,000F oblig. in seas. TV. Pets allowed. Heated pool. Garage parking. Telex 309623. Cards: V, AE, DC.

These spacious, well-conceived rooms have just been renovated. They offer direct access to the slopes and numerous facilities. Relais et Châteaux.

IN NEARBY **Mottaret**

(6 km S)

73550 Méribel-les-Allues - (Savoie)

Mont Vallon

79.00.44.00

Closed May 1-Dec. 1. 6 stes 1,000-1,500F (half-board). 57 rms 700-1,000F (half-board). TV. No pets. Heated pool. Telex 309192. Cards: V, AE, DC.

This huge, sumptuous chalet was recently opened on the edge of the ski slopes. Intimate wood decor, with warmth and elegance, extremely comfortable rooms and good facilities (swimming, squash). Restaurant.

Merville-Franceville-Plage

see Cabourg

Les Mesnuls

see Montfort-l'Amaury

Metz

57000 Metz - (Moselle)

Paris 313 - Nancy 59 - Strasbourg 157 - Luxembourg 60

Sights. Saint-Etienne cathedral (Gothic, with Chagall stained glass); Saint-Pierre-aux-Nonnains church (one of the oldest in France); Chapelle des Templiers (octagonal shaped); the old village granary (fifteenth century); pl. St-Louis (arched facades); Porte des Allemands (thirteenth and fifteenth centuries); Gare de Metz (William II style); Musée d'Art et d'Histoire (one of the best organized in the provinces, on the site of old Roman baths).

Eating on the Run. Les Amandines, 3 bis, quai Félix-Mal (nice tea salon); Buffalo Grill, 11, pl. de Chambre (excellent meats); Royal Pub, 15, rue du Petit-Paris (facing the Saint-Jacques center); Le Samovar, 3, rue des Parmentiers (tea salon).

Brasseries. ABC, 2, pl. du Général-de-Gaulle; A la Belle Epoque, 6, rue de la Tête-d'Or; Le Rallye, 20 bis, ave. Robert-Schuman; La République, 11, ave. Robert-Schuman.

Bars & Cafés. Bar de l'Altea, 29, pl. St-Thiébault (attractive and comfortable); Bar des Roches, 27, rue des Roches; Sofitel bar, Saint-Jacques commercial center, pl. des Paraiges (refined); Le Caveau, 23, ave. Foch (Royal Concorde bar).

Shops. *Bakeries:* Au Bon Pain de France, 27, pl. de Chambre; Doyotte, 34, rue des Clercs; Gilet, 66, rue Serpenoise. *Gourmet foods:* Carcano, 29, rue St-Livier. *Pastries:* Bourguignon, 31, rue de la Tête-d'Or; Koenig, 11, rue Pasteur (the best chocolates and ice cream); Moisson, 4, pl. du Général-de-Gaulle.

(13) Le Cambout

1, rue de Cambout - 87.74.56.16

Mme. Staub. Open until midnight. Closed Sat. lunch & Sun. Pets allowed. Cards: V, AE, DC, MC.

There is nothing very inviting about this immense building attached to Sainte-Blandine hospital. Inside, though, it's bright, warm and attractive, with comfortable bamboo furniture and beautiful china. The service is fine, and the list of offerings short but sweet. The no-frills modernism could benefit by a bit more generosity. Try the Scandinavian-style salmon, well seasoned and rolled in a light cream, and the pleasant blend of sweetbreads and kidneys in parsley butter. Desserts are uneven—the oranges aux oranges was rather uninteresting. Wine prices are on the steep side, like the rest of the offerings.

A la carte: 250-300F. Menus: 100F and 160F (wine incl.).

(14) Le Crinouc

79-81, rue du Général-Metman
87.74.12.46, 87.74.04.88

M. Lamaze. Open until 9:30 p.m. Closed Sat. lunch, Sun. dinner, Mon. & Aug. Pets allowed. Hotel: 9 rms 200-210F. Parking. Cards: V, AE, DC.

Ignore the gloomy suburban setting and the decor overwhelmed with velour and chandeliers. The rest will be worth it: a fine reception, devoted service and, particularly, the improving cuisine of the new owner, Jean-Claude Lamaze. His refinement, invention and perfect execution are explained by his training with some of the top chefs in France. Those qualities are evident in his dishes: red mullet salad chaud-froid, topped with a superb vinaigrette that's full of sunshine; sander with fresh noodles, highlighted with a simple, tart sauce; saddle of young rabbit with langoustines (a happy discovery). The chocolate parfait is plentiful, but it was its quality that reaffirmed the chef's reputation for outstanding desserts.

A la carte: 300F. Menus: 90F (weekdays only), 145F, 215F.

(15) La Dinanderie

2, rue de Paris - 87.30.14.40

MM. Piergiorgi. Open until 9:30 p.m. Closed Sun., Mon., Feb. school vacation & Aug. 8-31. Air cond. Pets allowed. Cards: V, AE.

An intimate atmosphere, beautiful china, beaded curtains surrounding the pretty round tables—the decor appears a bit dated, but it suffices. There is more evidence of good humor and simplicity at the table d'hôte, an open table where diners can taste whatever dishes they wish. Claude Piergiorgi is an innovative and skillful technician, and his refreshing young rabbit terrine in a vegetable aspic, thick salmon steak perfectly cooked in a fine chive-mustard sauce and accompanied by broad beans, and delicious kiwi "à la coque" with a banana-lime sorbet help maintain the stature of this spot (away from the center of town) as one of the best restaurants in the region. Don't miss the terrific foie gras and the dark-chocolate sorbet. Beautiful wines and a gracious, dedicated hostess of the house, Marthe.

A la carte: 300F. Menus: 115F (weekday lunch only), 160F (weekdays only), 215F, 300F.

> *Some establishments change their hours and annual closings without warning. It is always wise to call ahead.*

Foch

8, ave. Foch - 87.74.40.75, 87.75.56.42

Open year-round. 42 rms 109-226F. TV in 8 rms. Telex 860489. Cards: V, MC.

A nice, no-surprises way station on the plaza, near the fountain. No restaurant.

Royal Concorde

23, ave. Foch - 87.66.81.11

Open year-round. 6 stes 585-950F. 69 rms 305-485F. Half-board 470-682F. TV. Telex 860425. Cards: V, AE, DC, MC.

In this renovated turn-of-the-century building, some of the rooms are modern, some stylish, and all are comfortable and soundproofed. Two restaurants.

Meudon

see PARIS SUBURBS

Meximieux

01800 Meximieux - (Ain)
Paris 452 - Nantua 57 - Lyon 36 - Bourg 35 - Ambérieu 15

(14) Claude Lutz

17, rue de Lyon - 74.61.06.78

M. Lutz. Open until 9 p.m. Closed Sun. dinner, Mon., July 17- 24 & Oct. 16-Nov. 8. Pets allowed. Hotel: 16 rms 110-260F. Parking. Cards: V, AE.

Claude Lutz, a pupil of Paul Bocuse and the Troisgros, is an exemplary professional; his virtues, however, are consistency, sobriety and honesty more than imagination and personality. The chic Louis XIII decor made this place such a hit that he had to expand it. Food lovers in the region appreciate the artichoke-bottom salad with shrimp and foie gras, the frogs' legs on a bed of watercress with a mousseline accompaniment and the turbot stew with Gamay wine, among other dishes.

A la carte: 250F. Menus: 130F, 170F, 270F.

Meyrueis

48150 Meyrueis - (Lozère)
Paris 630 - Millau 42 - Florac 35 - Mende 58 - Le Vigan 56

Château d'Ayres

66.45.60.10

Closed Oct. 15-March 23. 3 stes 480-510F. 21 rms 260-510F. Half-board 260-385F. TV in 16 rms. Air cond. in 24 rms. Tennis. Parking. Cards: V, AE, DC.

A splendid twelfth-century Benedictine monastery, with superb exterior restoration, was transformed into a hotel with spacious rooms that have lodged the likes of Charles de Gaulle. It's set in a marvelous twelve-acre wooded estate with giant sequoias. Restaurant.

Millau

12100 Millau - (Aveyron)
Paris 640 - Béziers 125 - Albi 125 - Rodez 71 - Nîmes 166

(13) Capion

3, rue J.-F.-Alméras - 65.60.00.91
M. Airault. Open until 9:30 p.m. Closed Mon. & Feb. 15-March 15. Pets allowed. Cards: V, AE, DC, MC.

The people of this region, who have a reputation as being robust and penny-pinching, extol the virtues of the sort of abundant cuisine that is found in this sanctuary of tradition. Here is a chef who loves his trade and, even more so, his customers. But one doesn't come to dine on this cuisine for its lightness or refinement; rather, it is for the convivial atmosphere and the fine local duck confit, duck salmis (stew), Aveyron salad and delicious farm-raised squab cooked in garlic. Wonderful fixed-price menus offer enormous portions. The provincial oak-parquet decor is charming, and the regional wines are well chosen.

A la carte: 200-250F. Menus: 68F, 85F, 135F, 200F.

(13) International

1, pl. de la Tine - 65.60.20.66
M. Pomarède. Open until 9:30 p.m. Closed Sun. dinner & Jan.-mid-Feb. Air cond. Pets allowed. Garage parking. Telex 520629. Cards: V, AE, DC, MC.

This unusual eight-story hotel rises from the spectacular Aveyron mountains above the city's rooftops. The luxurious restaurant (on the ground floor, unfortunately) has won praise for its efficient and graceful staff, as well as for its veteran chef's steady, generous yet lightened regional cuisine: fine foie gras (weighed down a bit by the accompanying sweet brioche), langoustine gratin, pigeon salmis (stew) with pasta and interesting cakes. One of the finest wine cellars in the region.

A la carte: 230-250F. Menus: 100F, 250F.

International

(See restaurant above)
Open year-round. 8 stes 398-435F. 94 rms 168-370F. Half-board 178-271F. TV in 70 rms. Air cond. in 5 rms. Pets allowed.

An exemplary provincial hotel, well modernized, with pleasant and comfortable rooms. The top floors have breathtaking views, and the staff is exceptionally congenial and efficient.

(14) La Musardière

34, ave. de la République - 65.60.20.63
Mme. Canac. Open until 9 p.m. Closed Mon. & Nov. 4-April 1. Pets allowed. Hotel: 12 rms 300-500F; half-board 380-460F oblig. in seas. Parking. Cards: V, DC.

The graceful high-society crowd has adopted this elegant manor house, which was transformed by Gisèle Canac into a remarkably appealing Relais et Chatêaux. The restaurant owes its success to its salmon millefeuille with chives, duck liver with sherry, thinly sliced lamb with fresh pasta and divinely light and fresh pastries made by the former chef, Michel Dubois. Unfortunately, Dubois left quite recently, and his number two, who was put in charge, does not yet have the same light touch or lively imagination. The food is quite good nonetheless, particularly the mussel soup with saffron, pan-fried duck liver in sherry and the good classic desserts.

A la carte: 250-280F. Menus: 95F, 175F, 205F.

Mimizan

40200 Mimizan - (Landes)
Paris 676 - Bordeaux 108 - Dax 73 - Mont-de-Marsan 74

(15) Au Bon Coin du Lac

34, ave. du Lac - 58.09.01.55
M. Caule. Open until 10 p.m. Closed Sun. dinner, Mon. & Feb. Air cond. Garden dining. No pets. Hotel: 3 stes 320-550F; 5 rms 250-280F. Garage parking. Cards: V, AE.

The no-frills tone suggested from the sign outside is misleading. Enter and you find a large garden shaded with plane trees and white parasols and a luxurious dining room overlooking the lake. This is no workman's café, despite the look from outside. And Jean-Pierre Caule's cuisine attracts food lovers from as far away as Bordeaux. It's a nice out-of-the-way spot in any season, whether you're watching the pedal boats in summer or sitting by a roaring fire in winter. The sincere cuisine has a delicious Landaise accent: red mullet fricassée with fresh cèpes (a dream dish), a creative duck breast pâté with truffles and foie gras in a Saint-Crois-du-Mont wine sauce (a bit flat), crème brûlée "grandma-style." Fine Bordeaux vintages, but poor wine advice.

A la carte: 350-400F. Menus: 120F (weekdays only), 280F (weekends and holidays only), 230F, 300F.

Mionnay

01390 St-André-de-Corcy - (Ain)
Paris 454 - Bourg 42 - Lyon 19 - Meximieux 25

(19.5) Alain Chapel

N 83
78.91.82.02
M. Chapel. Open until 10 p.m. Closed Tues. lunch (except holidays), Mon. & Jan. Garden dining. Pets allowed. Parking. Telex 305605. Cards: V, AE, DC.

The "Blanc effect" has struck again. Georges Blanc was one of the first to understand that the French were becoming rather fussy. To be counted among the greatest restaurants in France, one could no longer afford to offer the simple decor and comfort of a family-style inn; gone were the days when one could bet everything on the quality of the cooking. When you're stuck out in the country or even in a provincial village, you have to have hotel rooms and, surrounding these rooms, oodles of charm, space, greenery and attractions interesting enough to keep guests longer than one meal. This is particularly true when you're part of the Relais et Châteaux chain, whose image is that of the epitome of the art of fine living.

Blanc set the example, and his peers were well obliged to follow his lead. After Marc Meneau, Michel Lorain, Bernard Loiseau, Pierre

Troisgros, Jean Bardet and Michel Trama, to name just a few, Alain Chapel is in turn setting out on this costly but inevitable path. Of course, Chapel didn't wait to see how his friend from Vonnas would fare before he transformed his small family hotel into a seductive establishment with an almost Provençal charm, created by the galleries of arcades surrounding an exquisite garden. Still, this hasn't been enough to lure in steady weekenders or short-vacationers. So he recently (and wisely) jumped at the chance to expand, and by 1991, Mionnay will be one of the most charming stopovers in France. By about the time this book is published, he should have completed the addition of a vast English garden and heated greenhouse enclosing a pool. After that, the facade of the hotel will get a pretty framework that resembles the one that brought great success to Blanc; and seven luxurious guest rooms, with elevator, will be remodeled and decorated.

The other good news, and for this there's no waiting, is that Chapel is at the peak of his art. He's a beaming, happy family man, and when a chef of his dimension is truly at peace with himself—which hasn't always been the case—and has perfect control over his restaurant, down to the smallest detail, his cooking can only soar. For us, meals at Chapel's have always bowed to an immutable ritual, and even when the setting changes, we won't deviate.

It always begins with a glass of wine—a rare and delightful bubbly Mâcon, perhaps—served in the garden or in the refinished salon filled with white woodwork. And while you give your mouth a little treat with morsels of fried perch, frogs' legs with herbs, and soft carp roe with mushrooms in crème fleurette, you work out the final details of the battle plan with Hervé, the charming dining room manager. Beware! This is serious work. You don't go to Chapel's for one course and coffee. A meal at Chapel's is put together like a symphony, and each movement deserves close study. Therefore, take your time to prepare for your pleasure, and then take the time to savor it.

At our last visit, our symphony was composed of seven movements. The first was a partially set pigeon aspic (the kitchen must have needed at least 50 birds to make it) flavored with anise and accompanied by a velouté of a purée of langoustines and chanterelles. Next was a cold dish of lotte liver and artichoke hearts sprinkled with a strong, pungent balsamic vinegar; then new potatoes stuffed with summer truffles that, in spite of their reputation for tastelessness, revealed an unexpected flavor. Exquisite and adorable petits pois were served in miniature pots and laced with smoked fish, morsels of spider crab and new onions, with salt serving as the only seasoning. Our fifth course was sea bass rolled with its skin as if it were stuffed, basking in a bouillon of watercress and asparagus (a blending of the ocean and the garden, punctuated by a glass of Ramonet Chassagne-Montrachet Les Ruchottes 1984, which had a vaguely honey flavor—truly a top-level meeting!). Then, along with a truly grand Echezeaux 1984 from Henry Jayer, came an astounding apple tart à la lyonnaise dotted with diced potatoes and flat parsley; the tart accompanied calves' liver and minuscule sweetbreads, sprinkled with the juices of a roast. Ecstasy! The sensation was discreetly prolonged by the final course, a broiled peach-and-rice pudding à la crème anglaise angelica, served with a glass of Muscat d'Alsace from that saint Hugel.

A standing ovation! Now it's your turn to dream, closing your eyes and anticipating the pleasures that await you on your next visit.

A la carte: 550-600F and up. Menus: 375F (weekday lunch only), 475F, 580F.

Alain Chapel

(See restaurant above)

Closed Mon. (except holidays) & Jan. 13 rms 600-750F. TV. Pets allowed.

At this writing, the hotel consisted of thirteen quite comfortable rooms on two stories, but an addition is well under way. Breakfast is magnificent. Valet parking should be in place by the time you visit. Relais et Châteaux.

Miramar

see Théoule-sur-Mer

Missillac

44780 Missillac - (Loire-Atlantique)
Paris 427 - Nantes 61 - Vannes 53 - Redon 24

Le Golf de la Bretesche

40.88.30.05

Closed Feb. 1-March 4. 27 rms 225-410F. Half-board 240-320F oblig. in seas. Heated pool. Tennis. Golf. Parking. Cards: V.

This restored castle, flanked by stately buildings and a 30-acre lake, sits on an eighteen-hole golf course. Stylish rooms. Restaurant.

Moëlan-sur-Mer

29116 Moëlan-sur-Mer - (Finistère)
Paris 514 - Concarneau 26 - Lorient 25 - Pont-Aven 16

Les Moulins-du-Duc

98.39.60.73

M. Quistrebert. Open until 10 p.m. Closed mid-Jan.-end Feb. Garden dining. Pets allowed. Parking. Telex 940080. Cards: V, AE, DC.

A hidden valley along the coast, an oyster-laden stream, a duck pond and the picturesque Breton countryside: such is the setting for the little cluster of slate-roofed granite cottages that make up this establishment. Unfortunately, the kitchen has had a revolving door recently. But it finally looks as if things might settle down, thanks to the promotion of sous-chef Thierry Quilfen, who also worked under Barrier in Tours. If he stays, we can probably look forward to the same sort of sober treatments of local ingredients that has characterized this house in the past, such as the sole in lobster cream and the pot-au-feu of native young pigeon. We'll find out soon, and in the meantime we wish them stability.

A la carte: 300-350F.

Les Moulins du Duc

(See restaurant above)

Closed mid-Jan.-end Feb. 5 stes 820-1,040F. 22 rms 400-630F. Half-board 475-590F. TV in 20 rms. Heated pool.

Several superb rooms are found in these little granite houses in a hamlet tucked away in a green valley. Some rooms are less attractive than others. Relais et Châteaux.

Le Molay-Littry

see Bayeux

Moltig-les-Bains

66500 Prades - (Pyrénées-Orientales)
Paris 978 - Quillan 53 - Prades 7 - Perpignan 50

Château de Riell

D 116 - 68.05.04.40

Mlle. Barthélemy. Open until 10 p.m. Closed Nov. 3-March 23. Garden dining. No pets. Parking. Telex 500705. Cards: V, AE, MC.

This marvelous feudal castle built at the end of the nineteenth century is the most showy spot in the mountains. Part of Michel Guérard's spa empire, the château offers a spectacular landscape of woods, snow-capped peaks, a mountain stream and flower beds; spa-goers delight in the extraordinary dining room pool that coils around a giant fir tree. A strange but warm and extravagantly refined interior decor has transformed this building into a luxurious, romantic retreat. The attractive Biche Barthélemy (daughter-in-law of Guérard) maintains a sense of relaxed grace here, while chef Marc Baurdy prepares a true Catalan cuisine: delicious "impromptu" salads, salmon millefeuille with artichoke chips, young duck served in two courses and tarte tatin made with Roussillon apricots.

A la carte: 400F. Menus: 275F, 395F.

Château de Riell

(See restaurant above)

Closed Nov. 3-March 23. 3 stes 1,330-1,365F. 18 rms 891-1,043F. Half-board 1,068-1,385F. TV in 9 rms. Pets allowed. Heated pool. Tennis.

The service is excellent and the comfort perfect, with a superb view of the mountains, a magnificent subdued decor, a thermal spa, two pools, two tennis courts and a private club. Relais et Châteaux.

Mondragon

84430 Mondragon - (Vaucluse)
Paris 646 - Avignon 46 - Bollène 6 - Pont-St-Esprit 8

La Beaugravière

N 7 - 90.40.82.54

M. Jullien. Open until 9:30 p.m. Closed Sun. dinner & Sept. 15-30. Terrace dining. Pets allowed. Hotel: 5 rms 125-295F; half-board 295-395F. Parking. Cards: V.

One of the richest wine cellars in France, stocked with some remarkable Côtes-du-Rhône, lies below this place. Owner Guy Jullien is an ardent wine lover, anxious to share his passion with others and to sell you a bottle for a song. The wine also finds its way into the fine regional cuisine: warm foie gras in Muscat, fresh salmon in Châteauneuf-du-Pape, beef filet in Fonsalette and duck in Gigondas. Also try the Richerenches truffles, which are generously served. Fine fixed-price menus, uninteresting decor but pleasant terrace.

A la carte: 200-300F (with truffles). Menus: 55F (weekdays only), 240F (wine incl.), 89F, 150F.

Montaigut-le-Blanc

63220 Champeix - (Puy-de-Dôme)
Paris 420 - Clermont-Ferrand 34 - Le Mont-Dore 34

Le Rivalet

Rte. de St-Nectaire - 73.96.73.92

M. Anglard. Open until 9:30 p.m. Closed Mon. & Tues. (except July-Aug.) & Jan. Air cond. Garden dining. Pets allowed. Hotel: 7 rms 165-200F; half-board 200-210F. Parking. Cards: V, AE, DC.

The landscape in this fortified burg is splendid, and it's peaceful enough to allow for a good night's rest. The dining room overlooking the countryside features an attractive muted decor. Gérard Anglard doesn't buy the traditional Auvergne lentils- and-sausage business; he prefers to create his own so-called "nouvelle cuisine auvergnate," which blends a light, modern touch with savory, genuine country flavors: fresh salmon in coriander served on a cabbage salad, red mullet with zucchini spaghetti and a carrot sauce, stuffed cabbage with pigeon, quail with cèpes, salad with a Cantal cheese feuilleté. Well-balanced wine cellar and affordable prices.

A la carte: 230-250F. Menus: 145F, 185F, 210F.

Montargis

42500 Montargis - (Loiret)
Paris 113 - Orléans 71 - Sens 51 - Fontainebleau 50

La Gloire

74, ave. du Général-de-Gaulle
38.85.04.69

M. Jolly. Open until 9:15 p.m. Closed Tues. dinner, Wed., Feb. 1-25 & Aug. 15-27. Air cond. No pets. Hotel: 13 rms 170-400F. Garage parking. Cards: V.

Located near the train station and the national highway, La Gloire has a decor that can best be described as bland bourgeois. But Jean-Louis Jolly is a meticulous professional, and his cuisine is a cautiously modernized version of the grand tradition: lobster aspic steeped with vegetables, red mullet filets with wild rice, young pigeon cooked in mild garlic and served with a cèpes crêpe, fine pastry desserts. Some wines are served for less than 100 francs, and good fixed-price menus are offered.

A la carte: 300F. Menus: 130F and 180F (weekdays only), 190F (weekends and holidays only), 260F.

The prices given in this guide reflect what restaurants and hotels were charging at press time.

IN NEARBY **Amily**
(5 km S on D 943)
45200 Montargis - (Loiret)

Auberge de l'Ecluse

14

Rue des Ponts - 38.85.44.24

M. Girault. Open until 9 p.m. Closed Sun. dinner, Mon., Thurs., 8 days end Aug. & 3 weeks at year end. No pets. Parking. Cards: V.

Jean-Luc Girault's cuisine is making progress—it's lighter, more modern and has more personality. His sauces have improved, too; they're finer but still vigorous. He uses delicious wild mushrooms year-round and makes desserts that are acclaimed throughout the region. The flat countryside is dotted with oil wells, but you don't see them from here; a pleasant terrace overlooks the melancholic beauty of the Briare canal. Try the wild girolle and asparagus salad, herbed sole fricassée and excellent pastries—strawberry cake, tarte tatin and tarte bourguignonne (raisin and black currant). Good Loire wines.

A la carte: 260-300F. Menus: 115F (weekdays only), 220F (weekends and holidays only), 155F.

Montauroux

83440 Fayence - (Var)
Paris 895 - Cannes 35 - Draguignan 40 - Grasse 20

Auberge du Puits Jaubert

13

5 km S on D 37 & VO,
Lac de St-Cassien - 94.76.44.48

M. Fillaprau. Open until 9:30 p.m. Closed Tues. & Jan. 10-Feb. 15. Garden dining. Pets allowed. Hotel: 8 rms 195F; half-board 205-225F. Parking. Cards: V, AE, MC.

Lost at the end of a road, in a pastoral setting near peaceful Saint-Cassien lake, is this delightful seventeenth-century inn with a splendid old vaulted dining room. The service is a bit rough, but the new owner's son creates a meticulous but modest cuisine that will leave you with happy memories: well-grilled salmon steak in a feuilleté with aromatic herbs, tender lamb noisettes in tarragon, delicate glazed pastry with seasonal fruit (though the coulis needs work). Nice regional wines.

A la carte: 250F. Menus: 150F, 210F.

Relais du Lac

D 562 - 94.76.43.65, 94.47.72.81

Open year-round. 37 rms 95-279F. Half-board 144-230F. TV in 10 rms. Pool. Parking. Telex 462392. Cards: V, AE, DC.

Comfortable, quiet rooms (the quietest face the landscape). Restaurant.

Montbazon

37250 Montbazon - (Indre-et-Loire)
Paris 247 - Châtellerault 59 - Chinon 41 - Tours 12

La Chancelière

16

1, pl. des Marronniers - 47.26.00.67

MM. Hatet & de Pous. Open until 9:30 p.m. Closed Sun. dinner, Mon. & Feb. 1-March 6. Air cond. Pets allowed. Cards: V.

Michel Gangneux's very modern cuisine doesn't ignore simple dishes or fine regional products, which is a good part of his charm. He is a remarkably skilled technician who can risk blending new, unexpected flavors, and his talent hasn't peaked yet; in fact, he appears to be headed for the top of the Touraine culinary heap. Try his oyster ravioli in Champagne, foie gras with figs, farm rabbit with morels, Loire salmon "en petite nage" and delicious desserts (blini soufflés with beurre d'orange, fresh-fruit sorbets). Otherwise, the staff is top-notch, the wine cellar well stocked, and the decor of the old village house in the greenery precious and elegant.

A la carte: 400F. Menus: 175F and 270F (weekday lunch only), 360F.

Château d'Artigny

16

Rte. d'Azay-le-Rideau - 47.26.24.24

M. Rabier. Open until 9:15 p.m. Closed Dec. 3-Jan. 13. Pets allowed. Garage parking. Telex 750900. Cards: V.

Americans, Japanese, the fur-and-diamond set, conference-goers and those who come for the famous musical weekends fill this restaurant overlooking the Indre valley. The rotunda dining room has raspberry-colored carpets, pistachio-colored walls and a golden-yellow light reflected from the eight columns that support the building—"French refinement" in a pompous and colossal fashion. (Perfume magnate René Coty built the place in 1912, and it swallowed up most of his fragrance money.) More attached to authentic flavors and simplicity (in fortunate contrast to the embellished decor), chef Francis Maignaut uses finesse and never lapses into excess: leek vinaigrette with foie gras shavings, eggs with lemon and coriander, roast pigeon and foie gras with Banyuls and tender, wild-strawberry macaroons with vanilla ice cream. One of the richest wine cellars in France (a shrine) is stocked with incomparable Loire vintages and great Armagnacs.

A la carte: 350-400F. Menus: 240F (weekday lunch only, wine incl.), 230F, 280F, 350F.

Château d'Artigny

(See restaurant above)

Closed Dec. 3-Jan. 13. 7 stes 720-1,300F. 46 rms 445-1,150F. Half-board 595-945F oblig. in seas. Air cond. in 2 rms. Pets allowed. Heated pool. Tennis. Golf.

One of France's most sumptuous hotels, with immense deluxe rooms, attracts wealthy Parisians and equally wealthy tourists, plus conference-goers from around the world and devotées of the château's musical weekends and golf packages. It's set on 60 acres of woods above the Indre valley.

L'Orangerie

14

2 km N on D 10 & N 287, Gués de Veigné
47.26.00.19

Mme. Olivereau-Capron. Open until 9 p.m. Closed Wed. lunch & Tues. (March & Oct. 15-Nov. 15) & Nov. 15-March 1. No pets. Parking. Telex 752186. Cards: V, MC.

The elongated dining room was recently redecorated with a fresh print fabric, and the room's view extends to the horizon of the spectacularly green landscape around Tours. Jean-Claude Laizé, the new chef, has already earned an extra point for his exquisite duck salad, braised sander with little tomatoes and spinach, delicious stewed veal in a sort of pot-au-feu of chamomile tea and marvelous little applesauce crêpes seasoned with hard cider. A beautiful selection of Loire wines is available, and the service is flawless.

A la carte: 300F and up. Menus: 150F (weekday lunch only), 195F.

Domaine de la Tortinière

(See restaurant above)

Closed Nov. 15-March 1. 7 stes 690-790F. 14 rms 290-630F. Half-board 370-610F. No pets. Heated pool. Tennis.

This fin-de-siècle château in a beautiful estate with century-old trees boasts comfortable rooms, several of which were redecorated recently.

Montbéliard

25200 Montbéliard - (Doubs)
Paris 483 - Besançon 82 - Belfort 22 - Basel 69

Ibis

Rue Jacques-Foillet - 81.90.21.58

Open year-round. 62 rms 210-240F. TV. Pets allowed. Parking. Telex 361555. Cards: V, MC.

Near an eighteen-hole golf course and the superhighway, the Ibis has bright little rooms that are simple and functional. Warm reception. Restaurant.

IN NEARBY **Sochaux**
(5 km NE)
25600 Sochaux - (Doubs)

(14) Luc Piguet

9, rue Belfort - 81.95.15.14

M. Piguet. Open until 9:15 p.m. Closed Sun. dinner, Mon. & Jan. 2-16 & Sept. 1-20. Pets allowed. Parking. Cards: V, AE, DC, MC.

Luc Piguet is a favorite of Peugeot executives, set as it is in the desolate outskirts of Sochaux, where the car factories are located. The manor house surrounded by a garden and the dining room dressed to the nines have a definite allure. The neo–Louis XV furniture is part of a strict, elegant bourgeois decor that well suits the chef, who is a fine technician strongly attached to tradition. The excellent salmon tartare is served with sour cream, a so-so blini and a glass of aquavit (eau-de-vie). And the tender, savory saddle of rabbit with thyme flowers is served with a blette (strawberry-spinach) gratin. Beautiful desserts, particularly the peach with Champagne and an orange à l'orange that's as good as Bocuse's. Wines aren't the strong point here.

A la carte: 280-300F. Menus: 100F, 150F, 210F, 320F.

Montbenoît

see Pontarlier

Montbonnot-Saint-Martin

see Grenoble

Montchenot

see Reims

Monte-Carlo

Monaco
Paris 955 - Nice 18 - Menton 9 - San Remo 44

Balmoral

12, ave. de la Costa - 93.50.62.37

Open year-round. 75 rms 300-600F. TV in 50 rms. Air cond. in 40 rms. Telex 479436. Cards: V, AE, DC, MC.

Some of the rooms show their age at this old hotel on the port, but the staff is obliging. Snack bar.

Beach Plaza

22, ave. Princesse-Grace - 93.30.98.90

Open year-round. 9 stes 2,037-3,183F. 320 rms 535-1,760F. TV. Air cond. Heated pool. Parking. Telex 479617. Cards: V, AE, DC, MC.

A truly grand hotel, with three pools and spacious, attractive rooms that have a certain air of refinement. The numerous amenities include a "sea club" offering water sports, a private beach and several restaurants.

12/20 Belle Epoque

Square Beaumarchais - 93.50.67.31

M. Rauline. Open daily until 10 p.m. Air cond. Terrace dining. No pets. Parking. Telex 479432. Cards: V, AE, DC, MC.

This sumptuous dining room (with a Gabriel Ferrier trompe l'oeil on the ceiling) could overshadow the cuisine. But fortunately, the likes of the fresh salmon with zucchini and the breast of duck with a truffle flan are skillfully done. The wine cellar is shared with the Hôtel de Paris.

A la carte: 500F. Menu: 260F.

Hermitage

(See restaurant above)

Open year-round. 16 stes 4,200-7,000F. 230 rms 1,000-1,900F. TV. Air cond. Pets allowed. Heated pool.

A venerable luxury hotel perched on its cliff, the Hermitage is a monument to Belle Epoque architecture. Its large rooms are pleasantly decorated. Large pool and fitness center.

12/20 Café de Paris

Pl. du Casino - 93.50.57.75

M. Grenier. Open daily until 2:30 a.m. Air cond. Garden dining. Pets allowed. Parking. Telex 469925. Cards: V, AE, DC, MC.

The most important development on the Côte d'Azur in recent years has been the renovation of the renowned Café de Paris, where you'll now find a game room, boutiques, slot machines and an immense brasserie in a very successful turn-of-the-century-style interior. State-of-the-art kitchens enable the chef, Roger Cuisinier (named by destiny!), to turn out a thousand meals per day without loss of quality. So we'll award another point for the excellent hot quail feuilleté and the fine roast rabbit in mustard. There's a superb terrace, and a late-supper menu is available after midnight.

A la carte: 220-250F. Menus: 160F to 280F.

La Coupole

1-3, ave. Princesse-Grace - 93.25.45.45

M. Sri. Open until 10:30 p.m. Closed lunch July-Aug. Air cond. No pets. Parking. Telex 479413. Cards: V, AE, DC, MC.

The ambience is a bit stiff, but the cuisine jumps nicely around Provence with pleasant aromas and a touch of modernity: fettuccine with langoustines, lobster in a Sauternes cream sauce with a leek fondue, and a surprisingly good red mullet matelote (stew) with olive oil. For customers sitting on the terrace overlooking the sea and the pool, the relaxed look is de rigueur.

A la carte: 400-450F. Menus: 225F and 340F (July-August only).

Mirabeau

(See restaurant above)

Open year-round. 10 stes 2,420-3,168. 101 rms 825-1,584F. Half-board 300F (plus room). TV. Air cond. Heated pool.

These rooms have exceptional amenities, including individual climate controls and beautiful terraces overlooking the ocean. Guests can enjoy the heated pool and all the activities of the Société des Bains de Mer: casino, beach, tennis, golf and more.

Le Foie Gras

Ave. des Spélugues - 93.50.65.00

M. Lorenzi. Open daily until 11:30 p.m. Air cond. No pets. Parking. Telex 479435. Cards: V, AE, DC.

At this chic, dressy nightspot for guests of the gigantic Loews hotel complex, the comfortable, vaguely Roaring Twenties decor complements rather nicely the scintillating silver and impeccable black-tie service. The cuisine is laudably enterprising, now more than ever: oyster gratin in Champagne butter served with broccoli, crayfish nage with yellow wine, roast lotte with sweet bell peppers and roast veal with wild rice. The prices are as upscale as the clientele.

A la carte: 500-600F. Menus: 270F, 325F and 425F (dinner only).

Loews

(See restaurant above)

Open year-round. 68 stes 1,300-8,500F. 637 rms 730-1,250F. Half-board 270F (plus room). TV. Air cond. Heated pool.

Loews is a city within a city, and one of the most famous hotels in the world. It comprises a casino, bars, shopping gallery, game rooms and much more. The cheerful rooms are done in an American Colonial style. Three restaurants: L'Argentin (grill), Le Pistou (on the roof terrace) and Le Foie Gras (see above).

Le Grill de l'Hôtel de Paris

(Hôtel de Paris)

Pl. du Casino - 93.50.80.80

M. Vanis. Open daily until 10:30 p.m. Air cond. Terrace dining. No pets. Parking. Telex 469925. Cards: V, AE, DC, MC.

The panoramic dining room provides a bird's-eye view of the sea, the rooftops and the casino cupola. And it's never been empty, even when the food was bad. Let's hope the beautiful people—who come to gossip and display their jewels—will notice not only the new neo-Venetian decor but the changes in the cuisine. The new chef is 26-year-old Sylvain Portay, who has worked with Alain Ducasse—who's now in charge of this entire operation—and with Maximin at Le Chantecler in Nice. With those credentials, one would assume that Portay has talent, an assumption that proves true when one tastes his crayfish pistou, Mediterranean bass steak with candied lemons, delicious langoustines from the Genoa Gulf with escargots butter, old-fashioned ravioli with a daube sauce, risotto with shellfish and his brochettes of various poultry and meats. Equally superb are the desserts—the velvety chocolate, the glazed millefeuille with citrus and vanilla, the crème brûlée and the soufflés—all credits to pastry chef Christian Lutzelschwab. Only pros are found in this kitchen now. And the wine cellar, which had fallen into a sorry state, has also been upgraded with the addition of such fine Provençal vintages as Domaine de Trévallon and Bandol Terre-Brune.

A la carte: 600-800F.

Le Louis XV

(Alain Ducasse)

(Hôtel de Paris)

Pl. du Casino - 93.50.80.80

Open until 10 p.m. Closed Wed. (except dinner July-Aug.), Tues. & Feb. 28-March 15. Air cond. Parking. Telex 469925. Cards: V, AE, DC, MC.

Did they eat so poorly because they were so rich? Or did they become so rich because they ate so poorly? In any case, for the past few decades the clients of the Hôtel de Paris have swallowed without flinching the most affected and expensive meals on the Côte d'Azur. But Prince Rainier, who likes real food, became rather upset, and the managers finally snared a rare bird: Alain Ducasse. Ducasse immediately put in a new chef at La Terrasse in Juan-les-Pins and set himself up at this little gem of grand luxury in Monte-Carlo. It's a breathtaking salon where, under the frescoes of a neo-eighteenth-century ceiling restored during the Third Republic, 50 place settings—not one more—are laid on linen tablecloths woven with gold thread. The silver-gilt dishes, sparkling crystal, sumptuous flower arrangements, rare silks and taffetas—the entire Louis XV decor is enough to make you swallow your set of jewels.

And, in a new development—or should we say undevelopment?—windows were reinstalled in the dining room after they had recently, and ludicrously, been walled up, thereby making the most sumptuous restaurant in the principality blind. So French doors once again open onto the place du Casino, and Louis XV's brief flirtation with a nightclub decor is history.

With or without windows, Ducasse's dazzling cuisine is indisputably full of light; it has attained a degree of perfection that leads one to believe that Monte-Carlo has been a magic potion for this 32-year-old chef. He used to be a very good chef; now he's a great one. He could have been happy reproducing his old menu without changing a thing, and that alone would have been a blessing for the Hôtel de Paris. But he decided to start from scratch, building an entirely new repertoire that is enriched by Florentine recipes dating from the nineteenth century, which were brought over by his assistant, Franck Cerutti, who worked at Enoteca Pinchiorri. Ducasse himself, who has far from the worst list of credits on his resumé (Guérard, pastry chef at Lenôtre's, Le Moulin de Mougins and Alain Chapel—"His talent had the greatest effect on me," he claims), managed to start over with exquisite, even breathtaking dishes whose quasi-rustic flavors are a delightful way to scorn ostentatious hotel cuisine. The menu includes—just to whet your appetite—a warm tourte of Provençal vegetables; sautéed frogs' legs and crayfish that couldn't be better; a bouillon au pistou (pesto) with local vegetables; foie gras and truffle ravioli in a chicken broth; lobster with fresh pasta; red snapper sautéed with new potatoes; a delicate ragoût of young rabbit and chicken wings with morels; and crayfish with chervil. Ravioli filled with purple artichokes and fresh goat cheese come on a bed of herbs. Pigs' feet and loin of baby pig are cooked in a juice seasoned with sage and served with a delicious polenta with cèpes. Tender sweetbreads are prepared in a sweet-and-sour sauce with capers and accompanied by sensational spinach and gnocchi made of baby goat cheese. We have also relished the brochette of leg of lamb from the Tende with fresh thyme, veal piccata with pine nuts and raisins à la florentine, and basmati rice in coconut milk.

We weren't happy just jotting down the names of these dishes. We ate them, savored them, leaving nary a crumb of the splendid aged Reggiano Parmigiano, the tiramisu, the coffee sabayon with shaved bitter chocolate, the warm wild-strawberry gratin with white pine nuts in a thyme sauce and the Louis XV cake with a praline crust. Nor could we resist the warm "coussinet" of pears, baked in honey and wrapped in a butter sauce with Alcool de Poire Brana (the best in France). And believe it or not, at the end of each meal (you couldn't possibly think we ate all this in one sitting!), we were practically ready to sit down to another one. We just can't get enough of this fine, intelligent and extremely light cuisine.

Ducasse brought with him Jean-Pierre Rous, whose clients at Jacques Chibois's Le Royal Gray in Cannes knew he was one of the top wine stewards on the Côte. He manages to pull out of an incredibly rich cellar bottles that won't force you to run to the bank, such as the Côtes-de-Provence, an excellent Château Realmartin Rouge 1982 for 110 francs.

A la carte: 500-1,000F and up. Menus: 460F, 530F.

Hôtel de Paris

(See restaurant above)

Open year-round. 39 stes 5,000-12,000F. 255 rms 1,200-2,200F. TV. Air cond. Heated pool. Tennis. Golf.

Since it opened in 1865, all the greats from throughout the world have paid a visit to this hotel, the last of the great European *palaces*. Now thoroughly modernized, the comfortable rooms are decorated in pastel tones in a turn-of-the-century English style. There are numerous luxury boutiques. The top three floors were recently completely remodeled.

11/20 Polpetta

2, rue Paradis - 93.50.67.84

MM. Guasco. Open until 11 p.m. Closed Tues., Feb. 15-March 5 & Oct. 15-30. Terrace dining. Pets allowed. Cards: V.

This is the beloved bistro of tennis stars, race-car drivers, Frank Sinatra, Roger Moore, Pavarotti and Monaco's upper crust—resident or transient. The brother-owners know this glittering crowd like the back of their hands, and their simple Italian cooking is a big hit: pasta, more pasta and good red wine.

A la carte: 200F. Menu: 90F.

12/20 La Potinière

Ave. du Bord-de-Mer, Saint-Roman, 06190 Roquebrune-Cap-Martin (1 km N on N 599) - 93.78.21.40

M. Maillet. Open until 9:30 p.m. Closed mid.-Sept.-early June. Terrace dining. No pets. Parking. Cards: V, AE, DC, MC.

Come here for beautiful seafood (praiseworthy hors d'oeuvres, seafood risotto and brochettes, steamed lotte escalopes with saffron). Jacket and tie are de rigueur in the elegant dining room, and relaxed summerwear reigns on the poolside terrace.

A la carte: 300-400F.

Monte-Carlo Beach Hôtel

(See restaurant above)

Closed Oct. 10-April 10. 46 rms 1,500-1,900F. TV. Air cond. Heated pool. Tennis. Golf.

These magnificently restored rooms, each with a superb loggia overlooking the surf, are home to millionaires from all over the world. They're attracted by the irresistible aura of the Roaring Twenties that emanates from the beautiful ocher facade and the perfect, old-world service. Excellent Olympic-size pool, luxury cabins and tents and lush foliage.

(13) Roger Vergé Café

Galerie du Sporting d'Hiver - 93.25.86.12

M. Vergé. Open until 11 p.m. Closed Sun. Air cond. No pets. Cards: V, AE, DC.

The luxurious Sporting d'Hiver gallery, marked by elegant blond wainscoting, is home to this café, which is really more a luxurious snack bar than a restaurant. But the cuisine has made progress following a hesitant start: curried poultry breast salad, good rabbit stew with lentils and less successful lasagne with cèpes. Not all of the wines served by the glass are scintillating. But the reception and the charming, efficient waitresses are always warm.

A la carte: 260-280F. Menus: 80F, 100F.

Montélimar

26200 Montélimar - (Drôme)
Paris 604 - Valence 46 - Marseille 182 - Lyon 145

Relais de l'Empereur

1, pl. Marx-Dormoy - 75.01.29.00
Closed Nov. 10-Dec. 22. 2 stes 640F. 38 rms 180-510F. TV in 10 rms. Pets allowed. Garage parking. Telex 345537. Cards: V, AE, DC, MC.

As the name implies, the emperor spent the night here in 1814. Americans adore it. Spacious rooms. Restaurant.

IN NEARBY **Malataverne**
(9 km S on D 144A)
26780 Malataverne - (Drôme)

Hostellerie du Mas des Sources

75.51.74.18
M. Picard. Open until 9:30 p.m. Closed Wed. (except in seas.), Sun. dinner & 3 weeks end Feb.-early March. Garden dining. No pets. Parking. Cards: V.

Jean-Marie Picard came here from his Paris wine shop to retire, but instead he transformed this farmhouse into a remarkably luxurious country inn, which combines rustic charm with a modern decor. His best idea, though, was to bring in young chef Bernard Leray, a pupil of Bernard Loiseau who creates a cuisine that, though still displaying a few mistakes, is full of freshness. And it's nicely adapted to the territory (it's based on truffles, asparagus, local suckling lamb and fresh garden vegetables). At twilight time, it's heavenly to sit on the terrace, particularly when dining on the poultry-liver fricassée in Tricastin wine, delicious Gard pigeon (though it's unusual to serve it with creamed corn) and glazed nougat with prune coulis served with a glass of Rasteau Noir. The fixed-price lunch menu is extremely regional, offering escargots soup, lamb with thyme and so on. Excellent southern Côtes-du-Rhône are served by the glass at unbeatable prices.

A la carte: 300F. Menus: 145F (weekdays only), 200F (weekday lunch only, wine incl.), 380F (wine incl.), 190F, 280F.

Hostellerie du Mas des Sources

(See restaurant above)
Closed Wed. (except in seas.) & 3 weeks end Feb.-early March. 2 stes 500F. 3 rms 250-350F. TV.

A delicious valley view and all the comforts of a country home, including chirping crickets. Tennis courts and a swimming pool are nearby.

Monteux

see Carpentras

Always remember to phone ahead!

Montfort-l'Amaury

78490 Montfort-l'Amaury - (Yvelines)
Paris 50 - Mantes 35 - Rambouillet 19 - Versailles 27

Les Préjugés

18, pl. Robert-Brault - 34.86.92.65
M. Scoffier. Open until 9:30 p.m. (10:30 p.m. in summer). Closed Jan. 2-Feb. 9. Garden dining. No pets. Cards: V, AE.

Jean-Pierre Scoffier, once a doctor in Cambodia, returned home with several adopted Cambodian children, who help him run this lovely village restaurant. One of the children, Henri, studied with the grand chefs and was so gifted that he has now taken over this ultra-functional kitchen. In a picturesque, cozy setting with a flower garden and fireplace, we found the most unexpected cuisine, original and subtle, with the taste of family-style cooking from both Asia and France: langoustines with watercress pulp, fresh salmon with oysters, veal filet mignon with ginger, bass in lettuce, spiced apple strudel. Good low-priced fixed menus.

A la carte: 400F. Menus: 190F (weekday lunch only), 190F, 275F, 390F.

IN NEARBY **Mesnuls**
(4 km SE)
78490 Montfort-l'Amaury - (Yvelines)

La Toque Blanche

12, Grande-Rue - 34.86.05.55
M. Philippe. Open until 9:30 p.m. Closed July 23-Sept. 1 & Dec. 24-Jan. 3. Garden dining. Pets allowed. Cards: V, AE.

With a bit more creativity, Jean-Pierre Philippe, the burly chef with the booming voice, could be considered one of the best chefs in the western Paris region. Still, he is impressive not only for his bulk but for his rigorous classicism, his generosity and his mastery of seafood and organ meats. Try his remarkable langoustines (scampi) with artichokes and shellfish, "symphony" of duck (filets and tiny sweetbreads) in a perfect wine sauce, popular tête de veau (calf's head), pear bavarois with a nice minty flavor and tasty sorbets. Pleasant flowery decor in a village-square setting.

A la carte: 300F and up.

Montignac

24290 Montignac - (Dordogne)
Paris 496 - Périgueux 47 - Brive 38 - Limoges 102

Château de Puy Robert

53.51.92.13
M. Parveaux. Open until 9:30 p.m. Closed mid-Oct.-early May. Pets allowed. Hotel: 5 stes 900-1,400F; 33 rms 350-900F; half-board 560-1,010F. Pool. Parking. Telex 550616. Cards: V, AE, DC, MC.

The Parveauxs, who own excellent hotels in the Alps and in this region, have just opened this Napoléon III–style castle along the marvelous Vézère river, with a graceful, fresh, rustic decor that seems to have leapt directly off the pages of a magazine. The Limoges china is superb, the staff attentive, and Philippe Lacour's cuisine delicate and refreshing: cold tomato soup with langoustines, lotte in a Cahors wine aspic (a bit flat), filet of sole with star anise, a fine fricassée of cèpes and an exquisite warm apple and almond tart. Excellent Cahors and Bergerac vintages.

A la carte: 320-350F. Menus: 170F, 280F, 390F.

Le Relais du Soleil d'Or

16, rue du 4-Septembre - 53.51.80.22

Closed Jan. 5-Feb. 15. 4 stes 440-470F. 34 rms 160-300F; half-board 230-270F. TV. Heated pool. Parking. Cards: V, AE, MC.

Renovated from top to bottom, this old relais has lovely new rooms and suites, all of which are comfortable and quiet, overlooking the splendid woods. Large heated pool, game room and salon. Restaurant.

Montpellier

34000 Montpellier - (Hérault)
Paris 760 - Marseille 164 - Perpignan 161 - Nîmes 51

Sights. Peyrou promenade (splendid terraces under plane trees); Jardin des Plantes (oldest in France); pl. de la Comédie (nerve center of Montpellier); Old Montpellier (magnificent mansions); Musée Fabre (a rich art museum, from primitive to twentieth-century works, including Greuze, Courbet and Delacroix); Musée Régional de Fougau (ethnography, Languedoc library); Musée Atger (French and Italian drawings from the seventeenth and eighteenth centuries); Saint-Pierre cathedral (fourteenth century nave and porch).

Eating on the Run. L'Assiette au Boeuf, 2 bis, rue de Verdun (a Parisian chain); Local Collation, rue de Faubourg-des-Flammes (homemade tarts, cakes); Le Quest, 1, rue des Soeurs-Noires (brunch, English lunch); Le Tire-Bouchon, 2, pl. Jean-Jaurès (pleasant wine bar).

Brasseries. Le Bistro Saint-Germain, pl. Jean-Jaurès (classic); La Grande Brasserie, pl. de la Comédie (a must).

Bars & Cafés. Bar du Métropole, 3, rue du Clos-René (pleasant hotel bar, musical ambience); Le Café Riche, pl. de la Comédie (*the* bar in Montpellier); Le Petit Nice, 1, pl. Jean-Jaurès, and Le Puits du Temple, 17, rue Soeurs-Noires (both très chic).

Nightlife. Le Copacabana, in La Grande-Motte (festive, relaxed atmosphere); Le Phébus, rte. de Palavas (for men only); Le Réganeous (Le Privé), rte. de Palavas (grill and swimming pool, luxurious and classic); Le Rimmel, rte. de Broussairolles (rather chic).

Altea Antigone

See Lou Païrol restaurant.

11/20 Le Bouchou

7, rue de l'Université - 67.66.26.20

M. Tabor. Open until 10 p.m. Closed Sun., Mon. & July 1-Aug. 15. Pets allowed.

A cramped spot with heated competition for tables, particularly at lunchtime, when an incredible budget fixed-price menu is offered. Ordering à la carte, we'd suggest the lamb's tongue, scorpionfish filet and chocolate-praline terrine.

A la carte: 180F. Menus: 43F (lunch only), 55F.

Le Chandelier

3, rue Leenhart - 67.92.61.62

M. Forest. Open until 9:30 p.m. Closed Mon. lunch, Sun., Aug. 1-16. Air cond. Pets allowed. Cards: V, AE, DC.

Montpellier food lovers are passionate about this place—they either adore it or despise it. That's proof this is no ordinary restaurant. The aggravation, we suspect, comes not from the bold cuisine but the bold prices. What we love here, aside from the perfect service and elegant pink decor, are the salmon-whitefish feuilletés with two sauces (creamy tomato and herbed), red mullet filets with a garlic cream sauce (nicely cooked with crushed walnuts) and herbed lobster lasagne, as well as the winks at regional cuisine: bourride en gélée, squid stuffed with an anise cream sauce, remarkable eggplant gratin with thinly sliced lamb. We also were lucky with some delicious desserts, notably the crêpe cake and the exquisitely fresh cinnamon tea–honey ice cream. Good wines.

A la carte: 350-400F. Menus: 110F (weekday lunch only), 230F, 300F.

Grand Hôtel du Midi

22, blvd. Victor-Hugo - 67.92.69.61

Open year-round. 50 rms 285-350F. TV. Air cond. in 28 rms. Telex 490752. Cards: V, AE, DC, MC.

This old (but renovated), pretty hotel has spacious rooms and a stylish, careful decor. No restaurant.

12/20 Le Louvre

2, rue de la Vieille - 67.60.59.37

M. Pillard. Open until 10 p.m. Closed Sun., Mon., May 15-31 & Nov. 1-15. Air cond. Terrace dining. No pets. Cards: V, DC.

Some dishes are uninteresting, but others have plenty going for them, such as the cod potée with aïoli, cassoulet with duck confit, Aveyron tripoux (tripe braised with cream and vegetables) and Roquefort tourte. Several good fish come from the daily market. Young, pleasant atmosphere.

A la carte: 180-200F. Menu: 98F (wine incl.).

Métropole

3, rue du Clos-René - 67.58.11.22

Open year-round. 4 stes 1,440F. 84 rms 390-650F. TV. Air cond in 20 rms. Pets allowed. Parking. Telex 480410. Cards: V, AE, DC, MC.

Modern comforts blend with an old-fashioned charm (antique furniture and objects). Attractive, quiet interior garden. Restaurant.

L'Olivier

12, rue Aristide-Olivier - 67.92.86.28

MM. Breton. Open until 9:30 p.m. Closed Sun., Mon., holidays & end July-end Aug. Pets allowed. Cards: V, AE, DC.

Michel Breton's cuisine is making progress in originality, in creating sturdy and perfect flavors and in the use of beautiful regional products. A toque for the duck terrine with foie gras, cooked with a confit sauce and served with coriander-seasoned mushrooms, for the red mullet filets with zucchini and tomatoes in a cold saffron sauce, for magnificent cheeses and for the strawberry feuilleté. Wonderful wine cellar and a new decor in the latest style. Service is uneven.

A la carte: 280-300F. Menus: 105F (lunch only), 168F.

Lou Païrol

(Le Polygone)
218, rue du Bastion-Ventadour
67.64.65.66

M. Blenet. Open until 9:30 p.m. Closed Sat. lunch & Sun. Air cond. Terrace dining. Pets allowed. Garage parking. Cards: V, AE, DC, MC.

Certain weaknesses and oversights must be corrected to retain the toque here—the chef's imagination appears to have gone to sleep, and the sauces have become heavy. The moëlle (marrow) wine sauce threatens to compromise the magnificent grilled beef filet by overloading it, and much the same can be said about the lemon confit sauce that accompanies the fine veal mignon. On the other hand, the fruit tarts are excellent and the cheeses well chosen. The blue decor could be freshened up, and service could stand some improvement.

A la carte: 250-280F. Menus: 120F, 190F.

Altea Antigone

(See restaurant above)

Open year-round. 1 ste 630F. 115 rms 275-435F. TV. Air cond. Pets allowed.

These beautiful rooms in the business district are perfectly equipped in the Frantel chain hotel style. Good facilities for conferences.

Sofitel

Le Triangle, allée Jules-Milhau
67.54.04.04, 67.58.45.45

Open year-round. 2 stes. 96 rms 490-610F. TV. Air cond. Pets allowed. Parking. Telex 480140. Cards: V, AE, DC, MC.

Here are some 100 perfectly comfortable modern rooms, the best ones fronting the esplanade. A copious breakfast is served, as well as room-service meals.

Montpinchon

50210 Cerisy-la-Salle - (Manche)
Paris 312 - Carentan 50 - St-Lô 22 - Coutances 12

Château de la Salle

33.46.95.19

Mme. Lemesle. Open until 9:30 p.m. Closed Nov. 13-March 20. Parking. Cards: V, AE, DC.

This is the place to come if you like lush, thick woods, a countryside where the farms aren't second homes for rich city dwellers, where the cows linger on the road and the postmen ride bicycles. It's a rather curious château surrounded by French-style lawns; inside is a somewhat solemn decor with exposed beams, a large fireplace and pretty lace tablecloths. The young Basque chef, Claude Esprebenss, has rebounded spectacularly after a disappointing start: fine langoustines fricassée with potatoes and generous truffle bits, excellent fisherman's stew in Sauternes, classic Norman-style farm chicken and tender glazed nougat that's a bit overwhelmed by a too-sweet raspberry coulis. The lady of the house is a gracious and affable hostess; her husband fills the wine cellar with excellent vintages.

A la carte: 350F. Menus: 145F, 210F.

Château de la Salle

(See restaurant above)

Closed Nov. 1-March 20. 11 rms 480-750F. Half-board 1,300F oblig. in seas. Pets allowed.

Large, elegant rooms in a pastoral setting have a fine old-fashioned decor (sometimes a bit heavy). Lovely estate. Relais et Châteaux.

Montreuil

see Dreux

Montreuil-sur-Mer

62170 Montreuil-sur-Mer - (Pas-de-Calais)
Paris 204 - Le Toquet 18 - Boulogne 37 - Lille 114

(15) Château de Montreuil

4, chaussée des Cappucins - 21.81.53.04

M. Germain. Open until 9:30 p.m. Closed Thurs. lunch (except July-Aug.) & mid-Dec.-early Feb. Garden dining. No pets. Parking. Telex 135205. Cards: V, AE, DC, MC.

It's going a bit far to call this country house a château. Nonetheless, some large, romantic rooms lurk behind the green shutters, and the good life has reigned here since Christian Germain took over several years ago, shaking the dust out of the decor and the cuisine. The garden is lovely and the dining room cheerful and rustic, though not very original. A pupil of the Roux brothers in England, Germain—assisted by his young British wife, Lindsay—creates a cuisine bursting with freshness. He is devoted to a pleasantly regionalized style that emphasizes herbs and vegetables from the garden, local products and fish from the Boulogne market. The British adore it and fill the place year-round, dining on escargots in a garden dressing, duck foie gras pot-au-feu and roast turbot with aromatic herbs and port. It's particularly pleasant in nice weather on the garden terrace.

A la carte: 300-350F. Menus: 250F (lunch only, wine incl.), 320F.

Château de Montreuil

(See restaurant above)

Closed mid-Dec.-early Feb. 14 rms 380-580F. Half-board 550F. No pets.

This large manor house (not quite a château) offers antique furniture, canopy beds, cretonne

> *Hotel prices are per room, not per person. The exceptions are half-board (price per person, including two meals a day) and full board (price per person, including three meals a day).*

linens and bathrooms worthy of starlets. Charm abounds, especially in the refurbished rooms facing the English garden. Relais et Châteaux.

La Grenouillère

La Madeleine-sous-Montreuil
21.06.07.22

M. Gauthier. Open until 9:15 p.m. Closed Tues. dinner, Wed. (except July-Aug.) & Dec. 15-Jan. 31. Garden dining. Pets allowed. Cards: V, AE, DC.

This wonderful old Picardie inn is meticulously maintained and boasts a rustic yet refined ambience. The decor inside, with its restored murals, is as pleasant as the courtyard set amid the garden's foliage (at the foot of the town's old ramparts). The menu is remarkable: sweetbreads salad with croutons, anise-seasoned lotte médaillons, outstanding poultry cooked in port and tulip-shaped sorbets with fresh fruit. Wines are a bit expensive but well selected.

A la carte: 300F and up. Menus: 190F, 250F.

IN NEARBY **Saint-Aubin**
(11 km SW on D 144E)
62170 Montreuil - (Pas-de-Calais)

Auberge du Cronquelet

Rte. de Montreuil - 21.94.60.76

Closed Wed. & Sept. 10-25. 5 rms 105-250F. Half-board 180-210F. Garage parking. Cards: V.

Absolute quiet can be found in these small but pleasant and impeccable rooms. Charming hosts. Restaurant.

Montrevel-en-Bresse

01340 Montrevel-en-Bresse - (Ain)
Paris 402 - Mâcon 26 - Bourg 17 - Tournus 36

Léa

74.30.80.84

M. Monnier. Open until 9 p.m. Closed Sun. & holiday dinner, Wed., Feb. school vacation & July. Pets allowed. Cards: V, DC.

Léa is the name of the Lyonnaise "mother" dear to the hearts of food lovers of the region. Louis Monnier bases his classic, generous cuisine on that same tradition: white liver gâteau, fresh duck liver, Bresse hen with morels, bitter-chocolate cake. The flowery inn decor is inviting, and good low-priced wines are served.

A la carte: 250-300F. Menus: 120F, 230F.

Montrichard

41400 Montrichard - (Loir-et-Cher)
Paris 204 - Tours 44 - Blois 32 - Romorantin 50

IN NEARBY **Chissay-en-Touraine**
(4 km W on N 76)
41400 Montrichard - (Loir-et-Cher)

Château de Chissay

54.32.32.01

Closed Jan. 5-March 15. 8 stes 890-1,350F. 19 rms 400-1,000F. Half-board 520-840F. TV in 10 rms. Heated pool. Telex 750393. Cards: V, AE, DC.

Sumptuous rooms with eighteenth-century furniture and mosaic- tile bathrooms were recently installed in this château, which dates from the twelfth and fifteenth centuries and which sits in the middle of woods and formal French gardens. The salons are magnificent. Restaurant. Relais et Châteaux.

Montrond-les-Bains

42210 Montrond-les-Bains - (Loire)
Paris 441 - Roanne 50 - St-Etienne 28 - Lyon 68

Gilles Etéocle

2, rue de St-Etienne - 77.54.40.06

MM. Etéocle. Open until 10 p.m. Closed Mon. dinner, Tues. lunch & Jan. 2-13. Air cond. Pets allowed. Garage parking. Cards: V, AE, DC.

This old thermal spa has a cheerful new look, and so the remarkable transformation continues: a contemporary bar and a rustic-classic decor in the dining room, with round tables, orange-and-blue curtains and a smart-looking red menu. An old postal relay station, the former La Poularde restaurant has been renamed for owner Gilles Etéocle, who took over several years ago from his father-in-law. He has disrupted the traditional, opulent tournedos-Rossini cuisine that long reigned here, yet we found the changes to be more superficial than real. Already graying at 38, Etéocle, named a Meilleur Ouvrier de France, remains torn between the new and the old. He has rediscovered some old, forgotten products, such as manioc, or cassava (the starchy root that goes into making tapioca), which accompanies salmon and langoustines. And he still clings to some old hotel recipes, trying such exotic things as sesame seeds and amber sauces, all with a rather rich and complicated taste. It's appetizing to read about but sometimes confusing on the palate.

The warm marinated salmon with anise and two kinds of sesame (one almost burnt, the other raw), the fisherman's specials (langoustines with a meat sauce, bass with beurre blanc, lobster à l'américaine), braised sweetbreads with celery, and duckling filets with almonds and juniper berries leave one with a mixed reaction. This sometimes unharmonious marriage of flavors is unfortunate, because the products are chosen with extreme care. Etéocle does offer some good standard fare, such as the old-fashioned veal blanquette and beef miroton (onion stew). Desserts also need some changes, but there is an excellent Montbrison cheese, served warm on oak leaves. With a few changes in its "philosophy," we could come to love this cuisine. We already love the four fixed-price menus, each more generous than the last, the excellent variety of Côtes-du-Rhône and the friendly, attentive service headed by the elegant Monique Etéocle.

A la carte: 450F. Menus: 240F (weekdays only, wine incl.), 140F to 200F (weekdays only), 300F to 395F.

La Poularde

(See restaurant above)

Closed Mon. & Jan. 2-15. 14 rms 190-370F. TV.

Although not very imaginative, these rooms are spacious, modern, pleasant and unpretentious.

The hotel is quiet and isolated and offers a perfect breakfast (mouth-watering brioches and jams). Relais et Châteaux.

Le Mont-Saint-Michel

50116 Le Mont-St-Michel - (Manche)
Paris 323 - Rennes 66 - St-Malo 52 - Fougères 47

(14) La Mère Poulard

33.60.14.01

M. Pierpaoli. Open daily until 9:30 p.m. Pets allowed. Telex 170197. Cards: V, AE, DC, MC.

The spectacular omelet—beaten before your eyes in a copper bowl and then grilled—is still king here. But the new chef is trying to rejuvenate the place with an excellent asparagus-oyster cassoulet, a good escalope of duck liver with an apple-cider vinegar, and spectacular oysters. However, the salad of langoustines and sweetbreads was lifeless and confused, and the John Dory in cider was just decent. A surprising (but expensive) variety of wines, perfect service, a new pale-blue decor and piano music at night to liven things up.

A la carte: 350F. Menus: 450F (dinner only), 135F, 220F, 310F.

La Mère Poulard

(See restaurant above)

Open year-round. 1 ste 1,250F. 26 rms 350-950F. TV.

The stairs creak and the flowery wallpaper is faded, but the view is breathtaking from some of the rooms.

Les Terrasses Poulard

Rue Principale - 33.60.14.09

Open year-round. 29 rms 230-800F. Half-board 310-560F. TV. Pets allowed.

Although new, this hotel fits in quite nicely with the town's old buildings. The rooms are smallish but pretty and bright, and they open onto either the sea or the town. The reception is excellent. Restaurant.

Mornac-sur-Seudre

17113 Mornac-sur-Seudre - (Charente-Maritime)
Paris 504 - Royan 13 - Saintes 36 - Rochefort 36

(13) La Gratienne

Rte. de Breuillet - 46.22.73.90

Mme. Forgerit. Open until 10 p.m. Open weekends only Dec.-March. Closed Wed. & Thurs. (except July-Aug.), Dec. 11-30 & April 4-27. Garden dining. Pets allowed. Cards: V.

Mireille Forgerit's place on the road to Oléron and the oyster beds is a hearty inn where one celebrates a regional cuisine with a nice personal touch (seaweed soup, sole with noodles, haddock with curry). A toque for the eel matelote (stew), eel fritters and fricasséed eels, as well as the calf's belly. Good desserts, fine low-priced local wines and a pretty, rustic decor.

A la carte: 220F. Menu: 100F.

Mortagne-sur-Sèvre

85290 Mortagne-sur-Sèvre - (Vendée)
Paris 358 - Cholet 10 - Bressuire 40 - Nantes 56

(15) La Taverne

4, pl. du Dr-Pichat - 51.65.03.37

M. Jagueneau. Open until 9:30 p.m. Closed Sat., Dec. 20-Jan. 6 & Aug. 1-13. Air cond. Pets allowed. Telex 711403. Cards: V, AE, DC, MC.

You'll find plenty of rustic charm in this extremely old postal relay station located next to a restored steam train called the Puy-du-Fou. It's an inviting stopover, comfortable and refined (President Clemenceau thought so, anyway), where the foliage hides a beautiful covered pool and an expansive, flowery garden, onto which the impressive dining room opens. After some recent lapses, chef Philippe Gaborit's cuisine is back in fine form: a bowl of hot oysters nicely presented with artichokes; homemade foie gras graced with a delicious onion confit; little smoked eels with young leeks; an entirely successful great classic dish, le colvert grand veneur (mallard hunter-style); and fine desserts (peach charlotte, chocolate cake). The service is most attentive.

A la carte: 300F. Menus: 140F, 190F, 295F.

Hôtel de France

(See restaurant above)

Closed Sat., Aug. 1-13 & Dec. 20-Jan. 6. 1 ste 380F. 24 rms 210-300F. Half-board 460F. TV. Air cond. in 6 rms. Heated pool.

Fine, classicly decorated rooms, some with lovely furniture and pleasant terraces opening onto the garden. Good facilities for small conferences. VCRs.

Morzine

74110 Morzine - (Haute-Savoie)
Paris 602 - Lyon 230 - Annecy 83 - Chamonix 71

(16) La Chamade

50.79.13.91

MM. Thorens. Open until 10 p.m. Closed May 1-June 17 & Sept. 15-Oct. 15. Air cond. Terrace dining. Pets allowed. Parking. Cards: V, AE, DC, MC.

La Chamade is a find that could shake the mountains—the Alps haven't seen anything this good in years. Mme. Thorens, an alluring beauty, left her hairdressing salon and, with her genius of a son, Thierry, put together a Hollywood-style decor with plaster columns, Venetian-style mirrors and a superb piano behind the large bay windows—you'd think you were at Graceland. After midnight, when his work is done, Thierry works at his hobby of creating unusual sugar sculptures. The 27-year-old Bocuse pupil displays plenty of creativity in the kitchen, too: The 230-franc fixed-price menu is a cornucopia that includes smoked salmon with a strongly flavored mousse filling and lemon, and poultry fricassée en croûte served in two courses—first a soup tureen with its pastry cap (which Thierry learned to make at Bocuse), then superb poultry livers in wine sauce with green cabbage. The young rabbit compote in a red wine sauce is unlike any other we've tried, the bass filet with saffron comes with zucchini vermicelli, fried parsley and an excellent mushroom sauce, and the dish of crab and shrimp has a tasty hazelnut flavor. Cheese comes with wonderfully fragrant and fresh bread. The desserts include a light-as-air anise-topped lemon feuilleté. By meal's end, we only wished we had the appetite to start all over again. Good wines, many served by the glass, and impeccable service make the experience all the more impressive. Thierry also helps out in his parents' bistro, which offers excellent 80-franc meals that include duck sausage, regional dishes and warm lemon feuilleté.

A la carte: 300F and up. Menus: 230F, 280F.

Le Dahu

50.79.11.12

Closed April 15-June 15 & Sept. 15-Dec. 15. 26 rms 150-420F. Half-board 300-420F oblig. in seas. Heated pool. Parking. Telex 309514. Cards: V.

Stylish, traditional and well-kept rooms, along with salons, a pool and theme evenings with entertainment. Restaurant.

IN NEARBY **Avoriaz**

(5 km NE, access by téléphérique)
74110 Morzine - (Haute-Savoie)

Les Dromonts

50.74.08.11

Mme. Sirot. Open until 9:30 p.m. Closed April 15-Dec. 15. Terrace dining. Pets allowed. Cards: V, AE, DC, MC.

The attractive chalet decor works well here, and the cuisine has a loyal following among the cosmopolitan ski set: langoustines and scallops with bacon, shellfish swimming in a court bouillon with ginger, choucroute with sander and juniper berries. Bistro-style cuisine at easier prices is served downstairs in La Taverne.

A la carte: 400F. Menus: 170F, 260F.

Les Dromonts

(See restaurant above)

Closed April 15-Dec. 15. 37 rms 555-1,090F. Half-board 550- 710F. TV.

This ultra-modern hotel was the first in this ski resort. There's an avant-garde decor in the rooms, all of which face the ski slopes. Sauna, massage, beauty center.

Les Hauts Forts

50.74.09.11

Closed April 20-June 1 & Sept. 1-Dec. 15. 50 rms 357-855F. TV. Pets allowed. Heated pool. Cards: V.

Right in front of the slopes is this beautiful, roomy hotel, which is modern, full of light and perfectly equipped for winter sports. Sauna, bar, boutiques, restaurant.

This symbol signifies hotels that offer an exceptional degree of peace and quiet.

Mosnac

see Pons

Le Mottaret

see Méribel-les-Allues

Moudeyres

43150 Le Monastier-sur-Gazeille - (Haute-Loire)
Paris 594 - Aubenas 63 - Le Puy 25 - Yssingeaux 35

Le Pré Bossu

71.05.10.70

M. Grootaert. Open until 9 p.m. Closed Tues. & Wed. lunch (off-seas.) & Nov. 11-Easter. No pets. Garage parking. Cards: V, AE, DC.

In the woodsy countryside in the clean air at 3,500 feet, this thatched cottage has the charm and warmth of a Flanders farm—a refined yet bucolic setting. Belgian native Carlos Grootaert, a big, affable, mustachioed man attracted to the rugged beauty of the Auvergne, prepares a cuisine that is principally French, with little reference to his native region, with the exception of waterzoï (fish casserole) with a verbena infusion (this area is paradise for verbena lovers). Try his a solid cabbage and cod terrine with a celery sauce, salmon in bouillon, frogs' legs with star anise, stuffed rabbit in an herbed pastry crust and a marvelous Velay plum soufflé. Good southwestern wines at popular prices.

A la carte: 250F. Menus: 105F (weekdays only), 155F, 178F, 198F, 290F.

Le Pré Bossu

(See restaurant above)

Closed Nov. 11-Easter. 10 rms 215-280F. Half-board 255-400F oblig. in seas. Pets allowed.

These simple but attractive, clean rooms make for tranquil nights. Inviting ambience, a salon with a fireplace and an excellent breakfast.

Mougins

06250 Mougins - (Alpes-Maritimes)
Paris 902 - Nice 32 - Grasse 11 - Cannes 8

Acanthe Hôtel

Val-de-Mougins,
95, ave. du Maréchal-Juin - 93.75.35.37

Open year-round. 26 rms 227-344F. TV. Garage parking. Cards: V, AE, DC, MC.

This new, pleasant little hotel is well maintained and equipped, with rooms that are not spectacular but are comfortable. Double windows. Restaurant.

L'Amandier de Mougins

Pl. du Commandant-Lamy - 93.90.00.91

MM. Vergé. Open until 10:30 p.m. Closed Sat. lunch & Wed. Terrace dining. Pets allowed. Telex 970732. Cards: V, AE, DC.

Roger Vergé and his wife, Denise, bought and fixed up this lovely old hill-country inn ten years ago, creating a beautiful vaulted dining room around an old millstone and filling it with antiques and charming knickknacks; then a hanging garden and enchanting terrace were added, providing a view of the countryside. A few years ago, they left the place in charge of an excellent manager, Yves Dallet, and a chef, Francis Chauveau. The problems we have complained about in the past—concerning the service, the wine cellar and the various upsets caused by the summer wave of tourists—have largely been corrected, but the food itself, unfortunately, is no longer worthy of two toques. Our crayfish with chanterelles was overpowered by a strong truffle butter that killed the taste of the crayfish, and the filet of lamb on an immense platter was much too fussy. As for the desserts: Simply put, they are unworthy of the house.

A la carte: 450F and up. Menu: 280F.

12/20 Le Bistrot de Mougins

Pl. du Village - 93.75.78.34

MM. Ballatore & Giordano. Open until 10 p.m. Closed Tues. & Wed. (except July-Aug.) & Dec. 1-Jan. 20. Air cond. Pets allowed. Cards: V.

A marvelous fixed-price menu (only one is offered) capturing the fragrance of Provence is served in a vaulted dining room: blette (strawberry-spinach torte), stuffed vegetables, seafood salad à la roquette (with Mediterranean spices), gnocchi au pistou and savory roast Alpine quail.

Menu: 135F.

16 La Ferme de Mougins

10, ave. St-Basile - 93.90.03.74

M. Sauvanet. Open until 9:30 p.m. Closed Sat. lunch, Thurs. & Feb. 1-March 10. Garden dining. Pets allowed. Parking. Telex 970643. Cards: V, AE, DC, MC.

If Henri Sauvanet's restaurant is being showered with praise, it's due chiefly to young chef Patrick Henriroux, who is precise, consistent, hard-working and in love with natural and simple food. Politicians, entertainers and film stars appreciate it (in winter they also flock to Sauvanet's other restaurant, in the Alps, where he boasts serving "the world's most expensive Raclette"). Try the coquilles St-Jacques in thyme sauce, bass poached in its skin with a verjuice (juice of unripened grapes) sauce, savory breast of lamb with an herbed salad (seasoned with excellent olive oil) and delicious glazed lavender-scented nougat. Charming hostess and a wonderful sommelier.

A la carte: 400-500F. Menus: 210F (until 9 p.m.), 380F.

Le Mas Candille

Blvd. Rebuffel - 93.90.00.85

Closed Jan. 3-16. 1 ste 1,000-1,150F. 22 rms 700-750F. Pets allowed. Pool. Parking. Cards: V, AE, DC.

Renovated from top to bottom, this exquisite family hotel is quietly tucked away on the Mougins hill. It offers comfortable rooms and absolute calm.

18 Le Moulin de Mougins

424, chemin du Moulin
(Quartier Notre-Dame-de-Vie)
93.75.78.24

M. Vergé. Open until 10:30 p.m. Closed Thurs. lunch, Mon. (except July 1-Sept. 15) & Jan. 29-March 20. Garden dining. Pets allowed. Parking. Telex 970732. Cards: V, AE, DC.

Nine times out of ten, don't you find restaurants terribly boring? If the cuisine isn't marvelous, all that pomp, so religiously executed, is intolerable. But when the food is excellent, you're thrilled to be able to enjoy it in inviting and clever surroundings. Thanks be to God, a few such places exist.

While Moulin de Mougins hardly lacks the accoutrements of a great restaurant, all that seems stuffy, intimidating and overwhelming in other contexts takes on a charming and entertaining tone here. Bursts of flowers greet you at the entrance, and on the simple white walls paintings by Muhl throw off rays of light. The enclosed garden, hidden from the street below, stands at the foot of a hill with fields spared by urban development. On summer nights, a smart, stylish crowd storms the two main dining rooms, managed marvelously by Sylvain and Christian, the two maîtres d', and a first-class wine steward.

Roger Vergé, who might as well be a movie star—he lives among them all year long, and doesn't he have the looks of an eternally young leading man?—has managed to imbue this haven of luxury with his simplicity and love for real things. He has attained an exceptional degree of success, and even if you visit to Le Royal Gray (Jacques Chibois) in Cannes or Le Louis XV (Alain Ducasse) in Monte-Carlo, you'll always be most anxious to return to Vergé's.

In such delightful surroundings, you naturally expect the cuisine to surprise you, to astound you, to take your breath away. Alas, once again, Vergé has wiped out old and marvelous memories by settling for being no more than extremely good. At a time when so many young chefs—those we mentioned above and many more—set off veritable skyrockets all year long and enlist prodigious amounts of imagination in the service of breathtaking technique, you find yourself forced to make distinctions. With the fricassée of fresh morels with cream and gnocchi niçoise, you're off to a good start. But when that's followed by stuffed artichokes with fava beans and purple aparagus; slightly overcooked breaded blanc de palangre (a French fish) on a bed of sorrel; roast breast of lamb with savory (an herb akin to mint) accompanied by eggplant, pleurotes (the most uninteresting of mushrooms) and—why Lord?—watercress; and, finally, a young Bresse chicken cooked Provençal style with tomatoes, zucchini, eggplant and onions... you say to yourself that all of this can indeed be eaten with pleasure and is quite honorable, but it can't in any way claim the title of one of the finest cuisines in France. You're forced to draw the logical conclusion when it's time to give a rating. And to hope Vergé understands that even the best of old friends can't be blind to all faults. So we must remove (with regret) Moulin de Mougins from the ultra-elite club of 19.5-ranking restaurants, to which it has belonged these last few years.

A la carte: 800F. Menu: 600F.

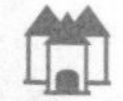

Le Moulin de Mougins

(See restaurant above)

Closed Jan. 29-March 20. 2 stes 1,300F. 3 rms 800-900F. TV. Air cond. Pets allowed.

The three rooms and two small suites above the garden are delightful and much less expensive than a room in some palace, but they're also more difficult to reserve than a ticket to heaven.

15 Le Relais à Mougins

Pl. de la Mairie - 93.90.03.47

M. Surmain. Open until 10:30 p.m. Closed Tues. lunch, Mon. (except July-Aug), Feb. 13-March 6 & Nov. 13-Dec. 4. Terrace dining. Pets allowed. Telex 462559. Cards: V.

André Surmain, former owner of Lutèce in New York (then "the world's most expensive restaurant"), is a master chef, but he spends most of his time keeping up his image as an attentively watching, knowledgeable professional. This prosperous bistro, which he launched a decade ago with a new garden-style decor, is a bit noisy but quite enchanting, and it's always crowded with Cannes's beautiful people. Predictably, it's quite expensive, especially at dinner, but you do get to sample Dominique Louis's culinary delights: three kinds of foie gras cooked "au torchon" (in cloth), seafood ravioli, lamb's sweetbreads in strawberry-spinach leaves. Delicious chocolate mousse dominates the dessert list, and generic vintages the wine list.

A la carte: 450-550F. Menus: 190F (dinner only), 215F (lunch only, wine incl.), 445F.

Moulins

03000 Moulins - (Allier)
Paris 292 - Vichy 57 - Nevers 54 - Bourges 98

16 Jacquemart

10, pl. de l'Hôtel-de-Ville - 70.44.32.58

M. Rauch de Roberty. Open until 9 p.m. Closed Sun. dinner, Mon., April 24-May 1 & July 31-Aug. 14. Air cond. Pets allowed. Cards: V, AE, DC.

Louis Rauch de Roberty gives credit where credit is due: The name of his mentor, Alain Senderens, is inscribed on his attractive menu. The decor is pretty and refined, utilizing pink and blue tones to highlight the remarkable fourteenth-century ceiling (a landmark). The cuisine, however, is up-to-date, with fine blends of tastes and a simple style. De Roberty, beginning to cut the umbilical cord and find his own personality, has come up with such dishes as warm escargots salad, a grilled "symphony" (beef filet, foie gras and potatoes) with crushed thyme-seasoned tomatoes, exceptional pan-fried veal kidneys and sweetbreads in curry with wild rice, and for dessert, a first-rate bitter-chocolate soufflé with pistachio cream and a biscuit. We do have reservations, however, about a few unnecessary additions (vanilla with sole, pleurotes with foie gras, port in the fritters). There are some excellent wines for about 100 francs and fine service directed by Anne-Françoise.

A la carte: 350F. Menus: 120F (weekdays only), 180F, 270F, 380F.

16 Hôtel de Paris ✪

21, rue de Paris - 70.44.00.58

M. Laustriat. Open until 9:30 p.m. Closed Sun. dinner & Mon. (except June-Sept.). Air cond. Pets allowed. Garage parking. Telex 394853. Cards: V, AE, DC, MC.

There's something for nearly everyone here: alluring provincial charm, a warm family atmosphere, a pleasant oak-paneled decor, a young, eager staff and a string of generous fixed-price menus for the budget-conscious. The young owners go to great pains to get things right and maintain their enthusiasm, despite a dining room that's often half empty (Moulins doesn't draw hordes of tourists, and it will become even more isolated now that the new superhighway is 30 miles away). Pascal Bouffety, who directs the kitchen, has added a personal touch to the regional Bourbonnaise cuisine that he inherited from the former chef: leg of lamb, tartoufle (potato) pâté and squab à la ficelle. He has his own creations as well, such as filet of sole in a saffron sauce, a mussel-shellfish ragoût and sweetbreads stuffed with fennel. The light strawberry millefeuille could, however, do without the warm spiced wine. Delicious petits fours and a fine selection of teas and coffees, not to mention the "reasonable" Burgundy vintages that sommelier Philippe Blanc will recommend.

A la carte: 350F. Menus: 85F, 150F, 170F, 240F, 290F.

Hôtel de Paris

(See restaurant above)

Open year-round. 8 stes 520F. 19 rms 225-440F. Half-board 480-780F. TV in 15 rms.

Attractive rooms and suites have pretty antique furniture. Special packages for hunting, golf and horseback riding were recently introduced. Perfect service. Relais et Châteaux.

Moustiers-Sainte-Marie

04360 Moustiers-Ste-Marie - (Alpes-de-Haute-Provence)
Paris 792 - Manosque 50 - Castellane 45 - Digne 48

14 Les Santons ✪

Pl. de l'Eglise - 92.74.66.48

MM. Albert & Fichot. Open until 9:30 p.m. Closed Mon. dinner (off-seas.), Tues. & Nov. 15-March 1. Terrace dining. Pets allowed. Cards: V, DC.

The owners of this odd-looking building—a former bakery next to a church and a stream—have created an attractive, flowery decor, featuring rustic tables covered with white linens. It's delightful, simple and fresh, as is the terrace along the babbling stream. André Albert's cuisine, using fine local produce, has a sunny flavor: gâteau of eggplant with duck and foie gras, vegetables with a sweet-pepper sauce, seafood panaché (mixture) wrapped in lettuce, veal kidneys in wine and desserts fragrant with seasonal fruit. It's a good idea to make reservations, since competition can be keen for the 35 place settings.

A la carte: 280F. Menus: 135F, 185F, 240F.

Mulhouse

68100 Mulhouse - (Haut-Rhin)
Paris 537 - Belfort 44 - Colmar 41 - Strasbourg 116

Sights. Musée National de l'Automobile (440 cars from around the world); Musée Français du Chemin de Fer (railroad museum, tops in France, rich and fascinating); Musée de l'Impression sur l'Etoffe (printed fabrics—ten million samples, largest in the world); Le Jardin des Senteurs (for the blind); zoological and botanical park (magnificent foliage and more than 1,000 animals); La Tour de l'Europe (tower with magnificent view).

Eating on the Run. Auberge du Vieux Mulhouse, 8, rue des Archives (Alsatian specialties, warm atmosphere); L'Esterel, 83, ave. de la 1re-D.B. (nice terrace, daily specials); Honk-Hong, 22, rue Engle-Dollfus (good Asian cuisine); La Marmite, 8, ave. Auguste-Wicky (popular); Le Pirée, 143, ave. de Colmar (little Greek spot); Relais de Stressla, 71, rue A.-Briand (Alsatian specialties); Le Saint-Michel, 1, pl. de l'Europe (a magnificent view of the town).

Bars & Cafés. L'Aiglon, 10, ave. Auguste-Wicky (for lonely guys); Bar de l'Altea, 4, pl. Charles-de-Gaulle; Le Moll, 6, pl. de la République (pleasant terrace, young crowd); Le Sunny Pub, 8, ave. de Lattre-de-Tassigny (informal, cosmopolitan).

Nightlife. Le Caesar, 192, rue Vauban (young, hip set); Le Club 1900, 3, rue des Halles (a Mulhouse institution, always in vogue); Piano Bar, 46, blvd. du Président Roosevelt (à la mode); Music-Hall Saint-Jacques, 47, rue de la Sinne (very lively).

(13) L'Alsace

4, pl. Charles-de-Gaulle - 89.46.01.23

M. Seitz. Open daily until 10 p.m. Terrace dining. Pets allowed. Parking. Telex 881807. Cards: V, AE, DC, MC.

The new interior is at least comfortable if not very warm and inviting, with its mirrors, ceiling lights and plants. The cooking, meanwhile, is coming along quite well, in the hands of the former chef at the famous Mère Poulard in Mont-Saint-Michel. He offers a balanced collection of fresh-flavored, well-executed dishes. The most expensive fixed-price menu, for example, brings an honest terrine of salmon and pike in a very good green sauce, scorpionfish stew in a well-balanced ginger and pimiento sauce, interesting cheeses and a selection of carefully prepared desserts. The reception is hardly friendly, and the waiters, though kindly, are often inept.

A la carte: 250F. Menus: 150F (wine incl.), 75F, 130F.

Altea

(See restaurant above)

Open year-round. 96 rms 240-395F. Half-board 380-515F. TV. Pets allowed.

Across from the main train station, the Altea offers comfortable, decent-sized rooms and a good breakfast. The service is perfunctory, but the tab is not.

Bourse

14, rue de la Bourse - 89.56.18.44

Closed Dec. 22-Jan. 3 & July 14-30. 50 rms 262-350F. Telex 881720. Cards: V, DC, MC.

The rooms, which are modern and spacious, have double windows (some overlook an interior garden). No restaurant.

Hôtel du Parc

26, rue de la Sinne - 89.66.12.22

Open year-round. 7 stes 1,200-2,900F. 69 rms 650-950F. TV. Air cond. Pets allowed. Telex 881790. Cards: V, DC, MC.

A Lebanese group poured a fortune into this former mansion of the Schlumpf brothers, the famous automobile collectors, keeping its exterior, which reeks of grand, provincial elegance, but completely redoing the interior. The results are tasteful and sober, a restoration of the art deco style that was contemporary to the original building. Excellent facilities, wonderful service and a restaurant.

(13) La Tissandière

6 km NE, Mulhouse-Sausheim, N 422A, 68390 Sausheim - 89.61.87.8

M. Melique. Open daily until midnight. Air cond. Garden dining. Pets allowed. Telex 881757. Cards: V, AE, DC, MC.

This place has a standard, cheery contemporary decor—the kind you expect in a big chain hotel—and an uninviting neighborhood on the edge of town. The service is fast but without much warmth. The new young chef makes a cuisine that's laudably light and inventive, whose only fault is that it's rather expensive (which, of course, is not his fault): pan-fried foie gras with olives and port (a good idea, but the sauce lacks subtlety), rather good duck breast with lime, fine salmon in parsley sauce and an excellent pear soufflé.

A la carte: 200-230F. Menus: 130F.

Mercure

(See restaurant above)

Open year-round. 2 stes 685F. 98 rms 335-390F. TV. Air cond. Heated pool. Tennis.

Excellent conference facilities and bright, spacious rooms with magnificent baths.

IN NEARBY **Illzach**
(6 km N)
68110 Illzach - (Haut-Rhin)

(13) Le Parc

8, rue Victor-Hugo - 89.56.61.67

M. Huffschmitt. Open until 9 p.m. Closed Sat. lunch, Sun. dinner, Mon., Feb. 20-March 6 & Aug. 14-28. Pets allowed. Parking. Cards: V.

Jean-Pierre Huffschmitt is an amiable, young, able chef, but he's still too shy, both with his customers and in the kitchen—we'd like to see him take a stronger stand. This isn't a reproach but an encouragement; he seems to have everything it takes to develop his own style. His cooking precision and light sauces are promising qualities, and now all he needs is a bit of boldness. We'll forget the lifeless foie gras and the bland young turbot, and instead remember the panaché of sander and salmon with mussels and saffron, the pigeon suprême and the mocha and mint desserts. The wines are surprisingly ordinary.

A la carte: 300-350F. Menus: 250F (dinner only, wine incl.), 175F (lunch only), 130F, 300F.

IN NEARBY **Steinbrunn-le-Bas**
(8 km S on D 21)
68440 Habsheim - (Haut-Rhin)

(16) Moulin du Kaegy

89.81.30.34

M. Bégat. Open until 10:30 p.m. Closed Sun. dinner, Mon. & Jan. Pets allowed. Parking. Cards: V, AE, DC.

Bernard Bégat swallows criticism and compliments in the same breath—and neither appears to have much of an effect on him. At 50, he still dances to rock music and considers himself a *bel homme*. Bégat remains a first-rate chef who turns out an incomparable foie gras (aged ten days in a stone pot without grease and rubbed with lemon), langouste rounds with new potatoes and chervil, poultry breast with foie gras and cabbage and such old standards as boeuf bourguignon and navarin. The extensive wine selection includes an excellent Clevner by the carafe. Children get a thrill going into the kitchen to choose their dishes. Quite steep à la carte prices.

A la carte: 400-500F. Menus: 170F (weekday lunch only), 275F (wine incl.), 230F, 400F.

Murbach

68530 Buhl - (Haut-Rhin)
Paris 480 - Gérardmer 65 - Guebwiller 6 - Colmar 31

(13) Hostellerie Saint Barnabé

25, rue de Murbach - 89.76.92.15

MM. Orban. Open until 9 p.m. Closed Sun. dinner & Mon. (off-seas.) & Jan. 15-March 1. No pets. Hotel: 4 stes 345-550F; 20 rms 225-480F; half-board 255-415F. Tennis. Parking. Telex 881036. Cards: V.

Eric Orban has come to breathe new life into this attractive, flowery inn in the fresh-air country of the Alsace mountains. His repertoire includes a foie gras mousseline made with well-aged Gewürztraminer (a dish with a pleasant aroma but a heavy consistency), pan-fried veal kidneys in a delicate sauce, a beautiful tarragon-essence salmon steak and a pear millefeuille that's uninspired but well made. His rating will undoubtedly rise once he displays a few new ideas and refines some current ones. The decor lacks character and could be more comfortable. Don't forget to meet the young, distinguished and attractive Alsatian patronne.

A la carte: 300F. Menus: 160F, 210F.

DON'T FORGET: Gault Millau also brings you The Best of Chicago, The Best of Hong Kong, The Best of Italy, The Best of London, The Best of Los Angeles, The Best of New England, The Best of New York, The Best of Paris, The Best of San Francisco *and* The Best of Washington, D.C.

Mur-de-Bretagne

22530 Mur-de-Bretagne - (Côtes-du-Nord)
Paris 455 - St-Brieuc 45 - Quimper 98 - Pontivy 16

(15) Auberge Grand'Maison

1, rue Léon-le-Cerf - 96.28.51.10

M. Guillo. Open until 9 p.m. Closed Sun. dinner, Mon., Feb. school vacation, June 23-30 & Sept. 25-Oct. 25. Pets allowed. Hotel: 12 rms 180-400F; half-board 300-400F. Cards: V, AE, DC.

Jacques Guillo's cuisine demonstrates his love for rich products and personal creations, such as foie gras profiteroles with a truffle coulis, lobster stew with poached eggs and lobster in a fricassée of creamed pink peppercorns. A disciple of Robuchon and other notables, he is a serious professional who's anxious to be perfect, but he also uses a lot of heart, spontaneity and fresh market produce. Notable recent creations are his thick smoked-salmon-and-potato galettes, turbot filet with a subtle fennel aroma and mouth-watering mandarin orange crêpes, among the best on the peninsula. The new decor—a rustic-modern style, with beams and Louis XV chairs—is much warmer than it once was. Mme. Guillo, with the unrelenting smile, is omnipresent. Good fixed-price menus.

A la carte: 250-300F. Menus: 130F (weekdays only), 190F, 250F, 350F.

Le Beau Rivage

6 km NW on D 767 & N 164, Caurel, Lac de Guerlédan - 96.28.52.15

Closed Mon. & Tues. (off-seas.) & Jan. 5-Feb. 15. 8 rms 150-280F. Half-board 250-320F. TV. Parking.

This small, well-kept hotel has newly refurbished rooms overlooking the lake. Restaurant.

Najac

12270 Najac - (Aveyron)
Paris 640 - Rodez 86 - Cahors 85 - Albi 50

(13) L'Oustal del Barry

65.29.74.32

M. Miquel. Open until 9 p.m. Closed Mon. (April & Oct., except holidays) & Nov. 1-March 31. Terrace dining. Pets allowed. Garage parking. Cards: V.

In a marvelous village at the foot of a proud château sits this inviting inn, where the cuisine is both modern and loyal to the territory: excellent cochonaille (sausage), asparagus flan with duck "ham," warm liver with a compote of capers and local Gaillac wine, and an astet najacois à l'aligot de Laguiole (potato-cheese melt). Good modest wine cellar.

A la carte: 250F. Menus: 98F, 160F, 225F.

L'Oustal del Barry

(See restaurant above)

Closed Mon. (April & Oct., except holidays) & Nov. 1-March 31. 4 stes 195-215F. 17 rms 160-215F. Half-board 165-200F. Pets allowed.

We suggest, in particular, the rooms that face the southwest. The decor is rather dated, but the plumbing's new.

Nançay

18330 Neuvy-sur-Barangeon - (Cher)
Paris 187 - Vierzon 20 - Bourges 35 - Salbris 14 - Giens 55

Auberge Les Meaulnes

48.51.81.15

M. Prat. Open until 9:30 p.m. Closed Tues. (off-seas.) & mid- Jan.-mid-March. Garden dining. Pets allowed. Cards: V, AE, DC.

The owners of this romantic country inn, former Parisian journalists, draw a clientele that is an ambitious mixture of press and showbiz types. The young new chef creates a simple and light cuisine: asparagus Solognote-style, spring trout with dried fruit, rabbit with vegetables in a subtle sweet-and-sour sauce and an excellent caramel sorbet with crunchy nougatine morsels.

A la carte: 300F and up. Menus: 185F, 245F.

Auberge Les Meaulnes

(See restaurant above)

Closed Tues. (off-seas.) & mid-Jan.-mid-March. 10 rms 340-420F. Half-board 500-550F.

Beautiful rooms have been redecorated with taste in an opulent, old-fashioned style. Plenty of peace and quiet, along with excellent service.

Nancy

54000 Nancy - (Meurthe-et-Moselle)
Paris 307 - Metz 57 - Epinal 69 - Lyon 385 - Reims 230

Sights. Pl. Stanislas (one of the most beautiful and harmonious in the world) and its two eighteenth-century "annexes": pl. de la Carrière and pl. d'Alliance; Musée de l'Ecole de Nancy (representing the Nancy school); Musée des Beaux-Arts; Musée Historique Lorrain; Aquarium (one of Europe's best); Musée de Fer (in Jarville).

Eating on the Run. Auberge du 20e Corps, 15, ave. du 20e Corps; Le Broadway, 39, rue des Maréchaux (dependable American food); Ducal, 71, Grande-Rue (abundant food, fun atmosphere, good prices); Le Gallé, 3, pl. Thiers (good railroad-station buffet); La Jouverte, 31, Grande-Rue (vegetarian).

Brasseries. Excelsior, 50, rue H.-Poincaré (a 1900 architectural marvel); Le Luxembourg, 4, pl. du Luxembourg (convenient, fast).

Bars & Cafés. Hôtel Albert 1er et Astoria, 3, rue de l'Armée Patton (cozy, intimate); L'Altea, 11, rue R.-Poincaré (perfect for business meetings), Grand Café Foy, 1, pl. Stanislas (to admire the setting); Stan, rue Ste-Catherine (excellent bar of the Grand Hôtel de la Reine).

Nightlife. Jean Lam, pl. Stanislas (a venerable institution); La Scala, rue St-Dizier (young).

Shops. *Butchers:* Branchu, 52, rue Stanislas (excellent quality); Rocher, 28, rue R.-Poincaré; Wolff, covered market (superb choice of poultry, game and foie gras). *Bakeries:* Collin, 125, Grande-Rue (don't let the long lines deter you). *Chocolate:* Michel Lalonde, 32, rue St-Jean, and 28, rue Héré (bergamots, macaroons and fine chocolates). *Cheese:* Michel Marchand, covered market. *Pastries:* Jean-Marie Génot, 129, rue St-Dizier (the most creative).

Les Agaves

2, rue des Carmes - 83.32.14.14

M. Durand. Open until 10:30 p.m. Closed Sun., Mon. dinner, 3 weeks in Feb. & 8 days end Oct. Pets allowed. Cards: V, AE, DC.

The new almond-green decor is bright, airy, comfortable and in good modern taste, but it's a bit cold, which could be remedied with a touch more effort and eagerness on behald of the staff. Gilles Durand, who came up from the Côte d'-Azur, knows his cuisine: salmon terrine highlighted with an anchovy flavor; a respectable brill steak with bacon and croutons, accompanied by perfect young vegetables; saddle of lamb with kidneys; and classic, well-made desserts (chocolate gourmandin with mint cream).

A la carte: 220F. Menus: 160F (holidays only), 79F, 99F, 145F.

Albert Ier et Astoria

3, rue Armée-Patton - 83.40.31.24

Open year-round. 126 rms 160-295F. TV. Garage parking. Telex 850895. Cards: V, AE, DC, MC.

Functional rooms, some just redone, without much character but overlooking a pleasant interior garden. Solarium, sauna, shiatsu massage. No restaurant.

Le Capucin Gourmand

31, rue Gambetta - 83.35.26.98

M. Veissière. Open until 10 p.m. Closed Sun. dinner, Mon. & Aug. Air cond. Cards: V, AE.

The 50ish Gérard Veissière, now joined in the kitchen by his eldest son, employs all of his talents and throws himself into his efforts to sustain his reputation as the most brilliant chef in Nancy. The attractive woodwork decor, some 60 years old, is in the most refined "Nancy school" style. Upon stepping into the cheerful dining room filled with precious knickknacks, we developed an appetite immediately and were happy to see listed such dishes as warm lobster salad with oil, bass filet cooked in its skin and served with a thick ginger sauce, salmon steeped with peppers, and simply grilled beefsteak with a leek gratin and a Muscadet wine sauce. Superb wines, remarkably generous fixed-price menus.

A la carte: 350-400F. Menus: 150F, 220F, 380F.

Central Hôtel

6, rue Raymond-Poincaré - 83.32.21.24

Open year-round. 68 rms 175-260F. TV. Pets allowed. Telex 850895. Cards: V.

An excellent hotel, renovated from top to bottom, the Central has a pleasant garden and double windows, which allow for a quiet night in the heart of town. No restaurant.

12/20 Le Comptoir des Maréchaux

1, pl. Vaudémont - 83.35.51.94

M. Tanesy. Open until 11 p.m. Closed Sun., Mon. (except dinner in summer), 1 week in Feb., 1 week at Easter & Sept. 1-15. Pets allowed. Cards: V.

This perfectly luxurious little bistro, firmly directed by Patrick and Josette Tanesy, welcomes Nancy's high society, which crowds in for the fine rural cuisine: tripe plate, grilled salmon, warm tarte tatin. Excellent wines by the glass.

Menus: 85F, 145F.

15 Le Goéland

27, rue des Ponts - 83.35.17.25

M. Mengin. Open until 10 p.m. Closed Mon. lunch. Air cond. Pets allowed. Cards: V, AE, DC.

The Pompadour tapestries have been stripped away, revealing cream-colored walls, which add to the refined geometric elegance here. With pale-green carpets, indirect lighting and varnished marble, it barely escapes coldness in being Nancy's first luxurious contemporary restaurant. Jean-Luc Mengin's almost exclusively seafood repertoire has loads of imagination, personality and subtlety; his problems with cooking precision seems to be over, and he has brought his desserts up to a level worthy of the rest of the cuisine (delicious strawberry gratiné with vanilla ice cream). Try the splendid fish aspic (really a fragrant terrine—the lumpfish caviar is superfluous), exquisite red mullet filets, oven-browned in their skin and topped with a fine caviar sauce, or the plentiful fine potée with cabbage. The affable lady of the house, Danièle Mengin, is a wine connoisseur. The prices, however, are hard to swallow.

A la carte: 300-400F. Menus: 120F, 180F.

Le Stanislas

2, pl. Stanislas - 83.35.03.01

M. Ziegler. Open daily until 10:30 p.m. No pets. Parking. Telex 960367. Cards: V, AE, DC, MC.

The locals barely had a chance to taste the delights of Yves Jury's cuisine before he left recently to go back to cook at his family's old hotel in Chaufailles. His number two, Pascal Walter, has worked very hard to pick up everything from his boss, but we haven't yet had the chance to see if the lessons were well learned. We hope that all is still well with the strudel of pigeon thighs, the crusty potatoes with foie gras and the layers of crisp crêpes and red fruits. In any case, the splendid dining room in this magnificent eighteenth-century home, which looks onto one of the prettiest squares in the world, is still in place, and it seems an unlikely place to find poor cooking, especially in the wake of a chef like Jury.

A la carte: 300-350F. Menus: 155F (wine incl.), 210F.

Grand Hôtel de la Reine

(See restaurant above)

Open year-round. 5 stes 650-1,450F. 46 rms 400-650F. TV. Golf.

This remarkable hotel, luxuriously decorated with antique furniture, is a perfect complement to the place Stanislas. Its salons and stairways are registered landmarks, and rooms have marvelous Louis XV decors, particularly those that open onto the place. Relais et Châteaux.

14 La Toison d'Or

11, rue Raymond-Poincaré - 83.35.61.01

M. Laxenaire. Open daily until 10:30 p.m. Air cond. Pets allowed. Garage parking. Telex 960034. Cards: V, AE, DC, MC.

Pinks and grays are peacefully blended in this new decor, where the tables are well spaced, the chairs comfortable, and the staff excellent. Fine products, many from the region, are treated with just the right touch of originality by young Bernard Denauw. He could certainly be a bit less timid and simpler in his execution, which is sometimes complicated: crab–wild mushroom gratin, perch feuillantine with broad beans, grilled breast of duck with pepper and grapefruit. Pastries are improving a bit.

A la carte: 250F. Menus: 135F (weekday only, wine incl.), 160F (weekends and holidays only, wine incl.), 220F.

Altea Thiers

(See restaurant above)

Open year-round. 4 stes 450-500F. 108 rms 305-400F. TV. Pets allowed.

Beautiful, spacious rooms, tastefully decorated. Excellent bar, sauna, weight room.

IN NEARBY **Flavigny-sur-Moselle**
(16 km NE on N 74 & N 57)
54630 Flavigny-sur-Moselle - (Meurthe-et-Moselle)

15 Le Prieuré

3, rue du Prieuré - 83.26.70.45

M. Roy. Open until 9:30 p.m. Closed Sun. dinner, Wed., holidays, Feb. school vacation & Nov. 1. No pets. Parking. Cards: V, AE, DC, MC.

Though not very alluring, this large manor house nevertheless has a comfortable and pleasing decor, particularly given its setting in an insignificant roadside village. This decor mixes bourgeois and peasant styles—no luxury but a nice, simple atmosphere and elegant tables. Joël Roy came to this austere part of the Lorraine not to be forgotten but to create one of the best places in the region (which currently has a dearth of good restaurants). Not one to make concessions, Roy was regarded cautiously by the locals when he introduced such imaginative and original dishes as a tartare of oysters or salmon, a salad of warm duck foie gras and langoustines, turbot viennoise with fresh noodles and tomatoes, and poached squab in red wine with foie gras ravioli. He finally won over disbelievers with his careful execution, which is neither weak nor colorless. Fine inexpensive fixed-price menus with a regional flavor make good use of local mirabelle plums and Meuse truffles and wink at the Lorraine with a warm crêpe of smoked sander, gratin of frogs' legs with fresh Xaintois goat cheese, and an escargots casserole with Toul wine brandy. Well-chosen wines.

A la carte: 300-350F. Menus: 155F (weekday lunch only), 210F, 270F.

Nans-les-Pins

83860 Nans-les-Pins - (Var)
Paris 811 - Toulon 61 - Aix 43 - Marseille 41

Domaine de Châteauneuf

N 560, Logis de Nans - 94.78.90.06

Closed Nov. 30-April 1. 6 stes 925-1,750F. 26 rms 420-630F. Half-board 430-1,100F oblig. in seas. TV. Heated pool. Tennis. Golf. Parking. Telex 400747. Cards: V, AE, DC, MC.

At this beautiful residence surrounded by a huge park, you'll find a pleasant terrace, eighteen-hole golf course and three tennis courts. The stylish rooms are not large, but they're well conceived. Relais et Châteaux.

Nantes

44000 Nantes - (Loire-Atlantique)
Paris 392 - Rennes 106 - Vannes 109 - Angers 87

Sights. Château of the Dukes of Brittany (tower of the golden crown, horseshoe tower, wells); museums (d'Art Populaire, d'Art Décoratif, de la Marine); Saint-Pierre and Saint-Paul cathedrals (Gothic arches); the eighteenth-century village (passage Pommeraye, rue Santeuil, cours Cambronne, pl. Graslin); Jardin des Plantes (beautiful exotic greenhouses); Musée des Beaux-Arts (exceptional paintings); Musée d'Archéologie Régionale; Palais Dobrée (Roman and Gothic treasures); the old Ile Feydeau (quai de la Fosse).

Eating on the Run. On the rue Kervégan: at number 28, Les Boucaniers (varied); at number 19, La Gratinée (soups); at number 13, Poivre et Sel (pleasant atmosphere); and at number 11, Le Roma (fine pasta). Chez Fanfan, 2, rue Suffren (good pizzas, a soccer players' hangout); Hanoi, 20, rue St-Léonard (good Chinese food); Le Petit Faitout, 2, rue Armand-Brossard (southwest cuisine); La Poissonerie, 4, pl. Neptune (fish, family-style cuisine); Rio-Sul, 19, allées Baco (Brazilian, hot spot until 6 a.m.); Au Vieux Quimper, 10, rue Bâclerie (excellent crêpes).

Brasseries. Les Arcades, 8, rue Racine (salads, daily specials); Le Molière, pl. Graslin (young, chic).

Bars & Cafés. Pullman, 3, rue du Dr-Zamenhof, and Sofitel, blvd. A.-Millerand (both on the Ile Beaulieu); Le Bouffray, 2, pl. du Bouffray; Café de la Place, 1, pl. du Bouffray (on market days); Le Delorme, 1, pl. Delorme (student spot); Le Marlowe, 1, pl. St-Vincent (piano bar, cocktails); Le Trianon, 11, pl. de la Bourse (beer, cocktails).

Nightlife. Le Balapapa, quai Fernard-Crouan; Le Fox Trot, 32 bis, rue de Crucy; L'Interdit, 14, rue Menou (men only); Le New Way, 4, pl. Emile-Zola (popular three-story spot); Pub Univers, 16, rue J.-J.-Rousseau (jazz); Le Speak Easy, 24, blvd. E.-Orieux (pleasant); Le Tie Break, 1, rue des Petites-Ecuries (piano bar, band).

Shops. *Bakeries:* Elie Brisson, le Petit-Chantilly, 3, ave. de la Corniche in Orvault (best brioche); La Huche à Pain, 23, rue des Carmes (50 varieties). *Charcuteries, caterers:* Brison, 7, rue Franklin (beautiful products); Chagneau, 4, rue du Général-de-Gaulle in Saint-Sébastien-sur-Loire (excellent); Hébel, 30, rue de la Bastille (for foie gras). *Chocolate:* Gauthier, 9, rue de la Fosse (superb 1900 decor). *Pastries:* La Brioche Vendéenne, blvd. des Pas-Enchantés in Saint-Sébastien-sur-Loire (special creations); Jamin, 15, rue Crébillon (undoubtedly the best). *Loire salmon:* Le Fumoir, La Marionnière in Champtoceaux (smoked salmon). *Wine:* Le Fief de Vigne, 16, rue Marceau (Muscadets and Vendée wines, among others).

Beaujoire Hôtel

Rue des Pays-de-la-Loire - 40.93.00.01

Open year-round. 41 rms 230-245F. TV. Pets allowed. Parking. Telex 701438. Cards: V, AE.

Spanking new, with functional, bright rooms in a pleasant building. Restaurant.

12/20 Café du Marché

1, rue de Mayence - 40.47.63.50

M. Le Nay. Lunch only. Closed Sat., Sun., last week in July & 1st 3 weeks in Aug. Pets allowed.

At this extraordinary and unchanging bistro from the former marketplace, the entire family is at work, making a delicious cuisine served with the best Muscadet wines at unbelievable prices: shellfish and langoustine salad, rabbit stew, potée (hot cabbage pot), remarkable calf's head, caramel rice.

Menu: 80F.

15 Le Colvert

14, rue A.-Brossard - 40.48.20.02

M. Macouin. Open until 10:30 p.m. Closed Sat. lunch, Sun. & Sept. Air cond. Pets allowed. Cards: V, MC.

Despite the fact that the Loire wines are delicious, the prices reasonable, the fixed-price menus sensational and the lady of the house charming, this place still hasn't gotten the credit it deserves. Perhaps the Nantais find the beige-and-wheat-colored decor too slack or poorly lit. (Local boy Didier Macouin does plan to spruce up the place.) But it's still more than worthwhile to visit for the little coquilles St-Jacques cooked in an oil sauce with zucchini and bell peppers, precisely pan-fried red mullet with two kinds of cream sauces (one with oysters, the other with foie gras), magnificent young pigeon roasted with lentils and a honey sauce, and a casserole of prunes and orange rind with a wonderful fragrance.

A la carte: 250-280F. Menus: 100F (lunch only), 120F, 170F to 240F.

L'Hôtel

6, rue Henri-IV - 40.29.30.31

Open year-round. 32 rms 295-370F. TV. Garage parking. Cards: V, AE, DC, MC.

All the rooms are attractive, cheerful and decorated with refinement, some with a pleasant terrace. Located on a nice spot near Beaulieu and the Jardin des Plantes. Excellent breakfast. No restaurant.

(13) Les Lions de Canton

10, blvd. Jean-XXIII - 40.76.72.27

MM. Gouon. Open until 10 p.m. Closed Sun. dinner, Mon. & Aug. 15-31. No pets. Cards: V, AE, DC.

Where does the touch of the Orient in the sophisticated salmon-tone decor (with stylish armchairs and cashmere hangings reflected in the mirrors) come from? Why, from the owners: two Eurasian brothers, Charles and François Gouon. You can hardly call this elegant restaurant Chinese—its short à la carte menu and its manner are robustly French. However, a scent of exoticism comes through in the light cuisine: salade gourmande with shrimp, fish and crab, lotte stew with a fine minty perfume, well-balanced honey-glazed duck and delicious (and ungreasy) fritters. Wonderful, extremely courteous service.

A la carte: 230F. Menus: 100F (weekdays only), 160F.

(16) Les Maraîchers

21, rue Fouré - 40.47.06.51

M. Pacreau. Open until 11 p.m. Closed Sat. (except by reserv.) & Sun. Air cond. Pets allowed. Cards: V, AE, DC.

Roguish and assertive Serge Pacreau is the most Parisian of the region's restaurateurs, and he's always full of wit and surprises. (Among his staff is 1984's Mr. France, a member of the muscular crew of waiters.) He is a master of paradoxes, humor and blunt statements. The cheerful ambience that results is of the sort rarely found in the provinces. It does, of course, irritate a few and cause some gnashing of teeth, but primarily from competitors. Nantes's high society crowds, particularly evident at night, enjoy the pretty dining room done up in red chintz, with contemporary paintings on the walls. (The second dining room, in beige and cream tones, is starting to show its age.) Therefore it seemed catastrophic when Pacreau lost his superb chef, Yves Benneteau, but the loss has proven to be not nearly so bad, thanks to the efforts of his able, promising sous-chef, Philippe Tisserat. Of course, Tisserat is still finding his style and lacks some of Benneteau's panache, but his cassolette of prawns with raspberries, timbale of spider crab and zucchini, and John Dory with periwinkles and excellent little vegetables are not dishes that in any way mar the reputation of this fine restaurant. And the pastry chef has made great strides: superlative apricot tart, and a lovely marriage of verveine (verbena) and green-tomato sorbets. The fine ambience remains the same, gentle and discreet at lunch, a little livelier at night, and always infused with Pacreau's great spirit.

A la carte: 350-400F. Menus: 175F, 230F and 350F (wine incl.).

(13) Le Tilbury

Blvd. A.-Millerand - 40.47.61.03

M. Bouclet. Open daily until 11 p.m. Air cond. Garden dining. Pets allowed. Garage parking. Telex 710990. Cards: V, AE, DC, MC.

A new name, a new two-level interior and a new chef can now be found at this restaurant facing the Loire. The result is a compromise in the cuisine, which now at least attempts to please everyone's tastes. It's well made and generous, including calf's head in a ravigote sauce (white wine, vinegar, shallot butter), stuffed sole à la royale with mushrooms, and saddle of lamb grilled with the bone in. Desserts are good, but the wine list is a bit weak.

A la carte: 250-280F. Menus: 95F to 140F.

Sofitel

(See restaurant above)

Open year-round. 2 stes 950-1,100F. 98 rms 490-650F. TV. Air cond. Heated pool. Tennis.

On the quiet isle of Beaulieu near the center of town is this fine soundproofed and air-conditioned hotel that's perfectly suited to conferences, with its modern facilities. Heated pool, terrace.

(13) Le Tillac

3, rue du Dr-Zamenhof - 40.47.10.58

M. Darenne. Open daily until 10:15 p.m. Garden dining. Pets allowed. Garage parking. Telex 711440. Cards: V, AE, DC, MC.

A resurrection has been accomplished here on all fronts. The somber, cold decor has been brightened up with flowers on the well-spaced tables and a pretty view of the countryside. Other additions include a cordial hostess, rapid service and a new chef, who hails from the Nikko hotel in Paris. His varied, light and pleasantly regionalized cuisine includes oyster stew with a well-balanced langoustine coulis, fish en papillote (cooked in foil), which was slightly overcooked but had an exquisite celery sauce (could be lighter), excellent lemon meringue tart.

A la carte: 250F. Menus: 130F (wine incl.), 68F, 180F.

Pullman Beaulieu

(See restaurant above)

Open year-round. 1 ste 900-1,100F. 149 rms 300-560F. TV. Pets allowed.

Indisputably the most beautiful hotel in Nantes today. All the rooms have been harmoniously and attractively renovated, featuring perfect amenities and soundproofing. Cheerful bellhop service and a good breakfast.

(16) Torigaï

Ile de Versailles - 40.37.06.37

M. Torigaï. Open until 10 p.m. Closed Sun. & Aug. Garden dining. Cards: V.

Shigeo Torigaï is the incontestable star of Japanese chefs in France. A former student of Michel Guérard, he was impressive at his restaurant in Bretagne; here, after a sojourn back home in Japan, he is astounding. It is a treat to crowd into this freshly decorated dining room with Nantes's chic set to be served such intelligent, such perfectly done and—yes—such French cooking. Torigaï achieves balance, clarity of flavors and inventiveness with startling ease. His coquilles St-Jacques on the half-shell scented with truffles; red snapper filets cooked in the pan with sea urchin butter and fried zucchini; noisettes of lamb roasted en croûte with eggplant; tropical fruit "ravioli"; and bitter- chocolate cake layered with raspberries can stand with anyone's. The wine list is diverse and full of lovely Bordeaux and good Loire bottles at very reasonable prices. And the fixed-price menus, including the Japanese one, are full of good things.

A la carte: 280-330F. Menus: 95F and 140F (weekdays only), 195F, 240F, 290F.

IN NEARBY **Basse-Goulaine**
(8 km E on D 119)
44115 Basse-Goulaine - (Loire-Atlantique)

14 Mon Rêve

Rte. des Bords-de-Loire - 40.03.55.50

M. Ryngel. Open until 9:30 p.m. Closed Wed. (off-seas.), Sun. dinner & Feb. school vacation. Garden dining. Pets allowed. Parking. Cards: V, AE, DC.

This nice country inn on the banks of the Loire reminds us of those blessed days when one could take a quiet stroll along the river, and it has pretty well withstood the ravages of time. Gérard Ryngel has obstinately but gently stood his ground, despite the highways and interchanges, retaining the charm of his lovely bourgeois house and its rhododendron garden. The cuisine is classic and well made, using fine products and radiating sincere generosity: warm salad of plump langoustines with tarragon, wild duck aiguillettes lightly cooked with a delicious blend of cèpes and girolles (wild mushrooms), eels with fresh, savory herbs and an original dessert made with a Muscadet flan, prunes and apples. The exceptional "gourmandise" fixed-price menu offers foie gras, salmon, leg of lamb and more. Exclusive Nantais wines are poured.

A la carte: 300F. Menus: 108F (weekdays only), 130F (weekdays only, wine incl.), 296F (wine incl.), 138F to 250F.

IN NEARBY **Bellevue**
(9 km E on D 68 & D 337)
44480 Ste-Luce-sur-Loire - (Loire-Atlantique)

15 Delphin

3, promenade de Bellevue - 40.25.60.39

MM. Delphin. Open until 9:30 p.m. Closed Sun. dinner & Mon. Pets allowed. Cards: V, AE, DC, MC.

If you like lovely starched tablecloths and table linens, silver candlesticks and little silver-gilt spoons, you'll find them here, along with such other old-fashioned treats as amuse-gueules (cocktail snacks), petits fours, mignardises (pastries) and service in the grand style (waiters who stand at attention, dressed in black, white and violet outfits). It's all terribly retro-French and nostalgically provincial, the creation of Joseph and Janie Delphin, champions of these delicious frills. Mirrors in the three sumptuous dining rooms reflect the beige-caramel tapestries, the view of the Loire and the gull-filled Nantais sky. The kitchen turns out a masterful French cuisine with superb sauces (though sometimes we wish they'd be more discreet). True, the presentation is pompous, but there's plenty of creativity, generosity and exactitude (Delphin has commercialized an efficient steam-cooking method). Try the warm lotte salad with turmeric, lobster with a hazelnut cream sauce, warm foie gras with honey and artichokes, red mullet and eels in Chinon wine, warm caramel soufflé and caramel ice cream. Excellent fixed-price menus and good-value Loire wines.

A la carte: 350F. Menus: 255F (weekday lunch only), 155F, 255F to 360F.

IN NEARBY **Orvault**
(7 km NW on N 137 & D 42)
44700 Orvault - (Loire-Atlantique)

Le Domaine d'Orvault

Chemin des Marais-du-Cens
40.76.84.02

M. Bernard. Open until 9:30 p.m. Closed Mon. lunch & 3 weeks in Feb. Garden dining. Pets allowed. Parking. Cards: V, AE, DC.

In this beautiful estate in the middle of a silent, lush-green countryside in the Cens valley, the decor is slightly solemn but not without elegance. The Bernard family is very attentive to details: Tables are set with refinement, the staff is one of the best in the region, and a pianist livens up the dinner atmosphere. The cuisine is subtle and sometimes a bit too complicated, but it's well studied and uses the most beautiful products: thyme-seasoned ragoût of artichokes and petits-gris (escargots) à la tomate, fresh herring terrine in a light mustard sauce, kidneys à la diable (flattened and grilled in a shallot sauce) with steamed rice and a hazelnut sauce, wild-strawberry gratin and a caramelized pear sauté. Excellent wines. Prices are going through the roof.

A la carte: 350-500F. Menus: 170F, 230F, 270F, 350F.

Le Domaine d'Orvault

(See restaurant above)

Open year-round. 1 ste 700F. 29 rms 270-520F. Half-board 450- 610F. TV. Pets allowed. Tennis.

Ten minutes from the center of Nantes is this oasis of calm in a large forest. Pleasant rooms with fine facilities. Relais et Châteaux.

IN NEARBY **Saint-Sébastien-sur-Loire**
(SE)
44230 St-Sébastien-sur-Loire - (Loire-Atlantique)

15 Manoir de la Comète

21, rue de la Libération - 40.34.15.93

MM. Thomas-Thomphime. Open until 10 p.m. Closed Sat. lunch, Sun., Feb. school vacation & July 25-Aug. 17. Garden dining. Pets allowed. Garage parking. Cards: V.

This fin-de-siècle manor house boasts the most attractive restaurant in the Nantes region, a place where, in nice weather, tables are set on a superb terrace overlooking the woods. The best of the two dining rooms, upstairs, has gray flannel on the walls, with contemporary paintings. You'll also find clear curtains with white quilting, lovely tables and a greeting from patronne Edith Thomas, who knows how to receive guests and is a connoisseur of wines. The wine list includes reasonably priced Bordeaux, excellent Burgundies and magnificent Anjou vintages. In the kitchen, Christian Thomas-Tromphine is on the right track, producing a variable list of offerings and quite "technical" dishes that respect their products and flavors (superb sauces): lobster-and-cèpes ravioli with beurre rouge; a zucchini-shellfish gâteau with olive oil; larded turbot; a cabbage aumonière (purse); and exciting and light desserts, such as strawberries in a lemon sabayon sauce and the "all-chocolate" dessert. An exceptionally good low-priced fixed menu is accompanied by regional wines in carafes.

A la carte: 300-350F. Menus: 160F and 340F (wine incl.), 110F, 215F, 275F.

Nantua

01130 Nantua - (Ain)
Paris 479 - Geneva 64 - Lyon 92 - Annecy 66

L'Embarcadère

Ave. du Lac - 74.75.22.28

Closed Dec. 20-Jan. 20 & May 1-8. 50 rms 200-280F. Half-board 235-245F. TV. Parking. Cards: V.

The lake is on one side, the forest on the other. The rooms don't look like much, but they have good facilities and are irreproachably maintained. Restaurant.

(13) Hôtel de France

44, rue du Dr-Mercier - 74.75.00.55

M. Pauchard. Open until 9 p.m. Closed Tues. Jan.-March, Fri. April-Oct. (open daily July-Aug.) & Nov. 1-Dec. 20. Pets allowed. Hotel: 19 rms 172-325F. Garage parking. Cards: V, MC.

The tables at this inviting hotel are the most attractively flowered in Nantua. The reception is always cheerful, the bourgeois decor full of charm, and the menu abundant with appetizing suggestions (though some aren't so great). Try the delicious lake trout à l'eclusière (shallots, cream and white wine), the fine vegetable terrine with herbs and the guinea-hen salmis served with gratin dauphinois. Beautiful cheeses (comté, bleu), rather ordinary but well-made desserts and a wine cellar rich in Jura vintages.

A la carte: 280F. Menus: 123F, 190F.

La Napoule

06210 Mandelieu - (Alpes-Maritimes)
Paris 850 - St-Raphaël 34 - Cannes 8 - Nice 41

Ermitage du Riou

3, blvd. du Bord-de-Mer - 93.49.95.56

Open year-round. 2 stes 870-1,460F. 40 rms 445-1,160F. Half- board 425-720F. TV. Air cond. in 30 rms. Pool. Pets allowed. Parking. Telex 470072. Cards: V, AE, DC, MC.

Rooms and suites—some with large terraces—face the ocean, the port, the golf course or the swimming pool. Beautiful flower garden. Restaurant.

This symbol stands for "Les Lauriers du Terroir," an award given to chefs who prepare noteworthy traditional or regional recipes.

Loews

Blvd. H.-Clews - 93.49.90.00

Open year-round. 25 stes 2,790-6,390F. 186 rms 675-730F. TV. Air cond. Pets allowed. Heated pool. Tennis. Telex 469820. Cards: V, AE, DC, MC.

Extremely handsome ultra-modern rooms facing the sea are freshly and alluringly decorated. Noteworthy conference facilities. Piano bar and restaurant.

L'Oasis

Rue Jean-Honoré-Carle

Closed.

We cannot see L'Oasis disappear without saluting Louis Outhier, who turned this old boarding house into one of the best and most prestigious restaurants in France (a 19.5 rating and 4 toques in previous editions of this guide). He surprised everyone when he announced its closing. He hasn't quite hung up his apron, though, since he has been asked to be a consultant around the world; he's supervising the Lafayette at the Drake Hotel in New York. Despite this unexpected departure, we hope to find him somewhere, someday, in the kitchen again.

Narbonne

11100 Narbonne - (Aude)
Paris 850 - Perpignan 62 - Béziers 27 - Carcassonne 56

La Résidence

6, rue du 1er-Mai - 68.32.19.41

Closed Jan. 2-30. 26 rms 265-320F. TV. Air cond. in 8 rms. Garage parking. Telex 500441. Cards: V.

Near the Saint-Just cathedral and the Archbishops' Palace. No restaurant.

(16) La Réverbère

4, pl. des Jacobins - 68.32.29.18

M. Giraud. Open until 9:30 p.m. Closed Sun. dinner & Mon. Air cond. Pets allowed. Cards: V, AE, DC.

Claude Giraud has installed an ultra-modern kitchen and a new decor (though we thought the old one was pleasant) in a cozy English style that's quite charming, with pretty green tones and monogrammed china sparkling on the damask tablecloths. This renovation hasn't improved Sabine Giraud's reception, which is still quite stiff, or the service, which borders on incompetence (despite the waiters' white gloves). But it did seem to help the cuisine, whose imagination has taken off. Girard's simpler techniques produce a violet-artichoke broth highlighted with fresh chives, superb petits-gris (escargots) from the nearby moor in a sort of pastry made of thin slices of potatoes and served with a light herb-oil sauce, crusty hen with spinach shoots and delicious tagliatelle pasta with poultry liver. Almost all the desserts are vibrant (try the marvelous tea cream with brown sugar and orange blossoms). The exceptional wines from all regions deserve a more informed sommelier.

A la carte: 400-500F. Menus: 160F (weekdays only), 200F, 320F, 450F.

IN NEARBY **Narbonne-Plage**
(15 km E on D 168)
11100 Narbonne-Plage - (Aude)

Hôtel de la Clape

Rue des Flots-Bleus - 68.49.80.15

Closed Nov. 6-Easter. 12 rms 155-210F. No pets. Parking.

This comfortable small hotel facing the sea has a relaxed atmosphere and pleasant owners. No restaurant.

Les Flots-Bleu

Pl. des Karantes - 68.49.83.47

Mme. Marty. Open until 10:30 p.m. Closed Tues. & Wed. (except July 1-Sept. 15) & Dec. 1-Feb. 15. Terrace dining. Pets allowed. Cards: V, MC.

At this opulent, cheerful place facing the sea, Rose-Marie Marty, the owner, grills superb fish (turbot, sole, lotte) caught by her husband, over wine-stock frames with great dexterity. She also prepares with sincerity such tasty dishes as eel civet au fitou (stew with local wine) and bass stuffed with a garlic cream. Good local wines. This place is modest, appealing and well worth its toque.

A la carte: 230F. Menus: 80F (except holidays), 150F.

IN NEARBY **Ornaisons**
(14 km W on N 113 & D 24)
11200 Lézignan-Corbières - (Aude)

Relais du Val d'Orbieu

D 24 - 68.27.10.27

M. Gonzalvez. Open until 9:30 p.m. Closed 1 week in Feb. Garden dining. Pets allowed. Parking. Cards: V, AE, DC, MC.

Set prettily among the vineyards, this former mill near the Corbières gates has begun attracting crowds since its new, very serious owner renovated and transformed it into a luxurious vacation hotel with a fine restaurant. His talented young chef has since left, but an impressive, solid veteran, Jean-Pierre Robert, was hired just before press time. Knowing him as we do (from Nice), we can confidently predict a delicious future for the Relais, along with a fine rating (once we have had the chance to get here).

A la carte: 300-330F. Menus: 150F, 230F, 320F.

Relais du Val d'Orbieu

(See restaurant above)

Closed 1 week in Feb. 7 stes 750-1,300F. 15 rms 380-660F. Half-board 540-650F oblig. in seas. Pets allowed. Pool. Tennis.

This pretty, squat house in the style of the region holds not-terribly-cheerful rooms that are nonetheless perfectly comfortable. The inn is quite well equipped, with a swimming pool, heliport, garden and more. Good breakfast and perfect reception.

Natzwiller

see Schirmeck

Neuilly-sur-Seine

see PARIS SUBURBS

Nevers

58000 Nevers - (Nièvre)
Paris 239 - Dijon 190 - Montargis 124 - Bourges 68

Sights. Saint-Cyr-et-Sainte-Julitte cathedral (with its double apse); the neighboring districts; the lovely palace of the Polish princesses; the square, with its small theater; the old streets leading up to Saint-Etienne church (extraordinary in its luminosity and purity of lines); the door of the Croux; the china collection at the Musée Municipal; and (for those who like such things) the shrine of Bernadette Soubirous (located in the chapel of Saint-Gildard convent).

Eating on the Run. Coquillat, 84, rue de Nièvre (for fish); La Grignote, 7, rue Ferdinand-Gambon; Istambul, 53, rue de la Barre (very good Turkish restaurant); San Remo, 12, rue du 14-Juillet (fine pizzeria).

Bars & Cafés. Black Horse, 37, rue de la Barre (beer and tasty meat dishes); Broadway, 7, rue du Fer (good music); Donalds, 3, rue du Commerce (a variety of good beer in a cordial atmosphere); Le Petit Verdot, 32, rue de Nièvre (excellent wine bar, hearty cuisine).

Nightlife. Le Privilège, at the Pougues casino (a lovely place); Le Relais Bleu, 63, blvd. Dagonneau (a new piano bar).

Château de la Rocherie

6 km N on N 7, Varennes-Vauzelles
86.38.07.21

MM. Reparet & Brunat. Open until 9:30 p.m. Closed Sun. & Jan. 1-15. Garden dining. Pets allowed. Parking. Cards: V, AE, DC.

The romanticism of this large nineteenth-century castle-style mansion had become a bit shabby, but it's been given new life, now that the dining room decor has been brightened and the general surroundings attended to. These days, owner Pierre Reparet (a former cook at Troisgros) can devote all his attention to the quality of his cuisine. Though a bit confused at times, it possesses a lovely and honest generosity: salad of pigeon, watercress and new onions, coquilles St-Jacques with corn salad and aiguillettes of duck garnished with a fricassée of radishes. There is a lovely short fixed-price menu; the wine cellar is being expanded judiciously; and the reception is extremely gracious.

A la carte: 280-300F. Menus: 85F (wine incl.), 150F, 200F, 270F.

Château de la Rocherie

(See restaurant above)

Closed Sun. & Jan. 1-15. 14 rms 150-260F. No pets.

The spacious rooms in this charming hotel are being renovated one by one, and though their decor is irregular, they are undeniably comfortable. The environment is peaceful, the service gracious, and the park superb.

La Porte du Croux

17, rue de la Porte-du-Croux
86.57.12.71

M. Gély. Open until 9:30 p.m. Closed Aug. 15-31. Garden dining. Pets allowed. Hotel: 2 rms 150-180F; half-board 245-320F. Parking. Cards: V, AE, DC, MC.

This lovely white house located in a quiet district of Nevers has a rustic, softly lit, delightfully quaint dining room that opens onto a flower garden, which is illuminated at night. In summer, the tasty, scrupulous cuisine—whose creativity lies solely with fresh fish obtained directly from the fishermen (sea bass sautéed with young turnips and turbot with creamed lettuce)—is served on the terrace. There is also a wonderful calf's head, some beautiful grilled meats and several splendid desserts, particularly the ice creams.

A la carte: 280-320F. Menus: 95F (except holidays), 190F.

Nice

06000 Nice - (Alpes-Maritimes)
Paris 943 - Lyon 475 - Marseille 188 - Turin 222

Note: The numbers following the telephone number in each review pinpoint the establishment's exact location on the accompanying map.

Sights. The promenade des Anglais; Old Nice; the cours Saleya (flower market and Monday antiques market); the fish market (on pl. St-François); the Acropolis; the Cimiez Arenas (home of the famous Jazz Festival); Musée des Beaux-Arts Jules Chéret (featuring nineteenth-century works); Musée Masséna (primitive-style paintings from the Nice region); Musée d'Art Naïf (one of the most beautiful collections in the world); Musée Chagall (its 450 paintings portray biblical themes); Musée Terra Amata (on the site of major paleontological discoveries); Musée Matisse; the regional primitive-style paintings at the Cimiez monastery; the Observatory.

Eating on the Run. Acchiardo, 38, rue Droite (regional dishes of Nice); Auberge de Théo, 52, ave. Cap-de-Croix (pizza and Italian specialties); La Datcha, 1 bis, rue Dalpozzo (caviar, smoked fish, vodka and pear cake); Fjord, 21, rue François-Guisol (lake-trout eggs and homemade gravlax); Grand Café de Turin, 5, pl. Garibaldi (shellfish); Chez Pipo, 13, rue Bavastro (deserving of its title, "king of the socca"); Puccini, 1, rue Louis-Gassin (sandwiches and salads, perfect for lovers of Old Nice); Restaurant du Théâtre de Nice (pre- and post-theater dinners); Scotch Tea House, 4, ave. Gustave-V (breakfast and daily specials in an artistic atmosphere); Le Tire-Bouchon, 19, rue de la Préfecture (wine bar, generous variety plate).

Brasseries. Berthet, 10, ave. Félix-Faure (daily specials); Félix-Faure, 12, ave. Félix-Faure (youthful, casual atmosphere); Le Koudou, 28, promenade des Anglais (extremely popular terrace); Kronenbourg, 55, rue Gioffredo (classical ambience); Le Mozart, 11 bis, ave. Baquis (quiet and discreet).

Bars & Cafés. Atlantic, 12, blvd. Victor-Hugo (Le New-Bar); L'Aventure, 12, rue Chauvain (piano bar, classic, fashionable atmosphere); Beach-Regency, 223, Promenade des Anglais (piano bar); La Bièrerie (Chez Nino), rue Trachel (130 different beers from around the world); House Bar, 26, blvd. Victor-Hugo (soft atmosphere, music, chess games); Park Hôtel, 6, ave. George-V; Pullman, 25, ave. Notre-Dame (lovely bar of the former Frantel); Scarlett-O'Hara, 22, rue Droite (piano bar, Irish coffee).

Nightlife. L'Accordéon, 36, rue de France (dancing in an upbeat atmosphere); L'Arlequin, Passage Emile-Négrin (fashionable, features "psychedelic" evenings); Blue Boy, 9, rue J. B. Spinetta (gay, but admits women on Wednesdays); La Camargue, 6, pl. Charles-Félix (popular club); Club des Ecossais, 6, rue Halévy (becoming fashionable, quiet atmosphere for singles and late-nighters); Le Grand Escurial, 29, rue Alphonse-Karr (energetic reception, young atmosphere, light show); Le Quartz, 18, rue du Congrès (classic); Ruby's Club, 8, descente Crotti (West Indian atmosphere).

Shops. *Bakeries:* André Espuno, 22, rue Vernier (for its Poilâne from Nice). *Charcuteries, caterers:* Calluaud, 2, rue Maccarini (the caterer for the *tout* Nice, a beautiful, well-stocked store); Germanetto, 13, rue Masséna (the best in the classic tradition); Julien et Fils, 8, rue de la Poissonnerie (authentic, traditional products). *Chocolate:* René Fontaine, 28, rue de la Liberté (one of the best chocolate makers on the Côte-d'Azur). *Gourmet foods:* Aux Allées de la Côte d'Azur, 1, rue St-François-de-Paule (superb fresh fruit and a wide selection of exotic and dried fruit); Ferme Saint-Isidore, 8, rue de France (Hédiard products and a lovely selection of wines and spirits). *Cheese:* L'Edelweiss, 55, rue de France (good ripened cheeses); La Ferme Fromagère, 13, rue Assalit. *Preserves and jams:* Auer, 7, rue St-François-de-Paule (an extraordinary store, opened in 1820); Confiserie du Vieux-Nice, 14, quai Papacino (lovely selection, delicious homemade preserves). *Olive oil and regional products:* Alziari, 14, rue St-François-de-Paule (purest olive oil in the world). *Fresh pasta:* Quirino, 10, rue Bavastro, and 22, rue de France. *Pastries:* Chéreau, 25, blvd. Gambetta; Raspail, 41, rue de France (Swiss specialties, perfect quality); Vogade, 1, pl. Masséna. *Wine and spirits:* Les Belles Années, 43, rue Trachel (huge selection).

Altea Masséna

58, rue Gioffredo - 93.85.49.25 / D5-3

Open year-round. 116 rms 270-570F. TV. Air cond. Pets allowed. Garage parking. Telex 470192. Cards: V, AE, DC, MC.

Only 500 meters from the sea, this is a decent, traditional hotel with quality modern equipment and good service, including room service 24 hours a day.

L'Ane Rouge

7, quai des Deux-Emmanuel
93.89.49.63 / F5-47

M. Vidalot. Open until 9:30 p.m. Closed Sat., Sun., holidays & July 14-Sept. 1. Terrace dining. Pets allowed. Cards: V.

The Vidalots are a couple of professionals who are so conscientious and attentive to the quality of their products, the consistency of their cuisine and the courtesy of their personnel that they have succeeded, apparently without the least difficulty,

1 - Le Palais Jamaï **R**
2 - Le Gourmet Lorrain **R**
3 - Altea Masséna **H**
4 - Barale **R**
5 - Le Tramway **R**
6 - Bong-Laï **R**
7 - Le Farniente (Westminster Concorde) **RH**
8 - La Mérenda **R**
9 - Relais de Rimiez **H**
10 - Windsor **H**
11 - La Rive Gauche **R**
12 - Plaza-Concorde **H**
13 - Hôtel-Club des Fleurs **H**
14 - Méridien **H**
16 - Hôtel Brice **H**
17 - Ville de Siena **R**
18 - Atlantic **H**
19 - Au Ciel d'Azur **R**
20 - Le Bistrot d'Antoine **R**
21 - Ruffel **R**
22 - Au Passage **R**
23 - Icardo **R**
24 - Chantecler et La Rotonde (Hôtel Negresco) **RH**
25 - Le Regency (Beach Regency) **RH**
26 - La Toque Blanche **R**
27 - Prince de Prusse **R**
28 - Hippopotamus **R**
29 - Asia **R**
30 - Les Dents de la Mer **R**
31 - Victoria **H**
32 - Au Chapon Fin **R**
33 - La Malmaison **H**
34 - Le Garac **R**
35 - La Pérouse **H**
36 - Boccaccio **R**
37 - La Chaumière **R**
38 - West-End **H**
39 - Napoléon **H**
40 - Georges **H**
41 - Le Champagne (Grand Hôtel Aston) **RH**
42 - L'Auberge de Théo **R**
43 - Park Hôtel **H**
44 - Holiday Inn **H**
45 - Sofitel-Splendid **H**
46 - Beau Rivage **RH**
47 - L'Ane Rouge **R** et L'Esquinade **R**
48 - Côte d'Azur **H**
49 - Pullman **H**
50 - L'Oasis **H**
51 - Elysée Palace **H**
52 - Le Cadaqués **R**
53 - Le Florian **R**
54 - Lou Balico **R**
55 - Mercure **H**

56 - Le Pot d'Etain **R**
57 - Aux Gourmets **R**
58 - Au Bon Coin Breton **R**
59 - Coco Beach **R**

61 - Vendôme **H**
64 - Petit Palais **H**
66 - Jacques Maximin **R** et Le Bistrot de Nice **R**

in keeping their high prices for specialties that *never* vary: stuffed mussels "Ane Rouge," lobster "Ane Rouge," sea perch braised in Champagne, Provençal bourride, rack of lamb with parsley. All this is ruinous to your bank balance, but the preparation is honest, serious and, in the end, delicious. The pastries are excellent.

A la carte: 400-450F.

12/20 Asia

12, rue Cassini - 93.56.80.83 / E5-29

M. Vu Van. Open until 10:30 p.m. Closed Sun. dinner, Mon. & June 8-30. Air cond. Pets allowed. Cards: V.

Alice and Nam, daughter and father, have been running this perfect little eating place for over three years now. Not only is it cute and lively, but its strictly (northern) Vietnamese repertoire is excellent: delicious nems à la tonkinoise, five-flavor duck, chicken saté.

A la carte: 180F.

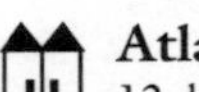

Atlantic

12, blvd. Victor-Hugo
93.88.40.15 / C4-18

Open year-round. 148 rms 350-650F. 2 stes 600-700F. Half-board 110-120F (plus rm). TV. Air cond. in 10 rms. Pets allowed. Parking. Telex 460840. Cards: V, AE, DC, MC.

A freshly renovated traditional hotel, with pleasant, well-equipped rooms. Restaurant and grill.

11/20 L'Auberge de Théo

52, ave. Cap-de-Croix
93.81.26.19 / D1-42

M. Mansi. Open until 10:30 p.m. Closed Wed. & Aug. 22-Sept. 8. Garden dining. Pets allowed. Cards: V.

The rough plaster decor is brand-new, and the pizzas come out of the oven crisp, velvety and fragrant. This good little Italian eating place also offers lovely pasta (seafood linguine) and generously served meats grilled over a wood fire.

A la carte: 160F.

10/20 Lou Balico

(Chez Adrienne)
20, ave. St-Jean-Baptiste - 93.85.93.71, 93.85.90.56 / E4-54

M. Issautier. Open daily until midnight. Air cond. Terrace dining. Pets allowed. Cards: V, AE, DC.

This popular bistro, which used to be a solid and authentic bastion of Nice-style cuisine, continues its inexorable decline. Stockfish, daube, white-beet pie—these names promise more than the actual dishes deliver.

A la carte: 200F. Menus: 125F, 150F.

13 Barale

39, rue Beaumont - 93.89.17.94 / F4-4

Mme. Barale. Open until 9 p.m. Dinner only (with reserv.). Closed Sun., Mon. & Aug.

Since last year we have all gotten one year older... and so has the delightful Hélène Barale. But her single, lengthy fixed-price menu, whose price has not increased one cent, remains completely faithful to her generous and painstaking authenticity. You haven't heard about Hélène's salade niçoise, her ravioli, her daube, her mesclun or her white-beet pies? Perhaps it's because you've never had the opportunity to dine on such splendid ravioli (stuffed with a fabulous blend of three meats) or such an authentic salade niçoise (so fresh and savory). The dining room is lively, crowded as it is by a thousand objects, including a player piano whose music often accompanies dessert.

Menu: 170F (wine incl.).

Beach Regency

See Le Regency restaurant.

13 Beau Rivage

24, rue St-François-de-Paule
93.80.80.70 / D5-46

M. Constant. Open daily until 10:30 p.m. Air cond. Terrace dining. Pets allowed. Parking. Telex 462708. Cards: V, AE, DC.

After a five-year closing, the reopening of this old, small luxury hotel from the grand days of Nice was truly a happy, lovely event. Matisse lived here for two years at the end of World War I; and it was here, a few feet away from the flower market, that Chekhov wrote *The Seagull.* Today the handsomely spruced up Beau Rivage seems almost brand-new behind its sober, graceful nineteenth-century facade. In its elegant, almost spare dining room, one can see lobster, a perfect rack of lamb, farm ducklings and crusty, savory Bresse chickens turning on the superb rôtisserie. Next to these flawless classic dishes, Jean-Pierre Retureau, the young chef placed here by his teacher, Roger Vergé, shows no hesitation in proposing an andouillette in white wine and grilled pigs' feet. Everything is delicious and generous, and the service is gracious. The wine list, however, should be expanded, and a bit more style should be given to the desserts. On Sundays, a vast and outstanding brunch is served.

A la carte: 300F.

Beau Rivage

(See restaurant above)

Open year-round. 10 stes 1,000-1,200F. 110 rms 600-1,000F. TV. Air cond. Pets allowed.

Its interior completely redone, this renovated old luxury hotel on a small scale features exquisite rooms. The decor—lovely fabrics, light woods and blond-marble bathrooms—is restrained yet bright, the management outstanding, and the service ever attentive. Private beach.

13 Le Bistrot d'Antoine

26, blvd. Victor-Hugo
93.88.49.75 / C4-20

M. Villa. Open until 9:30 p.m. Closed Sat. lunch & Sun. Terrace dining. Pets allowed. Cards: V.

Antoine and Dominique Villa's charming bistro is off to a wonderful start. The small, rose-colored dining room and adjacent terrace are often crowded with clients eager to taste Antoine's cuisine, filled with freshness and sunny flavors: fresh artichoke ravioli arranged simply atop ratatouille, chevreau (kid) roasted in fresh garlic juice, and a cake stuffed with black chocolate. So it's only right that Antoine retrieve the toque he was awarded at Frédante in Ajaccio. But

certain details should be improved: The cheeses are too predictable, the à la carte menu is not very well presented, and the fixed-price menu includes too many supplements. The service, performed graciously, is excellent.
A la carte: 200F. Menus: 75F (lunch only, except holidays), 110F (except holidays), 150F (dinner only, except holidays).

Le Bistrot de Nice

2-4 rue S.-Guitry - 93.80.70.10 / D5-66
M. Maximin. Open daily until 11:30 p.m. Air cond. Pets allowed. Cards: V, AE, DC, MC.
Adjoining Jacques Maximin's first-class restaurant, this pretty, wood-and-tile bistro, opening soon, will seat about 50 with a view of the main kitchens. Here Maximin plans to serve a menu of traditional niçoise cooking: ravioli and grilled fish and meat, with just a touch of Japanese, sushi-style. All this will go for 120 to 150 francs a head.
A la carte: 120-150F.

12/20 Boccaccio

7, rue Masséna - 93.87.71.76 / D5-36
M. Cannatella. Open daily until 11 p.m. Air cond. Terrace dining. Pets allowed. Cards: V, AE, DC.
Located in Nice's pedestrian zone, Boccaccio's large, air-conditioned dining rooms are decorated like luxury three-mast cabins. It's comfortable and entertaining, and the seafood is tasty: bouillabaisse, paella, langouste (spiny lobster) spaguettata, assorted seafood and shellfish plates.
A la carte: 300F.

11/20 Au Bon Coin Breton

5, rue Blacas - 93.85.17.01 / D4-58
M. Matray. Open until 10 p.m. Closed Sun. dinner, Mon. & Aug. Air cond. Pets allowed. Cards: V.
Despite the name, there's not one ounce of Brittany here—neither in the decor nor in the owner's unchanging, carefully prepared cuisine: homemade smoked or marinated salmon, breast of duck en croûte and fish fricassée. Attractive fixed-price menus.
A la carte: 250F. Menus: 75F (weekdays only), 140F, 165F.

12/20 Bong-Laï

14, rue Alsace-Lorraine
93.88.75.36 / C3-6
M. Costa. Open until 10 p.m. Closed Mon., Tues. & Dec. 5-27. Air cond. Pets allowed. Cards: AE, DC, MC.
This is the oldest Vietnamese restaurant on the Côte d'Azur. For more than 25 years, Eurasian André Costa has prepared a fresh, honest cuisine, based on delicious soups, crisp nems, fish with ginger and a remarkable duck with pineapple, which must be ordered several hours ahead of time.
A la carte: 200-230F. Menu: 145F.

Hôtel Brice

44, rue du Maréchal-Joffre
93.88.14.14 / C5-16
Open year-round. 61 rms 295-480F. Half-board 295-410F oblig. in seas. TV. Pets allowed. Telex 470658. Cards: V, DC, MC.
Two hundred meters from the promenade des Anglais, this quite comfortable hotel is surrounded by greenery and has a pleasant winter garden. Its rooms are furnished with Provençal-style furniture. Restaurant.

12/20 Le Cadaquès

8, quai des Docks - 93.89.41.76 / F6-52
M. Font-Puigferrer. Open daily until 10:30 p.m. Terrace dining. Pets allowed. Cards: V, DC.
Family-style, charming, with lots of flowers, this is the best Spanish restaurant in the Nice region, serving primarily Catalonian cuisine: paella, zarzuela, rabbit al ajillo and Catalonian cream. Alas, the menu also includes several rather absurd dishes, such as the salmon in Champagne. The list of Spanish wines, though brief, is superb and includes an exceptional Gran Coronas '79.
A la carte: 250F. Menu: 100F.

(14) Le Champagne

12, ave. Félix-Faure
93.80.62.52 / D5-41
M. Jolivet. Open daily until 10 p.m. Air cond. Garden dining. Pets allowed. Garage parking. Telex 470290. Cards: V, AE, DC, MC.
The regional accents and clever inventions on the menu can't conceal the solid, adroitly updated tradition behind this masterful cuisine. The fine ingredients, the careful preparations and the finesse of the sauces make for some lovely meals, start to finish, in this very comfortable wood-and-mirrored decor. Particularly noteworthy are the fricassée of prawns with cèpes, the sole in Champagne sauce with stuffed zucchini flowers, the exceptional rack of lamb with a niçoise stuffing, and the delicious pastries. These dishes deserve a big fat toque.
A la carte: 450F. Menus: 190F, 240F.

Grand Hôtel Aston

(See restaurant above)
Open year-round. 2 stes 920-1,120F. 158 rms 310-820F. Half- board 140F (plus rm). TV. Air cond. No pets.
A handsome hotel with recently renovated rooms, some of which overlook the luminous fountains on the square. A superb rooftop garden-terrace faces the sea.

Chantecler

37, promenade des Anglais
93.88.39.51 / B5-24
Mme. Augier. Open daily until 10 p.m. Closings vary. Air cond. Pets allowed. Parking. Telex 460040. Cards: V, AE, DC, MC.
The inevitable has occurred: Jacques Maximin has parted ways, amicably, with Chantecler. And who should arrive to take his place but our old friend Dominique Le Stanc, whom we have followed since his days in Alsace. Rigorously trained in the best apprenticeships, this dependable Breton professional has produced excellent food wherever he has been. He is certainly capable of putting the resources of the Hôtel Negresco to use. There is little chance that this lofty position will turn Le Stanc's head; he is as modest a chef as one is likely to meet. Chantecler is taking this

time during the changing of the guard to completely redo itself, and we look forward to seeing—and telling—all when it reopens.

Hôtel Negresco

(See restaurant above)

Closed Jan. 22-March 6. 20 stes 2,550-6,000F. 130 rms 1,150-1,850F. TV. Air cond. Pets allowed.

For years, Jeanne Augier has been filling the 6,000 square yards of the Negresco—its endless corridors, six floors and 150 rooms and suites—with paintings, furniture, fixtures and sculptures, which can never be sold or leave the old palace, now 66-plus years old. There is perhaps too much; it would be nice to find a little more harmony, particularly in the suites, where the mix is so great that it's often staggering. But a huge redecorating program has begun under the direction of Augier and her excellent general manager, Michel Palmer. The least that can be said of them is that they are the most active and passionate hotel people on the Côte.

13 Au Chapon Fin

1, rue du Moulin - 93.80.56.92 / D5-32

M. Loubés. Open until 10 p.m. (10:30 p.m. in summer). Closed Sun., holidays, June 19-July 2 & Dec. 22-Jan. 15. Terrace dining. Pets allowed. Cards: V, AE.

The owner/chef of this friendly new eating place likes to prepare the finest bistro-style fare. Whether local (daube, ravioli) or from the southwest (cassoulet), the cuisine contains some pleasant surprises, such as the lovely ravioli filled with red mullet.

A la carte: 250F. Menus: 103F, 160F.

13 La Chaumière

Les 4-Chemins, Grande-Corniche
384, blvd. de l'Observatoire
93.01.77.68 / G3-37

Mme. Cere. Dinner only. Open until 9:30 p.m. Closed Sun. & Oct. 15-Dec. 15. Pets allowed. Parking. Cards: V, AE.

La Chaumière's rustic decor is not without its charm, and its atmosphere is sincerely congenial, even if the prices are not what one would expect to pay in a simple cottage. There is neither an à la carte nor a fixed-price menu; you simply sit down to a full-course meal: excellent ham, duck terrine, salads, grilled beef and lamb and, to finish, a hot apple tart. To wash it down, there's a little red wine from the Var that you'll want to keep drinking forever.

Menu: 310F (wine incl.).

13 Au Ciel d'Azur

Aéroport de Nice (3rd floor)
93.21.36.36 / A6-19

M. Teissier. Open daily until 9:45 p.m. Air cond. Pets allowed. Telex 970011. Cards: V, AE, DC.

Au Ciel d'Azur is a bright, spacious, contemporary place with large windows facing the runways and the sea, blue carpeting, comfortable bucket chairs and extremely attentive service. A menu allows you to compose the meal of your choice; you pay according to the number of dishes ordered. For example, for 212 francs, you are entitled to delicious red-mullet filets with small vegetables, breast of duck in cider vinegar, cheeses and magnificent desserts. Everything is seasonal, meticulously prepared and generously served.

Menus: 175F, 215F, 235F.

14 Coco Beach

2, ave. Jean-Lorrain
93.89.39.26 / F7-59

Mme. Cauvin. Open until 9:30 p.m. Closed Sun., Mon., 2 weeks in mid-Sept. & 2 weeks in mid-Dec. Terrace dining. Pets allowed. Cards: V, AE, DC, MC.

This large house, built against the high rocks just above the sea, commands a boundless view from the large bay windows of its dining room. The classical decor, while somewhat stolid, is quite comfortable. The cuisine is prepared by Carmen Coco, who is adored by the gourmet jet set. She offers every fish from the Côte d'Azur, grilled or in bouillabaisse. Once you've selected your fish from the baskets, prices are set by the kilogram.

A la carte: 400F.

Côte d'Azur

57, blvd. Gambetta
93.96.10.10 / B4-48

Open year-round. 35 rms 290-350F. TV. Pets allowed. Telex 970225. Cards: V, AE, DC.

Functional, recently renovated rooms near the train station and the ocean. No restaurant.

12/20 Les Dents de la Mer

2, rue St-François-de-Paule
93.80.99.16 / D5-30

M. Bertoni. Hours & closings vary. Air cond. Terrace dining. Pets allowed. Cards: V, AE, DC.

The shipwreck decor, which looks like Walt Disney's version of something Captain Nemo might have dreamed up, allows you to admire the marine fauna. The seafood cooking, however, is nothing out of the ordinary: shellfish with fresh noodles, sea perch with a rosemary cream sauce.

A la carte: 300F and up.

Elysée Palace

59, promenade des Anglais
93.86.06.06 / B5-51

Open year-round. 2 stes 1,000-1,500F. 148 rms 550-900F. TV. Air cond. Pets allowed. Pool. Parking. Telex 462666. Cards: V, AE, DC.

A hotel group recently opened this luxury hotel by the beach, which sports a striking, modern facade replete with a giant bronze female silhouette. Perfectly comfortable inside, it also has a rooftop pool, piano bar, gym, sauna, conference room, private parking and beach access.

14 L'Esquinade

5, quai des Deux-Emmanuel
93.89.59.36 / F5-47

M. Béraud. Open until 11 p.m. Closed Mon. lunch, Sun. & Jan. 2-Feb. 8. Air cond. Terrace dining. Pets allowed. Parking. Cards: V, AE.

After a nasty fire, L'Esquinade has just reopened; it now features a new cozy, rustic decor and, above all, a talented young chef, Pascal

Roche, who spent six years with Jacques Maximin as the great chef's fish cook. So suddenly this place has become the brightest and most Parisian restaurant in Nice, where the celebrity clientele once again makes an appearance. But this time around they are dining on excellent fare: fresh sardine salad with apples and onions, mussel and saffron soup, lamb in olive butter with noodles, and a delicious hot apple-almond tart, all washed down with good Bandol wine. Of course, it's no great bargain, but it is good, and the greeting by the owners is quite friendly.

A la carte: 350F.

12/20 Le Farniente

27, promenade des Anglais
93.88.29.44 / C5-7

M. Gouirand. Open daily until 10 p.m. Closed Sun. (off-seas.). Air cond. Terrace dining. No pets. Telex 460872. Cards: V, AE, DC.

The expanse of the sea spreading out before the terrace that overlooks the promenade des Anglais promises luxurious idleness. The peach-toned decor is lovely; the cuisine needs more precision (it still includes some rather banal fare), but such dishes as the lobster ravioli and stuffed duck filet are encouraging. The wines are intelligently selected, the prices well maintained.

A la carte: 300F. Menu: 180F.

Westminster Concorde

(See restaurant above)

Open year-round. 110 rms 350-1,000F. Half-board 420-590F. TV. Air cond. Pets allowed.

This modernized old hotel is located right in the middle of the promenade des Anglais. Both the reception and the service have remained impeccably old-fashioned. Discotheque and bar.

Hôtel-Club des Fleurs

3, ave. des Fleurs - 93.96.84.29 / B5-13

Open year-round. 52 rms 160-280F. Half-board 160-255F. TV. No pets.

Located near the sea, this hotel is a "club"-style place that is unique in Nice. The comfort is excellent for its type, and many activities are available—video, evening entertainment, shows, outings, excursions and the like. Restaurant.

(15) Le Florian

22, rue Alphonse-Karr
93.88.86.60 / C4-53

M. Gillon. Open until 9:30 p.m. Closed Mon. lunch, Sun. & July 10-Aug. 20. Air cond. Pets allowed. Cards: V.

Although Claude Gillon has owned this bistro in downtown Nice for about four years (after managing a small restaurant in Mayenne), he has not yet succeeded in making it charming and attractive. The gloomy wainscoting, the standard rustic ornaments and the stark walls certainly haven't contributed to the popularity of his restaurant; rather, Le Florian owes all of its success to the delicious, refined cuisine of this outstanding professional. Gillon has instilled classical and bourgeois dishes with new life, and his mastery of the sauces, as well as his meticulousness, has done wonders for the preparation of the many splendidly light and personalized interpretations. Try the magnificently delicate zucchini-and-artichoke pie with foie gras; the gigot of rabbit navaraise in its own juice with rosemary, garnished with steamed cabbage, which possesses both a majestic subtlety and wonderfully forthright flavors; the simple grilled Challans duck; the sole stuffed with fresh chanterelles. These dishes all deserve two toques, even if many of the desserts (parfait in coffee sauce, croquant with raspberries) do not. Mme. Gillons's reception is extremely gracious.

A la carte: 350-400F. Menus: 150F (lunch only), 205F, 300F.

11/20 Le Garac

2, blvd. Carnot - 93.89.57.36 / F5-34

M. Treppoz. Open until 11 p.m. Closed Thurs. lunch, Mon. & July 5-20. Pets allowed. Cards: V, AE, DC.

The greenish decor and the cuisine still have a long way to go to reach the high standard set by the exceedingly friendly reception by the owners. Still, it rates a good mark for the fish soup and the curry sauce served with the (overcooked) sole.

A la carte: 300-350F. Menu: 140F.

Georges

3, rue Henri-Cordier
93.86.23.41 / A5-40

Open year-round. 18 rms 250-360F. TV. Cards: V, AE.

The rooms have been renovated; on the fourth floor, you can sunbathe and have breakfast on a terrace decorated with flowers. No restaurant.

12/20 Le Gourmet Lorrain

7, ave. Santa-Fior - 93.84.90.78 / C1-2

M. Leloup. Open until 9:30 p.m. Closed Sun. dinner, Mon., Jan. 1-10 & Aug. Air cond. Pets allowed. Hotel: 15 rms 130-180F; half-board 150-265F oblig. in seas. Cards: V, AE, DC.

Tasty dishes from around the world are served in this tiny but charming place. The central attraction of the house is its exceptional wine cellar: 50,000 rare or enticing bottles, at all prices.

A la carte: 260-300F. Menus: 70F (board), 90F (weekday lunch only), 150F, 160F.

11/20 Aux Gourmets

12, rue Dante - 93.96.83.53 / B5-57

M. Collison. Open until 9:15 p.m. Closed Sun. dinner, Mon. & July. Air cond. Pets allowed. Cards: V, AE, DC.

In this friendly small bistro with its meticulous inn decor, young uniformed waiters perform a zealous service. The generous cuisine is prepared by the owner, a native Scotsman: escargots en croûte, guinea-fowl émincé and lotte brochette.

A la carte: 230F. Menus: 120F, 193F.

10/20 Hippopotamus

16, ave. Félix-Faure
93.92.42.77 / D5-28

M. Guignard. Open daily until 1 a.m. Air cond. Terrace dining. Pets allowed. Cards: V.

Like all the Hippos in the chain, this one offers generous grilled meats, served swiftly and at reasonable prices until late into the night.

A la carte: 130F. Menus: 52F, 73F.

Holiday Inn

179, blvd. René-Cassin (Nice Airport)
93.83.91.92 / A6-44

Open year-round. 1 ste 2,000F. 150 rms 495-730F. TV. Air cond. Pets allowed. Pool. Parking. Telex 970202. Cards: V, AE, DC.

Perfectly representative of the gigantic and ubiquitous American chain. Excellent facilities for conferences. Its spacious, quite comfortable rooms are intelligently and generously equipped. Restaurant.

12/20 Icardo

234, rte. de Grenoble
93.83.17.30 / A6-23

M. Icardo. Lunch only. Closed Sun. & Aug. Terrace dining. Pets allowed. Parking. Cards: V, DC, MC.

Hiding behind a tobacconist/newspaper shop front, this bistro is much appreciated by the natives of Nice, especially for its exquisite pissaladière (onion and tomato tart)—prepared on order—and perfect homemade ravioli. Warm reception and service. There's a small shaded terrace set back from the street.

A la carte: 150F. Menus: 70F, 98F, 140F.

La Malmaison

48, blvd. Victor-Hugo
93.87.62.56 / C4-33

Open year-round. 46 rms 300-620F. Half-board 415-425F. TV. Air cond. Pets allowed. Telex 470410. Cards: V, AE, DC, MC.

This excellent modern hotel, located near the promenade des Anglais, features comfortable, well-equipped and soundproofed rooms, all tastefully decorated. Efficient service. Satellite television. Restaurant.

Jacques Maximin

2-4 rue S.-Guitry - 93.80.70.10 / D5-66

M. Maximin. Open daily until 10:30 p.m. Air cond. Pets allowed. Parking. Cards: V, AE, DC, MC.

Our "Napoléon of the range" has finally made the big leap, leaving behind the Chantecler restaurant in the capable hands of Dominique Le Stanc and setting out on his own campaign. We'll be able to judge his success soon, when he opens his new empire, which he has planned with grand confidence. The interior design has been entrusted to Jean-Michel Wilmotte (who did the Tokyo Opera, the Louvre pyramid, the Museum of Modern Art in Nice), who promises a ground floor done in a style très "La Scala Opera" and upper rooms each decorated by a different artist; all in all, it will house some 200 customers. The central kitchen will also put out catered food, banquet dinners and the food for Le Bistrot de Nice (see above).

This is truly an ambitious undertaking, though less mad than perhaps it seems, given the slice of conference and festival business that Nice has been carving out for itself. If Maximin can harness his sometimes turbulent passions, he'll be a great success, particularly with his projected check totals in the neighborhood of 500 francs per person (as opposed to the 700 or 800 francs he commanded at the Negresco).

Mercure

2, rue Halévy - 93.82.30.88 / C5-55

Open year-round. 124 rms 420-700F. TV. Air cond. Pets allowed. Telex 970656. Cards: V, AE, DC, MC.

The bright, spacious, modern rooms, all with a view of the sea, are well equipped and attractively decorated. Lovely buffet breakfast. No restaurant.

(13) La Mérenda

4, rue de la Terrasse - (no phone) / D5-8

M. Giusti. Open until 9:30 p.m. Closed Sat. dinner, Sun., Feb. & Aug. Air cond. Pets allowed.

A cramped, noisy and friendly setting, with simple tables, hard stools and a slate displaying the daily specials. With this unpromising material, Jean and Christiane Giusti have done wonders. Gracious hosts, they are civilized without affectation, and they convey their happiness simply by doing their job in good humor, without the convenience of a telephone... and without allowing their enormous success to go to their heads. The prices are wonderful, and the cuisine is still the best on the Côte d'Azur in the authentic, homemade Italian/niçoise style: magnificent salami and coppa, pizza, flower fritters, pasta in pistou, daube (stew) garnished with fresh string beans, andouillette, stuffed sardines, stockfish and so on. The only wine served is a fresh, simple red (or rosé) from the Var at 38 francs a bottle.

A la carte: 150F.

Méridien

1, promenade des Anglais
93.82.25.25 / C5-14

Open year-round. 22 stes 1,900-4,550F. 292 rms 800-1,550F. TV. Air cond. Pets allowed. Heated pool. Parking. Telex 470361. Cards: V, AE, DC, MC.

The beautiful, modern, attractively furnished rooms of the Méridien have superb views of the sea. The swimming pool and all the luxuries, including impeccable service, are all that one could possibly desire. Restaurant.

Napoléon

6, rue Grimaldi - 93.87.70.07 / C5-39

Open year-round. 1 stes 520F. 83 rms 300-410F. TV. Air cond. Pets allowed. Telex 460949. Cards: V, AE, DC, MC.

An imposing hotel not far from the Ruhl and the Albert-1er park, with spacious, fairly quiet rooms. No restaurant.

Hôtel Negresco

See Chantecler restaurant.

L'Oasis

23, rue Gounod - 93.88.12.29 / C4-50

Open year-round. 38 rms 300-350F. Telex 462705. Cards: AE, DC, MC.

An oasis of greenery in the center of town, with simply decorated, well equipped, perfectly comfortable rooms. No restaurant.

(13) Le Palais Jamaï

3, quai des Deux-Emmanuel
93.89.53.92 / F5-1

M. Bastide. Open until 10:45 p.m. Closed Tues. lunch, Mon. & July. Air cond. Terrace dining. Pets allowed. Cards: V, AE, DC.

The best Moroccan cooking on the Côte d'-Azur is served with a great deal of refinement in this pleasantly refreshing, almost luxurious decor. A young Moroccan woman prepares the food in the best Moroccan family "festive" tradition. You'll be even happier if you order, several hours in advance, the lamb shoulder méchoui, "choua" (delicious steamed lamb), Moroccan-style stuffed fish and "hagma," an extraordinary tagine of calf's feet. The à la carte menu offers excellent couscous and a light pigeon b'stilla (a sweet-savory pie). The impeccable service is supervised by the owner.

A la carte: 300F and up. Menus: 220F, 240F, 260F (wine incl.).

Park Hôtel

6, ave. de Suède - 93.87.80.25,
93.87.81.15 / C5-43

Open year-round. 2 stes 550-700F. 133 rms 280-650F. TV. Air cond. Pets allowed. Telex 970176. Cards: V, AE, DC.

The Park Hôtel is exceptionally well located; it faces the Albert-1er park. All of its rooms are perfectly equipped. Restaurant.

(13) Au Passage

11 bis, blvd. Raimbaldi
93.80.23.15 / D3-22

Mme. N'Guyen. Open until 10:30 p.m. Closed Sun. & Feb. 1-15. Air cond. Terrace dining. Pets allowed. Cards: V.

A Dutch-born French woman marries a French-born Vietnamese man. The result? A most original and savory Far Eastern cuisine, which has the additional virtue of closely following the fresh, seasonal market produce. Try the steamed lotte in fresh crab sauce, grilled gilthead in curry or ginger butter, sautéed gambas (large prawns) à la cantonaise in garlic sauce, breast of duck à la pékinoise, served with fried rice vermicelli, and Saigon-style shellfish with shallots. The desserts are also delicious, which is an unexpected treat in a Chinese restaurant.

A la carte: 230-250F. Menu: 60F (lunch only, wine incl.).

La Pérouse

11, quai Rauba-Capeu
93.62.34.63 / E6-35

Open year-round. 2 stes 990-1,500F. 63 rms 365-975F. TV. Air cond. in 50 rms. Pets allowed. Pool. Parking. Telex 461411. Cards: V, AE, DC.

The magnificent rooms of La Pérouse, one of the most pleasant hotels in Nice, are located around the gardens of an old castle; each has either a terrace or a balcony and a view of the sea. A panoramic solarium encloses a hydrotherapeutic swimming pool and sauna. Summer bar and grill.

Petit Palais

10, ave. E.-Bieckert
93.62.19.11 / E4-64

Open year-round. 25 rms 330-480F. Half-board 280-355F. TV. Pets allowed. Parking. Telex 462233. Cards: V, AE, MC.

This superb Belle Epoque edifice commands a view of Nice from its green hilltop site and boasts a stylish interior, attractive rooms, plush fabrics and deep armchairs. The rooms are perfectly equipped and many are graced with huge terraces and magnificent sandstone bathrooms. The service is thoughtful, and there is a restaurant.

Plaza-Concorde

12, ave. de Verdun - 93.87.80.41 / D5-12

Open year-round. 8 stes 1,400-2,200F. 200 rms 420-1,100F. Half-board 130F (plus rm). TV. Air cond. Pets allowed. Telex 460979. Cards: V, AE, DC, MC.

The Plaza-Concorde has a marvelous rooftop terrace, as well as lovely, modern, flawlessly equipped rooms and air-conditioned conference rooms. The hotel also features a bar and grill, boutiques and many services.

10/20 Le Pot d'Etain

12, rue Meyerbeer - 93.88.25.95 / C5-56

M. Lestarquit. Open until 11 p.m. Closed Sun. dinner. Air cond. Pets allowed. Cards: V, AE, DC.

Some good intentions... and some slipups (the desserts are distressing). The à la carte menu is endless and too expensive, but an attractive budget fixed-price menu includes escargots casserole, lamb chops, exceptional cheeses and dessert.

A la carte: 250F and up. Menus: 70F, 110F, 220F.

11/20 Prince de Prusse

Pl. du Jésus - 93.80.75.11 / E5-27

Open daily until midnight. Air cond. Terrace dining. Pets allowed. Cards: V, AE, MC.

The mustachioed owner of this picturesque wein- and bierstube across from the old Jésus church is a real character. Good Rhine wines and beers accompany the suckling pig berlinoise and the shank with Sauerkraut.

A la carte: 180-200F.

Pullman

28, ave. Notre-Dame
93.80.30.24 / D3-49

Open year-round. 1 ste 1,250F. 199 rms 395-890F. TV. Air cond. Heated pool. Parking. Telex 470662. Cards: V, AE, DC, MC.

This modern, well-equipped luxury hotel has two things in particular going for it: It is located in the center of Nice, and its rooms, featuring beds with multiple remote-control systems, are remarkably soundproofed. Indeed, it has all the comfort one expects of the chain. On the terraced roof, which overlooks the entire city and its hills, there is a Polynesian bar, a swimming pool and a sauna. No restaurant.

Le Regency
223, promenade des Anglais
93.83.91.51 / A6-25

M. Ligné. Open daily until 10:30 p.m. Garden dining. Pets allowed. Air cond. Parking. Telex 461635. Cards: V, AE, DC, MC.

The new manager of this big hotel has called in Gérard Ferri to take the cooking in hand. This is a great idea, for Ferri is a fine talent who has been wasting away a bit since he left Couletta d'Eze. Recently we were thrilled to rediscover the charms of his light and personal cooking, which is anchored in the best Niçois and Provençal traditions. The young rabbit served cold with a fragrant ratatouille, the smartly dressed lobster salad, the lamb sautéed in vinegar and honey and the roast pigeon with corn cakes will soon merit two toques for Ferri. The competent maître d' and the new sommelier are busy stocking the cellars, and it remains now the task of the owner to put a little life into the decaying luxury-hotel decor. The terrace/garden on the other hand is delightful, as is the luncheon fixed-price menu.

A la carte: 300-400F. Menus: 175F (weekday lunch only), 250F (dinner only).

Beach Regency
(See restaurant above)

Open year-round. 12 stes 1,500-5,500F. 320 rms 600-1,200F. TV. Air cond. Pool. Telex 461635. Cards: V, AE, DC, MC.

Facing the Baie des Anges, this superb, large, modern hotel has magnificent, spacious rooms with terraces. There is a pool on the roof; elsewhere there are such amusements as a sauna, piano bar, boutiques and two restaurants.

Relais de Rimiez
128, ave. de Rimiez
93.81.18.65 / E1-19

Open year-round. 24 rms 180-330F. TV. Air cond. Pets allowed. Cards: AE.

The lovely rooms are as comfortable as they are quiet. There are fantastic views from the large terraces. No restaurant.

12/20 La Rive Gauche
27, rue Ribotti - 93.89.16.82 / F4-11

M. Bouisset. Open until 10 p.m. Closed Sun. & Aug. Pets allowed. Cards: V, AE.

Friendly elbow-to-elbow atmosphere, a pleasant reception, fast service and traditional, well-prepared cuisine served in generous portions: octopus camargaise, fresh salmon with sorrel, leek quiche and lotte with saffron. Well-selected wine cellar (wines from the Var) and a good fixed-price menu for 90 francs.

A la carte: 160-180F. Menus: 100F, 130F.

12/20 La Rotonde
(Hôtel Negresco)
37, promenade des Anglais
93.88.39.51 / B5-24

Mme. Augier. Open until midnight. Closed Jan. 22-March 6. Air cond. Pets allowed. Parking. Telex 460040.

The decor is lively (there's a pink-and-blue merry-go-round), the clientele generally young, and the cooking well designed and well prepared—pink salmon terrine with cucumber confit, cheese ravioli, rabbit with fresh noodles—though we expected more, considering that Maximin is supervising it. Excellent desserts.

A la carte: 150-250F.

Ruffel
10, blvd. Dubouchage
93.62.05.45 / D4-21

M. Ruffel. Open until 11 p.m. Closed Mon. Garden dining. Pets allowed. Cards: V.

What weird fantasies apparently have overtaken the imagination of Didier Ruffel! The spontaneity of his fresh, light touch has given way to useless ornament and fussiness—in fact, to the kind of tricking-up that slits his fish down the back to fill them with who knows what silly stuff. Burdened by such laborious nonsense, his restaurant can no longer wear the second toque of last year despite the delicious seafood stew with coriander, the friendly reception, the reasonable prices and the more-than-charming garden.

A la carte: 250F.

Sofitel-Splendid
50, blvd. Victor-Hugo
93.88.69.54 / C4-45

Open year-round. 12 stes 850-1,200F. 118 rms 500-820F. TV. Air cond. Pets allowed. Heated pool. Parking. Telex 460938. Cards: V, AE, DC, MC.

All the rooms have air conditioning; from the upper floors, one has a lovely view of the town. The quality of the service is outstanding, and the hotel also features a beauty salon, an outside swimming pool, a solarium and a restaurant.

La Toque Blanche
40, rue de la Buffa - 93.88.38.18 / C5-26

M. Sandélion. Open until 9:30 p.m. Closed Sun. dinner, Mon. & July 15-Aug. 15. Air cond. Pets allowed. Cards: V.

Alain Sandélion, who moved into this attractively restored former vegetarian bistro in 1987, is already quite the experienced professional. This Grenoble native prepares with great dedication a cuisine guaranteed to please all tastes: a beautifully seasoned duck salad, lotte and bacon in a most subtle red-wine sauce and admirable noisettes of lamb à la provençal The gratin dauphinois is delicious, but the chocolate cake is less impressive. Prices are moderate, and Denise Sandélion is as gracious as she is pretty. No doubt this new restaurant (the opening of a good new restaurant is, alas, an event all too rare in Nice) will soon prove a great success. The wine cellar is small but judiciously selected.

A la carte: 300F. Menus: 130F (weekdays only), 150F, 250F.

11/20 Le Tramway
11, rue Lamartine - 93.62.16.74 / D4-5

M. Térèse. Open until 9:45 p.m. Closed Mon. dinner, Sat. lunch, Sun. & Aug. Air cond. Pets allowed. Cards: V.

The decor is still that of a 1910 tramway, despite the expansion and embellishment of this convivial bistro run by two brothers. The cooking

is one of the most serious of its kind in Nice: onglet, stockfish, roast peppers.
A la carte: 130F. Menu: 79F.

Victoria

33, blvd. Victor-Hugo
93.88.39.60 / C4-31

Open year-round. 39 rms 420-500F. TV. Pets allowed. Parking. Telex 461337. Cards: V, AE, DC, MC.

Some of the renovated rooms face a marvelous cool park. Its quiet atmosphere makes it an ideal hotel for relaxation and rest. Fast-food service.

12/20 Ville de Siena

10, rue St-Vincent - 93.80.12.45 / D5-17

M. Iorio de Marco. Open until 11 p.m. Closed Mon. lunch & Sun.; annual closing varies. Air cond. Terrace dining. Pets allowed. Cards: V, AE.

A bistro-style terrace opens up on sunny days onto a charming street in Old Nice. Its tables are much sought after, for the cooking is as tasty as it is typical: minestrone, maccherini alla siciliana, many varieties of fresh pasta and fresh, simple desserts.
A la carte: 150F.

West End

31, promenade des Anglais
93.88.79.91 / B5-38

Open year-round. 2 stes 1,000-1,600F. 98 rms 350-900F. TV. Air cond. in 50 rms. Pets allowed. Garage parking. Telex 460789. Cards: V, AE, DC, MC.

Half of these beautiful, spacious rooms have been renovated, and there's a lovely view of the sea. The atmosphere, though, is a bit dull. Sauna. Restaurant.

Westminster-Concorde

See restaurant Le Farniente.

Windsor

11, rue Dalpozzo - 93.88.59.35 / C5-10

Open year-round. 60 rms 300-460F. Half-board 430F. TV. Air cond. in 3 rms. Pets allowed. Parking. Telex 970072. Cards: V, AE, DC, MC.

The owner of the Windsor is a great art lover—collector's pieces are everywhere. The rooms are well equipped, and there are business offices, a pool in the shaded garden, a sauna and a lounge room. Restaurant.

IN NEARBY **Saint-Pancrace**
(8 km N on D 914)
06100 Nice - (Alpes-Maritimes)

---

(15) Rôtisserie de Saint-Pancrace

93.84.43.69

M. Teillas. Open until 10 p.m. Closed Mon. & Jan. 5-Feb. 5. Garden dining. Pets allowed. Garage parking. Cards: V.

In the early springtime, when the flowers begin to bloom in the exquisite gardens, and the hills in the backcountry turn green, one simply must make the climb to this large inn perched 300 meters up in the serenity of the Nice hills. Its cool terraces and magnificent view of the Var valley contribute significantly to its reputation (unfortunately, the interior decor has not aged well), as do the small refinements of an always diligent service and the rigorously consistent quality of the cuisine of the newly promoted chef, M. Prabonne. Prabonne is carrying on his former boss's work faithfully, while already beginning to introduce some welcome, discreet touches of his own. Discretion and gentle change have always been the watchwords here, but everything is fresh, well prepared, cooked to precision and filled with sunny flavors: terrine of fresh shrimp from the Adriatic Sea, marinière of shellfish salad with fresh pasta, lovely fish of the region grilled with care and an exceptional millefeuille in a vanilla sauce with candied chestnuts. A prestigious sommelier, Antoine Luciano, is in charge of one of the most handsome wine cellars on the Côte d'Azur.
A la carte: 400F. Menus: 175F (lunch only), 265F.

IN NEARBY **Saint-Romans-de-Bellet**
06200 Nice - (Alpes-Maritimes)

---

(14) Auberge de Bellet

93.37.83.84

M. Raybaud. Open until 10 p.m. Closed Tues. & Jan. 20-28. Terrace dining. Parking. Cards: V, AE, MC.

Whether it's winter—under the wooden beams of the large dining room, whose eccentric decor is absolutely charming—or summer—in the garden filled with flowers under the vine arbor—this old inn, which has remained faithful to the tradition of country restaurants, is a most delightful place far from the noisy crowds. To these seductive delights are added those of a cuisine whose originality and consistency are quite remarkable. (We might find it even lovelier were its inspiration simpler and its prices more affordable.) Among the lovely dishes: "crépazes" of smoked salmon in sevruga caviar butter, creamed beans with smoked goose and quail eggs, marinière of fowl garnished with frogs and asparagus, and a Bohemian-style rissolé of pork and lamb's brains. The wine cellar is stocked with all the wines of Bellet, and Jacqueline Raybaud's reception is delightful.
A la carte: 400F and up. Menus: 195F, 280F.

See also: **Beaulieu-sur-Mer**

Niedermorschwihr

see Colmar

Nieuil

16270 Roumazières-Loubert - (Charente)
Paris 430 - Angoulême 40 - Limoges 65 - Reffec 36

---

(15) Château de Nieuil

Rte. de Fontafie - 45.71.36.38

M. Bodinaud. Open until 9:30 p.m. Closed Nov. 6-April 27. Pets allowed. Garage parking. Telex 791230. Cards: V, AE, DC.

The doyen of Relais et Châteaux is not at all what it appears to be, nor are the Bodinauds the conservative, business-like hosts one expects to find in such an aristocratic place. The bearded Jean-Michel Bodinaud (to be more precise, goateed) is smiling and discreet; he loves his park, his kitchen garden, his collection of Aubusson tapestries and his priceless old Cognacs. He maintains with simplicity an almost home-like ambience that easily lends warmth to the slightly solemn atmosphere of his large, old-fashioned dining room, but without lessening the standard of the always efficient and flexible service. As for Luce, his wife, she is a passionate, self-taught cook who loves art (she teaches drawing) as much as she does cuisine and can speak ardently of both. In brief, this former hunting lodge of François I has soul; in fact, it's one of the rare restaurants of its kind where charm, simplicity and conviviality accompany the daily fixed-price menus, which include a "poule au pot" soup, sautéed lamb, a salad of nettle sprouts with foie gras, a marvelous calves' liver à la fermière with puréed onions, a light chocolate cake and a splendid orange tart (the recipe for which Jean-Michel Bodinaud's friend Girardet confided to him). The wonderfully simple seasonal à la carte menu composed by Luce explicitly distinguishes the rustic dishes from those of modern cuisine; recently, she has added several extremely light vegetarian creations to her repertoire. But we wish that Luce would pay more attention to her vegetable garnishes, which are often a bit ordinary, and that she would get rid of her battered old stainless-steel dish covers.

A la carte: 300F. Menus: 135F (weekday lunch only), 220F (weekends and holidays only), 190F, 245F.

Château de Nieuil

(See restaurant above)

Closed Nov. 6-April 27. 3 stes 950-1,400F. 12 rms 400-850F. Half-board 505-675F. TV in 10 rms. Pets allowed. Heated pool. Tennis.

The Château de Nieuil is stocked with lovely furniture, old paintings and a refined decor (it also features some annoying plumbing noises) and sits snugly in the midst of a beautiful, marvelously maintained park adjacent to a forest and pond (though the moat water is a bit vile smelling). The reception is delightful. Relais et Châteaux.

Nîmes

30000 Nîmes - (Gard)
Paris 712 - Lyon 249 - Marseille 123 - Montpellier 52

Sights. Nîmes la Romaine: the Arenas; Maison Carrée (built in 5 B.C.); the Magne Tower; Jardin de la Fontaine (the fountain is the real center of the town, but the gardens date from the eighteenth century); the Castellum (the terminus of the aqueduct); the Door of Arles (also called the Door of Augustus, built in 15 B.C.); the chapel and ancient college of the Jesuits, including the museums of natural history, prehistory and archaeology; the great férias (holidays) of the "French Madrid."

Eating on the Run. Les Vendanges, 1, rue de la Violette (wine bistro, boutiques and a bar).

Nightlife. Cotton Club, 11, sq. de la Couronne (not really faithful to its name); Le Moulin de la Ponche, rte. d'Avignon (wildly popular on Saturday nights).

(13) L'Alberguier

4, rue Racine - 66.36.13.22

M. Fraisse. Open until 10:30 p.m. Closed Sun. dinner. Air cond. Pets allowed. Cards: V, AE, DC, MC.

Some of the flavor combinations are not always successful, but that's a small price to pay for the appealing genius for experimentation that this young chef displays. That he is an extremely skilled cook is verified by his small cod (a light ragoût) garnished with cèpes or prepared in a tarragon sauce, and in his feuilleté of oysters with a shrimp coulis in Noilly-Prat. The croustade of lamb with langoustines is less convincing, but the white-chocolate-and-Kirsch sorbet is a delicious dessert. The stone-and-stucco decor is both pleasant and discreet. The service is diligent, and, since last year, the wine cellar has been judiciously expanded.

A la carte: 230-250F. Menus: 90F (weekdays only), 145F, 180F, 230F.

(15) L'Enclos de la Fontaine

Quai de la Fontaine - 66.21.90.30

Open until 9:30 p.m. Closed Sat. lunch. Air cond. Garden dining. Pets allowed. Parking. Telex 490635. Cards: V, AE, DC, MC.

Didier Thibaud, a young chef who studied with Jacky Fréon and Robuchon at the Nikko in Paris, has definitely abandoned the shy caution of his beginnings. Encouraged by the intelligent management of this refreshing, wonderful restaurant located in the center of Nîmes, he has clearly opted for a cuisine that is both luxurious and subtle (a style entirely appropriate for the 1930s-era dining room and its view of a flower-filled garden). At the same time, however, it is also brilliant, bold, precise and true to the tradition of its creators. It naturally deserves two toques, particularly the subtle bouillon of chilled langoustines flavored with dill, the splendid fresh cod bouillabaisse, the noisettes of young pork roasted in a lobster fumet, and the émincé of calves' liver with an onion compote and black currants, garnished with exquisite apple slices in Calvados. The repertoire of rustic dishes is interesting, but too limited and deserves expansion, and the quality of the desserts should be improved so that it matches the high standard of the rest of the cuisine. The wine list includes handsome Côtes-du-Rhône; unfortunately, they are not always recommended or served to advantage.

A la carte: 400F. Menus: 160F (weekday lunch only), 170F and 190F (weekend and holiday dinner only), 345F.

Impérator

(See restaurant above)

Open year-round. 3 stes 1,060-1,200F. 59 rms 290-630F. Half-board 160F (plus rm). TV. Air cond. Pets allowed.

Not far from the streets bustling with pedestrians, the Roman monuments and the La Fontaine gardens, this old, small luxury hotel has been perfectly modernized and is completely air conditioned; it also features an exquisite inner garden.

Mercure

Périphérique Sud, on D 42, Chemin de l'Hostellerie - 66.84.14.55

Open year-round. 2 stes 620F. 98 rms 350-400F. TV. Air cond. Pets allowed. Pool. Tennis. Parking. Telex 490746. Cards: V, AE, DC, MC.

The Mercure's rooms are outstanding: bright, spacious and soundproofed. Excellent service. Restaurant.

Niort

79000 Niort - (Deux-Sèvres)
Paris 412 - Poitiers 74 - Angers 149 - Angoulême 111

Motel des Rocs

Rte. de Paris (Chavagné), 79260 La Crèche - 49.25.50.38

Open year-round. 51 rms 310-330F. Half-board 320F. TV. Pets allowed. Heated pool. Tennis. Parking. Telex 790632. Cards: V, AE, DC, MC.

The rooms of the Motel des Rocs, which is located in a seventeen-acre park, are hospitable and well equipped, and the numerous services provided are quite decent. Recreational activities are offered. Helicopter landing. Two restaurants.

(15) Le Relais Saint-Antoine

Pl. de la Brèche - 49.24.02.76

Mme. Godon & M. Fichet. Open until 10 p.m. Closed Fri. dinner, Sat., July 1-22 & Feb. school vacation. Terrace dining. Pets allowed. Cards: V, AE, DC, MC.

Much more than a modern restaurant, Le Relais Saint-Antoine is an ultra-contemporary "space," to which the best of the fashionable design professionals (led by Philippe Starck) have given polish. Clever lighting from the halogen lamps lends black, white or silver shadings to the large, somewhat bare interior decorated with photographs by Doisneau and Man Ray. All this is perfectly executed, even if such modernism seems somewhat incongruous on this central square in Niort, which embodies the very spirit of provincialism. Thierry Fichet's cuisine is second to none in its modern, bold style. However, we have two minor complaints: His à la carte menu is too long, and the names of his dishes tend to ramble on in an affected style ("harvest from the sea"; "quintessence of langoustines"). But this is excusable, as it's due solely to an excess of enthusiasm and generosity.

The cuisine is lovely and alive with delicious ideas, such as the salmon sautéed with turmeric; the poached eggs à la fermière with split-pea biscuits and bacon; and the ravioli of sweetbreads and morels, garnished with spinach and cabbage. The desserts are exquisite.

A la carte: 380-400F. Menus: 135F, 175F, 370F.

We're always happy to hear about your discoveries and to receive your comments about ours. We want to give your letters the attention they deserve, so when you write to Gault Millau, please state clearly what you liked or disliked. Be concise but convincing, and take the time to argue your point.

Nocé

61340 Nocé - (Orne)
Paris 174 - Nogent-le-Rotrou 14 - Alençon 49 - Bellême 8

(14) Auberge des Trois J

Grande-Rue - 33.73.41.03

M. Joly. Open until 9 p.m. Closed Tues. dinner (except July & Aug.), Wed., 2 weeks in Feb. & 2 weeks in Sept. Pets allowed. Parking. Cards: V, AE.

This old, beautifully restored Perche-style house has nothing to do with the Trois J of Galeries Lafayette; the name refers to the three Jolys who manage it: the father, in charge of the wine cellar (to which he is very attentive); Thierry, who runs the lovely, rustic, wooden-beamed dining room; and Stéphane, who devotes himself to preparing an ornate, expressive, clever cuisine (which is quite surprising considering he's only 27 years old—most likely due to his high-quality training as a pastry chef with Lenôtre and Peltier). A respect for produce, a remarkable skill and a spirit of adventure characterize his masterful dishes: tomato soup with roast langoustines and coquilles St-Jacques, salmon with bacon served atop a potato pie, filet of lamb with basil, and a gratin of tomatoes and zucchini. And the astounding, exquisitely presented desserts—from the marbré of caramelized pears to the heavenly millefeuille minute with a creamy pistachio sauce and warm chocolate. The fixed-price menus are outstanding.

A la carte: 280F. Menus: 140F.

Nogent-le-Rotrou

28400 Nogent-le-Rotrou - (Eure-et-Loir)
Paris 151 - Le Mans 65 - Chartres 55 - Châteaudun 53

IN NEARBY **Condeau**
(10 km N on N 23, D 918 & D 10)
61110 Remalard - (Orne)

(14) Moulin de Villeray

33.73.30.22

M. Coldeboeuf. Open until 9 p.m. Closed Tues., Wed. lunch & Nov. 15-Feb. 15. Terrace dining. Pets allowed. Garage parking. Telex 171779. Cards: V, AE, DC, MC.

The bearded Roland Coldeboeuf, an authentic self-made man and an outstanding professional, includes few feuilleté dishes in his current repertoire. This is something rare indeed among chefs like Coldeboeuf who train strictly as pastry cooks—but once you've tried his marvelous warm boskoop (a variety of apple) tart, you'll truly appreciate the virtues of his discretion. Recently he made a serious effort to liven up the brief à la carte menu, with such dishes as the crown of scallops in sherry, the braised turbot with oysters and the pigeon à la fermière with cèpes. The fresh homemade pasta is still delicious, the farm cheeses are splendid, and homemade products are available for takeout. You can dine inside, in a room decorated with old mill equipment, or on the

terrace overlooking the bucolic grounds (water and a beautiful garden).
A la carte: 350-400F. Menus: 220F, 280F.

Moulin de Villeray

(See restaurant above)

Closed Tues. & Nov. 15-Feb. 15. 10 rms 540-640F. Half-board 625F. Pets allowed.

Located about ten kilometers from Nogent-le-Rotrou, this completely restored old mill contains ten rooms stocked with comfortable (though ornate) furniture. Relais et Châteaux.

Nouan-le-Fuzelier

41600 Lamotte-Beuvron - (Loir-et-Cher)
Paris 173 - Orléans 44 - Vierzon 35 - Blois 58

(13) Le Dahu

14, rue Henri-Chapron - 54.88.72.88

M. Germain. Open until 9:15 p.m. Closed Tues. dinner & Wed. (off-seas.) & Feb. 10-March 20. Garden dining. Pets allowed. Garage parking. Cards: V, AE, MC.

Jean-Luc Germain is more than a little proud: His lovely inn is now located on a street newly renamed for his great-uncle, the famous coach builder Henri Chapron. But all this has had no effect on his cuisine, which is the same as it's always been: fresh, authentically regional and skillfully prepared—whether it is the Sologne fritters or the rib of beef in a red Sancerre sauce. There are some delicious novelties, such as the escargots with a feuilleté of local asparagus and the ramekin of lobster from Brittany served with citrus fruit. When the weather is nice, the hostess serves meals in her exquisite garden. The wine list includes some good local wines.

A la carte: 230-250F. Menus: 95F (weekdays only), 125F, 170F, 210F.

Le Moulin de Villiers

Rte. de Chaon (3 km on D 44)
54.88.72.27

Closed Tues. & Wed. (Nov.-Dec.), Jan. 5-March 18 & Sept. 1-15. 20 rms 120-240F. Half-board 180-270F oblig in seas. No pets. Parking. Cards: V.

A quiet, charming old house with modest rooms, located in the midst of a forest, next to a pond. Restaurant.

IN NEARBY **Saint-Viâtre**
(8 km W on D 93)
41210 Neung-sur-Beuvron - (Loir-et-Cher)

Auberge de la Chichone

Pl. de l'Eglise - 54.88.91.33

Closed Wed. (off-seas.) & March. 7 rms 270F. Half-board 520F (for two). Pets allowed. Cards: V.

Located among the Sologne ponds, this old, quiet, absolutely delightful house has been entirely renovated and modernized. Its rooms and service ensure a comfortable stay. Restaurant.

Noves

13550 Noves - (Bouches-du-Rhône)
Paris 700 - St-Rémy-de-Provence 16 - Avignon 14

Auberge de Noves

On A 7 (toward Châteaurenard), Avignon-Sud exit - 90.94.19.21

M. Lalleman. Open until 10 p.m. Closed Wed. lunch & Jan. 3-March 1. Air cond. Garden dining. Pets allowed. Garage parking. Telex 431312. Cards: V, AE, MC.

The charming André Lalleman, more a private host than a hotel owner, prefers to speak of friends rather than clients. Of course, he presents them with a check at the end of their stay; but he does it so discreetly, and only after he has made them feel so welcome and brought them so much pleasure in his large Provençal manor among the pines and cypresses, that they accept the stiff prices without complaint. And why shouldn't they? The surrounding countryside is so beautiful, the swimming pool so refreshing, and the personnel so relaxed that the hours pass as though in a dream. Pascal Johnson's cuisine contributes subtly to this sense of contentment, with his rock fish bouillabaisse en gelée, his panaché of sea perch and red mullet, his veal kidney with tarragon and his crème brûlée in a pastry crust with licorice sauce. The wine list, excellent and rich, is presented with great clarity.

A la carte: 400-500F. Menus: 220F (weekday lunch only), 260F (weekday lunch only, wine incl.), 300F, 360F, 400F.

Auberge de Noves

(See restaurant above)

Closed Wed. & Jan. 3-March 1. 2 stes 1,350F. 21 rms 600-1,150F. Half-board 730-1,005F oblig. in seas. TV. Air cond. in 15 rms. Heated pool. Tennis.

This handsome, slightly austere Provençal manor is truly a dream house, despite the fact that the twenty rooms are not endowed equally with charm and comfort. Marvelous park. Relais et Châteaux.

Nuits-Saint-Georges

21700 Nuits-St-Georges - (Côte-d'Or)
Paris 330 - Beaune 16 - Dijon 22 - Chalon-sur-Saône 48

La Côte d'Or

37, rue Thurot - 80.61.06.10

M. Crotet. Open until 9:30 p.m. Closed Sun. dinner, Wed. & Feb. 6-March 9. Air cond. Pets allowed. Hotel: 1 ste & 6 rms 320-600F. Cards: V, MC.

Jean Crotet, the owner/chef, is leaving this big, in-town establishment to set up shop on the outskirts of nearby Beaune, and his sous-chef, Thierry Guyot, is taking charge here. We expect that this talented, 23-year-old chef, who has been with Bocuse and Lameloise and is full of ideas, will do fine things here, but at the moment we have yet to taste his work.

La Gentilhommière

14

13, vallée de la Serrée - 80.61.12.06

M. Vanroelen. Open until 9 p.m. Closed Mon. & Dec. Parking. Telex 350401. Cards: V, AE, DC.

For quite some time now, we have been waiting for a chef capable of luring us back to this elegiac restaurant located in the hollow of a hill. And now that Jack Vanroelen, the new owner and former assistant at Lorrain in Côte Saint-Jacques, has arrived, our wait is over. He is a solid, classical chef who is precise (but not to the point of obsession); he even could become quite famous in the region before long if he keeps making such dishes as the sautéed chanterelles with foie gras, roasted langoustines in a fine, well-seasoned cream sauce, perfect squab in truffle juice and a delicious peach terrine with black currants. However, the wine cellar isn't altogether original, and neither the service nor the reception could be called exceptional. The wide windows of the attractive dining room open onto a lovely natural landscape.

A la carte: 300F. Menus: 130F, 190F.

La Gentilhommière

(See restaurant above)

Closed Dec. 20 rms 270-290F. Air cond. Pets allowed.

This modern, motel-style building nevertheless blends well into the green scenery of the surrounding countryside. The spacious rooms are all on a single level.

Obenheim

67230 Benfeld - (Bas-Rhin)
Paris 465 - Strasbourg 33 - Sélestat 26 - Erstein 9

12/20 La Matelote

4, rue du Sand - 88.98.31.53

M. Ertel. Open until 8:30 p.m. Closed Mon. & Jan. Terrace dining. Pets allowed. Parking. Cards: V.

La Matelote is a veritable Alsatian temple dedicated to fish stew and freshwater fish, which are kept at their freshest in large ponds. Recently Robert Ertel added to his long à la carte menu a new matelote (stew) of carp, sander and sea pike (this time without bones), which is served in a pleasant dining room facing the Vosges mountains. The majestic brandies are among the rarest to be found. One more point in this edition.

A la carte: 250F.

Obernai

67210 Obernai - (Bas-Rhin)
Paris 486 - Strasbourg 27 - Sélestat 23 - Colmar 45

IN NEARBY **Ottrott-le-Haut**
(4 km W)
67530 Ottrott-le-Haut - (Bas-Rhin)

Beau Site

14

Pl. de l'Eglise - 88.95.80.61

MM. Schreiber. Open daily until 9:30 p.m. Garden dining. Pets allowed. Hotel: 10 stes 480-620F; 9 rms 310-400F; half-board 400-700F. Garage parking. Telex 870445. Cards: V, AE, DC, MC.

The Schreiber brothers and their wives have just one concern: that their cuisine match their reputation. That is no easy task, since their luxurious, flower-filled inn at the foot of Mont Saint-Odile has, for many years now, been an almost compulsory stop along the road to the wines (those in Ottrott are red). And if anything were amiss in this rustic yet refined dining room, with its many bouquets of flowers, the news would spread quickly through the whole of Alsace. But there is no sign of that: The reception and service are still exemplary, as are the rich Alsatian wine list and the splendid feast of game offered throughout the hunting season. A small selection of honest modern dishes balances the foie gras and Sauerkraut: creamed scallops with salmon eggs, sot-l'y-laisse (delicate poultry) with a parsley flan, filet of hogfish served without sauce and garnished with fried zucchini. There is a lovely selection of rustic dishes.

A la carte: 300-350F. Menus: 135F (weekdays only), 178F, 250F, 350F.

Offemont

see Belfort

Oléron (Ile d')

(Charente-Maritime)
Paris 500 - Marennes 10

IN **La Rémigeasse**
(10 km Pont d'Oléron)
17550 Dolus-d'Oléron - (Charente-Maritime)

Amiral

14

46.75.37.89

Mme. Moreau & M. Lemoine. Open until 9 p.m. Closed late Sept.-early April. Pets allowed. Parking. Telex 790395.

This large, sober, meticulously maintained building, which overlooks the sea across its garden and the verdant dunes, gives one the illusion that Oléron is still a deserted island, even at the height of the summer season. From the distinctively sedate and elegant dining room and its terrace, one can enjoy the serenity of this lovely scenery. Joël Lebeaupin's cuisine is as consistent and subtle as ever, though his repertoire is a bit overly ambitious and the names of his dishes a tad pretentious: warm terrine of filet of sole with tourteaux (crab), flan of duck and langoustine foie gras in a pink-pepper sauce, sea bass from the Atlantic with creamed oysters and truffles, and ice cream with a raspberry coulis.

A la carte: 350-400F. Menus: 140F (weekday lunch only), 195F, 295F.

Le Grand Large

(See restaurant above)

Closed late Sept.-early April. 4 stes 1,330-1,600F. 23 rms 460-1,330F. Half-board 540-985F oblig. in seas. TV. Pets allowed. Heated pool. Tennis.

Cozily nestled amid the dunes on the border of an immense sandy beach, this modern hotel provides a pleasant feeling of well-being, though the rooms not facing the sea are less attractive. Breakfast is excellent. Indoor pool. Relais et Châteaux.

IN **Saint-Georges-d'Oléron**
(20 km Pont d'Oléron)
17190 St-Georges-d'Oléron - (Charente-Maritime)

(14) Les Trois Chapons

240, rte. de St-Pierre - 46.76.51.51
M. Hayard. Open until 10 p.m. Closed Sun. dinner & Mon. (except holidays & school vacations) & Dec. 1-Feb. 1. Garden dining. Pets allowed. Parking. Cards: V, AE, DC.

Once chef of the nearby Amiral and more recently of the Richelieu in La Rochelle, Jean Hyart has recently taken on the difficult task of succeeding the talented Jack Rolland, who had established this place as the best restaurant on the island (15/20 in our last edition). The interior has been prettied up, including some paintings by a local painter/goatherd who also supplies the wonderful goat cheeses and chevreau (kid). Hyart is a good, solid cook, and here he lets his imagination go a bit with a sweetbreads turnover pan-fried with mushrooms, duck-breast slices deglazed in the local sherry and delicious fritters with lemon sorbet. The service, led by Mme. Hyart, makes up in charm what it lacks in efficiency.

A la carte: 350-400F. Menus: 130F, 180F, 350F.

IN **Saint-Trojan-les-Bains**
(8 km Pont d'Oléron)
17370 St-Trojan-les-Bains - (Charente-Maritime)

Novotel

Plage de Gatseau - 46.76.02.46
Open year-round. 80 rms 330-650F. Half-board 330-490F oblig. in seas. TV. Pets allowed. Heated pool. Tennis. Parking. Telex 790910. Cards: V, AE, DC, MC.

A fine place to stay, whether one is seeking recreation or simple rest: swimming pool, tennis courts, sauna, exercise room and windsurfing club. The decor of the rooms is rather severe but nevertheless pleasant. Restaurant.

Olivet

see Orléans

Onzain

41150 Onzain - (Loir-et-Cher)
Paris 199 - Tours 45 - Blois 16 - Amboise 20

(15) Domaine des Hauts de Loire

54.20.72.57
MM. Bonnigal. Open until 9 p.m. Closed Dec. 1-Feb. 5. Garden dining. No pets. Parking. Telex 751547. Cards: V, AE, MC.

A weekend at the Bonnigals' Domaine, among the gentle hills of Tours, will prove a welcome antidote to the carelessness and lack of personality that characterize today's representatives of the large-hotel industry. Hidden in a lush, 172-acre park between Blois and Amboise, this eighteenth-century country estate would deserve to be the single Relais et Châteaux inn should this chain, by some misfortune, lose all but one of its members. Gaston Bonnigal and his wife, son and daughter-in-law will quickly make you forget that you are staying in a hotel. They greet you with a warm simplicity seldom learned in restaurant schools. The house, its decor and furniture, its park, its pond (filled with carp and pike), its large Sologne-style pavilion where the rooms are located—all are the result of their work, and everything has been done with such exquisite taste and care that we wanted to stay there forever.

The cuisine of some other Relais et Châteaux places may be more elegant, but here the perfection of simplicity (relatively speaking) was quite enough for us. The roulade of salmon and gilthead with dill, the red mullet with herbs and the filet of lamb with thyme deserve special mention: Gérard Hummel, who worked with Girardet in Crissier, understands perfectly that it's best to do things properly, not excessively. With their wooden beams, tapestries, buttercup-yellow curtains and sparkling silverware, the dining rooms, overlooking the park, are delightful.

A la carte: 350-400F. Menu: 240F (wine incl., except at dinner).

Domaine des Hauts de Loire

(See restaurant above)
Closed Dec. 1-Feb. 5. 5 stes 1,200-1,500F. 24 rms 500-1,020F. Half-board 700-890F. TV. Tennis.

Mme. Bonnigal has decorated the rooms, suites and bathrooms with perfect taste. Their vast proportions, refinement and comfort are enchanting. We particularly recommend the "solognote" annex, where the most handsome suites are located. Fishing pond.

IN NEARBY **Seillac**
(7 km N)
41150 Onzain - (Loir-et-Cher)

Domaine de Seillac

54.20.72.11
Closed Sun. & Mon. (off-seas.) & Dec. 19-Jan. 5. 1 ste 500F. 82 rms 360-450F. Half-board 300-350F. TV. Pets allowed. Heated pool. Tennis. Parking. Telex 751315. Cards: V, AE, DC.

This attractive old building and its many adjacent bungalows (whose comforts are constantly improving) are located in a 59-acre park, which includes three tennis courts, a large swimming pool and various recreational facilities.

Orange

84100 Orange - (Vaucluse)
Paris 660 - Avignon 31 - Nîmes 55 - Carpentras 23

Arène

Pl. de Langes - 90.34.10.95
Closed Nov. 1-Dec. 15. 30 rms 210-280F. TV in 18 rms. Pets allowed. Garage parking. Telex 431195. Cards: V, AE, DC, MC.

Impeccable reception and service can be expected at this superb, serene hotel (whose decor is constantly being embellished) located in the center of historic Orange, across from a lovely square shaded by plane trees. No restaurant.

IN NEARBY **Rochegude**
(14 km NW on D 976, D 11 & D 117)
26790 Rochegude - (Drôme)

13 Château de Rochegude

75.04.81.88

M. Chabert. Open until 9 p.m. Closed Tues. & Wed. lunch (off-seas.) & Jan. 1-March 6. Air cond. No pets. Parking. Telex 345661. Cards: V, AE, DC.

This expensive château (built in the eleventh century, restored by Viollet-le-Duc and replete with antique furniture and vermilion-velvet tapestries) houses a huge dining room that overlooks some delightful gardens. Amid all this luxury, a new chef—the third in two years—is trying to recapture former glories. The results so far are encouraging, but he still needs to sharpen the regional accents and refine the preparations of such dishes as the ravioli and quenelles in pesto, the raw salmon in gazpacho and the fried red snapper. The desserts, on the other hand, are top-notch and the wine list excellent.

À la carte: 300F. Menus: 170F (weekday lunch only), 300F (weekend and holiday dinner only).

Château de Rochegude

(See restaurant above)

Closed Jan. 1-March 6. 4 stes 1,800-2,000F. 25 rms 400-1,500F. Half-board 300F (plus rm). TV. Air cond. Pets allowed. Heated pool. Tennis.

Facing the Ventoux and Tricastin mountains, the Château de Rochegude encompasses an immense park, a swimming pool, tennis courts, marble statues in every corner and expensive furniture in the spacious rooms. It's all very refined, from the outstanding personnel to the delicious breakfast. Relais et Châteaux.

Orcines

see Clermont-Ferrand

Orléans

45000 Orléans - (Loiret)
Paris 116 - Chartres 72 - Tours 113 - Blois 56

Sights. The Maison de Jeanne d'Arc (with dioramas); pl. du Martroi; the rue d'Escures; the Town Hall (where François I died in 1560, an intensively restored Renaissance-style building); the Sainte-Croix cathedral (built in Gothic style and reconstructed during the seventeenth and eighteenth centuries, handsome wood panels in the choir, interesting relics); the Hôtel Cabu (a historical museum); the floral park of La Source (eight kilometers southeast); Musée des Beaux-Arts (portraits by the French School from the seventeenth and eighteenth centuries).

Eating on the Run. Le Bannier, 13, Faubourg Bannier (good, hearty, tasty dishes); Le Khédive, rue des Carmes (a lively café, tobacconist, brasserie and newspaper shop); Les Mouettes Blanches, 2, quai de la Madeleine (brochettes, decent prices and service); La Pasta, 8, pl. du Martroi (many varieties of pasta, good pizza); Chez Tonio, 67, rue des Carmes (unbeatable prices, generous servings, quality that's more than fair); La Vieille Auberge, 2, Faubourg St-Vincent (good simmered dishes, speedy service, high prices).

Nightlife. L'Abbaye de l'Empereur, 28, rue de l'Empereur (young clientele, sumptuous decor); L'Arraldia, at St-Pryvé-St-Mesmin (ten kilometers toward Blois, a magnificent discotheque); Le Bugatti, 6, rue d'Avignon (comfortable, the rendezvous for 30- to 40-year-old all-nighters).

Shops. *Bakeries:* Plisson, rue Bannier (large loaves of country bread and onion, walnut and soy breads). *Charcuteries:* André Lenormand, 318, Faubourg Bannier (takeout deli dishes prepared by a Meilleur Ouvrier de France—terrines and pasta). *Chocolate, confections:* Chocolaterie Royale, 53, rue Royale (the oldest and best confiserie in town, pralines, crystalized fruit and, of course, the Orléans cotignacs—quince cheeses—so dear to Balzac); Thouveny, 8, rue des Carmes (for its chocolates). *Cheese:* Lavarenne, in the Châtelet market (a fine selection of good products). *Pastries:* Morin, 209, rue de Bourgogne (lovely cakes, ice creams and homemade chocolates).

Special Events. May 7 and 8: Jeanne d'Arc Festival.

15 Les Antiquaires

2-4, rue au Lin - 38.53.52.35

M. Pipet. Open until 9:30 p.m. Closed Sun., Mon., 1 week in April, 3 weeks in Aug. & Dec. 24-Jan. 2. Air cond. Pets allowed. Cards: V, AE, DC.

The second toque has been waiting to be awarded for some time now, on a corner of the piano... perhaps next to the tournedos Rossini and the vermouth sauces that the excellent Michel Pipet has finally and definitely discarded. It has become a real pleasure to read his handsome, clear, well-balanced à la carte menu, now that this outstanding professional has given both his imagination and savoir-faire more opportunity for expression. The shellfish soup with creamed tomatoes and sweet pepper, the cocotte of frogs' legs en croûte, the duckling tourte, the noisettes of young rabbit with small shellfish and the handsome cakes, such as the ananassier (pineapple) and the chocolate–morello cherry dessert—all these dishes have made Les Antiquaires one of the best restaurants in Orléans today. (It was already one of the most stylish, with its elegant decor of wooden beams, lovely lighting and beautiful china.) The wine list includes several handsome bottles of regional wines for about 60 francs; the two fixed-price menus are outstanding.

A la carte: 250-300F. Menus: 100F (weekdays only), 180F (wine incl.), 270F.

18 La Crémaillère

34, rue Notre-Dame-de-Recouvrance
38.53.49.17

M. Huyart. Open until 9:30 p.m. Closed Sun. dinner & Mon. Pets allowed. Cards: V, AE, DC.

The best chef in Orléans? That goes without saying. And why not declare Paul Huyart one of the best in France, since he is? He's an astounding fellow, this 50ish Breton who hides the soul of a young man and the sensitivity of an innovator behind his majestic plumpness and engraved culinary diplomas. He could have chosen, like so many chefs of his generation, to grow old peacefully, bathed in butter and crème fraîche, or to simply latch onto the latest cliché, just to show he was "with it." Instead, he chose an infinitely more difficult path—making his cuisine the dash between the Ancients and the Moderns, without the least concession to either. His imagination and his heart come through in his cuisine, affirming his personality. If we weren't afraid of sounding pompous, we'd say that his is cuisine d'auteur.

He's an author who plays with aromas, essences and the most subtle blendings of flavors. Take, for example, the langoustines royales, seasoned just so, served in a thin, crispy phyllo pastry over which is a sweet-and-sour sauce that is almost Chinese: perfect harmony. The gâteau de tourteau (crab) au confit d'oignon comes with a sliver of lime, enough to wake it up without overwhelming it. The turbot, thick and tender at the same time, comes enveloped in an extraordinary herb sauce where chives, parsley, chervil and spinach blend with the lightly peppered flavor of watercress. The pailleté of wild salmon with warm potatoes will renew your love of this noble fish, so often put to shame these days. Almost every restaurant seems to pull out a seafood pot-au-feu, but this is one of the few to successfully make it with each fish—from red snapper to turbot, lotte to sole—cooked to perfection and retaining its own flavor. We should mention all the fish and shellfish on the menu. In his homeland of Brittany (he's from Saint-Brieuc), Huyart has developed a network on the docks and thus has access to the best and freshest fish, which are brought to his restaurant daily. And we can guarantee you that a "tête-à-tête" with a sole, a fricassée of rouget-barbet (variety of red snapper) au verjuice (the juice of unripened grapes), a fresh cod in aromatic herbs and spices, or a steamed lobster is just as tender as any lovers' rendezvous.

La Crémaillère could easily pass for one of the finest fish restaurants in France if it weren't for its warm foie gras, admirably firm and resting on a bed of celery and apples. Or for the light touch of sesame oil that brings out unknown flavors in warm young rabbit. Or for the roast duck that is metamorphosed by a pinch of ginger.

Should we mention any flops? Of course. Having just showered Huyart with rosy praise, we're not going to shy away from telling him that his is no way to prepare a baby pigeon. His roast pigeon, too rare and tangled in leaves of foie gras and cabbage, is merely la vieille cuisine wrapped in a modern dressing, and it holds no interest. But we'll forget about that and move on to the desserts. In general, they're too sweet and not particularly inventive, except for the bitter-chocolate entremets with coffee sauce and an orange salad that is nothing less than a masterpiece. There is also a simple but enchanting rhubarb compote with wild strawberries.

The small disappointment is the wine cellar. Not because of its prices, which are reasonable—as are those of the main courses and the amazing 190-franc fixed-price menu—but the selection is rather meager. Surely Gérard Pelletier, the charming and clever maître d'hôtel/sommelier, could ask his boss to give him a wider range of Loire wines, as well as some private-label Burgundies, instead of just those from the large producers. Then everything would be perfect, since the greeting by Paul and his wife, who are the epitome of kindness and delicacy, is already flawless. We have yet to see any unhappy clients in the bright, appetizing main dining room, discreetly separated from the large table where Orléans's notables hold court.

A la carte: 250-400F. Menus: 190F, 330F.

Jackotel

18, rue Cloître-St-Aignan - 38.54.48.48

Open year-round. 40 rms 190-260F. TV in 20 rms. No pets. Garage parking. Cards: V, DC.

This decent small hotel located in front of place du Cloître looks much better than the sign implies: Its attractive rooms have been tastefully decorated, and it features a garden. No restaurant.

(14) Le Lautrec

26, pl. du Châtelet - 38.54.09.54

M. Boulais. Open until 10 p.m. Closed Sun., Feb. 15-28 & July 15-30. Terrace dining. Pets allowed. Cards: V, AE, DC, MC.

Bruno Boulais, a native of Tarn, prepares a lovely, modernized interpretation of the cuisine of his region that cannot be found anywhere else in the Orléans area. An admirer of Daguin and a former student of Gisèle Crouzier, today he is a completely independent cook as far as personality is concerned, and his execution is perfectly self-assured. He offers a short, versatile, well-balanced à la carte selection and an attractive fixed-price menu that follows the market: brochette of pink trout with prunes, salmon with a garlic confit, saddle of young rabbit browned in a caul and garnished with celery sticks, and a superb sorbet millefeuille. There are also several more classical successes, particularly the handsome cassoulet and the light Sologne tart (tarte tatin with apples and pears). The wine cellar, composed of wines from the southwest of France, is attractive; the collection of Armagnacs, from 1893 to the present (more than 60 vintages), is impressive; and the selection of coffees is quite fine. The new, adjacent wine bistro, Le Petit Boulais, serves well-prepared brasserie dishes from 9 a.m. to midnight. One more point with this edition.

A la carte: 260F. Menus: 120F, 180F, 260F.

(14) La Poutrière

8-10, rue de la Brèche - 38.66.02.30, 38.66.51.71

MM. Thomas & Saunier. Open until 10 p.m. Closed Sun. dinner & Mon. Garden dining. Pets allowed. Parking. Cards: V, AE, DC, MC.

The cuisine served in this old farmhouse, with its appealing decor of mirrors and old wooden beams, is becoming increasingly exotic. Marcel Thomas, the co-owner and chef (formerly a cook at La Transat) makes good use of foreign fruits and vegetables and endows the traditional, classic themes with a light and personal touch. Try the gray daurade cooked in a salt crust with a purée of sweet potatoes in nutmeg, the langoustines and soy rice crêpes flavored with basil, the splendid mignon of veal sautéed in honey and seasoned with vinegar and the warm mango tart. The wine cellar becomes richer and more handsome each year. The increase in prices, however, has been dramatic (though this may be understandable, since the owners are building a swimming pool). Good service.

A la carte: 300F and up. Menus: 140F (weekday lunch only, wine incl.), 180F.

(13) La Vénerie

44-46, quai Barentin - 38.62.17.39

M. Mornat. Open daily until 10:30 p.m. Terrace dining. Air cond. Pets allowed. Parking. Telex 780073. Cards: V, AE, DC, MC.

This is an excellent example of what a chain hotel can accomplish when it is managed intelligently. Professional judgment is as evident in the bright interior overlooking the pool as it is in the well-mannered service and the wonderful, even-handed technique of chef Michel Marolleau. His adept yet personal cooking style is at its best in the sweetbreads crêpe, the steamed pollock with jasmine and the filet of pork with raisins. In season the game is very good, and there are some delightful bottles of Loire wine in the cellar.

A la carte: 250-300F. Menus: 120F.

Sofitel

(See restaurant above)

Open year-round. 1 ste 860-920F. 108 rms 420-550F. TV. Pets allowed. Heated pool.

Here you'll find spacious, comfortable rooms on the banks of the Loire (and the ring road). Services include an express laundry service and satellite TV.

IN NEARBY **Olivet**
(5 km S on D 15)
45160 Olivet - (Loiret)

---

(13) Le Rivage

635, rue de la Reine-Blanche
38.66.03.30, 38.66.02.93

M. Béreaud. Open until 9:30 p.m. Closed Sun. dinner (Nov. 1-Palm Sun.) & Dec. 28-Jan. 15. Garden dining. No pets. Parking. Telex 760926. Cards: V, AE, DC, MC.

Chef Didier Benoit seems to be fascinated with the number three: His repertoire includes three fresh seasonal mousses in basil sauce, a small three-fruit tart, three fruit mousses in red sauce and more such trios. Aside from this curiosity, his cuisine offers the more substantial advantage of being skillful and quite personal: a tasty salad of young rabbit cut in round slices and served in a foie gras dressing (unfortunately a bit too thin), young pigeon (filet and grilled legs) served in an exquisite sauce (its vegetable garnish is a bit disappointing, however) and desserts of somewhat inconsistent quality. The selection of wines from the Loire (as well as from the Orléans region, which are more rare) is impressive. We prefer the magnificent terrace on the particularly lush banks of the Loiret to the majestic, somewhat melancholy interior.

A la carte: 250-300F. Menus: 100F, 140F, 200F.

Le Rivage

(See restaurant above)

Closed Dec. 28-Jan. 15. 21 rms 100-220F. Half-board 400-450F oblig. in seas. Pets allowed. Tennis.

The lovely white facade is reflected in the Loiret river, which several of the most attractive rooms overlook. Boating is available.

IN NEARBY **Saint-Jean-de-Braye**
(2.5 km E on N 60)
45800 St-Jean-de-Braye - (Loiret)

---

(14) La Grange

205, Faubourg de Bourgogne
38.86.43.36

M. Dupuy. Open until 9:30 p.m. Closed Sun. (except holiday lunch), Mon., Aug. & 1 week in Feb. Garden dining. Pets allowed. Parking. Cards: V.

The charming, wooden-beamed dining room opens onto a small, semienclosed small garden; the old furniture adds still more to the seductiveness of this intimate restaurant, well protected from the noise of the nearby highway. The art of Robert Dupuy, the chef/owner, lies in the execution and subtlety of his dishes, particularly his fine smooth and savory sauces and his judicious use of vegetable garnishes. During our last visit, the warm salad of green lentils and veal tongue, the feuilleté of asparagus with chives and the beautiful filet of lamb in a salt crust nearly merited two toques, but the desserts required improvement. The patronne's reception is attentive, though directed primarily toward the regular clientele. The wine cellar—Cahors and Beaujolais—is impressive.

A la carte: 260F. Menus: 85F and 125F (weekdays only).

Orly

see PARIS SUBURBS

Ornaisons

see Narbonne

Orthez

64300 Orthez - (Pyrénées-Atlantiques)
Paris 751 - Bayonne 66 - Pau 41 - Mont-de-Marsan 54

---

(14) Auberge Saint-Loup

20, rue du Pont-Vieux - 59.69.15.40

Mme. Saint-Pé. Open until 11 p.m. Closed Mon. & Oct. 2-16. Terrace dining. No pets. Cards: V, AE, DC.

Once you've passed the old Orthez bridge, you'll discover this former relais that a self-made industrialist transformed into a delightful family restaurant twelve years ago. You'll enjoy the old stones and beautiful wooden beams, the adorable little dining room with its corner fireplace (the other two dining rooms are less impressive) and the patio where meals are served in summer. And you'll especially relish the fascinating cuisine of Jacques Saint-Pé, who is assisted by his daughter, Sandrine. He successfully exhibits the boldness typical of self-taught cooks, but without the usual confused excesses. Taste the filet of sole in a cream sauce flavored with Jurançon wine, the sea pike braised with thyme and fennel and garnished with eggplant "caviar" and a sweet-pepper confit (the fish, which comes from a fishmonger in Saint-Jean-de-Luz, is magnificent) and the young lamb from the Pyrénées served with vegetable-stuffed zucchini. Excellent regional wines.

A la carte: 200-230F. Menus: 110F, 185F.

Orvault

see Nantes

Ottrot-le-Haut

see Obernai

Ouilly-du-Houley

see Lisieux

Pacy-sur-Eure

27120 Pacy-sur-Eure - (Eure)
Paris 84 - Rouen 62 - Évreux 18 - Mantes-la-Jolie 26

12/20 L'Etape

32.36.12.77

Mme. Angot. Open daily until 9 p.m. Terrace dining. Pets allowed. Hotel: 1 ste 210-313F; 8 rms 69-189F; half-board 160-190F. Parking. Cards: V, MC.

Located on the banks of the Eure, this handsome house has a garden and lush greenery overhanging the river—and a new chef who is committed to giving a nice élan to the cuisine. One more point for the sweetbreads with morels, the bourride of lotte with cabbage and the roast lamb sautéed in red wine.

A la carte: 220F. Menus: 81F (weekdays only), 132F, 185F.

IN NEARBY Douains

(On D 181)
27120 Pacy-sur-Eure - (Eure)

Château de Brécourt

32.52.40.50

M. Savry. Open daily until 9:30 p.m. Pets allowed. Garage parking. Telex 172250. Cards: V, AE, DC, MC.

This lovely seventeenth-century château, here at the gateway to Normandy, has always been one of the shining links in the Relais et Châteaux chain. We also used to be able to look forward to delicious, well-thought-out cooking served with the finest manners. This is not exactly—actually, not at all—true any longer; the sole pleasure left to us on recent visits has been the splendid dining room of old beams, polished brick-tile floor, beautivul table settings and a view of the Norman woods. Otherwise, we were offered a distracted reception and left to sloppy service amid a noisy crowd, and fed just barely adequate food: overjellied beef stew, rack of lamb without distinction, great cheeses and an acceptable hot tart. Attractive, reasonably priced wine list.

A la carte: 400F. Menus: 150F (weekday lunch only, wine incl.), 310F (Fri. dinner only), 205F, 315F.

Château de Brécourt

(See restaurant above)

Open year-round. 4 stes 900-1,100F. 20 rms 375-800F. Half- board 645-845F. Pets allowed. Heated pool. Tennis.

Amenities here include spacious, comfortable, stylishly furnished rooms (though the bathrooms are a bit small), new conference rooms and marvelous grounds. Relais et Châteaux.

Paimpol

22500 Paimpol - (Côtes-du-Nord)
Paris 491 - St-Brieuc 45 - Lézardrieux 4 - Lannion 33

Le Relais Brenner

Pont de Lézardrieux (4 km W on D 786)
96.20.11.05

M. Brenner. Open until 9:30 p.m. Closed Mon. (off-seas.) & Jan. 2-March 5. Pets allowed. Parking. Telex 740676. Cards: V, AE, DC, MC.

This restaurant, once venerable but more recently fading into banality, keeps getting new leases on life, apparently of the twelve-month variety; last year's promising young chef has given way to this year's newly arrived accomplished professional. He has brought with him dishes of which he is already a master, such as prawn-stuffed ravioli with rosemary, salmon en papillote with seaweed, a remarkable bass braised in parsley juices and a gratin of pears. All are excellently served under the supervision of an Italian maître d'. It's time for another point.

A la carte: 300F. Menus: 115F, 150F, 215F.

Le Relais Brenner

(See restaurant above)

Closed Mon. (off-seas.) & Jan. 2-March 5. 5 stes 620-820F. 23 rms 280-500F. Half-board 325-495F oblig. in seas. TV in 5 rms. Pets allowed.

Le Relais Brenner is admirably located in the midst of a splendid garden. The well-soundproofed rooms and the suites with balconies overlooking the sea are both comfortable and bright. Relais et Châteaux.

La Vieille Tour

13, rue de l'Eglise - 96.20.83.18

M. Rosec. Open until 9 p.m. Closed Sun. dinner & Wed.; annual closing varies. Pets allowed. Cards: V, DC.

The new second-floor dining room, with rose-colored fabrics and attractive lighting, is well suited to the cuisine prepared by Alain Rosec, a fine self-taught chef who once cooked at Paris's Le Pré Catelan. Over the years, he has learned everything there is to know from Vergé, Masraff and Coutanceau; his ideas are good, and their execution precise. (But he should be more attentive to his cooking when his lovely restaurant is filled in season.) Try the salad of warm foie gras with coquilles St-Jacques, red mullet with oysters and a sauce made of its own liver, and sweetbreads and kidneys with fresh pasta. The patronne is charming.

A la carte: 250-280F. Menus: 76F (weekdays only), 88F (weekends and holidays only), 150F, 240F, 340F (in season only).

IN NEARBY **Arcouest**
(6 km N on D 789)
22620 Ploubazlanec - (Côtes-du-Nord)

Le Barbu

96.55.86.98

Open year-round. 2 stes 400-500F. 20 rms 250-350F. Half-board 375-400F oblig. in seas. TV. Pets allowed. Heated pool. Parking.

The rooms in this small, delightful seaside hotel overlook either the greenery or the open sea, with views of the coast and the island of Bréhat. Restaurant.

IN NEARBY **Pléhédel**
(9 km S on D 7 & D 79)
22290 Lanvollon - (Côtes-du-Nord)

(15) Château de Coatguelen

96.22.31.24

M. de Boisgelin. Open until 9 p.m. Closed Wed. lunch, Tues. & Jan. 5-April 1 (except by reserv.). Garden dining. No pets. Parking. Telex 741300. Cards: V, AE, DC, MC.

Louis Le Roy is perhaps a slightly better theorist than a technician, and he devotes much time to his cookbooks and the study of cuisine. But he is an outstanding professional, too, capable of beautifully executed creations. We would swear that he has taken our (minor) criticisms to heart; today his cooking is much more masterful, boasting new, clever, lively, light dishes: quail eggs with foie gras in sea urchin shells, chartreuse of sole with potatoes, ragoût of shellfish with garlic and orange, and pastries that are, for the most part, exquisite and inventive. Under the management of Nicole de Morchoven, the service is both precise and attentive. Though it is true that the checks are quite steep, this is to be expected in such a magnificent château that opens onto the greenery of a golf course and the Goélo countryside. The Château de Coatguelen has become one of the best, most alluring restaurants in Brittany.

A la carte: 400F. Menus: 200F, 280F, 350F.

Château de Coatguelen

(See restaurant above)

Closed Jan. 5-April 1. 2 stes 950-1,250F. 14 rms 580-1,150F. Half-board 680-750F oblig. in seas. TV. Pets allowed. Pool. Tennis. Golf.

This appealing little castle nestled in an immense park in truly marvelous countryside has extremely comfortable rooms with excellent bathrooms; exquisite antique furniture is everywhere. Breakfast is delicious. Horseback riding, fishing and nine- and eighteen-hole golf courses (along with golf lessons) are available, as are cooking classes with Louis Le Roy. Relais et Châteaux.

Pau

64000 Pau - (Pyrénées-Atlantiques)
Paris 759 - Bordeaux 195 - Toulouse 195 - Tarbes 39

Sights. The blvd. des Pyrénées and its sublime terrace facing the mountains (which, according to Lamartine, is "the most beautiful sight in the world"); the château (birthplace of Henri IV, marvelous Flanders and Gobelins tapestries and a museum of the Béarn region); Musée des Beaux-Arts (primitive-style paintings from Aragon, numismatics); the parks: Beaumont Park (29 acres, English style), Lawrence Park (extraordinary trees) and the Royal Park (halfway between the château and the oldest golf course in Europe); the Hédas district (located in a ravine, Old Pau under restoration); the Sentiers du Roy (features a walk through the palm trees and rose laurels along the blvd. des Pyrénées).

Eating on the Run. L'Entrecôte, 26, rue Lamothe (pizza and grilled meats, open until 2 a.m.); Le Kamok, 20, rue Maréchal-Foch (bakery, pastry shop, tea salon, crowded at lunch); Au Petit Bab-el-Oued, 22, cours Lyautey (North African cuisine and atmosphere); La Picolette, 48, rue de Liège (daily specials for late-nighters); Tarte Julie, 30, rue Samonzet (serves tarts only).

Brasseries. L'Aragon, 18, blvd. des Pyrénées (the most popular terrace on sunny days); Le Berry, 4, rue Gachet (not very lively, but the best value in Pau); Le Mermoz, 39, ave. Jean-Mermoz (rendezvous for sophisticated late-nighters); Le Saint-Vincent, 4, rue Gassiot (a few feet away from the palace, a clientele composed largely of clergymen).

Bars & Cafés. Le Beaumont, at the Parc Beaumont casino (piano bar); Le Café de l'-Europe, 17, rue Maréchal-Foch (lively, all ages); L'Octave, 5, rue A.-de-Lassence (the most popular piano bar in town); Le Transat, sq. Georges V (state-of-the-art design).

Nightlife. Le Lagon Bleu, 26, rue du Moulin and 5, rue Sully (variety of rums); Le Paradis, 11, pl. du Foirail (discotheque); Le Royal, at the Parc Beaumont casino (the casino's disco); five quite popular discos outside of Pau: L'Auberge du Moulin in Soumoulou, Fun in Lescar, M3 in Serres-Castet and La Siesta and Tio Pepe in Idron.

Continental

2, rue du Maréchal-Foch - 59.27.69.31

Open year-round. 2 stes 700F. 100 rms 240-395F. Half-board 260-410F. TV. Pets allowed. Garage parking. Telex 570906. Cards: V, AE, DC.

This is Pau's prestige hotel, with 100 perfectly arranged and well-soundproofed rooms. Good facilities and attentive reception. Restaurant.

Paris

80, rue Emile-Garet - 59.27.34.39

Open year-round. 41 rms 285-420F. TV. Pets allowed. Garage parking. Telex 541595. Cards: V, AE, DC, MC.

The peaceful rooms face the courtyard; a breakfast buffet is served at no additional charge. Free parking in the building. No restaurant.

(14) Pierre

16, rue Louis-Barthou - 59.27.76.86

M. Casau. Open until 10 p.m. Closed Sat. lunch, Sun. & last 2 weeks of Feb. Pets allowed. Cards: V, AE, DC, MC.

Raymond, son of the mighty Roland Casau, is becoming a legend, too, thanks to his fine character, warmth and originality—Pau's elegant set all flock to his famous little spot. The Casau ladies are extremely attentive at the cash register or in the dining room. And Champagne flows steadily at the bar, where regulars usually stop for a moment before going to their tables—preferably on the main floor, with its narrow but charmingly provincial dining room, mahogany wainscoting and tables facing each other, which encourages conversations more than privacy... but that's the style of this establishment. As for the cuisine, it's not terribly versatile, being devoted primarily to regional dishes, though it is generous and hearty. The magnificent Béarn-style cassoulet is one of the best in France; the foie gras from the Landes is fine indeed; the grilled meats are exceptionally tasty; and the Prélat chocolate cake has been copied throughout the world. We feel, however, that this cuisine no longer warrants two toques.

A la carte: 250-300F.

Roncevaux

25, rue Louis-Barthou - 59.27.08.44

Open year-round. 40 rms 85-260F. TV. Pets allowed. Parking. Telex 570849. Cards: V, AE, DC, MC.

A fair hotel located in the center of Pau near the château entrance, with pleasant, comfortable rooms. No restaurant.

(15) Le Viking

33, blvd. Tourasse - 59.84.02.91

M. David. Open until 9:15 p.m. Closed Sat., Sun. & Aug. Garden dining. No pets. Parking. Cards: V, AE.

The friendly Hubert David, a first-class grumbler (and a veteran of the *France* and *Liberté* transatlantic liners) who moved to Pau six years ago, today is responsible for one of the best cuisines in town. His attractive new establishment is rustic, comfortable, intimate and neat. Quite wisely, David has limited his dining room to about twenty seats, which gives him ample time to refine his wonderful classic cuisine and to do everything himself, from smoking his exquisite fresh salmon to baking his petit fours and chocolate truffles. On the down side, the à la carte prices are quite stiff, and his imagination is still too much on the shy side. But we cannot complain too much—everything is impeccably executed and wonderfully generous, and the flavors are honest, particularly the splendid lotte-and-mussel terrine served with a little mayonnaise (without garlic) on the side, the salmon in a wonderfully light sorrel cream sauce, the braised young turbot, the hind brisket Saint-Anne (named after his wife) in a tasty Bordeaux sauce and the exquisite small fresh-fruit tarts. A fine selection of handsome Bordeaux wines and an extremely cordial atmosphere. Le Viking deserves a second toque in this edition.

A la carte: 350F. Menu: 130F.

The à la carte restaurant prices given are for a complete three-course meal for one, including a half-bottle of modest wine and service. Menu prices are for a complete fixed-price meal for one, excluding wine (unless otherwise noted).

IN NEARBY **Bosdarros**

(12 km S on D 285)

64290 Gan - (Pyrénées-Atlantiques)

(13) Auberge Labarthe

59.21.72.03

M. Morlaes. Open until 9:30 p.m. Closed Mon. & Tues. Pets allowed. Hotel: 8 rms 65-95F.

The three dining rooms (two downstairs and one upstairs) in this old Béarn house in the center of Bosdarros are constantly humming with the conversations of diners who have come from all parts of the region. Jean-Claude Morlaes, the owner, is a true champion of generous regional dishes, which he serves at most affordable prices. Come here to sample one of the best garbures (a soup of goose confit, cabbage and bacon) in Béarn, large portions of perfect foie gras, delicious duck confit with Béarnaise potatoes, cèpe omelets, breast of duck (of course!) and fair fruit tarts. Morlaes's cuisine may be irrevocably set, but since he's got it down, it's perhaps for the best. At any rate, he earns his toque. The service is quick and simple.

A la carte: 160F. Menus: 50F, 65F, 80F, 140F.

IN NEARBY **Gan**

(8 km S on N 134)

64290 Gan - (Pyrénées-Atlantiques)

(13) Le Tucq

Rte. de Laruns - 59.21.61.26

M. Rances. Open until 9 p.m. Closed Mon. dinner, Tues., Wed. & Sept. 28-Nov. 10. Terrace dining. Pets allowed. Parking. Cards: V.

The well-deserved success of this large, rustic restaurant has resulted in a threefold increase of its parking capacity. Luckily, this expansion has had no ill effect on the extraordinary prodigality of the cuisine (the 68-franc menu is impressive). The reception is cordial and the service informal; efficiency and a quick turnover of tables (up to three times on Sundays) enable the prices to stay low. Expect a tonic, hearty meal here, perhaps enjoyed on the attractive small terrace on the banks of the Neez: garbure Béarnaise, plate of cold meats, crudités, confits, rib of mutton, duck breasts and savory trout meunière with garlic and parsley. To accompany all of this, select one of the pleasant local wines listed on the à la carte menu.

A la carte: 160F. Menus: 52F (weekdays only), 75F.

IN NEARBY **Jurançon**

(2 km SW on N 134)

64110 Jurançon - (Pyrénées-Atlantiques)

(13) Chez Ruffet

3, ave. Charles-Touzet - 59.06.25.13

M. Larrouy. Open until 10 p.m. Closed Sun. dinner & Mon. Pets allowed. Cards: AE, DC.

Emile ("Milou") Larrouy has remained a faithful disciple of the rich, copious and savory cuisine of his region (Béarn): salade paysanne with duck skins and gizzards, Béarn ham, grilled duck hearts, fresh duck liver with caramelized apple slices, old-fashioned goose confit. Excellent local wines are served for about 60 francs. The convivial atmosphere of the warm, hospitable dining room conveys the feeling that everything at Chez Ruffet is running smoothly.

A la carte: 250F. Menu: 80F, 150F.

Paulx

44270 Machecoul - (Loire-Atlantique)
Paris 425 - Nantes 38 - La-Roche-sur-Yon 45 - Challans 19

13 Les Voyageurs

Pl. de l'Eglise - 40.26.02.26

M. Clavier. Open until 9:30 p.m. Closed Sun. dinner, Mon., Feb. school vacation & Aug. 27-Sept. 19. Pets allowed. Cards: V, AE, DC.

Located on the church square, Les Voyageurs is a solid, hospitable, well-maintained restaurant. Fine modern paintings adorn its dining room walls, which are hung with dark-red woollen fabric, and its tables are set in the best of taste. As you might have guessed, it's a serious place, run by an owner who is attentive to everything. A young chef who trained at Bocuse for three years is at the stoves, and if his repertoire lacks brilliance, it's nevertheless skillful and well executed. The sander vinaigrette with herbs, expertly cooked, is well garnished; the fish of the day—perhaps steamed turbot with a sweet-pepper mousse, stuffed zucchini and a slightly too creamy sauce—is good; and the crème brûlée is actually caramelized eggs in milk. The cellar holds handsome wines from the Loire. We award it one well-deserved toque.

A la carte: 260F. Menus: 95F (weekdays only), 175F, 270F.

Pérignat-lès-Sarliève

see Clermont-Ferrand

Périgueux

24000 Périgueux - (Dordogne)
Paris 528 - Bordeaux 120 - Limoges 101 - Angoulême 85

15 L'Oison

31, rue St-Front - 53.09.84.02

M. Chiorozas. Open until 9:30 p.m. Closed Sun. dinner, Mon. & Feb. 15-March 15. Air cond. Pets allowed. Cards: V, AE, DC.

Régis Chiorozas has done a magnificent job of refining his cuisine and improving the decor of this old building (where hosiery was once made) close to the cathedral. Today his bistro is one of the loveliest in Périgueux, and his à la carte menu is one of the most personal and lively in the province. His judicious use of products, his oh-so-subtle sauces and his masterful execution (the fish dishes are quite tasty and cooked to precision) have truly impressed us (an opinion now shared by the residents of Périgueux). Try the salmon marinière with lentils, warm duck tourte, fish panaché in spicy butter, confit of sweetbreads in onion milk and imaginative, personalized desserts, such as the glazed nougatine with pralines and the wild hazelnut ice cream. Brigitte Chiorozas greets her clients in a charming manner and with great efficiency handles the good, small wine cellar.

A la carte: 350-400F. Menus: 140F (weekdays only), 180F, 260F, 370F.

IN NEARBY **Antonne-et-Trigonant**
(10 km NE on N 21)
24420 Savignac-les-Eglises - (Dordogne)

L'Ecluse

Rte. de Limoges - 53.06.00.04

Closed Sat. (off-seas.) & 1-2 weeks in winter. 50 rms 180-225F. Half-board 190-320F. TV in 33 rms. Pets allowed. Parking. Telex 570382. Cards: V, AE, DC, MC.

This large, modern building has a pleasant terrace overlooking the Isle and the greenery. Fine conference facilities. Entertainment. Restaurant.

Pérouges

01800 Meximieux - (Ain)
Paris 454 - Bourg 37 - Lyon 36 - St-André-de-Corcy 20

12/20 Ostellerie du Vieux Pérouges

Pl. du Tilleul - 74-61.00.88

M. Thibault. Open until 9 p.m. Closed Wed. in winter. Terrace dining. Pets allowed. Garage parking. Cards: V.

Located in a medieval village, this is one of the oldest, loveliest and best-preserved inns in France. Period furniture, china and precious pewter objects compose an attractive setting for the serious, well-prepared local cuisine: salad with smoked carp filets, seafood platter with baby vegetables, roast Bresse chicken and, for dessert, galettes. Handsome wines.

A la carte: 250F. Menus: 150F to 320F.

Ostellerie du Vieux Pérouges

(See restaurant above)

Closed Wed. in winter. 3 stes 900F. 25 rms 390-800F. Half-board 550-800F. TV in 5 rms. Pets allowed.

Within these venerable fifteenth-century walls are spacious, comfortable and quiet rooms, which, with their beautiful regional period furniture and countless ornaments, are exceptionally appealing. Cozy family atmosphere.

Perpignan

66000 Perpignan - (Pyrénées-Orientales)
Paris 908 - Toulouse 208 - Béziers 93 - Foix 137

Sights. Le Castillet (with the wharves of the Basse and their flowers); the palace of the Kings of Majorca; Saint-Jean cathedral (with its famous "Pious Christ" crucifix); Saint-Jacques church; the Town Hall; the rue des Marchands; the train station (Dali called it an absolute masterpiece); Musée Rigaud (primitive-style fifteenth-, sixteenth- and nineteenth-century Catalonian paintings, ceramics); the Julia House (a typical Catalonian townhouse); the Hôtel Päms Library

(77,000 books, incunabula and manuscripts); Musée Puig (an outstanding numismatic collection).

Eating on the Run. Le Blé Noir, 14, rue Gustave-Flaubert (excellent crêperie); Les Expéditeurs, 13, ave. du Général-Leclerc; Le Palmarium, pl. Arago; Le Typhon, 22 bis, ave. du Général-de-Gaulle.

Brasseries. Brasserie de la Loge, pl. de la Loge; Le Café Catalan, pl. de Verdun; Le Vauban, 14, quai Vauban.

Bars & Cafés. Bar du Park Hôtel, 18, blvd. Jean-Bourrat (hospitable, comfortable); Bar Tarterie Le Quartz, galerie Centre Ville, quai Vauban; La Cafetière, 17, rue de l'Ange (fine selection of teas and coffees).

Nightlife. ABC Dancing, rue Dombasle (retro atmosphere); Cotton Club, 14, Traverse des Cardeurs (piano bar); Le Privé, pl. Arago.

Athéna

1, rue Queya - 68.34.37.63

Open year-round. 37 rms 90-200F. TV. Pets allowed. Pool. Garage parking. Cards: V, AE, DC, MC.

The quiet, comfortable rooms of the Athéna hotel overlook a leafy patio with a small swimming pool. No restaurant, but there is room service and a cafeteria.

15 Le Chapon Fin

18, blvd. J.-Bourrat - 68.35.14.14

M. Fernandez. Open until 9:30 p.m. Closed Sat. dinner, Sun., Dec. 25-Jan. 8 & Aug. 13-Sept. 4. Air cond. No pets. Garage parking. Telex 506161. Cards: V, AE, DC, MC.

This bright, spacious hotel restaurant is probably the most luxurious in Perpignan. Tourists flock here, having heard that its cuisine is the best in town. After being greeted most courteously, they are led to a comfortable, modern dining room (another room—Catalonian-style—is decorated with wood panels and ceramics). The dishes served include delicious anchovies from Collioures, escargots fricassée à la Catalane, superb gilthead "à la planche" with a warm sherry vinaigrette and a smooth cassoulet of small beans and goose confit, as well as splendid grilled fish, meats and fowl. Everything is skillfully prepared and tastefully presented by Claude Patry, a solid chef who was Roger Vergé's assistant for four years.

A la carte: 300F. Menus: 170F, 250F, 350F.

Park Hôtel

(See restaurant above)

Open year-round. 67 rms 200-400F. TV. Air cond. Pets allowed.

The rooms of this modern, almost new hotel are quiet, tasteful and stylishly decorated with rustic but beautiful antique furniture. Excellent reception by the entire Fernandez family.

15 Le Relais Saint-Jean

1, cité Bartissol - 68.51.22.25

M. Banyols. Open until 10 p.m. Closed Mon. lunch, Sun. & Feb. 15-28. Terrace dining. Pets allowed. Cards: V, AE, DC.

After a fantastic start, there was a slight drop in quality at Le Relais Saint-Jean. But quite recently it has regained the right rhythm with a fresh, lively and original cuisine impeccably served in the most attractive bistro setting in town. Perpignan's residents have fallen in love with the place, with its paved terrace shaded by the cathedral and its small, splendid dining rooms done in Second-Empire style. Marie-Louise Banyols, an active and charming hostess, is in charge of one of the best wine cellars in Roussillon. Her husband, Didier, delights his smart clientele with his dishes: small sautéed calamari with tomato pulp and basil, thyme-flavored ravioli filled with escargots, and a splendid chocolate and pistachio cake. The fixed-price menus are very good, and the prices have stabilized. Things are looking so good, in fact, that it's time to up the ranking to two toques.

A la carte: 300-350F. Menus: 130F (weekday lunch only), 180F, 260F.

Le Perreux

see PARIS SUBURBS

Perros-Guirec

22700 Perros-Guirec - (Côtes-du-Nord)
Paris 521 - St-Brieuc 76 - Guingamp 44 - Tréguier 20

France

14, rue Rouzig - 96.23.20.27

Closed Nov. 10-April 1. 30 rms 180-280F. Half-board 210-240F. No pets. Parking. Telex 740637. Cards: V.

This large house—which, beyond its park planted with pine trees, overlooks the ocean—offers traditional, pleasant rooms that are redecorated regularly. Solarium. Ping-Pong. Restaurant.

Printania

12, rue des Bons-Enfants - 96.23.21.00

Closed Dec. 15-Jan. 15. 1 ste 387F. 38 rms 200-387F. Half-board 265-343F oblig. in seas. TV. Pets allowed. Tennis. Parking. Telex 741431. Cards: V, AE, DC, MC.

The fine rooms of the Printania have superb views of the sea and the Sept-Iles islands. The beach is 750 feet away; tennis courts are located behind the building. Attentive reception and service. Restaurant.

Pertuis

84120 Pertuis - (Vaucluse)
Paris 747 - Cavaillon 45 - Aix-en-Provence 20

13 Le Sans Souci

60, rue Voltaire - 90.79.16.81

M. Tantini. Open until 10 p.m. Closed Sun. dinner & Mon. Terrace dining. Pets allowed. Cards: V.

Michel and Marie Tantini moved into this bright, hospitable house with its provincial terrace just about two years ago, and already their friendliness, moderate prices and lively cuisine have made them famous. Young Michel, an excellent saucier and skillful cook, is constantly seeking novelty, and his versatile à la carte menu lists lots of mouth-watering dishes: frog curry with a julienne of crisp cabbage, marinated breast of duck with walnuts and rhubarb sauce and some heavenly desserts, such as the extraordinary fig blinis with acacia and rosemary honey. Good selection of regional wines.

A la carte: 230F. Menus: 76F (lunch only), 94F, 140F, 180F.

Le Petit-Pressigny

see Le Grand-Pressigny

La Petite-Pierre

67290 Wingen-sur-Moder - (Bas-Rhin)
Paris 429 - Sarreguemines 45 - Haguenau 40 - Saverne 22

12/20 Auberge d'Imsthal

3, rue d'Imsthal - 88.70.45.21

M. Michaely. Open until 9 p.m. Closed Mon. dinner, Tues. & Nov. 25-Dec. 20. Terrace dining. No pets. Parking. Cards: V, AE, DC.

This large, attractive Alsatian house facing a pond and surrounded by splendid greenery in a cozy wooden setting serves a spirited, copious cuisine: pot-au-feu with horseradish, homemade foie gras and so on.

A la carte: 230F.

Auberge d'Imsthal

(See restaurant above)

Open year-round. 23 rms 140-300F. Half-board 190-260F. TV in 4 rms. Pets allowed.

These quiet, simple and attractive rooms face a pond (delightful for summer swimming).

Peyreleau

12720 Peyreleau - (Aveyron)
Paris 655 - Mende 80 - Rodez 85 - Millau 14

12/20 Grand Hôtel Muse et Rozier

65.62.60.01

M. Lucas de Leyssac. Open until 9:15 p.m. Closed Oct. 7-Easter. Terrace dining. No pets. Garage parking. Cards: V, AE, DC, MC.

The new chef at this extraordinary inn set in the wild surroundings of the Aveyron region prepares such dishes as marinated trout with fennel, salmon turnover with fresh mint, breast of duck with prunes and roast peaches with pistachios. The contemporary decor is very pretty; dinner is served on the terrace in summer.

A la carte: 250F. Menus: 140F, 180F.

Grand Hôtel Muse et Rozier

(See restaurant above)

Closed Oct. 7-Easter. 3 stes 560-590F. 35 rms 270-450F. Half-board 310-450F oblig. in seas. TV. Pets allowed. Tennis.

Lively, bright rooms, each with a view of the river and the lush green gorges.

Phalsbourg

57370 Phalsbourg - (Moselle)
Paris 430 - Sarrebourg 16 - Saverne 11 - Strasbourg 57

Notre-Dame

4 km E on N 4 & VO, Bonnes-Fontaine
87.24.34.33

Closed Jan. 9-28 & Feb. 11-20. 26 rms 150-280F. Half-board 170-270F. Pets allowed. Heated pool. Garage parking. Cards: V, AE, DC, MC.

You'll spend peaceful nights in these fine rooms surrounded by tall trees. Indoor swimming pool and sauna. Restaurant.

Au Soldat de l'An II

1, rte. de Saverne - 87.24.16.16

M. Schmitt. Open until 9:30 p.m. Closed Sun. dinner, Mon. & Jan. 2-30. Terrace dining. Pets allowed. Parking. Telex 890555. Cards: V.

In just a few years, George Schmitt has become a true professional: He gave up his career as a designer to throw himself with the enthusiasm of a neophyte into the intricacies of the culinary world. He went back to designing, though, to restore this old barn on the road to Savernes, in which he created a three-level restaurant that provides a harmonious combination of comfort and rustic warmth. The heavy tables dressed with pale-blue tablecloths are elegantly yet unpretentiously set (on the other hand, the chairs are worn). As for the cuisine, it's always honest and subtle, with a personal touch. A cordial, exuberant Alsatian filled with joie de vivre, Schmitt reveals his decorative concern in the names and presentations of his dishes, and some of his creations—young rabbit "à l'Impérial" (with truffles, foie gras, sweetbreads and pasta) and a paupiette of fowl stuffed with salmon and shellfish—may sound like an impossible challenge. But never fear: Schmitt's eyes, hands and generosity will soon earn him the title of best cook in these parts of Alsace and Lorraine; that is, as soon as he emphasizes his seasonings a touch more (our salmon tartare with ginger needed some vigor) and pays more attention to his vegetable garnishes, as well as other details (such as cheeses, bread and petit-fours), which are nonexistent or mediocre. Handsome cigars. Unfortunately, prices have rocketed.

A la carte: 300F and up. Menus: 135F (weekdays only), 200F (wine incl.), 165F to 235F.

Pisciatello

see CORSICA: Ajaccio

La Plaine-sur-Mer

44770 La Plaine-sur-Mer - (Loire-Atlantique)
Paris 453 - Nantes 58 - St-Nazaire 27 - Pornic 8

Anne de Bretagne

163, blvd. de la Tara - 40.21.54.72

M. Vételé. Open until 9:30 p.m. Closed Sun. dinner & Mon. (off-seas.) & Jan. 2-Feb. 4. Terrace dining. No pets. Parking. Telex 701912. Cards: V.

Young chef Philippe Vételé, whom we discovered a year or so ago in his large purple and pink house facing the Loire estuary, knows what he's doing and intends to do it well. So does his wife, who's in charge of the handsome Loire wine cellar and who won second prize recently in Brittany's sommelier competition. The prices are still moderate; the service a bit slow, but nevertheless well performed; and the cuisine tasty, despite several small errors. It includes an excellent combination of warm oysters and crayfish flavored with ginger, sea bass (slightly overcooked), lobster and red mullet in a delicate sauce, and a delicious praline cake. Unfortunately, our strawberry tart had a jam filling; and it would be better not to serve coquilles St-Jacques in the off-season (having been vacuum-packed, they had an unpleasantly fishy taste).

A la carte: 280-300F. Menus: 95F (weekdays only), 145F, 200F, 240F.

Anne de Bretagne

(See restaurant above)

Closed Sun. & Mon. (off-seas.) & Jan. 2-Feb. 4. 26 rms 220-320F. Half-board 250-340F. TV in 10 rms. No pets. Heated pool. Tennis.

One of the rare decent hotels in this coastal region, Anne de Bretagne has several well-redecorated rooms with ocean views (the ones overlooking the garden are less attractive). Delicious breakfast. Special weekend rates.

Plaisance-du-Gers

32160 Plaisance-du-Gers - (Gers)
Paris 740 - Condom 64 - Auch 54 - Tarbes 44 - Pau 64

16 Ripa-Alta

3, pl. de l'Eglise - 62.69.30.43

M. Coscuella. Open until 9:30 p.m. Closed Nov. Pets allowed. Hotel: 1 ste 350F; 11 rms 90-300F. Garage parking. Cards: V, AE, DC.

Rotund Maurice Coscuella draws his inspiration from the past, the future, the countryside, humor and poetry—sometimes simultaneously. His cuisine is the complete opposite of Gascon's folkloric cooking, which overflows with foie gras and magret (duck breast). As a matter of fact, "Coscu" was one of the chefs who taught Parisians that magret could be eaten grilled. As always, he's at his best with his foie gras from the Jura, fabulous goose tripe and very tender terrine of beef shanks listed on the à la carte menu in this old village inn (its rustic Louis XIIIth decor is not too exciting). And next to these traditional local dishes, this veteran of Point, Bocuse and Troisgros is enthusiastically inaugurating an evolutionary cuisine; his versatile, lively, daily-changing fixed-price menus based on fresh market produce include brilliant and copious dishes: smoked duck salad with green soy, lobster and foie gras; veal grenadine and a blanquette of calves' feet; with pink berries; and exquisite desserts, like the Pompadour tart. Try one of the delicious local wines served in pitchers (a half bottle of Côtes-de-Saint-Mont is just 12 francs!).

A la carte: 250-300F. Menus: 70F (wine incl.), 130F, 260F.

Remember to call or write in advance to reserve your room or your table.

Plancoët

22130 Plancoët - (Côtes-du-Nord)
Paris 385 - Lamballe 26 - Dinard 14 - Dinan 17

14 Chez Crouzil

Les Quais - 96.84.10.24

M. Crouzil. Open until 9:15 p.m. Closed Sun. dinner & Mon. Terrace dining. Pets allowed. Hotel: 8 rms 400F. Garage parking. Cards: V, MC.

The facade of this former bus station isn't exactly promising, but once you've passed through its front door you'll discover not only an attractive, rustic decor and elegant tables set with delicate china, but also beautiful, imaginative and copious dishes prepared with fresh products and cooked to precision. Jean-Pierre Crouzil goes out of his way to find and prepare good local products and seafood. Because he is almost always the first to arrive at the markets and fish auctions, he swiftly snatches up the best, which you'll be first to taste if you opt for the daily specials, which are listed on an outstanding 200-franc menu. We tried one of these meals, consisting of a filet of John Dory sautéed with fresh chanterelles, a tender roast young pigeon, a plate of steamed fish (sea bass, salmon, brill) and an exquisite crème brûlée à l'orange. New terrace; cordial patronne.

A la carte: 280-300F. Menus: 85F (weekdays only), 170F, 230F, 400F.

Plan-de-la-Tour

83120 Ste-Maxime - (Var)
Paris 868 - St-Tropez 17 - Ste-Maxime 10

12/20 Ponte Romano

Rte. de Grimaud (1 km S on D 44)
94.43.70.56

MM. Boatto & Jeunot. Open until 10 p.m. Closed Mon. (off-seas.) & Oct. 30-March 15. Garden dining. No pets. Parking. Cards: V, AE, MC.

Above the vineyards, the olive trees and the bay of Sainte-Maxime, Ponte Romano is a little corner of paradise planted with rare species of trees. The setting is charming, the hosts are lively, and the classic cuisine is most expensive: fresh homemade foie gras, shellfish en croûte and grilled fish. The service is performed by young, attentive waitresses.

A la carte: 350-400F. Menu: 230F (dinner only).

Ponte Romano

(See restaurant above)

Closed Oct. 30-March 15. 2 stes 500-600F. 8 rms 300-500F. Air cond. Pets allowed. Pool. Tennis.

This serene cluster of Provençal buildings forms one of the most delightful and comfortable hotels in the region. The garden is superb, and there's a lovely swimming pool and exquisite shade. The reception and service are equally charming.

Pléhédel

see Paimpol

Pléneuf-Val-André

22370 Pléneuf-Val-André - (Côtes-du-Nord)
Paris 417 - St-Brieuc 30 - St-Malo 54 - Dinan 43 - Erquy 9

(15) La Cotriade

Port de Piégu (1 km) - 96.72.20.26

M. Le Saout. Open until 9 p.m. Closed Mon. dinner, Tues. & Jan.-Feb. Pets allowed. Cards: V.

It was certainly not at New York's Lutèce, where he worked for a long time, that Jean-Jacques Le Saout learned to keep his prices so moderate. And anyway, why should one pay a fortune for a meal on this stretch of the Brittany coast, when the two fixed-price menus of this truly talented cook are so magnificent? His warm oysters and his marvelous warm coquilles St-Jacques with a watercress mousse are both subtle and light; the millefeuille of sole and the turbot are cooked to perfection in a red butter of a rare subtlety; and the fowl jambonnette with shellfish—such a difficult blend of flavors—is perfectly exquisite. There are several remarkable desserts, such as the small caramelized pear tarts, and the impressive wine list (fine selection of Bordeaux) is reasonably priced. In brief, each Le Cotriade meal (which takes place in a neorustic setting with rather mediocre furniture, which we don't really notice too much, absorbed as we are by what's on our plates and the superb view of the St-Brieuc bay) is a perfect adventure.

A la carte: 300-400F. Menus: 140F, 220F.

Grand Hôtel

80, rue Amiral-Charner - 96.72.20.56

Closed Nov. 12-March 23. 39 rms 230-305F. Half-board 289-319F oblig. in seas. TV in 21 rms. Pets allowed. Garage parking. Cards: V.

Some of these impeccably maintained rooms have a view of the sea. Restaurant.

Plérin-sous-la-Tour

see Saint-Brieuc

Plogoff

29113 Audierne - (Finistère)
Paris 606 - Douarnenez 37 - Pont-l'Abbé 47 - Quimper 50

Hôtel de la Baie des Trépassés

La Baie-des-Trépassés
(3 km on D 784& VO) - 98.70.61.34

Closed Jan. 5-Feb. 5. 27 rms 130-264F. Half-board 209-276F oblig. in seas. Pets allowed. Parking. Cards: V, MC.

An outstanding, end-of-the world setting fronting the ocean, with a view of the island of Sein. The reception is minimal. Restaurant.

> *Prices in red draw attention to restaurants that offer a particularly good value.*

Plouarzel

29229 Plouarzel - (Finistère)
Paris 611 - Brest 22 - Le Conquet 12 - St-Renan 9

(14) Auberge du Kruguel

7, rue de la Mairie - 98.84.01.66

M. Quesnel. Open until 9:15 p.m. Closed Thurs. lunch, Sun. dinner, Wed., Feb. 8-March 2 & Oct. 2-18. No pets. Parking. Cards: V, MC.

After working ten years at the stoves of the Auberge du Kruguel, Gabriel Quesnel now owns the place. Always concerned with improving his skills, he studied with Maximin, Delaveyne and Rostang. His cuisine is dedicated (though without excess) to seafood; he is renowned for his fish casserole. Depending on the catch of the day, the menu may also include a warm seafood salad, fresh salmon in coarse salt and a matelote of sole with leeks. Desserts are exquisite. Now and then, though, a little novelty in Quesnel's repertoire would be welcome. The bourgeois decor is pleasant, with lovely granite walls and rug-covered waxed floors.

A la carte: 250-300F. Menus: 140F, 230F, 270F.

Plounérin

22780 Longuivy-Poulgras - (Cotes-du-Nord)
Paris 510 - Morlaix 23 - Lannion 25 - St Brieuc 60

(16) Patrick Jeffroy

96.38.61.80

M. Jeffroy. Open until 9:30 p.m. Closed Sun. dinner (off-seas.) & Mon. Pets allowed.. Hotel: 3 rms 180-240F; half-board 240-380F. Parking.

It was just a short time ago that Patrick Jeffroy left his chefdom at the three-toque L'Europe six miles down the road to realize his dream, finally, of having his own restaurant. We dropped by soon after he had set up shop in these two pretty little rooms and tasted the hot oysters in an Alsatian sabayon sauce, the impressive roasted rock lobster, the pan-fried turbot in cider and green apples, the noisettes of lamb with bacon in a vegetable paella and the marvelously simple and delicious crispy layered raspberry pastry. After enjoying that meal, we can offer complete assurances that food like this will never have to go begging for customers—quite the contrary, particularly if he continues to keep his prices so attractive and to reinvent with such gusto the Breton culinary traditions of which he himself is a product. We're holding off on awarding him his third toque, simply to avoid burdening him with it during the cares and worries of setting up. But once the paint is dry...

A la carte: 280F. Menus: 82F (weekdays only), 120F, 180F, 250F.

Le Poët-Laual

see Dieulefit

Poincy

see Meaux

Poissy

78300 Poissy - (Yvelines)
Paris 38 - St-Germain-en-Laye 6 - Pontoise 17

(13) L'Esturgeon

6, cours du 14-Juillet - 39.65.00.04, 39.79.19.94

M. Soulat. Open until 9:30 p.m. Closed Thurs. & Aug. Pets allowed. Cards: V, AE, DC.

From the early 1900s, when men in striped waistcoats and straw hats came here to parade with lovely ladies carrying umbrellas, this luxurious little roadside inn has maintained some of its impressionist atmosphere (Corot and Renoir were regulars). The setting, with a terrace overlooking the river and a view of the ruins of the old bridge built by Saint-Louis, is picturesque. Unfortunately the cooking is sliding into a kind of dull oblivion where nothing ever changes and so nothing excites: tasty duckling badly presented, fish in beurre blanc and crêpes sprinkled with the local walnut liqueur.

A la carte: 350-400F.

Poitiers

86000 Poitiers - (Vienne)
Paris 338 - Tours 104 - Angoulême 109 - Niort 74

Sights. The churches: Notre-Dame-la-Grande (a real jewel, with a Romanesque facade, a place of pilgrimage in the Middle Ages), Sainte-Radegonde (eleventh-century apse and crypt), Saint-Jean-de-Montierneuf (eleventh and nineteenth centuries, much restored), the cathedral (completed in the fifteenth century) and the Saint-Jean Baptistry (one of the oldest Christian structures in France, standing oddly in the middle of a street); the Hôtel Fumé (Gothic facade, flamboyant windows); the Courts of Law (former palace of the Counts of Poitou, immense main room, triple fireplace); Musée Sainte-Croix (antique and medieval archaeology); the House of Science and Technology; Blossac Park (atop the ancient ramparts, with a view of the Clain, designed in the eighteenth century). In the surrounding area: the Futuroscope, ten kilometers north (with Kinémax, the largest screen in Europe at 85 by 70 feet, an alphanumeric theater with 6,000 seats overlooking a lake, and a technological garden); the recreational park of Bois-de-Saint-Pierre, seven kilometers south (308 acres, with swimming pool, animal park, fishing pond and sport fields).

Eating on the Run. Le Cappucino, 5, rue de l'Université, and Casa Nostra, 1, blvd. de Pont-Achard (two good pizzerias); O César, 55, pl. du Général-de-Gaulle; Pizzéria Le Florencia, 30, rue Sylvain-Drault; Le Roy d'Ys, 51, rue de la Cathédrale; La Taverne de Maître Kanter, 24, rue Carnot (quite fashionable); Vésuvio, 5, rue du Chaudron d'Or.

Nightlife. The best discotheques: Black House, 195, ave. du 8-Mai-1945; La Grande Goule, 46, rue du Pigeon-Blanc (the most intimate); also, Le Ren Bo is in the north of the town on the Nationale 10.

France

28, rue Carnot - 49.41.32.01

Open year-round. 86 rms 130-650F. TV in 32 rms. Pets allowed. Garage parking. Telex 790526. Cards: V, AE, DC, MC.

The quietest rooms of this pleasant hotel face an inner garden. Restaurant.

(14) Maxime

4, rue St-Nicolas - 49.41.09.55

M. Rougier. Open until 10 p.m. Closed Sat. lunch & Sun.; annual closing varies. Pets allowed. Cards: V, AE.

In less time than is necessary to write these words, the charming Christian Rougier left the stoves of the Beaugency abbey for those of the Château de l'Aubrière, near Tours, and finally moved into this old restaurant in the heart of Poitiers. Perhaps he will stay here for a while, since he owns the place. He proceeded at once to redecorate the facade of his restaurant in a chic Parisian style—with awnings and black lacquer—and is actively freshening up its attractive, imposing, 1930s-style interior decor of wood panels and frescoes. As for the cuisine, it's characterized more and more by enthusiasm tempered with experience as this excellent chef continues to progress. He deserves an additional point for his rich and delicious salad of foie gras and breast of duck, exquisite roast langoustines, superb little seafood stew with paprika, and saddle of rabbit served in a perfect Chardonnay sauce. Friendly and cheerful reception by the patronne, Jacqueline. Reasonable prices.

A la carte: 230-250F. Menus: 140F (weekdays only, wine incl.), 95F, 168F, 200F.

IN NEARBY **Buxerolles**
(4 km N on D 4)
86180 Buxerolles - (Vienne)

(13) Auberge de la Cigogne

20, rue Planty - 49.45.61.47

M. Kress. Open until 9:30 p.m. Closed Sun., Mon., 2 weeks at Easter & July 25-Aug. 14. Garden dining. No pets. Parking. Cards: V, AE, MC.

Charles Kress, who moved to these suburbs located 500 yards from the highway seven years ago, hasn't forgetten his Alsatian origin or his training. Consistent and experienced, he is also a good sauce maker. His eclectic repertoire includes many choucroutes, of course, and game in season (cooked Alsatian style), as well as a good, richly prepared bouillabaisse; chevreau (kid) à la Poitevine (with green garlic) served in the spring; smooth foie gras (prepared almost Alsatian-style) flavored with Armagnac; and his most famous dish, sander in Noilly wine (it was slightly overcooked). Catherine Kress is a cordial, very friendly patronne, and her establishment is impeccably maintained. There is a pleasant dining room terrace and a garden where meals are served in summer.

A la carte: 180-230F. Menus: 100F, 150F.

IN NEARBY **Croutelle**
(6 km S on N 10)
86240 Ligugé - (Vienne)

(14) Pierre Benoist

N 10 & A 10, exit Poitiers South
49.57.11.52

N. Benoist. Open until 9:30 p.m. Closed Sun. dinner, Mon. & July 24-Aug. 7. Garden dining. Pets allowed. Parking. Cards: V.

It's in this old, luxuriously arranged farmhouse amid serene green surroundings (located between the route Nationale and Highway 10 on the way to Angoulême) that Pierre Benoist delights the sophisticates of Poitiers and Poitou. A summer terrace faces the valley; the atmosphere of the two large dining rooms, with their lovely furniture and antique tiles, is more elegant than rustic, and beautiful china and silverware adorn the large round tables. The cuisine served is that of a well-experienced, confident cook. Having started at the Grand Véfour and Taillevent, Benoist believes in the excellence of tradition, which he lightens and personalizes: calves' liver served in a subtle sauce of acacia honey and lime, feuilleté of sweetbreads with morels (one of the most popular dishes of the restaurant), veal kidney grilled in its juice, excellent calf's head prepared in the traditional, old-fashioned style and a tasty strawberry charlotte. Handsome wine cellar (Loire and Bordeaux), and excellent small fixed-price menu.

A la carte: 300F and up. Menu: 150F (weekday lunch only).

Pons

17800 Pons - (Charente-Maritime)
Paris 495 - Bordeaux 96 - Cognac 23 - Saintes 22

(13) Auberge Pontoise

23, ave. Gambetta - 46.94.00.99

M. Chat. Open until 9 p.m. Closed Sun. dinner, Mon. (except for lunch in July-Aug.) & Jan. 2-Feb. 12. Air cond. Pets allowed. Garage parking. Cards: V, MC.

The Auberge Pontoise is *the* place to go in this area. Its provincial decor is a bit quaint but filled pleasantly with flowers (thanks to Mme. Chat's green thumb). Though often grumpy, the owner is nevertheless a fine cook; his cuisine (always the same) is prepared with lovely seasonal and local produce. We give it a well-deserved toque for the small oyster feuilletés in red butter, the traditional lamprey in Bordeaux served with leek whites and the escalope of duck liver sautéed with chanterelles. Alas, the prices have not improved.

A la carte: 350-400F. Menus: 95F (weekdays only), 155F, 240F.

Auberge Pontoise

(See restaurant above)

Closed Mon. (except July-Aug.), Sun. & Dec. 23-Jan. 31. 1 ste 480F. 21 rms 180-310F. Half-board 360F oblig. in seas. TV in 10 rms. No pets.

The fairly large rooms of the Auberge Pontoise were recently modernized; some of them, overlooking the courtyard, are quiet, but the ones on the street are noisy. UVA tanning center. Pleasant reception.

IN NEARBY **Mosnac**
(11 km S on N 137 & D 134)
17240 St-Genis-de-Saintonge - (Charente-Maritime)

(16) Le Moulin de Marcouze

46.70.46.16

M. Bouchet. Open until 10 p.m. Closed Wed. & Feb. 15-March 15. Air cond. Pets allowed. Parking. Cards: V, AE, DC, MC.

In the heart of Fins-Bois, just outside a small village with a beautiful Romanesque church, you'll discover these proud buildings located between a road and a river. One section is original, and the other has been tastefully re-created; upon entering it, you'll see the kitchen behind its windows. As for the flower-filled, wooden-beamed dining room, it has a hospitable and refined atmosphere and windows that open widely onto splendid, lush riverbank scenery. The cuisine is prepared in the same spirit: classic, discreet, light and fresh (even with the rustic dishes: jugged hare in four spices, leg of lamb à la cuillère and simmered young rabbit). The small tureen of creamed lobster we had was frankly aristocratic, and the quenelles of sea pike were light and exquisitely savory. The owner of this lovely place, Dominique Bouchet, a native of the region (where his parents are farmers), is the man who in just a few years gave a new spirit to La Tour d'Argent in Paris. The region, so lacking in good restaurants, has hit the jackpot with this one. The wines are well selected, and delicious little farm Cognacs are offered at reasonable prices.

A la carte: 280F. Menus: 110F (weekdays only), 160F, 210F.

Pontarlier

25300 Pontarlier - (Doubs)
Paris 452 - Belfort 125 - Besançon 58 - Geneva 120

(14) La Poste

55, ave. de la République - 81.46.47.91

M. Bertin. Open until 10 p.m. Closed Sun. dinner, Mon., March 1-15 & Nov. 15-30. Pets allowed. Garage parking. Cards: V.

The Bertins, who also manage a good restaurant in Besançon (La Péniche) took over this hotel restaurant not long ago, embellishing its original decor, which was that of a prosperous turn-of-the-century inn. Today its patterned carpet, embroidered tablecloths, velvet chairs, marble, bizarre period candelabra, wood panels and mirrors compose a slightly kitsch, but quite attractive, setting. The cuisine, prepared by one of the Bertins' sons, is much more sober—and conscientious—and some of the richer dishes are superb: exquisite salad of Jésus de Morteau with smoked salmon and potatoes, fresh foie gras sautéed in Sauternes, aiguillettes of young duck with morels. Excellent service.

A la carte: 400-500F. Menus: 120F (weekdays only), 220F (weekends and holidays only), 160F, 320F.

Pontaubert

see Avallon

Pont-Audemer

27500 Pont-Audemer - (Eure)
Paris 168 - Rouen 52 - Honfleur 24 - Lisieux 36

12/20 Belle Isle-sur-Risle

112, rte. de Rouen (1.5 km on N 185)
32.56.96.22

Mme. Yazbeck. Open until 10 p.m. Closed Sun. dinner, Mon. lunch & Jan. 3-Feb. 28. Garden dining. No pets. Parking. Cards: V, AE, DC.

Recently opened in the midst of a large park on a small island in the Risle river, Belle Isle-sur-Risle is an attractive, comfortable, tastefully furnished house filled with flowers. The patronne prepares a cuisine that, like her, is lively and generous: brouillade (stew) of hen, salmon and quail eggs, medallion of veal with sweet pepper, and a light apple feuilleté. The wine cellar still needs developing, and the fixed-price menus are a bit complicated.

A la carte: 280-300F. Menus: 139F (weekday lunch only), 189F (weekdays only), 210F and 280F (weekends and holidays only).

Belle Isle-sur-Risle

(See restaurant above)

Closed Jan. 3-Feb. 28. 1 ste 890F. 12 rms 390-760F. Half-board 460-660F. TV. No pets. Heated pool. Tennis.

Everything here is brand-new, clean and lovely. The spacious rooms are remarkably well equipped with elegant period furniture and attractive bathrooms. Serene and charming surroundings.

(13) Le Vieux Puits

6, rue Notre-Dame-du-Pré - 32.41.01.48

M. Foltz. Open until 9 p.m. Closed Mon. dinner, Tues., June 26-July 6 & Dec. 18-Jan. 18. Hotel: 12 rms 130-330F; half-board oblig. in seas. Parking. Cards: V, MC.

The old Norman style of Le Vieux Puits is certainly charming... provided you are not put off by the modern district in which this splendid cluster of sixteenth-century buildings is hidden. The restaurant, a former tannery, is exquisitely arranged with wooden beams, pewter ornaments, old earthenware, copper objects and weathered furniture; an inner courtyard is planted with very old willows. In brief, everything is absolutely enchanting. The reception by the patronne is delightful, and the service is attentive. If the pleasant, well-executed cuisine was a touch more imaginative, Le Vieux Puits could become one of the best little spots in Normandy. There is a fair salad maraîchère with seafood, which tastes a bit bland; a so-so trout Bovary (in a Champagne sauce); and an exquisite apple tart in cream.

A la carte: 280-300F. Menus: 150F (weekday lunch only), 240F.

IN NEARBY **Campigny**
(6 km S on D 810 & D 29)
27500 Pont-Audemer - (Eure)

(13) Le Petit Coq aux Champs

La Pommeray south - 32.41.04.19

MM. Pommier. Open daily until 9:30 p.m. Garden dining. Pets allowed. Parking. Telex 172524. Cards: V, AE, DC, MC.

Standing amid the fields, the Pommiers' cottage looks like a folkloric illustration of a languid, pastoral Normandy: authentic thatched roof, small window panes, a chimney smoking in the cloudy sky and a luxuriant garden. It's difficult not to fall madly in love with so much beauty, particularly since the Pommier family is also so charming; what makes it easier is the alarming trend, noted of late, of son Patrick's cooking—it is growing sloppy and unattractive. The warm goat cheese salad was uninspiring, the veal filet tough and overdone, and the warm apple crêpes lacked distinction. He who would sport even one toque must pay more attention than this.

A la carte: 350-400F. Menus: 200F (lunch only, wine incl.), 200F (weekdays only), 240F to 350F.

Le Petit Coq aux Champs

(See restaurant above)

Open year-round. 1 ste 1,200-1,410F. 11 rms 450-950F. Half-board 550-735F oblig. in seas. Pets allowed. Heated pool.

The newly redecorated rooms of Le Petit Coq aux Champs are attractive, bright and lively (though some of them are tiny). Breakfast is magnificent. Impeccable service.

Pont-Aven

29123 Pont-Aven - (Finistère)
Paris 522 - Lorient 36 - Concarneau 15 - Quimper 38

(16) La Taupinière

Rte. de Concarneau - 98.06.03.12

MM. Guilloux. Open until 9:15 p.m. Closed Mon. dinner (except July-Aug.), Tues. & Sept. 20-Oct. 20. Air cond. No pets. Parking. Cards: V, MC.

This large house looks exactly like the molehill described by its unimaginative sign: "A roadside inn just outside Pont-Aven, with parking lot and lawn." But how deceiving appearances are, for once inside, the decor is inviting, comfortable and bright; the tables are elegantly set; the view of the flower garden is lovely; and good local fish and ham are grilled and cooked in the large, blazing fireplace. Pierrette Guilloux, the patronne, isn't awaiting guests with a carbine, but with a large smile, and she'll offer you splendid wines (her cellar is one of the greatest in Brittany) and dazzlingly fresh seafood. Guy Guilloux, her husband and a friend of Jean Delaveyne, prepares it with a passion and a sense of the unexpected, typical of self-taught people, even when they have become, as is the case here, true and knowledgeable professionals. So, sample the decorticated shellfish in a leek fondue, crab (or spider crab) millefeuille, lotte in cider butter à la fermière, fricassée of cod jowls with baby vegetables, and light pastries.

A la carte: 300-350F. Menus: 220F, 280F, 360F.

Pontchartrain

78760 Jouars-Pontchartrain - (Yvelines)
Paris 40 - Dreux 44 - Rambouillet 21 - Versailles 17

(14) L'Aubergade

N 12 - 34.89.02.63

M. Ogier. Open until 9:30 p.m. Closed Tues. dinner (off-seas.), Wed. & Aug. Garden dining. Pets allowed. Cards: V.

Very few clients use the small heliport that Jean Bordier places at their disposal, which is a good thing for the serenity of the large garden marked by its dreamy luxuriant flower beds. Take a little walk on these delightful paths before joining the other guests seated in front of plates of foie gras in a sherry aspic, filet of sole miroton, salmon in Champagne and roast rack of lamb with gratin dauphinois. Nothing is really fancy in this cuisine, but its execution is exemplary, and the sauces are always light. The country-inn decor, with its large tables and red tablecloths, is truly superb.

A la carte: 300-350F.

Pont-de-l'Isère

see Valence

Pont-de-Vaux

01190 Pont-de-Vaux - (Ain)
Paris 379 - Bourg-en-Bresse 39 - Tournus 18 - Mâcon 19

(13) Le Commerce

5, pl. Joubert - 85.30.30.56

MM. Patrone. Open until 9 p.m. Closed May 30-June 15 & Nov. 19-Dec. 16. Pets allowed. Hotel: 11 rms 200-300F. Garage parking. Cards: V, AE, DC.

Peekaboo! Mme. Patrone is smiling again in her attractive, delightfully neat pink decor. Under the fierce eyes of Général Joubert's statue erected in front of their house, for more than twenty years she and her husband have been serving a cuisine brimming with the creamy generosity of Bresse: sautéed frogs, gâteau of poultry livers, escargots (in cream!), crayfish (in cream!) and Bresse fowl (in cream!). Everything is attentively prepared, well presented and not really light—of course—but controlled. Fine wine cellar.

A la carte: 280F. Menus: 110F to 260F.

Pont-du-Dognon

87340 La Jonchère - (Haute-Vienne)
Paris 379 - Bellac 52 - Limoges 26 - Bourganeuf 27

Le Rallye

St-Laurent-les-Eglises - 55.56.56.11

Closed Mon. (off-seas.) & Nov. 6-Palm Sun. 21 rms 110-240F. Half-board 170-260F. Parking. Cards: V, MC.

You'll enjoy a beautiful view of the Taurion and the lake from this small hotel, which, though rather plain, is nevertheless well equipped for aquatic activities. Pleasant walks in the area. Restaurant.

Ponte San Ludovico

see Menton

Le Pontet

see Avignon

Pontoise

see PARIS SUBURBS

Pornic

44210 Pornic - (Loire-Atlantique)
Paris 428 - Nantes 51 - St-Nazaire 29

(13) Gilles de Retz

70, quai Le Ray (Hôtel Beau Soleil)
40.82.34.58

M. Vételé. Open until 9:30 p.m. Closed Fri. (off-seas.) & Nov. 15-Feb. 28. Terrace dining. Pets allowed. Hotel: 15 rms 185-280F; half-board 250F oblig. in seas. Cards: V.

This large, handsome, modern building facing the old Pornic port is a most attractive spot. The Vételés are cordial, even hospitable, and their delicate, classic cuisine is enhanced by a charming presentation (especially the desserts, made by this former pastry maker). Try the langoustines with coriander, the panaché of coquilles St-Jacques and crayfish in two sauces and the delicious fondant with warm, creamy, authentic black chocolate and a subtle mint sabayon. The wine cellar houses handsome Burgundies.

A la carte: 230-250F. Menus: 135F, 170F, 255F.

Porquerolles (Ile de)

83400 Hyères - (Var)
Embarkation: Cavalaire, Hyères, Toulon

(15) Mas du Langoustier

94.58.30.09

Mme. Le Ber. Open until 9:30 p.m. Closed Nov. 15-March 15. Terrace dining. Pets allowed. Cards: V, AE, DC.

When Jean-Louis Vosgien left Mas de Chastelas in Saint-Tropez for Mas du Langoustier, a secret rendezvous hidden amid pine trees, the lodgers' customary fare underwent a complete change. And though they are still amazed at the delicious and imaginative food served on the partly shaded, partly sunny terrace facing the sea, they are not the only ones allowed to feast on the sardines with ginger, crayfish in orange butter, shellfish-stuffed ravioli with tarragon, red mullet sautéed in lemon juice, braised sea perch in urchin sauce, fowl fricassée in white wine and pistou, rack of lamb with cumin, and exquisite desserts. Mas du Langoustier is a sanctuary, but not a forbidden fortress; so, with a simple telephone reservation, they'll come get you at the port (if you're on a boat, a small craft will pick you up), and shortly afterward you'll be dining among the happy chosen ones. By the time you read this, extensive work will be under way: 22 new rooms will be built, and the dining room will be restored. After that, the Mas will be open for eight months during the year instead of the current four and a half. It will also accommodate group cooking courses, and M. Richard is even planning a helicopter shuttle service for his golfing clients to access the greens on the Côte d'Azur. Will the Mas du Langoustier turn into a luxury hotel like any other? Apparently not: "Nothing will be changed that might alter the spirit of the Mas!" protests Richard, who is shocked at the idea that one could suspect him of planning to commit such a sacrilege. In any case, he doesn't even want to raise his hotel rates: 760 francs a day for a room with television, private bathroom and three meals. And that's that!

A la carte: 350-400F. Menu: 200F.

Mas du Langoustier

(See restaurant above)

Closed Nov. 15-March 15. 5 stes 1,162F (full board). 60 rms 560-962F (full board). Pets allowed. TV. Tennis.

The Mas du Langoustier has an exceptional location at one end of the island. Its rooms are frequently renovated; 22 new ones are currently being built.

Les Portes-en-Ré

see Ré (Ile de)

Le Port-Marly

see PARIS SUBURBS

Poudenas

47170 Mézin - (Lot-et-Garonne)
Paris 659 - Mézin 5 - Sos 6 - Nérac 17 - Barbotan 23

A la Belle Gasconne

53.65.71.58

M. Gracia. Open until 9:30 p.m. Closed Sun. dinner (off-seas.), Mon., Dec. 1-15 & Jan. 1-15. Garden dining. Pets allowed. Parking. Cards: V, AE, DC.

Along the tumultuous banks of the Gélise, within a splendid sixteenth-century mill restored with perfect taste, Marie-Claude and Richard Gracia await, longing to have you share their enthusiasm for the rustic cuisine whose secrets and techniques they are reviving. Marie-Claude cooks with a big heart and an impulsive passion that neither years nor worries have shaken. Everything is lively, highly tasty, nobly rustic and most exciting: quail salad in melon vinegar, jugged duck cooked in its natural juices and Buzet wine, veal kidney in walnut wine with morels, tourte of sweetbreads, breast of duck in a pepper sauce and marvelous chocolate cake. As for Richard, the recently elected mayor of Mézin, he spends his time embellishing this surprising decor of ancient stones and authentic wooden beams (a marvelous setting for his wife's cuisine) and enriching his considerable collection of local and great wines from the southwest of France. In summer, you'll enjoy charming meals on the terrace. And the prices remain moderate. Exquisite foie gras can be purchased to take out (directly on the premises or by mail order).

A la carte: 250F. Menus: 100, 155F, 180F, 220F.

Pra-Loup

see Barcelonnette

Prémesques

see Lille

Le Pré-Saint-Gervais

see PARIS SUBURBS

Présilly

see Saint-Julien-en-Genevois

Prunoy

89120 Charny - (Yonne)
Paris 135 - Joigny 28 - Montargis 34

Château de Prunoy

86.63.66.91

Closed Jan.-Easter. 1 ste 600F. 11 rms 350-420F. Tennis. Parking. Cards: V, AE.

This lovely eighteenth-century castle, located in the heart of the Puisaye area, which was so dear to Colette, is surrounded by a 247-acre park dotted with ponds and woods. The owner, an antiques dealer, has stylishly furnished his château, whose twelve delightful rooms re-create the charm of an ancient family house. A small, rustic dining room can also be found within the château's walls.

Puligny-Montrachet

21190 Meursault - (Côte-d'Or)
Paris 327 - Autun 43 - Beaune 12 - Chagny 5

Le Montrachet

Pl. des Marronniers - 80.21.30.06

M. Gazagnes. Open until 9:30 p.m. Closed Dec. 1-Jan. 10. Terrace dining. Pets allowed. Parking. Cards: V, AE, DC, MC.

Located on a village square shaded by linden trees, Le Montrachet is a handsome house built in the local style. Its service is a bit informal, but this year the chef is paying more attention to his kitchen and has won back his toque with a superb turbot filet in a beautiful white Burgundy sauce and the best apple tart we've had in a long while. Exceptional wine list by the connoisseur owner.

A la carte: 300-350F. Menus: 130F, 195F, 310F.

Le Montrachet

(See restaurant above)

Closed Dec. 1-Jan. 10. 22 rms 310-390F. Pets allowed.

Bright, comfortable rooms, some of which are outfitted with lovely, rustic furniture. Wine-tasting tours are organized by the house sommelier.

Purpan

see Toulouse

Puteaux

see PARIS SUBURBS

Puyfond

see Aix-en-Provence

Puymirol

see Agen

Quarré-les-Tombes

89630 Quarré-les-Tombes - (Yonne)
Paris 246 - Saulieu 27 - Avallon 19 - Dijon 101

(13) Auberge de l'Atre

At Lavaults - 86.32.20.79

M. Salamolard. Open until 9 p.m. Closed Tues. dinner (off-seas.) & Wed., Jan. 10-Feb. 24. Terrace dining. Pets allowed. Parking. Cards: V, AE, DC, MC.

A couple of years ago, Francis Salamolard, an experienced chef, came to this granite house on a small country road. Having spent seven years in Relais et Châteaux kitchens, he knows his job remarkably well. The food he serves in his neat, hospitable inn filled with flowers seems to have been prepared effortlessly: roast langoustines in a sorrel and walnut butter, aiguillette of duck with cherries, feuilleté of sweetbreads with mousserons and chanterelles and delicious small tarts filled with local strawberries. Salamolard (a passionate man who loves to chat about his profession) and his charming wife actively contribute to the friendly atmosphere that prevails here. The wine cellar is stocked with handsome Bordeaux.

A la carte: 300F. Menus: 90F (weekdays only), 153F, 238F.

Questembert

56230 Questembert - (Morbihan)
Paris 423 - Redon 33 - Vannes 26 - Rennes 88

(18) Georges Paineau

13, rue St-Michel
97.26.11.12

M. Paineau. Open until 9:30 p.m. Closed Sun. dinner, Mon. (except July-Aug.) & Jan. 3-March 1. Terrace dining. Pets allowed. Garage parking. Cards: V, AE, DC.

From his distant voyages, Georges Paineau brought back a taste for Far Eastern meditation, as well as a collection of objects in bronze and gold that ring as true in his old Breton house as a concert of Breton bagpipes in a Zen temple. It is true that this collection, which, actually, is slowly being removed (and some of the paintings by Master Paineau should go the same route), is fortunately concentrated in the charming greenhouse that opens onto the garden (also Zen). And it is no less true that the Oriental influence has managed to find other means of expression, namely in the cuisine that comes straight from the heart of this charming, quietly exuberant chef. For example, the Chinese dumplings with a bit of coriander maintain a miraculous equilibrium of flavors. The barbotine de canard aux parfums thaïs is an extravagantly light duck bouillon that whispers the subtle perfume of ginger. It is becoming abundantly clear that Paineau will always be a better chef than painter, as evidenced by his small wrapped oysters steamed in tarragon, his truffled flan with turnip mousse and lamb juices, his creamy lobster ragoût, his lamb with eggplant and basil and his desserts, which are a marvel of invention and lightness and rank among the best in France. But let's not leave this old postal way station without mentioning how Michèle Paineau shows herself to be a well-informed lady of the house, capable of guiding the most timid clients through the labyrinth of pleasures that lay in store for them. Together they draw us into the inventive maelstrom of Paineau's beautiful cuisine. The restaurant's suave, alluring provincial dining room is marked by its oak woodwork, soft lighting and collection of antique glass and porcelain. And, amazingly, prices have not been on the rise of late.

A la carte: 300-500F. Menus: 150F, 185F, 295F, 395F.

Bretagne

(See restaurant above)

Closed Sun. & Mon. (except July-Aug.) & Feb. 1-March 15. 6 rms 290-560F. Half-board 680F. TV. Pets allowed.

All the rooms were redone recently with particularly comfortable bedding, pretty English furniture, thick carpeting and perfect soundproofing. Every detail has been seen to, the marvelous breakfast is served on a rolling table, and the service fulfills your every dream. Relais et Châteaux.

Quiberon

56170 Quiberon - (Morbihan)
Paris 498 - Lorient 52 - Vannes 46 - Auray 28

(14) Le Thalassa

Pointe de Goulvars - 97.50.20.00

M. Radtke. Open until 9:30 p.m. Closed Jan. No pets. Parking. Telex 730712. Cards: V, AE, DC, MC.

The low-calorie menu served in this large, cold dining room (which, fortunately, should have been renovated by the time you read this) facing the sea is intended for the distinguished paunches, bellies and fleshy hips of those undergoing the rough thalassotherapy treatments in the nearby institute. But chef Angelo Oriliéri has other things to propose than these dietetic treats. His light sauces and precise cooking enhance the exquisite quality of the seafood served here: jugged lobster, fresh salmon in coarse salt and brill steamed with basil. The feuilleté desserts and ice creams are irresistible; the service, a bit less so; the china, quite plain.

A la carte: 300F and up. Menus: 185F, 245F.

Sofitel Thalassa

(See restaurant above)

Closed Jan. 133 rms 690-1,248F. Half-board 760-1,050F. Heated pool. Pets allowed. Tennis. TV.

Located at the very end of Quiberon, the Sofitel Thalassa is isolated from the noise by a private road (for pedestrians only) and is connected to the thalassotherapy institute by an inner corridor. It features luxurious facilities, superb, renovated rooms (some with terraces or private patios) and outstanding facilities for conferences and groups.

Quimperlé

29130 Quimperlé - (Finistère)
Paris 513 - Concarneau 32 - Lorient 20 - Quimper 48

(13) Le Bistro de la Tour

2, rue Dom-Morice - 98.39.29.58

M. Cariou. Open until 9:30 p.m. (10 p.m. weekends). Closed Sat. lunch, Sun. dinner & Mon. No pets. Cards: V.

The owner/oenologist has turned his upstairs floor into a cozy, discreet Louis XIIIth–style dining room and hired a good assistant from Loiseau. Exquisite fish and duck dishes are served on the ground floor, which is done in an amusing decor. The tasty 125-franc fixed-price menu includes local salmon and langoustines. Fine wine cellar.

A la carte: 230-250F. Menus: 49F (weekday lunch only), 79F, 129F, 198F.

Rabastens-de-Bigorre

65140 Rabastens-de-Bigorre - (Hautes-Pyrénées)
Paris 798 - Auch 53 - Tarbes 19 - Aire-sur-l'Adour 60

12/20 Chez Yvonne

6, rue de l'Agriculture - 62.96.60.20

Mme. Dupui. Open until 9 p.m. Closed Fri. & Sun. dinner, May 1-8 & Oct. 15-Nov. 5. Terrace dining. Pets allowed. Hotel: 8 rms 55-105F. Parking. Cards: V.

Yvonne has redecorated her dining room (we haven't seen it yet), but she has kept the huge fireplace, as well as her famished local clientele. As for the chef, he prepares a simple, consistent and copious rustic cuisine: lamb's sweetbreads with cèpes, grilled duck breast with chanterelles, crayfish and so on.

A la carte: 160-180F. Menus: 50F, 60F, 65F, 70F.

Le Raincy

see PARIS SUBURBS

Raizeux

78120 Rambouillet - (Yvelines)
Paris 69 - Rambouillet 15 - Maintenon 15 - Epernon 2

(13) La Maison des Champs

At Chaises - 34.83.50.19

M. Lacourrège. Open until 9 p.m. Closed Mon. & Tues. dinner, Wed., Feb. & Aug. Pets allowed. Parking. Cards: V, AE.

The charming Mme. Lacourrège is no longer here to welcome us to her Maison des Champs, which is nestled in a small, delightful park at the edge of the Rambouillet forest. But her son-in-law, who has been at the stoves for several years, remains at his post, preparing an à la carte menu whose escargots with herbs, andouillette with cabbage, onglet with shallots, goose confit and chocolate charlotte always result in a simple, savory meal.

A la carte: 200-250F.

Ramatuelle

83350 Ramatuelle - (Var)
Paris 892 - Hyères 54 - St-Tropez 10 - Draguignan 53

Les Bergerettes

Rte. des Plages - 94.97.40.22

Closed Oct. 15-Easter. 29 rms 800-900F. Pool. Parking. Telex 460037. Cards: V.

This quiet new hotel located in a 27-acre pine forest has a view of the Pampelonne bay and the owner's vineyard. It is neat, clean and filled with flowers. Grill.

(15) La Terrasse du Baou

Ave. Georges-Clemenceau - 94.79.20.48

M. Sarraquigne. Open until 11 p.m. Closed Jan. 4-March 18 & Nov. 5-Dec. 20. Terrace dining. Pets allowed. Garage parking. Telex 462152. Cards: V, AE, DC, MC.

Thanks to a first-rate Japanese chef, the cuisine of this restaurant perched atop the Ramatuelle hill has definitely improved. Let's hope he'll still be there when you head for this lovely terrace to enjoy the splendid view and feast on the warm red-mullet salad, sea perch steamed with fennel, crayfish ravioli in a shellfish juice, filet of sole garnished with fresh fettuccine, gilthead royale fished locally, young duck in sweet garlic, gratin of prunes in Armagnac butter, and the plate of assorted chocolates. This subtle, clever cuisine blends all the wonderful flavors of Provence. The wine list offers a delicious "summer red," a Château Barbeyrolles, to drink cool, and one of the best rosés from Provence, the "Pétales de Roses."

A la carte: 350-450F. Menus: 250F, 360F.

Le Baou

(See restaurant above)

Closed Jan. 4-March 18 & Nov. 5-Dec. 20. 8 stes 920-1,150F. 28 rms 590-880F. Heated pool. Pets allowed. TV in 28 rms.

You'll face extraordinary scenery from the balconies of Le Baou's large, quite comfortable rooms. The hotel's facilities—including a Jacuzzi, solarium and bar and grill by the swimming pool—are outstanding.

Le Rayol - Canadel-sur-Mer

83820 Le Rayol - Canadel-sur-Mer - (Var)
Paris 893 - St-Tropez 25 - Le Lavandou 14 - Cavalaire 7

Bailli de Suffren

94.05.67.67

Closed Jan. 5-March 23. 4 stes 900-1,500F. 42 rms 600-1,000F. Half-board 150-250F (plus rm) oblig. in seas. Pets allowed. TV. Telex 420535. Cards: V, AE, DC, MC.

Facing the splendid scenery of the Levant Islands, the Bailli features stylish rooms (completely modernized), a lovely floral decor and comfortable terraces with ocean views. Restaurant.

Karlina Club Hôtel

Chemin du Plageron - 94.05.61.65

Closed Oct. 20-April 15. 1 ste 700F. 10 rms 350-750F. Half-board 420-650F. Pool. Parking. Cards: V, DC.

Nestled amid the palm and cork trees, this hotel overlooks the sea. Extras include a swimming pool, plenty of sports equipment and a restaurant.

Ré (Ile de)

(Charente-Maritime)
La Palice, 15-minute crossing - 46.85.61.48

IN **La Flotte-en-Ré**
17630 La Flotte-en-Ré - (Charente-Maritime)

15 Le Richelieu

44, ave. de la Plage - 46.09.60.70

M. Gendre. Open until 9:30 p.m. Closed Jan. 5-March 15. Air cond. Pets allowed. Parking. Telex 791492. Cards: V.

Now that the excellent M. Gendre has spent more than two million francs to get himself a futuristic, push-button chrome kitchen, it's obviously not the right time to dream of moderate prices at Le Richelieu. This superb vacation hotel is becoming an increasingly refined establishment with a well-trained staff and impeccable management. Its wonderful dining area, extended by a covered terrace facing the sea, ensures complete privacy from the summer crowds. Its wines (mostly Bordeaux) are marvelous, and its cuisine, while not particularly dazzling, is always quite tasty. Dominique Bourgeois, a chef who trained at Lucas-Carton and Taillevent, can cook just about anything: langoustines with ginger (the servings are a bit meager), filet of sole in an exquisite oyster sauce, grilled or roast lobster (which comes from an 800-gallon fish pond) and classic, perfect glazed nougat in strawberry sauce.

A la carte: 450-600F. Menus: 190F, 250F, 350F.

Le Richelieu

(See restaurant above)

Closed Jan. 5-March 15. 14 rms 250-950F. Half-board 450-1,000F oblig. in seas. Heated pool. Tennis.

Le Richelieu has a heated pool, tennis courts, a billiard room, elegant, brand-new banquet rooms and a splendid terrace facing the sea. Its extremely comfortable rooms are located in delightful pavilions scattered in a green park.

IN **Les Portes-en-Ré**
17880 Les Portes-en-Ré - (Charente-Maritime)

14 Le Chasse-Marée

1, rue Jules-David - 46.29.52.03

M. Frigière. Open until midnight. Closed Nov. 15-March 15. Terrace dining. Pets allowed. Cards: V, AE, DC.

You won't find many tourists here, at the ultimate refuge for Ile de Ré lovers fleeing the summer crowds. The restaurant is perfectly suited to Bernadette Frigière, the delightful patronne (we can't help but wonder why no film director has yet put her before a camera). With her husband, Pascal (an electrician), she has turned this old, traditional house into one of the most charming restaurants on the Atlantic coast. Intimate and warm, it's decorated with antique ornaments; the terrace set with four tables is the perfect place to enjoy a warm summer evening. Start with an exquisite strawberry wine, then make your selection from a cuisine that is creative, cooked to precision and well balanced: "sorbets" of vegetables, escalope of salmon with ginger and fish pot-au-feu with saffron. To crown your meal, try any of the superb desserts, especially the chocolate cake and the fresh-fruit mousse. A small but judicious selection of cigars is also offered.

A la carte: 250-300F. Menu: 120F.

IN **Rivedoux-Plage**
17940 Rivedoux-Plage - (Charente-Maritime)

13 Auberge de la Marée

55, rue Albert-Sarrault - 46.09.80.02

M. Bernard. Open until 9 p.m. Closed Mon. & Tues. lunch & Nov. 4-March 25. Pets allowed. Cards: V.

Daniel Bernard is a solid cook who has been awarded many diplomas. An excellent oyster grower as well, he has gradually transformed his restaurant, which faces the charming port of Rivedoux, into a large, hospitable, comfortable, almost luxurious inn with a patio, garden, swimming pool and solarium. His cuisine is ambitious—and his sauces are slightly on the rich side—but on the whole, everything is carefully prepared and well worth one toque. Sample the turbot with a sole mousseline, the langoustine consommé with ravioli and the aumonière of glazed nougat in orange sauce. The wine cellar is well stocked.

A la carte: 280F. Menus: 80F, 180F, 280F.

Auberge de la Marée

(See restaurant above)

Closed Nov.-March 25. 28 rms 280-400F. Half-board oblig. in seas. Pets allowed. Pool.

The Auberge de la Marée's rooms are attractive; some have a view of the Rivedoux-Plage port, while others overlook a delightful pool surrounded by flowers. The service is excellent.

IN **Saint-Clément-des-Baleines**
17590 Ars-en-Ré - (Charente-Maritime)

13 Le Chat Botté

2, rue de la Mairie - 46.29.42.09

MM. Massé. Open until 9 p.m. Closed Wed. (except in seas. & school holidays), Oct. 20-28 & Jan. 5-Feb. 5. Terrace dining. Pets allowed. Parking. Cards: V, MC.

Its loyal habitués seem to have staked out a permanent claim to the fresh, unpretentious summer-holiday decor of Le Chat Botté; for many years now, it has been one of the most famous places in town for those who want to sample (without going bankrupt) the magnificent fresh shellfish and several specialties of delicate fish that are served year-round. Daniel Massé prepares the turbot in half a dozen ways (braised, in buttered paper, grilled, in a feuilleté...), and the sea bass en croûte, the most popular dish in the restaurant, is matched with a delicious beurre blanc. The service is most courteous, and the wine cellar holds some small, pleasantly light vintages.

A la carte: 220F. Menus: 68F (weekdays only), 130F, 170F.

Le Chat Botté

(See restaurant above)

Closed Oct. 10-25. 23 rms 85-220F. Pets allowed.

Le Chat Botté's rooms are spotless, albeit somewhat nondescript. There is a flower garden, and the sea is less than half a mile away.

IN Sainte-Marie-de-Ré

17740 Sainte-Marie-de-Ré - (Charente-Maritime)

L'Atalante

46.30.22.44

Open year-round. 65 rms 290-560F. Half-board 385-520F oblig. in seas. Heated pool. Tennis. Parking. Cards: V, AE, DC, MC.

You can almost feel the water lapping at your feet. The rooms of this well-equipped hotel, pleasantly insulated from the tourist crowds, are bright and comfortable. Restaurant.

(13) Auberge de la Chauvetière

1, rue de la Beurelière - 46.30.21.56

M. Ducruet. Open until 9 p.m. Closed Wed. & Feb. 15-March 1. Pets allowed. Cards: V, AE, DC.

Amédée Ducruet, a wise, capable, experienced cook, has absolutely no trouble filling his plain little bistro, which is lit like a village café. The reasons are simple: His cuisine is appetizing and generous, his products are superb, and his prices are quite reasonable. We recommend the famous, classic dish of the house—fisherman's salad with warm oysters and a julienne of vegetables—as well as the ramekin of langoustines with basil and coriander and the rich filet of sole royal in morel juice, served with fresh pasta. Unfortunately, the homemade coffee ice cream parfait is much less impressive. The wine list includes some good Bordeaux, and the atmosphere is charming.

A la carte: 230-250F. Menus: 85F, 145F, 170F.

Réalmont

81120 Réalmont - (Tarn)
Paris 696 - Castres 22 - Albi 20 - Toulouse 75

(13) Noël

1, rue de l'Hôtel-de-Ville - 63.55.52.80

M. Galinier. Open until 9:30 p.m. Closed Sun. dinner & Mon. (off-seas.) & Feb. school vacation. Terrace dining. No pets. Parking. Hotel: 1 ste 250-285F; 14 rms 90-190F; half-board 210-290F. Cards: V, AE, DC.

M. Noël (Father Christmas!) had a son-in-law, and after spending more than 50 years at the stoves himself, he brought him to his small seaside hotel, which five generations of Galiniers have turned into an authentic, traditional family establishment. But don't be alarmed: It was not to start a subversive revolution with young vegetables and imaginative creations, but rather to keep alive such dishes as the pot-au-feu of calf's head, the lobster Newburg, the pascade with Roquefort, the famous three-meat cassoulet and the handsome daube with pork rind. With the lovely regional products, the generous portions, the smiles on everyone's faces and the lovely shaded terrace in sunny weather, each day is like Christmas in Réalmont.

A la carte: 260F. Menus: 120F, 190F, 220F.

Redon

35600 Redon - (Ille-et-Vilaine)
Paris 400 - La Baule 63 - Vannes 57 - Rennes 65

(13) La Bogue

3, rue des Etats - 99.71.12.95

MM. Hatté. Open until 9 p.m. Closed Tues. dinner, Wed. & Jan. 1-21. Pets allowed. Cards: V.

The blond Yvonne Hatté always seems to be smiling in her rustic, bourgeois dining room with its wooden beams and flooring. And not without reason: All of Redon comes here to sample the lovely, light, classic cuisine prepared by Philippe, her husband. The series of fixed-price menus he has composed are models of intelligent generosity, and they include almost all the dishes listed on his à la carte list. For 145 francs, for example, you'll enjoy a delicious, fresh homemade duck foie gras, followed by aiguillettes of duck in a lovely walnut wine sauce, salad, cheeses and a fresh-fruit gratin. The wine list is filled with fine little discoveries, such as a red Anjou from Château de Chamboureau (at 55 francs).

A la carte: 230-250F. Menus: 65F (weekday lunch only), 90F, 120F, 155F, 190F.

Jean-Marc Chandouineau

1, rue Thiers - 99.71.02.04

Closed Feb. school vacation & Aug. 9-20. 2 stes 400-520F. 5 rms 300-450F. TV.

The seven rooms of this pleasant and hospitable hotel have been completely redone, with double-glazed windows, thick carpets and good bathrooms.

(14) Le Moulin de Via

Rte. de La Gacilly - 99.71.05.15

MM. Chéneau. Open until 9 p.m. Closed Sun. dinner & Mon.; annual closings not available. Garden dining. Pets allowed. Parking.

Le Moulin de Via, a lovely house located just outside of town, is as pleasant in winter, with its wooden beams, fireplace and warm cheer, as it is in summer, when the attractive Claudine Chéneau sets tables on the large terrace. Jean-Paul, her husband, prepares a simple but personalized cuisine largely devoted to products from Brittany, Armor and Arvor: salted butter, exquisite pigeons from Carmoël, farm chèvres, oysters from Carnac and magnificent fish. The cooking is precise, the sauces light, and the presentations refined. Dishes cannot be ordered à la carte, but a series of lovely fixed-price menus include warm oysters with periwinkles, a plate of sea bass and red mullet, pigeon in a light sauce flavored with a wonderful brunoise of vegetables, an émincé of pears served with pear ice cream and an exquisite dish of caramel and orange. The wine list is well composed. An excellent new little restaurant.

Menus: 140F (weekdays only, wine incl.), 170F to 250F.

Reillanne

04110 Reillanne - (Alpes-de-Haute-Provence)
Paris 780 - Forcalquier 18 - Manosque 17 - Apt 27

(14) L'Auberge de Reillanne

92.76.45.95

Mme. Founès. Open until 9 p.m. Closed Wed. & Nov. 15-Dec. 15. Pets allowed. Parking. Cards: V, AE, DC.

A royal couple—Beaudoin and Fabiola—and a young prince—Albert of Monaco—were delighted *not* to be recognized here. Was it because of their hosts' complete indifference to current events, or because of their extraordinary good manners? Perhaps a little of both, for Florent and Anne-Marie Founès have wanted their large eighteenth-century farmhouse to be immune to time and the fashion of the moment. The short à la carte menu of Anne-Marie, a self-made cook, perfectly reflects her passions: She has a strong penchant for the freshest produce coming either from her own vegetable garden or from the local growers, and she is enamored of sweet-and-sour combinations and of the local wines. The latter deliciously enhance the salad of young pigeon with apples, the foie gras with a turnip confit flavored with crushed coriander, the small fowl (completely boned) with fennel, the duck breast glazed in honey and sesame seeds, the splendid chaud-froid of young pigeon à la royale, the marvelous cheeses obtained directly from a goatherd in Manosque, and the wonderful plate of desserts whose flavors are both fresh and complex.

A la carte: 300F and up.

L'Auberge de Reillanne

(See restaurant above)

Closed Nov. 15-Dec. 15. 7 rms 395F. Half-board 680-880F. No pets.

This marvelous old farmhouse, which has been cleverly turned into a charming inn, has seven large rooms that are soberly and impeccably furnished in the best regional taste. You'll enjoy perfectly peaceful days here, for there are neither radios nor television sets. A swimming pool should be built by the time you read this report.

Reims

51100 Reims - (Marne)
Paris 145 - Lille 212 - Metz 187 - Verdun 118

Sights. Notre-Dame, the cathedral where the kings of France were crowned (a marvel of thirteenth-century ogival art and statuary—see the Rose of Light, the Smiling Angel, the tapestries portraying the Life of the Virgin and, on summer days, the splendid audiovisual events); Musée Tau (the cathedral's treasures), Musée Saint-Remi (in the ancient abbey/church, history and archaeology); Musée Saint-Denis (paintings by Cranach, Corot and Boudin); the imposing Porte de Mars (a major Roman arch); the "Blue Bus" tours of the town (daily from June 21 to September 7, depart from the court in front of Notre-Dame); tours of the Champagne cellars (offered by many famous Champagne makers); Fort de la Pompelle (5 kilometers toward Châlons-sur-Marne, a handsome World War I museum).

Eating on the Run. On pl. d'Erlon: Aux Coteaux (tasty pizza, open from 6 p.m. to dawn); Le Glue Pot (serves grilled meat until 3 a.m.); Taverne de Maître Kanter (Sauerkraut and shellfish, open until midnight).

Bars & Cafés. Bar de l'Altea, 31, blvd. Paul-Doumer (modern and comfortable); Brigith's Club, 7, blvd. du Général-Leclerc (pleasant English bar in a winter garden); Waïda, 35, pl. d'Erlon (tea, ice cream, terrace).

Nightlife. L'Aquarium, 93, blvd. du Général-Leclerc (young, well-to-do clientele); La Bergerie, in Cernay-lès-Reims (rustic decor, disco); Brigith's Club, 7, blvd. du Général-Leclerc (lively disco); Club St-Pierre, 41, blvd. du Général-Leclerc (the most popular).

Shops. *Bakeries:* Collot, pl. de l'Hôtel-de-Ville (good yeast bread); Jactat, 52, rue de Mars (many varieties of bread—nut bread, poppy seed bread, sesame bread). *Charcuteries:* Au Cochon Sans Rancune, 105, rue de Vesle (Reims ham cooked in bread crumbs, white boudin and pâtés). *Cheese:* La Cave aux Fromages, 12, pl. du Forum (supplies the best restaurants in the region). *Mustards and condiments:* Charbonneaux-Brabant, 5, rue de Valmy (the supplier to Fauchon, outstanding selection and quality). *Pastries, confections:* Deléans, 20, rue Cérès (solid and serious, sells delicious "nélusko"); Fossier, 25, cours Langlet (for its croquignolles, marzipan and the famous Reims cookies, which are divine when fresh); La Petite Friande, 15, cours Langlet (chocolate Champagne corks and bottles). *Wine:* Délices et Arômes, 40, pl. Drouet-d'Erlon.

(16) L'Assiette Champenoise

40, ave. Paul-Vaillant-Couturier, 51430 Tinqueux - 26.04.15.56

M. Lallement. Open daily until 10 p.m. Pets allowed. Hotel: 2 stes 950F; 28 rms 560-760F. TV. Garage parking. Cards: V, AE, DC.

Ten days after the grand opening of L'Assiette Champenoise in the summer of 1987, all of Champagne—curious spectators and journalists alike—were already crowding its brand-new dining room, which opens onto a still-unfinished park. The main subject of conversation at the comfortably spaced tables concerned the chances of success of Jean-Pierre Lallement, whose pleasant, beaming demeanor chases away any thoughts of gloominess. His new house is located next to a freeway entrance, in a modern environment completely the opposite of the warm, intimate atmosphere in which he had worked in Châlons-sur-Vesle for twelve years. But Jean-Pierre has fulfilled everyone's expectations. Barely settled, he already seems in complete control, engaging quite naturally in the most perilous virtuoso performances with his sauces, tossing in quite casually some dishes with magnificent finishing touches. Obviously, one can only rejoice at the arrival of a cook of such caliber and ambition in this suburb just west of Reims; let's hope it will encourage healthy emulation rather than mean-spirited rivalry.

For the moment, the decor, which was planned and executed at great cost in this pleasant, typically turn-of-the-century chalet, still needs some polishing. The dining room is quite spacious, especially now that two wings have been added; its walls are covered with pink wallpaper, and its ceiling is a kind of vault, supported by columns that are strangely dressed in yellow fabric. On the whole, the style is modern, quite chilly and a bit incongruous (some of the paintings hanging on the walls are of questionable taste, contributing absolutely nothing to the place); it should be furnished more cozily and filled with flowers. That task we can entrust to Colette Lallement, who, livelier than ever, supervises with a gentle authority her crew of young, tuxedo-clad men and women.

As for the rest, let's leave it to Jean-Pierre to raise the stakes with his langoustines sautéed in grapefruit juice and served with an extraordinarily smooth sauce in small, hollow plates; his wonderful braised John Dory garnished with slightly warm oysters and leeks; and his kidneys and sweetbreads sautéed in anise. The desserts are good, if not brilliant (bitter-chocolate cake, glazed raspberry-mousse cake); we're sure that they will only get better. There is a worthwhile fixed-price menu based on products obtained fresh each day from the market. The wine cellar includes famous Champagnes and Bordeaux. The Lallements recently opened some 30 comfortable hotel rooms in the adjacent building.

A la carte: 400F. Menus: 185F (weekday lunch only), 360F.

Boyer

19

(Les Crayères)
64, blvd. Henry-Vasnier - 26.82.80.80

M. Boyer. Open until 9:30 p.m. Closed Tues. lunch, Mon. & Dec. 19-Jan. 10. Air cond. Terrace dining. Pets allowed. Parking. Telex 830959. Cards: V, AE, DC, MC.

Bardet, Taillevent, Gagnaire, Haeberlin and Loiseau. What do they have in common? Nothing, except that they all belong to the same family of four toques and ratings of 19/20. But their talents are of distinct, if not opposing, natures. Some are artists, modernists, creators, while others are classicists, traditionalists, cautious types. But reality, of course, is filled with more nuance than those black-and-white distinctions, and Gérard Boyer, who you would instinctively class with the latter group, actually has a much more modern spirit than a Loiseau or a Haeberlin.

While we detoured through this preface, you at least learned that the "Lord" of Crayères has received his fourth toque from us. Why now and not sooner? The answer is simple. When we visit a restaurant, we give each dish we've tasted a grade, and take the average. Clearly, for major restaurants, we go several times, in order to try various dishes. Boyer hit the jackpot when, after six recent meals (with the two of us, that makes for an impressive number of dishes!), the number 19 lit up.

We have followed Boyer since his beginnings in Reims, where he existed in the shadow of his charming father, who has since retired. We've been able to watch the development of a character that, while remaining thoughtful, even wary (after all, he's from the Auvergne), has blossomed to the point of taking on a liberated tone and a sensitivity that is reflected in both his establishment and his cuisine, which is elegant but never pompous. A classicist at heart—and that's not a flaw!—Boyer has managed to free himself of "saucy" cuisine and the latest fashions that threatened to close in on him. Today, his dishes denote a perfectly mastered imagination, and in addition to their extreme delicacy they have a sun-drenched touch that comes from particularly seductive herbs and spices. In short, Gérard Boyer has begun to make his cuisine sing, and that gives rise to quite a few nice concerts.

Here, we find a terrine of leeks and carrots "fattened" with foie gras and truffle oil; there, a pan of celeriac and truffles or, better yet, of truffles with asparagus (and not asparagus with truffles!). And again a bit of truffle—en jus—in the coquilles St-Jacques with endives, which is a masterpiece of balance and flavor, as is the lobster with chanterelles in a sauce corail (lobster roe) that floats like a cloud. And how could we hesitate to award a 19 to the warm foie gras with grapes and baby vegetables, the warm escalopes of sweetbreads on a salad of green beans, artichokes and tomatoes in an orange vinaigrette (and truffles, of course!), and the grenadins de veau, a bit too firm, perhaps, but softened by a peanut sauce with corn blintzes au foie gras? And we can't forget the saddle of young rabbit with langoustines, garden vegetables and basil, nor, above all, the exceptional dish that deserves a rating of 21/20: duck filets on a bed of thinly sliced black and green olives served with a dish of artichokes and fresh tomatoes, almost a purée. This dish, bathed in a Rivesaltes wine sauce, makes for an unforgettable bouquet of flavors with an angelic simplicity.

The desserts deserve less commentary. Clearly they're good, but not enough to make you fall over, except perhaps the iced nougat in a coulis of apricots and honey. But that's enough about the cuisine. It's not the only thing that made our hearts flutter. There are also some 120 Champagnes from an exceptional wine cellar that counts among its many strengths the ability to rouse the large, pensive Werner, the manager of the dining room, who is so dearly loved by his clients and so enamored of wine that you'd think he'd invented it. And then there's the sheer shock of finding, almost in the middle of town, this fairyland of greenery, well protected by high walls—fifteen acres of grass, trees, valleys and ravines, all created during the last century by Louise Pommery, the grande dame of Champagne. She was never even able to enjoy the whimsical quarters in the Louis XVI style that she built for herself at the top of the park. Restored by Xavier Gardinier, at the time the head of Pommery, this very "Elysian" abode, with a courtyard at one end and a huge white terrace set with tables at the other, is not at all pretentious. The high ceilings, enormous French doors, monumental stairway, period woodwork, heavy tapestries and candelabra in the dining rooms could intimidate or even elicit gasps, but just the opposite is true. You feel good, happy and relaxed. Rather than life in the château, it feels more like life with a loving family, because Boyer and his wife, Elyane, are just that—simple, kind, spontaneous and warm.

A la carte: 300-600F.

Boyer

(See restaurant above)

Closed Dec. 23-Jan. 15. 3 stes 1,530F. 16 rms 980-1,530F. TV. Air cond. Tennis.

Sixteen rooms and suites, all tastefully decorated and furnished in constrasting styles: classical, French, English, romantic and exotic. Elyane Boyer gives full attention to every detail, especially to the bathrooms. The breakfast is exquisite, the service is perfect, and all this goes for the price of a chain-hotel room overlooking the highway... you understand why foreign travelers do business in Paris and sleep here. It's only an hour and fifteen minutes from Paris by car (the Saint-Rémi exit on the autoroute, direction Luxembourg, then Châlons). Relais et Châteaux.

Bristol

76, pl. Drouet-d'Erlon - 26.40.52.25

Open year-round. 40 rms 170-245F. Parking. Pets allowed. TV. Telex 842155. Cards: V, MC.

The rooms of this centrally located, elegant hotel are a bit gloomy, but they are comfortable and well maintained. No restaurant.

Campanile

Val de Murigny, ave. Georges-Pompidou
26.36.66.94

Open year-round. 60 rms 205-225F. Half-board 294-310F. TV in 50 rms. Parking. Pets allowed. Telex 830262. Cards: V, MC.

This is a decent, quite peaceful hotel in which to spend the night; its rooms (twenty additional ones were recently built) are functional, and the restaurant is pleasant.

(14) Le Chardonnay

184, ave. d'Epernay - 26.06.08.60

M. Lange. Open until 9:30 p.m. Closed Sat. lunch, Sun., Dec. 22-Jan. 16 & July 29-Aug. 28. Pets allowed. Cards: V, AE, DC, MC.

Jean-Jacques Lange has purchased this warm, cheerful house from the Boyers. (It used to be their Chaumière, where he was both chef and sommelier.) Dominique Giraudeau, also a former chef for the Boyers, remains at the stoves of this solid and sensible (perhaps too much so) restaurant. The cuisine here has been consistent for years—it's serious, light and well prepared, but occasionally one meets up with a dish that's a bit ordinary. Sample the shrimp steamed in Champagne wine vinegar, the rib of beef enhanced by a magnificent Bouzy sauce and the filet of duck with morello cherries. The wine list includes some great Champagnes, as well as a number of wines served by the glass.

A la carte: 320-350F. Menus: 185F, 250F, 320F.

Red toques signify modern cuisine; black toques signify traditional cuisine.

(16) Le Florence

43, blvd. Foch - 26.47.12.70

M. Maillot. Open until 9:30 p.m. Closed Sun. dinner & July 25-Aug. 9. Garden dining. Pets allowed. Cards: V, AE, DC, MC.

A high ceiling, tall windows with flowing draperies, Regency chairs and lovely silverware: It's difficult to find a more elegant decor in the entire city of Reims—or a more attractive one, now that a lovely patio has been opened behind the salon. The restaurant's fine reputation is carefully maintained. The reception by the owners is in the latest style of provincial chic, and the service is impeccable. But it is the cuisine prepared by the discreet young chef, Yves Méjean (a former student of Guérard), that remains the lightest, most imaginative and most modern aspect of Le Florence. Its inspiration is sharp, its execution precise, and its presentations artful, especially the pot-au-feu of foie gras with puréed garlic, the boudin of John Dory in bread crumbs and lobster sauce, and the exceptional roast lamb with honey. The à la carte prices are reasonable, but take a look at the menu/carte intended "for the little gourmets." Its selection and generosity, as well as its moderate price, are absolutely outstanding. For 250 francs, including a half bottle of Champagne, you will dine on marinated salmon, lotte with a watercress cream sauce, cheeses and an glazed mint nougatine.

A la carte: 400F. Menus: 250F (Champagne incl.), 180F (weekdays only), 200F (weekends and holidays only), 340F.

(13) Le Foch

37, blvd. Foch - 26.47.48.22

M. Gonzalès. Open until 9 p.m. Closed Sun. dinner, Mon., Jan. 2-16 & July 17-31. Pets allowed. Cards: V, AE, DC, MC.

This former townhouse, tastefully decorated by its new owners, has quickly become one of the best addresses in Reims. The dining room, in pink and raspberry tones, has a lovely view of the trees lining the boulevard; the chairs are comfortable, the china lovely, and the bouquets of wildflowers as fresh as the pretty face of the young patronne. The cuisine prepared by Patrick Gonzalès, her husband, is personalized and light, almost to the point of affectation (he will have to watch that!)—but never at the sacrifice of his splendid generosity. Sample the pleasant salmon leaves with oysters in a subtle lemon sauce; the filet of brill (or sole) in a rather tasty vanilla sauce, which goes quite well with the small mushroom flan; the handsome cheeses, especially the Bries; and the tasty, though slightly too sweet, family-style desserts. All of this fully merits a toque. The wine cellar includes at least 100 Champagnes, some at reasonable prices.

A la carte: 280-300F. Menus: 175F and 250F (wine incl.), 130F, 175F.

La Paix

9, rue de Buirette - 26.40.04.08

Open year-round. 105 rms 280-430F. TV. Pets allowed. Pool. Garage parking. Telex 830974. Cards: V, AE, DC, MC.

Perfectly located between the train station and the cathedral, this hotel is the only one in Reims with a swimming pool (it also has a sauna and a gym). Well-equipped rooms. Restaurant.

12/20 **Les Relais Bleus**

12, rue Gabriel-Voisin - 26.82.59.79
Mme. Piedagnel. Open until 9:30 p.m. Closed Sun. dinner. Pets allowed. Terrace dining. Hotel: 40 rms 220-320F. Telex 841121. Cards: V, MC.

Les Relais Bleus, located in Reims's industrial district, has a bright, modern decor of wood and concrete; excellent comfort and good service; and a skillful, impressive new chef. Sample his ragoût of shrimp "en habit verts" (spinach), the perfectly grilled salmon with mushrooms and the glazed nougat in raspberry sauce (but we really would prefer not to have to get our desserts ourselves, as though we were in a cafeteria).

A la carte: 230F. Menus: 65F and 85F (weekdays only), 90F and 110F (weekends and holidays only).

IN NEARBY **Champigny**
(6 km NW on N 31 & D 275)
51370 St-Brice-Courcelles - (Marne)

(13) **Auberge de la Garenne**

Rte. de Soissons - 26.08.26.62
M. Laplaige. Open until 10 p.m. Closed Sun. dinner, Mon. & July 31-Aug. 20. Pets allowed. Parking. Cards: V, AE, DC.

This old inn, which saw both the glory and the decline of the Reims racing circuit, was recently taken over by a young chef, and in no time at all it has become the fashionable place for Reims gourmets, especially the VIPs of the huge Champagne business. Laurent Laplaige is not a mere cook of the moment; he spent six years with Boyer (among others) before taking on this old rundown place located next to a noisy highway, which he completely redecorated in a chic rustic style (dinners are served by candlelight). His cuisine is ambitious and full of promise: sander in Bordeaux (the sauce is a bit strong, but the vegetable garnish is wonderful), superb saddle of lamb with wild mushrooms, nage of salmon delicately cooked in Sauternes, and a delicious soup of fresh fruit served with an imaginative Champagne-flavored crème anglaise. Champagnes are also served by the glass.

A la carte: 280-300F. Menus: 95F, 170F.

IN NEARBY **Montchenot**
(11 km S on N 51)
51500 Rilly-la-Montagne - (Marne)

(14) **Auberge du Grand Cerf**

N 51 - 26.97.60.07
M. Guichaoua. Open until 9:30 p.m. Closed Tues. dinner, Wed. & Feb. 8-March 8. Garden dining. Pets allowed. Parking. Cards: V, AE.

Year-round, the residents of La Montagne (near Reims) who are partial to good food crowd this bright and luxurious suburban restaurant; they especially enjoy its comfortable, glassed-in terrace, which opens onto a charming garden. A lovely reception by Françoise Guichaoua and service that has improved considerably under the supervision of sommelier Hervé Launois add even more to the subtle pleasure of sampling Alain Guichaoua's cuisine. He seems to be increasingly at ease with fish and shellfish: We tasted an exquisite tian of lobster and fish (a brandade of fresh cod) in a Champagne dressing and a delicious estouffade of sea bass garnished with vegetables. There is a lovely selection of light, appetizing desserts. The wine cellar contains splendid Champagnes, with exceptional old vintages.

A la carte: 280-320F. Menus: 150F (weekdays only), 230F, 300F, 320F.

La Rémigeasse

see Ile d'Oléron

Rennes

35000 Rennes - (Ille-et-Vilaine)
Paris 348 - Brest 245 - Nantes 106 - St-Malo 69

Sights. The Old Rennes district (fifteenth and sixteenth centuries), including rue St-Guillaume (an ancient chapel and the Ti-Koz restaurant), rue du Chapitre (Hôtel de Blossac), rue St-Sauveur, rue St-Michel, pl. du Champ-Jacquet (old houses with leaning upper floors) and the intersection of rue du Champ-Jacquet and rue Le Bastard (note the superb Robien townhouse, built at the end of the sixteenth century, the great fire of 1720 stopped at its walls); pl. des Lices; pl. du Parlement (its seventeenth-century law courts were built by Salomon de Brosse); pl. de la Mairie (eighteenth century); Musée Beaux-Arts (it contains "The Newborn Infant" by Georges de La Tour); Musée de Bretagne (history and ethnography); Palais St-Georges; the Garden of Thabor.

Eating on the Run. La Bonne Pâte, 6, rue Derval (best crêperie in town, prices match quality); Le Café des Loges, 1, quai Lamennais (fast service, short fixed-price menus); La Cotriade, 40, rue St-Georges (pleasant decor, good fixed-price menus); L'Epicerie Russe, 42, rue Vasselot (caviar, blinis and vodka); La Korrigane, 26, rue du Dr-Joly (rustic decor, daily specials); Le Louisiane, 7, pl. St-Michel (good fixed-price menus); Le Mix-Grill, pl. de Bretagne (tasty meat dishes); L'Oudaya, 91, rue St-Hélier (excellent couscous); Le Picardy, 5, rue de Redon (reasonable prices); Le Shangaï, 8, rue Rallier-du-Baty (very good Chinese restaurant); Le Skipper, 39, rue St-Georges (maritime decor, interesting fixed-price menus); Le Tandoori, 12, rue Nantaise (Indian restaurant); La Théière, pl. du Champ-Jacquet (English cakes, apple pies); Le Verseau, rue Ste-Mélaine (vegetarian); Villa d'-Este, 1, rue de la Psalette (best Italian restaurant).

Brasseries. Le Bistrot des Canotiers, 35, ave. Janvier (honest, classic cuisine); La Chope, 3, rue de La Chalotais (a veritable institution in Rennes); Le Colombier, 9-11, rue Tronjolly (good grilled meats).

Bars & Cafés. L'Aventure, 5, imp. Rallier-du-Bary (attractive decor, student clientele); Le Bentley, 27, rue de la Monnaie (strong cocktails); Le Bob-Pub, 12, rue de la Parcheminerie (varied clientele, good cocktails); Le Café Carmès, 36, rue St-Georges (high-tech decor, hosts various exhibitions); La Contrescarpe, 5, pl. du Champ-Jacquet (pleasant atmosphere, piano).

Nightlife. Le Batchi, 34, rue Vasselot (men only); L'Espace, 45, blvd. de La Tour d'Auvergne (fashionable, very large); Le Pim's, 27, pl. du Colombier (more mature clientele); La Prison St-Michel, 7, imp. Rallier-du-Baty (attractive decor, young clientele); Le Stanley, at Le Haut-Val in Saint-Grégoire (quite hospitable, garden open in summer).

Shops. *Bakeries:* Blanchard, 18, rue St-Michel (tasty baguettes); Cochet, 51, rue St-Guéhenno (best bread in town). *Charcuteries, caterers:* Hesteau, 28, rue de Nemours. *Chocolate:* Gaudissard, rue La Fayette; Léonidas, 4, rue Hermine. *Pastries:* Coupel, 13, rue Vasselot (apple tarts); La Duchesse Anne, 3, rue de Toulouse (a veritable institution in Rennes, with excellent cakes and croissants). And, of course, the lively, colorful Lices street market on Saturday morning.

Altea

See La Table Ronde restaurant.

Central

6, rue Lanjuinais - 99.79.12.36

Open year-round. 1 ste 520-600F. 43 rms 150-290F. TV. Pets allowed. Parking. Telex 741259. Cards: V, AE, DC, MC.

The Central hotel, well located next to the wharf, features redecorated rooms, good facilities and a lovely breakfast. No restaurant.

(14) Le Corsaire

52, rue d'Antrain - 99.36.33.69

M. Luce. Open until 9:45 p.m. Closed Sun. dinner, Mon. lunch, Feb. school vacation & 3 weeks in Aug. Pets allowed. Cards: V, AE, DC, MC.

The result of Le Corsaire's recent renovation is impressive: The upstairs room has been wallpapered with light striped fabrics and hung with mirrors; the large salon now has bourgeois pink and bordeaux tones and a majestic crystal chandelier; the third room is decorated in a chic purple cashmere; and the downstairs bar has been wisely discarded. Antoine Luce, a veteran of Grand Véfour and Beau Rivage, is still impressing us with his solid savoir faire in a cuisine whose execution may be slightly routine but is always impeccable, light and dedicated to outstanding fish and shellfish: cabbage stuffed with mussels, ramekin of coquilles St-Jacques and duck livers in raspberry vinegar and a subtle filet of sea bass with an émincé of leeks. As for the desserts, they are a great success, despite their totally unappealing names ("pineapple delice" and the like). A handsome wine service is provided by Nelly Luce.

A la carte: 260F. Menus: 78F, 150F.

(13) Le Galopin Gourmet

21, ave. Jean-Janvier - 99.30.09.51, 99.31.55.96

M. Saday. Open until 10:30 p.m. Closed Sun. & July 14-Aug. 14. Air cond. Pets allowed. Cards: V, AE, DC.

This old Rennes brasserie has been transformed (at great expense) into an elegant restaurant decorated in peach and apricot tones, white furniture, large and colorful bouquets of flowers and clever indirect lighting. The new owner, who plays the role of an attentive maître d', has hired a young, adroit cook who already has won awards at various culinary competitions. Here, his delicious saffron-sauced coquilles St-Jacques from Erquy are prepared with a refined simplicity, and the salmon from Scotland is cooked to precision in coarse salt. Nonetheless, the sauces could be slightly lighter (and include fewer egg yolks), and the repertoire could be a bit bolder. But the desserts are wonderful, especially the sweet orange slices gratinéed in crémant (a slightly sparkling wine). The wine cellar lists several excellent Bordeaux at unusually reasonable prices.

A la carte: 250F. Menus: 86F, 119F, 156F.

Hôtel de Nemours

5, rue de Nemours - 99.78.26.26

Open year-round. 26 rms 180-260F. TV. Air cond. Telex 306022. Cards: V.

This small, central hotel on a busy street has been entirely renovated. Small restaurant.

(14) L'Ouvrée

18, pl. des Lices - 99.30.16.38

M. Langlais. Open until 10:30 p.m. Closed Sat. lunch & Mon. No pets. Cards: V, AE, DC, MC.

After the house burned down recently, L'Ouvrée got a brand-new decor. The four small salons are tastefully done in a style reminiscent of the '30s, with mirrored ceilings and retro candelabra. The chairs are comfortable, the silverware is lovely, and Gérard Hehannin, the chef, has returned to his stoves in high spirits. His semicooked foie gras in a light honey and soy sauce, his fresh, expertly cooked red mullet with a chive cream sauce, his filets of young pigeon roasted in lemon and his perfect vanilla ice cream with morello cherries still place his cuisine among the best in town. M. Langlais, the owner, greets his clientele in a friendly manner. He also tends to the wonderful cellar, home to Loire and Bordeaux wines.

A la carte: 250F. Menu: 120F.

(16) Le Palais

7, pl. du Parlement - 99.79.45.01

MM. Anfroy & Tizon. Open until 9:45 p.m. Closed Sun. dinner, Mon., Feb. school vacation & Aug. 7-30. Pets allowed. Cards: V, AE, DC, MC.

At this luxury hotel you'll see Marc Tizon and Bernard Anfray, two friends who met at the Lion d'Or in Liffré. Bernard Anfray supervises the service, which can sometimes get off to a rather slow start but is quite cordial. With its view of the incomparable Salomon Debrosse square and a serene decor—apricot wallpaper, soft lighting, attractive shades behind a screen of greenery, stylish etchings and tables discreetly adorned with fresh flowers and silverware—it's a delightful spot. As for Tizon, he's like a fire smoldering beneath the embers—beneath an apparent classicism, he hides a bold creativity. His is an enthusiastic cuisine that reveals his passion for fresh products. His à la carte menu may be short, but it is renewed three times a year and supplemented by daily specials created with products purchased fresh from the market that best display his brilliant style:

fresh cod with celery chips, oysters in a pumpkin mousse, salad "amuse-paysan" combining foie gras and sweetbreads in a sauce flavored with balsamic vinegar, wonderful sea bass cooked in its skin and in vinegar, and Flemish pistachio waffles. All these are personalized dishes that not only pique our interest but also attest to an authentic, fully mature talent. The wine cellar is well stocked, and the fixed-price menus are lovely.

A la carte: 280-300F. Menus: 95F and 160F (weekdays only), 175F (weekends and holidays only).

(15) Le Piré

18, rue du Maréchal-Joffre - 99.79.31.41

M. Angelle. Open until 9:45 p.m. Closed Sat. lunch, Sun., Aug. 22-Sept. 4 & Dec. 25-Jan. 1. Pets allowed. Cards: V, AE, DC.

We're not quite sure what to praise most about this small, hospitable establishment: the courtesy of the lively patronne, the brunette Agnès; the speedy service; the reasonable prices; the lovely porcelain; the newly decorated champagne-and-salmon-colored dining room that opens onto an arbor shaded by a tall ash tree; or the inventive and light cuisine of Marc Angelle. At any rate, with the exception of an uninspired "nectar of beetroots" that accompanied the langoustines, and cheeses that were not at their best, this outstanding technician who trained at Faugeron and Beauvilliers seemed to be in a state of grace when we last ate here. The imaginative Sainte-Maure ravioli in truffle juice, perfectly cooked foie gras, a delicious parmentier of oysters and leeks with salmon eggs (chosen from the "Ultra-Light-Slender" section of the menu), duck in a powerful arabica sauce and a wide variety of equally creative desserts (especially the chocolate ones) were some of the highlights. The wine cellar is rich in handsome, reasonable reds from the Loire, and the fixed-price menus are simply astounding.

A la carte: 250F. Menus: 84F (weekdays only), 110F, 260F.

(13) La Table Ronde

Pl. du Colombier - 99.31.54.54

M. Ladevèze. Open daily until 10:15 p.m. Air cond. Terrace dining. Pets allowed. Telex 730905. Cards: V, AE, DC, MC.

They have made an effort to arrange the tables a little more attractively in this huge room of rather more style than comfort. The table settings are pretty, the leather armchairs soft, and the maître d' as friendly as he is competent. The cooking of chef James Bruneau, however, has taken a careless turn: endives smothering the scallop salad, acceptable bass and celery in a beurre blanc, lovely but oversugared apple pastry. We'll leave the toque but take away the extra point for now. There's a nice summer terrace underneath a tent—but double-check that the place is open before visiting on a summer weekend, even if you have reservations (management shows a capricious side in this regard).

A la carte: 250F. Menus: 85F (weekday lunch only), 115F (weekdays only), 130F (weekday lunch only, wine incl.), 160F (weekends and holidays only).

Altea

(See restaurant above)

Open year-round. 140 rms 362-455F. TV. Pets allowed.

Located in the new district of the Colombier, not far from the center of Rennes, the Altea hotel features functional, pleasant, bright rooms, all of which are equipped with a four-program video circuit. Very hospitable.

IN NEARBY **La Bouëxière**
(16 km NE on N 12 & D 27)
35340 Liffré - (Ille-et-Vilaine)

(13) La Fontaine aux Perles

6, rue Jean-Marie-Pavy - 99.00.91.50

M. Gesbert. Open until 9:30 p.m. Closed Sun. dinner, Mon., Feb. school vacation & 10 days in Sept. Pets allowed. Cards: V, MC.

Within these former stables, named after a novel written by Paul Féval in this very village, Rachel Gesbert continues to keep her prices low, all the while searching her imagination and local rustic recipes for all kinds of tasty little dishes. The filet of haddock in a mustard cream, the filet of young cod in soy butter, the outstanding country pâté and the étuvée of lamb's tongue with fresh chanterelles are making her attractive, rustic floral restaurant known to all of Rennes' Sunday gourmets anxious for a feast at a budget price. The desserts have progressed, but so have the wine prices, it seems. The service, performed by Cathy Gesbert, is quite attentive.

A la carte: 180-200F. Menus: 60F (weekday lunch only), 78F (weekdays only), 100F to 150F.

IN NEARBY **Cesson-Sévigné**
(6 km E on N 157)
35510 Cesson-Sévigné - (Ille-et-Vilaine)

Germinal 

9, cours de la Vilaine - 99.83.11.01

Closed Aug. 1-20 & Dec. 24-Jan. 5. 20 rms 210-280F. Pets allowed. TV in 15 rms. Parking. Cards: V.

This small hotel has been arranged stylishly in an ancient mill set on a small island on the Vilaine. The scenery is quite charming, and the rooms are attractive. Restaurant. Another hotel, Floréal, is located next door.

Reuilly-Sauvigny

02130 Jaulgonne - (Aisne)
Paris 110 - Château-Thiery 17 - Reims 47 - Epernay 33

(13) Auberge Le Relais

23.70.35.36

M. Berthuit. Open until 9 p.m. Closed Tues. dinner, Wed., Feb. & Aug. 22-Sept. 6. Pets allowed. Hotel: 7 rms 228-380F. Parking. Cards: V, AE, DC, MC.

The Auberge Le Relais commands a lovely view of the Marne valley, and it has many of the charms of an engaging, stylish, well-maintained country inn. It's a treat indeed to sit at one of these tables, with a smiling patronne and an attentive staff fussing over you. Martial Berthuit is still a bit too shy as a cook, yet he has plenty of spirit and many good ideas. We had a small, subtle feast, ordering from a large menu that lists handsome foie gras cooked "au torchon" (preferable to the red-mullet salad), sander in a perfectly saffroned cream sauce and a duck aiguillette "à la bourguignonne," followed by several handsome cheeses and a lovely feuilleté of bitter chocolate and pistachio. The well-composed wine cellar is rich in Champagnes.

A la carte: 300-350F. Menus: 103F, 129F, 169F.

Ribeauvillé

68150 Ribeauvillé - (Haut-Rhin)
Paris 434 - Colmar 15 - Sélestat 15 - Mulhouse 57

12/20 Clos Saint-Vincent

Rte. de Bergheim - 89.73.67.65

M. Chapotin. Open until 8:30 p.m. Closed Tues., Wed. & Nov. 15-March 15. Terrace dining. Pets allowed. Parking. Cards: V, MC.

This is a large, luxurious chalet located in front of the vineyards. The chef has all the looks of a jovial cowboy, and his courteous wife supervises an attractive dining room that offers an expansive view of the countryside. The classic à la carte menu includes mignon of veal cooked in the traditional style, quenelles of pike and a number of versions of a tasty homemade foie gras.

A la carte: 350F. Menus: 130F (weekday lunch only), 180F (weekday lunch only), 230F.

Clos Saint-Vincent

(See restaurant above)

Closed Nov. 15-March 15. 3 stes 800-1,131F. 8 rms 500-829F. TV.

This very attractive inn faces the Rhine valley and the Alsace plains. Its rooms are lovely and spacious and provide perfect tranquility. Relais et Châteaux.

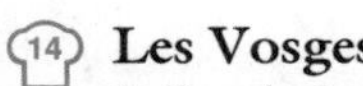

Les Vosges

2, Grande-Rue - 89.73.61.39

M. Matter. Open until 9:30 p.m. Closed Mon., Tues. lunch, Jan. 1-15 & March 1-15. Pets allowed. Hotel: 2 stes 240-460F; 18 rms 200-350F; half-board 272-300F oblig. in seas. Cards: V, AE, MC.

Hidden inside this large, nondescript building is the most elegant inn in town. Not long ago, the Matters completely renovated the decor, especially that of their dining room. Now the round tables are elegantly set, surrounded by comfortable oval-backed chairs and bathed in a soft brown and rose light. The atmosphere may be somewhat contrived, but the chef's intelligently updated traditional cuisine is both impeccable and lively: a mosaic of sweetbreads, salmon and foie gras, escargots ravioli in a soft garlic bouillon, matelote of pike with fresh pasta and a compote of young pigeon garnished with young vegetables. The thorough wine cellar is judiciously composed and includes some well-selected regional vintages whose prices are kept as reasonable as possible.

A la carte: 350F. Menus: 130F and 180F (weekdays only), 230F, 300F.

Riec-sur-Belon

29124 Riec-sur-Belon - (Finistère)
Paris 518 - Quimper 42 - Concarneau 19 - Quimperlé 13

Auberge de Kerland

3 km S on D 24, Domaine de Kerstinec
98.06.42.98

M. Chatelain. Open until 10 p.m. Closed Sun. dinner (Oct.-Easter) & Feb. school vacation. Garden dining. Pets allowed. Parking. Cards: V, MC.

The Chatelains first turned their old inn into a seafood bistro (L'Assiette du Pêcheur), and then they moved a mile or so away into this brand-new modern house set in a 42-acre park. There is an all-blue dining room on the main floor and another, more pleasant one upstairs, decorated in dark red and beige tones, with attractive bay windows overlooking the river. The cuisine is consistent, fresh, seasonal and personalized: salmon feuilleté served with a salmon-nutmeg sabayon, pot-au-feu of shellfish with a sorrel cream sauce, roast quail with its newly laid eggs poached, garnished with fresh pasta, and delicious desserts.

A la carte: 260-280F. Menus: 103F to 280F.

Auberge de Kerland

(See restaurant above)

Closed Sun. (Oct.-Easter) & Feb. school vacation. 2 stes 480-590F. 17 rms 280-590F. Half-board 340-420F. TV. Pets allowed.

Within the old stone walls of this renovated hotel (located behind the restaurant) are large, well equipped, soundproofed rooms; at river level, they offer lovely views.

Riquewihr

68340 Riquewihr - (Haut-Rhin)
Paris 437 - Colmar 13 - Ribeauvillé 5 - Sélestat 19

Auberge du Schoenenbourg

2, rue de la Piscine - 89.47.92.28,
89.49.01.11

M. Kiener. Open until 9:30 p.m. Closed Wed. dinner & Thurs. Garden dining. Pets allowed. Parking. Cards: V, MC.

All the signs erected by the local visitors bureau proclaim Riquewihr to be "one of the loveliest villages in France." Consequently, we were a bit disappointed to find that the best restaurant in the area is hidden inside such a plain house. But the terrace is absolutely charming (much more so than the spotless decor inside), perched as it is atop the ramparts overlooking the famous Schoenenbourg vineyards (which produce the best Riesling in the world). And the service is among the most friendly in all of Alsace. A discreet touch of imagination doesn't detract from the basically traditional nature of the cuisine (François Kiener is a veteran of Le Père Bise and L'Auberge de l'Ill), and that's a good thing, for the escargots ravioli with poppy seeds and the rack of lamb with lime are not exactly dishes destined for eternity. On the other hand, the sweetbreads grand-mère and the estouffade of coquilles St-Jacques are superbly executed classics, and the stuffed crêpes à l'Alsacienne is an interesting dessert. There is a good (though much too expensive) cuvée of Edelszwicker, vinified by the house.

A la carte: 300F. Menus: 170F (weekdays only), 270F.

Le Riquewihr

Rte. de Ribeauvillé - 89.47.83.13

Open year-round. 49 rms 180-255F. TV in 17 rms. Garage parking. Pets allowed. Telex 881720. Cards: V, AE, DC, MC.

The view of the slopes and vineyards offered by Le Riquewihr is splendid indeed. The hotel's spacious rooms have been attractively decorated in the local rustic style. Sauna. The bar stays open until 3 a.m., but there's no restaurant.

Le Schoenenbourg

Rue du Schoenenbourg - 89.49.01.11

Open year-round. 2 stes 470F. 23 rms 290-370F. TV in 19 rms. Parking. Cards: V, MC.

At the foot of a hill, this new, well-designed hotel has comfortable rooms furnished in a contemporary style.

Rive-de-Gier

42800 Rive-de-Gier - (Loire)
Paris 495 - Lyon 37 - St-Etienne 22 - Vienne 27

Georges Paquet

13

Combeplaine - 77.75.02.18

M. Paquet. Open until 9 p.m. Closed Sun. dinner, Mon. & July 12-Aug. 12. Pets allowed. Parking. Cards: V, MC.

In this small, quaint house in a busy village, it's a sure bet that you'll fall in love with at least one of the many fixed-price menus. For 135 francs, for example, you can dine on a salad of smoked duck breast, a mousseline of pike in a langoustine sauce, grilled duck leg, cheeses and desserts.

A la carte: 180-200F. Menus: 65F (weekdays only), 95F, 120F to 170F.

La Renaissance

15

41, rue Antoine-Marrel - 77.75.04.31

MM. Forest & Mounier. Open until 9:30 p.m. Closed Sun. dinner (Jan. 1-March 31). Garden dining. Pets allowed. Hotel: 8 rms 200-450F. Garage parking. Cards: V, AE, DC, MC.

The Laurents sold their famous three-toque restaurant to Jean-Paul Mounier before they left for Loué, and he has absolutely no intention of moping around among the memories they left, or indulging the old clientele's nostalgia in this already too-morose little town. After a rather difficult start, La Renaissance now fully justifies its name: Its facade has been repainted and its decor rejuvenated. Though a somewhat heavy-handed tone prevails for the upholstery in the dining room, it does offer perfect comfort, with elegantly set tables. And Michel Forest, the associate owner, supervises his young dining room staff well. In short, if the economy brightens up again in this area, La Renaissance will clearly be well on its way to success. Its cuisine will certainly prove no obstacle—our salmon marinated in dill was nicely balanced, the trilogy of fish was beautifully cooked in a lovely sauce, the lamb in curry was accompanied with an exquisite, exotic orange and banana garnish, the boned Giers pigeon was delicious, and the desserts were wonderful. The handsome wine cellar includes the best Saint-Josephs, Gigondas and Condrieus possible. All this, we feel, makes the second toque well deserved.

A la carte: 350-400F. Menus: 138F (weekdays only), 198F, 250F, 350F, 450F.

Rivedoux-Plage

see Ré (Ile de)

Roanne

42300 Roanne - (Loire)
Paris 390 - Lyon 88 - St-Etienne 77 - Mâcon 97

L'Astrée

13

17 bis, cours de la République
77.72.74.22

M. Falcoz. Open until 9:30 p.m. Closed Sat., Sun., 3 weeks in July-Aug. & 3 weeks in Dec.-Jan. Air cond. Pets allowed. Cards: V, AE, DC.

What an excellent cook Simon Falcoz is! He settled at L'Astrée (located across from the train station, not far from Troisgros) a few years ago, after working for two years at Le Lion d'Or in Romorantin as an assistant chef. This solid background makes itself felt in his handsome, personalized, rather decorative cuisine served at extremely moderate prices. The 145-franc fixed-price menu is well worth one toque, with its light feuilleté of langoustines generously garnished with fresh chanterelles, its veal kidney with sesame accompanied by excellent young vegetables and its outstanding classic chocolate prélat in coffee sauce. The patronne supervises the attentive staff in a warm dining room enlivened by multicolored draperies.

A la carte: 230-250F. Menus: 90F (weekdays only), 140F, 170F, 240F.

Troisgros

19.5

Pl. de la Gare
77.71.66.97

M. Troisgros. Open until 9:30 p.m. Closed Wed. lunch, Tues. & Jan. Air cond. Pets allowed. Parking. Telex 307507. Cards: V, AE, DC, MC.

Troisgros in the country in the midst of vineyards? Now that's news! This countryside is one that Pierre Troisgros (and we whispered this idea to him) made for himself in the courtyard once used to park cars. Out of this once-utilitarian space he has created a raised garden of some 400 square yards (a veritable Babylon) with everything needed to make birds sing (trees, flowers, even a birdbath). It's all above a hidden garage—easily the most beautiful in France—that looks like the entrance of a California mansion, with a small wine cellar and a large, climatized glass case filled with cigars. As for the vineyards, they're here as well, in the form of a gag: a dozen plants most representative of the French wine industry.

And who gets to luxuriate in all of this? You'll never guess: the cooks and dishwashers, who from their huge bay windows can now leisurely feast their eyes on this green landscape. But let's be fair. If you manage to get a table where you can catch a glimpse of the garden, you can share in this privilege. So the garden plan was a complete success, and the longtime regular customers who remember—with tears in their eyes—the old family-style hotel of Papa Jean-Baptiste are left gaping.

As for the rest, it'a all running smoothly. There will always be a few readers who drone on, like the one who doesn't care for the far dining room with its odd wall fixtures made of Gard stones cut to different heights (but the main dining room, recently redecorated in bright, cheerful tones, cannot elicit any complaints). Another reader will be bothered by smokers, and yet another by the pastries, which, it's true, are not always on a par with the rest and should be reexamined.

One might wonder if 30-year-old Michel Troisgros, a laughing little bearded Bacchus, has inherited his father's talent, not to mention that of his departed uncle Jean. When he took his place beside his father at the stove, it gave us cause to think that Troisgros's cuisine was no longer singing one song, but two—and that here and there it was hitting a false note. Michel had his own ideas, and they weren't always good ones.

We're sorry to repeat ourselves, but for modern cuisine, you're better off looking to Jean Bardet, Marc Meneau, Pierre Gagnaire, Michel Trama or Didier Clément. The Troisgros, both father and son, excel when sticking firmly to the spirit of their restaurant—they catch you and tease your tongue with deceptively everyday dishes, which are as crafty as the devil and astound you with their delicacy and intelligence. The red snapper with marrow is a miraculous and incredibly harmonious meeting of the Lyon style (Gamay sauce) and the Midi style (thyme and shallots). The Lorraine lamb has an unforgettable flavor, combining red beans and whole cloves of garlic (positively grandiose!). The pigeon in liver sauce comes with rose-shape fried potatoes resting on a fine bed of bread crumbs. The tête de veau ragoût with olives is an absolute masterpiece of everyday cooking interpreted by a great—make that superb—chef.

Consider yourself warned. There are conceptual errors, and not all the dishes deserve a 19.5, but since there are others that soar past 20/20, the overall rating is safe. And the rest counts for something, too. The sumptuous Burgundies, the unforgettable old Cognacs, the charm of the place (for now, quite beautiful), the feeling of gourmandise that floats in the air, Pierre's pleasing face and sense of humor, Michel's bursts of laughter and the Florentine looks of Olympe, smiling at her post. All of this has a single name: feast.

A la carte: 500F and up. Menus: 375F, 470F.

Troisgros

(See restaurant above)

Closed Tues. & Jan. 3 stes 800-900F. 20 rms 450-560F. TV in 21 rms. Air cond. Pets allowed.

There are a few small duplexes that have a view only of the train station but are otherwise delightful. But windows in many of the rooms open onto the famous courtyard/garden, whose charm and greenery nearly wipe out the grayness of the urban landscape dominated by warehouses. The Troisgros are crazy about contemporary style, and they serve up plenty of it, along with absolutely perfect comfort. And to start the feast early, they serve a breakfast that'll make you fall out of bed.

IN NEARBY **Coteau**
(3 km E on N 7)
42120 Le Coteau - (Loire)

(14) Auberge Costelloise

2, ave. de la Libération - 77.68.12.71

MM. Alex. Open until 9 p.m. Closed Sun., Mon., July 29-Aug. 29 & Dec. 25-Jan. 3. Air cond. Pets allowed. Cards: V.

Of course, the Auberge Costelloise isn't Troisgros (although he comes here as a friend and sends his clients), but all the same it's quite chic, with its capped facade and its modern, metallic entrance. The dining room, decorated in salmon-pink tones, is, happily, fresher and simpler than before and better suited both to the delightful reception given by the patronne and to the lively cuisine prepared by Daniel Alex, her husband. In his own way, Alex is trying to justify the large sign erected at the entrance of the town: "Roanne, the capital of contemporary cuisine." Despite a few errors, his creativity is generous, and ultimately, everything is good, especially the minute of sea bass and salmon with chervil, the warm foie gras with an onion preserve (a subtle sweet-and-sour blend that reminds us of some happy irreverences of English cuisine), the tasty tourte of sweetbreads in a morel sauce and the good desserts, both warm and cold. The wine cellar is well composed, especially in its selection of white wines. Prices are reasonable.

A la carte: 230F. Menus: 95F (weekdays only), 160F, 190F, 260F.

La Roche-Bernard

56130 La Roche-Bernard - (Morbihan)
Paris 441 - Vannes 41 - La Baule 31 - St-Nazaire 35

(16) Auberge Bretonne

2, pl. Du Guesclin - 99.90.60.28

M. Thorel. Open until 9 p.m. Closed Fri. lunch, Thurs. & Nov. 15-Dec. 15. Pets allowed. Hotel: 5 rms 180-250F. Cards: V, MC.

The Auberge Bretonne is not located in the most pleasant district of this attractive little port on the banks of the Vilaine, nor is it the most elegant restaurant in Brittany, with its large, rustic dining room, multicolored tiles, artificial stones and false wooden beams. So how can one explain the necessity of making reservations several days in advance? And by what miracle does this Breton decor become so warm and hospitable as soon as one sits down at a table? Perhaps it is simply the lovely presence of the sincere, attentive Solange Thorel and her crew of friendly, efficient, unpretentious young waiters, who take care to explain all the dishes. But no—the real reason is that here we are certain to discover one of the most brilliant cuisines in all of Brittany, prepared by 34-year-old Jacques Thorel, who suddenly is exalted by the critics (for once, unanimously—except for the Michelin guide, which graciously granted him two forks!) as the latest national revelation. The meals we had here in the restaurant's earlier days were sophisticated and superbly refined, yet without affectation. On a more recent visit, we discovered that the cuisine of this former cook at Ricordeau, Boyer, Taillevent and Robuchon is even more enthralling: Now it's stripped to the essentials, as faithful as possible to the products and showing a rare concern for finishing touches and fresh flavors. The system of fixed-price menus has not changed (there is no à la carte menu)—they are still as numerous, cleverly varied and incredibly generous as ever, from the most modest to the largest.

Our last meal nearly warranted three toques: exquisite small appetizer tarts (mackerel, langoustines and asparagus), a filet of red mullet seasoned with coriander and served with a small watercress salad (crisp, warm and flavorful), a "cultivateur" of lobster (a marvelous country soup of vegetables and lobster), an estouffade of turbot served with fish juice, enhanced with spices and slightly sweetened with carrots, perfect cheeses and a whole string of desserts ("Solange's Delights"), all equally delicate, particularly the wonderful caramelized cream of oats, which has an irresistible praline flavor. The exceptional wine cellar holds 15,000 bottles and 800 labels; it includes all the famous vintages from excellent years, as well as many local winegrowers' bottles for less than 100 francs. And the several new, spacious, well-equipped rooms allow you to prolong your pleasure.

Menus: 130F (weekday lunch only), 160F (weekdays only), 180F to 300F.

11/20 Auberge des Deux Magots

1, pl. du Bouffay - 99.90.60.75, 99.90.68.13

M. Morice. Open until 9:30 p.m. Closed Sun. dinner & Mon. (off-seas.) & Dec. 6-Jan. 15. No pets. Hotel: 15 rms 200-400F. Cards: V.

This decent, hospitable little Breton bistro still offers its lovely fixed-price menus. For 110 francs you'll be served fresh langoustines, hake in beurre blanc, grilled beef, cheeses and dessert. Local wines are served for about 40 francs.

A la carte: 230F. Menus: 50F (weekdays only), 75F, 120F, 180F.

Rochefort

17300 Rochefort - (Charente-Maritime)
Paris 465 - La Rochelle 30 - Saintes 37 - Royan 40

IN NEARBY **Soubise**
(8.5 km SW on D 733 & D 258 E)
17780 Soubise - (Charente-Maritime)

(14) Le Soubise

62, rue de la République - 46.84.93.36, 46.84.92.16

MM. Benoit. Open until 9 p.m. Closed Sun. dinner, Mon. (except July-Aug.), Jan. 15-31 & Oct. Air cond. Pets allowed. Parking. Telex 791171. Cards: V, AE, DC, MC.

The false beams painted on the facade give Le Soubise a somewhat kitschy look, but in the back, there is a lovely parking lot filled with flowers. Entering through the bistro, you literally fall into the waiting arms of the warm and hospitable René Benoit, a sweet, affable man who seats you immediately in his rustic dining room (it's not even old-fashioned anymore) and proceeds to prepare you for the truly delicious dishes that Lilyane, his wife, is busy cooking for you. For years, the program has remained much the same, but that's no reason not to tell you about it. The best dishes are devoted to seafood, which we chose at our last visit (as Benoit wisely says, "It would be stupid to come here to eat anything else"). Be sure to order the delicious mussels grand-mère sautéed in their own juice, the plate of warm shellfish, the blanquette of four fish, the cream of claire oysters or the éclade. The Bordeaux are handsome, and their prices are often outstanding.

A la carte: 320-350F. Menu: 140F.

Le Soubise

(See restaurant above)

Closed Sun. & Mon. (except July-Aug.), Jan. 1-15 & Oct. 1 ste 280F. 23 rms 135-270F. Half-board 300-360F. Pets allowed.

Le Soubise's modern rooms, located in the annex, are spacious and well equipped. There's a lovely garden, and all the serenity one finds in the Saintonges countryside.

Rochegude

see Orange

La Roche-l'Abeille

87800 Nexon - (Haute-Vienne)
Paris 412 - Limoges 31 - St-Yrieix 10 - Brive 72

(16) Moulin de la Gorce

2 km S on D 17 - 55.00.70.66

M. Bertranet. Open until 9 p.m. Closed Sun. dinner & Mon. (off-seas.) & Jan. 2-31. Garden dining. Pets allowed. Garage parking. Cards: V, AE, DC.

The hermit certainly chose the right hermitage: an adorable sixteenth-century mill that deserves an award for its charm, lost as it is in nature on the banks of a large, romantic pond. It's here Jean Bertranet retired after delighting Limoges's diners for more than twenty years. The sighs of the waterfall, the flight of the ducks overhead, the shade provided by the ash trees, the early evenings on the terrace—everything here is enchanting. The decor inside may be a bit much, but it's quite enjoyable to sit at one of the round tables in the dining room, where Mme. Bertranet greets her clients as if they were old friends—which most of them are, for the residents of nearby Limoges have made the Moulin de la Gorce their obligatory gourmet stop for many years.

Bertranet, who worked at the Elysée Palace under the presidency of Vincent Auriol, has abandoned the clichés of traiteur-style cuisine; he and Yves, his young son-in-law, delight their clientele with lovely dishes of well-defined flavors, executed with an impeccable technique. The general tone is rather classical, but the preparations are personal, and no dish will leave you indifferent. The sauces in particular are exquisite, and following a wonderful terrine of duck foie gras, one's pleasure continues with a sea bass served with tiny, crisp chanterelles; a filet of John Dory cooked in a light crust and served in a smooth sauce flavored with mustard seeds; a tender and juicy filet of Limousin beef with crushed pepper; and a young rabbit stuffed with its own liver (perhaps even overstuffed, but then the stuffing is so good) and garnished with fresh pasta and small diced vegetables.

Bertranet has not forgotten that he was the best pâtissier in his town; and you'll agree once you've tasted his marvelous chocolate-and-raisin truffé, his orange meringue and his morello-cherry ice cream (though we wish the latter would have more vanilla flavor).

The wine cellar is rich, the coffees are varied and well prepared, and the checks are reasonable. Everything, it seems, contributes to one's happiness—a happiness that would be complete if Bertranet would offer his versions of the local recipes, instead of staying clear of them. Indeed, wouldn't the Moulin de la Gorce be the ideal place to discover regional cuisine? Nevertheless, we'll move it up a point.

A la carte: 300-450F. Menus: 160F, 250F, 320F, 400F.

Moulin de la Gorce

(See restaurant above)

Closed Sun. & Mon. (off-seas.) & Jan. 9 rms 250-450F. Half-board 550-800F oblig. in seas. TV. Pets allowed.

Located between a pond and a trout stream, Moulin de la Gorce consists of nine rooms that are comfortable and wonderfully quiet, even if their antique decor is a bit forced. These rooms allow you to fully savor the charm of the Limousin countryside from the midst of a twelve-acre wooded park. There is a fishing pond nearby; tennis courts and a swimming pool are ten minutes away; and Pompadour's equestrian center is 30 minutes away.

La Rochelle

17000 La Rochelle - (Charente-Maritime)
Paris 475 - Nantes 146 - Bordeaux 188 - Angoulême 128

Sights. The Old Wharf (guarded by the famous towers of Saint-Nicolas and La Chaîne); Muséum d'Histoire Naturelle (one of the most beautiful in France); Musée Océanographique (port of the Minimes—sea mammals, shellfish); Musée des Automates (Automation); Musée du Nouveau-Monde (the New World); the fish market (go at 6 a.m. for the fish auction); an interesting and well-narrated excursion aboard the "histo-bus" sponsored by the Convention and Visitors Bureau (25 francs for one hour); the "Grand Pavois" (in mid-September, the best European boat show on the wharf); the Festival of Cinema (end of June to beginning of July, the Cannes Festival for true cinema fans); Francofolies (before July 14, Bastille Day, festival of francophile songs).

Eating on the Run. Café de la Poste, 1, pl. de l'Hôtel-de-Ville (in the midst of the pedestrian center); Le Coquelicot, 2, rue du Collège (music, cuisine from the Dauphiné); Le Riva, allées du Mail (pizzeria, faces the ocean).

Bars & Cafés. Le Crystal, pl. de la Chaîne (piano bar, serves ice cream and cocktails); La Grand'Rive, 24, quai Duperré (the port is at your feet); Le Mail, 16, allées du Mail (recommended for the evening, also a snack bar); Le Piano Pub, 12, cour du Temple (beer and jazz, open until 3 a.m.).

Nightlife. La Cotte de Mailles, rue Admyrault (thirteenth-century cellar, quiet); L'Oxford, plage de la Concurrence (comfortable, disco, all ages).

Les Brises 

Chemin de la Digue-Richelieu
46.43.89.37

Open year-round. 2 stes 650F. 46 rms 215-430F. Pets allowed. Cards: V.

This serene hotel is remarkably well maintained; its pleasant terrace has a lovely view of the islands of Ré, Aix and Oléron. No restaurant.

Le Champlain

20, rue Rambaud - 46.41.23.99

Closed Nov. 15-March 4. 4 stes 450F. 33 rms 260-340F. TV. Garage parking. Telex 790717. Cards: V, AE, DC, MC.

This ancient townhouse located in the heart of La Rochelle has comfortable rooms with lovely furniture and a pleasant flower garden. No restaurant.

16 Richard Coutanceau

Pl. de la Concurrence - 46.41.48.19

M. Coutanceau. Open until 9:30 p.m. Closed Mon. dinner & Sun. Air cond. Pets allowed. Parking. Cards: V, AE, DC.

Having settled on the Plage de la Concurrence ("Competition Beach") just outside La Rochelle five years ago, Richard Coutanceau has established himself as a modern, eclectic and original cook who is very good when it comes to purchasing his products and keeping his imagination alive. In short, he is the best cook in La Rochelle. Perhaps he's been told this too often, or perhaps he discovered it by himself—at any rate, Coutanceau has become more and more convinced of his superiority, it seems, and his checks proclaim it. But their steepness is justified: The blue and rose dining room, opening out onto the sea and the port entrance, is luxurious, the service, supervised by a patronne who knows her business, is that of a grand house, and the china is quite stylish. But people don't come here to admire the plates—they come to eat what's on them. Fortunately, the food doesn't disappoint. We especially liked the turbot and periwinkles in a curry cream (the turbot was thick, perfectly poached and served in a creamy sauce flavored with just the right touch of curry), the delicate gratin of frogs' legs with mushrooms, and the almost perfect sea bass (just a touch overcooked) served with small fried vegetables. But we can't say the same about the salad of langoustines and sole goujonnettes: The langoustines were not firm enough, and the sole was quite bland. Nor did we much care for the slices of foie gras, whose flavor doesn't blend well with that of seafood, even if Coutanceau is not the only chef who presents this mélange. The desserts are as admirable as always, particularly the wonderful feuilleté of pears caramelized in the oven. To sum up, since he came here in 1984, Coutanceau has overcome his initial hesitancy remarkably well, and the fully merited additional point should send him well along the path to glory.

A la carte: 350F. Menus: 170F, 340F.

François Ier

13, rue Bazoges - 46.41.28.46

Open year-round. 38 rms 130-260F. TV in 20 rms. No pets. Parking. Cards: V.

François Ier's fairly large rooms (some of them are quite attractive) are located inside a building of noble aspect in superb Old La Rochelle. No restaurant.

(14) La Marmite

14, rue St-Jean-du-Pérot - 46.41.17.03

M. Marzin. Open until 10 p.m. Closed Wed. & Jan. 15-31. Pets allowed. Cards: V, AE, DC, MC.

The tasty, substantial bourgeois feasts so enjoyed by the residents of La Rochelle take place without a hitch in the stylish Marmite. Everything is perfectly organized under the owner's watchful eye: in the tidy, not too personalized dining room, where the service is discreet and outstanding, as well as in the kitchen, where Louis Marzin, a remarkable professional, demands perfect execution of his dishes. And everything is truly wonderful, even if the quality of execution and the richness of the products often seem more important than the creativity. Sample the sole goujonnettes with morels, the filet of sea bass with truffles, the lobster in Sauternes and the marguerite of salmon and langoustines with grains of caviar (unnecessary) and lime.

A la carte: 300F. Menus: 150F, 230F, 330F.

(13) Le Richelieu

22, rue Gargoulleau - 46.41.34.66

Mme. Jouineau. Open until 10 p.m. Closed Sun. Terrace dining. Pets allowed. Garage parking. Telex 790717. Cards: V, AE, DC, MC.

These elegant dining rooms, remarkably well located in downtown La Rochelle, are also well isolated from the street noises by a charming inner garden. Everything is muted, luxurious and of large dimensions (both tables and spaces). The cuisine is good, though during our last visits we found the standard slightly lower than in previous years. The chiffonnade of ray wing in sweet-pepper vinaigrette is a fresh appetizer, though its sauce is a bit heavy; the sea bass with fennel hearts is generous and well cooked, but too salty; and the galette Charentaise with a Pineau cream and vanilla ice cream is not exactly overwhelming. Handsome wine cellar. The service is correct, but nothing more.

A la carte: 230-260F. Menus: 115F (weekdays only), 155F.

IN NEARBY **Aytré**
(5 km S on D 937)
17440 Aytré - (Charente-Maritime)

(14) La Maison des Mouettes

Rte. de la Plage - 46.44.29.12

M. Pouget. Open until 9 p.m. Closed Mon. (except holidays & July-Aug.), Feb. & Oct. 1-15. Terrace dining. Pets allowed. Parking. Cards: V, AE, MC.

A comfortable terrace just above the Aytré beach complements La Maison des Mouettes's large, rustic dining room. Owner Jacques Pouget is attentive to products and final touches, as evidenced by the artistic presentation of his warm salad of crayfish and cockles from the Ile de Ré, the precisely poached sole served with a shellfish sabayon and the imaginative grenadin of veal with roast goat cheese and fresh pasta. The menus are judiciously composed; choose one of the local wines from the Vendée, whose prices are much more moderate than those of the bottles on the handsome wine list.

A la carte: 300F. Menus: 110F, 170F, 320F.

La Roche-sur-Foron

74800 La Roche-sur-Foron - (Haute-Savoie)
Paris 565 - Annecy 30 - Geneva 25 - Bonneville 8

(14) Le Marie Jean

Amancy-Vozerier (2.5 km E)
50.03.33.30

M. Signoud. Open until 9:30 p.m. Closed Sun. dinner, Mon., 3 weeks in Aug., 1 week in Feb. and Dec. 25. Cards: V, AE, DC.

You won't easily forget Jean-Pierre Signoud, even if he's not so easy to find out in this countryside near the Swiss border. His flower-bedecked house is attractive, and the patronne is shy but hospitable. This meticulous cook uses lovely products to prepare his crayfish salad "sans manière," steamed filet of turbot, farm pigeons, superb game and delicious gratin of fruit in season (though his desserts don't have the same élan as the rest). Fine selection of Savoie wines.

A la carte: 280F. Menus: 120F, 145F, 180F, 200F.

Rodez

12000 Rodez - (Aveyron)
Paris 608 - Brive-la-Gaillarde 156 - Albi 78 - Aurillac 96

(13) Hostellerie de Fontanges

3 km N on rte. de Conques - 65.42.20.28

M. Charrié. Open daily until 10 p.m. Terrace dining. Pets allowed. Parking. Telex 521142. Cards: V, AE, DC, MC.

The decor and the à la carte menu are intended to impress. The former—Louis XIIIth-style—is a touch solemn; the latter—early modern cuisine—is pompous, but it should be more rigorously executed: The shellfish salad is plain, the émincé of lamb with its kidneys served atop a bed of cèpes is delicious but poorly presented, and the pear charlotte is good. The atmosphere is inviting within the thick old walls surrounded with lush greenery, and service is efficient and relaxed.

A la carte: 250F. Menus: 85F (weekdays only), 130F, 180F.

Hostellerie de Fontanges

(See restaurant above)

Open year-round. 4 stes 380-450F. 41 rms 250-280F. Half-board 280-380F. Pets allowed. TV. Heated pool. Tennis.

These simple yet comfortably furnished small rooms overlook either the park or the castle's courtyard. Indoor swimming pool. Reasonable rates.

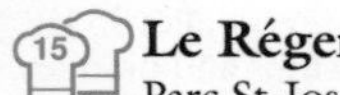

Le Régent

Parc St-Joseph, rte. de Rignac
65.67.03.30

M. Ferrié. Open until 10 p.m. Closed Jan. 4-Feb. 28. Garden dining. Pets allowed. Hotel: 2 stes 400-450F; 18 rms 290-400F. Parking. Cards: V, AE, DC, MC.

A former neighbor of Sacred-Heart church, Jean-François Ferrié didn't move too far away from God when he came to this former bishops' residence in a fourteen-acre park. The attractive tables, old wooden beams and windows opening onto a green panorama form a splendid and sober setting, one that is worthy of the ambitions of this whimsical cook. Imaginative and prepared with the best market products, Ferrié's cuisine is as free as air. It fully deserves a second toque, especially for the tasty sautéed sander served atop a salad of oak leaves and mint, the gilthead with spinach flavored with an exquisite orange sauce, the sweetbreads sautéed in a foie gras sauce and the best apricot feuilleté in the world. Exceptional wine cellar and cordial reception by Simone Ferrié. The prices are doing better than stabilizing—they're actually going down!

A la carte: 300F. Menus: 110F (weekdays only, wine incl.), 155F, 185F, 210F.

Le Saint-Amans

12, rue de la Madeleine - 65.68.03.18

M. Amat. Open until 9:30 p.m. Closed Sun. dinner, Mon. & Feb. 1-March 28. Air cond. Pets allowed. Cards: V.

Year after year, no one has ever left this serious restaurant feeling unhappy or hungry (the fixed-price menus are models of generosity). The service is as good and attentive as the decor is comfortable and warm, and Jacques Amat's long à la carte menu cleverly covers a wide range of prices. Sample the hot consommé of young vegetables and foie gras, the salmon in shellfish juice, the lamb shank with plums and the breast of duck. Excellent cheeses and judicious small wine cellar.

A la carte: 180-230F. Menus: 100F, 190F.

Roissy-en-France

see PARIS SUBURBS

Rolleboise

78270 Bonnières-sur-Seine - (Yvelines)
Paris 70 - Versailles 53 - Evreux 37 - Mantes 9 - Vernon 15

Château de la Corniche

5, rte. de la Corniche - 30.93.21.24

Mme. Ternova & M. Bourrier. Open until 9:30 p.m. Closed Sun. dinner & Mon. (off-seas.). Terrace dining. Parking. Telex 695544. Cards: V, AE, DC, MC.

Perched atop a little hill overlooking the vast Val de Seine scenery, Château de la Corniche is a charming manor for weekend getaways (Léopold II used it as a hideaway for his amorous intrigues). The new owners have entrusted the stoves to a young chef who trained with Garcia and Boyer. Thierry Descart's rather brief à la carte menu is devoted to rich, superb produce, simple preparations, vegetables in season and honest flavors—all enhanced by a straightforward, modern execution. Sample his beautifully seasoned (and superbly presented) crayfish salad with mushrooms and string beans, delicate young vegetable feuilleté, fresh, delicious and simple John Dory with chanterelles, and semicooked foie gras with figs. The dessert we had, a sabayon with fruit in season, was a bit plain. The reception is cordial in this large, bright dining room overlooking the valley beyond a summer terrace (but the white plastic chairs are unbelievably uncomfortable).

A la carte: 400-500F. Menus: 200F (weekdays only), 350F.

Château de la Corniche

(See restaurant above)

Closed Sun. & Mon. (off-seas.). 1 ste 1,200F. 37 rms 260-600F. Heated pool. Tennis.

The terrace of this turn-of-the-century "castle" perched atop the cornice commands a wonderful view of the Seine. Its rooms are lovely, quiet and cozy.

Romainville

see PARIS SUBURBS

Romans-sur-Isère

26100 Romans-sur-Isère - (Drôme)
Paris 558 - Grenoble 83 - Valence 18 - Die 72 - Vienne 71

IN NEARBY **Granges-les-Beaumont**
(6 km W on D 532)
26600 Tain-l'Hermitage - (Drôme)

Les Cèdres

75.71.50.67

M. Boissy. Open until 9:30 p.m. Closed Tues. dinner, Wed. & Aug. 22-31. Terrace dining. Pets allowed. Parking. Pool. Cards: V, AE.

Fine tables for sunny holidays, a terrace in the shade, a swimming pool, a large white dining room with flowers, ever-present smiles and courteous attention (even on hot summer days!)—it's all there waiting for you. Perhaps the cuisine could be lighter and more delicate, but chef Jean Boissy has at least the merit of being generous. His preference runs to hearty, savory dishes: pigeon feuilleté, fowl fricassée served with young vegetables (perhaps slightly overcooked) and a creamy gratin dauphinois, cakes and a delicious peach dessert in raspberry sauce. Good, reasonably priced Hermitage and Saint-Joseph wines.

A la carte: 300F. Menus: 98F, 160F, 210F, 280F.

Romorantin

41200 Romorantin - (Loir-et-Cher)
Paris 183 - Tours 92 - Orléans 68 - Bourges 65 - Blois 41

Grand Hôtel du Lion d'Or

69, rue Georges-Clemenceau
54.76.00.28

M. Barrat. Open until 9 p.m. Closed Jan.-mid-Feb. Garden dining. Pets allowed. Parking. Telex 750990. Cards: V, AE, DC, MC.

The lion isn't sleeping. He's going at it by leaps and bounds. And now he's captured his fourth toque. But Didier Clément is not a roaring lion. This 31-year-old boy with an open face and warm smile hates noise, clamor and hoopla. He is the complete opposite of the enthroned chef who strolls among the tables to snatch up compliments. He sees himself as a craftsman, and if he is undeniably also an artist, he's not the one who will tell you so.

Marie-Christine, whose parents, Alain and Colette Barrat, own this former relais de poste, plays an enormous role in his life—not only his personal life (she's his wife), but also his professional life. This young woman, so sweet, so delicate, so communicative and "gourmande," has a passion for the history of gastronomy, which she studies all year long. Curious about old recipes and long-forgotten products, she threw herself into a treasure hunt with her husband, which has resulted in their rediscoveries of dishes that he then prepares in his own way. They come up with unprecedented seasonings, like "kitchen tobacco" (the seventeenth-century name for a mixture of mushrooms ground into a powder), which gives an incredible flavor to his noisettes of lamb pré-salé. And the canny mixture of spices that Clément has ground by the village pharmacist transforms a dish of roast langoustines into a pure masterpiece. In the garden of Dame Leloup—a truculent character who looks like she popped straight out of the Middle Ages—they gather vegetables, herbs and even flowers that we've long lost touch with. They have thus created an evocative world of odors and perfumes, a magical world that has nothing imaginary about it, since it's right there for you to enter.

The decor invites you in. Behind a banal facade plopped in the middle of a main street is a flowered courtyard, in which it's nice to have a glass of Vouvray before going into the dining room. It is an elegant and infinitely harmonious room, with seventeenth-century woodwork, a Dutch chandelier, porcelain-blue wall hangings and draperies, a rose-colored ceiling, watercolors of a sleepy countryside in stunning frames and huge bouquets of artfully arranged flowers. You can't help but feel good here, and Colette Barrat works at making you feel that way. She may seem a bit standoffish at first, but once a rapport has been established, she reveals her liveliness and sharp wit. It's hard to get her off the topic of goat cheese (the finest examples come from this region). She never falters on the wine either, particularly Loire wines, always finding just the right one to complement her son-in-law's cuisine.

Gazing at the menu, you feel like a dog ready for the hunt. But since you're ready to try *everything*, how do you fix your target? Frogs' legs à la racambole (supremely delicate wild garlic) or a pan of cèpes with grilled eel? Filet of carp with red beets in a roquette (rocket) salad or marvelous little langoustines with purplane? Fricassée of escargots and artichokes with licorice or veal brains with nasturtium? At our last meal, we opted for the zucchini flowers with hermit crabs with tourteau (hermit crabs) and an aspic of rouget de roche (variety of red snapper) with sweet pickles. Ah, the art of condiments! But wait till you hear the rest. Skate with pomme d'amour (tomatoes) and melissa, suprême de brochet with the tang of tarragon, sweet-and-sour noix de coquilles St-Jacques, bar (sea bass) with sea urchins and oranges, roast salmon wrapped in lard... By chance, Clément had just received a fish that rarely makes its way to Romorantin: omble-chevalier, a member of the salmon family. He prepared it with a purplane salad butter, and if a contest of omble-chevalier dishes were organized in Annecy or Talloires, this one would win the crown. You'll also go to pieces over the Challans duck with a vegetable confit, roast pigeon with spiced foies blonds, noisettes of lamb in a salt crust and veal chops more tender than angel fish (you hardly ever see it any more) that come with baby leeks from Dame Leloup's garden. And the desserts could have been served at the table of Catherine de Médicis or Louis XIV: caramelized pears in red wine and elderberries, an apple and quince ice cream in a clémentine (akin to tangerine) aspic, wild strawberry waffles à la confiture de lait, prune soufflé à la crème de thé and tender macaroons with almond milk and hot chocolate.

Finally, if you want to learn to love game all over again, you'll rediscover its true taste here. Every amateur fan knows that come hunting season, you hurry to the Grand Hôtel to find a saddle of hare à la crème, young roast partridge with endives, noisettes of doe with fresh huckleberries, and venison with clémentines.

You can tell there's something going on in the Loir-et-Cher region. Like Palavas-les-Flots and Landerneau, Romorantin used to make people laugh. Now it makes them hungry.

A la carte: 350-500F. Menus: 260F (weekdays only), 420F.

Grand Hôtel du Lion d'Or

(See restaurant above)

Closed Jan.-mid-Feb. 6 stes 850-1,200F. 10 rms 550-650F. TV. Pets allowed.

This former wayside stopover, still bearing traces of the Renaissance, has been renovated and embellished to a remarkable degree by the current owners, the Barrats. They have created an Italian-style inner courtyard, full of flowers, above which the rooms and apartments are arranged. And the facade has been restored to its original, early look. A pianist gives recitals in the inviting salon on Friday nights. Relais et Châteaux.

Roquebrune-Cap-Martin

06190 Roquebrune-Cap-Martin - (Alpes-Maritimes)
Paris 953 - Nice 26 - Menton 5 - Monte-Carlo 7

13 Le Grand Inquisiteur

18, rue du Château - 93.35.05.37

M. Valente. Dinner only (in seas.). Open until 10 p.m. Closed Mon., March 1-16 & Nov. 13-Dec. 25. Air cond. No pets. Cards: V.

Le Grand Inquisiteur may look like a tourist trap, but don't let that deceive you. This superb nineteenth-century shepherd's house (with vaulted ceiling) illuminated by candlelight is in fact a serious, consistent restaurant with stable prices and a brief à la carte menu that is renewed four times a year. As a matter of fact, it deserves a toque for its potatoes stuffed with fresh escargots, tasty grilled chicken à la fermière in a garlic-flavored cream and gilthead with lemon confit and fennel. Good desserts and fruit in season.

A la carte: 250F. Menus: 115F, 195F.

Vista Palace

Grande-Corniche - 93.35.01.50

Closed Nov. 1-Jan. 31. 30 stes 1,500-5,000F. 46 rms 1,000-1,400F. TV. Air cond. Heated pool. Parking. Telex 461021. Cards: V, AE, DC, MC.

Overlooking an abyss and surrounded by breathtaking scenery, the Vistaero was on the verge of collapsing when the German group Gründig took it over. Its new manager, M. Wegener, tore down almost everything in order to turn the Vista Palace (its new name) into an impressive building of almost 70 rooms, with a recreation center that features a heated pool, Turkish bath, solarium, golf-practice facility, squash, archery and hiking. Its modern architecture is a success, its inside decor less so, though it's the latest in terms of comfort. And let's not forget the five suites complete with private pools.

As for the restaurant, at the time of this writing, the management was still looking for a chef worthy of the decor.

(16) Le Vistaero

Grande-Corniche - 93.35.01.50

M. Vanis. Open until 10:30 p.m. Closed Nov. 1-Jan. 31. Air cond. No pets. Parking. Telex 461021. Cards: V, AE, DC, MC.

The biggest news of late on the Côte d'Azur was the arrival of Bruno Caironi at Le Vistaero. Formerly with Roger Vergé and more recently Alain Ducasse, this great young chef has been able here to fully demonstrate his talent for intelligent cuisine, full-flavored and gracefully scented by Mediterranean traditions. Witness the country-style roast prawns with vegetables, the cream of polenta with fried parsley, the wonderful turbot with leeks and celeriac in a simple truffle sauce and the saddle of Pauillac lamb in a casserole. François Ducroux's pastries are marvelous, the bread a sheer delight, the regional wines wisely chosen, and the service charming while thoroughly professional. As if that were not enough, the dining room enjoys a breathtaking panorama of Monaco, the residents of which—driven away by some unhappy experiments in the past—are returning in droves to dine magnificently. All is well once again at the Vistaero, which in the superbly professional hands of Karl Vanis is turning over as smoothly as the engine in a Rolls-Royce.

A la carte: 450-600F. Menu: 420F.

Roquefort-les-Pins

06330 Roquefort-les-Pins - (Alpes-Maritimes)
Paris 935 - Nice 25 - Grasse 15 - Antibes 22 - Cannes 18

(14) Auberge du Colombier

Rte. de Grasse - 93.77.10.27

MM. Wolff. Open until 10 p.m. Closed Tues. (off-seas.) & Jan. 10-Feb. 10. Garden dining. Pets allowed. Parking. Telex 461942. Cards: V, AE, DC, MC.

The Auberge du Colombier offers a vast garden with lawns and flowers, a tennis court, a swimming pool and a terrace (with tables) that commands a marvelous view of the valley and the sea. Martine and Jacques Wolff, a couple of true professionals, are better than anyone else at anticipating and satisfying the wishes of their most demanding clients. The reception and service are most cordial, the cuisine generous and fresh, and the price of the fixed menu unbeatable. Lionel Goyard, the chef, has made noticeable progress lately in his execution and presentations: salmon pancake with trout tartare, lotte navarin in a shellfish sauce and chicken à la fermière with a basil-flavored cream sauce. An array of exquisite desserts is prepared by the new pastry chef. Fine wine cellar.

A la carte: 300F and up. Menu: 135F (weekdays only), 170F.

Auberge du Colombier

(See restaurant above)

Closed Jan. 10-Feb. 10. 1 ste. 550F. 18 rms 160-520F. Half-board 310-420F oblig. in seas. Pets allowed. TV. Pool. Tennis.

Though a bit small, the rooms of the Auberge du Colombier are quite lovely, as well as perfectly equipped, and they face a park planted with a wonderful variety of trees. Excellent service. Private discotheque.

Roquemaure

30150 Roquemaure - (Gard)
Paris 671 - Avignon 16 - Orange 11 - Nîmes 45 - Alès 69

(13) Château de Cubières

Rte. d'Avignon - 66.82.89.33, 66.82.64.28

M. Wagner. Open until 9 p.m. Closed Sun. dinner, Mon. & Tues. (Feb. 20-March 20). Garden dining. Pets allowed. Parking. Cards: V.

A few readers have complained about the reception, or the lack thereof, and we have found the service to be negligent. It's a shame, because the spacious terrace at the back of this restaurant, shaded by extraordinary old trees, is an irresistible place in summer (the somber flowered wallpaper in the dining room is not nearly as charming). And the menu prepared by Philippe Wagner, though not exactly generous, is quite imaginative: crispy scorpionfish with green peppers (the filets are wrapped in a rice pancake), an interesting émincé of leg of lamb (the thin strips are discreetly breaded), good dark-chocolate fondant. The service is amiable but incompetent.

Menus: 100F, 140F, 170F.

Château de Cubières

(See restaurant above)

Open year-round. 19 rms 185-290F. Half-board 274-294F.

The magnificent old grounds are always green, and the large rooms are quite comfortable. There are two bungalows with terraces facing the garden.

Roscoff

29211 Roscoff - (Finistère)
Paris 561 - Brest 63 - Morlaix 28 - Quimper 109

Brittany

Blvd. Ste-Barbe - 98.69.70.78

Closed Nov. 10-March 15. 2 stes 470-580F. 17 rms 290-380F. Half-board 290-390F. Pool. Parking. Telex 940397. Cards: V, AE.

The rooms in this handsome building behind a seventeenth-century manor are tastefully furnished.

(13) Gulf Stream

Rue Marquise-de-Kergériou
98.69.73.19

M. Greach. Open until 9 p.m. Closed Nov. 30-March 15. No pets. Parking. Cards: V, MC.

From the wide bay windows of this large, modern restaurant, one can take in an exceptional view, past the garden and out to the ocean. The cuisine, in addition to displaying a meticulous style of presentation, is showing signs of becoming more and more conscientiously prepared, with perfect cooking times that respect the superbly fresh seafood. So we'll award a toque for the sole vinaigrette with leeks, the fried foie gras with langoustes and artichokes, the baked medallions of lotte with thyme and bay leaves and the nice feuilleté desserts.

A la carte: 300-350F. Menus: 110F, 165F, 280F.

Gulf Stream

(See restaurant above)

Closed Nov. 30-March 15. 32 rms 280-330F. Half-board 262-369F oblig. in seas. Heated pool.

Most of the rooms in this comfortable hotel, well secluded amid the trees, have views of the sea.

Les Rosiers-sur-Loire

49350 Gennes - (Maine-et-Loire)
Paris 290 - Angers 30 - La Flèche 44 - Bressuire 64

(16) Auberge Jeanne de Laval

54, rue Nationale - 41.51.80.17

Mme. Augereau. Open until 10 p.m. Closed Mon. & Jan. 8-Feb. 18. Air cond. Pets allowed. Garage parking. Cards: V, AE, DC, MC.

Bruno Beugner, who decorated Faugeron, has redone the decor of this sanctuary of Anjou charms and has installed terraces (both covered and open-air) facing the flowering interior gardens. The new look is a total success. The inn hasn't lost an ounce of its gracious atmosphere, its light or that unique seductiveness for which it is known throughout the entire Loire valley. And it is also unique in its way of being both scrupulous and subtle in perpetuating the culinary traditions of this corner of old France. Michel Augereau, like his father before him, brings clarity and freshness and inimitable flavor to the fish of the Loire: sander (like perch), pike and salmon, accentuated with an incomparable beurre blanc or fried with parsley and lemon. His products are extraordinary, his execution faultless. The only grievance we have about Augereau is that he shies away from novelty. But you won't mind that once you've tasted the delicious braised sweetbreads, the roast wild duck with pears, the rich chocolate cake with meringue and the sublime apple tart. There are some intoxicating finds in the wine cellar—as many from the Loire as from Bordeaux.

A la carte: 350-500F. Menus: 170F (weekdays only), 270F, 320F.

Jeanne de Laval Ducs d'Anjou

(See restaurant above)

Closed Mon. (off-seas.) & Jan. 8-Feb. 18. 12 rms 280-480F. Half-board 480-550F oblig. in seas.

Overlooking the village church and a flower-filled garden, these pleasant rooms are spacious, well equipped and quiet. The service is excellent, and breakfast is marvelous.

Roubaix

59100 Roubaix - (Nord)
Paris 231 - Lille 12 - Tourcoing 14 - Tournai 19

Altea Grand Hôtel

22, ave. J.-B.-Lebas - 20.73.40.00

Open year-round. 15 stes 355-410F. 77 rms 240-360F. Telex 132301. Cards: V, AE, DC, MC.

Facing the lovely Roubaix town hall, this superbly renovated modern establishment offers functional, simple rooms and excellent conference facilities, but no restaurant.

(14) Le Caribou

8, rue Mimerel - 20.70.87.08

M. Siesse. Lunch only (except dinner Fri. & Sat. until 9 p.m.). Closed Sat. & Mon. lunch & July 10-Aug. 31. No pets. Parking. Cards: V, AE.

With its vast entrance, majestic paneling and superb fireplaces, this large manse is a reflection of the bourgeois splendors of days gone by, when the textiles of Roubaix still had a certain elegance. Christian Siesse carries on as if nothing has changed: Foie gras, morels and truffles are still obligatory ornaments of his cuisine. But he is a man of experience, with a rigorous execution and a good hand with sauces. Taste the prawn salad with raspberry vinegar, the turbot with mousseline and the saddle of lamb with hazelnuts.

A la carte: 350F. Menus: 168F (lunch only), 260F.

Rouen

76000 Rouen - (Seine-Maritime)
Paris 139 - Amiens 116 - Le Havre 88 - Tours 273

Sights. Pl. du Vieux-Marché and the new Sainte Jeanne-d'Arc church (1979); rue du Gros-Horloge (animated pedestrian walkway that passes under the great clock); the cathedral (thirteenth century, Renaissance stained glass); rue St-Romain (antique dealers); L'Hôtel de Bourgtheroulde; pl. St-Maclou (the St-Maclou church, a gem of flamboyant Gothic art); L'-Abbaye Saint-Ouen; Le Secq des Tournelles (museum with 12,000 pieces of ironware); Musée de la Céramique (school); Musée des Beaux-Arts (Claude Monet); Musée Départemental (antiques from the Middle Ages and Renaissance); Le Muséum (enthnography, prehistory); Le Palais de Justice (the Courthouse).

Eating on the Run. A l'1, 5, pl. de la Cathédrale (salads); Le Caraïbe, 32, rue des Fossés-Louis-VIII (West Indian); La Chaumière, 48, rue de la République (omelets, crêpes); Dame Tartine, 52, rue St-Romain (breakfast, snacks); Le Djurdjura, 121, rue Beauvoisine (couscous, tajines); L'Etoile d'Asie, 31, pl. de la Rougemare (Thai); Le Grill de l'Hôtel de Dieppe, pl. Bernard-Tissot; La Mère Michel, 33, rue des Carmes (pizzeria); La Petite Posada, 31, rue de l'Hôpital (Spanish); La Pizza Paï, 60, rue des Carmes (inexpensive); Le Restaurant des Beaux-Arts, 34, rue Damiette (couscous); Le Tabou, 5, rue de la Maladrerie (West Indian and African specialties); Les Tripes du Père Neveu, 157, rue du Gros-Horloge.

Bars & Cafés. Le Bar des Fleurs, 36, pl. des Carmes (lively terrace in the evenings); Big Ben, 30, rue des Vergetiers (young clientele, jumping until 2 a.m.); La Brasserie Paul, 1, pl. de la Cathédrale (for a late-night beer and a lovely view); Le Dieppe 1925, pl. de la Gare (cocktails, classy-conservative clientele); Le Michel Ange, 11, rue des Boucheries-St-Ouen (good cocktails); Pub Hamilton, 26, rue St-Etienne-des-Tonneliers; Pub Yesterday, 3, rue du Moulinet.

Nightlife. Le Bateau Ivre, 17, rue des Sapins (café-theater); Le Blues, 246, rue Martainville (piano bar); La Brocherie, in St-Thomas (popular for twenty years, two restaurants); Le Gaelic, 29, rte. de Bonsecours (pub).

15 Le Beffroy

15, rue Beffroy - 35.71.55.27

Mme. L'Hernault. Open until 9 p.m. Closed Sun., Mon., Feb. school vacation & Aug. 1-24. Pets allowed. Cards: V, AE.

By strange coincidence, the two best female chefs in Normandy come from the east. The first, from this side of the Rhine, is the Alsatian Odile Engel (at Le Pavé d'Auge in Beuvron-en-Auge). And the second, from across the Rhine, is the German Dorothée L'Hernault. Each has an extraordinary understanding of her new territory and a style that is both strongly Norman and personal. Like Engel, L'Hernault began with the discovery of the great products of the region: the Routo cider, the farm cheeses, the Duclair duck, the Dampierre pigeons (perhaps the best in France) and the Jumièges apples, not to mention the dairy products, the produce and the seafood that finds its way into her kitchen on certain days. And with her good humor, her sincerity, her heart and her appetite (she makes only things she likes), L'Hernault prepares such marvels as sweetbreads salad in a gazpacho sauce with ratatouille, turbot from the Auge valley, pigeon with garlic, and cherries with caramel ice cream. Her husband provides advice on making selections from the excellent wine cellar.

A la carte: 350F. Menus: 125F (weekday lunch only), 190F.

12/20 La Cache-Ribaud

10, rue du Tambour - 35.71.04.82

Mme. Maître. Open until 9:30 p.m. Closed Sun. dinner. Pets allowed. Hotel: 10 rms 68-98F; half-board 140-180F. Cards: V, AE, DC.

Mme. Maître offers old-fashioned decor and cuisine at her charming establishment. Her cooking is always generous and fresh: good terrines, a filet of John Dory with mushrooms, ham in cider. It's all rather unexciting but well prepared.

A la carte: 220F. Menus: 55F (weekday lunch only), 120F and 175F (weekends and holidays only), 70F, 100F.

12/20 Le Havre

27, rue Verte - 35.71.46.43

M. Carbonié. Open until 9 p.m. Closed Fri. dinner, Sat., 1 week in Feb., April 1-8 & July 15-Aug. 15. No pets. Hotel: 9 rms 125-186F; half-board 215-275F. Cards: V, MC.

Thérèse Carbonié is in charge of the ovens at this cute bistro near the train station, which is frequented by Rouen gourmands who enjoy her hot oysters, Henri IV soft-boiled eggs and fish stew with sweet wine, as well as the friendliness of the place.

A la carte: 230F. Menus: 69F and 88F (weekdays only), 128F.

14 Les P'tits Parapluies

46, rue du Bourg-l'Abbé - 35.88.55.26

M. Andrieu. Open until 10 p.m. Closed Sun. & Mon. lunch, Feb. school vacation & Aug. 7-21. Pets allowed. Cards: V, AE.

The construction of some old street-level shops was the inspiration for these two small dining rooms hidden beneath beams and behind a half-timbered facade. The light salmon-pink decor, brightened with turn-of-the-century posters and big flower bouquets, is intimate and charming, with large, well-spaced tables. Inventiveness, freshness and attention to the seasons are the principal qualities of the consistently good cuisine of Marc Andrieu, formerly of Beauvilliers. On the concise and well-presented menu you will find, for example, a parsleyed terrine of lobster and sweetbreads, fried John Dory with a gâteau of chanterelles, squab stew with new vegetables and, among the sometimes-too-sweet desserts, an exceptional fondant of chocolate and morello cherries. The wine cellar is excellent and the prices reasonable.

A la carte: 300F and up. Menus: 130F (lunch only), 190F, 255F.

Pullman Albane

Rue Croix-de-Fer - 35.98.06.98

Open year-round. 4 stes 750-950F. 121 rms 420-640F. TV. Air cond. Pets allowed. Parking. Telex 180949. Cards: V, AE, DC, MC.

Located in the heart of the walking quarter of old Rouen, this hotel provides sunny, modern rooms that are well equipped. The service is limited but efficient. No restaurant.

Le Réverbère

13

5, pl. de la République - 35.07.03.14

MM. Blondeau & Rato. Open until 10 p.m. Closed Sun. & Aug. 14-27. Pets allowed. Cards: V.

Le Réverbère's excellent formula includes an appetizer, dessert and wine in the price of the main dish, which is chosen from a well-diversified menu (sautéed lamb, beef bourguignon with fresh noodles, fish stew). The price range is vast. For 190 francs, for example, you can have scrambled eggs with oysters, veal kidneys in sherry, an apple-pear feuilleté and a half bottle of young Bordeaux. Thanks to the delicate execution and attentive service, you'll almost forget the extremely simple decor.

A la carte: 100F to 300F. Menus: 139F (lunch only, wine incl.), 265F (wine incl.).

Pascal Saunier

16

12, rue du Belvédère, 76130 Mont-St-Aignan - 35.71.61.06

M. Saunier. Open until 9 p.m. Closed Sun. dinner & Mon. Air cond. Terrace dining. Pets allowed. Parking. Cards: V.

After leaving the Orée du Bois in Auzouville-sur-Saône (which ranked 14/20), the still very young Pascal Saunier recently took possession of this large 1930s building in the university neighborhood. Plessis, the decorator used by Gilles Tournadre, has come up with a decor inspired by Louis XVI, with a high ceiling that would be a bit morose without the blazing fireplace and the smile of Maryse Saunier. Also impressive are the ultra-modern pianos and the wide, curved windows and bubble curtains that open onto a lovely garden, the town of Rouen and the Seine valley beyond.

Saunier has gone from a modern, well-thought-out style to an uncomplicated yet masterful cuisine that boasts an impressive execution. The menu dégustation is testimony to this excellence from beginning to end. It begins with duck liver marinated in Muscat served with fig confit and slices of brioche, and prawn salad in a lightly creamy oyster-and-spinach vinaigrette with tarragon. Then comes John Dory court bouillon served with a Pouilly Fumé beurre blanc and exquisite baby vegetables, and a stunning celery consommé (served boiling hot, between courses, renewing the appetite much more intelligently than the usual alcohol-doused sorbets). Next, local squab with chanterelles and shredded cabbage, loin of lamb au jus flavored with truffles, and the desserts, all light and not too sweet (bavaroise, glazed nougat, millefeuille), though in need of a little more imagination. In all, this is a near-great cuisine, prepared with much love and talent and already good enough to provide competition for Warin and Tournadre. And to think that just a few years ago it took great effort to find even a good, simple bistro in Rouen!

A la carte: 350F. Menus: 125F and 195F (weekday lunch only), 265F.

Bertrand Warin

16

7-9, rue de la Pie - 35.89.26.69

MM. Warin & Liberge. Open until 10 p.m. Closed Sun. dinner, Mon., 1st week in Jan. & last 3 weeks in Aug. Pets allowed. Cards: V, AE.

Not far from the house where Corneille was born, behind a carriage entrance off the place du Vieux-Marché, this sixteenth-century structure is one of the most beautiful in the neighborhood. Opening onto an always-green garden, the dining room has high beamed ceilings, delicate paintings and Second Empire mirrors that reflect the elegant tables and luscious bouquets. Bertrand Warin is barely 30 years old, and he can already take great pride in the success of his business. But if he wants it to continue, he'll have to work hard to keep up the spark of his debut, show less indifference to the products and repertoire of the region, vary his menu more often and not replace the spirit of invention with excess (for example, turbot and lobster with caviar and salmon eggs). This is gentle advice, not meant to diminish our expression of infatuation for this beautiful cuisine (inspired, perhaps too much so, by Michel Guérard)—even if our last meal, featuring rather dull baby zucchini with chanterelles and tough Duclair duckling, left us vaguely unsatisfied. Eric Liberge's reception isn't as relaxed as it used to be, and the service sometimes lacks attentiveness.

A la carte: 400-500F. Menus: 180F (weekday lunch only), 285F.

IN NEARBY **Bonsecours**
(3 km E on N 14)
76240 Le Mesnil-Esnard - (Seine-Maritime)

Auberge de la Butte

15

69, rue de Paris - 35.80.43.11

M. Hervé. Open until 9:30 p.m. Closed Wed. & Sun. dinner, Thurs. & Aug. Garden dining. Pets allowed. Cards: V, AE, DC.

If you passed by this inn, situated between a grocery store and a gas station in a morose Rouen suburb, ten times, it probably would never cross your mind to enter. You would be like us—that is, until recently, when we discovered that this lovely old Norman restaurant, behind its 1680 facade and pinnacle, hides a treasure of charm. Its rooms have imposing low beams, wood and brick walls, fireplaces, pleasant paintings and dish collections. But you won't appreciate it fully until you've experienced the talent of the chef, who for twenty years has consistently turned out an exceptional cuisine. Pierre Hervé possesses a rare modesty and swears that he never even thought of contacting guidebooks about his existence. But when he finally gained recognition at a recent chef's competition at the age of 46, he decided to abandon his discretion. And we broke our ignorant silence. Hervé isn't an innovator but a technician and a relentless hard worker who, without leaving his kitchen, watches over and does everything, including making several kinds of marvelous little breads and exquisite pastries. The basis of his cuisine is quite classic, but it is brilliant and modern in its execution, wisely using the best local products: fricassée of lobster in a perfect coral (lobster roe) sauce and flanked by seasonal vegetables, roast saddle of young rabbit stuffed with liver and served with an exceptional Bordeaux sauce and a puff pastry with celery, veal kidneys émincé in a savory-sweet Calvados sauce. Although the desserts are not masterpieces, they are quite good, from the hot apple tart to the fondant of bitter chocolate and orange sabayon.

Like her husband, Mme. Hervé seems a little timid when she greets you, but she has a friendly smile and manner of seeing to your needs. You will, however, need plenty of francs to pay the bill (unless you have selected the one fixed-price menu), which can climb frightfully if it includes one of the excellent wines.

A la carte: 350-400F. Menu: 180F.

IN NEARBY **Tourville-la-Rivière**
(11 km S on N 5 & D 7)
76410 Cléon - (Seine-Maritime)

Le Tourville

12, rue D.-Casanova - 35.77.58.79

M. Florin. Lunch only (except dinner Fri. & Sat. until 10 p.m.). Closed Mon. & Aug. Terrace dining. Pets allowed. Parking. Cards: V.

After 67 years on this planet, 51 of which have been spent in front of the stove, Michel Florin sees himself as heir to, and perpetuator of, the great cooking traditions. His repertoire certainly doesn't hide that image, but it's all prepared in a particular style. And the style of this wise man, son of a cook for Alphonse XIII, is sincerity, love for good products, generosity and a polished technique that extends even to the most classic of dishes and sauces. In addition, this large establishment facing the church is the contradiction of so many restaurants withering away in provincial stagnancy. It's rather elegant, with a beige-and-brown decor accented by romantic lithos; the atmosphere is gay, the service playful, and the pleasantly plump Madeleine Martin as energetic as she is charming. From the poultry-liver terrines to the genuine profiteroles to the magnificent sorbets (especially the grapefruit), passing along the way the salmon (smoked there), the duck with peas, the bass with beurre blanc and the roast rack of lamb with baby lima beans, everything is delicious and far from the usual perfunctory, gloomy presentation of this style of cuisine. The wine cellar is richly furnished with good bottles for less than 100 francs. This is the best old-style restaurant in Normandy, so a second toque is well deserved.

A la carte: 280-330F.

IN NEARBY **Val-de-la-Haye**
(10 km SW on D 51)
76830 Dieppedalle-Croisset - (Seine-Maritime)

La Muserolle

15, quai Napoléon - 35.32.40.85

Mme. Lecomte. Open until 9:15 p.m. Closed Sun. dinner, Mon., Feb. school vacation & mid-July-mid-Aug. Garden dining. Pets allowed. Parking. Cards: V.

On the banks of the Seine, this marvel of an old Norman structure (1610), a former hunting waystation, has a charming beamed dining room that looks out on a peaceful garden. The reception offered by Rosemonde Lecomte is sweet, and the short menu is prepared by a solid professional: excellent muserolle terrine (pork and veal, subtly spiced), good Alsatian-style escargots cassoulet with sorrel, Norman escalope (exquisite meat with a delicate sauce) and a tarte flamande (with apples and chocolate) that is a little strange but well made. Reasonable prices.

A la carte: 200-230F. Menus: 75F (weekdays only), 125F.

Rouffach

68250 Rouffach - (Haut-Rhin)
Paris 458 - Mulhouse 28 - Colmar 15 - Guebwiller 10

Les Tommeries

89.49.63.53

MM. Traversac & Dalibert. Open until 9:15 p.m. Closed early Jan.-early March. Garden dining. Pets allowed. Parking. Cards: V.

The director of this luxurious Relais et Châteaux inn overlooking the Alsatian plain got his hands on a young chef who comes from Loiseau and Lorain via Daguin and who has taken it upon himself to transform this good place into a great place. Two recent experiences moved us to encourage him with a second toque, in spite of a médaillon of sweetbreads with lime that was a bit muddled and a rather ordinary feuilleté of red fruits. We were inspired by the exquisite vegetable terrine with watercress cream; the extraordinarily tender fresh salmon, smoked on the premises over Alsatian fruit-tree wood; the whole turbot (for two) cooked to perfection and accompanied by a forcemeat (stuffing) with chanterelles and a lemon sauce; and, finally, the rhubarb-and-strawberry crème brûlée created with subtle talent by pastry chef Pascal Garnier. The new wine steward, a post office employee–turned-oenophile, has familiarized himself perfectly with the wine cellar and its excellent representation of regional labels, including a superb '83 Tokay. The large dining room has sunny yellow tones, sturdy furniture (the green-leather chairs are more comfortable than elegant), a large tapestry that we could do without and, refreshingly, a beautiful view of the vineyards, the old city and the plain.

A la carte: 400F. Menus: 530F (wine incl.), 200F, 280F.

Château d'Isenbourg

(See restaurant above)

Closed early Jan.-early March. 2 stes 1,085-1,320F. 38 rms 590-1,075F. Half-board 615-857F. Heated pool. Tennis.

Indoors you will find large, comfortable rooms with period decor; outdoors, tennis, swimming and horseback and bicycle riding (organized trips). Relais et Châteaux.

Les Rousses

39220 Les Rousses - (Jura)
Paris 474 - Lons-le-Saunier 69 - Nyons 25 - Gex 29

Hôtel de France

323, rue Pasteur - 84.60.01.45

M. Petit. Open until 9:30 p.m. Closed June 5-30 & Nov. 13-Dec. 15. Terrace dining. Pets allowed. Hotel: 34 rms 175-300F; half-board 242-300F. Parking. Cards: V, AE, DC, MC.

The decor of this large establishment in the center of a resort is not overflowing with charm. It's actually quite modest, and you might even find it depressing if you were not enraptured by the glorious mountain view from the bay windows. Another reason you'll be happy here is the cuisine of Roger Petit. He may be an old-school chef, but he is steadfast in bringing a light touch to his repertoire: ravioli with Bresse escargots, a duo of turbot and salmon au jus with mushrooms, rare roast pigeon with chicken livers, hot apple tart with caramel sauce. The fixed-price menus are excellent.

A la carte: 300-350F. Menus: 99F, 162F, 286F.

Roussillon

84220 Gordes - (Vaucluse)
Paris 727 - Cavaillon 27 - Apt 11 - Avignon 45

(13) Mas de Garrigon

Rte. de St-Saturnin-d'Apt - 90.05.63.22

M. Rech. Open until 9 p.m. Closed Sun. dinner, Mon. & Nov. 15-Dec. 27. Terrace dining. No pets. Parking. Cards: V, AE, DC, MC.

Twice recently we heard from readers who thought we were too easy on this superb place in the northern Lubéron. They admitted that they found the environment wonderful and the dining veranda seductive, but they were disappointed in the reception, which lacked grace. And they were hoping for more from Philippe Tur's cuisine, which doesn't seem to have diminished in quality though it still isn't up to par with the prices. But you surely will have a good meal, as we did, if you order the rack of Lubéron lamb, the boned and stuffed squab and the melon soup with basil.

A la carte: 400F. Menu: 155F (wine incl.).

Mas de Garrigon

(See restaurant above)

Open year-round. 1 ste 740F. 7 rms 585-600F. Half-board 550-750F oblig. in seas. Pool.

The eight Provençal-style rooms, not large but exquisitely charming, have terraces opening onto an immense panorama. The hotel also offers an inviting lounge with a fireplace, and the superb pool is well sheltered from the mistral winds.

Royan

17200 Royan - (Charente-Maritime)
Paris 490 - Bordeaux 124 - Saintes 37 - La Rochelle 70

12/20 Le Chay

Plage Le Chay - 46.38.51.99, 46.39.97.23

M. Riedel. Open until 11 p.m. Closed Sept. 15-June 15. Terrace dining. Pets allowed.

The menu of this friendly summer restaurant is lengthy, but no one looks at it. People come here to eat lobster and more lobster, which is grilled to perfection next to some beautiful pieces of fish. The owner is a character, jovial and charismatic.

A la carte: 250F. Menu: 260F.

Family Golf Hôtel

Grande-Conche, 28, blvd. Garnier
46.05.14.66

Closed Oct. 1-Easter. 33 rms 300-350F. Parking. Cards: V.

This pleasant hotel facing the beach recently was entirely modernized. No restaurant.

(13) La Jabotière

Pontaillac - 46.39.91.29

M. Auger. Open until 11 p.m. Closed Sun. dinner & Mon. (off-seas.) & Jan. 2-March 12. Terrace dining. Pets allowed. Parking. Cards: V, AE, DC, MC.

The lovely canopied terrace on the beach is an extension of a banal, though comfortable, dining room. In the kitchen, which can be seen from the bar area, the Japanese chef, Torigaï (formerly of Moulins du Duc), is now playing the role of culinary consultant; his assistant is responsible for the ovens. A few minor errors occurred during this changeover, but without significant detriment to the cuisine, which is always light and modern: salmon with seafood ravioli, grilled red mullet with a fennel compote, roast squab with sweet garlic.

A la carte: 300F. Menus: 120F (lunch only), 140F, 195F.

Résidence de Rohan

Rte. de St-Palais (3 km), Vaux-sur-Mer
46.39.00.75

Closed Nov. 15-April 1. 41 rms 250-600F. Tennis. Parking. Cards: V, AE.

This superb hotel is isolated on shaded grounds that border the beach (direct access). The attractive rooms have English and Empire-style furnishings. No restaurant.

Résidence de Saintonge

Conche de Pontaillac, Allée des Algues
46.39.00.00

Closed Sept. 30-March 15. 5 stes 380-420F. 35 rms 200-280F. Half-board 300-320F oblig. in seas. Parking. Cards: V.

Located in the residential quarter of town 100 yards from the beach, this hotel has a friendly atmosphere and renovated rooms. Restaurant.

IN NEARBY **Breuillet**

(14 km NW on D 733 & D 14)
17920 Breuillet - (Charente-Maritime)

(14) La Grange

46.22.72.64

M. Reversade. Open until 11 p.m. Closed Sept. 4-June 28. Garden dining. Pets allowed. Parking. Cards: V.

Guests at this huge hotel complex, who keep their tanned bodies busy on the tennis courts, at the pool, on the discotheque floor and in the movie theater, wouldn't normally think of going to the restaurant (open two and a half months of the year) for a good meal. However, Luc Reversade, the shrewd owner, is an expert at tracking down good seasonal cooks, and his excellent rapport with some of the great French chefs allows him to bring some of their best students to his restaurant for the season. The latest to date, André Chenu (who trained with Boyer, Rochédy and Daguin), is no exception. Try, for example, his mussel soup with vermicelli, his court bouillon with sole and green oysters or his green cod with tomato butter. The service on the terrace, at the pool or next to the barbecue, where fish and meat are grilled over fruit-tree wood, is as refined as it is in the comfortable and bright dining room.

A la carte: 300F. Menus: 100F (lunch only), 190F.

Royat

see Clermont-Ferrand

Roye

80700 Roye - (Somme)
Paris 105 - Amiens 41 - Compiègne 38 - Péronne 29

La Flamiche

20, pl. de l'Hôtel-de-Ville
20.87.00.56

Mme. Klopp & M. Borck. Open until 9:30 p.m. Closed Sun. dinner, Mon., July 9-18 & Dec. 21-Jan. 23. Air cond. Pets allowed. Cards: V, AE, DC, MC.

One hour from Paris, on the main highway at the edge of the Nord region, this friendly restaurant facing the brick town hall is the home of pure Picardie tradition. It has the tradition of hospitality (Marie-Christine Klopp and her associate, Gérard Borck, pour on the personalized treatment for their guests) and, more and more, the tradition of a daring cuisine, prepared by a 27-year-old chef who is showing no signs of cold feet. Wilfried Travet is encouraged by the directorial team, who put at his disposal a dazzling choice of produce, farm poultry and seafood. He offers, without complexity, some of the old, the modern and the eternal in his exquisitely flavorful and fresh dishes, which show the greatest respect for those fabulous products. Travet began working here at the age of 13, before going to Paris to join Gérard Pangaud and then to the Grand Monarque in Chartres, which are his only two references. But there are other influences on the spirit and style of this cuisine: for example, that of Robert Bardot, notably in the improvisations of themes from the north, and (even more so) that of Joël Robuchon, in the concern for light sauces and accompaniments. But these influences never encroach upon the personality of this exceptional cook, who is without a doubt our youngest three-toque French chef. Aside from a minor slippage in the desserts, everything we tried here recently was worth a salute—in particular, the pot-au-feu with duck foie gras poached in a basil bouillon, poached filet of turbot with artichoke hearts in a light anise sauce, oysters in a sea urchin and Sauternes aspic, red mullet with turnips and shallots, and aiguillettes of duck with avocado (a find!). Borck, who is in charge of the impressive wine cellar, lovingly favors the proprietary vintages, but the prices are as dear as his affection for them. The service is young and attentive, in a newly soundproofed dining room enriched with lovely old furniture and hung with Japanese weavings.

A la carte: 600F. Menus: 320F (weekends and holidays only), 300F (weekdays only, wine incl.), 175F, 230F, 380F.

Le Florentin

36, rue d'Amiens - 22.87.11.05

M. Devaux. Open until 9:30 p.m. Closed Sun. dinner, Mon., Dec. 23-Jan. 4 & March 5-13. Air cond. Pets allowed. Garage parking. Cards: V, DC.

This place is as extraordinary as it is unexpected, with its neoclassic decor: marble floor, painted columns and trompe l'oeil walls. In Roye, it had to be a risk to create a place like this! We'll give one toque to a cuisine that is discreetly fashionable yet simple, fresh and carefully prepared by a young, conscientious chef, Denis Devaux: duck liver with leeks, braised turbot with rhubarb, delicious langoustines in Sauternes and a rather uninteresting glazed nougat with strawberries. Danielle Devaux's smile is a selective one—diners "passing through town" are not always the best served.

A la carte: 220F. Menus: 65F (weekdays only), 160F (weekends and holidays only), 85F, 115F.

Rungis

see PARIS SUBURBS

Les Sables-d'Olonne

85100 Les Sables-d'Olonne - (Vendée)
Paris 450 - La Rochelle 100 - La Roche-sur-Yon 35

Beau Rivage

40, promenade Georges-Clemenceau
51.32.03.01

M. Drapeau. Open until 9:15 p.m. Closed Sun. dinner & Mon. (off-seas.), Oct. 2-12 & Dec. 18-Jan. 18. Air cond. Pets allowed. Hotel: 4 stes 550F; 17 rms 175-390F; half-board 260-450F oblig. in seas. Cards: V, AE, DC, MC.

This bright restaurant looks out at multicolored buoys and windsurfing sails. It is the only good place to eat on this long ribbon of sandy coast devoted to family fun in the sun. Owner/chef Joseph Drapeau has high standards and cuts no corners: His first fixed-price menu is at an embarrassingly low price for its generous good quality. The Loire wines are perfect and inexpensive, and Drapeau applies a personality all his own to the lessons in wisdom, freshness and precision he learned while chef at Barrier. From the impressively long menu, we recommend the lobster fricassée with foie gras, the sole and salmon stew, the brill with eggplant and ginger butter, the interesting fatted chicken with filet of sole and the perfect beuchelle tourangelle (veal kidneys and morels in a cream sauce, a specialty of Tours).

A la carte: 300-400F. Menus: 145F, 190F, 230F, 390F.

Saché

37190 Azay-le-Rideau - (Indre-et-Loire)
Paris 268 - Châtellerault 60 - Chinon 26 - Tours 25

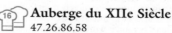

Auberge du XIIe Siècle

47.26.86.58

M. Niqueux. Open until 9:30 p.m. (10 p.m. in summer). Closed Tues. & Feb. Air cond. Garden dining. Pets allowed. Cards: V, AE, DC.

An immense Calder mobile agitates its appendages in an environment that remains fundamentally hostile to it: the heartland of France, a stone's throw from Tours, Langeais and Montbazon and alongside the château that houses the Balzac museum. Everything throbs with delicate light, and the interior garden of the four-century-old auberge is so charming in the warm season that people congregate there rather than in the gleaming, beamed dining room (which extends into a gallery and supplementary room). Maryline Niqueux is smiling and attentive, the wines are good (including a marvelous Chinon), and Jean-Louis Niqueux's cuisine is one of the best in the region. With a certain virtuosity it combines daring modernity with updated tradition: boiled egg with morels, oven-fried escalopes of lotte served with warm baby spinach in a vinaigrette with fines herbes, poached turbot in an oyster and periwinkle sauce and an exemplary beuchelle tourangelle (veal kidneys and morels in a cream sauce). The desserts (like chocolate-mint cake) are delicious but not quite on a par with the rest of the menu. Nevertheless, all of this is worth an additional point. The new wine steward, Michel Desroches, who comes from Artigny and the Grand Monarque, is a true connoisseur of Loire wines.

A la carte: 250F. Menu: 150F.

Saillagouse

66800 Saillagouse - (Pyrénées-Orientales)
Paris 1,000 - Perpignan 91 - Font-Romeu 12

Atalaya

Llo (2 km E on D 33) - 68.04.70.04

Closed Tues. (off-seas.), Mon. & Nov. 5-Dec. 20. 1 ste 470F. 9 rms 370-425F. Half-board 353-535F oblig. in seas. Parking. Golf. Cards: V, MC.

At this hotel, located at the edge of town on a small road where the houses cling to a mountainside, the reception is attentive and the rooms charming and calm. Good regional fare is served in the restaurant.

Saint-Antoine

38160 St-Marcellin - (Isère)
Paris 586 - Romans 20 - St-Marcellin 12 - Grenoble 67

(13) L'Abbaye

Rue Haute - 76.36.42.83

M. Blanc. Open until 9:30 p.m. Closed Mon. dinner, Tues. & Feb. 2-27. Terrace dining. Pets allowed. Cards: V, AE, DC.

When talking of Saint-Antoine, the guidebooks mention only the admirable medieval village with an abbey that is regarded as France's second-most-important repository of relics. But we would like to highlight once again this beautiful restaurant out of the Middle Ages, with its polished decor, antique furnishings and elegant dishes. As for the cuisine, it too is charming, flavorful and sincere, especially when it doesn't stray too far from simplicity: crayfish ravioli, filet of beef with goat cheese and chives, breast of farm chicken. There is a nice wine cellar, and a small terrace faces the church.

A la carte: 250-280F. Menus: 96F (weekdays only), 169F, 272F.

Saint-Aubin

see Montrevil-sur-Mer

Saint-Aubin-sur-Scie

see Dieppe

Saint-Aygulf

83600 Fréjus - (Var)
Paris 880 - Draguignan 33 - Ste-Maxime 14 - Fréjus 7

La Caravelle

94.81.24.03

Closed Oct. 16-March 18. 10 rms 174-362F. No pets. Cards: V.

This small, simple hotel has soundproofed rooms with lovely terraces overlooking the sea. No restaurant.

12/20 La Glycine

Pl. de la Poste - 94.81.30.23

M. Loudet. Dinner only in seas. Open until 9:30 p.m. (10:30 p.m. in summer). Closed Tues. & mid-Dec.-mid-Jan. Terrace dining. Pets allowed. Cards: V, AE, DC.

The owner, a fisherman's son and seafood expert, grills or bakes all of his locally caught fish. As is the rule in this area, the prices are substantial, but the fixed-price menu is still a good deal. You'll find a well-prepared bouillabaisse, reasonable wines and a pleasant dining room that extends out into an arbor.

A la carte: 250-350F. Menu: 90F, 200F.

Saint-Bonnet-le-Froid

43290 Montfaucon-en-Velay - (Haute-Loire)
Paris 558 - St-Etienne 59 - Annonay 26 - Tournon 53

(16) Auberge des Cimes

71.59.93.72

M. Marcon. Open until 9:30 p.m. Closed Nov. 15-April 1. Pets allowed. Parking. Cards: V, DC.

Since when has there been underground parking? Since 1987, when Régis Marcon found himself wearing two toques in his first appearance in the French-language edition of the Gault Millau guide. Ever since, he has been turning away enough people to fill up another restaurant. (In winter, when the temperature dips below freezing, he has some time to relax.) An incredible metamorphosis has arrived at this humble, once-fading village of 120 inhabitants, which straddles the departments of Ardèche and Haute-Loire. Drive around—there is virtually nothing to see except crudely constructed houses. But this sleepy town has two things going for it. The first is the miraculously beautiful surrounding countryside, an infinite stretch of prairies, forests and steep hills. The second bit of luck is that it is the home of the amazing Marcon family.

The parents gave up their struggling farm at the foot of the village without a franc in their pockets. The mother, an avid cook, decided she could use her skills to feed the local residents. The people took a liking to her cuisine, and the Marcons' bistro expanded into a little inn with rooms to rent. Régis, who saw himself as an illustrator, gave in to his mother's wishes. He was quickly hooked by the kitchen arts, and after venturing out for some experience in Lyon and in southern England, he returned to his native region to cook up a storm. This new talent in town seemed to awaken the village, which took the opportunity to start new businesses, including a combined restaurant/tea room/caterer. A second Marcon brother, the mayor of Saint-Bonnet, opened several economical chalets for tourists. And yet another brother has had great success welcoming hikers from throughout Europe to La Découverte, the hotel he converted from an old convent, from which he accompanies his guests on botanical jaunts.

Régis and his petite wife are in the midst of realizing another dream. They are transforming their lodgings for business travelers into an impressive Ardèche inn, even to the point of building some of the furniture themselves. We have compared this 31-year-old young man—in love with his region, nature and animals—to Michel Bras, whose acquaintance he finally made and whose cuisine enticed him. But be assured, Régis continues to have his own style. They are close in spirit, and even if Bras flies much higher—as much through inspiration as through technique—Régis has so many intelligent ideas and intense flavors that it would take many days, without ever slowing down, to discover all of these dishes, which you'll find nowhere else.

Try the Margaridou brochette of lamb giblets, foie gras, mountain ham and fresh morels; the slices of fatted chicken stuffed with cèpes and a sweet-and-sour marmalade of onion and Chinese artichoke; the gâteau of duck and pigs' feet in a red-wine aspic; or the tender, flavorful rabbit en croûte. And we can't forget to mention the buckwheat pancakes baked with herbs and the "couci-couça" (one slice of lamb au jus, another stuffed with thyme). And for dessert, sample the stunning pastries made with verbena, star anise, rosemary, almonds or roasted chicory, or the spice bread made incredibly moist with orange jam.

The wines (Ardèche and Côtes-du-Rhône) are delicious, inexpensive and touted by Christian, whose wine knowledge was acquired on the job. And the prices... look below and you will understand our enthusiasm.

Menus: 250-300F. Menus: 102F, 200F, 300F.

Auberge des Cimes

(See restaurant above)

Closed Nov. 15-April 1. 2 stes 350F. 7 rms 250-350F. Half-board 250-300F oblig. in seas. TV in 4 rms. Pets allowed.

At the time of this writing, the work was not quite completed, so we cannot give an exact description of the hotel, which is being entirely transformed to feature rooms and suites surrounding a patio. In addition, there will be a private room, smoking room and library, not to mention the kitchens and the dining room. It will all be done in a contemporary Ardèche style—not big on luxury but with loads of character. You can expect a superb breakfast.

La Découverte

71.59.94.42

Closed April 15-May 20 & Sept. 20-Dec. 15. 19 rms 120-250F. Pets allowed. Heated pool. Parking.

This hotel is like no other. André Marcon, brother of Régis (see Auberge des Cimes), has fixed up an ancient convent—with a splendid view of the Haute-Loire and Ardèche mountains—where he welcomes hikers and, in winter, cross-country skiers. He leads groups on treks through the forests and the high plains, and he has developed an enthusiastic and loyal French and English clientele. Restaurant.

Saint-Brieuc

22000 St-Brieuc - (Côtes-du-Nord)
Paris 445 - Brest 146 - Rennes 99 - Dinan 59 - Lorient 122

Sights. The cathedral-fortress (built at the end of the twelfth century, with an organ case that alone is worth the visit); the large pedestrian zone in the center of town and the restored historic quarter (the fifteenth-century Saint-Brieuc oratory and Saint-Brieuc fountain); the new prefecture in the garden facing the cathedral (see the St-Esprit tower); Basilique Notre-Dame-d'Espérance (monumental pulpit and nineteenth-century stained-glass windows); behind the Halles, handsome houses with corbeled construction; the pl. au Lin and the rue Fardel (with the house of the "dukes of Bretagne" and interesting sculptures); Vallée Gouédic, a calm, green section in the heart of the city.

Eating on the Run. La Couscousserie, 4, rue Gouët; Les Druides, 1 bis, rue des Trois-Frères-Le Goff (crêpes); Gargamelle, 7, rue Maréchal-Foch (small fixed-price menus, regional foods); Le Madure, 14, rue Quinquaine (grilled meats, open late, rustic setting); Mille Tartes, 4, rue de Bourg-Vasé (savory tarts); Le Porche, 9, rue St-Guillaume (crêpes, pleasant atmosphere); La Proue, 7, rue Fardel (delicious pizzas cooked over wood); Les Ribaudes, 1, pl. au Lin (good pizzas in a lovely fifteenth-century atmosphere); Le Sympatic, 9, blvd. Carnot (good grilled meats, open late).

Bars & Cafés. La Cigale, 2, pl. Blais-Bizoin (student clientele); L'Edwards, 21, rue Pierre-Le Gorrec (pretty decor, friendly); Le Melody Pub, 28, rue Jules-Ferry (nightclub, jazz evenings).

13 L'Amadeus

22, rue du Gouet - 96.33.92.44

M. Malotaux. Open until 9:30 p.m. Closed Sun. dinner & Mon. Pets allowed. Cards: V, AE.

This pleasant restaurant with a smiling hostess has tempting fixed-price menus that change every two weeks and a short, seasonal à la carte menu. For 110 francs you'll get salmon in a cockle stock, filet of duck breast with fruit, hot toast with fourme d'Ambert (a firm blue cheese) and pear gratin with almonds. Good Loire wines.

A la carte: 250F. Menus: 75F, 110F, 170F, 200F.

Le Griffon

Rue de Guernesey - 96.94.57.62

Closed Dec. 24-Jan. 8. 3 stes 345F. 42 rms 235-305F. Pool. Tennis. Garage parking. Telex 950701. Cards: V, AE, DC.

The rooms in this hotel at the edge of Saint-Brieuc are bright and spacious but without much character; the covered pool is lovely. Restaurant.

(14) Le Quatre Saisons

61, chemin des Courses - 96.33.20.38

M. Faucon. Open until 9:30 p.m. Closed Sun. dinner, Mon., Feb. 6-26 & Aug. 21-Sept. 30. Garden dining. Pets allowed. Cards: V.

In the old days, horse races were held on the beach at Cesson. Four years ago, the Restaurant des Courses (Restaurant of the Races) was completely transformed (and renamed) by its owner, Patrick Faucon. This former maître d'hôtel at Le Divellec has taken full advantage of his woodsy location, adding a ravishing, modern decor with stone walls and a lath ceiling. This new dining room looks out on a garden courtyard where meals are served on sunny days. At first helped out by a good chef, he now heads the kitchen himself, serving a true chef's cuisine: modern, light and well thought out, with inventive appetizers and delicate sauces. Fish from the Saint-Brieuc bay and local vegetables are the main attractions: mussel quenelles with a tomato purée, hot oysters in a cauliflower-mousseline sauce, hot bitter-chocolate soufflé and nice wines. You will be welcomed by the cheery Christiane Faucon.

A la carte: 300F. Menus: 120F, 160F, 220F.

IN NEARBY **Plérin-sous-la-Tour**

(3 km NE on D 24)

22190 Plérin - (Côtes-du-Nord)

---

(16) La Vielle Tour

75, rue de la Tour (Port de St-Brieuc, Le Légué) - 96.33.10.30

M. Hellio. Open until 9 p.m. Closed Sat. lunch, Sun., June 20-July 4 & Dec. 23-Jan. 5. Pets allowed. Parking. Cards: V, AE, DC.

After you walk up to the second floor, to the elegant dining room where the blue carpet complements to the salmon-lacquered walls, your attention will be stolen by the grandiose view of the Saint-Brieuc bay. Everything here is light, fresh and delicate—starting with the stunning cuisine of young, mustachioed Michel Hellio, who pays endless homage to the ocean and to the Breton region (fabulous vegetables) with his spirited inventiveness. This former student of England's Roux brothers likes only what is fresh, rare and good. The most beautiful fish from the Légué arrive in the kitchen still wriggling. Bread comes hot from the oven morning and night. And the exquisite ice creams are made to order. As for the menu, it changes nearly every week but always manages to include dishes that are balanced, appetizing and reasonably priced, like the cod with an onion-and-cabbage compote, the quail wings with salmon, the gilthead with carrots and fennel, the roast lobster with tarragon and the boned pigeon with a potato purée.

A la carte: 260-280F. Menus: 110F (weekdays only), 160F, 280F.

Saint-Cast

22380 St-Cast - (Côtes-du-Nord)

Paris 394 - Fougères 99 - St-Malo 34 - Dinan 33

12/20 Ar-Vro

10, blvd. de la Plage (2 km SE), La Garde 96.41.85.01

M. Levayer. Open until 9 p.m. Closed Sept. 4-June 4. Pets allowed. Parking. Cards: V, AE, DC, MC.

The terrace of this sprawling old Anglo-Norman chalet overlooks the beach and its bathing huts. A combination of English tourists and Brittany fanatics vacation here, where the prices are serious and the cuisine unchanging: John Dory pâté, foie gras, kidneys in mustard...

A la carte: 280F. Menus: 160F (weekends only), 170F (weekends and holidays only), 280F.

Ar-Vro

(See restaurant above)

Closed Sept. 4-June 4. 47 rms 240-400F. Half-board 360-390F oblig. in seas.

This vast, half-timbered villa is situated in the calm of the pines, right at the edge of the beach. Seven of the rooms overlook the ocean, and the service is good.

12/20 Hôtel des Dunes

Rue Primauguet - 96.41.80.31

MM. Féret. Open until 9 p.m. Closed Sun. dinner & Mon. (Oct.) & Nov. 13-March 18. No pets. Hotel: 2 stes 325-350F; 27 rms 120-240F; half-board 250-280F oblig. in seas. Tennis. Parking. Cards: V.

This hostelry at the beach far from worldly worries. The decor is bright and pleasantly modernized, and the cuisine is without pretension, generously distributed among a multitude of fixed-price menus (seafood, lotte braised with garlic, grilled lobster). The desserts are consistently good.

A la carte: 250F. Menus: 90F and 115F (weekdays only), 130F (weekends and holidays only), 195F, 285F.

Saint-Céré

46400 St-Céré - (Lot)

Paris 521 - Cahors 76 - Tulle 58 - Figeac 45 - Brive 54

---

(13) Le Coq Arlequin

1, blvd. du Dr-Roux - 65.38.02.13

M. Bizat. Open until 9 p.m. Closed Jan. 1-March 1. Garden dining. No pets. Garage parking. Hotel: 30 rms 150-350F; half-board 250-300F oblig. in seas. TV in 15 rms. Pool. Tennis. Pets allowed. Cards: V.

Five generations of Bizats have brought a true family ambience to this cheerful old hotel. The hosts will take you by the hand to show you the surroundings, give you cooking lessons and seat you, when the weather is right, at the pool, where you'll eat delicious grilled meats, pork with prunes, foie gras, truffles and confits. Eric, the youngest, prepares all these good things with a commendable spirit of freshness and simplicity. The wine cellar has some marvelous bottles from Cahors.

A la carte: 250F. Menus: 80F, 100F, 150F, 200F.

(13) France

Ave. F.-de-Maynard - 65.38.02.16

M. Lherm. Open until 9 p.m. Closed Sat. lunch & Sun. dinner (off-seas.) & Feb. & Christmas school vacations. Garden dining. Pets allowed. Hotel: 1 ste 350F; 22 rms 200-330F. Heated pool. Parking. Cards: V.

A student of Bocuse, Manière and Daguin, Patrick Lherm is also faithful to Quercy. So his cuisine is a delicious meeting of regional traditions and modern freedom. In the charming garden of his private home, you will taste smoked salmon with blinis and cream, terrine of duck foie gras cooked just until pink and breast of duck in honey and sherry. The Cahors wines are lovely, and there is an alluring pool to keep you there a little longer.

A la carte: 250F. Menus: 75F (weekdays only), 95F, 125F, 165F.

Saint-Clément-des-Baleins

see Ré (Ile de)

Saint-Cloud

see PARIS SUBURBS

Saint-Côme

30870 Clarensac - (Gard)
Paris 734 - Nîmes 15 - Sommières 16 - Lunel 24

(14) La Vaunage

66.81.33.29

M. Villenueva. Open until 9:30 p.m. Closed Mon., Tues., March 1-18 & Sept. 1-18. Terrace dining. No pets. Cards: V.

This venerable priory dating from the Middle Ages is a most exceptional place, thanks to the friendly host/chef, Guy Villenueva. His attractive summer patio facing an old loggia and the exemplary quality and vivacity of his cuisine, which is priced so reasonably, attracts all the gourmands in the Gard region. They come for the fresh cod with garlic cream, the scorpionfish with a light mustard cream and presented with cucumber "scales," the saddle of rabbit stuffed with its giblets in thyme butter and the superb glazed nougat with an apricot purée. A little effort to fill out the wine list, and everything will be perfect.

A la carte: 200F.

Saint-Cyprien

66750 St-Cyprien - (Pyrénées-Orientales)
Paris 920 - Perpignan 15 - Port-Vendres 20 - Céret 33

(13) Le Mas d'Huston

Golf de St-Cyprien - 68.21.01.71

M. Socquet. Open until 10 p.m. Closed Jan. 30-Feb. 24 & Nov. 27-Dec. 15. Air cond. Terrace dining. No pets. Parking. Telex 500834. Cards: V, AE, DC, MC.

This is the restaurant, unsurpassed in opulence, of the large Saint-Cyprien golf resort, with its eighteen holes, two pools, four tennis courts and morale-heightening cuisine. In the style of Michel Guérard, of whom the chef was a student in Asnières and in Eugénie-les-Bains, the dishes are both fresh and light: warm sweetbreads and lobster salad, filet of brill, fricassée of sweetbreads and chicken with wild mushrooms. The desserts are carefully prepared, and the small wine cellar offers numerous good bottles for less than 100 francs.

A la carte: 260-280F. Menus: 130F, 185F.

Le Mas d'Huston

(See restaurant above)

Closed Jan. 30-Feb. 24 & Nov. 27-Dec. 15. 50 rms 280-630F. Half-board 310-545F. Pool. Tennis. Golf.

Perfect for a luxuriously sporty and relaxing vacation, this resort has attractive though slightly noisy rooms, as well as a variety of shops.

Saint-Denis

see PARIS SUBURBS

Saint-Didier

see Carpentras

Saint-Didier-en-Velay

43140 St-Didier-en-Velay - (Haute-Loire)
Paris 544 - Annonay 48 - Le Puy 58 - St-Etienne 25

(13) Auberge du Velay

17, Grand-Place - 71.61.01.54

M. Caseres. Open until 9 p.m. Closed Sun. dinner, Mon. & Jan. 2-22. Pets allowed. Hotel: 6 rms 70-160F. Cards: V, AE.

Facing the fountain on the cobblestone square of this charming village, Auberge de Velay has an aging facade, but its country decor is most welcoming in its simplicity (beams, old wood paneling, tables with flowers). The young hostess is all smiles, and her husband, Jean-Luc Caseres, creates a cuisine with some small faults—it's not particularly light or clever—but also with good qualities: frankness, generosity and the flavor of fresh regional products, the latter quality is reflected in his salade gourmande with smoked bacon and frogs' legs, his hot chicken pâté (actually, a flavorful quenelle) and his feuilleté of lotte (though the fish is overcooked). He always offers a few variations on Velay lentils and a good homemade whole-grain bread.

A la carte: 250F. Menus: 78F (lunch only), 98F, 149F, 220F, 260F.

Saint-Emilion

33330 St-Emilion - (Gironde)
Paris 549 - Bordeaux 38 - Libourne 7 - Bergerac 56

(13) Hostellerie de Plaisance

Pl. du Clocher - 57.24.72.32

M. Quilain. Open daily until 9:15 p.m. Closed Jan. 2-31. Pets allowed. Parking. Cards: V, AE, DC, MC.

This former monastery overlooking the town's old roofs has been converted into an elegant hostelry for both business people and tourists. Accompanied by the excellent wines of Saint-Emilion, the generous fixed-price menus include such dishes as a salad of roasted lobster, turbot with mustard and boeuf mignon bordelaise.

Menus: 100F (weekdays only), 162F, 204F.

Hostellerie de Plaisance

(See restaurant above)

Closed Jan. 2-31. 1 ste 800-1,100F. 11 rms 400-600F.

This admirable residence above a troglodytic church has immense, bright, recently renovated rooms, some of which have terraces overlooking the valley.

Saint-Epain

37800 Ste-Maure-de-Touraine - (Indre-et-Loire)
Paris 281 - Ste-Maure 9 - Azay-le-Rideau 16 - Chinon 25

14 Château de Montgoger

S of Azay-le-Rideau - 47.65.54.22

M. Debat-Cauvin. Open daily until 9 p.m. Garden dining. Pets allowed. Garage parking. Telex 752380. Cards: V, AE, DC, MC.

Expansive grounds, the still-impressive ruins from the Duke of Choiseul's château and a bucolic glade with a 600-year-old oak tree are the surroundings for this recently opened, luxurious hostelry set up in a nineteenth-century orangerie. Christel and Jacques Debat-Cauvin have passionately transformed themselves into château-keepers. Their elegant dining room, although rather interior-decoratory in taste, is nevertheless cheerful and comfortable, looking out on a summer terrace shaded by linden trees. Christel takes charge of the cuisine with the authority and imagination of an autodidact who also happened to learn a few things under Clerc and Meneau: scallop court bouillon with truffle juice, crisp baby vegetables in a light sauce, duck foie gras steamed in spinach leaves, tureen of calf's head (a dressed-up country-style dish, with a feuilletage and truffle juice), simple, good desserts and an exceptional collection of Chinon wines. The service is distinguished but insufficient.

A la carte: 300F. Menus: 160F, 185F, 280F.

Château de Montgoger

(See restaurant above)

Open year-round. 2 stes 750F. 8 rms 400-550F. Half-board oblig. in seas.

Located in idyllic calm between the towns of Loches and Chinon, these seven rooms (more to come) are large and pleasantly decorated. The atmosphere is at once refined and simple, and breakfast is superb.

Saint-Etienne

42000 St-Etienne - (Loire)
Paris 520 - Marseille 318 - Lyon 59 - Le Puy 78

Sights. The Notre-Dame quarter (the old city); pl. de l'Hôtel-de-Ville (1882); pl. du Peuple; rue de la Ville; pl. Boivin; Eglise Saint-Louis; rue Léon Nautin; rue Dormand; rue des Martyrs-de-Vingré; Le Palais des Arts, including the Musée d'Art et d'Industrie and the Musée de la Mine (mining); Musée du Vieux Saint-Etienne; Musée de l'Armée (army); Pilat park; Le Barrage de Grandjean in St-Victor-sur-Loire.

Eating on the Run. La Coquille, 3, rue du Président-Wilson; Evohé, 10, pl. Villeboeuf (wine bar); Le Globe, 8, rue du Grand-Moulin; Le Praire, 14, rue Praire (fish); Le P'tit Zinc, Centre-Deux business center.

Bars & Cafés. Les Colonnes, 17, pl. Jean-Jaurès (until 1 a.m.); Le Grillon, 48, rue Gambetta; Meyrieux, 5, rue Pierre-Bécard (pub, good cocktails); Le Piccadilly Circus, 3, pl. Neuve; La Plage, 4, rue de la Convention (young atmosphere).

Nightlife. Le Grenier du Bistrot, 13, rue des Francs-Maçons (discotheque); Whisky Club, 1, rue Marengo (grill, nightclub).

Astoria

Le Rond-Point, rue Henri-Déchaud
77.25.09.56

Open year-round. 33 rms 195-270F. Garage parking. Telex 307237. Cards: V, AE, DC, MC.

Set in a garden near the highway, this small, modern hotel offers a friendly reception and is excellent within its category. No restaurant.

19 Pierre Gagnaire

3, rue Georges Teissier
77.37.57.93

M. Gagnaire. Open until 9:45 p.m. Closed Sun., Mon., Feb. school vacation & Aug. 13-Sept. 4. Pets allowed. Cards: V, AE, DC.

It's not an easy task to be the maître d' at Gagnaire's. In the morning you're told the ingredients of the latest dish to come out of that perpetually stewing pot, the boss's brain. You learn your lesson well, and just as you're about to recite it to a customer who's dying for an explanation, *whap!*—that big magician (who never stops laughing) has already reshuffled the cards, throwing out this and keeping that, or maybe he's pulled out of his hat a dish you've never heard of before. Flying between the kitchen and the dining room, you scurry to gather up the latest news from the front. What a dance!

Though some restaurant trade unions willingly grant the designation "Creator" to anyone who wants it, even promoting the grotesque project of granting patents to recipes you can find almost anywhere, the true creators can be counted on one hand, maybe two. Gagnaire is one of them—of the first order. And he's crazy, if you think like a manager. Passionate, extremely intelligent and a real artist, he takes too many risks not to miss from time to time, but the same risks produce sensational delights. Take our last meal: It made for truly great music without a single false note and was filled with the unexpected and the exquisite. A spinach tourte with Roquefort hosted a confrontation—victorious for both sides—between girolle mushrooms and beets. Beef in aspic with fresh goat cheese came with potatoes and red beets that made for a stupefying marriage of tastes and textures. What word could possibly describe the mousseline of smoked eel and salad with hazelnut oil? *Divine.* Huge langoustines are matched with almonds and pois gourmands.

What, do you think he's just rehashing the terrible trout amandine? No, no, no. It is a sheer wonder, and all you have to do is go see for yourself.

Let's get back to our meal. Sautéed lobster with thyme, citron (lemon) and crème de fanes de carottes (carrot tops). Pure heaven. A slice of braised cod with crushed tomatoes and a fondue of baby leeks and oysters, despite its sharp and blended flavors, fell a notch below. But then we took off to the heavens like Martians with a salad of apples, grapefruit and nuts. Gagnaire's version of a Normand standard? Perhaps, but regardless, it works, leaving your mouth revived and ready to welcome, with a glass of Banyuls, an inspired dish: a salmis de colvert (wild duck) in a sauce of the juices, bitter orange, black currants and a confiture of red currants. Beside this was a boulette made of the liver and other organs.

Bear with us a bit longer and we'll get to the end. Next came cheeses from la mère Richard—that says it all—with an exquisite 1984 Côte-Rotie de Bernard Burgard and a plate of four chocolates that, sorry Gaston, force Lenôtre's pastry chef to start over from scratch. Voilà. That's it.

But for those who have never been here, we should add a few details. First, you will surely be eating something else, since the menu changes all the time. Second, nothing is more unique and alluring than this former photographer's studio transformed by Gagnaire and his pretty wife, Gabrielle, into a sort of art gallery, where they've hung modern paintings under a skylight that allows a flood of light into the room. In the large new wine cellar there is a smoking room where you can puff your Havana cigar and sip an Armagnac or Cognac that Patrick Gerbaud, an excellent sommelier, will lead you to with a sure hand. Third, you'll meet the region's intelligentsia at Gagnaire's (you may not know it, but Saint-Etienne is quite active in the arts); along with people from all over, including the local notables, who, after hesitating a bit when confronted with this unusual decor and original cuisine, are not far from dedicating a statue to their wonder boy. Fourth, you'll discover that all this doesn't come for free, but it's close. The first fixed-price menu is an amazing value... and on that happy note, we'll leave you.

A la carte: 350-600F. Menus: 195F, 315F, 445F.

Midi

19, blvd. Pasteur - 77.57.32.55

Closed Aug. 33 rms 230-290F. Garage parking. Telex 300012. Cards: V, AE, DC, MC.

This modern, functional hotel at the southern edge of the city has new, well-equipped rooms. No restaurant.

(14) Le Monte-Carlo

19 bis, cours Victor-Hugo - 77.32.43.63

M. Barcet. Open until 9:30 p.m. Closed Wed. & Aug. 30-Sept. 13. Pets allowed. Cards: V, AE, DC.

The recipients of the coveted Meilleur Ouvrier de France (literally, Best French Worker) award are not all Paganinis, and André Barcet, honored in 1986, doesn't take sufficient advantage of his diploma to send a quiver throughout Saint-Etienne. His cuisine is good and remarkably executed, but unevenly inventive and too weak on vegetables. Nevertheless, it is worth a solid toque for its impromptu, fresh salad of smoked duck and salmon, its beef tenderloin in aspic, its impeccable fish combination with beurre blanc and its delicate desserts. Although the black-and-purple Napoléon III decor isn't very cheery, it's quite comfortable. Both the reception and the service could stand some added warmth. The à la carte prices are high, but the first two fixed-price menus are more easily digestible.

A la carte: 250-300F. Menus: 185F (weekdays only, wine incl.), 115F, 165F, 230F, 255F.

(14) Le Parc Fauriel

106, cours Fauriel - 77.41.13.94

M. Cartal. Open until 9:30 p.m. Closed Sun. dinner, Mon., Jan. 10-24 & Aug. Garden dining. Pets allowed. Cards: V.

One can't eat at Pierre Gagnaire's every day, so it's good to know about this excellent place set in a calm, ritzy neighborhood. A terrace surrounded by greenery awaits you when warm weather arrives. In the terribly chic beige dining room are Louis XV chairs and lace tablecloths, and the service is exquisitely polite. Chef Jean-Paul Cartal, a former student of Bocuse, is skilled, reasonable and not prone to mood swings. His two menu/carte formulas allow guests to enjoy generous, superbly priced meals that are classic but not dull. They include, for example, a bavarois of salmon and langoustines in a sorrel sauce, coquilles St-Jacques in a Champagne sauce, a tender filet of beef with truffle juice, a beautiful cheese platter and inventive and delicious desserts (Cartal started out as a pastry maker). Le Parc Fauriel is a good place to visit during the week, rather than Sunday, when the waiters can get overwhelmed.

Menus: 105F, 135F, 170F, 210F.

12/20 Le Régency

17, blvd. Jules-Janin - 77.74.27.06

M. Chabanny. Open until 10 p.m. Closed Sat., Sun. & Aug. 2-29. Air cond. Pets allowed. Cards: V, MC.

This rustic though slightly complicated decor is as serious as the owner's cuisine, which is pleasantly personal: crab ravioli, a warm salad of kidneys and sweetbreads and a flan of sea urchin and mushrooms. The reception is excellent.

A la carte: 200-230F. Menus: 95F, 115F, 165F.

Saint-Etienne-de-Baïgorry

64430 St-Etienne-de-Baïgorry - (Pyrénées-Atlantiques)
Paris 789 - St-Jean-de-Port 11 - Cambo 31 - Pau 114

(13) Arcé

59.37.40.14

MM. Arcé. Open until 8:45 p.m. Closed Nov. 13-March 11. Garden dining. Pets allowed. Garage parking. Cards: V.

This family establishment on the edge of the Nive river faces a marvelous landscape of Basque greenery. Young Pascal Arcé has gone full steam ahead with an ambitious and personal cuisine. He has nothing more to do with the tired regional dishes of days gone by. Rather, his cuisine includes a seafood mousse, trout filets marinated in lemon, lamb's sweetbreads sautéed with shallots, aiguillettes of duck breast with endive, and delicious desserts (thanks to training with Lenôtre). The reception given by this family of innkeepers is charming, and they go out of their way to make you fall in love with their region... and keep you there (tennis, swimming pool, jeep rides in the mountains and wood-pigeon hunting).

A la carte: 300F. Menus: 60F, 90F, 130F, 190F.

Arcé

(See restaurant above)

Closed Nov. 11-March 11. 4 stes 430-700F. 23 rms 270-420F. Half-board 270-420F. Heated pool. Tennis.

In one of the most seductive of the small Basque country hotels, Arcé's spacious rooms are decorated with warmth and look out on either the river or the Pyrénées.

Saint-Georges-d'Oléron

see Oléron (Ile d')

Saint-Germain-en-Laye

see PARIS SUBURBS

Saint-Gervais-en-Vallière

71350 Verdun-sur-le-Doubs - (Saône-et-Loire)
Paris 328 - Beaune 13 - Verdun-sur-le-Doubs 9

14 Moulin d'Hauterive

Hameau de Chaublanc - 85.91.55.56

M. Moille. Open until 9 p.m. Closed Sun. dinner & Mon. (except holidays) & Dec. 12-Feb. 5. Open weekends only Feb. 5-March 2. Garden dining. No pets. Parking. Telex 801391. Cards: V.

Formerly an oil mill run by the Cîteaux monks, this gray-stone structure stands tall and proud alongside a stream that could almost be called a river. You reach the end of an out-of-the-way road, park your car beneath some apple trees and find yourself stepping into an atmosphere befitting an elegy: a flower-bedecked room with a roaring fireplace, shiny paving stones, old furniture, odd trinkets, a big clock and the smell of polish. Christiane Moille is a driven woman who, by dint of studious training, has perfected a cuisine that is very much her own—a combination of country and modern that is generous but remains light. It could be even better if she would forgo her tendency for the complex and if she were more attentive to execution (we have witnessed some imprecise cooking times). Try the salmon mousse with lime, the fried foie gras with fruit and capers, the scrambled eggs with frogs' legs, the turbot with cabbage and marrow and the roasted whole veal kidneys. The wine cellar is progressing in selection, but also in price. And the reception is a little too "Parisian" and lax.

A la carte: 400F. Menus: 330F (dinner and Sunday lunch only), 200F, 250F.

Prices in red draw attention to restaurants that offer a particularly good value.

Moulin d'Hauterive

(See restaurant above)

Closed Sun. & Mon. (except holidays) & Dec. 12-Feb. 3. Open weekends only Feb. 5-March 2. 5 stes 600-700F. 17 rms 270-460F. Half-board oblig. in seas. TV. Heated pool. Tennis. Pets allowed.

This superb place is full of soul. Each room is delightfully furnished and unique. Quiet nights are punctuated by delicious breakfasts. Weekend fitness packages are available, as is a heliport.

Saint-Girons

09200 St-Girons - (Ariège)
Paris 798 - Toulouse 100 - Foix 44 - St-Gaudens 45

13 Eychenne

8, ave. Paul-Laffont - 61.66.20.55

M. Bordeau. Open until 9:15 p.m. Closed Dec. 22-Jan. 31. Pets allowed. Garage parking. Telex 521273. Cards: V, AE, DC, MC.

This is the archetype of the old, traditional establishment that perpetuates, without stagnating, the virtues of friendliness and generosity. You will receive an exemplary greeting from the owners in their old-fashioned dining room. Then Maurice Bordes, their devoted chef for more than 40 years, will offer you his lengthy menu enriched with a special section of suggestions from that day's marketing, especially fish. That is to say, the regional classics based on foie gras, confits and grilled salmon are proposed along with such less-common dishes as grilled red mullet and escalope of John Dory with sorrel. The desserts are lovely, and the wine cellar is substantial.

A la carte: 250F and up. Menus: 98F, 155F, 247F.

Eychenne

(See restaurant above)

Closed Dec. 22-Jan. 31. 48 rms 136-404F. Half-board 247-436F.

All the rooms in this remarkable family-run hotel are furnished with style. Reception and service are cheery.

Saint-Guénolé

29132 Penmarch - (Finistère)
Paris 585 - Quimper 33 - Pont-l'Abbé 14 - Douarnenez 43

14 La Mer

Rue François-Péron - 98.58.62.22

M. Sannier. Open until 9 p.m. Closed Sun. dinner & Mon. (off-seas.) & Jan. 15-Feb. 25. Hotel: 17 rms 135-230F; half-board 240-310F. Pets allowed. Garage parking. Cards: V.

The difficult succession of Loïc Sannier following the departure of his chef of twenty years, "Father" Donatien, seems to have gone smoothly. And the prices are leaping with joy. But it must be said that the products are superb and served with elegance and generosity. Note especially the freshwater lobster and crayfish (the latter steamed and served with an herb sauce—an extraordinary dish), the turbot with mustard or beurre blanc and the large langoustines caught inshore. The pastries are delicious, and the wine cellar is impressive. There is a view of the ocean from the second floor, which has an opulent Louis XIII decor, but we prefer the more cozy ground floor.

A la carte: 300F and up. Menus: 125F (weekdays only), 185F, 225F, 370F.

Saint-Hilaire-du-Rosier

38840 St-Hilaire-du-Rosier - (Isère)
Paris 580 - Grenoble 63 - Romans-sur-Isère 18

Bouvarel

3 km S on N 92 & N 531 - 76.36.50.87

Mme. Bouvarel. Open until 9:30 p.m. Closed Sun. dinner & Mon. (off-seas.) & Jan. Garden dining. Pets allowed. Garage parking. Cards: V, AE, DC, MC.

The legendary René Bouvarel hoisted this two-century-old auberge to glory. Today his wife, Lucette, takes sole responsibility for the enterprise, putting her extraordinary vigilance to use on all fronts. Tucked away between the towns of Drôme and Isère, Bouvarel, with its summer garden, ultra-rustic and comfortable decor, beautiful silver and attractive fixed-price menus (designed by Palayer), is a stop—or more precisely, a detour—that is absolutely essential. The superb cuisine prepared by Richard Ferrand celebrates the spirit of the region with consistent attention to honesty and lightness: salade gourmande, foie gras, delicious ravioli, salmon with green-pepper cream, partridge with garlic cloves. Nice wine list.

A la carte: 250-400F. Menus: 160F, 250F.

Bouvarel

(See restaurant above)

Closed Sun. & Mon. (off-seas.) & Jan. 14 rms 250-320F. Half-board 400-480F oblig. in seas.

The recently modernized rooms are quite inviting and well equipped, although the decor isn't always engaging.

Saint-Jean-Cap-Ferrat

06290 St-Jean-Cap-Ferrat - (Alpes-Maritimes)
Paris 945 - Cannes 43 - Nice 14 - Monte-Carlo 11

Brise Marine

58, ave. Jean-Mermoz - 93.76.04.36

Closed Oct. 31-Feb. 1. 15 rms 210-480F. Half-board 320F oblig. in seas. Cards: V.

The nice, large rooms are frequently redecorated and have ocean views. Gardens, terraces and a restaurant.

Le Grand Hôtel du Cap Ferrat

Blvd. du Général-de-Gaulle - 93.76.00.21

M. Reliance. Open until 10:30 p.m. Closed Sept. 19-April 20. Air cond. Garden dining. No pets. Parking. Telex 470184. Cards: V, AE, DC, MC.

The new management has completely redone this place but kept the same chef, Jean-Claude Guillon, who has been here since time began. It turned out to be a smart move, for Guillon has begun turning out some very good, dependably classic dishes, along with some lighter, more creative offerings, such as prawns in tarragon and a sea bass filet with a delicious grape sauce. Unfortunately, the complete remodeling has led to unreasonable prices.

A la carte: 500F.

Le Grand Hôtel du Cap Ferrat

(See restaurant above)

Closed Sept. 19-April 20. 7 stes 3,680-6,670F. 58 rms 1,620-3,250F. Half-board 400F (plus rm). TV in 10 rms. Air cond. Heated pool. Tennis. Pets allowed.

This luxury hotel dating from the turn of the century recently reopened after major construction. A previous renovation made the place exceptionally comfortable and luxurious (exotic gardens, terraces, sunbathing beach). The new building, which was unfinished at the time of this writing, houses 60 suites overlooking the ocean, and the decor of the main building has been completely redone.

Le Sloop

Port de Plaisance - 93.01.48.63

M. Therlicocq. Open until 11 p.m. Closed Sun. dinner & Wed. (off-seas.). Terrace dining. Pets allowed. Cards: V, AE, DC.

Moving from Switzerland to Zaire and from the kitchens of La Coupole in Paris to those of Jacques Maximin, Alain Therlicocq did a lot of navigating before dropping his Sloop's anchor at the Saint-Jean port. Success came quickly, because he's not the kind of chef who just throws things together. His ideas are numerous, very much his own and well realized: fresh salmon with aïoli, veal shank with a fennel aspic, breaded loin of lamb with pine nuts, tasty gratin of Golden Delicious apples with Marc wine from Provence. Régine Therlicocq will make you feel right at home on her lovely terrace shaded by umbrellas and facing the yachts.

A la carte: 300-350F. Menu: 155F.

La Voile d'Or

Port de Plaisance - 93.01.13.13, 93.76.13.13

M. Lorenzi. Open until 10:15 p.m. Closed Nov. 1-March 12. Air cond. Garden dining. Pets allowed. Parking. Telex 470317.

These last few years, much headway has been made in giving this marvelous Italian-style luxury hotel (see below) a cuisine that is finally on a par with the spirit and elegance of its decor and atmosphere. Jean Crépin can be seen each winter spending his free time in France's most prestigious kitchens, refining his technique while rubbing elbows with the best. His menu is certainly not a festival of imagination, but everything that it proposes, for a small fortune, is caressed by the touch of perfection: fresh salmon millefeuille with chervil butter, John Dory and lobster with beurre rouge and sorrel, mignon of veal in chive cream, crispy apples with cider butter. M. Lorenzi, the proprietor of this paradise for celebrities and millionaires, does everything in his power to allow them to eat in peace; even Madonna would go unnoticed. But everyone has the opportunity to gaze upon the spectacular view of the port and the sea from the garden terrace where the tables are set. The service has a marvelous and natural distinction.

A la carte: 600-800F. Menus: 320F (lunch only), 430F.

La Voile d'Or

(See restaurant above)

Closed Nov. 1-March 12. 4 stes & 41 rms 595-3,200F. Half-board 870-2,000F oblig. in seas. Air cond. Heated pool.

This marvelous hotel overlooking the port provides perfect comfort and refined elegance in a dream-like setting. Guests can take advantage of the flowering garden, two saltwater swimming pools, the sauna, massages, water sports and glass-bottom boats. Every peacefully quiet room was decorated by Jansen, like the rest of the hotel. The ambience is friendly, with as little stiffness as possible.

Saint-Jean-de-Braye

see Orléans

Saint-Jean-de-Luz

64500 St-Jean-de-Luz - (Pyrénées-Atlantiques)
Paris 760 - Biarritz 15 - Hendaye 13 - San Sebastian 33

Sights. The fishing port; the pl. Louis-XIV (with the Lohobiague house); La Maison de l'-Infante (on the wharf); Saint-Jean-Baptiste church (fourteenth century, where the marriage of Louis XIV was celebrated); the harbor; the beaches; la pointe Sainte-Barbe.

Eating on the Run. La Bodega, 3, rue Chauvin Dragon (at night); La Piazza, 13, pl. Louis-XIV; La Pizzéria, 1, rue Dornaldéguy.

Brasseries. La Banquise, 34, blvd. Thiers; Le Cosmopolitain, 5, pl. du Maréchal-Foch; Le Saint Jean, 30, blvd. Thiers.

Bars & Cafés. Bar Basque, Lloyd's, Le Madison and Le Vauban, all on blvd. Thiers; Majestic and Le Suisse, on pl. Louis-XIV.

Nightlife. Amphithéâtre (Grand Hôtel), 43, blvd. Thiers (cabaret/shows, the poshest spot in Saint-Jean-de-Luz); Le Boléro, on the Corniche in Hendaye; La Licorne, in Bidart (popular discotheque); Sun Set, in Bidart; Le Swing, on N 10 in Urrugne.

Chantaco

Golf de Chantaco - 59.26.14.76

Closed Oct. 30-April 1. 4 stes 1,110-1,250F. 20 rms 550-1,050F. Half-board 700-850F. TV. Pets allowed. Parking. Telex 540016. Cards: V, AE, DC, MC.

This opulent Basque hotel surrounded by greenery has been decorated with good taste. The lovely rooms are located on the garden, while the grounds overlook the famous golf course. Restaurant.

La Devinière

5, rue Loquin - 59.26.05.51

Open year-round. 8 rms 375-475F. No pets. Cards: V, MC.

This renovated family pension in the heart of town is full of charm. Its few rooms are deliciously decorated and furnished. The owners, he an ex-notary public and she a former antiques dealer, welcome their guests warmly. No restaurant.

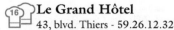

Le Grand Hôtel

43, blvd. Thiers - 59.26.12.32

M. Lagun. Open until 10:30 p.m. Closed Sun. dinner & Mon. (off-seas.) & Jan. 3-March 10. Air cond. Terrace dining. Pets allowed. Parking. Telex 571487. Cards: V, AE, DC, MC.

Jacques and Evelyne Lagun were real estate investors often taken by "love at first sight" deals (those sure to generate juicy operations). They finally found true love in the form of this King Alfonso XIII's home during the Belle Epoque. In renovating the fin-de-siècle edifice from top to bottom, they have created one of the best and most beautiful restaurants on the Basque coast. First they set up a large art deco dining room, vibrant with light and facing the bay dotted with sailboats and fishing craft. Then they introduced one of the most promising names in cuisine, Bruno Cirino, a fiesty young chef who for three months was the assistant to Jacques Maximin in Nice. He is a man who favors sharp tastes, fresh herbs, strong flavors and a sunny cuisine that brings a touch of Provence to the Basque country.

There was one error, however, in the five-course meal we sampled there recently: an Adour salmon that was played with too much and was overwhelmed by vinegar. But the rest was exquisite: the leeks stuffed with truffles, the red mullet with peppers and herbs, the milk-fed lamb's sweetbreads with mushrooms and the spit-roasted squab accompanied by crushed fresh peas (an inspired idea!). The pastry chef is no slouch either. Chocoholics are advised to try his coffee-and-chocolate macaroon with vanilla ice cream. Your bill will be moderately debilitating, unless you choose the first fixed-price menu or the special lunch, which is served on the Grill's terrace.

A la carte: 400-500F. Menus: 220F (weekday lunch only), 380F.

Le Grand Hôtel

(See restaurant above)

Closed Jan. 3-March 10. 2 stes 900-1,300F. 45 rms 400-1,100F. Half-board 285F (plus rm). TV. Pets allowed. Heated pool.

Real estate investor Jacques Lagun and his wife, Evelyne, fell in love with this great nineteenth-century structure on the beach. They decided to sell a part of it to pay for the extensive renovation work on the hotel. At what is now Le Grand Hôtel, they have made a luxurious hotel of 35 rooms and 6 suites. Fabric hangings adorn the walls, and the furniture is of bleached wood. Special touches, like feather pillows and chocolates, make for a pleasant stay.

Maria-Christina

13, rue P.-Gelos - 59.26.81.70

Open year-round. 13 rms 190-250F.

This old Basque residence, just 200 meters from the beach, comprises completely renovated cozy rooms. The reception is charming, and the breakfast delicious. As for the restaurant, the owner/chef recently ceded his place behind the stove to one of his helpers, and it remains to be seen whether the fresh, hearty seafood fare will maintain its former high level of quality.

(14) La Réserve

Rond-point de Ste-Barbe
(Hôtel Basque) - 59.26.04.24

Mme. Boutin. Open daily until 10 p.m. Garden dining. Pets allowed. Hotel: 1 ste 540F; 37 rms 130-400F; half-board 260-465F. Golf. Garage parking. Telex 540140. Cards: V, AE, DC, MC.

Henri Manterola, after having launched the excellent Amar Lur in Briscous before earning a toque at his Etxola here in town, has packed his bags once again and come to take over the kitchen of this vast hotel/motel on the sea. A remarkable professional, Manterola has taken advantage of his move to shift into high gear, lighten his sauces and seek out better products, all of which has earned him great success in the region. Attesting to this are the salmon marinated in herbs, the grilled langoustines with tarragon butter and the casserole of farm pigeon and cèpes. The desserts, such as the delicious vanilla ice cream poached in red wine with a fresh raspberry sauce, are eminently delicious. The wine list is short but nice. And in the two large, rustic dining rooms, you will be served efficiently while looking out on the terrace, the golf course and the ocean.

A la carte: 260-280F. Menu: 120F.

(14) Le Tourasse

25, rue Tourasse - 59.51.14.25

M. Basset. Open until 10:30 p.m. (10 p.m. in winter). Closed Tues. (off-seas.); annual closing varies. Air cond. Pets allowed. Cards: V.

In 1987, young Pascal Basset, who spent eighteen months with Dutournier at the Carré des Feuillants, took over this little restaurant, which had been lying dormant on a street lined with lovely old fishermen's houses. He has used the decor (a little cramped but cheerful) to its best advantage and has set out to create a light, flavorful and inspired cuisine that from the very beginning is worthy of a toque: marinated salmon with raw mushrooms, exquisite gilthead tartare with oyster sauce, juicy, perfectly boned red mullet with fresh pasta and a light fish-essence sauce, and a simple fish soup with Beaumes-de-Venise wine. Mme. Basset is a friendly hostess, and the prices are reasonable.

A la carte: 250F. Menus: 75F (weekdays only), 100F.

IN NEARBY Ciboure

(1 km SW)
64500 St-Jean-de-Luz - (Pyrénées-Atlantiques)

(14) Chez Dominique

Quai Maurice-Ravel - 59.47.29.16

M. Lafargue. Open until 9:30 p.m. Closed Sun. dinner, Mon., 1 week after Easter & Oct. Terrace dining. Pets allowed. Cards: V.

At this lovely Basque restaurant situated on the harbor, with a terrace overlooking the ocean, the prices seem rather severe. But Dominique Lafargue doesn't scrimp on the freshness of her products (which come exclusively from the sea) or on the generosity of her portions. Everything here is dazzling but without pretension, making this always-lively seaside setting clearly one of the best of its kind on the coast. To confirm its popularity are the herbed langoustines with a light lemon beurre blanc, the turbot baked in buttered paper (a thick portion served with olive oil), the magnificent fried red mullet and the simple ray with capers. We like to finish things off with the almond cake with raspberry sauce. The service is charming, but because the chef cooks everything to order, it's always a little slow.

A la carte: 300-350F.

Saint-Jean-du-Bruel

12230 La Cavalerie - (Aveyron)
Paris 677 - Lodève 45 - Millau 41 - Le Vigan 36

(13) Midi ✿

Pl. A.-Lemasse - 65.62.26.04

M. Papillon. Open until 9:30 p.m. Closed Nov. 11-March 18. Pets allowed. Hotel: 19 rms 65-164F; half-board 144-185F. Garage parking. Cards: V.

Everything is cheery in this bucolic, charming place facing the river and the Cévennes mountains—from the flower bouquets in the dining room to the frank cuisine that fills the plates: pickled duck cooked over a wood fire and garnished with cèpes, blanquette of weever (fish) with baby vegetables, strawberry gratin with a Sauternes sabayon. The prices are cheery, too.

A la carte: 200F. Menus: 61F (weekdays only), 89F, 104F, 113F, 163F.

Saint-Jean-Pied-de-Port

64220 St-Jean-Pied-de-Port - (Pyrénées-Atlantiques)
Paris 793 - Pau 102 - Bayonne 54 -San Sebastian 97

(18) Les Pyrénées ✿

19, pl. du Général-de-Gaulle
59.37.01.01

M. Arrambide. Open until 9 p.m. Closed Mon. dinner (off-seas.), Tues. (except holidays & school vacations), Jan. 7-27 & Nov. 20-Dec. 22. Air cond. Terrace dining. No pets. Parking. Cards: V, AE.

He looks as sweet as the cute baby lambs that graze in the Pyrénées mountains, but since he's donned his third toque, Firmin Arrambide has the ferocious energy of a lion. He began by getting rid of the roadside-inn look of his country hotel—he threw out the wrought iron, the wagon wheels and the housewifey curtains—so he could give his clients an elegant dining room in salmon tones with enameled ceilings and soft lighting, along with a flower-filled terrace. Then he redid the smart, comfortable hotel rooms and small suites. Now he's getting ready to fulfill his dream: to create a huge field of greenery on the other side of this beautiful stone building, which dates from the seventeenth century. The windows of more hotel rooms to be added to this future Relais et Châteaux will then open onto this garden. It's too soon to set a date for the completion of this work. Regardless, the day of his housewarming the reservation book will be filled, and we're already savoring the possibility of stretching out on a chaise longue alongside the pool and the enormous pleasure that comes from a meal in the Pyrénées.

At 41, Arrambide is an extremely sensitive chef, intelligent and passionately attached to his region and its products. Has his art peaked? We're not at all certain that he's uttered his last word, and since as he's perfecting the tools of his trade, we have every reason to think that his talent will only continue to make itself felt and develop even further. At our last meal we were as pleased as we had been on previous visits, as we enjoyed his admirable fresh duck foie gras au naturel (with a glass of Jurançon Clos Joliette 1975 that'll send you straight to high heaven), his warm terrine of cèpes with herbs, his louvine (striped bass) with thyme served on crushed fresh tomatoes, his incomparable Adour salmon in an incredibly light béarnaise sauce and his rabbit stuffed with vegetables. And Arrambide was not without new creations. The lobster-and-shellfish consommé with coriander, oysters gratinées à l'effiloché de légumes, ravioli with langoustines and caviar, baby peppers stuffed with cod, and long, thin slices of duck with ginger and other spices also enchanted us with their delicacy, distinct flavors and harmony.

The grand chocolate dessert, the white-peach chaud-froid with pistachios, and the glazed nougat with almonds and honey provide a beautiful finish to the finest meal you can find in the Basque region. Etienne Brana will bring you the best pear eau-de-vie in France and we look forward to the Irouleguy from the vineyards he has planted on the mountainside. Brana travels beyond the region to find the finest Bordeaux and delicious but inexpensive Spanish wines. With a split of Vina Contino, an exquisite terrine of young rabbit with an onion compote, lotte sautéed with fresh tomatoes and sweet pimiento, a baby chèvre, a red-orange sorbet and a warm sabayon, you won't spend more than 280 francs—and that's not the least of the charms of this inn of happiness.

A la carte: 350-500F. Menus: 150F (weekdays only), 220F, 280F, 350F.

Les Pyrénées

(See restaurant above)

Closed Mon. (off-seas.), Tues. (except holidays & school vacations), Jan. 7-27 & Nov. 20-Dec. 22. 3 stes 680-780F. 23 rms 260-580F. Half-board 350-450F. TV in 8 rms. No pets.

While we wait for the luxurious rooms to be built above the garden, those recently redecorated by Firmin and Anne-Marie Arrambide—a hostess as attractive as she is attentive—recently redecorated are charming and comfortable, despite being somewhat cramped. Relais et Châteaux.

IN NEARBY **Esterençuby**
(8 km SE on D 31)
64220 St-Jean-Pied-de-Port - (Pyrénées-Atlantiques)

Artzain-Etchea

3 km on VO - 59.37.11.55

Closed Wed. (off-seas.) & Jan. 4-April 2. 20 rms 125-180F. Half-board 155-160F oblig. in seas. Pets allowed. Parking. Cards: V, AE, DC, MC.

This small hotel tucked away in the trees has clean, bright, tranquil rooms. Restaurant.

Saint-Jorioz

see Annecy

Saint-Julien-de-Crempse

see Bergerac

Saint-Julien-en-Genevois

74160 St-Julien-en-Genevois - (Haute-Savoie)
Paris 536 - Annecy 34 - Geneva 9 - Annemasse 14

La Diligence

Rue de Genève - 50.49.07.55

MM. Favre. Open until 9:30 p.m. Closed Sun. dinner, Mon., July 3-24 & Dec. 26-Jan. 9. Air cond. Pets allowed. Cards: V, AE, DC.

Less than ten kilometers from this sumptuous hostelry is the center of Geneva, which sets the tone for La Diligence's chic decor, its loyal clientele and its prices. But the latter are not at all unjustified, considering the attention that the Favres, father and son, bring to the selection of their exceptional regional products, as well as to the execution of an ambitious yet careful cuisine. In their respective seasons, you'll find crayfish and morels and, all year, the best Bresse poultry (roast duckling with an onion confit), farm rabbits (with mustard) and turbot (cooked whole in seaweed), which assure well-deserved success for this traditionally provincial restaurant. Christiane Favre is a sublime hostess in her refurbished lower-level dining room with its elegant, round tables. There is also a pleasant adjoining brasserie.

A la carte: 400F. Menus: 150F (weekday lunch only), 200F, 250F.

IN NEARBY **Présilly**
(7 km S on N 201)
74160 St-Julien-en-Genevois - (Haute-Savoie)

Abbaye de Pomier

50.04.40.64

M. Mathon. Open until 9:30 p.m. Closed Tues. (except lunch July-Aug.), Wed. lunch & Jan. 3-March 3. Garden dining. Pets allowed. Parking. Cards: V, DC, MC.

The beautiful Swiss clientele is very much at home in this delicious decor set in the remains of an old abbey isolated in the middle of a natural setting. A stone's throw from the border, it has all the seductions of tasteful elegance (handsome furniture, nice dishes, pretty garden), plus Geneva prices. For six years the self-taught Pierre Mathon has led the life of a hermit in this solitary spot at the foot of the Salève, sharing it with a hostess who is both ravishing and discreet. His cuisine is whimsical, daring and more changeable than the Haute-Savoie sky. Sometimes this generous creativity results in a sad dish or an overzealous one. But you must take the risk (which is actually minimal), because the lobster with baby vegetables, the turbot in an infusion of pepper, the shellfish and vegetable fritters with coral butter, the fried lamb served with exceptional garlic crêpes and the very remarkable desserts are un-

questionably worth it.
A la carte: 350F. Menus: 140F (weekday lunch only), 240F, 290F.

Saint-Lambert-des-Bois

see Chevreuse

Saint-Laurent-du-Var

06700 St-Laurent-du-Var - (Alpes-Maritimes)
Paris 925 - Nice 10 - Cannes 27 - Antibes 16 - Cagnes 5

Hôtel Galaxie

Ave. Maréchal-Juin - 93.07.73.72
Open year-round. 28 rms 300-430F. TV. Air cond. Pets allowed. Telex 470431. Cards: V, AE, DC.

All new, this hotel's perfectly conceived rooms are equipped with good bathrooms and private terraces. Restaurant.

Le Mas Saint-Laurent

Magnolias, rue Plateau-Calliste
93.31.93.31
Open year-round. 2 stes 680-730F. 11 rms 300-480F. TV. Pets allowed. Telex 306022. Cards: V, AE, DC, MC.

Located in the heart of the countryside, this rich old Provençal establishment has been completely restored. The rooms are all different, all superb (including one for the handicapped) and as big as they are comfortable. Service is excellent. No restaurant.

Saint-Laurent-en-Grandvaux

39150 St-Laurent-en-Grandvaux - (Jura)
Paris 450 - Pontarlier 60 - Lons-le-Saunier 45

12/20 Moulin des Truites Bleues

N 5 - 84.60.83.03, 84.60.83.09
Mme. Perenet & M. Levavasseur. Open daily until 9:30 p.m. Pets allowed. Hotel: 20 rms 250-590F; half-board 470F. Parking. Telex 360443. Cards: V, AE, DC.

This is a fine place for lovers of the great outdoors and for trout fishing (there are innumerable lakes and gorges from the Lemme). The old-fashioned decor of this former Spanish fort is spectacular, and the menu comprises a festival of trout, as well as rich and expensive classic dishes (crayfish in yellow wine, Bresse chicken with morels).

A la carte: 350F. Menus: 115F (weekday lunch only), 185F, 285F.

Saint-Malo

35400 St-Malo - (Ille-et-Vilaine)
Paris 366 - Rennes 69 - Dinan 34 - St-Brieuc 76

Sights. A walk along the ramparts (indispensable, superb view of Saint-Servan, La Rance, Dinard, La Grande Passe and the sea); Le Grand Bé (accessible at low tide, the tomb of Chateaubriand); Le Fort National (the works of Vauban, lovely view of Saint-Malo); La Cour de la Houssaye (rue Chateaubriand, old interior courtyard); Musée de la Ville (devoted to the history of the city, known for its privateers, and to the Galerie Quic-en-Grogne) and Musée de Cire (wax museum), portraying the celebrated figures of Saint-Malo (pirates, navigators, writers, mathematicians), both of which are at the château; boat tours (Dinard, Le Cap Fréhel, La Rance, the Chausey islands and the Anglo-Norman islands).

Eating on the Run. L'Art-Caddy, 7, rue des Petits-Degrés (salads, intimate); Le Chalut, 8, rue de la Corne-aux-Cerfs (nice setting); Chez Gaby, rue de Dinan (tiny crêperie with nice puff-pastry cakes, inexpensive); Côté Jardin, 36, rue Dauphine (pretty view of the harbor, interior garden and good pizza "soufflé"); Pinocchio, 75, rue Ville-Pépin in Saint-Servan (good pizza); La Rose des Sables, 8, rue Am-Magon in Saint-Servan (couscous and exoticism); Tea-Time, 4, Grand-Rue; Ty Coz, 57, chaussée Sillon.

Brasseries. Brasserie de l'Ouest, 4, pl. Chateaubriand (rococo style, summer orchestra); Café de Paris, 4, pl. Guy-La Chambre (quick service); L'Univers, pl. Chateaubriand ("boat" decor, a favorite of locals).

Bars & Cafés. La Caravelle, 95, blvd. Rochebonne in Paramé (on the "little" dike, for a memorable experience, have an apéritif one evening at high tide); Le Cunningham's Bar, 2, rue des Hauts-Sablons in Saint-Servan (pub ambience, darts and billiards, view of the harbor); Cutty Stark, 20, rue Hers (best cocktails).

Nightlife. L'Angélus, 10, rue Puits-aux-Braies (subdued lighting, overstuffed seats, cellar bar open until 3 a.m., dinner on main floor); L'-Escalier, pointe de la Varde in Paramé (the latest fashionable nightclub, with a balcony overlooking the sea and Saint-Malo); L'Hippocampe, 34, rue Lecoufle (late-night dinners); Le Welcome, 3, Grand-Rue (open until 5 a.m., topless waitresses).

(14) Le Cap Horn

100, blvd. Hébert - 99.56.02.56
M. Raulic. Open until 9 p.m. Closed Jan. Air cond. No pets. Garage parking. Telex 740184. Cards: V, AE, DC, MC.

The new dining room, with its grand ocean view, is nicely dressed in a pinkish beige and gray (the mahogany furniture is less cheerful), and the service is alert and smiling. There's no question that Henry Reverdy's cuisine could be more inventive, but it is fresh, generous and executed with precision. That's enough for the happiness of the spa-goers, who are pampered by a management eager to please (a piano bar was recently added, as was a low-calorie menu created by a dietician). Taste the langoustine cassolette in a perfumed court bouillon with a touch of cream, all the fresh fish, the breast of duck with blackberries and the delicate almond cake flavored with lemon.

A la carte: 250F. Menus: 98F, 125F, 175F, 220F.

Les Thermes

(See restaurant above)
Closed Jan. 11 stes 720F. 90 rms 220-680F. Heated pool.

This modern seaside spa-hotel stands at the edge of the beach. Some of its rooms have been remarkably renovated, and guests can take advantage of the delicious breakfast and the covered saltwater pool.

Elizabeth

2, rue des Cordiers (walled city)
99.56.24.98

Open year-round. 17 rms 250-402F. TV. Pets allowed. Garage parking. Telex 730800. Cards: V, AE, DC, MC.

In the walled-in maze of the old city, this recently opened hotel is attractively set up behind its sixteenth-century facade. Three of its numerous suites were recently redone, and breakfast is excellent.

IN NEARBY **Saint-Servan**
(SE on N 137)
35400 St-Malo - (Ille-et-Vilaine)

Le Valmarin

7, rue Jean-XXIII - 99.81.94.76

Closed Dec. 24-March 1. 10 rms 330-470F. TV. Pets allowed. Parking. Cards: V.

This lovely piece of eighteenth-century Saint-Malo has been entirely renovated and faces small private grounds. You'll find the reception excellent and the rooms fairly large, pleasant and well soundproofed. No restaurant.

Saint-Martin-aux-Chartrains

see Deauville

Saint-Martin-de-Londres

34380 St-Martin-de-Londres - (Hérault)
Paris 785 - Le Vigan 38 - Montpellier 25 - Béziers 75

Les Muscardins

19, rte. des Cévennes - 67.55.75.90, 67.55.75.89

MM. Rousset. Open until 10 p.m. Closed Mon. (off-seas.) & Nov. 1-15. Pets allowed. Cards: V, AE, DC.

Georges Rousset left his restaurant in the hills—an austere and superb place—but he didn't feel at home there and didn't have the will or the means to keep it up as it deserved. So he set himself up at the edge of town in this small restaurant where he doesn't hide the fact that he is returning to simpler fare. The dining room is sober and welcoming, with white walls, pink curtains and large, well-spaced tables. And the cuisine remains one of the best in the Languedoc region. His wise technique, his knowledge of regional products and the presence of his enthusiastic 21-year-old son at his side give his dishes a stunning liberty. Combining daring inventiveness with powerful, rustic Languedoc flavors are escalopes of salmon fried with a light butter flavored with shallot juice and cardamom, an exquisite combination of three river fish (sander, salmon, pike) poached in a light red-wine sauce, fresh cod fried à la provençale (unfortunately much too salty), a pleasant and tender stew of baby pig, and lovely desserts (which could nevertheless be better and more original). The service is simple—almost too much so—and the prices are attractive, at least for the moment.

A la carte: 250-280F. Menus: 100F (weekdays only), 145F, 200F.

We're always happy to hear about your discoveries and to receive your comments about ours. We want to give your letters the attention they deserve, so when you write to Gault Millau, please state clearly what you liked or disliked. Be concise but convincing, and take the time to argue your point.

Saint-Martin-du-Fault

see Limoges

Saint-Martin-du-Var

06670 St-Martin-du-Var - (Alpes-Maritimes)
Paris 946 - Antibes 35 - Nice 27 - Vence 23 - Cannes 45

Issautier

(Auberge de la Belle Route)
N 202, St-Blaise - 93.08.10.65

M. Issautier. Open until 9:30 p.m. Closed Sun. dinner, Mon., Feb. school vacation & Oct. 28-Nov. 8. Pets allowed. Parking. Cards: V, AE, DC.

The "Belle Route" is route Nationale 202 and its shabbily elegiac surroundings, a few minutes from the Nice airport. But this old Provençal inn, whose name is reminiscent of Provence in the Greek glory of yesteryear, is a real beauty, with a rich decor in regional taste, just discreet enough to be seductive. Although fresh, bright and comfortable, the atmosphere is still betrayed by a somewhat stuffy feeling, which is inconsistent with the light, delicious dishes prepared by one of the best cooks in Provence. Jean-François Issautier is certainly not a newcomer among the frontrunners. For years this "adopted son" of Roger Vergé has been following a course that is slightly off the beaten track, as discreet as it is original. But now, with 43 years gone by, he is allowing his talents to pour forth, and his imagination (a great one) to run more freely. He is particularly inventive when working in the regional repertoire and with local products. The early crop of fruits and vegetables is incomparable, the fish are magnificent, and the olive oil, farm poultry, meats and mushrooms—all local—are the best to be found anywhere. To say nothing of the wines (like the white Bellet) that accompany the meunière of fresh langoustines with basil, the roasted aiguillettes of John Dory with an exquisite mustard sauce, the whole roasted veal kidneys with pickled red onions and the wise desserts from pastry chef Jean Meyer (whose brother is Issautier's assistant). A touch of generosity would be welcome (the dishes are sometimes more like samplings), considering the fierce prices.

A la carte: 400-500F. Menus: 235F, 385F.

Servotel

Castagniers-les-Moulins (6 km S on N 202) - 93.08.22.00

Open year-round. 43 rms 210-290F. Half-board 210-340F oblig. in seas. Pool. Tennis. Garage parking. Telex 461547. Cards: V, AE.

Ideal for travelers looking for leisure activities, this hotel has three tennis courts, a swimming pool and rooms with blooming terraces. Restaurant.

Saint-Méloir-des-Ondes

35350 St-Méloir-des-Ondes - (Ille-et-Vilaine)
Paris 355 - St-Malo 11 - Cancale 7 - Dol-de-Bretagne 18

(14) Hôtel Tirel

(Hôtel de la Gare)
Gare de la Gouesnière - 99.89.10.46

MM. Tirel & Guérin. Open until 9:30 p.m. Closed Sun. dinner (off-seas.) & Dec. 15-Jan. 15. Pets allowed. Garage parking. Telex 740896. Cards: V, AE, DC.

The little train station at La Gouesnière, between Dinan and Cancale, is a pleasant stopover in the Breton countryside. As soon as you've hopped off the train you'll find this large family-run establishment, a little frilly but quite comfortable, with its manicured garden shaded by willow trees and its festive tables, where you'll be seduced by the cuisine of Roger Tirel and his brother-in-law, Jean Luc Guérin. It is light, precise and of a generosity that never fails: salade "amoureuse" with quail, truffles and foie gras; Breton lobster cooked on the spot, red mullet seasoned with citronella oil, and sweetbreads. The Loire wines are good and reasonably priced.

A la carte: 280-300F. Menus: 90F (weekdays only), 110F, 180F.

Hôtel Tirel

(See restaurant above)

Closed Dec. 15-Jan. 17. 5 stes 420-450F. 52 rms 80-230F. Half-board 170-320F.

For rail travelers awaiting the next train for Saint-Malo, this hotel offers lovely rooms and a few luxurious suites, some on the garden.

Saint-Ouen

see PARIS SUBURBS

Saint-Palais

64120 St-Palais - (Pyrénées-Atlantiques)
Paris 801 - Bayonne 54 - Dax 55 - St-Jean-Pied-de-Port 31

(13) Dindart

23, rue Thiers - 59.65.72.42

M. Dindart. Open until 10 p.m. Closed May 15-30. Air cond. Terrace dining. Pets allowed. Cards: V, AE, DC, MC.

If you would like to become more familiar with magret (rare duck breast), salmis of wood pigeon and true Basque cooking with no tricks or phony folklore, come to this institution full of warmth, noise and cheer. The Dindart son, who followed in the footsteps of his father, is also a great sauce chef (eels in parsley sauce, grilled salmon with a delicious tarragon mousseline). The waitresses in traditional dress are the friendliest in the region, but the fixed-price menus have let themselves go a little.

A la carte: 180-200F. Menus: 50F, 75F, 120F.

Saint-Pancrace

see Nice

Saint-Pardoux-la-Croisille

19320 Marcillac-la-Croisille - (Corrèze)
Paris 510 - St-Céré 68 - Tulle 28 - Marcillac-la-Croisille 5

(13) Le Beau Site

55.27.85.44

M. Bidault. Open until 9 p.m. Closed Oct. 1-April 30. Air cond. No pets. Parking. Telex 590140.

Far from the automobile fumes and fashionable crowds, the Bidault family gallantly maintains the best traditions of vacation hotels. Here, it's all countryside, forest and walks in the clean air. But you'll also find tennis, swimming, a charming reception and the pleasure of a cuisine that is surprising in its originality and its faithfulness to the seasons. You'll drink first-rate wines (M. Bidault is from Burgundy) while partaking in the escalope of duck liver with cider vinegar, the sander with walnut essence, the sweetbreads with truffle juice and cèpes, and the cakes made with fruit from the region.

A la carte: 250F. Menus: 95F (weekdays only), 135F, 215F.

Le Beau Site

(See restaurant above)

Closed Oct. 1-April 30. 32 rms 190-250F. Half-board 170-235F. Pets allowed. Heated pool. Tennis.

The rooms are comfortable, with bathrooms that are adequate but no more: puny baths, paltry lighting. But breakfast is always perfect, and there are spacious grounds and various diversions.

Saint-Patrice

37130 Langeais - (Indre-et-Loire)
Paris 267 - Tours 34 - Saumur 33 - Langeais 9

(15) Château de Rochecotte

47.96.91.28, 47.96.90.62

Mlle. Pasquier. Open until 9:30 p.m. Closed Jan. 15-March 15. Pets allowed. Garage parking. Cards: V, AE, DC, MC.

Two years at this elegant Renaissance château seems to have been beneficial to young Thierry Marx, formerly with Taillevent. We're giving him two toques already, thanks to his rabbit's head in a Vouvray aspic; his exquisite ragoût of pigeon in truffle juice, topped with golden potatoes; his delicious salmon stuffed with smoked pigs' feet and his rhubarb ice cream "bombe"—our only possible response to the remarkably well-thought-out and unified cuisine of this talented young master. Why all this elegance goes unpatronized is a mystery to us, so hurry now to support the Pasquier sisters, to enjoy the beautiful Touraine countryside and, especially, to dine on such gems as the bold dish of chicken with prawns, the exquisite lotte stuffed with smoked salmon and served with creamed lentils, the roast lamb with a shallot and red-wine marmalade and the terrine of dark chocolate and dark-roasted coffee. You'll be so enraptured with the food on your plate that you'll be hard put to pay due attention to either the sumptuously sober dining room, with its lovely flowered curtains, fluted columns and superb tables, or the excellent selection of Loire wines.

A la carte: 300F. Menu: 160F.

Château de Rochecotte

(See restaurant above)

Open year-round. 2 stes 520-650F. 13 rms 300-480F. Half-board 530-620F. TV in 8 rms. Pets allowed.

On a hill overhanging the valley are a dozen extremely comfortable and perfectly equipped rooms, all decorated with ravishing, contemporary fabrics and modern furniture. You will be greeted by the entire family with more charm than professionalism. The grounds are immense.

Saint-Paul-de-Vence

06570 St-Paul-de-Vence - (Alpes-Maritimes)
Paris 925 - Cannes 27 - Nice 20 - Antibes 16 - Vence 5

Auberge du Soleil

1334, rte. de la Colle - 93.32.80.60

Closed Jan. 5-Feb. 10. 7 rms 325-395F. Half-board 330-385F oblig. in seas. TV. Pets allowed. Pool. Parking. Cards: V, MC.

From the large terrace and from some of the rooms, there is a marvelous view of the village of Saint-Paul. Restaurant.

12/20 La Colombe d'Or

Pl. du Général-de-Gaulle - 93.32.80.02

M. Roux. Open until 10 p.m. Closed Nov. 15-Dec. 20 & Jan. 10-20. Terrace dining. Pets allowed. Garage parking. Telex 970607. Cards: V, AE, DC, MC.

The memorabilia from the 1950s, the fascinating modern paintings (Picasso, Rouault, Miro, Léger) and the breathtaking terrace facing the valley are enough to attract celebrities and high society to this charming bistro. And everyone eats reasonably well here, from a cuisine that is banal, tremendously copious and pricey (turbot with fresh vegetables, Sisteron lamb).

A la carte: 300-400F.

La Colombe d'Or

(See restaurant above)

Closed Nov. 15-Dec. 20 & Jan. 10-20. 10 stes 1,020F. 15 rms 820F. Half-board 590-790F. TV. Air cond. Pets allowed. Heated pool.

This warmly welcoming Provençal hotel is decorated with a great deal of taste. A Braque mosaic and a Calder mobile are reflected in the swimming pool. The rooms are gorgeous, and the prices are reasonable for so much comfort.

(14) Mas d'Artigny

Rte. de La Colle - 93.32.84.54

M. Scordel. Open daily until 9:30 p.m. Terrace dining. Pets allowed. Garage parking. Telex 470601. Cards: V, MC.

This breeding ground for millionaires is a rural luxury hotel with astounding opulence: twenty wooded acres facing the walls of Saint-Paul-de-Vence, villas with patios and private lakes and, above the sumptuous pool, a terrace that allows you to turn your back on the rather pretentious dining room. The reception is discreet, the service greatly courteous, and Arthur Dorschner's cuisine, aside from a few unconvincing stabs at modern innovations, is consistent and perfectly realized. The Languedoc asparagus with a delicious lime mousseline, the grilled turbot with mustard and tarragon, and the rack of roast lamb are the daily fare at this princely cottage.

A la carte: 400-600F. Menus: 260F, 340F.

Mas d'Artigny

(See restaurant above)

Open year-round. 26 stes 1,340-2,280F. 59 rms 410-1,580F. Half-board 630-2,260F. TV. Air cond. in 77 rms. Pets allowed. Heated pool. Tennis.

In spite of a few unfortunate lapses in taste, this is a dream retreat for overworked executives. Twenty-five suites have private pools, the grounds are huge, and there is a marvelous view of the countryside and the bay. Relais et Châteaux.

IN NEARBY La Colle-sur-Loup

(3 km SW on D 7)
06480 La Colle-sur-Loup - (Alpes-Maritimes)

12/20 Bacchus

Rte. de Grasse - 93.32.83.53

M. Teisseire. Open until 10 p.m. Closed Sun. dinner & Mon. (except in seas.) & Dec. 20-March 1. Terrace dining. Pets allowed. Parking. Cards: V, AE, DC.

Out in the wilderness amid olive, pine and plane trees, this place is a festival of aggressive colors and provocative forms. The Parisian decorator, Pierre Sala, deserves credit for having succeeded with his interesting interior, whose vividness is surely more attractive than the usual neo-Provençal reconstitutions. The reception by the owner and his wife is quite friendly, and the hearty cuisine features a 150-franc fixed-price menu that includes a salad of young rabbit with olives, fresh cod with anchovy sauce, a green salad and a tasty apple tart.

Menus: 150F, 250F.

Hostellerie de l'Abbaye

Rte. de Grasse - 93.32.66.77

Open year-round. 13 rms 200-600F. Half-board 150F. TV. Pets allowed. Pool. Parking. Telex 462304. Cards: V, AE, DC.

This old winter residence of the Lérins monks houses luxurious rooms and a patio. Restaurant.

Marc-Hély

535, rte. de Cagnes - 93.22.64.10

Closed Nov. 15-March 1. 15 rms 260-360F. Parking. Cards: V, AE.

All of the rooms have double-glazed windows and terraces looking out on Saint-Paul-de-Vence. No restaurant.

Saint-Paul-Lez-Durance

13115 St-Paul-Lez-Durance - (Bouches-du-Rhône)
Paris 765 - Aix-en-Provence 25 - Manosque 27

(14) Le Fougassier de Saint-Paul

34, Grand-Rue - 42.57.42.43

M. Béchu. Open until 10 p.m. Closed Sun. dinner & Mon. Pets allowed. Cards: V, AE, DC, MC.

The old land-mine oven for which this restaurant is named is still visible in one of the charming dining rooms. The decor here combines Tuscan vaults, French ceilings and trompe l'oeil paintings. The owner is a perfectionist and a professional who, together with his young chef, has created a brief menu on which every item is a temptation, whether it's the vegetable terrine with duck liver, served with hot chive butter, the lotte "rissole" (turnover) with coriander, accompanied by green and red peppers, the leg of lamb en croûte or the exquisite sorbets. The wonderful wine cellar is exclusively regional. One more point is deserved.

A la carte: 280F. Menus: 125F (weekday lunch only), 185F.

Saint-Pée-sur-Nivelle

64310 Ascain - (Pyrénées-Atlantiques)
Paris 764 - Pau 131 - Bayonne 21 - St-Jean-de-Luz 13

Bonnet

59.54.10.26

Closed Mon. (off-seas.) & Nov. 11-Dec. 10. 60 rms 186-220F. Half-board 218-225F. TV in 5 rms. Heated pool. Tennis. Pets allowed. Parking. Telex 541104. Cards: V, AE, DC, MC.

Simple rooms overlook the lush Basque countryside. The reception is enthusiastic. Restaurant.

(14) Le Fronton

59.54.10.12

M. Daguerre. Open until 9:30 p.m. Closed Wed. (off-seas.) & Jan. 15-Feb. 15. Air cond. Garden dining. Pets allowed. Hotel: 12 rms 130-180F; half-board 170-190F oblig. in seas. Parking. Cards: V, AE, DC.

The cuisine of Jean-Baptiste Daguerre is constantly progressing. He deserves an additional point for his light sauces, his respect for products and his strides toward simplicity: delicious cold gazpacho with lobster and chervil, fried langoustines with cèpes and artichokes (perfectly balanced), filet of bass served with sautéed fresh chanterelles and a superb dessert plate (delicate and not too sweet). The wine cellar is lovely, as is Mme. Daguerre, and we hope that the dining room, which was being revamped at the time of this writing, will be equally as pleasing. There is also a nice terrace under the trees.

A la carte: 280-300F. Menus: 115F, 190F, 220F.

Saint-Père-sous-Vézelay

see Vézelay

Saint-Pierre-de-Boeuf

42410 St-Pierre-de-Boeuf - (Loire)
Paris 513 - Lyon 50 - St-Etienne 50 - Vienne 22

(13) La Diligence

Pl. de la Bascule - 74.87.12.19

M. Belle. Open until 8:30 p.m. Closed Sun. dinner, Mon. & 2 weeks in July. Cards: V, AE.

There is much to discover behind this discreet facade at the edge of the route Nationale. You will find a refined, flower-filled decor in peach tones, pleasantly partitioned by decorative screens. The welcome is always exemplary, and the young staff is efficient. Everything has an air of seriousness, and the cuisine prepared by Guy Belle does not belie this impression. It is classic at its roots, but nicely brought up-to-date and in step with the seasons: duck filets fried with peaches and served warm in a salad of julienned vegetables, filet of lemon sole with chives, émincé of veal with chanterelles, excellent gratins of in-season fruit (apricots, pears, raspberries). The Côtes-du-Rhône are good but too expensive.

A la carte: 200-220F. Menus: 85F (weekdays only), 132F, 192F, 220F.

Saint-Prest

see Chartres

Saint-Quentin

02100 St-Quentin - (Aisne)
Paris 155 - Amiens 73 - Lille 116 - Reims 96

Sights. The basilica (Gothic); Musée Antoine Lécuyer (exceptional collection of pastels by Maurice Quentin de La Tour); the town hall facade (late Gothic, early Renaissance); Musée d'Entomologie (only collection in Europe).

Eating on the Run. Le Brésilien, pl. du 8-Octobre (serves until midnight); Le Glacier, 28, pl. de l'Hôtel-de-Ville; Le Scampi, 25 bis, rue Dachery (Italian specialties).

Bars & Cafés. Le Carillon, 7, rue Croix-Belle-Porte (pleasant, recently renovated); Le Piano-Bar (Hôtel Diamant), pl. de la Basilique (mellow, British ambience).

Nightlife. Le Nymphée, rte. de Cambrai; Le Privé, rue Michelet; Le Xénon, 5 km toward Laon (one of the largest discotheques in Europe).

(13) Le Château

Neuville-St-Amand (3 km SE on D 12)
23.68.41.82

M. Meiresonne. Open until 9 p.m. Closed Wed. & Sun. dinner, Mon., Feb. school vacation, Aug. 1-21 & 1 week at Christmas. Pets allowed. Parking. Cards: V, AE, DC, MC.

This large, bourgeois structure is set amid fields and trees at the edge of town. When seated in the comfortable white and auburn dining room, you'll look out on the greenery through bay windows while the friendly owners serve you marvelous fish from Boulogne, good-quality meats (pan-fried beef, roast rack of lamb) and a delicious breast of duck cooked with cream and cider. The wine cellar is well composed (mainly Bordeaux and Champagnes), and all the bottles may be purchased to take with you.

Menus: 140F and 245F (weekdays only), 235F and 275F (weekends and holidays only).

France et Angleterre

28, rue Emile-Zola - 23.62.13.10

Open year-round. 28 rms 155-235F. TV. Pets allowed. Garage parking. Telex 140986. Cards: V, AE, MC.

Located some 200 meters from the cathedral, this hotel is convenient and well equipped. No restaurant.

Le Président

6-8, rue Dachery
23.62.69.77

M. Brochard & Mme. Morchayan. Open until 10 p.m. Closed Sun. dinner, Mon., Dec. 24-Jan. 9 & July 30-Aug. 22. Pets allowed. Parking. Telex 140225. Cards: V, AE, DC, MC.

On the questionnaire we send to all of our listed establishments, we ask if they offer "an interesting view." Mme. Morchayan, manager of Le Président, gave us a good laugh by responding, "Not really." You will understand why we laughed when you arrive in this train-station neighborhood, where boredom is the norm and where the eye searches desperately for anything with a little grace. But you must go there nevertheless, because behind the "not really" pleasant facade of the Grand Hôtel hides a ravishing little restaurant with white ceramics, salmon-hued hangings and soft light. And behind the kitchen doors bustles a sensational team of young cooks, whose average age is probably no more than 26 or 27. At its head is a young man who is so modest and timid that you would almost need an explosion in the oven to get him to venture into the dining room. But it must be said that Raymond Brochard has followed in the steps of his master, Joël Robuchon, the king of the "invisible" chefs. Devoured by anxiety, this perfectionist creates a cuisine with a modern spirit, full of finesse and intelligence. The à la carte menu is short, but given the fixed-price menus, the attention to the seasons and the daily specials, it is nearly impossible to eat the same thing in two visits. It's like a dream, here in little Saint-Quentin, compared to the big cities where so many restaurants—even the better ones—don't go to the trouble of changing their menus even twice a year.

Although at times it does slip into sameness, this most elaborate cuisine nearly always succeeds in giving the impression of simplicity to the richest ingredients and the most complex flavor combinations. At our last visit, we loved the lobster and salmon vinaigrette with radish cream; the tiny, quickly cooked chanterelles and chervil sauce in a truly airy feuilleté; the duo of lotte and lobster in a voluptuous Sauternes sauce; the simmered sweetbreads and lobster in morel juice (a reckless dish, but what splendor!); the milk-fed lamb stuffed with vegetables. And, of course, the desserts, the work of the extraordinary Dominique Cholin, who serves as both the maître d'hôtel and pastry chef. What a baker! His desserts of the day, his ice creams and his millefeuille of red fruit are staggeringly good. And then there is Franck Palm, who is 24 years old and already has an impressive knowledge of wines. His wine list is a model of clarity and quality. It includes not only the premier grand crus from Bordeaux and about 50 Champagnes, but also a selection of Loire vintages that sell for about 100 francs.

A la carte: 400F. Menus: 170F (weekdays only), 290F.

Grand Hôtel

(See restaurant above)

Open year-round. 24 rms 380-480F. TV. Pets allowed.

Recently, owner M. Roupioz completed a total transformation of his hotel. The rooms are small in number but big in charm and luxury. There is even an exterior elevator.

Saint-Raphaël

83700 St-Raphaël - (Var)
Paris 892 - Cannes 44 - Toulon 96 - Draguignan 33

La Chêneraie 

Blvd. des Gondins - 94.83.65.03

Closed Feb. 1-March 15. 10 rms 245-470F. Half-board 340-415F oblig. in seas. TV in 2 rms. Cards: V.

The ten large, modernized rooms are outfitted with much attention to comfort, down to the lovely bathrooms. From this tranquil setting the rooms have a view of the golf course or the Esterel. Restaurant.

Golf-Hôtel de Valescure 

Ave. Paul-Lermite - 94.82.40.31

Closed Jan. 8-31 & Nov. 16-Dec. 20. 40 rms 435-650F. Half-board 395-600F oblig. in seas. TV. Pets allowed. Air cond. in 2 rms. Pool. Tennis. Golf. Telex 461085. Cards: V, AE, DC, MC.

These pretty rooms are bright and comfortable; some face the golf course. Golf and tennis lessons are available, as well as archery. Restaurant.

L'Orangerie

Promenade René-Coty - 94.83.10.50

M. Porro. Open until 10 p.m. Closed Sun. dinner & Mon. Terrace dining. Pets allowed. Cards: V, AE, DC, MC.

This new restaurant on the promenade has a fresh decor illuminated by a multitude of plants, immense bouquets of dried flowers around a Wallace fountain and graceful, young waitresses. And the cuisine of Alain Couture, formerly with La Ferme Saint-Siméon in Honfleur, is also delightfully fresh: baby zucchini stuffed with a green-pepper flan, delicious ravioli of lamb's sweetbreads with herbs, veal kidneys with beans and artichokes. The pigeon was mediocre, but it was doubtless an accident. Desserts are beautiful.

A la carte: 250F. Menus: 90F (weekday lunch only), 150F.

Pastorel

54, rue de la Liberté - 94.95.02.36

M. Floccia. Open until 9:30 p.m. Closed Sun. dinner, Mon., Jan. & lunch in Aug. Garden dining. Cards: V, AE.

In low or high season, this old provincial restaurant with oak paneling is always filled with a clientele that has been irresistibly lured there by word of mouth. Charles Floccia enjoys a solid reputation, and we find that he is not at all overrated. His cuisine has the great virtue of consistency, and his fundamental classicism is not without a certain variation in repertoire. His specialties include Friday's great aïoli, filet of red mullet with tomatoes and basil, salmis (a ragoût) of squab and a chilled soufflé of mint and chocolate. And you will be served irreproachable meals at moderate prices, considering these inflationary times. The old-style service is excellent, and the wine cellar is well stocked.

A la carte: 280-300F. Menus: 140F, 190F.

(13) San Pedro

Ave. du Colonel-Brooke - 94.83.65.69, 94.40.57.40

M. Wateau. Open until 9:45 p.m. Closed Mon. (off-seas.) & Jan. 2-March 1. Air cond. Terrace dining. No pets. Parking. Telex 461360. Cards: V, AE.

The decor inside this luxurious hacienda isn't thrilling, so you won't be missing anything if you choose to sit under a sun umbrella on the terrace at one of the tables around the swimming pool. For the last year or so, the cuisine has been prepared by an excellent professional who came from La Crémaillère in Gréoux-les-Bains, where he was chef for six years. Philippe Troncy has perfected a short but interesting seasonal menu, from which we enjoyed the saveloy (sausage) of salmon on a bed of leeks, the cod with shellfish essence served with fresh pasta and, after some rather tired cheeses, the delicious "parchemin" (a crispy, light biscuit) with hazelnut ice cream. The greeting and service are of luxury-hotel quality.

A la carte: 300-350F. Menus: 150F (weekday lunch only), 180F, 300F.

San Pedro

(See restaurant above)

Closed Jan. 2-March 1. 28 rms 510-650F. TV. Pets allowed. Pool.

Close to the golf course and tennis courts of Valescure, this attractive, "parador"-style building is set in the middle of a large garden and pine forest. The rooms are pleasant, though more comfortable than enticing.

Saint-Rémy-de-Provence

13210 St-Rémy-de-Provence - (Bouches-du-Rhône)
Paris 710 - Marseille 91 - Arles 24 - Avignon 21 - Nîmes 42

Château de Roussan

Rte. de Tarascon (2 km on N 99)
90.92.11.63

Closed Oct. 30-March 15. 17 rms 350-500F. Parking. Cards: V.

This splendid eighteenth-century residence stands amid fifteen acres of flowers, ponds, waterways bordered with antique statues, rare fragrances and immense, 200-year-old plane trees. Offering a dozen irresistibly seductive rooms, this is without a doubt one of the most exquisite hotels in the south of France. No restaurant.

Château des Alpilles

D 31 - 90.92.03.33

Closed Jan. 3-March 20. 2 stes 910-1,100F. 17 rms 560-760F. TV. Pets allowed. Pool. Tennis. Parking. Telex 431487. Cards: V, AE, DC, MC.

Built at the beginning of the nineteenth century, this serene and lovely place is surrounded by 100-year-old trees. The rooms are huge and have been redecorated with impeccable taste. Here, at one of the most refined hotels in Provence, guests enjoy a true change of scenery. In summer there is a poolside grill.

(16) Domaine de Valmouriane

Rte. des Baux - 90.92.44.62

Mme. McHugo. Open daily until 10 p.m. Garden dining. No pets. Telex 431169. Cards: V, AE, MC.

This establishment perched on a white rock in the middle of an exquisite, green Provençal setting has just been completely remade into a luxurious inn by a British investor. He has entrusted the management of the place to his capable daughter, Catherine McHugo, and has left the cooking in the experienced hands of Jean-Claude Aubertin, who has been running fine restaurants for years. This conscientious native of the Champagne region has begun anew here by offering a simple menu based on Provençal flavors. Although scarcely underway at the time of our visit, the cooking was already flying high, with such dishes as the fricassée of lamb's trotters with truffles, the inventive and delicious guinea-fowl wings in cinnamon and cacao, the plate of foie gras with peaches and ginger, the rabbit slices in pesto (a three-toque dish, with its accompanying light giblet cakes) and such breathtaking desserts as the souffléed fig-and-cheese tart or the honey-mango puff pastry. It doesn't take a crystal ball to see a bright future for this gay and charming restaurant, especially once the weather allows for use of the tables and pretty parasols in the garden. The service is perfect, and the prices are well in line with the quality.

A la carte: 300F. Menus: 200F, 350F.

Domaine de Valmouriane

(See restaurant above)

Open year-round. 12 rms 705-1,310F. Half-board 905F. TV. Air cond. Pets allowed. Heated pool. Tennis.

This all-new plush little hotel offers spacious rooms (some with terraces) that have been completely equipped with the latest amenities. An impressive array of leasure activities is available on the eight acres of grounds: swimming, tennis, archery, golf putting and more.

(14) Vallon de Valrugues

1, ch. de Cato Cigalo - 90.92.04.40

M. Gallon. Open until 9:30 p.m. Closed Jan. 2-Feb. 28. Garden dining. Air cond. No pets. Parking. Telex 431677. Cards: V, AE, DC.

This big, rectangular fortress surrounded by parkland has just been turned into a small Provençal luxury hotel—a hotel that intends to also offer one of the best restaurants in the region. With enough resources to hire Jacky Morlon as chef, the corporation now ought to have enough vision to leave him free to run his own show. Certainly such a talented young chef—a former student of Michel Guérard—can do better than the timidly flavored marinated tuna with leeks and truffles, the good but unexceptional whiting and prawns with tomato and the too-clever desserts that we have encountered here. Nonetheless, it's an extremely well-run dining room in a vast expanse of white and salmon.

A la carte: 350-400F. Menus: 260F, 350F.

Vallon de Valruges

(See restaurant above)

Closed Jan. 2-Feb. 28. 10 stes 680-780F. 24 rms 430-580F. Half-board 560-610F oblig. in seas. TV. Air cond. Pets allowed. Heated pool. Tennis.

The luxurious style is a bit ostentatious, but it certainly is quiet and comfortable in the rooms, all of which have terraces, some facing the Alpilles mountains. In addition, there are tennis courts, a huge pool, a driving range and so on. Valet parking is provided, and the service in general is most accommodating.

Saint-Romans-de-Bellet

see Nice

Saint-Savin

see Argelès-Gazost

Saint-Sébastien-sur-Loire

see Nantes

Saint-Sernin-sur-Rance

12380 - St-Sernin-sur-Rance - (Aveyron)
Paris 702 - Albi 50 - Rodez 83 - St-Affrique 32

Carayon

Pl. du Fort - 65.99.60.26

M. Carayon. Open until 9 p.m. Closed Sun. dinner & Mon. (off-seas.). Terrace dining. Pets allowed. Hotel: 2 stes 250-325F; 38 rms 105-270F; half-board 189-269F. TV in 5 rms. Parking. Cards: V, AE, DC, MC.

For a cure-all of good humor, good food and good manners without pretense, consult Pierre Carayon. In all of Aveyron there is no other innkeeper as happy to do his job or as devoted to celebrating the treasures of his region. Behind his old inn (which each year is embellished, while maintaining a rustic simplicity), a magnificent terrace overhangs the green valley. Take a table there, and make your selection from the innumerable and equally appealing regional specialties. The young chef has a style that is both enthusiastic and generous (take a look at the fixed-price menus): crayfish in a court bouillon, old-fashioned stuffed cabbage, grilled mutton, squab salmis (ragoût) and Saint-Sernan cheeses ripened on the premises. You'll also have the chance to treat yourself to a marvelous Gaillac wine or even a good cigar.

A la carte: 200F. Menus: from 57F to 113F, 143F, 228F.

Saint-Servan

see Saint-Malo

Saint-Sylvain-d'Anjou

see Angers

Saint-Symphorien-le-Château

28700 Auneau - (Eure-et-Loir)
Paris 69 - Essarts 2 - Ablis 7 - Rambouillet 23 - Chartres 26

Château d'Esclimont

37.31.15.15

M. Spitz. Open daily until 9:30 p.m. No pets. Parking. Telex 780560. Cards: V.

René Traversac, who collects châteaux throughout France (Artigny, Isenbourg, Divonne and so on), chooses his managers and his cooks better than his decorators. He buys up these sumptuous mansions and puts them back into shape without skimping, but there is always something that's not quite right, perhaps machine-made tapestries or candy-pink silk. One day, we hope, he will stop using his family as decorators and go to a professional. Only then will the "château life" promised at each of his establishments be truly that, rather than just an approximation.

But enough criticism. This astonishing man—who would eat lion meat until his dying day—knew how to make this Renaissance château of the La Rochefoucaulds, vigorously revamped in the nineteenth century (the château, not the La Rochefoucaulds), one of the best spots for weekend getaways, since it's just 45 minutes from Paris. It boasts lavish grounds, a pond, a river, tennis courts, a pool... in brief, heaven. And let's not forget the musical evenings in the former seventeenth-century stables, which have been transformed into "trophy rooms."

The other attraction, which isn't negligible, is that the cuisine improves with each new chef. Far from making us miss his former excellent master, Patrick Guerry, who has just been promoted from being Jean-Michel Diot's number-two to being his successor, beguiles us in his own way. With his evident talent and what he has learned from his predecessors, Guerry is a real find for the manager of the château, Raymond Spitz. As a matter of fact, if we knew for sure that he would be here a year from now, that he would rewrite the menu with less frills, and that he would be a little more careful with his presentations, we would grant a third toque right away. For that's what several of the dishes we tried recently deserved—namely the incredibly light lobster lasagne with a truffle sauce, the roasted truffled local pigeon served with delicious braised cabbage, the wonderful fricassée of lotte with lentils and the dish of pears with cacao sorbet. The wine cellar is excellent—with even too many Burgundies—the service is perfect, and the ambience is pleasant in spite of the business breakfasts, receptions and conferences that seem to always be going on.

A la carte: 400-500F. Menus: 250F, 430F.

Château d'Esclimont

(See restaurant above)

Open year-round. 6 stes 1,430-2,100F. 48 rms 520-1,210F. TV. Pets allowed. Heated pool. Tennis.

The 48 rooms and six suites of this château are classic, comfortable and well situated in the middle of a 150-acre expanse of completely walled-in grounds at the bottom of a valley, which is traversed by a river and situated near the road that connects Rambouillet and Chartres. Guests can play tennis, swim in the heated pool and attend wintertime musical evenings, for which weekend packages are proposed at quite reasonable prices (less than 2,000 francs per couple). Relais et Châteaux.

Saint-Thégonnec

29223 St-Thégonnec - (Finistère)
Paris 550 - Châteaulin 52 - Morlaix 12 - Landivisiau 12

(14) Auberge Saint-Thégonnec

6, pl. de la Mairie - 98.79.61.18

M. Le Coz. Open until 9 p.m. Closed Sun. dinner, Mon. & Jan. 2-Feb. 14. Terrace dining. No pets. Hotel: 6 rms 100-250F; half-board 200-350F. Cards: V, AE, DC, MC.

This lovely stone structure is located directly across from the famous "enclos" (walled enclosure), one of the most beautiful in Brittany. The interior decor is simple and in good taste, with a few watercolors on the walls and a statue of Saint-Thégonnec in his stone niche giving his benediction to the excellent cuisine prepared by Alain Le Coz, worthy son of his mother, Manick (Hôtel de la Plage in Sainte-Anne-la-Palud). He has perfected several fixed-price menus of remarkable quality and generosity, as well as a large à la carte menu that is conservative but incorporates modern touches, on which you will find a Breton lobster braised in Muscadet, a delicious shellfish terrine with saffron under a pastry crust, a filet of beef fondant sautéed with pickled shallots, exquisite goat cheeses freshly made by goatherds in the Arrée mountains, a perfect apple tart caramelized with wild honey, and in May, freshly picked strawberries. The service is good, the atmosphere lively, and the wine cellar interesting.

A la carte: 250F. Menus: 70F (weekdays only), 120F, 160F, 300F.

Saint-Trojan-les-Bains

see Oléron (Ile d')

Saint-Tropez

83990 St-Tropez - (Var)
Paris 890 - Cannes 75 - Toulon 69 - Ste-Maxime 14

Sights. The old harbor, its yachts, its terraced bistros, its people and its painters; the citadel (Musée de la Marine and the marvelous panorama); L'Eglise (bust of Torpes); the chapels: Ste-Anne (mariners) and St-Joseph (pilgrimage of marine carpenters); the pl. des Lices (bocci players); the marvelous marine cemetery clinging to the hillside; the marketplace on pl. aux Herbes (mornings, truly Provençal).

Eating on the Run. Le Bar à Vins, 13, rue des Féniers (wine by the glass, snacks); Le Canastel, 1, rue des Féniers (pizza); L'Escoundu, 3, rue du Clocher (friendly bistro, until 11 p.m.); La Flo, 15, rue de la Citadelle (tarts); La Fraîche Grotte, rue François-Sibilli (in a cellar, reasonably priced, small fixed-price menus); La Marjolaine, 10, rue François-Sibilli (trattoria).

Bars & Cafés. On the harbor: Le Gorille (ice cream and motorcycle policemen) and Sénéquier (ice cream and dark glasses); on pl. des Lices: Le Café des Arts (stars and boules players) and Le Bistrot des Lices (cocktails and orchestra); Chez Nano, pl. de l'Hôtel-de-Ville (the most popular among locals, before and after dinner, especially in high season); bar at Hôtel Byblos (remarkable, welcoming), piano bar at Yaca, 1, blvd. d'Aumale.

Nightlife. L'Aphrodisiaque (fashionable, excellent music); Le Bal (gay/mixed clientele); Les Caves du Roy, at Hôtel Byblos (disco and private club run by music-business tycoon Eddie Barclay and Jacqueline Veyssière, who, with Régine, is co-queen of Saint-Tropez's nightlife); L'Esquinade (heterosexual, late-night); Le New Jimmy's, at the new harbor (challenger to Régine); Le Pigeonnier (gay, shows).

Shops. *Charcuteries:* Boix, 5, rue du Marché; Michel Miguel, 2 bis, rue des Commerçants. *Chocolate, confections:* Georget, 11, rue Allard (chocolates and pastes of almond, fig and dried fruits). *Gourmet foods:* Le Bouchon de l'Echalotte, 22, rue Seillon (foie gras, beer). *Ice cream:* Glace Alfred, rue François-Sibilli (46 flavors). *Pasta:* La Maison des Pâtes, 31, rue du Portail-Neuf (large selection, plus sauces). *Pastries:* Sénéquier, 4, pl. aux Herbes (best and most famous, for tarts, frangipanes and nougat).

La Bastide des Salins

Rte. des Saline - 94.97.24.57

Closed Jan. 5-Feb. 15. 4 stes 950-1,200F. 9 rms 650-1,200F. TV. Pets allowed. Pool. Parking. Cards: V.

This is one of the most charming new addresses in Saint-Tropez. The large rooms in this appealing hotel on private grounds have great personality. No restaurant.

(13) Bistrot des Lices

3, pl. des Lices - 94.97.29.00

M. Falcot. Open until 12:30 a.m. Closed Wed. (Nov.-Aug.). Air cond. Garden dining. Pets allowed. Cards: V.

From behind the scenes, Jacques Manière pulls the strings of this intelligent and fresh cuisine. Out of an old hangout for Saint-Tropez celebrities, he has created one of the most pleasant gathering spots in a town swelling with restaurants. The menu is the essence of clarity: a dozen main dishes whose prices—from 210 to 300 francs—include an appetizer and a dessert. The langoustines, the fresh duck liver, the salmon and the andouillette of red mullet are all good (with no tricks), generous and well worth a toque. The local wines are well chosen.

Menus: 300-350F.

Byblos

Ave. Paul-Signac - 94.97.00.04

Closed Nov.-Feb. 48 stes 1,790-3,420F. 59 rms 900-2,080F. TV. Air cond. Heated pool. Parking. Telex 470235. Cards: V, AE, DC.

In addition to the rooms (often cramped) and suites (more spacious), this hotel offers new boutiques, two conference rooms and a nightclub, outside of which the chic of Saint-Tropez wait in line. The enlarged parking lot is yet another sign that this a true hotel complex, but it is run so well that you'll hardly notice. The ambience is high-class, even down to the magnificent pool. Restaurant.

11/20 Café des Arts

Pl. des Lices - 94.97.02.25

Mme. Bain. Open until midnight. Closed Oct. 15-March 1. Air cond. Pets allowed.

The "arts" of the game of boules, chitchat and pastis (i.e., Pernod) are discussed at Café des Arts by the show-biz crowd. The kitchen turns out an honest, rustic cuisine.

A la carte: 200-220F. Menu: 160F (dinner only, wine incl.).

17 Chabichou

Ave. Foch
94.54.80.00

M. Rochedy. Open until 11:30 p.m. Closed Oct. 10-early May. Air cond. Terrace dining. Pets allowed. Telex 461051. Cards: V.

In three stirs of a spoon, the friendly Michel Rochedy has become the king of Saint-Tropez. Without playing up to the stars or making waves, he has conquered, with his amiable manner and the finesse of his cuisine, a gilt-edged public known for being one of the most difficult in the world. It was hardly a shoo-in. The people of Saint-Tropez, even with all their play money, actually are not interested in making a big production out of eating. Mainly they enjoy conviviality, groups of friends and joking around. From this point of view, Bistrot des Lices, Café des Arts, Bistrot de la Marine or even the peaceful Fifine are much more representative of the Saint-Tropez spirit than this luxurious restaurant where you see, through an immense aquarium, about twenty cooks moving about in a kitchen so spotless you could eat off the floor. In any case, the hostess, the elegant service, the lovely dishes and the almost Hollywood-style terrace compose a grand show that has succeeded in attracting spectators. Though rare at lunchtime, they are sufficiently numerous in the evenings for Rochedy to envision the future with optimism. He has also struck a gold mine with his most faithful supporter, Eddie Barclay. This Saint-Tropez music business celebrity not only has parties catered by Chabichou, but prefers to eat Rochedy's fare at home in his slippers instead of running around to restaurants. There isn't a big party or an event that takes place without Rochedy and his boys... with 100 percent success guaranteed.

Since this lovable snowman (in winter he is at Courchevel) has been spending six months of the year under the Provence sun, his style has become more pure and even taken on a certain southern grace. He is still a genius with olive oil. His glazed oysters, lightly seasoned with anise, are exquisitely fresh and subtle; his casserole of oysters, potatoes and chanterelles (the rye biscuits are a good idea but have no taste) is a superb dish with intense flavors, as are the escalope of turbot with celery and truffles, the cod with lentils and the sweetbreads on a spinach salad with truffle oil. And it is impossible not to succumb to Rochedy's desserts: feuillantine of caramelized pears, peach soup with Beaumes-de-Venise, licorice parfait, bitter-chocolate meringue cake. And if the great wines of the sumptuous cellar threaten to weigh down the bill, which already tends to be heavy, there is a choice of excellent Côtes-de-Provence—red and rosé Château Barbeyrolles, Château Minuty and so on. Besides, it's not fair that Chabichou is considered to have exorbitant prices; 180 francs for a duck ballottine with truffles, a rack of veal with wild mushrooms and a dessert, or 280 francs for a superb four-course meal, plus a thyme sorbet and petits fours—in Saint-Tropez, that's practically a gift!

A la carte: 500-800F. Menus: 135F (lunch only), 320F, 420F.

La Maison Blanche

Pl. des Lices - 94.97.52.66

Open year-round. 2 stes 1,200F. 6 rms 700-1,200F. TV. Air cond. Parking. Cards: V, AE, DC.

At this turn-of-the-century pavilion, with its garden and antique furniture, the service is most attentive and the atmosphere pleasant. No restaurant, but catering is available.

La Mandarine

Rte. de Tahiti - 94.97.21.00

Closed Oct. 21-March 23. 4 stes 2,200F. 39 rms 840-1,350F. TV in 30 rms. Air cond. in 2 rms. Heated pool. Parking. Telex 970461. Cards: V, AE, DC.

This group of small, pink houses is far from the buzz of town. The rooms are bright and modern, with lovely terraces. There is a private beach a few kilometers away in Pampelonne. Restaurant.

16 Le Mas de Chastelas

Rte. de Gassin, Quartier Bertaud
94.56.09.11

MM. Racine & Sulitzer. Open until 10:30 p.m. Closed late Sept.-mid-May. Garden dining. No pets. Parking. Telex 462393. Cards: V, AE, DC, MC.

A three-toque chef at Le Mas de Chastelas! To replace Alain Rondelli, Gérard Racine has hired Michel Gaudin, who, after spending fourteen years in Brittany at Le Château de Locguénolé, was lured away by the Mediterranean sun (not to mention his fondness for the flavors of Provence). And after all those years preparing a large menu and a particularly complex cuisine, he is now content with a more simple formula. It's just what he had been dreaming of: fifteen Provençal-style appetizers and main dishes for some 60 place settings on the terrace, under the arbor of this beautiful old building, where silkworms once were raised. The exquisite Paulette will continue to make her delicious tarts and chocolate cake. Everyone has been impatient to discover the new Gaudin, and we are just now in the happy posi-

tion, after several fine meals, to reconfirm the two toques that this establishment has justly worn for so long.
A la carte: 350-400F.

Le Mas de Chastelas
(See restaurant above)
Closed early Oct.-early April. 10 stes 1,650-2,000F. 21 rms 510-1,150F. TV in 11 rms. Heated pool. Tennis.
All pink and ocher, this eighteenth-century house in the vineyards is the most truly Tropezian hotel in town. We highly recommend it to those who crave calm and simplicity. The rooms (several of which are rather small) have their faithful following, but it is most pleasant to stay in one of the duplex villas set among the pine and oak trees. Guests are graciously received by Dominique Sulitzer and her staff. Whirlpool.

14 L'Olivier
Rte. des Carles (1 km) - 94.97.58.16
M. Aubrun. Open daily until 10:30 p.m. Closed Jan. 4-April 15 & Oct. 31-Dec. 18. Garden dining. Pets allowed. Parking. Telex 461516. Cards: V, AE, DC.
The dining room has finally been opened out onto the small park at the heart of the old city, and a new chef has just taken over the ovens. Francis Cardaillac is a newcomer to the region, and he is slowly getting the hang of Mediterranean cooking. His sautéed filets of red snapper and artichokes, the young rabbit with thyme flowers, the grilled bass steak with a shallot confit and the rack of lamb dressed with basil (lacking character) are still in need of balance and refinement, which this excellent chef is certain to master in time. Until then we are holding back the second toque, while encouraging him to seek simplicity (which can be seen in his magnificent duck cooked in honey and coarse salt). The charming young waiters are most attentive, making a fine pleasure out of eating either in the attractive dining room or on the exquisite garden terrace. The prices range from the reasonable to the ridiculous, and you will find little relief on the wine list.
A la carte: 250-300F.

Bastide de Saint-Tropez
(See restaurant above)
Closed Nov. 15-Dec. 15 & Jan. 4-Feb. 4. 8 stes 1,800-2,500F. TV. Air cond. Pool.
A luxurious country house and three smaller ones surround the superb pool. The rooms are decorated in pastel tones and offer modern comfort.

11/20 La Ponche
Pl. du Révelin - 94.97.02.53
Mme. Barbier. Open until midnight. Closed Oct. 15-April 1. Air cond. Terrace dining. Pets allowed. Telex 461516.
The strategically positioned terrace, which extends out from the stunning interior, witnesses the comings and goings of all the Saint-Tropez celebrities—as it has for the past 35 years. The clientele is always fashionable, and alongside the stiffly priced à la carte dishes, there is a fixed-price menu that includes fish soup, baked sardines with herbed onions, green peppers and tomatoes, and sorbets.
A la carte: 200-300F. Menus: 95F (lunch only), 160F.

La Ponche
(See restaurant above)
Closed Oct. 15-April 1. 23 rms 300-900F. TV in 10 rms. Air cond. in 17 rms. Pets allowed.
Looking out over the fortified square, this hotel offers a beautiful ocean view. The rooms are well maintained and, though decorated in outdated luxury, are full of charm.

12/20 La Ramade
Rue du Temple - 94.97.00.15
M. Aurelly. Open until 11 p.m. Closed Wed. & Nov. 15-April 15. Garden dining. No pets. Cards: V.
All summer long people swarm to this flower-filled garden shaded by mulberry trees. The fare includes fresh produce, meats and fish grilled over grapevine stalks and a respectable bouillabaisse served on weekends.
A la carte: 200-250F.

14 Résidence de la Pinède
Plage de la Bouillabaisse - 94.97.04.21
M. Delion. Open until 10:30 p.m. Closed Oct. 15-Easter. Air cond. Garden dining. Pets allowed. Parking. Telex 470489. Cards: V, AE, DC, MC.
It has always been enchanting to dine on the terrace here under the tall trees, facing the bay and the lights of Sainte-Maxime, and now that professional management has finally arrived, it is that much more inviting. With it comes a new chef, Pierre Roger, who is in the process of improving the cooking. He has yet to show a great deal of imagination, though everything is finely done—from the minced turbot with salmon eggs, to the stuffed sea bass in a crust, to the filet of lamb in layered pastry with tarragon, to the souffléed crêpes with red fruit. The young wine steward stocks reasonably priced, attractive wines from Provence. The bill at lunch isn't as frightening as that at dinner, and one lunches outdoors next to the pool. Service can be starchy.
A la carte: 400-500F. Menus: 150F (weekday lunch only), 200F (weekdays only), 300F (dinner only), 350F (weekends and holidays only).

Résidence de la Pinéde
(See restaurant above)
Closed Oct. 15-Easter. 5 stes 2,000-4,400F. 35 rms 1,000-2,400F. Half-board 1,800-2,800F. TV. Air cond. Pets allowed. Heated pool.
The highway is behind this hotel (but it can't be heard), and the Saint-Tropez golf course is in front (with direct access via the private beach). There is also the lovely kidney-shaped pool, the shade of the pines and the large rooms with ordinary but quite comfortable furnishings.

Hôtel Sube Continental
On the harbor - 94.97.30.04
Open year-round. 24 rms 300-1,200F. TV. Air cond. in 6 rms. Parking. Cards: V, AE, DC, MC.

If you like greenery, tranquility and birds singing, the oldest hotel in Saint-Tropez—and the only one directly on the harbor—won't be your cup of tea. If, on the other hand, you'd like to look out your window and watch the fascinating show of Saint-Tropez life, this place has the best seats in town. Here to welcome you is a well-known personality, Annie Bolloré (coming from Le Mas de Chastelas), who has taken over the management of this typically Tropezian hotel, whose reception area and rooms were undergoing renovation at the time of this writing. By the time you read this, another local celebrity—Picolette—is expected to be serving her cuisine in the large second-floor dining room that opens its windows above the lineup of the most famous yachts in France.

La Tartane

Rte. des Saline - 94.97.21.23

Closed Jan. 2-March 15 & Nov. 5-Dec. 20. 12 rms 520-700F. TV. Air cond. Pets allowed. Pool. Parking. Cards: V.

These remarkably furnished bungalows are charming, tranquil, surrounded by greenery and just steps from the pool. Other pluses are the comfortable terraces, swimming pool, whirlpool and attentive service. Restaurant (lunch).

Le Yaca

1, blvd. d'Aumale - 94.97.11.79

Closed Jan. 10-April 1 & Oct. 15-Dec. 20. 1 ste 2,300F. 22 rms 700-1,400F. TV. Air cond. Heated pool. Parking. Telex 462140. Cards: V, AE, DC, MC.

In the heart of Saint-Tropez, this ravishing little hotel has attractively decorated rooms (by Souleiado) and faces a pretty interior garden. Restaurant.

See also: **Gassin, Grimaud, Ramatuelle**

Saint-Valéry-en-Caux

76460 St-Valéry-en-Caux - (Seine-Maritime)
Paris 198 - Dieppe 32 - Fécamp 32 - Rouen 59

Les Terrasses

22, rue Le Perrey (at the oceanfront)
35.97.11.22

Closed Wed. & Dec. 20-Jan. 30. 12 rms 160-260F. Half-board 260-360F. Cards: V, DC, MC.

At the water's edge, this hotel has an austere facade but rather well-equipped rooms, some of which face the sea. Restaurant.

Saint-Viâtre

see Nouan-le-Fuzelier

This symbol signifies hotels that offer an exceptional degree of peace and quiet.

Saint-Vincent-Sterlanges

85110 Chantonnay - (Vendée)
Paris 408 - La Roche-sur-Yon 31 - Chantonnay 7

Auberge du Parc

51.40.23.17

M. Guilbaud. Open until 9:30 p.m. Closed Tues., March 1-15 & Oct. 1-15. Terrace dining. Pets allowed. Parking. Cards: V, AE, DC, MC.

It's hard to imagine how more than ten years on the team at Le Plazza could leave a cook with such a youthful touch and such respect for the products, for the seasons and for humor. These are the best qualities of Lionel Guilbaud, whose cuisine is both frank and impulsive. A native of the Vendée, he returned a few years ago to sing the praises of his region. The sober refinements of his decor make it one of the most beautiful restaurants in the west of France: a spectacular centuries-old relais with paving stones, beams and antique furniture. Its powerful charm is perhaps carried over from the dreamy simplicity of the old days, but also from a cuisine surprising for its contradictory qualities: conservative yet spontaneous, modern yet country style. We have given him one more point for the salad of sweetbreads and kidneys, which was worth three toques; following not far behind were the fricassée of eels with wild mushrooms, the subtle suprême of chicken with langoustines, the fresh-fruit tarts and the chaud-froid of fresh figs with almond milk. We can only recommend that Guilbaud not spread himself too thin: His menu is too long and needlessly weighted down with predictable dishes that are less convincing. The hostess welcomes her guests with a warm reception.

A la carte: 300F. Menus: 80F, 120F, 200F.

Sainte-Anne-la-Palud

29127 Plomodiern - (Finistère)
Paris 569 - Quimper 25 - Châteaulin 19 - Douarnenez 16

La Plage

98.92.50.12

Mme. Lecoz. Open until 8:45 p.m. Closed Oct. 10-March 24. No pets. Parking. Telex 941377. Cards: V, AE, DC.

At the tip of the Douarnenez bay, and at the end of a small road that makes its way to the ocean between sand dunes hemmed with the yellow flowers of gorse plants, you will find the Lecoz family's vast, modern establishment. The atmosphere of this deserted beach becomes even more solemn when the great gusts of wind blow from the west. But this impression of slightly austere solitude vanishes as soon as you cross the threshold of this Relais et Châteaux inn, whose large, shaded garden, heated pool and opulent dining room looking out at the sea spray immediately plunge you into an ambience of warmth and civility. Manick Lecoz, an energetic, natural and attentive hostess, along with her staff members (who are a little slow) and her son and his wife, gives a festive air to what remains one of the best kitchens in Brittany. The cuisine is prepared by a young Breton, Jean-Pierre Gloanec, who is as at ease with his repertoire from the sea as with dishes of the land. A few errors (a seafood platter that was incomprehensibly sparse, a banal marinated salmon) can't overshadow the good memories we have from the chartreuse of bass stuffed with langoustines, cabbage and baby vegetables; the admirable squab deprived of perfection by a sauce that was slightly too sour; and a succulent chaud-froid of apples and pears (but the apple tart was boring).

A la carte: 300F. Menus: 170F (Sunday dinner and weekdays only), 205F and 300F (weekends and holidays only).

La Plage

(See restaurant above)

Closed Oct. 10-March 24. 4 stes 700-1,000F. 26 rms 340-700F. Half-board 500-650F oblig. in seas. TV. Pets allowed. Heated pool. Tennis.

Stylish without being overdone, these rooms face the sublime spectacle of the sea. Both the comfort level and the reception are top-notch. A sauna, Ping-Pong and children's play area. Relais et Châteaux.

Sainte-Livrade-sur-Lot

47110 Ste-Livrade-sur-Lot - (Lot-et-Garonne)
Paris 613 - Agen 39 - Marmande 43

12/20 Le Midi

74, rue Nationale - 53.01.00.32

M. Benito. Open until 9:30 p.m. Closed Dec. 20-April 1. Air cond. Pets allowed. Hotel: 8 stes. 15 rms 120-220F. Garage parking. Telex 560800. Cards: V, AE, DC.

A master of foie gras and confits, the owner invites his guests into the kitchen for a lesson on fatted duck. Then he treats them to a mousseline of cod with green peppers or grilled aiguillettes of duck with ginger. The reception is warm, and the Duras and Buzen wines are well chosen.

A la carte: 200-250F. Menus: 62F (weekdays only), 85F, 115F, 160F.

Sainte-Magnance

see Avallon

Sainte-Marie-de-Ré

see Ré (Ile de)

Sainte-Marine

see Bénodet

Sainte-Maxime

83120 Ste-Maxime - (Var)
Paris 880 - Toulon 63 - St-Raphaël 23 - Cannes 61

(15) Amiral

Le Port - 94.43.99.36

M. Guerre. Open until 10 p.m. Closed Sun. dinner & Mon. (off-seas.) & Nov. 1-May 1. Air cond. Terrace dining. Pets allowed. Cards: V.

Have we ever found in Sainte-Maxime a more refined little place offering such fine food? The new owner, who leaves behind a place in eastern France, has put together all the elements of success here. Outside is a big terrace under a blue-and-white awning; inside is a pretty, light-wood-paneled dining room; and in the kitchen is an excellent chef, Bernard Mathis. He has quickly laid claim to the two toques he had previously earned elsewhere with his adroit and personal cooking. Watch in particular for his vegetable galettes, his beans and green olives in a crunchy crust, his impressive lamb filets with rosemary en croûte, his risotto with crab butter and cuttlefish ink, his scorpionfish in anchovy cream and all his perfect desserts, especially the bitter-chocolate fondue. The excellent regional wine list includes a very good Bandol red, Domaine de Cagueloup. The checks are as full-bodied as the wine.

A la carte: 300F. Menus: 135F, 195F.

Calidianus

Blvd. Jean-Moulin - 94.96.23.21

Closed Nov. 31-Feb. 1. 33 rms 390-470F. TV. Pool. Tennis. Parking.

This group of modern, Provençal-style houses is 200 meters from the ocean. The rooms are adorned with small terraces, and guests have access to a pool and garden. No restaurant.

La Croisette

2, blvd. des Romarins - 94.96.17.75

Closed Oct. 31-March 15. 20 rms 243-328F. Parking. Cards: V, MC.

Close to the beaches and nicely renovated, La Croisette is an ideal place to stay in winter, when the mimosas are flowering. The ocean is 200 meters away. No restaurant.

Hostellerie de Beauvallon

Beauvallon - 94.43.81.11

Closed Sept. 30-May 1. 25 rms 600F. Half-board 575-600F oblig. in seas. Pool. Tennis. Parking. Telex 970238. Cards: V.

These small Provençal-style buildings surround a large pool and overlook the Saint-Tropez golf course. The rooms are modern, bright and rather spacious. The service is excellent. Restaurant.

(14) Hostellerie de la Belle Aurore

4, blvd. Jean-Moulin - 94.96.02.45, 94.96.05.03

M. Goutille. Open until 9:30 p.m. Closed Oct. 15-March 15. Air cond. Terrace dining. Pets allowed. Hotel: 2 stes 950-1,200F; 14 rms 650-800F; half-board 700-780F oblig. in seas. Pool. Parking. Cards: V, AE.

Everything is going well for Raymond Goutille, a former transatlantic sailor who is celebrating his 60th year of life with the euphoria of success. And he deserves it. Seated on the terrace in his spacious roadside restaurant that overlooks a sumptuous panorama of blue water, tawny rocks and the city of Saint-Tropez, you'll have the impression of eating whith your toes dangling in the water. In spite of the rather uncalled-for prices (at the time of this writing the small fixed-price menu had gone up from 140 to 200 francs), the cuisine of this remarkable professional is always well prepared and pleasantly personal, though fundamentally classic: langoustine salad with marinated vegetables, lobster soufflé, ratatouille with loin of lamb, hot mango tart. A

few luxurious rooms face the pool and the private beach.
A la carte: 350F. Menus: 200F, 320F.

Hôtel de la Poste
7, blvd. F.-Mistral - 94.96.18.33
Closed Oct. 25-April 1. 24 rms 290-500F. Half-board 300-460F oblig. in seas. Pool. Cards: V, AE, DC.
This remarkable new hotel is elegant and filled with light. To accommodate families, some of the rooms are connected. The restaurant faces the terrace, pool and garden.

Marie-Louise
Hameau de Guerrevieille (2 km SW)
94.96.06.05
Open year-round. 14 rms 140-265F. Half-board 260F oblig. in seas. Parking. Cards: V, DC.
Five of the rooms in this tranquil, well-maintained hotel have windows overlooking the sea. Restaurant.

12/20 Le Sarrazin
7 pl. Colbert - 94.96.10.84
M. Quatrevaley. Open until 10 p.m. (11 p.m. in summer). Closed Tues. & Feb. 2-15. Terrace dining. Pets allowed. Cards: V, AE, DC, MC.
Don't let the view of the old quarter of the city keep you from noticing the handsome seventeenth-century china from Bresse in the cute rose-colored dining room. The worthwhile fixed-price menu at 100 francs includes some carefully cooked and generously served dishes. On the à la carte you will a find classic, sauce-based cuisine, as well as local-style lamb chops. The wine list features a good, inexpensive red wine from the domaine Sainte-Marie.
A la carte: 200-230F. Menus: 80F (lunch only), 100F, 160F.

Saintes
17100 Saintes - (Charente-Maritime)
Paris 465 - Bordeaux 118 - Royan 37 - Niort 67

14 Le Logis Santon
54, cours Genêt - 46.74.20.14
MM. Sorillet. Open until 9:30 p.m. Closed Mon. lunch, Sun. & Feb. 20-28. Terrace dining. Pets allowed. Parking. Cards: V, AE, DC, MC.
People no longer come to the house of the good Dr. Sorrilet to show him their eardrums or their tonsils, but rather to be cared for by his lively son, Alain, who prescribes émincés of sweetbreads, grilled brill filets with marjoram, loin of lamb with foie gras flavored with anise, and fresh terrines of citrus fruit with Champagne and an orange purée. Such is the cuisine of an autodidact (Alain previously managed a pharmacy and a bookstore) and of a master of execution (the sauces are superb). The attractively decorated old dining room has an inviting terrace that faces the garden. Wisely, the number of table settings is limited to about twenty. Mme. Sorillet offers a smiling greeting. Excellent Bordeaux and Cognacs.
A la carte: 300F. Menus: 85F, 155F.

Relais du Bois Saint-Georges
Rue de Royan-Cours Genêt - 46.93.50.99
Open year-round. 3 stes 790-950F. 27 rms 260-680F. Half-board 450-580F. TV. Heated pool. Garage parking. Telex 790488. Cards: V, MC.
At the entrance to Saintes and its amphitheaters, this hotel sits on seventeen acres of peaceful grounds, with a lovely view of the surrounding countryside. Recently renovated, the tastefully furnished rooms are charming and quite comfortable; some are located just off the garden. Restaurant and bar.

Les Saintes-Maries-de-la-Mer
13460 Les Stes-Maries-de-la-Mer - (Bouches-du-Rhône)
Paris 777 - Marseille 129 - Nîmes 53 - Montpellier 67

Mas de la Fouque
Rte. d'Aigues-Mortes (4 km)
90.47.81.02
Closed Jan. 3-March 15. 1 ste 2,000F. 13 rms 1,200-1,700F. Half-board 890-1,140F oblig. in seas. TV. Heated pool. Tennis. Golf. Parking. Telex 403155. Cards: V, AE, DC, MC.
Marvelously situated in the heart of the Camargue, some of these attractive rooms are nestled in a private garden. This hotel offers absolute tranquility and great comfort. Restaurant.

Mas du Clarousset
Rte. de Cacharel (7 km on D 85A)
90.47.81.66
Closed Tues. (except holidays). 10 rms 530-550F. Half-board 745-980F oblig. in seas. Pool. Garage parking. Cards: V, AE, DC.
These large rooms are superb and bright, with private terraces and a wonderful view of Camargue. Pleasant pool and terrace/solarium; courteous greeting and service. Restaurant.

Lou Mas du Juge
D 85 - 66.73.51.45, 66.73.51.42
Open year-round. 4 rms 350-400F. Half-board 500-850F oblig. in seas. Parking.
A private house offering very comfortable guest rooms, a convivial atmosphere and a friendly dinner table. Restaurant.

13 Mas du Tadorne
Chemin Bas (3 km N on N 570)
90.47.93.11
M. Fava. Open until 10:30 p.m. Closed Jan. 4-March 4. Terrace dining. Pets allowed. Garage parking. Telex 403700. Cards: V, AE, DC.
Bruno Fava, the chef here until recently, has given way to the young, technically well-trained Frédéric Joffrin. The influences of his excellent mentors, Christian Willer and Jacques Maximin, can be detected in such dishes as the consommé of sole with ginger, good marinated raw fish and interesting veal shank with shiitake mushrooms (which are now cultivated in these parts). In the pretty little dining room, diners suffer alternately

between closed windows and mosquito swarms.
A la carte: 280-300F. Menus: 150F and 350F (dinner only).

Mas du Tadorne

(See restaurant above)

Closed Jan. 4-March 4. 4 stes 1,200F. 11 rms 800F. Half-board oblig. in seas. TV. Air cond. Pool. Tennis.

The terraces of these luxurious rooms open right out onto the pool. The facilities are remarkable (whirlpool bathtubs, air conditioning, videotape recorders), the service perfect, the breakfast carefully prepared, and the leisure activities well conceived (horseback riding, fishing).

Salins-les-Bains

39110 Salins-les-Bains - (Jura)
Paris 410 - Besançon 45 - Poligny 25 - Lons-le-Saunier 52

Auberge du Val d'Héry

Rte. de Genève, D 467 (3 km)
84.73.06.54

M. Dupont-Oullier. Open until 9:45 p.m. Closed Mon. (Sept.-May) & Sun. dinner. Garden dining. Hotel: 5 rms 220-510F; half-board 294-340F. Pets allowed. Parking. Cards: V, AE.

A pleasant restaurant where guests are made to feel as if they are no trouble at all—unfortunately, this kind of place seems rare these days. But in the Auberge du Val d'Héry's classically beautiful dining room, the guest is greeted with attention, advised on a wine selection and served discreetly. The spirited regional cuisine features cream sauces and generous gratins, while remaining faithful to the Jura repertoire: soufflé "au comté de Salins," smooth and perfectly presented; trout from the Val d'Héry in yellow wine and walnuts, a fresh dish accented by a rich sauce; magnificent cheeses of the region; and well-made pastries. The honest, generous cuisine is created by a southern chef, Lionel Oullier, who appreciates distinctive flavors and has a talent for seasonings. The prices are exemplary.
A la carte: 180-230F. Menus: 76F, 120F, 220F.

Salon-de-Provence

13300 Salon-de-Provence - (Bouches-du-Rhône)
Paris 730 - Marseille 55 - Avignon 46 - Arles 40 - Nîmes 71

L'Abbaye de Sainte-Croix

Rte. du Val-de-Cuech (5 km NE on D 16)
90.56.24.55

Mme. Bossard. Open until 9:30 p.m. Closed Mon. lunch & Nov. 1-Feb. 28. Terrace dining. No pets. Parking. Telex 401247. Cards: V, AE, DC, MC.

Without a doubt, this restaurant has one of the most spectacular panoramas in the Provence countryside between the Alpilles and the Lubéron. And, to make the setting even better, the entire complex of old monastery buildings has been restored with infinite tact. In front of the endless greens and blues of nature and surrounded by the fragrance of 3,000 lavender plants, you will dine on a personal and serious cuisine prepared by the good chef Yves Sauret: fish soup, roast squab with garlic, aiguillette of bass with basil oil, salmon gâteau with leek fondue. The prices are rather fearsome, so we were glad to see the recent addition of a fixed-price lunch menu, which will finally put this paradise within most people's reach.
A la carte: 400-500F. Menus: 205F (wine incl.), 170F, 285F, 390F.

L'Abbaye de Sainte-Croix

(See restaurant above)

Closed Nov. 1-Feb. 28. 5 stes 930-1,460F. 19 rms 565-830F. Half-board 580-1,070F oblig. in seas. TV in 7 rms. Pets allowed. Pool. Tennis.

This stunning twelfth-century abbey is located in the foothills of the Alpilles, in a setting of absolute tranquillity with a sumptuous view. Lovely old furniture is featured in the rooms, and guests can avail themselves of the pool set in the scrublands and admirable breakfast offerings. Relais et Châteaux.

Francis Robin

1, blvd. Georges-Clemenceau
90.56.06.53

M. Robin. Open until 9 p.m. Closed Sun. dinner, Mon., Feb. school vacation & 10 days in Aug. Air cond. Pets allowed. Cards: AE, DC, MC.

The cuisine of Francis Robin completely escapes the somewhat cold and rigid atmosphere maintained by his old-fashioned provincial decor. The food is, on the contrary, light and, if not exactly daring, at least personal and up-to-date, especially in the huge fixed-price menus, which are often a mirror image of that day's marketplace. The à la carte menu isn't as flexible and is too long. But you can create a delicious meal by choosing, for example, the turbot with morels, the rich lobster stew, the aiguillette of duck with puréed olives, the perfect cheeses from Gérard Paul's shop across the street and any of the exceptional desserts that demonstrate Robin's passion for sweets.
A la carte: 300-350F. Menus: 150F (weekdays only), 230F, 320F.

Sanary-sur-Mer

83110 Sanary-sur-Mer - (Var)
Paris 828 - Marseille 54 - Toulon 12 - La Ciotat 27

L'Aricot

Baie de Bandol - 94.74.10.33

M. Beruti. Open until 10:30 p.m. Closed Mon. dinner & Tues. (off-seas.). Terrace dining. Pets allowed. Parking. Cards: V, DC.

How splendid it is to dip your feet in the water while looking out at the island of Bendor! The terrace is just above the ocean, well sheltered from the wind and even more so from the summer crowds. It extends out from a bright dining room ornamented with magnificent tanks of shellfish that, along with the best local fish, are the featured attraction on the small menu (whose prices are not as extravagant as one might fear). Try the filets of mostèle (a small cod) fried in a wine sauce (with light vegetable and oyster flans), nicely made bouillabaisse and grilled fish. It's simple and unpretentious, with service included in the price.
A la carte: 250F. Menu: 125F.

Sancerre

18300 Sancerre - (Cher)
Paris 201 - Bourges 46 - Cosne 16 - Nevers 50

Hôtel Panoramic

Rempart des Augustins - 48.54.22.44

Open year-round. 2 stes 700F. 55 rms 170-240F. Half-board 210F. TV. Pets allowed. Parking. Telex 783433. Cards: V, AE.

The building has no charm, but the clean, comfortable rooms look out on an extraordinary panorama of the Loire valley and the vineyards. Restaurant.

(13) La Tour

31, pl. de la Halle - 48.54.00.81

M. Fourvier. Open unil 9:30 p.m. Closings vary. Air cond. Pets allowed. Cards: V, AE.

The owner of this renovated restaurant with its view of the Sancerre vineyards makes constant efforts to create stunning fixed-price menus filled with freshness and new ideas. For 150 francs you will be served a grapefruit-and-smoked-salmon salad, a fricassée of scallops in lemon sauce, filet of beef, cheeses and dessert. The selection of Sancerre wines is extraordinary.

A la carte: 230-250F. Menus: 88F (weekdays only), 140F, 195F, 235F.

Sancy-lès-Meaux

see Meaux

Sare

64310 Ascain - (Pyrénées-Atlantiques)
Paris 776 - St-Jean-de-Luz 14 - Cambo 24 - Hendaye 27

(14) Arraya

59.54.20.46

M. Fagoaga. Open until 10 p.m. Closed Nov. 4-May 20. Terrace dining. Pets allowed. Parking. Cards: V, AE, DC.

For ages this former relais has maintained the exquisite atmosphere of an old bourgeois house, with its polished furniture and gracefully aging family knickknacks, in the heart of the most deliciously Basque of the small Basque villages. And Paul Fagoago, who attentively preserves the delicate charms of this house, is equally proficient as a restaurateur. His cuisine marries, sometimes even with a little daring, his personal inspiration and the traditions of the region, as in the charlotte of lettuce with sautéed preserved gizzards, the grilled fresh salmon in a stew with cèpes and baby onions, the bell peppers stuffed with hake rillettes in a crayfish sauce and the chartreuse of goose, sweetbreads and cèpes with cabbage. The choice of wines testifies to the same search for what is both good and original. A boutique of regional products sells the famous homemade gâteau Basque (chewy cake filled with pastry cream).

A la carte: 250-280F. Menus: 75F (weekday lunch only), 100F, 180F.

Arraya

(See restaurant above)

Closed Nov. 4-May 20. 21 rms 260-360F. Half-board 270-350F oblig. in seas.

Choose one of the eight rooms on the interior garden of this ravishing Basque residence furnished with confident good taste.

Sarlat-la-Canéda

24200 Sarlat-la-Canéda - (Dordogne)
Paris 535 - Périgueux 67 - Cahors 62 - Bergerac 74

La Hoirie

La Canéda (2 km S) - 53.59.05.62

Closed Nov. 15-March 15. 3 stes 420-470F. 12 rms 260-370F. Half-board 315-395F. Pool. Parking. Cards: V, AE, DC.

This tranquil, friendly hotel boasts a pool in its garden and fine rooms with impressive bathrooms. Restaurant.

(13) Hostellerie de Meysset

Rte. des Eyzies, Argentouleau
53.59.08.29

M. Brottier. Open until 9 p.m. Closed Oct. 17-April. Terrace dining. Hotel: 6 stes 420-580F; 20 rms 305-370F; half-board 315-360F oblig. in seas. Pets allowed. Parking. Cards: V, AE, DC.

This is the magic of the Périgord: friendly people, beautiful countryside, good food. An inviting terrace faces the grounds, and the cuisine of the young new chef comprises, with just enough personality, the classics of modern as well as regional cooking: foie gras, breast of duck with mango, mignon of veal with mustard seeds, homemade fresh-fruit sorbets and a walnut soufflé. The wines are a little expensive, though no more so than the rest of the menu.

A la carte: 300F and up. Menus: 85F (weekday lunch only), 160F, 200F.

(13) La Madeleine

1, pl. de la Petite-Rigaudie - 53.59.10.41

M. Melot. Open until 9:30 p.m. Closed Nov. 12-March 18. Terrace dining. Pets allowed. Telex 306022. Cards: V, MC.

The dining room of this noble old house got a coat of salmon paint a couple of years ago, and that alone was enough to bring out the beauty of the copperware on the walls and the decorative old grill. Mme. Melot is all smiles, and the cuisine seems to have gained recently in vigor: a beautiful terrine of baby vegetables with tomato purée; a delicious assortment of escalopes of lamb's sweetbreads, foie gras and goose gizzards served warm over leeks in a sauce of Chinon wine vinegar and olive oil; a serviceable pot-au-feu of duck confit; and a light walnut cake with crème anglaise. Nice wine cellar.

A la carte: 250-280F. Menus: 100F, 160F, 245F.

La Madeleine

(See restaurant above)

Closed Jan. 1-March 15. 3 stes 370F. 19 rms 268-330F. Half-board 295-370F oblig. in seas. TV. Air cond. in 14 rms.

This traditional, family-run hotel provides its guests with conscientious service. The large rooms may not have much in the way of decor, but they are quite comfortable.

Saulieu

21210 Saulieu - (Côte-d'Or)
Paris 255 - Dijon 73 - Beaune 70 - Autun 41 - Avallon 39

(13) La Borne Impériale

14-16, rue d'Argentine - 80.64.19.76

M. Bouché. Open until 9 p.m. Closed Wed. & Nov. 15-Dec. 15. Pets allowed. Hotel: 7 rms 92-195F. Parking. Cards: V.

Formerly the pastry chef at La Côte d'Or (where he created a marvelous chocolate cake in honor of the then-president of the republic), Pierre Bouché is an old-school cook whose 50 years in the business haven't deflated his enthusiasm or his rigor. We've enjoyed his delicious hot pâté en croûte, ham with morels, filet mignon of beef with shallots, salmon with a tomato fondue and, of course, the famous chocolate "Président" cake. He also serves an excellent, reasonably priced Beaujolais by the carafe.

A la carte: 200-230F. Menus: 88F, 145F, 195F.

(19) La Côte d'Or

(Bernard Loiseau)
2, rue d'Argentine - 80.64.07.66

M. Loiseau. Open daily until 10 p.m. Pets allowed. Parking. Telex 350778. Cards: V, AE, DC, MC.

When we start poking through letters from our readers, there are ones that make us think we're dreaming. Are they really referring to the same building, the same decor, the same cooking? One reader speaks of Bernard Loiseau's La Côte d'Or with boundless admiration and enthusiasm; another is so outraged you'd think his dinner had been served on the sidewalk. In any case, the inventor of "cuisine à l'eau" does not evoke lukewarm reactions. If you like him, you adore him; if you're not too crazy about him, you blast him.

Our attitude, and we've known him since the beginning, is calmer. We're well aware of the trouble spots. In the last three or four years, the former postal stop has seen quite a metamorphosis behind its facade, which was recently repainted in a pink-burgundy color. Loiseau built a beautiful entryway full of sumptuous flowers, opened a new dining room and freshened up the old one, fixed up a salon, redecorated the hotel rooms, built charming suites (each decorated in a different style) and tripled the kitchen area. (These guest quarters are located above a garden recently planted with trees, bushes and flower beds that are all starting to take shape.) All this is quite seductive, but it is still the unique talent of Loiseau, his mind-boggling technique, astonishing imagination and unparalleled subtleties that claim center stage. Where else can you find dishes so studiously prepared, so painstakingly built up from their own juices and so rich with the natural flavors of their ingredients? And with the little notes of explanation that Loiseau adds next to each menu item, diners can more easily comprehend the complexities of such dishes as the duck pan-fried with a velouté of caramelized cauliflower, the crab in herb juices, the incredible ragoût of vegetables with a meat aspic, the mushrooms and scrambled eggs in a sauce of the mushrooms' juices, the delicious whiting filets in veal sauce, the lobster and caramelized carrots moistened with onion juice and cloves, the crisp-skinned duck, and the lamb and organ meats in a sauce scented with walnuts.

Such explanations may ease the difficulty some people have appreciating this unique cuisine, which does away with butter and cream and tickles your nose with the famous "sauces à l'eau," about which more than a few stupidities have been written. In fact, Loiseau hasn't invented anything. He picked up the tried-and-true method used by chefs in days of old, who deglazed meats, fish and organs while forgetting all too often to degrease the meat ahead of time, which resulted in overly heavy dishes. As for the vegetables, if they are so fine, so crunchy and so flavorful, it isn't because he cooks them in water. The carrots, for example, start out being cooked in water, but he then caramelizes them in butter, carefully draining them on absorbent paper. Zucchini, conversely, starts out being cooked in butter on the skin side and is then deglazed with water. Whatever the procedure, fat is used only as a means of cooking to retain the authentic taste of the basic materials.

There isn't a single dish that doesn't have its own sauce. While, with so many of his colleagues, the same basic seasoning, added to different ingredients, comes back at you again and again, Loiseau manages to pull out of the cooking process the maximum amount of natural juices, which he then reduces to make his sauce.

His is a remarkable talent, as pure as the song of the nightingale. And even if every dish doesn't make trumpets blare and cymbals clang, it is still at La Côte d'Or that we have had some of our most unforgettable meals and tasted dishes that we will never forget, such as the lobster "rôti à l'eau," whose strong flavor of iodine and salt enveloped that of the cabbage, the vegetable fricassée with chervil, the soup of baby shrimp and fava beans, the breast of chicken rapidly cooked in its juices and the veal kidneys browned in their own fat and abundantly clarified with braised shallots. And at our last meal, we had a filet of carp—deboned thanks to a new tool—in an ultra-light wine sauce, and served with roe cooked in the same manner as brains, and with shallots and exquisite, slightly crunchy petits pois. Loiseau also cooked a fantastic Allier salmon in veal juices and served it with tiny wild asparagus. The vegetarian menu—artichoke bavarois in a tomato coulis, leeks and potatoes sprinkled with truffle vinegar (we dare you to pull that amazing secret recipe out of Loiseau), roast zucchini in pepper juice and a mushroom ragoût à l'oeuf cassé—is growing in popularity. Even if this converts you to vegetarianism, you'll want to break faith long enough to taste the most exquisite dish of rabbit livers cooked in their own juices and seasoned with sea salt, served as it should be with green cabbage. Its simplicity astounds.

The desserts, which we have found a little lacking in the past, have come alive with a fanfare. If the roast pear in a pear glaze with cardamom, the puff pastry of grapefruit and crushed pralines, the pastry layered with chocolate and orange coulis or the pineapple coated in crushed pistachios doesn't leave you begging for mercy, than the orange-marmalade sorbet that is served with a bitter-chocolate mousse and warm madeleines will send you to paradise. And Hubert, the maître d', will lead you down innumerable paths of Burgundy, directing you to some of its finest vintages.

The checks at La Côte d'Or don't reveal the same light touch as the cooking, but if you choose carefully (escargots soup, delicious fresh cod, potato purée with garlic and dessert) and settle for a delightful Irancy rouge, you can easily get out for less than 300 francs. Better still, try the lunch menu/carte, which is almost a gift.

A la carte: 500-800F. Menus: 250F (lunch only), 290F (vegetarian menu), 350F (dinner only), 490F.

La Côte d'Or

(See restaurant above)

Open year-round. 9 stes 800-2,200F. 15 rms 260-600F. TV in 18 rms. Pets allowed.

Three red houses house nine extremely appealing suites, which are decorated with antique furniture and paintings and with windows that open onto a large garden. The other rooms, grouped together in the main wing, don't offer the same amenities, but since they've been redone in fresh, cheerful colors, they are welcoming and comfortable. Relais et Châteaux.

12/20 La Poste

1, rue Grillot - 80.64.05.67

M. Virlouvet. Open daily until 10 p.m. Air cond. Pets allowed. Garage parking. Telex 350540. Cards: V, AE, DC.

The restaurant of this venerable hostelry, which reopened in 1986 with an opulent-looking decor, serves a carefully prepared cuisine at honest prices. The hard-working chef turns out such fare as a warm terrine of scorpionfish with saffron and a roast pigeon with truffle juice. The first fixed-price menu is excellent.

A la carte: 280-300F. Menus: 98F, 168F, 288F.

La Poste

(See restaurant above)

Open year-round. 3 stes 310-425F. 45 rms 230-345F. Half-board 280-400F. TV in 42 rms. Air cond.

This renovated seventeenth-century way station for horses is the oldest hotel in Saulieu. The decor is a little cluttered, but the rooms are comfortable and well soundproofed. Some overlook a pretty courtyard.

DON'T FORGET: Gault Millau also brings you The Best of Chicago, The Best of Hong Kong, The Best of Italy, The Best of London, The Best of Los Angeles, The Best of New England, The Best of New York, The Best of Paris, The Best of San Francisco *and* The Best of Washington, D.C.

Saumur

49400 Saumur - (Maine-et-Loire)

Paris 300 - Angers 53 - Poitiers 91 - Tours 65 - Nantes 127

IN NEARBY **Chênehutte-les-Tuffeaux**

(8 km NW on D 161 & D 751)

49350 Gennes - (Maine-et-Loire)

16 Le Prieuré

D 751 - 41.67.90.14

M. Traversac. Open until 9:30 p.m. Closed Jan. 8-March 4. Pets allowed. Parking. Telex 720379. Cards: V.

Dominating the slate roofs of this old village named for its volcanic rock (tuff), the fifteenth-century vestiges of this structure show clear signs of a turn-of-the-century, neo-Gothic restoration. But the rather thrown-together feeling disappears inside, where the young personnel are cheerful and attentive, and the glassed-in dining room affords a grandiose view of the undulating river. As for the cuisine, since Jean-Noël Lumineau took over a few years ago, it has gained in both confidence and lightness: court bouillon of lobster with thyme and lemon, a warm salad of sweetbreads and beans, curried roast skate with wild rice, and a white-chocolate-and-mint parfait. Good regional wines are offered at fair prices.

Menus: 200F (lunch only), 280F, 360F, 390F.

Le Prieuré

(See restaurant above)

Closed Jan. 8-March 4. 2 stes 980-1,750F. 33 rms 450-1,500F. Half-board 580-1,200F. TV in 20 rms. Heated pool. Tennis.

This old priory has been remarkably modernized and furnished. The huge rooms are opulent (albeit sometimes overdone) and look out on a marvelous river. For latecomers, there are a few fairly ugly bungalows scattered on the grounds.

Sauveterre-de-Comminges

31510 Barbazan - (Haute-Garonne)

Paris 776 - Luchon 36 - St-Gaudens 10 - Lannemezan 32

14 Hostellerie des Sept Molles

Gesset (3 km S on D 9) - 61.88.30.87

M. Ferran. Open until 9 p.m. Closed Mon. (off-seas.), Jan. 5-Feb. 1 & Nov. 15-Dec. 15. Pets allowed. Parking. Telex 530171. Cards: V, AE, DC.

The remarkable menu dégustation created at the whim of Gilles Ferran reveals all the charm of this beautiful family-run establishment—and it's reasonably priced to boot. For example: foie gras, mousseline of trout and salmon with herbs, filet of sole with coquilles St-Jacques ravioli, sorbet "commingeois" (with Armagnac), breast of duck with pink berries, cheeses and a millefeuille with light cream and prunes. The reception is perfect, and the evenings are cozy in front of the large fireplace.

A la carte: 260-280F. Menus: 135F, 220F.

Hostellerie des Sept Molles

(See restaurant above)

Closed Mon. (off-seas.), Jan. 5-Feb. 1 & Nov. 15-Dec. 15. 2 stes 600-880F. 17 rms 300-500F. Half-board 390-420F. TV. Heated pool. Tennis.

The old-style rooms are vast and well maintained. Outdoor activities include tennis, swimming and hiking. Relais et Châteaux.

Sauveterre-de-Rouergue

12800 Naucelle - (Aveyron)
Paris 644 - Albi 54 - Rodez 40 - Millau 95

Auberge du Sénéchal

65.47.05.78

M. Truchon. Open until 9:30 p.m. Closed Mon. & Tues. lunch (except July-Aug.) & Nov. 2-April 1. Terrace dining. No pets. Parking. Cards: V, AE, DC.

This admirable walled city, with its sprawling arcade, handsome old houses and inhabitants who exude joie de vivre, has nevertheless been an ungrateful place for this young restaurateur, who wants to survive, progress and make a name for himself. Michel Truchon has had a hard time and would appreciate it if you'd go cheer him up at his appealingly rustic inn, where he awaits you with first-rate fare. Native to the region, he is an excellent cook—you won't regret the detour—who creates superb fixed-price menus and a few varying à la carte selections that are at once modern and faithfully regional: duck liver fried in truffle juice with corn pancakes, fat langoustines en feuilleté with orange butter, roast pigeon au jus with local vegetables, and honey cake with walnuts and a tarragon sauce. The wine cellar houses an interesting regional selection.

A la carte: 200-250F. Menus: 90F (weekdays only), 140F, 200F, 280F.

Auberge du Sénéchal

(See restaurant above)

Closed Nov. 2-April 1. 15 rms 180-250F. Half-board 230-280F.

The small rooms are simple, cozy, nicely maintained and well equipped.

Sauze

see Barcelonnette

Schirmeck

67130 Schirmeck - (Bas-Rhin)
Paris 405 - Strasbourg 49 - St-Dié 39 - Molsheim 25

Neuhauser

Les Quelles - 88.97.06.81

Closed Wed. (except July-Aug.), Nov. 15-Dec. 1 & Jan. 15-30. 10 rms 150-270F. Half-board 180-230F. TV in 6 rms. Heated pool. Parking. Cards: V, AE, DC.

This large residence at the edge of the forest is a dream come true for travelers enamored with Alsace. The rooms are charming and carefully maintained. Restaurant.

Relais du Château de Barembach

Barembach (1 km E) - 88.97.97.50

Open year-round. 2 stes 1,000-1,100F. 13 rms 260-575F. Half-board 310-420F. TV in 7 rms. Pool. Tennis. Parking. Telex 880400. Cards: V, AE, DC.

In this opulent little mansion standing up against the Champ du Feu mountain, the rooms are silent and look out at a park. Restaurant.

IN NEARBY **Natzwiller**
(11 km SE on N 420, D 130 & D 530)
67130 Schirmeck - (Bas-Rhin)

Auberge Metzger

88.97.02.42

M. Metzger. Open until 9 p.m. Closed Mon. (except Feb., July & Aug.), Jan. 5-30 & March 15-31. Terrace dining. Pets allowed. Parking. Hotel: 10 rms 140-160F; half-board 160-170F.

Tucked away in a village in the Vosges amid mountains and forests, this prim, flower-bedecked auberge is a picture of hospitality and forthrightness. It boasts a lovely rustic dining room (impeccably clean), a small terrace for sunny days, a beautiful hostess and a classic cuisine, which is also inventive and delicately executed. The chef features lots of mushrooms and game, and such dishes as a filet of sander (a perch-like fish) with Riesling and a sirloin braised with onions and grenadine. The desserts are rather ordinary (and too alcoholic). A small toque of encouragement.

A la carte: 180F. Menus: 45F (weekdays only), 85F.

Ségos

see Aire-sur-l'Adour

Seillac

see Onzain

Sélestat

67600 Sélestat - (Bas-Rhin)
Paris 434 - Strasbourg 47 - Colmar 22 - St-Dié 46

IN NEARBY **Val-de-Villé**
(6 km NE on N 59)
67730 Châtenois - (Bas-Rhin)

Au Valet de Coeur

24, rte. de Villé - 88.85.67.51

M. Egert. Open until 9:15 p.m. Closed Sun. dinner & Mon. Pets allowed. Parking. Cards: V, AE, DC, MC.

As its name implies, Le Valet serves a cuisine from the heart; and it has good prospects for the future, as long as nothing gets in the way of the enthusiasm of the amiable owner, who takes your hand when you arrive, chats with you and offers you an after-dinner drink when regretfully bidding you farewell. And as long as the young Jean-Michel Eblin soon gets the recognition he deserves for his warm escalopes of salmon in a salad seasoned with hazelnut oil, his exemplary matelote with Riesling and fresh pasta, his delicate frogs'-leg ravioli with garlic cream and his fine desserts. Formerly with Haeberlin, Faugeron and Taillevent, this remarkable technician should soon become the talk of the region. The wine cellar is intelligent, and the setting, with its rustic ambience and flowers, is warm.

A la carte: 250-300F. Menus: 132F, 176F, 231F, 330F.

Sens

89100 Sens - (Yonne)
Paris 118 - Dijon 203 - Troyes 65 - Fontainebleau 53

Clos des Jacobins

(13) 49, Grande-Rue - 86.95.29.70

M. Bompay. Open until 9 p.m. Closed Tues. dinner, Wed., Feb. 25-March 10, Aug. 16-31 & Dec. 23-Jan. 2. Air cond. Pets allowed. Cards: V.

Success is confirmed—and justified—for this small place, with its sober, tasteful dining room decorated with beautiful bouquets. The resolute patronne manages a staff of two perfectly efficient waiters. As for the cuisine of M. Bompay, formerly with the neighboring Hôtel de Paris, it has progressed greatly and will continue to do so if it doesn't get dragged down with cumbersome sauces and confused side dishes. Already, the desserts are exceptional (chocolate tart with coffee sauce), and the kidneys with fresh pasta, as well as the breast of duck with mushrooms, deserve a toque. Weak wine list.

A la carte: 300F. Menus: 102F (weekdays only), 112F (weekends and holidays only).

IN NEARBY **Villeroy**
(6 km W on D 81)
89100 Sens - (Yonne)

Le Relais de Villeroy

(13) Rte. de Nemours - 86.88.81.77

M. Clément. Open until 9 p.m. Closed Sun. dinner, Mon., Dec. 20-Jan. 12 & July 30-Aug. 10. Pets allowed. Parking. Cards: V, AE, DC.

Continual renovation has transformed this old barn on the noisy highway into a pleasant auberge with a rustic Norman decor (beams, copperware, striped fabrics). The cuisine is a little too heavy, and the sauces could have more finesse: generous feuilleté of rabbit liver (too much cream), fresh asparagus salad, John Dory flavored with basil, rather sad cheeses and pastries that are a bit too sweet but well prepared. The wine cellar excels (for the region) in Bordeaux and Burgundies.

A la carte: 300F. Menus: 100F (weekdays only), 165F, 190F.

Le Relais de Villeroy

(See restaurant above)

Closed Sun., Mon., Dec. 20-Jan. 12 & July 30-Aug. 10. 8 rms 165-220F.

These new rooms, with their interior-decorator look, are spotless and equipped with perfect bathrooms. The more tranquil side of the hotel faces the countryside. Good breakfast.

Sept-Saulx

51400 Mourmelon-le-Grand - (Marne)
Paris 168 - Reims 23 - Châlons-sur-Marne 26 - Epernay 29

Le Cheval Blanc

Rue du Moulin - 26.03.90.27

Closed Jan. 15-Feb. 15. 2 stes 350-410F. 19 rms 220-350F. Half-board 455-520F oblig. in seas. TV. Pets allowed. Parking. Telex 830885. Tennis. Cards: V, AE, DC, MC.

In a glorious park traversed by the Vesle river, these pleasant rooms have been carefully decorated in rustic taste. The reception and service are perfect.

Sète

34200 Sète - (Hérault)
Paris 790 - Béziers 53 - Montpellier 35 - Lodève 72

L'Amandier

(13) Blvd. Joliot-Curie - 67.51.30.30

Open daily until 9:30 p.m. Terrace dining. Pets allowed. Parking. Cards: V, AE, DC.

This new bistro-style restaurant with a pretty, modern decor is sure to improve the gastronomic standing of Sète—even if Philippe Gilbert, still too recently arrived from his faraway Aurillac, doesn't seem, at least for the moment, as keenly inspired here as in the Auvergne. But it's good food, generously served: delicious foie gras, grilled breast of duck served with potato baskets and a cider-vinegar sauce, an exquisite gratin of figs and red fruit with a light Champagne sabayon.

A la carte: 220F. Menus: 60F, 90F, 150F.

Jacques Coeur

(13) 17, rue Paul-Valéry - 67.74.33.70

Mme. Page. Open until 10:30 p.m. Closed Sun. dinner. Air cond. Pets allowed. Cards: V, AE, DC.

The owner is a hostess who is more than just welcoming. She takes the time to be friendly to everyone, even when her modern, Oriental-style dining room in pink and blue is brimming with guests—which is quite often, thanks to the quality and generosity of her cuisine. The new chef can turn out classics with his eyes closed. There's nothing bold about his cooking, but he uses excellent products and has a mastery of execution: fricassée of lobster in a light cream sauce, gratin of oysters, sweetbreads à l'orange and perfect desserts (delicate sorbets, fresh-fruit tarts). A few good Loire wines (the owner is from Chinon).

A la carte: 250-280F. Menus: 89F (weekdays only), 130F.

Grand Hôtel

Quai de Lattre-De-Tassigny
67.74.71.77

Closed Dec. 23-Jan. 1. 4 stes 350-499F. 47 rms 169-350F. TV in 40 rms. Air cond. in 35 rms. Garage parking. Telex 480225. Cards: V, AE, DC, MC.

On the shore of a canal, this recently modernized hotel is both soundproofed and air conditioned. Pleasant winter patio/garden. Restaurant.

Sévignacq-Meyracq

64260 Arudy - (Pyrénées-Atlantiques)
Paris 795 - Pau 25 - Oloron-Ste-Marie 20 - Arudy 3

(13) Les Bains de Secours

59.05.62.11

M. Paroix. Open until 9 p.m. Closed Sun. dinner, Mon. & Jan. 1-Feb. 15. Terrace dining. Pets allowed. Hotel: 8 rms 95-115F; half-board 115F. Parking. Cards: V, MC.

This beautiful farm is the only survivor of the old constellation of micro-resorts in the Piedmont-like Béarn region. It still offers spa treatments, and the owner had the excellent idea of retaining his clients who come for the waters by offering them his personal and seasonal cuisine. So between sulphur-water baths you can try a good salad of filet of sole with cèpes, a gratinée of Scottish salmon with herbs and a chocolate fondant with mint ice cream. The wines are good and reasonably priced.

A la carte: 200F. Menus: 59F (weekdays only), 85F and 115F (weekends and holidays only).

Sierck-les-Bains

57480 Sierck-les-Bains - (Moselle)
Paris 359 - Luxembourg 33 - Thionville 17 - Metz 45

(13) La Vènerie

10, rue de la Porte-de-Trèves
82.83.72.41

M. Terver. Open until 9:30 p.m. Closed Wed. dinner, Mon. & Jan. 20-March 1. Terrace dining. Pets allowed. Cards: AE, DC.

In summer, the Germans and the Luxembourgers who frequent this elegant manor on the shores of the Moselle (the river crosses the grounds) are served on the new terrace. This is yet another seduction to strengthen their faithfulness to the good cuisine of Marcellin Terver, a former student of the Soustelle brothers at Lucas-Carton and at Martinez. He does nice work, with undaunted consistency: terrine of scorpionfish with herbs (fresh and flavorful, but with too much mayonnaise), exquisite lamb chops with potatoes dauphinoise and baby vegetables, feuilleté of strawberries (not great). The decor is lovely, the service irreproachable.

A la carte: 280-300F. Menus: 115F, 190F, 230F.

Sochaux

see Montbéliard

Soubise

see Rochefort

Souillac

46200 Souillac - (Lot)
Paris 525 - Cahors 67 - Brive 35 - Sarlat 29 - Figeac 74

12/20 La Vieille Auberge

1, pl. de la Minoterie - 65.32.79.43

M. Veril. Open until 9:30 p.m. Closed Jan. 1-March 15. Air cond. Pets allowed. Hotel: 20 rms 180-220F; half-board 250-270F oblig. in seas. Heated pool. Garage parking. Telex 533715. Cards: V, AE, DC, MC.

Regional tradition pervades this old inn, from the rustic decor to the warm reception to the generous cuisine: foie gras, escargots stew en croûte, aiguillette of squab with a garlic confit. Local products are sold on the premises, and organized excursions to the area's food sources are available.

A la carte: 250-300F. Menu: 100F, 180F.

See also: **Lacave**

Steinbrunn-le-Bas

see Mulhouse

Strasbourg

67000 Strasbourg - (Bas-Rhin)
Paris 488 - Metz 161 - Colmar 69 - Basel 137 - Lyon 489

Note: The numbers following the telephone number in each review pinpoint the establishment's exact location on the accompanying map.

Sights. The marvelous cathedral (twelfth and fifteenth centuries, made of red Vosges sandstone); Château des Rohan (1730, rich royal apartments, home of Musée des Beaux-Arts, Musée des Arts Décoratifs and Musée Archéologique); pl. Gutenberg (and its Renaissance-style Hôtel du Commerce); the pedestrian sector (with the picturesque Petite France quarter on the banks of the Ill); the grounds of the Orangerie and the Citadelle; Musée Zoologique (second largest in France); magnificent Musée Alsacien (arts and traditions); boat tours on the Rhine river (April-Oct.).

Eating on the Run. Typical Strasbourg "winstubs": L'Ami Fritz, 8, rue des Dentelles (intensely Alsatian); Le Clou, 3, rue du Chaudron (an institution, open very late); Le Coucou des Bois, 44, allée David-Goldschmidt (superb "tarte flambée"—thin tart with onions and cheese); Le Cruchon, 11, rue des Pucelles (picturesque); Le Tire-Bouchon, 5, rue des Tailleurs-de-Pierre (next to the flea market, minuscule); and, of course, those listed as restaurants: S'-Burjerstuewel, Pfifferbriader, Le Saint-Sépulcre, Winstub Strissel. Also the "bouchons," with their plats du jour: L'Ange d'Or, 9, rue des Orphelins (rather inventive); L'Evasion, 6, blvd. de Nancy (simple, fun dishes); Le Guetteur, 39, rue des Frères (classic, bar); Chez Olivier, 5, rue de la Mésange (Viennese ambience); Le Palais des Fêtes, 5, rue Sellénick (copious servings, spacious); La Salle à Manger, 3, rue Paul-Janet (fashionable, excellent value).

This symbol stands for "Les Lauriers du Terroir," an award given to chefs who prepare noteworthy traditional or regional recipes.

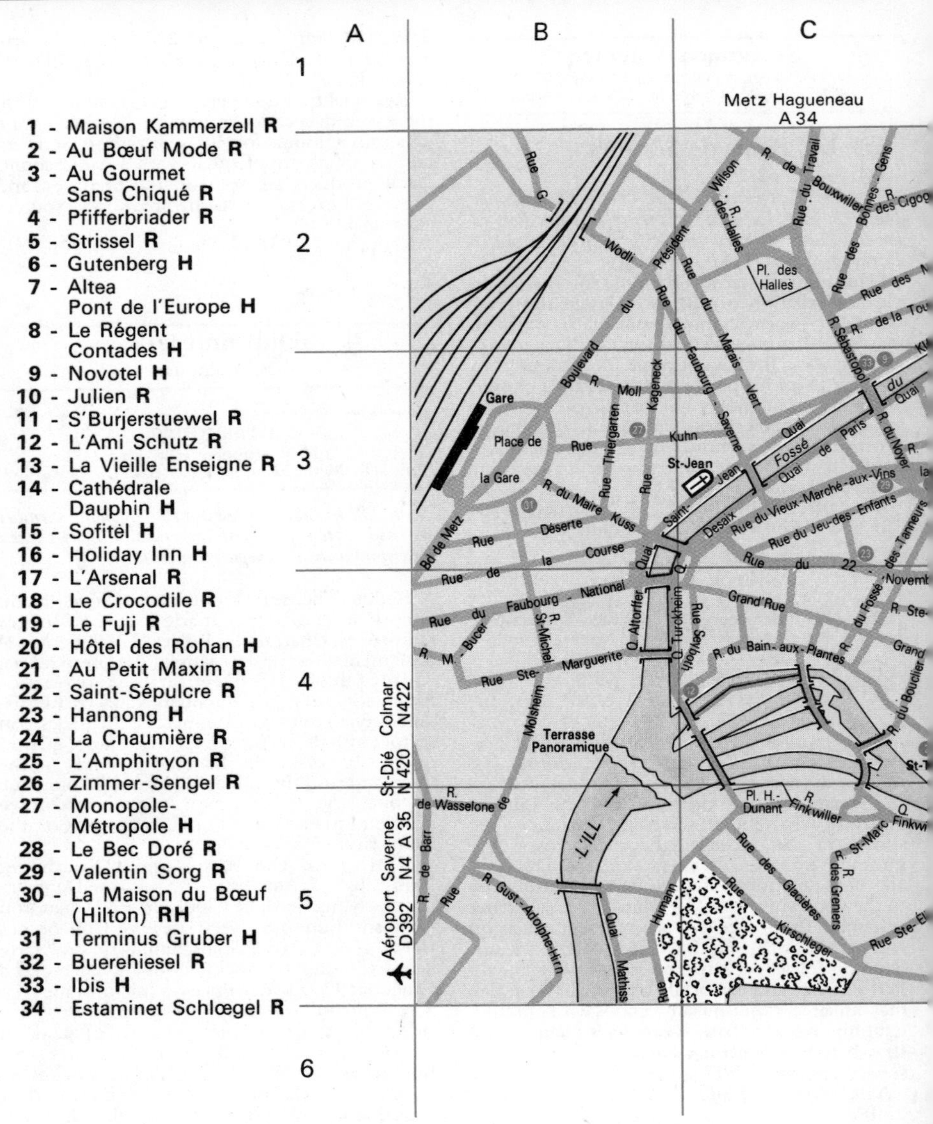

Brasseries. La Bague d'Or, 7, rue de l'Eglise (traditional); La Bourse, 1, pl. du Maréchal-de-Lattre-de-Tassigny (good Alsatian cuisine, tartes flambées); La République, 40, rue du Faubourg-National (good steak tartare); La Victoire, 1, quai des Pêcheurs (until 1 a.m.)

Bars & Cafés. Les Aviateurs, 12, rue des Soeurs (popular hangout); Le Bouchon, 6, rue Ste-Catherine (American-style bar, chic); Le Bugatti, ave. Herrenschmidt (Hilton bar, refined); Aux Douze Apôtres, rue Mercière (good beer selection); Le Gutenberg, 8, pl. Gutenberg (music and snacks); Le Petit Bois Vert, 3, quai de la Broche (pleasant shaded terrace on the Ill); Bar du Régent Contades, 8, ave. de la Liberté (good bartender); Bar du Sofitel, pl. St-Pierre-le-Jeune (mellow atmosphere, elegant).

Nightlife. Le Babouin, 8, rue du Faubourg-de-Pierre (trendy); Le Blue Hawaï, 19, rue du Marias-Vert (real change of scenery); Le Chalet, 376, rte. de la Wantzeneau; Le Charlie's, 24, pl. des Halles (always a good reputation); Le Funambule, 3, rue Klein (jazz bar, designer touches); Le Pub Nelson, rue des Couples (pub ambience, good beer).

Shops. *Bakeries:* Scholler, 10, pl. Broglie (best and most complete). *Charcuteries:* Frick-Lutz, 6, rue des Orfèvres (excellent smoked products); Klein, 28, blvd. d'Anvers (impressive choice of meat products and cheeses); Kraft, 25, rue des

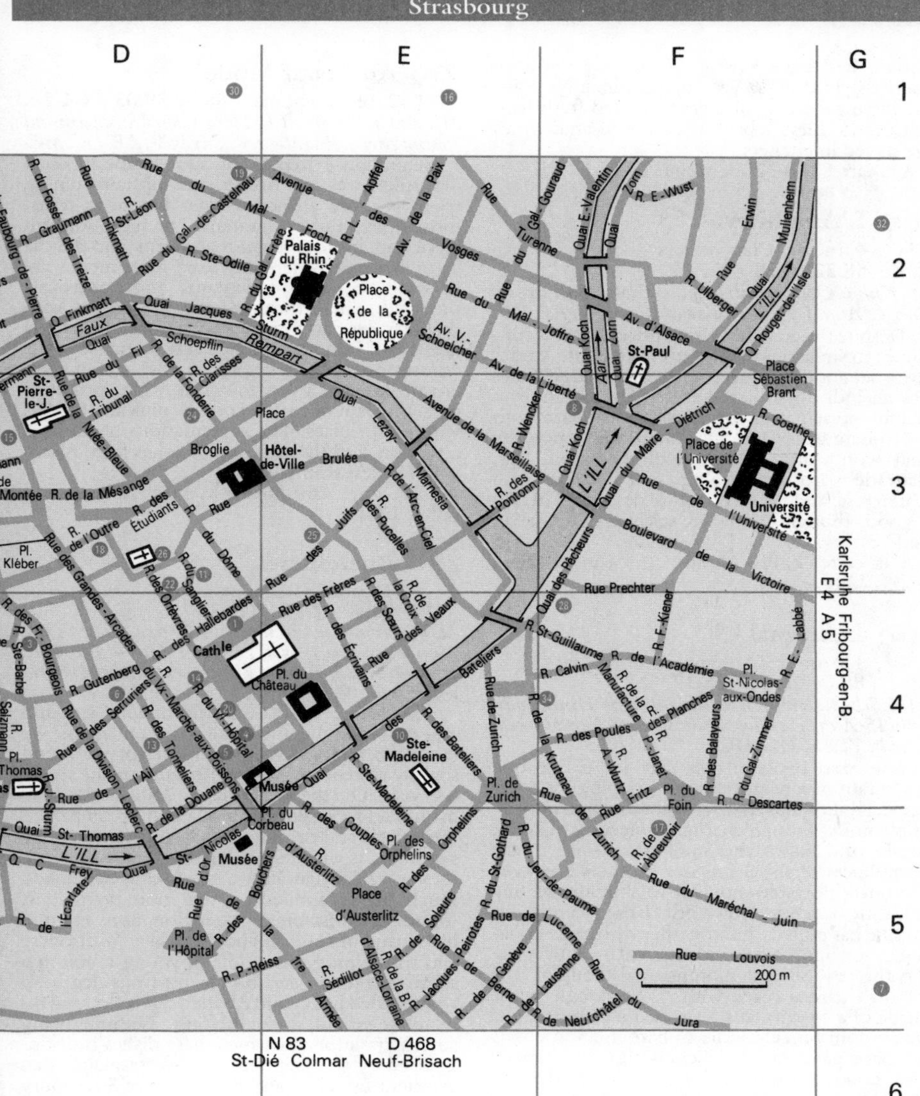

Hallebardes (local specialties). *Chocolate, pastries:* Falcinella, 17, rue du Général-de-Castelnau (tea room); Kubler, 29, ave. des Vosges (specializes in tiered cakes); Christian Meyer, 12, rue de l'Outre (truffles in fruit eau-de-vie, spectacular desserts, one of the great French chocolatiers). *Foie gras:* La Boutique du Foie Gras, 6, rue Friesé (half-cooked and canned, Strasbourg-style).

Altea Pont de l'Europe

Parc du Rhin - 88.61.03.23 / G5-7
Open year-round. 5 stes 545-565F. 88 rms 285-355F. Half-board 305-390F. TV. Pets allowed. Parking. Telex 870833. Cards: V, AE, DC, MC.

This large group of modern, not-terribly-attractive buildings is located in a park, just a stone's throw from the German border. The functional, well-equipped rooms were recently redecorated. Restaurant.

12/20 L'Ami Schutz

1, Ponts Couverts - 88.32.76.98 / C4-12
Mlle. Sevellec. Open until midnight. Closed Sun. & Mon. Terrace dining. Pets allowed. Telex 890221. Cards: V.

It's been a pleasure to reacquaint ourselves with the seductions of this adorable restaurant in Petite-France—the owner has gone to considerable trouble to improve L'Ami Schutz, whose cuisine had been sinking to a none-too-fussy tourist-style level. So we'll up the ranking a point for the escargots choucroute, roasted fresh ham hock and kidneys in beer. Excellent Alsatian wines are served in pitchers.

A la carte: 150-170F. Menu: 148F.

13 L'Amphitryon

4, rue des Charpentiers
88.22.63.30 / E3-25

M. Kuhn. Open until 10 p.m. Closed Sat. lunch, Sun. & Aug. 1-16. Pets allowed. Cards: V, AE, DC.

Despite the gradually rising prices, success continues to smile on this elegant restaurant. Attractively set and well spaced, each of the large tables has an individual light fixture. The cuisine is a skillful presentation of classic bistro fare with up-to-date tastes and a freshness and generosity that won't quit: compote of tenderloin tips, daurade with Pinot Noir, calf's brains with watercress, and rather exquisite desserts. There is a good, though expensive, selection of Alsatian and Loire wines.

A la carte: 250F. Menus: 75F (lunch only), 120F, 220F.

14 L'Arsenal

11, rue de l'Abreuvoir
88.35.03.69 / F5-17

MM. Schneider. Open until midnight. Dinner only July 15-Aug. 15. Closed Sat. & Sun. Pets allowed. Cards: V, AE, DC, MC.

Squeezed between two bars and a fast-food restaurant in a neighborhood grasping for some respectability, this Arsenal is not much to look at. It is a noisy, though charming, meeting place for locals who adore the smoky atmosphere, the friendliness of the Schneider brothers and even the uncomfortable shoulder-to-shoulder seating on rustic benches. After a brief lapse recently, the cuisine has pulled itself together with exact cooking times, light sauces and regional inventiveness. Try the exquisite and monumental "kouglof" (an Alsatian gâteau made with raised dough in the shape of a crown) with seasoned escargots and a mushroom purée; saddle of hare in an intensely aromatic game sauce; delicious pigs' feet in beer; and good, though not always light, desserts (notably the chocolate cake). They have made an astute choice of undiscovered wines.

A la carte: 230-250F. Menu: 150F.

12/20 Le Bec Doré

8, quai des Pêcheurs
88.35.39.57 / F4-28

M. Maria. Open until 10 p.m. Closed Mon., Tues., Feb. school vacation & 3 weeks in Aug. Pets allowed. Cards: V, AE, DC.

The short, talkative, bearded owner prepares a robust cuisine devoted to fowl: tarragon-flavored suprêmes, medallions à l'américaine, fowl served in salads and confits. His best specialty is the black-legged rooster with Chambertin, which is boned, stuffed and served with a delicious sauce. Desserts are nothing out of the ordinary; the brand-new decor, however, is stylish.

A la carte: 250F. Menus: 98F (weekday lunch only, wine incl.), 120F, 220F.

13 Au Boeuf Mode

2, pl. St-Thomas - 88.32.39.03 / C4-2

M. Letzter. Open until 11 p.m. Closed Sun.; annual closing varies. Pets allowed. Cards: V, AE, DC, MC.

Behind an extremely discreet facade lurks an old split-level weinstube (the upstairs dining room is more attractive) that has been transformed into a real restaurant. The reception and service are more efficient than warm, and the à la carte menu and the many fixed-price menus are devoted to beef, intelligently and generously prepared. These include large rib; onglet with shallots marinated in red wine; beef filet "à la ficelle"; T-bone; carpaccio; and particularly the "must prime rib," a savory piece of beef in a salt crust roasted at a very low heat, which produces meat that is at once well cooked, pink and tender, with all its juices. The presentations need more attention, and the selection of wines from Alsace could be less scanty.

A la carte: 250-300F. Menus: 120F (lunch only), 175F.

18 Buerehiesel

4, parc de l'Orangerie
88.61.62.24 / G2-32

M. Westermann. Open until 9:30 p.m. Closed Tues. dinner (in seas.), Wed., Dec. 21-Jan. 4, Feb. 2-15 & Aug. 10-23. Terrace dining. Pets allowed. Parking. Cards: V, AE, DC.

The goose liver caramelized with soy and vinegar—the Japanese-Alsatian endeavor we tasted on a recent visit, whose flavor we found slightly sickening—was still on the menu at our last visit. On the other hand, Antoine Westermann had replaced the vanilla that accompanied the lobster and the ginger that overwhelmed the sweetbreads with fennel. He did well to remove these very Parisian dishes, because his talent is so much better applied to the more frank, less sophisticated flavors of the region, as revealed in his terrine of venison and duck liver with celery and truffle juice, his saddle of young rabbit in a salad with lentils and bacon, his frogs'-leg soup with pearled barley and Alsatian quenelles, and his matelote of fish with Riesling. Without being strictly traditional, each of these dishes is distinguished by a personal touch. Westermann is an excellent fish chef, and the people of Strasbourg have always been fond of fish and are enraged at seeing their rivers decimated by pollution. They're enraptured here with, for example, the exquisite miniature escalopes of salmon covered by a thin layer of fresh herbs and a marvelous smoked-salmon butter with a touch of lime. Or by the bass with thyme cream accompanied by a tasty potato pancake. Or by the roast daurade with an onion confit and coriander. The desserts are a model of finesse (the strawberry millefeuille with white-chocolate mousse and the cold currant soufflé with an Alsatian crémant are little masterpieces). And to add to the charm of this 300-year-old farm, the wine list is one of the most sumptuous in Alsace.

Resurrected during the nineteenth century in the admirable park of the Orangerie, designed by Le Nôtre, the restaurant today is bathed in a peaceful light that shows off its charming, almost romantic decor and discreet folkloric nuances. Viviane Westermann, always smiling, welcomes the little princes who govern Europe and the members of Strasbourg society, who for many years have been dividing their dining-out time between Le Crocodile and the old Buerehiesel. It seemed to us, however, that although the service was quite courteous, it showed signs of fatigue: 34 minutes passed between the time they presented the menu to our anonymous envoy and the time they took his order.

A la carte: 460F. Menus: 230F (weekday lunch only), 240F (weekend and holiday dinner only), 390F.

Cathédrale Dauphin

12, pl. de la Cathédrale
88.22.12.12 / D4-14

Open year-round. 3 stes 490-590F. 29 rms 340-480F. TV. No pets. Telex 871054. Cards: V, AE, DC.

Entirely renovated in 1987, this luxurious little hotel presents one of the most beautiful spectacles in Europe: the cathedral, with its spires shooting up before your window. The lovely decor is modern and comfortable, with superb bathrooms and perfect soundproofing. You will be greeted with charm by a young and extremely courteous staff. Two conference rooms, as well as a fitness club 150 meters away. No restaurant.

11/20 La Chaumière

12, rue de la Fonderie
88.32.35.23 / D3-24

M. Greth. Open until 10 p.m. Closed Sat. lunch, Sun. & July 14-Aug. 15. Pets allowed. Cards: V, AE, DC, MC.

For ten years, a custom has been well established at La Chaumière: The owner waits on the tables, and his wife, in front of the fireplace, prepares a variety of generous grilled meats, as well as a good pot-au-feu. Lively little wines.

A la carte: 180F. Menu: 105F.

Le Crocodile

10, rue de l'Outre
88.32.13.02 / D3-18

M. Jung. Open until 10 p.m. Closed Sun., Mon., July 9-Aug. 7 & Dec. 23-Jan. 1. Air cond. No pets. Cards: AE, DC, MC.

For the first time since we've known him we had to gently scold Emile Jung for serving us a slightly disappointing meal. And since that coincided with a few lukewarm comments from our readers, we knocked him down a point in a recent edition of our French-language guide.

Since he's intelligent and very professional, Jung didn't waste his time with lamentations and recriminations, but apparently delved right into fixing what wasn't working. The result was that he strengthened his team, and today Le Crocodile is as good as ever. We were convinced of this by three meals seated before an enormous painting of a peasant feast in Strasbourg of the last century, in a beautiful closed dining room made both soft and voluptuous by marvelous yellow and rose lighting. Here we rediscovered the technical mastery and delicacy of flavors that are the mark of Jung in optimum shape. The chaud-froid de pintade (guinea-fowl) with champignons de couche was exquisite, as was the tureen of lamb consommé with marrow. The fresh foie gras au torchon et à l'ancienne revealed a master's seasoning and an aspic of a rare delicacy. The sautéed red snapper in a shellfish coulis made us believe that Strasbourg borders the Mediterranean. The calves' liver and kidneys in tarragon mustard came with zucchini stuffed with a vegetable purée, a broccoli mousseline and a small gratin, a perfectly harmonious blend. The veal mignon with kidneys cooked in sage and the pressed duck wrapped in a sumptuous and complex blood sauce were extraordinary. The dessert cart, an antique made of polished wood, shining silver, heavy glass shelves and columns, is laden with creations that will make your mouth water; the bread, baked on the premises, is wonderfully crunchy; the cheeses are delicious; and the service runs like clockwork, under the vigilant but always laughing eye of Bernard Epp. He's one of the finest maître d's in France and generously teaches students the secrets of his art. The wine list, for which you couldn't have a better guide than Gilbert Mestrallet, is so extensive that you'll have to stop to catch your breath. Every wine region parades before your eyes, even the most forsaken, and each bottle is from the best vineyard and of the finest vintage. But of course when we go to Le Crocodile, we drink Alsatian wines, and it's always a fabulous feast when a Riesling from Kienzler, a Tokay from Trimbach, a "Vendages Tardives" from Hugel or Beyer or a more modest but very good Pinot Noir from Turckheim ("modest" in that these wines don't come cheap and this red Alsatian wine is among the least expensive) appears at the table.

There is also Le Crocodile's most gracious smile that greets you when you enter the pretty dining room, among the elegantly set tables, swarms of flowers and green plants. It's the smile of the frail, lively and distinguished Mme. Jung, who, without seeming to, catches every detail as if she were using a magnifying glass.

A la carte: 420F. Menus: 230F (lunch only), 290F (dinner only).

(13) Estaminet Schloegel

19, rue de la Kruteneau
88.36.21.98 / F4-34

M. Deprez. Open until 10 p.m. Closed Sun., Mon., July 12-26 & Dec. 24-Jan. 7. Pets allowed. Cards: V.

In the trendy Kruteneau neighborhood, Gérard Deprez and his wife, Valentine, ensure a warm atmosphere in their small, attractive and friendly eighteenth-century house. A fine fixed-price menu offers, for example, an escalope of duck liver, squab breasts with juniper berries and dessert; à la carte, you can choose light, tasty dishes prepared by Gérard: crab ravioli with two sauces, sweetbreads with sorrel purée and lamb navarin with young vegetables.

A la carte: 280-300F. Menus: 130F (weekday lunch only), 180F.

11/20 Le Fuji

39, av. des Vosges - 88.35.54.75 / D2-19

M. Hermann. Open until 10:30 p.m. Closed Feb. 1-15. Pets allowed. Cards: AE, V, DC, MC.

This Japanese restaurant, adjoining an 18th-century building on the avenue des Vosges in Strasbourg, is the only place in France where patrons may enjoy all the authentic classics of Nippon cuisine—sushi, sukiyaki, tempura, brochettes, etc.—in the traditional fashion: without any napery, directly on the table. An attractive little menu featuring brochettes is offered at lunch.

A la carte: 150F. Menus: 55F (lunch only), 165F.

(13) Au Gourmet Sans Chiqué

15, rue Ste-Barbe - 88.32.04.07 / D4-3

M. Klein. Open until 10 p.m. Closed Mon. lunch, Sun., March 27-April 7 & July 24-Aug. 7. Pets allowed. Cards: V, AE, DC.

A young Alsatian couple has just taken over this delightful restaurant, modern and bright with the decor of an elegant bistro. Mme. Klein is charming, her brother-in-law is a talented maître d'hôtel/sommelier, and her husband, Daniel Klein (who trained with Boyer in Reims), previously was in charge of the kitchen at the remarkable Grange in Royan. Klein's cuisine is creative, tasty and unpretentious, unquestionably worthy of a solid toque, in spite of a few excessive sauces (to accommodate his German guests): escalope of fried salmon with a chive mousseline, pink and tender veal kidneys cooked with spices and accompanied by baby vegetables, so-so cheeses and a hot apple tart (light in itself, but with a caramel sauce that weighs it down a bit). There's a worthwhile fixed-price menu.

A la carte: 260-280F. Menus: 160F, 220F.

Gutenberg

31, rue des Serruriers
88.32.17.15 / D4-6

Closed Jan. 1-10. 50 rms 132-280F. TV in 4 rms. Cards: V.

The original furniture from this residence dating from 1750 still remains in the lounges and some of the rooms. No restaurant.

Hannong

15, rue du 22-Novembre
88.32.16.22 / C3-23

Closed Dec. 23-30. 70 rms 280-420F. TV. Pets allowed. Parking. Telex 890551. Cards: V, AE, DC, MC.

This classic hotel is named for the famous eighteenth-century earthenware with which it is decorated. Perfectly equipped for small conferences. Restaurant.

Holiday Inn

20, pl. de Bordeaux
88.35.70.00 / E1-16

Open year-round. 1 ste 1,650F. 169 rms 645-835F. TV. Air cond. Pets allowed. Heated pool. Tennis. Parking. Telex 890515. Cards: V, AE, DC, MC.

This handsome, modern, functional hotel located near the Music and Convention Center features a solarium, sauna and Turkish bath, as well as a discotheque, bank, travel agency and several restaurants.

Ibis

1, rue Sébastopol - 88.22.14.99 / C3-33

Open year-round. 97 rms 269F. TV. Pets allowed. Telex 880399. Cards: V.

Ibis's rooms are small, but brand-new, modern and comfortable. Restaurant.

(13) Julien

22, quai des Bateliers
88.36.01.54 / E4-10

M. Schaller. Open until 10 p.m. Closed Sat. lunch, Sun., Feb. school vacation & 1st 3 weeks in Aug. Pets allowed. Cards: V, AE, DC, MC.

This charming hotel on the banks of the Ill facing the Rohan château has all the little touches of early-twentieth-century Parisian decor. The mustachioed owner prepares a modern menu that sparkles with the savoir-faire of an excellent sauce chef and a highly personal head chef: cabbage stuffed with steamed langoustines, "pope's nose" (bird's tail) ragoût with truffle juice, feuilleté of Muenster cheese, morello cherry soup with semolina quenelles, and terrine of rhubarb and red fruits. The service is commendable in this little dining room with its abundant bouquets, and the respected wine growers of Alsace are honored in the wine cellar.

A la carte: 280F. Menu: 125F (lunch only), 160F to 250F.

(13) La Maison du Boeuf

Ave. Herrenschmidt
88.37.10.10 / D1-30

M. Zimmermann. Open until 10:15 p.m. Closed Sat., Sun., Feb. school vacation & July 29-Aug. 21. Air cond. No pets. Parking. Telex 890363. Cards: V, AE, DC, MC.

A clientele of business people, international conference attendees and European experts keeps this luxurious Hilton dining room going worry-free. But that doesn't necessarily stimulate an imaginative cuisine or an enthusiastic staff. It is difficult for us not to reveal that on our last visit the service was distracted and slow, the menu had hardly changed since our previous visit, and there were a few weaknesses that should be a warning signal to this restaurant that was, not long ago, one of the best in Strasbourg: A nice escalope of salmon with a chanterelle feuilleté was sullied with slightly overcooked fish, and a disastrous squab pot-au-feu with foie gras had raw vegetables and an aqueous sauce. But the desserts, notably the soup with oranges and red fruits, were exquisite. Though the selection of wines was admirable, the advice we received was poor.

A la carte: 350-400F. Menus: 155F (lunch only), 250F (dinner only).

Hilton

(See restaurant above)

Open year-round. 5 stes. 246 rms 620-780F. TV. Air cond.

Surrounded by wide-open greenery, these lovely rooms look out over the city and the cathedral. The hotel offers a sunny, tranquil terrace, as well as boutiques, a sauna and hot tubs.

(13) Maison Kammerzell

16, pl. de la Cathédrale
88.32.42.14 / D4-1

M. Baumann. Open until 1 a.m. Closed Feb. 1-15. Terrace dining. Pets allowed. Cards: V, AE, DC, MC.

With choucroute in hand, Guy-Pierre Baumann has settled at the doorstep of the pink cathedral in the extraordinary Maison Kammerzell, which dates from 1427 and is right out of a Victor Hugo story. The "Kammerzell institution," as it's called in Strasbourg, was in trouble. But the spirited Alsatian returned from Paris (he now divides his time between his restaurant on rue Marbeuf and this historic monument) and restored order to the kitchen by hiring the former assistant chef of Le Camélia in Bougival. He also instituted a single menu for all four floors—each one fixed up beautifully with polished furniture, wood paneling and stained-glass windows—where the previous management wasted its time combining Alsatian specialties and an allegedly classic-modern "grande cuisine." More wisely, Baumann has created a short menu that is heavy on fish, to which the locals are extremely partial, and that includes the famous choucroutes (fish, duck confit, Oriental) that made a name for him in Paris and aroused, in the beginning, the mistrust of the Alsatians.

At any rate, they would be ungracious to not recognize that Baumann's classic Alsatian choucroute is by far the best in town. Prepared in wide strips, crunchy and smooth, this Sauerkraut is accompanied by exquisite sausages (especially the boudin noir) and beats the pants off its rivals, whose aromas assail you at every street corner. Baumann also serves an excellent foie gras, superb oysters, good pastries and all varieties of Alsatian wines. His touristy clientele inundates the terrace and the first-floor dining room. Guests are greeted with a charming reception but served with some difficulty (because of the four floors). In all, the new Kammerzell is a brilliant recovery by an astute and untiring professional.

A la carte: 300F. Menus: 171F, 250F.

Monopole-Métropole

16, rue Kuhn - 88.32.11.94 / B3-27

Closed Dec. 25-Jan. 1. 94 rms 295-470F. TV. Pets allowed. Garage parking. Telex 890366. Cards: V, AE, DC, MC.

A lovely, traditional, well-maintained and centrally located hotel. Twelve TV channels. No restaurant.

Novotel

Quai Kléber - 88.22.10.99 / C3-9

Open year-round. 97 rms 450-500F. TV. Air cond. Parking. Telex 880700. Cards: V, AE, DC, MC.

A modern hotel that provides good value for its rates, Novotel is located in the midst of a large shopping center. Grill.

12/20 Au Petit Maximin

4, pl. de l'Homme-de-Fer - 88.23.05.00, 88.32.50.38 / C3-21

M. Schmitt. Open daily until 6 a.m. Air cond. Terrace dining. Pets allowed. Cards: V, AE, DC, MC.

The small entrance to this nightclub leads to three floors, each devoted to a different type of cuisine (Italian, traditional, weinstube). There's a good sander feuilleté with foie gras and fresh noodles, veal kidneys (too firm) and desserts. Service until 6 a.m. on the main floor.

A la carte: 180-230F. Menus: 58F, 78F, 104F, 128F.

12/20 Pfifferbriader

9, pl. du Marché-aux-Cochons
88.32.15.43 / D4-4

M. Heydmann. Open until 11 p.m. Closed Sun., 1 week in Feb. & Aug. Pets allowed. Cards: V, MC.

Tasty Alsatian-style pork cuts and Sauerkrauts, along with liver quenelles and ham en croûte. All varieties of Alsatian wines are offered by the carafe. An attractive weinstube-style place near the Museum of History.

A la carte: 150F.

Le Régent Contades

8, ave. de la Liberté - 88.36.26.26 / F3-8

Closed Dec. 23-Jan. 2. 1 ste 1,000-1,200F. 31 rms 550-905F. TV. Air cond. in 26 rms. Garage parking. Telex 890641. Cards: V, AE, DC.

Recently opened in a beautiful nineteenth-century structure, this hotel is located in the residential quarter at the edge of the Ill. The luxurious rooms are large, attractively decorated and well equipped, and the reception is particularly friendly. If you are looking for a Strasbourg hotel with charm, come here. Special features include a sauna, solarium, UVA tanning, a chic bar and room service.

Hôtel des Rohan

17-19, rue du Maroquin
88.32.85.11 / D4-20

Open year-round. 36 rms 250-500F. TV. Air cond. in 12 rms. Telex 870047. Cards: V.

This small hotel in the pedestrian zone is 50 meters from the cathedral. It has guaranteed calm and a relaxed atmosphere, but no restaurant.

10/20 Saint-Sépulcre

15, rue des Orfèvres
88.32.39.97 / D3-22

M. Lauck. Open until 9:30 p.m. Closed Sun., Mon. & July 14-Aug. 9. Cards: V, MC.

This is a great, classic Strasbourg-style weinstube (though a bit touristy), with a large oven, checkered tablecloths and a variety of pork cuts.

A la carte: 100-130F.

12/20 S'Burjerstuewel

(Chez Yvonne)
10, rue du Sanglier - 88.32.84.15 / D3-11

Mme. Haller. Open until midnight. Closed Mon. lunch, Sun., holidays & July 14-Aug. 10. Pets allowed. Cards: V.

Polished wood, small curtains, shiny copperware and an atmosphere as folkloric as it is smoky. Mme. Haller greets her guests warmly and offers a glass of white wine while you await more serious things, such as escargots, foie gras, Sauerkraut and liver quenelles. Wines from Alsace are served in flasks or pitchers.

A la carte: 130-150F.

Sofitel

Pl. St-Pierre-le-Jeune
88.32.99.30 / D3-15

Open year-round. 5 stes 1,800-3,600F. 158 rms 680-880F. Parking. Telex 870894. Cards: V, AE, DC, MC.

Well-situated on a quiet square in the center of town, these rooms are rather small but comfortable. Pleasant patio, boutiques, hair salon and restaurant.

12/20 Valentin Sorg

6, pl. de l'Homme-de-Fer
88.32.12.16 / C3-29

M. François. Open until 9:45 p.m. Closed Sun. dinner, Tues., Feb. 15-28 & Aug. 15-30. No pets. Cards: V, AE, DC, MC.

By day or night, the view of Strasbourg's old rooftops and the cathedral spire from this panoramic fifteenth-floor restaurant is breathtaking. The cuisine, however, is on an inexorable decline: a distressing suprême of sole Pyramide, dismal sweetbreads grenadine, Kirsch-flavored crêpes... A Prince Charming is certainly needed.

A la carte: 400F. Menus: 150F, 225F.

10/20 Strissel

5, pl. de la Grande-Boucherie
88.32.14.73 / D4-5

M. Schrodi. Open until 11 p.m. Closed Sun. (exc. hols.) and Mon., 10 days in Feb. and July 8-31. Air cond. Pets allowed. Cards: V, MC.

A major spring cleaning has considerably improved the appearance of this ancient (1385) building near the place Kléber. At the picturesque bar inside, two fleet-footed, cool-headed ladies serve drinks with incredible speed, along with moderately tasty onion tarts and smoked pork shoulder.

A la carte: 120F. Menus: 44F (weekdays only), from 54F to 86F.

Terminus Gruber

10, pl. de la Gare - 88.32.87.00 / B3-31

Open year-round. 8 stes 500-650F. 70 rms 220-500F. Half-board 300-600F. TV in 60 rms. Telex 870998. Cards: V, AE, DC, MC.

The decent well-soundproofed rooms face the train station esplanade. Remarkable comfort, attentive service. Restaurant and brasserie.

La Vieille Enseigne

9, rue des Tonneliers
88.32.58.50 / D4-13

M. Langs. Open until 10 p.m. Closed Sat. lunch, Sun. & 3 weeks in Aug. Air cond. Pets allowed. Cards: V, AE, DC.

The new, intimate bourgeois decor—light wood, rugs, stylish round tables and flowers—is an elegant success. The young dining room staff, supervised by the owner's attentive wife, is rather more courteous than experienced, and Franz Langs's cooking is serious and quite well finished (with perhaps too great a tendency to use expensive products): steamed salmon with ginger (its sauce is a bit too pungent), a perfectly roasted whole veal kidney served with beautiful broccoli, and unoriginal but well-prepared desserts (tarte tatin, sorbets).

A la carte: 300-350F. Menus: 150F (lunch only), 180F.

Zimmer-Sengel

8, rue du Temple-Neuf
88.32.35.01 / D3-26

M. Sengel. Open until 9:30 p.m. Closed Sun., Mon. lunch & Aug. 1-20. Terrace dining. Pets allowed. Cards: V, AE, DC.

The elegant Zimmer-Sengel is at the end of a peaceful alleyway in the middle of the city; inside is a bright, wood-paneled dining room decorated with flowers, interesting paintings and curious curtains. The old-pro maître d'hôtel and the beautiful silver lend an air of luxury to the restaurant, which the prices faithfully echo. Georges Sengel's cuisine is at once serious and inventive: delicious (but somewhat meager) foie gras, coquilles St-Jacques in a light sauce with mangetout peas (also a little stingy and without accompanying vegetables), good spiced lamb, admirable feuilleté of pistachios and pears. The wine cellar is fine but a bit pricey.

A la carte: 300-350F. Menus: 200F (wine incl.), 160F, 290F.

IN NEARBY **Fegersheim**
(13 km S on N 83)
67640 Fegersheim - (Bas-Rhin)

---

16 La Table Gourmande

43, rte. de Lyon - 88.68.53.54

M. Reix. Open until 9:30 p.m. Closed Sun. dinner, Mon., Dec. 24-Jan. 6 & Aug. 1-21. Pets allowed. Cards: V, AE, DC.

In the summer of 1987, Alain Reix was finally able to open the restaurant of his dreams, leaving behind a morose northern suburb for this cheerful southern one. His new, sophisticated dining room decor (gray tones) isn't very warm, in spite of the pleasant tables with flowers, but it does have a sober elegance as well as exemplary comfort. In the kitchen, which can be seen through a windowpane from the entryway, Reix still stirs up the salt-air breezes of the Atlantic. This native of La Rochelle came to the area a few years ago, with sea foam on his mustache and seaweed in his hair, to marry a woman from Strasbourg and to settle down in the land of choucroute and storks. But just glance at his lovely blue menu, designed like a wave, and you'll know that it's still sea gulls and spring tides that dance inside his head. All of Marennes and Boulogne, plus the best of Brittany, have inspired his delicate cuisine, which is both daring and precise and has no rival in Alsace: Atlantic tartare of fried duck liver, house-smoked turbot and salmon, shredded skate topped with a garlic sabayon and exquisitely presented with fresh baby vegetables, filet of red mullet with liver sauce. The desserts are on occasion brilliant, like the baked crêpes with prune mousse and a fig purée. And the wine list is perfectly eclectic. Our only hope is that in the future this exciting cuisine

will be served in less parsimonious portions.
A la carte: 350-400F. Menus: 180F (weekdays only), 250F, 350F.

IN NEARBY **La Wantzenau**
(13 km NE on D 468)
67610 La Wantzeneau - (Bas-Rhin)

(13) Zimmer
23, rue des Héros - 88.96.62.08
Mme. Zimmer. Open until 9:15 p.m. Closed Sun. dinner, Mon. & Aug. 1-17. Air cond. Garden dining. Pets allowed. Cards: V, AE, DC, MC.

The simple rustic decor in this row of dining rooms is a great improvement over the banal, decrepit building that houses them. And the classically rigorous cuisine is also a pleasant surprise: feuilleté of sweetbreads and escargots in a rich but good sauce, filet of lamb en croûte with fines herbes (good meat, but slightly overdone), uneven desserts. The Alsatian wines are excellent, but the recommendations are, unfortunately, off-base.
A la carte: 300F. Menus: 130F (except Saturday dinner and Sunday), 190F, 320F.

Super-Sauze
see Barcelonnette

Tain-l'Hermitage
26600 Tain-l'Hermitage - (Drôme)
Paris 550 - Grenoble 99 - St-Etienne 75 - Valence 18

(16) Restaurant Reynaud
82, ave. du Président-Roosevelt
75.07.22.10
M. Reynaud. Open until 9:30 p.m. Closed Sun. dinner, Mon. & Jan. Garden dining. No pets. Parking. Cards: V, AE, DC.

We have to hand it to Jean-Marc Reynaud, who is no longer content to play secondary roles in this corner of the Drôme: He revamped his beautiful dining room on the banks of the Rhône river (with a terrace for sunny days) with comfortable chairs, new silver and lovely Limoges china. In addition, he clarified the wine list; now Chapoutier comes up more than ever as the preferred wine of the house (tastings and snacks are offered in the bar). Improvements to the cuisine are no less evident, even if they are increasingly on the classic side. The just-pink squab, fricassée of lobster and émincé of quail are simply perfect dishes that reveal great talent. As for the desserts, they are divided between good, hearty cakes and such fine delicacies as strawberry-mint soup with sorbet. The à la carte prices are stable, and the fixed-price menus are always popular with the weekend crowds.
A la carte: 300-350F. Menus: 130F, 200F, 280F.

Talloires
see Annecy

Tancarville
76430 St-Romain-de-Colbosc - (Seine-Maritime)
Paris 200 - Rouen 70 - Deauville 43 - Le Havre 29

(14) La Marine
D 984 - 35.39.77.15
M. Sedon. Open until 8:45 p.m. Closed Sun. dinner, Mon. (except holidays), Feb. 15-March 2 & July 16-Aug. 10. Terrace dining. Pets allowed. Hotel: 8 rms 170-200F; half-board oblig. in seas. Parking. Cards: V.

The graceful Tancarville bridge, which straddles the Seine with a great leap over big blackened boats, is just above La Marine. This sight is the main attraction of the simple, comfortable dining room, whose large bay windows take in the river and the natural light. The cuisine is also simple and light, prepared by the young owner, Jean-Pierre Sedon. His menu is short and well composed, and nearly everything on it is mouth watering, from the Paimpol or Grandcamp oysters (inexpensive), to the grilled mix of bass and salmon in saffron sauce, to the local duck, to the precious desserts (lime soufflé with raspberry purée). Both fixed-price menus are generous.
A la carte: 300F. Menus: 125F (except holidays, wine incl.), 230F (holidays only), 160F.

Tarare
69170 Tarare - (Rhône)
Paris 467 - Roanne 43 - Lyon 65 - Villefranche 32

(16) Jean Brouilly
3 ter, rue de Paris - 74.63.24.56
M. Brouilly. Open until 9 p.m. Closed Sun., Mon., Feb. school vacation & Aug. 5-17. Air cond. Pets allowed. Parking. Cards: V, AE, DC.

The discreet, charming Jean Brouilly is just the man you need to see when you're at an equal distance from the superstars of Roanne and Collonges. He is, moreover, the only one capable of keeping you for a few hours in this big town with no charm, particularly since his nineteenth-century restaurant has blossomed with a pleasant garden, where perhaps he will be inspired to set up some tables when the weather is right. But the real attractions in this serious establishment are the friendly prices, the inventiveness, the excellent products (fish, poultry, vegetables) and the delicious Bordeaux. We were enraptured by one of the fixed-price menus: a perfect salad of duck aiguillettes, a ragoût of langoustines in a delicate orange sauce, rich tournedos of white poultry with truffle cream, cheeses and dessert.
A la carte: 300F. Menus: 120F, 180F, 240F, 280F.

Tarbes
65000 Tarbes - (Hautes-Pyrénées)
Paris 778 - Bordeaux 211 - Toulouse 155 - Auch 72

(15) L'Amphitryon
38, rue Larrey - 62.34.08.99
M. Ribardière. Open until 9:45 p.m. Closed Sat. lunch, Sun. & Aug. 5-21. Air cond. Pets allowed. Cards: V, AE, DC.

Christelle and Claude Ribardière have found success without upsetting the tradition of heaviness in the local food. They have accomplished this feat with a frankly modern cuisine, refined and on occasion daring, that abounds with the beautiful products of the region. The tartare of tuna and oysters, mosaic of leeks and eel, crispy smoked salmon with salmon roe, escalopes of fresh liver and loin of fatted duck with juniper-berry butter are dishes that won't be found everywhere and that show off a singularly inventive vitality. The carefully set large tables and the classic decor are accented with floral bouquets. The regional wines are excellent.

A la carte: 260F. Menus: 130F, 200F.

IN NEARBY **Juillan**
(6 km SW on N 21)
65290 Juillan - (Hautes-Pyrénées)

(14) La Caravelle

Tarbes airport - 62.32.99.96

M. Rouzaud. Open until 9:30 p.m. (10 p.m. in summer). Closed Sun. dinner, Mon., Jan. 9-Feb. 1 & July 3-19. Air cond. Pets allowed. Parking. Telex 531444.

The immense menu is still encumbered with old standbys that defy good sense (like filet of sole Thermidor, Noilly langoustines and flambéed kidneys). But Louis Rouzaud wants to please everyone and show that he can cook everything. In any case, his generosity is well intended and doesn't degrade the quality of the classic cuisine, which has made an intelligent move toward lightness: quail salad with foie gras, filet of bass in gazpacho, pigeon with truffles and foie gras in a port sauce, grilled salmon en papillote. The desserts are lovely and the Bordeaux interesting. The impeccable, air-conditioned dining room looks out at the ski runs and the mountains. Brasserie on the ground floor.

A la carte: 300F. Menus: 185F (weekends and holidays only), 135F, 220F.

Tavers

see Beaugency

Teteghem

see Dunkerque

Théoule-sur-Mer

06590 Théole-sur-Mer - (Alpes-Maritimes)
Paris 895 - St-Raphaël 36 - Cannes 10 - Nice 41

IN NEARBY **Miramar**
(6 km S on N 98)
06590 Théoule-sur-Mer - (Alpes-Maritimes)

12/20 Père Pascal

16, ave. du Trayas - 93.75.40.11

M. Cozzolino. Open until 10 p.m. Closed Thurs. (except July-Aug.) & Nov. 1-Jan. 30. Garden dining. Pets allowed. Parking. Cards: V, AE, DC.

The terraces at Père Pascal have marvelous views of the Théole coast and its yachts, but you'll pay dearly for these vistas. Dishes include lobster ravioli, beef with shallots and lotte stuffed with Provençal mushrooms.

A la carte: 350-400F. Menus: 105F (weekdays only), 180F.

Saint-Christophe

47, ave. de Miramar (on La Corniche d'Or) - 93.75.41.36

Closed Nov. 15-March 1. 1 ste 1,100-1,700F. 37 rms 355-870F. Half-board 380-540F oblig. in seas. TV. Air cond. in 10 rms. Pool. Garage parking. Telex 470878. Cards: V, AE, DC, MC.

Perched on rocks overlooking the sea, the pool and a private beach (direct access), this hotel offers numerous leisure activities, as well as many services (such as babysitting). Restaurant.

Thivars

see Chartres

Thoissey

01140 Thoissey - (Ain)
Paris 411 - Bourg 37 - Mâcon 16 - Lyon 56

(15) Au Chapon Fin

(Paul Blanc)

Rue du Champ-de-Foire - 74.04.04.74

MM. Blanc-Maringue. Open until 9:30 p.m. Closed Tues. (except dinner in seas.) & early Jan.-early Feb. Terrace dining. Pets allowed. Garage parking. Telex 305728. Cards: V.

Can it be that the Bresse region has put chef Jacques Lanusse to sleep? The menu from which we ordered recently drew its inspiration exclusively from a sort of middle-class regionalism—minus the flambé, and not just on the 190-franc fixed-price "regional" menu. When an ordinary plate of local products (as a first course), an uninteresting warm salad of lamb's sweetbreads and broccoli, a tiny serving of a delicious beef à la ficelle with little vegetables in vinegar, a handsome cheese platter and a choice of conventional desserts come to about 500 francs, one needs a digestive with the bill. Fortunately, the garden is still superb, the greeting warm, the reasonable list of Burgundies intact, and the lovely decor still includes the Lurat tapestries. But one less point in this edition; the second toque is hanging in the balance.

A la carte: 450-500F. Menus: 160F (weekday lunch only), 190F, 275F, 400F.

Au Chapon Fin

(See restaurant above)

Closed Tues. (off-seas.) & early Jan.-early Feb. 25 rms 210-600F. TV in 15 rms.

This comfortable, traditional residence is flanked by a modern annex of equal comfort, with loggia windows overlooking a shaded garden. Relais et Châteaux.

Remember to call or write in advance to reserve your room or your table.

Thonon-les-Bains

74200 Thonon-les-Bains - (Haute-Savoie)
Paris 575 - Geneva 33 - Evian 9 - Annecy 72

(15) Le Prieuré

68, Grande-Rue - 50.71.31.89

M. Plumex. Open until 10:30 p.m. Closed Mon. (except dinner July-Aug.) & Sun. dinner. Air cond. Pets allowed. Cards: V, AE, DC, MC.

A sort of creative exasperation seems to have seized the clever, bearded Charles Plumex for some time now. Hoping that he doesn't go too far in his pursuit of the amazing, we can say that for now it is a pleasure to partake of his cuisine, and Plumex's steady technique is able to keep the boldness under control. It is with the precarious balance of a tightrope walker that he combines, for example, vanilla with curry (oeufs à la neige—with oysters) or onions and orange peels (crayfish ragoût). But our feeling persists that this former chef at London's Saint-Quentin should, in the future, find a more peaceful path—especially more simplified—whereby his grand personality and his virtuous sauces will be able to fully express themselves. He has already broken that path here with such delicious dishes as the filets of perch marinated in herbs, the terrine of foie gras with leeks, the langoustine ravioli with thyme and the saddle of young rabbit in garlic juice. Business people can take advantage of a remarkable fixed-price menu at lunchtime.

A la carte: 350-400F. Menus: 180F (lunch only, wine incl.), 150F, 210F, 280F.

Thury-Harcourt

14220 Thury-Harcourt - (Calvados)
Paris 260 - Vire 45 - Caen 26 - Falaise 26 - Flers 31

(14) Relais de la Poste

Rue de Caen - 31.79.72.12

M. Foucher. Open until 9:30 p.m. Closed Dec. 1-Feb. 1. Pets allowed. Garage parking. Cards: V, AE, DC, MC.

Thanks to the beautiful old timbering of this long, airy dining room, you'll think you're dining under the overturned hull of a ship, surrounded by a sea of green and facing a magnificent garden. The owner, Philippe Foucher from the Touraine region (who keeps some lovely bottles of wine from the Loire valley in his cellar), is a self-taught cook, though that has been scarcely evident since he took over the kitchen after his chef left. The care that was taken when overhauling the menu and the attention to local traditions are revealed in the simple, unabashedly rustic and mouth-watering dishes: lotte peasant style, calf's head in cider, a local version of tripe and veal kidneys. The pear and apple tarts are divine, and the fixed-price menus are worth noting.

A la carte: 250F. Menus: 85F (weekday lunch only), 110F, 160F, 190F.

Relais de la Poste

(See restaurant above)

Closed Dec. 1-Feb. 1. 2 stes 320-360F. 9 rms 160-230F. Half-board 194-270F oblig. in seas. Pets allowed.

You'll find nine rooms completely made over, plus a sauna, solarium and a good breakfast. Excellent reception.

Tignes

73320 Tignes - (Savoie)
Paris 690 - Albertville 79 - Val-d'Isèere 13

(14) Le Ski d'Or

Val-Claret (2 km SW) - 79.06.51.60

MM. Bréchu. Open until 9:30 p.m. Closed May 1-Dec. 1. Pets allowed. Telex 375974.

The new chef hired by Jeanne and Claude Bréchu comes with good, dependable references. We immediately realized that he harbors no intention of reversing the traditional direction of this sober establishment, where everybody who's anybody in Tignes has always found one another. So we will continue to enjoy the hot oysters in melted sorrel butter, raw or smoked salmon with ginger, veal kidneys roasted and served with a watercress purée, and blueberry charlotte. Nothing earthshaking, but it's prepared in a thoroughly modern way using bold, uncomplicated flavors. The dining room is traditional French Alps and, being several stories up, commands a great view of the ski slopes and the mountains. Friendly, unpretentious reception, but hefty tabs.

A la carte: 300F and up. Menu: 100F (lunch only), 250F (dinner only).

Le Ski d'Or

(See restaurant above)

Closed May 1-Dec. 1. 22 rms. Half-board 750F oblig. in seas.

Comfortable rooms in a building that is nicely integrated with the rest of the village. Relais et Châteaux.

Tonnerre

89700 Tonnerre - (Yonne)
Paris 196 - Troyes 57 - Avallon 52 - Sens 73 - Auxerre 35

(17) L'Abbaye Saint-Michel

Montée de St-Michel
86.55.05.99

M. Cussac. Open until 9:15 p.m. Closed Mon. & Tues. lunch (off-seas.) & Jan. 2-Feb. 15. Pets allowed. Telex 801356. Cards: V, AE, DC.

We've been keeping an eye on Christophe Cussac, now 32 years old, since the moment he returned home to get the ovens of his father's place roaring after spending seven years under Joël Robuchon and a year with the brothers Troisgros. A year later we were predicting a third toque, and now it is a certainty.

Cussac is no mere Robuchon clone. He has his own style and personality, though the mark of the master is clearly felt in the rigorous selection of ingredients and techniques, in the elegant presentation, in the keen and clear flavors and above all in his concept of cooking. Cussac is not afraid to seek inspiration beyond traditional bounds. Witness, for example, the exquisite terrine of rabbit with savory and broad beans, the poached eggs in wine sauce with snails and sweet garlic, the pork shins in a meat pie à la benedictine, the Burgundy-style beef cheeks simmered in red wine, the breast of farm-bred chicken cooked in a bladder, the calf's head with garden vegetables, the wonderful crépinettes (small fresh sausages) of lamb, poached very slowly and served with a thyme-flavored, lightly creamy sauce. And, in another vein, consider the exceptional shellfish soup with orange rind, cod steaks pan-fried with artichokes, the lovely breaded sea bream on a purée of fresh tomato, the braised sweetbreads in verjuice (the juice of unripened grapes), and the mead-roasted pigeon with herbs. And though the desserts are less brilliant, the sorbet is nevertheless a delight. There is room for improvement in the wine list as well, though we have fond memories of an Epineuil, a red Burgundy. Under the Romanesque vaults of the old abbey, the dining room is truly lovely, even if we can't get too excited about the same old Louis XIII striped chairs, the turned wood lamps and the conspicuous display of culinary certificates. Be that as it may, we can be glad that there's yet another three-toque restaurant in Burgundy.

A la carte: 400-600F. Menus: 270F, 370F, 430F.

L'Abbaye Saint-Michel

(See restaurant above)

Closed Mon. & Tues. (off-seas.) & Jan. 2-Feb. 15. 6 stes 1,200-1,800F. 11 rms 600-900F. Half-board 600-1,360F oblig. in seas. TV. Pets allowed. Tennis.

This inn, the remains of a former abbey restored some twenty years ago by Daniel Cussac, has just been completely renovated and reappointed in order to join the luxurious ranks of the Relais et Châteaux group. The wrought iron, the machine-made tapestries and the local knick-knacks have not disappeared completely, but the general impression is a good deal more becoming than before. The ten rooms and six suites are done in a country style, fresh and pleasant, with windows overlooking eight acres of grounds at the top of a rise above the valley of the Armançon river and the Burgundy Canal.

Toul

54200 Toul - (Meurthe-et-Moselle)
Paris 283 - Metz 74 - Nancy 23 - Verdun 81

16 Le Dauphin

Rte. de Villey-St-Etienne - 83.43.13.46

M. Vohmann. Open until 10 p.m. Closed Sun. dinner, Mon., last 2 weeks of Jan. & 1st 2 weeks of Nov. Garden dining. Pets allowed. Parking. Cards: V.

Christophe Vohmann is without a doubt the Lorraine chef to watch if you don't want to miss the imminent arrival of a sure third toque. We'll leave it at that for now, except to award him an extra point, bringing him that much closer to the next rung of success. It's the least we can do in response to the progress of this young chef from eastern France, who possesses startling technical mastery and rare finesse and who is intent on the synthesis of classical and modern cuisine. Goodness knows it's not the industrially zoned neighborhood that draws you chez Vohmann. Nor is it the charm of the huge dining room made out of a former GI mess hall, even though it does have pretty tables, flowers, a sunny summer terrace and the equally sunny smile of Véronique Vohmann. On the contrary, the draw is the exquisite tempura of crayfish, the Japanese-style fritters in an extremely light batter, the fatted Bresse fowl with goose liver (perfectly prepared—17/20 for this dish), the rich panful of scallops and urchins, the farm-raised pigeon in a salt crust seasoned with local truffles, the commendable apple-and-date confit and the remarkable mango-flavored galette. Vohmann is proving to be less timid with his customers as he gets more familiar with his stoves, but he will have to become mindful of his prices, though the à la carte tab is still warranted despite a noticeable hike. You'll find lovely cheeses and a wine list obviously filled out (Bordeaux and local wines).

A la carte: 350-400F. Menus: 150F, 220F.

Toulon

83000 Toulon - (Var)
Paris 833 - Nice 152 - Aix 81 - Marseille 66 - St-Raphaël 96

Sights. The cours La Fayette and its lovely Provençal market; the old city and its "hot" quarter around the rue d'Alger; Musée de Toulon (Provençal paintings) and Musée de Vieille-Toulon (old manuscripts); the memorial of the Allied debarkment at Mount Faron (excellent view, get there by cable car); three museums of naval history (Musée de la Marine at the Arsenal, another in the cellars of the Mourillon fort and the third at Fort Balaguier in La Seyne, with exhibits from the old jail); boat tours (of the French Mediterranean fleet) and three-hour cruises on the *Toulonnaise II*, a big catamaran (meal served on board).

Eating on the Run. Le Chantilly, 5, pl. Puget (lively brasserie, salads, crêpes, steaks); Le Grill, 39, rue Victor-Micholet (plain but plenty).

Bars & Cafés. The bar at the Grand Hôtel and, above all, the bar at La Tour Blanche; L'Orangerie, 4, pl. de la Liberté (piano bar); La Tortue, 71, quai de la Sinze (comfortable, chic, lots of music).

Nightlife. Côté Jardin (very *Harper's Bazaar*, open until 2 a.m.) and La Lampe à Pétrole (young people), both recently opened on the beach at Mourillon and both instantly successful.

Altea La Tour Blanche

Blvd. Amiral-Vence - 94.24.41.57

M. Georges. Open year-round. 92 rms 290-600F. Half-board 370-520F. TV. Air cond. Pool. Cards: V, AE, DC.

Most of the rooms at this excellently located, recently renovated hotel above the beach are situated along a loggia overlooking the sea. The restaurant, La Tour Blanche, is well worth a stop.

15 La Corniche

1, littoral Frédéric-Mistral - 94.41.39.53

M. Suere. Open until 10:30 p.m. Closed Sun. dinner (except July-Aug.), Mon. & Feb. 20-27. Garden dining. Pets allowed. Garage parking. Telex 400479. Cards: V, AE, DC, MC.

In 1987 Patrick Suere left his hyper-Parisian-looking restaurant, Domaines (located off the Champs-Elysées in Paris), for this hotel and restaurant on the waterfront in Mourillon, and for its one-of-a-kind dining room built on the second floor around the trunks of three magnificent pines that grow right on up through the roof. After a cautious first season, which was spent not disturbing the status quo, he has been joined by young chef Eric Berthier, who has a background that belies his tender age: Paul et France, via Guy Savoy and Jacques Chibois. Thus the new menu is no real surprise: raw salmon perfectly marinated with the right touch of ginger, sautéed fresh langoustines served in a lentil-thickened ragoût along with little potatoes steamed over the langoustines, and salmis of red mullet, which could have done with a shade less cooking but that was delicately turned in a mild shallot purée. These are all dishes of admirable precision and clarity, as are the excellent desserts created under Berthier's leadership (even if we were not perfectly happy with the sugary pear gratin)—and it certainly deserves two toques. Now Suere has only to put in order his wine list, which shouldn't be too difficult a job for someone who used to maintain one of the best cellars of the Paris wine bars. He ought to redecorate the place as well, or at least improve the ambience—especially the dreadful lighting—in the sort-of-countrified dining room.

A la carte: 300-350F. Menus: 160F (lunch only), 198F (weekend and holiday dinner only), 260F (dinner only), 120F.

La Corniche

(See restaurant above)

Open year-round. 4 stes 280-410F. 18 rms 250-370F. TV. Pets allowed.

Facing the sea, in the superb surroundings of Mourillon, stands this little hotel with its fully equipped rooms, an interesting enough decor and a recent refurbishment.

Toulouse

31000 Toulouse - (Haute-Garonne)
Paris 681 - Lyon 534 - Marseille 400 - Bordeaux 249

Note: The numbers following the telephone number in each review pinpoint the establishment's exact location on the accompanying map.

Sights. The pl. du Capitole, the focal point of theater in Toulouse, with the famous Lyric Theatre inside the eighteenth-century Capitole; the cathedral of Saint-Etienne (twelfth and fifteenth centuries) and the basilica of Saint-Sernin (note the chevet and the spire); the Jacobean convent (founded by Saint Dominique, nicely restored); the old city and its walking district (lined with fine old homes); the quays along the canal; the many beautiful museums, including Musée de Vielle-Toulouse (folklore, pottery), Musée des Augustins (sculpture, painting) and, in the Jardin des Plantes, the important Musée d'-Histoire Naturelle; the antiques dealers' area (around the Daurade).

Eating on the Run. Aquarius, 10, blvd. de la Gare (the restaurant of a health club, fast and light); Bistro de la Maréchale, 47, rue de Metz (comfortable, modern setting, inexpensive); Café de l'Opéra, 1, pl. du Capitole (an easygoing, '30s-style bistro, lovely seafood and good home cooking); Les Ecuries de la Maréchale, 32 bis, ave. Honoré-Serres (beautiful fireplace, soft decor and excellent value); Le Jeu de l'Oie, 19, rue Gabriel-Péri (relaxed, good local dishes).

Bars & Cafés. On pl. du Capitole: the bar at the Grand Hôtel de l'Opéra (good cocktails, trendy happy-hour crowd), Le Bibent and Le Florida (two magnificent grand old-style cafés—marble, stucco, old paneling); on pl. St-Georges: the Van Gogh (lots of flowers, good selection of beers and wines by the glass, chic), Le Fil à la Patte (hip, exotic atmosphere); on pl. Wilson: Le Frégate and Le Capoul (lovely warm-weather terraces, both extremely popular); also, L'Eclusane, 39, rue de l'Eclusane (lively, rock, folk and jazz); Le Sylène, 60, rue de Metz (looks out on pl. St-Etienne, cocktails of all sorts).

Nightlife. L'Apocalypse, 9, rue Jean-Rodier; Le New Privé, 23, rue St-Rome (successful, all types); L'Ubu Club, 16, rue St-Rome (the undisputed inner sanctum of Toulouse nightlife for 25 years, not yet showing a wrinkle).

Shops. *Bakeries:* Cros, 204, rte. de Narbonne at Ramonville (excellent old-style breads); La Paysanne, 26, ave. Jean Rieux. *Charcuteries:* Cucq (for chicken-liver pâtés) and Chez Jacques, both in the Marché (market) des Carmes; Garcia, in Castelnau-d'Estrefonds (wonderful sausages). *Gourmet foods:* Comtesse du Barry, 8, pl. St-Etienne and Ducs de Gascogne, 79, blvd. Carnot (fresh and preserved products of the southwest); Germain, 6, rue de Rémusat (traditional); Le Jardin du Rempart, 13, rue Rempart-Villeneuve (exotic fruits and vegetables, as well presented as they are fresh). *Cheese:* La Pastorale, 10, pl. des Carmes (excellent cheese maturer and dealer); Xavier, 6, pl. Victor-Hugo (the best). *Pastries, confections:* Chiche, 3, rue St-Pantaléon, and 9, rue Rempart-Villeneuve (the best pastry in the city); Le Poussin Bleu, 45, rue du Languedoc (petits fours, chocolates, ice cream); Saux, 51, blvd. de Strasbourg (an institution). *Wine:* Domaine de Lastours, 44, rue de Languedoc (the oldest wine merchants in Toulouse).

12/20 L'Abbaye

20, rue Peyrolières - 61.22.72.40 / D4-7

M. Gleyses. Open until 10:30 p.m. Closed Sun., Mon., 1st week of Jan., 1 week at Easter & Aug. 1-21. Air cond. Pets allowed. Cards: V, AE, DC, MC.

A Toulousian temple of "la cuisine au fromage." The brick decor is quite pleasant, and the owner skillfully prepares such tasty classics as Roquefort tart, Emmenthal soufflé and tournedos au pont-l'évêque. Good choice of inexpensive wines.

A la carte: 250F. Menus: 63F (lunch only), 115F.

Airport Hôtel

176, rte. de Bayonne
61.49.68.78 / A2-29

Open year-round. 48 rms 264-294F. TV in 30 rms. Air cond. in 20 rms. Pets allowed. Garage parking. Telex 521752. Cards: V, AE, DC, MC.

Modern and charmless, but well soundproofed and perfectly equipped. Free airport shuttle. No restaurant.

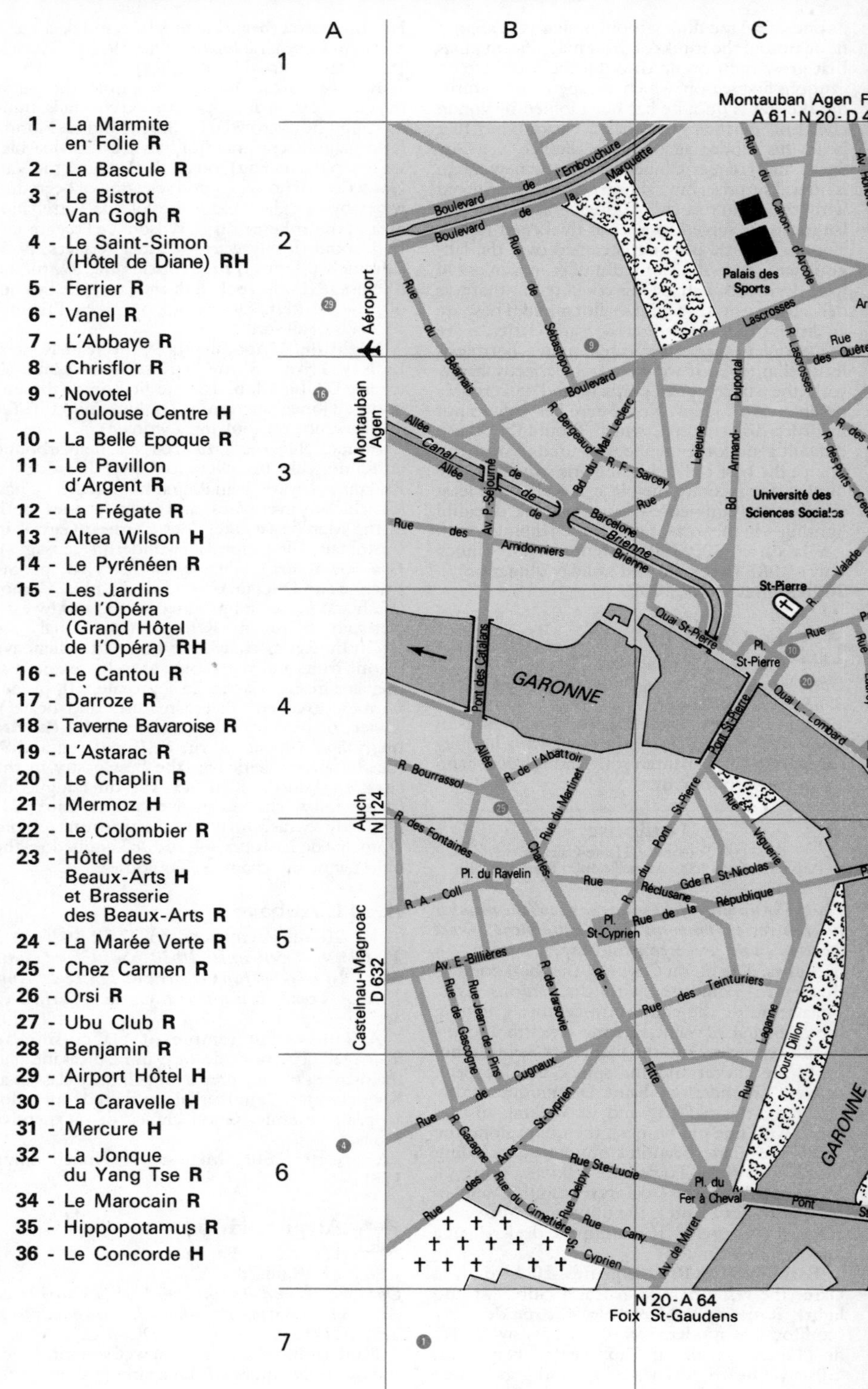
1 - La Marmite en Folie R
2 - La Bascule R
3 - Le Bistrot Van Gogh R
4 - Le Saint-Simon (Hôtel de Diane) RH
5 - Ferrier R
6 - Vanel R
7 - L'Abbaye R
8 - Chrisflor R
9 - Novotel Toulouse Centre H
10 - La Belle Epoque R
11 - Le Pavillon d'Argent R
12 - La Frégate R
13 - Altea Wilson H
14 - Le Pyrénéen R
15 - Les Jardins de l'Opéra (Grand Hôtel de l'Opéra) RH
16 - Le Cantou R
17 - Darroze R
18 - Taverne Bavaroise R
19 - L'Astarac R
20 - Le Chaplin R
21 - Mermoz H
22 - Le Colombier R
23 - Hôtel des Beaux-Arts H et Brasserie des Beaux-Arts R
24 - La Marée Verte R
25 - Chez Carmen R
26 - Orsi R
27 - Ubu Club R
28 - Benjamin R
29 - Airport Hôtel H
30 - La Caravelle H
31 - Mercure H
32 - La Jonque du Yang Tse R
34 - Le Marocain R
35 - Hippopotamus R
36 - Le Concorde H
A
B
C
1
2
3
4
5
6
7
Aéroport
Montauban Agen
Auch N 124
Castelnau-Magnoac D 632
Montauban Agen
A 61 - N 20 - D 4
N 20 - A 64
Foix St-Gaudens
Boulevard de l'Embouchure
Boulevard de la Marquette
Palais des Sports
Rue du Canon d'Arcole
Boulevard Lascrosses
R. Lascrosses
Rue des Quêteurs
Rue de Sébastopol
Rue du Béarnais
Bd du Mal-Leclerc
R. Bergeaud
R. F.-Sarcey
Rue Lejeune
Bd Armand-Duportal
Allée de Barcelone
Allée de Brienne
Canal de Brienne
Av. P.-Séjourné
Rue des Amidonniers
Université des Sciences Sociales
St-Pierre
Quai St-Pierre
Pl. St-Pierre
Quai L.-Lombard
Pont des Catalans
GARONNE
Pont St-Pierre
R. de l'Abattoir
R. Bourrassol
Rue du Martinet
R. des Fontaines
Pl. du Ravelin
R. A.-Coll
Rue du Pont St-Pierre
Rue Viguerie
Gde R. St-Nicolas
Rue de la République
Pl. St-Cyprien
Av. E.-Billières
Rue de Gascogne
Rue Jean-de-Pins
R. de Varsovie
Rue des Teinturiers
Rue Laganne
Cours Dillon
Rue de Cugnaux
R. Gazagne
Rue des Arcs-St-Cyprien
Rue Ste-Lucie
Rue Delpy
Rue du Cimetière St-Cyprien
Rue Cany
Av. de Muret
Pl. du Fer à Cheval
Pont
GARONNE

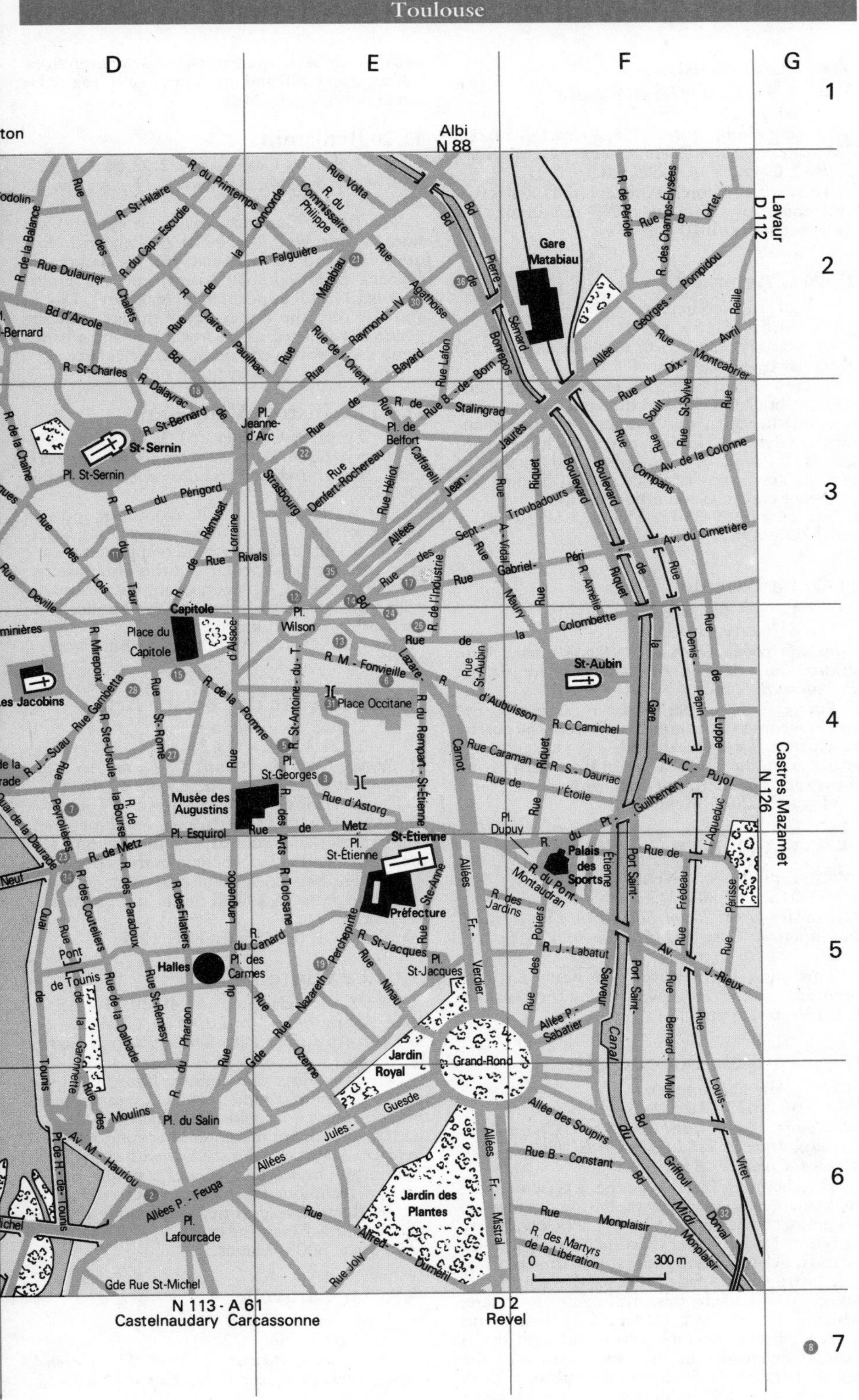

Altea Wilson

7, rue Labéda (at pl. Wilson)
61.21.21.75 / E4-13

Open year-round. 4 stes 755F. 91 rms 495-625F. TV. Air cond. Pets allowed. Garage parking. Telex 530550. Cards: V, AE, DC, MC.

This excellent hotel in the center of town is very well equipped. Piano bar. No restaurant, but room service until 10 p.m.

12/20 L'Astarac

21, rue Perchepinte
61.53.11.15 / E5-19

Mme. Manavit. Open until 11 p.m. Closed Sun. & Aug. Air cond. Pets allowed. Cards: V.

There's a new sign out front but the same pleasant brick interior and the same owner, Martine, with her open, southwestern provincial manners and deft hand in the kitchen: duck livers with grapes, a confit of cèpes, the local version of poelée (stew), old-fashioned stuffed chicken and prune ice cream. Good little wine list.

A la carte: 200-230F. Menus: 65F (weekday lunch only), 95F, 160F, 230F.

11/20 La Bascule

14, ave. Maurice-Hauriou
61.52.09.51 / D6-2

Mme. Maccagno. Open until 10 p.m. Closed Mon. dinner, Sun. & Aug. Air cond. Terrace dining. Pets allowed. Cards: V.

For years the owner has been nourishing the most ravenous of the gourmands from the nearby newspaper, *La Dépêche*, with a good, generous regional cuisine: roast saddle of lamb with thyme flower and aiguillettes of duck with cèpes.

A la carte: 250F. Menu: 95F.

Hôtel des Beaux-Arts

1, pl. du Pont-Neuf
61.23.40.50 / D5-23

Open year-round. 20 rms 300-495F. TV. Air cond. Pets allowed. Telex 532451. Cards: V, AE, DC, MC.

This nice little hotel has been entirely renovated, with rooms overlooking the Garonne river. No restaurant.

La Belle Epoque

3, rue Pargaminières
61.23.22.12 / C4-10

M. Roudgé. Open until 10:30 p.m. Closed Sun., holidays, Mon. & Sat. lunch & July. Air cond. Pets allowed. Cards: V, AE, DC.

The charming Pierre Roudgé, a Gascon and a rugbyman, is no longer here, having made good his desire to decamp to Vanel (see below, where he is now Lucien Vanel's second chef). But don't be too quick to give up your table in this comfortable bistro with its faded turn-of-the-century interior. You'd likely miss Roudgé's stout fare, which is now being perfectly interpreted by his protégé, Bruno Besson, who cooks with much Gascon generosity in the best manner of the updated traditions of the rural southwest: duck liver with figs, wild-game pie, turbot with cèpes and duck breast with caramelized Belgian endives.

A la carte: 400F and up. Menu: 135F (weekday lunch only), 200F, 240F.

12/20 Benjamin

7, rue des Gestes - 61.22.92.66 / D4-28

M. Lemercier. Open daily until 11 p.m. Pets allowed. Cards: V.

The daring (lumpfish caviar en cocotte) sits side by side with the banal (sirloin with Roquefort); and in between are the laughable (banana flambéed with bacon) and the multiregional (veal à la normande, leek tart). Day in and day out, the dishes never change. But the generosity is there, as are low prices and a handsome decor with a certain modern elegance.

Menus: 68F (weekday lunch only), 99F.

12/20 Le Bistrot Van Gogh

21, pl. St-Georges - 61.21.03.15 / E4-3

M. Baron. Open until 11 p.m. Closed Sun. Air cond. Terrace dining. Pets allowed. Cards: V, AE, DC, MC.

This is one of the loveliest outdoor spots in Toulouse, here on the always lively place Saint-Georges. The young new owners apparently want to restore the good cooking of this old brasserie: excellent seafood, a pigeon confit with cabbage, grilled meats and duck breasts—and a nice little fixed-price menu at lunch.

A la carte: 250F. Menus: 60F (lunch only), 110F.

11/20 Brasserie des Beaux-Arts

1, quai de la Daurade
61.21.12.12 / D5-23

M. Peyrat. Open daily until 1:30 a.m. Air cond. Terrace dining. Pets allowed. Cards: V, AE, DC.

The Brasserie Flo has come down to Toulouse! This new place has a superb decor—walnut paneling, mirrors—that goes back to the beginning of the century and a chef who comes from Boeuf sur le Toit. The brasserie cuisine is like that of Paris's Flo: good seafood, grilled meats and pitchers of Riesling.

A la carte: 230F. Menus: 88F, 129F.

12/20 Le Cantou

98, rue Velasquez - 61.49.20.21 / A3-16

Mme. Mouls. Open until 10 p.m. Closed Sat. & Sun. Garden dining. Pets allowed. Parking. Cards: V, AE, DC.

This truly agreeable country house is all the more pleasant in summer, when one can dine on the cool terrace in a lovely garden. Inside is a modern dining room centered around an open fireplace. The chef, who studied with the famous Paladin way back when, creates a simple cuisine in which technique takes a back seat to the use of fine products: foie gras maison, fondue of lotte with zucchini. Fine wine cellar.

A la carte: 300F. Menus: 78F, 185F.

La Caravelle

62, rue Raymond-IV
61.62.70.65 / E2-30

Open year-round. 30 rms 310-390F. TV. Air cond. Garage parking. Telex 530438. Cards: V, AE, DC, MC.

Centrally located and well maintained, La Caravelle features soundproofing and air conditioning in all its rooms. No restaurant.

(13) Le Chaplin

56, rue des Blanchers
61.22.82.25 / C4-20

M. Belkadi. Open until 11 p.m. Closed Mon. & week of Aug. 15. Pets allowed. Cards: V, AE, DC.

This truly self-taught cooking is turned out by Yacine Chaplin in a pretty little bistro, where the gourmets of Toulouse come to escape their normal culinary habitat. In other words, the cooking is enthusiastic and bold—if a bit scattered and confused—and certainly warm and likable. And it is also growing increasingly skillful and accomplished. Witness the charlotte of sole, the scallops with leeks, the sauté of veal in a white-rum and banana purée, and the rolled salmon and spring vegetables with a cream of broccoli sauce. Nice little list of wines from both hereabouts and elsewhere. Warm welcome from Huguette, the owner.

A la carte: 250F. Menu: 125F, 165F, 240F (dinner only).

11/20 Chez Carmen

(Café des Abbatoirs)
97, allées Charles-de-Fitte
61.42.04.95 / B4-25

M. Carmen. Open until 10:30 p.m. Closed Mon. dinner, Sun. & Aug. Air cond. Terrace dining. Pets allowed. Parking. Cards: V.

Olé! In this temple of carnivorism, butchers from the nearby abbatoir (slaughterhouse) feast on superb organ meats (tripe, brains with chives) and generous meats, not to mention the sausages (boudin, andouillette). The service is prompt and smiling, and the ambience is quite jolly in the evening.

A la carte: 180-200F. Menus: 60F (weekday lunch only, wine incl.), 70F (wine incl.).

12/20 Chrisflor

26, ave. St-Exupéry - 61.53.12.86 / G7-8

Mme. Pezet. Open until 9:30 p.m. Closed Sat. lunch, Sun. & Mon. dinner & Aug. Air cond. No pets. Cards: V, DC.

In this small, often-packed family bistro, Paul Pezet remains eternally faithful to his grandmother's recipes, producing an unchanging repertoire of generous bourgeois dishes enriched with daily specials inspired by the marketplace: fried baby sole, brill with an eggplant purée, lamb's sweetbreads with fresh pasta. Also be sure to try the excellent foie gras maison, the confit of pork knuckle and the duck breast forestier. Nice wine cellar.

A la carte: 220F. Menu: 220F (weekend and holiday dinner only).

12/20 Le Colombier

14, rue Bayard - 61.62.40.05 / E3-22

M. Zasso. Open until 10 p.m. Closed Sat., Sun., 1 week at Easter, 3 weeks in Aug. & Dec. 24-Jan. 2. Air cond. Pets allowed. Cards: V, AE.

The mustachioed Gérard Zasso is a pillar of cassoulet toulousain, which he's been preparing forever with a fine goose confit. This cassoulet is one of the best dishes of the house, along with the excellent grilled meats and the foie gras. Nice little wine cellar.

A la carte: 250F. Menus: 75F, 93F, 180F.

Le Concorde

16, blvd. Bonrepos - 61.62.48.60 / E2-36

Open year-round. 97 rms 430-600F. Half-board 530-580F. TV. Air cond. Pets allowed. Garage parking. Telex 531686. Cards: V, AE, DC, MC.

On the whole, spacious rooms with luxurious if not exactly lively appointments. Some have kitchenettes. Restaurant.

(16) Darroze

19, rue Castellane - 61.62.34.70 / E3-17

M. Darroze. Open until 11 p.m. Closed Sat. lunch, Sun., 1 week in Feb. & 3 weeks in July-Aug. Air cond. No pets. Cards: V, AE, DC.

Just recently, Pierre Darroze, the patriarch of this fine establishment, took sudden leave of us at 76 years of age with the same courage and panache that marked the old musketeer's life. But for several years prior to that, this great, ardent chef took the time to hand down his know-how to his daughter-in-law, Viviane Darroze, who acquired it at his side in front of the stove. Employing her father-in-law's noble tutelage, Viviane continues to manifest the same fresh and impetuous spirit, and we have every confidence in her ability to maintain the rating. From now on, she is taking charge of putting together the daily menu, which admirably balances the renewed traditions of the region with the old market cuisine. From the former come the scrambled eggs with truffles from Lalbenque, the foie gras of Chalosse duck, the preserved Chalosse ham and the best Basque piperade anywhere. From the latter we find a salad of lamb's sweetbreads and white truffles, lotte simmered with vegetables and Gascon duckling cooked with turnips. All this is served by Henri Darroze, Pierre's son, who is assisted by his sister—nothing has changed in this regard—in a comfortable, provincial setting at tables set well apart. The same Henri is also king of the richly endowed wine cellar, which includes a fabulous collection of proprietary Armagnacs that he ages himself in oak. Ordering à la carte can get quite expensive, but the fixed-price menus, even the most expensive, are reasonable and certainly copious.

A la carte: 300-350F. Menus: 140F, 240F, 300F.

Hôtel de Diane

See Le Saint-Simon restaurant.

(14) Francis Ferrier

13, pl. St-Georges - 61.21.05.56 / E4-5

M. Ferrier. Open until 10:30 p.m. Closed Sun., Mon. & Dec. 24-Jan. 9. Air cond. Terrace dining. Pets allowed. Cards: V, AE, DC.

Some exotic spirit prompted the normally sensible Francis Ferrier to go Chinese when, a year ago, he opened a sort of barge/restaurant on the Midi Canal (La Jonque Chinoise), which, in summer, resembles a floating garden and is always packed. But let's get back to the more serious elements that continue to make this establishment (where Ferrier concentrates his efforts) such a pleasant and interesting place. On the second floor of the two-level restaurant, meat dishes and regional specialties (superb cassoulet, duck breasts grilled over wood) are served, while down on the ground floor one finds beautiful seafood (pollack and salmon marinated in lime and ginger, grilled calamari, a lotte bourride). Interesting wine list and service that is always cheerful. A good, consistent restaurant.

A la carte: 230-250F. Menus: 95F (lunch only), 145F.

12/20 La Frégate

1, rue d'Austerlitz - 61.21.59.61 / E3-12

M. Fernandez. Open daily until 10 p.m. Air cond. Pets allowed. Telex 530879. Cards: V, AE, DC, MC.

The menu is priced as if this place were a little "grande maison," but the two lovely fixed-price menus are much more reasonable. They also sing of Gascony and are truly generous: foie gras, cassoulet, cheeses and pastries. The pleasant dining rooms are spread over two levels overlooking the trees. Good choice of regional wines.

A la carte: 280F.

10/20 Hippopotamus

1, blvd. de Strasbourg
61.23.20.71 / E3-35

M. Guignard. Open daily until 1 a.m. Air cond. Terrace dining. Pets allowed. Cards: V.

Good charcoal-grilled meats—like at all the Hippos in France—are served in a pleasant, functional setting until late at night.

A la carte: 130-150F. Menus: 52F, 73F.

(16) Les Jardins de l'Opéra

1, pl. du Capitole - 61.23.07.76,
61.21.82.66 / D4-15

M. Turin. Open until 9:30 p.m. Closed Aug. 6-20. Air cond. Garden dining. Pets allowed. Telex 521998. Cards: V, AE, DC.

The young Dominique Toulousy, established here since 1984, has devoted himself to a cuisine that draws on regional traditions, originality and whimsy. This devotion, along with his knowledge of regional produce and his passion for simplicity, work wonders. The startling progress he has made in technique (admirable sauces) and in grounding his inventiveness has placed this upstart in the forefront of Toulouse's chefs. And the allure of the cooking is matched by the charm of the cook—one would like to see him more often out front. He is an intelligent young man who doesn't (yet) take himself too seriously, enjoys life and attends to his craft honestly and humbly. Taste the foie gras ravioli in truffle sauce, the gâteau of blond livers caramelized in port wine, the baked sea bream with simmered mushrooms and potatoes in their jackets, the exemplary cassoulet toulousain, his small fresh sausages (crêpinettes) of compote of duck and of pigs' trotters served with delicious young vegetables lightly cooked in goose fat, and the hot pear pie or the orange bavarois stuffed with chocolate truffles. Then you'll better understand the fondness, despite a regrettable tendency toward smaller portions, that Toulousians have for these six rooms, which are decorated with precious striped fabric and which face the garden and the terrace with its fountain. Despite a very good regional section, the wine list could stand some filling out.

A la carte: 500F. Menus: 180F (dinner only), 250F, 380F.

Grand Hôtel de l'Opéra

(See restaurant above)

Open year-round. 15 stes 880-1,050F. 48 rms 350-700F. TV. Air cond. Pets allowed. Pool.

A hotel with character in the middle of town, including a little garden, a pool (albeit a tiny pool) and air-conditioned rooms, tastefully appointed and for the most part quiet and well maintained (take one on the back side). Excellent service and reception.

12/20 La Jonque du Yang Tse

Canal du Midi, Port St-Sauveur
61.20.74.74 / F6-32

M. Ferrier. Open until 10 p.m. Closed Mon. lunch & Sun. Air cond. Terrace dining. Pets allowed. Parking. Cards: V, AE.

The Canal du Midi has taken on a mad air of exoticism thanks to the gleam of the lanterns and dragons on this deluxe Chinese junk ("jonque") fixed up by Francis Ferrier. He has manned his ovens with Szechwan cooks charged with the mission of preparing Chinese food that is simple (fixed-price menus, a short à la carte list) and authentic. Taste the morsels of beef with coriander and the crab ravioli. Pleasant atmosphere in the evening.

Menus: 110F (weekday lunch only), 135F (weekday lunch only, wine incl.), 138F (weekend and holiday lunch only), 185F (weekends and holidays only).

12/20 La Marée Verte

52, blvd. Carnot - 61.62.10.29 / E4-24

M. Solomiac. Open daily 24 hours. Air cond. Terrace dining. Pets allowed. Cards: V, AE, DC.

The new chef at this comfortable, welcoming, upscale brasserie has put his own stamp on the fresh, seafood-based cuisine promised by the sign outside. The cuisine includes plenty of fresh grilled fish, along with an interesting salmon millefeuille with a chervil butter and an honest seafood blanquette. We'll kick the ranking up another point.

A la carte: 250F. Menus: 100F (lunch only, wine incl.), 115F and 160F (wine incl.).

(13) La Marmite en Folie

28, rue Paul-Painlevé - 61.42.77.86,
61.59.57.36 / B7-1

M. Brandolin. Open until 10:15 p.m. Closed Sat. lunch & Sun. Garden dining. Pets allowed. Cards: V.

Marc Brandolin is a fine self-taught chef whose years of experience have helped him develop excellent culinary reflexes. His cuisine is undoubtedly original, yet it is also consistent and skillfully prepared, as evidenced by the eggplant gâteau with a duck stuffing, the broccoli flan with langoustines and the veal sauté with a vinegar, cider and shallots sauce. The desserts are quite delicate, and the wine list has some choice discoveries at

reasonable prices. Pleasant setting on two floors in a handsome suburban house.
A la carte: 250F.

12/20 Le Marocain
47, rue des Couteliers
61.53.28.01 / D5-34
M. Boualami. Open until 11 p.m. Closed Mon. Air cond. Garden dining. Cards: V, AE, DC, MC.
Zohra Taimi tends the ovens in this luxurious Toulousian Arabian Nights-reminiscent house, with its elegant decor and charming patron. As one would expect from the restaurant's name, the cuisine comprises all the Moroccan classics: couscous, tahine, pigeon b'stilla, grilled pigeon à la marocaine.
A la carte: 180-200F.

Mercure
Rue St-Jérome - 61.23.11.77 / E4-31
Open year-round. 170 rms 430-490F. Telex 520760. TV. Air cond. Pets allowed. Cards: V, AE, DC, MC.
Modern and central, the Mercure is located near the business district. Excellent breakfast. Various sorts of restaurants.

Mermoz
50, rue Matabiau - 61.63.04.04 / E2-21
Open year-round. 1 ste 980F. 52 rms 390-450F. TV. Air cond. Pets allowed. Garage parking. Telex 532427. Cards: V, AE, DC, MC.
The newest hotel in Toulouse is an interesting structure, modern along '30s lines but with the tranquility of huge interior courtyards. The beautiful rooms are quite out of the ordinary, functional and well equipped. No restaurant.

Novotel Toulouse Centre
1, pl. Alphonse-Jourdain
61.21.74.74 / B2-9
Open year-round. 6 stes 700F. 125 rms 450-490F. TV. Air cond. Pets allowed. Parking. Telex 532400. Cards: V, AE, DC.
All new and remarkably well designed and equipped, the Novotel has convenient underground parking and an excellent breakfast. No restaurant.

14 Orsi
(Le Bouchon Lyonnais)
13, rue de l'Industrie
61.62.97.43 / E4-26
M. Orsi. Open until 11 p.m. Closed Sun. (except holidays) & Aug. 15-30. Air cond. Pets allowed. Cards: V, AE, DC, MC.
Recently Laurent Orsi has been enlarging the wine cellar of his restaurant to accommodate 10,000 bottles, improving the lavatories and cloakrooms and redoing the not-so-old interior. Now you can rediscover the 1900 bistro dressed up to 1930, with mirrored walls, leather seats, bronze statues and a beautiful oak floor. As for the food, there's still a good selection of the great classics of Burgundian tradition, such as the gratin of tripe and andouillette from Fleurie. But it is, above all, the seafood dishes that are the premier attraction of this fine establishment, especially the salmon in coarse salt, the lotte in a pot, the civet of turbot, the grilled red mullet and the lamprey eel à la bordelaise. The desserts are superb, especially the candied orange in chocolate sauce. The high-caliber service is quite professional.
A la carte: 260-300F. Menus: 142F, 152F, 183F.

12/20 Le Pavillon d'Argent
43, rue du Taur - 61.23.36.48 / D3-11
M. Nguyen. Open until 10 p.m. Closed Sun. & Aug. Air cond. No pets. Cards: V, AE, DC.
In a pleasant decor comprising brick, flowers and a cheerful little interior garden, the charming Etienne Nguyen serves a light, delicate Saigon-style cuisine: beef salad, cuttlefish pâté with a piquant sauce, chicken with ginger, pork à la saigonaise.
A la carte: 130-150F.

10/20 Le Pyrénéen
14, ave. Franklin-Roosevelt
61.23.38.88 / E3-14
M. di Pietro. Open daily 24 hours. Closed Aug. Air cond. Pets allowed. Cards: V.
One of the best seafood brasseries in Toulouse, Le Pyrénéen serves good plates of shellfish followed by such comforting grilled dishes as breast of duck.
A la carte: 180-200F.

12/20 Le Saint-Simon
3, rte. de St-Simon - 61.07.59.44 / A6-4
M. Chagnon. Open until 10 p.m. Closed Sat. lunch, Sun. & holidays. Air cond. Garden dining. No pets. Garage parking. Telex 530518. Cards: V, AE, DC, MC.
Evidently the dullness of routine is catching up with the folks here. Ten years behind the same stove is enough for anyone, and frankly our last meal was pretty frayed around the edges: considerably overcooked sole and mushrooms and, for dessert, a lifeless coffee marquise. Nice people serving, but they're not exactly excited about their work.
A la carte: 250F. Menus: 122F, 160F.

Hôtel de Diane
(See restaurant above)
Open year-round. 35 rms 310-395F. Half-board 270-415F. TV. Pets allowed. Pool. Tennis.
A lovely hotel made over from a large building from the last century, the Diane sits in the middle of a park with lots of flowers. Adjacent is a comfortable motel with covered parking. Pool and five tennis courts (pay to play).

12/20 Taverne Bavaroise
59, blvd. de Strasbourg
61.21.54.46 / D3-18
M. Chaffre. Open until 11 p.m. Closed Dec. 25. Terrace dining. Pets allowed. Cards: V.
This proper Munich-style brasserie menu starts with Westphalian ham and ends with Black Forest cake; in between are a generous choucroute (with excellent charcuterie from the Aríege, like the owner), schnapps and German beer. Pleasant decor, slow service.
A la carte: 160-180F.

(13) Ubu Club

16, rue St-Rome - 61.23.26.75 / D4-27

M. Fernandez. Dinner only. Open until 2 a.m. Closed Sun. Air cond. Pets allowed. Telex 521150. Cards: V, AE, DC.

Heading for twenty-eight years of success, the ever unperturbable Honoré Guilhem is still preparing his excellent dishes of fish, duck breasts and confits. So there's still plenty more lovely evenings ahead for Toulousian nightlife here in their indestructible temple, with its great service, excellent ingredients, nice little wine cellar and delicious desserts.

A la carte: 300-350F.

(18) Vanel

22, rue Maurice-Fonvielle
61.21.51.82 / E4-6

M. Vanel. Open until 11 p.m. Closed Sun. Air cond. Pets allowed. Cards: AE, MC.

The charming Mme. Vanel, who had some health problems, is back in shape, and her husband, Lucien, is back in emotional shape. He no longer talks about going to join a colony of hermits or, at least for now, of giving up the best restaurant in Toulouse.

Lighter and younger than ever, this little man, who with his clear eyes under a halo of gray hair would make for a perfect saint in a stained-glass window, continues to rally his team with a singing voice that occasionally shifts into bellowing, more or less real, in the best Gascon tradition. Does he ever manage to spoil a meal? Two or three readers have claimed he has, and it must be true, since even the best of cooks has an off day every now and then. But don't get it into your head to tell us that this marvelous man has no right to his toques and fame, because then we'll really get mad. That creative daring leads him to take chances all year long, tossing onto his menu a swarm of new dishes with delicate taste and frank flavors that almost always reveal a touch of the peasant. For us and for all who have followed his career since he began in Toulouse, he is a permanent source of surprise and pleasure. It is somehow blessed, this bright cuisine; even the heaviest foods seem to take flight. Lord knows that a stew of oxtails and pigs' feet, a pot-au-feu of calf's tongue with lamb's brains (a recipe from his late dear friend and client Doumeng) or even a little squab roasted with foie gras rarely have wings. But Vanel has a knack, and though his cooking is made up of quite diverse elements, it has a spirit and a unity that allows you to shift easily from a rustic tarte of rabbit livers and scrambled eggs to lettuce stuffed with oysters, from a crêpe stuffed with cèpes to coquilles St-Jacques braised with a watercress purée, from escargots aux noix to eggs with clams, from a confit aux pommes sarladaise to artichoke hearts with mussels and the zest of blood oranges (not necessarily in that order!). Vanel even knows how to turn a pain perdu (french toast) into an undiscovered masterpiece. And then there are his wines, every one delicious, from Bordeaux or the southwest, each weighing as little as possible on the bill.

Of course, you can dream of a building covered with virgin vines in the middle of a vast garden, of a nicer dining room than this ground floor with modern furniture, of more attentive service and even of a sommelier who would refill your glass. But that's the way Vanel is. Take it or leave it. As for ourselves, we've seen enough, and we're takers!

A la carte: 250-400F. Menus: 140F (lunch only), 200F (lunch only, wine incl.), 300F (wine incl.), 420F.

IN NEARBY **Sainte-Livrade**
(33 km NW on N 124, D 42 & D 87)
31530 Lévignac - (Haute-Garonne)

---

(15) Restaurant d'Azimont

61.85.61.13

Mme. Delieux. Open until 9:45 p.m. Closed Mon. Garden dining. Pets allowed. Parking. Telex 532467. Cards: V, AE, DC.

When this establishment opened recently it was the event of the year (of sorts) around Toulouse. The enormous brick-and-wood house, vintage 1880, is surrounded by five acres of gardens all in flower and impeccably maintained. The winter garden is a delight, and the huge dining room is strikingly original in its appointments (large tapestries, bits of ruins scattered about, rather crude lighting). They'll certainly need to warm up the room a bit, with all its tile floors and garden-style chairs (no friend of the fanny these), especially during the months when the garden's enchantments are unavailable. The charming owner of this country house, Marie-Joseph Delieux, was an overnight hit with the Toulousians, and she has hired Bernard Bordaries to run the kitchen. A very good cook, he trained at Maxim's and the Oasis, and this new setting has obviously proven to be an inspiration to him. To witness this inspiration for yourself, try the puff tarts of fennel and brebis (sheep's cheese), croquettes of puréed foie gras with artichokes and langoustines in a lentil cream, sander roasted with beurre rouge, galette of duck confit with turnips and pine nuts and original desserts (chocolate-glazed mousse flavored with licorice). Such efforts have lifted this food to the two-toque level. Knowledgeable sommelier and attentive service.

A la carte: 300F. Menus: 145F, 215F, 340F.

Hôtel d'Azimont

(See restaurant above)

Open year-round. 10 stes 890-1,200F. 8 rms 500-800F. TV. Pets allowed. Pool. Tennis.

These big, beautiful yet snug rooms are enlivened with cheerful, pretty fabrics and furnished in a modern, comfortable and elegant manner. Superb salons, bar, billiard room.

IN NEARBY **Vieille-Toulouse**
(8.5 km S on D 4)
31320 Castanet-Tolosan - (Haute-Garonne)

La Flânerie

Rte. de Lacroix-Falgarde - 61.73.39.12

Open year-round. 12 rms 160-420F. TV in 8 rms. Pets allowed. Garage parking. Telex 531666. Cards: V, AE, DC.

This lovely house perched on a rise comes complete with a ravishing view of the Garonne river valley, old or period furnishings, a delightful reception and huge grounds, but no restaurant.

IN NEARBY **Vigoulet-Auzil**
(12 km S on D 35, Ramonville exit)
31320 Castanet-Tolosan - (Haute-Garonne)

(14) Auberge de Tournebride

Near the Club Hippique - 61.73.34.49

M. Nony. Open until 10 p.m. Closed Sun. dinner, Mon., 3 weeks in Jan. & 2 weeks in Aug. Cards: V, AE, DC.

Pierre and Gilberte Nony's place, pleasantly located high in the Pech-David hills a stone's throw from golf and equestrian clubs, overlooks the rolling country south to the Pyrénées. It is undoubtedly the most alluring restaurant in the countryside surrounding Toulouse. The interior is refined and comfortable, the huge summer terrace that runs the length of the picture windows in front is magnificent, and the young staff is expertly supervised by Gilberte. High-quality regional produce and a revival of tradition characterize the cooking of Pierre Nony, who after 57 years has not lost one iota of his zeal for research and his attention to the seasons. Taste, for instance, the rabbit aspic with little vegetables, fresh-caught red mullet à la bohémienne, fresh sausages of lamb's sweetbreads and fresh liver, Pauillac lamb served with little farcis (stuffings), and fresh figs in Banyuls wine. Lovely selection of wines from Bordeaux.

A la carte: 300F. Menu: 220F (Sunday lunch only).

Le Touquet

62520 Le Touquet - (Pas-de-Calais)
Paris 222 - Arras 97 - Boulogne 32 - Lille 132

(15) Flavio-Club de la Forêt

1, ave. du Verger - 21.05.10.22

M. Flavio. Open until 9:30 p.m. (10 p.m. on weekends). Closed Wed. (off-seas.), Jan. & Feb. Terrace dining. Pets allowed. Cards: V, AE, DC, MC.

This velvety, affected decor, flooded with flowers and light, attracts loads of rich Brits for whom Flavio is the greatest thing on France's channel coast. For his part, the loquacious and colorful Flavio shares this opinion with his wealthy clientele, primarily owners of second or third homes strung out along the fairways, the race course and the pretty Touquet forest, which Flavio's refreshing terrace overlooks. It's quickly evident that this precious little restaurant, chic with a wee touch of kitsch, is (as the name suggests) a sort of club where the tone is set by the silver, the lobster dinners, the fine wines and the sheikh-worthy tabs. Flavio recently spent a bundle on improvements, including a huge custom-made carpet, but ironically, the once delicious fare of son-in-law Guy Delmotte has fallen on dull times. Perhaps Delmotte was just taking a rest that day; in any case, after a remarkable bisque, the excellent salmon arrived with leeks burnt to a crisp and the delicate flavor of scallops buried under too much pepper. Happily the strawberry genoise was perfect. It's still worth two toques but not for long unless somebody tends to the lapses. Excellent wines.

A la carte: 500-600F. Menus: 230F, 360F, 480F.

Novotel-Thalamer

Ave. Louison-Bobet (on the beach)
21.09.85.00

Open year-round. 8 stes 475-660F. 96 rms 350-540F. TV. Pets allowed. Heated pool. Parking. Telex 160480. Cards: V, AE, DC, MC.

This big contemporary structure is located right on the beach, and its sunny, inviting rooms are decorated in the style of the Novotel chain. The hotel connects directly to a saltwater therapy spa. Great views. Sauna. Restaurant.

12/20 Le Restaurant

Ave. du Verger - 21.05.48.48

M. Flament. Open until 9:30 p.m. Closed Mon. dinner, Tues. & Nov. 30-March 1. Terrace dining. No pets. Garage parking. Telex 160439. Cards: V, AE, DC, MC.

A beautiful dining room tended by an impeccable luxury-hotel staff, and a coffee shop that features an excellent grill, with mildly priced items. The menu is a little short on originality, but the execution is earnest and the ingredients top-notch (sweetbreads Saint-Hubert, turbot in Sauternes, duck confit with mushrooms).

A la carte: 230-280F. Menus: 150F, 190F.

Westminster

(See restaurant above)

Closed Nov. 30-March 1. 2 stes 1,100F. 113 rms 430-850F. TV. Pets allowed. Heated pool.

Close to both the forest and the casino, this beautiful luxury hotel of pink brick was recently done over completely. Very pleasant atmosphere, perfect comfort and complete facilities (covered pool, sauna, solarium, squash and so on).

Tournus

71700 Tournus - (Saône-et-Loire)
Paris 360 - Mâcon 30 - Chalon 27 - Bourg-en-Bresse 53

(16) Greuze

1, rue Albert-Thibaudet - 85.51.13.52

M. Ducloux. Open until 9:45 p.m. Closed Dec. 1-10. Air cond. Pets allowed. Parking. Cards: V, AE.

Jean Ducloux, that thundering young fellow of 65 years (or thereabouts), holds onto his principles as stubbornly as a mule. One might criticize him for it, but the distinctive, if mad, bounty of his fare is worth holding one's tongue for. A living monument to the bygone tradition of eating well, the good Ducloux ages without wrinkles, like the fabulous Burgundies in his cellar—or like the vintage-1947 warmth, richness and good nature of his dining room. You'll dine here on a kind of ecstasy (if not excess) of dishes that virtually no one these days knows how, or dares, to execute: the best pike quenelles in the world with crayfish sauce, pâté Alexandre Dumaine, the galette with truffles Dodin-Bouffant, sweetbreads Grand-

Mère Ducloux and other most learned examples of the Great Tradition, prepared from extraordinary ingredients and served with neither fuss nor dotty frills. And besides, there is the incomparable atmosphere of this great road house, where everyone who works there carries wayside-inn dining ("It's the route," as Ducloux would say) to a kind of perfection whose passing, some day, we will dearly mourn.

A la carte: 400-500F. Menus: 215F (weekdays only), 420F.

Hôtel de Greuze

5, pl. de l'Abbaye - 85.40.77.77

Open year-round. 2 stes 1,660F. 19 rms 500-1,050F. TV. Air cond. Pets allowed. Parking. Telex 351055. Cards: V, AE, DC, MC.

This old mansion fronting the abbey contains twenty rooms, all of different sizes and appointments: huge beds with embroidered sheets, magnificent bathrooms, deep carpets and lovely furniture. You can expect a fire in the fireplace, perfectly correct service and a wonderful breakfast. Completely equipped and ultra-modern. No restaurant.

Tours

37000 Tours - (Indre-et-Loire)
Paris 234 - Angers 105 - Orléans 113 - Poitiers 103

Sights. Old Tours, admirably restored around the pl. Plumereau (pedestrian-only streets, remarkable old homes, lots of tourists and nightlife); Saint-Gatien cathedral (Gothic features, marvelous stained glass) and the old cobblestone streets around the Musée des Beaux-Arts (in the old archbishop's palace, paintings from the Middle Ages to the twentieth century); the Historial de Touraine (in the Château of Tours, a "Madame Tussaud's-on-the-Loire"); Musée du Compagnonnage ("Museum of Guilds," tools, masterpieces produced to gain membership, documents, unique in all the world); Musée du Germail (in the Hôtel Rimbault, astonishing glass paintings); Musée des Vins de Touraine (in the cellar of the Saint-Julien abbey); the lovely parks and gardens (botanical, at the archbishop's palace, along the promenade du Lac).

Eating on the Run. Il Capuccino, 14, rue du Grande-Marché (pizza); La Grange, 22, rue Lavoisier (good crêpes and galettes); Le Grill du Roy, 16, rue du Grand-Marché (salads and grill in a pretty, medieval-Moorish decor); Chez Plum'reau, 6, rue du Grand-Marché (tiny crêperie at the spectacular pl. Plumereau); Tart Annie, 15, rue du Grand-Marché (homey feel, sweet and savory tarts); Le Taste-Vin, 33, rue du Grand-Marché (regional wines and good food at any hour).

Brasseries. L'Universe, 8, pl. Jean-Jaurès (oldest in Tours, superb glasswork, circa 1900).

Bars & Cafés. Le Corsaire, 187, ave. de Grammont (countless excellent cocktails); Le Duke, pl. Plumereau (jazz in an original decor); Le Palais de la Bière, 29, pl. Gaston-Pailhou (200 beers and 60 whiskies); La Touraine, 5, blvd. Heurteloup (yuppie hangout, slick bartender); Les Trois Rois, pl. Plumereau (pub, English beers and good whiskies); Le Vieux Murier, pl. Plumereau (an institution in old Tours).

Nightlife. L'Excalibur, 35, rue Briçonnet (twelfth-century cellar); Le Pym's, 170, ave. de Grammont (big dance floor); Les Trois Orfèvres, 6, rue des Trois-Orfèvres (café/theater in a medieval cellar).

Jean Bardet

19

57, rue Groison
47.41.41.11

M. Bardet. Open until 9:30 p.m. Closed Sun. dinner, Mon. (except holidays) & Oct. 15-March 1. Garden dining. Pets allowed. Garage parking. Telex 752463. Cards: V, AE, DC, MC.

The Baron of Châteauroux has become the Prince of Tours. Will Jean Bardet ever succeed in convincing his frugal mayor, Jean Royer, of the pleasures of gourmet dining? In any case, the mayor of Tours made a smart move in welcoming with open arms this admirable chef, who before he was ever known or recognized had wrapped up his four toques with a whopping 19/20. And the transplant from Châteauroux to Tours has worked out beautifully.

Sophie and Jean Bardet had the unheard-of luck to find in the center of town a bit of country, hidden from view by high walls and 100-year-old sequoias. The early-nineteenth-century villa lies in the middle of a seven-acre park planted with rare essences and dotted with ponds, which was restored during the Second Empire by an Englishman with a green thumb. Onto this romantic setting Bardet's architect grafted a two-story building that, with its balconies set atop white pillars, evokes the Louisiane style of the Touraine and yet gives the impression that it's always been there. The chimneys, moldings and painted ceilings were all carefully preserved, and Michel Marchand—who had so much success with the room he did for Marc Meneau at L'Espérance—created a fresh English decor. And he did so inexpensively, for even if his work creates a strong effect, it is not meant to be sumptuous. In any event, it fits this laughing couple to a tee, with its bright rugs woven in England, its pale-wood furniture (either painted or varnished), its wall hangings and its armchairs and sofas in every color from fresh-butter yellow to beef-blood red. But aside from two or three combinations that are a bit too violent, an astounding harmony emerges from this mosaic of colors; and better than a hotel, it's a home that's easy to live in, one that welcomes with open arms. A small waiting room, the floor covered by a green carpet with red and violet borders, precedes the dining room, which is on the same level as the garden and is a perfect success. Round tables are draped with yellow tablecloths over burgundy undercloths, black and gold chairs are upholstered with blue fabric and set on a blue carpet with touches of pink, and walls are painted a pale lemon yellow edged with white. The dishes, the silver, the flower bouquets—Sophie hasn't missed a single detail, and everything here, including her bursts of laughter, witty comebacks and clever advice, is intended to wake up the senses and prepare guests for the sensitive and sensual cuisine. Only a lead palate would fail to grasp the harmonic unity.

The langoustine soup with girolle mushrooms and chives, the fine ragoût of Marennes oysters on a mousse of watercress strengthened with

Muscadet, the confit of duck foie gras in its own fat, the fricassée of Vendée eel (the fatty side miraculously disappeared), the stew of lobster and small shellfish in Vouvray spiced with fresh ginger and lime, the salmon steamed in soy, the inspired meeting of roast lobster and duck gizzards with a concentrated coulis of Graves wine, the sweetbreads with a lemon-rind confit, the warm yellow-plum tart, the vanilla ice cream with caramelized brown sugar, and the China tea sorbet perfumed with the aromas of mango and jasmin—all these dishes are clearly superior to anything Bardet cooked at Châteauroux. Here they send you flying through the air. We are, by the way, still willing to bet that Bardet's talent will come into full bloom and climb up another notch.

But what makes Bardet happiest is his vineyard and his wine cellar. Harvesting won't take long, since he has nothing more than a few grape plants alongside the herb garden and vegetable greenhouse. He wants to make his own wine, and the idea alone is enough to make him squirm with glee like a young child. Until then, Jean-Jacques, the young sommelier from Châteauroux who followed Bardet enthusiastically, can find either here in the huge vaulted cellars or in Vouvray (where Bardet recently bought magnificent cellars), the Burgundies, Bordeaux and the exquisite and sometimes rare Loire wines that make the flavors of this artist's cuisine mellifluous.

By the way, Sophie and Jean, along with their friend Jacques Puisais, are planning to organize introductory wine courses. That holds the promise of many happy evenings!

A la carte: 350-700F. Menus: 250F (lunch only, apéritif, wine and coffee incl.), 195F, 290F, 380F, 480F.

Jean Bardet

(See restaurant above)

Open year-round. 6 stes 1,100-1,600F. 9 rms 470-800F. TV. Pets allowed. Heated pool.

Along the facade on the garden side are six suites with terraces, each different from the others and nicely decorated with wallpapers and fabrics in delicate gay colors. They have an English feel to them, which you'll also find in the nine rooms found in the back of the building, whose windows open onto the greenery. The bathrooms, all in gray marble, are of an exceptional quality. Every detail is considered, including the provision of Alka-Seltzer packets. Breakfast is superb, with an indecent serving of breads, croissants, brioches, homemade jams and eggs.

Barrier

17

101-103, ave. de la Tranchée
47.54.20.39

M. Barrier. Open until 9:45 p.m. Closed Sun. Air cond. Pets allowed. Parking. Cards: V.

After every sort of mishap—closing, a false start, tax audits, the specter of prison and enough fallen-through deals to daunt many an entrepreneur in the prime of life—Charles Barrier, with his 70-some years, has set forth on another adventure. To everyone's amazement, he is reopening the same restaurant (old-timers still call it "Le Nègre") that he had once hoisted to the top rank of tables in France. The most likely reason for this intrepid and astounding comeback is not so much to make a buck as to put to rest the lies by any so-and-sos who were a little too quick to bury papa Barrier. He has thus set himself up, more modestly than before, to be sure, in a little 35-seat dining room put together from the waiting room of his old Nègre. The pink decor and flowered fabrics are smart and pleasant, the service is a good deal less muddled than before, and the cooking, true to form, is all in the best taste and of masterly execution.

A former chef in some of the great houses (Rothschild and the Prince of Monaco, among others), Barrier knows absolutely all of the grand repertoire of French cuisine, but also quite a bit from his own region of Touraine, whose best suppliers he has long been familiar with. His menu, wisely reduced, evinces, in a restrained manner, these two sources: stewed beef cheeks and lamb's tongues, stuffed pigs' trotters, grilled black pudding with mashed potatoes, Loire eel stewed in local wine, incomparable roast Challans duck, young pigeon roasted in garlic inside a bread crust (Barrier's bread is still marvelous) and, to finish, the tasty desserts of yesteryear, such as the airy baba au rhum and the good fruit sorbets. Lovely list of Loire wines, including incomparable Vouvrays.

A la carte: 400F. Menus: 200F, 335F.

Le Jardin du Castel

14

(Hôtel de Groison)

10, rue Groison - 47.41.94.40

MM. Lironville, Tricon & André. Open until 9:30 p.m. Closed Sat. lunch & Wed. Garden dining. Pets allowed. Hotel: 2 stes 575-600F; 8 rms 320-420F; half-board 360-450F. Garage parking. Cards: V, AE, DC.

Since competition has arrived to liven things up on this little Tours side street (in the form of Jean Bardet and his restaurant), the owners of this big establishment have amicably taken up the challenge. As before, they possess an irresistible attraction: a large garden in which one dines under beautiful white parasols in the shade of an extraordinary Virginia tulip tree. In addition, there is the attraction (despite a noticeable increase in prices since they did away with fixed-price menus alone) of Guy Tricon's earnest but delicate cooking: lovely plates of raw salmon, sander and pike with coarse salt and olive oil; bundles of chicken breast in cabbage leaves with an excellent cream and Vouvray wine sauce; crusty pan-fried pike (preferable to the skate in a caviar butter that was thoroughly bungled); and delicate strawberries in puff pastry. The wine list is oriented wisely toward Loire wines, with Gamay and Sauvignon served in carafes. Perfect welcome by Jean André, one of the faithful partners, who is greatly responsible for the allure of this delightful place.

A la carte: 350F. Menus: 185F, 300F.

Le Lys

15

63, rue Blaise-Pascal - 47.05.27.92

MM. Aubrun & Jimenez. Open until 10:30 p.m. Closed Sun. dinner. Pets allowed. Cards: V.

Having fallen asleep some time ago as a town of good hotel food, Tours is waking up as a gastronomic capital. The reason for this is talent welling up from all sources: An old master like

Barrier reliving his youth, a national star like Jean Bardet setting up shop here, and ambitious young cooks coming to town to cut their teeth. That last scenario is the story of Thierry Jimenez and Xavier Aubrun, both formerly of La Barrière restaurant in Clichy and both skillful practitioners of vacuum cookery. These enthusiastic colleagues began practicing their trade here to great and unexpected success—in staid Tours, that's not to be taken for granted. They are interchangeable in the kitchen of a most Parisian, up-to-the-minute restaurant (a stone's throw from the train station), with a flecked ceiling and walls that are mirrored and lacquered in grayish tones. Their cooking is lively and bold, in the highly technical style current among the younger masters of the culinary arts, and it adds just the right amount of sophistication to the spirit of regional revival. In any case, it merits a second toque, and it may soon merit even more, if the two chefs keep turning out such successful dishes as the langoustines with snap peas, sole with tomato marmalade, roasted young pigeon with truffles, and apple gratin with apricot.

A la carte: 250-280F. Menus: 90F, 135F, 270F.

(14) La Roche Le Roy

55, rte. de St-Avertin - 47.27.22.00

MM. Couturier. Open until 10 p.m. Closed Sun. & Aug. 1-20. Garden dining. Pets allowed. Parking. Cards: V.

Alain Couturier, who was successful with his restaurant Poivrière on the rue du Change, recently set himself up in this superb sixteenth-century house near the south exit from the highway. It was, despite the well-publicized arrival on the scene of Charles Barrier and Jean Bardet, the big news in Tours. This enchanting, flower-filled house gives Couturier, formerly with Barrier and Le Gavroche in London, a much more appropriate setting in which to display his abilities. The salad of red mullet with saffron, the breast of young pigeon, pink and tender, with gently braised cabbage, the small salmon steaks with a leek confit and an orange-flavored sauce and the apple tart (delicious despite the overabundance of red-fruit coulis) are all part of a cuisine that from now on will be one of the best in Tours. A good, young service staff is managed by owner Marilyn Couturier, a charming native of the north of England.

A la carte: 260-300F. Menu: 148F, 220F.

(13) Rôtisserie Tourangelle

23, rue du Commerce - 47.05.71.21

MM. Duguet. Open until 10 p.m. Closed Sun. dinner, Mon. (off-seas.) & March 1-15. Terrace dining. Pets allowed. Cards: V, AE, DC.

At the edge of the admirably restored old city of Tours, with a quiet summer terrace on the garden of François I, this well-run old establishment is one of the truly serious places of its kind in Tours. Marked by a discreet elegance, it is a place of good, sensible cooking. The tables are well spaced, with pretty 1900-style table lamps, and the room is filled with soft armchairs. Jacques Arrayet does not neglect the seasons or new ideas: local asparagus in puff pastry with a mint-flavored mousseline, sander in a Vouvray sabayon and farm-raised pigeon roasted with garlic and honey. Prices are holding fairly steady.

A la carte: 280F. Menus: 110F (weekdays only), 150F, 215F.

(13) La Touraine

5, blvd. Heurteloup - 47.05.37.12

Open until 9:15 p.m. Closed Sat. Pets allowed. Garage parking. Telex 751460. Cards: V, AE, DC, MC.

This big mahogany room (a bit stuffy, we must admit) was one of the most famous and popular restaurants in Tours in the days of Cécil Sorel and Edmond Rostand. Today, its food doesn't deserve the cold shoulder it gets from the guidebooks. Gérard Clément, formerly of Barrier, has proven to be a devotee of lighter cooking (though mindful of tradition), with such adept creations of his own as sole in orange butter, beef cooked in local wine and veal kidneys in a cream of shallots. An excellent fixed-price menu.

A la carte: 230F. Menu: 125F.

L'Univers

(See restaurant above)

Open year-round. 91 rms 313-420F. TV. Pets allowed.

Almost all the rooms face the inner courtyard and are therefore fairly quiet. There are some newly added rooms for meetings and receptions. Indoor parking.

(14) Les Tuffeaux

19, rue Lavoisier - 47.47.19.89

M. Marsollier. Open until 9:30 p.m. Closed Mon. lunch & Sun. Pets allowed. Cards: V.

Finally, the end of bashfulness! At the door, the young woman of the house, Jocelyne, is charming and at ease. And in the kitchen, Gildas Marsollier, from Brittany, is trying hard to be bold and to remember that he earned a ranking of 16/20 while chef at Château de Brécourt. For all the regional accent that his cooking may have lost since he's been here (which hasn't been long), it has gained from his seeking of new and modern ways: a salad of lightly cooked sweetbreads with asparagus (a shade overdone), a well-prepared lamb stew, thick, smooth salmon infused with fennel and remarkable desserts (especially the Saint-Eve, an almond cookie with pistachio butter that's rich and skillful). The stone interior is warmed up with russet-colored fabric, and it is not far to the Mirabeau bridge, under which flows the Loire river.

A la carte: 250F. Menu: 150F.

IN NEARBY **La Membrolle-sur-Choisille**

(6 km NE on N 138)

37390 La Membrolle-sur-Choisille - (Indre-et-Loire)

Château de l'Aubrière

Rte. de Fondette - 47.51.50.35

Open year-round. 3 stes 500-550F. 8 rms 385-420F. Half-board 405-550F. TV. Pets allowed. Telex 750020. Cards: V, AE, MC.

There are eleven huge rooms in this building, which is nicely set in 40 acres of grounds. Sauna, solarium and courteous reception. Restaurant.

IN NEARBY **Montlouis-sur-Loire**
(12 km E on D 751)
37270 Montlouis-sur-Loire - (Indre-et-Loire)

(16) Roc en Val

Pl. Courtemanche - 47.50.81.96

M. Regnier. Open until 10 p.m. Closed Sun. dinner, Mon. (except Mon. dinner in seas.) & Feb. 20-March 15. Garden dining. Pets allowed. Parking. Cards: V, AE, DC, MC.

From the day it opened, Roc en Val displayed talent, professionalism, youth and enthusiasm, picking up two toques right off the bat. Certainly everything needed for success came together for Thierry Regnier and his sister Laurence when they turned their old family house on the banks of the Loire into a luxurious and charming restaurant. Inside, the pretty, beige and pale-pink dining room opens splendidly onto the river. Outside is a wonderful terrace under a 300-year-old sequoia, elegant tables and a superb wine cellar in a cave at the end of the grounds. A young sommelier from Artigny has joined the brother-and-sister team to watch over the treasures (incomparable Vouvrays from 1921 and 1947). Above all, they found a remarkable chef, Franck Graux, a student of Marc Meneau and Michel Guérard and an enthusiastic disciple of Alain Chapel. However much Graux may defend himself against the charge, it is to the most lucid and authentic presentation of nouvelle cuisine that he aspires, through a small seasonal menu that is delicate yet appealing. He is already bringing to his cooking some personality, obviously having thoroughly digested the lessons of his formidable teachers. All of his food is creative, carefully done and true to the lighter-cuisine gospel—yet at the same time it is flavorful, simplified and mindful of regional traditions. Indeed, Graux is capable of out-and-out country cooking: oxtail stew with foie gras, a small filet of bass flavored with star anise and orange juice, exquisite foie gras with steamed baby leeks, a subtle coconut tart accompanied by a light sorbet of thyme or lemon. The least costly fixed-price meal is excellent.

A la carte: 300F. Menus: 145F (except holidays), 180F (weekday lunch only, wine incl.), 235F, 295F.

IN NEARBY **Rochecorbon**
(5 km E on N 152)
37210 Vouvray - (Indre-et-Loire)

(15) L'Oubliette

34, rue des Clouets - 47.52.50.49

M. Duhamel. Open until 9:30 p.m. Closed Sun. dinner & Mon.; annual closing varies. Pets allowed. Parking. Cards: V, MC.

A former apprentice to the great Barrier, Thierry Duhamel completed his training by going the traditional journeyman rounds throughout France. For several years now he has been established in this pretty (if rather strange and cave-like) restaurant whose dining room is carved into solid tufa rock halfway up a slope. A lively and delightful place, it is decorated with elegant simplicity and fronted by a pleasant summer terrace. Duhamel's style and technique are straightforward, not given to excess; the result is an attractive, short but nicely balanced menu: sliced foie gras in honey vinegar, gently braised langoustines with star anise, filet of lotte with marjoram, pigeon with confit of shallots. We certainly could stand seeing a few new items and, at the same time, a little more focus on regional fare. Beautiful pastries and a wine cellar housing some irresistible Vouvrays.

Menus: 165F, 220F, 310F.

Tourtour

83690 Salernes - (Var)
Paris 860 - Draguignan 20 - Aups 10 - Salernes 11

12/20 Bastide de Tourtour

94.70.57.30

M. Laurent. Open until 9 p.m. Closed Mon (off-seas.), Tues. lunch & Nov. 1-March 1. Garden dining. Pets allowed. Parking. Telex 970827. Cards: V, AE, DC, MC.

At the end of an old village 650 meters up in the hills sits a little corner of paradise that commands one of the most spectacular views in Provence—from Fréjus west to the Alpilles (the hills at the mouth of the Rhône near Arles). Here one finds a large, modern Provençal country house that blends nicely into the surroundings. It remains one of the meccas for the wealthy and the tasteful branch of the beautiful people, who find here the things they demand of a hotel and restaurant: unfailing luxury, impeccable service and hosts who are painfully attentive to their well-being. The new chef, on the other hand, does not appear to have found his stride yet. Between the delicious warm salad of artichoke and foie gras and the fine desserts arrived a braised sea bass that was completely dried out and a saddle of rabbit in lavender honey that sparked absolutely no interest. We're knocking the place down a point in this edition.

A la carte: 350-400F. Menus: 140F (weekday lunch only), 250F, 330F.

Bastide de Tourtour

(See restaurant above)

Closed Nov. 1-March 1. 25 rms 330-1,000F. Half-board 490- 810F oblig. in seas. TV. Pets allowed. Heated pool. Tennis.

This huge Provençal traditional country home is nestled on luxurious grounds overlooking 60 miles of Varois landscape. Jacuzzi, workout gym and lots of pine trees. Relais et Châteaux.

(14) Les Chênes Verts

2 km on rte. de Villecroze - 94.70.55.06

M. Bajade. Open until 9 p.m. Closed Tues. dinner, Wed. & Jan. 1-Feb. 20. Pets allowed. Parking.

It's nearly an impossible trick, but Paul Bajade has succeeded. He manages to maintain the country simplicity and naturalness of this hideaway among the pines and green oaks despite the proximity of Tourtour, the most sophisticated village in the upper Var region. This naturalness, however, carries over into the chilly dining room that Bajade imposes on his customers, with its drab curtains and clichéed rough-plaster walls. The tables, it must be admitted, are truly elegant, and the food is full of an open warmth and lightness, from the salad of quail and pine nuts, to the filet of turbot in shellfish butter, to the simple but magnificent saddle of lamb for two. The restaurant hosts a truffle festival in season, and year-round it serves a lovely local wine.

A la carte: 300F. Menus: 160F and 300F (wine incl.).

Hostellerie Les Lavandes

1.5 km on D 51 - 94.70.57.11

Closed Oct. 1-June 1. 16 rms 235-280F. Pets allowed. Pool. Tennis. Parking.

From this pretty Provençal house set in 70 acres of its own grounds and surrounding lavender fields, there is a panoramic view across the Maures hills. Restaurant.

Tourville-la-Rivière

see Rouen

Trébeurden

22560 Trébeurden - (Côtes-du-Nord)
Paris 519 - Perros-Guirec 13 - Lannion 9 - St-Brieuc 72

Manoir de Lan Kerrelec

Allée Centrale - 96.23.50.09

M. Daubé. Open until 9:30 p.m. Closed Mon. & Tues. (except June 15-Sept. 15) & Nov. 15-March 15. Garden dining. Pets allowed. Parking. Telex 741172. Cards: V, AE, DC.

Here is a perfect view of the ocean, the rocky shoreline and the sunset from one of the most beautiful interiors along this coast: a stunning and luxurious round dining room that looks like a meticulously crafted ship's hull turned upside down. (The room is, in fact, graced by a beautiful model ship.) We're glad that the Daubes are now anxious to resume their fine efforts in this beautiful hunting lodge, built on this rocky point in the last century (by Gervaise, architect of the Grand Palais in Paris). At the door, Gilles and his wife envelop you with smiles and warmth and civil chat. Meanwhile the young chef, Jean-Luc Danjou, has pulled himself together to produce, for example, a salade royale of shellfish (though it lacked the truffle sauce), a perfect turbot roasted with an onion confit, a well-prepared émincé of duckling (though the spinach was accidentally pickled) and a delicious hot apple tart. The wines are well chosen and reasonably priced.

A la carte: 300F. Menus: 125F (weekday lunch only), 185F (dinner only), 235F, 285F.

Manoir de Lan Kerellec

(See restaurant above)

Closed Nov. 15-March 15. 2 stes 960-1,360F. 11 rms 500-960F. Half-board 470-700F. TV. Pets allowed. Tennis.

All of the rooms are turned toward the sea, looking out to the islands, and some of them have terraces. It's all elegantly appointed, discreet and refined. Relais et Châteaux.

Ti Al Lannec

Allée de Mézo-Guen - 96.23.57.26

M. Jouanny. Open until 9:15 p.m. Closed Mon. lunch & Nov. 13-March 16. No pets. Parking. Telex 740656. Cards: V, AE.

This large floral dining room boasts an ocean-facing terrace, pretty tables, strikingly beautiful lighting and soft music somewhere in the background. The service is attentive to everything, yet the atmosphere remains relaxed. The new chef, trained in the best Parisian establishments, takes obvious pains over a well-thought-out modern menu. One of its more thoughtful features is the pride of place given to such lesser-reputed fish as skate, rock salmon and whiting, which are all perfectly cooked and sauced with, for example, saffron and little seasonal vegetables (slight danger of too much cream). You can also try the delicate shrimp mousse with a purée of langoustines, superb shellfish and the ultra-thin hot apple tart deliciously done in light puff pastry. Interesting, reasonably priced wine list (especially Champagnes).

A la carte: 250F. Menus: 100F (weekday lunch only), 210F and 150F to 368F.

Ti Al Lannec

(See restaurant above)

Closed Nov. 13-March 16. 8 stes 425-530F. 15 rms 270-530F. Half-board 370-450F oblig. in seas. TV. Pets allowed.

Eight of these rooms are suites that have either a porch or a terrace facing south toward the magnificent coastline. The atmosphere is hush-hush quiet. French-style billiard room.

Trelly

50660 Quettreville-sur-Sienne - (Manche)
Paris 340 - Avranches 39 - St-Lô 39 - Coutances 12

Verte Campagne

Au Hameau Chavelier - 33.47.65.33)

Closed Sun. & Mon. (off-seas.), Feb. 13-28 & Nov. 13-30. 1 ste 270F. 7 rms 150-300F. Half-board 310-460F. No pets. Cards: V, AE.

Green? You bet! In fact, you are deep among the little fields and coppices of Normandy, surrounded by nothing but birds, herds and tremendous silence. The rooms in this charming little inn are pretty and well maintained. Restaurant.

Trémolat

24510 St-Alvère - (Dordogne)
Paris 530 - Périgueux 54 - Sarlat 46 - Bergerac 34

Le Vieux Logis

53.22.80.06

M. Giraudel-Destord. Open daily until 10 p.m. Garden dining. Pets allowed. Garage parking. Telex 541025. Cards: V, AE, DC, MC.

Smack in the middle of the village, virtually at the foot of the old church, you'll stumble onto a perfectly adorable cluster of old houses that have been restored to a tee and are surrounded by showcase lawns and blooming flower beds. Everything visible is refined and peaceful, beckoning you to make a civilized stopover. You won't be sorry if you acquiesce. The dining room, designed by owner Bernard Giraudel, is also distinctive and surprisingly inviting, despite its dimensions, and it lies open to the light and green of the garden. Giraudel himself is another lure, particularly his spontaneity, even toward children, whom he takes to play in the garden while their parents linger à table. And who wouldn't linger at such a table! The kitchen crew is now built around the excellent chef, Pierre-Jean Duribreux, and the food is getting ever better. Duribreux is developing a perfect balance of modern cuisine on the one hand, and paying attention to regional tradition on the other: foie gras with a fig preserve, remarkable salmon with tomato butter, a potato stuffed with truffled sweetbreads and lightly crusted in the oven—a stunning success—roast beef served with thin slices of foie gras and a few coriander seeds, and beautiful, classic desserts, including simple fruit tarts in season. The wine list has been built up, particularly with bottles from Bordeaux. Yet another point.

A la carte: 300-350F. Menus: 120F, 175F, 240F.

Le Vieux Logis

(See restaurant above)

Open year-round. 5 stes 790F. 15 rms 595-660F. Half-board 585-678F. TV. Pets allowed.

The decorator of this very old Périgord-style house, Jean Dive, was savvy enough to outfit it elegantly, with no loss of charm. The combination of lovely fabrics, an unbelievable garden and perfect comfort makes for an allure that's utterly irresistible. Relais et Châteaux.

La Trinité-sur-Mer

56470 La Trinité-sur-Mer - (Morbihan)
Paris 482 - Auray 12 - Carnac 5 - Vannes 30 - Quiberon 22

15 Les Hortensias

4, pl. Yvonne-Sarcey - 97.55.73.69

MM. Flé & Bellance. Open until 9:30 p.m. Closed Tues. & Wed. (off-seas.), 1st week of Oct. & Nov. 30-March 1. Terrace dining. Pets allowed. Parking. Cards: V, AE, MC.

The hydrangeas (*les hortensias*) are in evidence everywhere. Planted in big pots, their pink plumes stand out against the blue of the sky, the sea and of the tablecloths and awnings that grace the new terrace. A white-tiled floor, big bay windows that let in great shafts of Breton light, halogen lighting and bougainvillea make up the sophisticated but successful interior. Likewise, the cuisine at times seems to reach the outer bounds of complexity while managing to remain delicate, balanced and skillfully prepared. This is the work of Patrick Le Guen, a student of Michel Gaudin, who recently won his second toque for his savory and aromatic marinated small sardines with a zucchini mousse, his red mullet salad (barely cooked in the pan and served sauceless) with foie gras, his toothsome turbot-and-potato galette with brown sauce and his crusty pastry of raspberries and light cream. The wine list is well done but pricey. You can count on a lovely reception by Henri Flé, the friendly owner, ringleader and overseer of the young service staff, who are pretty comical in their all-white sailor suits.

A la carte: 300-350F. Menus: 140F, 190F.

Les Trois-Epis

68410 Les Trois Epis - (Haut-Rhin)
Paris 450 - Gérardmer 50 - Munster 17 - Colmar 12

14 Le Hohlandsbourg

Pl. de l'Eglise - 89.49.80.65

M. Riehm. Open daily until 9 p.m. Terrace dining. Pets allowed. Parking. Telex 880229. Cards: V, AE, DC, MC.

This big hotel at the head of a valley welcomes year-round an international clientele eager for the great outdoors but deeply attached to luxury and comfort. We've found them in all their splendor here, in this recently refurbished dining room with woodwork up to the ceiling, flowers everywhere, soft carpets and strange ergonomic chairs designed by the owner. Once seated in one of these chairs, one is quite unaware of the passing of time. All the same, the big attraction is uncontestably the marvelous view—one of the best in Alsace—of the Vosges mountains and the plain below. It is as lovely in winter as in summer. The menu is quite short, almost too short, but nonetheless well balanced and carefully seasonal. We found on it dishes that are prettily turned out and remarkably consistent: a fine and simple salad of quail and red cabbage, thin slices of lamb with sweet garlic and excellent potato fritters, darnier of salmon and sole, and interesting desserts (among them a chocolate-and-egg-liqueur parfait). The extensive wine list is eclectic but serious. The hotel also has a cozy pub with a table d'hôte and good Alsatian dishes.

A la carte: 350F.

Le Grand Hôtel

(See restaurant above)

Open year-round. 1 ste 1,700F. 49 rms 380-950F. Half-board 485-770F. TV in 30 rms. Pets allowed. Heated pool.

This is a grand hotel of lovely rooms, unfailing modern appointments and a sort of sophisticated, dude-ranch mountaineer motif. Facilities include a covered pool, solarium, sauna, massage service and a splendid terrace for viewing the Vosges. A very nice reception. One of the best hotels in Alsace.

Villa Rosa

89.49.81.19

Closed Nov. 15-Feb. 3. 2 stes 210F. 7 rms 120-160F. Half-board 160-220F oblig. in seas. Pets allowed. Heated pool. Parking. Cards: V.

Very peaceful and quiet, this little inn sits by the edge of the Vosges forest. A good place for a stop. Restaurant.

Troyes

10000 Troyes - (Aube)
Paris 158 - Amiens 276 - Dijon 151 - Nancy 186

Sights. The cathedral (Gothic, thirteenth to seventeenth centuries, one of the biggest in France, a marvel of stained glass and a testimony to the high art of the master glassworkers of thirteenth-century Troyes, Saint-Pierre tower—67 meters high—its statuary, the cathedral's treasure). The churches: Sainte-Madeleine (twelfth century, remarkable rood screen of carved stone, Champagne-school stained glass); Saint-Jean (fourteenth century, Girardon reredos, interesting minaret); Saint-Rémy (fourteenth century, statues from the Troyes school); Saint-Nizier (sixteenth century, glazed roof tiles, beautiful stained-glass windows); Saint-Martin-lès-Aires (sixteenth century, double-dome clock tower, stained glass, restored organ from the sixteenth century); Saint-Pantheléon (sixteenth century, Renaissance Gothic, a virtual museum of statues and stained glass); Basilica Saint-Urbain (a celebration of Gothic art, established by Pope Urban IV, twelfth-century glasswork, statuary—Madonna with grapes). Museums: Abbey of Saint-Loup (important natural history and regional archaeology museum, medieval sculpture, painting from the fifteenth to twentieth centuries); the beautiful Musée d'Art Moderne Pierre-Levy (prestigious collection of impressionist works—350 paintings, 1,300 drawings, 100 sculptures—glasswork collection—the jewel box alone is worth the trip); historical museums of Troyes and Champagne; Musée de la (Hosiery) Bonneterie (Hôtel de Vauluisant, 4,500 pieces); Maison de l'Outil et de la Pensée Ouvrière ("House of the Tool and the Workingman's Idea," Hôtel de Mauroy, built in 1560, restored by the Compagnons du Devoir, 500 hand tools of all trades, 2,000 volumes of worker literature); Pharmacie de l'Hôtel Dieu (twelfth century, beautiful apothecary collection). Also architectural details in the carved wood of certain houses, and "Bouchon de Champagne," one of the oldest preserved urban areas in Europe.

Eating on the Run. Le Croco, ave. du Maréchal-Joffre (salads, grill); Grill Saint-Jean, 21, rue Champeaux (grill, andouillettes); La Marée, 35, rue Emile-Zola (seafood); Tartatou, 1, cours Mortier-d'Or (tarts at all hours); Il Theatro, 35, rue Emile-Zola (good pizza).

Bars & Cafés. Café du Musée, 59, rue de la Cité (handy beer bar, near the cathedral); for their outdoor seating: Café de Foy, 13, pl. du Maréchal-Foch, and Le Grand Café, 4, rue Champeaux.

Brasseries. L'Europe, 3, rond-point de l'Europe; Le Gambetta, 4, blvd. Gambetta; La Paix, 52, rue du Général-de-Gaulle; La Vosgienne, 18, pl. du Maréchal-Foch.

Nightlife. L'Aquarium, 14, blvd. Carnot; Le Caprice, rue Roger-Salengro (discotheque); Le Capricorne, 28, rue Georges-Clemenceau (discotheque, shows); Le Caveau, in the train station (the most popular nightspot in town); Le Strauss, 17, pl. de la Libération.

La Poste

1-3, rue Raymond-Poincaré
25.73.05.05

M. Deroussis. Open daily until 10 p.m. Air cond. Pets allowed. Telex 840995. Cards: V, AE.

This little hotel complex has just been renovated; the former grand dining room was cut in two to house a modern seafood bistro (La Marée) that is done up like a mahogany stateroom. More importantly, the other half, La Poste, is an opulent restaurant with marble, thick carpeting and contemporary paintings under a great-looking lighted ceiling. This is unarguably *the* fancy restaurant in Troyes. Pierre Roger, the chef, who had brought his entire crew from the Hostellerie de Pont-Sainte-Marie, has left, and his sous-chef is now in command. This change was too recent for a rating in this edition, but we expect to see the same updated classical repertoire, featuring a beautiful salad of frogs' legs and asparagus tips, simmered bass with little vegetables, local andouillette enriched with sweetbreads and foie gras, and an exceptional layered pastry with fresh fruit (mango, kiwi, strawberries). Excellent traditional service.

A la carte: 300F. Menus: 179F (lunch only), 185F (dinner only).

La Poste

(See restaurant above)

Open year-round. 3 stes 400-600F. 24 rms 250-350. TV. Air cond. in 3 rms. Pets allowed.

This modern, nicely renovated hotel is in the center of town. Its rooms are hardly big, but they're comfortable.

Royal Hôtel

22, blvd. Carnot - 25.73.19.99

Closed Sun. & Dec. 16-Jan. 9. 37 rms 200-235F. Half-board 235-320F. TV. Pets allowed. Telex 841015. Cards: V, AE, DC, MC.

A most comfortable hotel, partly renovated and with beautiful bathrooms. Restaurant.

(14) Le Valentino

Cour de la Rencontre - 25.73.14.14

M. Vattier. Open until 9:45 p.m. Closed Sun. dinner, Mon., Feb. school vacation & Aug. 16-Sept. 9. Air cond. Garden dining. Pets allowed. Cards: V, AE, DC, MC.

This restaurant boasts not only a lovely interior but a delightful exterior environment: the peaceful streets of old Troyes. Inside it is elegant, flowered, comfortable and flanked on one side by a terrace on the inner courtyard. In addition, a most professional owner, Alain Vattier, wages a mighty struggle to raise Troyes from the gastronomic torpor into which it has sunk. The results are encouraging, and Vattier, with the help of his young chef, has established a fairly refined menu based heavily on seafood and on the surprises of the daily market (which he visits personally). His 200-franc fixed-price menu (including wine) is superb: marinated salmon with mint and lemon confit, filet of sea trout perfectly cooked with a cider sauce (but it would be better to peel the potatoes), good Chaource cheese and pleasant desserts (though no knockouts) from the best pastry chef in Troyes. Vattier purchases some lovely wines directly from the producer.

A la carte: 300F. Menus: 200F (wine incl.), 290F.

Tulle

19000 Tulle - (Corrèze)
Paris 480 - Limoges 87 - Clermont-Ferrand 145

Limouzi

16, quai de la République - 55.26.42.00

Closed Jan. 1-8. 50 rms 135-235F. Half-board 200-240F. TV in 25 rms. Pets allowed. Garage parking. Cards: V, AE, DC, MC.

At this good, big downtown hotel near the cathedral, the rooms are unusually well equipped. Restaurant.

(14) La Toque Blanche

29, rue Jean-Jaurès - 55.26.75.41

M. Valentin. Open until 9 p.m. Closed Sun. (except holidays & in seas.) & Jan. 10-31. Air cond. Pets allowed. Hotel: 10 rms 110-180F; half-board 195-210F. Cards: V, AE.

With the help of his adopted son, Bruno Estival, old Jean Valentin seems content to prepare good food that's always a pleasure to eat. His more-or-less regional cooking is bold in its flavors and turned out in a hearty but never heavy manner. Try the simmered pot of local snails, frogs' legs and trout; the pike in beurre blanc; the slices of duck breast in honey and sherry vinegar; and the toothsome desserts (mint-chocolate bavarois). The wine list is wonderfully regional and easy on the budget. The delightful Mme. Valentin keeps busy overseeing the pleasant little bourgeois dining room.

A la carte: 250-300F. Menus: 105F.

Unac

see Ax-les-Thermes

Urt

64240 Hasparren - (Pyrénées-Atlantiques)
Paris 732 - Pau 97 - Cambo 28 - Peyrehorade 25

(15) Auberge de la Galupe

Pl. de Port - 59.56.21.84

Mme. Aliaga. Open until 10 p.m. Closed Sun. dinner (off-seas.), Mon., Feb. school vacation & Nov. 1. Pets allowed. Cards: V.

The new owner of this pretty little Basque place on the banks of the Adour river is in a hurry to realize her ambition of creating one of the best restaurants in the Basque country. The restaurant is already one of the most charming, with its authentic and polished basco-béarnais decor. The cooking of her chef, Christian Parra, is also making forward strides in imagination and lightness. Hence another point, earned by his langoustines, still firm and served with a light beurre blanc with a faintly smoky flavor, his red mullet boned with tweezers and barely cooked in a sauce made from red mullet meat, his straightforward and perfect Basque milk-fed lamb roasted with thyme and his magnificent caramelized thin apple tart. The service staff is young and competent, and the wine list worthwhile.

A la carte: 260F. Menu: 120F.

Ustaritz

see Bayonne

Vaison-la-Romaine

84110 Vaison-la-Romaine - (Vaucluse)
Paris 670 - Avignon 46 - Montélimar 65 - Carpentras 28

Hostellerie Le Beffroi

Rue de l'Evêché - 90.36.04.71

Closed Jan. 4-March 15 & Nov. 14-Dec. 15. 1 ste 415F. 20 rms 120-395F. Half-board 220-317F. TV in 12 rms. Pets allowed. Parking. Telex 306022. Cards: V, AE, DC, MC.

This is one of the loveliest sixteenth-century residences in the heart of old Vaison. There are terraced gardens, and some of the rooms command breathtaking views of the countryside. Half of the rooms are located in an equally beautiful wing.

IN NEARBY **Séguret**
(10 km SW on D 88)
84110 Vaison-la-Romaine - (Vaucluse)

(14) La Table du Comtat

Le Village - 90.46.91.49

M. Gomez. Open until 9 p.m. (9:30 p.m. in summer). Closed Tues. dinner, Wed. (except July-Aug.), Feb. & Nov. 21-Dec. 7. Air cond. No pets. Parking. Cards: AE, DC, MC.

This house, formerly a hospital from the sixteenth century, is perched high in this marvelous village, one of the most beautiful in Provence. The Provençal dining room opens onto a breathtaking panorama of the plain below, the vineyards and the peaks of Montmirail. What good fortune that such an enticing spot should be owned by such friendly people and staffed by a crew that can still smile (even in the summer at the tourists)! It is even more fortunate that it shelters the steadily improving cuisine of earnest Frank Gomez: a soufflé of julienned truffles, salmon lightly simmered with mushrooms, rognonnade of lamb in salt crust (with exquisite wild rice) and good, generous, classical desserts. Both Châteauneuf and Gigondas are available, surprisingly, by the carafe. The prices have stiffened seriously. We'll give it another point.

A la carte: 350-450F. Menus: 190F (weekday lunch only), 240F, 380F.

La Table du Comtat

(See restaurant above)

Closed Tues. & Wed. (except July-Aug.), Feb. & Nov. 21-Dec. 7. 1 ste. 7 rms 350-550F. Pets allowed. Pool.

Simple but attractive, these eight rooms are furnished in the Provençal way and boast big, wonderful views. You'll find a friendly reception by the owner and a small swimming pool in the rock ledge.

Red toques signify modern cuisine; black toques signify traditional cuisine.

Val-de-la-Haye
see Rouen

Val-de-Villé
see Sélestat

Val-d'Isère
73150 Val-d'Isère - (Savoie)
Paris 690 - Chambéry 133 - Albertville 85 - Briançon 158

Le Blizzard
79.06.02.07
Closed May 8-Dec. 1. 5 stes 500-900F. 105 rms 300-700F. Half-board 320-663F. TV. Pets allowed. Telex 309662. Cards: V, AE, DC.

One of the dependable establishments in the resort town of Val-d'Isère, Le Blizzard offers refurbished rooms, a discotheque and a restaurant.

12/20 El Cortijo
Rue Principale - 79.06.03.25
M. Henrypierre. Open until 10:30 p.m. Closed May 5-July 1 & Sept. 15-Dec. 1. Terrace dining. Pets allowed. Cards: V, AE, DC.

Since El Cortijo is the best place to eat in Val-d'Isère, its mezzanines are packed daily. Along with the rustic decor, you'll enjoy the simple, well-done cuisine of Breton chef Joseph Kerouel, particularly the trout filets in tarragon, the rack of lamb, the excellent stewed pork and the good mussels in saffron. We only wish the service was on the same level as the owner's warm reception.

A la carte: 280F. Menus: 70F (winter lunch only), 91F (summer dinner only).

12/20 Grand Paradis
79.06.11.73.
M. Korosec. Open until 10 p.m. Closed May-June & Sept.-Nov. Terrace dining. No pets. Parking. Telex 309731. Cards: V, AE, DC.

The new manager has redone the huge dining room, using hand-painted wood paneling from his native Austria. You'll find plenty of charm, grace and good feeling, as well as a young chef who will merit a toque once he has mastered his preparations and cooking times. The foie gras in raspberry vinegar, medallions of lotte with tomato and zucchini and fruit tarts are all good.

A la carte: 300-350F. Menus: 110F, 220F.

Savoyarde
79.06.01.55
Closed May 5-Dec. 1. 2 stes 885-1,005F (half-board). 44 rms 500-750F. Half-board 546-585F oblig. in seas. TV. Pets allowed. Parking. Telex 309274. Cards: V, AE, DC, MC.

Located 100 yards from the ski lifts, this big traditional chalet offers appealing rooms furnished in natural wood and equipped with attractive paneled bathrooms. Sauna and restaurant.

Sofitel
79.06.08.30
Closed May 5-July 1 & Aug. 28-Dec. 1. 5 stes 1,250-2,800F. 48 rms 605-1,080F. Half-board 580-710F. TV. Pets allowed. Heated pool. Garage parking. Telex 980558. Cards: V, AE, DC, MC.

Excellent modern rooms with bay windows are located in a completely equipped whirlpool therapy center. Restaurant.

Tsanteleina
79.06.12.13
Closed May-June & Sept.-Nov. 40 stes 400-510F. 20 rms 280-470F. Half-board 390-460F oblig. in seas. TV. Pets allowed. Tennis. Parking. Telex 980175. Cards: V, AE, DC.

You can take in a view of the entire resort from the beautiful terraces here, or relax in the comfortable rooms. Restaurant.

Valençay
36600 Valençay - (Indre)
Paris 230 - Blois 55 - Châteauroux 41 - Issoudun 44

Hôtel d'Espagne
9, rue du Château - 54.00.00.02
M. Fourré. Open until 9:30 p.m. Closed Sun. dinner, Mon. (Nov. 15-March 15) & Jan. 5-March 5. Garden dining. Pets allowed. Parking. Telex 751675. Cards: V, AE, MC.

Behold 100 years and four generations of earnest and perfectionist hoteliers, just a stone's throw from Talleyrand's huge château. Maurice Fourré, the owner, is honored with a great-grandfather who was cook to the Prince of Sagan; he himself was trained at the Ritz and Lucas-Carton. All of this has led to a cuisine that is in no way Spanish but that perpetuates in a lofty way the restaurant's old, involved repertoire (sliced duck liver with grapes, lobster stew with beurre rouge, sweetbreads Baron d'Aignan). The decor is fairly opulent, with lots of flowers, inside a large home buried in greenery.

A la carte: 350-400F. Menus: 130F, 180F.

Hôtel d'Espagne
(See restaurant above)
Closed Sun. & Mon. (Nov. 15-March 15) & Jan. 5-March 5. 16 rms 350-500F. TV. Pets allowed. Pool. Tennis.

The fine manners of yesteryear still thrive at this Relais et Châteaux hotel, at least when the owner is in a good mood. The grand-siècle interior is exceptionally comfortable.

Valence
26000 Valence - (Drôme)
Paris 560 - Lyon 100 - Grenoble 99 - Marseille 215

Pic
285, ave. Victor-Hugo
75.44.15.32
M. Pic. Open until 9:30 p.m. Closed Sun. dinner, Wed., 10 days during Feb. school vacation & Aug. Air cond. Garden dining. Pets allowed. Garage parking. Cards: V, AE, DC.

Happy chefs, like happy lovers, have no stories to tell, and Jacques Pic has less to tell than anyone else. On our part, there's never a reproach, and on his, never a blunder, an uneven emotional state, an impetuous pronouncement or a publicity stunt. He's a great artist, and no gust of wind will ever manage to swell his toque. But by constantly repeating the same thing about him (his fantastic kindness, his modesty, his impeccable technique, his clockwork timing), we run the risk of creating the impression that nothing new ever happens inside the walls of this temple of provincial virtues. In fact, nothing could be further from the truth. Soon, we'll no longer refer to "Pic," but to the "Pics," as we all already speak of the "Troisgros" or the "Lorains," referring to father-and-son teams. Alain—with a beard enveloping his timid smile—is now at his father's side, forming a complicit and affectionate duo. Sensitive and imaginative, this amateur painter is not yet ready for a solo. But he is a link in the chain of Pics, and through him the tradition will live on. But it is just as likely that he will bring with him—you can feel it already—his own ideas and personality, which surely will strengthen the combination of tradition and evolution that is the trademark of this restaurant.

Therefore, everything is working toward creating your happiness: the exquisite welcome of Mme. Pic, whose smile sweeps you away upon arrival, the quiet calm of the dining room decorated in ripe apricot tones, the refreshing sight of mounds of flowers and greenery from the interior garden, the courtesy and lively humor of the professional personnel, who also know how to establish a rapport of confidence if not complicity, the wonders of the endless wine cellar, where Côtes-du-Rhône shun patent letters of nobility, and finally, the irreproachable quality of the cuisine, which seems to get better every year.

If you want to seriously sample this cuisine, you'd better arrive with a completely empty stomach. Run a vacuum through it if you have to. At the top of the ladder is the menu Rabelais, which is not designed to let you eat like a bird. Seven courses, and not small portions, allow you to discover a feast of full flavors and subtle aromas. Rounds of langoustines with artichokes are sprinkled with a vinaigrette with petits pois. This appetizer is followed by a mosaic of sea bass and salmon with saffron; next comes a combination of red snapper and baudroie (lotte) in an eggplant cream, and then an eau-de-vie sorbet, which is not a good idea (distilled alcohol kills the appetite instead of whetting it). Then comes an exquisite crépinette (a sort of sausage) made of sweetbreads and zucchini buds, along with pigeon breasts with fava beans in an astounding carrot juice, which is more than just a dish, it is an opus! The chèvre cheeses came in every stage of ripeness. And since we still had one little empty spot left in our stomachs, a swarm of desserts and dainty morsels, neither too sweet nor not sweet enough, arrived. In short, they were delicious. If your appetite isn't up to all that, you can try a salad of langoustines and sautéed foie gras, turbot steamed with truffles—a masterpiece of delicacy—strips of beef in a marvelous sauce of marrow and garlic, or Drôme lamb with vine peaches (a divine mix).

A la carte: 500F and up. Menus: 260F (weekday lunch only), 380F, 480F.

Pic

(See restaurant above)

Closed Wed., Sun., 10 days during Feb. school vacation & Aug. 2 stes 550-700F. 2 rms 380-400F. TV. Air cond. Pets allowed.

Two suites and two rooms—this is not exactly a convention hotel. If you manage to get yourself a bed, you'll sleep wonderfully and wake up to birds singing in the garden and a sumptuous breakfast tray. Relais et Châteaux.

IN NEARBY **Granges-lès-Valence**

(3 km on N 533)

07500 Granges-lès-Valence - (Ardèche)

---

14 Auberge des Trois Canards

565, ave. de la République - 75.44.43.24

M. Giffon. Open until 9:30 p.m. Closed Sun. dinner, Mon. & 3 weeks in Aug. Terrace dining. Pets allowed. Parking. Cards: V, AE, DC.

The Giffon family has for some time displayed its generous hospitality not far from here in Grane. They left to come to this place on the highway that one of the brood, Jean-Philippe, took over a couple of years ago. You don't come here for the interior decorating—though it has been spruced up a bit—but to sit down at a table and "get your money's worth." We promise: You won't be disappointed. The fixed-price menus are a giveaway, and the à la carte menu is no slouch either: superb oysters, blanquette of seafood, platter of fish and shellfish in a light boil, roast beef in truffle sauce.

A la carte: 300F. Menus: 92F (weekdays only), 130F, 150F, 185F, 220F.

IN NEARBY **Pont-de-l'Isère**

(9 km N on N 7)

26600 Tain-l'Hermitage - (Drôme)

---

18 Chabran

Ave. du 45e-Parallèle (N 7)
75.84.60.09

M. Chabran. Open until 10 p.m. Closed Sun. dinner & Mon. (off-seas.). Air cond. Pets allowed. Parking. Telex 346333. Cards: V.

Life is cruel. There are worthless chefs in enchanting places, and superbly talented ones stuck along the national highway. Unfortunately for him, Michel Chabran counts himself among the disenfranchised, stuck as he is in the heart of a thankless village, right under the nose of cars whizzing along the route Nationale 7, not at all resembling the one Charles Trenet sang about—but let's not dirty the picture needlessly. Over the years, the old family inn where the village men would go for a drink has become unrecognizable. To say that it has developed an enchanting charm would be excessive, but the shingled facade is not lacking in elegance, nor is the salon, the stopover for a predinner drink, even though its ostensibly modern decor is nothing less than intimate. And though the dining room, with walls covered in Swedish pine and a brushed-steel chimney, is in good taste, the derisively smiling little garden where a few tables are set up in the shade of a pine tree and two cyprus trees would still remind you a bit of some huge hotel chain.

Chabran—who looks like a young leading man and has a remarkable sense of contact and a kindness that embraces everyone, even the most distant and solitary clients—has big projects in mind. They are utterly achievable, and, without a doubt, one of these days we'll be surprised to find behind the facade a real "relais de campagne" with a huge garden, little birds to cheerfully wake us in the morning, and charm to spare. It's simply a question of money. And it's just the right moment to bring him your money, because Chabran the chef has never been in such rare form. Three recent meals proved it to us.

He is a modern chef in the best sense of the word. He possesses a great knack for bending flavors while maintaining the character of each ingredient; a lot of imagination that is never wasted on useless inventions; and a personal way of translating the fruits of the land. You'll surely appreciate the way he enhances the respective tastes of lobster, pigs' feet and ears, and Nyons olives in a sesame-oil salad, where soy sauce and lobster juice blend marvelously. The acidity of his frogs sautéed with rich tomatoes is equally exquisite. The filets of canette (duckling), served warm on a crunchy salad, could not be better spiced or seasoned. The langoustines royales in a blanched garlic sauce (which is called a saint-joseph "rouge," not "blanc") with fried parsley, the pan of cuttlefish and mussels in olive oil, the grilled salmon in a vegetable fricassée with mustard cream, the filets of red snapper sautéed with fettuccine in a ham and soy sauce, and the effeuillé of fresh cod with zucchini buds and beurre blanc flavored with curry not only affirm that Jose Ferrer is the best fisherman in the region, but that Chabran is a virtuoso of the sea.

Faced with meat or fowl, he is equally clever. The lamb filet, wrapped in its crackling fat and stuffed with vegetables, is a true marvel. The only criticism you could possibly level at Chabran is that the curry sauce is a bit too heavy and the girolles uncalled for. On the other hand, the thin strips of beef with potatoes amandine (on the menu since the restaurant opened) have a sauce au vieil hermitage that is at once strong, thick and extraordinarily delicate. Also exquisite, but in a completely different vein, is the simple juice of the roast squab en cocotte, which Chabran serves with a morel flan.

As for the numerous desserts presented by the pretty and charming Rose-Marie Chabran, they are sumptuous. Forced to choose from the millefeuille with wild strawberries, the "ugly" bitter-chocolate cake (it is indeed ugly, but boy is it good), the lemon tart, the chestnut charlotte... well, you just won't know what to do.

It's difficult to cite the names of all the dishes and desserts, because Chabran changes the menu constantly in order, he says, not to fall asleep on the job. He has also put the final touches on a most clever "carte-club," made up of six first courses and six main courses priced from 55 to 200 francs, that allows you to order an excellent meal that's quick, light and well priced. And it comes with a choice of Côtes-du-Rhône for about 75 francs, selected from an astounding wine list where the best of the Rhône Valley and Burgundy are offered in every price range.

A la carte: 450F. Menus: 190F (carte-club), 280F, 390F.

Chabran

(See restaurant above)

Closed Sun. & Mon. (off-seas.). 12 rms 300-690F. TV. Air cond. Pets allowed.

The small, well-equipped, quite comfortable rooms are done in a unique modern style; some are rather refined, some rather bizarre. Exquisite breakfast.

Valence-d'Agen

82400 Valence-d'Agen - (Tarn-et-Garonne)
Paris 760 - Agen 26 - Cahors 66 - Moissac 17

---

(15) La Campagnette

Rte. de Cahors - 63.39.65.97

M. Lerchundi. Open until 9:30 p.m. (10 p.m. in summer). Closed Mon. (except July-Aug.), Sun. dinner & Sept. 1-10. Garden dining. Pets allowed. Parking. Cards: V.

The Lerchundis have enlarged their cute little Campagnette and spruced up the decor, while also fixing up the garden out back to serve meals on nice days. Gérard Lerchundi is an inventive chef who is quite concerned with the directness and lightness of his food (he's a former student of Guillot). He often changes his menu; we last found on it a bundle of warm oysters with a shallot vinaigrette, potato and salmon en croûte with horseradish sauce, and a young pigeon roasted in the local red wine and honey. There are many excellent desserts, and the wine list has been filled out, primarily with Bordeaux and Burgundies.

A la carte: 280F. Menus: 80F (weekday lunch only), 145, 235F.

Valenciennes

59300 Valenciennes - (Nord)
Paris 205 - Brussels 102 - Cambrai 32 - St-Quentin 70

---

(14) L'Albéroi

Pl. de la Gare - 27.46.86.30

M. Benoist. Open daily until 10 p.m. Pets allowed. Cards: V, AE, DC, MC.

Long before François Benoist did this place over from the basement to the rafters—now modern and comfortable and well lit, with pretty paintings—he held the blue ribbon for French train-station restaurants. He is now more than ever concerned about maintaining his reputation, recruiting top-notch chefs (the current one, Lionel Accolas, is as adept as he is consistent) and, as always, fussing about the quality of the ingredients and the recipes from his region, the Nord. As a result, you'll find beef tongue Lucullus, kidneys in old gin, marvelous andouillette from Cambrai and local cheeses. And there are also dishes that reflect Benoist's attention to the seasons and to the times. Nice little fast-food annex, La Dodenne.

A la carte: 350F. Menus: 150F, 220F.

Val-Suzon

see Dijon

Val-Thorens

73440 St-Martin-de-Belleville - (Savoie)
Paris 670 - Chambéry 110 - Albertville 70 - Moûtiers 36

Fitz Roy

79.00.04.78

Closed May-June & Sept.-Oct. 3 stes 1,000-1,500 (half-board). 36 rms 800-900F (half-board). TV. Pets allowed. Pool. Parking. Telex 309707. Cards: V, AE, DC.

In this huge, luxuriously done, modern chalet, the rooms are large, comfortable, more-or-less tastefully furnished and accessed by a panoramic elevator. The pool and the beauty salon are excellent. Restaurant.

Le Sherpa

79.00.00.70

Closed May 3-Dec. 15. 40 rms 260-400F (half-board). Parking. Telex 309279.

Lovely rooms with balconies overlooking the mountains can be found inside this hotel, a modern structure right on the ski trails. Restaurant.

Vannes

56000 Vannes - (Morbihan)
Paris 454 - Quimper 117 - Lorient 56 - Nantes 109

La Marebaudière

4, rue Aristide-Briand - 97.47.34.29

Closed Sun. (Nov. 1-Palm Sunday) & Dec. 18-Jan. 5. 41 rms 215-275F. Half-board 205-330F oblig. in seas. Parking. Cards: V, AE, DC, MC.

You'll find lots of peace and quiet here, along with plenty of room outside. The Breton-style service is well mannered and wonderfully kind and efficient. Restaurant.

Le Pressoir

37, rue de l'Hôpital (in St-Avé, 5 km N on D 767) - 97.60.87.63

M. Rambaud. Open until 9:30 p.m. Closed Sun. dinner, Mon., March 1-15 & Oct. 1-15. Pets allowed. Parking. Cards: V, AE, DC, MC.

The food served in this pleasant interior of fieldstone set off with garnet-colored fabrics has become more savvy and more consistent. Bernard Rambaud, trained at the Beau Rivage restaurant (at the seashore in Vendée), is proving to be adept and inventive, and our last meal merited another point from the appetizers (warm oysters with quail egg and caviar) to the after- dinner dainties. In between we tried the blanquette of oysters with lime, a Breton lobster roasted with scallop-coral butter and a hot apple tart dressed up with a fine apricot sauce. The wine list is interesting and the owner pleasant.

A la carte: 250F. Menus: 100F (weekdays only) and 130F to 250F.

Le Richemont

Pl. de la Gare - 97.42.61.41

M. Mahé. Open until 9:30 p.m. Closed Sun. dinner & Mon. Pets allowed. Cards: V, AE.

Will this restaurant at the train station make Vannes as famous a gastronomic whistle-stop as the station at Roanne (where the Troisgros brothers' restaurant is located)? We hope the best for Roger Mahé, the former assistant to Jacques Maximin in the south of France who then did so well in Paris before deciding to return here to the country. We must say, however, that the space he has taken over won't make it easy for him, with its aging, heavy neo-Renaissance decor. But he is already making the best of it with elegant, gaily dressed tables, pretty flowers and a charming if somewhat shy reception staff. More than anything, it is, of course, the brilliant cooking (still marked by southern accents) of the best chef this area has ever seen that makes the place such a success.

We promise that you'll be thrilled by this increasingly regional cuisine, featuring an exquisite mixture of rabbit and foie gras with tarragon; marinated sole and red snapper with asparagus tips; twice-cooked lamb, first roasted in rosemary and then cooked in a mixed grill with delicious juices, little onions and wonderful potatoes; and, finally, caramelized pears in puff pastry and little chocolate and caramel sweets. And all this is on the fixed-price menu at just 150 francs!

Should you venture up to the 200-franc menu or over onto the à la carte list, you'll come upon such dishes as the red snapper and artichoke soup with little grapes, bass grilled to perfection and served in a seaweed vinaigrette with a julienne of endive, salmis of duck surrounded by marvelous vegetables, and, for dessert, a crispy galette in an orange-vanilla sauce with a touch of chocolate. We are convinced—Brittany now boasts a talent of the first rank. Let us hope that it recognizes this and comes here to enjoy and support this fine achievement.

A la carte: 250-300F. Menus: 90F (weekday lunch only), 150F, 200F.

Le Roof

Presqu'île de Conleau - 97.63.47.47

Closed Jan. 10-Feb. 20. 13 rms 150-240F. Half-board 230-250F oblig. in seas. Parking. Cards: V, AE, DC, MC.

This quiet hotel facing the golf course at Morbihan is a handy jumping-off place for discovering the south coast of Brittany. At press time, Le Roof had closed temporarily to facilitate an extensive remodeling, so it would be wise to call before visiting. Restaurant.

This symbol signifies hotels that offer an exceptional degree of peace and quiet.

See also: **Questembert**

Les Vans

07140 Les Vans - (Ardèche)
Paris 669 - Alès 43 - Aubenas 37 - Mende 84 - Privas 67

Château Le Scipionnet

Rte. de Joyeuse, D 104A - 75.37.23.84
Closed Oct. 1-March 14. 2 stes 460-530F. 24 rms 300-430F. Half-board 380-420F oblig. in seas. Pool. Tennis. Parking. Cards: V, MC.

This big Napoléon III château will seduce you with its tranquility, the kindliness of its hosts and its large, prettily furnished rooms. Terrace and poolside grill in the summer. Restaurant.

Varces

see Grenoble

Varennes-Jarcy

see PARIS SUBURBS

Varetz

see Brive-la-Gaillarde

Vars

05560 Vars - (Hautes-Alpes)
Paris 737 - Gap 72 - Briançon 47 - Barcelonnette 37

Caribou

92.46.50.43
Closed April 9-Dec. 21. 35 rms 340-500F. Half-board 340-440F oblig. in seas. TV. Pets allowed. Garage parking. Cards: V, DC, MC.

You can ski directly from this big chalet, with its terrace, solarium and various diversions. The rooms are pleasant and well appointed. Restaurant.

Vauchoux

70170 Port-sur-Saône - (Haute-Saône)
Paris 354 - Epinal 88 - Gray 55 - Vesoul 15

(16) Château de Vauchoux

Rte. de la Vallée-de-la-Saône
84.91.53.55
M. Turin. Open until 9:30 p.m. Closed Tues. lunch, Mon. & Feb. Garden dining. Pets allowed. Tennis. Garage parking. Telex 361476. Cards: V, AE, DC, MC.

Jean-Michel Turin—of elfish mien, enormous energy and optimism to spare—announces with an air of certainty that there is no better calling than to feed your neighbor, and of course to feed him the best cooking possible. Therefore, nothing can be too lovely or too good for the hosts of this château, purchased in a state of ruin twelve years ago (Louis XV, it is said, used to come here to hunt deer and beautiful princesses). Over the course of time, it has become the most beautiful restaurant in the upper Saône area. The 42-year-old Turin has an insatiable curiosity for everything that lives and moves and has its being in the culinary world: new techniques, knowledge of ingredients, the search for elements of opposition and winning combinations of flavors. A tireless worker, Turin does not leave his kitchens except to head off to Rungis, the wholesale market center near Paris, or to visit small producers in the region.

The plate of hot Breton oysters, the smoked turbot with béarnaise sauce, the steamed bass filet with vermouth, the lamb sautéed until pink with a touch of garlic, the roast young pigeon and the almond-chocolate profiteroles are what constitute the framework of a cuisine devoted to the best ingredients prepared in a studiously simple style. The tariff, it is true, is fairly high, particularly for this region, but this can be explained, at least partially, by the bountiful helpings and the many gestures of helpfulness and attention that are lavished on guests throughout the meal. This is the case even if you stick to the least expensive fixed-price menu, which is served exactly the same as the most costly one, under the same watchful and engaging eye of Franceline Turin. And, of course, it's served in the same beautiful dining room done in pastel tones in a soothing Louis XVI style. The windows of the dining room open onto the grounds and the pool.

A la carte: 400-500F. Menus: 140F (weekdays only), 220F, 340F, 380F.

Vaux

see Auxerre

Venasque

see Carpentras

Vence

06140 Vence - (Alpes-Maritimes)
Paris 925 - Nice 22 - Cannes 30 - Antibes 19 - Grasse 27

(13) Château des Arômes

2618, rte. de Grasse - 93.58.70.24
M. Mosiniak. Open until 9:30 p.m. Closed Sun. dinner, Mon. & Jan. 9-Feb. 25. Air cond. Garden dining. Pets allowed. Parking. Cards: V, AE, DC.

The high, light-colored walls of the ancient eleventh-century abbey rise in a superb garden overlooking the Cagnes bay, among the captivating fragrances of aromatic plants. It is here that the perfumers of Grasse established the little museum of their scents. And it is here that Gérard Mosiniak, the new chef/manager, is staging—with a certain degree of success—an absolutely original experiment. He is replacing or enhancing certain ingredients with their natural distillates or essences. He has assembled more than 40 different aromas, from the most common to the most rare: onion or truffles, chives or lobster, peppermint or lime and so on. When Mosiniak came from London, where he spent ten years at La Grenouille, he had to promise he would use extensively in his cooking all these little flasks, and clearly it has been an extraordinary novelty for him. The results already are encouraging, at least in terms of the central idea of using and balancing the flavors. It remains to develop a preparation that is on the whole lighter, especially in the sauce department. Some of the dishes you're likely to run into here are a feuilleté of chanterelles with a cream of morels, scallops baked in a pastry shell with crunchy cabbage, filet of beef with cardamom, warm goat cheese with a cumin aspic, and a gratin of red fruit with a rose-liqueur-flavored sabayon. The service is impeccable, whether on the terrace or in the beauty of the Provençal interior of the abbey.

A la carte: 300-400F. Menus: 120F (weekday lunch only), 200F (vegetarian), 170F, 250F.

Château Saint-Martin

Rte. de Coursegoules - 93.58.02.02

Mlle. Brunet. Open until 9:30 p.m. Closed Wed. (off-seas.) & Nov. 15-March 15. Garden dining. Pets allowed. Parking. Telex 470282. Cards: V, AE, DC, MC.

Five hundred meters high, on the ruins of a castle of the Knights Templars—where legend has it there is a fabulous hidden treasure—sits this former millionaire's residence. The spot is delightfully sheltered from the mistral (the wind from the north) among splendid cypress and olive groves. The residence has been converted by the owner into a luxury hotel for the rulers of today's world. At least, they were the ones cultivated for the place, but they have had to share it with the less blue-blooded, for whom the beauty of the surroundings, the high-quality staff, the blue water of the pool sunk in the greenery, the antiques and the rich tapestries hanging in lofty state are worth any price. Even if the view constitutes the principal attraction of the dining room (facing the Esterel and Cap d'Antibes), we cannot deny the true talent of Dominique Ferrière. He is a smart and adept chef who knows how to prepare an up-to-date, straightforward cuisine without being untrue to the house style. His successes include baked scallops with saffron, savarin of langoustines with chanterelles, a ragoût of fresh pasta and truffles, and lamb with herbs in a salt crust.

A la carte: 600F. Menus: 390F, 450F.

Château Saint-Martin

(See restaurant above)

Closed Nov. 15-March 15. 11 stes 2,500-3,000F. 14 rms 1,550-2,180F. Half-board 460F (plus rm). TV. Pets allowed. Heated pool. Tennis.

An absolute jewel of a Relais et Châteaux inn set on 35 gorgeous acres at an altitude of 500 meters. The pool is lovely, and the rooms are of the sort one dreams of, set about in little villas commanding unbroken vistas across the hills.

Miramar

Plateau St-Michel - 93.58.01.32

Closed Oct. 31-March 1. 18 rms 243-326F. Pets allowed. Parking. Telex 470673. Cards: V, AE.

This small hotel gazes at the sea and the Alps across the tops of palm fronds. The rooms, for the most part redone, are quite pretty. The bar specializes in beer. No restaurant.

Relais Cantemerle

258, ch. de Cantemerle - 93.58.08.18

Closed Oct. 15-March 15. 18 stes 750F. 1 rm 550F. Half-board 170F (plus rm). TV. Pets allowed. Pool. Parking. Cards: V, AE, DC, MC.

Nearly all the rooms here are duplexes whose ground floors are at pool and garden level. The decorating scheme is circa 1925; the furnishings come from the former Palais de la Méditerranée. In summer a grill and restaurant are open for business.

La Roseraie

Ave. Henri-Giraud - 93.58.02.20

M. Ganier. Open until 9:30 p.m. Closed Tues. & Wed. (off-seas.) & Jan. Garden dining. Pets allowed. Hotel: 12 rms 230-330F. Pool. Parking. Cards: V, AE.

A surprising and likable little place devoted to the good food of the southwest, La Roseraie has a pretty, neo-1900s setting freshened by superb semitropical suroundings. A giant magnolia, a huge cedar and palm, grapefruit, mandarin, orange and kumquat trees enclose the splendid terrace, which faces the Baous of Vence and the old city. The cuisine's ingredients, shipped in each week from Landes farms, are perfectly lovely, and the classical finish given them by Maurice Ganier is seriously done: superb terrine of half-cooked duck livers, fresh salmon in a sweet white wine of the southwest, duck breast "riche Gascon" (cèpes and foie gras) and red fruit in white Jurançon wine. Excellent waitresses and a wonderful collection of southwestern wines, including an exceptional late-harvest Jurançon.

A la carte: 260-300F. Menus: 110F (weekday lunch only), 170F, 260F.

Verneuil-sur-Avre

27130 Verneuil-sur-Avre - (Eure)
Paris 118 - Evreux 43 - Alençon 76 - Chartres 56

Le Clos

98, rue de la Ferté-Vidame - 32.32.21.81

M. Simon. Open until 9 p.m. Closed Mon. & Nov. 1-Feb. 1. Garden dining. Pets allowed. Parking. Telex 172770. Cards: V, AE, DC, MC.

This little manor is done up in a cushy, Belle Epoque interpretation of Louis XIII. Everything is delightful, from the pretty brick and the delicate slate to the dazzling garden and the new, quite pleasant Regency dining room (we especially went for the accompanying terrace). Patrick Simon, formerly of Nandron, is inspired by classical cuisine, but follows his inspiration with pizzazz, finesse, style and a little touch of Normandy that's most effective: cold salmon with horseradish sauce, grilled bass with verjuice (the juice of unripened grapes), braised sweetbreads à la Normande. The desserts are dainty masterpieces (chocolate genoise, kiwi on the half shell).

A la carte: 350-400F. Menus: 160F (weekdays only), 220, 260F.

Le Clos

(See restaurant above)

Closed Mon. (Oct.-Easter) & Dec. 1-Feb. 1. 2 stes 680-750F. 9 rms 480-620F. Half-board 700-850F. TV. Pets allowed. Tennis.

You'll find beautiful rooms (ravishing bathrooms), some of which have private gardens. There are also two lovely suites that were recently completely made over, and lovely grounds and flowers. Relais et Châteaux.

Versailles

see PARIS SUBURBS

Vervins

02140 Vervins - (Aisne)
Paris 175 - St-Quentin 52 - Laon 37 - Reims 71

14 La Tour du Roy

45, rue du Général-Leclerc - 23.98.00.11

Mme. Desvignes. Open until 9 p.m. Closed Jan. 15-Feb. 15. Pets allowed. Parking. Cards: V, AE, DC, MC.

The taste for baronial splendors persists today, four centuries after Henri IV and Philippe II met right at this very spot (though at the time they did without the double bathtub in the "royal" duplex). This baronial style has continued almost as much in the decor of this old and noble house as in certain dishes on the menu, such as lobster mousseline with escargots "caviar" or the foie gras soufflé with essence of truffles. For our part, we prefer it when Anne Desvignes draws directly from the regional repertoire she knows so well (Picardie) to produce such dishes as a velouté of Maroilles cheese, young rabbit en gelée and delicious locally inspired pastry. The wonderful wines are purchased by the impassioned owner of the house.

A la carte: 350F. Menus: 140F, 220F, 300F.

La Tour du Roy

(See restaurant above)

Closed Jan. 15-Feb. 15. 1 ste 350F. 15 rms 120-400F. Half-board 325-650F. TV.

Some of these good renovated rooms command a view of the superb countryside and the roofs of the old town. The justly renowned breakfast includes farmhouse butter and homemade preserves. Some worthwhile weekend deals are available.

Le Vésinet

see PARIS SUBURBS

Vétheuil

95510 Vétheuil - (Val-d'Oise)
Paris 70 (Pte de St-Cloud) - Pontoise 40

13 Auberge Saint-Christophe

1, Grande-Rue - 34.78.11.50

M. Boizette. Open until 9:15 p.m. Closed Wed., Feb. school vacation & Aug. 16-Sept. 6. Pets allowed. Cards: V, AE, DC.

Just a stone's throw from the big church Monet painted, and on the way to the Monet museum in Giverny, Michel Boizette's restaurant keeps decidedly pleasant company. One dines here under the vaulted ceiling of a pretty room; even the food is trying hard to leave behind its once insipid guise and become more attractive. The à la carte menu may force your pocketbook to do something it had not intended, but both of the fixed-price menus are remarkable. Picture this meal: warm salad of fish and crustaceans, filet of beef with three peppers, green salad, cheese and a bavarois with raspberry coulis. Good little wines are available from 35 francs.

A la carte: 230F. Menus: 149F, 179F.

Veules-les-Roses

76980 Veules-les-Roses - (Seine-Maritime)
Paris 200 - Dieppe 24 - Rouen 57 - St-Valéry-en-Caux 8

15 Les Galets

3, rue Victor-Hugo - 35.97.61.33

M. Plaisance. Open until 9 p.m. Closed Tues. dinner, Wed. & Feb. Pets allowed. Parking. Cards: V.

This is the country of the pebbled strand (and not many roses) and chalk cliffs above a rolling sea, with an unflagging breeze to work the lungs. Not exactly a mild environment, mind you, but it is bracing. This is also where the smallest river in France comes to its mouth on the English Channel, and the biggest chef hereabouts rewards the hungry mouths that come to him. Inside, it's modern, comfortable, full of flowers and rich with an air of luxury that is verified by the à la carte prices. The tab, however, corresponds to the elegance of the tables, the high level of service, the increasing hoard in the wine cellar and, of course, to the cooking of Jacques Manière's old crony, Gilbert Plaisance. You look out at the ocean while reading a menu that is a hymn to its bounty, and to masterful execution: scalded lobster with leeks, filet of sole sautéed with shallots and a basil sauce, turbot poached with aromatic herbs. The beautiful pastries are fresh and dainty (for example, crusty layers with red fruit and a coulis of raspberries).

A la carte: 400-500F. Menus: 160F (lunch only), 200F, 310F.

We're always happy to hear about your discoveries and to receive your comments about ours. We want to give your letters the attention they deserve, so when you write to Gault Millau, please state clearly what you liked or disliked. Be concise but convincing, and take the time to argue your point.

Vézelay

89450 Vézelay - (Yonne)
Paris 221 - Clamecy 23 - Avallon 13 - Auxerre 52

Résidence Hôtel Le Pontot

86.33.24.40

Closed Nov. 15-Easter. 3 stes 650-800F. 7 rms 450-600F. Pets allowed. Parking. Cards: V, AE, MC.

The eight rooms of this charming old fortified house in the middle of the village were put together with a great deal of taste (and antique furniture). The terrace provides one of the most stunning views we've seen of the Vézelay countryside. No restaurant.

IN NEARBY **Saint-Père-sous-Vézelay**
(3 km SE on D 957)
89450 Vézelay - (Yonne)

Marc Meneau

86.33.20.45

M. Meneau. Open until 9:30 p.m. Closed Wed. lunch, Tues. & early Jan.-mid-Feb. Air cond. Pets allowed. Telex 800005. Cards: V, AE, MC.

What lucky dogs, those Soviet cosmonauts who will get to eat "à la Meneau" thousands of miles from Earth! With his friend Patrick Baudry, who didn't have fond memories of military "cuisine," Marc Meneau worked for months preparing "four-toque" dishes for space flight. His crème de crevettes, duck filet in aspic and squab with lentils (all canned, tubed or dehydrated, of course) made the Russians' mouths water so much that they'll carry them on board on their next mission.

Happily for us, we don't have to go as far to fly to such heights. Two and a half hours by car from Paris and there we are in front of the hill of Vézelay, our feet safely on the ground in L'Espérance's winter garden, above the well-manicured park crossed with streams where mallards cackle away. Some days there are so many people that Françoise Meneau, aware of the murmurs of clients who failed to make reservations, sets up a few tables in the new salon, where guests are served an apéritif around the piano and, later, liqueurs and cigars. Marc, busy as a bee back in his kitchen, grumbles a bit at the unannounced visitors but always rises to the occasion. Never is there a longer-than-reasonable wait for the next course, and Françoise, who scurries about like a mouse, always finds the time to care for each client as if he were the only one.

The composition of the menu, which is always and everywhere an important factor, is particularly critical here, since Meneau's cuisine, full of nuances and subtleties, requires a perfect harmony of flavors, dishes and wines. And in the domain of wines, Françoise Meneau (née Plaisir, or pleasure) is a virtuoso.

But her husband hardly leaves her time to breathe. No sooner has he finished creating one new dish than he's started on the next. In the past he has amazed us with oysters in aspic, a dish that everyone now copies, with cromequis (crunchy dumplings that explode in your mouth, flowing with a liquid foie gras), with roe beignets and with an epigramme of milk-fed lamb, where the breaded skin, sauced collar and grilled chops made for an admirable "ménage à trois." At our most recent meal he surprised us again with a red snapper dish in which he blends in the liver with red-beet juice (a memorable meeting), a skate in a mustard sauce, capers and ground hazelnuts, a wild salmon in tarragon sauce accompanied by sea urchins stuffed with a lobster cream, and fabulously simple sweetbreads dotted with lard and cooked on an open grill with the best petit pois you could possibly imagine. (For ages now, Meneau has coveted this open grill. Now he can roast an admirably thick, larded calves' liver, basting it in its juices enlivened with a touch of Xérès—sherry vinegar.) We had lobster whose flavor was without equal, and leg of baby lamb that was nothing less than a work of art, with its crackling skin, delicacy and rich aromas permeating its clear juices.

Still, we keep asking ourselves if one of these days this artist won't botch a dish or two. In fact, his utter perfection was starting to bother us, and then bam! morels stuffed with fowl, completely mushy, showed up to reassure us. Thanks be to God, Meneau is not infallible. Neither were Renoir, Mozart and Shakespeare. But rather than rant and rave as some people do when a chef of this stature slips up, shouldn't we thank him for all the moments of true happiness he has brought us? Isn't it a bit unreasonable to follow the example of one of our readers—who was otherwise thrilled with her meal—and split hairs over the fact that Meneau served alongside his desserts (a delicious pain perdu, a browned pear with anise ice cream, a cake of apple confit à l'orange) "too many sweets" that, according to her, "dispelled her desire." Or another reader, who, having found the morning coffee too bitter (we won't dispute him on this point), decided to knock L'Espérance off his list entirely!

Well, that's what happens when you get too spoiled from living in a country populated with the likes of Meneau. But since you, most fortunately, have nothing in common with these petty complainers, you can go to this bright Burgundy countryside inn to seek the just rewards of your "gourmandise."

A la carte: 500-800F. Menus: 280F (weekday lunch only), 520F.

L'Espérance

(See restaurant above)

Closed early Jan.-mid-Feb. 3 stes 1,050-1,950F. 18 rms 580-1,000F. TV. Pets allowed.

On the upper floors of this staunch bourgeois home covered with ivy are charming little country rooms done in fresh colors. Three hundred yards away are more rooms in a pretty, old restored mill. Most notable is a marvelous suite in the mill with an interior staircase. Breakfast is delicious. Relais et Châteaux.

This symbol stands for "Les Lauriers du Terroir," an award given to chefs who prepare noteworthy traditional or regional recipes.

Vialas

48220 Le Pont-de-Montvert - (Lozère)
Paris 650 - Mende 77 - Florac 40 - Génolhac 9

Le Chantoiseau

66.41.00.02

M. Pagès. Open until 10:30 p.m. Closed Tues. dinner, Wed. & Nov. 20-March 20. No pets. Hotel: 15 rms 220-320F; half-board 250- 280F. Parking. Cards: AE, DC, MC.

The beautiful, almost otherworldly, landscape of the Cevennes mountains, rough and invigorating, spreads out around this old stagecoach stop that looks out on Mount Lozère. The fieldstone interior is plain, but warm and inviting. And Patrick Pagès's cooking, ever better, whistles a lovely regional tune. It's full of the joy of tradition as embodied in his seasoned mushrooms, half-cooked foie gras, chicken terrine en gelée with Maury wine, magnificent tripe gratin, herbed and roasted leg of lamb and delicious desserts (note the exquisite thyme-and-honey bavarois). The wines are exceptional, and Pagès is eloquent on their behalf.

A la carte: 300F. Menus: 95F, 165F, 220F, 290F, 360F.

Vichy

03200 Vichy - (Allier)
Paris 348 - Clermont-Ferrand 59 - Lyon 160 - Roanne 74

Aletti Thermal Palace

3, pl. Joseph-Aletti - 70.31.78.77

Closed end Sept-early May. 3 stes 505-570F. 54 rms 325-495F. Cards: V, DC, MC.

A large, pleasant hotel with a wonderfully calming view of the grounds from both the wide-angle bar and the solarium/terrace. No restaurant.

Pavillon Sévigné

10-12, pl. Sévigné - 70.32.16.22

M. Thenard. Open daily until 10 p.m. Garden dining. Pets allowed. Parking. Telex 990393. Cards: V, AE, DC, MC.

Three managers and three chefs in three years have been through the heralded Pavillon, with its luxurious decor, rich history (from Madame de Sévigné to Marshall Pétain) and view across a green park. Even though the place has been put up for sale, the professionalism of the dining room staff is noteworthy, and the new chef, Jean-Francois Delanné, is quite good. Formerly with some of the better Relais et Châteaux restaurants, Delanné turns out quality food: a terrine of fresh foie gras (delicious but poorly presented), asparagus in puff pastry (slightly overweight but accompanied by a perfect hollandaise), delightful lobster mousse and a delicious apple tart.

A la carte: 300F and up. Menus: 160F (lunch only), 200F (weekends and holidays only), 250F (dinner only), 180F.

Pavillon Sévigné

(See restaurant above)

Open year-round. 60 rms. TV. Pets allowed.

This charming hotel contains magnificent salons, some superb and tasteful rooms and others that at least aspire to be.

Régina

4, ave. Thermale - 70.98.20.95

Closed Oct. 1-May 2. 90 rms 190-430F. Half-board 260-530F. Pets allowed. Cards: V.

A lovely luxury spa, this place is meticulously maintained in its state of obsolescent charm, but with superb modern facilities and great comfort. Restaurant.

Le Violon d'Ingres

Rue du Casino - 70.98.97.70

M. Muller. Open until 9:30 p.m. Closed Sun. dinner. Air cond. Terrace dining. Pets allowed. Parking. Cards: V, AE, DC, MC.

Two enormous rococo chandeliers high above this big dining room (in the heart of the casino) light up the green carpet, the blue foliage on the beige wallpaper and the damask table linens—not exactly a cozy spot, but it's comfortable and amusing. And the lapses by the friendly but lax young service staff will allow you plenty of time to take it all in. Jacques Muller, a cook who spends a little too much time in the dining room, is responsible for some uneven, perplexing dishes: delicious foie gras tricked up in an unconvincing mishmash of apples and raspberries, nice salmon with a lettuce cream sauce clad in an embarrassing puff pastry, perfect little langoustine pastries and desserts of likewise jagged quality (watery apricot sorbet, wonderful chocolate cake).

Menus: 150F, 225F, 290F.

Vienne

38200 Vienne - (Isère)
Paris 488 - Grenoble 86 - Lyon 31 - Valence 70

La Pyramide

Blvd. Fernand-Point - 74.53.01.96

M. Berrier. Open until 9:30 p.m. Air cond. Terrace dining. No pets. Hotel: 30 rms 500F. Garage parking. Cards: V, AE, DC.

By the time you read this report, this landmark of French cuisine, home of the late, great Fernand Point, should be reopening under new management. Point's widow ran it as a kind of shrine to the memory of the Master, but with her death the restaurant has passed into the hands of Parisian investors. The plans called for a tiny four-star hotel to be constructed in the garden, as well as for the refurbishment of the restaurant. The figureheads among the staff will likely remain, but there's lots of new blood. Of course, the menu's immortal classics will remain in hallowed place: pike quenelles, sole with morels, turbot in Champagne and fatted fowl in a bladder.

A la carte: 700F. Menus: 300F, 480F, 600F.

Prices in red draw attention to restaurants that offer a particularly good value.

IN NEARBY **Chonas-l'Amballan**
(9 km S on N7)
38121 Reventin-Vaugris - (Isère)

13 Le Marais Saint-Jean

74.58.83.28
M. Heugas. Open until 8:45 p.m. Closed Tues. dinner, Wed., Jan. 31-March 4 & Nov. 1-10. Terrace dining. Pets allowed. Parking. Cards: V, AE, DC, MC.

After several years' effort, Suzanne and Christian Heugas have finished their conversion of this lovely old farm hidden among the greenery. The pretty dining room is gracious and countrified beneath its beams, and in the courtyard there are several tables under parasols. All this, along with the well-cared-for grounds and especially the increased confidence of Christian Heugas in the kitchen, makes for a tremendously comfortable country inn. Heugas's cooking is classically founded, lightened and based on seasonal possibilities, resulting in such dishes as an artichoke salad with smoked salmon and sorrel sauce on the side, stuffed guinea-fowl with fresh onions, and nice layered pastries. Great selection of the better Côtes-du-Rhône.

A la carte: 250-300F. Menus: 130F, 220F, 300F.

Le Marais Saint-Jean

(See restaurant above)
Closed Tues., Wed., Jan. 31-March 4 & Nov. 1-10. 10 rms 450F. Pets allowed.

This well-restored old farm, with its pretty, unpretentious, quiet and comfortable rooms, is located on the vacation route.

La Vigerie

see Angoulême

Villefranche-sur-Mer

06230 Villefranche-sur-Mer - (Alpes-Maritimes)
Paris 935 - Monte-Carlo 15 - Nice 6 - Cannes 39

11/20 Carpaccio

Promenade des Marinires - 93.01.72.97
M. Garney. Open until 11 p.m. Closed Tues. Terrace dining. Pets allowed. Cards: V, AE.

The location is stunning: a sun-drenched terrace just steps from the sea but well removed from the bustling port. The food is eclectic (pizza, lobster feuilleté, duck breast with foie gras). Stiff prices, smiling service.

A la carte: 250-300F.

12/20 Le Saint-Pierre

1, quai Courbet - 93.76.76.93
M. Galbois. Open until 10 p.m. Closed Nov. 20-Dec. 19. Air cond. Terrace dining. No pets. Garage parking. Telex 470281. Cards: V, AE, DC, MC.

This is one of the most alluring spots around for a vacation lunch or dinner, thanks to its location right on the waterfront, with a glassed-in terrace overlooking the boats and the ocean. Of course, this lovely setting takes its toll on the bill, but at least the service is charming, and the food is fresh and dependable: escargots and cèpes in a light puff pastry, langoustines with saffron and roasted filet of lamb with zucchini.

A la carte: 350F. Menus: 155F, 215F, 325F.

Welcome

(See restaurant above)
Closed Nov. 20-Dec. 19. 32 rms 270-700F. Half-board 310-530F oblig. in seas: TV in 5 rms. Air cond. Pets allowed.

This establishment was recently renovated with care from top to bottom. The lovely air-conditioned and comfortable rooms face the harbor. Excellent homemade croissants are served at breakfast.

Villefranche-sur-Saône

69400 Villefranche-sur-Saône - (Rhône)
Paris 436 - Lyon 31 - Mâcon 41 - Bourg-en-Bresse 51

Château de Chervinges

Chervinges, 3 km W - 74.65.29.76
Closed Jan. 6 stes 1,000-1,800F. 11 rms 600-850F. TV in 7 rms. Heated pool. Tennis. Parking. Telex 380772. Cards: V, AE, DC.

In the middle of the Beaujolais vineyards, this luxurious establishment occupies its own gardens and holds beautifully decorated suites composed of huge rooms. Restaurant.

IN NEARBY **Fareins**
(5 km NE)
01480 Jassans - (Ain)

15 Fouillet

Jassans-Riottier - 74.67.91.94
M. Fouillet. Open until 9:30 p.m. Closed Mon. dinner, Tues. & Jan. 4-30. Air cond. Terrace dining. Parking. Cards: V, AE, DC.

Thoroughly modern cooking in a boldly original style is plied by Jean Fouillet in his new pink restaurant. He has been responsible for captivating (an easy task, if truth be told) many an overeager restaurant critic. This, of course, hasn't hurt business any, and for that we are glad, since we're quite fond of his daring salmon sausages with caviar and black tea, baked turbot with ginger and Château-Chalon wine, rillettes of Bresse chicken, and frozen anise parfait. And even if the food were not so delightful, to be so kindly served by such charming hosts in this plush little bourgeois house with its comfortable feminine decor (enlivened by a brushed-steel fresco by neighbor Mick Micheyl) would be more than enough for a pleasant evening. A lovely and intelligent wine list has been put together by a finalist for Best French Sommelier, the woman of the house, Dalia Fouillet. Come summer, you can

Some establishments change their hours and annual closings without warning. It is always wise to call ahead.

dine on a pleasant terrace amid the flowers.

A la carte: 300F. Menus: 108F (weekdays only), 145F, 180F, 218F, 270F, 328F.

Villefranque

see Bayonne

Villeneuve-de-Marsan

40190 Villeneuve-de-Marsan - (Landes)
Paris 690 - Eauze 35 - Mont-de-Marsan 17

Francis Darroze

Grand-Rue - 58.45.20.07

M. Darroze. Open until 9:30 p.m. Closed Mon. (off-seas., except holidays) & Jan. 2-31. Terrace dining. Pets allowed. Parking. Telex 560164. Cards: V, AE, DC.

Up there behind the pearly gates, Papa Darroze, the late "Caesar of the southwest," is undoubtedly throwing one of his legendary tantrums. For one who could make such a commotion over moving a piece of furniture, the complete revamping of the kitchen, dining room, rest rooms, reception area and guest rooms must be traumatic. Francis Darroze, in addition to being the innkeeper here, is a positive Sherlock Holmes when it comes to finding unfindable Armagnacs, and now he's also in search of a tourist trade for his southwestern-French (and now charming) inn, which boasts handsome grounds and poolside dining.

When the tourists leave, you can look forward to a nice nap after eating your fill of foie gras, salmis of ringdove, young pigeons with cream of meadow mushrooms, all kinds of game (except the recently protected woodcock and bunting) and all the traditional and modern tasty dishes prepared by Jean-Yves Lasserre, who was trained in the best restaurants of the southwest. As for the wine list, well, it isn't a wine list so much as a directory. From little 50-franc Madirans to the 1928 Château Yquem (the noblest Sauternes), it is an astounding travel guide to every vineyard from Bordeaux to the Pyrénées. And that's not to mention the agony of choice it presents in the Armagnac section, where there are so many so good. We're happy to report that at last, after some difficult years, Darroze, a flower in the heart of the southwest, is in the process of reblooming.

A la carte: 350-500F. Menus: 130F, 180F, 230F, 280F.

Francis Darroze

(See restaurant above)

Closed Mon. (off-seas., except holidays) & Jan. 2-31. 3 stes 600-680F. 27 rms 280-450F. Half-board 550-600F. TV. Pets allowed. Heated pool.

All these rooms and suites are new and strikingly comfortable. One almost forgets that one is in a village, given the lovely grounds, pool and nearby golf course (ask about the golf package deal). Darroze is a new member of Relais et Châteaux.

L'Europe

Pl. de la Boiterie - 58.45.20.08

M. Garrapit. Open daily until 9:30 p.m. Pets allowed. Hotel: 15 rms 100-250F; half-board 210-250F oblig. in seas. Pool. Parking. Cards: V, AE, DC, MC.

"Fantastic," wrote one reader. "Even our little poodle was welcomed and spoiled with treats." Despite grave health problems that have taken Robert Garrapit out of the kitchen, his house clearly remains the house of Gascony's gods. That is to say, the house of kindliness, liveliness and abundance. But don't get the idea that the food is to be taken lightly—this is hearty regional fare of the best preparation. But for all its robustness and traditional vigor, the food is creative, in its own way and in its own genre: salad of cèpes and smoked goose, spicy salad of lentils, bacon and preserved gizzards (a little too salty), a tremendous cassoulet "just for friends" and perfectly delicious desserts, like the baba à l'armagnac and the cream of almonds. The fixed-price menus are excellent, and Maithé Garrapit offers a spirited welcome to her two dining rooms (Louis XVI and modern rustic), both of which are chic and well maintained.

A la carte: 230-250F. Menus: 80F, 180F, 230F.

Villeneuve-lès-Avignon

see Avignon

Villeroy

see Sens

Villers-Cotterêts

02600 Villers-Cotterêts - (Aisne)
Paris 75 - Soissons 23 - Château-Thierry 48

Le Retz

Vertes-Feuilles (11 km E on N 2, toward Soissons) - 23.96.01.42

Mme. Lemoine. Open until 9:30 p.m. Closed Mon. dinner & Tues. Garden dining. Pets allowed. Parking. Cards: V.

The owner of this good-size, turn-of-the-century house on its own grounds is elegant though perhaps a little too preoccupied to adequately welcome her customers. The light and pretty 1930s-style decor deserves more graciousness, as does the food that has been served since the recent arrival of a new young chef, Eric Germain, whose cooking is modern yet nonconforming, ample and deliberately unpretentious. Le Retz is unarguably a discovery to be made, especially on a fine day, when tables are set outside facing the beautiful trees and lawns. You'll have a chance to sample the lobster salad, the pieds et paquets (sheep's feet and bundled tripe) with pig's-head ravioli, the filet of beef with a superb caper sauce and the delightful nougat glazed with maple syrup.

A la carte: 280F. Menu: 140F.

Prices in red draw attention to restaurants that offer a particularly good value.

Villers-le-Lac

25130 Villers-le-Lac - (Doubs)
Paris 459 - Besançon 72 - Salin-les-Bains 79 - Morteau 6

Hôtel de France

13

8, pl. M.-Cupillard - 81.68.02.46

M. Droz. Open until 9 p.m. Closed Sun. dinner, Mon. & Nov. 14-Jan. 15. Pets allowed. Parking. Cards: V, AE, DC, MC.

Switzerland, so nearby, could easily envy the watch museum on the second floor of this big village house. The owner of the house is also the chef, though his son throws in his two cents regarding the regional but not heavy repertoire: grilled local sausage (Morteau) with a gin sauce, apples and shallots; artichoke hearts with chopped morel mushrooms; and prime rib done in a marrow sauce. Droz's cooking is neither boring nor ponderous nor petty. And you can accompany it with some lovely Jura wines and enjoy it in a charming family atmosphere.

A la carte: 230-250F. Menus: 120F, 160F, 210F, 280F.

Vinay

see Epernay

Vire

14500 Vire - (Calvados)
Paris 272 - Caen 59 - Fougères 67 - Bayeux 59 - St-Lô 39

Manoir de la Pommeraie

13

2 km SE (rte. de Paris), Roullours
31.68.07.71

M. Lesage. Open daily until 9:30 p.m. Garden dining. Pets allowed. Parking. Cards: V, AE, DC.

The beautiful trees surrounding this elegant country mansion are, like the house itself, a good 100 years old. Georges Lesage, a talented professional chef from the region (lower Normandy), has been running the kitchen here for a couple of years. He and his wife have completely renovated the place, setting up two lovely dining rooms that are light and pleasant in tones of white, gray and blue. The service is adept and efficient, and Lesage turns out fairly traditional yet personal fare that is skillfully prepared, with clear flavors and an attention to detail: a generous warm langoustine salad with raspberry vinegar, turbot cooked with lettuce (less successful), perfect sweetbreads served with lovely vegetables and golden fried apples, and an excellent warm lemon tart that is nicely balanced between tart and sweet. The prices are going up, and the more reasonable fixed-price menus offer little choice.

A la carte: 280-330F. Menus: 102F, 145F, 265F.

Hotel prices are per room, not per person. The exceptions are half-board (price per person, including two meals a day) and full board (price per person, including three meals a day).

Vittel

88800 Vittel - (Vosges)
Paris 334 - Epinal 43 - Nancy 70 - Belfort 129

L'Aubergade

265, ave. des Tilleuls - 29.08.04.39

M. Meresse. Open until 9:30 p.m. Closed Sun. dinner (off-seas.), Mon. & Jan. Air cond. Pets allowed. Parking. Cards: V, AE.

This luxurious place facing the grounds of the Vittel natural springs is clearly the most elegant restaurant/hotel around for those taking the cure. The pink-violet and light-cream neoclassical decor can become tedious despite its refinement. As for the good food that we had become accustomed to here—its survival depends on the new chef, whose work remains to be tasted.

A la carte: 300-350F. Menus: 180F, 240F, 285F.

L'Aubergade

(See restaurant above)

Open year-round. 9 rms 250-390F. Half-board 471-581F. TV. Air cond. Pets allowed.

The rooms here are fairly big, classically appointed and well equipped, though they're not quite soundproof, and more care could be taken with the breakfast.

Vonnas

01540 Vonnas - (Ain)
Paris 419 - Mâcon 19 - Lyon 66 - Villefranche 39

Georges Blanc

19.5

(La Mère Blanc)
74.50.00.01

M. Blanc. Open until 9:30 p.m. Closed Thurs. (except dinner June 15-Sept. 15), Wed. & Jan. 2-Feb. 10. Air cond. Pets allowed. Parking. Telex 380776. Cards: V, AE, DC.

Soon it will no longer be Blanc in the town of Vonnas, but the town of Blanc-sur-Vonnas!

Georges's father, when he was mayor of this meager, rather thankless village plopped between Bresse and Dombe, made his first official act that of covering the town with flowers. For that alone he deserves a medal. Then Georges transformed the family homestead, famous for its poulet à la crème, into a superb inn in the wood-and-brick style typical of the region. In a shed a hundred yards from the main building, he set up his mail-order wine business. On the other side of the street, he opened a nice boutique where he sells his pastries, preserves, sausages, wines and elegant tableware. And most recently, just next door, he financed the construction of a small public square filled with flowers and a huge fountain. Now he plans to attack a block of old houses interspersed with gardens, out of which he'll make a hotel, with lower prices but no less charm or comfort than at his other hotel, La Mère Blanc. On top of all that, if you happen to have a helicopter at your disposal, you can park it a few feet from the pool. Blanc likes to show off his village from every angle.

You won't hear any complaints about his improvements. Quite the contrary, for without Georges Blanc, who'd have ever heard of Vonnas? Today, people come from every corner of the globe: Television viewers in Tokyo, New York and Munich have seen on their screens the bridge covered with flowers, the duckweed floating on the stream, the sparkling kitchens and the old Bresse furnishings in the dining room. And not a meal goes by without some Japanese, American or French visitor asking him to autograph one of his books.

There you have it. The "petit Blanc"—as he was dubbed by Paul Bocuse, who also said, "He's the best chef I know"—has become a star. But if all stars were as modest and reasonable, the tabloid *France-Dimanche* would have to close up shop. He has never lost touch with the people of his region. On the weekend, you'll see entire families piling in, with mom, dad and all the kids in their Sunday best, who've come to celebrate a birthday or some other happy occasion. To the locals, Blanc is one of them, and his home is their home. It's no accident that the Bresse growers asked Blanc, a chef, to become president of their appellation contrôlée (registered trademark).

This complicity owes a lot to the warm, good-natured and not at all touristy atmosphere of the establishment. As friendly as it is, every detail has been considered, and the entire place moves like clockwork. If you haven't visited for a while, you'll find some changes. The reception area was enlarged and made more beautiful, an enclosed garage (free) was constructed, a terrace was fixed up above the Veyle, and apéritifs and coffee are served in a salon with a glass roof.

And were there also changes in the kitchen? It's been so good for so many years that it's hard to see the need for improvements. But, yes, one was made. Blanc, undoubtedly tired of not seeing himself classed in the "imaginative" crowd, started playing the game. If you spend three days in a row here, you will be amazed by the creative spirit he's been revealing for some time now, a spirit that results in a delicious grecque of baby vegetables with caviar; warm red snapper vinaigrette with fresh goat-cheese quenelles; coquilles St-Jacques prepared with cèpes, curry and soy sauce; lobster and celery with caviar aspic, whole salmon in Pinot Rouge; squab with a confit of turnips, carrots and pearl onions, served with white grapes; and lamb marinated in tapenade (the Provençal sun shines through in more and more of his dishes). Blanc is even becoming slightly crazy about the vegetables he hunts out in the surrounding countryside, so much so that he recently devoted an entire book to vegetables, *La Nature dans l'Assiette* (published by Robert Laffont), with photographs by Christophe Baker. And nothing gives Blanc greater pleasure, if requested in advance, than preparing a quasi-vegetarian meal or even a meal made up entirely of tomatoes. This could include a tomato disguised as a ladybug with olives, eggs mimosa and red snapper, a fantastic crème de tomates with crayfish, a no-less-exquisite tomato stuffed with escargots, mushrooms, watercress and parsley, a tomato confit like we've never tasted before, with the most tender morsels of Bresse chicken and mustard seeds, and, finally, a fabulous tomato with Tahitian vanilla that has an astoundingly rich and peppery taste. But the list is far from complete. From the "poor man's" asparagus (leeks with beluga caviar!) to the spring herb cake with fava beans and pois gourmands, to the green flageolets with a trout-and-chive soufflé, garden cooking has found an unfailing defender in Georges Blanc.

And we never thought it would ever come to pass when we wrote that if Blanc began to sell his pastries, desserts, sorbets and petits fours in a shop, they would become the rage. Well, he's selling them in the shop across the street, and people come from miles around to stock up.

When we add that the wise and kind Marcel Perinet hasn't lost his touch or his nose (one of the finest in France for digging out a Burgundy utterly above suspicion or a mouth-watering Montagnieu), that this talented and friendly British sommelier hasn't left to open a wine bar in New York, and that you will surely find Jacqueline Blanc, Georges' wife, just as busy and adorable as ever, we will feel that we've completed our mission. Now you know everything about the Grande Maison de Blanc.

A la carte: 500-700F. Menus: 330F, 490F.

La Mère Blanc

(See restaurant above)

Closed Jan. 2-Feb. 10. 1 ste 1,850F. 29 rms 420-1,350F. TV. Air cond. Pets allowed. Heated pool. Tennis. Golf.

A putting green has been set up in the two-and-a-half-acre park that borders the terrace of the "Prestige" suite, the most luxurious suite in this most charming hotel. Soon to be added is an annex with extremely comfortable but less costly rooms. Breakfast is delicious. Two "Georges Blanc" boutiques across the street sell fresh gourmet foods, wines, alcohol and household goods. Relais et Châteaux.

La Wantzenau

see Strasbourg

Wimille

see Boulogne-sur-Mer

FOOD TERMS

Menu Savvy

The following is a list of culinary terms which often appear on French restaurant menus.

A

Aiguillette: long, thin slice (of duck breast, for example); also, top part of beef rump.

Aïoli or aïlloli: garlicky mayonnaise; also, in Provence, an entire dish composed of cod, snails and vegetables served with aïoli.

Américaine or armoricaine: sauce of white wine, Cognac, tomatoes and butter.

Andouille: smoked tripe sausage, usually served cold.

Andouillette: chitterling sausage, smaller than andouille, and usually served hot.

Anglaise (à l'): food dipped in beaten eggs and coated with breadcrumbs; also, boiled meats or vegetables.

Anguille au vert: eels cooked with white wine and a variety of green (vert) herbs, served hot or cold.

Argenteuil: refers to any dish which includes asparagus.

Aurore: béchamel sauce flavored with tomato (named by Brillat-Savarin after his mother).

B

Baba: sponge cake with raisins, soaked in rum or Kirsch.

Ballottine: boned, stuffed and rolled poultry.

Bavarois: creamy dessert made of egg yolks and whipped cream, flavored with fruit or chocolate.

Béarnaise: sauce made of shallots, tarragon, vinegar and egg yolks, thickened with butter.

Béchamel: sauce made of flour, butter and milk.

Bercy: sauce made with fish stock, shallots, white wine and butter.

Beurre blanc: sauce of wine and vinegar boiled down with minced shallots, then thickened with butter.

Beurre d'escargots: butter seasoned with shallots, garlic and parsley.

Beurre maître d'hôtel: melted butter with parsley and lemon.

Beurre marchand de vin: butter flavored with shallots and red wine.

Beurre de Montpellier: butter seasoned with olive oil, herbs, garlic and anchovies.

Beurre noir: browned butter with vinegar and capers.

Beurre noisette: lightly browned butter.

Bigarade: bitter orange used in sauces and marmalade.

Billy By: creamy mussel soup—a specialty of Maxim's.

Bisque (crayfish, lobster, etc.): rich, velvety soup, usually made with crustaceans, flavored with white wine and Cognac.

Blinis: small, thick crêpes made with eggs, milk and yeast.

Boeuf au gros sel: boiled beef, served with simmered vegetables and coarse salt.

Bohémienne: a garnish usually composed of rice, tomatoes and fried onion slices.

Bombe glacée: molded ice-cream dessert.

Bordelaise: fairly thin brown sauce of shallots, red wine and tarragon.

Borscht: thick Eastern European soup of beets and boiled beef, often garnished with a dollop of sour cream.

Boudin noir: blood sausage.

Bouquetière: garnish composed of artichoke bottoms, carrots, turnips, green beans, peas and cauliflower florets.

Bourdaloue: poached pear coated with vanilla frangipane cream and crushed macaroons; tart Bourdaloue is a pear tart with pastry cream.

Brandade de morue: puréed salt cod thickened with oil and milk; usually heavily seasoned with garlic.

C

Caille (or faisan or perdreau) Souvaroff or Souvarov: quail (or pheasant or young partridge) baked in a sealed casserole with truffles and foie gras.

Canard à la presse: duck that has been suffocated, not bled, briefly roasted for a fairly short period. The thighs are served grilled; the breast is cut into aiguillettes (slivers); the carcass is pressed to express juice and blood, to which butter and the pounded duck's liver are added and (optionally) red wine and Cognac.

Canard à la rouennaise: duck, identical to canard à la presse, but the carcass is stuffed with liver, onions and bacon.

Carottes vichy: sliced carrots boiled in Vichy water and served with butter and parsley.

Carpe à la juive: braised carp, marinated and served in aspic.

Charcutière: sauce of onions, white wine, beef stock and gherkins.

Charlotte: dessert of flavored creams and/or fruit molded in a cylindrical dish lined with

ladyfingers (if served cold) or strips of buttered bread (if served hot).
Chasseur: brown sauce made with shallots, white wine and mushrooms.
Chèvre (fromage de): goat cheese.
Chevreuil: venison; also, a sauce of vegetable stock, red wine and sometimes currant jelly.
Choron: béarnaise sauce with tomato.
Chou-fleur (à la polonaise): cauliflower (poached, breaded and baked).
Civet de lièvre: hare stewed in red wine, withlardoons and onions; the sauce is thickened with the animal's blood.
Clafoutis: cherries baked in batter.
Clamart: a garnish of green peas.
Colin (à la grenobloise): hake (with butter, capers and lemon).
Condé (à la): poached fruit on rice pudding, covered with fruit syrup.
Confit: pork, goose, duck, turkey or other meat cooked and sealed in its own fat.
Coquilles St-Jacques: sea scallops.
Côtelettes de mouton champvallon: mutton chops baked between layers of potatoes and sautéed onions.
Coulibiac de saumon: hot pâté of salmon with rice, mushrooms, hard-boiled eggs and onions baked in pastry.
Coulis: thick sauce or purée, often of vegetables or fruit.
Court bouillon: a somewhat acidic stock in which fish, meat and poultry are cooked.
Crécy: a garnish of carrots.
Crème chantilly: sweetened whipped cream.
Crêpe Suzette: crêpe stuffed with sweetened butter mixture, Curaçao, tangerine juice and peel.
Croquant: a crunchy petit four.
Croque-monsieur: grilled ham and cheese sandwich.
Croustade: puff-pastry case for creamy dishes; also, a fruit pastry.
Croûte: pastry crust.
Crudité: raw vegetable.
Cultivateur (potage): vegetable soup with bread and (optionally) cubes of bacon.

D

Daube: beef braised in red wine.
Dieppoise (à la): fish cooked in white wine, with cream, shrimp, mussels and mushrooms.
Diplomate: pudding of custard, candied cherries and rum- or Kirsch-soaked ladyfingers, served with vanilla custard sauce.

E

Emincé: sliced; also, thinly sliced meat covered with a sauce and reheated.
Entrecôte mirabeau: grilled rib steak, topped with anchovy filets and served with anchovy butter; garnished with pitted olives.
Escalope: slice of meat or fish, flattened slightly and sautéed.
Escalope (de veau) milanaise: breaded, sautéed veal scallop garnished with pasta in tomato sauce.
Escalope (de veau) viennoise: breaded, sautéed veal scallop garnished with lemon.
Escargots à la bourguignonne: snails with herbed garlic butter.
Escargots à la chablisienne: snails, as above, but with white wine.

F

Financière: Madeira sauce enhanced with truffle juice.
Florentine: with spinach.
Foie (gras): liver (of a specially fattened goose or duck).
Foie de veau à l'anglaise: grilled calf's liver, with slices of bacon.
Fondue: in addition to the well-known dishes, where food is cooked in a boiling liquid, the term also refers to vegetables cooked at length in butter and thus reduced to pulp.
Forestière: garnish of sautéed mushrooms and lardons.
Foyot: béarnaise sauce flavored with a meat glaze.
Frangipane: almond pastry cream; used to fill thick crêpes.

G

Galantine: boned poultry or meat, stuffed and pressed into a symmetrical form, cooked in broth and coated with aspic.
Gâteau: cake.
Gelée (en): in aspic (gelatin usually flavored with meat, poultry or fish stock).
Génoise: sponge cake.
Germiny (potage): garnish of sorrel (creamy sorrel soup).
Grand veneur: sauce for game made with stock, white wine, pepper, vinegar, currant jelly and cream.
Granité: lightly sweetened fruit ice.
Gratin dauphinois: sliced potatoes baked in milk, sometimes with cream and/or grated Gruyère.
Gribiche: sauce served with cold fish; mayonnaise with chopped hard-boiled eggs, capers, pickles and various herbs.
Gros sel: coarse salt.

H

Haricots blancs à la bretonne: white beans with onions, tomato, garlic and herbs.
Hollandaise: egg-based sauce thickened with butter and flavored with lemon.
Homard (and langouste) à la parisienne: lobster or langouste cut into scallops and placed in the shell; served cold with mayonnaise.
Homard (and langouste) Newburg: pieces of lobster or langouste with Cognac, Madeira or sherry and cream.
Homard (and langouste) Thermidor: lobster or langouste split in two lengthwise; served gratinéed with wine sauce.

I

Ile flottante: "floating island": caramelized poached meringue served in a "sea" of custard sauce with crushed, grilled almonds. It can also refer to a biscuit (or cookie) soaked in Kirsch and layered with apricot marmalade, covered with crème chantilly and "floating" in vanilla custard.

J

Joinville: sauce for fish, with egg yolk, cream, crayfish purée and (sometimes) small diced truffles.
Julienne: a vegetable soup made from a clear consommé, or any shredded food.

L

Lièvre à la royale: hare stuffed with foie gras and truffles.

Lotte: monkfish or anglerfish; sometimes called "poor man's lobster."

M

Macédoine: diced raw or cooked mixture of fruit or vegetables, served hot or cold.
Madrilène (à la): clear broth (or other dishes) garnished with raw, peeled tomatoes.
Magret: breast of fattened duck, cooked with the skin on; usually grilled.
Maltaise (sauce): blood orange; (hollandaise flavored with juice of a blood orange).
Marcassin à la Saint-Hubert: roasted cutlets of young boar, with a stuffing of boar meat and field mushrooms, wrapped in caul with breadcrumbs.
Médaillon: food, usually meat, fish or foie gras, cut into small, round "medallions."
Merlan (en colère): whiting (fried, with its tail pulled through its mouth.
Meurette: red-wine sauce served with freshwater fish or poached eggs.
Miroton: stew made with cooked meat and onions.
Montmorency (à la): garnished with cherries.
Mornay: béchamel flavored with cheese.
Moules marinière: mussels cooked in the shell with white wine, shallots and parsley.
Moules poulette: mussels on the half shell with sauce poulette (white sauce with lemon and parsley).
Mousseline: hollandaise, lightened with stiffly beaten egg whites.

N

Nage (à la): cooked in a seasoned court bouillon.
Nantua: sauce of crayfish, white wine, butter and cream with a touch of tomato.
Navarin: ragoût of lamb or mutton with small onions, potatoes and (optionally) carrots, turnips and peas (it is then called "à la printanière").
Noisettes: hazelnuts; also, small, round pieces of meat (especially lamb or veal).
Nougat: sweet made with roasted almonds, egg whites and honey.

O

Oeufs à la neige: small mounds of beaten egg whites poached in milk and served with vanilla custard sauce.
Omelette norvégienne: sweet souffléed omelet filled with ice cream ("baked Alaska").

P

Pannequet: rolled crêpe with jam.
Parfait: sweet or savory mousse; layered ice-cream dessert.
Parisienne: garnish of fried potato balls.
Parmentier: with potatoes.
Paupiettes: thin slices of meat stuffed with forcemeat and shaped into rolls.
Pauvre homme: "poor man's" sauce with onions, vinegar, mustard and tomato.
Paysanne: meat or poultry, usually braised, garnished with sliced, lightly cooked carrots and turnips; or a garnish of onions, bacon and potatoes.
Périgueux: truffled brown sauce.
Pigeon en crapaudine: pigeon, flattened slightly and grilled.
Piquante: sauce of shallots, white wine, vinegar, gherkins and herbs.
Pirojki: small croquettes of cheese or minced game, fish or vegetables.
Pochouse: a wine-flavored stew made of freshwater fish (especially eel), in a butter-thickened sauce.
Plombière: vanilla ice cream with, Kirsch, candied fruit and crème chantilly.
Pommes de terre allumettes: fried matchstick potatoes.
Pommes de terre à l'anglaise: boiled or steamed potatoes.
Pommes de terre Anna: flat cake of sliced, layered potatoes, fried in butter.
Pommes de terre boulangère: sliced potatoes baked with onions.
Pommes de terre château: whole, fairly small potatoes sautéed in butter.
Pommes (de terre) darphin: grated potatoes shaped into pancakes.
Pommes de terre dauphine: breaded, fried croquettes of potato purée and chou pastry.
Pommes de terre duchesse: potato puréed with egg yolks, glazed with egg and baked.
Pommes de terre lyonnaise: sliced potatoes sautéed with onions.
Pommes de terre macaire: potato purée mixed with butter, shaped into balls and baked or fried as a flat cake.
Pommes de terre mousseline: potato purée with whipped cream.
Pommes de terre noisette: like pommes château, but smaller—the size of hazelnuts (noisettes).
Pommes de terre pailles: fried julienned potatoes.
Pommes de terre Pont-Neuf: elegant designation for french fries.
Pommes de terre en robe de chambre or robe des champs: potatoes boiled or baked in their skin.
Pommes de terre sarladaise: sliced potatoes cooked in the oven with goose fat and (optionally) truffles.
Portugaise: garnish of peeled tomatoes cooked with garlic and onions.
Poulette: velouté sauce with lemon juice, parsley and (sometimes) mushrooms.
Printanier: garnish of diced carrots or turnips, blanched, with peas and French beans.
Profiteroles: small balls of chou pastry filled with custard, ice cream or whipped cream, covered with chocolate or other sauce.
Provençale (à la): with garlic or tomato and garlic.

R

Ravigote: sauce of white wine, vinegar, onion, lemon juice, parsley, shallot butter and herbs.
Rémoulade: mayonnaise with capers, onions, parsley, gherkins and herbs.
Rillettes: pork, rabbit or goose cooked in its own fat, pounded into a paste and served cold.
Riz créole: boiled rice.
Riz à l'Impératrice: rice pudding flavored with vanilla, custard cream and candied fruit soaked in Kirsch.
Riz pilau or pilaf: chopped onions and rice browned in butter, then cooked.
Robert: sauce of onions, white wine, vinegar and mustard.
Rognons vert pré: kidneys grilled with butter and parsley; garnished with watercress.
Rougets à la niçoise: grilled or fried red mullet with tomatoes, anchovy filets and black olives.

S

Sabayon: fluffy whipped egg yolks, sweetened and flavored with wine or liqueur; served warm.
Sablé: buttery shortbread.
Saint-Germain: purée of split or whole peas with croutons.
Saint-Pierre: John Dory; a white-fleshed Mediterranean fish.
Salade "folle": "crazy" salad; the only nouvelle-cuisine term widespread in culinary usage; a salad most often made of lightly cooked green beans, foie gras and shellfish.
Salade francillon: warm salad of mussels, potatoes marinated in Chablis and truffles, with vinaigrette.
Salade lorette: salad of lamb's lettuce, celery and beets.
Salade russe: salad of mixed diced vegetables, bound with mayonnaise.
Savarin: crown-shaped sponge cake, soaked in flavored syrup and doused with rum or Kirsch.
Santé (potage): (soup) garnished with potatoes and sorrel.
Selle de veau matignon: saddle of veal baked while covered with a thick layer of "matignon" (vegetable fondue), bacon or ham and caul fat.
Selle de veau Orloff: slices of saddle of veal alternating with a purée of onions, mushrooms and truffles.
Soissons: garnish of haricot beans.
Sole cardinal: poached filet of sole with a cream sauce made with crayfish.
Sole Dugléré: sole with a sauce of tomatoes, parsley, onion, shallots, butter and (sometimes) béchamel.
Sole marguery: sole in a white-wine sauce, accompanied by mussels and shrimp.
Sole (or truite) meunière: sole or trout dipped in flour and sautéed in butter with parsley and lemon.
Sorbet: sherbet (dessert ice usually made of fruit); sometimes mixed with frozen Italian meringue.
Soubise: béchamel with onion.
Spoom: sorbet with lots of Italian meringue (stiffly beaten sweetened egg whites).
Steak au poivre: pepper steak; steak covered in crushed peppercorns, browned in a frying pan, flambéed with Cognac; sauce deglazed with cream.
Suprême: chicken velouté sauce with cream.

T

Tartare: cold sauce for meat or fish: mayonnaise with hard-boiled egg yolks, onions and chopped olives.
Tête de veau en tortue: calf's head; see Tortue.
Tomates à la provencale: halved tomatoes baked with a sprinkling of parsley and garlic.
Tortue: sauce made with various herbs, tomato, Madeira; or a consommé of beef, chicken and turtle, with herbs including basil and sage.
Tournedos Henri IV: tournedos accompanied by a béarnaise sauce with reduced stock added.
Tournedos à la monégasque: tournedos sautéed in butter, served with a slice of eggplant and garnished with a fondue of tomatoes and black olives.
Tournedos Rossini: tournedos sautéed in butter, then the pan juices poured over them; garnished with foie gras.
Truffes sous la cendre: truffles wrapped in oiled paper or aluminum foil and cooked in ashes; or wrapped in dough and baked; or wrapped in a thin slice of fresh bacon and oiled paper and cooked in ashes.
Truffes à la serviette: truffles cooked with Madeira or Champagne and presented in a timbale or casserole placed in the middle of a folded napkin.
Truite au bleu: trout boiled live in water with vinegar; the fish turns "blue."

V

Vacherin: ice cream served in a meringue shell; also, creamy, pungent cheese from Switzerland or eastern France.
Vallée d'auge: sauce of Calvados and cream.
Veau marengo: veal sautéed in oil with tomatoes, onions and mushrooms.
Verjus: verjuice; juice of unripened grapes, used in sauces.

Z

Zingara: garnish for veal and fowl made of white wine, mushrooms, tomato sauce and ham.

Regional Foods

We certainly don't claim to have drawn up a complete inventory of all the regional dishes and ingredients in France. Instead, we have attempted to explain briefly in this little lexicon the composition and preparation of France's more commonly seen dishes, charcuterie and cakes, whose names are sometimes mysterious. What, for example, is a badrée, a cambajou, a fiouse? The definitions of the 500 dishes we list below are subject to discussion. One reader will denounce us for a certain spelling, or a chef will criticize a recipe we give. Our inventory is by necessity arbitrary, imperfect and incomplete—although, as it stands, its preparation required the work and devotion of a monk. You'll also notice that, while we have included many little-known dishes, we have, on the other hand, left out some that speak for themselves, such as coq au Riesling (Alsace), bass poached in cider (Normandy) and omelet with truffles (in all the regions known for truffles). Please note that the name of each dish in French is followed by the region or town in which it is found, in parentheses.

A

Accuncciatu (Corsica): a ragoût of horse meat, lamb and mutton with potatoes.

Aïgo bouido or boulido or bullido (Provence, Rouergue, Vivarais): garlic soup with oil served over slices of bread.

Aïgo saou or sau (Provence): sort of bouillabaisse, or fish soup with potatoes; the bouillon is poured over slices of bread.

Aïoli or aïlloli (Provence): aïloli sauce (mayonnaise with garlic) has lent its name to this dish of dried cod, various vegetables, snails and hard-boiled eggs.

Aligot (Auvergne, Rouergue): mashed potatoes combined with garlic and Cantal or fresh Tomme cheese; has a very elastic consistency.

Alose (Gironde): shad, a fish used particularly often in the Bordelais, stuffed with sorrel (the herb has the ability to dissolve the small bones of the fish) and grilled.

Alycot or alycuit, alicuit (Béarn, Languedoc): ragot of fowl giblets and gizzards.

Anchoïade (Provence): purée of anchovy filets combined with garlic and olive oil; accompanies crudités.

Andouille de Guémené (Brittany): andouille (pork sausage) with a characteristic marking of concentric rings.

Andouille de Jargeau (Loiret): sausage (sometimes aromatic) made from the shoulder and brisket of pork.

Andouille de Vire (Calvados): andouille (pork tripe sausage) with irregular marbling.

Andouillette de Cambrai (Nord): small andouille made of veal (caul, rennet and belly).

Andouillette de Troyes (Aube): small andouille made of pork in rather broad and alternating strips.

Anguille à la ploërmelaise (Ploërmel, Morbihan): eel marinated, then cooked suspended over a wood fire.

Anguille aux pruneaux (Brittany, Pays Nantais): pieces of eel sautéed in butter and cooked with white wine and onions; prunes are added at the end.

Anguille au vert (Lille): eel flavored with thirteen herbs.

Anisbrod (Alsace): anise-flavored macaroons.

Artichauts à la brétonne (Brittany): slices of artichoke simmered in oil and butter with diced onions and cider in a shallow frying pan.

Attereau (Burgundy): large meatballs made of pork's liver, kidneys and fat, wrapped in caul and baked.

Attignole (Normandy): small meatballs of ground meat, pork fat, bread and seasonings; baked, then served cold, coated in aspic.

B

Baba (Lorraine): sort of kugelhopf soaked in a rum syrup; said to have been invented by King Stanislas Leczinsky.

Badrée (Berry): marmalade of a mixture of apples and pears.

Baeckeoffe (Alsace): hot terrine made with alternating layers of pieces of beef, mutton and pork, marinated in Alsatian wine with slices of potatoes and onions.

Bardatte (Brittany): cabbage stuffed with hare, cooked in a terrine with white wine and served with steamed chestnuts and roast quail.

Bareuzai (à la, Burgundy): a meat preparation using wine; the word derives from "bas rouge"— referring to the red feet of grape pickers who pressed the grapes with their feet.

Beignets au caillé (Bourbonnais): dessert fritters made with curdled (caillé) milk.

Beignets de fleurs de courge (Provence, Nice): squash blossoms (pistils removed) dipped in batter and deep fried.

Berlingueto (Maillance, Provence): chopped spinach garnished with hard-boiled eggs.

Besugo (Pays Basque): regional name for red mullet.

Beugnons (Berry, Orléanais): small, crown-shape dessert fritters.

Beurre blanc nantais (Nantes, Loire, Anjou): sauce consisting of minced shallots cooked in a reduction of Muscadet and/or vinegar, with butter whisked in until the consistency is perfectly creamy; most often accompanies pike. The sauce often lends its name to the dish itself.

Beursades (Nivernais, Morvan): pieces of pork browned in lard, then baked with thyme and bay leaves in a casserole covered with water. Stored in stoneware pots and eaten hot.

Biche (Vivarais): mutton tripe and sliced potatoes, placed in layers one on top of the other; named for the container used to bake it in.

Bignons (Bourbonnais): small dessert fritters (beignets).

Biguenée (Brittany): slice of ham sandwiched between two layers of crêpes, fried on both sides in butter.

Bireweck (Alsace): sweet, moist bread studded with dried fruit, flavored with Kirsch and spices.

Blanchaille frite (Bordelais): fritter made of small fish.

Boeuf bourguignon (Burgundy): beef ragoût with red wine, onions and lardons.

Boeuf gardiane (Camargue): marinated beef sautéed with bacon, onions, garlic, tomatoes, olives and red wine.

Boles de picoulat (Roussillon): meatballs made of minced beef, pork, garlic and eggs, accompanied by parslied tomatoes.

Bottereaux or Bottreaux (Nantes, Charentes): a type of dessert fritter.

Boudin blanc havrais (Normandy and all of France): sausage of pork fat, milk, eggs, bread, starch and rice flour; often includes truffles, trimmings or leftover fowl.

Boudin de Brest (Brest): sausage made with cream, lardons and onions.

Boudin de Poitou (Poitou): a sausage made with minced spinach, bread, cream, eggs, milk and sugar.

Boudin de Saint-Romain (Seine-Maritime): large sausage made with cream.

Boudin de Strasbourg or alsatien (Alsace): smoked sausage made with onion, pork rind and bread soaked in milk.

Bougnette (Castres, Tarn): a sausage-like stuffing of pork, bread and eggs, eaten hot or cold.

Bouillabaisse (Provence): various fish (including scorpionfish) in a soup of olive oil, tomatoes, garlic and saffron.

Bouilleture or bouilliture (Anjou, Aunis): stewed eel with red wine, onions or shallots, prunes and, (optionally) garlic and egg yolk.

Bouillinade (Roussillon): a sort of bouillabaisse made of pieces of fish (lotte, turbot, John Dory, sea bass) with potatoes, oil, onions and garlic; the bouillon is thickened with egg yolk and oil.

Bouillon de boeuf aux quenelles de moëlle (Alsace): the bouillon from pot-au-feu, with small poached dumplings made of beef marrow mixed with semolina, breadcrumbs and eggs.

Boulaigou (Limousin): a thick crêpe; related to the sanciau (Bourbonnais), grapiau (Niverne) and chanciau (Berry).

Boumiane or bohémienne (Avignon): pieces of eggplant cooked in an earthenware casserole with onions, garlic and tomatoes.

Bouquettes aux pommes de terre (Bourbonnais): grated potatoes mixed with flour and egg whites and fried in small, thin cakes.

Bourdelot (Normandy): apple turnover (with whole apples); related to the douillon (also Normand) and rabotte (Picardie).

Bourride (Provence): a sort of bouillabaisse usually made with large white fish (lotte, turbot). The creamy bouillon is thickened with aïoli; served over slices of bread.

Bourriol (Auvergne): buckwheat pancake cooked in a frying pan, eaten savory or sweet.

Boutifare or boutifaron (Catalogne, Roussillon): boudin with bacon and herbs.

Brandade de morue (Nîmes): salt cod puréed with olive oil, truffles (optional) and milk or cream.

Braou bouffat (Roussillon): soup made with rice and cabbage.

Brassadeaux (Provence): rings of dough that are boiled then baked; reminiscent of craquelins (Brittany).

Bréjaude or bregeaude (Limousin): soup of cabbage, leeks, celeriac, potatoes, bacon, pork rind and bouillon; must be steeped and is often served with rye bread. The name derives from bréjou, the pork rind.

Brési (Jura): smoked, salted and dried beef, sliced very thin, like the viande des Grisons.

Bretzels (Alsace): interlacing rings of dough, dotted with aniseed.

Brioche tressée or tordée (Lorraine): bread in the shape of a braided crown.

Brocciu (Corsica): square-shaped, very mild white sheep's-milk cheese.

Broufado (Provence): layers of thin slices of marinated beef and chopped onions with vinegar, capers and anchovies. This seaman's recipe has a counterpart in Condieu (see Grillades des mariniers de condrieu).

Bugnes (Lyonnais, Burgundy): a type of dessert fritter made of rolled dough and fried in oil.

C

Cabassol (Languedoc): lamb tripe.

Cagouille or luma (Charentes): local name for snail; (cagouillard, the nickname for natives of the Charentes, comes from cagouille).

Caille à la vigneronne (Burgundy): quails with grapes and marc de Bourgogne.

Caillette (Ardèche, Drôme): chopped spinach, chard, onion, parsley, garlic, bread, pork and egg formed into fist-sized balls, baked and served hot or cold.

Caillette varoise (Var): layers of thinly sliced pork liver and a coarse stuffing made of breast and loin of pork, baked in a terrine.

Cambajou (Haute-Garonne): knuckle of salt pork.

Canard au Muscadet (Pays Nantais): roast duck served with a Muscadet sauce with shallots and (optionally) cream.

Canard à la presse (Rouen): duck that is suffocated rather than bled, roasted and cut into aiguillettes. The thighs are served grilled; the carcass is pressed to express the juice and blood, to which butter, the pounded duck's liver and (optionally) red wine and Cognac are added.

Canard à la rouennaise (Rouen): duck identical to canard à la presse, but stuffed with liver, onion and bacon.

Canistro finuchiettu (Corsica): cake with aniseed.

Capouns (Nice): Swiss chard or cabbage leaves stuffed with sausage meat, eggs, rice and grated cheese; formed into balls and baked.

Caqhuse (Picardie): fresh pork braised with onions.

Carbonnade (Flanders): pieces of lean beef, first sautéed then stewed with onions and beer.

Cardons à la moëlle (Lyonnais): cardoons, cut into pieces, boiled, then cooked au gratin with slices of marrow.

Cargolade (Languedoc, Roussillon): snails simmered in wine, or cooked over charcoal, with salt and pepper, flavored with bacon fat.

Carpe à la neuvic (Neuvic, Dordogne): carp stuffed with a mixture of pork, foie gras, truffles, minced shallots, bread and egg yolk, then baked with white wine.

Casse rennais (Rennes): casserole of head of pork or calf, calf's intestinal membrane and trotters cooked in bouillon, then cut in pieces; mixed with pork rind, slices of pâté de campagne, bacon and bouillon with white wine.

Casserons en matelote (Ile de Ré, Charente-Maritime): squid in a sauce of red wine (from the island), garlic, shallots, a bit of sugar and butter.

Cassoulet (Toulouse, Castelnaudary and other regions): white Cazères or Pamiers beans and various meats (mutton, preserved goose or duck, sausage, salt brisket, pig's trotters) cooked at length in an earthenware casserole.

Catigot (or catigau) d'anguilles (Camargue): eels cut into sections and cooked with garlic, onion, tomato and red wine.

Caudière or chaudrée (Flanders): fish soup with potatoes; there are numerous recipes. (It is the origin of American chowder.)

Cèpes à la bordelaise (Bordelais): cèpes (mushrooms) sautéed in oil with chopped shallots and parsley; several preparations.

Cervelas de Lyon (Lyonnais): fat, short pork sausage, often made with truffles or pistachios and placed in a brioche crust.

Cervelas de Strasbourg (Alsace): sausage in a red-colored casing cooked in fine pastry, eaten hot or cold (in a salad).

Cervelle de canut (Lyonnaise): white cheese mixed with shallots, herbs and chives, cream, white wine and a bit of oil. A treat for canuts (workers who specialize in silk weaving) in the Croix-Rouge.

Chargouère or chergouère (Bourbonnais): prune or plum turnover.

Chaudé (Lorraine): a large plum tart (damson, cherry plum).

Chaudrée (Argoumis, Poitou, Saintonge, Aunis): soup or ragout of various fish cooked in white wine, with shallots, garlic and butter.

Chevrettes (Charente-Maritime): local name for shrimp (crevettes).

Chevreuil (cuissot de) aux poires (Alsace): haunch of venison roasted with dried pears (schnitzen).

Chichi frégi (Marseille): round, sausage-shaped fritter with cinnamon; used to be sold throughout the streets of Marseille and Aix.

Chipirons à l'encre (Pays Basque): cuttlefish stuffed with onions, bread and cuttlefish meat, served in a sauce of its own ink with tomatoes.

Cholande aux pommes (Lorraine): a sort of apple tart.

Choquart (Brittany): a large turnover of flaky pastry filled with minced apples and cinnamon.

Chorlatte (Burgundy): balls of flour, eggs, cream and squash pulp, wrapped in cabbage leaves and browned in the oven.

Chotenn (Pays Bigouden): pig's head baked in earthenware with a little water and garlic.

Choucroute (Alsace): sauerkraut; thin strips of salted and fermented (soured) cabbage; often served with sausages, smoked bacon, pork loin and potatoes.

Chou rouge à l'alsacienne (Alsace): red cabbage cut into strips and cooked in a casserole with lard, smoked bacon, onions, vinegar and bouillon.

Chou rouge à la flamande (Flanders): red cabbage cut into strips and cooked in a casserole with butter, diced pippins, onion, red wine and a dash of vinegar.

Chouée (Angoumois, Poitou, Anjou): green cabbage fried in butter or boiled; sometimes served with potatoes.

Civelles or pibales (Bordelais): young eels raised in captivity.

Civet de tripes d'oies au vinaigre (Gascogne): civet of goose tripe sautéed in fat with onions, shallots and garlic, then cooked in wine vinegar diluted with water; the sauce is thickened with the bird's blood.

Confidous or coufidous (Rouergue): beef rago, tomato purée, garlic and onions.

Confit (Périgord, Quercy, Béarn): wings, thighs and other pieces of duck, pork or goose (or, rarely, turkey or chicken), cooked in their own fat and stored in a stoneware jar.

Coppa (Corsica): very dry ham served like a sausage.

Coq au vin jaune (Franche-Comté): cut-up chicken cooked in white Arbois wine, thickened with cream and often garnished with morels.

Cornics (Brittany): type of croissant.

Corniottes (Bordelais): triangles of dough stuffed with white cheese beaten with cream and eggs, browned in the oven; can also be eaten sweet. The Burgundian version is very similar.

Cotriade (Brittany): fisherman's soup or marine pot-au-feu, infinitely variable, composed of delicate fish boiled in water with potatoes, onions, garlic, parsley and butter; served over croutons.

Cou d'oie farci (Périgord): mixture of sausage meat, duck liver and a small amount of minced truffles, stuffed in the skin of a fatted goose. The whole is cooked in boiling fat, like a confit and eaten hot or cold, accompanied by a salad with walnut oil.

Coudenat (Southwest): pork sausage; like sabodet (Lyon, Dauphin).

Coudenou (Mazamet, Tarn): sausage with pork rind and a panade with eggs, poached in water.

Courraye (Normandy): boudin made from offal.

Cousina or cousinat (Vivarais, Auvergne): chestnut soup made with cream, butter, onions and leeks, or sometimes with prunes or apples.

Cousinat (Pays Basque): ragoût of cubes of Bayonne ham, small artichokes, beans, carrots, tomatoes and various other vegetables.

Crapiau (Nivernais, Morvan): fruit (often apple) crêpe.

Craquelin (Artois): oval-shaped brioche.

Craquelins (Brittany): rounds of yeast dough with eggs, boiled, then placed in the oven. They can be filled with apples. Similar to brassadeaux (Provence).

Craquelot (Flanders): herring smoked over walnut leaves.

Créat (Charentes): local name for tarragon.

Crème aux algues (Brittany): sweetened milk cooked with seaweed, which makes it set.

Crémet (Angers, Maine-et-Loire): whipped cream and stiffly beaten egg whites placed in a mold lined with muslin; served with cream and sprinkled with sugar.

Crémet (Nantes): curdled milk boiled, strained and molded and covered with sweetened whipped cream. Normandy has an almost identical recipe for white cheese that bears the same name.

Crêpes dentelle (Brittany): crêpes that are extremely thin, almost like lace (dentelle), and flaky, served rolled up. Originally from Quimper.

Crépiau (Burgundy): crêpe.

Criques (Vivarais): grated potatoes mixed with eggs and fried like pancakes. Related to the râpée and grapiau (Morvan) and truffiat (Berry).

Croquant (Auvergne): small dry pancake with honey.

Cruchade (Béarn, Pays Basque): corn-flour dessert fritter (or, in the Charente, a small corn-flour and wheat crêpe).

Cul de veau clamecyçoise (Clamecy, Nièvre): rump of veal wrapped in caul fat then boiled with vegetables; eaten cold.

D

Daube (Aude, Vaucluse and others): ragoût of beef or mutton marinated in red wine with oil and onions, then braised in earthenware.

Deffarde or défarde (Crest, Drôme): lamb's tripe, innards and trotters cooked like a pot-au-feu with carrots, onions and leeks, then simmered in the oven in a terrine with white wine and tomato purée.

Demoiselle de Cherbourg (Cherbourg): small lobster cooked in court bouillon, served in its cooking juice.

Dents de lion or grouin d'âne (Lyonnaise): salad of a dandelion typical of the area; prepared with small browned lardons and croutons.

Diots (Savoie): sausages made with chard, spinach, cabbage and leeks, with pork and pork fat; they are preserved in oil and are often cooked in white wine with shallots and minced onions.

Douillon (Normandy): (whole) pear turnover. Related to bourdelot (also Normand).

E

Echaudés (Auvergne): squares of dough cooked briefly in boiling water then baked.

Eclade de moules or fumée or térée (Saintonge): mussels laid out on a board with their tips up, roasted over a fire of pine needles.

Ecrevisses (gratin de queues d') (Dauphiné, Bugey): crayfish poached in a court bouillon (flavored stock), shelled, then covered in a béchamel sauce with cream when served in the Dauphiné region, or with a sauce nantua (with crayfish butter) in the Bugey region.

Eierkuchas (Alsace): small crêpes made of flour, eggs and cream.

Elzekaria (Pays Basque): soup of dried beans, cabbage, onion and garlic.

Embeurré de chou (Poitou): garden cabbage cooked in salted water and then crushed with butter.

Enchaud (Périgord): terrine of filet of pork with garlic and pigs' trotters.

Escargots à l'alsacienne (Alsace): snails cooked in a bouillon made with Alsatian wine; the shells are filled with spiced butter and herbs.

Escargots à la bourguignonne (Burgundy): snails stuffed with butter, garlic and parsley.

Escargots à la chablisienne (Chablis, Yonne): snails stuffed with shallots, white wine and butter with garlic and parsley.

F

Fagot (Charentes): medium-size meatballs made of a mixture of strips of liver and fat, wrapped in intestinal membranes, tied and cooked in pork fat.

Fallette (Rouergue): breast of veal stuffed with chard, bacon, eggs, bread and milk.

Falue (Normandy): long pancake.

Farée (Angoumois): stuffed cabbage.

Farci poitevin (Poitou): pâté of greens (spinach, chard, sorrel, cabbage) mixed with bacon and eggs, wrapped in cabbage leaves and cooked in bouillon; eaten hot or cold.

Farcis niçois (Nice): squash, eggplant, tomatoes and onions stuffed with their own pulp mixed with chopped pork or veal, eggs and garlic, then baked in the oven with oil.

Farcidure (Limousin): boulettes of wheat or buckwheat flour mixed with eggs and possibly chopped greens (sorrel, chard, cabbage, leek), then cooked in bouillon; may accompany a potée aux choux. Also a pancake of grated po~ta~toes, flour, eggs, and chopped bacon.

Farçon (Auvergne): large pancake made of sausage meat, sorrel, onions, eggs, flour and white wine; cooked in a frying pan.

Farçon (Savoie): potatoes, bacon, prunes and eggs, or mashed potatoes, milk and eggs, mixed and gratinéed in the oven.

Farinette (Auvergne): omelet with a touch of flour.

Fars (Brittany): various sorts of buckwheat and wheat porridge boiled in water in canvas bags, or baked in the oven in an earthenware dish. Savory or sweet, they can be mixed with bacon, cabbage, rutabaga, prunes and/or raisins.

Faude (Cantal): veal and mutton accompanied with various sauces; eaten hot or cold.

Faverolles (Lorraine): variously shaped dessert fritters.

Favouilles (Provence): smooth-shelled crabs used in fish soup.

Féchun (Franche-Comté): stuffed cabbage.

Ferchuse (Burgundy): pig's fry (heart, lungs and liver) cut into pieces and cooked in red wine with potatoes and onions.

Ficelle normande (Normandy): crêpes stuffed with a creamed mixture of mushrooms or ham.

Ficelle picarde (Picardie): crêpe rolled with ham, mushrooms and grated cheese, gratinéed in the oven.

Figatelli (Corsica): sausage made of pork liver.

Fiouse (Lorraine): bread made with onions, eggs, cream, oil and diced smoked bacon.

Flamery (Lorraine): semolina cake with raisins and preserved fruit.

Flamique or flamiche (Picardie): sort of tart-flan with leeks, onion or squash.

Flammekueche or tarte flambée (Alsace): a rectangle of bread dough with raised edges, filled with cream, bacon, onions and (sometimes) white cheese, then baked.

Flamusse (Nivernais, Morvan): fruit (often apple) omelet.

Flognarde or flaugnarde (Auvergne): a type of flan.

Fouace (Touraine): a country pancake (wheat) that is baked. Rabelais praised its merits.

Fougasse (Vivarais, Provence): rustic dough cakes baked in different shapes (such as a palm leaf).

Fougassette (Provence): oval-shaped bread with oil and orange or lemon rind perfumed with orange blossoms.

Fressure vendéenne (Vendée): terrine of pork (head, lung, rind and blood) with onions and bread.

Fricassin (Nivernais): calf's caul with cream.

Frittons (Southwest: Quercy, Rouergue, Lauragais): meat left over from confits mixed with pieces of kidney, head and heart of pork or goose and cooked in fat.

Frottée (Lorraine): tart with lardons and eggs, resembling a quiche.

G

Gâche (Vendée): brioche.

Galabart (Albigeois, Southwest): large blood sausage made of pig's head, lung and heart and often bread.

Galettes and crêpes (Brittany): galettes are made of buckwheat flour and are usually savory. Crêpes are made of wheat flour and are usually sweet.

Galette charentaise (Charentes): round and fairly thin pancake; a regional classic.

Galette aux griaudes or grillaudes (Morvan, Nivernais): crown-shaped brioche with lardons or bits of browned pork fat. A cousin of the pompe aux grattons (Bourbonnais).

Galimafrée (Gascony): fried meat, especially fowl, in a sauce with verjuice.

Galimafrée à la vauban (Morvan): shoulder of mutton stuffed with bacon, sliced mushrooms and garlic, then roasted and served with sauce ravigote (shallots, white wine, vinegar and gherkins).

Galopiaux (Flanders, Artois, Picardie): small crêpe.

Galopin (Flanders, Artois, Picardie): thick crêpe made of pieces of eggs and brioche or milk bread soaked in milk and crushed.

Garbure (Southwest): soup prepared with fat (sometimes with streaky bacon and sausage), green beans, thinly sliced cabbage, beans, garlic, marjoram, thyme and parsley; a piece of preserved duck, turkey, goose or pork (tromblon or trébuc) is served alongside; bouillon is served over slices of bread.

Gargouillau (Burgundy, Limousin): a type of clafoutis with pears.

Gâteau Basque (Pays Basque): thick torte stuffed with créme pâtissière (milk, eggs, sugar and flour).

Gâteau battu or wattieu (Flanders, Artois, Picardie): type of brioche.

Gâteau breton (Brittany): type of pound cake or a large, somewhat hard and crumbly cake.

Gâteau de foies blonds de volaille (Bugey): foies blonds (chicken livers) that are pounded, mixed with foie gras, eggs and cream, then cooked in a double saucepan; the gâteau (cake) is accompanied by a sauce with truffles or a purée of crayfish.

Gâteau au fromage (Auvergne): torte made with curdled milk.

Gaude (Franche-Comté, Burgundy, Bresse, Morvan, Nivernais): porridge of cornstarch, oats or buckwheat (depending on the region), enriched with cream.

Gaufres (Flanders, Artois): waffles.

Gigorit or gigourit, gigoret, tantouillet (Poitou, Angoumois, Morvan, Aunis, Saintonge): ragoût of pig's head cooked in blood and red wine; several regional variations.

Gigot brayaude (Auvergne, Bourbonnais): leg of lamb cooked for five or six hours in white wine or bouillon with bacon, onions and herbs; accompanied by red beans, braised cabbage and chestnuts; also called cassette, from the name of the high-sided stoneware dish in which it's cooked.

Gigot "pourri" (Rouergue): leg of lamb cooked in a clay cooker with unpeeled cloves of garlic; the latter are sucked to extract their pulp, from which the characteristic scent of garlic has practically disappeared.

Gimblette (Albi): a small, hard, dry, ring-shape pastry.

Gnocchi à la niçoise (Nice): small potato-and-flour dumplings poached in boiling water.

Gogues (Anjou): types of crépinettes made of equal amounts of herbs and vegetables (chard, spinach, onions), diced fat, lean pork and blood.

Gouère or guéron (Berry, Nivernais, Morvan): type of apple clafoutis.

Gouéron (Berry): cake of goat cheese and eggs.

Gouerre or gouère (Bourbonnais): savory cake of mashed potatoes, flour, eggs and white cheese, baked in a pie plate.

Gouerre au cirage (Bourbonnais): prune tart.

Gougère (Burgundy): ball (about the size of a small fist) of chou pastry with a cream filling of eggs and Gruyère.

Gouguenioche (Vendée): egg and chicken turnover.

Goyère (Valencienne, Nord): tart with Maroilles cheese.

Graisserons (Béarn): large rillettes.

Grapiau (Morvan): thick pancakes made of grated potatoes Related to râpée (also Morvan), criques (Vivarais) and truffiat (Berry).

Grattons (Bordelais): a mixture of lean meat and pieces of pork fat cut into cubes. Grattons de Lormont (Gironde) often accompany oysters in the Bordelais.

Grattons (Lyonnais): rillettes; browned but not molded cubes of bacon.

Grenouilles à la mode de Boulay (Lorraine): breaded frogs' legs baked with lemon, shallots and chopped parsley.

Grillade des mariniers de Condrieu (Lyonnais): layered beef scallops and minced onion with a mixture of oil, vinegar, anchovies, minced garlic and parsley placed on top; cooked in a covered earthenware casserole. An almost identical recipe is broufado (Provence).

Grillons (Périgord): bits of goose (or pork) meat left over from preparation of confit.

Guenilles (Auvergne): not rags, as the name suggests, but a type of doughnut.

H

Hachua (Pays Basque): ragoonne-style ham (or beef or veal), with onions and peppercorns.

Harengs marinés à la fécampoise (Fécamp, Seine-Maritime): marinated herrings placed on a bed of carrots, onions and lemon slices and preserved in a mixture of boiling vinegar and white wine; eaten cold.

Haricots blancs à la bretonne (Brittany): white beans in a sauce of onions, tomatoes, garlic and shallots.

Hochepot (Flanders): sort of pot-au-feu with oxtails.

Hogue vosgien (Lorraine): ball-shaped cake with rye flour and damson plums.

Homard à l'armoricaine (Brittany): or à l'américaine; the epithets have been the subject of numerous debates. Lobster is cut into sections, then browned in oil in a shallow frying pan with shallots, minced onions, tomato sauce and muscadet; many variations.

Huîtres à la bordelaise (Bordelais): gravette oysters from the Bassin (Arcachon), accompanied by crépinettes (sausages with optional truffles).

Hure blanche (Alsace): large sausage of pig's head and knuckle of ham cut into cubes, with pork rind added to form an aspic.

Hure à la parisienne (Paris): molded pig's or calf's tongue in aspic.

Hure rouge (Alsace): a large sausage of smoked pig's head cheese, beef forcemeat, aspic and rind.

I

Imbrucciate (Corsica): white cheese tart.

J

Jambon braisé à la lie de vin (Burgundy): ham boiled whole in water, then braised in red wine or wine lees (sediment), with onions, garlic and bouquet garni.

Jambon persillé (Burgundy): ham cooked in white wine, cut into pieces and mixed with aspic and parsley; served cold molded in a salad bowl.

Jambonette (Vivarais): minced fat and lean of ham wrapped in an intestine, formed in the shape of a ham or pear, then salted and dried.

Jésus de Morteau (Franche-Comté): sausage made of pork liver.

Jésus de Morteau (Morteau, Doubs): large pork sausage with a small wooden peg at one end—a sign that it has been smoked over pine and juniper.

Jonchée (Brittany): heart-shaped cheese of curdled milk.

Judru (Chagny, Saône-et-Loire): large dried sausage molded in the large intestine of a pig; the meat is soaked in marc de Bourgogne and cut into small pieces.

K

Kaleréi (Alsace): pâté made of pigs' trotters, ears and tail.

Knepfen (Alsace): sort of quenelle (meat dumpling).

Kouign amann (Douarnenez, Brittany): large pancake containing lots of butter.

Kugelhopf (Alsace): a sort of brioche with raisins and almonds, cooked in a characteristic round, fluted mold with a hole in the center, and unmolded before serving.

Kunpods (Brittany): balls of dough with eggs and raisins, boiled in a bouillon.

L

Lait ribot (Brittany): churned milk (a sort of thin yogurt).

Lamproie à la bordelaise (Bordeaux): sections of lamprey eel browned in oil and garnished with sliced whites of leek also browned in oil; with strained sauce of red Bordeaux, carrots, garlic, onions, green of leeks, thickened with the lamprey's blood.

Langouste en civet au Banyuls (Roussillon): sections of rock lobster browned in oil, then cooked in Banyuls wine with onion, shallot, garlic, tomato and cubes of ham.

Langues d'avocat (Bordelais): "lawyer's tongues"—the local name for small sole.

Lapin à l'artésienne (Artois): rabbit stuffed with sheep's trotters and boiled in beer.

Lapin à la flamande (Flanders): sectioned rabbit marinated in red wine and vinegar, then braised with onions and prunes.

Lard nantais (Nantes): pork rind, liver, lung and spleen, cut into pieces and boiled, pork cutlets are laid on top, then baked in an earthenware dish.

Leberknepfen (Alsace): quenelles of calf's liver, bread, shallots and eggs, poached in boiling water then fried.

Lièvre à la broche (Bourbonnais and other regions): hare marinated in a mixture of oil, vinegar or wine, onions and spices, then roasted on a spit.

Lièvre en cabessal or chabessal (Poitou, Périgord, Rouergue, Limousin): hare stuffed with bacon and garlic, then cooked for six hours in white or red wine with Armagnac.

Limaces (or escargots) à la suçarelle (Provence, Arles): snails covered in salt, then cooked with onion, garlic chopped tomato, sausage meat and white wine in an earthenware casserole; the mollusk is then sucked out (sucer).

Longeole (Savoie): rustic sausage.

Lonzo (Corsica): charcuterie (a sort of raw, salted ham) made from a boned filet of pork, left to macerate in aromatic brine, then dried.

M

Madeleine de Commercy (Lorraine): small, fluted and domed cake; said to have been created by King Stanislas Leczinsky's cook, Madeleine.

Magret or maigret (entire Southwest, where fowl is raised for foie gras): filet of fattened duck breast, usually grilled with its skin on and served rare. (A fairly recent and now very common dish.)

Migisca (Corsica): smoked filet of goat.

Migourée (Aunis): pieces of lotte, skate, mullet and cuttlefish, browned briskly then cooked in a bouillon of white wine, garlic, onion and chopped shallots.

Mijot or miot (Nivernais): soup made with red wine, bread and (optionaly) sugar.

Milchstriwle or milchstreevele (Alsace): small round noodles made of thick crêpe batter poached in milk, then arranged in layers with grated cheese, cream and butter, or simply served with melted butter.

Millas (Ariège): corn-flour pancakes (savory or sweet) browned in fat. May be served in cabbage soup.

Millas (Charentes): sort of corn-flour flan.

Millassou (Béarn, Pays Basque): a sort of corn-flour flan.

Millat or milla, milliard (Bourbonnais, Auvergne): sort of cherry clafoutis.

Millia (Périgord): a pumpkin-and-corn-flour flan. A very similar dish is made in Limousin.

Mique (Périgord, Limousin): originally, larded balls of dough which often replaced bread; now, a mixture of corn flour and wheat flour or stale bread, with eggs, formed into balls, poached in boiling water or bouillon; often sliced, dipped in beaten eggs and fried. Accompanies civets, salt pork with cabbage.

Mirliton (Rouen, Normandy): a small tart garnished with a sort of flan.

Miton or mitonée (Rennes): bread soup with onions, milk and egg yolk.

Mogette or mojette, Mougette, Mohjette (Angoumois): a small bean that reminds natives of Charente of the humble, curled-up posture of a nun (mougette) at prayer.

Mongetado (Saint-Gaudens, Haute-Garonne): a dish with beans.

Morue en raito (Provence): sections of soaked salt cod, fried and coated with a purée of tomato, onion and garlic.

Mouclade (Charentes): mussels with cream, egg yolks, white wine and butter, to which Pineau des Charentes can also be added.

Mourtayrol or mourtairol (Auvergne, Rouergue): saffron-flavored soup with a base of chicken stock; also, a sort of pot-au-feu made of beef, chicken, ham and various vegetables; the bouillon, to which saffron has been added, is poured over slices of coarse bread and the meat is served on the side.

Murçon (Privas, Ardèche): home-style sausage, eaten hot.

N

Nieulles (Flanders): a type of small round pancake.

Noces (Brittany): oat porridge.

O

Oeufs durs à la tripe (Normandy): sliced hard-boiled eggs, covered with minced onion and cooked in Norman beef suet and bouillon.

Oie à la flamande (North): goose that is (optionally) stuffed, braised and garnished with braised cabbage, carrots and turnips.

Omelette brayaude (Auvergne, Bourbonnais): omelet with bacon, cream, potatoes and cheese.

Omelette crespeu (Provence): omelet with smoked pork or potatoes, or a "cake" made of layers of omelet alternated with minced vegetables (tomatoes, peppers).

Omelette aux jets de houblon (Alsace): omelet with hops shoots that have been boiled and sautéed in butter.

Omelette de la Mère Poulard (Mont-Saint-Michel, Manche): omelet of beaten eggs, butter and various closely guarded ingredients; or eggs (yolks and whites beaten separately) to which cream is added. Named for the famous restaurant in Mont-Saint-Michel.

Oreilles et pieds de porc à la Sainte-Menehould (Sainte-Menehould, Marne): pronounced "menou"; pig's trotters and ears cooked at length in a court bouillon with white wine, then breaded and grilled.

Oreillettes (Provence): rectangular dessert fritters flavored with orange-blossom water.

Ouillade (Roussillon): potée with bacon, Catalan boudin, leeks, carrots and potatoes.

Oulade (Rouergue, Auvergne): soup with goose or pork fat, with onions and various vegetables; named after the oule (cooking pot).

Ouliat (Béarn): onion or bean soup, usually covered with varying amounts of cheese.

Oyonnade (Bourbonnais): sort of civet of goose with blood and crushed liver, cooked with wine and eau-de-vie.

P

Pachade (Auvergne): sort of omelet with flour and prunes.

Pan bagna (Nice): a round loaf of bread soaked with olive oil and garnished with anchovy filets, onions, black olives and celery.

Panisses (Provence): chickpea flour made into a porridge, then fried in oil.

Panzarotti (Corsica): fritters flavored with eau-de-vie, with a lemon-flavored cheese filling.

Papeton (Avignon): eggplant fried then baked, originally in a tiara-shaped mold; this dish was supposedly invented for a pope (pape).

Pascade (Rouergue): savory crêpe.

Pastis (Pays Basque): cake flavored with orange-blossom water.

Pâté de Beaucaire or pastissoun (Provence): pâté stuffed with candied citron, lemon rind and beef suet, flavored with orange-blossom water.

Pâté de canard d'Amiens (Amiens, Somme): duck pâté en croûte; several varieties.

Pissaladière (Nice): tart with onions, black olives and anchovy filets.

Pissalot (Provence, Nice): purée of anchovies and young fish, seasoned with cloves and thinned with oil.

Pistache (Saint-Gaudens, Haute-Garonne): dish of mutton and beans.

Pithiviers (Orléannais): puff-pastry cake filled with almond paste.

Pogne (Dauphiné): brioche loaf with candied fruit.

Poirat (Berry): pear torte.

Poires belle dijonnaise (Dijon, Côte-d'Or): poached pears served with black currant ice cream, coated with black-currant purée.

Poires vigneronne (Burgundy): pears cooked in red wine with sugar.

Pommes de terre sarladaise (Périgord): raw potatoes cut into thin slices and baked with goose fat and (optional) truffles.

Pompe (Auvergne, Nivernais, Morvan): sort of torte turnover with fruit (such as apples).

Pompe aux grattons (Bourbonnais): crown-shaped, savory "cake" made of a mixture of flour, eggs, milk and pork cracklings. A relative of the galette aux griaudes (Morvan-Nivernais).

Pompe de Noël or gibassié (Provence): bread with oil and orange rind or lemon, perfumed with orange-blossom water.

Porché (Dol, Ille-et-Vilaine): ears, trotters, rind and bone of pork covered in water in an earthenware dish and cooked at length in the oven.

Porchetta (Nice): a small pig stuffed with its offal mixed with herbs and garlic, then roasted on a spit.

Pormonier (Savoie): sausage with herbs.

Potage à la jambe de bois (Lyonnais): sort of pot-au-feu made of a piece of beef thigh with its bone as well as veal, chicken, game and vegetables.

Potage aux marrons (Brittany, Redon and other regions, including Vivarais and Auvergne): soup of chestnuts reduced to a purée; milk, cream and butter are added.

Potage aux noques (Alsace): liquid bouillon from a pot-au-feu, thickened with a roux, egg yolks and cream; served with noques (small quenelles).

Potage à la soissonnaise (Soissons, Aisne): soup with soissons (haricot beans).

Potée (multiregional): various vegetables and meats boiled together.

Potjevleish (Dunkirk, Nord): terrine of veal, pork and rabbit.

Poularde demi-deuil or de la Mère Filloux (Lyonnais): poularde stuffed with a fine, truffled farce, with strips of truffles inserted under the skin, then poached in bouillon.

Poularde en vessie (Lyonnais): fattened chicken soaked in water (to keep its meat very white), stuffed with truffles and foie gras, wrapped in a pork bladder and poached in bouillon; served with potatoes, carrots, turnips and whites of leeks.

Poulet (or coq) en barbouille (Berry): sectioned chicken or cock browned with onions and lean bacon; red-wine sauce thickened with blood.

Poulet basquaise (Pays Basque): sectioned chicken cooked in a casserole with tomatoes, peppers, peppercorns, mushrooms and wine.

Poulet à la crème et aux morilles (Franche-Comté): chicken with cream and morels; a popular dish.

Poulet vallée d'auge (Normandy): chicken with cream and Calvados.

Poulet au vinaigre (Lyonnais): sectioned chicken cooked with shallots, tomatoes, white wine and vinegar; the sauce is thickened with cream.

Pountari (Auvergne): minced bacon in cabbage leaves; or a type of large sausage, also wrapped in cabbage leaves.

Pounti (Auvergne): minced bacon and chard with a bit of flour, according to some; others say it's a soufflé of chard. Eggs or cream can also be added, or grapes, prunes and herbs.

Poutargue (Martigues, Saintes-Maries-de-la-Mer, Bouches-du-Rhône): red or gray mullet roe, salted, pressed and served in the form of slightly flattened sausages.

Poutine or putina (Provence, Nice): young anchovies raised in captivity, sardines and nonats used in omelets, fritters and other dishes.

Pouytrolle (Vivarais): pig's intestines stuffed with chopped spinach, chard, onions, pork and seasonings, then baked.

Presskopf or tête roulée (Alsace): cubes of pork's head or veal and pieces of pork in aspic with Riesling and (optionally) shallots and gherkins. Often served with a vinaigrette with fines herbes.

Prisultre (Corsica): raw ham.

Q

Quenelles (Lyonnais, Bugey, Alsace): fowl or pike made with a mousseline stuffing thickened with eggs and shaped into small cylinders.

Quiche (Lorraine): tart of eggs, bacon and cream.

Quichet or quiché (Provence): large slice of crusty bread with the soft part soaked in oil, several anchovies placed on top, and baked.

R

Râble de lapin à la moutarde (Dijon): saddle of rabbit brushed with mustard and roasted; cream is added to the cooking juice.

Rabotte or rabote, boulot, talibur (Champagne, Picardie): turnover with a whole apple. Related to bourdelot (Norman).

Raisiné (Aunis, Saintonge, Burgundy): jam made with grape juice or must, reduced until it has the consistency of jelly or marmalade.

Ramequin douaisien (Douai, Nord): rolls made with milk, stuffed with minced veal kidney, bread, chives and parsley, then baked.

Rapée or rapis (Morvan): thick crêpes or croquettes made from a mixture of grated potatoes, eggs, a bit of flour, butter, Gruyère or white cheese (or both). Related to grapiau (also Morvan), criques (Vivarais) and truffiat (Berry).

Ratatouille (Provence): a stew of eggplant, tomatoes, peppers, zucchini, onion and garlic, all sautéed in oil.

Ravioles (Dauphiné): pasta stuffed with goat cheese.

Ravioli à la niçoise (Nice): pasta stuffed with meat (veal, pork, or beef), poached and minced chard and a bit of grated cheese.

Reguigneu (Provence, Arles): slices of raw ham dipped in beaten egg and fried.

Rigodon (Burgundy): sort of flan made with leftover brioche, nuts, hazelnuts or fruit.

Rillettes du Mans (Sarthe): pale rillettes; rather big pieces.

Rillettes de Tours (Touraine): slightly brownish rillettes, rather delicate texture. Often contains pork liver.

Rillons or rillauds (Touraine, Anjou): pieces of pork brisket and shoulder cut into large cubes and cooked in pork fat.

Rimottes (Périgord): porridge made from corn flour.

Rissoles (Bugey-Savoie): type of small pie filled with forcemeat.

Rosette (Lyonnais): large dry sausage of pure pork (usually wrapped in a net).

Rougets à la niçoise (Nice): grilled or fried mullets (not gutted), coated with a purée of anchovies, fried tomatoes and black olives.

Rouille (Provence): sort of mayonnaise with pepper, garlic bread soaked in bouillon, olive oil and possibly saffron; often accompanies bouillabaisse and other fish dishes.

Rouyat or roulat, roulotte, robate (Lorraine): turnover enclosing a whole apple. Yet another relation of the rabotte (Picardie) and bourdelot (Norman).

Royan (Arcachon basin): local name for sardines.

S

Salade niçoise (Nice): salad of sweet peppers, celery, tomatoes, hard-boiled egg, anchovy filets, tuna and black olives from Nice; many different versions, some with green beans, potatoes, basil, onions and/or broad beans.

Salade des vendangeurs (Burgundy): salad of wild chicory or lamb's lettuce and dandelions with small browned lardons.

Saladier lyonnais (Lyonnais): salad of sheep's trotters, chicken livers, hard-boiled eggs and herring.

Salamis de Strasbourg (Alsace): type of smoked beef and pork sausage.

Salmis de palombes (Béarn, Pays Basque, Bordelais): stew of wood pigeon in a red wine sauce with small onions, cubes of ham and mushrooms.

Sardines à l'escabèche (Provence): layers of fried sardines and fried onion with garlic and a dash of vinegar; served cold as an hors d'oeuvre.

Sardines farcies aux épinards (Provence): baked sardines with a stuffing of spinach that has been poached, minced and browned in a frying pan with a bit of flour, milk and garlic.

Sartagnado (Provence): macédoine of small fish fried like a crêpe in oil and seasoned with vinegar.

Sauce de pire (Aunis): various parts of a pig cooked in white wine and thickened with blood.

Saucisse de bière (Alsace): cooked sausage, red meat and small pieces of bacon in a calf or pork bladder. Despite the name, there is no beer in it.

Saucisse de Strasbourg (Alsace): beef and pork sausage.

Soupe à la graisse (Cotentin): soup of beef suet with onion, cloves, leeks, parsley and celery, cooked for fifteen hours in a cast-iron pot, then stored in stoneware pots; completed with vegetables (including potatoes) and stale bread.

Soupe aux grenouilles (Alsace): soup of frogs' legs that have been cooked in a court bouillon with white wine. Egg yolks and cream are added just before serving.

Soupe de moules à la rochaise (La Rochelle, Aunis): soup of various fish, mussels, red wine, garlic, onions, tomatoes and saffron.

Soupe d'orge (Vivarais): barley soup with various vegetables simmered for a long time.

Soupe au pistou (Provence): soup with basil (pistou), green and other beans (fresh and dried, white and red), potatoes, tomatoes and zucchini, whose pulp serves as a binding. Small pasta is added during cooking, and at the end the pistou is crushed with garlic and tomato.

Spätzle (Alsace): round noodles, sometimes made from egg.

T

Tablier de sapeur (Lyonnais): pieces of tripe browned and cut into triangles, from the part known as the "nids d'abeille" (bee hives), dipped in beaten eggs, then breaded; often served with snail butter or with mayonnaise containing shallots and tarragon.

Tapenade (Provence): black olives from Nice, capers and anchovies, crushed in a mortar with lemon juice and pepper. Can be eaten as an hors d'oeuvre on toast, or used as a stuffing for hard-boiled eggs.

Tapinette (Montargis, Loiret): cheese tart.

Tapinette (Nivernais, Morvan): tart made with curdled milk.

Tarte à la courge (Provence): sweet dessert tart made with squash. Lemon rind and orange water are added.

Tarte à l'écoloche (Flanders): tart filled with a mixture of apple compote (peppered and caramelized) and vanilla flan, topped with browned, caramelized apples.

Tarte aux épinards (Provence): sweet dessert tart made with spinach; typical Christmas dish.

Tarte au m'gin or megin, mougin, mengin (Lorraine): dessert tart made with white cheese.

Tarte au quemeu (Champagne): tart filled with flan.

Tarte Tatin or solognote (Lamotte-Beuvron, Loir-et-Cher): upside-down apple tart invented by the maiden Tatin sisters.

Tartibas (Bourbonnais): pancake with raisins.

Tartine (Hucqueliers, Pas-de-Calais): sort of coarse country dessert bread made with cream, eggs and raisins.

Tartinette or weiche mettwurst (Alsace): a sausage spread made of a mixture of beef and fat pork.

Tartisseaux (Charentes): a type of dessert fritter.

Tartouillat (Morvan, Nivernais, Burgundy): rustic flan with quartered apples.

Telline (Camargue): a long, flat-shelled mollusk, common in the Camargue. Prepared many different ways.

Tergoule or teugoule, torgoule, terrinée (Normandy): rice with sweetened milk, a dash of cinnamon, baked for a long time in an earthenware dish.

Terrine de lapin aux pruneaux (Touraine): rabbit meat (optionally with veal and pork) mixed with eggs, Vouvray and prunes that have been soaked in Vouvray wine.

Terrinée (Rennes): pork rind, bones and meat, baked at length in a terrine with various vegetables.

Tourin or tourain (entire Southwest): onion soup made with bacon and a small clove of garlic, thickened with egg yolk and a dash of vinegar, then poured over thin slices of stale homemade bread.

Touron (Languedoc, Roussillon): sort of almond paste, with different flavors, containing pistachios, hazelnuts or candied fruit. Originally Spanish.

Tourte (and tourton) de blettes (Nice): a stuffing made of chard, eggs and grated cheese sandwiched between two layers of bread.

Tourte aux grenouilles (Lorraine): a garnish of boned frogs' legs sautéed in butter, with a sauce of cream and eggs.

Tourte à la lorraine (Lorraine): torte of marinated pork and veal, cooked in a thin pastry crust with cream and eggs.

Tourte aux pavots (Lorraine): torte filled with crushed poppyseeds mixed with semolina, eggs and cream.

Tourteau fromagé (Poitou): a round cheesecake with a very dark brown top.

Tourtière au poulet et aux salsifis (Périgord): torte (dough on top and bottom) with pieces of chicken browned in goose fat and cooked in a thick sauce (like a roux with white wine) with salsify.

Tourtou (Limousin): thick crêpe of buckwheat flour (or buckwheat mixed with wheat).

Tourtous (Corrèze): buckwheat pancakes.

Treize desserts de Noël (Provence): traditionally served at Christmas Eve parties, they are actually much more numerous than thirteen: almonds, marzipan, candied citrons, dates, dried figs, fougasse, various candied fruits, hazelnuts, nuts, dark nougat, quince pastry, winter pears, apples, Brignoles plums, raisins and so on.

Trénels (Rouergue): see Manouls.

Tripes au Banyuls (Roussillon): tripe moistened with Banyuls and white wine with tomato paste, carrots, onions and garlic.

Tripes de la Ferté-Macé (Orne): tripe cooked on a skewer; small bundles are held together by a stick called a billette.

Tripes à la mode de Caen (Caen, Calvados): made with the four beef stomachs, cooked (for about twelve hours) with trotters, onions, carrots, bouquet garni (herb bundle) and (optionally) Calvados, in a clay tripière (pot).

Tripes à la niçoise (Nice): beef tripe cooked with white wine, onions, carrots, garlic.

Tripes à la paloise (Pau): calf's tripe with white wine and Bayonne ham.

Tripes à la provençale (Provence): beef and pork tripe and pig's head with tomato sauce.

Tripes à la rébouleto (Provence): mutton tripe with vinaigrette.

Tripes de thon en daube (Martigues, Bouches-du-Rhône, Palavas, Hérault): tuna innards cooked in a court bouillon, then in a casserole with water, white wine, onion, bay leaf and pepper.

Tripotch or tripotcha (Pays Basque): a sort of blood sausage made from the tripe, lung and blood of mutton or lamb.

Tripoux or tripous (Auvergne, Rouergue, Cévennes): mutton or calf's tripe in the shape of small bundles, stuffed with meat from the trotters, cloves and lots of pepper.

Truffade (Auvergne): a large pancake of sautéed potato, with or without lardons, and Tomme cheese; another recipe calls for the Tomme to be served separately, cut into cubes.

Truffiat (Berry): grated potato mixed with flour, eggs and butter, then baked. Related to criques and râpée (Vivarais) and grapiau (Morvan).

Truite aux lardons (Rouergue): trout with lardons of lean pork brisket.

Trulet (Nice): blood sausage typical of Nice, made with pork's blood, chard, onion, sweetbreads and lardons.

Ttoro (Pays Basque): slices of various fish baked or fried with minced onion, tomato and garlic.

Turbot or barbue à la cancalaise (Cancale, Ile-et-Villaine): baked turbot or bass with cream sauce and poached Cancale oysters.

V

Ventrèche (Rouergue): salted or smoked pork brisket.

Visitandines (Lorraine): small round or oval cakes with crushed almonds; said to have been invented by nuns in Lorraine.

Vitalons (Picardie): a sort of flavored pastry quenelle, poached in sweetened milk.

W

Waterzooï or waterzoï de poissons (Flanders): freshwater fish bouillinade in a highly seasoned sauce with lots of butter.

Waterzooï or waterzoï de poulet (Flanders): chicken braised with whites of leek, bouillon, cream and egg yolk.

Z

Zewelmai (Alsace): minced onion gently cooked in a frying pan, combined with cream and beaten eggs, then baked in a charlotte mold. In another recipe, this mixture is cooked in a pie crust and served hot.

Zungenwurst or boudin de langue (Alsace): sausage made of beef or pork tongue.

CITIES INDEX CLASSIFIED BY *DEPARTEMENTS*

R: *restaurants with or without toques* - H: *hotels*

16 Charente

17 Charente-Maritime

18 Cher

19 Corrèze

20 Corse

In the guide these cities are listed under "Corse (Corsica)"

21 Côte-d'Or

22 Côtes-du-Nord

24 Dordogne

25 Doubs

26 Drôme

27 Eure

28 Eure-et-Loire

29 Finistère

30 Gard

31 Haute-Garonne

32 Gers

33 Gironde

34 Hérault

35 Ille-et-Vilaine

36 Indre

37 Indre-et-Loire

38 Isère

39 Jura

40 Landes

41 Loir-et-Cher

42 Loire

43 Haute-Loire

44 Loire-Atlantique

Orvault *(see Nantes)* ..... R ♔♔ .. H
Paulx ..... R ♔
La Plaine-sur-Mer ..... R ♔ ... H
Pornic ..... R ♔
Saint-Sébastien-sur-Loire *(see Nantes)* ..... R ♔♔ .....

45 Loiret

Amilly *(see Montargis)* ..... R ♔
Beaugency ..... R ..... H
Les Bézards ..... R ♔♔♔ . H
Gien ..... R ♔
Montargis ..... R ♔
Olivet *(see Orléans)* ..... R ♔ ... H
Orléans ..... R ♔♔♔ . H
Saint-Jean-de-Braye *(see Orléans)* ..... R ♔
Tavers *(see Beaugency)* ..... R ♔ ... H

46 Lot

Cabrerets ..... R ♔♔ .. H
Cahors ..... R ♔ ... H
Figeac ..... R ♔ ... H
Lacave ..... R ♔ ... H
Lamagdelaine *(see Cahors)* ..... R ♔
Mercuès *(see Cahors)* ..... R ♔ ... H
Saint-Céré ..... R ♔ ... H
Souillac ..... R ♔ ... H

47 Lot-et-Garonne

Agen ..... R ♔ ... H
Cancon ..... R ♔ ... H
Casteljaloux ..... R ♔ ... H
Poudenas ..... R ♔♔ .. H
Puymirol *(see Agen)* ..... R ♔♔♔♔
Sainte-Livrade-sur-Lot ... R
Villeneuve-sur-Lot ..... R ..... H

48 Lozère

Aumont-Aubrac ..... R ♔♔ .. H
Ispagnac ..... R ♔
Meyrueis ..... R ..... H
Vialas ..... R ♔♔ .....

49 Maine-et-Loire

Angers ..... R ♔♔♔ . H
Champtoceaux ..... R ♔
Cheffes-sur-Sarthe ..... R ..... H
Chênehutte-les-Tuffeaux *(see Saumur)* ..... R ♔♔ .. H
Cholet ..... R ♔♔ .. H
Fontevraud-l'Abbaye ..... R ♔♔
Les Rosiers-sur-Loire ..... R ♔♔ .. H
Saint-Sylvain-d'Anjou *(see Angers)* ..... R ♔ ... H
Saumur ..... R ♔ ... H

50 Manche

Barneville-Carteret ..... R ♔ ... H
Carentan ..... R ♔♔
Cherbourg ..... R ♔ ... H
Coutainville ..... R ♔
Montpinchon ..... R ♔ ... H
Le Mont-Saint-Michel ..... R ♔ ... H
Trelly ..... R ..... H

51 Marne

Châlons-sur-Marne ..... R ♔ ... H
Champigny *(see Reims)* ..... R ♔
Champillon *(see Epernay)* ..... R ♔ ... H
Epernay ..... R ♔ ... H
L'Epine *(see Châlons-sur-Marne)* ..... R ♔ ... H
Montchenot *(see Reims)* ..... R ♔
Reims ..... R ♔♔♔♔ H
Sept-Saulx ..... R ♔ ... H
Vinay *(see Epernay)* ..... R ♔ ... H

53 Mayenne

Javron-les-Chapelles ..... R ♔
Laval ..... R ♔♔ .. H

54 Meurthe-et-Moselle

Belleville ..... R ♔♔
Bouxières-aux-Chênes ..... R ♔
Flavigny-sur-Moselle *(see Nancy)* ..... R ♔♔
Liverdun ..... R ♔♔
Lunéville ..... R ♔♔ .. H
Nancy ..... R ♔♔ .. H
Toul ..... R ♔♔ ....

56 Morbihan

Arz (Ile d') ..... H
Auray ..... R ♔♔ .. H
Belle-Ile-en-Mer ..... R ♔ ... H
Billiers ..... R ♔♔ .. H
Bubry ..... H
Carnac ..... H
Erdeven ..... H
Hennebont ..... R ♔♔♔ . H
Lorient ..... R ♔ ... H
Questembert ..... R ♔♔♔ . H
Quiberon ..... R ♔ ... H
La Roche-Bernard ..... R ♔♔
La Trinité-sur-Mer ..... R ♔♔
Vannes ..... R ♔♔ .. H

57 Moselle

Forbach ..... R ♔♔
Metz ..... R ♔♔ .. H
Phalsbourg ..... R ♔♔ .. H
Sierck-les-Bains ..... R ♔ .....

58 Nièvre

La Charité-sur-Loire ..... R ♔ ... H
Magny-Cours ..... R ♔♔ .. H
Nevers ..... R ♔ ... H

59 Nord

Avesnes-sur-Helpe ..... R ♔
Bavay ..... R ♔ ... H
Cassel ..... R ♔♔
Douai ..... R ♔ ... H
Dourlers ..... R
Dunkerque ..... R ..... H
Lille ..... R ♔♔♔ . H
Marcq-en-Baroeul *(see Lille)* ..... R ♔ ... H
Prémesques *(see Lille)* ..... R ♔
Roubaix ..... R ♔ ... H
Teteghem *(see Dunkerque)* ..... R ♔♔ .. H
Valenciennes ..... R ♔ .... H

60 Oise

Chantilly ..... R ♔ .... H
Compiegne
Elincourt-Ste-Marguerite *(see Compiègne)* ..... H
Lamorlaye *(see Chantilly)* ..... H

61 Orne

L'Aigle ..... R ♔ .... H
Alençon ..... R ♔ .... H
Condeau *(see Nogent-le-Rotrou)* ..... R ♔ .... H
Nocé ..... R ♔ .....

62 Pas-de-Calais

Ardres ..... R ♔ .... H
Arras ..... R ♔ .... H
Boulogne-sur-Mer ..... R ♔ .... H
Calais ..... R ♔ .... H
Lumbres ..... R ♔ .... H
Montreuil-sur-Mer ..... R ♔♔ .. H
Pont-de-Briques *(see Boulogne-sur-Mer)* ..... R ♔
Saint-Aubin *(see Montreuil-sur-Mer)* ..... H
Le Touquet ..... R ♔♔ .. H
Wimille *(see Boulogne-sur-Mer)* ..... R ♔ .....

63 Puy-de-Dôme

Besse-en-Chandesse ..... R ♔♔ .. H
Chamalières *(see Clermont-Ferrand)* R ♔♔♔
Châtelguyon ..... R ..... H
La Chaulme ..... H
Clermont-Ferrand ..... R ♔♔ .. H
Durtol *(see Clermont-Ferrand)* ..... R ♔♔
Lezoux ..... R ..... H
Montaigut-le-Blanc ..... R ♔♔
Orcines *(see Clermont-Ferrand)* ..... R ♔ .... H
Pérignat-lès-Sarliève *(see Clermont-Ferrand)* ..... R ♔♔ .. H
Pontaumur ..... R ♔
Royat *(see Clermont-Ferrand)* ..... R ♔ .... H

64 Pyrénées-Atlantiques

Aïnhoa ..... R ♔♔ .. H
Anglet ..... R ♔ .... H
Bayonne ..... R ♔♔ .. H
Biarritz ..... R ♔♔ .. H
Bidart ..... R ♔♔ .. H
Biriatou *(see Hendaye)* ..... R ♔
Bosdarros *(see Pau)* ..... R ♔
Ciboure *(see Saint-Jean-de-Luz)* ..... R ♔
Espelette ..... R
Esterençuby *(see Saint-Jean-Pied-de-Port)* ..... H
Gan *(see Pau)* ..... R ♔
Hendaye ..... R
Jurançon *(see Pau)* ..... R ♔
Lestelle-Bétharram ..... R ♔

65 Hautes-Pyrénées

66 Pyrénées-Orientales

67 Bas-Rhin

68 Haut-Rhin

69 Rhône

70 Haute-Saône

71 Saône-et-Loire

72 Sarthe

73 Savoie

74 Haute-Savoie

76 Seine-Maritime

77 Seine-et-Marne

78 Yvelines

79 Deux-Sèvres

80 Somme

81 Tarn

82 Tarn-et-Garonne

83 Var

84 Vaucluse

85 Vendée

86 Vienne

87 Haute-Vienne

88 Vosges

89 Yonne

90 Territoire-de-Belfort

91 Essonne

92 Hauts-de-Seine

In the guide these cities are listed under "PARIS SUBURBS"

93 Seine-Saint-Denis

In the guide these cities are listed under "PARIS SUBURBS"

94 Val-de-Marne

In the guide these cities are listed under "PARIS SUBURBS"

95 Val-d'Oise

Andorre (Principauté d')

In the guide these cities are listed under "ANDORRE"

Monaco (Principauté de)

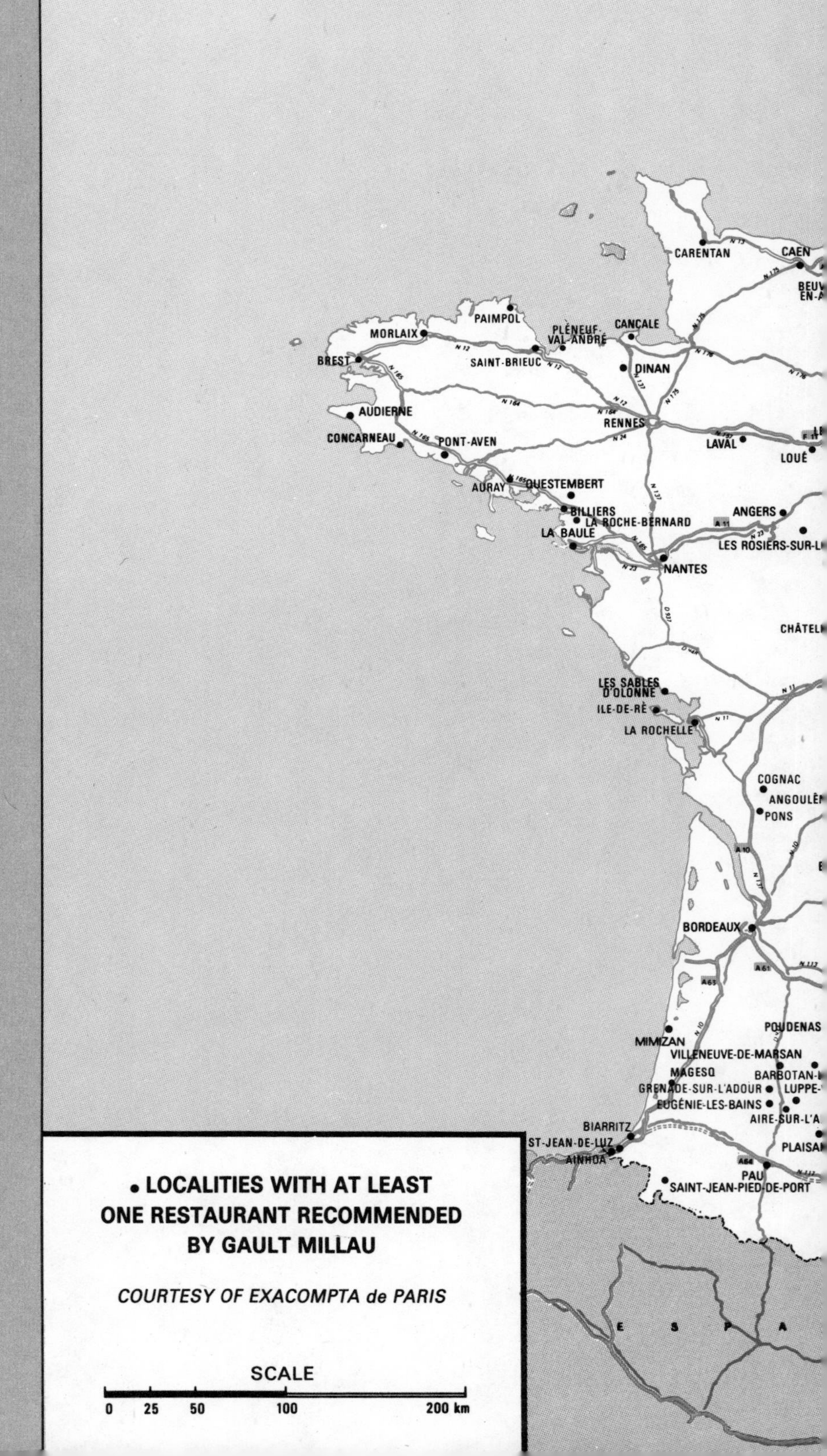

CARENTAN
CAEN
PAIMPOL
MORLAIX
PLÉNEUF-VAL-ANDRÉ
CANCALE
BREST
SAINT-BRIEUC
DINAN
AUDIERNE
RENNES
CONCARNEAU
PONT-AVEN
LAVAL
LOUÉ
AURAY
QUESTEMBERT
BILLIERS
LA ROCHE-BERNARD
ANGERS
LA BAULE
NANTES
LES SABLES D'OLONNE
ILE-DE-RÉ
LA ROCHELLE
COGNAC
PONS
BORDEAUX
MIMIZAN
POUDENAS
VILLENEUVE-DE-MARSAN
MAGESQ
GRENADE-SUR-L'ADOUR
EUGÉNIE-LES-BAINS
BIARRITZ
ST-JEAN-DE-LUZ
AINHOA
PAU
SAINT-JEAN-PIED-DE-PORT
N 12
N 165
N 164
N 137
N 175
N 24
N 23
D 937
N 11
N 10
A 10
A 11
A 61
A 63
A 64
• LOCALITIES WITH AT LEAST ONE RESTAURANT RECOMMENDED BY GAULT MILLAU
COURTESY OF EXACOMPTA de PARIS
SCALE
0
25
50
100
200 km

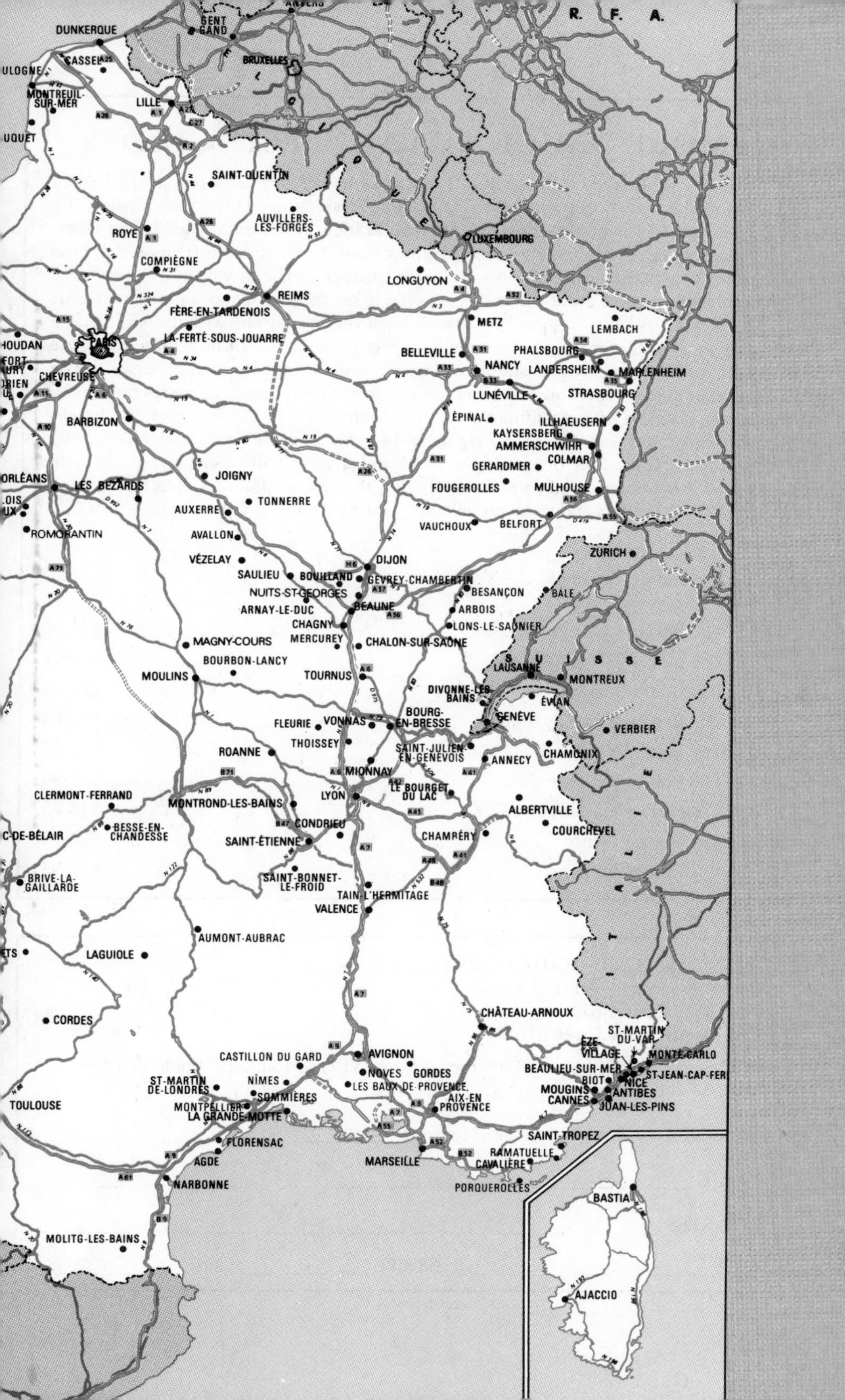

R. F. A.
DUNKERQUE
GENT GAND
CASSEL
BRUXELLES
MONTREUIL-SUR-MER
LILLE
SAINT-QUENTIN
AUVILLERS-LES-FORGES
ROYE
LUXEMBOURG
COMPIÈGNE
LONGUYON
REIMS
FÈRE-EN-TARDENOIS
METZ
LEMBACH
PARIS
LA-FERTÉ-SOUS-JOUARRE
HOUDAN
BELLEVILLE
PHALSBOURG
NANCY
LANDERSHEIM
MARLENHEIM
CHEVREUSE
LUNÉVILLE
STRASBOURG
BARBIZON
ÉPINAL
ILLHAEUSERN
KAYSERSBERG
AMMERSCHWIHR
COLMAR
GERARDMER
JOIGNY
ORLÉANS
LES BEZARDS
FOUGEROLLES
MULHOUSE
TONNERRE
AUXERRE
VAUCHOUX
BELFORT
ROMORANTIN
AVALLON
ZURICH
VÉZELAY
DIJON
SAULIEU
BOUILLAND
GEVREY-CHAMBERTIN
NUITS-ST-GEORGES
BESANÇON
BALE
ARNAY-LE-DUC
BEAUNE
ARBOIS
CHAGNY
LONS-LE-SAUNIER
MAGNY-COURS
MERCUREY
CHALON-SUR-SAÔNE
BOURBON-LANCY
SUISSE
LAUSANNE
MONTREUX
TOURNUS
MOULINS
DIVONNE-LES-BAINS
ÉVIAN
GENÈVE
FLEURIE
VONNAS
BOURG-EN-BRESSE
VERBIER
THOISSEY
SAINT-JULIEN-EN-GENEVOIS
ROANNE
ANNECY
CHAMONIX
MIONNAY
LE BOURGET DU LAC
CLERMONT-FERRAND
LYON
MONTROND-LES-BAINS
ALBERTVILLE
CONDRIEU
COURCHEVEL
C-DE-BÉLAIR
BESSE-EN-CHANDESSE
CHAMBÉRY
SAINT-ÉTIENNE
BRIVE-LA-GAILLARDE
SAINT-BONNET-LE-FROID
TAIN-L'HERMITAGE
VALENCE
AUMONT-AUBRAC
LAGUIOLE
CHÂTEAU-ARNOUX
CORDES
ST-MARTIN-DU-VAR
EZE-VILLAGE
MONTE-CARLO
CASTILLON DU GARD
AVIGNON
NOVES
GORDES
BEAULIEU-SUR-MER
ST-JEAN-CAP-FER
ST-MARTIN-DE-LONDRES
NÎMES
LES BAUX DE PROVENCE
BIOT
NICE
MOUGINS
ANTIBES
CANNES
JUAN-LES-PINS
TOULOUSE
SOMMIÈRES
MONTPELLIER
AIX-EN PROVENCE
LA GRANDE-MOTTE
SAINT-TROPEZ
FLORENSAC
MARSEILLE
RAMATUELLE
CAVALIÈRE
AGDE
PORQUEROLLES
NARBONNE
BASTIA
MOLITG-LES-BAINS
AJACCIO